Pope John

POPE JOHN PAUL II

IN MY OWN WORDS

Compiled and edited by
Anthony F. Chiffolo

Liguori

LIGUORI, MISSOURI

Library of Congress Cataloging-in-Publication Data

John Paul II, 1920–
   In my own words / Pope John Paul II ; compiled
and edited by Anthony F. Chiffolo. — 1st ed.
      p.   cm.
   ISBN 0-7648-0264-X
   1. John Paul II, Pope, 1920—Quotations. 2.
Christian life—Catholic authors. I. Chiffolo, Anthony F., 1959– . II. Title.
   BX1378.5.J574 1998
   282—dc21   98-7743

The editor and publisher gratefully acknowledge
permission to reprint/reproduce copyrighted works
granted by the publishers/sources listed on pages 114–
15.

Printed in the United States of America
98 99 00 01 02   5 4 3 2 1
First Edition

Friends: I greet you and

all those dear to you,

I bless you and

I encourage you not to

grow faint as you travel

the right road.

———

GREETING, SOUTH BRONX, 1979

Contents

Introduction IX

God the Father, Son, and Holy Spirit ... 1

Prayer 11

Faith, Hope, and Love 17

Salvation 25

Truth and Freedom 31

The Christian Life 39

The Sanctity of Life 55

Marriage and the Family 61

Solidarity and Human Relationships... 67

Progress and the Modern World 75

The Church 93

The Sacraments..................................... 99

The Priesthood 105

Mary 109

Permissions and Acknowledgments 115

$\mathcal{I}$NTRODUCTION

Who among us has not been touched in some small way by Pope John Paul II, has not seen on television his celebration of the Mass or read in the newspapers his statements about various current issues or simply heard news of his travels? He is, perhaps, the most visible pope the Catholic Church has ever had. Wherever he appears, he is greeted with the adulation normally accorded pop stars or royalty. Perhaps this is because he is "The Pilgrim Pope," the most widely traveled pope in the history of the papacy. Speaking many different languages and motoring around in his "popemobile," he is the first to bring the pope's love to people across the globe. Indeed, he is the first pope ever to have visited a number of countries, including, recently, Cuba.

Born Karol Wojtyla on May 18, 1920, in Wadowice, Poland, Pope John Paul II studied literature and drama in Kraków. During the Nazi occupation he worked in a stone quarry and a chemical plant, and he also began studying secretly for the priesthood in 1942.

He was ordained in 1946 and then earned a doctorate in theology at the Angelicum in Rome.

Afterward, from 1948 to 1951, he served as a parish priest in Kraków, then spent a year studying philosophy at the Jagiellonian University. From 1952 to 1958 he taught social ethics at the Kraków seminary, and he also served as professor at the University of Lublin.

Consecrated auxiliary bishop in Kraków in 1958 and archbishop in 1964, Karol Wojtyla attended all four sessions of the Second Vatican Council. He is said to have written *Gaudium et Spes,* the Pastoral Constitution on the Church in the Modern World, and to have played a prominent role in the formulation of *Dignitatis Humanae*, the Declaration on Religious Liberty. And his apologetic of the traditional Catholic teaching about marriage, *Love and Responsibility,* inspired Pope Paul VI to rely extensively on Archbishop Wojtyla's counsel during the writing of *Humanae Vitae*. Following the council, Karol Wojtyla was appointed cardinal in 1967.

As bishop and then as cardinal in Kraków, Karol Wojtyla provided inspirational leadership to Polish Catholics during the atheistic Communist regime, championing human rights and humankind's need to seek and know God. His support of Solidarity and fervent opposition to Communism hastened its downfall in Europe.

Karol Wojtyla was elected pope on October 16, 1978—the first non-Italian pope in more than four hundred years. To emphasize his commitment to continue the reforms of the Second Vatican Council, he took the names of his predecessors: John, Paul, and John Paul. He is the 262d successor of Saint Peter.

As pope, John Paul II has traveled around the world to meet and teach and minister to millions of Catholics—in locations as diverse as cathedrals, baseball stadiums, schools, and soup kitchens. But Pope John Paul II is much more than a jet-setting celebrity. During the course of his papacy he has emerged as perhaps the world's most important moral leader, unafraid to testify to the truth in both word and deed. He has written myriad letters, addresses, and encyclicals to the bishops, priests, and faithful of the Church, emphasizing the sacredness of life, the splendor of truth, and the love of God, as the selections in this collection demonstrate. And he authorized the preparation of the *Catechism of the Catholic Church*, the first universal catechism to be issued in more than four hundred years, to make the doctrines of the Church known in modern terms to a worldwide audience.

But what makes Pope John Paul II such a beloved leader is the constancy of his example. He speaks what he knows to be true, whether he's saying Mass at Yankee Stadium or addressing the General Assembly at the United Nations. Wherever he travels, he takes time to pray—especially the rosary—and he shares his prayers with millions via television and radio, as well as videocassettes and audio recordings. Each place he has visited he has consecrated to the Blessed Virgin Mary. And he has demonstrated the true meaning of love, having forgiven the man who wounded him during an unsuccessful assassination attempt.

Thus when he asserts, "Jesus is a demanding friend," or explains, "Love is the gift of self," or advises, "Be faithful to your daily prayers," or exhorts, "Do not be afraid!" it is clear that his are not empty words, for they arise out of his lived experience. And trusting these admonitions, we come to trust the pope's greatest message, words so many find so hard to believe: "God loves you." It is this message, so eloquently and often expressed, that has enabled him to touch the hearts of millions.

—AFC

GOD THE FATHER, SON, AND HOLY SPIRIT

We must go to this Child, this Man,
the Son of God, at whatever inconvenience,
at whatever risk to ourselves, because to know
and love him will truly change our lives.

HOMILY AT CENTRAL PARK, 1995

"*Life*" is one of the most beautiful titles which the Bible attributes to God. He is the living God.

MESSAGE TO PONTIFICAL ACADEMY
OF SCIENCES, 1996

*G*od created man as rational and free, thereby placing Himself under man's judgment. *The history of salvation is also the history of man's continual judgment of God.* Not only of man's questions and doubts but of his actual judgment of God.

CROSSING THE THRESHOLD OF HOPE

*E*very time Christ exhorts us to have no fear, He has both God and man in mind. He means: *Do not be afraid of God,* who, according to philosophers, is the transcendent Absolute. Do not be afraid of God, but invoke Him with me: "Our Father" (Mt 6:9). *Do not be afraid to say "Father"!* Desire to be perfect just as He is, because He is perfect.

CROSSING THE THRESHOLD OF HOPE

$\mathcal{G}$od's love for us is freely given and unearned, surpassing all we could ever hope for or imagine. He does not love us because we have merited it or are worthy of it. God loves us, rather, because he is true to his own nature. As Saint John puts it, "God is love, and he who abides in love abides in God, and God in him" (1 Jn 4:16).

ADDRESS AT MISSION DOLORES, 1987

$\mathcal{C}$hrist offers you his friendship. He gave his life so that those who wish to answer his call can indeed become his friends. His is a friendship which is deep, genuine, loyal, and total, as all true friendship must be.

MESSAGE TO YOUNG PEOPLE, CAMAGÜEY, CUBA, 1998

$\mathcal{W}$e always feel unworthy of Christ's friendship. But it is a good thing that we should have a holy fear of not remaining faithful to it.

TO PRIESTS, 1988

$\mathcal{I}$t is Christ who made man's way his own, and who guides him, even when he is unaware of it.

CENTESIMUS ANNUS

$\mathcal{T}$he goal and target of our life is he, the Christ, who awaits us—each one singly and all together—to lead us across the boundaries of time to the eternal embrace of the God who loves us.

MESSAGE TO YOUNG PEOPLE,
WORLD YOUTH DAY, 1996

$\mathcal{T}$his poor Babe, for whom "there was no room in the inn," in spite of appearances, is the sole Heir of the whole of creation. He came to share with us this birthright of his, so that we, having become children of divine adoption, might have a part in the inheritance that he brought with him into the world.

"URBI ET ORBI," 1995

*W*hat really matters in life is that we are loved by Christ, and that we love him in return. In comparison to the love of Jesus, everything else is secondary. And without the love of Jesus, everything else is useless.

PRAYER AT ST. PETER'S, PHILADELPHIA, 1979

*T*here is no evil to be faced that Christ does not face with us. There is no enemy that Christ has not already conquered. There is no cross to bear that Christ has not already borne for us, and does not now bear with us.

HOMILY IN ORIOLES PARK AT CAMDEN YARDS, 1995

*C*hrist himself carried a burden, and his burden—the cross—was made heavier by the sins of us all. But Christ did not avoid the cross; he accepted it and carried it willingly. Moreover, he now stands beside those weighed down by trials and persecutions, remaining beside them to the end. It is for all people and with all people that he carries the cross to Calvary, and it is there that for all of us he is nailed to his cross. He dies the death of a criminal, the most humiliating death known to the world at that time. That is why to those in our own century who carry terrible burdens he is able to say: "Come to me! I am your Brother in suffering. There is no humiliation or bitterness which I do not know!"

HOMILY AT AQUEDUCT RACETRACK, 1995

*J*esus Christ has taken the lead on the way of the cross. He has suffered first. He does not drive us toward suffering but shares it with us, wanting us to have life and to have it in abundance.

MEETING WITH THE SICK AND SUFFERING, 1998

*T*he name of Jesus, like the Word of God that he is, is a two-edged sword. It is a name that means salvation and life; it is a name that means a struggle and a cross, just as it did for him. But it is also the name in which we find strength to proclaim and live the truth of the Gospel: not with arrogance, but with confident joy; not with self-righteousness, but with humble repentance before God; never with enmity and always with charity.

ADDRESS AT LOS ANGELES, 1987

The splendor of Christ's glory is reflected in the face of every human being, and is even more so when that face is emaciated by hunger, saddened by exile, or oppressed by poverty and misery.

CATHOLIC RELIEF SERVICES MESSAGE, 1995

The Incarnation of the Son of God attests that God goes in search of man. Jesus speaks of this search as the finding of a lost sheep. It is a search which begins in the heart of God....If God goes in search of man, created in his own image and likeness, he does so because he loves him eternally in the Word, and wishes to raise him in Christ to the dignity of an adoptive son. God therefore goes in search of man who is his special possession in a way unlike any other creature.

TERTIO MILLENNIO ADVENIENTE

With man—with each man without any exception whatever—Christ is in a way united, even when man is unaware of it.

REDEMPTOR HOMINIS

$\mathcal{M}$aterialistic concerns and one-sided values are never sufficient to fill the heart and mind of a human person. A life reduced to the sole dimension of possessions, of consumer goods, of temporal concerns will never let you discover and enjoy the full richness of your humanity. It is only in God—in Jesus, God made man—that you will fully understand what you are. He will unveil to you the true greatness of yourselves: that you are redeemed by him and taken up in his love; that you are made truly free in him who said about himself: "If the Son frees you, you will be free indeed" (Jn 8:36).

MESSAGE TO STUDENTS,
THE CATHOLIC UNIVERSITY, 1979

$\mathcal{T}$he Spirit instills in us a desire for the world to come, but he also inspires, purifies, and strengthens those noble longings by which we strive to make earthly life more human.

HOMILY AT AQUEDUCT RACETRACK, 1995

The Holy Spirit is given to the Church as the source of strength to conquer sin. Only God has the power to forgive sins, because he alone sees right into the human person and can measure human responsibility completely. Sin remains, in its psychological depth, a secret which God alone has the power to enter, in order to say to a person the efficacious words: "Your sins are forgiven you, you are pardoned."

MASS WITH YOUTH,
HRADEC KRÁLOVÉ, CZECH REPUBLIC, 1997

The modern technological world can offer us many pleasures, many comforts of life. It can even offer us temporary escapes from life. But what the world can never offer is lasting joy and peace. These are the gifts which only the Holy Spirit can give.

MEETING WITH YOUTH,
NEW ORLEANS, 1987

$\mathcal{M}$ay the Holy Spirit,
The Spirit of Pentecost,
help you to clarify what is ambiguous,
to give warmth to what is indifferent,
to enlighten what is obscure,
to be before the world true and generous
witnesses of Christ's love,
for "no one can live without love."

PRAYER AT INSTITUTE CATHOLIQUE, PARIS, 1980

$\mathcal{P}$RAYER

*If you follow Jesus' advice and pray to God
constantly, then you will learn to pray well.
God himself will teach you.*

MEETING WITH YOUTH, NEW ORLEANS, 1987

What is prayer? It is commonly held to be a conversation. In a conversation there are always an "I" and a "thou" or "you." In this case the "Thou" is with a capital T. If at first the "I" seems to be the most important element in prayer, prayer teaches that the situation is actually different. *The "Thou" is more important, because our prayer begins with God.*

CROSSING THE THRESHOLD OF HOPE

We begin to pray, believing that it is our own initiative that compels us to do so. Instead, we learn that it is always God's initiative within us....

CROSSING THE THRESHOLD OF HOPE

It is a beautiful and salutary thought that, wherever people are praying in the world, there the Holy Spirit is, the living breath of prayer. It is a beautiful and salutary thought to recognize that, if prayer is offered throughout the world, in the past, in the present and in the future, equally widespread is the presence and action of the Holy Spirit, who "breathes" prayer in the

heart of man in all the endless range of the
most varied situations and conditions.

DOMINUM ET VIVIFICANTEM

*T*he Holy Spirit is the gift that comes into
man's heart together with prayer. In prayer he
manifests himself first of all and above all as the
gift that "helps us in our weakness." This is the
magnificent thought developed by Saint Paul
in the Letter to the Romans, when he writes:
"For we do not know how to pray as we ought,
but the Spirit himself intercedes for us with
sighs too deep for words" (8:26). Therefore, the
Holy Spirit not only enables us to pray, but
guides us "from within" in prayer: he is present
in our prayer and gives it a divine dimension.

DOMINUM ET VIVIFICANTEM

*M*any times, through the influence of the
Spirit, prayer rises from the human heart in
spite of prohibitions and persecutions and even
official proclamations....Prayer always remains
the voice of all those who apparently have no
voice....

DOMINUM ET VIVIFICANTEM

*P*rayer...brings the saving power of Jesus Christ into the decisions and actions of everyday life.

GREETING IN ST. PATRICK'S CATHEDRAL, 1995

*B*e faithful to your daily prayers; they will keep your faith alive and vibrant.

MESSAGE TO SEMINARIANS, CHICAGO, 1979

*C*hrist remains primary in your life only when he enjoys the first place in your mind and heart. Thus you must continuously unite yourself to him in prayer....Without prayer there can be no joy, no hope, no peace. For prayer is what keeps us in touch with Christ.

MESSAGE TO RELIGIOUS WOMEN,
WASHINGTON, D.C., 1979

*W*hat enormous power the prayer of children has! This becomes a model for grownups themselves: praying with simple and complete trust means praying as children pray.

LETTER OF THE POPE TO THE CHILDREN
IN THE YEAR OF THE FAMILY

$\mathcal{I}$f you really wish to follow Christ, if you want your love for him to grow and last, then you must be faithful to prayer. It is the key to the vitality of your life in Christ. Without prayer, your faith and love will die. If you are constant in daily prayer and in the Sunday celebration of Mass, your love for Jesus will increase. And your heart will know deep joy and peace, such as the world could never give.

MEETING WITH YOUTH, NEW ORLEANS, 1987

$\mathcal{P}$rayer can truly change your life. For it turns your attention away from yourself and directs your mind and your heart toward the Lord. If we look only at ourselves, with our own limitations and sins, we quickly give way to sadness and discouragement. But if we keep our eyes fixed on the Lord, then our hearts are filled with hope, our minds are washed in the light of truth, and we come to know the fullness of the Gospel with all its promise and life.

MEETING WITH YOUTH, NEW ORLEANS, 1987

*O*nly the human person, created in the image and likeness of God, is capable of raising a hymn of praise and thanksgiving to the Creator. The Earth, with all its creatures, and the entire universe call on man to be their voice.

HOMILY AT SAN ANTONIO, 1987

FAITH, HOPE, AND LOVE

People cannot live without love.
They are called to love God
and their neighbor, but in order
to love properly they must be certain
that God loves them.
God loves you, dear children!
This is what I want to tell you. . . .

LETTER OF THE POPE TO THE CHILDREN
IN THE YEAR OF THE FAMILY

$\mathcal{I}$n the very search for faith an implicit faith is already present, and therefore the necessary condition for salvation is already satisfied.

CROSSING THE THRESHOLD OF HOPE

$\mathcal{F}$aith is always demanding, because faith leads us beyond ourselves. It leads us directly to God. Faith also imparts a vision of life's purpose and stimulates us to action....Christ has commanded us to let the light of the Gospel shine forth in our service to society. How can we profess faith in God's word, and then refuse to let it inspire and direct our thinking, our activity, our decisions, and our responsibilities toward one another?

HOMILY IN ORIOLES PARK AT CAMDEN YARDS, 1995

$\mathcal{B}$y the practice of your religion you are called to give witness to your faith. And because actions speak louder than words, you are called to proclaim, by the conduct of your daily lives, that you really do believe that Jesus Christ is Lord!

MESSAGE TO HIGH SCHOOL STUDENTS, MADISON SQUARE GARDEN, 1979

*W*ithout faith in God, there can be no hope, no lasting, authentic hope. To stop believing in God is to start down a path that can lead only to emptiness and despair.

YOUTH TELECONFERENCE, LOS ANGELES, 1987

*T*o evangelize is to give an account to all of the hope that is in us.

MESSAGE FOR WORLD MIGRATION DAY, 1997

*W*e cannot live without hope. We have to have some purpose in life, some meaning to our existence. We have to aspire to something. Without hope, we begin to die.

YOUTH TELECONFERENCE, LOS ANGELES, 1987

*H*ope comes from God, from our belief in God. People of hope are those who believe God created them for a purpose and that he will provide for their needs.

YOUTH TELECONFERENCE, LOS ANGELES, 1987

To become like a little child—with complete trust in the Father and with the meekness taught by the Gospel—is not only an ethical imperative; it is a reason for hope. Even where the difficulties are so great as to lead to discouragement and the power of evil so overwhelming as to dishearten, those who can rediscover the simplicity of a child can begin to hope anew.

MESSAGE FOR WORLD DAY OF PEACE, 1996

In our bodies we are a mere speck in the vast created universe, but by virtue of our souls we transcend the whole material world. I invite you to reflect on what makes each one of you truly marvelous and unique. Only a human being like you can think and speak and share your thoughts in different languages with other human beings all over the world, and through that language express the beauty of art and poetry and music and literature and the theater, and so many other uniquely human accomplishments.

And most important of all, only God's precious human beings are capable of loving.

HOMILY AT CENTRAL PARK, 1995

$\mathcal{L}$ove can overcome great obstacles, and God's love can totally transform the world.

MEETING WITH CHARITIES,
SAN ANTONIO, 1987

$\mathcal{I}$nner peace comes from knowing that one is loved by God and from the desire to respond to his love.

"WOMEN: TEACHERS OF PEACE," 1995.

$\mathcal{G}$enuine love…is demanding. But its beauty lies precisely in the demands it makes. Only those able to make demands on themselves in the name of love can then demand love from others.

MESSAGE TO YOUNG PEOPLE,
CAMAGÜEY, CUBA, 1998

$\mathcal{L}$ove is the gift of self. It means emptying oneself to reach out to others. In a certain sense, it means forgetting oneself for the good of others.

"TRUE HUMAN LOVE REFLECTS THE DIVINE," 1993

*L*ove is the force that opens hearts to the word of Jesus and to his Redemption: love is the only basis for human relationships that respect in one another the dignity of the children of God created in his image and saved by the death and Resurrection of Jesus; love is the only driving force that impels us to share with our brothers and sisters all that we are and have.

HOMILY AT GRANT PARK, CHICAGO, 1979

*W*e cannot live without love. If we do not encounter love, if we do not experience it and make it our own, and if we do not participate intimately in it, our life is meaningless. Without love we remain incomprehensible to ourselves.

MESSAGE TO RELIGIOUS WOMEN,
WASHINGTON, D.C., 1979

$\mathcal{L}$ife is a talent entrusted to us so that we can transform it and increase it, making it a gift to others. No man is an iceberg drifting on the ocean of history. Each one of us belongs to a great family, in which he has his own place and his own role to play. Selfishness makes people deaf and dumb; love opens eyes and hearts, enabling people to make that original and irreplaceable contribution which, together with the thousands of deeds of so many brothers and sisters, often distant and unknown, converges to form the mosaic of charity which can change the tide of history.

MESSAGE FOR WORLD YOUTH DAY, 1996

SALVATION

Ultimately, only God can save man, but He expects man to cooperate. The fact that man can cooperate with God determines his authentic greatness. The truth according to which man is called to cooperate with God in all things, with a view toward the ultimate purpose of his life—his salvation and divinization—found expression in the Eastern tradition in the doctrine of synergism. With God, man "creates" the world; with God, man "creates" his personal salvation. The divinization of man comes from God. But here, too, man must cooperate with God.

CROSSING THE THRESHOLD OF HOPE

*A*wareness of our own sinfulness, including that which is inherited, is the first condition for salvation; the next is the confession of this sin before God, who desires only to receive this confession so that He can save man. *To save means to embrace and lift up with redemptive love*, with love that is *always greater* than any sin.

CROSSING THE THRESHOLD OF HOPE

*N*o human sin can erase the mercy of God, or prevent him from unleashing all his triumphant power, if we only call upon him.

VERITATIS SPLENDOR

*T*he power of Christ's Cross and Resurrection is greater than any evil which man could or should fear.

CROSSING THE THRESHOLD OF HOPE

*T*he precepts of the Lord are a gift of grace entrusted to man always and solely for his good, for the preservation of his personal dignity and the pursuit of his happiness.

EVANGELIUM VITAE

*T*hrough Christ's sacrifice on the Cross, the victory of the Kingdom of God has been achieved once and for all. Nevertheless, the Christian life involves a struggle against temptation and the forces of evil. Only at the end of history will the Lord return in glory for the final judgment with the establishment of a new heaven and a new earth; but as long as time lasts, the struggle between good and evil continues even in the human heart itself.

CENTESIMUS ANNUS

*T*he true and proper meaning of mercy does not consist only in looking, however penetratingly and compassionately, at moral, physical or material evil: mercy is manifested in its true and proper aspect when it restores to value, promotes and draws good from all the forms of evil existing in the world and in man.

DIVES IN MISERICORDIA

*A*n act of merciful love is only really such when we are deeply convinced at the moment that we perform it that we are at the same time receiving mercy from the people who are accepting it from us. If this bilateral and reciprocal quality is absent, our actions are not yet true acts of mercy, nor has there yet been fully completed in us that conversion to which Christ has show us the way by his words and example, even to the Cross, nor are we yet sharing fully in the magnificent source of merciful love that has been revealed to us by him.

Dives in Misericordia

Christ, in revealing the love-mercy of God, at the same time demanded from people that they also should be guided in their lives by love and mercy. This requirement forms part of the very essence of the messianic message, and constitutes the heart of the Gospel *ethos*.

Dives in Misericordia

Forgiveness demonstrates the presence in the world of the love which is more powerful than sin. Forgiveness is also the fundamental condition for reconciliation, not only in the relationship of God with man, but also in relationships between people. A world from which forgiveness was eliminated would be nothing but a world of cold and unfeeling justice, in the name of which each person would claim his or her own rights vis-à-vis others....

DIVES IN MISERICORDIA

*M*ercy in itself, as a perfection of the infinite God, is also infinite. Also infinite therefore and inexhaustible is the Father's readiness to receive the prodigal children who return to his home. Infinite are the readiness and power of forgiveness which flow continually from the marvelous value of the sacrifice of the Son. No human sin can prevail over this power or even limit it. On the part of man only a lack of good will can limit it, a lack of readiness to be converted and to repent, in other words persistence in obstinacy, opposing grace and truth, especially in the face of the witness of the Cross and Resurrection of Christ.

DIVES IN MISERICORDIA

$\mathcal{W}$hen it comes to salvation in the kingdom of God, it is not a question of just wages, but of the undeserved generosity of God, who gives himself as the supreme gift to each and every person who shares in divine life through sanctifying grace.

HOMILY AT DETROIT, 1987

$\mathcal{E}$ach of us is an individual, a person, a creature of God, one of his children, someone very special whom God loves and for whom Christ died. This identity of ours determines the way we must live, the way we must act, the way we must view our mission in the world. We come from God, we depend on God, God has a plan for us—a plan for our lives, for our bodies, for our souls, for our future. This plan for us is extremely important—so important that God became man to explain it to us.

MEETING WITH YOUTH, NEW ORLEANS, 1987

$\mathcal{T}$RUTH AND FREEDOM

You cannot insist on the right to choose,
without also insisting on the duty to choose
well, the duty to choose the truth.

HOMILY AT COLUMBIA, SOUTH CAROLINA, 1987

*T*he Gospel contains a *fundamental paradox:* to find life, one must lose life; to be born, one must die; to save oneself, one must take up the cross. This is the essential truth of the Gospel, which always and everywhere is bound to meet with man's protest.

Always and everywhere the Gospel will be a challenge to human weakness. But precisely in this challenge lies all its power. Man, perhaps subconsciously waits for such a challenge; *indeed, man feels the inner need to transcend himself.* Only in transcending himself does man become fully human....

CROSSING THE THRESHOLD OF HOPE

*M*an cannot be forced to accept the truth. He can be drawn toward the truth only by his own nature, that is, by his own freedom, which commits him to search sincerely for truth and, when he finds it, to adhere to it both in his convictions and in his behavior.

CROSSING THE THRESHOLD OF HOPE

It is quite human for the sinner to acknowledge his weakness and to ask mercy for his failings; what is unacceptable is the attitude of one who makes his own weakness the criterion of the truth about the good, so that he can feel self-justified, without even the need to have recourse to God and his mercy.

VERITATIS SPLENDOR

Man remains above all a being who seeks the truth and strives to live in that truth, deepening his understanding of it through a dialogue which involves past and future generations.

CENTESIMUS ANNUS

Jesus Christ meets the man of every age, including our own, with the same words: "You will know the truth, and the truth will make you free" (Jn 8:32). These words contain both a fundamental requirement and a warning: the requirement of an honest relationship with regard to truth as a condition for authentic freedom, and the warning to avoid every kind of illusory freedom, every superficial unilateral freedom, every freedom that fails to enter into the whole truth about man and the world.

REDEMPTOR HOMINIS

*B*ecause by its nature the content of faith is meant for all humanity, it must be translated into all cultures.…The expression of truth can take different forms. The renewal of these forms of expression becomes necessary for the sake of transmitting to the people of today the Gospel message in its unchanging meaning.

ET UNUM SINT

*A*t the heart of every culture lies the attitude man takes to the greatest mystery: the mystery of God. Different cultures are basically different ways of facing the question of the meaning of personal existence.

CENTESIMUS ANNUS

$\mathcal{A}$lthough each individual has a right to be respected in his own journey in search of the truth, there exists a prior moral obligation, and a grave one at that, to seek the truth and to adhere to it once it is known.

VERITATIS SPLENDOR

$\mathcal{R}$evelation teaches that the power to decide what is good and what is evil does not belong to man, but to God alone. The man is certainly free, inasmuch as he can understand and accept God's commands. And he possesses an extremely far-reaching freedom, since he can eat "of every tree of the garden." But his freedom is not unlimited: it must halt before the "tree of the knowledge of good and evil," for it is called to accept the moral law given by God. In fact, human freedom finds its authentic and complete fulfillment precisely in the acceptance of that law. God, who alone is good, knows perfectly what is good for man, and by virtue of his very love proposes this good to man in the commandments.

VERITATIS SPLENDOR

*J*esus' message applies to all the areas of life. He reveals to us the truth of our lives and all aspects of this truth. Jesus tells us that the purpose of our freedom is to say yes to God's plan for our lives. What makes our yes so important is that we say it freely; we are able to say no. Jesus teaches us that we are accountable to God, that we must follow our consciences, but that our consciences must be formed according to God's plan for our lives. In all our relationships to other people and to the world, Jesus teaches us what we must do, how we must live in order not to be deceived, in order to walk in truth.

MEETING WITH YOUTH, NEW ORLEANS, 1987

*B*e faithful to the truth and to its transmission, for truth endures; truth will not go away. Truth will not pass or change.

MESSAGE TO U.N. JOURNALISTS, 1979

*N*owadays it is sometimes held, though wrongly, that freedom is an end in itself, that each human being is free when he makes use of freedom as he wishes, and that this must be our aim in the lives of individuals and societies. In reality, freedom is a great gift only when we know how to use it consciously for everything that is our true good. Christ teaches us that the best use of freedom is charity, which takes concrete form in self-giving and in service.

REDEMPTOR HOMINIS

*F*reedom negates and destroys itself, and becomes a factor leading to the destruction of others, when it no longer recognizes and respects its essential link with the truth. When freedom, out of a desire to emancipate itself from all forms of tradition and authority, shuts out even the most obvious evidence of an objective and universal truth...then the person ends up by no longer taking as the sole and indisputable point of reference for his own choices the truth about good and evil, but only his subjective and changeable opinion or, indeed, his selfish interest and whim.

EVANGELIUM VITAE

*W*hile it is true that the taking of life not yet born or in its final stages is sometimes marked by a mistaken sense of altruism and human compassion, it cannot be denied that such a culture of death, taken as a whole, betrays a completely individualistic concept of freedom, which ends up by becoming the freedom of "the strong" against the weak who have no choice but to submit.

EVANGELIUM VITAE

O Lord, bestow on your faithful the Spirit of truth and peace, that they may know you with all their soul, and generously carrying out what pleases you, may always enjoy your benefits.
Through Christ our Lord.
Amen.

GENERAL AUDIENCE, ROME, 1980

𝒯HE CHRISTIAN LIFE

*𝒯he true success of our lives consists
in knowing and doing the will of 𝒥esus,
in doing whatever 𝒥esus tells us.*

MEETING WITH YOUTH, NEW ORLEANS, 1987

*E*veryone has a vocation: parents, teachers, students, workers, professional people, people who are retired. Everyone has something to do for God.

HOMILY AT GIANTS STADIUM, 1995

*T*he search and discovery of God's will for you is a deep and fascinating endeavor. It requires of you the attitude of trust expressed in the words of the Psalm…"you will show me the path to life, fullness of joy in your presence, the delights at your right hand forever" (16:11). Every vocation, every path to which Christ calls us, ultimately leads to fulfillment and happiness, because it leads to God, to sharing in God's own life.

MESSAGE TO YOUTH

*T*rue holiness does not mean a flight from the world; rather, it lies in the effort to incarnate the Gospel in everyday life, in the family, at school and at work, and in social and political involvement.

TO CATHOLIC CHARISMATICS, 1996

*G*od can use our weakness as easily as our strength in order to accomplish his will.

MEETING WITH PRIESTS, MIAMI, 1987

*D*o not be afraid! Life with Christ is a wonderful adventure. He alone can give full meaning to life, he alone is the center of history. Live by him!

MASS WITH YOUTH, HRADEC KRÁLOVÉ, CZECH REPUBLIC, 1997

*T*he whole of the Christian life is like a great pilgrimage to the house of the Father, whose unconditional love for every human creature, and in particular for the "prodigal son," we discover anew each day. This pilgrimage takes place in the heart of each person, extends to the believing community and then reaches to the whole of humanity.

TERTIO MILLENNIO ADVENIENTE

Conversion to God always consists in discovering his mercy, that is, in discovering that love which is patient and kind as only the Creator and Father can be....Conversion to God is always the fruit of the "rediscovery" of this Father, who is rich in mercy.

Authentic knowledge of the God of mercy, the God of tender love, is a constant and inexhaustible source of conversion, not only as a momentary interior act but also as a permanent attitude, as a state of mind. Those who come to know God in this way, who "see" him in this way, can live only in a state of being continually converted to him.

DIVES IN MISERICORDIA

The Gospel is certainly demanding. We know that Christ never permitted His disciples and those who listened to Him to entertain any illusions about this. On the contrary, He spared no effort in preparing them for every type of internal or external difficulty, always aware of the fact that they might well decide to abandon Him. Therefore, if He says, "Be not afraid!" He certainly does not say it in order to nullify in some way that which He has required. Rather, by these words He confirms the entire truth of the Gospel and all the demands it contains. At the same time, however, He reveals that *His demands never exceed man's abilities*. If man accepts these demands with an attitude of faith, he will also find in the grace that God never fails to give him the necessary strength to meet those demands.

CROSSING THE THRESHOLD OF HOPE

The way Jesus shows you is not easy. Rather, it is like a path winding up a mountain. Do not lose heart! The steeper the road, the faster it rises toward ever wider horizons.

MESSAGE FOR WORLD YOUTH DAY, 1996

It is true: Jesus is a demanding friend. He points to lofty goals: he asks us to go out of ourselves in order to meet him, entrusting to him our whole life: "Whoever loses his life for my sake and that of the gospel will save it" (Mk 8:35). The proposal may seem difficult, and, in some cases, frightening. But—I ask you—is it better to be resigned to a life without ideals, to a world made in our image and likeness, or rather, generously to seek truth, goodness, justice, working for a world that reflects the beauty of God, even at the cost of facing the trials it may involve?

MESSAGE FOR WORLD YOUTH DAY, 1996

In order to hold fast to the fundamental values which keep them sinless, Christians sometimes have to suffer marginalization and persecution—at times heroically—because of moral choices which are contrary to the world's behavior....This is the cost of Christian witness, of a worthy life in the eyes of God. If you are not willing to pay this price, your lives will be empty....

HOMILY AT CAMAGÜEY, CUBA, 1998

*C*hristians, like all people of good will, are called upon under grave obligation of conscience not to cooperate formally in practices which, even if permitted by civil legislation, are contrary to God's law.

EVANGELIUM VITAE

Those who live "by the flesh" experience God's Law as a burden, and indeed as a denial or at least a restriction of their own freedom. On the other hand, those who are impelled by love and "walk by the Spirit" (Gal 5:16), and who desire to serve others, find in God's Law the fundamental and necessary way in which to practice love as something freely chosen and freely lived out. Indeed, they feel an interior urge—a genuine "necessity" and no longer a form of coercion—not to stop at the minimum demands of the Law, but to live them in their "fullness."

Veritatis Splendor

To imitate and live out the love of Christ is not possible for man by his own strength alone. He becomes capable of this love only by virtue of a gift received....Christ's gift is his Spirit....

Veritatis Splendor

The Father puts in our hands the task of beginning to build here on earth the "kingdom of heaven" which the Son came to announce and which will find its fulfillment at the end of time.

It is our duty then to live in history, side by side with our peers, sharing their worries and hopes, because the Christian is and must be fully a man of his time. He cannot escape into another dimension, ignoring the tragedies of his era, closing his eyes and heart to the anguish that pervades life. On the contrary, it is he who, although not "of" this world, is immersed "in" this world every day, ready to hasten to wherever there is a brother in need of help, a tear to be dried, a request for help to be answered. On this will we be judged.

MESSAGE FOR WORLD YOUTH DAY, 1996

In children there is something that must never be missing in people who want to enter the kingdom of heaven. People who are destined to go to heaven are simple like children, and like children are full of trust, rich in goodness and pure. Only people of this sort can find in God a Father and, thanks to Jesus, can become in their own turn children of God.

LETTER OF THE POPE TO THE CHILDREN IN THE YEAR OF THE FAMILY

$\mathcal{P}$eace is a gift of God; but men and women must first accept this gift in order to build a peaceful world. People can do this only if they have a childlike simplicity of heart. This is one of the most profound and paradoxical aspects of the Christian message: to become childlike is more than just a moral requirement but a dimension of the mystery of the Incarnation itself.

The Son of God did not come in power and glory, as he will at the end of the world, but as a child, needy and poor. Fully sharing our human condition in all things but sin, he also took on the frailty and hope for the future which are part of being a child. After that decisive moment for the history of humanity, to despise childhood means to despise the One who showed the greatness of his love by humbling himself and forsaking all glory in order to redeem mankind.

MESSAGE FOR WORLD DAY OF PEACE, 1996

$\mathcal{B}$ut how are you to be recognized as true disciples of Christ? By the fact that you have "love for one another" (Jn 13:35) after the example of his love: a love that is freely given, infinitely patient and denied to no one. Fidelity to the new commandment will be the guarantee that you are consistent with respect to what you are proclaiming....In this world you are called to live fraternally, not as a utopia but as a real possibility; in this society you are called, as true missionaries of Christ, to build the civilization of love.

MESSAGE FOR WORLD YOUTH DAY, 1996

*Y*our great contribution to the evangelization of your own society is made through your lives. Christ's message must live in you and in the way you live and in the way you refuse to live....Your lives must spread the fragrance of Christ's Gospel throughout the world.

MEETING WITH LAITY, SAN FRANCISCO, 1987

*I*t is through the free gift of self that one truly finds oneself. This gift is made possible by the human person's essential "capacity for transcendence."...As a person, he can give himself to another person or to other persons, and ultimately to God, who is the author of our being and who alone can fully accept our gift. Man is alienated if he refuses to transcend himself and to live the experience of self-giving and of the formation of an authentic human community oriented toward his final destiny, which is God.

CENTESIMUS ANNUS

$\mathcal{N}$ever forget that blindly following the impulse of our emotions often means becoming a slave to our passions.

MESSAGE TO YOUNG PEOPLE, CAMAGÜEY, CUBA, 1998

$\mathcal{T}$here is no room in the world for selfishness. It destroys the meaning of life; it destroys the meaning of love; it reduces the human person to a subhuman level.

MEETING WITH YOUTH, NEW ORLEANS, 1987

$\mathcal{W}$hat does it mean to remain sinless? It means living your life according to the moral principles of the Gospel which the Church sets before you.

HOMILY AT CAMAGÜEY, CUBA, 1998

*I*ndifference in the face of human suffering, passivity before the causes of pain in the world, cosmetic remedies which lead to no deep healing of persons and peoples: These are grave sins of omission, in the face of which every person of good will must be converted and listen to the cry of those who suffer.

MEETING WITH THE SICK AND SUFFERING, 1998

*C*hrist is very clear: When we ourselves are without sympathy or mercy, when we are guided by "blind" justice alone, then we cannot count on the mercy of that "Great Creditor" who is God—God, before whom we are all debtors.

HOMILY AT NEW ORLEANS, 1987

*C*hrist responds neither directly nor abstractly to human questioning about the meaning of suffering. Human beings come to know his saving response in so far as they share in the sufferings of Christ. The response which comes from this sharing is before all else a call. It is a vocation. Christ does not explain in some abstract way the reasons for suffering, but says first of all: "Follow me," "Come," with your suffering share in this work of salvation of the world, which is realized through my suffering, by means of my Cross.

SALVIFICI DOLORIS

*T*hose who suffer are no burden to others, but with their suffering contribute to the salvation of all.

MEETING WITH THE SICK AND SUFFERING, 1998

*T*he eloquence of the parable of the Good Samaritan, as of the entire Gospel, is in real terms this: Human beings must feel personally called to witness to love in the midst of suffering.

MEETING WITH THE SICK AND SUFFERING, 1998

*T*he distinctive mark of the Christian, today more than ever, must be love for the poor, the weak, the suffering. Living out this demanding commitment requires a total reversal of the alleged values which make people seek only their own good: power, pleasure, the unscrupulous accumulation of wealth. Yes, it is precisely to this radical conversion that Christ's disciples are called.

MESSAGE FOR WORLD DAY OF PEACE, 1998

*D*o not be afraid, I say, because great courage is required if we are to open the doors to Christ, if we are to let Christ enter into our hearts so fully that we can say with Saint Paul, "The life I live now is not my own; Christ is living in me" (Gal 2:20)....You need courage to follow Christ, especially when you recognize that so much of our dominant culture is a culture of flight from God....

ADDRESS AT VESPERS, ST. JOSEPH'S SEMINARY, 1995

*B*e generous in giving your life to the Lord. Do not be afraid! You have nothing to fear, because God is the Lord of history and of the universe. Let grow in you the desire for great and noble projects. Nourish a sense of solidarity: these are the signs of the divine action in your hearts. Place at the use of your communities the talents which Providence has lavished on you. The more ready you are to give yourselves to God and to others, the more you will discover the authentic meaning of life. God expects much of you!

MESSAGE FOR WORLD DAY OF PRAYER
FOR VOCATIONS, 1996

THE SANCTITY OF LIFE

Man is called to a fullness of life which far exceeds the dimensions of his earthly existence, because it consists in sharing the very life of God. The loftiness of this supernatural vocation reveals the greatness and the inestimable value of human life even in its temporal phase.

EVANGELIUM VITAE

The life which God gives man is quite different from the life of all other living creatures, inasmuch as man...is a manifestation of God in the world, a sign of his presence, a trace of his glory....Man has been given a sublime dignity, based on the intimate bond which unites him to his Creator: in man there shines forth a reflection of God himself....The life which God offers to man is a gift by which God shares something of himself with his creature.

EVANGELIUM VITAE

The deliberate decision to deprive an innocent human being of his life is always morally evil and can never be licit either as an end in itself or as a means to a good end. It is in fact a grave act of disobedience to the moral law, and indeed to God himself, the author and guarantor of that law.

EVANGELIUM VITAE

I do not hesitate to proclaim before you and before the world that all human life—from the moment of conception and through all subsequent stages—is sacred, because human life is created in the image and likeness of God. Nothing surpasses the greatness or dignity of a human person. Human life is not just an idea or an abstraction; human life is the concrete reality of a being that lives, that acts, that grows and develops; human life is the concrete reality of a being that is capable of love, and of service to humanity....

Human life is precious because it is the gift of a God whose love is infinite; and when God gives life, it is forever.

HOMILY, CAPITOL MALL, WASHINGTON, D.C., 1979

All human beings ought to value every person for his or her uniqueness as a creature of God, called to be a brother or sister of Christ by reason of the Incarnation and the universal Redemption. For us, the sacredness of human life is based on these premises. And it is on these same premises that there is based our celebration of life—all human life. This explains our efforts to defend human life against every influence or action that threatens or weakens it, as well as our endeavors to make every life more human in all its aspects.

HOMILY, CAPITOL MALL, WASHINGTON, D.C., 1979

The human person is a unique composite—a unity of spirit and matter, soul and body, fashioned in the image of God and destined to live forever. Every human life is sacred, because every human person is sacred. It is in the light of this fundamental truth that the Church constantly proclaims and defends the dignity of human life from the moment of conception to the moment of natural death.

MESSAGE TO HEALTH WORKERS, PHOENIX, 1987

The Church counters the culture of death with the culture of love.

AD LIMINA APOSTOLÒRUM—
BISHOPS' CONFERENCE OF BRAZIL, 10

Life is entrusted to man as a treasure which must not be squandered, as a talent which must be used well. Man must render an account of it to his Master....

EVANGELIUM VITAE

*R*espect for life and for the dignity of the human person extends also to the rest of creation, which is called to join man in praising God.

"THE ECOLOGICAL CRISIS," 1990

ℳARRIAGE AND THE FAMILY

The witness to Christ of the entire Christian community has a greater impact than that of a single individual. How important, then, is the Gospel witness of every Christian community, but especially the most fundamental of them all, the Christian family. In the face of many common evils, the Christian family that truly lives the truth of the Gospel in love is most certainly a sign of contradiction; and at the same time it is a source of great hope for those who are eager to do good.

HOMILY AT SAN FRANCISCO, 1987

$\mathcal{M}$arriage, with its character as an exclusive and permanent union, is sacred because its origin is in God. Christians, in receiving the sacrament of marriage, share in God's creative plan and receive the graces they need to carry out their mission of raising and educating their children, and to respond to the call to holiness. It is a union different from any other sort of human society, for it is based on the mutual giving and receiving of husband and wife in order to become "one flesh" (Gn 2:24), living in a community of life and love, the vocation of which is to be a "sanctuary of life." By their faithful and persevering union, the couple contributes to the good of the institution of the family and shows that a man and a woman are capable of giving themselves to one another forever....

HOMILY AT SANTA CLARA, CUBA, 1998

$\mathcal{C}$ontemporary society has a special need of the witness of couples who persevere in their union as an eloquent, even if sometimes suffering, "sign" in our human condition of the steadfastness of God's love. Day after day, Christian married couples are called to open their hearts ever more to the Holy Spirit, whose power never fails and who enables them to love each other as Christ has loved us.

HOMILY AT COLUMBIA, SOUTH CAROLINA, 1987

*T*he family is the first school of living, and the influence received inside the family is decisive for the future development of the individual.

MESSAGE FOR WORLD DAY OF PEACE, 1998

*A*lthough people are rightly worried—though much less than they should be—about preserving the natural habitats of the various animal species threatened with extinction…too little effort is made to safeguard the moral conditions for an authentic "human ecology."…man too is God's gift to man. He must therefore respect the natural and moral structure with which he has been endowed.…

The first and fundamental structure for "human ecology" is the family, in which man receives his first formative ideas about truth and goodness, and learns what it means to love and to be loved, and thus what it actually

63

means to be a person. Here we mean the family founded on marriage....

It is necessary to go back to seeing the family as the sanctuary of life. The family is indeed sacred: it is the place in which life—the gift of God—can be properly welcomed and protected against the many attacks to which it is exposed, and can develop in accordance with what constitutes authentic human growth. In the face of the so-called culture of death, the family is the heart of the culture of life.

CENTESIMUS ANNUS

The Church and the family are each in its own way living representations in human history of the eternal loving communion of the three persons of the Most Holy Trinity. In fact, the family is called the Church in miniature, "the domestic church," a particular expression of the Church through the human experience of love and common life. Like the Church, the family ought to be a place where the Gospel is transmitted and from which the Gospel radiates to other families and to the whole of society.

HOMILY AT COLUMBIA, SOUTH CAROLINA, 1987

Catholic parents must learn to form their family as a "domestic Church," a church in the home as it were, where God is honored, his law is respected, prayer is a normal event, virtue is transmitted by word and example, and everyone shares the hopes, the problems, and sufferings of everyone else.

HOMILY AT AQUEDUCT RACETRACK, 1995

The family is the first setting of evangelization, the place where the good news of Christ is first received and then, in simple yet profound ways, handed on from generation to generation.

MEETING WITH AFRICAN AMERICANS,
NEW ORLEANS, 1987

It is above all in the home that, before ever a word is spoken, children should experience God's love in the love which surrounds them. In the family they learn that God wants peace and mutual understanding among all human beings, who are called to be one great family.

MESSAGE FOR WORLD DAY OF PEACE, 1996

$\mathcal{L}$ord God, from you every family in heaven and on earth takes its name. Father, you are Love and Life.

Through your Son, Jesus Christ, born of woman, and through the Holy Spirit, the fountain of divine charity, grant that every family on earth may become for each successive generation a true shrine of life and love.

Grant that your grace may guide the thoughts and actions of husbands and wives for the good of their families and of all the families in the world.

Grant that the young may find in the family solid support for their human dignity and for their growth in truth and love.

Grant that love, strengthened by the grace of the sacrament of marriage, may prove mightier than all the weaknesses and trials through which our families sometimes pass.

Through the intercession of the Holy Family of Nazareth, grant that the Church may fruitfully carry out her worldwide mission in the family and through the family.

We ask this of you, who are Life, Truth, and Love with the Son and the Holy Spirit. Amen.

PRAYER FOR THE 1980 SYNOD OF BISHOPS

SOLIDARITY AND HUMAN RELATIONSHIPS

Much to be envied are those who can give
their lives for something greater than
themselves in loving service to others.
This, more than words or deeds alone,
is what draws people to Christ.

ADDRESS AT CARMEL MISSION, MONTEREY, 1987

*P*eople need to be treated individually as persons, in the knowledge that Christ shed all his Precious Blood for each of them.

AD LIMINA APOSTOLORUM—
BISHOPS' CONFERENCE OF BRAZIL, 10

*T*rue happiness lies in giving ourselves in love to our brothers and sisters.

MESSAGE TO YOUNG PEOPLE,
CAMAGÜEY, CUBA, 1998

*N*o one can consider himself extraneous or indifferent to the lot of another member of the human family. No one can say that he is not responsible for the well-being of his brother or sister.

CENTESIMUS ANNUS

*E*very man is his "brother's keeper," because God entrusts us to one another.

EVANGELIUM VITAE

$\mathcal{T}$he path of human solidarity is the path of service; and true service means selfless love, open to the needs of all, without distinction of persons, with the explicit purpose of reinforcing each person's sense of God-given dignity.

MEETING WITH CHARITIES, SAN ANTONIO, 1987

$\mathcal{S}$olidarity is not a feeling of vague compassion or shallow distress at the misfortunes of so many people, both near and far. On the contrary, it is a firm and persevering determination to commit oneself to the common good; that is to say to the good of all and of each individual, because we are all really responsible for all....

The exercise of solidarity within each society is valid when its members recognize one another as persons. Those who are more influential, because they have a greater share of goods and common services, should feel responsible for the weaker and be ready to share with them all they possess. Those who are weaker, for their part, in the same spirit of solidarity, should not adopt a purely passive attitude or one that is destructive of the social fabric, but, while claiming their legitimate rights, should do what they can for the good of all. The intermediate groups, in their turn, should not selfishly insist on their particular interests, but respect the interests of others.

SOLLICITUDO REI SOCIALIS

The poor…are your brothers and sisters in Christ. You must never be content to leave them just the crumbs from the feast. You must take of your substance, and not just of your abundance, in order to help them. And you must treat them like guests at your family table.

HOMILY AT YANKEE STADIUM, NEW YORK, 1979

Other people are not rivals from whom we must defend ourselves, but brothers and sisters to be supported. They are to be loved for their own sakes, and they enrich us by their very presence.

EVANGELIUM VITAE

A society of genuine solidarity can be built only if the well-off, in helping the poor, do not stop at giving from what they do not need. Moreover, offering material things is not enough: what is needed is a spirit of sharing, so that we consider it an honor to be able to devote our care and attention to the needs of our brothers and sisters in difficulty....Those living in poverty can wait no longer: they need help *now* and so have a right to receive *immediately* what they need.

MESSAGE FOR WORLD DAY OF PEACE, 1998

*M*erciful love is absolutely necessary, in particular, for people who are close to one another: for husbands and wives, parents and children, and among friends....We must ask ourselves whether human relationships are being based, as they should be, on the merciful love and forgiveness revealed by God in Jesus Christ. We must examine our own heart and see how willing we are to forgive and to accept forgiveness in this world as well as in the next.

HOMILY AT NEW ORLEANS, 1987

*T*he more you cling to Jesus, the more capable you will become of being close to one another....

Message for World Youth Day, 1996

*K*eep Jesus Christ in your hearts, and you will recognize his face in every human being. You will want to help him out in all his needs: the needs of your brothers and sisters. This is the way we prepare ourselves to meet Jesus, when he will come again, on the last day, as the judge of the living and the dead....

Address, Shea Stadium, New York, 1979

*J*esus is living next to you, in the brothers and sisters with whom you share your daily existence. His visage is that of the poorest, of the marginalized who not infrequently are victims of an unjust model of development, in which profit is given first place and the human being is made a means rather than an end. Jesus' dwelling is wherever a human person is suffering because rights are denied, hopes betrayed, anxieties ignored. There, in the midst of humankind, is the dwelling of Christ, who asks you to dry every tear in his name, and to remind whoever feels lonely that no one whose hope is placed in him is ever alone.

MESSAGE FOR WORLD YOUTH DAY, 1996

*T*oday perhaps more than in the past, people are realizing that they are linked together by a common destiny, which is to be constructed together, if catastrophe for all is to be avoided...the good to which we are all called and the happiness to which we aspire cannot be obtained without an effort and commitment on the part of all, nobody excluded, and the consequent renouncing of personal selfishness.

SOLLICITUDO REI SOCIALIS

*I*t can hardly be hoped that children will one day be able to build a better world, unless there is a specific commitment to their education for peace. Children need to "learn peace": it is their right, and one which cannot be disregarded.

MESSAGE FOR WORLD DAY OF PEACE, 1996

$\mathscr{P}$eace is not a utopia, nor an inaccessible ideal, nor an unrealizable dream.

War is not an inevitable calamity.

Peace is possible.

And because it is possible, peace is our duty: our grave duty, our supreme responsibility.

Certainly peace is difficult; certainly it demands much good will, wisdom, and tenacity. But man can and he must make the force of reason prevail over the reasons of force....

And since peace, entrusted to the responsibility of men and women, remains even then a gift of God, it must also express itself in prayer to Him who holds the destinies of all peoples in His hands.

"NEGOTIATION," 1982

$\mathscr{S}$pirit of God, pour your light and your love into human hearts to achieve reconciliation between individuals, within families, between neighbors, in cities and villages, and within the institutions of civil society!

HOMILY AT THE NAVAL BASE ESPLANADE, LEBANON, 1997

$\mathcal{P}$ROGRESS AND THE MODERN WORLD

Men and women are made in the image and likeness of God. So people may never be regarded as mere objects, nor may they be sacrificed for political, economic, or social gain. We must never allow them to be manipulated or enslaved by ideologies or technology. Their God-given dignity and worth as human beings forbid this.

GREETING TO U.N. STAFF, 1995

$\mathcal{M}$an lives at the same time both in the world of material values and in that of spiritual values. For the individual living and hoping man, his needs, freedoms, and relationships with others never concern one sphere of values alone, but belong to both.

ADDRESS TO U.N. GENERAL ASSEMBLY, 1979

$\mathcal{M}$odern man easily forgets the proportion, or rather, the lack of proportion between what he has received and what he is obliged to give. He has grown so much in his own eyes and is so sure that everything is the work of his own genius and of his own "industry," that he no longer sees the One who is the Alpha and the Omega, the Beginning and the End, the One who is the First Source of all that is as well as its Final End, the One in whom all that exists finds its proper meaning.

HOMILY AT NEW ORLEANS, 1987

$\mathcal{D}$emocracy cannot be idolized to the point of making it a substitute for morality or a panacea for immorality. Fundamentally, democracy is a "system" and as such is a means and not an end. Its "moral" value is not automatic, but depends on conformity to the moral law to which it, like every other form of human behavior, must be subject....

EVANGELIUM VITAE

From bitter experience, we know that the fear of "difference," especially when it expresses itself in a narrow and exclusive nationalism which denies any rights to "the other," can lead to a true nightmare of violence and terror. And yet if we make the effort to look at matters objectively, we can see that, transcending all the differences which distinguish individuals and peoples, there is a fundamental commonality. For different cultures are but different ways of facing the question of the meaning of personal existence....Every culture is an effort to ponder the mystery of the world and in particular of the human person: it is a way of giving expression to the transcendent dimension of human life. The heart of every culture is its approach to the greatest of all mysteries: the mystery of God.

Our respect for the culture of others is therefore rooted in our respect for each community's attempt to answer the question of human life....

To cut oneself off from the reality of difference—or, worse, to attempt to stamp out that difference—is to cut oneself off from the possibility of sounding the depths of the mystery of human life....The "difference" which some find so threatening can, through respectful dialogue, become the source of a deeper understanding of the mystery of human existence.

ADDRESS TO U.N. GENERAL ASSEMBLY, 1995

*E*very person has the right to hear the "Good News" of the God who reveals and gives himself in Christ, so that each one can live out in its fullness his or her proper calling.

REDEMPTORIS MISSIO

*W*hen the Church demands religious freedom she is not asking for a gift, a privilege, or a permission dependent on contingent situations, political strategies, or the will of the authorities. Rather, she demands the effective recognition of an inalienable human right....It is not simply a matter of a right belonging to the Church as an institution, it is also a matter of a right belonging to every person and every people. Every individual and every people will be spiritually enriched to the extent that religious freedom is acknowledged and put into practice.

Meeting with Cuban Bishops, 1998

*R*eligious tolerance is based on the conviction that God wishes to be adored by people who are free: a conviction which requires us to respect and honor the inner sanctuary of conscience in which each person meets God.

Greeting in Baltimore Cathedral, 1995

*P*rogress usually tends to be measured according to the criteria of science and technology....Even so, this is not the only measure of progress, nor in fact is it the principal one. Much more important is the social and ethical dimension, which deals with human relations and spiritual values. In this area...society certainly owes much to the *"genius of women."*

Letter to Women

$\mathcal{W}$omanhood expresses the "human" as much as manhood does, but in a different and complementary way....It is only through the duality of the "masculine" and the "feminine" that the "human" finds full realization.

LETTER TO WOMEN

$\mathcal{T}$he disabled person is one of us and participates fully in the same humanity that we possess. It would be radically unworthy of man, and a denial of our common humanity, to admit to the life of the community, and thus admit to work, only those who are fully functional. To do so would be to practice a serious form of discrimination, that of the strong and healthy against the weak and sick.

LABOREM EXERCENS

$\mathcal{H}$owever true it may be that man is destined for work and called to it, in the first place work is "for man" and not man "for work."...in the final analysis it is always man who is the purpose of the work, whatever work it is that is done by man—even if the common

scale of values rates it as the merest "service,"
as the most monotonous, even the most
alienating work.

LABOREM EXERCENS

*I*t is a strict duty of justice and truth not to
allow fundamental human needs to remain
unsatisfied, and not to allow those burdened by
such needs to perish.

CENTESIMUS ANNUS

*W*hen the scale of values is inverted and
politics, the economy, and social activity are no
longer placed at the service of people, the
human person comes to be viewed as a means
rather than respected as the center and end of
all these activities, and man is made to suffer in
his essence and in his transcendent dimension.
Human beings are then seen simply as
consumers, and freedom is understood in a very
individualistic and reductive sense, or men and
women are seen as mere producers with little
room for the exercise of civil and political
liberties. None of these social and political

models fosters a climate of openness to the transcendence of the person who freely seeks God.

MEETING WITH CUBAN BISHOPS, 1998

*J*ustice will never be fully attained unless people see in the poor person, who is asking for help in order to survive, not an annoyance or a burden, but an opportunity for showing kindness and a chance for greater enrichment. Only such an awareness can give the courage needed to face the risk and the change involved in every authentic attempt to come to the aid of another.

CENTESIMUS ANNUS

*L*et us work together so that everyone may have bread.

ADDRESS TO WORLD FOOD SUMMIT, 1996

*T*he poor have needs which are not only material and economic, but also involve liberating their potential to work out their own

destiny and to provide for the well-being of
their families and communities.

WELCOME ADDRESS, NEWARK
INTERNATIONAL AIRPORT, 1995

$\mathcal{J}$t is manifestly unjust that a privileged few
should continue to accumulate excess goods,
squandering available resources, while masses
of people are living in conditions of misery at
the very lowest level of subsistence. Today, the
dramatic threat of ecological breakdown is
teaching us the extent to which greed and
selfishness—both individual and collective—
are contrary to the order of creation, an order
which is characterized by mutual inter-
dependence.

"THE ECOLOGICAL CRISIS," 1990

$\mathcal{J}$t is not wrong to want to live better; what
is wrong is a style of life which is presumed to
be better when it is directed toward "having"
rather than "being," and which wants to have
more, not in order to be more but in order to
spend life in enjoyment as an end in itself. It is
therefore necessary to create lifestyles in which

the quest for truth, beauty, goodness and communion with others for the sake of common growth are the factors which determine consumer choices, savings and investments.

CENTESIMUS ANNUS

I wish to appeal with simplicity and humility to everyone, to all men and women without exception. I wish to ask them to be convinced of the seriousness of the present moment and of each one's individual responsibility, and to implement—by the way they live as individuals and as families, by the use of their resources, by their civic activity, by contributing to economic and political decisions and by personal commitment to national and international undertakings—the measures inspired by solidarity and love of preference for the poor.

SOLLICITUDO REI SOCIALIS

*T*he poor ask for the right to share in enjoying material goods and to make good use of their capacity for work, thus creating a world that is more just and prosperous for all. The advancement of the poor constitutes a great opportunity for the moral, cultural and even economic growth of all humanity.

CENTESIMUS ANNUS

*T*he best kind of assistance is that which encourages the needy to become the primary artisans of their own social and cultural development.

CATHOLIC RELIEF SERVICES MESSAGE, 1995

*P*olitical leaders, and citizens of rich countries…especially if they are Christians, have the moral obligation, according to the degree of each one's responsibility, to take into consideration, in personal decisions and decisions of government,…this inter-dependence which exists between their conduct and the poverty and under-development of so many millions of people.

SOLLICITUDO REI SOCIALIS

$\mathcal{D}$evelopment must not be understood solely in economic terms, but in a way that is fully human. It is not only a question of raising all peoples to the level currently enjoyed by the richest countries, but rather of building up a more decent life through united labor, of concretely enhancing every individual's dignity and creativity, as well as his capacity to respond to his personal vocation, and thus to God's call. The apex of development is the exercise of the right and duty to seek God, to know him and to live in accordance with that knowledge.

<small>CENTESIMUS ANNUS</small>

$\mathcal{S}$ide-by-side with the miseries of underdevelopment, themselves unacceptable, we find ourselves up against a form of *superdevelopment*, equally inadmissible, because like the former it is contrary to what is good and to true happiness. This superdevelopment, which consists in an excessive availability of every kind of material goods for the benefit of certain social groups, easily makes people slaves of "possession" and of immediate gratification, with no other horizon than the multiplication or continual replacement of the things already owned with others still better. This is the so-called civilization of "consumption" or "consumerism," which involves so much "throwing-away" and "waste." An object already owned but now superseded by something better is discarded, with no thought of its possible lasting value in itself, nor of some other human being who is poorer.

All of us experience firsthand the sad effects of this blind submission to pure consumerism: in the first place a crass materialism, and at the same time a radical dissatisfaction, because one quickly learns—unless one is shielded from the flood of publicity and the ceaseless and tempting offers of products—that the more one possesses the more one wants, while deeper aspirations remain unsatisfied and perhaps even stifled.

SOLLICITUDO REI SOCIALIS

To "have" objects and goods does not in itself perfect the human subject, unless it contributes to the maturing and enrichment of that subject's "being," that is to say unless it contributes to the realization of the human vocation as such....

There are some people—the few who possess much—who do not really succeed in "being" because, through a reversal of the hierarchy of values, they are hindered by the cult of "having"; and there are others—the many who have little or nothing—who do not succeed in realizing their basic human vocation because they are deprived of essential goods.

The evil does not consist in "having" as such, but in possessing without regard for the quality and the ordered hierarchy of the goods one has. Quality and hierarchy arise from the subordination of goods and their availability to man's "being" and his true vocation.

SOLLICITUDO REI SOCIALIS

*P*art of the teaching and most ancient practice of the Church is her conviction that she is obliged by her vocation—she herself, her ministers and each of her members—to relieve the misery of the suffering, both far and near, not only out of her "abundance" but also out of her "necessities." Faced by cases of need, one cannot ignore them in favor of superfluous church ornaments and costly furnishings for divine worship; on the contrary it could be obligatory to sell these goods in order to provide food, drink, clothing and shelter for those who lack these things....here we are shown a "hierarchy of values"...between "having" and "being," especially when the "having" of a few can be to the detriment of the "being" of many others.

SOLLICITUDO REI SOCIALIS

The best legacy you can leave to future generations will be to pass on the higher values of the Spirit. It is not a matter of merely preserving some of these, but rather of promoting an ethical and civic training which will help people to accept new values and to reshape their own character and the heart of society on the basis of an education for freedom, social justice, and responsibility.

MESSAGE TO YOUNG PEOPLE, CAMAGÜEY, CUBA, 1998

Social injustice and unjust social structures exist only because individuals and groups of individuals deliberately maintain or tolerate them. It is these personal choices, operating through structures, that breed and propagate situations of poverty, oppression, and misery. For this reason, overcoming "social" sin and reforming the social order itself must begin with the conversion of our hearts.

Meeting with Charities, San Antonio, 1987

The purpose of a business firm is not simply to make a profit, but is to be found in its very existence as a community of persons who in various ways are endeavoring to satisfy their basic needs, and who form a particular group at the service of the whole of society. Profit is a regulator of the life of a business, but it is not the only one; other human and moral factors must also be considered which, in the long term, are at least equally important for the life of a business.

Centesimus Annus

When man turns his back on the Creator's plan, he provokes a disorder which has inevitable repercussions on the rest of the created order. If man is not at peace with God, then earth itself cannot be at peace.

"The Ecological Crisis," 1990

*W*hen man disobeys God and refuses to submit to his rule, nature rebels against him and no longer recognizes him as its "master," for he has tarnished the divine image in himself. The claim to ownership and use of created things remains still valid, but after sin its exercise becomes difficult and full of suffering.

SOLLICITUDO REI SOCIALIS

*T*he dominion granted to man by the Creator is not an absolute power, nor can one speak of a freedom to "use and misuse," or to dispose of things as one pleases. The limitation imposed from the beginning by the Creator himself and expressed symbolically by the prohibition not to "eat of the fruit of the tree" shows clearly enough that, when it comes to the natural world, we are subject not only to biological laws but also to moral ones, which cannot be violated with impunity.

SOLLICITUDO REI SOCIALIS

$\mathcal{W}$e must not be afraid of the future. We must not be afraid of man. It is no accident that we are here. Each and every human person has been created in the "image and likeness" of the One who is the origin of all that is. We have within us the capacities for wisdom and virtue. With these gifts, and with the help of God's grace, we can build in the next century and the next millennium a civilization worthy of the human person, a true culture of freedom. We can and must do so! And in doing so, we shall see that the tears of this century have prepared the ground for a new springtime of the human spirit.

ADDRESS TO U.N. GENERAL ASSEMBLY, 1995

THE CHURCH

*The Church's fundamental function
in every age and particularly in ours is to
direct man's gaze, to point the awareness and
experience of the whole of humanity toward
the mystery of Christ, to help all men to be
familiar with the profundity of the
Redemption taking place in Christ Jesus.*

REDEMPTOR HOMINIS

The Church wishes to serve this single end: that each person may be able to find Christ, in order that Christ may walk with each person....

REDEMPTOR HOMINIS

The Church is catholic...because she is able to present in every human context the revealed truth, preserved by her intact in its divine content, in such a way as to bring it into contact with the lofty thoughts and just expectations of every individual and every people.

SLAVORUM APOSTOLI

The Church has endured for 2000 years. Like the mustard seed in the Gospel, she has grown and become a great tree, able to cover the whole of humanity with her branches.

TERTIO MILLENNIO ADVENIENTE

The Gospel of Jesus Christ, which is the great gift of God's love, is never in contrast with what is noble and pure in the life of any tribe or nation, since all good things are his gifts.

MEETING WITH NATIVE AMERICANS, PHOENIX, 1987

In the Church there are many different gifts. There is room for many different cultures and ways of doing things. But there is no room in the Church for selfishness.

MEETING WITH YOUTH, NEW ORLEANS, 1987

Salvation, which comes as a free gift of divine love in Christ, is not offered to us on a purely individual basis. It comes to us through and in the Church. Through our communion with Christ and with one another on earth, we are given a foretaste of that perfect communion reserved for heaven. Our communion is also meant to be a sign or sacrament which draws other people to Christ, so that all might be saved.

MEETING WITH LAITY, SAN FRANCISCO, 1987

The unity of all divided humanity is the will of God....On the eve of his sacrifice on the Cross, Jesus himself prayed to the Father for his disciples and for all those who believe in him, that they might be one, a living communion....How is it possible to remain divided, if we have been "buried" through Baptism in the Lord's death, in the very act by which God, through the death of his Son, has broken down the walls of division?

ET UNUM SINT

Ecumenism, the movement promoting Christian unity, is not just some sort of "appendix" which is added to the Church's traditional activity. Rather, ecumenism is an organic part of her life and work, and consequently must pervade all that she is and does; it must be like the fruit borne by a healthy and flourishing tree which grows to its full stature.

ET UNUM SINT

$\mathcal{L}$et us make no mistake about it: as if by some evangelical instinct, the humble and simple faithful spontaneously sense when the Gospel is being served in the Church and when it is eviscerated and asphyxiated by other interests.

OPENING ADDRESS, PUEBLA CONFERENCE, 1979

$\mathcal{I}$f there is one challenge facing the Church and her priests today, it is the challenge of transmitting the Christian message whole and entire, without letting it be emptied of its substance. The Gospel cannot be reduced to mere human wisdom. Salvation lies not in clever human words or schemes, but in the Cross and Resurrection of our Lord Jesus Christ.

ADDRESS AT VESPERS, ST. JOSEPH'S SEMINARY, 1995

$\mathcal{T}$HE SACRAMENTS

*In Christ, the Holy Spirit makes us God's
beloved children. The Incarnation of the
Son of God happened once, and is
unrepeatable. Divine adoption goes on all the
time, through the Church, the Body of Christ,
and particularly through the Sacraments,
through Baptism, Penance, the Eucharist,
and of course the Sacrament of Pentecost
that we call Confirmation.*

HOMILY AT CENTRAL PARK, 1995

On the day of our Baptism, we received the greatest gift God can bestow on any man or woman. No other honor, no other distinction will equal its value. For we were freed from sin and incorporated into Christ Jesus and his Body, the Church.

MESSAGE TO RELIGIOUS WOMEN,
WASHINGTON, D.C., 1979

Baptism is not simply a seal of conversion, a kind of external sign....Rather, it is the sacrament which signifies and effects rebirth from the Spirit, establishes real and unbreakable bonds with the Blessed Trinity, and makes us members of the Body of Christ, which is the Church.

REDEMPTORIS MISSIO

Confession is an act of honesty and courage; an act of entrusting ourselves, beyond sin, to the mercy of a loving and forgiving God. It is an act of the prodigal son who returns to his Father and is welcomed by him with the kiss of peace.

HOMILY AT SAN ANTONIO, 1987

$\mathcal{I}$t is a mark of greatness to be able to say: "I have made a mistake; I have sinned, Father; I have offended you, my God; I am sorry; I ask for pardon; I will try again because I rely on your strength and I believe in your love. And I know that the power of your Son's paschal mystery—the death and resurrection of our Lord Jesus Christ—is greater than my weaknesses and all the sins of the world. I will come and confess my sins and be healed, and I will live in your love!"

HOMILY AT SAN ANTONIO, 1987

$\mathcal{I}$n faithfully observing the centuries-old practice of the Sacrament of Penance—the practice of individual confession with a personal act of sorrow and the intention to amend and make satisfaction—the Church is therefore defending the human soul's individual right: man's right to a more personal encounter with the crucified forgiving Christ, with Christ saying, through the minister of the Sacrament of Reconciliation: "Your sins are forgiven" (Mk 2:5); "Go, and do not sin again" (Jn 8:11). As is evident, this is also a right on Christ's part with regard to every human being redeemed by him:

his right to meet each one of us in that key moment in the soul's life constituted by the moment of conversion and forgiveness.

REDEMPTOR HOMINIS

*I*n our celebration of the Word of God, the mystery of Christ opens up before us and envelops us. And through union with our Head, Jesus Christ, we become ever more increasingly one with all the members of his Body. As never before, it becomes possible for us to reach out and embrace the world, but to embrace it with Christ: with authentic generosity, with pure and effective love, in service, in healing, and in reconciliation.

MORNING PRAYER, ST. PATRICK'S CATHEDRAL, 1979

*I*n the Eucharist, the Son, who is of one being with the Father, the One whom only the Father knows, offers himself in sacrifice to the Father for humanity and for all creation. In the Eucharist Christ gives back to the Father everything that has come from him. Thus there is brought about a profound *mystery of justice on the part of the creature towards the Creator*. Man needs to honor his Creator by offering to him, in an act of thanksgiving and praise, all that he has received. *Man must never lose sight of this debt,* which he alone, among all other earthly realities, is capable of acknowledging and paying back as the one creature made in God's own image and likeness. At the same time, given his creaturely limitations and sinful condition, man would be incapable of making this act of justice towards the Creator, had not Christ himself, the Son who is of one being with the Father and also true man, first given us the Eucharist.

GIFT AND MYSTERY

The Eucharist...shows us...what value each person, our brother or sister, has in God's eyes, if Christ offers himself equally to each one, under the species of bread and wine. If our Eucharistic worship is authentic, it must make us grow in awareness of the dignity of each person....

Christ comes into the hearts of our brothers and sisters and visits their consciences. How the image of each and every one changes, when we become aware of this reality, when we make it the subject of our reflections!

DOMINICAE CENAE

*E*ucharistic worship is not so much worship of the inaccessible transcendence as worship of the divine condescension, and it is also the merciful and redeeming transformation of the world in the human heart.

DOMINICAE CENAE

THE PRIESTHOOD

If we take a close look at what contemporary men and women expect from priests, we will see that, in the end, they have but one great expectation: they are thirsting for Christ. Everything else—their economic, social, and political needs—can be met by any number of other people. From the priest they ask for Christ! And from him they have the right to receive Christ, above all through the proclamation of the word.

GIFT AND MYSTERY

$\mathcal{I}$ am convinced that a priest…should… have no fear of being "behind the times," because the human "today" of every priest is included in the "today" of Christ the Redeemer. For every priest, in every age, the greatest task is each day to discover his own priestly "today" in the "today" of Christ.…

GIFT AND MYSTERY

$\mathcal{W}$hat does it mean to be a priest? According to Saint Paul, it means above all to be *a steward of the mysteries of God*.…The steward is not the owner, but the one to whom the owner entrusts his goods so that he will manage them justly and responsibly. In exactly the same way the priest receives from Christ the treasures of salvation, in order duly to distribute them among the people to whom he is sent. These treasures are those of faith.…No one may consider himself the "owner" of these treasures; they are meant for us all. But, by reason of what Christ laid down, the priest has the task of administering them.

GIFT AND MYSTERY

Christ needs holy priests! Today's world demands holy priests! Only a holy priest can become, in an increasingly secularized world, a resounding witness to Christ and his Gospel. And only thus can a priest become a guide for men and women and a teacher of holiness. People, especially the young, are looking for such guides. A priest can be a guide and teacher only to the extent that he becomes an authentic witness!

GIFT AND MYSTERY

If Christ—by his free and sovereign choice, clearly attested to by the Gospel and by the Church's constant Tradition—entrusted only to men the task of being an "icon" of his countenance as "shepherd" and "bridegroom" of the Church through the exercise of the ministerial priesthood, this in no way detracts from the role of women, or for that matter from the role of the other members of the Church who are not ordained to the sacred ministry, since *all* share equally in the dignity proper to the "common priesthood" based on Baptism.

These role distinctions should not be viewed in accordance with the criteria of functionality typical in human societies. Rather they must be understood according to the particular criteria of the *sacramental economy*, i.e., the economy of "signs" which God freely chooses in order to become present in the midst of humanity.

LETTER TO WOMEN

ℳARY

Like Mary, you must not be afraid to allow the Holy Spirit to help you become intimate friends of Christ. Like Mary, you must put aside any fear, in order to take Christ to the world in whatever you do—in marriage, as single people in the world, as students, as workers, as professional people. Christ wants to go to many places in the world, and to enter many hearts, through you. Just as Mary visited Elizabeth, so you too are called to "visit" the needs of the poor, the hungry, the homeless, those who are alone or ill. . . .

HOMILY AT CENTRAL PARK, 1995

This woman of faith, Mary of Nazareth, the Mother of God, has been given to us as a model in our pilgrimage of faith. From Mary we learn to surrender to God's will in all things. From Mary, we learn to trust even when all hope seems gone. From Mary, we learn to love Christ, her Son and the Son of God. For Mary is not only the Mother of God, she is Mother of the Church as well.

MESSAGE TO PRIESTS, WASHINGTON, D.C., 1979

At Cana in Galilee there is shown only one concrete aspect of human need, apparently a small one and of little importance ("They have no wine"). But it has a symbolic value: this coming to the aid of human needs means, at the same time, bringing those needs within the radius of Christ's messianic mission and salvific power. Thus there is a mediation: Mary places herself between her Son and mankind in the reality of their wants, needs and sufferings. She puts herself "in the middle," that is to say she acts as a mediatrix not as an outsider, but in her position as mother. She knows that as such she can point out to her son the needs of mankind, and in fact, she "has the right" to do so. Her mediation is thus in the nature of

110

intercession: Mary "intercedes" for mankind. And that is not all. As a mother she also wishes the messianic power of her son to be manifested, that salvific power of his which is meant to help man in his misfortunes, to free him from the evil which in various forms and degrees weighs heavily upon his life....

Another essential element of Mary's maternal task is found in her words to the servants: "Do whatever he tells you." The Mother of Christ presents herself as the spokeswoman of her Son's will, pointing out those things which must be done so that the salvific power of the Messiah may be manifested. At Cana, thanks to the intercession of Mary and the obedience of the servants, Jesus begins "his hour."

REDEMPTORIS MATER

O blessed Virgin, Mother of God, Mother of Christ, Mother of the Church, look upon us mercifully at this hour!

Virgo fidelis, faithful Virgin, pray for us! Teach us to believe as you believed! Make our faith in God, in Christ, in the Church, always to be limpid, serene, courageous, strong and generous.

Mater amabilis, Mother worthy of love! Mater pulchrae dilectionis, Mother of fair love, pray for us! Teach us to love God and our brothers, as you loved them: make our love for others to be always patient, kindly, respectful.

Causa nostrae laetitiae, Cause of our joy, pray for us! Teach us to be able to grasp, in faith, the paradox of Christian joy, which springs up and blooms from sorrow, renunciation, and union with your sacrificed Son: make our joy to be always genuine and full, in order to be able to communicate it to all! Amen.

PRAYER AT LOURDES GROTTO, VATICAN GARDENS, 1979

$\mathcal{I}$ leave you now with this prayer: that the Lord Jesus will reveal himself to each one of you, that he will give you the strength to go out and profess that you are Christian, that he will show you that he alone can fill your hearts. Accept his freedom and embrace his truth, and be messengers of the certainty that you have been truly liberated through the death and Resurrection of the Lord Jesus. This will be the new experience, the powerful experience, that will generate, through you, a more just society and a better world.

God bless you and may the joy of Jesus be always with you!

MESSAGE TO STUDENTS,
THE CATHOLIC UNIVERSITY, 1979

$\mathcal{P}$ERMISSIONS AND ACKNOWLEDGMENTS

The compiler wishes to express his gratitude to the following for granting permission to reproduce material of which they are the publisher or copyright holder:

Selections from *Crossing the Threshold of Hope* by His Holiness Pope John Paul II: Translation copyright © 1994 by Alfred A. Knopf, Inc. Reprinted by permission of the publisher.

Selections from *Centesimus Annus*, *Dives in Misericordia*, *Dominicae Cenae*, *Dominum et Vivificantem*, *Et Unum Sint*, *Evangelium Vitae*, *Laborem Exercens*, *Letter of the Pope to the Children in the Year of the Family*, *Letter to Women*, *Redemptor Hominis*, *Redemptoris Mater*, *Redemptoris Missio*, *Salvifici Doloris*, *Slavorum Apostoli*, *Sollicitudo Rei Socialis*, *Tertio Millennio Adveniente*, and *Veritatis Splendor* are reprinted by permission of Libreria Editrice Vaticana, 00120 Città del Vaticano.

Selections from the Holy Father's speeches, homilies, addresses, prayers, and greetings are reprinted by permission of *L' Osservatore Romano*.

Interior illustrations by Christine Kraus.

Photos

page ii: Pope John Paul hugs two children
upon his arrival in Baltimore, Maryland, in
1995. *(CNS photo)*

page v: Pope John Paul II pauses to pray at
the National Shrine of the Basilica of the
Assumption in Baltimore, 1995. *(CNS photo by
Michael Okoniewski)*

page 113: Pope John Paul II distributes
Communion at the Mass for World Youth Day,
1989. *(CNS photo by Arturo Mari)*

ANNUAL REVIEW OF MICROBIOLOGY

EDITORIAL COMMITTEE (1991)

ANNUAL REVIEW OF MICROBIOLOGY

VOLUME 45, 1991

L. NICHOLAS ORNSTON, *Editor*

Yale University

ALBERT BALOWS, *Associate Editor*

Centers for Disease Control, Atlanta

E. PETER GREENBERG, *Associate Editor*

University of Iowa, Iowa City

ANNUAL REVIEWS INC.   4139 EL CAMINO WAY   P.O. BOX 10139   PALO ALTO, CALIFORNIA 94303–0897

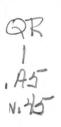

QR
1
.A5
N.45

International Standard Serial Number: 0066–4227
International Standard Book Number: 0–8243–1145-0
Library of Congress Catalog Card Number: 49-432
Annual Review and publication titles are registered trademarks of Annual Reviews
Inc.

∞ The paper used in this publication meets the minimum requirements of American National Standard for Information Sciences—Permanence of Paper for Printed
Library Materials, ANSI Z39.48-1984.

Typesetting by Kachina Typesetting Inc., Tempe, Arizona; John Olson, President
Typesetting Coordinator, Janis Hoffman

PRINTED AND BOUND IN THE UNITED STATES OF AMERICA

PREFACE

There is no dearth of information in our age. Indeed, the abundance of accessible data could be regarded as a protective covering that hides knowledge from our view. Should one have any doubts about this, ask any student what represents the greatest obstacle to learning. What knowledge is likely to be most important? How do we bring it forth without leaving behind something that is even more important? The driving force in this quest must be curiosity. The quality of science, as it is learned or as it is taught, is determined by the quality of the questions posed.

A good scientist, nascent or established, asks bold questions and tests them rigorously. In this context, existing information is called upon and new information gained. Perhaps the most difficult lesson for students is that present knowledge is not absolute. After years of taking multiple choice tests, students are not prepared to recognize that an insight challenging established knowledge is a source of delight. One way to trigger their curiosity is to introduce a simple concept with myriad consequences. For example, creatures with small size and limited genome are likely to be specialists that enter into consortia with other organisms.

One can ask the student, as an act of imagination, to become the microorganism: From the perspective of its niche, review the creature's requirements and opportunities, and allocate resources to optimize survival. Abandon preconceptions. A microorganism may behave very badly (when viewed from its host's perspective), but the imaginary microorganism's role should be acted with zeal. Remember that anyone who has attempted to lead a good and decent life is entitled to a few hours playing the villain. Furthermore, a visit to the soul of a villain may give valuable insight into the cause of villainous behavior. There are no recorded instances of microorganisms possessing souls, but a visit to the world-view of a microorganism may prove enlightening to the microbiologist. Such visits make vivid the diversity of microorganisms and their essential role in the balance of Nature.

The sources of delight within this volume were selected by the members of the Editorial Committee of the *Annual Review of Microbiology*. Good actors all, they have visited distant places and returned to tell the tale. They had questions that demanded the information provided in the review articles, and this information was shaped into knowledge by questions posed by both the

(*continued*)   v

reviewers and the authors of the reviewed articles. All of these individuals deserve our gratitude.

Guests of the editorial board in the planning of this volume were Edward Katz, Gary Sayler, and Simon Silver. Their contributions are deeply appreciated. Production of this volume remains in the highly capable hands of Amanda Suver. Rosemarie Hansen has assumed the difficult task of organizing the editor, and her successes are testament to remarkable skill.

L. Nicholas Ornston
EDITOR

Annual Review of Microbiology
Volume 45, 1991

CONTENTS

MY KIND OF BIOLOGY, *Ralph S. Wolfe*   1

SERINE β-LACTAMASES AND PENICILLIN-BINDING PROTEINS,
   Jean-Marie Ghuysen   37

GENETICALLY ENGINEERED BACULOVIRUSES AS AGENTS FOR PEST
   CONTROL, *H. Alan Wood and Robert R. Granados*   69

TECHNIQUES FOR SELECTION OF INDUSTRIALLY IMPORTANT
   MICROORGANISMS, *D. Bernie Steele and Mark D. Stowers*   89

CONTROL OF CARBON AND NITROGEN METABOLISM IN *BACILLUS
   SUBTILIS*, *Susan H. Fisher and Abraham L. Sonenshein*   107

POLYMERASE CHAIN REACTION: Applications in Environmental
   Microbiology, *R. J. Steffan and R. M. Atlas*   137

MSDNA AND BACTERIAL REVERSE TRANSCRIPTASE, *Masayori Inouye
   and Sumiko Inouye*   163

PUTATIVE VIRULENCE FACTORS OF *CANDIDA ALBICANS*,
   Jim E. Cutler   187

REGULATION OF HUMAN IMMUNODEFICIENCY VIRUS REPLICATION,
   Bryan R. Cullen   219

VIRUSES OF THE PROTOZOA, *A. L. Wang and C. C. Wang*   251

VARICELLA-ZOSTER VIRUS LATENCY, *Kenneth D. Croen and
   Stephen E. Straus*   265

BIOCHEMICAL DIVERSITY OF TRICHLOROETHYLENE METABOLISM,
   B. D. Ensley   283

THE UNIVERSALLY CONSERVED GROE (HSP60) CHAPERONINS, *Jill
   Zeilstra-Ryalls, Olivier Fayet, and Costa Georgopoulos*   301

RNA EDITING IN TRYPANOSOMATID MITOCHONDRIA, *K. Stuart*   327

PLANT GENETIC CONTROL OF NODULATION, *Gustavo
   Caetano-Anollés and Peter M. Gresshoff*   345

CHAPERONE-ASSISTED ASSEMBLY AND MOLECULAR ARCHITECTURE OF
   ADHESIVE PILI, *Scott J. Hultgren, Staffan Normark, and Soman
   N. Abraham*   383

(*continued*)   vii

viii   CONTENTS   (*continued*)

GENE AMPLIFICATION IN *LEISHMANIA*, *Stephen M. Beverley*   417

IVERMECTIN AS AN ANTIPARASITIC AGENT FOR USE IN HUMANS,
William C. Campbell   445

HEPADNAVIRUSES AND HEPATOCELLULAR CARCINOMA, *Averell H.
Sherker and Patricia L. Marion*   475

MECHANISMS OF NATURAL RESISTANCE TO HUMAN PATHOGENIC
FUNGI, *Juneann W. Murphy*   509

NUCLEAR FUSION IN YEAST, *Mark D. Rose*   539

PROKARYOTIC OSMOREGULATION: Genetics and Physiology, *Laszlo
N. Csonka and Andrew D. Hanson*   569

PROPER AND IMPROPER FOLDING OF PROTEINS IN THE CELLULAR
ENVIRONMENT, *Björn Nilsson and Stephen Anderson*   607

INDEXES

SUBJECT INDEX   637

CUMULATIVE INDEX OF CONTRIBUTING AUTHORS, VOLUMES 41–45   649

CUMULATIVE INDEX OF CHAPTER TITLES, VOLUMES 41–45   651

OTHER REVIEWS OF INTEREST TO MICROBIOLOGISTS

From the *Annual Review of Biochemistry*, Volume 60 (1991)

The Enzymology of Protein Translocation Across the Escherichia coli *Plasma Membrane*, William Wickner, Arnold J. M. Driessen, and Franz-Ulrich Hartl
Bacteriophage Lambda DNA Maturation and Packaging, Helios Murialdo
Signal Transduction Pathways Involving Protein Phosphorylation in Prokaryotes, Robert B. Bourret, Katherine A. Borkovich, and Melvin I. Simon
The Biochemistry of AIDS, Yashwantrai N. Vaishnav and Flossie Wong-Staal

From the *Annual Review of Biophysics and Biophysical Chemistry*, Volume 20 (1991)

Bacterial Chemotaxis and the Molecular Logic of Intracellular Signal Transduction, Jeffry B. Stock, Gudrun S. Lukat, and Ann M. Stock
Chloramphenicol Acetyltransferase, W. V. Shaw and A. G. W. Leslie

From the *Annual Review of Cell Biology*, Volume 7 (1991)

Development of the Legume Root Nodule, Nicholas J. Brewin
Structures of Bacterial Photosynthetic Reaction Centers, J. Deisenhofer and Harmut Michel
Cell Cycle Regulation in the Yeasts Saccharomyces cerevisiae *and* Schizosaccharomyces pombe, Susan L. Forsburg and Paul Nurse
Activation of Replication Origins Within Yeast Chromosomes, Walton L. Fangman and Bonita J. Brewer
Signal Transduction During Pheromone Response in Yeast, Lorraine Marsh, Aaron M. Neiman, and Ira Herskowitz
Analyses of the Cytoskeleton in Saccharomyces cerevisiae, Frank Solomon

From the *Annual Review of Genetics*, Volume 25 (1991)

Gene Transfer Between Distantly Related Bacteria, Philippe Mazodier and Julian Davies
Regulation of Bacterial Oxidative Stress Genes, Bruce Demple
Regulation of Gene Expression in Fermentative and Respiratory Systems in Escherichia coli *and Related Bacteria*, E. C. C. Lin and S. Iuchi
Restriction and Modification Systems, Geoffrey G. Wilson and Noreen E. Murray

(*continued*)   ix

x   OTHER REVIEWS OF INTEREST   (*continued*)

Genetic Analysis of Yeast Phospholipid Biosynthesis, D. Michele Nikoloff and Susan A. Henry

Mechanisms and Biological Effects of Mismatch Repair, Paul Modrich

Modulation of Mutagenesis by Deoxyribonucleotide Levels, Bernard A. Kunz and Susanne E. Kohalmi

Spontaneous Mutation, John W. Drake

Regulation of Expression of the Late Genes of Bacteriophage T4, E. Peter Geiduscheck

From the *Annual Review of Medicine,* Volume 42 (1991)

Latency of the Human Herpesviruses, Kenneth D. Croen

Antiviral Therapy of HIV Infection, Douglas D. Richman

Non-AIDS Retroviral Infections in Humans, Dale E. McFarlin and William A. Blattner

Resistance of Viruses to Antiviral Drugs, A. G. Freifeld and J. M. Ostrove

Infectious Diarrhea, Mitchell J. Rubinoff and Michael Field

For the convenience of readers, a detachable order form/envelope is bound into the back of this volume.

Ralph S. Wolfe

Annu. Rev. Microbiol. 1991. 45:1–35

MY KIND OF BIOLOGY

Ralph S. Wolfe

Department of Microbiology, University of Illinois, Urbana, Illinois 61801

KEY WORDS: methanogenic bacteria, ferredoxin, Archaebacteria, coenzymes of
methanogenesis, interspecies hydrogen transfer

CONTENTS

Toward Microbiology 1
Ferredoxin.. 5
Methanobacillus omelianskii... 7
Interspecies Hydrogen Transfer.. 8
Coenzyme M, the Terminal Methyl Carrier 10
Archaebacteria 11
Coenzyme F$_{420}$, the Deazaflavin... 14
Factor 342, Methanopterin, the Coenzyme of C$_1$ Transfer............................... 14
Coenzyme F$_{430}$, the First Nickel Tetrapyrrole 15
Methanofuran, the Coenzyme of Formylation.. 16
7-Mercaptoheptanoylthreonine Phosphate (HS-HTP), the Coenzyme That
        Donates Electrons to the Methylreductase 17
Enzymology of Methanogenesis from CO$_2$ and H$_2$... 17
Microbial Diversity.. 20
Reflections.. 26

Because the rigid format of scientific publishing renders the published product nearly sterile of the fun of doing science, I have attempted to provide here some background and perspective on the contributions to science in which my laboratory played a part.

Toward Microbiology

I was 25 years old before I saw a living bacterial cell. As an undergraduate, I had majored in biology at Bridgewater College in Virginia, a small liberal arts college. Undergraduate biology at that time was mostly descriptive, but "Doc" Jopson in the biology department insisted that I take organic chemistry

1

0066-4227/91/1001-0001$02.00

and minor in chemistry; this advice was sound. I had been raised on the campus of a small college where my father taught religion and philosophy. He would go to the campus, present a lecture, and return home to work in his shop or garden. His summers were free of college obligations. To me in my late teens, this seemed an ideal way to spend one's life. The pay was poor, but the freedom was fantastic—especially with a three-month summer. After I had taught high school for a brief period, a friend who had just received his Master's degree in history at the University of Pennsylvania recommended Penn as a "good university"; so I hitchhiked to Philadelphia intent on getting a MS degree and then teaching in a small college. (I never reached the small college.)

In my youth, I had been fascinated by petrified bones and had thought that working in a museum or digging up petrified skeletons would be exciting. In Philadelphia, I went to the Academy of Natural Sciences, visited the paleontology research area of the museum, and talked to a curator. The experience was rather sobering. Here was an investigator in a dimly lit area working under a light bulb, surrounded by what seemed to be acres of petrified bones. I remember thinking on my way out that I would have to find something more alive than this.

A fixture at many universities are frustrated individuals who enjoy keeping graduate students in line. When I inquired at the graduate college office of the university about the possibility of doing graduate work in biology, I was told, "We don't have a department of biology. We have a department of botany and a department of zoology; now which will it be?" Off the top of my head I blurted out, "botany." "Well in that case, you must go to McFarlane Hall and talk with Dr. Schramm." Professor Schramm was a white-haired kindly man who seemed interested in me. Instead of asking what courses I had taken, he inquired as to what I knew about various subjects. One question in particular stands out in my memory: "Do you know anything about bacteriology?" I replied that I knew nothing, but that I had often thought that might be an interesting subject. So, he signed me up for general bacteriology. This was the only course I could take because I needed to find employment to support myself, and I asked him if any jobs were available in the department. A job in the herbarium involved mounting pressed flowers on sheets of paper; would I be interested? A job was a job, and since I was to be a student in botany this seemed to be an ideal way to learn the names of flowers. Besides, I could set my own hours. So my career as a graduate student in botany was launched.

I was enthusiastic, and on my way to the first class in bacteriology I wondered if I would get to see a living bacterial cell. I did; I was fascinated. As the laboratory course unfolded, the fact that one could start to grow these living cells in the afternoon and the next morning could read the results seemed incredible to me. This was my kind of biology. The course was taught by W. G. Hutchinson, and he turned me on to bacteriology. I did well—after all I was only taking one course—and when an opening occurred for a teaching assistant in bacteriology, Professor Hutchinson invited me to assist him. I was elated and did not hesitate to leave the job of mounting flowers. It had become painfully obvious to me that something was wrong; I could not remember the names of the plants! In contrast, I had no trouble remembering the names of bacteria.

So as my second year in graduate school began, I moved to the old public health laboratory on 34th Street where Professor Hutchinson introduced me to a young assistant professor, D. J. O'Kane, who had just arrived from Cornell and was setting up his laboratory. I was to be a teaching assistant in general bacteriology and would take a new course being developed by O'Kane to give students some exposure to biochemical activities of microbes. I never had a formal course in biochemistry, and sometimes it shows.

As a teaching assistant, I soon found that a successful laboratory course was based on thorough preparation. The degree of success depended on attention to details; everything must be checked: the cultures, the media, the glassware, the incubator. Assume nothing! It was great when everything worked. I especially enjoyed being a teaching assistant with W. G. Hutchinson. However, his interests were not in the area of bacterial physiology and metabolism, an area that was on the forefront at the time and that seemed attractive to me. So O'Kane accepted me as a graduate student, one intent on getting a terminal Master of Science degree. I worked on the enzyme hippicurase, from *Streptococcus*, a hydrolytic enzyme that cleaved a peptide-like bond and was considered of interest because the mechanism of peptide bond synthesis was unknown at the time. My initial attempts at research were rather painful for my professor, I'm afraid, especially when I didn't even know how to plot the data I generated. I needed to be spoonfed. Eventually, I found that doing the experiment on my own without letting my professor know was fun. When I thought I had established a scientific fact, we would talk. I liked this system; the thrill of discovery on one's own is the best motivating force.

After receiving a MS degree, I decided to take a year off from graduate school. Graduate students were paid $950 for nine months, so it was necessary to save enough money during that period to live during the summer. I wanted to see what nonacademic life was like and try to shore up my financial condition. I accepted a position as a technician in Ruth Patrick's laboratory at the Academy of Natural Sciences. She had become interested in devising ways for assaying the toxicity of stream pollutants. This work broadened my appreciation of biology. My professors at Penn encouraged me to continue graduate studies toward a PhD degree, but before returning to the university, my life became complete; Gretka Young, who worked for the American Friends Service Committee, and I were married in September, 1950. My goal of teaching in a small college would become untenable in the next three years as my professors made me aware that the PhD degree was a research degree, that to do research one needed proper equipment, and that adequate facilities were rarely found in a small college. I eventually would realize that I had been scientifically seduced.

Professor O'Kane offered me a choice of two thesis topics involving a new factor, the pyruvate oxidation factor, which he had worked on in the laboratory of I. C. Gunsalus at Cornell. This factor was later identified as lipoic acid. He wanted to know whether lipoic acid was involved in the oxidation of pyruvate by *Escherichia coli* and *Clostridium butyricum*. I instantly chose the clostridial system because it seemed challenging and unknown. I was able to show with treated extracts that diphosphothiamin, coenzyme A, and ferrous ions were required for the oxidation of pyruvate, but I could find no role for lipoic acid (166). Various dyes could be used as electron acceptors to bypass hydrogenase; however, I could not make progress on the natural electron acceptor. Exchange of $^{14}CO_2$ with the carboxyl group of pyruvate occurred readily (167). These experiments introduced me to the use of radioisotopes. I completed my thesis work in June 1953, a few months after our first child, Danny, was born.

The event that encouraged me to consider the possibility of an academic position in a research environment involved the preparation of my first manuscript from part of my thesis. I was apprehensive about submitting a manuscript to the *Journal of Biological Chemistry* because I lacked confidence in writing. However, I carefully patterned the manuscript in the style of the journal and gave it to my professor. He returned it and announced, "I think this is fine, Ralph; let's send it in." We did, and it was accepted! This was the first time anyone had ever expressed approval of my writing and gave me confidence that perhaps I could become successful at scientific writing. I owe much to D. J. O'Kane, who made me appreciate the importance of hard data in nailing down a concept as well as the importance of freedom in exploring and making discoveries. Later, I would use this same philosophy in running my own laboratory.

Very few academic jobs were available in the summer of 1953. I had two interviews, one at a small college, which had only a case-full of student microscopes as equipment, and one at the University of Illinois. I was hired as an instructor at Urbana by H. O. Halvorson. My case had been presented in a sufficiently positive way through the efforts of my scientific grandfather, I. C. Gunsalus (known to everyone as Gunny). The Department of Bacteriology was an exciting place; with recent appointments of Halvorson, Spiegleman, Luria, Gunsalus, and Juni, the department was considered one of the best in the country, and I was fortunate to join it. A heavy teaching load didn't leave much time for research, and my program was rather slow in evolving. Before

I started anything, I was determined to prepare a manuscript for publication from the last part of my thesis. So I closed my office door whenever I had a chance and worked on the manuscript.

This action was interpreted as inaction but led to a revelation of one of the truisms of academic life. One day there was a knock on my office door. Professor Halvorson entered, sat down, and in a very concerned manner said, "I just want to tell you one thing—you are paid to teach; you get promotions for doing research." He departed immediately, and I pondered these words of wisdom. They are as true today as they were 38 years ago.

The faculty wanted to augment their specialties with someone who had a real interest in diverse organisms and who would want to teach a van Niel–type course. Largely through persuasion by Gunny, van Niel accepted me as an observer in his course at Pacific Grove for the summer of 1954. The class was a fantastic experience that opened my eyes to a microbial world of unfamiliar organisms and made it possible for me to attempt to fill the niche for which I had been hired at Urbana. I returned to Illinois with many ideas from van Niel that, together with some from Gunny, Luria, Sherman, and myself, became an organisms course that would be taught for nearly three decades.

When I left Penn, O'Kane generously allowed me to take the pyruvate clastic system with me to serve as a basis for my research program. In response to an inquiry about equipment that I would need to get started, I had suggested to Professor Halvorson a colorimeter, a vacuum pump (with which to freeze dry cell extracts) and a Warburg apparatus. He seemed a little dismayed by this, and I thought his response was a bit curious, for the request seemed modest to me. A year later, I was told, "We have enough biochemists around here; I hired you because I thought you weren't one." The message was clear—I had better begin visibly studying unusual organisms or I did not have a future at Illinois. Having a mandate to study such organisms was great, but I also instinctively knew that to gain the respect of the scientific community I must be involved in an in-depth study of a biochemical phenomenon. Isolation and cultivation of "funny bugs" (although challenging and rewarding) alone was not enough. I knew my abilities would limit how far I could go, but I was determined to become a respectable microbiologist.

Ferredoxin

As a graduate student I poured ferredoxin down the sink for three years. Fortunately, much later one of my own graduate students was involved in its discovery. At the time of my studies, the research community knew that clostridia did not possess cytochromes. Because no other protein electron carriers were known, we assumed that the unknown electron acceptor for pyruvate oxidation would be a soluble cofactor. Formation of carbon dioxide and acetyl phosphate from pyruvate could readily be followed in treated cell extracts upon addition of dyes, but I could find no evidence for a coenzyme that could play a role similar to nicotinamide adenine dinucleotide (NAD) or flavin adenine dinucleotide (FAD). When I accepted my first graduate student, Robert Mortlock, at Urbana, I suggested that he identify the electron acceptor and study the reversal of the reaction. He obtained convincing evidence for synthesis of pyruvate from acetate and carbon dioxide (99, 100). The nature of the electron acceptor remained obscure, however.

In the summer of 1957, an undergraduate student, Raymond Valentine, expressed an interest in learning about research with bacteria, and I suggested that he begin by helping Mortlock with studies on the pyruvate clastic reaction. Valentine was highly motivated, and the two developed an isopropanol precipitate of crude cell extract that actively decarboxylated pyruvate with methyl-viologen as electron acceptor. He realized the significance of this resolved extract and wanted to pursue study of the natural electron acceptor for a thesis.

One of the most difficult decisions in science is deciding when to quit one line of research and start a new one. There is always the possibility that one more cast might do it. I had been casting for a strike on the electron acceptor for about eight years and was eager to try something new. So, much to Valentine's disappointment, we dropped the clastic reaction and began to study anaerobic allantoin degradation. To augment Valentine's training, arrangements were made for him to spend a summer working on organic synthesis with Roe Bloom, an organic chemist with whom I was acquainted at the DuPont Company in Wilmington, Delaware. In the meantime, a paper by the DuPont nitrogen fixation group headed by Carnahan appeared. Mortenson had found that the addition of pyruvate to extracts of *Clostridium pasteurianum* greatly stimulated nitrogen fixation. We realized that the electron acceptor from pyruvate oxidation for which we had an assay might be the electron donor for nitrogenase, and Valentine communicated this to Gunny, who was a consultant to DuPont at the time. Gunny picked up the phone and arranged for Valentine to join the nitrogen fixation group for the summer. He applied the isopropanol precipitation procedure developed in Urbana to extracts of *C. pasteurianum* and produced a methyl-viologen-dependent pyruvate clastic reaction. With this assay, he began to test various nitrogenase preparations and fractions. Mortenson suggested that he should test a brown preparation stored in a certain refrigerator, a fraction prepared by Ralph Hardy before he left the company. When he opened the refrigerator, he found two bottles, each of which contained a brown fluid. The first one tested instantly denatured the proteins of the assay mixture; it turned out to be chromate cleaning solution. A sample from the second complemented the resolved enzyme preparation; the electron carrier had been located and could donate electrons to hydrogenase. (The first name considered for the carrier was "co-hydrogenase.") Under Mortenson's leadership, the protein was fractionated, purified, and shown to be an iron-sulfur protein, a new type of electron carrier. The naming group at the DuPont Company named this new product ferredoxin.

Upon returning to Urbana, Valentine wanted to pursue ferredoxin as a thesis, but I felt that the discovery had been made in DuPont laboratories, and to continue to study the ferredoxin of a saccharolytic *Clostridium* in my laboratory would be inappropriate. However, looking for ferredoxin in other anaerobes would not be a problem. We used the finding of ferredoxin in *Micrococcus lactilyticus* as a lever with which to pry the original proprietary data on *C. pasteurianum* into publication, and the papers were published back-to-back (98, 139). In the next 10 years, hundreds of papers on this new type of iron sulfur protein electron carrier, ferredoxin, appeared. We explored several ferredoxin-dependent reactions (18, 19, 136, 137, 140, 145).

I wished to know if the pyruvate reactions in *Bacillus macerans*, one of the sugar-fermenting members of the genus *Bacillus*, were similar to those of *C. butyricum*. Raymond Hamilton (65) studied the exchange reactions of CO_2 and of formate with the carboxyl group of pyruvate and found that the CO_2 exchange reaction was similar to that in *C. butyricum*, but that a separate formate-pyruvate exchange reaction also occurred.

Methanobacillus omelianskii

In 1960, I arranged to spend my first sabbatical leave in the laboratory of Sidney Elsden at Sheffield, England. He had been a student of Marjorie Stephenson and C. B. van Niel and was interested in microbial physiology. I thought he would be an ideal sounding board for the major purpose of my sabbatical, which was to write a guide to the isolation of unusual organisms from nature, for which I had received a Guggenheim Fellowship. After about a month in the library, I realized that this project wasn't much fun, so I threw down the pencil and moved to a lab bench. We decided that methane bacteria would be a good project. H. A. Barker kindly sent us a culture of *Methanobacillus omelianskii*, which I was able to culture. Our purpose was to study the synthesis of amino acids from [^{14}C]-labeled CO_2 and acetate by this unusual anaerobe. We got off to a good start; the labeling patterns were definitive on several amino acids, and Martin Knight continued the project for his thesis (85).

I returned to Urbana convinced that *M. omelianskii* could be mass cultured, and that the time was ripe to go after the biochemistry of methanogenesis. My colleague, M. J. Wolin, in the Department of Dairy Science, was interested in this subject, so I invited him to collaborate. We hired Eileen Wolin to initiate cultures and scale them to the 3-liter–florence flask stage. They were then brought to my laboratory where carboys were inoculated. We developed a production line so that we could harvest a carboy of cells at least three times a week, each carboy yielding enough cells for one experiment. Cells were immediately broken in a Hughes press, and a dark brown cell extract was prepared. Norman Ryckman played an essential role in growing and harvesting cells and in preparing cell extracts. Old Warburg flasks fitted with serum stoppers served as reaction vessels, and samples of the flask's atmosphere were transferred by syringe to a gas chromatograph to test for methane formation. The first extract was tested in October 1961, and for the next five months the recorder pen never moved from the baseline except to respond to a standard injection of methane. Extracts refused to oxidize ethanol or acetaldehyde and reduce CO_2 to methane under any condition. In March, out of desperation, I tipped my old friend, pyruvate, into the extract. I shall never forget the zing of the recorder as the pen soared to the top of the chart and back precisely at the time methane should elute from the column. The first formation of methane by a cell-free extract had occurred (171).

This assay allowed us to optimize the system and to show that the role of pyruvate was to provide electrons, carbon dioxide, and ATP. The discovery by Blaylock & T. Stadtman (11) that the methyl group of methylcobalamin could be reduced to methane by extracts of *Methanosarcina* in the presence of pyruvate was a major breakthrough. M. J. Wolin synthesized methylcobalamin, and we showed the ATP-dependent reduction of the methyl group to methane by extracts of *M. omelianskii* (172) and that B_{12r} was the product (173). John Wood (178) studied the reaction and showed that the cobamide derivatives, methyl-Factor B, and methyl-Factor III also were effective methyl donors for methanogenesis (180). The ferredoxin-dependent conversion of formate or acetaldehyde was worked out by Winston Brill (18, 19), and Wood (176) showed that the methyl group of methyl-tetrahydrofolate was reduced to methane. Additional studies suggested that carbon-3 of serine was a precursor of methane via conventional C_1-tetrahydrofolate intermediates (175). Wood also obtained evidence for alkylation (177) and propylation (179) of a cobamide enzyme involved in methanogenesis. Wolin (170) found that viologen dyes were potent inhibitors of methanogenesis. These experiments were exciting as we groped to figure out how extracts of "*M. omelianskii*" made methane from carbon dioxide. The laboratory of T. Stadtman was the only other group actively working on this project.

Interspecies Hydrogen Transfer

In the summer of 1965, I asked Marvin Bryant, who had recently joined the Department of Dairy Science, if he would teach me the Hungate technique. For the roll tube experiment, he suggested that we carry out an agar dilution series using *M. omelianskii* because one of his colleagues was not satisfied that the culture met the criteria of a pure culture. We decided to use a rich medium that contained rumen fluid to encourage the growth of any contaminants. In one series of roll tubes, we added H_2 and CO_2. We picked isolated colonies back into the ethanol carbonate medium of Barker, but nothing grew—not an unusual observation when working with methanogenic bacteria at that time. Soon the summer was over, and we returned to other duties. About seven months later, Bryant found a rack of roll tubes from our experiments in the incubator. One tube contained a large isolated colony, and, when he removed the rubber stopper, he found a strong negative pressure. The organism oxidized hydrogen, and a serial dilution in agar roll tubes established that the culture was pure and that it made methane. The organism was labeled strain M.o.H. and would not grow in the ethanol medium of Barker, so Hungate suggested to Bryant that the original culture must contain a companion organism that used ethanol as a substrate, and he should go after it. After many difficulties, Bryant succeeded in isolating the S organism, which was inhibited by the hydrogen that it produced.

M. J. Wolin realized what was going on. He blew the dust from his physical chemistry book and calculated the free energy change for the oxidation of ethanol to acetate and hydrogen vs the partial pressure of hydrogen. *M. omelianskii* was a symbiotic association of two organisms. The S organism oxidized ethanol to acetate and hydrogen; the methanogen, *Methanobacterium* strain M.o.H., lowered the partial pressure of hydrogen by oxidizing it to reduce CO_2 to CH_4; this allowed the anaerobic oxidation of ethanol by the S organism to become thermodynamically favorable. Thus, interspecies hydrogen transfer (the importance of the partial pressure of hydrogen in anaerobic biodegradation), one of the first principles of anaerobic microbial ecology, had been discovered. We thought this paper would be a suitable way to honor C. B. van Niel (22).

With the discovery that *M. omelianskii* was a mixed culture, the roof of my research program more or less collapsed. Much of Winston Brill's thesis could not be published because we did not know which enzymes came from which organism. During this work, I could not figure out why such a bright, dedicated student was having so much difficulty with variability of cell extracts. I have always regretted this and feel that I should have been more astute about the culture. Much of Abdel Allam's thesis could not be published, and Richard Jackson's work with Lovenberg on the amino acid sequence of ferredoxin was in doubt concerning which organism produced the iron sulfur protein. Five years of work on methanogenesis by extracts of *M. omelianskii* needed to be reinterpreted.

The real challenge now was to develop a mass culture technique and a method for growing cells on H_2 and CO_2. I accepted this challenge, but all attempts to culture strain M.o.H. by sparging gas through a liquid medium failed. In desperation, I developed a closed system in which a diaphram pump recirculated the gas atmosphere over heated copper and back into the culture vessel. I named this gadget the gaspirator. (Spiegleman referred to it as Wolfe's last gaspirator.) It provided a few good runs, but its performance was erratic, and it was abandoned. However, I developed a system for slowly shaking 200 ml of medium under a gas atmosphere of H_2 and CO_2 in a flask with a small continuous addition of gas (21). I was delighted that the inoculum grew when transferred to a 12-liter fermentor and could then be harvested or used to inoculate a 200-liter fermentor. Soon we had kilogram quantities of cells. This work could not have been done without Marvin Bryant, who patiently provided us with inocula of strain M.o.H. Langenberg (87) documented the electron microscopy of strain M.o.H. Anthony Roberton (109) studied the ATP requirement for methanogenesis from methylcobalamin by cell extracts of strain M.o.H. He showed that intracellular pools of ATP increased when cells were oxidizing hydrogen and carrying out methanogenesis, but decreased when hydrogen was removed (110).

Coenzyme M, the Terminal Methyl Carrier

Barry McBride arrived from the University of British Columbia, Vancouver, at a propitious time. A technology for growing cells on H_2 and CO_2 had been developed; he was able to contribute to the mass culture of cells at the 12-liter stage and was the first one to have the courage to grow a 200-liter batch of strain M.o.H on H_2 and CO_2. He discovered a new cofactor that was required for the formation of methane from the methyl group of methylcobalamin by cell extracts. Evidence suggested that this cofactor was involved in methyl transfer, so we named it coenzyme M (CoM) (94). He found a curious inhibition of methanogenesis by DDT (95). In testing various buffers to optimize the assay for CoM, he noticed that a strong garlic-like odor was produced in arsenate buffer, and we (96) documented the synthesis of dimethylarsine by cell extracts from methylcobalamin and arsenate. His work opened up a new era in the biochemistry of methanogenesis, one that we would follow for 20 years. We owe much to Barry McBride, who later pioneered use of the Frêter chamber for handling methanogens, the growth of methanogens on Petri dishes, the fluorescence of methanogen colonies, the use of the epifluorescence microscope to detect individual cells of methanogens, and the bright fluorescence of protozoa. Unfortunately, he did not receive proper acknowledgment for the discovery that individual cells of methanogens fluoresce.

The study of CoM was taken up by Craig Taylor, who over a five-year period purified the factor to homogeneity and determined its structure as 2-mercaptoethanesulfonic acid (128). He showed that the coenzyme was methylated on the reduced sulfur atom to form 2-(methylthio)ethanesulfonic acid, CH_3-S-CoM. Both forms of the coenzyme were chemically synthesized. CoM was identified as the unknown growth factor required by *Methanobrevibacter ruminantium* (126). Later, William Balch (8) studied its transport. A simplified enzymatic assay was developed for the synthesis of CH_3-S-CoM with methylcobalamin as the methyl donor, and the transmethylase that catalyzed this reaction was purified (127).

Because CH_3-S-CoM served as the substrate for methane formation in the absence of methylcobalamin, we considered both methylcobalamin and the transmethylase to be outside the natural pathway of methanogenesis. Attention now became focused on the CH_3-S-CoM methylreductase reaction, and Robert Gunsalus pursued this reaction as a thesis topic (64). He collaborated with James Romesser in synthesizing a variety of CoM analogues (59). We wanted to know just how specific the coenzyme was, and of all the derivatives tested only ethyl-CoM showed a positive effect, producing ethane at 20% of the rate of methane. We had noted that certain preparations of CH_3-S-CoM would not serve as a substrate for the methylreductase reaction, and we did not understand why until bromethanesulfonate (BES) was found to be a potent inhibitor of methanogenesis (59). We then made sure that any excess BES, the starting compound for the synthesis, was removed from preparations of CH_3-S-CoM.

Archaebacteria

As a result of graduate training and exposure to ideas of the Delft school, I had become a firm believer in the unity of biochemistry for the biological world. In my own laboratory, the 1926 paper by Kluyver & Donker (84) had a special impact on students during our studies on electron transport in clostridia, especially since we felt we were a part of the family tree to Kluyver through contact with van Niel. Perhaps students today should be made more aware that they are part of a continuum—that their experiments have scientific roots! For vitamins and coenzymes, the case for biochemical unity was particularly strong.

The discovery of coenzyme M and the elucidation of its structure revealed a chance to document the distribution of a new vitamin-coenzyme relationship with a classic microbial growth–dependent assay. Not since lipoic acid had there been such an opportunity. Perhaps CoM would have a similar distribution as well as an important role in methylation reactions. However, growing a hydrogen-oxidizing methanogen using the Hungate technique was difficult. Each tube had to be opened and regassed with H_2 and CO_2 more than twice a day for 4 or 5 days. The negative pressure developed inside each tube made it especially difficult to prevent contamination by O_2 and bacteria when the stopper was removed. The single figure (126) showing that CoM was the growth factor for *M. ruminantium* represented efforts made over a large portion of a year. Assay after assay failed in Bryant's laboratory, and finally the master himself took his spring break to generate the data. I thought there must be a better way. I suggested to a new student, William Balch, who was tooling up to document the distribution of CoM in the biological world for part of his thesis work, that to avoid the pitfalls of this assay (which only an expert like Bryant could handle) we should try to develop a system in which cells could be grown in a pressurized atmosphere.

Macy, Snellen, & Hungate (93) had pioneered the use of syringes for the transfer of oxygen-sensitive bacteria in the Hungate technique. Miller & Wolin (97) extended the use of syringes to the inoculation of media contained in a standard serum bottle with an aluminum-crimped seal. In addition, they had the manufacturer put the serum vial top on standard culture tubes. This procedure worked well for fermentative microbes, which produced gas, but the seal was not designed to hold for organisms such as methanogens that created a negative pressure during growth. Balch replaced the standard serum rubber seal with a solid rubber stopper, and pressurized the H_2 and CO_2 atmosphere above the medium to 2 atm. More carbonate was added to the medium to increase the buffering capacity. The medium was inoculated by use of a syringe, and the atmosphere could be repressurized aseptically so that a standard growth curve was produced. Contamination was no longer a problem. A special stopper with a lip was designed, and Bellco Glass agreed to market it (6). The Balch modification of the procedures of Macy & Hungate and Miller & Wolin became standard procedure for the field (3), and in the hands of Karl Stetter proved to be equally valuable for isolation of extremely thermoacidophilic archaebacteria (163).

In Balch's hands, the CoM growth-dependent assay became routine and could easily detect 10 pmol. With this sensitive assay, over the next two years he tested animal tissues of all types as well as a wide range of plants and microbes (7). The answer was clear-cut: the new vitamin-coenzyme was present only in methanogens! I was disappointed; not only had the unity of biochemistry thesis let me down, but it appeared as if we had spent two years on a fruitless endeavor. However, Balch had thoroughly documented a fact that later would become important and had perfected the new system for growing methanogens in a pressurized atmosphere. His expertise would soon reap unexpected collaborative discoveries that otherwise might not have been possible. Carl Woese and I had been discussing a proposed analysis of the 16S rRNA of methanogens. Because a sealed reliable growth procedure had been developed, we entered into a collaboration in which the ability to label the nucleic acids of methanogens with high ^{32}P-specific activity was the limiting parameter.

Woese had found that growth of slow-growing organisms could easily cease because of radiation damage before sufficient label could be incorporated. Balch, with his pressurized atmosphere technique, had the key to success in coaxing each methanogen to take up sufficient label before dying. He developed a close working relationship with George Fox in Woese's laboratory, and each methanogen was a special challenge. When I asked Woese about the results of the first attempt to label the 16S rRNA of a methanogen, he replied that something had gone wrong with the extraction— perhaps they had isolated the wrong RNA. The experiment was repeated with special care, and this time Carl's voice was full of disbelief when he said, "Wolfe, these things aren't even bacteria."

When we started these experiments in 1976, Woese's laboratory had previously analyzed the T_1 endonuclease–generated 16S rRNA oligonucleotides of 60 species of microbes representing a wide variety. Against this wealth of background information, the data from the methanogens were perceived to be clearly different. Analysis of other methanogenic species supported the conclusion that methanogens were only distantly related to typical bacteria with regard to their 16S rRNA (54). And now the curious coenzymes assumed special importance. CoM had been shown to be unique to methanogens, and Dudley Eirich had just finished working out the structure of the first natural deazaflavin, the unique coenzyme F_{420}.

So the concept that methanogens represented an ancient divergence in evolution was initially a two legged stool—one leg supporting the concept was the 16S rRNA oligonucleotide data and the other was the "crazy coenzymes." We needed more legs on the stool, and I thought that if methanogens were this different in these areas, they also should exhibit other unusual properties. I wrote to Otto Kandler in Munich asking if he would be interested in examining cell walls of methanogens that we could send to him. He was enthusiastic for the project, and his laboratory soon showed that, indeed, *Methanobacterium* species not only lacked the typical peptiodglycan cell wall structure, which was known to be a characteristic of all bacteria except the mycoplasma, but possessed instead a pseudomurein; other methanogens had no peptidogylycan at all. We now had a third leg on the stool supporting the concept that methanogens were only distantly related to typical bacteria (4). Soon, many legs would support the concept, but all of these data only made sense when Carl Woese proposed that methanogens, extreme halophiles, and certain thermoacidophiles belonged to a distinct phylogeny, the archaebacteria (161), now known as the Archaea (162).

Many researchers were sceptical about this concept and about the the use of 16S rRNA to establish a phylogeny for the microbial world. We were fortunate at Illinois to have Marvin Bryant, who had written the section on methanogenic bacteria for *Bergey's Manual of Determinative Bacteriology*, as a colleague. The acceptance of the methanogens as a distinct group was controversial; the popular press did not help by calling them a "third form of life."

We decided to prepare an article for *Microbiological Reviews* in which all evidence that supported the uniqueness of the methanogens could be evaluated readily by the scientific community (3). The backbone of the paper was the oligonucleotide analysis prepared in Woese's laboratory. This article gained the the respect of the scientific community. Working with Carl Woese was a unique experience, one of the high points in my scientific life. I gained respect and admiration for him, one of the most dedicated scientists I have known.

Coenzyme F_{420}, the Deazaflavin

While fractionating cell extracts of strain M.o.H., Paul Cheeseman observed an abundant yellow compound that exhibited a bright blue-green fluorescence under UV light. He purified this compound to homogeniety and Ann Toms Wood continued these studies (27). The compound was named factor-420 (F_{420}) because of the strong absorption maximum at 420 nm. Godfried Vogels chose to study the fluorescence spectra and other properties of F_{420} during a sabbatical leave at Urbana. In Bryant's laboratory, extracts of *M. ruminantium* grown on formate as substrate exhibited both formic dehydrogenase and hydrogenase activity. During fractionation, NADP reduction by hydrogenase was found to require an unknown factor. A sample of our preparation of F_{420} substituted; the K_m for F_{420} was 5×10^{-6} M (133). A similar story developed for the F_{420}-dependent reduction of NADP by formic dehydrogenase in which the enzyme also showed a high specificity for F_{420} (132). These papers documented the role of F_{420} as an electron carrier in methanogens.

I suggested to Dudley Eirich that the structure of F_{420} would make a good thesis topic. After a course in organic qualitative analysis, he began to analyze hydrolytic fragments of F_{420}, and after a five-year dedicated effort, he had a structure in hand (36). The kind interest of K. L. Rinehart, Jr. as well as his willingness to be a sounding board were essential to the success of the project. The coenzyme is the N-(N-L-lactyl-γ-L-glutamyl)-L-glutamic acid phosphodiester of 7,8-didemethyl-8-hydroxy-5-deazariboflavin 5' phosphate. The distribution of F_{420} and properties of its hydrolytic fragments were published (37). F_{420} was the first naturally occurring deazaflavin to be described. In contrast to CoM, it is found in certain organisms other than methanogens, although the quantities in methanogens may be vastly greater.

Factor 342, Methanopterin, the Coenzyme of Methyl Transfer

When fractionating cell extracts by column chromatography, Robert Gunsalus noted a compound that fluoresced bright blue under UV light (63). This compound was named factor 342 (F_{342}) because of its absorption at 342 nm. No role was found for the factor, but Vogel's laboratory showed that it was a pterin derivative. James Romesser started another line of investigation when he began to study methanogenesis from formaldehyde. Hydroxymethyl-CoM, which was readily synthesized from formaldehyde and HS-CoM, was proposed as an intermediate in methanogenesis (112). The compound was found to hydrolyze in water to yield HS-CoM and formaldehyde, but the rate was much slower than the rate of methanogenesis from hydroxymethyl-CoM catalyzed by cell extracts, so we believed at the time that it was an intermediate. Later, Jorge Escalante showed that, because formaldehyde was removed from solution by methanogenesis, the equilibrium was drastically displaced toward hydrolysis; hydroxymethyl-CoM was not an intermediate in methanogenesis (48).

However, Escalante discovered a factor that was required for methanogenesis from formaldehyde that was named the formaldehyde activation factor (FAF). The factor was purified anaerobically to homogeniety; in the reduced form it had a molecular weight of 776, whereas that of the oxidized form was 772 (45, 46). The factor had properties very similar to methanopterin described by Vogel's laboratory (83), and Escalante showed that FAF was tetrahydromethanopterin (45, 46, 49). Escalante documented the role of the methenyl, methylene, and methyl derivatives of tetrahydromethanopterin in methanogenesis (47). In Neijmegen, the structure of the yellow fluorescent compound of Daniels' was firmly established to be methenyl-tetrahydromethanopterin (146). Mark Donnelly (33, 34) documented the role of 5-formyl-tetrahydromethanopterin as a C_1 intermediate in methanogenesis. So the blue fluorescent compound F_{342} led to the discovery of the central C_1 carrier of methanogenesis.

Coenzyme F_{430}, the First Nickel Tetrapyrrole

In 1977, we sent some frozen cells of *Methanobacterium* to Gregory Ferry, who was pursuing postdoctoral studies with Harry Peck at Athens, Georgia. Somehow an extract of these cells ended up in the hands of Jean LeGall. He communicated to us the presence of a yellow nonfluorescent compound in these extracts and provided us with a sample, stating that he had a hunch the compound might be a cobamide derivative. Robert Gunsalus repeated the isolation, but the compound was uninteresting to me: when added to extracts, it neither inhibited nor stimulated methanogenesis. I thought it might be a carotenoid. We named it factor 430 (F_{430}) because of its dramatic absorption at 430 nm (63). Later, William Whitman submitted F_{430} for neutron activation analysis, and the results suggested that the compound contained one nickel atom per molecule (152). This finding was of considerable interest, and we were pondering experiments when we received a note from Rolf Thauer saying that F_{430} contained nickel and that the incorporation of ^{63}Ni into F_{430} during growth was documented (29). In addition, his laboratory produced convincing evidence for the incorporation of δ-aminolevulinic acid into F_{430}

(28). This work stimulated Eschenmoser's group to document the structure of F_{430} as a pentaacid tetrahydrocorphin (92, 107). But we still had no role for F_{430} until William Ellefson observed that homogeneous CH_3-S-CoM methylreductase was yellow and had an absorption maximum at 425 nm. Ellefson & Whitman grew cells with [63]Ni in the medium, and when the homogeneous radioactive methylreductase was allowed to react with specific antibodies in an immunodiffusion plate, the precipitated protein-antibody band was labeled with [63]Ni. The methylreductase contained two molecules of F_{430} per M_r 300,000 protein (38). So F_{430}, the compound that wouldn't do anything, now is considered to be at the very heart of methanogenesis. Recently, Karl Olson collaborated with Michael Summers in Baltimore on the 2D and 3D NMR analysis of native F_{430}, the 12-13 dieprimer, and the reduced derivative F_{560} (106, 174).

Methanofuran, the Coenzyme of Formylation

Although progress had been made in other areas of C_1 reduction, nothing was known in 1980 about the activation and reduction of CO_2 to the formyl level. James Romesser observed that cell extracts could be resolved for a factor that was required for the reduction of carbon dioxide to methane after passage through a short Sephadex G-25 column. This factor was partially purified and named the carbon dioxide reduction factor, CDR (113). John Leigh took up the study of this factor for his thesis project, a study that would take five years. He resolved the fraction from methanopterin and showed that the CDR factor had properties that were quite distinct (91), including the lack of absorption in the visible or long UV spectrum. This finding meant that each fraction from column chromatography had to be tested in a methanogenic assay to locate the active fraction, a laborious and time consuming process. After analysis of its hydrolytic fragments, a structure for the coenzyme was proposed (89) as 4[N-(4,5,7-tricarboxyheptanoyl-γ-L-glutamyl-γ-L-glutamyl)-ρ-(β-aminoethyl)phenoxymethyl]-2-(aminomethyl)furan.

The counsel of K. L. Rinehart, Jr. was essential to the success of the project. The compound was essentially a long linear molecule with a hydrophilic tetracarboxylic acid moiety on one end and a furan ring with a primary amine on the other end. Aharon Oren suggested the name methanofuran, and we liked it. Later, the methanofuran of *Methanosarcina barkeri* was found to contain glutamyl units instead of the tetracarboxylic acid structure (12). But how did the compound function? John Leigh thought it might be involved in electron transport. But now and then I would ask, "John, ol' boy, does CDR carry a C_1 group?" It was great fun when he showed that formyl-methanofuran was the product of CO_2 activation and reduction (90) and that the formyl group was carried on the primary amine of the furan moiety. A new method of CO_2 fixation had been discovered.

7-Mercaptoheptanoylthreonine Phosphate, the Coenzyme That Donates Electrons to the Methylreductase

Robert Gunsalus & S. Tandon developed a successful procedure for anaerobic column chromatography of cell extract at room temperature (60). Gunsalus separated the methylreductase system into three fractions, each of which was required for reconstruction of the methylreductase reaction from CH_3-S-CoM and molecular hydrogen (64). Component A consisted of large oxygen-sensitive, heat-labile protein complexes with hydrogenase activity. Component B was an oxygen-labile, heat resistant, dialyzable cofactor. Component C was an oxygen-stable, heat-labile protein. Over 10 years passed between the discovery of component B and elucidation of its structure, the most frustrating experience of my academic life. Component B, the small, heat-stable molecule that was absolutely required for reconstitution of the methylreductase reaction was rather stable in crude preparations. However, the factor proved to be highly unstable on fractionation. Ralph Tanner invested several years in attempts to purify the factor to homogeneity but finally had to settle for a partially characterized compound. Kenneth Noll then continued studies on component B with four years of discouraging results. As with methanofuran, no spectral properties were available that could be used to follow the compound during fractionation. The only assay available was methanogenesis by the reconstituted methylreductase system. Years of frustration centered around loss of activity during fractionation. A complex molecule appeared to be decomposing during fractionation, but no conditions could be found to prevent the decomposition. One day, Kenneth Noll showed me a recording from HPLC that exhibited an isolated peak about 2 mm high, and he said with an air of resignation in his voice, "That's B." This was what I had been waiting for. We increased the manpower and ran the column repeatedly until we had enough material to make some measurements.

The breakthrough had been made. We would eventually find that the compound was not decomposing; instead it was forming heterodisulfides during fractionation with any HS-compound that was available. Elucidation of the structure by Ken Noll as 7-mercaptoheptanoylthreonine phosphate, HS-HTP (103), with the counsel of K. L. Rinehart and its confirmation through chemical synthesis by Noll & Mark Donnelly (102) were rewarding experiences after 10 years of frustration. Tanner studied the growth factor required by *Methanomicrobium mobile* (124), and my last graduate student, Carla Kuhner, extended these studies to show that the unknown growth factor is HS-HTP.

Enzymology of Methanogenesis from CO_2 and H_2

Weaving the role of these six new coenzymes into a metabolic pathway for the reduction of carbon dioxide to methane was an intriguing experience that spanned about 15 years. Some of the coenzymes were C_1 carriers; others were electron carriers. It became evident that nature had chosen the strategy of keeping the C_1 group bound to a coenzyme as it was sequentially reduced. The first reaction of the methanogenic pathway to be studied was the CH_3-S-CoM methylreductase reaction (62, 64, 94, 127). Component C was shown to be a protein of M_r 300,000 with an $\alpha_2\beta_2\gamma_2$ subunit configuration with 2 mol of F_{430} (38, 39). The enzyme contained CoM, and later Patricia Hartzell determined by the *M. brevibacter* assay that a preparation of component C prepared in Walsh's laboratory contained 2 mol of bound CoM per mol of protein (71). Hartzell et al (66) could find no stoichiometry for CoM incorporation into component C. Kenneth Noll showed that component C also contained bound component B (HS-HTP) (104). Although we could find no evidence for cobamides or corrins in component C, Whitman (155) found that the addition of corrins to the reaction mixture activated the methylreductase reaction. He studied the activation of the methylreductase by ATP (153) as well as its inhibition by corrins (154). Hartzell performed a comparative study of component C from various methanogens and revealed minor differences (68). Later, Pierre Rouvière used the variation in the subunits of component C to construct a taxonomy for the methanogens (118) that is in remarkable agreement with that derived from analysis of 16S rRNA.

Because component C from *Methanobacterium thermoautotrophicum* strain ΔH required component A proteins for conversion to the active state, Hartzell was able to dissociate and purify separately the α, β, and γ subunits as well as F_{430}. She then showed that these constitutents could be reassembled into component C, which in the presence the A proteins showed a 70% recovery of the methylreductase activity (69). F_{430} was absolutely required, showing for the first time that it really was a coenzyme in the methylreductase reaction. Homogeneous component C from strain ΔH required protein fraction component A and coenzyme component B for activity (64). In a series of very demanding experiments, David Nagle (101) separated component A into three protein fractions, A1, A2, and A3. This was an especially difficult task because the only assay available was the reconstituted methylreductase system. Each fraction that was purified required three other active fractions for its assay. Fraction A3 was found to be specifically inhibited by 2',3'dialdehyde of ATP (119). Later, fraction A3 was separated into two protein fractions, and A2 was purified to homogeneity by Rouvière (117, 121). So far, no specific enzymatic reaction has been assigned to these fractions, but A2 and A3 appear to be involved in converting inactive component C (C_i) to its active form (C_a) (120). Attempts to simplify the assay (67) or study the reductive activation (116) did not produce a breakthrough. A breakthrough had occurred when Ankel-Fuchs in Thauer's laboratory prepared an active form of component C from the Marburg strain. These ex-

pointed to one, "This is an important paper. Unfortunately it is in Russian, but it has a good German summary." He loved to remind American students of their language limitations. *Gallionella* secretes a twisted ribbon-like sessile stalk of ferric hydroxide, and van Niel had suggestions about setting up enrichments in Carrell flasks. I followed his suggestions, and, in a few weeks, had my first successful enrichments; van Niel seemed impressed. These cultures did not survive the return trip to Illinois, so I was anxious to find a source of organisms.

During a weekend at Turkey Run State Park in Indiana, Gret saved the day by finding rusty patches along the Rocky Hollow trail; these proved to be an excellent source of *Gallionella*. Al Vatter took some electron micrographs that showed that the stalks were not solid ribbons but were composed of many strands secreted from one side of the cell (149). We developed a defined medium, and Sonia Kucera worked on *Gallionella* for her MS thesis (86). I prepared an article on iron bacteria for the *Journal of the American Water Works Association* (164); over the years I would take some kidding from scientific colleagues for publishing in this "prestigious" journal. I used this article to encourage water plant operators to send me samples of problem organisms. A beautiful example of the chlamydobacterium, *Crenothrix*, arrived from Sweden (165), but I could not cultivate it. Another sample contained a large *Leptothrix*. Because of problems with obtaining pure cultures and with mass culture, these organisms had to be abandoned as serious research subjects, but iron bacteria continue to be a scientific hobby. Our children continue to send me samples of rusty deposits they find in nature.

Phototrophs, my favorite enrichments in the organism course, were always fun to isolate, and, when Al Vatter became interested in the ultrastructure of *Rhodospirillum rubrum*, I suggested that we collaborate on a study of representative photosynthetic bacteria to discern their cellular anatomy. We published a pioneering article on the structure of photosynthetic bacteria, showing that *R. rubrum*, *Rhodopseudomonas sphaeroides*, and *Chromatium* all contained differentiated membranes, chromatophores (150). We also showed that *Chlorobium* was different, but we missed the chlorosome. While on a summer fellowship at the University of Washington, I set up enrichments for *Rhodomicrobium vannielii*, a most unusual phototroph discovered by Howard Douglas. We were surprised to find that the organism was motile (35) and that it contained lamellae rather than chromatophores (148). When Robert Uffen arrived for postdoctoral study, I suggested that he set up enrichments for methanogens that could grow on carbon monoxide. A technique was developed for streaking enrichment cultures on agar in bottle plates to which we could add an atmosphere of carbon monoxoide. Much later an improved bottle plate was developed and Bellco Glass produced it (74). Uffen could detect no methane in the bottle plates, but one plate contained a large red colony. I knew that Howard Gest and other investigators had been trying to grow phototrophs anaerobically in the dark without success. The organism proved to be *Rhodopseudomonas palustris*, a purple nonsulfur phototroph. A very careful study to insure that utilizable radiation was not available to the cells revealed that by use of pyruvate and H_2, representative nonsulfur phototrophs also could be cultured anaerobically in the dark indefinitely and that their photosynthetic apparatus could not be differentiated from that of anaerobic light-grown cells (134). Mutants also were studied (134a).

Beggiatoa, with its gliding trichomes stuffed with sulfur, was a fascination for me. I thought it would be fun to isolate, mass culture, and study the metabolism of this organism. We followed the method of Cataldi for isolation by allowing a trichome to glide over an agar surface; a cut-out agar block with the trichome on it was then transferred to sterile medium. Lois Faust developed a defined medium for the organism. By 1959, I realized that it was unrealistic to ever expect to mass culture this organism in quantities required for enzyme studies, so I documented its characteristics with photographs and motion pictures (50) and used these in teaching for many years.

Sarcina ventriculi, which carries out an alcoholic fermentation of sugar at pH 2.5, was studied by Ercolé Canale-Parola, my second PhD student. The organism was isolated from sediments of Boneyard Creek, a somewhat polluted stream that runs through our campus. The real challenge was to maintain the organism, for it could die quickly if the culture was not transferred properly. He developed a stock culture technique (24), evolved a synthetic medium (25), and studied the localization of cellulose (23) as well as its synthesis (26).

Streptococcus allantoicus was isolated by Ray Valentine from a duck pond at Monticello, Ill., to study allantoin degradation. H. A. Barker had discovered the organism and suggested that possibly one of the ureido groups of allantoin could be cleaved in an energy-yielding reaction. Valentine discovered the enzyme, oxamic transcarbamylase (141), and showed that the phosphorolysis of oxalurate yielded oxamate and carbamyl phosphate, the latter compound donating a phosphate group to ADP in a kinase reaction to yield ATP (142). In studying the phosphate-dependent degradation of urea, ureidoglycolate was found to be an intermediate (143, 144), and its NAD-dependent oxidation to oxalurate was proposed as the only oxidative step carried out by the organism when it grew anaerobically on allantoin (135). Elizabeth Gaudy (55, 58) characterized the enzyme ureidoglycolate synthetase for her thesis and implicated the enzyme in the allantoin degradation pathway. Robert Bojanowski & Gaudy (17) characterized the oxamic transcarbamylase, and Valentine & Harvey Drucker (138) documented the conversion of glyoxylate to tartronic semialdehyde and CO_2.

Sphaerotilus natans was studied by Elizabeth Gaudy for her MS thesis. In rich media, sheath formation by this chlamydobacterium ceased and the organism produced copious amounts of slime (56). The slime was purified and found to be composed of equal amounts of fucose, galactose, glucose, and glucuronic acid; we suggested that the latter two components occurred as an aldobiuronic acid (57). We then received a letter from Michael Heidelberger, who suggested that the aldobiuronic acid could be identified using antibodies that he had. The aldobiuronic acid precipitated with Type III and Type VII antipneumococcal horse sera and was identified as cellobiuronic acid (73).

Arthrobacter crystallopoietes was brought to my laboratory by a postdoctoral student, Jerald Ensign. *Arthrobacter* goes through a rod to coccus differentiation during growth, and he wished to study this phenomenon. He developed a chemically defined medium in which the organism grew only in the coccoid form. He discovered that addition of certain amino acids or organic acids to the defined medium resulted in the formation of the rod-shaped stage (42).

Myxobacter strain AL-1 was isolated by Ensign (43) by placing soil inocula on a lawn of *Arthrobacter*, where the myxobacter produced large clear areas; the lytic enzyme was found to readily lyse a number of gram-positive species (43). The enzyme was found to be a small protease that hydrolyzed proteins as well as peptide bonds in the glycosaminopeptide of cell walls (44). Richard Jackson studied the amino acid composition and characterized the enzyme (78). Strominger found the enzyme, Myxobacter AL-1 Protease I, to be valuable in determining the structure of the cell walls of gram-positive bacteria. A second protease, Myxobacter AL-1 Protease II, was discovered when the enzyme crystallized in certain fractions as it eluted from a column. We were somewhat stunned; usually an enzyme yields to crystallization only after a battle, but here we had crystals and no assay. Marilyn Wingard (158) determined that the enzyme was a protease that had the unusual specificity to cleave the peptide bond on the amino side of lysine. A third enzyme was discovered when in the course of dialyzing myxobacter extracts the dialysis tubing disintegrated. Allan Hedges (72) showed that this enzyme had both β-1,4 gluconase as well as chitosanase activity.

Clostridium tetanomorphum was studied by Robert Twarog, who showed that the organism makes only 1 mol of ATP per mol of glutamate and that ATP is generted via phosphostransbutyrylase and butyrate kinase reactions (130, 131).

Geodermatophilus was brought to the laboratory by Edward Ishiguro; he had found the organism in soil obtained from the lower reaches of Mt. Everest. From a clump of large coccoid cells, certain cells differentiated small motile rods, which multiplied as rods but later differentiated to cocci, forming large clumps. He studied this phenomenon and found that the life cycle could be controlled; a factor in certain batches of Tryptose (Difco) was required for differentiation to the motile-rod form (76). This factor was difficult to purify because the growth-differentiation assay was not easy to quantify. After a few years, the factor was in hand and the assay was reproducible (77), but Ishiguro was rather depressed; the factor was an inorganic cation (NH_4^+) and other inorganic as well as organic cations induced morphogenesis.

Methanobacterium thermoautotrophicum was isolated by Gregory Zeikus. In 1970, Leon Campbell encouraged me to set up some enrichments for thermophilic methanogens. These enrichments readily produce methane, but I could not pursue a successful isolation at the time. When Zeikus came to the laboratory, I suggested that he continue this project of isolating a thermophilic methanogen. He proceeded to enrich and isolate an organism from sewage sludge that grew well at 60–65°C. In spite of our poor latin scholarship (181), isolation of this organism, *Methanobacterium thermoautotrophicum* strain ΔH, was a major breakthrough. The organism had an interesting ultrastructure (182). Strain ΔH became the backbone of my research program. It could be readily scaled up to the 200-liter fermentor stage, it grew more rapidly than mesophilic strains, and, above all, enzymes were stable at room temperatures, 40° below the optimal growth temperature.

Methanogenium cariacii and *Methanogenium marisnigri* were isolated by James Romesser (115). Since I was a child, I have had an unfortunate propensity for motion sickness, so when Holger Jannasch invited me to join an expedition to the Cariaco Trench and later to the Black Sea, I was forced to decline. However, Romesser was pleased at the possibility for adventure and returned with samples from water columns of these anaerobic habitats.

Methanococcus voltae was sent to us by J. M. Ward, who had isolated it for his MS thesis, and we decided to name it after Alessandro Volta, who first described the formation of "combustible air" in sediments (3). Whitman and colleagues defined its nutrition and carbon metabolism (151) as well as its plating efficiency (82). We suggested that this organism might be the organism of choice for initiating genetic studies with methanogens.

Methanococcus jannaschii was isolated by John Leigh from samples obtained by Holger Jannasch at a geothermal vent on the east Pacific rise by use of the submersible, Alvin. This unusual organism grew optimally at 85°C with a generation time of 25 min. Its properties were reported by Jones et al (81).

Methanogenium thermophilum was isolated by Friedrich Widdel. He had stunned the field by showing that methanogens could oxidize alcohols and reduce CO_2 to CH_4. In Urbana, he isolated mesophilic and thermophilic alcohol-oxidizing methanogens and with Rouvière studied their taxonomy (156). He showed that F_{420} served as an electron acceptor for alcohol dehydrognease (157).

Acetobacterium woodii was discovered in enrichments set up for methanogens in which a gas mixture of 80% H_2:20% CO_2 was bubbled through a series of tubes that had been inoculated with sediment from Crystal Lake, Urbana, Ill. To save gas, the effluent of one tube was connected to the inlet of the next tube. The tubes were placed in a fume hood. About a month later, I happened to notice these tubes with their slowly bubbling contents; I had forgotten them. I could find no evidence of methane formation, but the black rubber stoppers were swollen and gnarled, and the amount of acetic acid coming out of the tubes was fantastic. This was obviously not the way to enrich for methanogens! At that time, no H_2-oxidizing, CO_2-reducing acetogen was in culture. One summer at Woods Hole, we set up enrichments from sediments at Oyster Pond Inlet, and Balch succeeded in isolating a cocco-bacillus-like organism. We named the organism after Harland Wood (5), who had spent 20 years trying to figure out how acetic acid was synthesized from CO_2, and presented him with a picture of the organism on his 70th birthday. Siegfried Schoberth thoroughly documented the substrate range and properties of the organism, and Ralph Tanner determined the presence of tetrahydrofolate enzymes in the organism (125). *A. woodii* opened the modern era of hydrogen-oxiding acetogens, the ecological importance of which is becoming increasingly appreciated. Later, John Leigh isolated a thermophilic acetogen on H_2 and CO_2 from sediments of Lake Kivu, Africa. We named this organism *Acetogenium kivui* (88).

Methanospirillum hungatei, strain JF, was isolated by Gregory Ferry from a stable consortium of cells that degraded benzoate anaerobically to CH_4 and CO_2 (52). He resolved the culture into three organisms. One was a pseudomonad that used benzoate as its substrate. Another organism was a spiral-shaped methanogen that grew on H_2 and CO_2 or formate. The other organism could not be isolated but was an acetophilic methanogen. The spirillum was similar to one described by Paul Smith in an abstract, but a publication never appeared, so we collaborated on its description and named the organism *Methanospirillum hungatei*, in honor of Robert Hungate (51). Later, the nutritional and biochemical characteristics of *M. hungatei* were described (53).

Josef Winter joined the laboratory and achieved complete degradation of carbohydrate to methane by a syntrophic culture of *A. woodii* and *M. barkeri* (160). In another study, he followed methane formation from fructose by *A. woodii* and other methanogens in a chemostat (159). I believe he was the first person to use a chemostat to study methanogens. He returned to Otto Kandler's laboratory and trained his colleagues to use the techniques developed by Balch. One brilliant pupil was Karl Stetter. Other consortia were studied by Jack Jones and Jean Pierre Guyot (80).

While on sabbatical leave in 1975, Norbert Pfenning suggested that I should isolate and study a spirillum-like organism that was persistent in enrichment cultures of *Desulfuromonas*. We named the organism spirillum 5175 and found that it could grow anaerobically by the oxidation of formate with the reduction of fumarate to succinate. It could also use H_2S as electron donor for this reaction. In addition, it could anaerobically oxidize hydrogen or formate and reduce elemental sulfur, thiosulfate, or sulfite, but not sulfate. Since *Chlorobium* does not use formate, we set up a syntrophic culture in which the spirillum oxidized formate and reduced elemental sulfur to H_2S; *Chlorobium* used the H_2S as its electron donor, producing elemental sulfur. Sulfur was limiting in the medium and was recycled through H_2S and elemental sulfur, so neither organism could grow alone, but together they grew beautifully (168).

Richard Blakemore discovered magnetotactic bacteria in sediments that had been collected at Woods Hole, but he was unable to pursue their isolation. Before his arrival in Urbana as a postdoctoral student, I spent the summer studying the survival of these organisms from enrichments in various media and conditions. Their survival was a matter of minutes or hours not days. When he arrived in September, 1976, I suggested that we set Christmas as a goal for achieving the first pure culture; by February he had a magnetic spirillum in hand (10). It would be 10 years before a second species would be captured by others. While on a von Humboldt Fellowship in Germany, I continued the study of magnetic bacteria; why were they so difficult to isolate? An undergraduate student in Rolf Thauer's laboratory, Alfred Spormann, was interested, and we found an excellent natural enrichment. Using reducing agents, we showed that chemotaxis could maintain a magnetically oriented cell at a certain oxygen tension, explaining why certain magnetotactic cells may not follow the magnetic lines of force deep into anaerobic sediments (123). I was able to perfect a capillary racetrack method for separating magnetic bacteria from typical bacteria (169), but an appropriate medium for their culture could not be formulated.

Reflections

Some believe it takes as much work to study an unimportant problem as an important one, so one should only work on important problems. Perceived important problems are usually in good hands, which means that most of us, fortunately, have the freedom to work on what interests us, and sometimes this turns out to be important. My goal has been to get as many persons as possible interested in working on methanogens. After a sabbatical leave in Urbana, Godfried Vogels returned to start his own program on methanogens at Nijmegen. Rolf Thauer became interested in methanogens after a two-week visit to Urbana. Josef Winter returned to Kandler's laboratory in Munich. Ziegfried Schoberth returned to Gottschalk's laboratory at Göttingen. Many individuals were trained by Balch, including visitors from Ottawa. Chris Walsh, Orme-Johnson, and students visited from MIT. John Reeve and students visited from Columbus. Jordan Konisky was encouraged to start his own program at Urbana. By 1982, there was a critical mass of investigators, and we began to organize our first Gordon Conference on methanogenesis.

During the years of teaching the organisms course at Urbana, I was frequently reminded of the limitations of formal laboratory scheduling where a two- to three-hour laboratory is wedged between classes, and where students have limited opportunities to make discoveries. I had always wanted to try a van Niel–type summer course, so when the opportunity came to be Director of the Microbiology Course at the Marine Biological Laboratory at Woods Hole, I asked Peter Greenberg, who would bring genetic and molecular components to the course, to join me as codirector with the purpose of starting a 1985 version of a van Niel–type summer organisms course. He agreed. We asked Bernhard Schink from Konstanz to join us for the first summer, and Carrie Harwood was course coordinator. Holger Jannasch was instrumental in urging students on the national and international scene to take the course. In subsequent years, we were joined by Norbert Pfenning, Friedrich Widdel, Bernhard, and Andrew Kropinski as course coordinator. We found that the Volta experiment on the third evening of the course not only focused interest on anaerobic physiology but was a great social mixer for students and staff. Student response and faculty dedication made these five summers the most satisfying teaching experiences of my academic career.

Over the years, I have formulated a few truisms that I refer to as Wolfe's Laws of Thermodynamics: 1st Law: Unpublished data do not improve with age. 2nd Law: If you are first on the scene, it is easy to make discoveries. 3rd Law: The emotion generated in scientific discussion increases proportionally with the softness of the data being discussed. 4th Law: If you join a parade, you become one of the marchers. Graduate students like to join highly visible parades, to be part of the current scene, not realizing that their visibility is reduced by the number of marchers. As an independent investigator, each should realize the importance of choosing a problem that isn't moving and move it.

Throughout my academic life, I have more or less been driven in some manner "to go back to the lab." This common syndrome of persons in science needing to be in the lab could be simply a security blanket or a necessary component of scientific survival. I have felt that, for me, the latter was the case, coupled with a feeling that possibly my presence somehow might encourage students. Gret has spent many lonely evenings sharing her life with the lab, and her support was pivotal. Our children, Danny, Jon, and Sue, shared a portion of their lives with the lab. However, one of the enjoyable aspects of academic life is the sabbatical; we have had interesting sabbaticals in England, Hawaii, France, and Germany. My last sabbatical, a short one, was spent with John Breznak, where I was introduced to the fascinating world of anaerobic protozoa from termites.

As these scientific memoirs have shown, I was fortunate to have a series of talented graduate and postdoctoral students to work with me. I thank them, my colleagues, Gret, and our children for making this experience a rewarding one. In operating my laboratory, my purpose has not been to play the role of the brilliant intellectual leader, but rather to stay in the background and try to create an atmosphere in which students could develop into independent investigators; this, for me, is what it's all about.

Literature Cited

1. Ankel-Fuchs, D., Böcher, R., Thauer, R. K., Noll, K. M., Wolfe, R. S. 1986. 7-Mercaptoheptanoylthreonine phosphate functions as component B in ATP-independent methane formation from methyl-CoM with reduced cobalamin as electron donor. *FEBS Lett.* 213:123–27

2. Ankel-Fuchs, D., Huster, R., Mörschel, E., Albracht, S. P. J., Thauer, R. K. 1986. Structure and function of methylcoenzyme M reductase and of factor F_{430} in methanogenic bacteria. *Syst. Appl. Microbiol.* 7:383–87

3. Balch, W. E., Fox, G. E., Magrum, L. J., Woese, C. R., Wolfe, R. S. 1979. Methanogens: reevaluation of a unique biological group. *Microbiol. Rev.* 43:260–96

4. Balch, W. E., Magrum, L. J., Fox, G. E., Wolfe, R. S., Woese, C. R. 1977. An ancient divergence among the bacteria. *J. Mol. Evol.* 9:305–11

5. Balch, W. E., Schoberth, S., Tanner, R. S., Wolfe, R. S. 1977. *Acetobacterium*, a new genus of hydrogen-oxidizing CO_2-reducing anaerobic bacteria. *Int. J. Syst. Bacteriol.* 27:355–61

6. Balch, W. E., Wolfe, R. S. 1976. New approach to the cultivation of methanogenic bacteria: 2-mercaptoethanesulfonic acid (HS-CoM)-dependent growth of *Methanobacterium ruminantium*. *Appl. Environ. Microbiol.* 32:781–91

7. Balch, W. E., Wolfe, R. S. 1979. Specificity and biological distribution of coenzyme M (2-mercaptoethanesulfonic acid). *J. Bacteriol.* 137:256–63

8. Balch, W. E., Wolfe, R. S. 1979. Transport of coenzyme M (2-mercaptoethanesulfonic acid) in *Methanobacterium ruminantium*. *J. Bacteriol.* 137:265–73

9. Baresi, L., Wolfe, R. S. 1980. Levels of coenzyme F_{420}, coenzyme M, hydrogenase and methylcoenzyme M methylreductase in acetate-grown *Methanosarcina*. *Appl. Environ. Microbiol.* 41:388–91

10. Blakemore, R. P., Maratea, D., Wolfe, R. S. 1979. Isolation and pure culture of a freshwater magnetic spirillum in chemically defined medium. *J. Bacteriol.* 140:720–29

11. Blaylock, A. B., Stadtman, T. C. 1963. Biosynthesis of methane from the methyl moiety of methylcobalamin. *Biochem. Biophys. Res. Commun.* 11:34–38

12. Bobik, T. A., Donnelly, M. I., Rinehart, K. L. Jr., Wolfe, R. S. 1987. Structure of a methanofuran derivative found in cell extracts of *Methanosarcina barkeri*. *Arch. Biochem. Biophys.* 254:430–36

13. Bobik, T. A., Olson, K. D., Noll, K. M., Wolfe, R. S. 1987. Evidence that the heterodisulfide of coenzyme M and 7-mercaptoheptanoylthreonine phosphate is a product of the methyl-reductase reaction in *Methanobacterium*. *Biochem. Biophys. Res. Commun.* 149:455–60

14. Bobik, T. A., Wolfe, R. S. 1988. Physiological importance of the heterdisulfide of coenzyme M and 7-mercaptoheptanoylthreonine phosphate in the reduction of carbon dioxide to methane of *Methanobacterium*. *Proc. Natl. Acad. Sci. USA* 85:60–63

15. Bobik, T. A., Wolfe, R. S. 1989. Activation of formylmethanofuran synthesis in cell extracts of *Methanobacterium thermoautotrophicum*. *J. Bacteriol.* 171:1423–27

16. Bobik, T. A., Wolfe, R. S. 1989. An unusual thiol-driven fumarate reductase in *Methanobacterium* with the production of the heterodisulfide of coenzyme

M and N-(7-Mercaptoheptanoyl)threo-
nine-O^3-phosphate. *J. Biol. Chem.* 264:
18714–18
17. Bojanowski, R., Gaudy, E., Valentine,
R. C., Wolfe, R. S. 1964. Oxamic
transcarbamylase of *Streptococcus allantoicus*. *J. Bacteriol.* 87:75–80
18. Brill, W. J., Wolfe, R. S. 1966. Acetaldehyde oxidation by *Methanobacillus*—
a new ferredoxin-dependent reaction.
Nature 212:253–55
19. Brill, W. J., Wolin, E. A., Wolfe, R. S.
1964. Anaerobic formate oxidation a
ferredoxin-dependent reaction. *Science*
144:297–98
20. Deleted in proof
21. Bryant, M. P., McBride, B. C., Wolfe,
R. S. 1968. Hydrogen-oxidizing methane bacteria. I. Cultivation and methanogenesis. *J. Bacteriol.* 95:1118–23
22. Bryant, M. P., Wolin, E. A., Wolin, M.
J., Wolfe, R. S. 1967. *Methanobacillus
omelianskii*, a symbiotic association of
two species of bacteria. *Arch. Mikrobiol.* 59:20–31
23. Canale-Parola, E., Borasky, R., Wolfe,
R. S. 1961. Studies on *Sarcina ventriculi*. III. Localization of cellulose. *J. Bacteriol.* 81:311–18
24. Canale-Parola, E., Wolfe, R. S. 1960.
Studies on *Sarcina ventriculi*. I. Stock
culture method. *J. Bacteriol.* 79:857–59
25. Canale-Parola, E., Wolfe, R. S. 1960.
Studies on *Sarcina ventriculi* II. Nutrition. *J. Bacteriol.* 79:860–62
26. Canale-Parola, E., Wolfe, R. S. 1964.
Synthesis of cellulose by *Sarcina ventriculi*. *Biochim. Biophys. Acta* 82:403–5
27. Cheeseman, P., Toms-Wood, A.,
Wolfe, R. S. 1972. Isolation and properties of a fluorescent compound, Factor
420, from *Methanobacterium* strain M.
o.H. *J. Bacteriol.* 112:527–31
28. Diekert, G., Jaenchen, R., Thauer, R.
K. 1980. Biosynthetic evidence for a
nickel tetrapyrrole structure of factor
F_{430} from *Methanobacterium thermoautotrophicum*. *FEBS Lett.* 119:118–20
29. Diekert, G., Klee, B., Thauer, R. K.
1980. Nickel, a component of factor
F_{430} from *Methanobacterium thermoautotrophicum*. *Arch. Microbiol.* 124:
103–6
30. DiMarco, A. A., Bobik, T. A., Wolfe,
R. S. 1990. Unusual coenzymes of
methanogenesis. *Annu. Rev. Biochem.*
59:355–94
31. DiMarco, A. A., Donnelly, M. I.,
Wolfe, R. S. 1986. Purification and
properties of the 5,10-methenyltetrahy-
dromethanopterin cyclohydrolase from
*Methanobacterium   thermoautotrophi-
cum*. *J. Bacteriol.* 168:1372–77

32. DiMarco, A. A., Sment, K. A., Konisky, J., Wolfe, R. S. 1990. The formylmethanofuran: tetrahydromethanopterin
formyltransferase from *Methanobacterium thermoautotrophicum* ΔH. *J. Biol.
Chem.* 265:472–76
33. Donnelly, M. I., Escalante-Semerena, J.
C., Rinehart, K. L. Jr., Wolfe, R. S.
1985. Methenyl-tetrahydromethanopterin cyclohydrolase in cell extracts of
Methanobacterium. *Arch. Biochem.
Biophys.* 242:430–39
34. Donnelly, M. I., Wolfe, R. S. 1986.
The role of formylmethanofuran: tetrahydromethanopterin   formyltransferase
in methanogenesis from carbon dioxide.
J. Biol. Chem. 261:16653–59
35. Douglas, H. C., Wolfe, R. S. 1959.
Motility of *Rhodomicrobium vannielii*.
J. Bacteriol. 78:597–98
36. Eirich, L. D., Vogels, G. D., Wolfe, R.
S. 1978. Proposed structure for coenzyme F_{420} from *Methanobacterium*.
Biochemistry 17:4583–93
37. Eirich, L. D., Vogels, G. D., Wolfe, R.
S. 1979. Distribution of coenzyme F_{420}
and properties of its hydrolytic fragments. *J. Bacteriol.* 140:20–27
38. Ellefson, W. L., Whitman, W. B.,
Wolfe, R. S. 1982. Nickel-contain-
ing factor F_{430}: Chromophore of the methylreductase   of   *Methanobacterium*.
Proc. Natl. Acad. Sci. USA 79:3707–
10
39. Ellefson, W. L., Wolfe, R. S. 1981.
Component C of the methylreductase
system of *Methanobacterium*. *J. Biol.
Chem.* 256:4259–62
40. Ellerman, J., Hederich, R., Böcher, R.,
Thauer, R. K. 1988. The final step in
methane formation: investigations with
highly purified methyl-CoM reductase
(component C) from *Methanobacterium
thermoautotrophicum* (strain Marburg).
Eur. J. Biochem. 172:669–77
41. Ellerman, J., Kobelt, A., Pfaltz, A.,
Thauer, R. K. 1987. On the role of
N-7-mercaptoheptanoyl-O-phospho-L-
threonine (component B) in the enzymatic reduction of methyl-coenzyme M to
methane. *FEBS Lett.* 220:358–62
42. Ensign, J. C., Wolfe, R. S. 1964. Nutritional control of morphogenesis in
Arthrobacter crystallopoietes. *J. Bacteriol.* 87:924–32.
43. Ensign, J. C., Wolfe, R. S. 1965. Lysis
of bacterial cell walls by an enzyme isolated from a myxobacter. *J. Bacteriol.*
90:395–402
44. Ensign, J. C., Wolfe, R. S. 1966.
Characterization of a small proteolytic
enzyme which lyses bacterial cell walls.
J. Bacteriol. 91:524–34

45. Escalante-Semerena, J. C. 1983. *In vitro methanogenesis from formaldehyde. Identification of three C₁ intermediates of the methanogenic pathway.* PhD thesis. Urbana: Univ. Ill. 229 pp.

46. Escalante-Semerena, J. C., Leigh, J. A., Rinehart, K. L. Jr., Wolfe, R. S. 1984. Formaldehyde activation factor, tetrahydromethanopterin, a coenzyme of methanogenesis. *Proc. Natl. Acad. Sci. USA* 81:1976–80

47. Escalante-Semerena, J. C., Rinehart, K. L. Jr., Wolfe, R. S. 1984. Tetrahydromethanopterin, a carbon carrier in methanogenesis. *J. Biol. Chem.* 259:9447–55

48. Escalante-Semerena, J. C., Wolfe, R. S. 1984. Formaldehyde oxidation and methanogenesis. *J. Bacteriol.* 158:721–26

49. Escalante-Semerena, J. C., Wolfe R. S. 1985. Tetrahydromethanopterin-dependent methanogenesis from non-physiological C₁ donors in *Methanobacterium. J. Bacteriol.* 161:696–701

50. Faust, L., Wolfe, R. S. 1961. Enrichment and cultivation of *Beggiatoa alba. J. Bacteriol.* 81:99–106

51. Ferry, J. G., Smith, P. H., Wolfe, R. S. 1974. *Methanospirillum,* a new genus of methanogenic bacteria, and characterization of *Methanosprillum hungatii* sp. nov. *Int. J. Syst. Bacteriol.* 24:465–69

52. Ferry, J. G., Wolfe, R. S. 1976. Anaerobic degradation of benzoate to methane by a microbial consortium. *Arch. Microbiol.* 107:33–40

53. Ferry, J. G., Wolfe, R. S. 1977. Nutritional and biochemical characterization of *Methanospirillum hungatii. Appl. Environ. Microbiol.* 34:371–76

54. Fox, G. E., Magrum, L. J., Balch, W. E., Wolfe, R. S., Woese, C. R. 1977. Classification of methanogenic bacteria by 16S ribosomal RNA characterization. *Proc. Natl. Acad. Sci. USA* 74:4537–41

55. Gaudy, E. T., Bojanowski, R., Valentine, R. C., Wolfe, R. S. 1965. Ureidoglycolate synthetase of *Streptococcus allantoicus.* I. Measurement of glyoxylate and enzyme purification. *J. Bacteriol.* 90:1525–30

56. Gaudy, E. T., Wolfe, R. S. 1962. Factors affecting filamentous growth of *Sphaerotilus natans. Appl. Microbiol.* 9:580–84

57. Gaudy, E., Wolfe, R. S. 1962. Composition of an extracellular polysaccharide produced by *Sphaerotilus natans. Appl. Microbiol.* 10:200–5

58. Gaudy, E. T., Wolfe, R. S. 1965. Ureidoglycolate synthetase of *Strepto-*

coccus allantoicus. II. Properties of the enzyme and reaction equilibrium. *J. Bacteriol.* 90:1531–36

59. Gunsalus, R. P., Romesser, J. A., Wolfe, R. S. 1978. Preparation of coenzyme M analogues and their activity in the methylcoenzyme M reductase system of *Methanobacterium thermoautotrophicum. Biochemistry* 17:2374–77

60. Gunsalus, R. P., Tandon, S. M., Wolfe, R. S. 1980. A procedure for anaerobic column chromatography employing an anaerobic Freter-type chamber. *Anal. Biochem.* 101:327–31

61. Gunsalus, R. P., Wolfe, R. S. 1977. Stimulation of CO₂ reduction to methane by methylcoenzyme M in extracts of *Methanobacterium. Biochem. Biophys. Res. Commun.* 76:790–95

62. Gunsalus, R. P., Wolfe, R. S. 1978. ATP activation and properties of the methyl-coenzyme M reductase system in *Methanobacterium thermoautotrophicum. J. Bacteriol.* 135:851–57

63. Gunsalus, R. P., Wolfe, R. S. 1978. Chromophoric factors F342 and F430 of *Methanobacterium thermoautotrophicum. FEMS Microbiol. Lett.* 3:191–93

64. Gunsalus, R. P., Wolfe, R. S. 1980. Methyl coenzyme M reductase from *Methanobacterium thermoautotrophicum:* resolution and properties of the components. *J. Biol. Chem.* 255:1891–95

65. Hamilton, R. D., Wolfe, R. S. 1959. Pyruvate exchange reactions in *Bacillus macerans. J. Bacteriol.* 78:253–58

66. Hartzell, P. L., Donnelly, M. I., Wolfe, R. S. 1987. Incorporation of coenzyme M into component C of methylcoenzyme M methylreductase during in vitro methanogenesis. *J. Biol. Chem.* 262:5581–86

67. Hartzell, P. L., Escalante-Semerena, J. C., Bobik, T. A., Wolfe, R. S. 1988. A simplified methylcoenzyme M methylreductase assay with artifical electron donors and different preparations of component C from *Methanobacterium thermoautotrophicum. J. Bacteriol.* 170:2711–15

68. Hartzell, P. L., Wolfe, R. S. 1986. Comparative studies of component C from the methylreductase system of different methanogens. *Syst. Appl. Microbiol.* 7:376–82

69. Hartzell, P. L., Wolfe, R. S. 1986. Requirement of the nickel tetrapyrrole F₄₃₀ for in vitro methanogenesis: Reconstitution of methylreductase component C from its dissociated subunits. *Proc. Natl. Acad. Sci. USA* 83:6726–30

70. Hartzell, P. L., Zvilius, G., Escalante-

Semerena, J. C., and Donnelly, M. I. 1985. Coenzyme F_{420} dependence of the methylene H_4MPT dehydrogenase. *Biochem. Biophys. Res. Commun.* 133:884–90

71. Hausinger, R. P., Orme-Johnson, W. H., Walsh, C. 1984. The nickel tetrapyrrole cofactor F_{430}: comparison of the forms bound to methyl-S coenzyme M methylreductase and protein-free in cells of *Methanobacterium thermoautotrophicum.* *Biochemistry* 23:801–4

72. Hedges, A., Wolfe, R. S. 1974. Extracellular enzyme from myxobacter AL-1 that exhibits both β-1, 4-gluconase and chitosanase activities. *J. Bacteriol.* 120:844–53

73. Heidelberger, M., Gaudy, E., Wolfe, R. S. 1964. Immunochemical identification of the aldobiuronic acid of the slime of *Sphaerotilus natans.* *Proc. Natl. Acad. Sci. USA* 51:568–69

74. Hermman, M., Noll, K. M., Wolfe, R. S. 1986. Improved agar bottle plate for isolation of methanogens or other anaerobes in a defined gas atmosphere. *Appl. Environ. Microbiol.* 51:1124–26

75. Hoyt, J. C., Oren, A., Escalante-Semerena, J. C., Wolfe, R. S. 1986. Tetrahydromethanopterin-dependent serine transhydroxymethylase from *Methanobacterium thermoautotrophicum.* *Arch. Microbiol.* 145:153–58

76. Ishiguro, E. E., Wolfe, R. S. 1970. Control of morphogenesis in *Geodermatophilus:* ultrastructural studies. *J. Bacteriol.* 104:566–80

77. Ishiguro, E. E., Wolfe, R. S. 1974. Induction of morphogenesis in *Geodermatophilus* by inorganic cations and by organic nitrogenous cations. *J. Bacteriol.* 117:189–95

78. Jackson, R. L., Wolfe, R. S. 1968. Composition, properties, and substrate specificities of Myxobacter AL-1 protease. *J. Biol. Chem.* 243:879–88

79. Jones, W. J., Donnelly, M. I., Wolfe, R. S. 1985. Evidence of a common pathway of carbon dioxide reduction to methane in methanogens. *J. Bacteriol.* 163:126–31

80. Jones, W. J., Guyot, J. -P., Wolfe, R. S. 1984. Methanogenesis from sucrose by defined immobilized consortia. *Appl. Environ. Microbiol.* 47:1–6

81. Jones, W. J., Leigh, J. A., Mayer, F., Woese, C. R., Wolfe, R. S. 1983. *Methanococcus jannaschii* sp. nov., an extremely thermophilic methanogen from a submarine hydrothermal vent. *Arch. Microbiol.* 136:254–61

82. Jones, W. J., Whitman, W. B., Fields, R. D., Wolfe, R. S. 1983. Growth and plating efficiency of methanococci on agar media. *Appl. Environ. Microbiol.* 46:220–26

83. Keltjens, J. T., Huberts, M. J., Laarhoven, W. H., Vogels, G. D. 1983. Structural elements of methanopterin, a novel pterin present in *Methanobacterium thermoautotrophicum.* *Eur. J. Biochem.* 130:537–44

84. Kluyver, A. J., Donker, H. J. L. 1926. Die Einheit in der Biochemie. *Chem. Zelle Gewebe* 13:134–90

85. Knight, M., Wolfe, R. S., Elsden, S. R. 1966. Synthesis of amino acids by *Methanobacterium omelianskii.* *Biochem. J.* 99:76–86

86. Kucera, S., Wolfe, R. S. 1957. A selective enrichment method for *Gallionella ferruginea.* *J. Bacteriol.* 74:344–49

87. Langenberg, K. F., Bryant, M. P., Wolfe, R. S. 1968. Hydrogen-oxidizing methane bacteria. II. Electron microscopy. *J. Bacteriol.* 95:1124–29

88. Leigh, J. A., Mayer, F., Wolfe, R. S. 1981. *Acetogenium kivui,* a new thermophilic hydrogen-oxidizing acetogenic bacterium. *Arch. Microbiol.* 129:275–80

89. Leigh, J. A., Rinehart, K. L. Jr., Wolfe, R. S. 1983. Structure of methanofuran (carbon dioxide reduction factor) of *Methanobacterium.* *J. Am. Chem. Soc.* 106:3636–40

90. Leigh, J. A., Rinehart, K. L. Jr., Wolfe R. S. 1985. Methanofuran (carbon dioxide reduction factor), a formyl carrier in methane production from carbon dioxide in *Methanobacterium.* *Biochemistry* 24:995–99

91. Leigh, J. A., Wolfe, R. S. 1983. Carbon dioxide reduction factor and methanopterin, two coenzymes required for CO_2 reduction to methane by extracts of *Methanobacterium.* *J. Biol. Chem.* 258:7435–40

92. Livingston, D. A., Pfaltz, A., Schreiber, J., Eschenmoser, A., Ankel-Fuchs, D., et al. 1984. Zur kenntnis des faktors F_{430} aus methanogenic bakterien: Struktur des proteinfreien faktors. *Helv. Chim. Acta* 67:334–51

93. Macy, J. M., Snellen, J. E., Hungate, R. E. 1972. Use of syringe methods for anaerobiosis. *Am. J. Clin. Nutr.* 25:1318–23

94. McBride, B. C., Wolfe, R. S. 1971. A new coenzyme of methyl transfer, coenzyme M. *Biochemistry* 10:2317–24

95. McBride, B. C., Wolfe, R. S. 1971. Inhibition of methanogenesis by DDT. *Nature* 234:551–52

96. McBride, B. C., Wolfe, R. S. 1971. Biosynthesis of dimethylarsine by

Methanobacterium. Biochemistry 10: 4312–17
97. Miller, T. L., Wolin, M. J. 1974. A serum bottle modification of the Hungate technique for cultivating obligate anaerobes. *Appl. Microbiol.* 27:985–87
98. Mortenson, L. E., Valentine, R. C., Carnahan, J. E. 1962. An electron transport factor from *Clostridium pasteurianum. Biochem. Biophys. Res. Commum.* 7:448–52
99. Mortlock, R. P., Valentine, R. C., Wolfe, R. S. 1959. Carbon dioxide activation in the pyruvate clastic system of *Clostridium butyricum. J. Biol. Chem.* 234: 1653–56
100. Mortlock, R. P., Wolfe, R. S. 1959. Reversal of pyruvate oxidation in *Clostridium butyricum. J. Biol. Chem.* 234: 1657–58
101. Nagle, D. P. Jr., Wolfe, R. S. 1983. Component A of the methyl coenzyme M methylreductase system of *Methanobacterium:* Resolution into four components. *Proc. Natl. Acad. Sci. USA* 80:2151–55
102. Noll, K. M., Donnelly, M. I., Wolfe, R. S. 1987. Synthesis of 7-mercaptoheptanoylthreonine phosphate and its activity in the methylcoenzyme M methylreductase system. *J. Biol. Chem.* 262:513–15
103. Noll, K. M., Rinehart, K. L. Jr., Tanner, R. S., Wolfe, R. S. 1986. Structure of component B (7-mercaptoheptanoyl-threonine phosphate) of the methylcoenzyme M methylreductase system of *Methanobacterium thermoautotrophicum. Proc. Natl. Acad. Sci. USA* 83: 4238–42
104. Noll, K. M., Wolfe, R. S. 1986. Component C of the methylcoenzyme M methylreductase system contains bound 7-mercaptoheptanoylthreonine phosphate (HS-HTP). *Biochem. Biophys. Res. Commun.* 139:889–95
105. Noll, K. M., Wolfe, R. S. 1987. The role of 7-mercaptoheptanoylthreonine phosphate in the methylcoenzyme M methylreductase system from *Methanobacterium thermoautotrophicum. Biochem. Biophys. Res. Commun.* 145: 204–10
106. Olson, K. D., Won, H., Wolfe, R. S., Hare, D. R., Summers, M. F. 1990. Stereochemical studies of coenzyme F_{430} based on 2D NOESY back calculations. *J. Am. Chem. Soc.* 112:5884–86
107. Pfaltz, A., Jaun, B., Fassler, A., Eschenmoser, A., Jaenchen, R., et al. 1982. Zur Kenntnis des Faktors F_{430} aus methanogenen Bakterien: Struktur des

porphinoiden Ligandsystems. *Helv. Chim. Acta* 64:828–65
108. Poirot, C. M., Kengen, S. W. M., Valk, E., Keltjens, J. T., van der Drift, C., Vogels, G. D. 1987. Formation of methylcoenzyme M from formaldehyde by cell-free extracts of *Methanobacterium thermoautotrophicum.* Evidence for the involement of a corinoid-containing methyltransferase. *FEMS Microbiol. Lett.* 40:7–13
109. Roberton, A. M., Wolfe, R. S. 1969. ATP requirement in methanogenesis in cell extracts of *Methanobacterium. Biochem. Biophys. Acta.* 192:420–29
110. Roberton, A. M., Wolfe, R. S. 1970. Adenosine triphosphate pools in *Methanobacterium. J. Bacteriol.* 102:43–51
111. Romesser, J. A. 1978. *Activation and reduction of carbon dioxide to methane in* Methanobacterium thermoautotrophicum. PhD thesis. Urbana: Univ. Ill. 183 pp.
112. Romesser, J. A., Wolfe, R. S. 1981. Interaction of coenzyme M and formaldehyde in methanogenesis. *J. Biochem.* 197:565–71
113. Romesser, J. A., Wolfe, R. S. 1982. CDR factor, a new coenzyme required for CO_2 reduction to methane. *Zentralbl. Bakteriol. Parasitenkd. Infektionskr. Hyg. Abt. 1: Orig.* C3:271–76
114. Romesser, J. A., Wolfe, R. S. 1982. Coupling of methylcoenzyme M reduction with carbon dioxide activation in extracts of *Methanobacterium. J. Bacteriol.* 152:840–47
115. Romesser, J. A., Wolfe, R. S., Mayer, F., Spiess, E., Walther-Mauruschat, A. 1979. *Methanogenium,* a new genus of marine methanogenic bacteria, and characterization of *Methanogenium cariaci* sp. nov. and *Methanogenium marisnigri* sp. nov. *Arch. Microbiol.* 121:147–53
116. Rouvière, P. E., Bobik, T. A., Wolfe, R. S. 1988. Reductive activation of the methylcoenzyme M methylreductase system of *Methanobacterium thermoautotrophicum. J. Bacteriol.* 170:3946–52
117. Rouvière, P. E., Escalante-Semerena, J. C., Wolfe, R. S. 1985. Component A2 of the methylcoenzyme M methylreductase system from *Methanobacterium thermoautotrophicum. J. Bacteriol.* 162: 61–66
118. Rouvière, P. E., Wolfe, R. S. 1987. Use of subunits of the methylreductase protein for taxonomy of methanogenic bacteria. *Arch. Microbiol.* 148:253–59
119. Rouvière, P. E., Wolfe, R. S. 1987.

2',3' dialdehyde of ATP: a specific, irreversible inhibitor of component A3 of the methylreductase system of *Methanobacterium thermoautotrophicum*. *J. Bacteriol.* 169: 1737–39

120. Rouvière, P. E., Wolfe, R. S. 1988. Novel biochemistry of methanogenesis. *J. Biol. Chem.* 263:7913–16

121. Rouvière, P. E., Wolfe, R. S. 1989. Component A3 of the methylcoenzyme M methylreductase system of *Methanobacterium thermoautotrophicum* ΔH: Resolution into two components. *J. Bacteriol.* 171:4556–62

122. Shapiro, S., Wolfe, R. S. 1980. Methylcoenzyme M, an intermediate in methanogenic dissimilation of C_1 compounds by *Methanosarcina barkeri*. *J. Bacteriol.* 141:728–34

123. Spormann, A. M., Wolfe, R. S. 1984. Chemotactic, magnetotactic and tactile behavior in a magnetic spirillum. *FEMS Microbiol. Lett.* 22:171–77

124. Tanner, R. S., Wolfe, R. S. 1988. Nutritional requirements of *Methanomicrobium mobile*. *Appl. Environ. Microbiol.* 54:625–28

125. Tanner, R. S., Wolfe, R. S., Ljungdahl, R. S. 1978. Tetrahydrofolate enzyme levels in *Acetobacterium woodii* and their implication in the synthesis of acetate from CO_2. *J. Bacteriol.* 134:668–70

126. Taylor, C. D., McBride, B. C., Wolfe, R. S., Bryant, M. P. 1974. Coenzyme M, essential for growth of a rumen strain of *Methanobacterium ruminantium*. *J. Bacteriol.* 120:974–75

127. Taylor, C. D., Wolfe, R. S. 1974. A simplified assay for coenzyme M ($HSCH_2CH_2SO_3$). *J. Biol. Chem.* 249: 4886–90

128. Taylor, C. D., Wolfe, R. S. 1974. Structure and methylation of coenzyme M ($HSCH_2CH_2SO_3$). *J. Biol. Chem.* 249:4879–85

129. TeBrömmelstroet, B. W., Hensgens, C. M. H., Keltjens, J. T., van der Drift, C., Vogels, G. D. 1990. Purification and properties of 5,10-methylenetetrahydromethanopterin reductase, a coenzyme F_{420}-dependent enzyme, from *Methanobacterium thermoautotrophicum* strain ΔH. *J. Biol. Chem.* 265: 1852–57

130. Twarog, R., Wolfe, R. S. 1962. Enzymatic phosphorylation of butyrate. *J. Biol. Chem.* 237:2474–77

131. Twarog, R., Wolfe, R. S. 1963. Role of butyryl phosphate in the energy metabolism of *Clostridium tetanomorphum*. *J. Bacteriol.* 86:112–17

132. Tzeng, S. F., Bryant, M. P., Wolfe, R. S. 1975. Factor 420-dependent pyridine nucleotide linked formate metabolism of *Methanobacterium ruminantium*. *J. Bacteriol.* 121:192–96

133. Tzeng, S. F., Wolfe, R. S., Bryant, M. P. 1975. Factor 420-dependent pyridine nucleotide linked hydrogenase system of *Methanobacterium ruminantium*. *J. Bacteriol.* 121:184–90

134. Uffen, R. L., Wolfe, R. S. 1970. Anaerobic growth of purple nonsulfur bacteria under dark conditions. *J. Bacteriol.* 104:462–72.

134a. Uffen, R. L., Wolfe, R. S. 1971. Mutants of *Rhodospirillum rubrum* obtained after long-term anaerobic dark growth. *J. Bacteriol.* 108:1348–56

135. Valentine, R. C., Bojanowski, R., Gaudy, E., Wolfe, R. S. 1962. Mechanism of the allantoin fermentation. *J. Biol. Chem.* 237:2271–77

136. Valentine, R. C., Brill, W. J., Wolfe, R. S. 1962. Role of ferredoxin in pyridine nucleotide reduction. *Proc. Natl. Acad. Sci. USA* 48:1856–60

137. Valentine, R. C., Brill, W. J., Wolfe, R. S., San Pietro, A. 1963. Activity of PPNR in ferredoxin-dependent reactions of *Clostridium pasteurianum*. *Biochem. Biophys. Res. Commun.* 10:73–78

138. Valentine, R. C., Drucker, H., Wolfe, R. S. 1964. Glyoxylate fermentation by *Streptococcus allantoicus*. *J. Bacteriol.* 87:241–46

139. Valentine, R. C., Jackson, R. L., Wolfe, R. S. 1962. Role of ferredoxin in hydrogen metabolism of *Micrococcus lactilyticus*. *Biochem. Biophys. Res. Commun.* 7:453–56

140. Valentine, R. C., Mortenson, L. E., Mower, H. F., Jackson, R. L., Wolfe, R. S. 1963. Ferredoxin requirement for reduction of hydroxylamine by *Clostridium pasteurianum*. *J. Biol. Chem.* 238:857–58

141. Valentine, R. C., Wolfe, R. S. 1960. Biosynthesis of carbamyl oxamic acid. *Biochem. Biophys. Res. Commun.* 2: 384–87

142. Valentine, R. C., Wolfe, R. S. 1960. Phosphorolysis of carbamyl oxamic acid. *Biochim. Biophys. Acta.* 45:389–91

143. Valentine, R. C., Wolfe, R. S. 1961. Glyoxylurea. *Biochem. Biophys. Res. Commun.* 5:305–08

144. Valentine, R. C., Wolfe, R. S. 1961. Phosphate-dependent degradation of urea. *Nature* 191:925–26

145. Valentine, R. C., Wolfe, R. S. 1963. Role of ferredoxin in the metabolism of

34   WOLFE

molecular hydrogen. *J. Bacteriol.* 85:1114–20
146. van Beelen, P., Stassen, A. P. M., Bosch, J. W. G., Vogels, G. D., Guijt, W., Haasnoot, C. A. G. 1984. Elucidation of the structure of methanopterin, a coenzyme from *Methanobacterium thermoautotrophicum,* using two-dimensional-nuclear-magnetic reasonance techniques. *Eur. J. Biochem.* 138:563–71
147. Deleted in proof
148. Vatter, A. E., Douglas, H. C., Wolfe, R. S. 1959. Structure of *Rhodomicrobium vannielii. J. Bacteriol.* 77:812–13
149. Vatter, A. E., Wolfe, R. S. 1956. Electron microscopy of *Gallionella ferruginea. J. Bacteriol.* 72:248–52
150. Vatter, A. E., Wolfe, R. S. 1958. The structure of photosynthetic bacteria. *J. Bacteriol.* 75:480–88
151. Whitman W. B., Ankwanda, E., Wolfe, R. S. 1982. Nutrition and carbon metabolism of *Methanococcus voltae. J. Bacteriol.* 149:852–63
152. Whitman, W. B., Wolfe, R. S. 1980. Presence of nickel in Factor F_{430} from *Methanobacterium bryantii. Biochem. Biophys. Res. Commun.* 92:1196–201
153. Whitman, W. B., Wolfe, R. S. 1983. Activation of the methylreductase system from *Methanobacterium bryantii* by ATP. *J. Bact.* 154:640–49
154. Whitman, W. B., Wolfe, R. S. 1987. Inhibition by corrins of the ATP-dependent activation and CO_2 reduction by the methylreductase system in *Methanobacterium bryantii. J. Bacteriol.* 169:87–92
155. Whitman, W. B., Wolfe, R. S. 1985. Activation of the methylreductase system from *Methanobacterium bryantii* by corrins. *J. Bacteriol.* 164:165–72
156. Widdel, F., Rouvière, P. E., Wolfe, R. S. 1988. Classification of secondary alcohol-utilizing methanogens including a new thermophilic isolate. *Arch. Microbiol.* 150:477–81
157. Widdel, F., Wolfe, R. S. 1989. Expression of secondary alcohol specific enzyme from *Methanogenium thermophilum* strain TCI. *Arch. Microbiol.* 152:322–28
158. Wingard, M., Matsueda, G., Wolfe, R. S. 1972. Myxobacter AL 1 protease II: specific peptide bond cleavage on the amino side of lysine. *J. Bacteriol.* 112:940–49
159. Winter, J., Wolfe, R. S. 1980. Methane formation from fructose by syntrophic associations of *Acetobacterium woodii* and different strains of methanogens. *Arch. Microbiol.* 124:73–79

160. Winter, J., Wolfe, R. S. 1979. Complete degradation of carbohydrate to carbon dioxide and methane by syntrophic cultures of *Acetobacterium woodii* and *Methanosarcina barkeri. Arch. Microbiol.* 121:97–102
161. Woese, C. R., Fox, G. E. 1977. Phylogenetic structure of the prokaryotic domain: the primary kingdoms. *Proc. Natl. Acad. Sci. USA* 74:5088–90
162. Woese, C. R., Kandler, O., Wheelis, M. L. 1990. Towards a natural system of organisms: proposal for the domains Archaea, Bacteria, and Eucarya. *Proc. Natl. Acad. Sci. USA* 87:4576–79
163. Woese, C. R., Wolfe, R. S., eds. 1985. *The Archaebacteria,* Vol. 8, *The Bacteria,* ed. I. C. Gunsalus, J. R. Sokatch, L. N. Ornston. Orlando: Academic. 582 pp.
164. Wolfe, R. S. 1958. Cultivation, morphology and classification of the iron bacteria. *J. Am. Water Works Assoc.* 50:1241–49
165. Wolfe, R. S. 1960. Observations and studies of *Crenothrix polyspora. J. Am. Water Works Assoc.* 52:915-18
166. Wolfe, R. S., O'Kane, D. J. 1953. Cofactors of the phosphoroclastic reaction of *Clostridium butyricum. J. Biol. Chem.* 205:755–65
167. Wolfe, R. S., O'Kane, D. J. 1955. Cofactors of the carbon dioxide exchange reaction of *Clostridium butyricum. J. Biol. Chem.* 215:637–43
168. Wolfe, R. S., Pfennig, N. 1977. Reduction of sulfur by spirillum 5175 and syntrophism with *Chlorobium. Appl. Environ. Microbiol.* 33:427–33
169. Wolfe, R. S., Thauer, R. K., Pfenning, N. 1987. A "capillary racetrack" method for isolation of magnetotactic bacteria. *FEMS Microbiol. Ecol.* 45:31–35
170. Wolin, E. A., Wolfe, R. S., Wolin, M. J. 1964. Viologen dye inhibition of methane formation by *Methanobacillus omelianskii. J. Bacteriol.* 87:993–98
171. Wolin, E. A., Wolin, M. J., Wolfe, R. S. 1963. Formation of methane by bacterial extracts. *J. Biol. Chem.* 238:2882–86
172. Wolin, M. J., Wolin, E. A., Wolfe, R. S. 1963. ATP-dependent formation of methane from methylcobalamin by extracts of *Methanobacillus omelianskii. Biochem. Biophys. Res. Commun.* 12:464–68
173. Wolin, M. J., Wolin, E. A., Wolfe, R. S. 1964. The cobalamin product of the conversion of methylcobalamin to CH_4 by extracts of *Methanobacillus omelianskii. Biochem. Biophys. Res. Commun.* 15:420–23

174. Won, H., Olson, K. D., Wolfe, R. S., Summer, M. F. 1990. Two-dimensional NMR studies of native coenzyme F_{430}. *J. Am. Chem. Soc.* 112:2178–84

175. Wood, J. M., Allam, A. M., Brill, W. J., Wolfe, R. S. 1965. Formation of methane from serine by extracts of *Methanobacillus omelianskii*. *J. Biol. Chem.* 240:4564–69

176. Wood, J. M., Wolfe, R. S. 1965. Formation of CH_4 from N^5-methyltetrahydrofolate monoglutamate by cell extracts of *Methanobacillus omelianskii*. *Biochem. Biophys. Res. Commun.* 19: 306–11

177. Wood, J. M., Wolfe, R. S. 1966. Alkylatin of an enzyme in the methaneforming system of *Methanobacillus omelianskii*. *Biochem. Biophys. Res. Commun.* 22:119–23

178. Wood, J. M., Wolfe, R. S. 1966. Components required for the formation of CH_4 from methylcobalamin by extracts of *Methanobacillus omelianskii*. *J. Bacteriol.* 92:696–700

179. Wood, J. M., Wolfe, R. S. 1966. Propylation and purification of a B_{12} enzyme involved in methane formation. *Biochemistry* 5:3598–603

180. Wood, J. M., Wolin, M. J., Wolfe, R. S. 1966. Formation of methane from methyl Factor B and methyl Factor III by extracts of *Methanobacillus omelianskii*. *Biochemistry* 5:2381–84

181. Zeikus, J. G., Wolfe, R. S. 1972. *Methanobacterium thermoautotrophicus* sp.n., an anaerobic, autotrophic, extreme thermophile. *J. Bacteriol.* 109: 707–13

182. Zeikus, J. G., Wolfe, R. S. 1973. Fine structure of *Methanobacterium thermoautotrophicus:* effect of growth temperature on morphology and ultrastructure. *J. Bacteriol.* 113:461–67

Annu. Rev. Microbiol. 1991. 45:37–67

SERINE β-LACTAMASES AND PENICILLIN-BINDING PROTEINS

Jean-Marie Ghuysen

Centre d'Ingénierie des Protéines, Université de Liège, Institut de Chimie, B6, B-4000 Sart Tilman (Liège 1), Belgium

KEY WORDS: bacterial wall peptidoglycan, β-lactam antibiotics, emergence of resistance, enzyme catalysis, serine peptidases, divergent evolution, molecular modeling, protein engineering

CONTENTS

The Penicillin-Interactive, Active-Site Serine Protein Family 37
The Low-Mr PBPs 45
The β-Lactamases and the Penicillin Sensory-Transducer BLAR 47
The Atomic-Level Enzyme-Ligand Interactions 50
The High-Mr PBPs of Class A and B 54
Intrinsic Resistance by Emergence of Altered High-Mr PBPs 58

The Penicillin-Interactive, Active-Site Serine Protein Family

In the bacterial world, hundreds, perhaps thousands, of distinct proteins catalyze rupture of the lactam amide bond of penicillin and transfer the penicilloyl moiety to an essential serine, forming a serine ester-linked acyl derivative (Figure 1). The reaction is analogous to the catalyzed rupture of a peptide bond by the serine peptidases of the trypsin and subtilisin families. It

37

0066-4227/91/1001-0037$02.00

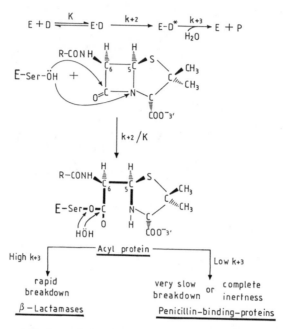

Figure 1 The penicillin-interactive, active-site serine proteins. Reactions with β-lactam carbonyl donors. E = protein; D = β-lactam carbonyl donor; E·D = Michaelis complex; E-D* = acyl protein; P = reaction product (penicilloate); K = dissociation constant; k_{+2} and k_{+3} = first-order rate constants. The acyl enzyme mechanism was proposed in 1965 (112). Involvement of an essential serine was demonstrated in 1976 for reaction with the *Streptomyces* R61 penicillin-binding protein (36) and in 1979–1981 for reaction with several β-lactamases (17, 20, 35, 71). The concept of a penicillin-interactive, active-site serine protein family was put forward in 1988 (66).

involves initial binding of the ligand to the enzyme (K), enzyme acylation (k_{+2}) and, in a third step, enzyme deacylation (k_{+3}). A common substrate requirement is that a negative charge must occur at the 3' position in the penicillins and the 4' position in the cephalosporins (this group is usually a carboxylate, but a sulfonate is found in the monobactams), and the acyl side chain borne by the β-lactam ring must be on the β face in a *cisoid* position relative to the thiazolidine or dihydrothiazine ring. As a result of these requirements, the scissile amide bond in the β-lactam ring is equivalent to a carboxy-terminal peptide bond extending between two carbon atoms with the D configuration

Given the endocyclic nature of the scissile bond, acylation of the active-site serine generates a bulky leaving group that remains part of the acyl enzyme through the C5-C6 bond (Figure 1) and thus cannot diffuse away. As a result of this occupancy, only water has access to the active site and can attack the acyl enzyme, release the penicilloyl moiety, and concomitantly recover the enzyme. This mechanism is general. However, with the β-lactamases, water has a facile access to the active site and is an excellent attacking nucleophile. The β-lactamases turn over rapidly and hydrolyze effectively the β-lactam substrates into biologically inactive metabolites. With the penicillin-binding proteins (PBPs), the acyl enzyme is almost hydrolytically inert. The higher the k_{+2}/K and the smaller the k_{+3} are, the lower the antibiotic concentration required to immobilize completely a given PBP as acyl enzyme at the steady-state of the reaction (46, 78).

The fact that the acyl enzymes are sufficiently stable to be analyzed with SDS gel electrophoresis has led to the development of a convenient procedure for the detection of the individual PBPs as radioactively labeled proteins (104). All the bacteria possess multiple PBPs. Each bacterial species has its own assortment of PBPs. The PBPs occur in a small number of copies per cell, from a few hundred to one or two thousand. Their affinities for penicillin and other β-lactam antibiotics vary widely, and their molecular masses range from 25,000 to 100,000.

The penicillin-interactive proteins fall into three groups: the β-lactamases, the low-Mr PBPs, and the high-Mr PBPs. The β-lactamases and the low-Mr PBPs are monofunctional catalytic entities. The active-site serine resides close to the amino terminus of the protein. The high-Mr PBPs possess a several-hundred–amino acid domain that is fused to the amino terminus of the penicillin-binding domain per se, which is assumed to start 60 residues upstream from the essential serine. Pair-wise comparison of amino acid sequences leads to the conclusion that each of these groups falls into several classes (Figure 2). Members of a given class are related in the primary structure. However, proteins that lack relatedness may fulfill similar functions. Whether they belong to class A, C, or D, the β-lactamases are β-lactam antibiotic-hydrolyzing enzymes. Conversely, similarity in the primary structure does not necessarily reflect similarity in the physiological function. The *Streptomyces* K15 low-Mr PBP of class A is related to the staphylococcal β-lactamase of class A, and the *Streptomyces* R61 low-Mr PBP of class B is related to the *Citrobacter freundii* β-lactamase of class C by a low but significant similarity index of about 7. The carboxy-terminal, penicillin-binding domain of the class C high-Mr PBP BLAR of *Bacillus licheniformis* is related to the Oxa-2 β-lactamase of class D by a high-similarity index of 40.

Divergent evolution implies that proteins of the same family evolved from a common ancestor. Depending on the evolutionary distance, they may have acquired very different amino acid sequences and distinct functionalities and specificities while conserving the same polypeptide scaffolding. The case of a divergent evolutionary relationship between the penicillin-interactive, active-site serine proteins and domains is supported by a bulk of experimental data and predictional studies.

The three-dimensional structures are known for the class A β-lactamases of

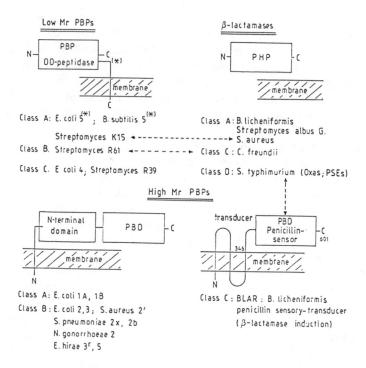

Figure 2 The penicillin-interactive, active-site serine proteins. Groups, classes, and membrane topology. PBP/PBD, penicillin-binding protein/domain; (*), membrane-bound; PHP, penicillin-hydrolyzing protein. Many β-lactamases other than those listed are of known primary structure. ↔ indicates similarity in the primary structure. The algorithm used for homology searches (66) generates the best alignment for each pair of amino acid sequences and expresses the extent of similarity by a score. This score is the sum of the individual scores obtained for each pair of amino acids minus a penalty of 8 for each gap introduced. Pair-wise comparison of members of a given class generates scores that are at least 5 but may be as high as 50 standard deviations above that expected from a run of 20 randomized pairs of proteins with the same amino acid compositions as the two proteins under consideration. This standard deviation defines a similarity index. Figure 7 shows pair-wise comparison of the amino-terminal and carboxy-terminal domains of the high-Mr PBPs of class A and B.

Staphylococcus aureus (56), *Streptomyces albus* G (25, 62), and *B. licheniformis* (82); the class C β-lactamase of *C. freundii* (89); and the class B low-Mr PBP of *Streptomyces* R61 (70, 72). They have a unique signature in the form of several amino acid groupings that occur along their amino acid sequences (66, 103) (Figure 3): the tetrad active-site serine-X-X-lysine (S*XXK), where X is a variable amino acid; the triad serine or tyrosine-X-asparagine [S(Y)XN]; a peptide segment (D/E) that contains two dicarboxylic amino acids; and the triad lysine or histidine-threonine or serine-glycine [K(H)T(S)G]. As a result of the folding of the polypeptide chain, these four

Class	Low-Mr PBPs	NH_3^+	↔	S*XXK	↔	S(Y)XN	↔	D/E	↔	K(H)T(S)G	↔	COO^-	Ref.
A	E.coli 5	D30	42	S73LTK	62	S139 GN	41	D183,D204	37	K242 TG	158	403	15
	B.subtilis 5	?	?	S36MTK	63	S100 AN	43	E144, D179	47	K227 TG	181	412	115
	Streptomyces K15	V30	33	S64TTK	57	S125 GC	41	D169, D172	69	K242 TG	46	291	(*)
B	Streptomyces R61	A32	60	S93VTK	93	Y190 SN	63	D256,STEQ	69	H329 TG	74	406	30
C	E.coli 4	A21	40	S62TQK	240	S306DN	38	D347,D355	61	K427 TG	57	477	83
	Actinomadura R39	R50	47	S98NMK	245	S347NN	44	D394,D411	46	K458TG	77	538	(*)
β-Lactamases													
A	S.aureus	K25	37	S63TSK	54	S121DN	33	E*157,TELN	65	K225 SG	53	281	19
	Streptomyces albus G	G40--S47	41	S89VFK	60	S153DN	35	E*189PELN	65	K257 TG	52	312	23
	B.licheniformis	S35--E45	40	S86TIK	54	S144DN	35	E*180,PELN	67	K248 TG	56	307	87
C	C.freundii	A21	42	S84VSK	82	Y170AN	64	D217 AEAY	65	K335 TG	45	381	79
D	Oxa-2	Q23	44	S68TFK	74	Y146GN	12	E161	48	K210 TG	62	275	22
High-Mr PBPs													
A	E.coli 1A	M1	463	S465NIK	55	S524KN	32	E559	156	K716 TG	131	850	14
	E.coli 1B	M1	508	S510LAK	58	S572MN	26	D601, E620	77	K698 TG	143	844	14
B	E.coli 2	M1	328	S330TVK	53	S387 AD	34	E424,D447	96	K544 SG	86	633	5
	E.coli 3	M1	305	S307TVK	48	S359 SN	34	E396,D409	84	K494 TG	91	588	86
	S.aureus 2'	M1	403	S405TIK	55	S464DN	25	E492,D511	87	K599 SG	68	670	
	N.gonorrhoeae 2	M1	308	S310A1K	48	S362SN	34	E399,E414	82	K497 TG	81	581	100
	S.pneumoniae 2x	M1	335	S337TMK	54	S395 SN	34	E432,D440	106	KS47 SG	200	750	74
	S.pneumoniae 2b	M1	383	S385VVK	53	S442 SN	32	E475, E483	130	K614 TG	62	679	28
	E.hirae 5	M1	420	S420TFK	54	S480DN	25	E508, E542	74	K617 TG	58	678	33
C	B.licheniformis BLAR	M1	400	S402TYK	70	Y476 GN	11	D490	48	K539 TG	59	601	73

Figure 3 The penicillin-interactive, active-site serine proteins. Location of the motifs S*XXK, S(Y)XN, D/E, and K(H)T(S)G along the amino acid sequences. The amino acid numbering refers to the protein precursors. The low-Mr PBPs and the β-lactamases are manufactured with a cleavable signal peptide. Cleavage may produce a mature protein that has a ragged amino terminus (NH_3^+). The amino acid sequence of the *Streptomyces albus* G β-lactamase (23) has been corrected by deleting Gly128 and substituting the dyad Gln141-Leu142 by Met (4, 67). In the ABL numbering scheme for the β-lactamases of class A (4), S* of the S*XXK motif is at position 70, S of the SDN motif is at position 130, E* of the E/D motif is at position 166, and K of the KT(S)G motif is at position 234. The *E. coli* PBP1B is a mixture of two major proteins resulting from the use of alternative sites for the initiation of translation. The numbering refers to the largest form. (*), Unpublished data (see text). Reference 86 should read 85.

motifs are brought close to each other, generating an active-site at the junction between an all-α domain and an α-β domain whose five-stranded β-sheet is protected by additional α-helices on both faces (Figure 4). In this structure, the serine of the S*XXK motif is at the amino terminus of helix α2 of the all-α domain and occupies a central position in the cavity. The S(Y)XN motif connects helices α4 and α5 of the all-α domain and forms one side of the cavity. The D/E motif resides at the entrance of the cavity. The K(H)T(S)G motif on the innermost β3 strand of the β-sheet forms the other side of the cavity. Using the *S. aureus* β-lactamase as reference, one finds that the differences in length in the *S. albus* G β-lactamase, the *C. freundii* β-lactamase, and the *Streptomyces* R61 PBP are associated with surface loops, small helices, and β-strands that occur away from the active site and that connect conserved structures (Figure 5). In this proposed scheme, the conserved secondary structures have the same numbering.

Superimposition experiments lead to the result that the β3 strand is sim-

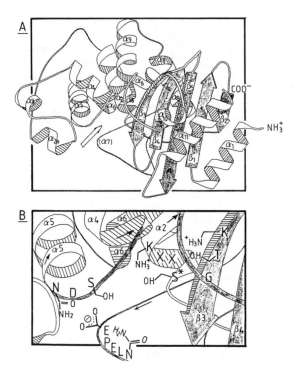

Figure 4 Structure of the *Streptomyces albus* G β-lactamase of class A. Polypeptide folding (*A*) and disposition of the conserved motifs (*B*). The active site is indicated by the white arrow in A and is threefold enlarged in B. Adapted from References 25, 62, 67.

ilarly situated with respect to the S*XXK motif in the three-dimensional structures. However, the Y(A or S)N motif in the β-lactamase of class C and the PBP is about 4–5 Å farther away from the K(H)T(S)G motif than the corresponding SDN motif in the β-lactamases of class A. As a consequence of this displacement, the phenolic oxygen of the tyrosine of the Y(A or S)N motif and the γ-OH of the serine of the SDN motif are similarly disposed with respect to the γ-OH of the active-site serine of the S*XXK motif. Superimposition experiments also highlight noticeable differences at the level of the D/E motif. Site-directed mutagenesis (49) and molecular modeling (J. Lamotte-Brasseur, G. Dive, O. Dideberg, J.-M. Frére, & J.-M. Ghuysen, in preparation) support the view that the glutamic acid E* of the sequence E*XELN (Figures 3 and 4) of the class A β-lactamases is essential and that a water molecule bound to this glutamic acid acts as proton abstractor-donor in catalysis. The corresponding sequences DAEAY in the *C. freundii* β-lactamase and DSTEQ in the *Streptomyces* R61 PBP (Figure 3) have a spatial

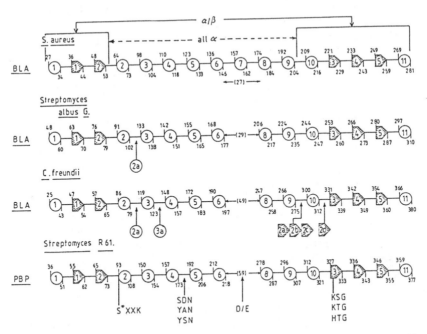

Figure 5 Occurrence of the conserved motifs and secondary structures along the amino acid sequences of the *S. aureus* β-lactamase of class A (56), the *Streptomyces albus* G β-lactamase of class A (25, 62, 67), the *C. freundii* β-lactamase of class C (89), and the *Streptomyces* R61 PBP (70, 72). *Circles*, α-helix; *pointing boxes*, β-strand. BLA = β-lactamase. The amino acid numbering is that of the protein precursors.

disposition that is not compatible with such a role in catalysis. Yet alterations of the D/E motif of the *C. freundii* β-lactamase [DAEAY −> DAKAY and DAEAY −> (E, K or T)AEAY] modify the specificity profile of the enzyme and extend its hydrolytic activity to oxyimino-cephalosporins (117, 118).

All the β-lactamases, the low-Mr PBPs, and the pencillin-binding domains of the high-Mr PBPs possess, along their amino acid sequences, the same four motifs as those found in the penicillin-interactive proteins of known three-dimensional structure (Figure 3). Identification of the S*XXK, S(Y)XN, and K(H/R)T(S)G motifs (66, 103) is not, most often, an issue of controversy [HTG occurs in the *Streptomyces* R61 PBP (30) and RSG in the PSE-4 carbenicillinase (10)], and analysis, at the molecular level, of protein mutants (see below) leads to the conclusion that these motifs are elements of the active sites. Given that several dicarboxylic amino acids occur approximately at the expected distances in the primary structures, identification of the D/E motif is hypothetical unless the importance of the predicted motif is demonstrated experimentally. As shown by site-directed mutagenesis, Asp444 in the high-Mr PBP2 of *Escherichia coli* is probably the homolog of the glutamic acid E* of the β-lactamases of class A (H. Adachi, M. Ishiguro, S. Imajo, T. Ohta, & H. Matsuzawa, personal communication).

The penicillin-interactive, active-site serine proteins and domains exhibit endless variations. Predictional studies suggest that the 275 amino acid β-lactamases of class D, which are the smallest known β-lactamases, have a shorter connection between the YDN and KTG motifs and that the homologous 477–amino acid PBP4 of *E. coli* (83) and 538–amino acid PBP of *Actinomadura* R39 (B. Granier, C. Duez, S. Lepage, J. Van Beeumen, S. Englebert, et al, in preparation), which are the largest known low-Mr PBPs/ DD-peptidases, have an additional 180– to 190–amino acid insert located between the S*XXK and SDN motifs and occurring on the surface of the protein. Deletion by genetic engineering of a substantial part of this insert from PBP4 produces a truncated protein that still binds penicillin (H. Mottl & W. Keck, personal communication). Several β-lactamases and low-Mr PBPs are susceptible to thiol reagents. The *Streptomyces* K15 PBP has two cysteines. One of them occurs in the active-site as a result of the replacement of the usual S(Y)XN motif by a SDC motif, and the other occurs at the tenth position downstream from the lysine of the KTG motif, i.e. probably on strand β4 (P. Palomeque-Messia, M. Leyh-Bouille, M. Nguyen-Distèche, C. Duez, S. Houba, et al, in preparation). Derivatization of one of these cysteines by para-chloromercuribenzoate greatly decreases but does not abolish the enzymatic activities of the PBP (77).

The wall peptidoglycan is an essential polymer of the bacterial cell. Its structure and biosynthesis are well-known (Figure 6). The peptidoglycan precursors are lipid-transported disaccharide (N-acetylglucosaminyl-N-acetylmuramyl)-L-Ala-γ-D-Glu-L-Xaa-D-Ala-D-Ala pentapeptide units. Depending on the bacterial species, L-Xaa is a diamino acid whose ω amino group is either free or substituted by additional amino acids. These precursors, the end products of the cytoplasmic and membrane cycles of the biosynthetic pathway, are transported onto the outer face of the plasma membrane for final peptidoglycan assembly, a process that requires a glycan chain elongation and interpeptide crosslinking machinery.

The penicillin-interactive, active-site serine proteins fulfill multiple functions. The low-Mr PBPs and the high-Mr PBPs of class A and B are involved, in one way or another, in peptidoglycan assembly. They are the targets of penicillin action. The β-lactamases are defensive enzymes that the bacteria synthesize to protect their PBPs from the deleterious effects of penicillin. β-Lactamase synthesis is not always constitutive. The high-Mr PBP BLAR of class C acts as a penicillin sensory-transducer involved in the specific inducibility of β-lactamase synthesis.

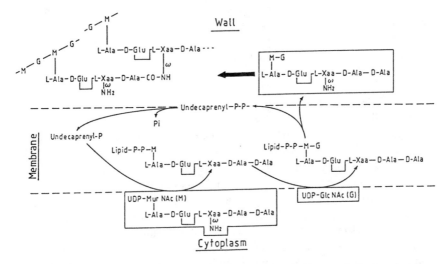

Figure 6 Bacterial wall peptidoglycan assembly from lipid-transported disaccharide-pentapeptide units. The final steps *(heavy arrow)* are made by transglycosylation and peptide crosslinking.

The Low-Mr PBPs

The low-Mr PBPs are manufactured with a cleavable signal peptide. Some low-Mr PBPs do not possess transmembrane segments. The *E. coli* PBP4 and the *Streptomyces* K15 PBP somehow interact with the membrane surface and are isolated as membrane components. Overproducing strains produce a high proportion of the PBPs in a water-soluble form. The PBP of *Streptomyces* R61 and that of *Actinomadura* R39 are excreted in the medium during growth. When compared to the excreted protein, the 406–amino acid precursor of the *Streptomyces* R61 PBP possesses both a cleavable peptide signal and a cleavable 26-amino acid carboxy-terminal extension (30). Should it not be removed during protein maturation, this carboxy-terminal extension might function as a stop transfer sequence.

All the other known low-Mr PBPs are membrane-bound (97) (Figure 2). The polypeptide chain does not terminate approximately 60 residues downstream from the KT(S)G motif as observed with the soluble PBPs, but has an ~50- to 100–amino acid carboxy-terminal extension (Figure 3), the end of which contains a signal-like peptide segment that serves as membrane anchor. As a consequence, the bulk of the protein is on the outer face of the membrane. Catalytically active, water-soluble derivatives that lack the membrane anchor can be produced by proteolytic treatment of isolated membranes (33, 123) and by engineering the encoding genes (34, 61).

The low-Mr PBPs are DD-peptidases. They catalyze acyl transfer reactions from D-alanyl-D-alanine–terminated peptides and depsipeptide analogs. Thus, rupture of the carboxy-terminal peptide (or ester) bond of acetyl$_2$-L-Lys-D-Ala-D-Ala (or Ac$_2$-L-Lys-D-Ala-D-lactate) involves transfer of the Ac$_2$-L-Lys-D-alanyl moiety to the active-site serine with formation of a serine-ester linked acyl (Ac$_2$-L-Lys-D-alanyl) enzyme, and then to an exogenous acceptor (45, 46, 88). Because the scissile bond is acyclic, the leaving group D-Ala (or D-lactate) does not remain part of the acyl enzyme and, as a corollary, the acyl enzyme is short-lived. The efficacy with which the low-Mr PBPs/DD-peptidases perform hydrolysis vs transpeptidation of the carbonyl donor depends on the efficacy with which water, the leaving group D-Ala, and an exogenous, suitably structured peptide H$_2$N-X can attack the acyl enzyme (Figure 7). This picture, however, is an oversimplification (40, 44, 47, 48, 88, 94). Hydrolysis and transpeptidation do not proceed through strictly identical pathways. The amino acceptor does not behave as a simple alternate attacking nucleophile of the acyl enzyme. It also influences both the initial binding of the D-alanyl-D-alanine-terminated carbonyl donor to the enzyme and the ensuing enzyme acylation step. An excess of amino acceptor can inhibit the DD-peptidase activity.

Most of the known low-Mr PBPs/DD-peptidases act mainly as DD-carboxypeptidases. The *Streptomyces* K15 PBP/DD-peptidase, however, is peculiar in that the relative acceptor activity for attack of the acyl enzyme is H$_2$O $\ll$ D-Ala $\ll$ H$_2$N-X (88). As a consequence, hydrolysis of Ac$_2$-L-Lys-D-Ala-D-Ala, in the absence of H$_2$N-X, is negligible because breakdown of the acyl enzyme by the leaving group D-Ala regenerates the original tripeptide. The enzyme turns over but is, seemingly, silent. In the presence of an amino compound H$_2$N-X of high acceptor activity, Ac$_2$-L-Lys-D-Ala-D-Ala

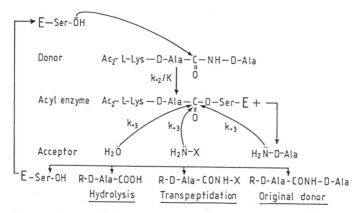

Figure 7 DD-peptidase–catalyzed reactions with Ac$_2$-L-Lys-D-Ala-D-Ala carbonyl donor. E-Ser-OH: enzyme and the active-site serine.

is quantitatively converted into the transpeptidated product Ac$_2$-L-Lys-D-Ala-CONH-X. This PBP functions as a strict transpeptidase.

Ac$_2$-L-Lys-D-Ala-D-Ala and β-lactam antibiotics are competing substrates of the low-Mr PBPs/DD-peptidases. The β-lactam antibiotics, however, are suicide substrates or mechanism-based inactivators: they immobilize the essential serine in the form of a stable ester-linked acyl enzyme (Figure 1). Yet the inertness of the acyl (benzylpenicilloyl) PBP is not absolute. Slow attack of the penicilloyl moiety by water generates penicilloate, which is the degradation product of β-lactamase action on penicillin. Alternatively, a slow and rate-limiting intramolecular rearrangement of the penicilloyl moiety can rupture the bond between C5 and C6 (Figure 1) and release the leaving group (3, 37–39, 80, 121). As a result of the vacancy thus created in the active site, the newly formed acyl (phenylacetylglycyl) enzyme undergoes immediate breakdown. Attack by water gives rise to phenylacetylglycine; attack by an amino compound NH$_2$-X gives rise to the transpeptidated product phenylacetylglycyl-CONH-X.

Ac$_2$-L-Lys-D-Ala-D-Ala is an analog of the carboxy-terminal tripeptide moiety of the peptidoglycan precursors (Figure 6). As with the reactions that they catalyze, the low-Mr PBPs/DD-carboxypeptidases help control the extent of peptidoglycan crosslinking (8a). They hydrolyze the carboxy-terminal D-alanyl-D-alanine peptide bond of peptidoglycan precursors and, in those bacterial species where peptidoglycan crosslinking is mediated by a carboxy-terminal D-alanyl-(D)-*meso*-diaminopimelic acid linkage, they hydrolyze bonds previously made through transpeptidation. All the bacteria possess one or several low-Mr PBPs. *Streptococcus pneumoniae* PBP3-negative mutants are severely affected in cell division and show highly altered morphology (99a). A 10-fold overproduction of the *E. coli* PBP5 causes conversion of the rod-shaped cells into round cells (106). The sporulation-specific PBP5a is temporally and spatially regulated in *B. subtilis*. It is detected in large amounts only during spore peptidoglycan synthesis from stage II to stage V (16, 113).

The β-Lactamases and the Penicillin Sensory-Transducer BLAR

The β-lactamases are secretory proteins. They are excreted in the growth medium (gram-positive bacteria) or they accumulate in the periplasm (gram-negative bacteria). The β-lactamase III of *Bacillus cereus* and that of *B. licheniformis* contain a diacylglyceride that is thioether-linked to the amino terminal cysteine and a fatty acid that is amide-linked to the same cysteine (57). This hydrophobic moiety functions as the anchor of the protein to the plasma membrane. In fact, these β-lactamases have membrane-bound and secretory forms.

The only known function of the β-lactamases is hydrolysis of the β-lactam antibiotics. β-Lactamases show hysteretic kinetics (99). A unique conformation is induced in the enzymes by each of several closely related β-lactam substrates, and the enzymes can adjust to unfavorable modifications in the substrate.

The β-lactamases lack DD-peptidase activity and thus do not interfere with wall peptidoglycan metabolism. However, they catalyze acyl transfer reactions on noncyclic depsipeptides (2, 91–93) with, for some of them, complex steady-state kinetics comparable to those shown by the low-Mr PBPs/DD-peptidases. Like the PBPs, the β-lactamases may give rise to long-lived acyl enzymes (42) and long-lived acyl enzymes may undergo various types of intramolecular rearrangements (18). Rupture of the bond between S1 and C5 in the acyl enzyme formed by reaction with the penam sulfones and 6-β-bromo(iodo)penicillanate or rupture of the bond between O1 and C5 in clavulanate is an integral part of the β-lactamase inactivation process. The established common feature is that of a branched pathway in which β-elimination leads to a hydrolytically inert acyl enzyme and, sometimes, to further modification of some residues of the active site.

The β-lactamases are dispensable enzymes, while the low-Mr PBPs/DD-peptidases fulfill functions in wall peptidoglycan metabolism. A possible mechanism that may explain the emergence of β-lactamases is the excretion of one or several low-Mr PBPs/DD-peptidases by bacteria exposed to lactam antibiotics. Further improvement of this detoxication mechanism results in the conversion of these water-soluble PBPs into β-lactam-hydrolyzing enzymes (69). Hence, the presumed features of evolution are catalysis of deacylation of the acyl enzyme formed with cyclic amide compounds, i.e. the β-lactam antibiotics, and loss of productive binding of planar acyclic amides, i.e. loss of DD-peptidase activity. Productive binding of planar acyclic esters has no physiological significance; it is conserved to varying extent.

Emergence of new β-lactamases can be achieved by altering a limited number of amino acids in the direct environment of the active site. A key mutation in the decreased cephalosporinase activity of the *S. albus* G β-lactamase of class A is the conversion of the SDN motif into SDS (62, 63). This single change has little effect on the hydrolytic activity towards good penicillin substrates but results in a drastically decreased hydrolytic activity towards the cephalosporins. Yet the presence of a SDN or SDS motif in the β-lactamases of class A does not, by itself, determine the specificity profile of the enzyme. The β-lactamase III of *B. cereus* possesses a SDS motif (57). It does not exhibit as strong a preference for penicillins as does the *S. albus* G β-lactamase SDS mutant.

A key step in the increased cephalosporinase activity of the R-TEM β-lactamases of class A is alteration of the β3 strand. The first mutant of this type, obtained through selective pressure on the *E. coli* host cells (51), has one single change just after the KSG motif (KSGA $->$ KSGT) (66). R-TEM β-lactamase mutants from clinical isolates exhibiting high hydrolyzing capacity towards third-generation cephalosporins have more than one alteration (21, 101). Thus, for example, the TEM-5 enzyme, which confers resistance to ceftazidime, has two changes in the β3 strand (KSGAGE $->$ KSGTGK) and one additional change upstream from the D/E motif (DRWE* $->$ DSWE*, where E* is the essential glutamic acid). The TEM-4 enzyme, which confers resistance to both cefotaxime and ceftazidime, has one change in the β3 strand (KSGAG $->$ KSGAS), one change at position 26 upstream from the SDN motif (VEY $->$ VKY; note that the 25–amino acid stretch that extends between this tyrosine and the SSN motif controls the specificity profile of some high-Mr PBPs, see below) and two other changes close to the amino (L19 $->$ F) and carboxy (T261 $->$ M) terminus of the mature protein.

Some β-lactamases are produced in maximal amounts only in the presence of β-lactam antibiotics. The locus *blaR*, required for the induction of β-lactamase synthesis in *B. licheniformis*, encodes the 601–amino acid BLAR protein (125). This high-Mr PBP of class C (Figure 2) acts as penicillin sensory-transducer. A likely organization of BLAR (68) is that the 346–amino acid amino-terminal region, i.e. the transducer, has the same membrane topology as that found in some chemotactic transducers, with an extracellular domain responsible for signal reception and a cytosolic domain responsible for the generation of an intracellular signal. The 255–amino acid carboxy terminal region of BLAR, i.e. the penicillin sensor, extends on the outer face of the plasma membrane and is fused to the transducer by means of an additional transmembrane segment; this fusion is a direct consequence of the absence of periplasm in *B. licheniformis*.

The penicillin sensor of BLAR can be produced in *E. coli* as a periplasmic, stable water-soluble low-Mr PBP (68). This PBP, which now has the amino acid numbering M1 . . . R255, possesses the four markers S*56TTK, Y130GN, D144, and K193TG. It is very similar, in the primary structure, to the β-lactamases of class D, in particular to the *Salmonella typhimurium* Oxa-2 β-lactamase (homology index > 40). It lacks detectable β-lactamase, DD-peptidase, or esterase activity. Its only function is to bind penicillin. In all likelihood, conformational changes induced by penicilloylation of the active-site serine give rise to a signal that, in the intact BLAR, is transmitted to the extracellular domain of the transducer and, from this, to the intracellular domain.

β-Lactamase inducibility is a more refined defensive mechanism than β-lactamase constitutivity. The BLAR penicillin sensor might have evolved from a class-D β-lactamase. The presumed features are loss of deacylation of acyl enzyme, no acquisition of DD-peptidase activity, and fusion to a trans-membrane transducer.

The Atomic-Level Enzyme-Ligand Interactions

Serine peptidase–catalyzed rupture of a peptide bond is carried out by several enzyme reagents that fulfill the required functions of an electrophile or oxyanion hole, a proton abstractor-donor, and a nucleophile (Figure 8). In each of the serine peptidases of the trypsin and subtilisin families, two backbone NH groups, one of which belongs to the active-site serine, create the oxyanion hole environment; a histidine adjacent to the essential serine (and in interaction with a buried aspartic acid) is involved in proton abstraction-donation; and one side of the active site generates a nucleophilic suction-pump in the immediate vicinity of the essential serine (75). Reaction-rate enhancement, when compared to that of the analogous uncatalyzed reaction, depends on the goodness of fit of the ligand in the active site and on its correct positioning with respect to the enzyme functional groups.

Geometry optimization, superimposition searches, and conformational analysis of lactam compounds belonging to different chemical families (penicillins, 6-epoxy-spiropenicillins, cephalosporins, thienamycin, γ-lactams,

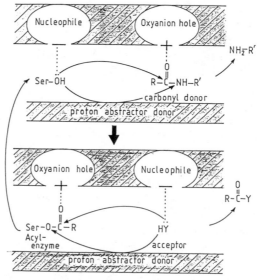

Figure 8 Serine peptidase-catalyzed rupture of a peptide bond. The oxyanion hole polarizes the C = O bond; the nucleophile enhances the reactivity of the serine hydroxyl or the acceptor HY; and the proton abstractor-donor achieves nucleophilic attack.

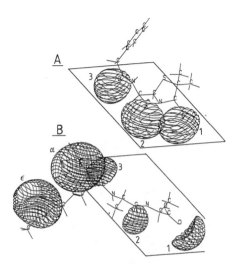

Figure 9 Coplanarity of the binding entity of benzylpenicillin (*A*) and the most stable, extended conformer of Ac$_2$-L-Lys-D-Ala-D-Ala (*B*). Electrostatic potential isocontours at −10 kcal/mol. 1, COOH; 2, CO of the scissile CONH bond (i.e. the electrophilic center); 3, CO of the exocyclic carbonyl (penicillin) or the L-Lys-D-Ala peptide bond (tripeptide). Distances and dihedral angles are given in Reference 76. The increased volume of well 2 of penicillin when compared to well 2 of Ac$_2$-L-Lys-D-Ala-D-Ala expresses the increased intrinsic reactivity of a β-lactam amide bond when compared to an acyclic peptide bond. The two additional wells seen in the tripeptide are generated by the acetyl carbonyl groups that substitute the α and ϵ lateral chains of lysine. The views are shown along the plane of the scissile amide bond. The α and ϵ side chains of lysine are above and below the reference plane, respectively.

lactivicin) have led to the concept of a productive binding entity (76). To confer activity to these compounds (either as substrates of the β-lactamases or inactivators of the PBPs), the triad formed by the carbon atom of the carboxylate, the carbonyl of the scissile amide bond (i.e. the electrophilic center C = O) and the oxygen atom of the exocyclic carbonyl (or COH in thienamycin) must fulfill rather strict spatial requirements—one of which is an almost coplanar disposition of these four atoms (Figure 9A). In the most stable extended conformer of Ac$_2$-L-Lys-D-Ala-D-Ala, the triad formed by the carboxylate, the C = O of the scissile D-Ala-D-Ala peptide bond, and the C = O of the L-Lys-D-Ala peptide bond has a spatial disposition comparable to that of the equivalent triad of the biologically active lactam compounds (Figure 9B). These functional groups generate a typical electronic property, and this electronic distribution gives rise to an electrostatic potential of defined shape and volume. Isosterism, however, is partial. The Ac$_2$-L-Lys moiety of Ac$_2$-L-Lys-D-Ala-D-Ala and the side-chain of the lactam ring in the antibiotics are oriented differently (79). The spatial disposition adopted by the Ac$_2$-L-Lys moiety relative to the D-alanyl-D-alanine dipeptide in the tripeptide can be visualized using the negative electrostatic wells generated by the carbonyl groups of the two acetyl substituents (Figure 9B).

The active site of the β-lactamases of class A and C and that of the *Streptomyces* R61 PBP/DD-peptidase are dense hydrogen bonding networks (Figure 10A). One important feature of the enzyme-ligand interactions (lactam compound-β-lactamase; lactam compound-PBP; Ac$_2$-L-Lys-D-Ala-D-Ala-PBP) is an antiparallel hydrogen bonding between the innermost β3 strand of the β-sheet and the binding entity of the ligand (Figure 10B) (25, 56, 62, 67, 70, 72, 82, 89). The carbonyl oxygen of the scissile bond forms hydrogen bonds to the backbone NH group of the active-site serine itself and to the backbone NH of the alanine (the class A β-lactamase), serine (the class C β-lactamase), or threonine (the PBP) immediately downstream from the K(H)TG motif of the β-strand, in a way reminiscent of the oxyanion-hole hydrogen bonds found in the peptidases of the trypsin family. The NH and CO of the exocyclic amide bond borne by the lactam ring or the equivalent groupings of the L-Lys-D-Ala peptide bond of Ac$_2$-L-Lys-D-Ala-D-Ala are in hydrogen bond interactions with the backbone carbonyl of the same alanine, serine, or threonine of the β-strand and with the side chain of the asparagine of the S(Y)XN motif, respectively. The carboxylate (sulfonate in the monobactams) head of the ligand interacts with the OH group of the threonine of the K(H)TG motif and is oriented towards the lysine or histidine of the same motif.

Optimal positioning of the electrophilic center of the ligand relative to the γ-OH of the active-site serine also depends much on the appendages borne by the binding entity. Structural variations in the acyl side chain of the lactam ring, or the R-L-Xaa moiety of the R-L-Xaa-D-alanyl-D-alanine-terminated peptides, cause wide variations in the value of the second-order rate constant (k_{+2}/K) of protein acylation. These effects are both protein and ligand specific (41, 45). In the emerging picture, the *Streptomyces* R61 PBP possesses a subsite that specifically interacts with the side chain borne by the lactam ring and another subsite that specifically interacts with the ϵ side chain of the L-lysine residue of the tripeptide Ac$_2$-L-Lys-D-Ala-D-Ala. As a corollary, these side-chains are not interchangeable (9). Also according to the picture, the α side chain of Ac$_2$-L-Lys-D-Ala-D-Ala extends to the exterior of the enzyme cavity and, thereby, binding of glycan-substituted pentapeptides to the active-site would be mediated mainly by the C-terminal tripeptide moiety.

Though we are learning much, microbiologists still seek answers to questions regarding the distinction between the PBPs and the β-lactamases in terms of stability vs lability of the acyl enzymes formed by reaction with the lactam antibiotics, the inability of the β-lactamases to perform acyl transfer reactions on acyclic carbonyl donor peptides, and the mechanism of

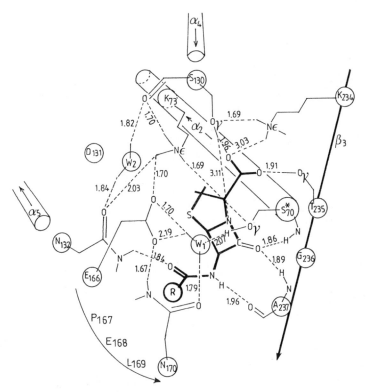

Figure 10 Hydrogen bonding interactions between penicillin and the active site of the *Streptomyces albus* G β-lactamase of class A (25, 62, 67; J. Lamotte-Brasseur, G. Dive, O. Dideberg, J.-M. Frère, J. M. Ghuysen, in preparation). S*70 = active-site serine. The amino acid numbering follows the ABL scheme (4). S*70K73 is S89K92 in the precursor (Figure 3). Similarly, S130DN132 is S153DN155; E166PELN170 is E189PELN193; K234TGA2375 is K257TGA260. Two water molecules W1 and W2 are shown. Distances are given in Å. The acyl side chain of penicillin is represented by CO-Ⓡ. W1, W2, E166, and S130 would be involved in proton abstraction-donation. Attack of the carbonyl carbon of the β-lactam scissile bond by the Oγ of S*70 occurs on the well-exposed α face. Similar hydrogen bonding networks are proposed for the *S. aureus* (56) and *B. licheniformis* (82) β-lactamases of class A, the *C. freundii* β-lactamase of class C (89), and the *Streptomyces* R61 PBP (70, 72).

transpeptidation by the PBPs/DD-peptidases. Recent advances, however, have shed light on the mechanism of proton abstraction-donation.

Site-directed mutagenesis (49) and molecular modeling (J. Lamotte-Brasseur, G. Dive, O. Dideberg, J.-M. Frère, & J. M. Ghuysen, in preparation) support the view that the essential glutamic acid E* of the E*XELN sequence, i.e. the E/D motif, activates, via a bound water molecule, the essential serine of the class A β-lactamases (Figure 10) and that the serine of the SDN motif may be involved in proton shuttle. This serine has a homolog in the tyrosine of the YAN motif in the β-lactamases of class C, but the spatial disposition of the D/E motif in these β-lactamases is not compatible with the role of a general base in catalysis. Superimposition of class C *C. freundii* β-lactamase onto trypsin, using the active-site serine and the oxyanion hole as reference points, results in the phenolic oxygen of the tyrosine of the YAN motif in the β-lactamase being < 0.5 Å from the Nϵ2 position of the essential histidine in trypsin, indicating that the tyrosine, as its anion, might act in a way similar to the essential histidine in trypsin (89). The constellation of two positively charged lysines around this tyrosine would sufficiently lower its pK$_a$ value.

The High-Mr PBPs of Class A and B

The high-Mr PBPs of class A and B have two functional domains that are fused to each other and that operate in a concerted manner (Figure 2). An amino terminal domain several hundred amino acids long is linked on its carbonyl side to the penicillin-binding domain per se. The penicillin-binding domain is assumed to start 60 residues upstream from the S*XXK motif and to terminate 60 residues downstream from the KT(S)G motif. In most high-Mr PBPs, but not in all, this domain bears a tail in the form of a ~100–amino acid carboxy terminal extension (Figure 3).

The high-Mr PBPs are not synthesized as preproteins but have a highly hydrophobic region close to the amino terminus that acts as a noncleaved signal-like segment, both to translocate the bulk of the protein to the periplasm and to anchor the protein in the plasma membrane (1, 6, 12, 31, 32, 96). The *E. coli* PBP3 has been suggested to be a lipoprotein (84) because the sequence L26LCGC30 is similar to the consensus sequence for the modification and processing of bacterial lipoproteins. However, only a small fraction of PBP3 appears to be lipid-modified, at least under conditions of protein overexpression. The PBP3 undergoes maturation by eliminating a cleavable 10-amino acid carboxy-terminal stretch, from I578 to S588, in a way reminiscent of that observed with the low-Mr PBP of *Streptomyces* R61. Short hydrophobic regions upstream from Leu558 in the carboxy terminal tail are important for the functioning and/or stability of the protein (52, 84).

The simple mode of membrane insertion of the high-Mr PBPs allows the production of water-soluble forms through proteolytic treatment of isolated membranes (32, 96). Genetic constructs aimed at removing the membrane anchor from high-Mr PBPs also yield truncated proteins that are sufficiently stable to be isolated (1, 6, 31). They may require high salt concentrations to remain soluble and to retain their penicillin-binding capacity. A gene fusion that removes the amino terminal domain of the *E. coli* PBP3 and links the carboxy-terminal domain to the amino-terminal of the β-galactosidase leads to a chimeric protein that binds penicillin but is unstable (55). Expression of that portion of the gene that encodes only the carboxy-terminal domain of the

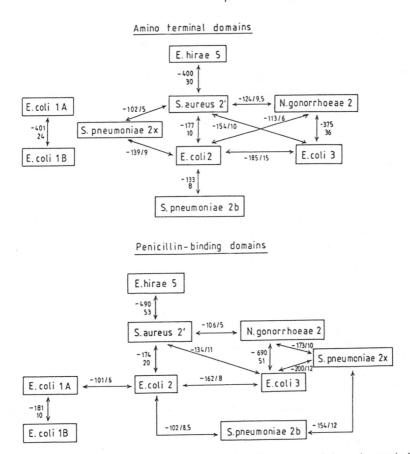

Figure 11 Search of homology between the amino acid sequences of the amino-terminal domains and penicillin-binding, carboxy-terminal domains of the high-Mr PBPs of class A and B. Comparison scores *(negative values)* and significance in standard deviations *(positive values)* are shown. For more details, see the legend of Figure 2. The *E. coli* PBPs 1A and 1B are of class A. The other PBPs are of class B.

PBP yields the expected polypeptide as evidenced by immunological tests and penicillin binding, but this polypeptide is very unstable. Similar observations have been made with other high-Mr PBPs. In addition, no simple in vitro assays are available that would allow one to monitor the enzymatic activities related to peptidoglycan synthesis of the high-Mr PBPs. To all appearances, all high-Mr PBPs lack activity on Ac$_2$-L-Lys-D-Ala-D-Ala, the standard substrate analog of the low-Mr PBPs.

The distinction between the two classes A and B (Figures 2 and 11) derives from homology searches. The *E. coli* PBPs 1A and 1B of class A and the *E. coli* PBPs 2 and 3 of class B have received much attention.

The 850–amino acid PBP1A (encoded by *ponA* in the 73.5-min region of the chromosome map) and the 799– to 844–amino acid PBP1B (encoded by *ponB* in the 3.3-min region of the map) are bifunctional, peptidoglycan-synthesizing enzymes (59, 85, 107, 108). Their amino terminal domain is a penicillin-insensitive transglycosylase that catalyzes glycan chain elongation, and their penicillin-binding carboxy-terminal domain is a transpeptidase that catalyzes peptidoglycan crosslinking. Their bifunctionality is revealed by the reaction products that they generate upon incubation with the lipid-linked precursor N-acetylglucosaminyl-N-acetylmuramyl (D-alanyl-D-alanine–terminated pentapeptide) diphosphoryl-undecaprenol. The overall reaction, however, proceeds with a low turnover number, suggesting that the in vitro conditions poorly mimic the in vivo situation. PBP1A and PBP1B show differences in reaction conditions for optimal activity. They may compensate for each other according to the cell culture conditions. Selective inactivation of the transpeptidase domain of both PBP1A and PBP1B by derivatization of the essential serine by β-lactam antibiotics causes cell death by cell lysis. Deletion of both *ponA* and *ponB* genes has also that effect.

The interplay between the two catalytic domains of PBP1B is well documented. Penicillin inhibits peptide crosslinking and, under certain conditions, greatly increases formation of uncrosslinked peptidoglycan, suggesting that the uncoupling of the two reactions stimulates the transglycosylase activity. Moenomycin, which inhibits the transglycosylase (120), strongly inhibits or prevents peptide crosslinking, suggesting that transpeptidation requires prior or concomitant glycan chain elongation. Studies with monoclonal antibodies also suggest that transpeptidation depends on the product of transglycosylation and that PBP1B has only one type of pentapeptide (donor)/ tetrapeptide (acceptor) transpeptidase activity (24). Membrane components act as effectors of the catalyzed reaction and strongly stimulate the polymerization reaction.

The 633–amino acid PBP2 (encoded by *pbpA* at the 14-min region of the map) and the 588–amino acid PBP3 [encoded by *pbpB* (also called *ftsI*) at the 2-min region] of class B fulfill essential functions in cell morphogenesis, in connection with other membrane proteins. The 14-min region contains, in addition to the PBP2-encoding *pbpA* gene, other genes required for cell-wall elongation and maintenance of the rod shape of the cell. In particular, *rodA* encodes the 370–amino acid integral membrane protein RodA (81), and *dacA* encodes the low-Mr PBP5 (15). Inactivation of *dacA* does not cause growth defects, but a 10-fold overproduction of PBP5 results in spherical cells. Inactivation of PBP2 by the amidinopenicillin mecillinam causes *E. coli* to grow and divide as round-coccal cells. Mutations in either *pbpA* or *rodA* also have that effect and confer resistance to mecillinam.

The 2-min region of the chromosome map contains, in addition to the PBP3-encoding *pbpB* gene, other genes required for the synthesis of the peptidoglycan precursors *(murE, murF, murG, murC, ddl)* and for cell division and septum formation *(ftsW, ftsQ, ftsA, ftsZ)* (109). Selective inactivation of PBP3 either by mutation of *pbpB* or by reaction with, for example, the monobactam aztreonam, leads to filamentous growth of the cells. FtsW is an intrinsic membrane protein very similar to RodA (similarity index: 40). Mutations in FtsW also cause defects in cell division (58). The 420–amino acid FtsA protein is though to participate in the construction of the septum (98, 116). It must be synthesized during a short period just before division for cell division to be completed. High-level expression of FtsA inhibits cell septation. The 383–amino acid FtsZ protein (124) probably regulates the frequency of cell division. It is the target of the SOS-induced inhibitor SfiA (64). Overexpression of FtsZ leads to a hyperdivision activity displayed as the minicell phenotype (122). The relative levels of FtsZ and trigger factor, an abundant cytosolic 543–amino acid protein that might act as a chaperone, probably control initiation of cell division (50).

The pair RodA-PBP2 is involved in formation of the rod-shape of the cell (81). The pair FtsW-PBP3 may be involved in cell division (58), but interaction between RodA and PBP3 has also been suggested (8). The complex RodA-PBP2 appears to be linked to the ribosomes via the *lov* gene product and to the cyclic AMP (cAMP)-receptor protein (CAP) complex via the adenylate cyclase-encoding *cya* gene and the CAP-encoding *crp* gene (11, 90). The cAMP-CAP complex is involved in the transcriptional regulation of many operons. Mutations in either *cya* or *crp* confer high-level resistance to mecillinam, associated with a slow growth rate. All these data suggest that the intrinsic membrane proteins RodA and FtsW (and perhaps FtsA and FtsZ) link PBP2 and PBP3 at the surface of the cell to structures, chaperones, and/or enzymes in the cytosol, and that correct functioning of these networks is essential for cell morphogenesis.

A connection between PBPs and intracellular components is a feature that is not unique to *E. coli*. In the course of sporulation, the PBP profile of *Bacillus subtilis* undergoes profound remodeling with a sporulation-specific increase in vegetative PBPs and a de novo synthesis of PBPs (114). SpoVE, which is extremely similar in the primary structure to the pair RodA-FtsW of *E. coli* (58, 65), seems to be involved in this process. Mutations in the *spoVE* locus cause a blockage at stage V of sporulation (95), and *spoVE* mutants are grossly deficient in cortex, which consists of a sporulation-specific peptidoglycan. *B. subtilis* also contains homologs of the *E. coli* cell division genes *ftsA* and *ftsZ*. Expression of these *B. subtilis* homologs in *E. coli* results in filamentation and cell death (7).

The use of *E. coli* strains overproducing PBP2 and RodA (60) or PBP3 and FtsW (M. Matsuhashi, personal communication) supports the view that these PBPs catalyze transpeptidation reactions. Assignment of a peptidoglycan transpeptidase activity to the penicillin-binding, carboxy-terminal domain of the high-Mr PBPs is also supported by the study, at the molecular level, of the resistance to β-lactam antibiotics acquired through emergence of altered PBPs with a much decreased affinity for the drugs (see below). A remodeling of the penicillin-binding–transpeptidase site that results in a decreased affinity for the drug should presumably affect the specificity profile of the enzyme for the carbonyl donor and/or amino acceptor peptides involved in transpeptidation and, thereby, should cause structural modifications of the wall peptidoglycan. The analysis of the peptidoglycans of penicillin-sensitive and penicillin-resistant pneumococci has confirmed the prediction (43).

The question of which enzymatic function the amino terminal domains of the high-Mr PBPs of class B perform is still a matter of controversy. These domains (at least some of them) possess several conserved amino acid groupings not found in the transglycosylase domain of the *E. coli* PBPs 1A and 1B of class A (96). These groupings might be the signature of an active site whose function would be different from that of a transglycosylase. One should remember that PBPs are involved, directly or indirectly, in the average glycan chain length of the peptidoglycan, in the extent of peptidoglycan O-acetylation, and in the amounts of peptidoglycan-attached lipoprotein. None of these observations has received a satisfactory explanation.

Intrinsic Resistance by Emergence of Altered High-Mr PBPs

Assuming that a given high-Mr PBP is the most sensitive killing target of a lactam antibiotic, conversion of this PBP into an altered PBP whose penicillin-binding domain has acquired a decreased affinity for the drug, but has retained the capacity of performing its physiological (transpeptidase) function, causes an increased resistance of the bacterial cell to this particular antibiotic.

Alterations affecting amino acids located away from the active site may be neutral or they may stabilize the protein in response to changes occurring within or close to the active site. Study of an altered PBP2X of a *S. pneumoniae* laboratory mutant with a decreased affinity for cefotaxime shows that such distal alterations may be of real significance (74). By reference to the PBP2X of the cefotaxime-sensitive strain, the two mutations G597 −> D and G601 −> V, occurring about 50 residues downstream from the KTG motif, are responsible for the first level of resistance to the drug. One may hypothesize that these amino acid alterations cause changes in the conformation and thereby, changes in the specificity profile of the penicillin-binding domain.

The acquisition of resistance through alterations affecting the active site is well documented. Many β-lactamases of class A have a tyrosine approximately 25 residues upstream from the SDN motif (4). Alterations of the equivalent peptide stretches Tyr334-S359SN of the *E. coli* PBP3, Tyr337-S362SN of the *Neisseria gonorrhoeae* PBP2, and Tyr419-S447SN of the *S. pneumoniae* PBP2B profoundly modify the specificity profile of these PBPs. Cephalexin, at the minimum inhibitory concentration (MIC), kills *E. coli* by inactivating PBP3. *E. coli* laboratory mutants have been obtained whose PBP3 has a much decreased affinity for cephalexin and other cephalosporins but not for penicillins and aztreonam (53, 54). These PBP3 mutants have either a Val344 −> Gly substitution (occurring approximately in the middle of the Tyr334-S359SN sequence) or an Asn361 −> Ser substitution (converting the SSN motif into a SSS motif). This latter mutant has some degree of functional impairment that causes the formation of *E. coli* cells with pointed polar caps (110). Maximal level of resistance to cephalexin, however, is achieved by combining four changes: the conversion SSN −> SSS, the substitution Glu349 −> Lys (which also occurs approximately in the middle of the Tyr −> SSS stretch), and the substitutions Val530 −> Ile and Tyr541 −> Ser (about 50 to 40 residues upstream from the carboxy terminus of the 388–amino acid protein). Penicillin kills *N. gonorrhoeae* by inactivating PBP2. The PBP2 of clinical isolates that have a decreased affinity for penicillin differs from the PBP2 of the penicillin-sensitive strains only in the insertion of an additional aspartic acid (Asp345A) between Arg345 and Asp346, thus affecting the Tyr337-S362SN sequence (13). However, a *penA* gene containing only the Asp345A codon insertion does not transform a penicillin-sensitive gonococcus to as high a level of resistance to penicillin as the *penA*[R] genes from other non-lactamase-producing, chromosomally mediated resistant gonococcal strains. The PBP2 of these strains contains not only the inserted Asp345A but numerous other amino acid changes in the penicillin-binding domain. Similarly, a *S. pneumoniae* PBP2B mutant obtained from clinical isolates exhibiting a >1000-fold increased resistance to penicillin has 17 amino acid substitutions (27). Seven of these changes are within the Tyr231-S249SN sequence and another change affects the amino acid immediately downstream from the SSN motif.

Acquired resistance may emerge through recombinational events that recruit portions of homologous genes from related species and result in the creation of mosaic genes encoding hybrid PBPs (26, 29, 102, 105). Such horizontal gene transfers occur between species that are naturally transformable such as *Neisseria* and *Streptococcus* spp. The gene encoding the penicillin-resistant PBP2 of *Neisseria meningitidis* consists of regions almost identical to the corresponding regions of the penicillin-sensitive strains and of two regions that are very different from them. These two blocks of altered sequence have resulted from the replacement of meningococcal sequences with the corresponding sequences of the *penA* gene of *Neisseria flavescens*.

The resulting altered form of PBP2, when compared to that of the penicillin-sensitive *N. meningitidis* strain, contains 44 amino acid substitutions and 1 amino acid insertion. *N. gonorrhoeae* also produces altered forms of PBP2, whose part of the *penA* gene has been replaced by the corresponding region of the *N. flavescens* gene.

Methicillin-resistant *S. aureus* strains have imported an inducible high-Mr PBP2' of low affinity for the drug (100). The PBP2'-encoding *mecA* gene may have evolved through recombination of a PBP gene of some bacterium and a β-lactamase inducible gene. The promoter and close upstream region of *mecA* are similar to those of the staphylococcal β-lactamase inducible gene, and the *mecR* region has two main open reading frames, one of which encodes a putative protein that has strong similarity in the primary structure to the penicillin sensory-transducer BLAR of *B. licheniformis* (111; B. Berger-Bächi, personal communication). The *mecA* gene is linked to the *aadD* gene that encodes the 4',4'' adenyltransferase responsible for tobramycine resistance (119). The two linked genes are carried on a moving element and may have emerged in *S. aureus* through transposition.

The staphylococcal PBP2' has two homologs, PBP5 (32) and PBP3R (96), in the penicillin-resistant *Enterococcus hirae* strains. Complete derivatization of these PBPs by penicillin or cefotaxime requires conditions under which serum albumin is partially acylated. These PBPs can take over the functions needed for wall peptidoglycan assembly under conditions in which all the other PBPs are inactivated. Though they have conserved the characteristic motifs of the penicillin-interactive proteins, their active site has acquired a configuration that almost completely discriminates between penicillin and D-alanyl-D-alanine–terminated peptides, the ultimate achievement in intrinsic penicillin resistance.

ACKNOWLEDGMENTS

It gives me great pleasure to acknowledge the contribution of the colleagues who, at the University of Liège, carried out the work described here: Drs. P. Charlier, J. Coyette, D. Dehareng, O. Dideberg, G. Dive, C. Duez, J. Dusart, J.-M. Frère, B. Joris, J. Lamotte-Brasseur, M. Leyh-Bouille, M. Nguyen-Distèche, and C. Piron-Fraipont. I also thank Dr. J. Van Beeumen of the University of Ghent, Belgium, and Drs. J. Kelly and J. Knox of the University of Connecticut, Storrs, USA. The work at Liège has been supported by the *Fonds de la Recherche Scientifique Médicale*, the *Fonds National de la Recherche Scientifique*, the Belgian Government, the Government of the Walloon Region, and the *Fonds de Recherche de la Faculté de Médecine*, Université de Liège.

Literature Cited

1. Adachi, H., Ohta, T., Matsuzawa, H. 1987. A water-soluble form of penicillin-binding protein 2 of *Escherichia coli* constructed by site-directed mutagenesis. *FEBS Lett.* 226:150–54
2. Adam, M., Damblon, C., Plaiton, B., Christiaens, L., Frère, J. M. 1990. Chromogenic depsipeptide substrates for β-lactamases and penicillin-sensitive DD-peptidases. *Biochem. J.* 270:525–29
3. Adriaens, P., Meesschaert, B., Frère, J.-M., Vanderhaege, H., Degelaen, J., et al. 1978. Stability of D-5,5-dimethyl-Δ^2-thiazolidine-4-carboxylic acid in relation to its possible occurrence as a degradation product of penicillin by the exocellular DD-carboxypeptidase-transpeptidase from *Streptomyces* R61 and the membrane-bound DD-carboxypeptidase from *Bacillus stearothermophilus*. *J. Biol. Chem.* 253:3660–65
4. Ambler, R. P., Frère, J.-M., Ghuysen, J.-M., Jaurin, B., Levesque, R. C., et al. 1991. A standard numbering scheme for the class A β-lactamases. *Biochem. J.* In press
5. Asoh, S., Matsuzawa, H., Ishino, F., Strominger, J. L., Matsuhashi, M., et al. 1986. Nucleotide sequence of the *pbp*A gene and characteristics of the deduced amino acid sequence of penicillin-binding protein 2 of *Escherichia coli* K12. *Eur. J. Biochem.* 160:231–38
6. Bartholomé-De Belder, J., Nguyen-Distèche, M., Houba-Herin, N., Ghuysen, J.-M., Maruyama, I. N., et al. 1988. Overexpression, solubilization and refolding of a genetically engineered derivative of the penicillin-binding protein 3 of *Escherichia coli* K12. *Mol. Microbiol.* 2:519–25
7. Beall, B., Lowe, M., Lutkenhaus, J. 1988. Cloning and characterization of *Bacillus subtilis* homologs of *Escherichia coli* cell division genes *fts*Z and *fts*A. *J. Bacteriol.* 170:4855–64
8. Begg, K. J., Spratt, B. G., Donachie, W. D. 1986. Interaction between membrane proteins PBP3 and RodA is required for normal cell shape and division in *Escherichia coli*. *J. Bacteriol.* 167:1004–8
8a. Begg, K. J., Takasuga, A., Edwards, D. H., Dewar, S. J., Spratt, B. G., et al. 1990. The balance between different peptidoglycan precursors determines

whether *Escherichia coli* will elongate or divide. *J. Bacteriol.* 172:6697–6703
9. Bentley, P. H., Stachulski, A. V. 1983. Synthesis and biological activity of some fused β-lactam peptidoglycan analogues. *J. Chem. Soc. Perkin Trans.* 1:1187–92
10. Boissinot, M., Levesque, R. C. 1990. Nucleotide sequence of the PSE-4 carbenicillinase gene and correlations with the *Staphylococcus aureus* PC1 β-lactamase crystal structure. *J. Biol. Chem.* 265:1225–30
11. Bouloc, P., Jaffé, A., D'Ari, R. 1989. The *Escherichia coli* lov gene product connects peptidoglycan synthesis, ribosomes and growth rate. *EMBO J.* 8:317–23
12. Bowler, L. D., Spratt, G. D. 1989. Membrane topology of penicillin-binding protein 3 of *Escherichia coli*. *Mol. Microbiol.* 3:1277–86
13. Brannigan, J. A., Tirodimos, I. A., Zhang, Q.-Y., Dowson, C. G., Spratt, B. G. 1990. Insertion of an extra amino acid is the main cause of the low affinity of penicillin-binding protein 2 in penicillin-resistant strains of *Neisseria gonorrhoeae*. *Mol. Microbiol.* 4:913–19
14. Broome-Smith, J. K., Edelman, A., Yousif, S., Spratt, B. G. 1985. The nucleotide sequences of the *pon*A and *pon*B genes encoding penicillin-binding proteins 1A and 1B of *Escherichia coli*. *Eur. J. Biochem.* 147:437–46
15. Broome-Smith, J. K., Ioannidis, I., Edelman, A., Spratt, B. G. 1988. Nucleotide sequences of the penicillin-binding protein 5 and 6 genes of *Escherichia coli*. *Nucleic Acids Res.* 16:1617
16. Buchanan, C. E., Neyman, S. L. 1986. Correlation of penicillin-binding protein composition with different functions of two membranes in *Bacillus subtilis* forespores. *J. Bacteriol.* 165:498–503
17. Cartwright, S. J., Coulson, A. E. W. 1980. Active-site of staphylococcal β-lactamase. *Phil. Trans. R. Soc. London* B289:370–72
18. Cartwright, S. J., Waley, S. G. 1983. β-Lactamase inhibitors. *Med. Res. Rev.* 3:341–82
19. Chan, P. T. 1986. Nucleotide sequence of the *Staphylococcus aureus* PC1 β-lactamase gene. *Nucleic Acids Res.* 14:5940
20. Cohen, S. A., Pratt, R. F. 1980. In-

activation of *Bacillus cereus* β-lactamase I by 6β-bromopenicillanic acid. Mechanism. *Biochemistry* 19:3996–4003

21. Collatz, E., Labia, R., Gutman, L. 1990. Molecular evolution of ubiquitous β-lactamases toward extended-spectrum enzymes active against newer β-lactam antibiotics. *Mol. Microbiol.* 4:1615–20

22. Dale, J. W., Godwin, D., Mossakouska, D., Stephenson, P., Wall, S. 1985. Sequence of the Oxa-2 β-lactamase: comparison with other penicillin-reactive enzymes. *FEBS Lett.* 191:39–42

23. Dehottay, P., Dusart, J., De Meester, F., Joris, B., Van Beeumen, J., et al. 1987. Nucleotide sequence of the gene encoding the *Streptomyces albus* G β-lactamase precursor. *Eur. J. Biochem.* 166:345–50

24. den Blaauven, T., Aarsman, M., Nanninga, N. 1990. Interaction of monoclonal antibodies with the enzymatic domains of penicillin-binding protein 1b of *Escherichia coli.* *J. Bacteriol.* 172:63–70

25. Dideberg, O., Charlier, P., Wéry, J. P., Dehottay, P., Dusart, J., et al. 1987. The crystal structure of the β-lactamase of *Streptomyces albus* G at 0.3 nm resolution. *Biochem. J.* 245:911–13

26. Dowson, C. G., Hutchison, A., Brannigan, J. A., George, R. C., Hansman, D., et al. 1989. Horizontal transfer of penicillin-binding protein genes in penicillin-resistant clinical isolates of *Streptococcus pneumoniae.* *Proc. Natl. Acad. Sci. USA* 86:8842–46

27. Dowson, C. G., Hutchison, A., Spratt, B. G. 1989. Extensive re-modelling of the transpeptidase domain of penicillin-binding protein 2B of a penicillin-resistant South African isolate of *Streptococcus pneumoniae.* *Mol. Microbiol.* 3:95–102

28. Dowson, C. G., Hutchison, A., Spratt, B. G. 1989. Nucleotide sequence of penicillin-binding protein 2B gene of *Streptococcus pneumoniae* strain R6. *Nucleic Acids Res.* 17:7518

29. Dowson, C. G., Hutchison, A., Woodford, N., Johnson, A. P., George, R. C., et al. 1990. Penicillin-resistant *viridans* streptococci have obtained altered penicillin-binding protein genes from penicillin-resistant strains of *Streptococcus pneumoniae.* *Proc. Natl. Acad. Sci. USA* 87:5858–62

30. Duez, C., Piron-Fraipont, C., Joris, B., Dusart, J., Urdea, M. S., et al. 1987. Primary structure of the *Streptomyces*

R61 extracellular DD-peptidase. 1. Cloning into *Streptomyces lividans* and nucleotide sequence of the gene. *Eur. J. Biochem.* 162:509–18

31. Edelman, A., Bowler, L., Broome-Smith, J. K., Spratt, B. G. 1987. Use of a β-lactamase fusion vector to investigate the organization of penicillin-binding protein 1B in the cytoplasmic membrane of *Escherichia coli.* *Mol. Microbiol.* 1:101–6

32. El Kharroubi, A., Jacques, P., Piras, G., Coyette, J., Van Beeumen, J., et al. 1991. The penicillin-binding proteins 5 of *Enterococcus hirae* R40 and the penicillin-binding protein 2' of the methicillin-resistant *Staphylococcus aureus* are homologs. *J. Bacteriol.* In press

33. El Kharroubi, A., Piras, G., Jacques, P., Szabo, I., Van Beeumen, J., et al. 1989. Active-site and membrane topology of the DD-peptidase/penicillin-binding protein n°6 of *Enterococcus hirae (Streptococcus faecium)* ATCC9790. *Biochem. J.* 262:457–62

34. Ferreira, L. C. S., Schwarz, U., Keck, W., Charlier, P., Dideberg, O., et al. 1988. Properties and crystallization of a genetically engineered, water-soluble derivative of the penicillin-binding protein n°5 of *Escherichia coli* K12. *Eur. J. Biochem.* 171:11–16

35. Fisher, J., Charnas, P. L., Bradley, S. M., Knowles, J. R. 1981. Inactivation of the RTEM β-lactamase from *Escherichia coli.* Interaction of penam sulfones with enzyme. *Biochemistry* 20:2726–31

36. Frère, J.-M., Duez, C., Ghuysen, J.-M., Vandekerkhove, J. 1976. Occurrence of a serine residue in the penicillin-binding site of the exocellular DD-carboxypeptidase-transpeptidase from *Streptomyces* R61. *FEBS Lett.* 70:257–60

37. Frère, J.-M., Ghuysen, J.-M., Degelaen, J., Loffet, A., Perkins, H. R. 1975. Fragmentation of benzylpenicillin after interaction with the exocellular DD-carboxypeptidase-transpeptidases of *Streptomyces* R61 and R39. *Nature* 258:168–70

38. Frère, J.-M., Ghuysen, J.-M., De Graeve, J. 1978. Fragmentation of penicillin catalysed by the exocellular DD-carboxypeptidase-transpeptidase of *Streptomyces* R61. Isotopic study of hydrogen fixation on carbon 6. *FEBS Lett.* 88:147–50

39. Frère, J.-M., Ghuysen, J.-M., Vanderhaeghe, H., Adriaens, P., Degelaen, J. 1976. Fate of thiazolidine ring during

fragmentation of penicillin by exocellular DD-carboxypeptidase-transpeptidase of *Streptomyces* R61. *Nature* 260:451–54

40. Frère, J.-M., Ghuysen, J.-M., Perkins, H. R., Nieto, M. 1973. Kinetics of concomitant transfer and hydrolysis reactions catalysed by the exocellular DD-carboxypeptidase-transpeptidase of *Streptomyces* R61. *Biochem. J.* 135:483–92

41. Frère, J.-M., Joris, B. 1985. Penicillin-sensitive enzymes in peptidoglycan biosynthesis. *CRC Crit. Rev. Microbiol.* 11:299–396

42. Galleni, M., Amicosante, G., Frère, J.-M. 1988. A survey of the kinetic parameters of class C β-lactamases. *Biochem. J.* 255:119–22

43. Garcia-Bustos, J., Tomasz, A. 1990. A biological price of antibiotic resistance: major changes in the peptidoglycan structure of penicillin-resistant pneumococci. *Proc. Natl. Acad. Sci. USA* 87:5415–19

44. Ghuysen, J.-M. 1977. The bacterial DD-carboxypeptidase-transpeptidase enzyme system. A new insight into the mode of action of penicillin. *E. R. Squibb Lectures on Chemistry of Microbial Products,* series ed. W. E. Brown. Tokyo: Univ. Tokyo Press. 162 pp.

45. Ghuysen, J.-M., Frère, J.-M., Leyh-Bouille, M., Coyette, J., Dusart, J., et al. 1979. Use of model enzymes in the determination of the mode of action of penicillins and Δ³-cephalosporins. *Annu. Rev. Biochem.* 48:73–101

46. Ghuysen, J.-M., Frère, J.-M., Leyh-Bouille, M., Nguyen-Distèche, M., Coyette, J. 1986. Active-site serine D-alanyl-D-alanine-cleaving peptidases-catalysed acyl transfer reactions. Procedures for studying the penicillin-binding proteins of bacterial plasma membranes. *Biochem. J.* 235:159–65

47. Ghuysen, J.-M., Leyh-Bouille, M., Campbell, J. N., Moreno, R., Frère, J.-M., et al. 1973. Structure of the wall peptidoglycan of *Streptomyces* R39 and the specificity profile of its exocellular DD-carboxypeptidase-transpeptidase for peptide acceptors. *Biochemistry* 12:1243–51

48. Ghuysen, J.-M., Reynolds, P. E., Perkins, H. R., Frère, J.-M., Moreno, R. 1974. Effects of donor and acceptor peptides on concomitant hydrolysis and transfer reactions catalysed by the exocellular DD-carboxypeptidase-transpeptidase from *Streptomyces* R39. *Biochemistry* 13:2539–47

49. Gibson, R. S., Christensen, H., Waley, S. G. 1990. Site-directed mutagenesis of β-lactamase I. Single and double mutants of Glu166 and Lys73. *Biochem. J.* 272:613–19

50. Gutherie, B., Wickner, W. 1990. Trigger factor depletion and overproduction causes defective cell division but does not block protein export. *J. Bacteriol.* 172:5555–62

51. Hall, A., Knowles, J. R. 1976. Directed selective pressure on a β-lactamase to analyse molecular changes involved in development of enzyme function. *Nature London* 264:803–4

52. Hara, H., Nishimura, Y., Kato, J. I., Suzuki, H., Nagasawa, H., et al. 1989. Genetic analysis of processing involving C-terminal cleavage in penicillin-binding protein 3 of *Escherichia coli.* *J. Bacteriol.* 171:5882–89

53. Hedge, P. J., Spratt, B. G. 1985. Resistance to β-lactam antibiotics by remodelling the active site of an *E. coli* penicillin-binding protein. *Nature* 318:478–80

54. Hedge, P. J., Spratt, B. G. 1985. Amino acid alterations that reduce the affinity of penicillin-binding protein 3 of *Escherichia coli* for cephalexin. *Eur. J. Biochem.* 151:111–21

55. Hedge, P. J., Spratt, B. G. 1988. A gene fusion that localises the penicillin-binding domains of penicillin-binding protein 3. *J. Bacteriol.* 170:5392–95

56. Herzberg, O., Moult, J. 1987. Bacterial resistance to β-lactam antibiotics: crystal structure of β-lactamase from *Staphylococcus aureus* PC1 at 2.5 Å resolution. *Science* 236:694–701

57. Hussain, M., Pastor, F. I. J., Lampen, J. O. 1987. Cloning and sequencing of the *blaZ* gene encoding β-lactamase III, a lipoprotein of *Bacillus cereus* 569/H. *J. Bacteriol.* 169:579–86

58. Ikeda, M., Sato, T., Wachi, M., Jung, H. K., Ishino, F., et al. 1989. Structural similarity among *Escherichia coli* FtsW and RodA proteins and *Bacillus subtilis* SpoVE protein, which function in cell division, cell elongation, and spore formation, respectively. *J. Bacteriol.* 171:6375–78

59. Ishino, F., Mitsui, S., Tamaki, S., Matsuhashi, M. 1980. Dual enzymatic activities of cell wall peptidoglycan synthesis, peptidoglycan transglycosylase and penicillin-sensitive transpeptidase in purified preparations of *Escherichia coli* penicillin-binding protein 1A. *Biochem. Biophys. Res. Commun.* 97:287–93

60. Ishino, F., Park, W., Tomioka, S.,

Tamaki, S., Takase, I., et al. 1986. Peptidoglycan synthetic activities in membranes of *Escherichia coli* caused by overproduction of penicillin-binding protein 2 and RodA protein. *J. Biol. Chem.* 262:7024–31

61. Jackson, M. E., Pratt, J. M. 1988. Analysis of the membrane-binding domain of penicillin-binding protein 5 of *Escherichia coli*. *Mol. Microbiol.* 2:563–68

62. Jacob, F., Joris, B., Dideberg, O., Dusart, J., Ghuysen, J.-M., et al. 1990. Engineering of a novel β-lactamase by a single point mutation. *Protein Eng.* 4:223:6427–37

63. Jacob, F., Joris, B., Lepage, S., Dusart, J., Frère, J.-M. 1990. Role of the conserved amino acids of the "SDN" loop in a class A β-lactamase studied by site-directed mutagenesis. *Biochem. J.* 271:399–406

64. Jones, C. A., Holland, I. B. 1985. Role of the SfiB (FtsZ) protein in division inhibition during the SDS response in *E. coli*. FtsZ stabilizes the inhibitor SfiA in maxicells. *Proc. Natl. Acad. Sci. USA* 82:6045–49

65. Joris, B., Dive, G., Henriques, A., Piggot, P. J., Ghuysen, J.-M. 1990. The life-cycle proteins RodA of *Escherichia coli* and SpoVE of *Bacillus subtilis* have very similar primary structures. *Mol. Microbiol.* 4:513–17

66. Joris, B., Ghuysen, J.-M., Dive, G., Renard, A., Dideberg, O. et al. 1988. The active-site serine penicillin-recognizing enzymes as members of the *Streptomyces* R61 DD-peptidase family. *Biochem. J.* 250:313–24

67. Joris, B., Ledent, P., Dideberg, O., Fonzé, E., Lamotte-Brasseur, J., et al. 1991. A comparison of the sequences of class A β-lactamases and of the secondary structure elements of penicillin-recognizing proteins. *Biochem. J.* In press

68. Joris, B., Ledent, P., Kobayashi, T., Lampen, J. O., Ghuysen, J.-M. 1990. Expression in *Escherichia coli* of the Met346-Arg601 carboxy terminal domain of the BLAR sensory transducer protein of *Bacillus licheniformis* as a water-soluble 26,000-Mr penicillin-binding protein. *FEMS Microbiol. Lett.* 70:107–14

69. Kelly, J. A., Dideberg, O., Charlier, P., Wéry, J. P., Libert, M., et al. 1986. On the origin of bacterial resistance to penicillin. Comparison of a β-lactamase and a penicillin target. *Science* 231:1429–37

70. Kelly, J. A., Knox, J. R., Zhao, H.,

Frère, J.-M., Ghuysen, J.-M. 1989. Crystallographic mapping of β-lactams bound to a D-alanyl-D-alanine peptidase target enzyme. *J. Mol. Biol.* 209:281–95

71. Knott-Hunziker, V., Waley, S. G., Orlek, B. S., Sammes, P. G. 1979. Penicillinase active sites: labelling of serine-44 in β-lactamase I by 6β-bromopenicillanic acid. *FEBS Lett.* 99:59–61

72. Knox, J. R., Pratt, R. F. 1990. Different modes of vancomycin and D-alanyl-D-alanine peptidase binding to cell wall peptide and a possible role for the vancomycin resistance protein. *Antimicrob. Agents Chemother.* 34:1342–47

73. Kobayashi, T., Zhu, Y., Nicholls, N., Lampen, J. O. 1987. A second regulatory gene, BLAR1, encoding a potential penicillin-binding protein required for induction of β-lactamase in *Bacillus licheniformis*. *J. Bacteriol.* 169:3873–78

74. Laible, G., Hakenbeck, R., Sicard, M. A., Joris, B., Ghuysen, J.-M. 1989. Nucleotide sequences of the *pbpX* genes encoding the penicillin-binding proteins 2X from *Streptococcus pneumoniae* R6 and a cefotaxime resistant mutant, C50G. *Mol. Microbiol.* 3:1337–48

75. Lamotte-Brasseur, J., Dive, G., Dehareng, D., Ghuysen, J.-M. 1990. Electrostatic potential maps at the quantum chemistry level of the active sites of the serine peptidases, α-chymotrypsin and subtilisin. *J. Theor. Biol.* 145:183–98

76. Lamotte-Brasseur, J., Dive, G., Ghuysen, J.-M. 1991. Conformational analysis of β- and -lactam antibiotics. *Eur. J. Med. Chem.* In press

77. Leyh-Bouille, M., Nguyen-Distèche, M., Bellefroid-Bourguignon, C., Ghuysen, J.-M. 1987. Effects of thiol reagents on the *Streptomyces* K15 DD-peptidase-catalysed reactions. *Biochem. J.* 241:893–97

78. Leyh-Bouille, M., Nguyen-Distèche, M., Pirlot, S., Veithen, A., Bourguignon, C., et al. 1986. *Streptomyces* K15 DD-peptidase-catalysed reaction with suicide β-lactam carbonyl donors. *Biochem. J.* 235:177–82

79. Lindberg, F., Normark, S. 1986. Sequence of the *Citrobacter freundii* chromosomal *ampC* β-lactamase gene. *Eur. J. Biochem.* 156:441–45

80. Marquet, A., Frère, J.-M., Ghuysen, J.-M., Loffet, A. 1979. Effects of nucleophiles on the breakdown of the benzylpenicilloyl-enzyme complex EI* formed

between benzylpenicillin and the ex-ocellular DD-carboxypeptidase-transpeptidase of *Streptomyces* strain R61. *Biochem. J.* 177:909–16

81. Matsuzawa, H., Asoh, S., Kunai, K., Muraiso, K., Takasuga, A., et al. 1989. Nucleotide sequence of the *rod*A gene, responsible for the rod shape of *Escherichia coli: rod*A and the *pbp*A gene, encoding penicillin-binding protein 2, constitute the *rod*A operon. *J. Bacteriol.* 171:558–60

82. Moews, P. C., Knox, J. R., Dideberg, O., Charlier, P., Frère, J.-M. 1990. β-Lactamase of *Bacillus licheniformis* 749/C at 2 Å resolution. *Proteins Struct. Funct. Genet.* 7:156–71

83. Mottl, H., Terpstra, P., Keck, W. 1991. Penicillin-binding protein 4 of *Escherichia coli* shows a novel type of primary structure among penicillin-interacting proteins. *FEMS Microbiol. Lett.* 78:213–20

84. Nagasawa, H., Sakagami, Y., Suzuki, A., Suzuki, H., Hara, H., et al. 1989. Determination of the cleavage site involved in C-terminal processing of penicillin-binding protein 3 of *Escherichia coli. J. Bacteriol.* 171:5890–93

85. Nakagawa, J.-I., Tamaki, S., Matsuhashi, M. 1979. Purified penicillin-binding protein 1Bs from *Escherichia coli* membranes showing activities of both peptidoglycan polymerase and peptidoglycan crosslinking enzyme. *Agric. Biol. Chem.* 43:1379–80

86. Nakamura, M., Maruyama, I. N., Soma, M., Kato, J. I., Suzuki, H., et al. 1983. On the process of cellular division in *Escherichia coli:* nucleotide sequence of the gene for penicillin-binding protein 3. *Mol. Gen. Genet.* 191:1–9

87. Neugebauer, K., Sprengl, R., Shaller, H. 1981. Penicillinase from *Bacillus licheniformis:* nucleotide sequence of the gene and implications for the biosynthesis of a secretory protein in a Gram-positive bacteria. *Nucleic Acids Res.* 9:2577–88

88. Nguyen-Distèche, M., Leyh-Bouille, M., Pirlot, S., Frère, J.-M., Ghuysen, J.-M. 1986. *Streptomyces* K15 DD-peptidase-catalysed reactions with ester and amide carbonyl donors. *Biochem. J.* 235:167–76

89. Oefner, C., D'Arcy, A., Daly, J. J., Gubernator, K., Charnas, R. L., et al. 1990. Refined crystal structure of β-lactamase from *Citrobacter freundii* indicates a mechanism for β-lactam hydrolysis. *Nature* 343:284–88

90. Ogura, T., Bouloc, P., Niki, H., D'Ari, R., Horaga, S., et al. 1989. Penicillin-binding protein 2 is essential in wild-type *Escherichia coli* but not in *lov* and *cya* mutants. *J. Bacteriol.* 171:3025–30

91. Pazhanisamy, S., Govardhan, C. P., Pratt, R. F. 1989. β-Lactamase-catalysed aminolysis of depsipeptides: amine specificity and steady-state kinetics. *Biochemistry* 28:6863–70

92. Pazhanisamy, S., Pratt, R. F. 1989. β-Lactamase-catalysed aminolysis of depsipeptides: proof of the nonexistence of a specific D-phenylalanine/enzyme complex by double-label isotope trapping. *Biochemistry* 28:6870–75

93. Pazhanisamy, S., Pratt, R. F. 1989. β-Lactamase-catalysed aminolysis of depsipeptides: peptide inhibition and a new kinetic mechanism. *Biochemistry* 28:6875–82

94. Perkins, H. R., Nieto, M., Frère, J.-M., Leyh-Bouille, M., Ghuysen, J.-M. 1973. *Streptomyces* DD-carboxypeptidases as transpeptidases. The specificity for amino compounds acting as carboxyl acceptors. *Biochem. J.* 131:707–18

95. Pigott, J. J., Coote, J. G. 1976. Genetic aspects of bacterial endospore formation. *Bacteriol. Rev.* 40:908–62

96. Piras, G., El Kharroubi, A., Van Beeumen, J., Coeme, E., Coyette, J., et al. 1990. Occurrence and characterization of a penicillin-binding protein 3 of low penicillin affinity in *Enterococcus hirae. J. Bacteriol.* 172:6856–62

97. Pratt, J. M., Jackson, M. E., Holland, I. B. 1986. The C-terminus of penicillin-binding protein 5 is essential for localisation to the *E. coli* inner membrane. *EMBO J.* 5:2399–2405

98. Robinson, A. C., Begg, K. J., Sweeney, J., Condie, A., Donachie, W. D. 1988. Mapping and characterization of mutants of the *Escherichia coli* cell division gene, *fts*A. *Mol. Microbiol.* 2:581–88

99. Samuni, A., Citri, N. 1979. How specific is the effect of penicillins on the conformation of penicillinase? An experimental model. *Mol. Pharmacol.* 16:250–55

99a. Schuster, C., Dobrinski, B., Hakenbeck, R. 1990. Unusual septum formation in *Streptococcus pneumoniae* mutants with an alteration in the D, D-carboxypeptidase penicillin-binding protein 3. *J. Bacteriol.* 172:6499–6505

100. Song, M. D., Wachi, M., Doi, M., Ishi-

no, F., Matsuhashi, M. 1987. Evolution of an inducible penicillin-target protein in methicillin-resistant *Staphylococcus aureus* by gene fusion. *FEBS Lett.* 221:167–71

101. Sougakoff, W., Petit, A., Goussard, S., Sirot, D., Bure, A., et al. 1989. Characterization of the plasmid genes *bla*T-4 and *bla*T-5 which encode the brood-spectrum β-lactamases TEM-4 and TEM-5 in Enterobacteriaceae. *Gene* 78:339–48

102. Spratt, B. G. 1988. Hybrid penicillin-binding proteins in penicillin-resistant strains of *Neisseria gonorrhoeae*. *Nature* 332:173–76

103. Spratt, B. G., Cromie, K. D. 1988. Penicillin-binding proteins of Gram-negative bacteria. *Rev. Infect. Dis.* 10:699–711

104. Spratt, B. G., Pardee, A. B. 1975. Penicillin-binding proteins and cell shape in *E. coli*. *Nature* 254:516–17

105. Spratt, B. G., Zhang, Q.-Y., Jones, D. M., Hutchison, A., Brannigan, J. A., et al. 1989. Recruitment of a penicillin-binding protein gene from *Neisseria flavescens* during the emergence of penicillin-resistance in *Neisseria meningitidis*. *Proc. Natl. Acad. Sci. USA* 86:8988–92

106. Stoker, N. G., Broome-Smith, J. K., Edelman, A., Spratt, B. G. 1983. Organization and subcloning of the *dac*A-*rod*A-*pbp*A cluster of cell shape genes in *Escherichia coli*. *J. Bacteriol.* 155:847–59

107. Suzuki, S., van Heijenoort, Y., Tamura, T., Mizoguchi, J., Hirota, Y., et al. 1980. *In vitro* peptidoglycan polymerization catalysed by penicillin-binding protein 1b of *Escherichia coli* K12. *FEBS Lett.* 110:245–49

108. Tamaki, S., Nakajima, S., Matsuhashi, M. 1978. Thermosensitive mutation in *Escherichia coli* simultaneously causing defects in penicillin-binding protein-1Bs and in enzyme activity for peptidoglycan synthesis *in vitro*. *Proc. Natl. Acad. Sci. USA* 74:5472–76

109. Taschner, P. E. M., Huls, P. G., Pas, E., Woldringh, C. L. 1988. Division behavior and shape changes in isogenic *fts*Z, *fts*Q, *fts*A, *pbp*B and *fts*E cell division mutants of *Escherichia coli* during temperature shift experiments. *J. Bacteriol.* 170:1533–40

110. Taschner, P. E. M., Ypenburg, N., Spratt, B. G., Woldringh, C. L. 1988. An amino acid substitution in penicillin-binding protein 3 creates pointed polar caps in *Escherichia coli*. *J. Bacteriol.* 170:4828–37

111. Tesch, W., Ryffel, C., Strässle, A., Kayser, F. H., Berger-Bächi, B. 1990. Evidence of a novel staphylococcal *mec*-encoded element (*mec*R) controlling expression of penicillin-binding protein 2'. *Antimicrob. Agents Chemother.* 34:1703–6

112. Tipper, D. J., Strominger, J. L. 1965. Mechanism of action of penicillins: a proposal based on the structural similarity to acyl-D-alanyl-D-alanine. *Proc. Natl. Acad. Sci. USA* 54:1131–41

113. Todd, J. A., Bone, E. J., Ellar, D. J. 1985. The sporulation-specific penicillin-binding protein 5a from *Bacillus subtilis* is a D-carboxypeptidase *in vitro*. *Biochem. J.* 230:825–28

114. Todd, J. A., Bone, E. J., Piggot, P. J., Ellar, D. J. 1983. Differential expression of penicillin-binding protein structural genes during *Bacillus subtilis* sporulation. *FEMS Microbiol. Lett.* 18:197–202

115. Todd, J. A., Roberts, A. N., Johnston, K., Piggot, P. J., Winter, G., et al. 1986. Reduced heat resistance of mutant spores after cloning and mutagenesis of the *Bacillus subtilis* gene encoding penicillin-binding protein 5. *J. Bacteriol.* 167:257–64

116. Tormo, A., Vicente, M. 1984. The *fts*A gene product participates in formation of the *Escherichia coli* septum structure. *J. Bacteriol.* 157:779–84

117. Tsukamoto, K., Kihura, R., Ohno, R., Sawai, T. 1990. Substitution of aspartic acid-217 of *Citrobacter freundii* cephalosporinase and properties of the mutant enzymes. *FEBS Lett.* 264:211–14

118. Tsukamoto, K., Ohno, R., Saway, T. 1990. Extension of the substrate spectrum by an amino acid substitution at residue 219 in the *Citrobacter freundii* cephalosporinase. *J. Bacteriol.* 172:4348–51

119. Ubukata, K., Nonoguchi, R., Matsuhashi, M., Song, M. D., Konno, M. 1989. Restriction maps of the regions coding for methicillin and tobramycin resistances on chromosomal DNA in methicillin-resistant staphylococci. *Antimicrob. Agents Chemother.* 33:1624–26

120. van Heijenoort, Y., Leduc, M., Singer, H., van Heijenoort, J. 1987. Effect of moemycin on *Escherichia coli*. *J. Gen. Microbiol.* 133:667–74

121. Varetto, L., Bellefroid-Bourguignon, C., Frère, J.-M., Nguyen-Distèche, M., Ghuysen, J.-M., et al. 1987. The pH-dependence of the active-site serine DD-

peptidase of *Streptomyces* R61. *Eur. J. Biochem.* 162:525–31

122. Ward, J. E., Lutkenhaus, J. F. 1985. Overproduction of FtsZ induces minicells in *Escherichia coli*. *Cell* 42:941–49

123. Waxman, D. J., Strominger, J. L. 1981. Primary structure of the COOH-terminal membranous segment of a penicillin-sensitive enzyme purified from two Bacilli. *J. Biol. Chem.* 256:2067–77

124. Yi, Q. M., Lutkenhaus, J. F. 1985. The nucleotide sequence of the essential cell division gene *ftsZ*. *Gene* 36:241–47

125. Zhu, Y. F., Curran, I. J., Joris, B., Ghuysen, J.-M., Lampen, J. O. 1990. Identification of BlaR, signal transducer for β-lactamase production in *Bacillus licheniformis* as a penicillin-binding protein with strong homology to the Oxa-2 β-lactamase (class D) of *Salmonella typhimurium*. *J. Bacteriol.* 172:1137–41

Annu. Rev. Microbiol. 1991. 45:69–87

GENETICALLY ENGINEERED BACULOVIRUSES AS AGENTS FOR PEST CONTROL

H. Alan Wood and Robert R. Granados

Boyce Thompson Institute for Plant Research at Cornell University, Tower Road, Ithaca, New York 14853

KEY WORDS: field release, genetic engineering, pesticides, microbial control

CONTENTS

INTRODUCTION 69
BACULOVIRUS BIOLOGY AND LIFE CYCLE 70
   Classification and General Properties 70
   Infection and Replication in Insects 71
BACULOVIRUSES AS VIRAL INSECTICIDES 74
FACTORS CONSTRAINING GREATER USE OF BACULOVIRUS PESTICIDES ... 75
GENETICALLY ENHANCED VIRAL PESTICIDES 76
ENGINEERING STRATEGIES 78
ENVIRONMENTAL ISSUES 80
FIELD-RELEASE TESTING 81
FUTURE: PROMISES AND PITFALLS 84

INTRODUCTION

Baculoviruses constitute one of the largest and most diverse groups of insect-pathogenic viruses. The first record of a baculovirus disease of insects was the description of the "jaundice disease" of the silkworm, *Bombyx mori,* in 1527 (2). In 1856, the Italian scientists Maestri and Cornelia were the first to

69

establish a correlation between the presence of refractive crystals (viral occlusion bodies) and the symptoms of jaundiced silkworms, and by 1947 Bergold (3) had convincingly demonstrated the viral nature of the baculovirus disease of silkworms. Following World War II, research on baculoviruses intensified with the realization that these relatively virulent insect-specific viruses were widespread in nature among economically important insect pests and had potential utility in pest control programs.

Numerous experimental field trials between 1950 and 1960 demonstrated the usefulness of baculoviruses as viral insecticides (25); however, with the concurrent advent of numerous synthetic pesticides with broad-spectrum, low cost, and high insecticidal activity, viral insecticides failed to become a commercial success (7). During the late 1970s and throughout the 1980s, it became clear that our overdependence on chemical pesticides for pest control created numerous unacceptable agricultural, environmental, and human-health problems (30). These factors, combined with the increasing difficulty of discovering new classes of chemicals, have encouraged the search for alternative methods for insect control.

Despite the need for new environmentally sound biological pesticides such as baculoviruses, the majority of these viruses possess an inherent property of slow speed of kill that does not afford growers an economic level of pest control. However, published results of studies on the molecular biology of baculoviruses (6, 13, 40) have recently indicated that engineering these viruses to alter their host range and virulence is now feasible. In this review, we examine the current status of pesticidal baculoviruses, their genetic improvement, and the field-release testing of modified viruses.

BACULOVIRUS BIOLOGY AND LIFE CYCLE

Classification and General Properties

Baculoviruses constitute a large family of invertebrate viruses with a double-stranded DNA genome of 88–153 kilobase pairs (kbp) (36). The family Baculoviridae has a single genus, *Baculovirus*, which is divided into three subgroups. Subgroup A contains the nuclear polyhedrosis viruses (NPVs), which have many virions (enveloped nucleocapsids) occluded within intranuclear protein crystals known as polyhedra or occlusion bodies. These polyhdra are usually 1–10 μm in size and up to 30 or more may be produced in infected cells (6, 16, 20). The polyhedra have a crystalline protein lattice, comprised primarily of a single viral-encoded protein with a molecular weight of 29 kilodaltons (kd). This protein, named polyhedrin, accounts for about 95% of the mass of the polyhedra. The virions are present within the polyhedra as singly enveloped nucleocapsids (SNPV) or bundles of multiply enveloped nucleocapsids (MNPV). Subgroup B contains the granulosis viruses (GVs) that occur as singly enveloped nucleocapsids and are individually occluded with small (0.1 to 1.0 μm) capsule-shaped polyhedra termed granules. The GV occlusion body protein, termed granulin, also has a molecular weight of 29 kd. Unlike the NPVs, which replicate in the nucleus, GVs undergo replication in both the nuclear and cytoplasmic components of an infected cell (16). Subgroup C represents a small group of baculoviruses that have one nucleocapsid per envelope and are not occluded at any stage in their life cycle.

Baculoviruses have a restricted host range and have been isolated only from arthropods. While the majority of baculoviruses (over 600) have been reported from insects, several have also been reported from crustaceans and arachnids (35). Baculoviruses are primarily pathogens of insects in the order Lepidoptera (moths and butterflies) but also infect species in Hymenoptera, Diptera, Coleoptera, and Trichoptera. Claims of baculovirus infections in Orthoptera (1) and Isoptera (14) remain unconfirmed. Within the insects, baculoviruses have been observed to infect only holometabolus insects (those that undergo complete metamorphosis). GVs and MNPVs are found only in Lepidoptera, whereas the SNPVs have been described from all orders from which baculoviruses have been reported (50). NPVs have the widest insect host range and many of them have been grown in insect cell cultures (19). In particular, the MNPV from the alfalfa looper, *Autographa californica* (AcMNPV), has a host range of over 30 insect species and can grow in several permissive insect cell lines. The NPVs have been the most intensively studied insect viruses in recent years and are the primary focus of this review.

Infection and Replication in Insects

In nature, baculoviruses can be isolated from plant foliage, plant debris, and soil. The virus-containing polyhedra are relatively stable and persist in the soil environment for many years (26). Natural epizootics due to NPV or GV infection are common and result when insect larvae feed on plant foliage contaminated with polyhedra. Upon ingestion, the proteinaceous polyhedra are subjected to the high pH of the insect midgut and are rapidly solubilized, thereby releasing the highly infectious virions that may infect susceptible midgut epithelial cells. Baculoviruses are unusual in that two structurally different but genetically identical virion phenotypes are produced during their life cycle (Figure 1). Those virions, found in the polyhedra, are termed polyhedra-derived virus (PDV), and the other form, which is found in the hemolymph of infected insects, is termed budded virus (BV). The PDV is primarily responsible for horizontal transmission between insects and appears to be specialized for infection of epithelial cells of the insect midgut, whereas the BV is believed to facilitate systemic infection of virus within the insect hemocoel (61).

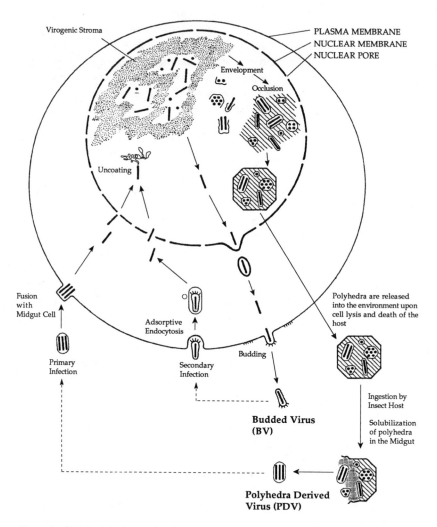

Figure 1   Cellular infection cycle of a nuclear polyhedrosis virus. Polyhedra are ingested by a susceptible insect and solubilized within the insect midgut. The polyhedra-derived virus (PDV) phenotype is released and enters midgut cells by fusion with microvilli. Uncoating of the DNA, followed by gene expression and viral DNA replication, takes place in the nucleus. Progeny nucleocapsids (NCs) are observed assembling within and around the virogenic stroma. Some progeny NCs leave the nucleus and bud through the cytoplasmic membrane into the hemocoel, acquiring a modified virus envelope. These budded virions (BV) have the phenotypes specialized for the systemic spread of virus to other host cells. Other NC progeny become enveloped within the nucleus and are occluded within polyhedra. Upon insect death and cell lysis, the polyhedra are released into the environment. Diagram is reproduced with permission from Blissard & Rohrmann (4).

Dissolution of the polyhedra within the midgut lumen is facilitated by the highly alkaline digestive juices (pH 9.0 to 11.5) and possibly by some enzymatic degradation (48). Released PDV are susceptible to inactivation by midgut juices (59) and must also traverse a relatively nonporous lining of the intestinal tract known as the peritrophic membrane. This noncellular membrane is a secreted sheath, composed primarily of chitin and proteins, and probably serves as a mechanical barrier to pathogenic microorganisms including baculoviruses (8). Some baculoviruses overcome this barrier by producing a viral-encoded protein that degrades the peritrophic membrane, thereby assisting in the passage of virions and enhancing the infection of midgut cells (11, 15, 17). Similar proteins may also function in mediating the adsorption and fusion of virion envelopes with the microvillar membranes of gut cells (58).

NPV infections of lepidopteran hosts are generally polyorganotropic and, soon after infection of midgut cells, general dispersion of virus occurs (18, 19). Secondary rounds of replication lead ultimately to the formation of polyhedra within the nucleus of most larval tissues. Tissue liquification and rupture of fragile epidermis upon death liberates masses of viral polyhedra. Under ideal conditions, a late-instar larva can produce 6×10^9 polyhedra before death. The duration before death of infected larvae in the field can range from 3 to 15 days or more depending on the virus type and host species involved. Other important factors related to virus virulence include virus dose, metamorphic stage of the insect, and temperature. In general, infected larvae continue to feed until shortly before death.

The genetics and molecular basis of baculovirus pathogenesis in insect larvae is poorly understood (16, 29, 62), and broader knowledge of the genetic and molecular factors involved in the mode of action of these viruses will greatly facilitate their genetic improvement. Recently, O'Reilly & Miller (43) reported the presence of an AcMNPV gene (*egt*) that inactivates the ecdysteroid insect molting hormone and blocks the molting of infected larvae. This interruption of the normal development of the larva may provide the virus with a selective advantage. Kuzio et al (31) reported a gene believed to be essential for virulence of AcMNPV polyhedra to cabbage looper (*Trichoplusia ni*) larvae. The gene product was identified as a 74-kd protein but the function of this factor in viral pathogenesis was not determined. The gene encoding the viral-enhancing protein from *T. ni* GV (TnGV) was cloned and sequenced (17; Y. Hashimoto, B. G. Corsaro, & R. R. Granados, unpublished data). In addition to significantly enhancing the infectivity of NPVs, this enhancing factor can decrease the time of larval death by 10 to 63 hours (15). These reports suggest that baculoviruses have evolved novel strategies by which they can infect and replicate in their host. Certainly, other viral gene products important for viral infection and replication in insects will

Table 1 Baculoviruses commercialized or registered in North America

Country	Product name	Registrant and year of registration	Current use pattern
United States	Elcar	Sandoz—1975	Experimental field trials on cotton bollworm, *Heliothis zea.*
United States	Tm-BioControl-1	USDA Forest Service—1976	Toll processed by Espro, Inc., for use on Douglas-fir tussock moth, *Orgyia pseudotsugata.*
United States	Gypchek	USDA Forest Service—1978	Produced by Espro Inc., for use on gypsy moth, *Lymantria dispar.*
United States	Noecheck	USDA Forest Service—1983	For European pine sawfly, *Neodiprion sertifer,* control. No current use.
Canada	Virtuss	Forestry Canada—1983	Experimental field trials on Douglas-fir tussock moth.
Canada	Lecontivirus	Forestry Canada—1983	For operational control by Canadian FS on red-headed pine sawfly, *Neodiprion leconti.*
Canada	Tm-BioControl-1	Forestry Canada—1985	Experimental field trials on Douglas-fir tussock moth, *O. pseudotsugata.*

be described and their genes will be useful in the genetic enhancement of the pesticidal properties of baculoviruses.

BACULOVIRUSES AS VIRAL INSECTICIDES

In North America, the United States and Canada have registered a total of seven baculoviruses for use against forest and agricultural insect pests (Table 1). Of these seven, only two—Gypchek, for control of the gypsy moth (*Lymantria dispar*) and Tm-BioControl-1, for control of the Douglas-fir tussock moth (*Orgyia pseudotsugata*)—are commercial products. In 1990, over 600 acres of forest were treated with Gypchek produced by Espro, Inc., Columbia, Md., and approximately 150,000 acre equivalents of Tm-BioControl-1 have been toll processed for use in the northwestern United States (D. M. K. Hirsch & A. Hutchins, personal communication).

In Western Europe, at least four baculoviruses are commercial products but their use is limited (46). In Russia, eight viral insecticides have been registered but their commercial use is not known (32). In China, numerous baculoviruses have been field tested and the first commercial viral pesticide was reported in 1989. This baculovirus is used against cotton pests of the genus *Heliothis* and sales for the treatment of 25,000 acres were expected in 1989 (22). By far, the most successful commercial baculovirus in terms of total acres treated is the NPV of the velvetbean caterpillar (*Anticarsia gemmatalis*), a major pest of soybean in Brazil. This product, known as Multigen, was manufactured and sold by Agroggen, São Paulo, Brazil. In 1988–1989, the amount of Multigen sold was adequate to spray approximately 200,000 acres (O. H. Pavan, personal communication). The virus-treated areas could increase to over four million acres within three to four years (41).

FACTORS CONSTRAINING GREATER USE OF BACULOVIRUS PESTICIDES

Although numerous naturally occurring NPVs have been field tested, and in a few cases commercialized (Table 1), the worldwide use of these viruses for pest control is insignificant. Recent figures estimate that the total sales of biological control agents account for less than 1% of world pesticide sales (27), and baculoviruses account for only 0.2% of that. Clearly, the limited commercial penetration of the global market by viral insecticides suggests that major factors constrain their wider use. Several key reasons explain the restricted use of viral pesticides. These include: (*a*) virulence, (*b*) host range, (*c*) persistence, (*d*) production, (*e*) product stability, and (*f*) registration and patentability (45, 46). While all these factors are important constraints, virulence and host range are serious deficiencies. First, lack of virulence is commonly thought to contribute to the variable or ineffective field control of pests. Growers find it difficult to accept the slower speed of kill of baculoviruses because chemical pesticides provide broad-spectrum activity and rapid knockdown and kill. Second, naturally occurring baculoviruses have a high host specificity, which is seen as advantageous in conserving beneficial insects. However, the natural host range of these viruses often limits the market potential for their use, and the limited amount of revenues anticipated from the small market size is a major disincentive to commercial development of baculoviruses by large agrochemical companies.

Knowledge of the molecular biology and genetics of baculoviruses has accelerated greatly in recent years, and this database will enable the genetic manipulation of these viruses. The introduction of new genes into the baculovirus genome, which could deliver some deleterious gene product in the insect larva, could greatly increase the speed of kill or host range (34, 40). As discussed below, biotechnological approaches have recently been applied to increase the pesticidal properties (e.g. virulence) of baculoviruses, and the results suggest that genetic improvement of these viruses will be possible.

GENETICALLY ENHANCED VIRAL PESTICIDES

As a means of improving the commercial attributes of baculovirus insecticides, several types of foreign pesticidal genes have been proposed for
insertion into viral genomes. They include insect-specific toxins, hormones,
hormone receptors, metabolic enzymes, growth regulators, and so on. Expression of these foreign products would be aimed at enhancing the speed
with which infected larvae are killed or stop feeding. The selection of a
pesticidal-enhancing gene will have to be made both on the basis of its
pesticidal properties and its potential environmental impact.

In 1988, Carbonell et al (9) reported on the properties of a baculovirus
containing the gene coding for the scorpion *Buthus eupeus* insect toxin-1
(BeIt). BeIT is an insect-specific paralytic neurotoxin and was selected on the
basis of its perceived potential to halt feeding. The BeIT gene was synthesized
based on the amino acid sequence (21) using the codon preferences exhibited
in the AcMNPV polyhedrin and p10 genes. The synthetic gene was inserted
into the AcMNPV genome under the control of the polyhedrin gene promoter.
High levels of BeIT gene transcription but only small amounts of the gene
product were detected. When infection-paralytic assays were performed with
the wax moth, *Galleria mellonella*, and *T. ni* host larvae, no paralytic activity
was detected and the infected insects died at times expected with wild-type
AcMNPV infections. The lack of biological activity was considered to result
from either low toxin concentrations (inefficient translation) or instability of
the protein.

Merryweather et al (38) have inserted the delta-endotoxin gene from *Bacillus thuringiensis* (*Bt*) ssp. *kurstaki* HD-73 into the AcMNPV genome. During
sporulation, the gram-positive *B. thuringiensis* produces crystalline inclusions
containing the protoxin. When ingested, the protoxin is cleaved in the insect
midgut, producing an active toxin that causes an immediate cessation of
feeding and eventual death of susceptible host larvae. Several *Bt* strains are
commercially available and used to control numerous insect pests (10). The *Bt*
HD-73 protoxin gene was inserted into the AcMNPV genome under the
control of the polyhedrin and the p10 gene promoters. Biologically active
protoxin was expressed following virus replication in both insect cell cultures
and *T. ni* larvae. Insect bioassays were problematic with *Bt* inocula produced
with recombinant viruses because the inoculum exhibited feeding deterrent
properties. This observation probably resulted from small amounts of endotoxin in the inocula. In bioassays with second-instar *T. ni* larvae, the dosage
required to kill 50% of the larvae (LD_{50}) and the time required to kill 50% of
the larvae (LT_{50}) with the *Bt*-recombinant and wild-type viruses were not
significantly different. The insertion and expression of the active toxin sequences rather than the protoxin may effect faster death of infected larvae.

Although expression of the protoxin did not lead to a detectable enhancement of pesticidal properties, the *Bt* toxin produced in the larvae would contaminate plant tissue following death. Under field conditions, both the progeny virus and *Bt* toxin produced in these larvae would contaminate plant tissues and might significantly enhance the potential for secondary control.

In 1989, Maeda (34) reported replacement of the *Bombyx mori* nuclear polyhedrosis virus (BmMNPV) polyhedrin gene with the diuretic hormone gene from the tobacco hornworm, *Manduca sexta*. Insect diuretic and anti-diuretic hormones probably play vital roles in the strict regulation of water balance in response to environmental changes. Hemolymph-volume and mortality assays were performed with fifth-instar silkworm larvae infected with the diuretic hormone-containing BmMNPV (BmDH5). At three days post-infection (p.i.), the BmDH5-infected larvae had lower hemolymph volumes as compared to control larvae and larvae infected with wild-type virus. At four days p.i., all BmDH5-infected larvae were dead, whereas most larvae infected with wild-type virus died at five days p.i. This was the first positive report of a foreign gene product that enhanced the pesticidal properties of a baculovirus. These observations await confirmation by other investigators.

Hammock et al (24) inserted the juvenile hormone esterase (JHE) gene from the tobacco hornworm, *Heliothis virescens*, genome into AcMNPV genome. In last-instar lepidopterous larvae, juvenile hormone (JH) is inactivated by a dramatic increase in JHE levels. This reduction in JH titres initiates metamorphosis to the pupal stage and to a cessation of feeding. The polyhedrin gene of AcMNPV was replaced with the JHE gene under the control of the polyhedrin gene promoter. Expression of JHE following infection of first-instar *T. ni* larvae resulted in a significant reduction in feeding and growth as compared to the control or wild-type virus–infected larvae. Infections of later instar larvae showed no significant differences in feeding or growth. The investigators (24) speculated that this level of JHE may not be sufficient to overcome the level of hormone biosynthesis in later stages.

Hammock et al (24) also considered that the AcMNPV-induced production of the ecdysteroid UDP-glucosyl transferase (EGT) may have reduced the effect of JHE in later instar larvae. O'Reilly & Miller (43, 44) reported that the AcMNPV genome contained a gene coding for the enzyme EGT. This enzyme inactivates ecdysteroids by a transfer of glucose from UDP-glucose to ecdysteroids. Ecdysteroids are a family of steroid hormones involved in both larval-to-larval and larval-to-pupal molts. O'Reilly & Miller (43) showed that most fourth-instar larvae of the fall armyworm, *Spodoptera frugiperda*, infected with the wild-type AcMNPV did not molt to the fifth instar. However, all larvae infected with an EGT-minus mutant molted. Two characteristics of impending molts, feeding cessation and wandering, were noted with EGT-minus–infected larvae but no data were presented regarding any alteration in the pesticidal properties of the EGT mutant virus. Other baculoviruses may carry EGT genes. Dougherty et al (12) found reduced ecdysteroid titres and prolonged larval stages in *T. ni* larvae infected with a granulosis virus (GV). EGT-minus baculoviruses, by themselves or with foreign gene inserts such as the JHE gene, may be useful in the development of enhanced viral pesticides.

Another viral gene that affects the pesticidal activity of baculoviruses is the viral-enhancing factor (VEF) gene of *T. ni* GV described by Derksen & Granados (11). The VEF has biological properties similar to a *Pseudaletia unipuncta* GV synergistic factor reported by Tanada (54) in 1959 and recently reviewed by Tanada (55). The VEF is a component of the polyhedra (granules of GV). Following dissolution of polyhedra in the midgut of host larvae, the VEF disrupts the integrity of the peritrophic membrane, which lines the gut cavity. The removal of this barrier significantly increases the efficiency of virus infections (11, 15). Addition of VEF resulted in more than 10-fold reductions in the LD_{50}. In addition, the increased efficiency of infection led to increased numbers of virion particles infecting larvae, which resulted in a reduced LT_{50}. The overexpression and/or increased occlusion of VEF in polyhedra or granules would significantly reduce the amount of field inocula required to achieve high rates of infection.

Many gene products may be used to enhance the pesticidal properties of baculoviruses. From an environmental standpoint, the use of host gene products that are expressed at inappropriate developmental stages, in new cell types and/or in excessive amounts, is presently attractive. Metabolic enzymes, hormones, and their receptors are likely candidates. Keeley & Hayes (28) have proposed the use of "antipeptides," which would bind to neurohormones, thereby blocking their physiologic functions. The introduction of naturally occurring viral pesticides that have been engineered to express host proteins should pose few if any toxicological problems.

ENGINEERING STRATEGIES

A commonly used strategy for insertion and expression of foreign genes in baculoviruses is the baculovirus expression vector system (47, 53). The basis of this system is the replacement of the polyhedrin gene–coding region with a foreign gene sequence. As described above, the polyhedrin gene is nonessential for the replication of infectious, nonoccluded virions. Recombinant viruses are produced by allelic transplacement following cotransfection of insect cells with viral DNA and plasmid DNA containing the foreign gene sequences, the polyhedrin gene promoter, and flanking sequences. The foreign gene is inserted under the transcriptional control of the strong polyhedrin gene promotor. Recombinant viruses are isolated based on the lack of polyhedra in infection foci. Because of the ease and high expression levels achieved in this system, dozens of foreign genes (33) have been expressed in the baculovirus expression vector system.

Occlusion of the baculovirus particles within polyhedra is required for persistence of biological activity in nature. In the absence of polyhedron occlusion, the nonoccluded PDV are rapidly inactivated in the soil and on plant tissues (5) as well as in dead larval tissues (23). Therefore, genetically engineered viruses lacking a functional polyhedrin gene (poly-minus) cannot persist in the environment—a highly desirable ecological trait. The problem with this strategy is that the nonoccluded virions are so unstable that they could not be delivered to the field in an active state. To deal with this problem, alternative strategies have been proposed and are discussed below.

In order to occlude poly-minus baculovirus particles in polyhedra and thereby stabilize infectivity, host cells can be co-infected with both wild-type and poly-minus virus isolates (23, 39, 51, 64). Late in the replication cycle, the wild-type virus produces polyhedrin protein that occludes both the wild-type and poly-minus virus particles. This co-occlusion process provides a method for delivering a poly-minus baculovirus to the field in an infectious form. Persistence of a co-occluded, poly-minus virus in a virus population is determined by the probability of co-infection of individual larvae and cells with both virus types as the virus is passed from insect to insect. The level of persistence was studied under laboratory conditions by determining the amount of occluded poly-minus AcMNPV progeny produced following larval infections with different virus inoculum dosages and with inocula containing varying ratios of co-occluded poly-minus and wild-type virions (23, 64). The results indicated that a poly-minus virus would not persist in a virus population under natural conditions. Based on these data, researchers at the Boyce Thompson Institute for Plant Research at Cornell University were granted permission by the US Environmental Protection Agency to conduct the first field introduction of a genetically engineered virus in 1989 (discussed below).

Vlak et al (60) have proposed the replacement of the p10 gene with foreign gene inserts. Like the polyhedrin gene, the p10 gene is not essential for virus replication and has a strong late promoter. Recombinant viruses lacking the p10 gene produce polyhedra lacking a polyhedral envelope. These polyhedra exhibit significantly reduced LD_{50} values as compared to wild-type AcMNPV. Vlak et al hypothesized that the absence of p10 protein reduced the stability of polyhedra, resulting in an increased efficiency of virion release. Williams et al (63) showed that the physical integrity of the mutant polyhedra was sensitive to disruption by physical stress. The data suggest that p10-minus AcMNPV polyhedra have a lower environmental stability as compared to wild-type virus. If this is the case, poly-plus baculoviruses with pesticidal gene inserts in the p10 region would provide a product that was sufficiently stable for commercial use and also environmentally unstable.

The polyhedrin and p10 genes are both expressed late in the replication cycle. Therefore, foreign genes under the transcriptional control of either promoter will be expressed approximately 10 hours p.i. To shorten this time, Miller (40) suggested the use of an early viral gene promoter to control the expression of the foreign gene and to retain polyhedrin expression. Although early gene promoters are not very strong, the early expression of the pesticidal gene might compensate for the reduction in expression levels. If immediate early promoters are used, the new gene might be expressed during semipermissive or nonpermissive infections, and the host-range specificity might be lost (37). An alternative to the use of early viral gene promoters might be use of a constitutive host promoter. This approach could achieve high expression levels soon after infection.

Another containment strategy might be to replicate poly-minus recombinants in transgenic insects that contain integrated polyhedrin promoter and coding sequences. Virus progeny replicated in the transgenic host would be occluded; however, replication in field insects would produce only nonoccluded virions that would be rapidly inactivated following death of the target pest.

ENVIRONMENTAL ISSUES

Besides improving the commercial attributes of viral pesticides, the genetic modifications to baculoviruses must also be evaluated in relationship to ecological and environmental issues such as those outlined by Tiedje et al (57). The field release of engineered viral pesticides in the US is governed by the US EPA under the Federal Insecticide, Fungicide, and Rodenticide Act. If federal monies are used to sponsor the release, the sponsoring agency must also perform a review under the National Environmental Policy Act. In addition, several states now have legislation governing the release of engineered materials.

Among the issues that need to be addressed prior to the release of a genetically altered baculovirus are host-range attributes. One of the attractive attributes of baculoviruses is that their host ranges are limited to a few invertebrate hosts. Although host-range expansion might be commercially attractive, care will be needed to ensure that genetic alterations do not extend host ranges to include beneficial insects or vertebrates.

Another consideration in the release of a genetically enhanced virus will be its potential to displace wild-type virus populations in nature. Displacement of natural virus populations, particularly in nonagricultural settings, could result in unanticipated ecological perturbations over large areas. Accordingly, release of engineered viruses that have a selective advantage over natural virus isolates either with respect to persistence in the environment or efficiency of infection may be unwise.

Despite the meticulous risk assessments mandated prior to the release of any genetically engineered organism, the remote possibility always exists that the engineered organism may possess unforseen properties that would dictate mitigation. Removal of an engineered virus from the environment would be difficult because baculoviruses can survive for years in the soil (56). Therefore, engineering strategies that limit survival in nature are extremely attractive and appropriate at the present time.

Another area of concern with the release of modified organisms is genetic transfer or reassortment. The engineered virus should have stable genetic properties. In addition, evaluation of the frequency and possible consequences of gene transfer to related and unrelated naturally occurring baculoviruses is important.

FIELD-RELEASE TESTING

As discussed below, field testing of genetically modified forms of the AcMNPV began in 1986. Approval for these tests were granted only after extensive reviews by regulatory authorities. In addition, considerable efforts were made to inform the public about the nature and benefits of this research. The tests to date have not been performed with viruses with enhanced pesticidal properties. Rather, the tests have been designed to gather information regarding the nature of engineered baculoviruses in the environment and to evaluate any potential hazards that future releases may pose.

In 1986, the Natural Environment Research Council's (NERC) Institute of Virology in Oxford, UK, began a series of field trials with genetically altered forms of the AcMNPV (5). The first test was undertaken with a genetically marked AcMNPV isolate that had an 80-bp insert downstream of the AcMNPV polyhedrin–gene coding region. The inserted sequence contained translation stop codons in all six reading frames, contained no ATG codon, and did not affect gene expression or replication. Initial studies showed that the marked and parental isolates had an identical host range, genetic stability in cell culture, and stability in soil.

The release site was in a field approximately 0.5 km from the nearest human population and was constructed to provide a high degree of physical containment. The test site was surrounded by a two-meter-high fence to prevent access by large animals. The ten-meter-square facility was enclosed within a net to prevent access by birds and to restrict arthropods from entering or leaving the facility. To prevent entry by moles and rodents, wire netting was inserted into the ground all around the enclosure. Precautions were also taken to control carabids and spiders.

For the 1986 test, third-instar *Spodoptera exigua* larvae were inoculated in the laboratory with ten times the LD_{50} dose of the marked virus. The infected larvae were then released onto sugar beet plants in a plexiglass enclosure within the field containment facility. All of the infected larvae died within one week p.i. Over the next six months, plant and soil samples were analyzed to determine the persistence of the marked virus. The marked virus was detected on plant leaves by feeding the tissues to *T. ni* larvae and analyzing the progeny virus. Persistence of the virus in the soil was determined by growing cabbage seedings in the soil samples and then feeding the plants to *T. ni* larvae. The marked virus was detected in the plant and soil samples throughout the six-month sampling period. Although the number of biologically active polyhedra was not quantified, the test indicated that the marked virus probably had a survival capacity in nature equal to that of the parental virus polyhedra.

At the end of test, the field site was decontaminated by removal and sterilization of all vegetation. The soil was decontaminated with three 5% formalin treatments. The treated soil was used to propagate cabbage seedings, which were subsequently fed to *T. ni* larvae. No virus infections were detected using this method.

In 1987, the NERC Institute of Virology conducted a second release with a different AcMNPV isolate. The polyhedrin gene (promoter and open reading frame) had been removed from the genome and replaced with a 100-bp insert. In the absence of the polyhedrin gene, the virus particles do not become occluded and therefore were unprotected. Preliminary studies were conducted to assess the persistence of the nonoccluded virus particles in sterile soil. Using tissue culture assay procedures, nonoccluded virus titres decreased more than two logs after three days in sterile soil.

Based on this lack of environmental stability, the second test was designed to evaluate the environmental persistence of polyhedrin-minus virus produced in insects. Again the insects were infected in the laboratory and then placed on sugar beet plants in the field enclosure. All of the infected larvae died within one week p.i., and virus infectivity could not be detected in foliage or samples taken one week later. Therefore, the marked polyhedrin-minus virus was "self-destructive" (5) and could not persist in nature.

In 1989, researchers at the Boyce Thompson Institute for Plant Research at Cornell University conducted the first uncontained field application of a genetically altered baculovirus (64). The release was conducted to test the environmental persistence of an AcMNPV isolate whose genome lacked the polyhedrin gene open reading frame and that had been occluded through replication in cells also infected with wild-type AcMNPV (co-occlusion process discussed above). No DNA marker inserts were used. The poly-minus virus was detected based on the reduced size of a single restriction enzyme fragment. The ratio of the complete to smaller fragment was used to determine the amount of occluded altered virus in progeny polyhedra isolated from individual larvae.

As discussed above, the co-occlusion process allowed for delivery of inoculum virus in a stable form. However, laboratory data (23) indicated that the polyhedrin-minus mutant could not persist in a virus population under natural conditions because of the low probability of co-infection of individual larvae and larval cells. Therefore, although the strategy was similar to the self-destructive process employed in the UK release, the loss of the polyhedrin-minus virus from the environment would be slow. The field release was designed to test the rate at which the engineered virus would be eliminated from the environment.

Because of the biological containment provided by the removal of the polyhedrin gene and lack of foreign gene inserts, physical containment of the test was minimal. The test was conducted in a circular, two-acre cabbage plot at Cornell University's New York State Agricultural Experiment Station in Geneva, N.Y. Access to the farm site was limited, so no fences or physical barriers were constructed. Because of the lack of barriers, careful monitoring of naturally occurring insect populations was conducted.

The center of the test plot was seeded with 2700 third-instar *T. ni* larvae prior to each of three virus applications during the summer of 1989. Each virus application was made with a backpack sprayer at a rate of 3×10^{12} polyhedra per acre. The polyhedra inocula contained equal numbers of occluded wild-type and poly-minus virus particles. All of the test larvae died following each application. The progeny polyhedra isolated from these larvae contained, on average, 42% poly-minus virus particles. At the end of the 1989 growing season, the test site was estimated to contain approximately 10^{14} progeny AcMNPV polyhedra per acre.

During 1990, the field was replanted with cabbage seedings. In order to monitor the persistence of the poly-minus virus, soil and tissue samples were assayed for virus. Three times during the summer, the plants were inoculated with *T. ni* larvae. Prior to pupation, the larvae were collected and placed on artificial diet until pupation. Unlike the UK release, very little infectious virus was detected on the foliage. Soil samples collected from the test site in 1990 contained significant amounts of infectious virus. The amount and composition of this virus population is being quantitated to evaluate the persistence of the polyhedrin-minus virus with time.

Monitoring of the field will continue through 1991 to obtain an estimate of the rate of loss of the engineered virus within the virus population. Little, if any, virus will probably be detectable in 1992.

FUTURE: PROMISES AND PITFALLS

A joint committee of the National Academy of Sciences, the National Academy of Engineering, and the Institute of Medicine recently concluded that "biological control can and should become the primary method used in the United States to ensure the health and productivity of important plant and animal species" (42). The emergence of recombinant DNA technology has provided the most significant impetus thus far for the continued growth of biological control research. Understanding the genes and gene products important to biological control has enabled the genetic alteration of microbial agents for pest control.

From an environmental and health-safety standpoint, baculovirus pesticides are outstanding alternatives to synthetic chemical pesticides. At present, the field performance and production costs of baculovirus pesticides, as well as other microbial control agents, have significantly limited their use. The short-term pesticidal efficacy of baculoviruses is certainly a goal achievable through genetic engineering. A major factor in the commercialization of baculoviruses will be the willingness of government agencies or industry to invest the resources needed to conduct the required safety testing and to address other regulatory issues. Accordingly, the development of appropriate governmental regulatory policies will significantly impact the development and release of genetically enhanced pesticides.

Industrial-scale methods for the production of viral pesticides is an additional limiting factor. At present, in vivo production methods must be used. This involves a large commitment in facility development and, in some cases, the invention of commercial procedures. The recent development of serum-free media for tissue-culture production procedures and the development of novel bioreactors presents an attractive commercial alternative (52).

The species specificity of viral pesticides is considered a positive attribute from an environmental standpoint but a deterrent to commercial development. Restrictive host ranges limit the market potentials of many baculoviruses. However, selected insect pest species in major crop systems can be targeted. In addition, as synthetic pesticides become unusable because of resistance or nonrenewal of registration, viral pesticides may play a more important role in integrated pest management systems of major crops and as viable options in minor crop management.

Clearly, the widespread use of viral pesticides in agriculture and forestry is a desirable goal in several pest management systems. To reach this goal, the cost/benefit ratios of microbial versus synthetic pesticides must be improved. The costs associated with registration, production, and efficacy will continue to influence the difference between these ratios. The determinations of the cost/benefit ratios of microbial control agents have been restricted to agricultural production costs. Certainly, this ratio would be significantly reduced and the value placed on this technology would increase if socio-economic and environmental costs and benefits were factored into the evaluation process.

ACKNOWLEDGMENTS

The preparation of this manuscript was supported in part through grant CR-815831-01-0 from the US Environmental Protection Agency, grant no. 88-37263-3700 from the USDA Competitive Research Grants Program, and grant no. 23-243 from the USDA Forest Service.

Literature Cited

1. Bensimon, A., Gerassi, E., Hauschner, A., Harpaz, I., Sela, I. 1987. "Dark Cheeks", a lethal disease of locusts provoked by a lepidopterous baculovirus. *J. Invertebr. Pathol.* 50:254–60
2. Benz, G. A. 1986. Introduction: Historical perspectives. See Ref. 18, 1:1–35
3. Bergold, G. H. 1947. Die isolierung des polyeder-virus und die natur der polyeder. *Z. Naturforsch. Teil B,* 2:122–43
4. Bishop, D. H. L. 1986. UK release of genetically marked virus. *Nature* 323: 496
5. Bishop, D. H. L., Entwistle, P. F., Cameron, I. R., Allen, C. J., Possee, R. D. 1988. Field trials of genetically-engineered baculovirus insecticides. In *The Release of Genetically-Engineered Micro-organisms,* ed. M. Sussman, C. H. Collins, F. A. Skinner, D. E. Stewart-Tull, pp. 143–79. New York: Academic. 306 pp.
6. Blissard, G. W., Rohrmann, G. F. 1990. Baculovirus diversity and molecular biology. *Annu. Rev. Entomol.* 35: 127–55
7. Bohmfalk, G. T. 1986. Practical factors influencing the utilization of baculoviruses as pesticides. See Ref. 18, 2(2):223–35
8. Brandt, C., Adang, M., Spence, K. 1978. The peritrophic membrane: Ultrastructural analysis and function as a mechanical barrier to microbial infection in *Orgyia pseudotsugata. J. Invertebr. Pathol.* 32:12–24
9. Carbonell, L. F., Hodge, M. R., Tomalski, M. D., Miller, M. K. 1988. Synthesis of a gene coding for an insect-specific scorpion neurotoxin and attempts to express it using baculovirus vectors. *Gene* 73:409–18
10. Carlton, B. 1988. See Ref. 49, pp. 38–43
11. Derksen, A. C. G., Granados, R. R. 1988. Alteration of lepidopteran peri-

trophic membrane of baculoviruses and enhancement of viral infectivity. *Virology* 167:242–50
12. Dougherty, E. M., Kelly, T. J., Rochford, R., Forney, J. A., Adams, J. R. 1987. Effects of infection with a granulosis virus on larval growth, development and ecdysteroid production in the cabbage looper, *Trichoplusia ni. Physiol. Entomol.* 12:23–30
13. Faulkner, P., Carstens, E. B. 1986. An overview of the structure and replication of baculoviruses. *Curr. Top. Microbiol. Immunol.* 131:1–19
14. Fazairy, A. A., Hassan, F. A. 1988. Infection of termites by *Spodoptera littoralis* nuclear polyhedrosis virus. *Insect Sci. Appl.* 9:37–39
15. Gallo, L. G., Corsaro, B. G., Hughes, P. R., Granados, R. R. 1991. In vivo enhancement of baculovirus infection by the viral enhancing factor of a granulosis virus of the cabbage looper, *Trichoplusia ni* (Lepidoptera: Noctuidae). *J. Invertebr. Pathol.* In press
16. Granados, R. R. 1980. Infectivity and mode of action of baculoviruses. *Biochem. Bioengineer.* 22:1377–405
17. Granados, R. R., Corsaro, B. G. 1990. Baculovirus enhancing proteins and their implication for insect control. *Proc. Int. Coll. Invertebr. Pathol., 5th, Adelaide, Australia, 1990,* pp. 174–78. Adelaide, Australia: Soc. Invert. Pathol.
18. Granados, R. R., Federici, B. A., eds. 1986. *The Biology of Baculoviruses,* Vols. 1–2. Boca Raton, FL: CRC
19. Granados, R. R., Hashimoto, Y. 1989. Infectivity of baculoviruses to cultured cells. In *Invertebrate Cell System Applications,* ed. J. Mitsuhasi, 2:3–13. Boca Raton, FL: CRC. 303 pp.
20. Granados, R. R., Williams, K. A. 1986. In vivo infection and replication of baculoviruses. See Ref. 18, 1:89–108
21. Grishin, E. V. 1981. Structure and func-

tion of *Buthus eupeus* scorpion neuro-toxins. *Int. J. Quantum Chem.* 19:291–98
22. Guangyu, Z. 1989. The first commercial viral pesticide in China. *IPM Pract.* 11:13
23. Hamblin, M., van Beek, N. A. M., Hughes, P. R., Wood, H. A. 1990. Co-occlusion and persistence of a baculovirus mutant lacking the polyhedrin gene. *Appl. Environ. Microbiol.* 56:3057–62
24. Hammock, B. D., Bonning, B. C., Possee, R. D., Hanzlik, T. N., Maeda, S. 1990. Expression and effects of the juvenile hormone esterase in a baculovirus vector. *Nature* 344:458–61
25. Ignoffo, C. M. 1973. Development of a viral insecticide: Concept to commercialization. *Exp. Parasitol.* 33:380–406
26. Jaques, R. P. 1977. Stability of entomopathogenic viruses. In *Environmental Stability of Microbial Insecticides*, ed. D. L. Hostetter, C. M. Ignoffo, 10:99–117. 119 pp.
27. Jutsum, A. R. 1988. Commercial application of biological control: Status and prospects. *Phil. Trans. R. Soc. London Ser. B.* 318:357–73
28. Keeley, L. L., Hayes, T. K. 1987. Speculations on biotechnology applications for insect neuroendocrine research. *Insect Biochem.* 17:639–51
29. Kelly, D. C. 1982. Baculovirus replication. *J. Gen. Virol.* 63:1–13
30. Kirschbaum, J. B. 1985. Potential implication of genetic engineering and other biotechnologies to insect control. *Annu. Rev. Entomol.* 30:51–70
31. Kuzio, J., Jaques, R., Faulkner, P. 1989. Identification of p74, a gene essential for virulence of baculovirus occlusion bodies. *Virology* 173: 759–63
32. Lipa, J. J. 1990. Update: microbial pest control in Eastern Europe. *IPM Pract.* 12:1–5
33. Luckow, V. V., Summers, M. D. 1988. Trends in the development of baculovirus expression vectors. *Bio/Technology* 6:47–55
34. Maeda, S. 1989. Expression of foreign genes in insects using baculovirus vectors. *Annu. Rev. Entomol.* 34:351–72
35. Martignoni, M. E., Iwai, P. J. 1986. A catalog of viral diseases of insects, mites, and ticks. *USDA Forest Service PNW-195.* Washington, DC: USGPO. 50 pp.
36. Matthews, R. E. F. 1982. Classification and nomenclature of viruses. Fourth report of the International Committee on Taxonomy of Viruses. *Intervirology* 17: 1–199
37. McClintock, J. T., Dougherty, E. M.,

Weiner, R. M. 1986. Semipermissive replication of a nuclear polyhedrosis virus of *Autographa californica* in a gypsy moth cell line. *J. Virol.* 57:197–204
38. Merryweather, A. T., Weyer, U., Harris, M. P. G., Hirst, M., Booth, T., Possee, R. D. 1990. Construction of genetically engineered baculovirus insecticides containing the *Bacillus thuringiensis* ssp. *kurstaki* HD-73 delta endotoxin. *J. Gen. Virol.* 71:1535–44
39. Miller, D. W. 1988. Genetically engineered viral insecticides: Practical considerations. In *Biotechnology for Crop Protection*, ed. P. A. Hedin, R. M. Hollingworth, J. J. Mann, pp. 405–21. Washington, DC: Am. Chem. Soc. 471 pp.
40. Miller, L. K. 1988. Baculoviruses as gene expression vectors. *Annu. Rev. Microbiol.* 42:177–99
41. Moscardi, F. 1988. Production and use of entomopathogens in Brazil. See Ref. 49, pp. 53–60.
42. National Academy of Sciences, National Academy of Engineering, Institute of Medicine. 1987. *Research Briefings: Report of the Research Briefing Panel of "Biological Control in Managed Ecosystems"*. Washington DC: National Academic Press. 12 pp.
43. O'Reilly, D. R., Miller, L. K. 1989. A baculovirus blocks insect molting by producing ecdysteroid UDP-glucosyl transferase. *Science* 245:1110–12
44. O'Reilly, D. R., Miller, L. K. 1990. Regulation of expression of a baculovirus ecdysteroid UDP-glucosyl transferase gene. *J. Virol.* 64:1321–8
45. Payne, C. C. 1988. Insect pest management concepts: The role of biological control. See Ref. 49, pp. 1–7
46. Payne, C. C. 1988. Pathogens for the control of insects: Where next? *Phil. Trans. R. Soc. London Ser. B.* 318:225–48
47. Pennock, G. D., Shoemaker, C., Miller, L. K. 1984. Strong and regulated expression of *Escherichia coli* beta-galactosidase in insect cells with a baculovirus vector. *Molec. Cell. Biol.* 4: 399–406
48. Pritchett, D. W., Young, S. Y., Yearian, W. C. 1982. Dissolution of *Autographa californica* nuclear polyhedrosis virus polyhedra by the digestive fluid of *Trichoplusia ni* (Lepidoptera: Noctuidae) larvae. *J. Invertebr. Pathol.* 39:354–61
49. Roberts, D. W., Granados, R. R., eds. 1988. *Biotechnology, Biological Pesticides and Novel Plant-Pest Resistance*

for *Insect Pest Management. Proc. Int. Conf. Ithaca, N.Y.*. Ithaca, NY. 175 pp.

50. Rohrmann, G. F. 1986. Evolution of occluded baculoviruses. See Ref. 18, 10:203–15

51. Shelton, A. M., Wood, H. A. 1989. Microbial pesticides. *World & I* 4:358–65

52. Shuler, M. L., Cho, T., Wickham, T., Ogonah, O., Kool, M., et al. 1990. Bioreactor development for production of viral pesticides on heterologous proteins in insect cell cultures. *Ann. NY Acad. Sci.* 589:399–422

53. Smith, G. E., Summers, M. D., Fraser, M. J. 1983. Production of human beta interferon in insect cells infected with a baculovirus expression vector. *Molec. Cell. Biol.* 3:2156–65

54. Tanada, Y. 1959. Synergism between two viruses of the armyworm *Pseudaletia unipuncta* (Haworth) (Lepidoptera: Noctuidae). *J. Insect Pathol.* 1:215–31

55. Tanada, Y. 1985. A synopsis of studies on the synergistic property of an insect baculovirus: A tribute to Edward A. Steinhaus. *J. Invertebr. Pathol.* 45:125–38

56. Thompson, C. G., Scott, D. W., Wickham, B. E. 1981. Long term persistence of the nuclear polyhedrosis virus of the Douglas-fir tussock moth, *Orgyia pseudotsugata*, (Lepidoptera:Lymantriidae) in forest soil. *Environ. Entomol.* 10:254–55

57. Tiedje, J. M., Colwell, R. K., Grossman, Y. L., Hodson, R. E., Lenski, R. E., et al. 1989. The planned introduction of genetically engineered organisms: ecological considerations and recommendations. *Ecology* 70:298–315

58. Uchima, K., Harvey, J. P., Omi, E. M., Tanada, Y. 1988. Binding sites on the midgut cell membrane for the synergistic factor of a granulosis virus of the armyworm (*Pseudaletia unipuncta*). *Insect Biochem.* 18:645–50

59. Vail, P. V., Romine, C. L., Vaughn, J. L. 1979. Infectivity of nuclear polyhedrosis virus extracted with digestive juices. *J. Invertebr. Pathol.* 33:328–30

60. Vlak, J. M., Klinkenberg, F. A., Zaal, K. J. M., Usmany, M., Klinge-Roode, E. C., et al. 1988. Functional studies on the p10 gene of *Autographa californica* nuclear polyhedrosis virus using a recombinant expressing a p10-beta-galactosidase fusion gene. *J. Gen. Virol.* 69:765–76

61. Volkman, L. E. 1986. The 64K envelope protein of budded *Autographa californica* nuclear polyhedrosis virus. *Curr. Top. Microbiol. Immunol.* 131:103–18

62. Volkman, L. E., Koddie, B. A. 1990. Nuclear polyhedrosis virus pathogenesis. *Semin. Virol.* 1:249–56

63. Williams, G. V., Rohel, D. Z., Kuzio, J., Faulkner, P. 1989. A cytopathological investigation of *Autographa californica* nuclear polyhedrosis virus p10 gene function using insertion/deletion mutants. *J. Gen. Virol.* 70:187–202

64. Wood, H. A., Hughes, P. R., van Beek, N., Hamblin, M. 1990. An ecologically acceptable strategy for the use of genetically engineered baculovirus pesticides. In *Insect Neurochemistry and Neurophysiology, 1989.* ed. A. B. Borkovec, E. P. Masler, pp. 285–88. Clifton, NJ: Humana. 480 pp.

Annu. Rev. Microbiol. 1991. 45:89–106

TECHNIQUES FOR SELECTION OF INDUSTRIALLY IMPORTANT MICROORGANISMS

D. Bernie Steele

Department of Botany and Microbiology and Alabama Agricultural Experiment Station, Auburn University, Alabama 36849

Mark D. Stowers

Monsanto Company, St. Louis, Missouri 63198

KEY WORDS: bioactive metabolites, microbial products, biocatalysts, industrial screening

CONTENTS

INTRODUCTION 89
HISTORICAL PERSPECTIVE 90
MICROORGANISMS AND PRODUCTS 91
SELECTION STRATEGY AND TECHNIQUES 91
    Sources of Microorganisms 94
    Enrichment and Isolation 95
    Primary Screening 98
FUTURE POTENTIAL AND NEEDS 102
SUMMARY 102

INTRODUCTION

Since prehistoric times, humans have exploited microorganisms for their own use. By means of trial and error, people developed strains of microbes that were used in the production of beverages, food, textiles, and antibiotics

89

without knowing that microbes were the responsible agent. With the discovery that microorganisms existed, and the subsequent development of culture methods, came the birth of modern biological technology or *biotechnology*. Expanded development of microbial screening and cultural techniques has brought us to a point where microbially produced products are a major part of our life. While production of food, drink, and textiles remains a large part of the biotechnology industry, the discovery of penicillin in the first half of this century revolutionized microbial screening for other useful products such as antibiotics, enzymes, and specialty chemicals.

During the past 40–50 years, screening of industrially important microorganisms has evolved steadily, although somewhat haphazardly, while still relying on the original underlying techniques of enrichment, pure culture, mutagenesis, and sheer labor. Classical methods are still used extensively with modifications resulting from the use of chemical analogs, coupled colorimetric reactions, membrane technology, immunological techniques, and advances in instrumentation.

This review focuses on the development of primary screening techniques during the past two decades through modifications of classical techniques, coupled with advances in the basic understanding of microbial physiology and growth.

HISTORICAL PERSPECTIVE

While many people have contributed to the advancement of microbiology, some have been particularly instrumental in the development of ideas and techniques that are crucial to modern industrial microbiology.

The beginnings of industrial microbiology are rooted in Louis Pasteur's discovery that microorganisms were responsible for the fermentative process, which rendered the theory of spontaneous generation invalid. Pasteur went on to make contributions to the science of food and beverage production, including the discovery that heat could be used to kill contaminating microorganisms.

A contemporary of Pasteur, Robert Koch, developed the first solid-culture media, thus providing the means to easily obtain pure cultures of bacteria. Koch also provided proof that microorganisms are the causative agents of many diseases, firmly establishing the germ theory of disease. Koch's postulates regarding the isolation of disease-causing microorganisms and subsequent reinfection of a host have tremendously impacted not only medical microbiology but other areas as well. This concept of associating specific activities with pure cultures of microorganisms is the basis of modern microbiological research. One of Koch's coworkers, Paul Ehrlich, used this concept in conducting one of the first systematic searches for selection of specific antimicrobial substances.

No discussion of microbial diversity and the selection of specific organisms would be complete without mention of the contributions of the Delft School and such men as Martinis W. Beijerinck and Albert J. Kluyver. Our understanding of the microbe's role in nature began with Beijerinck's introduction of the concept of enrichment culture. Kluyver's concept of comparative biochemistry opened the door to understanding the relatedness of all living things and initiated the first true studies into microbial physiology. These concepts have profoundly affected the science of microbiology, particularly in relation to isolation of bacteria that occupy specific niches in the environment.

Martinis Beijerinck's principle of enrichment culture allowed the isolation of microbes with specific metabolic properties. Others, including Sergei Winogradsky, spread and utilized his ideas, resulting in an explosion of information concerning the microbe's role in geochemical conversions in the environment. The concept and utilization of enrichment culture continues to grow and is now a cornerstone of many modern microbiological screening programs. While some programs may include simple screening of existing culture collections, enrichment culture has proven to be a reliable technique for isolation of microbes exhibiting specific traits. Usually, the more stringent the requirement, the more successful the enrichment will be at eliminating nontarget organisms.

MICROORGANISMS AND PRODUCTS

Microorganisms are used to produce hundreds of commercial products valued in the tens of billions of dollars worldwide. Table 1 shows a sampling of the types of products manufactured by microbiological means. Products produced by naturally occurring microbes have the advantage of being considered "natural" themselves and therefore are more easily approved for marketing than genetically manipulated organisms. For this reason, most industries favor the selection of naturally occurring microorganisms for production purposes, making a viable and efficient screening program a necessity. The diversity of microorganisms holds the promise of many new technologies, including remedies for diminishing environmental pollution, that could substantially impact our standard of living. The belief that the microbe holds the solution to many problems is exemplified by Perlman's "laws of applied microbiology" (47), in which he states that microorganisms are capable of any task, and that, "If you take care of your microbial friends, they will take care of your future."

SELECTION STRATEGY AND TECHNIQUES

The selection of industrial microorganisms is systematically approached using a strategy similar to the one shown in Figure 1. The key elements of a

Table 1 Microorganisms and commercial applications

Product	Microorganism
Enzymes	
Amylase	*Bacillus* spp.
	Aspergillus spp.
Cellulase	*Aspergillus* spp.
	Trichoderma spp.
Lactase	*Aspergillus* spp.
	Kluyveromyces spp.
Lipase	*Mucor* spp.
	Aspergillus spp.
Protease	*Bacillus* spp.
	Aspergillus spp.
Rennet	*Mucor* spp.
Chemicals	
Citric acid	*Aspergillus* spp.
Ethanol	*Saccharomyces* spp.
Dextran	*Leuconostoc* spp.
Vitamins and Amino Acids	
B$_{12}$	*Pseudomonas* spp.
L-Lysine	*Corynebacterium* spp.
Pharmaceuticals	
Antibiotics	*Penicillium* spp.
	Streptomyces spp.
	Bacillus spp.
Insulin	*E. coli* (Recombinant)
Steroid transformation	*Arthrobacter* spp.

selection strategy are (*a*) defining the activity of interest; (*b*) surveying known microbes with that activity; (*c*) developing enrichment and screening protocols; (*d*) identifying sources for new microorganisms; and (*e*) developing screening methodology. Primary screening is predominantly a qualitative endeavor in which a large population of organisms is screened either directly or indirectly for a specific type of activity. Secondary screening is both

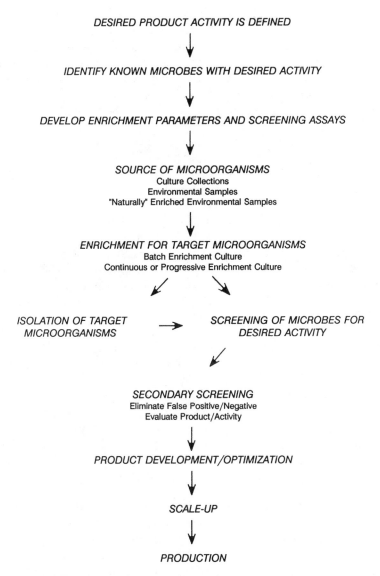

Figure 1   General schematic of an industrial screening program.

qualitative and quantitative in that its objective is to determine the precise activity of the organisms, to verify production or degradation of compounds, and to evaluate the production potential of the organisms identified in the primary screen.

While new techniques for screening specific microbes have been developed during the past two decades, the majority are modifications of classical techniques, such as enrichment culture and enzymatic or chemical assays coupled to colorimetric reactions. Highly sophisticated analytical techniques using gas chromatography and mass spectrometry have also evolved, and while many remain slow, cumbersome, and expensive, they are the only techniques available in some instances for detection of specific metabolic activities. A discussion follows of some of the more prominent techniques being used, their evolution, and their potential for the future. Space allocations preclude citation of all the techniques in use, but we have attempted to give an overview of representative concepts and techniques.

Sources of Microorganisms

The most promising trend in enrichment culture is perhaps the move toward investigation of novel environments. Instead of enriching from anonymous soil or water samples, investigators are increasingly seeking out natural enrichments in the environment, such as thermal springs, glacier ice, or industrial-waste-treatment facilities, where populations of microorganisms are in abundance because of physical or chemical pressure. These environments provide an ongoing enrichment and natural selection of organisms adapted to specific conditions. Cheetam (9) speculates that probably < 1% of the Earth's microorganisms have been identified and characterized. Thus a vast array of potentially useful organisms probably still await discovery. In our experience, when a new environment is sampled using multiple variations of culture media and enrichments, novel organisms are isolated more often than not.

Our laboratory and others have explored Yellowstone National Park for several years in search of unique microorganisms. Although this area has been studied by other groups in great detail (4–6, 11), we have isolated many previously unknown microorganisms including thermophiles, acidophiles, and alkalophiles, many producing useful enzymes and other products. One such organism is a gram-positive, spiral-shaped bacterium that may represent a new genus (58).

Many novel environments like Yellowstone await examination. Our laboratory was one of the first to search the microbial diversity of bat-inhabited caves for microorganisms with industrial potential. Sites such as Bracken Cave in south-central Texas offer a unique example of such an ecosystem. Twenty million female Mexican free-tailed bats (*Tadarida brasiliensis*) use this location as a nursery cave each summer. These bats eat an estimated 250,000 lbs of insects each night and have been depositing guano for tens of thousands of years, resulting in a 10-meter deep, nutrient-rich cave floor. This site is rich in alkalophilic, ammonia oxidizing, and chitinase-producing microorganisms (57).

One of our recent projects involved the search for microorganisms exhibiting "ice biological" activity such as ice nucleation or antifreeze activity. In this endeavor, we traveled to the High Andes of Peru and Bolivia where the environment is subjected to daily freeze-thaw extremes from night to day, providing a natural enrichment for organisms with freeze-thaw protective mechanisms. This project has resulted in the isolation of a diverse group of microorganisms now undergoing secondary evaluation for novel ice-nucleating abilities and antifreeze activity.

Natural enrichment sources are not always as exotic as the spectacular thermal areas of Yellowstone or the High Andes. Many researchers, including us, have successfully isolated target organisms from industrial waste treatment facilities (9, 18). Wastes from potato and fruit processing facilities have yielded organisms producing amylases with industrial potential (17, 37). Lauff et al (33) used inoculum from a facility treating photographic waste to enrich for and to isolate a pure culture capable of degrading ethylenediamine-tetraacetic acid (EDTA), a component of photographic waste. Many such facilities have been in operation for decades and provide an ongoing enrichment for organisms capable of producing many useful enzymes and possessing degradative capabilities.

Enrichment and Isolation

Enrichment culture as a concept has not varied much since the days of Beijerinck and Winogradsky. Variations on its use have evolved, however, in the screening for industrially important microorganisms. In essence, enrichment is the process of providing a suitable environment for the growth and reproduction of a specific microbe while being inhibitory or lethal for non-target organisms.Growth-media formulation for the selection of desired traits is most prominently employed. These include the use of particular compounds as sole carbon sources when screening for utilization or degradation of such compounds, inhibitors for blocking specific biochemical pathways, pH adjustments, etc. One of the most straightforward approaches to the isolation of new organisms is the use of a specific carbon and/or energy source for the selection of organisms specific for their utilization of these compounds. This method has yielded organisms capable of utilizing or degrading such compounds as chlorinated hydrocarbons (42, 54, 59), benzene (56), aniline (2), and other recalcitrant compounds. As mentioned earlier, our own laboratory used the same technique for the isolation of a novel *Agrobacterium* sp. capable of degrading ferric EDTA at concentrations as high as 100 mM (33). EDTA is used as a metal chelator in many industrial products and, owing to its recalcitrance, represents a substantial influx of chemical oxygen demand as part of industrial waste effluent. Initial studies show that this organism also has potential in treating nuclear-waste material by degrading EDTA bound to radionuclides, thus inhibiting the migration of these compounds from storage sites.

Although the recalcitrance of EDTA made isolation difficult (only one positive culture was obtained from over 100 enrichments), Shirai (56) illustrates the diversity of microorganisms and the potential of enrichment culture by using benzene as the sole carbon source in an enrichment for benzene-assimilating organisms. From 150 samples taken from rice fields, vegetable gardens, and forests, Shirai observed microbial growth in 102 enrichments and isolated 95 strains of benzene-assimilating organisms.

One of the inherent problems with enrichment and selection of utilization of a compound as sole carbon source is the concomitant enrichment of carbon dioxide–fixing bacteria. Strotmann & Roschenthaler (59) circumvented this problem by developing an assay that exploited the liberation of protons during degradation of chlorinated hydrocarbons by bacteria. By incorporating the pH indicator bromthymol blue in the growth medium, they monitored release of protons and drop in pH to identify degradation.

While some organisms are readily isolated in batch culture, others may require more intensive selection. Often, a population of microbes may contain a relatively small number of organisms with the targeted genotype, the organisms may exhibit a low expression of a particular enzyme, or organisms may be inhibited by the compound one is seeking to degrade. In such cases, gradual adjustments to a chemostatic or continuous culture may be used to enrich slowly for a specific organism. In this way, one may select for organisms in small numbers and/or may exploit mutations in the general population. This progressive enrichment is tedious, possibly requiring months of continuous culture, but may be the most effective technique in certain cases. Investigators have successfully used chemostatic culture to select a specific microbe from a mixed population to isolate microbes capable of growth on certain herbicides (29) and halogenated alkanes (28, 30, 58).

Manipulation of pH has proven useful in the isolation of organisms capable of growing at extremes of pH. Alkaline media (pH < 10) is routinely employed (31, 52, 58) for the isolation of alkalophilic bacteria. Organisms capable of producing alkaline active enzymes have tremendous industrial potential in such areas as laundry detergent formulation, pulp and paper production, and food processing (23, 31). Our laboratory used an alkaline enrichment (pH 10.5) to isolate a *Bacillus* sp. from a thermal spring that produces a unique protease exhibiting a high specific activity against elastin and other insoluble proteins (M. Fiske, D. B. Steele, & S. Middlebrook, in preparation). Other researchers successfully isolated a wide array of alkalophilic organisms from a variety of environments that produce many alkaline active and stable enzymes including proteases (12, 62), amylases (22), lipases (63), cellulases (16, 24), and xylanases (21, 26). The isolation of acidophiles has achieved equal success, uncovering organisms capable of growing and producing enzymes active at low pH levels (9, 27).

An incomplete understanding of metabolic and physiological requirements can greatly impede progress when designing screening procedures. In the presence of a Na^+/H^+ antiporter system, the growth of certain obligate alkalophiles depends on the presence of sodium in the growth medium (31, 38). Similar requirements may be necessary for the growth of other types of organisms when using particular carbon or energy sources. A lack of calcium required for enzymatic stability of certain proteases could obscure positive cultures during enrichment and subsequent screening. Different genera of organisms may predominate in enrichments from the same environment using the same medium at the same pH, simply by changing the buffering system (D. B. Steele, unpublished data). Such seemingly minor differences underscore the importance of understanding the physiological mechanisms operating in these organisms. Indeed, advancement of knowledge in the area of microbial physiology is paramount to the future improvement and success of enrichment-culture technology (9, 41, 46, 48). Research on produc on of L-phenylalanine by Hummel et al (25) exemplifies how knowledge of microbial physiology can aid a screening program. Previous work had established that acetamidocinnamic acid (ACA) was an intermediate in the chemical synthesis of phenylalanine; therefore it was expected that an ACA acylase could be used in an alternate production scheme. Using ACA as a sole carbon source enrichment proved fruitless. A double screen that yielded organisms capable of growing on ACA and L-phenylalanine (indicating catabolism of the aromatic compound via phenylpyruvate) was successful in isolating several *Brevibacterium* sp. that produced the desired ACA-acylase.

Physical parameters such as temperature may be manipulated for the isolation of psychrophiles and thermophiles. Enzymes that are stable and active at temperature extremes are very much in demand for various industrial processes. Thermostable enzymes are useful in various conversion processes used for fruit and vegetable processing, starch processing, and the stereospecific reduction of alcohols (9). An immobilized thermo-active penicillin-acylase is presently produced on a large scale (66). A particular problem with the isolation and cultivation of thermophiles is that agar is a poor solidifying agent at high temperatures ($< 70°C$). Development of new solidifying agents such as the *Pseudomonas*-produced gellan gum, Gelrite ®, are facilitating the isolation of such organisms (36).

Perhaps the greatest stride being made in enrichment technique is progress in the understanding of various metabolic traits of microorganisms. As more is learned of specific pathways of degradation, for example, microbes may be selected using specific enzyme assays, or enrichments may be modified to take advantage of specific knowledge of biochemical pathways or energetic mechanisms. Understanding of life under low nutrient and other harsh conditions is advancing (19, 32, 70). The development of so-called starvation media and other advances have enabled the isolation of new and novel bacteria from extreme environments such as oligotrophic Antarctic lakes (40). Innovative enrichment culture techniques involve the combination of all possible elements in creating the most stringent environment for selection of the desired microorganism.

Primary Screening

Assays for screening a particular activity play a major role in selection of specific microorganisms. Aspects to consider when selecting a screening assay are simplicity, cost, speed, and specificity. This is often the step that will determine if a screening program fails or succeeds. Most assay methods can be categorized as being either direct (specific identification of the target product) or indirect, such as enzyme detection via a coupled colorimetric or fluorimetric reaction resulting from enzymatic activity.Advances in the understanding of microbial physiology coupled with development of new chromogenic and fluorogenic enzyme substrates have improved indirect assays, while advances in analytical instrumentation are responsible for most of the improvements for direct detection of specific compounds.

INDIRECT ASSAYS   The basic principles of simplicity and specificity in the development of an appropriate assay are exemplified by primary screening assays such as those employed for hydrolytic enzymes such as proteases and amylases. An agar-plate medium with the subject compound included is used for growth of the organism. Either a hydrolytic clear zone (i.e. the hydrolysis of casein) or a zone enhanced by some colorimetric reaction (i.e. the reaction of starch and iodine to produce a purple color) is used to determine qualitative activity. Similar procedures have been used with great success in isolation and screening of organisms producing industrial enzymes. In these assays, manipulating such parameters as temperature, pH, and even the effect of inhibitors is simple. Consequently, screening may be accomplished quickly and inexpensively on many organisms.

In some cases, the specificity or sensitivity of this type of assay is inadequate. Lipase detection presents a particular problem because of the apparent lack of specificity in known lipases, and problems with the distinction between true lipases and esterases. Often tributyrin was used as an assay substrate, even though it is not specific for lipase activity, simply because it was easier to disperse in water than more desirable substrates such as triolein. Tweens are also used as substrates. Some lipase assays depend on the reaction of freed fatty acids with calcium compounds to form a precipitate; however, if the organism can use the free fatty acids as well, false negative results occur. While investigators continue to develop new combinations of substrates and dyes (51), the lipase plate screen remains a problem.

Many other enzymes are screened with similar techniques that examine hydrolytic activity on agar plates, often coupled with stains, including cellulases (10) and uricases (34). Once again, caution must be used in devising such an assay. An example is the widespread use of congo-red to stain cellulose and various hemicelluloses in determining degradation of these compounds. Sharma et al (55) found that some minor media components, mainly certain metal chlorides, could interfere with the assay resulting in either false negatives or false positives. Similarly, Zitomer & Eveleigh (68) found that iodine staining of cellulose produced artifactual activity because of contaminating starch in commercial agar. These examples exemplify the need for careful scrutiny of the mechanisms involved in particular assays and for the appropriate caution and control one must use in adaptation of an assay to a new situation.

In a more positive light, some novel plate screening methods have been recently developed. Wikstrom (67) developed a protease screen in which a fine layer of the substrate is sprayed onto the inner surface of a plastic petri dish, which is then covered with the appropriate growth medium. Following growth, the agar is removed, and protease activity is indicated by increased wettability of the plastic dish. The main advantages of this method are the reduced amount of substrate needed, resulting in reduced cost, and the ability to use any growth medium required. The incompatibility of some substrates with certain growth media makes this technique particularly useful.

Colorimetric or fluorescent reactions often provide a simple and effective means of identifying microbial products both in plate assays and in analysis of fermentation broths. Assays are being widely used to identify microbes producing enzymes such as glucose-2-oxidase that are capable of generating hydrogen peroxide via their catalyzed reactions with a subsequent color production from a coupled peroxidase reaction (US Patent no. 4,568,638: Nabisco Brands, Inc., Parsippany, N.J.).

O'Connor & Somers (44) developed a method for detection of angiotensin-converting enzyme inhibitors in a plate assay in which the putative inhibitor was applied to an enzyme-containing layer and then overlaid with an agar layer containing the substrate p-nitrobenzyl-oxycarbonylglycyl-(S-4-nitrobenzo-2-oxa-1,3-diazole)-L-cysteinyl-glycine. Subsequent flooding of the plate with NaOH generated a color reaction that could be read and photographed. This system was also adaptable to a quantitative spectrophotometric assay for analyzing fermentation broths.

Baker (3) exploited a difference in fluorescence intensity of 6-aminopenicillinic acid (6-APA) with fluorescamine at pH 4 to develop an improved screening technique for penicillin amidase. Prior to this work, such reactions had been utilized at pH 7; however, the strong reactions of amino acids and polypeptides at neutral pH often interfered with the assay. The new procedure proved more sensitive and simpler to perform than previous assays.

When looking for zones of activity on an agar plate, the thickness of the substrate may reduce sensitivity. A technique commonly used to overcome this is the double-layer technique, in which a thin layer of substrate is overlaid onto an agar-solidified growth medium. Although this development is not particularly recent, variations of this method have been used extensively to screen for enzyme activities as well as for the production of specialty chemicals such as lysine (35).

Modifications of overlay techniques include the use of micropore membranes in separating layers and in separating the bacterial culture from the substrate. In 1983, a patent was granted to Eberhard Breuker (US Patent no. 4,421,849) for a device in which bacteria imbedded in an agar layer were separated from an agar-based reaction layer. Metabolites from the bacteria could diffuse through the membrane barrier and subsequent reactions could be noted in the bottom layer. Many researchers have developed variations of this technique. A European patent application (No. 83110397.3) was filed by Miles Laboratories, Inc. (Elkhart, Ind.) in 1983 for a similar technique in which bacteria were cultured on top of a membrane overlaying an agar nutrient medium with indicator compounds. This particular modification consisted of lysing the bacteria in situ on top of the membrane, allowing the detection of nonextracellular enzyme production.

BIO-ASSAYS   Bio-assays are continuously being developed for the selection of organisms exhibiting antibiotic and antitumor activity. Omura (46) and White (65) have contributed excellent current reviews of this material. Of interest in these areas is the new focus on specific targets of activity such as cell wall synthesis (45) and metabolic or biosynthetic activities (46). Rake et al (49) describe an example of such an approach in which the investigators employed a bacterial cell wall receptor mimetic to detect glycopeptide antibiotics at a high efficiency. Novel compounds were detected at a rate of 1 in every 320 organisms screened using this technique, opposed to the usual screening estimate of 10,000–100,000 organisms for one novel compound.

Another area of novel application of bio-assays is in the detection of insecticidal agents. Such screening has successfully yielded microbial insecticides such as nikkomycins (15), milbemycins (61), tetranactin (1), and avermectins (8). Fabre et al (13) described a twofold approach in which antibacterial activity is coupled with insecticidal activity to reduce the number of organisms screened and eliminate detection of toxic and known antimicrobial agents possessing insecticidal activity.

Researchers at Boeringer Mannheim received a patent for a screening method developed for the detection of cephalosporin C acylase activity. In the assay, an indicator organism is used that is sensitive to 7-aminocephalosporanic acid but resistant to cephalosporin C. The indicator organism is incubated on an agar nutrient medium containing a tolerable amount of cephalosporin C and the test broth from the organism being screened. Production of cephalosporin C acylase results in the inhibition of the indicator organism. Meevootisom et al (39) devised a similar method in which penicillin acylase–producing bacteria were screened using a *Serratia marcescens* sensitive to 6-aminopenicillanic acid but resistant to benzylpenicillin.

Screening for production of biosurfactants has long been a tedious process involving surface tension measurements of culture broths. Following the observation that the *Bacillus subtilis* lipopeptide surfactin would rupture erythrocytes, Mulligan et al (43) developed an assay employing blood agar plates for the screening of surfactant production by microorganisms. Although some false positives occurred because of hemolysin producers, the assay greatly reduced the number of organisms to be verified through surface tension reduction.

DIRECT ASSAYS   While this review is concerned with primary screening techniques, some comment is warranted relative to secondary screening. Secondary screening is an important process in the selection of industrial microorganisms. During this process, one must eliminate false negative and false positive organisms quickly before the more costly endeavors of production optimization and scale-up are performed. In this regard, advances in analytical instrumentation have the greatest impact. The progressive advances in development of analytical and micro-instrumentation during the past 20 years profoundly affect one's ability to screen for specific compounds. Micro-instrumentation is useful both in secondary screening and in primary screening when simpler techniques are not available. Instrumentation such as high-performance liquid chromatography (HPLC), gas chromatography (GC), mass spectrometry (MS), nuclear magnetic resonance spectrometry (NMR), and others allow more rapid, selective, and highly sensitive detection of metabolic products. An example is Fiedler's use of HPLC coupled with a photodiode array detector to screen new microbial metabolites (14). This technique compares the UV-visible spectra of all peaks from the HPLC elution profile in a single chromatographic run, yielding a vast amount of useful information, including Fiedler's discovery of six potentially new nikkomycins.

Inductively coupled plasma detectors coupled with ion chromatography and ultrasonic nebulizers now routinely allow various metal detection in the range of 5-10 parts per billion. This equipment and many other types are being coupled with more advanced and "smarter" autosampling devices that provide rapid analysis 24 hours a day. Autosampling technology has evolved in some instances into more advanced robotic systems that not only sample but perform enzyme assays, staining procedures, and other routine tasks tirelessly. This type of technology is very efficient and productive in instances where vast numbers of samples must be screened.

FUTURE POTENTIAL AND NEEDS

The exciting progress being made in the areas of protein and genetic engineering will hopefully substantially impact screening programs in the future. For now, genetic engineering and protein engineering have a greater impact on industrial microbiology at the level of product optimization. Microbial proteins such as the alkaline protease subtilisin have been engineered for increased stability (7, 69) and changes in substrate specificity (64). Takagi et al (60) successfully used site-directed mutagenesis to develop enhanced activity in a subtilisin protease. Many corporations are working extensively to develop enhanced genetic promoters for increased gene expression and subsequent increased product formation.

An example of the type of techniques that may prove useful for screening is the utilization of colony hybridization by Sayler et al (53) to detect DNA sequences specific for hydrocarbon-catabolic pathways. A similar screen based on hybridization of DNA extracted from environmental samples (dot blot) can be used to look for microbes with particular DNA sequences (20). New developments with polymerase chain reactions should increase the sensitivity of such techniques in the future.

The potential of microbial screening for industrial products lies in the tremendous microbial diversity of the earth. The organisms are there; we must develop the techniques to select for and isolate them. The largest impediment to this is the lack of research programs dedicated to the development of screening techniques. This is a multidisciplinary problem that requires the expertise of chemists and engineers as well as microbiologists.

SUMMARY

The screening of microorganisms for the production of useful products continues to be an important aspect of biotechnology. Although advances in instrumentation, genetics, and microbial physiology are having an impact, screening programs are still primarily based on so-called classical techniques of enrichment and mutagenesis. One area that needs strengthening is the advancement of knowledge in microbial physiology. Recent surveys indicate that industry leaders see trained microbial physiologists as being the limiting factor in development of biotechnology in the coming decade.

The largest impediment to development of new screening techniques is the ironic lack of programs specifically directed at developing new techniques. Too much emphasis is placed on using available techniques and relying on sheer labor and screening of vast numbers of organisms to produce novel products. In this respect, the Japanese are the exception and have proven that the establishment of new programs is worth the cost and effort. They are undoubtedly the world leaders in development of screening techniques and consequently the discovery of novel products.

The isolation of microbes from novel and extreme environments holds tremendous promise in two areas. First, as Omura (46) and others (9, 48, 65) state, novel organisms will yield novel products. Second, such organisms serve as models for the understanding of structure and function that will facilitate the genetic manipulation of organisms and advance our ability to engineer novel enzymes. Hopefully such advances will enable genetic and protein engineering to have a greater impact on screening programs and techniques in the future.

The earth holds a vast amount of varied and unique environments, from natural extremes such as high-altitude deserts and thermal springs, to man-made environments such as industrial-waste-treatment facilities, from which, with the appropriate methods and techniques, we may isolate and evaluate new potential products.

ACKNOWLEDGMENTS

The authors wish to express their gratitude to Eastman Kodak Company, BioProducts Division; Genencor International; and Symbion, Inc. for support of our microbial screening programs and for their support of the preparation of this manuscript.

Literature Cited

1. Ando, K., Oishi, H., Hirano, S., Okutomi, T., Suzuki, K., et al. 1971. Tetranactin, a new miticidal antibiotic. I. Isolation, characterization and properties of tetranactin. *J. Antibiot.* 24:347–52
2. Aoki, K., Ohtsuka, K., Shinke, R., Nishira, H. 1984. Rapid biodegradation of aniline by *Frateuria* species ANA-18 and its aniline metabolism. *Agric. Biol. Chem.* 48:865–72
3. Baker, W. L. 1984. A sensitive procedure for screening microorganisms for the presence of penicillin amidase. *Aust. J. Biol. Sci.* 37:257–65
4. Brock, T. D. 1967. Life at high temperatures. *Science* 158:1012–19
5. Brock, T. D., Brock, M. L. 1971. *Life in the Geyser Basins.* Yellowstone, WY: Yellowstone Library and Museum Assoc. and the Natl. Park Serv., US Dept. of the Interior. 29 pp.
6. Brock, T. D., Darland, G. K. 1970. The limits of microbial existence: Temperature and pH. *Science* 169:1316–18
7. Bryan, P. N., Rollence, M. L., Pantoliano, M. W., Wood, J., Finzel, B. C., et al. 1986. Proteases of enhanced stability: characterization of a thermostable variant of subtilisin. *Proteins: Struct. Funct. Gene* 1:326–34
8. Burg, R. W., Miller, B. M., Baker, E. E., Birnaum, J., Currie, S. A., et al. 1979. Avermectins, new family of potent anthelmintic agents: Producing organism and fermentation. *Antimicrob. Agents Chemother.* 15:361–67

9. Cheetham, P. S. J. 1987. Screening for novel biocatalysts. *Enzyme Microb. Technol.* 9:194–213

10. Creswell, M. A., Attwell, R. W., Dempsey, M. J. 1988. Detection of cellulolytic actinomycetes using cellulose-azure. *J. Microbiol. Methods* 8: 299–302

11. Doemel, W. N., Brock, T. D. 1970. The upper temperature limit of *Cynidium caldarium*. *Arch. Mikrobiol.* 72:326–32

12. Durham, D. R., Stewart, D. B., Stellwag, E. J. 1987. Novel alkaline- and heat-stable proteases from alkalophilic *Bacillus* sp. strain GX6638. *J. Bacteriol.* 169:2762–68

13. Fabre, B., Armau, E., Etienne, G., Legendre, F., Tiraby, G. 1988. A simple screening method for insecticidal substances from actinomycetes. *J. Antibiot.* 41:212–19

14. Fiedler, H.-P. 1984. Screening for new microbial products by high-performance liquid chromatography using a photodiode array detector. *J. Chromatogr.* 316:487–94

15. Fiedler, H.-P., Kurth, R., Langharig, J., Delzer, J., Zahner, H. 1982. Nikkomycins: microbial inhibitors of chitin synthase. *J. Chem. Technol. Biotechnol.* 32:271–80

16. Fukumori, F., Kudo, T., Horikoshi, K. 1985. Purification and properties of a cellulase from alkalophilic *Bacillus* sp. No. 1139. *J. Gen. Microbiol.* 131: 3339–45

17. Gee, J. M., Lund, B. M., Metcalf, G., Peel, J. L. 1980. Properties of a new group of alkalophilic bacteria. *J. Gen. Microbiol.* 117:9–17

18. Grueninger, H., Sonnleitner, B., Fiechter, A. 1984. Bacterial diversity in thermophilic aerobic sewage sludge: III. A source of organisms producing heat-stable industrially useful enzymes, e.g., α-amylases. *Appl. Microbiol. Biotechnol.* 19:414–21

19. Harder, W., Dijkhuizen, L. 1983. Physiological responses to nutrient limitation. *Annu. Rev. Microbiol.* 37:1–23

20. Holben, W. E., Jansson, J. K., Chelm, B.K., Tiedje, J. M. 1988. DNA probe method for the detection of specific microorganisms in the soil bacterial community. *Appl. Environ. Microbiol.* 54:703–11

21. Honda, H., Kudo, T., Ikura, Y., Horikoshi, K. 1985. Two types of xylanases of alkalophilic *Bacillus* sp. No. C-125. *Can. J. Microbiol.* 31:538–42

22. Horikoshi, K. 1971. Production of alkaline enzymes by alkalophilic microorganisms: Part II. Alkaline amylase produced by *Bacillus* No. A-40-2. *Agric. Biol. Chem.* 35:1783–91

23. Horikoshi, K., Akiba, T. 1982. *Alkalophilic Microorganisms.* New York: Springer-Verlag. 213 pp.

24. Horikoshi, K., Nakao, Y., Kurono, Y., Sashihara, N. 1984. Cellulases of an alkalophilic *Bacillus* strain isolated from soil. *Can. J. Microbiol.* 30:774–79

25. Hummel, W., Schutte, H., Schmidt, E., Kula, M. R. 1987. Isolation and characterization of acetamidocinnamate acylase, a new enzyme suitable for production of L-phenylalanine. *Appl. Microbiol. Biotechnol.* 27:283–91

26. Ikura, Y., Horikoshi, K. 1987. Stimulatory effect of certain amino acids on xylanase production by alkalophilic *Bacillus* sp. *Agric. Biol. Chem.* 51: 3143–45

27. Jensen, B. F., Norman, B. E. 1984. *Bacillus acidopullulyticus* pullulanase: application and regulatory aspects for use in the food industry. *Process Biochem.* 19:129–34

28. Keuning, S., Janssen, D. B., Witholt, B. 1985. Purification and characterization of hydrolytic haloalkane dehalogenase from *Xanthobacter autotrophicus* GJ10. *J. Bacteriol.* 163:635–39

29. Kilbane, J. J., Chatterjee, D. K., Karns, J. S., Kellogg, S. T, Chakrabarty, A. M. 1982. Biodegradation of 2,4,5-trichlorophenoxyacetic acid by a pure culture of *Pseudomonas cepacia*. *Appl. Environ. Microbiol.* 44:72–78

30. Kohler-Staub, D., Leisinger, T. 1985. Dichloromethane dehalogenase of *Hyphomicrobium* sp. strain DM2. *J. Bacteriol.* 162:676–81

31. Krulwich, T. A., Guffanti, A. A. 1990. Alkalophilic bacteria. *Annu. Rev. Microbiol.* 43:435–63

32. Kuznetsov, S. I., Dubinina, G. A., Lapteva, N. A. 1979. Biology of oligotrophic bacteria. *Annu. Rev. Microbiol.* 33: 377–87

33. Lauff, J. J., Steele, D. B., Coogan, L., Breitfeller, J. M. 1990. Degradation of the ferric chelate of EDTA by a pure culture of *Agrobacterium* sp. *Appl. Environ. Microbiol.* 56:3346–53

34. Lehejckova, R., Demnerova, K., Kralova, B. 1986. Screening of microorganisms with uricase activity. *Biotechnol. Lett.* 8:341–42

35. LiMuti, C. M., Paulson, T. C. 1989. Colorimetric detection of microbially excreted lysine directly on agar plates. *J. Microbiol. Methods* 9:129–37

36. Lin, Ch.-Ch., Casida, L. E. 1984. Gelrite as a gelling agent in media for the

growth of thermophilic microorganisms. *Appl. Environ. Microbiol.* 47:427–29

37. Madi, E., Antranikian, G., Ohmiya, K., Gottschalk, G. 1987. Thermostable amylolytic enzymes from a new *Clostridium isolate. Appl. Environ. Microbiol.* 53:1661–67

38. McLaggan, D., Selwyn, M. J., Dawson, A. P. 1984. Dependence on Na$^+$ of control of cytoplasmic pH in a facultative alkalophile. *FEBS* 165:254–58

39. Meevootisom, V., Somsuk, P., Prachaktam, R., Flegel, T. W. 1983. Simple screening method for isolation of penicillin acylase-producing bacteria. *Appl. Environ. Microbiol.* 46:1227–29

40. Mikell, A. T. Jr., Parker, B. C., Gregory, E. M. 1986. Factors affecting high oxygen survival of heterotrophic microorganisms from an antarctic lake. *Appl. Environ. Microbiol.* 52:1236–41

41. Monaghan, R. L., Tkacz, J. S. 1990. Bioactive microbial products: focus upon mechanism of action. *Annu. Rev. Microbiol.* 44:271–301

42. Motosugi, K., Esaki, N., Soda, K. 1982. Bacterial assimilation of *d*- and l-2-chloropropionates and occurrence of a new dehalogenase. *Acta Microbiol.* 131:179–83

43. Mulligan, C. N., Cooper, D. G., Neufeld, R. J. 1984. Selection of microbes producing biosurfactants in media without hydrocarbons. *J. Ferment. Technol.* 62:311–14

44. O'Connor, S., Somers, P. 1985. Methods for the detection and quantitation of angiotensin converting enzyme inhibitors in fermentation broths. *J. Antibiot.* 38:993–96

45. Omura, S. 1981. Screening of specific inhibitors of cell wall peptidoglycan synthesis. An approach to early identification of new antibiotics. In *The Future of Antibiotherapy and Antibiotic Research*, ed. L. Ninet, P. E. Bost, D. H. Bouanchand, J. Florent, p. 389–405. New York: Academic

46. Omura, S. 1986. Philosophy of new drug discovery. *Microbiol. Rev.* 50: 259–79

47. Perlman, D. 1980. Some problems on the new horizons of applied microbiology. *Dev. Ind. Microbiol.* 21:xv–xxiii

48. Porter, N. 1985. Discovering new secondary metabolites: a view from the pharmaceutical industry. *Pestic. Sci.* 16: 422

49. Rake, J. B., Gerber, R., Mehta, R. J., Newman, D. J., Oh, Y. K., et al. 1986. Glycopeptide antibiotics: a mechanism-based screen employing a bacterial cell wall receptor mimetic. *J. Antibiot.* 39: 58–67

50. Roszak, D. B., Colwell, R. R. 1987. Survival strategies of bacteria in the natural environment. *Microbiol. Rev.* 51: 365–79

51. Samad, M. Y. A., Razak, C. N. A., Salleh, A. B., Yunus, W. M. Z. W., Ampon, K., et al. 1989. A plate assay for primary screening of lipase activity. *J. Microbiol. Methods* 9:51–56

52. Sato, M., Beppu, T., Arima, K. 1983. Studies on antibiotics produced at high alkaline pH. *Agric. Biol. Chem.* 47: 2019–27

53. Sayler, G. S., Shields, M. S., Tedford, E. T., Breen, A., Hooper, S. W., et al. 1985. Application of DNA-DNA colony hybridization to the detection of catabolic genotypes in environmental samples. *Appl. Environ. Microbiol.* 49:1295–303

54. Scholtz, R., Schmuckle, A., Cook, A., Leisinger, T. 1987. Degradation of eighteen 1-monohaloalkanes by *Arthrobacter* sp. strain HA1. *J. Gen. Microbiol.* 133:267–74

55. Sharma, P., Pajni, S., Dhillon, N., Vadehra, D. V., Dube, D.K. 1986. Limitations of the congo-red techniques for the detection of cellulolytic activities. *Biotechnol. Lett.* 8:579–80

56. Shirai, K. 1986. Screening of microorganisms for catechol production from benzene. *Agric. Biol. Chem.* 50:2875–80

57. Steele, D. B. 1989. Bats, bacteria and biotechnology. *BATS* 7:3–5

58. Steele, D. B., Steele, B. P., Kelley, V. C. 1989. Isolation and characterization of a novel spiral-shaped alkalophilic bacterium. *Abstr. Annu. Meet. SE Branch Am. Soc. Microbiol., Orange Beach*, p. 50

59. Strotmann, U., Roschenthaler, R. 1987. A method for screening bacteria: aerobically degrading chlorinated short-chain hydrocarbons. *Curr. Microbiol.* 15:159–63

60. Takagi, H., Morinaga, Y., Ikemura, H., Inouye, M. 1988. Mutant subtilisin E with enhanced protease activity obtained by site-directed mutagenesis. *J. Biol. Chem.* 263:19592–96

61. Takaguchi, Y., Mishima, H., Okuda, M., Terao, M., Aoki, A., et al. 1980. Milbemycins, a new family of macrolide antibiotics: Fermentation, isolation and physico-chemical properties. *J. Antibiot.* 33:1120–27

62. Tsai, Y. C., Lin, S. F., Li, Y. F., Yamasaki, M., Tamura, G. 1986. Characterization of an alkaline elastase

from alkalophilic *Bacillus* Ya-B. *Biochim. Biophys. Acta* 883:439–47

63. Watanabe, N., Ota, Y., Minoda, Y., Yamada, K. 1977. Isolation and identification of alkaline lipase producing microorganisms, cultural conditions and some properties of crude enzymes. *Agric. Biol. Chem.* 41:1353–58

64. Wells, J. A., Powers, D. B., Bott, R. R., Graycar, T. P., Estell, D. A. 1987. Designing substrate specificity by protein engineering of electrostatic interactions. *Proc. Natl. Acad. Sci. USA* 84:1219–23

65. White, R. J. 1982. Microbiological models as screening tools for anticancer agents: potentials and limitations. *Annu. Rev. Microbiol.* 36:415–33

66. Wiegel, J., Ljungdahl, L. G. 1986. The importance of thermophilic bacteria in biotechnology. *CRC Crit. Rev. Biotechnol.* 3:39–107

67. Wikstrom, M. B. 1983. Detection of microbial proteolytic activity by a cultivation plate assay in which different proteins adsorbed to a hydrophobic surface are used as substrates. *Appl. Environ. Microbiol.* 45:393–400

68. Zitomer, S. W., Eveleigh, D. E. 1987. Cellulase screening by iodine staining: an artefact. *Enzyme Microb. Technol.* 9:214–16

69. Zukowski, M., Stabinsky, Y., Narhi, J., Mauck, J., Stowers, M., et al. 1990. An engineered subtilisin with improved stability: applications in human diagnostics. In *Genetics and Biotechnology of Bacilli*, Vol 3, ed. A. Ganesan, J. Hock, M. Zukowski, pp. 157–62. San Diego: Academic

Annu. Rev. Microbiol. 1991. 45:107–35

CONTROL OF CARBON AND NITROGEN METABOLISM IN *BACILLUS SUBTILIS*

Susan H. Fisher

Department of Microbiology, Boston University School of Medicine, Boston, Massachusetts 02118

Abraham L. Sonenshein

Department of Molecular Biology and Microbiology, Tufts University Health Sciences Campus, Boston, Massachusetts 02111

KEY WORDS: catabolite repression, sporulation, gram-positive bacteria, sugar metabolism

CONTENTS

CARBON CATABOLITE REPRESSION 108
 Sugar Transport 109
 Mutants Affected in Carbon Catabolite Repression 112
 Carbohydrate Metabolism Genes 113
 Other Genes Subject to Carbon Catabolite Repression 119
NITROGEN CATABOLITE REPRESSION 119
 Ammonia Assimilation Systems 120
 Other Genes Induced by Nitrogen-Source Limitation 123
 Regulation by Amino Acids 123
CATABOLITE REPRESSION OF SPORULATION 124

Bacteria are renowned for their metabolic efficiency and adaptability. They have evolved complex, interlocking regulatory networks that respond to nearly every imaginable environmental condition. To respond quickly and appropriately, bacteria must closely monitor the availability of essential nutrients (e.g. sources of carbon, nitrogen, phosphorus, sulfur, trace metals,

107

0066-4227/91/1001-0107$02.00

cations, and anions). Bacteria react to their environment by measuring extracellular concentrations, intracellular pools, or fluxes in those pools and transmitting that information to regulatory proteins. For *Escherichia coli* and its close relatives, many such information-transfer systems have been worked out in detail, revealing that most genes whose products provide fuel or precursors for cell growth are regulated in more than one way. The instantaneous rate of transcription of a given gene in cells in a particular environment is the complex product of multiple forms of regulation.

CARBON CATABOLITE REPRESSION

When offered a mixture of carbon energy sources, bacteria preferentially utilize those they can metabolize most rapidly. For the majority of bacteria, including *Bacillus subtilis,* the preferred carbon energy source is glucose. As long as rapidly metabolizable carbon sources are available, expression of genes whose products code for transport and metabolism of other carbon energy sources is greatly reduced. This phenomenon, first observed as diauxic growth, is known as catabolite repression (67, 72).

One important aspect of carbon catabolite repression in *E. coli* is well understood at the molecular level. Genes for utilization of carbon sources other than glucose generally depend on a positive regulatory protein (catabolite activator protein; CAP) and its activating metabolite, cyclic AMP, for their maximal expression (67). Some genes less directly involved in carbon-source metabolism are also subject to CAP-cAMP control. When glucose is available, the intracellular pool of cAMP is greatly reduced because adenyl cyclase activity is low. This exact mechanism does not appear to be relevant to *B. subtilis* because efforts to find measurable amounts of cAMP in *B. subtilis* cells in balanced growth have been unsuccessful (103). [There is a report of detectable cAMP in *B. subtilis* cells suspended under anaerobic conditions (66).] In general, carbon catabolite repression is much less well understood for gram-positive bacteria, of which *Bacillus* species are the best-studied examples (for an overview, see 28). Our knowledge of nonenteric gram-negative bacteria in this respect is also rudimentary. Moreover, the CAP-cAMP system cannot be the only mechanism governing carbon catabolite control even in *E. coli* because repression cannot be fully overcome by feeding cAMP to wild-type cells and mutants defective in cAMP synthesis or CAP proteins are still subject to partial catabolite repression (22, 120). In addition, transcription of a set of genes turned on by carbon deprivation is independent of cAMP (71). Other organisms that have detectable levels of this metabolite, such as *Streptomyces venezuelae,* show no correlation between cAMP pools and catabolite repression (17). Nonetheless, catabolite repression in *Streptomyces* is mediated at the level of gene transcription by a mechanism that has yet to be identified (14, 33, 105, 119). The universality of the CAP-cAMP model for carbon catabolite repression is highly improbable.

For *Bacillus*, rapidly metabolizable carbon sources clearly limit the expression of enzymes required for utilization of other carbon sources (Table 1), raising the possibility that many carbon utilization genes fall under a common regulatory umbrella. In fact, current evidence, detailed below, suggests that catabolite-repressed genes are controlled by multiple mechanisms rather than by a single, global regulatory system. Unfortunately, none of these systems is understood in great detail at the molecular level. Because the CAP-cAMP system does not seem to operate in *B. subtilis*, one has to consider alternative models of both positive and negative regulation. For example, one could imagine that cells in an environment with an excess of the carbon source sense that their growth rate is limited by some other (e.g. nitrogen-containing or phosphate-containing) metabolite. In that case, accumulation of carbon catabolites could trigger the activity of negative regulatory proteins. In the few cases in which sufficient information is available (α-amylase or aconitase synthesis; see below), a negative regulatory protein is implicated. Negative regulation is an important contrast to the *E. coli* paradigm.

Genes for utilization of most carbon sources other than glucose are inducible by their substrates. Because glucose interferes with entry of many such substrates (inducer exclusion), it may appear to repress expression of utilization genes. One can distinguish between inducer exclusion and other mechanisms of regulation in several ways. By isolating a mutant that does not require the substrate (inducer) for expression (i.e. a constitutive mutant), one can test whether apparent catabolite repression is independent of entry of the substrate. Such an approach has been used for a few *B. subtilis* systems [genes for utilization of histidine (16), arabinose (96), sucrose (60)] and has provided evidence for effects of glucose other than inducer exclusion. Alternatively, one can mutate the site of action of the operon-specific regulator and then test whether carbon source regulation is still intact. A third approach is to titrate the operon-specific repressor by placing the operator site on a high-copy plasmid. This method creates phenotypic constitutivity, allowing a test of the effect of carbon sources that is independent of operon-specific repression. Such an analysis for the gluconate and xylose utilization operons revealed residual repression by glucose (40, 45), suggesting that inducer exclusion cannot be the sole mechanism by which rapidly metabolizable carbon sources regulate these genes (see below).

Sugar Transport

The phosphoenolpyruvate-dependent sugar phosphotransferase (PTS) system catalyzes the phosphorylation of certain sugars concomitant with their translocation across the cytoplasmic membrane (72). The PTS system has two

Table 1 Repression by carbon sources in *Bacillus subtilis*

Nutritional source	Relevant enzymes tested	Carbon sources that repress strongly[a]	Other repressing carbon sources[a]	Reference
Acetoin	Acetoin dehydrogenase	Glucose (300) Mannitol (300)	Mannose (5.5) Glycerol (4)	63–65
Arabinose	Arabinose isomerase	Glucose (4)		13, 96
Arginine (plus glucose)	Arginase	Glutamine (11)		7
	Ornithine amino transferase	Glutamine (61)		7
Citrate	Aconitase	Glucose plus glutamine (20) Glycerol plus glutamine (20)	Glucose (2)	94
	Citrate transport	Glucose (6)		123
Glucitol	Glucitol dehydrogenase		Glucose (3.5)	65, 97
	Glucitol transport	Glucose (6)		97
Gluconate	Gluconate kinase	Glucose (10) Fructose (5) Mannitol (5)	Glycerol (2) Mannose (2) Glucitol (2) Sucrose (2) Trehalose (2)	79
	Gluconate permease	Glucose (6)	Glycerol (3.5)	8
Glycerol	Glycerol kinase	Glucose (5)		61
	Glycerophosphate dehydrogenase	Glucose (27)		61
Histidine (plus citrate)	Histidase	Glucose (20–40) Glycerol (22) Malate (16)	Maltose (3.5) Arabinose (3.5)	16
Inositol	Inositol dehydrogenase	Glucose (20–300) Glycerol (300) Fructose (300) Mannose (300) Mannitol (300) Glucitol (300) Sucrose (300)	Trehalose (10)	5, 16, 65, 79
Malate	Malate transport		Glucose (3.5)	38

Table 1   (*Continued*)

Nutritional source	Relevant enzymes tested	Carbon sources that repress strongly[a]	Other repressing carbon sources[a]	Reference
Maltose	α-Glucosidase	Glucose (210)		16, S. Fisher[b]
Mannitol	Mannitol-1-P dehydrogenase	Glucose (4–9)	Fructose (2.5) Glucitol (2)	54, 97
	Mannitol transport		Glucose (2.5)	97
Starch	α-Amylase	Glucose (200)		51
Sucrose	Sucrase	Glucose (100)[c]		60
Xylose	Xylose isomerase	Glucose (8)		45

[a] Numbers in parentheses refer to repression ratios observed in media containing inducer and repressing sugar vs inducer alone.
[b] Unpublished data.
[c] Measured in a *sacT*[c] mutant.

classes of components, the general cytoplasmic proteins (Enzyme I and HPr, required for transport of all PTS-dependent sugars) and the sugar-specific proteins (Enzyme II and Enzyme III). During sugar transport, Enzyme I catalyzes transfer of phosphate from phosphoenolpyruvate (PEP) to a histidine residue of HPr. Phosphorylated HPr then donates its phosphate to Enzymes III and II. These enzymes transfer their phosphates to their specific sugars as the sugars pass through the cytoplasmic membrane.

The *E. coli* PTS system plays a central role in regulation of carbon metabolism. If glucose is available, glucose-specific Enzyme III is primarily in the dephosphorylated form and causes inducer exclusion by inhibiting the transport of other sugars (72, 95). In the absence of glucose, glucose-specific Enzyme III is phosphorylated and stimulates the activity of adenyl cyclase (72, 95). These two activities of glucose-specific Enzyme III account for major aspects of catabolite repression.

The *B. subtilis* genes encoding Enzyme I and HPr (*ptsI* and *ptsH*, respectively) form an operon (49). An adjacent gene (*ptsG*) encodes a single polypeptide with both glucose-specific Enyzme II and Enzyme III activities (49, 114). (By contrast, the corresponding enzymes from *E. coli* are coded for by independent, unlinked genes.) In the cases studied to date, genes for some other *B. subtilis* Enzyme II and Enzyme III activities are encoded in operons specific for metabolism of particular sugar substrates (34, 69). The sucrose-specific Enzyme II has no Enzyme III counterpart, however (34, 35, 114). The Enzyme II of sucrose must compete with glucose-specific Enzyme II for interaction with the Enzyme III domain of PtsG (114) for sucrose to be transported. This competition may be the basis of inducer exclusion by glucose in this case. In addition, the PTS pathway may be involved in regulating transport of non-PTS sugars because a *ptsI* mutant has enhanced sensitivity of glycerol uptake to inhibition by several PTS substrates (89).

A phenomenon called inducer expulsion may protect various species of gram-positive cells from accumulation of toxic amounts of the phosphorylated forms of slowly metabolized sugars (72, 90, 91). In the presence of PTS sugars, efflux of these phosphorylated compounds is stimulated (90). Study of this phenomenon led to the discovery that HPr can be phosphorylated at a serine residue by an ATP-dependent protein kinase (90). This kinase is found in various gram-positive bacteria but is absent in *E. coli*. HPr-ser-P is a very poor substrate for phospho-Enzyme I in vitro and is therefore expected to be inactive in PTS transport (90). HPr-his-P, the intermediate in PTS phospho-transfer, is a poor substrate for the serine protein kinase (90). These findings led to the hypothesis that serine phosphorylation of HPr is a key element in regulation of PTS function and inducer expulsion. As noted above, a different mechanism is responsible for the preferential uptake of glucose relative to sucrose, however (114). Replacement of the phosphorylatable serine residue of *B. subtilis* HPr by alanine caused a decrease in growth yield (but not growth rate) on PTS sugars (26, 92) and led to failure of glucose to exert catabolite repression of glucitol dehydrogenase and gluconate kinase (J. Deutscher & J. Reizer, personal communication). Thus, while HPr serine phosphorylation appears to be important in the regulation of carbon metabolism in *B. subtilis,* its precise role in this regulation remains to be identified.

Mutants Affected in Carbon Catabolite Repression

Several mutations at diverse genetic loci cause at least partial relief of carbon catabolite repression. These mutations are of particular interest because they could potentially identify proteins that regulate many catabolite-repressed genes. For instance, the *cdh-3* mutation partially relieves carbon catabolite repression of aconitase, α-amylase, α-glucosidase, and histidase (29). The molecular basis of this phenotype has not been determined, but the mutant is defective neither in glucose transport (29) nor in inducer exclusion (G. Chambliss, personal communication). Because intracellular pools of pyruvate and 2-ketoglutarate are reduced in this mutant, glucose metabolism may be partially blocked (29). The mutant probably fails to generate or respond to a common signal for many carbon-regulated genes.

Mutations in the glutamine synthetase (*glnA*) gene partially relieve carbon catabolite repression of aconitase, citrate synthase, histidase, and α-glucosidase (32). These mutants are also derepressed for *glnA* transcription with respect to the nitrogen source (102; see below). Because, in these mutants, the pool of glucose-6-phosphate is reduced (32), the mutations may cause a defect in glucose transport. This interesting observation would suggest that the key enzyme of ammonium assimilation plays a role in balancing carbon and nitrogen metabolism.

Mutations called *crs* allow cells to sporulate in the presence of high concentrations of glucose (115). At least some of these mutations, which map at several loci, also affect carbon catabolite repression of metabolic genes. For instance, the *crsA* mutation causes synthesis of acetoin dehydrogenase and aconitase to be relatively insensitive to glucose repression (115; D. W. Dingman & A. L. Sonenshein, unpublished data). Interestingly, *crsA* is an allele of *rpoD*, the gene for the major vegetative σ factor of *B. subtilis* RNA polymerase (87). The basis of the Crs$^-$ phenotype is unclear; in the case of *crsA* it seems to cause a decreased rate of glucose metabolism (D. W. Dingman & A. L. Sonenshein, unpublished data).

Other mutations (*gra, spo0A, hpr, degU, degS*) that affect catabolite repression of sporulation or metabolism or both are discussed below.

Carbohydrate Metabolism Genes

In the following section, we discuss selected systems of carbon source utilization in *B. subtilis* that have been the subject of detailed analyses of regulation. A recent review by Klier & Rapoport (57) provides additional information about these and other carbon utilization pathways.

SUCROSE AND SUCROSE POLYMERS   Metabolism of sucrose and polymeric sugars depends on the products of several operons subject to overlapping regulation. Sucrose is transported and metabolized by the products of the *sacPA* operon, a sucrose-specific Enzyme II of the PTS system and a sucrase (34, 35). Synthesis of these enzymes is induced by sucrose and repressed by glucose and by glycerol (Table 1). Induction requires the product of a neighboring gene, *sacT*, which seems to encode a polypeptide similar to BglG, the positive regulator of the *bgl* operon of *E. coli* (2). BglG is an antiterminator protein that allows RNA polymerase to bypass transcriptional termination sites within the *bgl* operon (2). It is inactivated when it is phosphorylated by the β-glucoside–specific Enzyme II of the PTS system. In the presence of substrate, BglG is dephosphorylated and stimulates transcription of the operon (2). By analogy, nonphosphorylated SacT may be an antiterminator that acts (not necessarily specifically) at the *sacPA* operon. In fact, DNA sequence analysis suggests the existence of a transcriptional termination site just upstream of the *sacP* gene (21). In this model, SacP would sense sucrose availability, transferring phosphate received from Enzyme I and HPr to sucrose, if it is present, or to SacT, if sucrose is absent.

This model is consistent with the observation that mutations in the gene for Enzyme I (*ptsI*) cause constitutive transcription of *sacPA* (21, 47). (SacT would always be in the active state in these mutants.) Some evidence indicates that SacY can function in place of SacT in *sacPA* regulation (see below), but this evidence is inconclusive (21, 110).

Because sucrose is both the substrate and the inducer, interference by glucose with sucrose uptake could explain glucose repression of the *sacPA* operon. Mutations in *sacT* that cause constitutivity do not abolish glucose repression, however, indicating the existence of a glucose effect independent of inducer exclusion (60). No specific mechanism of catabolite repression of *sacPA* has been described.

The *sacB* gene, encoding a secreted levansucrase, is induced by high concentrations of sucrose or fructose and is controlled by SacY, another homolog of BglG (18, 104, 109, 130). SacY appears to act at a potential termination site located just upstream of *sacB* (at a site previously defined genetically as *sacR*) (111). The activity of SacY is modulated by SacX (apparently an Enzyme II of unknown specificity) and can be partially replaced by SacT (110). SacX and SacY are products of an operon that is not linked to any other known *sac* genes. Transcription of *sacB* is not repressed by glucose or glycerol (60). It is subject to an additional level of control, however. Mutations in *degU, degS,* and *degQ* alter expression of *sacB*, as they do for other genes coding for secreted enzymes (57, 104; see below).

A third example of potential regulation at the level of transcription termination is found in the operon for metabolism of extracellular β-glucans (12). The gene for β-glucanase is preceded by a sequence that could form part of a stem-loop structure and is highly homologous to the proposed terminator structures of the *E. coli bgl* and *B. subtilis sacB* and *sacPA* operons (15, 21, 75, 99). Moreover, the putative product of the gene upstream of the β-glucanase coding region (only partly sequenced to date) is very similar to *E. coli* BglG and *B. subtilis* SacY (15, 99).

A complex operon (*levDEFG sacC*), inducible by low concentrations of fructose, encodes fructose-specific PTS enzymes and a levanase. A current model for regulation is that Enzyme III^{Fru} (LevDE) phosphorylates and thereby inactivates a positive regulator (LevR, the product of an upstream gene) when substrate is limiting (68, 69). No evidence suggests that LevR works by antitermination; in fact, it has sequence similarity to NifA, a positive regulator from gram-negative bacteria that stimulates transcription by the σ^{54} form of RNA polymerase (21a). Interestingly, the *lev* promoter has consensus sequences for σ^{54}-containing RNA polymerase, and its utilization in *E. coli* depends on σ^{54} (21a). (No evidence yet indicates a σ^{54} homolog in *B. subtilis*.) Glucose or high concentrations of fructose repress *lev*. Repression by glucose is partially relieved in a *ccpA* (formerly, *gra-26*) mutant (68).

This gene was originally identified as a locus at which mutations relieve glucose repression of α-amylase expression (see below).

GLUCONATE   After transport into the cell by gluconate permease (GntP), gluconate is converted to gluconate-6-phosphate by gluconate kinase (GntK) and metabolized through the pentose cycle (57). GntP and GntK are encoded in an operon (*gntRKPZ*), which also includes genes for the repressor (GntR) and GntZ, a protein that is homologous to mammalian gluconate-6-phosphate dehydrogenases (42; J. Reizer, personal communication).

The *gnt* operon is induced by gluconate and subject to carbon catabolite repression (Table 1). In the absence of gluconate, GntR binds to an operator sequence that overlaps the −10 region of the *gnt* promoter and prevents transcription (41, 43). Inactivation of GntR by gluconate leads to an increase in *gnt* mRNA (41, 42). Little is known about catabolite repression of *gnt*. The presence of glucose clearly causes decreased transcription of the operon (41, 42). A promoter-containing DNA fragment corresponding to positions −100 to +123 with respect to the transcription start point has at least some of the sequences at which catabolite repression is exerted because a fusion of this fragment to a reporter gene is subject to threefold repression in the presence of glucose (40). This fusion was tested as part of a high-copy plasmid, a condition in which gluconate was not required for expression. Thus, glucose repression and gluconate induction appear to be separable.

XYLOSE   Enzymes for degradation of xylose and xylose polymers are induced by growth in xylose-containing medium and repressed when rapidly metabolized carbon sources are available (Table 1). Most of the xylose metabolism genes are organized in two neighboring operons, *xynCB* and *xylAB*, that are separated by *xylR*, the gene whose product regulates both operons (50). Because mutations in *xylR* cause constitutive expression, XylR appears to be a negative regulator (58). The operator sites are nearly identical 25-bp sequences that include a 10-bp inverted repeat; they are centered at approximately position +15 with respect to the start points for *xylAB* and *xynCB* transcription (58). Very little is known about catabolite repression of these genes. Inducer exclusion cannot be totally responsible, however, because the *xyl* promoter, when present on a high-copy plasmid, is constitutive with respect to xylose but repressed threefold by glucose (45). The target of glucose repression of *xylAB* is near the 5' end of the *xylA* gene (W. Hillen, personal communication).

STARCH   Synthesis of α-amylase, a secreted enzyme that degrades starch to metabolizable sugars, is regulated by several factors, at least some of which act independently. Cells grown in a nutrient broth medium synthesize and secrete the enzyme only as the cells enter stationary phase, a phenomenon referred to as temporal regulation (78). Stationary-phase expression of *amyE*, the structural gene for α-amylase, does not occur if the medium contains high concentrations of glucose or glycerol (Table 1). Cells grown in minimal-glucose medium do not express α-amylase unless the carbon source becomes limiting for growth (51, 77; G. Chambliss, personal communication).

A dyad symmetry sequence, called *amyO*, located between positions −3 and +11 with respect to the transcription start site, is necessary for the glucose effect (78, 121). This sequence is very similar to the operator sites for the *lac* and *gal* repressors of *Escherichia coli* (78, 121). Mutations in this sequence cause transcription of *amyE* to be insensitive to glucose and other sugars (76), leading to the suggestion that catabolite repression of *amyE* involves a negative regulatory protein (78, 121). These mutations have no effect on temporal regulation, however (78, 121).

Researchers have sought repressor proteins that interact with *amyO* in two ways. First, a series of transposon-insertion mutations that overcome the glucose effect was identified. Such mutations map to at least three different loci on the *B. subtilis* chromosome (76). The wild-type allele of one of these mutations (originally called *gra-26;* renamed *ccpA*) has been cloned and sequenced. The putative gene product (CcpA) is a 36,900 M_r polypeptide very similar to the *lac* and *gal* repressor proteins (52). This finding strongly suggests that CcpA represses *amyE* by binding to *amyO*, although it may actually act indirectly by controlling expression of the true regulator of *amyE*. [As mentioned above, CcpA is also involved in regulation of levanase gene expression; it is implicated in control of acetoin accumulation as well (see below).] CcpA, however, is not responsible for repression of *amyE* by glycerol or for temporal regulation because a *ccpA* mutant grown in nutrient broth medium is repressed by glycerol and expresses *amyE* only in stationary phase whether glucose is present or not (52).

A second approach was to purify proteins that bind to *amyO*. Crude extracts of *B. subtilis* were shown to slow the electrophoretic mobility of *amyO*-containing DNA fragments (124). During gel filtration, this activity separated into at least four distinct fractions. A polypeptide purified to homogeneity from one of these fractions binds tightly to *amyO* (124). This activity may not be the product of the *ccpA* gene, however. Preliminary results suggest that it is present in extracts of a *ccpA* null mutant (G. Chambliss, personal communication). This raises the interesting possibility that the purified protein and CcpA are repressors that bind to overlapping sites but respond to different effectors. The purified protein, for instance, might respond to glycerol rather than to glucose.

Starch, the substrate of α-amylase, is not an inducer of *amyE* in *B. subtilis* and no other external inducer has been found (80). Thus, catabolite repression in this case cannot result from inducer exclusion. One can speculate that in *B.*

subtilis carbon catabolites act as corepressors; induction would require either that the concentrations of these catabolites drop below critical levels or that a metabolite produced intracellularly compete with them for binding to the repressor.

Temporal regulation of *amyE* expression is clearly independent of glucose/ glycerol repression but its mechanism is otherwise mysterious. Interestingly, stationary-phase induction of *amyE* depends at least in part on some of the same regulatory proteins (e.g. DegU, DegS, DegQ) that control other station-ary-phase phenomena, such as competence for transformation, motility, and sporulation (57, 76). Given the multitude of genes whose products are necessary for glucose repression of *amyE* and the multitude of proteins that bind to the *amy* regulatory region, a full understanding of this system will probably reveal a complex interplay of regulatory proteins that respond to partially overlapping signals and bind to partially overlapping sites.

ACETOIN   When grown in media that contain rapidly metabolizable sugars as primary carbon energy sources, *B. subtilis* metabolizes these sugars to pyruvate through the glycolytic pathway. Rather than pass the pyruvate molecules through the Krebs Cycle, the cells convert pyruvate to various two- and three-carbon compounds, many of which are excreted. These compounds are transported back into the cell and further metabolized only when the sugars are used up (108). An example of this phenomenon is the synthesis and degradation of acetoin:

$$\text{2 pyruvate} \xrightarrow{\text{ALS}} \text{acetolactate} \xrightarrow{\text{ALD}} \text{acetoin} \xrightarrow{\text{ADH}} \text{acetyl CoA} + \text{acetaldehyde.}$$

Acetolactate synthase (ALS; coded for by *alsS*) carries out the same reaction as does acetohydroxy acid synthase, the product of *ilvB* (126). (Synthesis of acetolactate is the first step in the pathway to valine.) ALD (acetolactate decarboxylase; encoded by *alsD*) is an extracellular protein; synthesis of acetoin occurs outside the cell (23). Synthesis of acetoin dehydrogenase (ADH), an intracellular enzyme, is repressed by glucose, fructose, mannose, and glycerol (Table 1).

Acetoin is probably the inducer of ADH synthesis (63). Catabolite control could be mediated by regulation of acetoin transport, but the extent of inducer exclusion by glucose or other carbon sources is insufficient to explain catabo-lite repression in this case (64). Mutations in *alsA*, now known to be allelic to *ccpA*, cause a marked change in acetoin accumulation (52, 127). That is, these mutants do not accumulate acetoin in glucose medium but continue to do so in glycerol medium (52). One interpretation of these results is that CcpA is the glucose-responsive repressor of ADH synthesis. As a result, a *ccpA* mutant would be constitutive for acetoin degradation and fail to accumulate acetoin in the medium. An alternative hypothesis is that CcpA is a positive regulator of *alsS* (127). In this case, the *ccpA* mutant would simply fail to make acetoin. To distinguish between these hypotheses, one must test whether synthesis of ADH is derepressed in a *ccpA* mutant. CcpA seems to play a critical role in glucose repression of at least three operons. Direct action on any of these genes has yet to be shown, however. Moreover, CcpA cannot be the sole regulatory protein involved in catabolite repression because it is dispensable for catabolite repression of histidase (S. Fisher, unpublished data).

CITRATE   The Krebs Cycle serves two functions—energy production and provision of biosynthetic precursors (e.g. 2-ketoglutarate, succinyl CoA, oxaloacetate). Not surprisingly, when a cell is provided with a highly favorable energy source and good sources of precursors, it expresses Krebs Cycle genes at low levels. Such is the case for the aconitase *(citB)* gene of *B. subtilis*.

Cells grown in a medium containing glutamine and glucose or glycerol (with or without citrate added) have a very low level of *citB* mRNA (Table 1). Glutamine has no repressive effect in the absence of a rapidly metabolizable carbon source; glucose has a small repressive effect in the absence of glutamine (24, 94). Interestingly, glucose also represses the arginine catabolic enzymes, but only if glutamine is present (7). Whether this reflects any commonality with the mechanism of catabolite repression of *citB* is unknown.

Detailed analysis of the *citB* promoter region has revealed that a sequence centered at 66 bp upstream of the transcriptional start point is essential for the glucose-glutamine effect (36, 37). It is also essential for repression by glycerol. This sequence, which has dyad symmetry, appears to be the binding site for a negative regulatory protein. In fact, an extract of glucose-grown cells was shown to contain a factor that retards the electrophoretic mobility of the *citB* promoter region DNA; mutations in the dyad symmetry sequence greatly reduced this interaction (36). Because this site is rather far from the RNA polymerase binding site, a working model has been advanced that takes advantage of the existence of a halfsite for the putative negative regulator at position -27. The repressor protein is thought to bind tightly to the dyad sequence (position -66) and less well to the site at position -27. This latter binding, which is essential for inhibition of transcription, is stabilized by protein-protein interaction. Such a conformation would only be possible if the DNA were to bend, permitting the protein molecules bound at positions -66 and -27 to interact. The sequence around position -42 fits the consensus for IHF, a DNA-bending protein from *E. coli*. Interaction of IHF with the *citB* promoter region has been shown (S.-F. Jin & A. L. Sonenshein, unpublished data), but no evidence indicates that an IHF-like protein exists in *B. subtilis*.

Given this model, catabolites derived from glucose or from glutamine or both (30) could provoke repression by binding to repressor and stabilizing the protein-protein interaction. Alternatively, an inducing metabolite might disrupt the protein-protein interaction. A candidate for such an inducer is citrate, the substrate for aconitase. In this latter case, glucose could control *citB* by preventing intracellular accumulation of citrate by inhibiting both citrate uptake (123) and intracellular production of citrate. Clearly intracellular accumulation of citrate is necessary for *citB* expression because a mutant defective in citrate synthase activity cannot transcribe *citB* unless supplied with citrate (24, 36).

A striking parallel to the *citB* regulatory system is found in the operon for lactose metabolism in *Staphylococcus aureus*. As for *citB*, negative regulation of the *lac* promoter region depends on a region of dyad symmetry located at approximately position −70 (82). A halfsite resides at position −26, near a potential binding site for IHF. The *lac* repressor has been identified; it appears to be inactivated by galactose-6-phosphate produced intracellularly when cells are fed either lactose or galactose (82). Interestingly, the sites involved in repression and catabolite repression appear to be overlapping, but separable genetically (82).

Other Genes Subject to Carbon Catabolite Repression

HISTIDINE   Histidine utilization requires the products of four genes organized in a single operon (*hutHUIG*) (16, 56, 81). An open reading frame (*hutP*) immediately downstream of the *hut* promoter may encode a positive regulator of *hut* transcription (81). Because the 5' untranslated region of *hut* mRNA contains a sequence that could form a stem-loop structure, regulation of *hut* transcription may be subject to termination-antitermination control (81).

Transcription of *hut* is induced by histidine (16) and repressed by rapidly metabolized carbon sources (Table 1). The effect of glucose on *hut* expression does not result from inducer exclusion because a constitutive mutant is repressed 20-fold by glucose (16). As detailed below, *hut* is also repressed by a mixture of amino acids. Since a mutant that is insensitive to glucose repression is still repressed by amino acids, the mechanism of amino acid repression is independent of carbon catabolite repression.

NITROGEN CATABOLITE REPRESSION

Just as bacteria have favored carbon energy sources, they also have favored sources of nitrogen. Reduced nitrogen (as found in ammonium ions, amino groups, or amide groups) is the form utilized in biosynthesis. The preferred source is usually ammonium ion or glutamine. For *E. coli* and its relatives, ammonium ion is the favored nitrogen source (glutamine is poorly transported) (88). When ammonium ion is available in excess, genes for glutamine synthetase and for transport and degradation of ammonium-generating compounds (e.g. certain amino acids) are expressed at low levels (88). When ammonium becomes limiting, the NtrC protein is activated and serves as a positive regulator for transcription of the glutamine synthetase gene and for some other nitrogen metabolism genes (88). NtrC is activated by phosphorylation by NtrB, a protein kinase-phosphatase, in response to a decrease in the intracellular concentration of glutamine relative to that of 2-ketoglutarate (88). For some nitrogen metabolism operons, the action of NtrC is indirect. For example, during nitrogen limitation, NtrC stimulates synthesis of Nac, which acts in turn as a positive regulator for the *Klebsiella aerogenes hut* operon (9).

The NtrB and NtrC proteins are members of the two-component family of bacterial regulatory proteins (88). Several members of that family regulate the expression of stationary phase and sporulation genes of *B. subtilis* (106), but none of these proteins has been associated directly with global control of nitrogen metabolism.

In *B. subtilis*, glutamine is the preferred nitrogen source and the precursor of all nitrogen-containing compounds. *B. subtilis* has no assimilatory glutamate dehydrogenase activity (55). As a result, ammonium ion can only be assimilated through the activity of glutamine synthetase; glutamate synthase alone directs glutamate biosynthesis. Because some enzymes (e.g. glutamine synthetase, asparaginase, urease) are more active when cells are grown in a poor nitrogen source (Table 2), many nitrogen metabolism genes may have a common mechanism of regulation. The genes for these enzymes and other genes depend on the *glnA* gene for regulation (see below), so they are likely to respond to a common signal. Not all nitrogen metabolism genes have these properties, however; nitrogen limitation does not significantly derepress synthesis of enzymes for degradation of histidine and proline (5; S. Fisher, unpublished data).

Ammonia Assimilation Systems

GLUTAMINE SYNTHETASE   Transcription of *glnA*, the structural gene for glutamine synthetase (GS), is highest when cells are grown with a poor nitrogen source or when growth is limited by depletion of the nitrogen source (4, 5, 31, 32, 83). Transcriptional regulation seems to be the most important factor controlling GS enzymatic activity. Although the enzyme is subject to inhibition by a variety of metabolites in complex combinations, it is not susceptible to the rapid modification (adenylylation) characteristic of glutamine synthetases from gram-negative bacteria (32, 88).

The *glnA* gene is the second gene of a dicistronic operon (100, 112). The promoter-proximal gene codes for a small protein, GlnR (100). Mutations in

Table 2 Repression by nitrogen sources in *Bacillus subtilis*

Enzyme or gene tested[a]	Strongly repressing nitrogen sources[b]	Other repressing nitrogen sources[b]	Reference
Asparaginase	16 AA mix[c] plus ammonium (>14) Ammonium (>14) Arginine (>14) Urea (9)	Aspartate (2) Asparagine (2)	4
Glutamate synthase	Glutamate (10)	Glutamine (2.5)	10, 83
Glutamine synthetase	16 AA mix[c] plus glutamine (10) Glutamine (10) Ammonium plus arginine plus glutamine (14) Ammonium (4)		4, 5, 83
Histidase[d]	16 AA mix[c] (>60) Ammonium plus arginine plus glutamine (12)	Ammonium (4) Glutamine (7)	5
nrg-21	Glutamine (25) Ammonium (25) Asparagine (20)		4
nrg-29	Glutamine (>4000) Asparagine (>4000) Ammonium (>4000) Urea (22)		4
Proline oxidase[e]	16 AA mix[c] (>10)		5
Urease	16 AA mix[c] plus glutamine (>25) Ammonium (>25) Asparagine (>25) Arginine (20)	Urea (2)	4

[a] Enzyme activity or gene expression tested in cells grown in minimal-glucose medium containing glutamate and other nitrogen sources as indicated. For measurements of proline oxidase and glutamate synthase, ammonium was substituted for glutamate.
[b] Numbers in parentheses refer to repression ratios observed in media containing indicated nitrogen source vs the least-repressing nitrogen source.
[c] A mixture of 16 amino acids (alanine, arginine, aspartic acid, cysteine, glutamic acid, glycine, isoleucine, leucine, lysine, methionine, phenylalanine, proline, serine, threonine, tryptophan, valine) (5).
[d] Tested under inducing conditions (i.e. with histidine added).
[e] Tested under inducing conditions (i.e. with proline added).

glnR cause transcription from the *glnRA* promoter to be constitutive with respect to the nitrogen source (100). Purified GlnR specifically inhibits transcription of the *glnRA* operon in vitro and binds with high affinity (apparent $K_d = 10^{-11}$ M) to a sequence located between positions -60 and -20 of the *glnRA* promoter region (S. Brown & A. L. Sonenshein, unpublished data). This region contains a large, inverted repeat sequence (centered at position -50) and a series of short, directly repeated sequences. Deletions and point mutations that affect the dyad symmetry sequence cause constitutive expresson of the operon (H. Schreier, personal communication). Thus, GlnR appears to be a repressor of the *glnRA* operon. GlnR is not known to regulate any other gene.

The simplest model for *glnRA* regulation, that GlnR senses the intracellular concentration of glutamine and represses transcription appropriately, does not fit the available data. First, mutations in the *glnA* gene also cause constitutivity of transcription (even when glutamine is provided in high concentration and enters the cells efficiently) (20, 32, 102). Second, nitrogen source–dependent regulation of the *B. subtilis glnRA* operon (as reconstructed with cloned genes in *E. coli*) requires the wild-type versions of both *glnR* and *glnA* genes (44, 100, 101). Thus, GlnR, although able to bind to the *gln* promoter and repress transcription, probably cannot by itself respond appropriately to the available nitrogen source. The facts suggest that GS monitors the availability of a critical nitrogen metabolite and signals GlnR by interaction or modification. No evidence for such interaction or modification has yet been obtained. Evidence does indicate that GS also plays a role in regulation of other genes. Mutations in *glnA* that cause constitutive transcription of the *gln* operon (with respect to the nitrogen source) also cause constitutive expression of genes normally activated by nitrogen limitation (see below) and, as described above, partial relief of glucose repression of other genes. GS may interact with multiple regulatory proteins, informing them of the relative abundances of key carbon and nitrogen-containing compounds.

The *glnRA* operon may be regulated by other factors as well. A mutation in *outB* prevents cell growth and the activation of *glnRA* transcription in a medium containing slowly metabolized nitrogen sources (1). The derived amino acid sequence of the putative *outB* product is similar to that of an *E. coli* gene that complements Ntr-like mutants of *Rhodobacter capsulatus* (1). Identification of the precise physiological defect in the *outB* mutant should help determine whether its gene product participates in *glnRA* regulation directly or indirectly.

GLUTAMATE SYNTHASE   The genes coding for the two subunits of glutamate synthase (*gltA* and *gltB*) appear to be organized as an operon. Under derepressing conditions (i.e. absence of glutamate; Table 2), transcription of *gltAB* is stimulated by GltC, a member of the LysR family of regulatory proteins (10, 11). The *gltC* gene is located upstream of *gltAB* and transcribed in the opposite orientation (11). Its transcription is repressed by GltC, but is not responsive to the nitrogen source (11). GltC is not known to control any genes other than *gltAB* and *gltC*.

Because the start points for transcription of *gltC* and *gltAB* are only 52 bp apart (11), GltC may act as a negative regulator for *gltC* and a positive regulator for *gltAB* by virtue of binding to a single site. Two types of potential regulatory sites have been found. A 9-bp sequence is repeated seven times in the *gltC*-*gltAB* regulatory region; homologs of this sequence have also been found in the regulatory regions of genes controlled by other LysR family members (11). No experimental evidence links these sequences with regulation, however. A dyad symmetry sequence is centered at position +13 with respect to *gltC* transcription. A double mutation in this site derepressed *gltC* transcription (P. Janssen & A. L. Sonenshein, unpublished results).

Other Genes Induced by Nitrogen-Source Limitation

UREASE, ASPARAGINASE, AND THE *nrg* GENES   The levels of urease and asparaginase are derepressed 25-fold and 20-fold, respectively, when cells are grown in media containing poor sources of nitrogen (4) (Table 2). Asparaginase expression is also regulated by nitrogen availability in *Bacillus licheniformis* (48). Additional genes that respond to nitrogen availability were isolated by seeking Tn*917*-*lac* insertions that express β-galactosidase only when nitrogen is limiting (4). Two such loci were found. The insertions *nrg-21*::Tn*917*-*lac* and *nrg-29*::Tn*917*-*lac* were derepressed 26-fold and 4000-fold, respectively, by growth in media containing poor nitrogen sources (Table 2).

Expression of urease, asparaginase, and the *nrg* genes appears to be subject to a global system of regulation involving the product of the *glnA* gene. Although these genes and enzymes are unaffected by *glnR* mutations, they are constitutive in *glnA* mutants (4). Thus, GlnR may be a regulator specific to the *glnRA* operon, but GS may transmit information about nitrogen availability to multiple regulatory proteins. This observation suggests that a common metabolic signal gives rise to multiple regulatory responses that are probably mediated by different regulatory proteins.

Regulation by Amino Acids

An additional, recently described, phenomenon may reflect regulation by nitrogen availability. Expression of several genes and operons, including those for histidine degradation (5), proline degradation (5), aconitase (36), and nutrient transport (*dciA,* see below), is repressed when the medium contains a mixture of amino acids. Effective mixtures contain those amino acids that are sources of glutamate (glutamate, glutamine, arginine, proline) or those derived from aspartate (aspartate, asparagine, lysine, methionine, leucine, isoleucine, valine) (5). The combined mixtures cause the most severe repression.

Although the molecular basis of this repression is unknown, in two cases (expression of histidase and aconitase), repression by amino acids is independent of carbon catabolite repression. For the aconitase gene, promoter-region mutants deleted for a dyad symmetry sequence critical for carbon catabolite repression are still subject to amino acid repression (36). These amino acid mixtures strongly repress mutants of the *hut* operon that are insensitive to carbon catabolite repression, indicating again that carbon repression and amino acid repression are genetically separable mechanisms (5). Amino acid repression of *hut* is not related to the stringency phenomenon because a *relA* mutant responds normally to amino acid mixtures (S. Fisher, unpublished data).

Regulation by amino acids is also independent of the products of the *glnR* and *glnA* genes. Expression of *hut* and proline oxidase is not subject to *glnA*-dependent repression under conditions of nitrogen excess but is repressed by the combined mixtures of amino acids (5). Moreover, amino acid mixtures decrease expression of urease and *nrg*-21, which is sensitive to *glnA*-dependent repression, even in cells in which *glnR* or *glnA* is mutated (S. Fisher, unpublished data). In addition, expression of asparaginase and *nrg*-29 is subject to *glnA*-dependent regulation but is insensitive to repression by amino acids (S. Fisher, unpublished data). The mechanism of amino acid regulation, therefore, is clearly different from that of the *glnA*-dependent repression seen under conditions of nitrogen excess.

In summary, amino acid mixtures affect expression of many genes by a mechanism that is distinct from those that control these same genes in response to carbon or nitrogen availability.

CATABOLITE REPRESSION OF SPORULATION

The landmark papers of Schaeffer et al (98) and Dawes & Mandelstam (19) established that cells of *B. subtilis* become committed to sporulate when growth is slowed by limitation of the carbon or nitrogen source. This apparent overlap with regulation of carbon and nitrogen utilization pathways is intriguing, but whether sporulation is regulated by the same mechanisms that control metabolism is not yet clear. Each of the conditions that induce sporulation, such as exhaustion of individual carbon or nitrogen sources, exhaustion of a nutrient broth medium, or inhibition of guanine nucleotide synthesis, also leads to induction of some metabolic genes. But few metabolic genes respond to all of the conditions that induce sporulation. Instead, early sporulating cells express different, overlapping sets of genes depending on the specific environmental conditions used to initiate the spore-formation process. Therefore, sporulation seems to be a response provoked by multiple signals and is likely to be subject to multiple regulatory factors (107).

Conditions that induce sporulation in *B. subtilis* are similar, if not identical, to those that provoke all bacteria to enter stationary phase. These conditions elicit a variety of responses that range from turning off certain biosynthetic pathways to induction of extracellular macromolecule–degrading enzymes, chemotaxis, motility, and competence to import DNA. These typical stationary-phase phenomena seem designed to permit the cell to utilize alternative nutritional sources. In *B. subtilis,* such adaptations may delay or prevent an irreversible step in sporulation.

Some insight into the relationship between regulation of sporulation and regulation of other phenomena has come from the use of an antibiotic, decoyinine, to induce sporulation. Decoyinine inhibits GMP synthetase, thereby causing a rapid decrease in the intracellular pool of guanine nucleotides (39, 117). Such a decrease has been associated with the onset of sporulation (62), although the cause-effect relationship has not been proved. When cells are in balanced exponential growth in a glucose-glutamine-phosphate medium, addition of decoyinine causes them to break off growth and initiate sporulation (39). This treatment also causes the cells to induce certain catabolite-repressed genes, such as *citB* (24, 117). Thus, decoyinine seems to override glucose-glutamine repression of *citB,* as if it were interfering with the mechanism of carbon catabolite repression of this gene. This is not the case for sugar-metabolism genes, however. Inositol dehydrogenase, acetoin dehydrogenase, and sorbitol dehydrogenease activities continue to be repressed in glucose medium despite the addition of decoyinine (65). In other words, decoyinine may interfere with carbon catabolite repression of certain genes, but does not block any global mechanism of catabolite repression. It also does not override repression of *citB* caused by amino acids (36). On the other hand, decoyinine does overcome amino acid represson of *hut,* but cannot circumvent glucose repression of *hut* or *amyE* (77; M. Atkinson & S. Fisher, unpublished data). Clearly, decoyinine affects different genes in different ways, reinforcing the notion that catabolite repression of genes expressed in stationary phase involves many factors.

One may view the complexity of early sporulation events and their overlap with metabolic regulation by focusing on the postulated role of guanine nucleotides as indicators of sporulation-inducing conditions. Thus, exhaustion of the carbon source would relieve catabolite repression of sugar metabolism genes by depleting carbon catabolities, but would induce sporulation by reducing the rate of formation of precursors for guanine nucleotide synthesis. Analogous scenarios would occur upon exhaustion of nitrogen or phosphorus sources. Decoyinine would short-circuit this process by decreasing guanine nucleotides without necessarily reducing the pools of catabolites. As a result, decoyinine would only induce those genes that respond directly or indirectly to guanine nucleotide levels and only under conditions in which those genes are not repressed by catabolites.

Many regulatory proteins for early sporulation (stationary phase) events have been identified. The SpoOA protein is a transcriptional regulator (86). It can be phosphorylated by a protein kinase encoded by the *spoIIJ (kinA)* gene in a series of reactions in which SpoOF-phosphate is probably an intermediate (84; J. Hoch, personal communication). [SpoOA, SpoOF, and KinA are members of the two-component family of regulatory proteins (3, 84, 106, 116).] Phosphorylated SpoOA exerts at least some of its effects by repressing transcription of *abrB,* whose product is a repressor of many early sporulation genes (86, 113). Repression of *abrB* is not the only role of SpoOA, however, because a *spoOA abrB* double mutant cannot sporulate, and inhibition of AbrB synthesis may not be sufficiently rapid to explain the turn-on of early genes. SpoOA is synthesized during exponential growth in nutrient broth medium, but its expression increases as cells enter stationary phase; the combination of glucose and glutamine inhibits this increase (125; E. Dubnau & I. Smith, personal communication). Glucose and glutamine also inhibit similar increases in *spoOF* and *spoIIJ* transcription (6; E. Dubnau & I. Smith, personal communication).

The ComA and ComP proteins are also members of the two-component family (122). They were initially identified as necessary for expression of competence genes, but they are also required for transcription of some other stationary phase genes, such as *degQ* (74) and *gsiA* (see below). Moreover, ComP, a putative protein kinase, seems to overlap in specificity with KinA. Individual mutations in *comP* or *kinA* have little effect on sporulation; a double mutation greatly inhibits spore formation (122). Other two-component family members are DegU and DegS (53, 59, 74a). DegU, when phosphorylated by DegS, acts as a positive regulator of genes that code for secreted enzymes (e.g. levansucrase, alkaline protease, α-amylase) and acts, in its dephosphorylated form, as a positive regulator of competence genes (73, 104). Some of the effects of DegU may be mediated by DegQ, a small protein whose synthesis is positively controlled by DegU, ComA, and ComP (73, 74). We cannot be certain of this mediation until direct binding of purified proteins to specific DNA sequences has been tested. Transcription of *degQ* is induced by limitation of the carbon or nitrogen or phosphorus source (73). Another regulatory protein, Sin, seems to repress alkaline protease and sporulation genes, but acts as a positive regulator of motility and competence genes (46). The Hpr protein appears to repress sporulation and protease production (85). Perhaps significant is that certain mutations in *hpr, degU, degS,* and *spoOA* allow cells to sporulate in the presence of excess glucose (107). Thus, proteins known to play regulatory roles with respect to sporulation respond to nutritional conditions, but in an as yet undefined way.

The alkaline protease (*aprE*) gene is induced as cells initiate sporulation and is subject to regulation by many of these proteins (118). AbrB represses this gene by binding to a broad region surrounding position −20 of the promoter site (113). Regulation by a series of other proteins occurs at upstream sites. For example, DegU and DegQ stimulate trancription by acting near position −150 (27); Sin represses transcription by binding near position −240 (46); Hpr appears to bind upstream of position −200 and represses transcription (27). Each of these regulators presumably responds to a different set of environmental signals, but none of these signals has been identified.

Several genes expressed during vegetative growth in minimal media containing slowly metabolized carbon sources are repressed in nutrient broth media; as cells in nutrient broth reach stationary phase, however, these genes are induced. Examples include genes for aconitase, histidine utilization, and proline oxidase (24; M. Atkinson & S. Fisher, unpublished data). Because these same genes are repressed in minimal medium by a mixture of amino acids, their regulation in nutrient broth probably reflects amino acid repression. For the *citB* gene, promoter-region mutants that are totally constitutive with respect to glucose repression are still fully repressed in nutrient broth or by mixtures of amino acids (36, 37). Stationary-phase induction of *citB* is independent of Spo0A, KinA, DegU, and DegS (A. Fouet & A. L. Sonenshein, unpublished data).

In cells in nutrient broth medium, *hut* expression is repressed during exponential growth and completely derepressed when cells enter stationary phase (M. Atkinson & S. Fisher, unpublished data). This derepression is independent of the Spo0A, Spo0F, DegU, DegS, ComA, ComP, and Sin proteins (M. Atkinson, P. Rice, & S. Fisher, unpublished data), but is prevented by the presence of glucose. During exponential growth in minimal medium containing slowly metabolized carbon sources, expression of histidase (and arabinose isomerase) is partially derepressed and elevated further in mutants blocked early in sporulation (*spo0* mutants) (13). The enhancing effect of a *spo0A* mutation on *hut* is reversed by a second mutation in *abrB* (M. Atkinson & S. Fisher, unpublished data). By these criteria, AbrB apparently acts as a positive regulator of *hut* expression under slow-growth conditions.

The *spoVG* gene is one of the earliest expressed genes whose product is necessary for formation of normal spores. Its expression depends on Spo0A-KinA, but not on ComA-ComP or DegU-DegS (128, 129; E. Dubnau & I. Smith, personal communication). AbrB represses the gene, but, even in the absence of this protein, induction requires that the cells enter stationary phase (129). This induction is sensitive to nutritional conditions. Cells in a nutrient broth medium that contains high concentrations of glucose and glutamine enter stationary phase but do not express *spoVG* (6; P. Zuber, personal communication). Whether this observation results from a direct effect on *spoVG* or from reduction in transcription of *spo0A, spo0F,* and *spoIIJ* is unknown (E. Dubnau & I. Smith, personal communication). Neither glucose nor glutamine acting alone has as great an effect. In minimal glucose-glutamine medium, *spoVG* is repressed, but can be induced rapidly by addition of decoyinine (129). Mutations called *ggr* overcome repression of *spoVG* by glucose and glutamine (D. Frisby, C. D'Souza, M. Nakano, & P. Zuber, personal communication). These same *ggr* mutations overcome glucose-glutamine repression of *srfA* as well (75a).

A high glutamine concentration in the medium also inhibits development of competence (25, 93), a phenomenon that may be induced by nitrogen limitation. The glutamine effect depends on the simultaneous presence of excess glucose and is expressed at the level of transcription of *com* genes. Since ComA and ComP are thought to monitor environmental conditions in order to induce competence genes appropriately, glutamine concentration may be the signal the proteins react to (25). Mutations in the *mec* genes overcome repression by glutamine and make competence independent of ComA-ComP (93). Whether the *mec* gene products normally monitor nutrient availability or represent a mechanism for bypassing the ComA-ComP pathway is unknown.

A different perspective on the interrelationships of nutritional responses characteristic of stationary phase and early sporulation came from isolation of genes turned on very early after nutrient limitation or treatment with decoyinine. The dicistronic *gsiA* operon is induced rapidly by deprivation of the carbon, nitrogen or phosphorous source, by treatment with decoyinine, or by exhaustion of a nutrient broth medium; the *gsiB* gene is induced by many of the same conditions, but is particularly responsive to phosphate deprivation (J. Mueller & A. L. Sonenshein, in preparation). The specific functions of these genes are unknown. Induction of these genes depends on ComA and ComP, but is independent of later components of the *com* pathway, as well as of Spo0A-KinA and DegU-DegS. A *gsiA* null mutant has a Crs^- phenotype, indicating that this mutant, unlike its wild-type parent, sporulates in media containing high concentrations of glucose. In cells in nutrient broth medium, the *gsiA* operon is induced transiently as cells enter stationary phase. Certain mutations that block sporulation at an early stage (e.g. *spo0A* or *kinA* mutations) prevent the normal shut-off of *gsiA*. A particular *spo* mutation, at a locus called *gsiC*, causes overexpression of *gsiA* and *gsiB*, but its sporulation defect can be suppressed by a null mutation in *gsiA*, suggesting that overexpression of *gsiA* interferes with sporulation. These results have led to the hypothesis that *gsiA* (and possibly *gsiB*) codes for products that direct the nutritionally stressed cell toward adaptation pathways as alternatives to sporulation. These genes are expressed transiently under sporulation conditions because they must be turned off for sporulation to be successful. In other words, this adaptation pathway and sporulation appear to be antithetical.

The *dciA* operon is induced by decoyinine, by deprivation of carbon or phosphorus sources, and by exhaustion of amino acid–containing medium

(70; F. Slack, J. Mueller, M. Strauch, J. Hoch, & A. L. Sonenshein, unpublished data). In addition, this operon is repressed during growth in minimal-glucose medium or amino acid-containing medium, but expressed constitutively in minimal-succinate medium. On the basis of its DNA sequence, this operon has been identified as a member of a family of genes that encode binding protein-dependent transport systems (C. Mathiopoulos, F. Slack, J. Mueller, C. Murphy, & A. L. Sonenshein, unpublished data). Expression of the *dciA* operon presumably allows the cell to attempt adaptation to nutritional stress conditions by scavenging low concentrations of a transportable nutrient. Expression of the *dciA* operon depends on Spo0A, indicating that it probably responds to the same initial nutritional signals as does the sporulation pathway (70; C. Mathiopoulos, F. Slack, J. Mueller, C. Murphy, & A. L. Sonenshein, unpublished data).

In summary, the various environmental conditions that induce sporulation also turn on several other responses that may allow the cell under nutritional stress to assess several alternative pathways. Such a cell can choose to sporulate or not in a judicious way. It is not surprising, therefore, that genes expressed very early during stationary phase depend on a large, overlapping set of regulatory proteins. The fact that a cell can distinguish among sporulation genes, antisporulation genes, stationary-phase genes, and catabolite-repressed vegetative genes probably reflects its ability to sort through combinations of signals, some of them contradictory, by using multiple regulatory proteins to control each of its relevant genes.

ACKNOWLEDGMENTS

We thank G. Chambliss, M. Débarbouillé, J. Deutscher, E. Dubnau, T. Henkin, W. Hillen, J. Hoch, J. Reizer, H. J. Schreier, I. Smith, and P. Zuber for permission to cite their results before publication and J. Mueller and L. Wray for helpful comments on the manuscript. Unpublished work from the authors' laboratories was supported by research grants from the US Public Health Service (AI23168 to S. H. F. and GM36718 and GM42219 to A. L. S.).

Literature Cited

1. Albertini, A. M., Galizzi, A. 1990. The *Bacillus subtilis outB* gene is highly homologous to an *Escherichia coli ntr*-like gene. *J. Bacteriol.* 172:5483–85

2. Amster-Choder, O., Houman, F., Wright, A. 1989. Protein phosphorylation regulates transcription of the β-glucoside utilization operon in *E. coli.* *Cell* 58:847–55

3. Antoniewski, C., Savelli, B., Stragier, P. 1990. The *spoIIJ* gene, which regulates early developmental steps in *Bacillus subtilis,* belongs to a class of environmentally responsive genes. *J. Bacteriol.* 172:86–93

4. Atkinson, M. R., Fisher, S. H. 1991. Identification of genes and gene products whose expression is activated during nitrogen-limited growth in *Bacillus subtilis.* *J. Bacteriol.* 173:23–27

5. Atkinson, M. R., Wray, L. V., Fisher, S. H. 1990. Regulation of histidine and

proline degradative enzymes by amino acid availability in *Bacillus subtilis. J. Bacteriol.* 172:4758–65

6. Bai, U., Lewandoski, M., Dubnau, E., Smith, I. 1990. Temporal regulation of the *Bacillus subtilis* early sporulation gene *spoOF. J. Bacteriol.* 172:5432–39

7. Baumberg, S., Harwood, C. R. 1979. Carbon and nitrogen repression of arginine catabolic enzymes in *Bacillus subtilis. J. Bacteriol.* 137:189–96

8. Baxter, L., Torrie, S., McKillen, M. 1974. D-Gluconate transport in *Bacillus subtilis. Biochem. Soc. Trans.* 2:1370–72

9. Bender, R. A., Snyder, P. M., Bueno, R., Quinto, M., Magasanik, B. 1983. Nitrogen regulation system of *Klebsiella aerogenes:* the *nac* gene. *J. Bacteriol.* 156:444–46

10. Bohannon, D. E., Rosenkrantz, M. S., Sonenshein, A. L. 1985. Regulation of *Bacillus subtilis* glutamate synthase genes by the nitrogen source. *J. Bacteriol.* 163:957–64

11. Bohannon, D. E., Sonenshein, A. L. 1989. Positive regulation of glutamate biosynthesis in *Bacillus subtilis. J. Bacteriol.* 171:4718–27

12. Borriss, R., Suss, K.-H., Suss, M., Manteuffel, R., Hofemeister, J. 1986. Mapping and properties of *bgl* (β-glucanase) mutants of *Bacillus subtilis. J. Gen. Microbiol.* 132:431–42

13. Boylan, S. A. Chun, K. T., Edson, B. A., Price, C. W. 1988. Early-blocked sporulation mutations alter expression of enzymes under carbon control in *Bacillus subtilis. Mol. Gen. Genet.* 212:271–80

14. Buttner, M. J., Smith, A. M., Servin-Gonzalez, L., Bibb, M. J. 1988. RNA heterogeneity and the agarase gene *(dagA)* of *Streptomyces coelicolor* A3(2). In *Biology of Actinomycetes '88,* ed. Y. Okami, T. Beppu, H. Ogawara, pp. 41–46. Tokyo: Jpn. Sci. Soc.

15. Cantwell, B. A., McConnell, D. J. 1983. Molecular cloning and expression of a *Bacillus subtilis* β-glucanase gene in *Escherichia coli. Gene* 23:211–19

16. Chasin, L. A., Magasanik, B. 1968. Induction and repression of the histidine-degrading enzymes of *Bacillus subtilis. J. Biol. Chem.* 243:5165–78

17. Chatterjee, S., Vining, L. C. 1982. Catabolite repression in *Streptomyces venezuelae.* Induction of β-galactosidase, chloramphenicol production, and intracellular cyclic adenosine 3',5'-monophosphate concentrations. *Can. J. Microbiol.* 28:311–17

18. Crutz, A.-N., Steinmetz, M., Aymer-

ich, S., Richter, R., Le Coq, D. 1990. Induction of levansucrase in *Bacillus subtilis:* an antitermination mechanism negatively controlled by the phosphotransferase system. *J. Bacteriol.* 172:1043–50

19. Dawes, I. W., Mandelstam, J. 1970. Sporulation of *Bacillus subtilis* in continuous culture. *J. Bacteriol.* 103:529–35

20. Dean, D. R., Hoch, J. A., Aronson, A. I. 1977. Alteration of the *Bacillus subtilis* glutamine synthetase results in overproduction of the enzyme. *J. Bacteriol.* 131:981–87

21. Débarbouillé, M., Arnaud, M., Fouet, A., Klier, A., Rapoport, G. 1990. The *sacT* gene regulating the *sacPA* operon in *Bacillus subtilis* shares strong homology with transcriptional terminators. *J. Bacteriol.* 172:3966–73

21a. Débarbouillé, M., Martin-Verstraete, I., Klier, A., Rapoport, G. 1991. The transcriptional regulator LevR of *Bacillus subtilis* has domains homologous to both sigma 54- and PTS-dependent regulators. *Proc. Natl. Acad. Sci. USA.* In press

22. Dessein, A., Schwartz, M., Ullman, A. 1978. Catabolite repression in *Escherichia coli* mutants lacking cyclic AMP. *Mol. Gen. Genet.* 162:83–87

23. Diderichsen, B., Wetsed, U., Hedegaard, L., Jensen, B. R., Sjoholm, C. 1990. Cloning of *aldB*, which encodes α-acetolactate decarboxylase, an exoenzyme from *Bacillus brevis. J. Bacteriol.* 172:4315–21

24. Dingman, D. W., Rosenkrantz, M. S., Sonenshein, A. L. 1987. Relationship between aconitase gene expression and sporulation in *Bacillus subtilis. J. Bacteriol.* 169:3068–75

25. Dubnau, D., Roggiani, M. 1990. Growth medium-independent genetic competence mutants of *Bacillus subtilis. J. Bacteriol.* 172:4048–55

26. Eisermann, R., Deutscher, J., Gonzy-Treboul, G., Hengstenberg, W. 1988. Site-directed mutagenesis with the *ptsH* gene of *Bacillus subtilis. J. Biol. Chem.* 263:17050–54

27. Ferrari, E., Henner, D. J., Perego, M., Hoch, J. A. 1988. Regulation of post exponential gene expression: transcriptional control of the subtilisin gene. See Ref. 43a, 2:39–44

28. Fisher, S. H. 1987. Catabolite repression in *Bacillus subtilis* and *Streptomyces.* See Ref. 89a, pp. 365–85

29. Fisher, S. H., Magasanik, B. 1984. Isolation of *Bacillus subtilis* mutants pleiotropically insensitive to glucose

catabolite repression. *J. Bacteriol.* 157:942–44

30. Fisher, S. H., Magasanik, B. 1984. 2-Ketoglutarate and the regulation of aconitase and histidase formation in *Bacillus subtilis. J. Bacteriol.* 158:379–82

31. Fisher, S. H., Rosenkrantz, M. S., Sonenshein, A. L. 1984. Glutamine synthetase gene of *Bacillus subtilis. Gene* 32:427–38

32. Fisher, S. H., Sonenshein, A. L. 1984. *Bacillus subtilis* glutamine synthetase mutants pleiotropically altered in glucose catabolite repression. *J. Bacteriol.* 157:612–21

33. Fornwald, J. A., Schmidt, F. J., Adams, C. W., Rosenberg, M., Brawner, M. E. 1987. Two promoters, one inducible and one constitutive, control transcription of the *Streptomyces lividans* galactose operon. *Proc. Natl. Acad. Sci. USA* 84:2130–34

34. Fouet, A., Arnaud, M., Klier, A., Rapoport, G. 1987. *Bacillus subtilis* sucrose-specific enzyme II of the phosphotransferase system: Expression in *Escherichia coli* and homology to enzymes II from enteric bacteria. *Proc. Natl. Acad. Sci. USA* 84:8773–77

35. Fouet, A., Arnaud, M., Klier, A., Rapoport, G. 1989. Genetics of the phosphotransferase system of *Bacillus subtilis. FEMS Lett.* 63:175–82

36. Fouet, A., Jin, S.-F., Raffel, G., Sonenshein, A. L. 1990. Multiple regulatory sites in the *Bacillus subtilis citB* promoter region. *J. Bacteriol.* 172:5408–15

37. Fouet, A., Sonenshein, A. L. 1990. A target for carbon source-dependent negative regulation of the *citB* promoter of *Bacillus subtilis. J. Bacteriol.* 172:835–44

38. Fournier, R. E., McKillen, M. N., Pardee, A. B., Willecke, K. 1972. Transport of dicarboxylic acids in *Bacillus subtilis. J. Biol. Chem.* 247:5587–95

39. Freese, E., Heinze, J., Galliers, E. M. 1979. Partial purine deprivation causes sporulation of *Bacillus subtilis* in the presence of excess ammonium, glucose and phosphate. *J. Gen Microbiol.* 115:193–205

40. Fujita, Y., Fujita, T. 1986. Identification and nucleotide sequence of the promoter region of the *Bacillus subtilis* gluconate operon. *Nucleic Acids Res.* 14:1237–52

41. Fujita, Y., Fujita, T. 1987. The gluconate operon *gnt* of *Bacillus subtilis* encodes its own transcriptional negative regulator. *Proc. Natl. Acad. Sci. USA* 84:4524–28

42. Fujita, Y., Fujita, T., Miwa, Y.,

Nihashi, J., Aratani, Y. 1986. Organization and transcription of the gluconate operon, *gnt*, of *Bacillus subtilis. J. Biol. Chem.* 261:13744–53

43. Fujita, Y., Miwa, Y. 1989. Identification of an operator sequence for the *Bacillus subtilis gnt* operon. *J. Biol. Chem.* 264:4201–6

43a. Ganesan, A. T., Hoch, J. A., eds. 1988. *Genetics and Biotechnology of Bacilli*, Vol. 2. New York: Academic

44. Gardner, A., Aronson, A. I. 1984. Expression of the *Bacillus subtilis* glutamine synthetase gene in *Escherichia coli. J. Bacteriol.* 158:967–71

45. Gartner, D., Geissendorfer, M., Hillen, W. 1988. Expression of the *Bacillus subtilis xyl* operon is repressed at the level of transcription and is induced by xylose. *J. Bacteriol.* 170:3102–9

46. Gaur, N. K., Oppenheim, J., Smith, I. 1991. The *Bacillus subtilis sin* gene, a regulator of alternate developmental processes, codes for a DNA binding protein. *J. Bacteriol.* 173:678–86

47. Gay, P., Cordier, P., Marquet, M., Delobbe, A. 1973. Carbohydrate metabolism and transport in *Bacillus subtilis*. A study of *ctr* mutations. *Mol. Gen. Genet.* 121:355–68

48. Golden, K. J., Bernlohr, R. W. 1985. Nitrogen catabolite repression of the L-asparaginase of *Bacillus licheniformis. J. Bacteriol.* 164:938–40

49. Gonzy-Treboul, G., Zagorec, M., Rain-Guion, M.-C., Steinmetz, M. 1989. Phosphoenol pyruvate: sugar phosphotransferase system of *Bacillus subtilis*: nucleotide sequence of *ptsX*, *ptsH* and the 5' end of *ptsI* and evidence for a *ptsHI* operon. *Mol. Microbiol.* 3:103–12

50. Hastrup, S. 1988. Analysis of the *Bacillus subtilis* xylose region. See Ref. 43a, pp. 79–83

51. Heineken, F., O'Connor, R. 1972. Continuous culture studies on the biosynthesis of alkaline protease, neutral protease, and α-amylase by *Bacillus subtilis* NRRL-B3411. *J. Gen. Microbiol.* 73:35–44

52. Henkin, T. M., Grundy, F. J., Nicholson, W. L., Chambliss, G. 1991. Catabolite repression of α-amylase gene expression in *Bacillus subtilis* involves a *trans*-acting gene homologous to the *Escherichia coli lacI* and *galR* repressors. *Mol. Microbiol.* In press

53. Henner, D. J., Yang, M., Ferrari, E. 1988. Localization of *Bacillus subtilis sacU*(Hy) mutations to two linked genes with similarities to the conserved procaryotic family of two-component

signalling systems. *J. Bacteriol.* 170: 5102–9

54. Horwitz, S. B., Kaplan, N. O. 1964. Hexitol dehydrogenases of *Bacillus subtilis. J. Biol. Chem.* 239:830–38

55. Kane, J. F., Wakim, J., Fischer, R. S. 1981. Regulation of glutamate dehydrogenase in *Bacillus subtilis. J. Bacteriol.* 148:1002–5

56. Kimhi, Y., Magasanik, B. 1970. Genetic basis of histidine degradation in *Bacillus subtilis. J. Biol. Chem.* 245:3545–48

57. Klier, A. F., Rapoport, G. 1988. Genetics and regulation of carbohydrate catabolism in *Bacillus. Annu. Rev. Microbiol.* 42:65–95

58. Kreuzer, P., Gartner, D., Allmansberger, R., Hillen, W. 1989. Identification and sequence analysis of the *Bacillus subtilis* W23 *xylR* gene and *xyl* operator. *J. Bacteriol.* 171:3840–45

59. Kunst, F., Débarbouillé, M., Msadek, T., Young, M., Mauel, C., et al. 1988. Deduced polypeptides encoded by the *Bacillus subtilis sacU* locus share homology with two-component sensor-regulator systems. *J. Bacteriol.* 170: 5093–5101

60. Lepesant, J.-A., Kunst, F., Pascal, M., Kejklarova-Lepesant, J., Steinmetz, M., Dedonder, R. 1976. Specific and pleiotropic regulatory mechanisms in the sucrose system of *Bacillus subtilis* 168. See Ref. 98a, pp. 58–69

61. Lindgren, V., Rutberg, L. 1974. Glycerol metabolism in *Bacillus subtilis:* gene-enzyme relationships. *J. Bacteriol.* 119:431–42

62. Lopez, J. M., Dromerick, A., Freese, E. 1981. Response of guanosine 5'-triphosphate concentration to nutritional changes and its significance for *Bacillus subtilis* sporulation. *J. Bacteriol.* 146: 605–13

63. Lopez, J., Fortnagel, P. 1972. The regulation of the butanediol cycle in *Bacillus subtilis. Biochim. Biophys. Acta* 279:544–60

64. Lopez, J. M., Thoms, B. 1977. Role of sugar uptake and metabolic intermediates on catabolite repression in *Bacillus subtilis. J. Bacteriol.* 129:217–24

65. Lopez, J. M., Uratani-Wong, B., Freese, E. 1980. Catabolite repression of enzyme synthesis does not prevent sporulation. *J. Bacteriol.* 141:1447–49

66. Mach, H., Hecker, M., Mach, F. 1988. Physiological studies on cAMP synthesis in *Bacillus subtilis. FEMS Microbiol. Lett.* 52:189–92

67. Magasanik, B., Neidhardt, F. C. 1987. Regulation of carbon and nitrogen utilization. See Ref. 75b, pp. 1318–25

68. Martin, I., Débarbouillé, M., Klier, A., Rapoport, G. 1989. Induction and metabolite regulation of levanase synthesis in *Bacillus subtilis. J. Bacteriol.* 171:1885–92

69. Martin-Verstraete, I., Débarbouillé, M., Klier, A., Rapoport, G. 1990. Levanase operon of *Bacillus subtilis* includes a fructose-specific phosphotransferase system regulating the expression of the operon. *J. Mol. Biol.* 214:657–71

70. Mathiopoulos, C., Sonenshein, A. L. 1989. Identification of *Bacillus subtilis* genes expressed early during sporulation. *Mol. Microbiol.* 3:1071–81

71. Matin, A., Auger, E. A., Blum, P. H., Schultz, J. E. 1989. Genetic basis of starvation survival in nondifferentiating bacteria. *Annu. Rev. Microbiol.* 43:293–316

72. Meadow, N. A., Fox, D. K., Roseman, S. 1990. The bacterial phosphoenolpyruvate:glycose phosphotransferase system. *Annu. Rev. Biochem.* 59:497–542

73. Msadek, T., Kunst, F., Henner, D. J., Rapoport, G., Dedonder, R. 1990. Signal transduction pathway controlling synthesis of a class of degradative enzymes in *Bacillus subtilis:* expression of the regulatory genes and analysis of mutations in *degS* and *degU. J. Bacteriol.* 172:824–34

74. Msadek, T., Kunst, F., Klier, A., Rapoport, G. 1991. DegS/DegU and ComA/ComP modulator/effector pairs control expression of the *Bacillus subtilis* pleiotropic regulatory gene *degQ. J. Bacteriol.* In press

74a. Mukai, K., Kawata, M., Tanaka, T. 1990. Isolation and phosphorylation of the *Bacillus subtilis degS* and *degU* gene products. *J. Biol. Chem.* 265:20000–6

75. Murphy, N., McConnell, D. J., Cantwell, B. A. 1984. The DNA sequence of the gene and genetic control sites for the excreted *B. subtilis* enzyme β-glucanase. *Nucleic Acids Res.* 12:5355–66

75a. Nakano, M. M., Zuber, P. 1989. Cloning and characterization of *srfB*, a regulatory gene involved in surfactin production and competence in *Bacillus subtilis. J. Bacteriol.* 171:5347–53

75b. Neidhardt, F. C., ed. 1987. *Escherichia coli and Salmonella typhimurium: Cellular and Molecular Biology*, Washington, DC: Am. Soc. Microbiol.

76. Nicholson, W. L. 1987. *Regulation of α-amylase synthesis in* Bacillus subtilis. PhD thesis. Madison: Univ. Wis. 322 pp.

77. Nicholson, W. L., Chambliss, G. H. 1987. Effect of decoyinine on the regulation of α-amylase synthesis in *Bacillus subtilis. J. Bacteriol.* 169:5867–69
78. Nicholson, W. L., Park, Y.-K., Henkin, T. M., Won, M., Weickert, M., et al. 1987. Catabolite repression–resistant mutations of the *Bacillus subtilis* α-amylase promoter affect transcription levels and are in an operator-like sequence. *J. Mol. Biol.* 198:609–18
79. Nihashi, J.-I., Fujita, Y. 1984. Catabolite repression of inositol dehydrogenase and gluconate kinase synthesis of *Bacillus subtilis. Biochim. Biophys. Acta* 798:88–95
80. Nomura, M., Maruo, B., Akabori, S. 1956. Studies on α-amylase formation by *Bacillus subtilis.* I. Effect of high concentrations of polyethylene glycol on amylase formation by *Bacillus subtilis. J. Biochem. Tokyo* 43:143–52
81. Oda, M., Sugishita, A., Furukawa, K. 1988. Cloning and nucleotide sequence of histidase and regulatory genes in the *Bacillus subtilis hut* operon and positive regulation of the operon. *J. Bacteriol.* 170:3199–3205
82. Oskouian, B., Stewart, G. C. 1990. Repression and catabolite repression of the lactose operon of *Staphylococcus aureus. J. Bacteriol.* 172:3804–12
83. Pan, F. L., Coote, J. G. 1979. Glutamine synthetase and glutamate synthase activities during growth and sporulation of *Bacillus subtilis. J. Gen. Microbiol.* 112:373–77
84. Perego, M., Cole, S. P., Burbulys, D., Trach, K., Hoch, J. A. 1989. Characterization of the gene for a protein kinase which phosphorylates the sporulation-regulatory proteins Spo0A and Spo0F of *Bacillus subtilis. J. Bacteriol.* 171:6187–96
85. Perego, M., Hoch, J. A. 1988. Sequence analysis and regulation of the *hpr* locus, a regulatory gene for protease production and sporulation in *Bacillus subtilis. J. Bacteriol.* 170:2560–67
86. Perego, M., Spiegelman, G. B., Hoch, J. A. 1988. Structure of the gene for the transition state regulator, *abrB:* regulator synthesis is controlled by the *spo0A* sporulation gene in *Bacillus subtilis. Mol. Microbiol.* 1:689–99
87. Price, C. W., Doi, R. H. 1985. Genetic mapping of *rpoD* implicates the major sigma factor of *Bacillus subtilis* RNA polymerase in sporulation initiation. *Mol. Gen. Genet.* 201:88–95
88. Reitzer, L. J., Magasanik, B. 1987. Ammonia assimilation and the biosynthesis of glutamine, glutamate, aspartate, asparagine, L-alanine and D-alanine. See Ref. 75b, pp. 302–20
89. Reizer, J., Novotny, M. J., Stuiver, I., Saier, M. H. 1984. Regulation of glycerol uptake by the phosphoenolpyruvate-sugar phosphotransferase system in *Bacillus subtilis. J. Bacteriol.* 159:243–50
89a. Reizer, J., Peterkofsky, A., eds. 1987. *Sugar Transport and Metabolism in Gram-Positive Bacteria.* Chichester, UK: Horwood
90. Reizer, J., Peterkofsky, A. 1987. Regulatory mechanisms for sugar transport in gram-positive bacteria. See Ref. 89a, pp. 333–64
91. Reizer, J., Saier, M. H. Jr., Deutscher, J., Grenier, F., Thompson, J., Hengstenberg, W. 1988. The phosphoenolpyruvate:sugar phosphotransferase system in gram-positive bacteria: properties, mechanism, and regulation. *CRC Crit. Rev. Microbiol.* 15:297–338
92. Reizer, J., Sutrina, S. L., Saier, M. H. Jr., Stewart, G. C., Peterkofsky, A., Reddy, P. 1989. Mechanistic and physiological consequences of Hpr(ser) phosphorylation on the activities of the phosphoenolpyruvate:sugar phosphotransferase system in gram-positive bacteria: studies with site specific mutants of HPr. *EMBO J.* 8:2111–20
93. Roggiani, M., Hahn, J., Dubnau, D. 1990. Suppression of early competence mutations in *Bacillus subtilis* by *mec* mutations. *J. Bacteriol.* 172:4056–63
94. Rosenkrantz, M. S., Dingman, D. W., Sonenshein, A. L. 1985. *Bacillus subtilis citB* gene is regulated synergistically by glucose and glutamine. *J. Bacteriol.* 164:155–64
95. Saier, M. H. Jr. 1989. Protein phosphorylation and allosteric control of inducer exclusion and catabolite repression by the bacterial phosphoenolpyruvate:sugar phosphotransferase system. *Microbiol. Rev.* 53:109–20
96. Sa-Nogueira, I., Paveia, H., de Lencastre, H. 1988. Isolation of constitutive mutants for L-arabinose utilization in *Bacillus subtilis. J. Bacteriol.* 170:2855–57
97. Sasjima, K., Kumada, T. 1981. Change in the regulation of enzyme synthesis under catabolite repression in *Bacillus subtilis* pleiotropic mutant lacking transketolase. *Agric. Biol. Chem.* 45:2005–12
98. Schaeffer, P., Millet, J., Aubert, J.-P. 1965. Catabolite repression of bacterial sporulation. *Proc. Natl. Acad. Sci. USA* 54:704–11
98a. Schlessinger, D., ed. 1976. *Microbiol-*

ogy—1976. Washington, DC: Am. Soc. Microbiol.

99. Schnetz, K., Toloczyki, C., Rak, B. 1987. β-glucosides *(bgl)* operon of *Escherichia coli* K-12: nucleotide sequence, genetic organization and possible evolutionary relationship to regulatory components of two *Bacillus subtilis* genes. *J. Bacteriol.* 169:2579–90

100. Schreier, H. J., Brown, S. W., Hirschi, K. D., Nomellini, J. F., Sonenshein, A. L. 1989. Regulation of *Bacillus subtilis* glutamine synthetase gene expression by the product of the *glnR* gene. *J. Mol. Biol.* 210:51–63

101. Schreier, H. J., Fisher, S. H., Sonenshein, A. L. 1985. Regulation of expression from the *glnA* promoter of *Bacillus subtilis* requires the *glnA* gene product. *Proc. Natl. Acad. Sci. USA* 82:3375–79

102. Schreier, H. J., Sonenshein, A. L. 1986. Altered regulation of the *glnA* gene in glutamine synthetase mutants of *Bacillus subtilis. J. Bacteriol.* 167:35–43

103. Setlow, P. 1973. Inability to detect cyclic AMP in vegetative or sporulating cells or dormant spores of *Bacillus megaterium. Biochem. Biophys. Res. Commun.* 52:365–72

104. Shimotsu, H., Henner, D. J. 1986. Modulation of *Bacillus subtilis* levansucrase gene expression by sucrose and regulation of the steady state mRNA level by *sacU* and *sacQ* genes. *J. Bacteriol.* 168:380–88

105. Smith, C. P., Chater, K. F. 1988. Cloning and transcriptional analysis of the entire glycerol utilization *(glyABX)* operon of *Streptomyces coelicolor* A3(2) and identification of a closely associated transcriptional unit. *Mol. Gen. Genet.* 211:129–37

106. Smith, I. 1989. Initiation of sporulation. See Ref. 106a, pp. 185–210

106a. Smith, I., Slepecky, R. A., Setlow, P., eds. 1989. *Regulation of Prokaryotic Development.* Washington, DC: Am. Soc. Microbiol.

107. Sonenshein, A. L. 1989. Metabolic regulation of sporulation and other stationary-phase phenomena. See Ref. 106a, pp. 109–30

108. Speck, E. L., Freese, E. 1973. Control of metabolite secretion in *Bacillus subtilis. J. Gen. Microbiol.* 78:261–75

109. Steinmetz, M., Aymerich, S., Gonzy-Treboul, G., Le Coq, D. 1988. Levansucrase induction by sucrose in *Bacillus subtilis* involves an antiterminator. Homology with the *Escherichia coli bgl* operon. See Ref. 43a, pp. 11–15

110. Steinmetz, M., Le Coq, D., Aymerich,

S. 1989. Induction of saccharolytic enzymes by sucrose in *Bacillus subtilis:* evidence for two partially interchangeable regulatory pathways. *J. Bacteriol.* 171:1519–23

111. Steinmetz, M., Le Coq, D., Aymerich, S., Gonzy-Treboul, G., Gay, P. 1985. The DNA sequence of the gene for the secreted *Bacillus subtilis* enzyme levansucrase and its genetic control sites. *Mol. Gen. Genet.* 200:220–28

112. Strauch, M. A., Aronson, A. I., Brown, S. W., Schreier, H. J., Sonenshein, A. L. 1988. Sequence of the *Bacillus subtilis* glutamine synthetase gene region. *Gene* 71:257–65

113. Strauch, M. A., Spiegelman, G. B., Perego, M., Johnson, W. C., Burbulys, D., Hoch, J. A. 1989. The transition state transcription regulator *abrB* of *Bacillus subtilis* is a DNA binding protein. *EMBO J.* 8:1615–21

114. Sutrina, S. L. Reddy, P., Saier, M. H., Reizer, J. 1990. The glucose permease of *Bacillus subtilis* is a polypeptide chain that functions to energize the sucrose permease. *J. Biol. Chem.* 265:18581–89

115. Takahashi, I. 1979. Catabolite repression-resistant mutants of *Bacillus subtilis. Can. J. Microbiol.* 25:1283–87

116. Trach, K. A., Chapman, J. W., Piggot, P. J., Hoch, J. A. 1985. Deduced product of the stage 0 sporulation gene *spo0F* shares homology with the *spo0A, ompR,* and *sfrA* proteins. *Proc. Natl. Acad. Sci. USA* 82:7260–64

117. Uratani-Wong, B., Lopez, J. M., Freese, E. 1981. Induction of citric acid cycle enzymes during initiation of sporulation by guanine nucleotide deprivation. *J. Bacteriol.* 146:337–44

118. Valle, F., Ferrari, E. 1989. Subtilisin: a redundantly temporally regulated gene? See Ref. 106a, pp. 131–46

119. Virolle, M. J., Bibb, M. J. 1988. Cloning, characterization and regulation of an α-amylase gene from *Streptomyces limosus. Mol. Microbiol.* 2:197–208

120. Wanner, B. L., Kodaira, R., Neidhardt, F. C. 1978. Regulation of *lac* operon expression: reappraisal of the theory of catabolite repression. *J. Bacteriol.* 136:947–54

121. Weickert, M., Chambliss, G. 1990. Site-directed mutagenesis of a catabolite repression operator sequence in *Bacillus subtilis. Proc. Natl. Acad. Sci. USA* 87:6238–42

122. Weinrauch, Y., Penchev, R., Dubnau, E., Smith, I., Dubnau, D. 1990. A *Bacillus subtilis* regulatory gene product for genetic competence and sporulation resembles sensor protein members of the

bacterial two-component signal-transduction systems. *Genes Dev.* 4:860–72

123. Willecke, K., Pardee, A. B. 1971. Inducible transport of citrate in a gram-positive bacterium, *Bacillus subtilis*. *J. Biol. Chem.* 246:1032–40

124. Won-Song, M., Takova, T., Chambliss, G. 1991. Purification of a possible catabolite repressor protein from *Bacillus subtilis*. *J. Bacteriol*. In press

125. Yamashita, S., Yoshikawa, H., Kawamura, F., Takahashi, H., Yamamoto, T., et al. 1986. The effect of *spo0* mutations on the expression of *spo0A*- and *spo0F-lacZ* fusions. *Mol. Gen. Genet.* 205:28–33

126. Zahler, S. A., Benjamin, L. G., Glatz, B. S., Winter, P. F., Goldstein, B. J. 1976. Genetic mapping of the *alsA, alsR, thyA, kauA,* and *citD* markers in *Bacillus subtilis*. See Ref. 98a, pp. 35–43

127. Zahler, S. A., Najimudin, N., Kessler, D. S., Vandeyar, M. A. 1990. α-Acetolactate synthesis in *Bacillus subtilis*. In *Biosynthesis of Branched Chain Amino Acids,* ed. Z. Barak, D. M. Chipman, J. V. Schloss, pp. 25–42. Weinheim: VCH Verlagsgesellschaft

128. Zuber, P., Losick, R. 1983. Use of a *lacZ* fusion to study the role of the *spo0* genes of *Bacillus subtilis* in developmental regulation. *Cell* 35:275–83

129. Zuber, P., Losick, R. 1987. Role of *abrB* in *spo0A*- and *spo0B*-dependent utilization of a sporulation promoter in *Bacillus subtilis*. *J. Bacteriol.* 169: 2223–30

130. Zukowski, M. M., Miller, L., Cosgwell, P., Chen, K., Aymerich, S., Steinmetz, M. 1990. Nucleotide sequence of the *sacS* locus of *Bacillus subtilis* reveals the presence of two regulatory genes. *Gene* 90:153–55

Annu. Rev. Microbiol. 1991. 45:137–61

POLYMERASE CHAIN REACTION:
Applications in Environmental
Microbiology

R. J. Steffan[1]

Gesellschaft für Biotechnologische Forschung mbH, Braunschweig, Germany

R. M. Atlas

Department of Biology, University of Louisville, Louisville, Kentucky 40292

KEY WORDS: PCR, gene probes

CONTENTS

INTRODUCTION 138
THE POLYMERASE CHAIN REACTION 138
   PCR Reaction Mixture 138
   PCR Reaction Conditions 140
   Multiplex PCR 141
   Enhancing PCR Efficiency 141
ISOLATION OF ENVIRONMENTAL NUCLEIC ACIDS FOR PCR 142
   Isolation of Nucleic Acids from Aquatic Environments 142
   Isolation of Nucleic Acids from Soil and Sediment 143
DETECTION OF PCR PRODUCTS 144
   Capture Probes—Reverse Hybridization 146
USE OF PCR TO DETECT MICROORGANISMS IN ENVIRONMENTAL SAMPLES 147
   Detection of Genetically Engineered Microorganisms 147
   Detection of Indicator Organisms and Pathogens 148
QUANTITATION OF PCR-AMPLIFIED PRODUCT 149
   Quantification of DNA Target Sequence 149
   Quantification of mRNA 150
USE OF PCR TO ISOLATE AND CLONE SPECIFIC DNA SEQUENCES 152
   Use of PCR to Analyze Ribosomal RNA Sequences 152
   Cloning DNA and Creating Gene Probes Using Degenerate Primers ... 153
CONCLUSION 155

[1]Current address: Envirogen Inc., Lawrenceville, New Jersey 08648.

0066-4227/91/1001-0137$02.00

INTRODUCTION

The development of the polymerase chain reaction (PCR) in 1983 (71–73a) was a major methodological breakthrough in molecular biology. The method has found its way into nearly every type of laboratory interested in molecular biology from forensics to ecology and diagnostics to pure research (22, 42). PCR permits the in vitro replication of defined sequences of DNA whereby gene segments can be amplified. Perhaps the most obvious application of this technique is to enhance gene probe detection of specific gene sequences. By exponentially amplifying a target sequence, PCR significantly enhances the probability of detecting rare sequences in heterologous mixtures of DNA. In this review, we describe some of the recent work in environmental microbiology that has been done with the aid of PCR as well as some uses of PCR that may be applicable to answering future questions in molecular microbial ecology.

THE POLYMERASE CHAIN REACTION

PCR involves three stages: 1. the DNA is melted to convert double-stranded DNA to single-stranded DNA; 2. primers are annealed to the target DNA; and 3. the DNA is extended by nucleotide addition from the primers by the action of DNA polymerase. The oligonucleotide primers are designed to hybridize to regions of DNA flanking a desired target gene sequence. The primers are then extended across the target sequence using DNA polymerase (currently almost exclusively *Taq* DNA polymerase) in the presence of free deoxynucleotide triphosphates, resulting in a duplication of the starting target material. Melting the product DNA duplexes and repeating the process many times result in an exponential increase in the amount of target DNA (Figure 1).

PCR Reaction Mixture

The essential components of the PCR reaction mixture are *Taq* DNA polymerase, oligomer primers, deoxynucleotides (dNTPs), template DNA, and magnesium ions. The recommended concentration range for *Taq* DNA polymerase is 1.0–2.5 units per 100 μl (58). If the enzyme concentration is too high, nonspecific background products often form. If the enzyme concentration is too low, the amount of desired product made is insufficient. The *Taq* DNA polymerase has an optimum activity around 70°C and is not inactivated by short incubations at temperatures at which PCR-generated fragments will denature (usually 90–95°C).

Primer concentrations of 0.1–0.5 μM are recommended. Higher primer concentrations may promote nonspecific product formation and in particular may increase the generation of a primer-dimer. Nonspecific products and

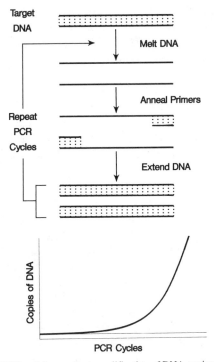

Figure 1   The stages of PCR and the resultant amplification of DNA copies of the target region.

primer-dimer artifacts are substrates for PCR and result in a lower yield of the desired product. Typical primers are 18 to 28 nucleotides in length with 50–60% G + C composition. The primers must have similar melting temperatures (Tms). One must avoid complementarity at the 3' ends of primer pairs as this arrangement favors the formation of primer-dimer and reduces the yield of the desired product. Also, three or more Cs or Gs at the 3' ends of primers may promote mispriming at G + C–rich sequences and should be avoided. Avoiding primers with 3' overlaps reduces the incidence of primer-dimer formation. Palindromic sequences within primers likewise must be avoided. Where possible, primers should have a G + C content of around 50% and a random base distribution. Secondary structure in the target template DNA and in the primers likewise should be minimized.

dNTP concentrations should be 20–200 μM to give optimal specificity and fidelity. The four dNTPs should be used at equivalent concentrations to minimize misincorporation errors. The lowest dNTP concentration appropriate for the length and composition of the target sequence should be used to minimize mispriming at nontarget sites and reduce the likelihood of extending misincorporated nucleotides (44). Twenty μM of each dNTP in a 100 μl reaction is theoretically sufficient to synthesize 2.6 μg of a 400-bp sequence.

PCRs should contain 0.5 to 2.5 mM magnesium over the total dNTP concentration. The presence of EDTA or other chelators in the primer stocks or template DNA may disturb the apparent magnesium optimum. The magnesium ion concentration affects primer annealing, DNA melting temperatures, and enzyme activity.

The recommended buffer for PCR is 10- to 50-mM Tris-HCl (pH 8.3–8.8). Up to 50-mM KCl can be included in the reaction mixture to facilitate primer annealing. KCl >50 mM inhibits *Taq* DNA polymerase activity (44). Gelatin or bovine serum albumin (100 μg/ml) and nonionic detergents such as Tween 20 can be used to stabilize the *Taq* DNA polymerase.

PCR Reaction Conditions

PCR involves repetitive cycling between a high temperature to melt the DNA, a relatively low temperature to allow the primers to hybridize (anneal) with the complementary region of the target DNA, and an intermediate temperature for primer extension. The temperature cycling can be achieved using an automated thermal cycler.

The temperature and length of time required for primer annealing depend upon the base composition, length, and concentration of the amplification primers (43). The annealing temperature generally is 5°C below the true Tm of the primers. Annealing temperatures in the range of 55 to 72°C generally yield the best results. At typical primer concentrations of 0.2 μM, annealing requires only a few seconds. Increasing the annealing temperature enhances discrimination against incorrectly annealed primers and reduces addition of incorrect nucleotides at the 3' end of the primers. Stringent annealing temperatures, especially during the first several cycles, help increase specificity. If the temperature is lower than the optimum, the reaction products frequently include additional DNA fragments that can be visualized using agarose gel electrophoresis and ethidium bromide staining.

The range of enzyme activity varies by two orders of magnitude between 20 and 85°C (26). Extension time depends upon the length and concentration of the target sequence and upon temperature. Primer extensions typically are performed at 72°C, which is optimal for *Taq* DNA polymerase. Low extension temperature together with high dNTP concentrations favors extension of misincorporated nucleotides. Using longer primers and only two temperatures, e.g. 55 to 75°C for annealing and extension and 94°C for DNA melting, can yield better results (52).

Typical denaturation conditions are 94–95°C for 30–60 s (43). Lower temperatures may result in incomplete denaturation of the target template and/or the PCR product and failure of the PCR. In contrast, denaturation steps that are too high and/or too long lead to unnecessary loss of enzyme activity.

The half-life of *Taq* DNA polymerase activity is 40 min at 95°C. Too many cycles can increase the amount and complexity of nonspecific background products. Too few cycles give low product yield.

Multiplex PCR

One can amplify several DNA segments simultaneously using multiple pairs of primers. Chamberlain et al (11) developed this procedure, called multiplex PCR, to detect human genes. Bej et al (7) modified the approach of simultaneous PCR amplification to detect gene sequences associated with different groups of bacteria in environmental samples. Multiplex PCR amplification of two different *Legionella* genes, one specific for *Legionella pneumophila* *(mip)* and the other for the genus *Legionella* (5S rRNA), was achieved by staggered additions of primers. Multiplex PCR amplification using differing amounts of primers specific for *lacZ* and *lamB* genes permitted the detection of coliform bacteria and those associated with human fecal contamination, including the indicator bacterial species *Escherichia coli* and enteric pathogens *Salmonella* and *Shigella*.

Enhancing PCR Efficiency

One way of enhancing the probability of successful and specific amplification of environmental DNA is to dilute the sample (1 : 10 to 1 : 200) after the first few cycles of PCR (73, 89) or after a completed reaction (81), and then perform an additional round of PCR. This process may effectively dilute potential inhibitors to an acceptable level and allow for successful amplification. The diluted DNA will also contain relatively high ratios of target sequences to total, nontarget, background DNA.

The second round of PCR may be performed with the same primer set, or with nested primers designed to recognize regions within the initial amplified region (35, 73). Using nested primers provides an additional level of specificity and increases amplification efficiency by minimizing nonspecific primer annealing (35), which is particularly useful in detecting organisms in environmental samples in which the exact specificity or uniqueness of the primers is not known.

Ruano et al (83) described a diphasic amplification strategy, termed booster PCR, to improve the efficiency of amplifying target sequences present in low numbers. Initial PCR cycles are performed with a low concentration (2.5–8.3 pM) of primers; after 20 PCR cycles, primer concentrations are increased to 0.1 μM and up to 50 more PCR cycles are performed. This methodology minimizes the formation of primer dimers that may result from primer excess (86) in the early PCR cycles and compete for polymerase molecules. Using this method, one can amplify and detect as few as 5 to 10 copies of a specific human DNA target.

ISOLATION OF ENVIRONMENTAL NUCLEIC
ACIDS FOR PCR

For PCR analysis of DNA from environmental samples, the DNA must be isolated and may have to undergo extensive purification. Purification procedures can be any combination of CsCl-EtBr ultracentrifugation (40, 81, 102), hydroxylapatite or affinity chromatography (76, 81, 102, 108), phenol/chloroform extractions, ethanol precipitations (24), dialysis, or repeated polyvinylpolypyrrolidone (PVPP) treatments (40, 81, 102, 117). For the isolation of RNA, humic-contaminated pellets may be resuspended in a solution of guanidine-hydrochloride and then subjected to ethanol precipitation and phenol extraction (33, 34). Unfortunately, standard purification protocols will probably not work with every environmental sample, and the required conditions must be ascertained on an individual basis.

Isolation of Nucleic Acids from Aquatic Environments

In general, water samples are the easiest environmental matrix from which to isolate nucleic acids. In many cases, water samples need only be filtered to collect microorganisms that may then be lysed to isolate their nucleic acids (8, 24, 30, 95). In some cases, filter-collected cells can be analyzed directly. The cells may be lysed directly on specific filters, e.g. by freeze-thaw cycling, and the PCR can be run without removing the filters (A. K. Bej, personal communication). Alternately, filtered cells may first be subjected to enzymatic lysis, and/or phenol-chloroform extraction procedures, to yield adequate DNA for PCR analysis. Sommerville et al (95) demonstrated a simple method for isolating nucleic acids from aquatic samples that allows filtering relatively large volumes of water. Cell collection and lysis are performed in a single filter cartridge, and chromosomal DNA, plasmid DNA, and speciated RNA can be selectively recovered. Dissolved and particulate DNA may also be isolated from aquatic environments for direct PCR analysis (19, 81).

In aquatic studies, microbial nucleic acids of sufficient purity for enzymatic analysis have also been isolated from algal mats (115, 117) and filtered algal (81) and cyanobacterial cells (125). Paul et al (81) reported that with certain algal DNA preparations, and all preparations of environmental DNA, purification by CsCl-EtBr ultracentrifugation was required for successful amplification of target genes. Multiple PVPP treatment was required to recover purified rRNA from microbial mats (117). In other studies, multiple phenol or phenol:chloroform extractions have produced sufficiently pure DNA from cyanobacteria (125) or planktonic microorganisms (24, 61).

We (100–102) observed that adding solid ammonium acetate to cell lysates from aquatic sediments to a final concentration of 2.5 M, followed by high speed centrifugation and then ethanol precipitation of the DNA in the supernatant, also removed great amounts of organic impurities from the recovered DNA. This treatment was necessary to obtain pure DNA even if additional purification treatments, such as ultracentrifugation or hydroxyapatite chromatography, were used.

Isolation of Nucleic Acids from Soil and Sediment

Two approaches have been used to recover DNA from soils and sediments: isolation of microbial cells followed by cell lysis and nucleic acid purification (cell extraction) and direct lysis of microbial cells in the environmental matrix followed by nucleic acid purification (direct extraction).

Balkwill et al (4) and Goksøyr and colleagues (23, 107) first demonstrated cell extraction methods, and several groups have since used cell extraction, with some modifications, to isolate DNA from soil (3, 40, 45, 102, 106, 108) or sediment (99, 102). Hahn et al (33) used a similar approach to recover rRNA from soils to detect *Frankia* sp. One simple but significant improvement of this approach is the inclusion of a PVPP treatment to decrease sample humic content prior to cell lysis (40, 102), thereby simplifying DNA purification.

Ogram et al (76) were first to describe direct extraction. In this method, cells are lysed while still within the soil matrix by incubation with SDS followed by physical disruption with a bead beater. The DNA is then extracted using alkaline phosphate buffer. This method has successfully recovered DNA from sediments (76, 102) and soil (102). B. Olson (personal communication) has developed an alternate direct DNA extraction procedure in which DNA is released through treatment with lysozyme and freeze-thaw disruption to lyse bacterial cells followed by phenol-chloroform extraction. The extracted DNA is then purified, e.g. by centrifugation or chromatography. One may also separate DNA from impurities by using gel electrophoresis (J. Armstrong, personal communication; B. Olson, personal communication). PVPP treatments may also be incorporated into this procedure to reduce the great amounts of humic materials inherently co-extracted during the treatment of soil or sediment with hot SDS (102).

Significantly higher yields of DNA are recovered with the direct extraction method, but the DNA may contain impurities that can inhibit enzymatic manipulation (102). Because the yield is so great, however, more purification steps (e.g. CsCL-EtBr centrifugation, hydroxyapatite chromatography, or affinity chromatography) may be incorporated with a lower percentage of DNA loss. Also, both eukaryotic and prokaryotic DNA can be recovered. With the cell extraction method, extracted bacterial cells can be separated and washed to remove impurities before cell lysis, but one might recover only DNA from easily extractable cells.

DETECTION OF PCR PRODUCTS

Gibbs (27) has estimated that, if PCR was performed at 100% of its theoretical maximum efficiency, one could generate 100 μg of a 1-kb unique human DNA fragment from 100 ng of total human DNA in only 25 PCR cycles. Generally, however, only a few μg of target are produced, even under the most controlled conditions. Paul et al (81) commented that they have never been able to generate enough amplified target from environmental DNA to visualize it on an EtBr-stained agarose gel, but the product was readily detectable following Southern blotting and probe hybridization. We (99) also made this observation during our studies with sediment DNA in which the amplified product was sufficient for detection with dot blot analysis but not with direct gel visualization.

To explain this inability to directly visualize amplified DNA, let us pose the following hypothetical scenario. First we will assume all cells in a sediment or soil have the same genome size (5×10^6 bp) and extractability by the cell-extraction procedure. Let us also assume that the sediment or soil sample has 10^{10} cells/g as determined by direct counting, and that we have added 1 target cell/g, each of which contains a single copy of a 500-bp target fragment. Our target cell and its genome thus represent 10^{-10} of the total cells and genomes present in the sample.

Now we extract the cells and DNA from 100 g of this sample and recover 100 μg of the highly purified DNA. The target genome represents 10^{-10} of the DNA, or 10^{-8} μg of DNA. Because the total genome size of the target cell is 5×10^6 bp and the target fragment is 500 bp (10^{-4} of the total genome), the total target in the extracted DNA is 10^{-12} μg. Now, if we perform PCR with 1 μg (10^{-2} of the total) of the extracted DNA, the sample will contain 10^{-14} μg (0.01 ag) of target DNA.

If we assume that 0.1 ng of a 500 bp fragment can be detected in an EtBr-stained agarose gel, we would require a 10^{10}-fold (approximately 2^{33}) amplification to see the fragment (assuming the entire sample is run on the gel). Gene probes, however, can detect target DNA in the 0.1 pg range (40), thus requiring only a 10^7-fold amplification (approximately 2^{24}). The gene-probe detection limit observed without amplification is generally in the range of 10^3 to 10^4 cells/g of soil or sediment (40, 98, 99). With PCR amplification and approximately 30 cycles, however, single target cells can be detected using gene probes (2).

Because of the great amounts of target DNA generated by PCR amplification, detection methods no longer need rely on the ability to produce strong signals using radiolabeled probes for the identification of minimal copies of target (62). This breakthrough has allowed the development of several nonradioactive detection methods that have many advantages over radioactive methods (9). PCR-based nonradioactive detection methods can be grouped into three categories: 1. use of nonradioactively labeled probes to detect amplified product (77); 2. the direct incorporation of label into the amplified product for use as a probe (18); and 3. the direct incorporation of label into the PCR product for probe or capture-mediated detection of amplified product (18, 51, 87, 104).

In the first case, analysis can be performed using standard dot-blot (68) or Southern blot procedures (96), and the methodology does not differ greatly from previous methods. Increased detection sensitivity results from the production of great quantities of target, and also the increase in target to nontarget sequence ratio. An additional advantage of PCR methodology is that it provides two levels of stringency; primer annealing and probe hybridization.

The latter cases have allowed for the development of several new techniques with great potential for the rapid screening of large numbers of environmental samples. Primers can be labeled with either biotin (89, 104), horseradish peroxidase or alkaline peroxidase (62), or fluorescent dyes (13), or they can include sequences specifically recognized by DNA binding proteins (109). Following amplification, each copy of the amplified product has the specific label. Similarly, one primer can contain a sequence to facilitate capture (i.e. biotin or DNA binding protein attachment site) while the opposite primer contains a label to facilitate detection (89).

Label can also be incorporated into the amplified product by performing PCR in the presence of labeled deoxyribonucleotides such as biotin-11-dUTP (2, 8, 18, 64) or digoxigenin-labeled nucleotides (56). Day et al (18) performed extensive studies to evaluate the parameters necessary to successfully incorporate biotinylated nucleotides (biotinylated-dNTP, where n is the number of carbons in the biotin-nucleotide spacer arm) into PCR products, and they evaluated how these incorporated biotinylated-dNTPs affect the efficiency of hybridization to these amplified products. Initial concentrations of biotin-11-dUTP from 1.5 to 200 μM were incorporated into a 123-bp product through 30 cycles of PCR. Greatest biotin incorporation occurred when the reaction was performed in the presence of 200 μM biotin-11-dUTP (total replacement of dTTP), but this level of biotin incorporation significantly affected both mobility on an agarose gel, and hybridization to a radiolabeled probe. Hybridization inhibition was also observed with 100-μM biotin-11-dUTP, but it decreased below 50 μM. Replacement of dTTP with biotin-7-dUTP or biotin-16-dUTP at concentrations greater than 180 μM inhibited primer extension, suggesting that the C_{11} spacer arm may be optimal for successful amplification.

Capture Probes—Reverse Hybridization

Potentially, any number of target sequences may be amplified in a single reaction mixture, or a number of samples could be screened for the presence of a specific sequence in a single hybridization assay and the resulting products could be screened against a bank of immobilized capture probes. Saiki et al (87) described a reverse hybridization procedure utilizing immobilized capture probes for detection of several specific allelic mutations in human HLA-DQA DNA types. One could achieve high incorporation of biotin by incorporating biotin-labeled nucleotides rather than using 5'-end labeled biotinylated primers during PCR amplifications, thereby reducing 10-fold the amount of biotin-labeled DNA that could be detected using the immobilized capture probes. Abbott et al (1) reported similar findings. The biotin-labeled amplified product is captured by an immobilized nonlabeled probe—the reverse of the typical reaction in which the target is immobilized and the probe is labeled.

One can use several methods to immobilize hybridization probes. In a relatively simple approach, long homomeric tails are added to the 3' end of oligomeric probes by the use of terminal deoxyribonucleotydltransferase and the tailed probes are then attached to nylon membranes through UV irradiation (7, 87). Because the tails are much longer than the probe, they are preferentially bound to the membrane and the probes function normally. Single-base-pair differences can still be detected (87). In general, long poly (dT) tails of several hundred bases produce the most efficient immobilization because of the efficiency at which light-activated thymidine reacts with primary amines present in nylon. However, when the intensity of the UV light source cannot be carefully controlled, less-reactive poly (dC) tail may be more desirable for preventing excessive binding of the tail to the membranes.

Bej et al (7) used hybridization to immobilize poly-dT-tailed capture probes with a dot- or slot-blot approach to detect *Legionella* and coliform bacteria in environmental waters. Hybridization of biotin-labeled amplified DNA, in which the biotin was incorporated during PCR amplification from biotinylated-dUTP, to immobilized 400-dT-tailed capture probes permitted specific and sensitive detection of target gene sequences. The sensitivity of colorimetric detection achieved by PCR amplification of target DNA was equivalent to 1–2 bacterial cells, which is the same level of sensitivity obtained with radioactive detection.

Running & Urdea (84) linked oligomeric probes to polystyrene plates by first coating the plates with the polypeptide poly (Lys-HBr, Phe) and then coupling an oligomeric probe synthesized with an alkylamine linker to the coated plate. Immobilizing probes in this fashion made them available for direct hybridization. Using a different approach that doesn't require a probe, Kemp et al (51) generated a peptide fusion between glutathione S-transferase

(GST) and the GNC4 DNA, binding the protein from *Saccharomyces cerevisiae* (GST-GNC4), and coated it onto microtiter wells. PCR was performed with one primer containing the consensus sequence recognized by GNC4 and another containing a biotin molecule. After PCR amplification, the amplified product was introduced into the GST-GNC4-coated wells where GNC4 bound amplified product containing the incorporated consensus binding sequence. The biotin of the second primer was then detected using a standard colorimetric detection system.

Because these methods utilize microtiter plates and colorimetric detection methods, robotic techniques can be used to dispense reagents, wash the wells, and perform the color-generating reaction (91). Positive reactions can be rapidly determined and the data analyzed using an automated spectrophotometric plate reader. Large numbers of environmental samples (e.g. standard water quality analysis) could be processed rapidly with a great degree of reproducibility.

USE OF PCR TO DETECT MICROORGANISMS IN ENVIRONMENTAL SAMPLES

Detection of Genetically Engineered Microorganisms

We (98) used the polymerase chain reaction (PCR) to amplify a 1.0-kilobase (kb) probe-specific region of DNA from the herbicide-degrading bacterium *Pseudomonas cepacia* AC1100 to increase the sensitivity of dot-blot detection of the organism. The 1.0-kb region was an integral portion of a larger 1.3-kb repeat sequence present as 15 to 20 copies on the *P. cepacia* AC1100 genome. PCR was performed by melting the target DNA, annealing 24-base oligonucleotide primers to unique sequences flanking the 1.0-kb region, and performing extension reactions with DNA polymerase. After extension, the DNA was again melted, and the procedure was repeated for a total of 25 to 30 cycles. After amplification, the reaction mixture was transferred to nylon filters and hybridized against radiolabeled 1.0-kb fragment probe DNA. Amplified target DNA was detectable in samples initially containing as little as 0.3 pg of target. The addition of 20 μg of nonspecific DNA isolated from sediment samples did not hinder amplification or detection of the target DNA. The detection of 0.3 pg of target DNA showed that the sensitivity of gene-sequence detection had increased at least 10^3-fold compared with dot-blot analysis of nonamplified samples. PCR performed after bacterial DNA was isolated from sediment samples permitted the detection of as few as 100 cells of *P. cepacia* AC1100 per 100 g of sediment sample against a background of 10^{11} diverse nontarget organisms; that is, *P. cepacia* AC1100 was positively detected at a concentration of 1 cell per gram of sediment. This observation represented a 10^3-fold increase in sensitivity compared with nonamplified samples.

Chaudhry et al (12) also used PCR for detecting genetically engineered microorganisms (GEMs). They cloned 0.3-kb napier grass *(Pennisetum purpureum)* genomic DNA that did not hybridize to DNAs isolated from various microorganisms, soil sediments, and aquatic environments into a derivative of a 2,4-dichlorophenoxyacetic acid–degradative plasmid, pRC10, and transferred the construct into *E. coli.* This genetically altered microorganism was seeded into filter-sterilized lake and sewage-water samples (10^4/ml). The PCR method amplified and detected the 0.3-kb DNA marker of the GEM even after 10 to 14 days of incubation. The PCR method required only picogram amounts of DNA and had an advantage over the plate count technique, which can detect only culturable microorganisms. They concluded that the method may be useful for monitoring GEMS in complex environments, where discrimination between GEMs and indigenous microorganisms is either difficult or requires time-consuming tests.

Detection of Indicator Organisms and Pathogens

PCR is useful for the identification of clinically important pathogens (10, 36, 55) and can be similarly applied for environmental surveillance (2). Bej et al (8) used PCR amplification and gene probe detection of regions of two genes, *lacZ* and *lamB,* to detect coliform bacteria in environmental waters. Amplification of a segment of the coding region of *E. coli lacZ* using a PCR-primer annealing temperature of 50°C detected *E. coli* and other coliform bacteria (including *Shigella* spp.) but not *Salmonella* spp. and noncoliform bacteria. Amplification of a region of *E. coli lamB* using a primer annealing temperature of 50°C selectively detected *E. coli* and *Salmonella* and *Shigella* spp. PCR amplification and radiolabeled gene probes detected as little as 1 to 10 fg of genomic *E. coli* DNA and as few as 1 to 5 viable *E. coli* cells in 100 ml of water. Thus, they demonstrated the potential use of PCR amplification of *lacZ* and *lamB* as a method to detect indicators of fecal contamination of water. They showed that amplification of *lamB* in particular permits detection of *E. coli* and enteric pathogens (*Salmonella* and *Shigella* spp.) with the necessary specificity and sensitivity for monitoring the bacteriological quality of water so as to ensure the safety of water supplies.

They also developed a method for the detection of the fecal coliform bacterium *E. coli* using PCR and gene probes based upon amplifying regions of the *uid* gene that code for β-glucuronidase—expression of which forms the basis for fecal coliform detection by the commercially available Colilert method (A. K. Bej, personal communication). Amplification and gene probe detection of four different regions of *uid* specifically detected *E. coli* and *Shigella* species including β-glucuronidase–negative strains of *E. coli;* no amplification was observed for other coliform and nonenteric bacteria.

Starnbach et al (97) reported the detection of *Legionella pneumophila* using amplification of a fragment of DNA of unknown function from *Legionella* spp. using PCR. The sensitivity of detection was equivalent to 35 colony-forming units detected by viable plating. Mahbubani et al (67) developed a method for the detection of *Legionella* spp. in environmental water sources based upon PCR and gene probes. All species of *Legionella,* including all 15 serogroups of *L. pneumophila* tested, were detected using PCR amplification of a 104-bp DNA sequence that codes for a region of 5S rRNA followed by radiolabeled oligoprobe hybridization to an internal region of the amplified DNA. Strains of *L. pneumophila* (all serogroups) were specifically detected based upon amplification of a portion of the coding region of the macrophage infectivity potentiator *(mip)* gene. *Pseudomonas* spp. that exhibit antigenic cross-reactivity in serological detection methods did not produce positive signals in the PCR-gene probe method using Southern blot analyses. Single-cell, single-gene *Legionella* detection was achieved with the PCR-gene probe methods.

M. H. Mahbubani (personal communication) investigated the ability of PCR-gene probe methods to detect viable *L. pneumophila* in water by examining bacterial cells exposed to biocide or elevated temperature for varying times. Both viable culturable and viable nonculturable cells of *L. pneumophila,* formed during exposure to hypochlorite, showed positive PCR amplification, whereas nonviable cells did not. Viable cells of *L. pneumophila* were also specifically detected using *mip* mRNA as the target, reverse transcription to form cDNA, and PCR to amplify the signal. When cells were killed by elevated temperature, only viable culturable cells were detected, and detection of these cells corresponded precisely with positive PCR amplification.

QUANTITATION OF PCR-AMPLIFIED PRODUCT

Quantification of DNA Target Sequence

Quantitative estimates of a target population based on PCR reaction products are hampered by the fact that the amount of PCR products formed during the reaction increases exponentially; therefore, minute differences in any of the parameters that affect the efficiency of amplification can dramatically affect the outcome of the reaction. Gilliland et al (28, 29) developed a competitive PCR scheme in which target DNA is quantified by co-amplifying target DNA in the presence of known quantities of a competitive DNA. In effect, they used an internal standard that competes for the same reagents as the target templates. In their work, competitive DNA (chromosomal) was amplified by the same primer set as the target DNA (cDNA), but it contained a small internal sequence and, thus, produced a larger reaction product. Because the primers and their sites on the two templates are identical, the two DNAs should be amplified with the same efficiency, provided the amplification of the competitive DNA is not affected by the presence of the intervening sequences.

By titrating unknown amounts of target DNA against a dilution series of competitor, one can reliably and reproducibly quantify the amount of target DNA in the original sample. One quantifies target DNA by performing PCR in the presence of one radiolabeled nucleotide, separating the products by electrophoresis, and quantifying the radioactivity in the resulting bands. Activity differences caused by the difference in the lengths of the two templates and, thus, the resulting PCR product, are adjusted for by multiplying the activity of the target band by the ratio of competitive DNA to target DNA length. Quantitation does not depend on cycle number or on concentration of primers or dNTPs. This approach could easily be applied to the quantitation of the number of target sequences in an environmental sample by first inserting a small transposon, such as those developed by Herrero et al (38), into a cloned copy of the target DNA. If enough amplified product is obtained, the sample can simply be resolved using electrophoresis and the intensity of the ethidium bromide–stained bands quantitated using videodensitometry.

Gilliland et al (28, 29) also demonstrated the possibility of using PCR-mediated site-directed mutagenesis (37, 39, 47) to insert or destroy a unique restriction site in the competitive DNA. The amplified competitive DNA could then be easily distinguished from target DNA following restriction enzyme digestion after competitive amplification. Again, this method could easily be adapted to environmental analysis by mutating a cloned copy of the target sequence. One limitation of this approach is that under conditions in which priming is rate limiting (i.e. late PCR cycles), the sequence similarities between the target and competitive DNA may allow for the formation of heteroduplex molecules that will not be digested by the restriction endonuclease (74).

Quantification of mRNA

Several groups have also used PCR to quantify mRNA (6, 28, 29, 93, 113). These mRNA levels may provide a valuable estimate of gene expression and/or cell viability under different environmental conditions (50). Singer-Sam et al (93) first converted mRNA into cDNA by treatment with reverse transcriptase directly in a PCR reaction mixture in the presence of specific primers, and then performed PCR to amplify the desired target. They then determined relative amounts of initial mRNA by separating the products using electrophoresis and comparing the resulting bands by videodensitometry or by autoradiography after Southern transfer (96) and hybridization to a specific radioactive probe. A linear response in activity was observed over a 1000-fold dilution range, from 0.02 to 2.00 μg of total mouse-liver mRNA, with an average deviation of 40% from the best-fit line. The linear response to template concentration could only be maintained if primer, nucleotide, and polymerase concentrations remained in excess. Consequently, the appropriate number of PCR cycles for adequate quantitation must be empirically determined for each sample because the number of cycles required to reach saturation depends on priming efficiency and the abundance of target transcript.

Other reported mRNA quantitation methods (6, 28, 29, 113) are essentially the same as the previously described method for DNA quantitation by competitive PCR. Competitor RNA can be generated by cloning a mutant (either with a deletion or intervening sequence or with an inserted or deleted restriction site) copy of the target DNA into a vector containing a RNA polymerase promoter (70, 99). Large amounts of RNA templates can then be easily produced by in vitro transcription with RNA polymerase for use as competitor in these reactions. Alternately, PCR primers can be designed that amplify the mutated copy of competitive DNA while at the same time insert a copy of a RNA polymerase promoter sequence (88, 116). PCR results in the production of large quantities of promoter-containing templates that can then be used for the production of RNA transcripts. This method eliminates the need for subcloning of the mutant template, for plasmid isolation, and for restriction digestion, and it allows for tailoring the length of the resulting RNA transcript without restriction enzyme digestion.

To quantify the specific mRNA, both the target and the competitor must first be converted to cDNA by the use of reverse transcriptase. This process can be done in a separate reaction (6, 118), or directly in the PCR reaction mixture by adding 5 U/μg RNA of AMV reverse transcriptase to the reaction mixture, incubating for an appropriate amount of time at 37–50°C, and then performing normal cycles of PCR (93). Alternately, *Taq* polymerase may also be used to reverse transcribe the RNA directly, circumventing the use of a separate reverse transcriptase (46, 110). The ultimate advantage of utilizing the reverse transcriptase activity of this enzyme is that the reaction can be performed at an elevated temperature (68°C) to overcome problems of transcribing RNAs with stable secondary structure. The amplified cDNA is then quantitated as previously described for competitive DNA amplification.

To demonstrate the sensitivity of this method, Becker-André & Hahlbrock (6) mixed samples of 50 pg of target mRNA with 100 pg of mutant competitor mRNA, diluted it to 10^{-4}, added 2.0 μg of nonspecific carrier mRNA, and subjected the samples to reverse transcription and PCR. At the 10^{-4} dilution, approximately 100 copies of target mRNA were present, and quantitative detection was still accurate. Similar results were obtained in the absence of carrier RNA. The method was, therefore, quantitative, whether the target RNA was present as a small portion of a large amount of total RNA or as a large proportion of a small amount of RNA. These investigators estimated the accuracy of the method at ±10% by analyzing portions of an identical titration mixture, but they observed considerable variation with fewer than 100 target molecules.

In an interesting adaptation of this technique, Wang et al (113, 114) developed a synthetic competitive gene that could be amplified by any of a large set of primers. The synthetic gene was constructed in a RNA polymerase promoter vector by PCR-mediated oligonucleotide overlap extension (39) and contained target sites for at least 12 sets of PCR primers that flanked an internal linker region and that were the same as those on the target DNA. This gene allowed them to use the same competitive RNA to quantitate many specific mRNA transcripts. This method could provide environmental microbiologists with a simple tool to study the relative expression of many environmentally important genes without developing separate competitive genes for each target.

USE OF PCR TO ISOLATE AND CLONE SPECIFIC DNA SEQUENCES

A potentially useful application of PCR is the direct cloning of genomic DNA sequences (25, 90). Historically, genes have been cloned from organisms of interest by first generating a gene library of the organism in either a λ phage or cosmid vector (68) and then screening the library (usually in *E. coli*) for expression of the desired phenotype by selective plating, the use of specific antibodies, or detection of the cloned sequence with gene probes. PCR provides a relatively simple alternative to these procedures that may be utilized in many cases in which specific or related sequence information (e.g. highly conserved DNA/amino acid regions) is known. This feature makes PCR particularly attractive for cloning and analyzing mutants of known genes (87), for cloning similar genes from different organisms (125), for subcloning genes or regions of genes where the nucleotide sequence is known (90), and even for isolating genes directly from natural environments (81). Several applications of PCR provide mechanisms by which only limited (48, 82) or virtually no specific sequence information is known (103, 105, 119). Likewise, PCR procedures have been described for directly cloning or analyzing genes that have been disrupted by the insertion of a transposon (21), and PCR has even been used to construct new gene sequences (41, 124), add expression sequences (e.g. promoters) (65, 121), and to insert or delete sequences (39, 49) in cloned genes.

Use of PCR to Analyze Ribosomal RNA Sequences

The use of ribosomal RNA (rRNA) sequences for identification and phylogenetic characterization of microorganisms has been a major advancement in the study of microbial ecology (5, 20, 30, 33, 34, 78, 79, 115, 117, 125). Generally, the methodology used to study these sequences has relied upon the successful isolation of rRNAs followed by direct sequencing with reverse transcriptase and chain terminators. To sequence both strands of the DNA coding for these transcripts, the genes must first be located within a gene library of the organism by using gene probes and then subcloned and sequenced. Alternately, double-stranded cDNA can be generated and subcloned for sequencing (115, 117).

PCR allows one to specifically amplify the region of DNA to be sequenced without developing gene libraries or performing extensive screening. The wealth of information presently available concerning highly conserved and variable regions within 5S and 16S rRNAs (17) allows for relatively simple selection of primer target sites for amplifying desired rRNA gene sequences (5). These specific amplified sequences may then be subcloned for conventional sequencing (30) or directly sequenced using any of the many currently available methods (32, 54, 92, 122, 123). Ginovannoni et al (30) utilized these techniques to isolate and characterize rRNA sequences from Sargasso Sea bacterioplankton.

Cloning DNA and Creating Gene Probes Using Degenerate Primers

Because of the degeneracy inherent the genetic triplet code (16), the exact nucleic acid sequence of a given piece of DNA cannot be deduced from the amino acid sequence alone. For PCR amplification, however, degenerate primers can be developed so that every possible combination of nucleic acid sequence that could code for a given amino acid sequence can be generated and used as a primer mixture to amplify the desired DNA fragment (15, 31, 60, 120, 125). Because of the speed of the *Taq* polymerase (approximately 150 nucleotides/s per enzyme molecule) (26, 43), only instantaneous annealing of the primer is needed to begin transcription, and an authentic copy of the intervening region is produced (60, 120). The thermal stability of *Taq* polymerase also allows the polymerase reaction to be performed at an elevated temperature that may prevent priming by highly mismatched primers, thus increasing the probability of producing authentic transcripts (60).

Several parameters are important for amplifying DNA using degenerate primers (14, 59, 60, 66, 80, 94, 120). Generally, short oligomeric primers ($\leq$ 20 nucleotides) with a limited degeneracy ($<$ 64-fold) appear to provide the most satisfactory amplification results, but longer primers ($>$ 30 nucleotides) with greater degeneracies (to 535-fold) may also provide adequate amplification in some instances (14, 94, 120). Primers with degeneracies as high as 516-fold have been successfully used for PCR (14). With primers of 17–20 nucleotides, great degrees of degeneracy may be acceptable provided the first three nucleotides on the 3' end are a perfect match (94). The degeneracy of primers may be compensated for by substituting deoxynucleotide analogs such as deoxyinosine at ambiguous positions (53, 80).

When using DNA polymerase I Klenow fragment to perform PCR reactions, temperatures must remain low, and yields of authentic clones as low as 2% can be expected (59). The *Taq* polymerase, however, allows the use of much higher primer annealing temperatures that potentially limit priming by highly mismatched primers (31). The first few cycles of PCR can be performed by using low annealing temperatures to ensure priming, and later cycles can be performed at a higher annealing temperature. Alternately, the ramping rate from annealing temperature to extension temperature can be decreased to allow for adequate priming (14). When short degenerate primers are used, annealing temperatures greater than the calculated Tm of the primers may produce sufficient amplification (66).

Degenerate primer methods may be useful for creating DNA probes based on N-terminal amino acid sequences. In many instances, native proteins may be easier to isolate and sequence than their respective genes, and the resulting amino acid sequence can be translated into its original nucleic acid sequence for use as a probe to screen a gene library (57). When little is known about an environmental isolate, however, nothing may be known about the organism's preferred codon usage, and probes must be developed with a very high degree of degeneracy. The short length and great degeneracy of these sequences may prevent their use as probes because of thermodynamic instability of the resulting mismatched duplexes (69, 85). The use of PCR circumvents this problem by allowing one to generate authentic transcripts of the sequenced region (59, 60, 120). By generating the amplified product from a cloned library with one degenerate primer and one primer targeted towards a known region flanking the cloning site in the vector, even regions with very little known sequence can be amplified. The nonprobe (vector) DNA can be trimmed away by digesting the amplified product with the restriction enzyme used to generate the library.

Degenerate primer PCR procedures have been applied to environmental samples, and several methods performed with nonenvironmental samples may also be directly applicable to this type of analysis. Zehr & McReynolds (125) used degenerate oligonucleotide primers to amplify nitrogen fixation *(nif)* genes from the marine cyanobacterium *Trichodesmium thiebautii*, an organism that has never been maintained in pure culture. By analyzing known amino acid sequence information for *nif* gene products of other nitrogen-fixing organisms, including the heterocystous cyanobacteria *Anabaena* and several other nitrogen-fixing eubacteria, they identified regions of conserved amino acid sequence, and subsequently translated the amino acid sequence into a potential DNA sequence. They selected regions with less than 200-fold degeneracy and designed mixed PCR primers (17-mers) to account for all possible nucleotide combinations for the conserved amino acid region. *T. thiebautii* bundles were isolated from the west Caribbean Sea by using plankton tows and were then washed in buffer and frozen for later analysis. DNA was isolated from the bundles using a phenol/chloroform extraction protocol, and then subjected to PCR amplification with a degenerate primer mixture of 126 and 96 oligomers for the up- and downstream primers, respectively. The resulting amplified product was resolved by electrophoresis, cloned into a M13 cloning/sequencing vector, and later subjected to sequence analysis.

Although this method allows for sequencing of only a portion of the total gene or operon (i.e. the area between the conserved-sequence-directed primers), several chromosomal walking techniques (63, 75) will allow amplification and sequencing of regions up- and downsteam of the initially sequenced region. Tung et al (111) used such a method to clone an exocrine protein gene from the salivary gland of a South American bat by first constructing a cDNA library in λ gt22. One PCR primer was then targeted against the SP6 promoter of the phage DNA, and a set of degenerate primers (containing 256 degeneracies) was targeted against a region of DNA coding for a known amino acid sequence. PCR resulted in the production of a 450–base pair region that was subsequently sequenced. Once this nucleic acid sequence was known, new PCR primers targeted towards the now known sequence were developed. Subsequent PCR reactions were performed with these primers and primers targeted towards the SP6 and T7 promoters flanking the cloning sites. Sequence information derived from this amplified DNA could then be used to walk along the DNA in either direction to clone or sequence DNA flanking the target DNA. This method should be applicable to microorganisms of environmental significance, such as cloning catabolic genes from isolated organisms or from DNA isolated from environments shown to exhibit a specific catabolic activity.

CONCLUSION

The polymerase chain reaction permits the amplification of specified DNA sequences. The reaction involves melting DNA (e.g. at 94°C), annealing oligomeric primers (approximately 20-mers at 50–70°C) to sites flanking the region to be amplified, and extending from the primers by deoxynucleotide addition using *Taq* DNA polymerase. The PCR cycle is repeated to increase exponentially the amplified DNA product. The process requires relatively purified DNA that can be obtained from environmental samples by cell extraction followed by cell lysis and DNA purification or by cell rupture within the environmental matrix followed by DNA extraction and purification. Removal of humic material is critical in the purification process. PCR amplification permits the detection of as few as 100 cells per 100-g sample and is useful for tracking genetically engineered microorganisms and monitoring indicator populations and pathogens in waters, soils, and sediments. The PCR product can be quantified, permitting estimates of organisms and specific mRNAs in environmental samples. PCR is useful for measuring gene expression by viable microorganisms as well as detecting specific populations based upon diagnostic gene sequences. PCR is also useful for cloning genes, permitting sequencing of genes, even from environmentally important microorganisms that cannot yet be cultured. Thus, PCR promises to have a wide range of applications in microbial ecology and environmental molecular microbial analyses.

Literature Cited

1. Abbott, M. A., Poiesz, B. J., Byrne, B. C., Kwok, S., Sninsky, J. J., Ehrlich, G. D. 1988. Enzymatic gene amplification: qualitative and quantitative methods for detecting proviral DNA amplified in vitro. *J. Infect. Dis.* 158:1158–69

2. Atlas, R. M., Bej, A. K. 1990. Detecting bacterial pathogens in environmental water samples by using PCR and gene probes. See Ref. 42, pp. 399–407

3. Bakken, L. R. 1985. Separation and purification of bacteria from soil. *Appl. Environ. Microbiol.* 49:1482–87

4. Balkwill, D. L., Labeda, D. P., Casida, L. E. Jr. 1975. Simplified procedure for releasing and concentrating microorganisms from soil for transmission electron microscopy viewing as thin-section and frozen-etched preparations. *Can. J. Microbiol.* 21:252–62

5. Barry, T., Powell, R., Gannon, F. 1990. A general method to generate DNA probes for microorganisms. *Bio/Technology* 8:233–36

6. Becker-André, M., Halbrock, K. 1989. Absolute mRNA quantification using the polymerase chain reaction (PCR). Novel approach by a PCR-aided transcript titration assay (PATTY). *Nucleic Acids Res.* 17:9437–46

7. Bej, A. K., Mahbubani, M. H., Miller, R., DiCesare, J. L., Haff, L., Atlas, R. M. 1990. Multiplex PCR amplification and immobilized capture probes for detection of bacterial pathogens and indicators in water. *Mol. Cell. Probes* 4:353–65

8. Bej, A. K., Steffan, R. J., DiCesare, J., Haff, L., Atlas, R. M. 1990. Detection of coliform bacteria in water by polymerase chain reaction and gene probes. *Appl. Environ. Microbiol.* 56:307–14

9. Bugawan, T. L., Saiki, R. K., Levenson, C. H., Watson, R. M., Erlich, H. A. 1988. The use of non-radioactive oligonucleotide probes to analyze enzymatically amplified DNA for prenatal diagnosis and forensic HLA typing. *Bio/Technology* 6:943–47

10. Byrne, B. C., Li, J. J., Sninsky, J., Poiesz, B. J. 1988. Detection of HIV-1 RNA sequences by in vitro DNA amplification. *Nucleic Acids Res.* 16:4165

11. Chamberlain, J S., Gibbs, R. A., Ranier, J. E., Nguyen, P. N., Cashey, C. T. 1988. Deletion screening of the Duchenne muscular dystrophy locus via multiplex DNA amplification. *Nucleic Acids Res.* 16:11141–56

12. Chaudhry, G. R., Toranzos, G. A., Bhatti, A. R. 1989. Novel method for monitoring genetically engineered microorganisms in the environment. *Appl. Environ. Microbiol.* 55:1301–4

13. Chehab, F. F., Kan Y. W. 1989. Detection of specific DNA sequences by fluorescence amplification: A color complementation assay. *Proc. Natl. Acad. Sci. USA* 86:9178–82

14. Compton, T. 1990. Degenerate primers for DNA amplification. See Ref. 42, pp. 39–45

15. Cooper, D. L., Isola, N. 1990. Full-length cDNA cloning utilizing the polymerase chain reaction, a degenerate oligonucleotide sequence and a universal mRNA primer. *BioTechniques* 9:60–64

16. Crick, F. H. C. 1965. The origin of the genetic code. *J. Mol. Biol.* 38:367–79

17. Dams, E., Hemdricks, L., Van der Peer, Y., Neifs, J. B., Smits, G., et al. 1988. Compilation of small ribosomal subunit RNA sequences. *Nucleic Acids Res.* 16(Suppl.):r87–r173

18. Day, P. J. R., Bevan, I. S., Gurney, S.

J., Young, L. S., Walker, M. R. 1990. Synthesis in vitro and application of biotinylated DNA probes for human papilloma virus type 16 by utilizing the polymerase chain reaction. *Biochem. J.* 267:119–23

19. DeFlaun, M. F., Paul, J. H., Davis, D. 1986. Simplified method for dissolved DNA determination in aquatic environments. *Appl. Environ. Microbiol.* 52: 654–59

20. Delong, E. F., Wickham, G. S., Pace, N. R. 1989. Phylogenetic stains: ribosomal RNA-based probes for the identification of single cells. *Science* 243:1360–63

21. Earp, D. J., Lowe, B., Baker, B. 1990. Amplification of genomic sequences flanking transposable elements in host and heterologous plants: a tool for transposon tagging and genomic characterization. *Nucleic Acids Res.* 18:3271–79

22. Erlich, H. A., ed. 1989. *PCR Technology: Principles and Applications for DNA Amplification.* New York: Stockton. 246 pp.

23. Faegri, A., Torsvik, V. L., Goksoyr, J. 1977. Bacterial and fungal activities in soil: separation of bacteria by a rapid centrifugation technique. *Soil Biol. Biochem.* 9:105–12

24. Fuhrman, J. A., Comeau, D. E., Hagström, A., Cham, A. M. 1988. Extraction from natural planktonic microorganisms of DNA suitable for molecular biological studies. *Appl. Environ. Microbiol.* 54:1426–29

25. Fuqua, S. A. W., Fitzgerald, S. D., McGuire, W. L. 1990. A simple polymerase chain reaction method for detection and cloning of low-abundance transcripts. *BioTechniques* 9:206–11

26. Gelfand, D. H., White, T. J. 1990. Thermostable DNA polymerases. See Ref. 42, pp. 129–41

27. Gibbs, R. A. 1990. DNA amplification by the polymerase chain reaction. *Anal. Chem.* 62:1202–14

28. Gilliland, G., Perrin, S., Blanchard, K., Bunn, H. F. 1990. Analysis of cytokine mRNA and DNA: Detection and quantitation by competitive polymerase chain reaction. *Proc. Natl. Acad. Sci. USA* 87:2725–29

29. Gilliland, G., Perrin, S., Bunn, H. F. 1990. Competitive PCR for quantitation of mRNA. See Ref. 42, pp. 60–69

30. Giovannoni, S. J., Britschgi, T. B., Moyer, C. L., Field, K. G. 1990. Genetic diversity in Sargasso Sea bacterioplankton. *Nature* 345:60–62

31. Girgis, S. I., Alevizaki, M., Denny, P., Ferrier, G. J. M., Legon, S. 1988.

Generation of DNA probes for peptides with highly degenerate codons using mixed primer PCR. *Nucleic Acids Res.* 16:10371

32. Gyllensten, U. 1989. Direct sequencing of in vitro amplified DNA. See Ref. 22, pp. 45–60

33. Hahn, D., Kester, R., Starrenburg, M. J. C., Akkermans, A. D. L. 1990. Extraction of ribosomal RNA from soil for the detection of *Frankia* with oligonucleotide probes. *Arch. Microbiol.* 154: 329–35

34. Hahn, D., Starrenburg, M. J. C., Akkermans, A. D. L. 1990. Oligonucleotide probes that hybridize with rRNA as a tool to study *Frankia* strains in root nodules. *Appl. Environ. Microbiol.* 56: 1342–46

35. Haqqi, T. M., Sarkar, G., David, C. S., Sommer, S. S. 1988. Specific amplification with PCR of a refractory segment of genomic DNA. *Nucleic Acids Res.* 16:11844

36. Hart, C., Schochetman, G., Spira, T., Lifson, A., Moore, J., et al. 1988. Direct detection of HIV RNA expression in seropositive persons. *Lancet* 2:596–99

37. Hemsely, A., Arnheim, N., Toney, M. D., Cortopassi, G., Galas, D. J. 1989. A simple method for site-directed mutagenesis using the polymerase chain reaction. *Nucleic Acids Res.* 17:6545–51

38. Herrero, M., de Lorenzo, V., Timmis, K. N. 1990. Transposon vectors containing non-antibiotic resistance markers for cloning and stable chromosomal insertion of cloned DNA in gram-negative bacteria. *J. Bacteriol.* 172:6557–67

39. Ho, S. N., Hunt, H. D., Horton, R. M., Pullen, J. K., Pease, L. R. 1989. Site-directed mutagenesis by overlap extension using the polymerase chain reaction. *Gene* 77:51–57

40. Holben, W. E., Jansson, J. K., Chelm, B. K., Tiedje, J. M. 1988. DNA probe methods for the detection of specific microorganisms in the soil bacterial community. *Appl. Environ. Microbiol.* 54:703–11

41. Horton, R. M., Hunt, H. D., Ho, S. N., Pullen, J. K., Pease, L. R. 1989. Engineering hybrid genes without the use of restriction enzymes: gene splicing by overlap extension. *Gene* 77:61–68

42. Innis, M., Gelfand, D., Sninsky, D., White, T., eds. 1990. *PCR Protocols: A Guide to Methods and Applications.* New York: Academic. 482 pp.

43. Innis, M. A., Gelfand, D. H. 1990. Optimization of PCRs. See Ref. 42, pp. 3–12

44. Innis, M. A., Myambo, K. B., Gelfand,

D. H., Brow, M. A. D. 1988. DNA sequencing with *Thermus aquaticus* DNA polymerase and direct sequencing of polymerase chain reaction-amplified DNA. *Proc. Natl. Acad. Sci. USA* 85:9436–40

45. Jansson, J. K., Holben, W. E., Tiedje, J. M. 1989. Detection in soil of a deletion in an engineered DNA sequence by using gene probes. *Appl. Environ. Microbiol.* 55:3022–25

46. Jones, M. D., Foulkes, N. S. 1989. Reverse transcription of mRNA by *Thermus aquaticus* DNA polymerase. *Nucleic Acids Res.* 17:8387–88

47. Kadowaki, H., Kadowaki, T., Wondisford, F. E., Taylor, S. I. 1989. Use of the polymerase chain reaction catalyzed by *Taq* DNA polymerase for site-specific mutagenesis. *Gene* 76:161–66

48. Kalman, M., Kalman, E. T., Cashel, M. 1990. Polymerase chain reaction (PCR) with a single specific primer. *Biochem. Biophys. Res. Commun.* 167:504–6

49. Kammann, M., Laufs, J., Schell, J., Gronenborn, B. 1989. Rapid insertional mutagenesis of DNA by polymerase chain reaction (PCR). *Nucleic Acids Res.* 17:5404

50. Kawasaki, E. S., Wang, A. M. 1989. Detection of gene expression. See Ref. 22, pp. 89–97

51. Kemp, D. J., Smith, D. B., Foote, S. J., Samaras, N., Peterson, M. G. 1989. Colorimetric detection of specific DNA segments amplified by polymerase chain reaction. *Proc. Natl. Acad. Sci. USA* 86:2423–27

52. Kim, H.-S., Smithies, O. 1988. Recombinant fragment assay for gene targeting based on the polymerase chain reaction. *Nucleic Acid Res.* 16:8887–8903

53. Knoth, K., Roberts, S., Poteet, C., Tamkun, M. 1988. Highly degenerate, inosine-containing primers specifically amplify rare cDNA using the polymerase chain reaction. *Nucleic Acids Res.* 16:10932

54. Kusukawa, N., Uemori, T., Kato, I. 1990. Rapid and reliable protocol for direct sequencing of material amplified by the polymerase chain reaction. *BioTechniques* 9:66–72

55. Kwok, S., Ehrlich, G., Poiesz, B., Kalish, R., Sninsky, J. J. 1988. Enzymatic amplification of HTLV-1 viral sequences from peripheral blood mononuclear cells and infected tissues. *Blood* 72:1117–23

56. Lanzillo, J. J. 1990. Preparation of dioxigenin-labeled probes by the polymerase chain reaction. *BioTechniques* 8:621–22

57. Lathe, R. 1985. Synthetic oligonucleotide probes deduced from amino acid sequence data. Theoretical and practical considerations. *J. Mol. Biol.* 183:1–12

58. Lawyer, F. C., Stoffel, S., Saiki, R. K., Myambo, K., Drummond, R., Gelfand, D. H. 1989. Isolation, characterization and expression in *Escherichia coli* of the DNA polymerase gene from *Thermus aquaticus*. *J. Biol. Chem.* 264:6427–37

59. Lee, C. C., Wu, X., Gibbs, R. A., Cook, R. G., Munzy, D. M., et al. 1988. Generation of cDNA probes directed by amino acid sequence: cloning of Urate oxidase. *Science* 239:1288–91

60. Lee, C. C., Caskey, C. T. 1990. cDNA cloning using degenerate primers. See Ref. 42, pp. 47–53

61. Lee, S., Fuhrman, J. A. 1990. DNA hybridization to compare species compositions of natural bacterioplankton assemblages. *Appl. Environ. Microbiol.* 56:739–46

62. Levenson, C., Chang, C. 1990. Nonisotopically labeled probes and primers. See Ref. 42, pp. 99–112

63. Lin, C.-S., Aebersold, R. H., Leavitt, J. 1990. Correction of the N-terminal sequences of the human plastin isoforms by using anchored polymerase chain reaction: identification of a potential calcium-binding domain. *Mol. Cell. Biol.* 10:1818–21

64. Lo, Y.-M. D., Mehal, W. Z., Fleming, K. A. 1990. Incorporation of biotinylated dUTP. See Ref. 42, pp. 113–18

65. MacFerrin, K. D., Terranova, M. P., Schreiber, S. L., Verdine, G. L. 1990. Overproduction and dissection of proteins by the expression-cassette polymerase chain reaction. *Proc. Natl. Acad. Sci. USA* 87:1937–41

66. Mack, D. H., Sninsky, J. J. 1988. A sensitive method for the identification of uncharacterized viruses related to known virus groups: Hepadnavirus model system. *Proc. Natl. Acad. Sci. USA* 85:6977–81

67. Mahbubani, M. H., Bej, A. K., Miller, R., Haff, L., DiCesare, J., Atlas, R. M. 1990. Detection of *Legionella* with polymerase chain reaction and gene probe methods. *Mol. Cell. Probes* 4:175–87

68. Maniatis, T., Fritsch, E. F., Sambrook, J. 1982. *Molecular Cloning: A Laboratory Manual*. Cold Spring Harbor, NY: Cold Spring Harbor Lab.

69. McGraw, R. A., Steffe, E. K., Baxter, S. M. 1990. Sequence-dependent oligonucleotide-target duplex stabilities:

Rules from empirical studies with a set of twenty-mers. *BioTechniques* 8:674–78

70. Melton, D. A., Krieg, P. A., Rebagliati, M. R., Maniatis, T., Zinn, K., et al. 1984. Efficient in vitro synthesis of biologically active RNA and RNA hybridization probes from plasmids containing a bacteriophage SP 6 promoter. *Nucleic Acids Res.* 12:7035–56

71. Mullis, K., Faloona, F., Scharf, S., Saiki, R., Horn, G., et al. 1986. *Cold Spring Harbor Symp. Quant. Biol.* 51:263–73

71a. Mullis, K. B. 1987. *US patent No. 4,683,195*

72. Mullis, K. B. 1990. The unusual origin of the polymerase chain reaction. *Sci. Am.* 262(4):56–65

73. Mullis, K. B., Faloona, F. A. 1987. Specific synthesis of DNA in vitro via a polymerase-catalyzed chain reaction. *Methods Enzymol.* 155:335–51

73a. Mullis, K. B., Erlich, H. A., Arnheim, N., Horn, G. T., Saiki, R. K., Scharf, S. J. 1987. *US patent No. 4,683,202*

74. Myers, R. M., Sheffield, V. C., Cox, D. R. 1989. Mutation detection by PCR, GC-clamps, and denaturing gel electrophoresis. See Ref. 22, pp. 71–88

75. Ochman, H., Ajioka, J. W., Garza, D., Hartl, D. L. 1989. Inverse polymerase chain reaction. See Ref. 22, pp. 105–111

76. Ogram, A., Sayler, G. S., Barkay, T. 1987. The extraction and purification of microbial DNA from sediments. *J. Microbiol. Methods* 7:57–66

77. Olive, D. M., Atta, A. I., Setti, S. K. 1988. Detection of toxigenic *Escherichia coli* using biotin-labelled DNA probes following enzymatic amplification of the heat labile toxin gene. *Mol. Cell. Probes* 2:47–57

78. Olson, G. S., Lane, D. J., Giovannoni, S. J., Pace, N. R., Stahl, D. A. 1986. Microbial ecology and evolution: a ribosomal RNA approach. *Annu. Rev. Microbiol.* 40:337–65

79. Pace, N. R., Stahl, D. A., Lane, D. J., Olsen, G. J. 1986. The analysis of natural microbial populations by ribosomal. RNA sequences. *Adv. Microb. Ecol.* 9:1–55

80. Patil, R. V., Dekker, E. E. 1990. PCR amplification of an *Escherichia coli* gene using mixed primers containing deoxyinosine at ambiguous positions in degenerate amino acid codons. *Nucleic Acids Res.* 18:3080

81. Paul, J. H., Cazares, L., Thurmond, J. 1990. Amplification of the rbcL gene from dissolved and particulate DNA from aquatic environments. *Appl. Environ. Microbiol.* 56:1963–66

82. Roux, K. H., Dhanarajan, P. 1990. A strategy for single site PCR amplification of dsDNA: priming digested cloned or genomic DNA from an anchor-modified restriction site and a short internal sequence. *BioTechniques* 8:48–57

83. Ruano, G., Fenton, W., Kidd, K. K. 1989. Biphasic amplification of very dilute DNA samples via "booster" PCR. *Nucleic Acids Res.* 17:5407

84. Running, J. A., Urdea, M. S. 1990. A procedure for protective coupling of synthetic oligonucleotides to polystyrene microtiter wells for hybridization capture. *BioTechniques* 8:276–77

85. Rychilk, W., Rhoads, R. E. 1989. A computer program for choosing optimal oligonucleotides for filter hybridization, sequencing and in vitro amplification of DNA. *Nucleic Acids Res.* 17:8543–51

86. Saiki, R. K. 1989. The design and optimization of the polymerase chain reaction. See Ref. 22, pp. 7–22

87. Saiki, R. K., Walsh, P. S., Leverson, C. H., Erlich, H. A. 1989. Genetic analysis of amplified DNA with immobilized sequence-specific oligonucleotide probes. *Proc. Natl. Acad. Sci. USA* 86:6230–34

88. Sarkar, G., Sommer, S. S. 1989. Access to a messenger RNA sequence or its protein product is not limited by tissue or species specificity. *Science* 244:331–34

89. Sauvaigo, S., Fouqué, B., Roget, A., Livache, T., Bazin, H., et al. 1990. Fast solid support detection of PCR amplified viral DNA sequences using radioiodinated or hapten labelled primers. *Nucleic Acids Res.* 18:3175–83

90. Scharf, S. J., Horn, G. T., Erlich, H. A. 1986. Direct cloning and sequence analysis of enzymatically amplified genomic sequences. *Science* 233:1076–78

91. Schofield, J. P., Vaudin, M., Kettle, S., Jones, D. S. C. 1989. A rapid semi-automated microtiter plate method for analysis and sequencing by PCR from bacterial stocks. *Nucleic Acids Res.* 17:9498

92. Shyamala, V., Ames, G. F.-L. 1989. Amplification of bacterial genomic DNA by the polymerase chain reaction and direct sequencing after asymmetric amplification: application to the study of periplasmic permeases. *J. Bacteriol.* 171:1602–8

93. Singer-Sam, J., Robinson, M. O.,

Bellvé, A. R., Simon, M. I., Riggs, A. D. 1990. Measurement by quantitative PCR of changes in HPRT, PGK-1, PGK-2, APRT, MTase, and Zfy gene transcripts during mouse spermatogenesis. *Nucleic Acids Res.* 18:1255–59

94. Sommer, R., Tautz, D. 1989. Minimal homology requirements for PCR primers. *Nucleic Acids Res.* 17:6749

95. Sommerville, C. C., Knight, I. T., Straub, W. L., Colwell, R. R. 1989. Simple, rapid method for direct isolation of nucleic acids from aquatic environments. *Appl. Environ. Microbiol.* 55:548–54

96. Southern, E. M. 1957. Detection of specific sequences among DNA fragments separated by gel electrophoresis. *J. Mol. Biol.* 98:503–17

97. Starnbach, M. N., Falkow, S., Tompkins, L. S. 1989. Species specific detection of *Legionella pneumophila* in water by DNA amplification and hybridization. *J. Clin. Microbiol.* 27:1257–61

98. Steffan, R. J., Atlas, R. M. 1988. DNA amplification to enhance the detection of genetically engineered bacteria in environmental samples. *Appl. Environ. Microbiol.* 54:2185–91

99. Steffan, R. J., Atlas, R. M. 1990. Solution hybridization assay for detecting genetically engineered microorganisms in environmental samples. *BioTechniques* 8:316–18

100. Steffan, R. J., Breen, A., Atlas, R. M., Sayler, G. S. 1989. Application of gene probe methods for monitoring specific microbial populations in freshwater ecosystems. *Can. J. Microbiol.* 35:681–85

101. Steffan, R. J., Breen, A., Atlas, R. M., Sayler, G. S. 1989. Monitoring genetically engineered microorganisms in freshwater microcosms. *J. Ind. Microbiol.* 4:441–46

102. Steffan, R. J., Goksoyr, J., Bej, A. K., Atlas, R. M. 1988. Recovery of DNA from soils and sediments. *Appl. Environ. Microbiol.* 54:2908–15

103. Steigerwald, S. D., Pfeifer, G. P., Riggs, A. D. 1990. Ligation-mediated PCR improves the sensitivity of methylation analysis by restriction enzymes and detection of specific DNA strand breaks. *Nucleic Acids Res.* 18:1435–39

104. Syvanen, A.-C., Bengtstrom, M., Tenhunen, J., Soderlund, H. 1988. Quantification of polymerase chain reaction products by affinity-based hybrid collection. *Nucleic Acids Res.* 16:11327–38

105. Timblin, C., Battey, J., Kuehl, W. M. 1990. Application for PCR technology to subtractive cDNA cloning: identification of genes expressed specifically in murine plasmacytoma cells. *Nucleic Acids Res.* 18:1587–93

106. Torsvik, V. L. 1980. Isolation of bacterial DNA from soil. *Soil Biol. Biochem.* 12:15–21

107. Torsvik, V. L., Goksoyr, J. 1978. Determination of bacterial DNA in soil. *Soil Biol. Biochem.* 10:7–12

108. Torsvik, V. L., Goksoyr, J., Daae, F. L. 1990. High diversity in DNA of soil bacteria. *Appl. Environ. Microbiol.* 56:782–87

109. Triglia, T., Argyropoulos, V. P., Davidson, B. E., Kemp, D. J. 1990. Colourimetric detection of PCR products using the DNA binding protein TyrR. *Nucleic Acids Res.* 18:1080

110. Tse, W. T., Forget, B. G. 1990. Reverse transcription and direct amplification of cellular RNA transcripts by *Taq* polymerase. *Gene* 88:293–96

111. Tung, J.-S., Daugherty, B. L., O'Neal, L., Law, S. W., Han, J., et al. 1989. PCR amplification of specific sequences from a cDNA library. See Ref. 22, pp. 99–104

112. Deleted in proof

113. Wang, A. M., Doyle, M. V., Mark, D. F. 1989. Quantitation of mRNA by the polymerase chain reaction. *Proc. Natl. Acad. Sci. USA* 86:9717–21

114. Wang, A. M., Mark, M. V. 1990. Quantitative PCR. See Ref. 42, pp. 70–75

115. Ward, D. W., Weller, R., Bateson, M. M. 1990. 16S rRNA sequences reveal numerous uncultured microorganisms in a natural community. *Nature* 345:63–65

116. Weier, H.-U., Rossette, C. 1990. Generation of clonal DNA templates for in vitro transcription without plasmid purification. *BioTechniques* 8:252–57

117. Weller, R., Ward, D. M. 1989. Selective recovery of 16S rRNA sequences from natural microbial communities in the form of cDNA. *Appl. Environ. Microbiol.* 55:1818–22

118. Wieder, K. J., Walz, G., Zanker, B., Sehajpal, P., Sharma, V. K., et al. 1990. Physiologic signaling in normal human T-cells: mRNA phenotyping by Northern blot analysis and reverse transcription-polymerase chain reaction. *Cell. Immunol.* 128:41–51

119. Wieland, I., Bolger, G., Asouline, G., Wigler, W. 1990. A method for difference cloning: gene amplification follow-

ing subtractive hybridization. *Proc. Natl. Acad. Sci. USA* 87:2720–24

120. Wilks, A. F., Kurban, R. R., Hovens, C. M., Ralph, S. R. 1989. The application of the polymerase chain reaction to the cloning of the protein tyrosine kinase family. *Gene* 85:67–74

121. Wilson, E. M., Franke, C. A., Black, M. E., Hruby, D. E. 1989. Expression vector pT7:TKII for the synthesis of authentic biologically active RNA encoding vaccinia virus thymidine kinase. *Gene* 77:69–78

122. Wilson, R. K., Chen, C., Hood, L. 1990. Optimization of asymetric polymerase chain reaction for rapid fluorescent DNA sequencing. *BioTechniques* 8:184–89

123. Winship, P. R. 1989. An improved method for directly sequencing PCR amplified material using dimethyl sulphoxide. *Nucleic Acids Res.* 17:1266

124. Yon, J., Fried, M. 1989. Precise gene fusion by PCR. *Nucleic Acids Res.* 17:4895

125. Zehr, J. P., McReynolds, L. A. 1989. Use of degenerate oligonucleotides for the amplification of the nifH gene from the marine cyanobacterium *Trichodesmium thiebautii. Appl. Environ. Microbiol.* 55:2522–26

Annu. Rev. Microbiol. 1991. 45:163–86

msDNA AND BACTERIAL REVERSE TRANSCRIPTASE

Masayori Inouye and Sumiko Inouye

Department of Biochemistry, Robert Wood Johnson Medical School, University of Medicine and Dentistry of New Jersey at Rutgers, Piscataway, New Jersey 08854

KEY WORDS: retroelements, mobile elements, retron

CONTENTS

INTRODUCTION 164
msDNA 164
   Discovery 164
   Structure 166
   General Features 168
   Genetic Locus 170
BIOSYNTHESIS OF msDNA 171
   Requirement for Reverse Transcriptase 171
   Biosynthetic Pathway 172
   General Features 173
REVERSE TRANSCRIPTASE 175
   Genetic Locus 175
   Structural Diversity 176
   Enzymatic Specificity 178
   Codon Usage 178
RETRON 178
   Structure and Distribution 178
   Chromosomal Integration Site 180
   Phylogenetic Relationship and Origin 181
   Function 183
SUMMARY AND PROSPECTS 183

163

0066-4227/91/1001-0163$02.00

INTRODUCTION

In the fields of biology and biochemistry, unusual compounds of unknown function have often been discovered accidentally during the course of experiments, and these compounds are later found to be very important for the living cell. Multicopy single-stranded DNA (msDNA) may be one such compound, although its functions have not yet been completely elucidated. This type of DNA was first found in *Myxococcus xanthus,* a gram-negative soil bacterium. The more recent discoveries of various msDNAs in *Escherichia coli* and the requirement of reverse transcriptase (RT) for msDNA synthesis add an exciting dimension to this discovery.

In particular, researchers have long believed that RT is specific to eukaryotic organisms and does not exist in the prokaryotes (36, 37). Retroelements that encode RT have been identified in various forms, including retroviruses, retrotransposons, introns, and plasmids, and are widely dispersed among the eukaryotes such as mammals, insects, plants, and fungi (2). No compelling evidence has demonstrated the existence of retroelements in the prokaryotes, despite sporadic reports claiming the existence of RT activity in *E. coli* (1, 39) and in a halobacterium (20). However, bacterial RTs associated with msDNA biosynthesis are structurally related to retroviral RTs (7, 42).

Thus, the existence of retroelements in the prokaryotes, the requirement of RT for msDNA synthesis, and the unusual structure—a 2',5' phosphodiester linkage between RNA and DNA of msDNA—offer formidable challenges for elucidating the evolutionary origin of retroelements, molecular mechanisms of msDNA biosynthesis, and functions and roles of msDNA in cells. Although a few review articles on msDNA (14, 22, 27, 36, 37) have been published, the present article provides a comprehensive review, emphasizing recent data on RT and the genetic element associated with it.

msDNA

Discovery

Myxobacteria are unique among bacteria in their ability to undergo multicellular development. Upon starvation of nutrients, cells migrate by gliding to form multicellular aggregation centers, which then, in some species, develop into sophisticated fruiting bodies containing spores (32, 33). Because of these unique properties, myxobacteria have been used as a model system for studying developmental biology.

During the course of experiments characterizing chromosomal DNA from two myxobacterial strains, *Myxococcus xanthus* and *Stigmatella aurantiaca,* a significant fraction of the DNA was found to reassociate with rapid, unimolecular kinetics, indicating the presence of large amounts of snapback structures (44). However, an attempt failed to isolate this snapback material using an S1 nuclease technique, which had been successfully employed to isolate rapid-renaturing structures from several enterobacteria (31).

The snapback material detected by optical reassociation analysis exclusively resulted from low-molecular-weight extrachromosomal DNA. When the chromosomal DNA from *M. xanthus* was analyzed using electrophoresis on a 5% acrylamide gel, a distinct satellite band was observed with a mobility corresponding to approximately 180 bp. This band was found to be a highly structured single-stranded DNA consisting of approximately 160 bases. This satellite DNA had 500–700 copies per genome in the *M. xanthus* cell. Thus, it was designated multicopy single-stranded DNA (msDNA). Similar msDNA was identified in *S. aurantiaca* (43) as well as in several other myxobacteria strains such as *Myxococcus coralloides, Cystobacter virolaceus, Cystobacter ferrugineus,* and *Nannocystis exedens* (4). Furthermore, msDNA was detected in nine independently isolated strains of *M. xanthus* as well as in *Flexibacter elegans,* a *Cytophaga*-like gliding bacterium distantly related to mxyobacteria. Although msDNA was not detected in some myxobacterial strains such as *Cystobacter fuscus* and *C. ferrugineus,* the evidence suggested that msDNA may have originated in an ancestral myxobacterium (4).

No msDNA was detected using ethidium bromide staining after polyacrylamide gel electrophoresis of DNA from an *E. coli* K12 strain, *Edwardsiella tarda, Salmonella typhimurium, Shigella dysenteriae, Serratia marcescens, Erwinia amylovora, Citrobacter freundi, Klebsiella aerogens, Proteus mirabilis, Pseudomonas aeruginosa, Neisseria gonorrhoeae,* or *Bacillus subtilis* (43). Because of this result, many believed for a long time that *E. coli* does not contain msDNA. However, a recent discovery revealed that *E. coli* B does contain msDNA in contrast to *E. coli* K12 strains (26). Furthermore, 6% of clinical *E. coli* strains (23, 34), 13% of wild *E. coli* strains (10), and certain serotypes of *E. coli* (25) also contain msDNA. Therefore, msDNA appears to be widely distributed among different bacterial species.

The discovery of msDNA in *E. coli* B was a surprise and came serendipitously, while Lim & Maas (26) were attempting to identify mRNA for an arginine biosynthetic enzyme by a primer extension. They detected a "cDNA" band even without the addition of a primer when a RNA preparation was used from *E. coli* B but not from strain K12. They speculated that this cDNA band might have resulted from reverse transcriptase–catalyzed extension of the DNA strand of msDNA using the RNA molecule linked to the msDNA as a template. Indeed, they identified a specific msDNA molecule in *E. coli* B as described in the next section.

Structure

As shown in Figure 1, the structure of six msDNAs are determined at present; three from myxobacteria and three from *E. coli*. These msDNAs are identified by two letters representing the host organism in which the msDNA is found and by the size of the single-stranded DNA (23).

The determination of the msDNA structure took some effort and time because of its unexpected structure, a 2',5' phosphodiester linkage between RNA and DNA molecules. When msDNA was first discovered in *M. xanthus* (43), a RNA molecule was found attached at the 5' end of msDNA even after treatment with ribonucleases T1 and A. A thorough study to determine the complete structure of the RNA molecule (called msdRNA) was carried out with msDNA from *S. aurantiaca* (8, 9). This myxobacterium contains a msDNA of 163 bases that is highly homologous (81%) to msDNA-Mx162 from *M. xanthus*. The msDNA-Sa163 contains 21 base substitutions, 5 insertions, and 4 deletions when compared with msDNA-Mx162. However, almost all of these base substitutions are in the stem region of the DNA strand in such a way that the secondary structure is conserved (see Figure 1).

Researchers (8) isolated msDNA-Sa163 from *S. aurantiaca* cells treated with ribonucleases A and T1 (RNaseA and RNaseT1, respectively) to remove RNA from the preparation. The remaining DNA was then labeled at the 5' end using T4 polynucleotide kinase and $[\gamma\text{-}^{32}P]ATP$. However, the 5' label was unstable after treatment with 0.2 M NaOH, releasing an adenine ribonucleoside 5' monophosphate. In addition, after this treatment, msDNA could no longer be labeled with kinase, indicating that rA is associated with, but not directly linked to, the 5' end of msDNA-Sa163. Thus, the investigators proposed that a branched RNA is linked to the 5' end of msDNA, which resembles the branch point of a lariat RNA, an intermediate structure formed during RNA splicing. Indeed, a triribonucleotide, 5'A-G-(C or U)3' was released when msDNA was treated with a debranching enzyme from HeLa cells (8). Because the G residue at the second position was identified only after the treatment with the debranching enzyme, the researchers concluded that the 5'-end residue of the single-stranded DNA of msDNA is branched out from the 2'-OH position of the G residue, forming a 2',5'-phosphodiester

---

→

Figure 1   The proposed structures of various msDNAs from *M. xanthus, S. aurantiaca,* and *E. coli.* Boxes enclose msdRNA, and the branched rG residues are circled. The 5'-end RNA sequence of msDNA-Mx65 was determined as UGA through direct sequencing (5). However, on the basis of the facts discussed in the text, an additional 13-base sequence probably exists at the 5' end of the primary product of msDNA-Mx65. Similarly, the 5'-end RNA structure of msDNA-Ec73 is considered to have a sequence of 15 bases, which has not been determined by RNA sequencing (35). Other sequences cited are: msDNA-Mx162 (6), msDNA-Sa163 (9), msDNA-Ec67 (23), and msDNA-Ec86 (26).

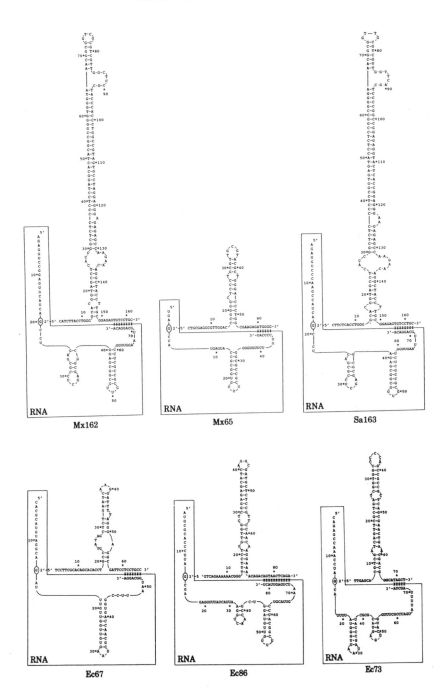

linkage. The 5' end of msDNA was also identified as deoxyribocytosine (dC), which was detected only after treatment with the debranching enzyme. Using msDNA-Sa163 prepared without ribonuclease treatment, Furuichi et al (9) subsequently determined the structure of the full-length RNA molecule. As shown in Figure 1, it consists of a RNA molecule of 76 bases, with the branched G residue located at the 19th position. In the 3' end of the sequence after the branched G residue are two stable stem-loop structures. In addition, the 3' end of the RNA is complementary to the 3' end of the DNA molecule, forming an 8-bp RNA-DNA hybrid. The existence of the hybrid structure was confirmed by demonstrating its sensitivity to ribonuclease H (9). Because of the unique structure of msDNA, it can be labeled at three different sites; the 3' end of the RNA molecule with [5'-^{32}P]pCp and RNA ligase, the 5' end of the RNA molecule with [γ-^{32}P]ATP and T4 polynucleotide kinase, and the 3' end of the DNA molecule with [α-^{32}P]ddATP and terminal deoxynucleotidyl transferase (9).

General Features

Except for msDNA-Mx162 and msDNA-Sa163, the msDNAs shown in Figure 1 share virtually no sequence similarities. Surprisingly, in addition to msDNA-Mx162, *M. xanthus* was found to contain another completely different msDNA, msDNA-Mx65 (5). However, in spite of the extensive diversity of msDNAs found so far, a few structural features are common to all msDNAs. (*a*) The most distinctive characteristic is the short single-stranded DNA (65 to 163 bases) linked at its 5' end to the 2'-OH group of an internal rG residue by a 2',5'-phosphodiester linkage. The G residue is specific because substitution of this G residue with A or C eliminates msDNA synthesis (12). (*b*) Stable secondary structures are present in both DNA and RNA molecules. (*c*) The complementary 3'-end sequences (5 to 8 bases) of DNA and RNA molecules form a stable DNA-RNA hybrid.

Table 1 summarizes general structural features of known msDNA molecules. Extensive open reading frames cannot be assigned in any one of the DNA and RNA molecules. Because many msDNA molecules exist in a cell (Table 1), msDNA appears stable in spite of the fact that the molecule consists of single-stranded RNA and DNA. Indeed, no decrease in the amount of msDNA-Sa163 was observed during a 270-min pulse-chase experiment (9). This stability probably results from the branched structure that protects the 5' end of the DNA molecule, the RNA molecule after the branched G residue, and the 3'-end DNA-RNA hybrid structure that blocks degradation of both RNA and DNA molecules from the 3' ends. The secondary structures in RNA and DNA molecules are also likely to be important for stability. Research has demonstrated that msDNA-Mx162 (38) and msDNA-Ec67 (24) form a complex with proteins in the cell. In the case of msDNA-Ec67, the complex

Table 1 Summary of the structure of msDNA

| | Structure of msDNA[a] | | | | | Reverse transcriptase | | |
Length of msDNA (nt)	Length of msdRNA (nt)	3'-end overlap length (nt)	Inverted[b] repeat length (nt)	Position of the branched G	Copy number per cell[c]	RT ORF	Distance between *msd* and RT ORF	Reference
Mx162	162	77	8	34	G-20	500–700	485	77	6, 43
Mx65	65	49 (62)[d]	6	15	G-4 (G-17)[d]	100	427	28	5
Sal63	163	76	8	33	G-19	500	ND	ND	8, 9
Ec67	67	58	7	13	G-15	500	586	51	23
Ec86	86	82	11	12	G-14	500	320	19	26
Ec73	73	75	5	13	G-15	ND	316	53[e]	35

[a]See Figure 1.
[b]The length of the a1 and a2.
[c]Copy numbers are estimated approximately.
[d]On the basis of the inverted repeat structures, the primary product is considered to have a longer 5' arm of 13 bases.
[e]The distance beteen *msd* and the first *orf*. The RT gene overlaps by 4 codons (35).

contains reverse transcriptase required for the synthesis of the msDNA (24) (see below).

The 5' arms (the position of the RNA molecule upstream of the branched G) of msDNA-Mx162 and msDNA-Sa163 are 20 and 19 bases in length, respectively (Figure 1). These sequences are a part of the sequences that form inverted repeats found in the msDNA coding region on the chromosome (see below). In the case of msDNA-Sa163, however, this 5' arm has been shown to be processed, or cleaved away, leaving a very stable msDNA with a 5' arm of only three bases (9). The fact that msDNA-Mx65 has a 5' arm of three bases (Figure 1) probably results from similar secondary processing of the RNA molecule. On the basis of the DNA sequence of the msDNA-coding region and the fact that the RNA molecule is processed at one base upstream of the a2 inverted repeat sequence (from msDNA-Ec67 and -Ec86; see the next section), the primary product of msDNA-Mx65 probably has a 5' arm of 16 bases (5) (see the legend of Figure 1). By the same principle, msDNA-Ec73 is considered to have a 5' arm of 14 bases (Figure 1) (35).

Genetic Locus

A DNA fragment coding for msDNA was first cloned for msDNA-Mx162 using the msDNA molecule labeled at the 5' end as a probe (43). The probe detected only one region of the *M. xanthus* chromosomal DNA that has the sequence identical to the DNA sequence of msDNA. Later, the coding regions for msDNA (*msd*) and msdRNA (*msr*) were cloned and sequenced for msDNA-Sa163 (8, 9), msDNA-Mx65 (5), msDNA-Ec67 (23), msDNA-Ec86 (26), and msDNA-Ec73 (35). From these studies, one can make the following conclusions:

1. Only one locus resides on the bacterial chromosome for each msDNA.
2. Sequences identical to msDNA and msdRNA are found in this locus.
3. The coding region for msdRNA (*msr*) resides downstream of the coding region for msDNA (*msd*) in such a way that these coding regions are in opposite orientation, overlapping by 5 to 8 bases at their 3' ends (see the top position of Figure 2).
4. Within the sequence of *msd* are a set of inverted repeats corresponding to the stem-loop structure of msDNA (b1 and b2 in Figure 2). In addition, msDNA and msdRNA share another set of inverted repeats, a1 and a2; a1 is immediately upstream of *msd*, and a2 is immediately upstream of the branched G residue within *msr*. As discussed in the next section, these inverted repeats are essential for msDNA biosynthesis because they allow the primary RNA transcript to form a stem structure (see Figure 2). The length and nucleotide sequence of the repeats are quite different for different msDNAs (Table 1).

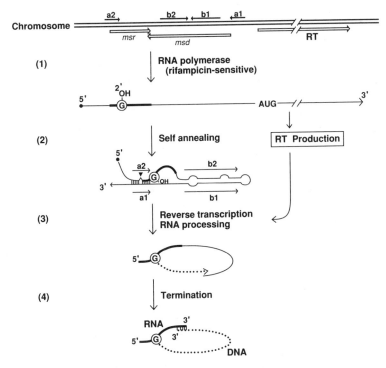

Figure 2 Biosynthetic pathway of msDNA synthesis. The retron region consisting of the *msr-msd* region and the gene for reverse transcriptase (RT) is shown on the top of the figure. Solid arrows indicate the locations of two sets of inverted repeats (a1 and a2, and b1 and b2). Open arrows indicate the genes for msdRNA (*msr*), msDNA (*msd*), and RT. The primary transcript is considered to encompass the upstream region of *msr* through the RT gene, which is shown by a thin line at step 1. The thick region in the RNA transcript corresponds to the final msdRNA. The branched G residue is circled, and the intiation codon for RT is also shown. On the folded RNA, a triangle indicates the 5'-end processing site at the mismatching base. The dotted lines at steps 3 and 4 represent DNA strands. The figure is modified from one by Dhundale et al (6).

5. The promoter for the *msr-msd* region is upstream of *msr*, and transcription is from left to right, encompassing the entire region including the RT gene (see Figure 2 and the next section).

BIOSYNTHESIS OF msDNA

Requirement for Reverse Transcriptase

The first indication suggesting that msDNA synthesis is quite different from chromosomal DNA synthesis came from labeling *S. aurantiaca* cells with [³H]-thymidine (9). In this system, msDNA-Sa163 synthesis was inhibited by rifampicin (20 μg/ml) and chloramphenicol (100 μg/ml) but not by nalidixic acid (100 μg/ml). These results indicate that msDNA requires rifampicin-sensitive RNA polymerase and a labile protein factor(s) but does not require DNA gyrase whose activity is known to be blocked by nalidixic acid. The same results were obtained for msDNA-Mx162 (6).

How does the priming of DNA synthesis occur at the 2'OH of the G residue? If the primary transcriptional product from the *msr-msd* region is much longer at both the 5' and 3' ends than msdRNA itself, a partial duplex or stem structure may form between the sequences corresponding to the a1 and a2 inverted repeats. The G residue at the end of the stem structure may serve as a primer for msDNA synthesis, which uses the same RNA transcript as a template for RT.

Synthesis of msDNA does indeed proceed according to this proposal. A primary product of the msdRNA for msDNA-Mx162 was identified by S1 nuclease mapping to be approximately 375 bases in length, much longer at both 5' and 3' ends (6). Furthermore, a system utilizing permeabilized cells treated with phenethyl alcohol was established and [α-^{32}P]dCTP was incorporated into msDNA-Mx162 (23). In this study, intermediate structures were identified by interrupting the synthesis of msDNA-Mx162 with dideoxyribonucleotides. The [α-^{32}P]dCTP-labeled products in the presence of ddGTP, ddATP, or ddTTP migrated during electrophoresis at the same position as the full-sized msDNA in acrylamide gels. However, treatment with ribonuclease A prior to gel electrophoresis resulted in many different-sized bands, indicating that, during the labeling, intermediates are produced in which single-stranded DNAs of various lengths are associated with a compensatory length of RNA such that the total number of nucleotides for each intermediate is identical. These results provide clear evidence for msDNA synthesis by RT to support the model proposed by Dhundale et al (6). In addition, the results indicate a precise coupling mechanism of RT and ribonuclease H.

A cell-free system was also established with use of a sonic extract of *E. coli* B cells to examine the synthesis of msDNA-Ec86 (26). Researchers have demonstrated that the in vitro DNA product is linked to a RNA, and, when ddTTP was used, all the chain termination products were larger than msDNA itself. After ribonuclease A treatment, a typical sequencing ladder appeared, indicating that the formation of the RNA-DNA linkage between msdRNA and msDNA is not a postsynthetic reaction but most likely the first step in msDNA synthesis.

Biosynthetic Pathway

Figure 2 summarizes the biosynthetic pathway according to the results described above. As discussed later, the primary transcript (pre-msdRNA) appears to contain an open reading frame for RT downstream of *msr*. This transcript is probably processed between the *msr-msd* region and the RT ORF, producing a stable shorter RNA molecule, which is then folded by self-annealing at step 2. The resulting stable structure serves not only as a primer but also as a template. The G residue that will form the branched linkage with msDNA resides at the very end of the stem formed by the a1 and a2 sequences in such a way that the G residue is readily accessible for priming msDNA synthesis. After the priming reaction at the 2'OH group of the G residue by a yet unknown mechanism, DNA synthesis proceeds using the same RNA molecule as a template (step 3). As DNA synthesis proceeds, the template RNA is processed by ribonuclease H activity until msDNA synthesis is completed (step 4).

General Features

INITIATION SITE OF THE RNA TRANSCRIPT   The 5' end of pre-msdRNA for msDNA-Mx162 resides approximately 75 bases upstream of *msr* (6). Thus, the promoter for the RNA transcript is at least 75 bp upstream of the *msr* locus. In the case of msDNA-Ec67, the promoter (-10 and -35 regions) was assigned approximately 185 bp upstream of the *msr* locus (23). However, a recent primer-extension experiment indicates that the transcription starts much closer to the *msr* locus (M. Hsu, M. Inouye, & S. Inouye, unpublished results). On the other hand, msDNA-Ec86 from *E. coli* B could still be synthesized, even if the region upstream of *msr* was deleted up to residue -14 ($+1$ for the first residue of msdRNA) (26). S1 nuclease mapping demonstrated that the major transcript started at position $+1$, the first base of msdRNA, and included the *msr-msd* region as well as the downstream RT gene. Therefore, the promoter for msDNA-Ec86 is probably located very close to the *msr* locus. When the *lacZ* gene was fused within the RT gene for msDNA-Ec86, β-galactosidase activities were 0.2 U and 1.2 U for the deletion of the *msr* upstream region up to residue -14 and the deletion up to residue -170, respectively. These results suggest the possible existence of an enhancer sequence between -170 and -14 residues (26). The *lacZ*-RT fusion with a *tac* promoter fused at residue -14 produced 26.5 U of β-galactosidase activity, indicating that the promoter for msDNA-Ec86 is extremely weak.

RNA PROCESSING   Intermediates detected in a cell-free system migrated at the same position as the full-sized RNA-linked msDNA in gel electrophoresis (see above) (21). This indicates that pre-msdRNA is probably processed by an endo- or exonuclease, removing the upstream part of msdRNA at a very early stage of msDNA synthesis. An extra nucleotide resides at the 5' end of msdRNA in addition to the a2 sequence for msDNA-Ec67 (23) and msDNA-Ec86 (26). For msDNA-Sa163 (9) and msDNA-Mx162 (6), cleavage of the 5' end of the RNA transcript appeared to occur at a base mismatch site within the a1-a2 stem structure, again leaving an extra nucleotide at the 5' end of msdRNA. At the 3' end, ribonuclease H digests msdRNA base by base as DNA elongation proceeds along the RNA template (21).

RNA STRUCTURE NEAR THE BRANCHED rG RESIDUE   The stem structure immediately upstream of the branched G residue is essential (12). When three-base mismatches were introduced into the stem structure immediately upstream of the branched G residue, the synthesis of msDNA-Mx162 was almost completely blocked (mutation A or B in Figure 3). However, if additional three-base substitutions were made on the other strand to resume the complementary base pairing, msDNA production was restored (double mutation A and B in Figure 3). Hsu et al (12) also found that the G residue could not be replaced with either C or A, while a dG residue could substitute

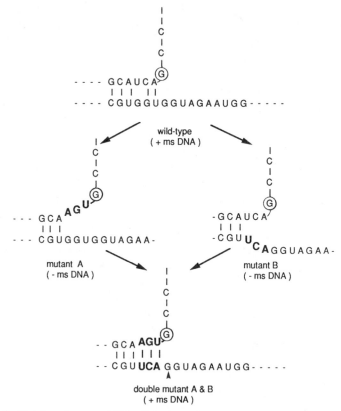

Figure 3 Mutations in pre-msdRNA. Only the region around the branched rG residue for msDNA-Mx162 is shown. The results are from Hsu et al (12). The branched rG residue is circled. Bold face indicates bases changed by mutagenesis, and an arrowhead indicates the conserved G residue paired with the branched rG residue.

for the 5' end (dC) of msDNA-Mx162. In all these cases, the same amount of pre-msdRNA was produced. Interestingly, all msDNAs have an extra base between the stem structure and the residue complimentary to the 5' end of msDNA on the template strand. This extra base, which corresponds to the branched G residue, is always a G residue (arrowhead in Figure 3).

TERMINATION OF msDNA SYNTHESIS   The in vivo synthesis of msDNA terminates 49, 39, 49, 36, 57, and 55 bases before reaching the branched G residue for msDNA-Mx162, -Mx65, -Sa163, -Ec67, -Ec86, and -Ec73, respectively (see Figure 1). Molecules of msDNA can serve as substrates in vitro for retroviral RTs to further extend the msDNA strand to the G residue once these molecules have been extracted from the cells and treated with phenol to remove proteins (10, 23, 24, 26, 35). This precise termination does not appear to result from the inherent specificity of bacterial RTs because bacterial RT preparations were also able to extend the DNA strand when phenol-extracted msDNAs were used as substrates (24, 26). Furthermore, the RT for msDNA-Ec67 was found to be purified with msDNA-Ec67, which could serve as a substrate for the RT so that the RT could complete the DNA extension to the branched rG residue in vitro (24). These results indicate that a protein factor(s) may block the RT reaction at a very precise position in vivo before it reaches the branched G residue. Because the DNA fragments containing only the *msr-msd* region and the RT gene are sufficient for msDNA production in K12 strains (23, 26, 35), the gene for this protein factor does not seem to be associated with the genetic locus for the msDNA-synthesizing system. This protein factor is probably bound to the stem-loop structure of msdRNA, which prevents RT from further extension.

On the other hand, RT has been shown to be associated with the msDNA molecule in the cell, forming an approximately 19S complex in a glycerol gradient (23). Thus, one can assume that msDNA exists in the cell as a complex with RT and a RT-termination factor, and that the RT remains bound to the RNA-DNA hybrid of msDNA. One study (38) showed that msDNA-Mx162 exists as a 14S complex with protein factors. This experiment showed that the sequence of msDNA from residue 60 to 101 is protected from dimethyl sulfate modification.

REVERSE TRANSCRIPTASE

Genetic Locus

Dhundale et al (3) observed significant reduction in msDNA production in a deletion mutation at the region 100 bp upstream of the *msd* region for msDNA-Mx162 (in other words, downstream of the *msr* region) and an insertion mutation at a site 500 bp upstream of *msd*. These observations indicate that a *cis*- or *trans*-acting positive element required for msDNA synthesis is in this region. DNA sequencing led to the identification of an open reading frame (ORF) downstream of *msr* coding for a polypeptide of 485 amino acid residues, which showed sequence similarity with retroviral RTs (16). Similarly, an ORF for RT has been identified for all msDNAs shown in Figure 1 (see also Table 1).The distances between the initiation site for *msd* and the ORF may vary from 19 to 77 bp, and the sizes of the RT ORF also vary from 316 to 586 residues (Table 1).

The RT ORF is essential for synthesis of msDNA-Ec67 (23), msDNA-Ec86 (26), and msDNA-Ec73 (35). DNA fragments required for msDNA synthesis can be cloned into a K12 strain of *E. coli,* resulting in production of msDNA in the K12 strain. These include fragments of 3.9 kb for msDNA-Ec67 (23), 3.5 kb for msDNA-Ec86 (26), and 3.5 kb for msDNA-Ec73 (35). A *lacZ* fusion with the RT ORF showed that the upstream *msr-msd* region and the downstream RT gene share the same promoter (23, 26). However, these two loci do not have to be in the same operon. If an appropriate promoter is added in front of a RT gene, the RT gene can be separated from the *msr-msd* region to support msDNA synthesis (35).

In the case of msDNA-Ec73, an extra ORF (*orf316*) is in front of the RT ORF. These two overlap by four codons (35). The gene *orf316* is dispensable for msDNA synthesis, and the RT ORF appears to have its own Shine-Dalgarno sequence.

Structural Diversity

The extensive size differences of the RT ORFs (Table 1) reflect the diversity of their domain structures. As summarized in Figure 4A, all bacterial RTs are quite different from eukaryotic RTs except for RT for msDNA-Ec67, which consists of a RT domain, a tether domain, and a RNase H domain. Both mxyobacterial RTs contain a large amino-terminal domain of an unknown function, and the RTs for msDNA-Ec86 and -Ec73 consist of only the RT domain.

Even within the RT domains, sequence similarities between the bacterial RTs are surprisingly few, as shown in Figure 4B. However, bacterial RTs share some common features indicating evolutionary relationships with retroviral RTs (see below) (42). In particular, all the RT domains contain the YXDD sequence, the highly conserved sequence in all known RTs (boxed in Figure 4B). Interestingly, the X position is A in all bacterial RTs (see Figure 4B). One finds within the RT domains of 250 to 260 residues 33 identical residues (solid circles in Figure 4B), out of which 11 residues are shared with eukaryotic RTs. The RT sequence alignment has many gaps. The two myxobacterial RTs appear to be more closely related. However, even within the RT domains, their identity is less than 50%. *E. coli* RTs do not show closer

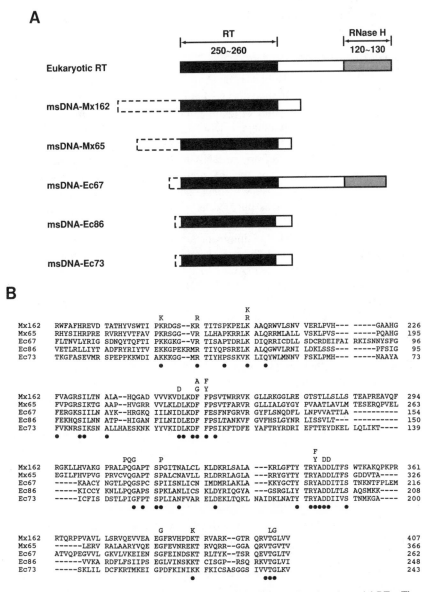

Figure 4 Comparison of bacterial RTs. (*A*) Domain structures of various bacterial RTs. The regions with closed bars and with stipled bars represent the RT and RNase H domains, respectively. (*B*) Amino acid sequence alignment of bacterial RTs. Sequence alignment was carried out according to Xiong & Eickbush (42). Amino acids highly conserved in eukaryotic RTs are shown on the top of the sequence. Amino acids conserved in five bacterial RTs are marked (•). Numbers on the left indicate the amino acid positions from the amino terminus for each RT. Sources for the sequences are: MX162 (16), Mx65 (15), Ec67 (23), Ec86 (26), and Ec73 (35).

relatedness to any particular RTs. For example, RT-Ec73 shows 30, 27, 26, and 25% identity to RT-Mx162, -Ec67, -Mx65, and -Ec86, respectively (35).

Enzymatic Specificity

Because DNA polymerase I has been shown to have intrinsic RT activity (28, 30), earlier claims for the existence of RT in bacteria remained rather obscure (1, 20, 39). Therefore, to identify the RT activity for msDNA-Ec67, a *polA* strain (DNA polymerase I-deficient) was used (23). In this experiment, $[\alpha\text{-}^{32}P]dGTP$ was incorporated when poly(rC)·oligo(dG) was used as a template-primer system. RT for msDNA-Ec86 was partially purified using column chromatography, and the RT preparation extended msDNA to the branched rG residue in the same manner as a retroviral RT (M-MuLV) (26).

RT for msDNA-Ec67 was purified as a large-molecular-weight complex with msDNA (24). The complex sedimented in a glycerol gradient at an S value greater than 19. The predominant protein species copurified with RT activity in the complex and had a molecular weight of 65 kilodaltons (kd), which is close to the expected size of 67,227 for RT-Ec67. The purified RT could produce single-stranded cDNA and double-stranded DNA as well, indicating that the bacterial RT can probably synthesize double-stranded DNA in vivo from mRNA like retroviral RTs.

Codon Usage

Table 2 shows codon usages of five bacterial RTs. One can see that codon biases are very similar to other genomic genes of *M. xanthus* for both myxobacterial RTs, while the codon usage of *E. coli* RTs are substantially different from that of other genomic genes of *E. coli*. These facts have very important implications for the evolution of these RTs as discussed in the next section.

RETRON

Structure and Distribution

Essential components required for msDNA synthesis can be confined to a short DNA sequence of 2 to 3 kb on the bacterial chromosome, although one cannot exclude the possible requirement of other cellular components. The *msr-msd* region and the RT gene belong to a single operon (see the previous section). One can consider this operon as a primitive retroelement, containing only a RT gene in contrast to other retroelements such as retroviruses [RT, integrase, long terminal repeats (LTR), and virions], retrotransposons (RT, integrase, and LTR), retroposons (RT and integrase), and pararetroviruses (RT, LTR, and virions). Thus, Temin (36) proposed the name *retron* to describe the element required for msDNA synthesis.

Table 2 Codon usage of the *M. xanthus* and *E. coli* reverse transcriptases

aa	Codon	M. Xanthus			E. Coli			
		Mx162[a]	Mx65[b]	Other[c] Gene %	Ec67[d]	Ec86[e]	Ec73[f]	Other[g] Gene %
Ala	GCU	4	1	9.3	15	6	8	20.2
	GCC	25	17	51.2	0	2	2	23.3
	GCA	2	3	3.1	9	5	7	21.6
	GCG	43	20	36.4	3	2	0	34.9
Arg	CGU	3	3	13.0	3	4	1	50.3
	CGC	25	26	64.1	1	2	1	37.9
	CGA	1	5	0	3	2	4	3.9
	CGG	15	27	15.2	4	2	0	5.1
	AGA	0	0	3.3	13	8	7	1.7
	AGG	1	1	4.3	7	4	0	1.0
Asn	AAU	1	1	7.6	29	9	10	32.3
	AAC	5	5	92.4	9	7	5	67.7
Asp	GAU	0	3	16.5	34	9	18	54.2
	GAC	24	14	83.5	7	1	2	45.8
Cys	UGU	0	0	0	8	4	2	42.1
	UGC	1	2	100	3	1	2	57.9
Gln	CAA	0	1	3.6	10	5	4	28.0
	CAG	16	11	96.4	2	3	2	72.0
Glu	GAA	5	2	15.7	19	10	9	71.4
	GAG	25	21	84.3	7	4	4	28.6
Gly	GGU	0	1	16.2	9	7	3	42.8
	GGC	28	23	75.2	4	3	1	41.1
	GGA	1	3	4.3	13	6	5	6.2
	GGG	2	5	4.3	6	3	2	10.0
His	CAU	0	2	14.3	8	6	7	44.3
	CAC	15	10	85.7	0	2	3	55.7
Ile	AUU	2	0	16.3	18	13	16	41.3
	AUC	5	4	81.3	7	3	2	55.1
	AUA	0	0	2.5	19	12	12	3.6
Leu	UUA	0	0	0	16	12	10	8.5
	UUG	2	3	7.3	15	10	3	10.1
	CUU	0	0	0	14	4	6	8.2
	CUC	12	15	33.9	2	12	4	9.5
	CUA	0	0	1.8	3	5	3	2.4
	CUG	35	36	56.9	5	3.	3	61.3
Lys	AAA	0	0	5.8	44	22	32	76.0
	AAG	38	15	94.2	23	9	8	24.0
Met	AUG	3	6	–	11	5	9	–
Phe	UUU	0	0	2.9	28	11	16	43.7
	UUC	14	11	97.1	4	2	2	56.3
Pro	CCU	1	0	12.9	9	6	5	12.5
	CCC	10	15	37.1	1	0	0	7.4
	CCA	0	3	0	7	5	4	17.6
	CCG	16	8	50.0	2	1	2	62.5
Ser	UCU	1	0	1.3	11	14	6	20.5
	UCC	12	8	40.0	4	1	0	20.4
	UCA	1	1	0	9	8	9	8.9
	UCG	7	4	20.0	1	1	2	12.9
	AGU	0	1	1.3	5	6	2	9.8
	AGC	5	5	37.3	5	2	4	27.5

Table 2 (*continued*)

aa	Codon	M. Xanthus Mx162[a]	Mx65[b]	Other[c] Gene %	E. Coli Ec67[d]	Ec86[e]	Ec73[f]	Other[g] Gene %
Thr	ACU	0	1	4.3	14	6	6	21.2
	ACC	7	10	60.0	3	4	1	48.6
	ACA	0	1	1.4	16	4	9	9.2
	ACG	22	16	34.3	5	1	2	21.0
Trp	UGG	9	3	-	0	2	3	-
Tyr	UAU	0	1	3.1	28	12	14	47.7
	UAC	3	11	96.9	2	2	1	52.3
Val	GUU	0	1	2.8	17	11	6	31.8
	GUC	7	16	43.5	0	1	1	17.6
	GUA	0	0	0	7	1	2	17.7
	GUG	31	25	53.7	5	2	2	32.9
Total	a.a	485	427		586	320	316	

[a]Inouye et al (16).
[b]Inouye et al (15).
[c]Average from 5 *M. xanthus* genes (16).
[d]Lampson et al (23).
[e]Lim & Maas (26).
[f]Sun et al (35).
[g]Average from 199 *E. coli* genes (29).

All retrons so far identified exist at only one copy per chromosome. *M. xanthus*, however, has two independent retrons, retron-Mx162 (6, 16) and retron-Mx65 (15). In contrast to *M. xanthus*, a minor population of *E. coli* strains contains retrons as judged by the ability to produce msDNA. The fact that msDNA is produced in *E. coli* B but not K12 (26) suggests that some other *E. coli* strains may produce msDNA. When 113 clinical isolates of *E. coli* were tested for msDNA, 7 strains were found to contain msDNA (34). Of these strains, two have been characterized so far, one for retron-Ec67 (23) and the other for retron-Ec73 (35). Distribution of retrons in *E. coli* strains is not restricted to clinical strains. Strains isolated from healthy people as well as wild strains isolated from their natural habitats contain msDNA (10).

Chromosomal Integration Site

Because of the extensive diversity of retrons in *E. coli*, it is interesting to know where and how retrons are integrated into the *E. coli* chromosome. Retron-Ec67 was mapped at a position equivalent to 19 min of the K12 chromosome (11). The element containing the retron consisted of a unique 34-kb sequence that was flanked by 26-bp direct repeats. This observation suggests that the 34-kb foreign DNA fragment containing retron-Ec67 was integrated into the *E. coli* genome as a movable element. Interestingly, the 34-kb fragment contained an ORF of 285 residues that has 44% identity with the *E. coli* Dam methylase.

Retron-Ec73 was found to be a part of a 12.7-kb foreign DNA fragment flanked by 29-bp direct repeats and integrated into the gene for selenocystyl tRNA (*selC*) at 82 min on the K12 chromosome (35). Except for the 2.4-kb retron region, the foreign DNA fragment showed remarkable sequence similarity to most of the bacteriophage P4. Among the phage genes, however, the integrase gene had rather low identity (40%) to P4 integrase. This cryptic prophage was excised from the host chromosome when phage P2 infected the host strain (17). Phage P4 is known to require a helper genome such as phage P2 to provide the late gene functions for lytic growth. The excised prophage genome was then packaged into an infectious virion. The newly formed phage designated retronphage φR73 closely resembles P4 as a virion and in its lytic growth. Most importantly, retronphage φR73 could also lysogenize a new host strain, reintegrating its genome into the *selC* gene of the host chromosome and enabling the newly formed lysogen to produce msDNA-Ec73. Thus retron-Ec73 is associated with a mobile element and can be transferred from cell to cell.

Some ORFs in the 34-kb foreign fragment containing retron-Ec67 are similar to genes of phage P186 (M. Hsu, M. Inouye, & S. Inouye, unpublished data), suggesting that this fragment may also be a cryptic prophage. Retron-Ec86 appears to be integrated at 19 min on the *E. coli* B chromosome (D. Lim & W. Maas, personal communication).

Phylogenetic Relationship and Origin

One should note the distinct differences between myxobacterial retrons and *E. coli* retrons. First, retron-Mx162 is found in all natural isolates of *M. xanthus* so far examined. Twenty strains isolated throughout the world (New York, California, Fiji Island, Spain, Italy, Poland, France, Germany, Turkey, and Greece) were tested for the presence of msDNA-Mx162 and the gene for RT-Mx162 using Southern blot analysis (B. C. Lampson, M. Inouye, & S. Inouye, unpublished results). Without exception, all strains contain retron-Mx162. In addition, *S. aurantiaca*, a different species of myxobacteria, also contains a highly homologous msDNA, msDNA-Sa163 (9) (see Figure 1). Most of the base substitutions between msDNA-Mx162 and -Sa163 occurred such that the stable secondary structure in msDNA is maintained. These facts clearly suggest that both retron-Mx162 and -Sa163 share a common progenitor retron, which existed in a common ancestral bacterium prior to the divergence of the two myxobacterial species. The fact that the codon usage of

RT-Mx162 is almost identical to those found in other *M. xanthus* genes (Table 2) supports the notion that the *M. xanthus* RT gene is as old as other genomic genes (15).

The mxyobacteria are believed to have diverged from their nearest bacterial relatives about 2×10^9 years ago (19). This belief leads to the argument that myxobacterial RTs are ancient and existed before eukaryotes evolved (16). In contrast, only a minor population of wild *E. coli* strains (13%) (10) contains retrons, and these retrons are extensively different from each other with regard to their msDNA and RT structures (10, 23, 26, 35). These facts indicate that *E. coli* retrons were more recently acquired from some foreign sources that remain to be identified.

Xiong & Eickbush (42) have constructed a phylogenetic tree of 82 different RTs from animals, plants, protozoans, fungi, and bacteria. From this tree, they proposed that retrotransposons are most likely progenitors of all current retroelements, from which the LTR branch and the non-LTR branch were derived. They also suggested that non-LTR retrotransposons are the oldest group of retroelements, and bacterial RTs were captured from the non-LTR retrotransposons later during evolution. This hypothesis conflicts with the proposal above in which the mxyobacterial RTs are the oldest. This discrepancy is considered to stem from the assumption in the latter hypothesis that all the retroelements are subject to an extremely error-prone system arising from the poor fidelity of DNA synthesis by RT (14). However, the RT genes in myxobacteria are part of the chromosomal DNA and are replicated not by their own gene product (RT), but rather by a DNA-dependent DNA polymerase of high fidelity. Therefore, the mutations in the contemporary myxobacterial RT genes are considered to have accumulated at far slower rates than those for eukaryotic RT genes, which have been replicated by highly error-prone RTs. If this consideration is taken into account, a substantially different phylogenetic tree could be established.

A puzzling fact, however, is that *E. coli* msDNAs and RTs are widely divergent, suggesting that before the integration of the retrons into the *E. coli* genome, they were replicated by a highly error-prone system. Thus, it is tempting to speculate that RTs were used for the retron's reproduction in that system. The recent discovery of retronphage ϕR73 may help provide an answer to this question (17, 35). Although retronphage ϕR73 has its own DNA primase gene, the phage genome may be replicated under certain circumstances by its own RT using selenocystyl tRNA and/or msDNA-Ec73 as primers (17). If such an event happens in the life cycle of retronphage ϕR73, many mutations would accumulate in the gene for RT-Ec73. An alternative hypothesis proposed that *E. coli* retrons might have ancient origins, having existed in other organisms before their relatively recent (in terms of evolutionary time) transfer to certain *E. coli* strains by several independent events (14).

Function

The fact that for all retrons so far characterized there is only one per genome suggests that they are not selfish DNA. Furthermore, the fact that all natural isolates of *M. xanthus* contained retron-Mx162 indicates that cells with the retron have some selective advantage in natural habitats over cells without the retron. However, under laboratory conditions, no phylogenetic differences were detected between the wild-type strain and a mutant strain that could not produce both msDNA-Mx162 and -Mx65 (5).

In all msDNA molecules examined (Figure 1), RT does not elongate msDNA all the way to the branched G residue, thus leaving unused template RNAs of 40 to 80 bases in length. The sites of this blockage are very precise for all msDNA molecules, but the blockage is eliminated if msDNA molecules are treated with phenol to remove protein components. These facts suggest that the 3'-end structure of msDNA may be important for its function. Multicopy single-stranded DNA may serve as a primer for cDNA synthesis from a specific mRNA template if the mRNA contains a sequence complementary to the 3'-end sequence of the msDNA. In *M. xanthus*, such an event might happen in a specific stage of cellular differentiation of the bacterium.

SUMMARY AND PROSPECTS

During the past seven years since the discovery of msDNA, a substantial amount of knowledge has accumulated concerning its structure and biosynthesis. However, as we learn more about msDNA, more questions seem to appear. Some of the major questions can be summarized as follows:

1. How is DNA synthesis primed at the 2'OH group of the rG residue? Bacterial RTs use their own template RNAs as primers, while retroviral RTs require cellular tRNAs as primers for the initiation of DNA synthesis. Such a self-priming function of a template RNA appears to be an attractive feature for a primitive RT or primitive DNA synthesis. Therefore, to know whether the priming reaction is enzymatic or nonenzymatic is important. Recently, a debranching enzyme was found to be required for efficient in vivo transposition of yeast Ty1 elements (K. B. Chapman & J. D. Boeke, personal communication). This observation may indicate that DNA initiation for Ty1 elements occurs at a 2'OH position; failure to debranch this linkage may reduce transposition efficiency.

2. How widely is the 2'OH priming reaction used? And how widely are retrons and RTs distributed, not only in other prokaryotes besides myxobacteria and *E. coli*, but also in archaebacteria and eukaryotes? The discovery of RT in the prokaryotes raises an important question with regard to the origin of RT, particularly if the RNA world preceded our current DNA world at a very early stage of life (18, 40). If earlier genomes were composed of RNA, RT could have played an essential role in their conversion to DNA. The bacterial RT's associated retrons may be closely related to the original RT.

3. Why are msDNA and bacterial RTs so diverse? Although the retrons found so far are integrated into bacterial genomes and replicated by DNA polymerase but not by RT, they are considered to have existed in highly error-prone systems before they settled in the bacterial genomes. What are these systems? The recent discovery of retronphage ϕR73 can explain how retrons can be transferred from cell to cell, but does not explain the diversity of bacterial RTs. It seems likely that retron-Ec73 was acquired by the genome of a P4-like phage, suggesting that the retron itself may be a mobile element. Recently, a retron smaller than 2 kb was found. It is directly integrated into the *E. coli* chromosome without flanking repeats (P. Herzer, M. Inouye, & S. Inouye, unpublished data).

Retronphage ϕR73 has its own attachment site (*attP*) derived from the 3'-end region of the gene for selenocystyl tRNA and its own integrase different from P4 *attP* and integrase, respectively (17, 35). To know whether these changes result from integration of the retron into the phage genome would be interesting.

4. What are the functions and roles of the retron? As discussed in the text, msDNA may function as a primer for cDNA production. If so, what is the role of the cDNA? As speculated for the eukaryotes (41), RT is believed to have played an important role in the evolution of bacterial genomes. But what is the contemporary role of the retron in the cell? Could msDNA be an enzyme (deoxyribozyme) (13)?

5. Can msDNA be used as a vector? In the cell, msDNA is a very stable molecule in spite of its single-stranded structures in both RNA and DNA. One can design artificial msDNAs, which could be used as antisense RNAs and/or ribozymes. Because of its stability, msDNA may serve as a very effective vector for these functions. Similarly, the DNA portion of msDNA could be used as a vector for antisense DNA if the single-stranded region of msDNA is used, or for amplification of a specific gene, or as a double-stranded DNA if the double-stranded region of msDNA is used.

ACKNOWLEDGMENTS

The authors thank Drs. J. D. Boeke, W. Maas, and D. Lim for making information available to us for this article before publication. We also thank

Drs. B. C. Lampson, C. Lerner, and P. Herzer for critical reading of this article. This work was supported by grants from the US Public Health Service, GM26843 and GM44012.

Literature Cited

1. Beljanski, M., Beljanski, M. 1974. RNA-bound reverse transcriptase in *Escherichia coli* and in vitro synthesis of a complementary DNA. *Biochem. Genet.* 12:163–80
2. Boeke, J. D., Corces, V. G. 1989. Transcription and reverse transcription of retrotransposons. *Annu. Rev. Microbiol.* 43:403–34
3. Dhundale, A., Furuichi, T., Inouye, M., Inouye, S. 1988. Mutations that affect production of branched RNA-linked msDNA in *Myxococcus xanthus. J. Bacteriol.* 170:5620–24
4. Dhundale, A., Furuichi, T., Inouye, S., Inouye, M. 1985. Distribution of multicopy single-stranded DNA among myxobacteria and related species. *J. Bacteriol.* 164:914–17
5. Dhundale, A., Inouye, M., Inouye, S. 1988. A new species of multicopy single-stranded DNA from *Myxococcus xanthus* with conserved structural features. *J. Biol. Chem.* 263:9055-58
6. Dhundale, A., Lampson, B., Furuichi, T., Inouye, M., Inouye, S. 1987. Structure of msDNA from *Myxococcus xanthus:* evidence for a long, self-annealing RNA preccursor for the covalently linked, branched RNA. *Cell* 51:1105–12
7. Doolittle, R. F., Feng, D.-F., Johnson, S., McClure, M. A. 1989. Origins and evolutionary relationships of retroviruses. *Q. Rev. Biol.* 64:1–30
8. Furuichi, T., Dhundale, A., Inouye, M., Inouye S. 1987. Branched RNA covalently linked to the 5' end of a single-stranded DNA in *Stigmatella aurantiaca:* structure of msDNA. *Cell* 48: 47–53
9. Furuichi, T., Inouye, S., Inouye, M. 1987. Biosynthesis and structure of stable branched RNA covalently linked to the 5' end of multicopy single-stranded DNA of *Stigmatella aurantiaca. Cell* 48:55–62
10. Herzer, P. J., Inouye, S., Inouye, M., Whittam, T. S. 1990. Phylogenetic distribution of branched RNA-linked multicopy single-stranded DNA among natural isolates of *Escherichia coli. J. Bacteriol.* 172:6175–81
11. Hsu, M. Y., Inouye, M., Inouye, S. 1990. Retron for the 67-base branched-

RNA-linked multicopy DNA from *Escherichia coli:* A potential transposable element encoding both reverse transcriptase and Dam methylase functions. *Proc. Natl. Acad. Sci. USA* 87:9454–58
12. Hsu, M. Y., Inouye, S., Inouye, M. 1989. Structural requirements of the RNA precursor for the biosynthesis of the branched RNA-linked msDNA of *Myxococcus xanthus. J. Biol. Chem.* 264:6214–19
13. Inouye, M., Delihas, N. 1988. Small RNAs in the prokaryotes: a growing list of diverse roles. *Cell* 53:5-7
14. Inouye, M., Inouye, S. 1991. Retroelements in bacteria. *TIBS* 16:16–21
15. Inouye, S., Herzer, P. J., Inouye, M. 1990. Two independent retrons with highly diverse reverse transcriptase in *Myxococcus xanthus. Proc. Natl. Acad. Sci. USA* 87:942–45
16. Inouye, S., Hsu, M. Y., Eagle, S., Inouye, M. 1989. Reverse transcriptase associated with the biosynthesis of the branched RNA-linked msDNA in *Myxococcus xanthus. Cell* 56:709–17
17. Inouye, S., Sunshine, M. G., Six, E. W., Inouye, M. 1991. Intercellular transfer and site-specific integration of retron Ec73, a retroelement associated with a temperate bacteriophage in *Escherichia coli. Science.* In press
18 Joyce, G. F. 1989. RNA evolution and the origins of life. *Nature* 338:217–24
19. Kaiser, D. 1986. Control of multicellular development: dictyostelium and myxococcus. *Annu. Rev. Genet.* 20: 539–66
20. Kohiyama, M., Nakayama, M., Mahrez, K. B. 1986. DNA polymerase and primase-reverse transcriptase from holobacterium. *Syst. Appl. Microbiol.* 7:79–82
21. Lampson, B. C., Inouye, M., Inouye, S. 1989. Reverse transcriptase with concomitant ribonuclease H activity in a cell-free system of branched RNA-linked msDNA of *Myxococcus xanthus. Cell* 56:701–7
22. Lampson, B. C., Inouye, S., Inouye, M. 1991. Branched RNA-linked msDNA of bacteria. In *Progress in*

Nucleic Acid Research and Molecular Biology, ed. W. E. Cohn, K. Moldave. Orlando: Academic. In press

23. Lampson, B. C., Sun, J., Hsu, M. Y., Vallejo-Ramirez, J., Inouye, S., Inouye, M. 1989. Reverse transcriptase in a clinical strain of *Escherichia coli:* production of branched RNA-linked msDNA. *Science* 243:1033–38

24. Lampson, B. C., Viswanathan, M., Inouye, M., Inouye, S. 1990. Reverse transcriptase from *Escherichia coli* exists as a complex with msDNA and is able to synthesize double-stranded DNA. *J. Biol. Chem.* 265:8490–96

25. Lim, D., Gomes, T. A. T., Maas, W. K. 1990. Distribution of msDNAs among serotypes of enteropathogenic *E. coli* strains. *Mol. Microbiol* 4:1711–14

26. Lim, D., Maas, W. K. 1989. Reverse transcriptase-dependent synthesis of a covalently linked, branched DNA-RNA compound in *E. coli* B. *Cell* 56:891–904

27. Lim, D., Maas, W. K. 1989. Reverse transcriptase in bacteria. *Mol. Microbiol.* 3:1141–44

28. Loeb, L. A., Tartof, K. D., Travaglini, E. C. 1971. Copying natural RNAs with *E. coli* DNA polymerase I. *Nat. New Biol.* 242:66–69

29. Maruyama, T., Gajobori, T., Aota, S., Ikemura, T. 1986. Codon usage tabulated from the GenBank genetics sequence data. *Nucleic Acids Res.* 14: r151–r89

30. Modak, M. J., Marcus, S. L., Cavalieri, L. F. 1973. DNA complementary to rabbit globin mRNA made by *E. coli* polymerase I. *Biochem. Biophys. Res. Commun.* 55:1–7

31. Ohtsubo, H., Ohtsubo, E. 1977. Repeated DNA sequences in plasmids, phages, and bacterial chromosomes. In *DNA Insertion Elements, Plasmids, and Episomes*, ed. A. I. Bukhari, J. A. Shapiro, L. Adhya, pp. 49-63. New York: Cold Spring Harbor Lab.

32. Rosenberg, E. 1984. *Myxobacteria: Development and Cell Interaction.* New York: Springer Verlag

33. Shimkets, L. J. 1990. Social and developmental biology for the myxobacteria. *Microbiol. Rev.* 54:473–501

34. Sun, J., Herzer, P. J., Weinstein, M. P., Lampson, B. C., Inouye, M., Inouye, S. 1989. Extensive diversity of branched RNA-linked multicopy single-stranded DNAs in clinical strains of *Escherichia coli. Proc. Natl. Acad. Sci. USA* 86: 7208–12

35. Sun, J., Inouye, M., Inouye, S. 1991. Association of a retroelement with a P4-like cryptic prophage integrated into the selenocystyl tRNA gene of *Escherichia coli. Science.* Submitted

36. Temin, H. M. 1989. Retrons in bacteria. *Nature* 339:254–55

37. Varmus, H. E. 1989. Reverse transcription in bacteria. *Cell* 56:721–24

38. Viswanathan, M., Inouye, M., Inouye S. 1989. *Myxococcus xanthus* msDNA-Mx162 exists as a complex with proteins. *J. Biol. Chem.* 264:13665–71

39. Vorob'eva, N. V., Nebrat, L. T., Potapov, V. A., Romashchenko, A. G., Salganik, R. I., Yushkova, L. F. 1983. Reverse transcription of heterologous RNA with the help of RNA-dependent DNA polymerase of *Escherichia coli. Mol. Biol.* 17:770–75

40. Waldrop, M. M. 1989. Did life really start out in an RNA world? *Science* 246:1248–49

41. Weiner, A. M., Deininger, P. L., Epstratadis, A. 1986. Nonviral retroposons: genes, pseudogenes, and transposable elements generated by the reverse flow of genetic information. *Annu. Rev. Biochem.* 55:631–61

42. Xiong, Y., Eickbush, T. H. 1990. Origin and evolution of retroelements based upon their reverse transcriptase sequences. *EMBO J.* 9:3353–62

43. Yee, T., Furuichi, T., Inouye, S., Inouye, M. 1984. Multicopy single-stranded DNA isolated from a gram-negative bacterium, *Myxococcus xanthus. Cell* 38:203–9

44. Yee, T., Inouye, M. 1981. Reexamination of the genome size of myxobacteria, including the use of a new method for genome size analysis. *J. Bacteriol.* 145:1257–65

Annu. Rev. Microbiol. 1991. 45:187–218

PUTATIVE VIRULENCE FACTORS OF *CANDIDA ALBICANS*

Jim E. Cutler

Department of Microbiology, Montana State University, Bozeman, Montana 59717

KEY WORDS: adherence, morphogenesis, acid proteinase, adhesins, phospholipases, receptors

CONTENTS

INTRODUCTION 187
   Hypothetical Set of Virulence Genes 188
   Commensal or Opportunistic Pathogen? 188
   Purpose of Review 189
HYPHAL PRODUCTION 190
   Early Observation 190
   Inherent Experimental Difficulties 191
   Recent Observations 193
   Other Approaches 197
PROTEINASE ACTIVITY 197
   Is There Only One Proteinase? 198
   Evidence For and Against Proteinase 199
ADHERENCE 203
   Classification of Receptor-Ligand Molecules 204
   How Many Receptor-Ligand Molecules on C. albicans *Are There?* 205
   Virulence Role 206
VARIABILITY 207
   Chromosomal Instabilities 208
   Antigenic Variability 208
OTHER ATTRIBUTES 209
   Suppression-Activation of Host-Acquired Specific Immunity 209
CONCLUDING REMARKS 209

INTRODUCTION

The expanding population of immunocompromised individuals has focused attention on the importance of *Candida albicans* as an opportunistic fungal pathogen. *C. albicans* is the primary etiologic agent of candidiasis, a disease

187

0066-4227/91/1001-0187$02.00

that can vary from superficial mucosal lesions to life-threatening systemic or disseminated disease. The increasing incidence of *C. albicans*–related illness highlights the difficulty of diagnosing and treating candidiasis in the immunocompromised patient. Overcoming these difficulties requires a better understanding of host–*C. albicans* interactions. An important aspect of these interactions is the virulence attributes of the fungus.

Recent basic genetic observations on *C. albicans* are startling. This strictly asexual organism appears locked into a quasidiploid state with an impressively plastic genome that apparently gives it genetic variability not afforded through meiotic recombination. This plasticity explains in part the rapidity with which the organism can change its morphologic and antigenic expression, which likely play a major role in host–*C. albicans* interactions. Surging interest in *C. albicans* has sparked a large volume of research data that, in simplest terms, may be summarized by stating that *C. albicans* is a very complex parasite presenting the host with several factors that contribute to the parasite's ability to cause disease.

Hypothetical Set of Virulence Genes

Genomic variability may account for varied virulence properties among and within strains of *C. albicans*. One can view virulence traits as belonging to a set of genes with a given isolate expressing a finite number or subset of traits making up the composite virulence phenotype of that particular strain. A single trait of the set is not sufficient for virulence, and not all genes within the set are necessary. Different strains may express qualitatively and quantitatively similar and dissimilar traits from the set. However, each isolate must express a critical number of genes that act in concert and enable the given strain to cause disease. Accordingly, one would expect to find substantial virulence variability among strains, and changes in virulence could occur within a given isolate. Indeed, variability of individual strain characteristics is becoming the rule rather than the exception. The virulence-set hypothesis represents an attempt to explain why, despite intense searching, no one character of *C. albicans* has been found to be "the" virulence factor.

Commensal or Opportunistic Pathogen?

In medicine, *C. albicans* is commonly viewed as an opportunistic fungal pathogen. On the normal host, the fungus has evolved to become a successful commensal. It expresses variant traits critical for existence on mucosal surfaces where constant but dynamic interplay occurs between innate and acquired host-defense mechanisms. In the abnormal host, these same traits become virulence characteristics accounting for invasive abilities as the delicate balance of *C. albicans* with the host shifts in favor of the fungus. The traits would be expected to be multiple, variant, and subtle. As with saprophytes (158), a single genetic expression should not make *C. albicans* pathogenic. The nature of disease resulting from tissue invasion by this organism is a complex issue, dependent not only on a variety of possible underlying physical and physiological abnormalities of the host, but capabilities of specific candidal strains as well. These various capabilities of *C. albicans* that allow commensalism or tissue invasion are regarded in this review as the proposed virulence set.

Purpose of Review

This review evaluates cellular features of *C. albicans* that belong to the virulence set. Numerous basic characteristics of all pathogenic microorganisms capable of living on and traversing the skin and mucous membranes are not covered, such as the ability to grow at 37°C or resistance of the cell wall to host-derived degradative enzymes. The review focuses on characteristics more germane to *C. albicans* as a pathogenic entity. This coverage should include growth rates as a potential virulence consideration, but the lack of data precludes their review. Various aspects of *C. albicans* virulence traits have received recent attention and are cited under appropriate sections. I avoid overt redundancies and cataloging of information. Rather, I critically evaluate works leading to acceptance of various *C. albicans* attributes as virulence determinants.

At the onset, two general points are made. First, many investigators preferentially use pet strains or isolates of *C. albicans* in their studies, while others use type strains obtained from culture collections such as the American Type Culture Collection. Whereas use of type strains has been heralded as the way to obtain results that are comparable among laboratories, apart from insuring that *C. albicans* is the organism under study, use of a type strain does not guarantee consistency of characteristics. *C. albicans* isolates vary with time, environmental conditions, and other unknown factors. Perhaps none of this information surprises the reader because of the apparent genetic instability of *C. albicans* (152, 159, 190), which is not a characteristic restricted to this species (114). In fact, variability of *C. albicans* has been noted for many years. In 1948, George & Plunkett (51) observed and wrote, "Since *C. albicans* undergoes dissociation when it is maintained for long periods under laboratory conditions, we must recognize the possibility that type cultures received from type culture collections may exhibit dissociative characteristics and consequently may no longer correspond with the original description."

The second point is related to increasing evidence that some virulence traits may be important at specific tissue sites and not others. Whereas intravenous (i.v.) inoculation of experimental animals is generally used as a standard to compare pathogenic characteristics of various strains, presentation of *C. albicans* by this route may not necessarily test for attributes such as attachment, penetration, and evasion of local host defenses. Fortunately other approaches, including cutaneous, mucosal, and organ-specific models of candidiasis, are now available (17, 26, 26a, 39, 44, 46, 48, 76, 122, 125, 142, 153, 155, 171, 189).

HYPHAL PRODUCTION

Possibly no other aspect of *C. albicans*–host interactions has prompted as much literature, confusion, and speculation as the relationship between virulence and the ability of *C. albicans* to undergo a yeast-to-hyphal-form transformation. Unlike other dimorphic fungi, such as *Histoplasma capsulatum, Blastomyces dermatitidis,* or *Paracoccidioides brasiliensis* in which the yeast tissue phase is almost exclusively different from the mold free-living form, candidal lesions are usually typified by the presence of yeast and hyphae (pseudo- and true hyphae) (127). So the question ensues as to whether the ability to produce hyphae represents a virulence trait of *C. albicans*. The answer is important because: the two morphological forms may produce different antifungal-susceptibility test results (154) that one should consider during in vitro antifungal drug susceptibility testing; new therapeutic strategies might include agents that target hyphal development; and hyphal-specific antigens or antibodies could be a signal of active disease (133). As indicated below, this experimentation is inherently difficult, and the question of hyphae-related virulence has not been definitively answered.

For purposes of this review, the terms hyphal production, germ tubes, and germinative ability all relate to the same process and are used interchangeably. These developmental forms produce true septa as defined by others (66, 127). Elongated blastoconidial development without formation of septa results in pseudohyphae as discussed below.

Early Observation

One of the first documentations of events occurring upon interaction of yeast and hyphal forms with host cells in vivo led to conclusions largely retained today. In 1958, Young (197) recounted events occurring in the peritoneal cavity of mice inoculated intraperitoneally (i.p.) with viable yeast forms of the fungus. At various times after infection, the emergence of germ tubes from yeast cells was observed, and the tendency of filamentous forms to clump was noted. Furthermore, the hyphae appeared able to penetrate mononuclear cells of the host and invade host pancreatic tissue. Young concluded that the hyphal forms were the infective elements of the fungus and postulated that this observation may result from the inability of phagocytic cells to ingest hyphae. Despite the descriptive nature of the report, Young correlated disappearance of yeast cells with appearance of neutrophils and correctly concluded that neutrophils could destroy *C. albicans* yeast forms.

HYPHAE ESCAPE PHAGOCYTOSIS?   Although the potential size of hyphal forms of *C. albicans* precludes ingestion by individual neutrophils, as observed by Young, the importance of this apparent host defense limitation may be contested. Diamond and coworkers (35–37) have produced in vitro evidence that ingestion is not requisite for neutrophils to kill *C. albicans* hyphae and pseudohyphae. Mere attachment of neutrophils to viable fungal filaments, resulting in frustrated phagocytosis, promotes a respiratory burst and degranulation apparently at the site of contact with the hypha and results in death of the fungal cell (37, 107). Although neutrophils probably also kill hyphae in vivo, the event has not been directly tested and thus the efficiency of this form of candidacidal activity is speculative. Germ tubes per se do not seem to provide the fungus with special resistance to fungicidal mechanisms of neutrophils (186), and germ tubes might be even more vulnerable to killing mechanisms than yeasts (25).

The ability of yeast to germinate upon ingestion by phagocytic cells may be viewed as a virulence trait. Investigators have reported that formation of germ tubes by yeasts after ingestion could represent a means of escape from phagocytic cells (3, 106, 176). When different phagocyte populations encounter *C. albicans*, their efficiency of killing ingested yeast varies (3, 101, 102, 112). Likewise, isolates of *C. albicans* vary with regard to resistance to candidacidal effects of phagocytes (3, 8, 144, 186). Variabilities of *C. albicans* strains and phagocytes make interpretation of experimental data difficult. Whether yeast cause disruption of microbicidal mechanisms of the phagocyte, resulting in germination of ingested yeast or if germination is destructive to the phagocyte is debatable. In support of the former, some evidence indicates that ingested yeasts secrete hydrolases toxic to phagocytic cells, an effect independent of germination (8). Whether yeast cells escape an inept phagocyte by way of germination and extension to an adjacent tissue site or become liberated upon dissolution of the phagocytic cell may be unimportant in terms of invasive potential of that fungal element.

Inherent Experimental Difficulties

The argument that hyphae represent an advantage in tissue invasion seems obvious and widely accepted, but again definitive experimental evidence is lacking. Several inherent problems make resolution of this question difficult.

DIFFICULTY IN OBTAINING SUITABLE MUTANTS   The diploid nature of *C. albicans* (129, 145, 192, 193) would be expected to confound attempts to select mutants with specific lesions. Induced hyphal- and yeast-form variants may have multiple gene defects, and complete sets (parent, mutant, and revertant) often are not available, making interpretation of comparative virulence data essentially impossible. Molecular approaches for obtaining specific mutant strains are now being applied (79, 80, 95, 96). These methods, however, are technically demanding and although theoretically appealing may also yield strains with multiple defects. For example, recombination of a genetic element may not be limited to a single genomic location, which could result in gene disruption at unrelated loci, or pleiotropic effects may occur if the element has regulatory function that affects more than one gene.

Despite expected difficulties in obtaining a set of morphological mutants, a recently described inexpensive and simple selection procedure appears promising (20, 177). In this approach, stationary-phase yeasts of a given strain are allowed to germinate and the filaments are removed by filtration. Then the nongerminative yeast are collected, grown to stationary stage, placed in germination conditions, and yeast forms are again physically selected. This process is repeated several times until yeasts are isolated that have become stabilized and have lost the ability to germinate. In principle, this method is not unlike the antibody-specific agglutination selection method first used on *Saccharomyces cerevisiae* (135). For *C. albicans*, nonagglutinating cells are propagated, cells nonreactive with specific antibody again selected, and this cycle repeated until stable nonantibody reactive cells are obtained. The resultant spontaneous mutants are deficient in production of the specific cell surface determinant in question (191), but as with all mutants other defects may be present.

In view of difficulties in obtaining an array of *C. albicans* auxotrophic mutants in the absence of mutagenic agents (58, 159), the ease of obtaining spontaneous morphologic or surface epitope mutants may at first appear perplexing. However, the selection protocols described above allow one to select many ($> 10^8$) yeast cells during each cycle, thus increasing the probability of selecting a recessive homozygote for a given trait. Other factors or mechanisms are involved, however, because these selection protocols may not work with all strains of *C. albicans* (191). In addition to the simplicity of these approaches and advantage of not using mutagenic agents, some morphological mutants obtained by physical selection give rise to revertants (177) that would be of use in virulence studies.

YEAST VERSUS HYPHAL INOCULA   Virulence comparisons of yeasts with hyphal forms are difficult because of unsuitable methods to prepare comparable inocula. Yeast growth occurs by enlargement of a mother cell followed by formation of blastoconidia, usually resulting in reasonably homogeneous cell suspensions when obtained from slants or broth culture. Cell concentration can thus be assessed by direct microscopic counting. Hyphal development, however, occurs by extension of germ tubes from the original yeast mother cell. Such tubes often are sticky (as discussed later), resulting in clumps of hyphae in nonhomogenous suspensions. Each filament may be comprised of several cells, defined by the presence of septa, which leaves one wondering whether each cell unit has equal potential for initiating disease.

In addition, induction of yeast or hyphal growth requires conditions of one or more of the following combinations: shifting the nutritional medium while keeping temperature constant; keeping the nutritional environment constant and shifting the temperature of incubation; or shifting both the nutritional environment and temperature of growth (126). Investigators have tended to focus on pathogenic comparisons between yeast and hyphal forms with little control for effects on virulence because of the induction method chosen. For example, temperature of growth alters the physiology of candidal cells in ways that may be expected to influence virulence (68). *C. albicans* yeasts grown at 25°C have different surface properties than yeasts grown in the same medium at 37°C, and cells grown at 25°C are more virulent (2). Although the cause of differences in virulence of yeasts as compared to hyphal forms are undetermined, they could result from conditions of growth rather than the form of the fungus. The use of appropriate morphological mutants would theoretically circumvent this objection, but so far such studies show limitations (see below).

NOT SIMPLY YEAST OR HYPHAE   In addition to yeast and hyphal forms, *C. albicans* can develop chains and branches of elongated blastoconidia termed pseudohyphae. Pseudohyphae are heterogeneous in form and character. They may be composed of relatively short elongated blastoconidia or may be so long as to be confused with germ tubes or septate hypha. Often hyphal development may initiate as a germ tube from a blastoconidial mother cell, and then produce blastoconidia or pseudohyphae from the apex of growth or from a septum that developed in the germ tube. The surface characteristics of pseudohyphae vary from nonsticky to sticky autoagglutinating hyphal-like cells. Under similar conditions of growth, variations are noted among strains as to their propensity to produce one or more of these various forms and characteristics. The same strain may often behave differently in different laboratories, or even within the same laboratory (J. E. Cutler, unpublished findings). For example, differences in separate laboratories were reported (see below) for growth and virulence characteristics of mutant strains hOG301 (154, 163) and MM2002 (20, 154). Of even greater consternation is that a given strain may vary under seemingly identical experimental conditions, making morphological predictions unreliable (J. E. Cutler, unpublished data).

Recent Observations

Despite inherent problems, virulence comparison studies on yeast and hyphal forms continue. Investigators have approached the question of hyphal virulence by use of morphological mutants and single strains grown under different conditions. Hyphal elements have also been found to express surface characteristics that differ from yeasts.

USE OF MORPHOLOGICAL MUTANTS   Sobel et al (169) compared the ability of a wild-type strain of *C. albicans* with a variant derivative to cause vaginitis in rats. The wild-type (B311-10) and variant (B311V6) were isolated previously (16), and both were reported to produce hyphae at 25°C. At 37°C, however, B311-10 produced hyphae in various defined media but B311V6 did not (16). Whereas both strains adhered to human vaginal epithelial cells in vitro at 37°C, all five rats infected with 10^4 yeast forms of the wild-type developed vaginitis, but only 8 of 14 rats developed vaginitis owing to B311V6. Even at an infection dose of 10^6, 2 of 14 rats infected with the mutant did not develop vaginitis (169). In addition, the disease tended to be less severe and more transient in rats infected with the nongerminative variant. The fact that the variant was a spontaneous mutant, thus reducing the chances of multiple gene lesions, strengthens these observations. The results do not, however, preclude the possibility that the mutation resides within a regulatory sequence and may have pleiotropic effects. In fact, although a revertant was isolated that regained virulence along with the ability to germinate, at least one other gene lesion associated with a nutritional requirement was detected (15). The investigators compared adherence properties but did not address other factors such as proteinase activity, comparative growth kinetics of the three strains in various media at 37°C, and so on. The B311-10, V6, and the revertant set of strains should be investigated further to substantiate a cause-and-effect relationship between the ability to produce hyphae and virulence.

Shepherd (163) compared virulence of wild-type strain ATCC 10261 with derived mutants isolated after nitrosoguanidine treatment. Mutants of particular relevance were hOG301, which produces only mycelia (hyphae), and CA2, which only produces yeasts. The method of testing involved i.v. inoculation of the particular strain into mice and a determination of mortality rate by 21 days. Inocula were determined by cell counts when yeast forms were injected, but for hOG301 a weight of mycelia equivalent to the weight of a known number of yeasts was used. These observations are limited because the induced mutants likely have more than one genetic defect, revertants to wild-type phenotype were not obtained, dry weight of mycelia cannot be extrapolated to yeast cell counts, and testing virulence by i.v. inoculation may circumvent potentially important virulence attributes. This study is, nonetheless, of interest because the mutants retained their respective phenotypes in vivo, and both morphological types were virulent to mice. The mean survival of mice infected with the wild-type, mycelial mutant, and yeast mutant were 6.4 (SE ±1.4), 13.0 (±4.0), and 9.3 (±2.1) days, respectively. Shepherd concluded that yeasts and mycelial forms can adhere, invade, and proliferate in the experimental host.

Ryley & Ryley (154) also used the mutants CA2 (yeast only) and hOG301 (hyphae only) and the ATCC 10261 parent wild-type, as well as a spontaneous yeast mutant strain MM2002 selected by Cannon (20) and its wild-type strain MEN. In careful and tedious observations on i.v. infected mice, LD_{50} determinations were made; colony-forming units from homogenized kidney counts were assessed at different times after infection; and histopathological evaluation was made of the pathogenesis of each strain within the kidney as a function of time.

These painstaking studies yielded interesting observations, some of which were different from those of Shepherd & Cannon. Strain CA2 characteristically grew strictly as a yeast in vitro and in vivo, but it was not as lethal as wild-type strains, and tended to cause chronic infection. The strain hOG301 produced only pseudohyphae instead of mycelia, as reported by Shepherd, and was essentially nonpathogenic by the LD_{50} measure. The yeast mutant, MM2002, produced a low percent of hyphae in vitro, although Cannon (20) found this strain to be strictly a yeast. The MM2002 strain was just as lethal for mice as its germinative wild-type strain MEN. However disease produced by the mutant was slower and correlated with initial infection limited to the renal cortex, as compared to all wild-type strains that attacked cortical and medullary areas of the kidney during early infection. As the disease progressed, strain MM2002 produced an abundance of yeast and hyphae; the renal pelvis became invaded by hyphal forms, while CA2 remained as yeast forms chronically associated with the kidney tissue. The investigators concluded that hyphae are not required for initiation of kidney disease nor for chronic renal candidiasis. However, mycelia may be important for lesion development within the pelvis. Although these interpretations are limited because of unknown mutations in the strains, this work suggests hyphae may contribute to virulence only at specific tissue locations. Furthermore, these observations show the variability potential of strains of *C. albicans*.

HYPHAL-READY YEASTS ARE MORE VIRULENT   *C. albicans* yeasts grown at 25°C are more hydrophobic as compared to yeasts grown at 37°C (62), a feature that may result from presence of a surface protein (69). A change to hydrophobicity is an event that also precedes germination of yeast cells grown as hydrophilic cells at 37°C prior to germination induction (62). Logically, hydrophobic yeasts germinate more quickly than yeasts that begin as hydrophilic cells. Further, hydrophobic yeasts are more virulent than hydrophilic ones in mice (2). When hydrophobic cells are inoculated i.v. into mice, within one hour the majority of *C. albicans* in kidneys are germinative forms, whereas only yeast forms are found in the spleen. When hydrophilic yeasts are inoculated i.v., only yeast forms are present in kidney and spleen (J. E. Cutler & K. C. Hazen, unpublished data). Although one can speculate that increased virulence of hydrophobic cells results from their rapid ability to germinate, this interpretation is tempered by other properties of hydrophobic cells, including increased adherence (63, 65).

OTHER ATTRIBUTES OF HYPHAE   In addition to physical attributes of filamentation that some believe give *C. albicans* an advantage in its encounter with the host, expression of various cell-surface antigens by these forms could contribute to virulence.

Adherence properties of germ tubes are well established (83, 147, 148, 156, 169) and may relate to loss or degradation of cell-wall molecules (69, 182) and movement or reorganization of preexisting molecules (22, 182) during germination. Recent data support the assertion that mobility of cell-wall components not only occurs during germination, but is a requirement (22). Fab fragments, but not intact immunoglobulin molecules, of an IgG1 monoclonal antibody (MAb 4C12) specific for a 260-kilodalton (kd) mycelial-specific mannoprotein (21) suppressed germination by 81%. The determinant that MAb 4C12 recognizes was confluently expressed along developing germ tubes, but showed a punctate distribution in cells exposed to the antibody during germination-induction attempts (22). This exciting observation awaits confirmation, which could include an additional control. Negative-control Fab fragments prepared in the investigators' laboratory, rather than from a commercial source, will control for trace nonspecific inhibitors of germination that can be found in laboratory reagents (J. E. Cutler, unpublished data).

In support of the observation that specific antibody may affect germination, Grappel & Calderone (61) reported in 1976 that a rabbit hyperimmune antiserum prepared against *C. albicans* inhibited oxygen consumption during yeast-to-hyphal induction and retarded germ-tube production. These workers obtained similar results with a gamma globulin fraction of the serum. The effects were observed with intact immunoglobulins. These results, therefore, differ fundamentally from those reported by Cassanova et al (22), who found germination to be affected by Fab fragments only. However, Siu et al (165) showed that Fab fragments of a monoclonal antibody specific for a cell-surface glycoprotein of *Dictyostelium discoideum* blocks development in that organism. At any rate, Cassanova et al (22) suggest that the antibody fragments interfere with *C. albicans* cell-wall reorganization, which is required for the germination event. A relationship between such reorganization and adherence remains to be determined.

In addition to adherence, other activities usually associated with hyphal and pseudohyphal forms may be important. One report indicates that coordination of physical and enzymatic processes of *C. albicans* hyphae is involved in invasion of host epithelial cells (134). Hydrophilic and hydrophobic molecules, enzymes, and receptors for various host cell proteins may be more heavily expressed on hyphal and pseudohyphal forms than on yeast forms.

The association of these various molecules with hyphae does not necessarily mean yeast forms are less virulent because at least some of these molecules are expressed by both forms. Yeasts produce acid proteinase(s) (54, 131). Other molecules, such as the CR2-like mannoprotein, at first believed to be hyphal-specific, are highly expressed in deep cell-wall layers and in small quantities on the yeast cell surface (78). Depending on nutritional factors, such as carbohydrate source, yeast forms of *C. albicans* may also produce adhesins (28, 118). Using whole vascular strips as in an in vitro model, workers found adherence and penetration of the endothelium by yeast forms independent of germination (87).

Other Approaches

Rather than addressing the question of hyphal virulence by seeking isolation of appropriate morphological mutants, investigators could use wild-type strains alone if infected animals were treated with agents that specifically suppress a yeast-to-hyphal transformation. Such an inhibitor would have to fulfill at least three criteria: specificity must be limited to suppression of *C. albicans* morphogenesis without affecting yeast function; a parenterally administered inhibitor must be able to reach the fungal cells in vivo; and the inhibitor should not affect the host.

Drugs, such as the azoles, markedly suppress germinative ability of *C. albicans* (128) and have been used in studies on hyphal virulence (154). Indeed, some have proposed that the triazoles, fluconazole and itraconazole, and amphotericin B may assist the host by blocking germination of macrophage-ingested *C. albicans* yeast cells (185). Because the effect of these antifungal agents is not limited to inhibition of candidal morphogenesis, the use of such agents in experiments designed to show the importance of germinative ability in relation to pathogenesis is limited.

Another possible agent is a substance purified from yeast forms that suppresses germination of yeast cells grown at 37°C (66, 67). This suppressive factor, termed morphogenic autoregulatory substance (MARS), does not interfere with replication of yeast cells, but other metabolic considerations have not been examined. MARS has yet to be tested in vivo.

Perhaps the best candidate is the Fab antibody preparation that suppresses germination (22) as discussed above. If yeast metabolic functions such as growth rates are normal in the presence of the specific Fab, to determine in vivo effects of these antibody fragments would be of great interest. A possible limitation of the use of MARS and the Fab fragments is that neither completely blocks germination.

PROTEINASE ACTIVITY

The role of microbial extracellular enzymes in pathogenesis of many bacterial diseases of man has served as the paradigm by which investigators have sought to uncover comparable virulence traits of *C. albicans*. Surprisingly few extracellular enzymes have been described, but at least one, an aspartyl acid proteinase, has received intense attention.

Staib (173, 174) first reported *C. albicans* could use serum proteins as a source of nitrogen and the proteolytic activity related to relative strain pathogenicity. Over the next few years, however, the proteinase was pursued primarily for purposes of developing a serological test for invasive candidiasis (175). Macdonald & Odds (109) continued along the serologic test theme, but also modified a protocol (143) for proteinase purification, raised antisera specific for the protein, and demonstrated that the proteinase was in fact produced in vivo. These studies, along with the isolation of a low virulent proteinase-deficient mutant (110), set the stage for the current surge of interest in proteinase as a virulence factor.

This review is restricted to *C. albicans*. However, acid proteinase secretion has also been reported to correlate with the potential of *Candida parapsilosis* to cause vaginitis (33, 34).

Is There Only One Proteinase?

The enzyme receiving essentially all of the attention as a possible virulence factor is a secreted aspartyl acid proteinase. Although the literature covers mostly this proteinase, others could be important. In early work, different strains of *C. albicans* were found to secrete proteinases of similar molecular mass, but differed in properties such as pH optima, substrate specificity, and isoelectric point (151). That is, evidence was produced for strain-specific proteinases. A single protein band of 43 kd was detectable using Western blots of vaginal fluid from patients with candidal vaginitis (32), but whether this represents a single molecular species, or if other proteinases may be produced at other body sites, is unknown.

At least three proteinases have been found associated with intracellular compartments of *C. albicans* (131). These enzymes have distinctly different pH optima and other distinguishing characteristics. One of the proteinases has many similarities with the secreted aspartyl acid proteinase being considered as the virulence factor. Like the secreted enzyme (139, 143, 149), the intracellular one is also an aspartyl acid proteinase that can act on a wide variety of proteins, is not inhibited significantly by phenylmethylsulfonyl fluoride, is inhibited by pepstatin, and is a glycoprotein. The differences are molecular weight and pH optimum. The intracellular form is reported as a 60-kd molecule (131) whereas the secreted proteinase is 40–45 kd (143, 149). The pH optima are approximately 5.0 and 2.2–4.5 for the intracellular and secreted forms, respectively.

Secretion of the intracellular proteinases is a reasonable possibility because intracellular pools of the putative virulence–associated aspartyl proteinase have been detected (146). Release of these enzymes would also be expected from dying cells. Because two of the intracellular proteinases have pH optima of 7.5 and 8.0, if released, they may function by assisting invasion of *C. albicans* at tissue sites near neutral pH. An inherent limitation of the action of the secreted aspartyl acid proteinase is that its low pH optimum precludes activity in such tissues. Therefore, the relevance of this enzyme may be restricted to sites of acute inflammatory changes likely to have a local drop in pH, presumably sites of neutrophil glycolysis (60), or on the skin surface, which tends to be acidic (6) . In fact, the acid proteinase is not only inactive at neutral pH, but at pH 7.5 or greater irreversible denaturation may occur (141), which correlates with evidence that the acid proteinase does not play a role in oral candidiasis (52, 53).

DIFFERENT SEQUENCE DATA   Existence of multiple proteinases might explain discrepancies between research groups on the primary structure of the secreted enzyme. Records on the identification of the N-terminal amino acid of the aspartyl proteinase differ (105, 141, 149). The sequence of a gene possibly coding for the secreted aspartyl acid proteinase and flanking regions was obtained from a *C. albicans* genomic library cloned into EMBL3 (105). The researchers identified the segment by hybridization to a *S. cerevisiae* probe specific for the *pep4* gene, which codes for a vacuolar enzyme, proteinase A (1, 85). The *S. cerevisiae* proteinase A is an intracellular enzyme that is also an aspartyl proteinase, and whether it is similar to either the intracellular aspartyl proteinase of *C. albicans* (131) or the secreted putative virulence factor is not known. However, the cloned *C. albicans* gene may not code for the secreted proteinase. The estimated molecular mass of the nonglycosylated product of the cloned gene calculates, by this reviewer, to approximately 41 kd, which is in the estimated range of the secreted glycosylated proteinase. Therefore, the cloned gene is larger than expected depending on the extent of glycosylation in the final product. Furthermore, whereas the nucleotide sequence of the cloned gene indicates high (85%) amino acid homology to the *pep4* gene product of *S. cerevisiae* (105), no homology was found with the first 24 amino acids of purified secreted aspartyl proteinase (141). These discrepancies could be explained if the enzymatically active secreted proteinase is a cleavage product of a larger precursor molecule. Completion of planned (105) expression experiments of the *C. albicans* cloned gene in *S. cerevisiae* should resolve this issue. Regardless of which proteinase was cloned, the gene will be useful in sorting out proteinases that may participate in pathogenesis.

Evidence For and Against Proteinase

Secretion of a proteinase is a common characteristic of *C. albicans*. Of 103 randomly selected clinical isolates, proteinase activity was detected from all of them, although quantitative and qualitative differences were noted among the strains (151). Proteinase production is also not limited to strains causing disease. *C. albicans* vaginal isolates were obtained from 22 women with candidal vaginitis and 17 women carriers (23). All isolates produced detectable quantities of the acid proteinase, but the highest producers were strains from patients with vaginitis. The ability to produce proteinase may not be a stable characteristic because one studied strain exhibited a high frequency of spontaneous proteinase-negative mutations (27).

The evidence is both for and against the secreted aspartyl acid proteinase as a virulence factor. As with experiments on hyphae, definitive experimentation is difficult and is likely confounded by multiple factors responsible for virulence and strain differences, as reported and discussed by Kondoh et al (92). Proteinase activity may also be more important as a virulence factor in selected body sites, and, as discussed below, may not necessarily function enzymatically.

PATHOGENIC ROLE   *C. albicans* proteinases probably did not evolve for purposes of pathogenesis. The secreted proteinase is an inducible enzyme produced when proteins are the primary source of nitrogen. Intracellular proteinases may function for fungal metabolic needs by recycling vacuolar reserves of amino acid nitrogen (194) and may also act in development as has been speculated for *C. albicans* (184) and other fungi (198). The broad substrate specificity of the secreted proteinase, therefore, is not surprising and makes in vivo function possible. For example, secretory IgA on epithelial surfaces may serve as a host defense against candidal invasion (115, 195) perhaps by limiting adherence of the fungus to host cells (47, 188). The secreted proteinase degrades heavy chains of human IgA (149). At low pH (pH 4), salivary proteins are degraded; but according to some investigators this may not be of significance in oral candidiasis because degradation of the proteins does not occur at pH 6 or above (53). Salivary pH, however, should fluctuate depending on nutrition and oral microbial activity throughout the day. Keratinolytic activity was described as a characteristic of the secreted proteinase (123), and this activity was found to copurify with the enzyme (139). The secreted acid proteinase may thus aid invasion through the keratin protective layer and facilitate initiation of cutaneous candidiasis.

The proteinase apparently can also cause limited proteolysis of Hageman factor, leading to activation of the kallikrein-kinin system, which in turn generates bradykinin and causes increased vascular permeability (77). This effect occurs in vivo and thus may lead to inflammatory reactions associated with the presence of *C. albicans*. Relative importance of kinin generation compared with release of inflammatory mediators through cell wall–induced complement activation via the alternative cascade (93, 121, 136), or direct production of a neutrophil chemotactic attractant by the fungus (29), is unknown. One may argue, however, that acute inflammation will more likely benefit the host rather than the fungus (4, 5, 35, 50, 74), except in patients with abnormal phagocytic cell function.

Most investigators have studied possible effects of the secreted proteinase on the host. However, proteinase activity, as cited below, also correlates with ability of strains to adhere to host tissue. Possible roles of the proteinase may thus extend to nonenzymatic activities as well.

To explain a role of the proteinase in adherence, the following hypotheses may be considered. (*a*) The proteinase is located on the surface of *C. albicans* and, as a mannoprotein, functions as a ligand for attachment to host cells. (*b*) The proteinase modifies cell membranes of the host to accept attachment of the fungus. (*c*) The proteinase modifies the cell surface of *C. albicans* in a way that promotes attachment. The first possibility may occur under conditions not conducive for enzyme function, such as at pH values greater than 6.0. Although the enzyme is referred to as secreted, investigators have demonstrated an association with the cell surface of *C. albicans* (7). The latter two possibilities would depend on enzyme activity. Modification of the host cell membrane could occur in an acidic environment, but under such conditions general proteolytic activity and dissolution of host-cell membranes may be more important than adherence considerations. Modification of the cell surface of *C. albicans*, however, may proceed if the surface pH is lowered because of carbohydrate utilization and production of acidic by-products. Proteolytic action on the candidal cell surface alters hydrophobicity (69), which would also affect adherence (65, 98).

EVIDENCE FOR VIRULENCE ROLE   Postulated pathogenic roles for the secreted proteinase do not prove its virulence-associated status. Perhaps the strongest evidence for the acid proteinase as a virulence factor is invasion of keratinized skin by *C. albicans* and correlation with adherence of the organism. The average pH of young adult male healthy skin varies depending on the specific site, but ranges between 4.37–4.67 (6), and within the reported pH optimum of purified acid proteinase (139). A similar enzyme has been isolated from *Trichophyton mentagrophytes* and a virulence role in dermatophytosis has been postulated (183).

Ray & Payne (138) observed effects of placing *C. albicans* blastoconidia on the skin of 1- to 2-day-old mice. The inoculum was applied by saturating a small cotton patch and retaining the patch on the new-borne-mouse skin by use of an occlusive dressing. Occlusive dressings have been used by others to initiate cutaneous candidiasis in guinea pigs (170). At various times for up to 48 h, mice were sacrificed and *C. albicans*–skin interactions were observed using scanning electron microscopy. Ability of yeast to adhere to skin was correlated with strains capable of acid proteinase production. By 4 h after application of the blastoconidia, depressions or cavitations were noted in the corneocyte surface in association with the yeast cells. Adherence was less and no cavitations were formed when *Candida* species negative for acid proteinase secretion or pepstatin-suppressed *C. albicans* were used. These cavitations are similar to adherence sites of yeast forms on endothelial surfaces of porcine vascular strips (87). Whether these observations are representative of human disease is not known.

In similar studies on nonkeratinized human buccal epithelia obtained by biopsy from healthy subjects, acid proteinase–producing strains of *C. albicans* were found to correlate more with adherence of yeasts than to production of cavitations (7). Others have also observed correlation of adherence properties to proteinase production (48a, 54). Although the studies on buccal epithelia (7) were done on human tissue, they were in vitro experiments and probably do not reflect conditions in the oral cavity. As indicated above, the importance of the secreted enzyme in development of oral candidiasis in humans has been challenged (53).

The literature abounds with other observations suggesting a positive or negative relationship between acid proteinase production and virulence of *C. albicans*. Basic physical-chemical characteristics of purified enzyme and possible relation to virulence have been recently reviewed (140, 141), thus a comprehensive review is not indicated here. Table 1 summarizes a few

Table 1   Selected evidence for proteinase as a virulence factor of *C. albicans*

Observation (limitation or alternative consideration)	Reference
CAP positive[a] *C. albicans* strains are more virulent for mice (other strain attributes could account for virulence)	174
C. albicans produces CAP during human and experimental candidiasis (does not prove a cause-and-effect relationship)	92, 108, 109, 137, 150
CAP-deficient mutants are less virulent than wild-type parent strains (mutants were obtained after exposure to mutagenic agents; other genetic lesions may account for decreased virulence)	97, 110, 146
CAP-deficient mutants that revert to CAP sufficiency regain virulence (changes in expression of more than one gene could have occurred in the revertant; CAP production may simply be a marker of expression of a set of coordinately regulated genes)	97
CAP production is correlated with adherence to tissue and tissue cavitation (has not been demonstrated in human disease)	7, 87, 138
CAP is produced during phagocytosis of *C. albicans* (experiments were in vitro and mouse thioglycollate–elicited macrophages were used; relevance to in vivo conditions is unknown)	8

[a]CAP is *C. albicans* acid proteinase.

Table 2   Selected evidence against proteinase as a virulence factor

Observation (limitation or alternative consideration)	Reference
The low pH optimum of CAP may preclude activity in various tissues (specific tissue sites, such as skin and areas of inflammation, may satisfy the pH requirement; individual patients may have lower than normal pH values at selected tissue sites; CAP may have nonenzymatic functions, such as adherence)	52
The level of CAP production by strains of *C. albicans* did not correlate with invasiveness of the isolates (a single attribute of *C. albicans* will unlikely explain its virulence potential; host factors must also be considered)	160
Low-virulence mutant of *C. albicans* produced CAP at levels equal to or greater than virulent parent (the mutant may grow more slowly than the parent in vivo and may have other differences; this example may support the idea that one characteristic does not make *C. albicans* pathogenic)	42
Strain WO-1 expresses white-opaque (W-O) switch phenotypes, W is high virulence and low producer of CAP, O is low virulence and high CAP (possibly another example that one characteristic does not make *C. albicans* a pathogen)	140, 141

observations from works purporting that the secreted proteinase is a virulence factor. The table also indicates possible limitations or alternative explanations for each observation. Table 2 was constructed in similar fashion except that data are presented that indicate the proteinase may not be associated with virulence.

Various evidences in both tables underscore the difficulty in considering a single characteristic as having a role in virulence. As alluded to earlier, multiple factors likely act in concert to account for relative pathogenicity of *C. albicans* isolates. For example, in some strains, and perhaps at specific sites on or in certain individuals, proteinase activity may act by destroying membrane barriers and facilitating hyphal penetration of cells, as suggested by Borg & Ruchel (8), or of tissue as suggested by Tanaka and coworkers (91, 92, 164).

ADHERENCE

Information relating adherence of *C. albicans* to virulence and studies of mechanisms of adherence emerge at an impressive rate since the report by King et al (84) only about ten years ago. In addition to studying *C. albicans* adherence to epithelial cells, fibrin platelets, endothelial cells, skin, and plastic surfaces (19), investigators are examining characteristics of adherence to subendothelial extracellular matrix glycoproteins (89) and splenic and lymph node nonendothelial sites (30). Several cell-surface molecules have been identified as possible adhesins, and perhaps all are mannoproteins.

The literature in this area is extensive and has received several recent reviews (19, 40, 57, 81, 147) to which the reader is referred. This review considers only a few points of summary or recent findings that are apropos to this topic. Adherence seems of obvious significance to virulence, but supportive information is scant and mostly correlative in nature. The extensive literature is devoted more to identification of receptor-ligand molecules involved in the adherence phenomenon.

Classification of Receptor-Ligand Molecules

Calderone & Braun (19) placed the ligand-receptor (adhesins) candidates of *C. albicans* into three categories. Whether all of these function as adhesin molecules has not been determined. The first category encompasses molecules involved in interactions between the protein portion of a mannoprotein of *C. albicans* and the protein portion of a host glycoprotein. Examples are the CR3-like and β_1-integrin-like (113) molecule(s) of *C. albicans*, which binds host glycoproteins with arginine-glycine–aspartic acid (RGD) sequences such as iC3b (196), fibronectin (86, 89, 166), laminin (10, 86), types I and IV collagen (86), and fibrinogen and fibrin (9, 130). A CR2-like molecule on *C. albicans* that binds C3d (18, 43, 71) appears to fit into this category (157), but participation of this molecule in adherence is uncertain. The second category includes molecules involved in lectin activity in which the protein portion of a *C. albicans* surface molecule recognizes sugar moieties, such as fucose or N-acetyl-glucosamine, of host-cell membrane glycoproteins (41). Sugar specificity varies depending on the *C. albicans* isolate. The third category encompasses the carbohydrate portion of a molecule that recognizes an unidentified host-cell membrane receptor-ligand. This putative adhesin is typified by the factor 6 moiety of *C. albicans* (49, 120).

Production of the secreted acid proteinase correlates with adherence properties of *C. albicans* but, as proposed above, may or may not act directly as an adhesin molecule. Thus, more information is required before assigning the proteinase to one of the proposed categories.

I suggest a fourth category to include hydrophobic interactions between a candidal cell-surface protein component and unknown receptor-ligand molecules of the host. Hydrophobicity of *C. albicans* varies depending on the strain (63), growth conditions, and morphogenesis (62, 70, 82). Hydrophobicity correlates with adherence properties of *C. albicans* to plastic (88, 119, 147) and human epithelial cells (63). Also, *C. albicans* yeast forms grown at room temperature to promote high expression of the hydrophobic molecule(s) bind impressively throughout mouse spleen and lymph node tissue in an ex vivo binding assay (65) as compared to yeast cells grown at 37°C, which bind specifically to splenic marginal zones rich in macrophages and to macrophage-rich areas of lymph nodes (30). Although the less specific

binding patterns have not been definitively shown to result from hydrophobicity, the correlation is striking, and mutants of *C. albicans* strongly
hydrophobic even at 37°C also bind throughout the tissues (65). In addition,
germ tubes, which tend to be highly adherent, are strongly hydrophobic
(104). The hydrophobic molecule appears to be a protein, and mannosylation
of the same or neighboring molecules was proposed to engender hydrophilicity to the cell surface (69). The relative importance of cell-wall lipids (56) in
hydrophobic interactions is unknown.

Host-cell receptors specific for *C. albicans* adhesins are beginning to be
identified, and some possibilities may be extrapolated from the preceding
paragraph. In addition, a recent report claims that *C. albicans* and other fungi
specifically bind to the widely distributed mammalian cell membrane glycosphingolipid lactosylceramide (75). If this material is important in binding of
C. albicans, it may pertain only to yeast forms because hyphae did not bind
the glycosphingolipid in their in vitro assay. If confirmed, this observation
would indicate that at least one adhesin is yeast specific.

How Many Receptor-Ligand Molecules on C. albicans Are There?

Although categories have been proposed and activities of adhesin-candidate
molecules are seemingly quite disparate, experiments have not been done to
determine if a limited number or even a single cell-surface molecular species
accounts for all of the observations. That is, the carbohydrate moiety of a
mannoprotein may have adherence or binding qualities that differ from the
protein portion of the same molecule. Further, various regions of the molecule
nonspecifically bind host molecules that generally satisfy a few conformational or charge constraints. Strain specificity of some binding activities may be a
function of glycosylation changes on the same peptide or protein backbone,
thus still limiting the number of genes dedicated to adherence capabilities.
Invoking the idea that *C. albicans* can make many specific surface molecules
that represent human molecular mimicry (116) seems unnecessary.

A potential danger in identifying specific host-like molecules on *C. albicans* by use of monoclonal antibodies is that each monoclonal antibody may
have physical-chemical characteristics that differ from other monoclonals
even of the same class or subclass. For example, the IgM monoclonal
antibody H9 is readily inactivated at 60°C (11). Other monoclonals have been
isolated against *C. albicans* that bind nonspecifically to a wide variety of
antigens and surfaces (D. L. Brawner & J. E. Cutler, unpublished data). The
point is, a negative or irrelevant monoclonal antibody control may be im-
practical. Before one identifies new putative receptors by use of a monoclonal
antibody, one should use Fab fragments of the antibody and attempt to

demonstrate specificity by the inability to block binding with antibodies that have supposed specificity to unrelated *C. albicans* surface determinants.

Virulence Role

Adherence would seem important in colonization of *C. albicans* to appropriate epithelial surfaces and seeding of tissue sites during fungemia. Whether colonization should be considered a virulence characteristic may depend on the site of colonization. Seeding of tissue during fungemia is likely important in pathogenesis of candidiasis. However, if adherence to host cells limits growth of *C. albicans*, attachment may work in favor of the host rather than *C. albicans*. The overall importance of adherence on host–*C. albicans* interactions probably depends on the subset of virulence characteristics of the strain of *C. albicans* involved, the tissue site of the interaction, and the immunologic status of the host. A virulence consideration of one or more of the variously described functions of mannoproteins necessitates demonstration of *C. albicans* in vivo expression of the receptor-ligand in question. This demonstration is important because of the influence of environment and morphogenesis on antigenic expression of *C. albicans*. Experimental and clinical evidence shows that the secreted acid proteinase is produced by *C. albicans* under in vivo conditions (92, 109, 150). In experimental animals, the CR2-like receptor that binds C3d is produced (78) and recent in vivo studies indirectly indicate that the integrin-like molecule (or molecules) is also expressed (90).

In mouse models of disseminated candidiasis, *C. albicans* presented as a fungemia results in adherence to areas in lymphoid organs rich in macrophages, as well as other nonlymphoid organs, as demonstrated by ex vivo and in vivo experimentation (30). Association with areas rich in macrophages may represent a favorable association for the host because lymphoid lesions rarely occur in an otherwise normal mouse infected i.v. with *C. albicans*. In immunocompromised humans, disseminated candidiasis may result in hepatosplenic abscesses (187, 189). Studies on mice extrapolated to humans suggest that human hepatosplenic candidiasis is the result or indication of an underlying phagocytic cell dysfunction.

Observations on association of adherence with virulence have yielded mostly correlative information. For example, species of *Candida* more commonly associated with disease tend to show greater adherence characteristics. A corollary is that strains with reduced adherence properties, either naturally or because of conditions of growth (19, 40) or mutation (100), are less virulent in experimental infections (40, 100). At least some receptor molecules may have functions in addition to probable adherence properties. As cited above, the secreted proteinase may act as an adhesin in addition to having proteolytic activity. The iC3b receptor of *C. albicans* may also suppress phagocytosis by neutrophils (59).

Investigators have attempted to demonstrate the importance of adherence by blocking attachment in vivo and determining the susceptibility of the experimental animals to candidiasis. If attachment favors the host by associating the fungus with phagocytic cells or favors *C. albicans* by association with other tissue sites, as proposed by Douglas (40), then inhibiting attachment of *C. albicans* might have different effects depending on the tissue site. For example, adherence properties might be expected to be especially important in establishment of candidal colonization at sites of potential tissue invasion, such as in the mouth, esophagus, and vaginal tract. Importantly, Segal et al (161) found that a chitin soluble extract prepared in a cream and applied intravaginally could significantly reduce establishment of candidal vaginitis in mice kept in estrus by estradiol therapy. In related work, these investigators previously showed that the chitin extract blocks adhesion of *C. albicans* to vaginal epithelium and suppresses short-lived vaginitis in mice (99, 162). Interestingly, chitin administered i.p. to mice was found to prolong the survival of mice challenged i.v. with *C. albicans* as compared to mice that received only the fungus (178).

Along these lines, Klotz et al (90) obtained an exciting result in experiments on the role of adherence in disseminated candidiasis. A nontoxic RGD-containing peptide, administered i.v. to rabbits at the same time as administration of viable *C. albicans* by the same route, caused marked reduction four hours later in recoverable *C. albicans* from heart, liver, spleen, and kidneys, but not lungs, as compared to rabbits who received only the fungus. Furthermore, at 72 h, animals treated with the RGD peptide had one-fifth the number of renal cortical abscesses owing to *C. albicans*. If the RGD peptide blocks attachment to vascular endothelium, as suggested by the authors (90), to determine whether *C. albicans* could still associate with other tissue sites such as macrophage-rich areas in spleen and lymph nodes would be interesting.

VARIABILITY

Relatively recent information indicates that *C. albicans* has an impressive variability potential. Although this characteristic likely relates to virulence by defining the virulence set of characters, in vivo experiments and clinical observations are scant. The basis for this variable nature may be gross genetic alterations responsible for chromosomal instabilities in individual strains and more usual coarse and fine controls responsible for qualitative and quantitative changes in expression of hyphal production, acid proteinase secretion, and adherence properties. Such mechanisms may be under as yet undiscovered environmental influences. At the very least, variability adds an extra dimension to thoughts on the virulence set. Expression of putative virulence factors is not an all-or-none situation. Strains vary with regard to extent of hyphal or pseudohyphal development, amount of acid proteinase secreted, and degree of adherence properties.

Chromosomal Instabilities

Negroni (124) reported variant colonial morphologies of *C. albicans* in 1935, and numerous, but sporadic, accounts substantiated those observations over the following 35 years (154a). In 1948, Slutsky et al (167) reported the high frequency with which colonial morphological shifts may occur. This startling observation, in conjunction with subsequent reports (179, 181) on ploidy variation, correlation between colonial morphotypes, and chromosomal rearrangements (180) and with the finding that high frequency switch strains can be isolated from patients with candidal vaginitis (172), has kindled speculation on the relationship of chromosomal rearrangement to virulence. Chromosomal instabilities may not only relate to colonial morphotype variations, but perhaps also to variations in germination potential within each strain of *C. albicans*.

Although the few virulence correlations observed so far in this new area of investigation have been disappointing, this attribute seems too profound to be trivial. So far, cells from normal or common colonial morphotypes appear more virulent than their variants. Eisman et al (45) in 1953 reported that the usual smooth colonial forms of *C. albicans* are more virulent than rough colonial variants. Similar results were recently observed by others (41a). In the white-opaque–switch phenotype system first reported by Slutsky et al (168), the white or common form of *C. albicans* is more virulent even though opaques produce more proteinase (141). Recent information on genetics of *C. albicans* and high-frequency switching has been thoroughly reviewed (84a, 159, 190).

Antigenic Variability

Initial contact of *C. albicans* with the host involves cell-wall surface components and secreted soluble substances. The ability to rapidly alter the surface composition may be a means to evade recognition by specific host immune mechanisms.

ENVIRONMENTAL INFLUENCES   The cell surface of *C. albicans* undergoes topographical variation dependent on the carbon source in the nutritional environment (94). The carbon source influences whether blastospore formation is lateral or multipolar, the nature of the bud scar, and the appearance of strands making up intercellular bridges. As might be expected, carbon source also sways receptor-ligand production and adherence properties of *C. albicans* (64, 73, 111, 117).

Differences in antigen expression were found to vary in vitro as a function of nutritional sources, growth phase and morphogenic form, temperature of incubation, and strain (11–13, 24, 72, 103, 132). The relation of these changes to virulence is unknown, but in one study, similar variations occurred in vivo (14). Mice were infected either subcutaneously or intravenously, and *C. albicans* was recovered from lesions and examined for the presence of specific surface antigens by use of monoclonal antibodies and immunocolloidal gold electron microscope techniques. Essentially identical variations in expression were noted from cells developed under these in vivo conditions as previously described for in vitro–grown cells.

OTHER ATTRIBUTES

Several other attributes of *C. albicans* have virulence potential, but information on these is either limited or experimentation has not focused on pathogenicity relationships. These include phospholipases, high- and low-molecular-weight toxic substances, and secretion of a cell-surface mucin-like material. The strongest case can be made for phospholipases, and Ghannoum (55) has hypothesized that the function of these enzymes is primarily related to pathogenicity. Some of these attributes are difficult to study. For example, high-molecular-weight cell-wall component(s) have endotoxic-like activities, but are much less toxic than bacterial endotoxin (31). Because of the relatively low toxicity, exclusion of minor bacterial contaminants is essential in such studies, which makes work on these components extremely tedious. Information on these various attributes is developing slowly, and current knowledge has been recently well reviewed (55).

Suppression-Activation of Host-Acquired Specific Immunity

Clinical and experimental evidence indicates that *C. albicans* modulates immune responses of the host in positive and negative ways. Cell-wall mannans responsible for such activities should be considered on the list of putative virulence factors, but the contribution to pathogenesis of candidiasis is still speculative. This aspect was the subject of a recent review (38).

CONCLUDING REMARKS

Evidence suggests that many factors are responsible for the virulence potential of *C. albicans*. To understand this potential, the researcher should determine a virulence profile of isolates before choosing strains for study. The appropriate profile and conditions of various assays require defining. Assessments could include: growth rates, germinative ability, adherence properties, quantitative determination of secreted acid proteinase, phospholipase quantification, and restriction fragment length polymorphism (RFLP) biotype analysis.

Other biotyping methods have been reviewed (118a) and may also be considered. Because evidence indicates that importance of virulence characters could be tissue related, information on type of lesion and location on the patient may also prove useful. Determination of the relative importance of one particular trait could then be made provided that the two given strains under study differ primarily in only the one characteristic of interest. Because of the tendency for instabilities, strains could be chosen that are relatively stable and/or experimentation could be done on cultures started from frozen stocks, rather than cultures continuously passaged in the laboratory or slants kept under refrigeration. Periodic profile checks throughout the experimental time would also be indicated.

An exciting potential of this experimentation is advancement of treatment strategies for candidiasis and efficient diagnostic tests for disseminated candidiasis. Understanding the relative role of *C. albicans* virulence traits in specific tissue invasion and metabolic pathways of trait expression could lead to development of highly selective antifungal therapies. Detection of candidiasis may be more effectively determined by assays for multiple candidal products or host antibodies against such products like secreted and intracellular proteinases, adhesin molecules, or phospholipases.

ACKNOWLEDGMENTS

I am especially grateful to Kevin C. Hazen and Richard A. Calderone for criticisms of the manuscript and for the opportunity to have stimulating exchanges of scientific ideas with them, and to Thomas L. Ray and Steven A. Klotz for sharing manuscripts in press. I thank also Pati M. Glee, Ren-Kai Li, Marcia Riesselman, and Toshio Kanbe who critiqued the manuscript and made many very helpful suggestions. During the writing of this review, work in my laboratory was supported by USPHS grants AI24912 and RR08218 (MBRS) and a grant from Ortho Pharmaceutical Corporation.

Literature Cited

1. Ammerer, G., Hunter, C. P., Rothman, J. H., Saari, G. C., Valls, L. A., Stevens, T. H. 1986. *Pep4* gene of *Saccharomyces cerevisiae* encodes proteinase A, a vacuolar enzyme required for processing of vacuolar precursors. *Mol. Cell. Biol.* 6:2490–99

2. Antley, P. P., Hazen, K. C. 1988. Role of yeast cell growth temperature on *Candida albicans* virulence in mice. *Infect. Immun.* 56:2884–90

3. Arai, T., Mikami, Y., Yokoyama, K. 1977. Phagocytosis of *Candida albicans* by rabbit alveolar macrophages and guinea pig neutrophils. *Sabouraudia* 15:171–77

4. Baghian, A., Lee, K. W. 1989. Systemic candidosis in beige mice. *J. Med. Vet. Mycol.* 27:51–55

5. Bistoni, F., Baccarini, M., Blasi, E., Marconi, P. F., Puccetti, P., Garaci, E. 1983. Correlation between in vivo and in vitro studies modulation of resistance to experimental *Candida albicans* infection by cyclophosphamide in mice. *Infect. Immun.* 40:46–55

6. Blank, I. H. 1939. Measurement of pH of the skin surface. *J. Invest. Dermatol.* 2:75–79

7. Borg, M., Ruchel, R. 1988. Expression of extracellular acid proteinase by proteolytic *Candida* spp. during exper-

imental infection of oral mucosa. *Infect. Immun.* 56:626–31

8. Borg, M., Ruchel, R. 1990. Demonstration of fungal proteinase during phagocytosis of *Candida albicans* and *Candida tropicalis. J. Med. Vet. Mycol.* 28:3–14

9. Bouali, A., Robert, R., Tronchin, G., Senet, J. M. 1987. Characterization of binding of human fibrinogen to the surface of germ-tubes and mycelium of *Candida albicans. J. Gen. Microbiol.* 133:545–51

10. Bouchara, J., Tronchin, G., Annaix, V., Robert, R., Senet, J. M. 1990. Presence of laminin receptors on *Candida albicans* germ tubes. *Infect. Immun.* 58:48–54.

11. Brawner, D. L., Cutler, J. E. 1984. Variability in expression of a cell surface determinant on *Candida albicans* as evidenced by an agglutinating monoclonal antibody. *Infect. Immun.* 43:966–72

12. Brawner, D. L., Cutler, J. E. 1986. Variability in expression of cell surface antigens of *Candida albicans* during morphogenesis. *Infect. Immun.* 51:337–43

13. Brawner, D. L., Cutler, J. E. 1986. Ultrastructural and biochemical studies of two dynamically expressed cell surface determinants on *Candida albicans. Infect. Immun.* 51:327–36

14. Brawner, D. L., Cutler, J. E. 1987. Cell surface and intracellular expression of two *Candida albicans* antigens during in vitro and in vivo growth. *Microb. Pathogen.* 2:249–57

15. Buckley, H. R., Daneo-Moore, L., Ahrens, J. C., Sobel, J. D. 1986. Isolation of a germ-tube-forming revertant from *Candida albicans* B311V6. *Infect. Immun.* 53:13–15

16. Buckley, H. R., Price, M. R., Daneo-Moore, L. 1982. Isolation of a variant of *Candida albicans. Infect. Immun.* 37:1209–17

17. Burke, V., Gracey, M. 1980. An experimental model of gastrointestinal candidiasis. *J. Med. Microbiol.* 13:103–10

18. Calderone, R., Linehan, L., Wadsworth, E., Sandberg, A. L. 1988. Identification of C3d receptors on *Candida albicans. Infect. Immun.* 56:252–58

19. Calderone, R. A., Braun, P. C. 1991. Adherence and receptor relationships in *Candida albicans. Microbiol. Rev.* In press

20. Cannon, R. D. 1986. Isolation of a mycelial mutant of *Candida albicans. J. Gen. Microbiol.* 132:2405–7

21. Casanova, M., Gil, M. L., Cardenoso, L., Martinez, J. P., Sentandreu, R.

1989. Identification of wall-specific antigens synthesized during germ tube formation by *Candida albicans. Infect. Immun.* 57:262–71

22. Casanova, M., Martinez, J. P., Chaffin, W. L. 1990. Fab fragments from a monoclonal antibody against a germ tube mannoprotein block the yeast-to-mycelium transition in *Candida albicans. Infect. Immun.* 58:3810–12

23. Cassone, A., DeBernardis, F., Mondello, F., Ceddia, T., Agatensi, L. 1987. Evidence for a correlation between proteinase secretion and vulvovaginal candidosis. *J. Infect. Dis.* 156:777–83

24. Chaffin, W. L., Skudlarek, J., Morrow, K. J. 1988. Variable expression of a surface determinant during proliferation of *Candida albicans. Infect. Immun.* 56:302–9

25. Cockayne, A., Odds, F. C. 1984. Interactions of *Candida albicans* yeast cells, germ tubes and hyphae with human polymorphonuclear leukocytes in vitro. *J. Gen. Microbiol.* 130:465–71

26. Cole, G. T., Lynn, K. T., Seshan, K. R. 1990. Evaluation of a murine model of hepatic candidiasis. *J. Clin. Microbiol.* 28:1828–41

26a. Cole, G. T., Lynn, K. T., Seshan, K. R., Pope, L. M. 1989. Gastrointestinal and systemic canidiosis in immunocompromised mice. *J. Med. Vet. Mycol.* 27:363–80

27. Crandall, M., Edwards, J. E. 1987. Segregation of proteinase-negative mutants from heterozygous *Candida albicans. J. Gen. Microbiol.* 133:2817–24

28. Critchley, I. A., Douglas, L. J. 1987. Isolation and partial characterization of an adhesin from *Candida albicans. J. Gen. Microbiol.* 133:629–36

29. Cutler, J. E. 1977. Chemotactic factor produced by *Candida albicans. Infect. Immun.* 18:568–73

30. Cutler, J. E., Brawner, D. L., Hazen, K. C., Jutila, M. A. 1990. Characteristics of *Candida albicans* adherence to mouse tissue. *Infect. Immun.* 58:1902–8

31. Cutler, J. E., Friedman, L., Milner, K. C. 1972. Biological and chemical characterization of toxic substances from *Candida albicans. Infect. Immun.* 6:616–27

32. De Bernardis, F., Agatensi, L., Ross, I. K., Emerson, G. W., Lorenzini, R., et al. 1990. Evidence for a role for secreted aspartate proteinase of *Candida albicans* in vulvovaginal candidiasis. *J. Infect. Dis.* 161:1276–83

33. De Bernardis, F., Lorenzini, R., Verticchio, R., Agatensi, L., Cassone, A.

1989. Isolation, acid proteinase secretion, and experimental pathogenicity of *Candida parapsilosis* from outpatients with vaginitis. *J. Clin. Microbiol.* 27: 2598–2603

34. De Bernardis, F., Morelli, L., Ceddia, T., Lorenzini, R., Cassone, A. 1990. Experimental pathogenicity and acid proteinase secretion of vaginal isolates of *Candida parapsilosis*. *J. Med. Vet. Mycol.* 28:125–37

35. Diamond, R. D., Clark, R. A., Haudenschild, C. C. 1980. Damage to *Candida albicans* hyphae and pseudohyphae by the myeloperoxidase system and oxidative products of neutrophil metabolism in vitro. *J. Clin. Invest.* 66:908–17

36. Diamond, R. D., Krzesicki, R. 1978. Mechanisms of attachment of neutrophils to *Candida albicans* pseudohyphae in the absence of serum, and of subsequent damage to pseudohyphae by microbicidal processes of neutrophils in vitro. *J. Clin. Invest.* 61:360–69

37. Diamond, R. D., Krzesicki, R., Wellington, J. 1978. Damage to pseudohyphal forms of *Candida albicans* by neutrophils in the absence of serum in vitro. *J. Clin. Invest.* 61:349–59

38. Domer, J. E. 1989. Candida cell wall mannan: a polysaccharide with diverse immunologic properties. *CRC Crit. Rev. Microbiol.* 17:33–51

39. Domer, J. E., Moser, S. A. 1978. Experimental murine candidiasis: cell-mediated immunity following cutaneous challenge. *Infect. Immun.* 20:88–98

40. Douglas, L. J. 1987. Adhesion of *Candida* species to epithelial surfaces. *CRC Crit. Rev. Microbiol.* 15:27–43

41. Douglas, L. J. 1991. Adhesion of *Candida albicans* to host surfaces. In *Proceedings of FEMS symposium on Candida and candidamycosis*, ed. E. Tumbay, H. Seelinger, O. Ang. New York: Plenum. In press

41a. Dutton, S., Penn, C. W. 1989. Biological attributes of colony-type variants of *Candida albicans*. *J. Gen. Microbiol.* 135:3363–72

42. Edison, A. M., Manning-Zweerink, M. 1988. Comparison of the extracellular proteinase activity produced by a low-virulence mutant of *Candida albicans* and its wild-type parent. *Infect. Immun.* 56:1388–90

43. Edwards, J. E., Gaither, T. A., O'Shea, J. J., Rotrosen, D., Lawley, T. J., et al. 1986. Expression of specific binding sites on *Candida* with functional and antigenic characteristics of human complement receptors. *J. Immunol.* 137: 3577–83

44. Edwards, J. E., Montgomerie, J. Z., Ishida, K., Morrison, J. O., Guze, L. B. 1977. Experimental hematogenous endophthalmitis due to *Candida:* species variation in ocular pathogenicity. *J. Infect. Dis.* 135:294–97

45. Eisman, P. C., Geftic, S. G., Mayer, R. L. 1953. Virulence in mice of colonial variants of *Candida albicans*. *Proc. Soc. Exp. Biol. Med.* 82:263–64

46. Ekenna, O., Sherertz, R. J. 1987. Factors affecting colonization and dissemination of *Candida albicans* from the gastrointestial tract of mice. *Infect. Immun.* 55:1558–63

47. Epstein, J. B., Kimura, L. H., Menard, T. W., Truelove, E. L., Pearsall, N. N. 1982. Effects of specific antibodies on the interaction between the fungus *Candida albicans* and human oral mucosa. *Arch. Oral Biol.* 27:469–74

48. Field, L. H., Pope, L. M., Cole, G. T., Guentzel, M. N., Berry, L. J. 1981. Persistence and spread of *Candida albicans* after intragastric inoculation of infant mice. *Infect. Immun.* 31:783–91

48a. Frey, C. L., Barone, J. M., Dreyer, G., Koltin, Y., Petteway, S. R., Drutz, D. J. 1990. Synthetic protease inhibitors inhibit *Candida albicans* extracellular acid protease activity and adherence to endothelial cells. *Proc. Am. Soc. Microbiol.* Abstr. F–102

49. Fukazawa, Y., Nishikawa, M., Suzuki, M., Shinoda, T. 1980. Immunochemical basis of the serological specificity of the yeast: immunochemical determinants of several antigenic factors of yeast. *Zentralbl. Bakteriol. Parasitenkd. Infectionskr. Hyg. Abt. 1: Orig.* 8:127–35

50. Gelfand, J. A., Hurley, D. L., Fauci, A. S., Frank, M. M. 1978. Role of complement in host defense against experimental disseminated candidiasis. *J. Infect. Dis.* 138:9–16

51. George, B. S., Plunkett, O. A. 1948. Dissociation in *Candida albicans*. *J. Invest. Dermatol.* 10:327–442

52. Germaine, G. R., Tellefson, L. M. 1981. Effect of pH and human saliva on protease production by *Candida albicans*. *Infect. Immun.* 31:323–26

53. Germaine, G. R., Tellefson, L. M., Johnson, G. L. 1978. Proteolytic activity of *Candida albicans:* Action on human salivary proteins. *Infect. Immun.* 22:861–66

54. Ghannoum, M., Abu, E. K. 1986. Correlative relationship between proteinase production, adherence and pathogenicity

of various strains of *Candida albicans*. *J. Med. Vet. Mycol.* 24:407–13

55. Ghannoum, M. A., Abu-Elteen, K. H. 1990. Pathogenicity determinants of *Candida*. *Mycoses* 33:265–82

56. Ghannoum, M. A., Burns, G. R., Elteen, K. A., Radwan, S. S. 1986. Experimental evidence for the role of lipids in adherence of *Candida* spp. to human buccal epithelial cells. *Infect. Immun.* 54:189–93

57. Ghannoum, M. A., Radwan, S. S. 1990. Candida *Adherence to Epithelial Cells*. Boca Raton, FL: CRC

58. Gil, C., Pomes, R., Nombel, C. 1990. Isolation and characterization of *Candida albicans* morphological mutants derepressed for the formation of filamentous hypha-type structures. *J. Bacteriol.* 172:2384–91

59. Gilmore, B. J., Retsinas, E. M., Lorenz, J. S., Hostetter, M. K. 1988. An iC3b receptor on *Candida albicans*: structure, function, and correlates for pathogenicity. *J. Infect. Dis.* 157:38–46

60. Grant, L. 1965. The sticking and emigration of white blood cells in inflammation. In *The Inflammatory Process*, ed. B. W. Zweifach, L. Grant, R. T. McCluskey, pp.197–244. New York: Academic

61. Grappel, S. F., Calderone, R. A. 1976. Effect of antibodies on the respiration and morphology of *Candida albicans*. *Sabouraudia* 14:51–60

62. Hazen, B. W., Hazen, K. C. 1988. Dynamic expression of cell surface hydrophobicity during initial yeast cell growth and before germ tube formation of *Candida albicans*. *Infect. Immun.* 56:2521–25

63. Hazen, K. C. 1989. Participation of yeast cell surface hydrophobicity in adherence of *Candida albicans* to human epithelial cells. *Infect. Immun.* 57:1894–1900

64. Hazen, K. C. 1990. Cell surface hydrophobicity of medically important fungi, especially *Candida* species. In *Microbial Cell Surface Hydrophobicity*, ed. R. J. Doyle, M. Rosenberg, pp.249–95. Washington, DC: Am. Soc. Microbiol.

65. Hazen, K. C., Brawner, D. L., Riesselman, M. H., Jutila, M. A., Cutler, J. E. 1991. Differential adherence between hydrophobic and hydrophilic yeast cells of *Candida albicans*. *Infect. Immun.* In press

66. Hazen, K. C., Cutler, J. E. 1979. Autoregulation of germ tube formation by

Candida albicans. *Infect. Immun.* 24:661–66

67. Hazen, K. C., Cutler, J. E. 1983. Isolation and purification of morphogenic autoregulatory substance produced by *Candida albicans*. *J. Biochem.* 94:777–83

68. Hazen, K. C., Hazen, B. W. 1987. Temperature-modulated physiological characteristics of *Candida albicans*. *Microbiol. Immunol.* 31:497–508

69. Hazen, K. C., Lay, J. G., Hazen, B. W., Fu, R. C., Murthy, S. 1990. Partial biochemical characterization of cell surface hydrophobicity and hydrophilicity of *Candida albicans*. *Infect. Immun.* 58:3469–76

70. Hazen, K. C., Plotkin, B. J., Klimas, D. M. 1986. Influence of growth conditions on cell surface hydrophobicity of *Candida albicans* and *Candida glabrata*. *Infect. Immun.* 54:269–71

71. Heidenreich, F., Dierich, M. P. 1985. *Candida albicans* and *Candida stellatoidea*, in contrast to other *Candida* species, bind iC3b and C3d but not C3b. *Infect. Immun.* 50:598–600

72. Hopwood, V., Poulain, D., Fortier, B., Evans, G., Vernes, A. 1986. A monoclonal antibody to a cell wall component of *Candida albicans*. *Infect. Immun.* 54:222–27

73. Hostetter, M. K., Lorenz, J. S., Preus, L., Kendrick, K. E. 1990. The iC3b receptor on *Candida albicans*: Subcellular localization and modulation of receptor expression by glucose. *J. Infect. Dis.* 161:761–68

74. Hurtel, B., LaGrange, P. H., Michel, J. C. 1980. Systemic candidiasis in mice. II. Main role of polymorphonuclear leukocytes in resistance to infection. *Ann. Immunol.* 131:105

75. Jimenez-Lucho, V., Ginsburg, V., Krivan, H. C. 1990. Cryptococcus neoformans, *Candida albicans,* and other fungi bind specifically to the glycosphingolipid lactosylceramide (Gal1B1-4GlcB1-1Cer), a possible adhesion receptor for yeasts. *Infect. Immun.* 58:2085–90

76. Jones, J. H., Adams, D. 1970. Experimentally induced acute oral candidosis in the rat. *Br. J. Dermatol.* 83:670–73

77. Kaminishi, H., Tanaka, M., Cho, T., Maeda, H., Hagihara, Y. 1990. Activation of the plasma kallikrein-kinin system by *Candida albicans* proteinase. *Infect. Immun.* 58:2139–43

78. Kanbe, T., Li, R. K., Calderone, R. A., Cutler, J. E. 1991. Evidence for expression of C3d receptor of *Candida albi-*

cans in vitro and in vivo by immunofluorescence and immunoelectron microscopy. *Infect. Immun.* In press

79. Kelly, R., Miller, S. M., Kurtz, M. B. 1988. One-step gene disruption by cotransformation to isolate double auxotrophs in *Candida albicans*. *Mol. Gen. Genet.* 214:24–31

80. Kelly, R., Miller, S. M., Kurtz, M. B., Kirsch, D. A. 1987. Directed mutagenesis in *Candida albicans:* one-step gene disruption to isolate *ura3* mutants. *Mol. Cell. Biol.* 7:199–207

81. Kennedy, M. J. 1988. Adhesion and association mechanisms of *Candida albicans*. *Curr. Top. Med. Mycol.* 2:73–169

82. Kennedy, M. J., Sandin, R. L. 1988. Influence of growth conditions on *Candida albicans* adhesion, hydrophobicity and cell wall ultrastructure. *J. Med. Vet. Mycol.* 26:79–92

83. Kimura, L. H., Pearsall, N. N. 1980. Relationship between germination of *Candida albicans* and increased adherence to human buccal epithelial cells. *Infect. Immun.* 28:464–68

84. King, R. D., Lee, J. C., Morris, A. L. 1980. Adherence of *Candida albicans* and other *Candida* species to mucosal epithelial cells. *Infect. Immun.* 27:667–74

84a. Kirsch, D. R., Kelly, R., Kurtz, M. B., eds. 1990. *The Genetics of* Candida. Boca Raton, FL: CRC

85. Klionsky, D. J., Banta, L. M., Emr, S. D. 1988. Intracellular sorting and processing of a yeast vacuolar hydrolase: Proteinase A propeptide contains vacuolar targeting information. *Mol. Cell. Biol.* 8:2105–16

86. Klotz, S. A. 1990. Adherence of *Candida albicans* to components of the subendothelial extracellular matrix. *FEMS Microbiol. Lett.* 68:249–54

87. Klotz, S. A., Drutz, D. J., Harrison, J. L., Huppert, M. 1983. Adherence and penetration of vascular endothelium by *Candida* yeasts. *Infect. Immun.* 42:374–84

88. Klotz, S. A., Penn, R. L. 1987. Multiple mechanisms may contribute to the adherence of *Candida* yeasts to living cells. *Curr. Microbiol.* 16:119–22

89. Klotz, S. A., Smith, R. L. 1991. A fibronectin receptor on *Candida albicans* mediates adherence of the fungus to extracellular matrix. *J. Infect. Dis.* In press

90. Klotz, S. A., Smith, R. L., Stewart, B. W. 1990. RGD-containing peptide inhibits metastatic lesions arising from I.

V. administration of *Candida albicans*. *Proc. ICAAC*. p.135. (Abstr.)

91. Kobayashi, I., Kondoh, Y., Shimizu, K., Tanaka, K. 1989. A role of secreted proteinase of *Candida albicans* for the invasion of chick chorio-allantoic membrane. *Microbiol. Immunol.* 33:709–19

92. Kondoh, Y., Shimizu, K., Tanaka, K. 1987. Proteinase production and pathogenicity of *Candida albicans*. II. Virulence for mice of *C. albicans* strains of different proteinase activity. *Microbiol. Immunol.* 31:1061–69

93. Kozel, T. R., Brown, R. R., Pfrommer, G. S. 1987. Activation and binding of C3 by *Candida albicans*. *Infect. Immun.* 55:1890–94

94. Kulkarni, R. K., Hollingsworth, P. J., Volz, P. A. 1980. Variation in cell surface features on *Candida albicans* with respect to carbon sources. *Sabouraudia* 18:255–60

95. Kurtz, M. B., Cortelyou, M. W., Kirsch, D. R. 1986. Integrative transformation of *Candida albicans*, using a cloned *Candida* ADE2 gene. *Mol. Cell. Biol.* 6:142–49

96. Kurtz, M. B., Cortelyou, M. W., Miller, S. M., Lai, M., Kirsch, D. R. 1987. Development of autonomously replicating plasmids for *Candida albicans*. *Mol. Cell. Biol.* 7:209–17

97. Kwon-Chung, K. J., Lehman, D., Good, C., Magee, P. T. 1985. Genetic evidence for role of extracellular proteinase in virulence of *Candida albicans*. *Infect. Immun.* 49:571–75

98. Lee, J. C., King, R. D. 1983. Characterization of *Candida albicans* adherence to human vaginal epithelial cells in vitro. *Infect. Immun.* 41:1024–30

99. Lehrer, N., Segal, E., Barr-Nea, L. 1983. In vitro and in vivo adherence of *Candida albicans* to mucosal surfaces. *Ann. Microbiol.* 134B:296–306

100. Lehrer, N., Segal, E., Cihlar, R. L., Calderone, R. A. 1986. Pathogenesis of vaginal candidiasis: studies with a mutant which has reduced ability to adhere in vitro. *J. Med. Vet. Mycol.* 24:127–31

101. Lehrer, R. I., Cline, M. J. 1969. Interaction of *Candida albicans* with human leukocytes and serum. *J. Bacteriol.* 98:996–1004

102. Lehrer, R. I., Ferrari, L. G., Patterson-Delafield, J., Sorrell, T. 1980. Fungicidal activity of rabbit alveolar and peritoneal macrophages against *Candida albicans*. *Infect. Immun.* 28:1001–8

103. Li, R. K., Cutler, J. E. 1991. A cell surface/plasma membrane antigen of *Candida albicans*. *J. Gen. Microbiol.* 137:455–64

104. Lis, H., Sharon, N. 1986. Lectins as molecules and as tools. *Annu. Rev. Biochem.* 55:35–67

105. Lott, T. J., Page, L. S., Boiron, P., Benson, J., Reiss, E. 1989. Nucleotide sequence of the *Candida albicans* aspartyl proteinase gene. *Nucleic Acids Res.* 17:1779

106. Louria, D. B., Brayton, R. G. 1964. Behavior of *Candida* cells within leukocytes. *Proc. Soc. Exp. Biol. Med.* 115: 93–98

107. Lyman, C. A., Simons, E. R., Melnick, D. A., Diamond, R. D. 1987. Unopsonized *Candida albicans* hyphae stimulate a neutrophil respiratory burst and a cytosolic calcium flux without membrane depolarization. *J. Infect. Dis.* 156:770–76

108. Macdonald, F., Odds, F. C. 1980. Purified *Candida albicans* proteinase in the serological diagnosis of systemic candidosis. *JAMA* 243:2409–11

109. Macdonald, F., Odds, F. C. 1980. Inducible proteinase of *Candida albicans* in diagnostic serology and in the pathogenesis of systemic candidosis. *J. Med. Microbiol.* 13:423–35

110. Macdonald, F., Odds, F. C. 1983. Virulence for mice of a proteinase-secreting strain of *Candida albicans* and a proteinase-deficient mutant. *J. Gen. Microbiol.* 129:431–38

111. Macura, A. B., Tondyra, E. 1989. Influence of some carbohydrates and concanavalin A on the adherence of *Candida albicans* in vitro to buccal epithelial cells. *Zentralbl. Bakteriol. Parasitenkd. Infectionskr. Hyg. Abt. 1: Orig.* 272: 196–201

112. Maiti, P. K., Kumar, R., Mohapatra, L. N. 1980. Candidacidal activity of mouse macrophages in vitro. *Infect. Immun.* 29:477–82

113. Marcantonio, E. E., Hynes, R. O. 1988. Antibodies to the conserved cytoplasmic domain of the integrin B1 subunit react with proteins in vertebrates, invertebrates, and fungi. *J. Cell Biol.* 106: 1765–72

114. Masel, A., Braithwaite, K., Irwin, J., Manners, J. 1990. Highly variable molecular karyotypes in the plant pathogen *Colletotrichum gloeosporioides*. *Curr. Genet.* 18:81–86

115. Mathur, S., Koistinen, J., Kyong, C. U., Horger, E. O., Virella, G., Fudenberg, H. H. 1977. Antibodies to *Candida albicans* in IgA-deficient humans. *J. Infect. Dis.* 136:436–38

116. Mayer, C. L., Diamond, R. D., Edwards, J. E. 1990. Recognition of binding sites on *Candida albicans* by monoclonal antibodies to human leukocyte antigens. *Infect. Immun.* 58:3765–69

117. McCourtie, J., Douglas, L. J. 1981. Relationship between cell surface composition of *Candida albicans* and adherence to acrylic after growth on different carbon sources. *Infect. Immun.* 32: 1234–41

118. McCourtie, J., Douglas, L. J. 1985. Extracellular polymer of *Candida albicans:* Isolation, analysis and role in adhesion. *J. Gen. Microbiol.* 131:495–503

118a. Merz, W. G. 1990. *Candida albicans* strain delineation. *Clin. Microbiol. Rev.* 3:321–24

119. Minagi, S., Miyake, Y., Inagaki, K., Tsuru, H., Suginaka, H. 1985. Hydrophobic interaction in *Candida albicans* and *Candida tropicalis* adherence to various denture base resin materials. *Infect. Immun.* 47:11–14

120. Miyakawa, Y., Kagaya, K., Kuribayashi, T., Suzuki, M., Fukazawa, Y. 1989. Isolation and biological characterization of antigenic mutants of *Candida albicans,* serotype A. *Symposium on Yeasts. 7th Symposium on Yeasts,* pp. 5225–29. New York: Wiley

121. Morrison, R. P., Cutler, J. E. 1981. In vitro studies of the interaction of murine phagocytic cells with *Candida albicans*. *J. Reticuloendothel. Soc.* 29:23–34

122. Myerowitz, R. L. 1981. Gastrointestinal and disseminated candidiasis. *Arch. Pathol. Lab. Med.* 105:138–43

123. Negi, M., Tsuboi, R., Matsui, T., Ogawa, H. 1984. Isolation and characterization of proteinase from *Candida albicans:* Substrate specificity. *J. Invest. Dermatol.* 83:32–36

124. Negroni, P. 1935. Variacion hacia el tipo R de *Mycotorula albicans*. *Rev. Soc. Argent. Biol.* 11:449–53

125. Nishikawa, T., Hatano, H., Ohnishi, N., Sasaki, S., Nomura, T. 1969. Establishment of *Candida albicans* in the alimentary tract of the germ-free mice and antagonism with *Escherichia coli* after oral inoculation. *Jpn. J. Microbiol.* 13:263–76

126. Odds, F. C. 1988. Morphogenesis in *Candida albicans*. *CRC Crit. Rev. Microbiol.* 12:45–93

127. Odds, F. C. 1988. Candida *and Candidosis*. London: Bailliere Tindall

128. Odds, F. C., Cockayne, A., Hayward, J., Abbott, A. B. 1985. Effects of im-

idazole- and triazole-derivative anti-fungal compounds on the growth and morphological development of *Candida albicans* hyphae. *J. Gen. Microbiol.* 131:2581–89

129. Olaiya, A. F., Sogin, S. J. 1979. Ploidy determination of *Candida albicans*. *J. Bacteriol.* 140:1043–49

130. Page, S., Odds, F. C. 1988. Binding of plasma proteins of *Candida* species in vitro. *J. Gen. Microbiol.* 134:2693–2702

131. Portillo, F., Gancedo, C. 1986. Purification and properties of three intracellular proteinases from *Candida albicans*. *Biochim. Biophys. Acta* 881:229–35

132. Poulain, D., Hopwood, V., Vernes, A. 1985. Antigenic variability of *Candida albicans*. *CRC Crit. Rev. Microbiol.* 12:223–70

133. Quindos, G., Ponton, J., Cisterna, R., Mackenzie, D. W. R. 1990. Value of detection of antibodies to *Candida albicans* germ tube in the diagnosis of systemic candidosis. *Eur. J. Clin. Microbiol. Infect. Dis.* 9:178–83

134. Rajasingham, K. C., Challacombe, S. J. 1987. Processes involved in the invasion of host epithelial cells by candidal hyphae. *Microbios Lett.* 36:157–63

135. Raschke, W. C., Kern, K. A., Antalis, C., Ballou, C. E. 1973. Genetic control of yeast mannan structure. Isolation and characterization of yeast mannan mutants. *J. Biol. Chem.* 248:4660–66

136. Ray, T. L., Hanson, A., Ray, L. F., Wuepper, K. D. 1979. Purification of a mannan from *Candida albicans* which activates serum complement. *J. Invest. Dermatol.* 73:269–74

137. Ray, T. L., Payne, C. D. 1987. Detection of *Candida* acid proteinase (CAP) antibodies in systemic candidiasis by enzyme immunoassay. *Clin. Res.* 35:711A

138. Ray, T. L., Payne, C. D. 1988. Scanning electron microscopy of epidermal adherence and cavitation in murine candidiasis: a role for *Candida* acid proteinase. *Infect. Immun.* 56:1942–49

139. Ray, T. L., Payne, C. D. 1990. Comparative production and rapid purification of *Candida* acid proteinase from protein-supplemented cultures. *Infect. Immun.* 58:508–14

140. Ray, T. L., Payne, C. D. 1990. *Candida albicans* acid proteinase: a role in virulence. In *Microbial Determinants of Virulence and Host Response*, ed. E. M. Ayoub, G. H. Cassell, W. C. Branche, T. J. Henry, pp.163–78. Washington, DC: Am. Soc. Microbiol.

141. Ray, T. L., Payne, C. D. 1991. *Candida albicans* acid proteinase: characterization and role in candidiasis. In *Structure and Function of the Aspartic Proteinases: Genetics, Structure, Mechanisms*, ed. B. M. Dunn. New York: Plenum. In press

142. Ray, T. L., Wuepper, K. D. 1976. Experimental cutaneous candidiasis in rodents. *J. Invest. Dermatol.* 66:29–33

143. Remold, H., Fasold, H., Staib, F. 1968. Purification and characterization of a proteolytic enzyme from *Candida albicans*. *Biochim. Biophys. Acta* 167:399–406

144. Richardson, M. D., Smith, H. 1981. Production of germ tubes by virulent and attenuated strains of *Candida albicans*. *J. Infect. Dis.* 144:565–69

145. Riggsby, W. S., Torres-Bauza, L. J., Wills, J. W., Townes, T. M. 1982. DNA content, kinetic complexity, and the ploidy question in *Candida albicans*. *Mol. Cell. Biol.* 2:853–62

146. Ross, I. K., De Bernardis, F., Emerson, G. W., Cassone, A., Sullivan, P. A. 1990. The secreted aspartate proteinase of *Candida albicans*: physiology of secretion and virulence of a proteinase-deficient mutant. *J. Gen. Microbiol.* 136:687–94

147. Rotrosen, D., Calderone, R. A., Edwards, J. E. 1986. Adherence of *Candida* species to host tissues and plastic. *Rev. Infect. Dis.* 8:73–85

148. Rotrosen, D., Edwards, J. E., Gibson, T. R., Moore, J. C., Cohen, A. H., Green, I. 1985. Adherence of *Candida* to cultured vascular endothelial cells: mechanisms of attachment and endothelial cell penetration. *J. Infect. Dis.* 152:1264–74

149. Ruchel, R. 1981. Properties of a purified proteinase from the yeast *Candida albicans*. *Biochim. Biophys. Acta* 659:99–113

150. Ruchel, R. 1983. On the role of proteinases from *Candida albicans* in the pathogenesis of acronecrosis. *Zentralbl. Bakteriol. Parasitenkd. Infektionskr. Hyg. Abt. 1: Orig. Reihe A* 255:524–36

151. Ruchel, R., Tegeler, R., Trost, M. 1982. A comparison of secretory proteinases from different strains of *Candida albicans*. *Sabouraudia* 20:233–44

152. Rustchenko-Bulgac, E. P., Sherman, F., Hicks, J. B. 1990. Chromosomal rearrangements associated with morphological mutants provide a means for genetic variation of *Candida albicans*. *J. Bacteriol.* 172:1276–83

153. Ryley, J. F., McGregor, S. 1986. Quantification of vaginal *Candida albi-

cans infections in rodents. *J. Med. Vet. Mycol.* 24:455–60

154. Ryley, J. F., Ryley, N. G. 1990. *Candida albicans*—do mycelia matter? *J. Med. Vet. Mycol.* 28:225–39

154a. Saltarelli, C. G. 1989. Candida albicans: *The Pathogenic Fungus*. New York: Hemisphere

155. Sande, M. A., Bowman, C. R., Calderone, R. A. 1977. Experimental *Candida albicans* endocarditis: Characterization of the disease and response to therapy. *Infect. Immun.* 17:140–47

156. Sandin, R. L., Rogers, A. L., Patterson, R. J., Beneke, E. S. 1982. Evidence for mannose-mediated adherence of *Candida albicans* to human buccal cells in vitro. *Infect. Immun.* 35:79–85

157. Saxena, A., Calderone, R. A. 1990. Purification and characterization of the extracellular C3d-binding protein of *Candida albicans. Infect. Immun.* 58: 309–14

158. Schafer, W., Straney, D., Ciuffetti, L., Van Etten, H. D., Yoder, O. C. 1989. One enzyme makes a fungal pathogen, but not a saprophyte, virulent on a new host plant. *Science* 246:247–50

159. Scherer, S., Magee, P. T. 1990. Genetics of *Candida albicans. Microbiol. Rev.* 54:226–41

160. Schreiber, B., Lyman, C. A., Gurevich, J., Needham, C. A. 1985. Proteolytic activity of *Candida albicans* and other yeasts. *Diagn. Microbiol. Infect. Dis.* 3:1–5

161. Segal, E., Gottfried, L., Lehrer, N. 1988. Candidal vaginitis in hormone-treated mice: Prevention by a chitin extract. *Mycopathologia* 102:157–63

162. Segal, E., Soroka, A., Lehrer, N. 1984. Attachment of *Candida* to mammalian tissues-clinical and experimental studies. *Zentralbl. Bakteriol. Parasitenkd. Infektionskr. Hyg. Abt. 1: Orig. Reihe A* 257:257–65

163. Shepherd, M. G. 1985. Pathogenicity of morphological and auxotrophic mutants of *Candida albicans* in experimental infections. *Infect. Immun.* 50:541–44

164. Shimizu, K., Kondoh, Y., Tanaka, K. 1987. Proteinase production and pathogenicity of *Candida albicans*. I. Invasion into chorioallantoic membrane by *C. albicans* strains of different proteinase activity. *Microbiol. Immunol.* 31:1045–60

165. Siu, C. H., Lam, T. Y., Choi, A. H. C. 1985. Inhibition of cell-cell binding at the aggregation stage of *Dictyostelium discoideum* development by monoclonal antibodies directed against an 80,000-

dalton surface glycoprotein. *J. Biol. Chem.* 260:16030–36

166. Skerl, K. G., Calderone, R. A., Segal, E., Sreevalsan, T., Scheld, W. M. 1984. In vitro binding of *Candida albicans* yeast cells to human fibronectin. *Can. J. Microbiol.* 30:221–27

167. Slutsky, B., Buffo, J., Soll, D. R. 1985. High frequency switching of colony morphology in *Candida albicans. Science* 230:666–69

168. Slutsky, B., Staebell, M., Anderson, J., Risen, L., Pfaller, M., Soll, D. R. 1987. "White-opaque transition": a second high-frequency switching system in *Candida albicans. J. Bacteriol.* 169: 189–97

169. Sobel, J. D., Muller, G., Buckley, H. R. 1984. Critical role of germ tube formation in the pathogenesis of candidal vaginitis. *Infect. Immun.* 44:576–80

170. Sohnle, P. G., Frank, M. M., Kirkpatrick, C. H. 1976. Mechanisms involved in elimination of organisms from experimental cutaneous *Candida albicans* infections in guinea pigs. *J. Immunol.* 117:523–30

171. Sohnle, P. G., Hahn, B. L. 1989. Effect of immunosuppression on epidermal defenses in a murine model of cutaneous candidiasis. *J. Lab. Clin. Med.* 113: 700–7

172. Soll, D. R., Langtimm, C. J., McDowell, J., Hicks, J., Galask, R. 1987. High-frequency switching in *Candida* strains isolated from vaginitis patients. *J. Clin. Microbiol.* 25:1611–22

173. Staib, F. 1965. Serum-proteins as nitrogen source for yeastlike fungi. *Sabouraudia* 4:187–93

174. Staib, F. 1969. Proteolysis and pathogenicity of *Candida albicans* strains. *Mycopathol. Mycol. Appl.* 37:346–48

175. Staib, F., Mishra, S. K., Abel, T. 1977. Serodiagnostic value of extracellular antigens of an actively proteolysing culture of *Candida albicans. Zentralbl. Bakteriol. Parasitenkd. Infektionskr. Hyg. Abt. 1: Orig. Reihe A* 238:284–87

176. Stanley, V. C., Hurley, R. 1969. The growth of *Candida* species in cultures of mouse peritoneal macrophages. *J. Pathol.* 97:357–66

177. Stewart, E., Hawser, S., Gow, N. A. R. 1989. Changes in internal and external pH accompanying growth of *Candida albicans:* studies of non-dimorphic variants. *Arch. Microbiol.* 151:149–53

178. Suzuki, K., Okawa, Y., Hashimoto, K., Suzuki, S., Suzuki, M. 1984. Protecting effect of chitin and chitosan on ex-

perimentally induced murine candidiasis. *Microbiol. Immunol.* 28:903–12

179. Suzuki, T., Kanbe, T., Kuroiwa, T., Tanaka, K. 1986. Occurrence of ploidy shift in a strain of the imperfect yeast *Candida albicans. J. Gen. Microbiol.* 132:443–53

180. Suzuki, T., Kobayashi, I., Kanbe, T., Tanaka, K. 1989. High frequency variation of colony morphology and chromosome reorganization in the pathogenic yeast *Candida albicans. J. Gen. Microbiol.* 135:425–34

181. Suzuki, T., Nishibayashi, T., Kuroiwa, T., Kanbe T., Tanaka, K. 1982. Variance of ploidy in *Candida albicans. J. Bacteriol.* 152:893–96

182. Tronchin, G., Bouchara, J. P., Robert, R. 1989. Dynamic changes of the cell wall surface of *Candida albicans* associated with germination and adherence. *Eur. J. Cell Biol.* 50:285–90

183. Tsuboi, R., Ko, I.-J., Takamori, K., Ogawa, H. 1989. Isolation of a keratinolytic proteinase from *Trichophyton mentagrophytes* with enzymatic activity at acidic pH. *Infect. Immun.* 57:3479–83

184. Tsuboi, R., Kurita, Y., Negi, M., Ogawa, H. 1985. A specific inhibitor of keratinolytic proteinase from *Candida albicans* could inhibit cell growth of *C. albicans. J. Invest. Dermatol.* 85:438–40

185. Van't Wout, J. W., Meynaar, I., Linde, I., Poell, R., Mattie, H., van Furth, R. 1990. Effect of amphotericin B, fluconazole and itraconazole on intracellular *Candida albicans* and germ tube development in macrophages. *J. Antimicrob. Chemother.* 25:803–11

186. Vecchiarelli, A., Bistoni, F., Cenci, E., Perito, S., Cassone, A. 1985. In-vitro killing of *Candida* species by murine immuneffectors and its relationship to the experimental pathogenicity. *Sabouraudia: J. Med. Vet. Mycol.* 23:377–87

187. von Eiff, M., Essink, M., Roos, N., Hiddemann, W., Buchner, T., van de Loo, J. 1990. Hepatosplenic candidiasis, a late manifestation of *Candida septicaemia* in neutropenic patients with haematologic malignancies. *Blut* 60:242–48

188. Vudhichamnong, K., Walker, D. M.,

Ryley, H. C. 1982. The effect of secretory immunoglobulin A on the in vitro adherence of the yeast *Candida albicans* to human oral epithelial cells. *Arch. Oral Biol.* 27:617–21

189. Walsh, T. J., Aoki, S., Mechinaud, F., Bacher, J., Lee, J., et al. 1990. Effects of preventive, early, and late antifungal chemotherapy with fluconazole in different granulocytopenic models of experimental disseminated candidiasis. *J. Infect. Dis.* 161:755–60

190. Whelan, W. L. 1987. The genetics of medically important fungi. *CRC Crit. Rev. Microbiol.* 14:99–170

191. Whelan, W. L., Delga, J. M., Wadsworth, E., Walsh, T. J., Kwon-Chung, K. J., et al. 1990. Isolation and characterization of cell surface mutants of *Candida albicans. Infect. Immun.* 58:1552–57

192. Whelan, W. L., Partridge, R. M., Magee, P. T. 1980. Heterozygosity and segregation in *Candida albicans. Mol Gen. Genet.* 180:107–13

193. Whelan, W. L., Soll, D. R. 1982. Mitotic recombination in *Candida albicans:* Recessive lethal alleles linked to a gene required for methionine biosynthesis. *MGG* 187:477–85

194. Woolford, C. A., Daniels, L. B., Park, F. J., Jones, E. W., van Arsdell, J. N., Innis, M. A. 1986. The Pep4 gene encodes an aspartyl protease implicated in the posttranslational regulation of *Saccharomyces cerevisiae* vacuolar hydrolases. *Mol. Cell. Biol.* 6:2500–10

195. Wray, D., Felix, D. H., Cumming, C. G. 1990. Alteration of humoral responses to *Candida* in HIV infection. *Br. Dent. J.* 168:326–29

196. Wright, S. D., Reddy, P. A., Jong, M. T. C., Erickson, B. W. 1987. C3bi receptor (complement receptor type 3) recognizes a region of complement protein C3 containing the sequence Arg-Gly-Asp. *Proc. Natl. Acad. Sci. USA* 84:1965–68

197. Young, G. 1958. The process of invasion and the persistence of *Candida albicans* injected intraperitoneally into mice. *J. Infect. Dis.* 102:114–20

198. Yuan, L., Cole, G. T., Sun, S. H. 1988. Possible role of a proteinase in endosporulation of *Coccidioides immitis. Infect. Immun.* 56:1551–59

Annu. Rev. Microbiol. 1991. 45:219-50
Copyright © 1991 by Annual Reviews Inc. All rights reserved

REGULATION OF HUMAN IMMUNODEFICIENCY VIRUS REPLICATION

Bryan R. Cullen

Howard Hughes Medical Institute and Department of Microbiology and Immunology, Duke University Medical Center, Box 3025, Durham, North Carolina 27710

KEY WORDS: retrovirus, HIV-1, AIDS, gene regulation

CONTENTS

INTRODUCTION... 219
THE RETROVIRAL LIFE CYCLE: A BRIEF OVERVIEW.............................. 221
THE HIV-1 REPLICATION CYCLE.. 223
   Proviral Synthesis and Integration 223
   The Role of Cellular Transcription Factors 225
   Early HIV-1 Gene Expression.. 227
   The Transition to Viral Structural Gene Expression....................... 232
   HIV-1 RNA Expression Patterns... 236
   HIV-1 Virion Assembly and Release 239
HIV-1 AS A PROTOTYPIC COMPLEX RETROVIRUS 240
CONCLUDING REMARKS 243

INTRODUCTION

In 1981, several groups reported an outbreak of severe opportunistic infections among previously healthy male homosexuals (50, 97). This newly described disease, subsequently termed acquired immunodeficiency syndrome (AIDS), spread rapidly into several other risk groups, including intravenous drug abusers and recipients of contaminated blood or blood prod-

219

0066-4227/91/1001-0219$02.00

ucts. More recently, AIDS has become the most significant infectious disease
in many parts of the world, including North America.

The pattern of disease transmission observed for AIDS strongly suggested
that the causative agent was a blood-borne viral pathogen. This expectation
was fulfilled in 1983 with the isolation of a novel retrovirus from the
lymphocytes of AIDS patients that has since become known as human
immunodeficiency virus type 1 (HIV-1) (7, 114). The importance of HIV-1 as
a human pathogen led to the rapid cloning and sequencing of several full-
length replication-competent HIV-1 proviral clones (102, 115, 123, 150).
Although these results clearly showed that HIV-1 was in many ways a typical
retrovirus, they revealed an unusually complex genomic organization when
compared to the prototypic mammalian retrovirus murine leukemia virus
(MLV) (Figure 1). Subsequently, HIV-1 has been shown to encode at least six
proteins in addition to the *gag*, *pol*, and *env* gene products characteristic of all
replication-competent retroviruses (23). These auxiliary viral proteins regulate both the quantity and quality of HIV-1 gene expression and also play an
important role in the morphogenesis and release of infectious HIV-1 virions.

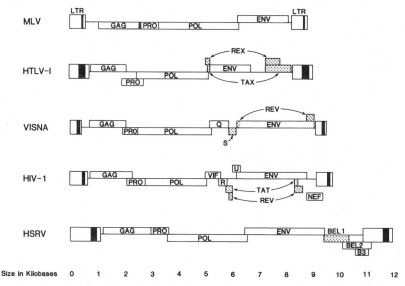

Figure 1 Retroviral genomic organization. This figure compares the proviral genomic organization seen in MLV, a representative simple retrovirus, with that seen in HIV-1 and other members
of the proposed complex-retrovirus classification. While all known viral genes are named and
drawn to scale, this listing should not be considered complete. Stippling indicates known
transcriptional activators, while hatching denotes known posttranscriptional regulators. LTRs are
indicated by large terminal boxes with the R region in black. R, Vpr; U, Vpu; B3, Bel-3
(reproduced with permission from Ref. 22).

More recently, it has become clear that HIV-1 is a member of a whole class of complex retroviruses that can be distinguished from simple retroviruses such as MLV and the avian leukemia viruses (ALV) by criteria based not only on their more complex genomic organization but, more specifically, on the pattern of viral gene expression detected in the infected host cell (22). Nevertheless, the canonical retroviral replication cycle depicted in Figure 2 remains an accurate, if simplified, description of the life cycle of both MLV and HIV-1.

I begin this review by briefly outlining the retroviral replication cycle as it has been described for MLV and other simple retroviruses (148). I then describe the life cycle of HIV-1 in detail, focusing particularly on the distinguishing aspects of this virus. Finally, I discuss the similarities between HIV-1 and other complex retroviruses and suggest that HIV-1 should be viewed as a representative member of this retroviral class.

THE RETROVIRAL LIFE CYCLE: A BRIEF OVERVIEW

The first step in the retroviral life cycle is the specific interaction of the virion envelope glycoprotein with a host-cell surface receptor protein (152) (Figure 2). The envelope protein also facilitates the subsequent intracytoplasmic penetration of the virion core to generate what has been termed the viral "nucleoprotein complex" (148). This nucleoprotein complex then initiates the synthesis of the double-stranded DNA proviral intermediate from the single-stranded viral RNA genome, utilizing the virion associated reverse transcriptase. The linear proviral DNA intermediate then migrates to the nucleus where the viral integrase enzyme acts to covalently link the retroviral genome to the

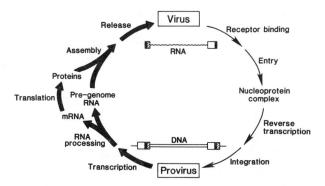

Figure 2   Overview of the retroviral replication cycle. Preintegration events are indicated by light arrows while postintegration events are denoted by thick arrows. See text for detailed discussion. Reproduced from Ref. 148 with permission.

host chromosomal DNA, thereby forming the retroviral provirus (148). Proviral integration appears to be an essential step in the retroviral life cycle (127).

Once stably linked to the host-cell genome, the provirus is in essence similar to any other host-cell gene. The provirus is replicated as if it were a normal part of the host genome and is transmitted to any progeny cells that result from division of the host cell. The host-cell RNA polymerase II transcribes the provirus to yield both progeny RNA genomes and viral mRNAs. These RNAs are posttranscriptionally processed (i.e. capped, spliced, polyadenylated, etc) by host-cell proteins and are translated by the host protein synthesis machinery to yield the viral proteins (148).

In its simplest form, as seen for example in MLV, retroviral replication requires only three distinct virally encoded genes (Figure 1). These are the *gag* gene, which encodes the virion structural proteins; the *pol* gene, which encodes the virion-associated reverse transcriptase and integrase enzymes; and *env*, which encodes the envelope glycoprotein. (The viral protease may be encoded in *pol* or may form part of *gag*.) In the integrated DNA provirus, these three genes are invariably arranged in the same order (5'-*gag-pol-env*-3') and flanked by the characteristic long terminal repeats (LTRs) generated during the process of reverse transcription. The LTRs contain enhancer and promoter elements required for efficient transcription of the retroviral genome and also contain sequences important for efficient mRNA polyadenylation within the 3' LTR (12, 148). In the case of MLV and other simple animal retroviruses, the integrated provirus encodes only two distinct transcripts. The full-length retroviral RNA transcript serves both as the genome of progeny virions and as the mRNA for synthesis of the Gag and Gag-Pol polyproteins. The level of Gag-Pol expression is set at ~5% of the level of expression of Gag and is regulated, depending on the retrovirus, by either the inefficient suppression of a stop codon located at the end of Gag (e.g. MLV) or by an inefficient ribosomal frame shift in the region where the *gag* and *pol* open reading frames overlap (e.g. ALV) (36, 66, 67). The full-length MLV transcript, which contains a single splice acceptor and splice donor combination, also serves as the precursor for the spliced viral *env* mRNA. The low frequency of this unusually inefficient splicing event appears to be regulated by *cis*-acting RNA sequences present within the viral genome and does not depend on the expression of virally encoded proteins (3, 74).

Retroviral virion formation and release remain rather poorly understood. In the case of MLV, virion assembly occurs adjacent to the plasma membrane and involves the ordered assembly of the Gag and Gag-Pol polyproteins (28, 148). These proteins are targeted to the inside of the host plasma membrane by myristylation of their N termini (124). This posttranslational modification, which is performed by host-cell proteins, is therefore essential for the formation of functional virions. During the process of virion assembly, two copies of the single-stranded retroviral RNA genome are incorporated into the virion by a process that involves the sequence-specific interaction of a zinc-finger motif located in the nucleocapsid component of the viral Gag protein with a packaging signal located within the leader region of the genomic RNA (28, 148). Subsequently, the retroviral cores bud through regions of the plasma membrane that bear high concentrations of the viral Env proteins. Assembly of Env onto the virion core may be facilitated by an interaction between the transmembrane domain of Env and the viral Gag proteins (45, 111). During or shortly after budding, the virion protease is activated, resulting in the ordered cleavage of the Gag and Gag-Pol polyproteins into the mature virion structural proteins. This maturation event, which involves a detectable change in virion morphology, is essential for virion infectivity (28, 73).

The life cycle of MLV and other simple retroviruses is therefore both highly streamlined and efficient. Viral gene products serve structural or enzymatic functions while regulation of viral gene expression, be it at the transcriptional or posttranscriptional level, is controlled entirely by the interplay of *cis*-acting viral DNA or RNA sequences with *trans*-acting factors encoded by the host cell. As we shall see, it is the direct participation of virally encoded proteins in the regulation of viral gene expression that most clearly distinguishes HIV-1 and other complex retroviruses from simple retroviruses such as MLV and ALV.

THE HIV-1 REPLICATION CYCLE

Proviral Synthesis and Integration

The initial events of the HIV-1 replication cycle, when examined in activated primary human CD4$^+$ T lymphocytes or in human T-cell lines, are similar to the initial events in the life cycle of MLV in infected fibroblasts. HIV-1 replication begins with the specific interaction of the gp120 or outer membrane (OMP) component of the viral envelope protein with the CD4 receptor found on human helper T-cells (25, 79, 98). The subsequent internalization of the HIV-1 virion core to form an activated viral nucleoprotein complex is mediated by the gp41 or transmembrane (TMP) component of the envelope protein (139). The enzymatic activities required for the synthesis of the HIV-1 DNA proviral intermediate and the eventual integration of this proviral intermediate into the host genomic DNA appear comparable for HIV-1 and MLV (30).

The human CD4$^+$ T lymphocyte forms a primary target for HIV-1 infection in vivo. However, unless activated by the presentation of appropriate antigen, these T-cells remain in the GO phase of the cell cycle. In this resting state, lymphocytes do not permit the replication of HIV-1, even though HIV-1 can bind to the CD4 receptor molecules displayed on the surface of these cells and also appears able to efficiently penetrate the cell cytoplasm (141, 154,

155). However, the HIV-1 nucleoprotein complex thus formed appears unable to complete the biosynthesis of the proviral DNA intermediate and no integrated proviruses are therefore observed (141, 154). Resting cells are similarly nonpermissive for the replication of many animal retroviruses (40). For example, MLV cannot productively infect nondividing murine fibroblasts, again owing to blockage of provirus synthesis and/or integration (149).

Infection of resting T-cells may therefore produce a form of latent HIV-1 infection that reflects the absence of certain cellular factors. A major unanswered question is how long these eclipsed HIV-1 virions can be maintained in the resting T-cell before they irreversibly lose their ability to respond to cellular activation. Zack et al (154) reported that these proviral intermediates are quite labile and lose viability with a half-life of approximately one day. Stevenson et al (141), in contrast, have reported that these extrachromosomal forms of the HIV-1 genome can persist for several weeks after infection of resting T-cells and, following T-cell activation, proceed normally through proviral integration to the generation of progeny virions.

In vivo, the majority of circulating T-cells are in a resting, quiescent state. Activation of T-cells, and the resultant cellular proliferation, is normally a rare event that occurs only after presentation of specific antigen or other appropriate immunological stimulus. A circulating HIV-1 virion would therefore appear far more likely to encounter a resting rather than a replicating T-cell. The vast majority of these infectious events are therefore predicted to result in the formation of nonproductive, extrachromosomal forms of the HIV-1 genome. If these forms are labile, as suggested by Zack et al (154), then the majority of these infections would be abortive. In contrast, if these nonintegrated viral forms are stable (141), then HIV-1 infection could lead to the establishment of a large reservoir of latently infected T-cells that would, upon their eventual activation, become active producers of further infectious HIV-1 virions. Resolution of this important question is clearly essential to an understanding of the factors that regulate HIV-1 spread and latency in the infected patient.

Although helper T-cells provide a primary target for HIV-1 replication in vivo, they are not the only, or perhaps even the most important, host cell. Significant evidence suggests that this distinction belongs instead to cells of the monocyte/macrophage lineage and particularly to the mature mononuclear phagocyte (99). Although HIV-1 replication in these cells is not as well understood as in T-cells, it is nevertheless clear that significant differences exist at the level of virion entry, at the level of proviral synthesis and integration, and in the effect of HIV-1 infection on the host cell.

Although all HIV-1 isolates appear able to replicate in activated primary human T-cells, the ability of different viral strains and proviral clones to replicate in macrophages differs greatly. For example, the related HTLV-IIIB and LAV isolates of HIV-1, which are the standard laboratory strains, replicate very poorly in primary macrophage cultures while other cloned HIV-1 isolates, such as JR-FL and Ba-L, replicate ~1000-fold more efficiently (44, 78, 99, 107). Recent studies showed that this viral tropism results from the inability of some strains to effectively penetrate into the macrophage cell (78, 107). Macrophage tropism appears to be determined by a region of the viral gp120 envelope protein that is distinct from those involved in binding to CD4 (107). Therefore, while infection of both T-cells and macrophages by HIV-1 requires the functional interaction of gp120 with the cell surface CD4 receptor (19, 25, 79, 98), productive infection of macrophages may also require a second, distinct interaction of gp120 with a currently unknown cell-surface molecule (107).

A second distinction between T-cell and macrophage infection by HIV-1 occurs subsequent to entry. As noted above, resting, nonreplicating T-cells are refractory to productive infection by HIV-1. In contrast, although human macrophages are end-stage, differentiated cells that rarely undergo cell division, they can nevertheless be efficiently infected by HIV-1 strains of appropriate tropism. In fact, HIV-1 infection of nonproliferating macrophages results in the production of full-length DNA proviral intermediates that integrate into the genomic DNA of the cell and serve as effective templates for the production of progeny virions (J. B. Weinberg, M. H. Malim, & B. R. Cullen, submitted). The reason for this difference between nonreplicating T-cells and macrophages is unknown, but tissue macrophages, while nondividing, cannot be considered metabolically resting cells. In any event, the observation that macrophages can be productively infected by HIV-1 without any requirement for replication or immunologic activation is consistent with observations suggesting that these cells form highly important reservoirs for the virus in vivo (99). This finding may also reflect the third major difference between the HIV-1 replication cycle in T-cells and macrophages—i.e. that the HIV-1 replication cycle in the former is normally a lytic cycle marked by high level, short-term production of virus (137), while HIV-1 infection of macrophages generally results in a chronic or persistent infection marked by the longer-term but lower-level production of progeny virions (44, 99). Currently, it remains unclear to what degree in vivo infection of macrophages by HIV-1 results in reduced long-term viability or disruption of essential effector functions (6, 99). It is, however, tempting to suggest that such effects might underlie several of the long-term cytopathic changes observed in HIV-1 infected patients.

The Role of Cellular Transcription Factors

Host transcription factors act upon the integrated HIV-1 provirus, as they do on all other retroviral proviruses. The recognition sequences for several constitutively expressed or inducible host-cell transcription factors have been identified within the HIV-1 LTR promoter element (Figure 3). Of particular importance are the binding sites for Spl and for the TATA factor TFIID, as well as for the inducible transcription factor NF-κB (42, 58, 69, 104). In addition, the HIV-1 LTR contains binding sites for the nuclear transcription factors NFAT-1, USF, AP-1, and LBP (42, 70, 88).

The constitutively expressed cellular transcription factors Spl and TFIID play an important role in mediating promoter function in many cellular and viral genes. The HIV-1 promoter possesses three adjacent functional Spl binding sites as well as a typical TATA element (42, 58, 70). Both the Spl and TFIID binding interactions appear critical for HIV-1 LTR promoter function as deletion of these binding domains results in a defective HIV-1 provirus (58, 68, 86).

The inducible transcription factor NF-κB serves as a pleiotropic mediator of both tissue-specific and inducible gene expression in a wide range of different human cells types (85). Recently, NF-κB was shown to belong to a family of eukaryotic regulatory proteins that also includes the *rel* oncogene and the *Drosophila* dorsal gene product (47). Activation of NF-κB, which occurs upon treatment of resting human T-cells with either lectin or specific antigen, is also a key step in the activation of T-cell specific genes such as interleukin-2 (IL-2) and the α-chain of the IL-2 receptor (11). Although the two NF-κB binding sites observed in the HIV-1 LTR are important for maximal expression, they do not appear essential for viral replication in vitro (86). Indeed, the deletion of both LTR NF-κB recognition sites reportedly only modestly affects the ability of HIV-1 to replicate in activated primary blood lymphocytes. Clearly, however, the functional interaction of NF-κB with its target sequence in the HIV-1 LTR does result in the enhanced expression of linked genes when measured in either T-cells or macrophages (52, 104). Therefore, the NF-κB motifs present in the HIV-1 LTR most likely serve primarily to increase the rate of viral gene transcription in response to the activation of NF-κB.

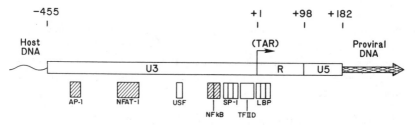

Figure 3   The HIV-1 LTR promoter element. Scale representation of the unique 3' (U3), repeat (R), and unique 5' (U5) subregions of the HIV-1 proviral LTR. Basepair coordinates are given relative to the transcription start site, which is designated as +1. Boxes indicate DNA binding sites for known cell transcription factors, and hatching shows inducible factors (reproduced with permission from Ref. 24).

A second nuclear factor induced by activation of T-cells, termed NFAT-1, also interacts with a specific binding site within the HIV-1 LTR (Figure 3). While NFAT-1 may also play a role in the activation of HIV-1 gene expression, little evidence regarding the functional significance of NFAT-1 currently exists (88). Similarly, the importance of a binding site for the inducible transcription factor AP-1, located towards the 5' end of the LTR U3 region, remains to be established (88).

Two additional constitutive HIV-1 DNA:protein binding interactions have also been defined (Figure 3). These involve binding of the cellular transcription factors USF and LBP (42, 70). Both protein:DNA binding events are readily detectable in vitro, using gel retardation and DNase footprinting analysis, and in vivo, using DNase hypersensitivity analysis (42, 59, 91). However, the functional significance of these interactions remains unclear, although some data suggest that USF may act as a modest silencer of the HIV-1 LTR, thus giving rise to the earlier term NRF (negative regulatory factor) (42, 88). Mutational analyses have so far failed to demonstrate any direct role for the tripartite LBP interaction in regulating HIV-1 specific gene expression in vivo (91).

In addition to transcription factors encoded by the host cell itself, superinfecting viruses may also encode factors able to enhance HIV-1–specific gene expression *in trans*. Viral gene products encoded by the human T-cell leukemia virus type I (HTLV-I), the human spumaretrovirus (HSRV), several members of the herpes virus family, the adenoviruses, and hepatitis-B virus all enhance HIV-1 LTR–dependent gene expression in transfected cells (46, 48, 75, 100, 105, 130, 132). Because of the somewhat narrow cell tropism of HIV-1, whether any of these observed activation events have any relevance to the spread of HIV-1 in vivo is unclear. Two viruses known to infect human T-cell populations, and hence strong candidates as cofactors in the pathogenesis of HIV-1–induced disease, are HTLV-I and human herpes virus 6 (HHV-6). The HTLV-I Tax *trans*-activator induces NF-κB activity in HTLV-I–infected T-cells (132), while herpes virus early gene products are believed to activate HIV-1 LTR–specific gene expression via both NF-κB-dependent and -independent pathways (48, 105). Of particular importance is the observation that dual infection of cultured CD4$^+$ human T-cells with HHV-6 and HIV-1 results in enhanced replication of HIV-1 and in accelerated cell death (89).

Early HIV-1 Gene Expression

The cellular transcription factors described above are sufficient to induce a low, basal level of HIV-1 gene expression in infected cells. Evidence suggests that these initial transcripts reach the infected cell cytoplasm exclusively in the form of the fully spliced, 2-kb class of viral mRNAs that encode the viral regulatory proteins Tat, Rev, and Nef (see below). The viral Tat *trans*-

activator then dramatically increases HIV-1 LTR directed gene expression, thereby establishing a powerful positive-feedback loop that can lead to very high levels of HIV-1 specific RNA and protein synthesis (4, 135, 137). A functional copy of the viral *tat* gene is essential for HIV-1 replication in vitro as is an intact copy of the *cis*-acting viral sequence responsive to Tat, the so-called *trans*-activation response (TAR) element (27, 38).

The *tat* gene is divided into two coding exons that together predict the synthesis of an 86–amino acid protein. However, the 72–amino acid first coding exon of Tat, which is flanked at its 3' end by a conserved translation termination signal, is sufficient to encode a fully active Tat protein (20, 102). At least two distinct functional domains have been identified in Tat. A highly conserved motif containing seven cysteine residues has been proposed to bind metal ions and may mediate protein:protein interactions in vivo (39, 41, 122). A C-terminal domain rich in lysine and arginine residues is required for the nuclear and nucleolar localization of Tat in expressing cells and will also direct heterologous proteins to the nucleolus when present *in cis* (60, 122, 133). This basic motif also serves as the RNA binding domain of Tat (see below).

The TAR element is a 59-nucleotide RNA stem-loop structure located at the 5' end of all HIV-1 transcripts (102, 118) (Figure 4). Both the location and orientation of TAR are critical for function (59, 112, 118, 128). Extensive mutational analyses support the hypothesis that the double-stranded RNA segments present in TAR primarily serve a structural role in the appropriate presentation of essential primary sequence information located in and immediately adjacent to the six-nucleotide terminal loop and the three-nucleotide bulge of TAR (9, 35, 59, 68, 121, 128). The fact that alteration of nonessential flanking sequences to create competing RNA secondary structures can dramatically inhibit TAR function provides further evidence for TAR function at the RNA level (10). Although the hypothesis that the TAR element acts as the RNA target sequence for Tat has been generally accepted, the importance of several cellular proteins that were proposed to bind to TAR remained unclear. This question was recently addressed using chimaeric proteins consisting of Tat fused to heterologous RNA (Rev, MS2 coat protein) or DNA (c-jun) binding domains (8, 129, 138). The TAR element was then replaced with the appropriate RNA (RRE, MS2 operator) or DNA (AP-1) target sequence. In each case, the novel sequence specificity conferred on Tat by fusion to these heterologous nucleic acid binding domains permitted transcriptional *trans*-activation of the HIV-1 LTR via the appropriate introduced target sequence, i.e. independently of TAR. One can draw two conclusions from this observation. The first is that the only role of TAR is to act as the target sequence for the Tat *trans*-activator. The second is that cellular TAR binding proteins are probably not important for Tat function except insofar as they act to mediate the interaction of Tat with TAR.

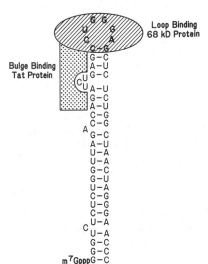

Figure 4 The Tat/TAR interaction. The sequence and structure of the 59-nucleotide TAR RNA element are shown together with the putative binding sites of Tat and of a cellular 68-kilodalton (kd) protein. This cooperative interaction is hypothesized to be essential for in vivo Tat function (reproduced with permission from Ref. 20).

Dingwall et al (29) provided the initial evidence that Tat possessed the ability to directly and specifically bind to the TAR RNA stem loop. However, attempts to correlate the effect of TAR mutations on in vivo function with their effect on Tat binding in vitro met with mixed success. Mutations that disrupted the TAR stem structure or that affected the three-nucleotide bulge reduced both in vivo function and in vitro Tat binding. However, because mutations in the terminal loop of TAR that were equally deleterious in vivo had little or no effect on Tat binding in vitro (29, 35), the physiological relevance of this interaction remained unclear. This concern has now been resolved by the demonstration that the interaction between Tat and TAR occurs entirely at the site of the three-nucleotide bulge (120, 151) (Figure 4). The basic domain of Tat is both necessary and sufficient for binding to TAR (120, 151), thus placing Tat into the arginine-rich class of sequence-specific RNA binding proteins that also includes the HIV-1 Rev *trans*-activator (84).

Despite the general agreement that Tat shows sequence-specific binding to TAR in vitro, several lines of evidence suggest that this direct interaction constitutes only one of the components involved in the in vivo interaction of Tat with TAR. The most significant of these is the finding, noted above, that mutations to the terminal loop of TAR that strongly inhibit in vivo function have little or no effect on in vitro Tat binding. In contrast, in the case of chimaeric Tat fusion proteins, binding to a heterologous RNA target sequence was found to be fully sufficient for in vivo *trans*-activation. Therefore, a second, cellular factor is probably involved in mediating the Tat:TAR interaction in vivo. The best current candidate for this role is a nuclear factor of ~68 kilodaltons (kd) that binds specifically to the terminal loop sequence of TAR in vitro (96). Mutations of the terminal loop that affect in vivo TAR function were observed to result in an appropriate reduction in the in vitro binding affinity of p68 for TAR. In addition, partially purified p68 protein was observed to enhance the in vitro *trans*-activation of HIV-1 LTR–specific transcription by Tat (95). It is therefore hypothesized that Tat *trans*-activation of the HIV-1 LTR requires the cooperative binding of both Tat and a 68-kd cellular protein to two different, adjacent loop structures present near the apex of the TAR RNA element (Figure 4).

Many studies have shown that Tat increases the steady-state level of transcripts derived from genes linked to the HIV-1 LTR (20, 102, 112, 153). This increase is generally agreed to be the result of an enhancement in the rate of transcription of such genes, rather than of the specific stabilization of mRNAs containing TAR (61, 68). However, the mechanism by which Tat enhances the rate of transcription has been more controversial. One hypothesis is that Tat acts to increase the rate of transcription initiation, thus making TAR the RNA equivalent of a DNA enhancer sequence (131). An alternative proposal is that Tat could function to prevent premature termination of transcripts initiated within the HIV-1 LTR (72). This hypothesis originally derived from the observation that Tat had little effect on the level of RNA polymerase density adjacent to the site of transcription initiation but dramatically increased the rate of transcription of sequences distal to the HIV-1 LTR (72). These authors also reported that the basal HIV-1 LTR promoter produced a large number of prematurely terminated, ~59-nucleotide TAR RNAs that were reduced upon coexpression of the Tat *trans*-activator (72, 128). They proposed that Tat therefore activated the HIV-1 LTR by relieving a specific block to transcription elongation through the TAR sequence. Unfortunately, the obvious prediction of this hypothesis, i.e. that deletion of TAR should enhance the level of HIV-1 LTR–dependent gene expression, proved invalid (59, 118, 128). However, the observation that Tat promotes elongation has now been confirmed both in vivo and in vitro (83, 95). These more recent results indicate that the transcription termination observed in the absence of Tat occurs at multiple, possibly random locations in viral or heterologous sequences linked to the HIV-1 LTR, thus suggesting that Tat acts by increasing processivity rather than by preventing a specific termination event (83, 95). The accumulation of short TAR-specific RNAs in the absence of Tat is now thought to result from the resistance of these structured RNAs to the action of a 3' exonuclease believed to degrade the heterogeneous, prematurely terminated RNA species transcribed from the basal HIV-1 LTR promoter (128).

The results discussed above suggest that transcription complexes initiating in the HIV-1 LTR elongate only poorly through adjacent DNA templates. This lack of elongation competence is somehow rectified by the interaction of the Tat protein with the nascent TAR element and, potentially, with the transcription complex itself (8). Neither the reason for the high incidence of premature termination nor the mechanism by which rescue of these transcription complexes occurs is currently understood. However, this poor elongation competence probably must be encoded within the HIV-1 LTR promoter element itself (8). It remains unclear whether the HIV-1 LTR simply lacks the ability to assemble a complete transcription complex or whether one or more factors that interact with LTR promoter sequences specify inefficient elongation. Tat, in combination with TAR, however, can at least modestly *trans*-activate transcription from such standard promoters as the LTR of Rous sarcoma virus, the SV40 early promoter, and the cytomegalovirus immediate-early promoter (20, 112, 118). Therefore, the poor processivity observed during basal HIV-1 LTR–driven transcription may simply be an extreme example of a relatively general phenomenon.

Although results from several groups support the hypothesis that transcriptional *trans*-activation by Tat results primarily from enhanced transcription elongation, evidence has also been presented suggesting that Tat can, in at least some experimental settings, also significantly increase the level of transcription initiation (83). Hence, the increased processivity of transcription complexes formed in the presence of Tat might be correlated with an increased ability to assemble a functional transcription complex at the HIV-1 LTR promoter—i.e. to enhance HIV-1 LTR transcription initiation via an interaction with the TAR RNA element (131). The question of whether Tat affects mRNA synthesis at both the level of initiation and elongation and, more importantly perhaps, whether these two effects are somehow functionally interlinked, clearly awaits full resolution. The recent demonstration of an in vitro transcription system that appears to faithfully reproduce the TAR-dependent *trans*-activation of the HIV-1 LTR by Tat appears likely to represent a key step towards the eventual unraveling of the mechanism of action of this novel regulatory protein (95).

While activation of viral RNA transcription is the major action of Tat in most experimental systems, it is clearly not the only effect of this small *trans*-activator. Several reports have noted that the effect of Tat on expression of genes linked to the viral LTR, when measured at the protein level, can be significantly more than the effect determined at the level of steady-state mRNA (20, 32, 117, 153). Although the molecular basis for this second, posttranscriptional component of the bimodal action of Tat remains unclear, it also appears to be mediated by the sequence specific interaction of Tat with the viral TAR RNA element (59). Results obtained using microinjection of preformed TAR-containing RNA molecules into *Xenopus laevis* oocytes show that this posttranscriptional effect occurs in the cell nucleus yet can be segregated from the transcriptional action of Tat (13). Thus far, Tat has not been shown to modulate the nuclear export of TAR-containing RNA species, and thus a more complex mechanism of action appears likely (13, 61). One hypothesis is that Tat could affect the cytoplasmic compartmentalization, and hence the translational utilization, of TAR-containing transcripts (13).

A second early gene product of HIV-1, termed Nef, is a 27-kd myristylated phosphoprotein associated with cytoplasmic membrane structures in expressing cells (57). Nef reportedly possesses the GTPase, autophosphorylation, and GTP-binding properties typical of the G-protein family of signal transduction proteins (54), but this observation remains unconfirmed (71). Unlike Tat and Rev, the Nef gene product is not required for HIV-1 replication in culture. In fact, one proposal is that expression of Nef results in an inhibition of HIV-1 LTR–specific gene expression and viral replication (1, 15, 106). However, these negative effects of Nef remain controversial as others have observed no effect of the Nef protein on either viral replication or gene expression (5, 57, 77). The role of the *nef* gene product in the HIV-1 replication cycle therefore remains unclear. However, the fact that the Nef open reading frame is reasonably conserved in all primate lentiviruses suggests that this protein likely plays a significant role in the viral life cycle in the infected host. Recent data suggest that a functional *nef* gene product can markedly enhance viral replication and pathogenicity in rhesus macaques infected with a cloned isolate of simian immunodeficiency virus (SIV) (H. Kestler & R. Desrosiers, personal communication).

The Transition to Viral Structural Gene Expression

The HIV-1 genome encodes two classes of viral mRNAs that can be distinguished based on their temporal expression during the HIV-1 replication cycle (Figure 5). The early class of viral mRNAs consists of the multiply spliced, ~2-kb mRNA species that encode the viral regulatory proteins Tat, Nef, and Rev. The late class of viral mRNAs consists of the unspliced (~9 kb) and singly spliced (~4 kb) transcripts that encode the virion structural proteins. In the absence of functional Rev protein, only the fully spliced class of HIV-1 mRNAs is expressed (32, 34, 92, 134) (Figure 5). In fact, Rev mutants of HIV-1 cannot induce the synthesis of the viral structural proteins and are, therefore, replication defective (145). An analysis of the time course of HIV-1 infection of human T-lymphocytes reveals a similar phenomenon (76). Initially, one detects only the 2-kb class of viral mRNAs in the cytoplasm of HIV-1 infected cells, but as the level of viral gene expression increases (resulting from the action of the Tat protein), one observes a switch to the synthesis of the viral structural gene mRNAs. This effect, which reflects the action of the viral Rev *trans*-activator, occurs concomitantly with an essentially equivalent reduction in the synthesis of the fully spliced mRNA species that encode the viral regulatory proteins (33, 92) (Figure 5). There-

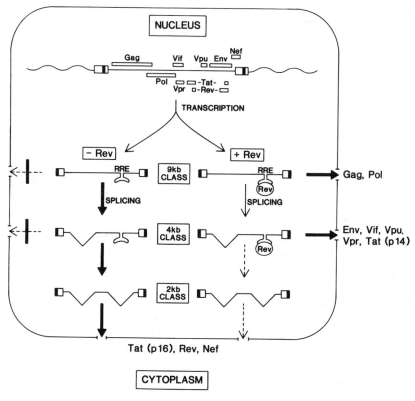

Figure 5 Schematic representation of HIV-1 Rev function. The pattern of HIV-1 mRNA and protein expression observed in the absence of Rev (i.e. early gene expression) and in the presence of Rev (i.e. late gene expression) is indicated. *Tat (p16)* represents the full length, two-exon form of Tat while *Tat (p14)* represents the truncated, one-exon form of Tat. See text for detailed discussion.

fore, Rev functions as a negative regulator of its own synthesis and also mediates the establishment of an equilibrium between viral structural and regulatory protein synthesis.

The switch from the early, regulatory phase of HIV-1 gene expression to the late, structural phase appears to require the expression of a critical level of the Rev protein (113). Several cell lines nonproductively infected by HIV-1 constitutively express a low level of viral mRNA that is primarily of the 2-kb class. Treatment of these cells with agents that result in activation of the HIV-1 LTR also induces the expression of the viral structural proteins (113). Therefore, latency in this context is hypothesized to result from the expression of a subcritical level of the Rev *trans*-activator, a level that in turn reflects a lack of cellular transcription factors critical for efficient HIV-1 LTR–

dependent gene expression (113). The primary role of the Rev regulatory pathway may therefore be to prevent the premature progression of the viral replication cycle to the late or lytic phase in cells that cannot support the required level of viral mRNA and protein synthesis.

While Rev is absolutely required for the cytoplasmic expression of unspliced HIV-1 RNA species, it appears to have little effect on the pattern of HIV-1 RNA expression in the cell nucleus (31, 34, 56, 93). In particular, high levels of unspliced viral transcripts can be detected in the nucleus even in the absence of Rev (Figure 5). While the splice sites present in HIV-1, like the splice sites present in other retroviral transcripts, are apparently inefficiently utilized by the splicing machinery of the cell (14, 93), why these incompletely spliced viral transcripts remain sequestered in the cell nucleus in the absence of Rev is unclear. One hypothesis suggests that the *gag*, *pol*, and *env* genes might contain multiple copies of a *cis*-acting repressive (CRS) sequence that functions to retain these RNAs in the nucleus in the absence of Rev (31, 119). An alternative hypothesis argues that it is, in fact, the intact splice sites present in these incompletely spliced mRNAs that act as nuclear retention signals (14, 93). One suggestion is that splicing factors may be able to assemble on the primary HIV-1 transcript but are then only poorly able to carry out the actual splicing step. Instead, this interaction results in the retention of incompletely spliced viral transcripts within the nucleus (14, 93). The Rev protein is believed to function by activating the nuclear export of these sequestered viral RNA species either by antagonizing their interaction with these splicing factors (14) or by directly facilitating their interaction with a component of a cellular RNA transport pathway (34, 93). In contrast, in the absence of Rev, viral mRNAs are eventually fully spliced prior to their transport to the cytoplasm.

The action of the Rev *trans*-activator is specific for unspliced HIV-1 transcripts and thus far has not been shown to affect the splicing or transport of cellular RNAs. The specificity of this response is conferred by a highly structured 234-nucleotide RNA target sequence, the Rev response element or RRE, which is located within the envelope gene of HIV-1 (55, 93, 119) (Figure 6). The Rev protein binds to the RRE with high affinity in vitro (26, 110, 156). Although the entire 234-nucleotide RRE is required for full biological activity in vivo, a 66-nucleotide stem-loop subdomain of the RRE is both necessary and sufficient for high-affinity binding of Rev and for partial biological activity in vivo (62, 64, 94) (Figure 6). The remainder of the RRE probably stabilizes the RNA structure of the Rev binding site and/or facilitates presentation of this RNA sequence in vivo (94).

The *rev* gene consists of two coding exons that together predict a protein of 116 amino acids. Rev is localized to the nuclei and, particularly, the nucleoli of expressing cells (16, 34, 82, 90). Rev is phosphorylated at two serine

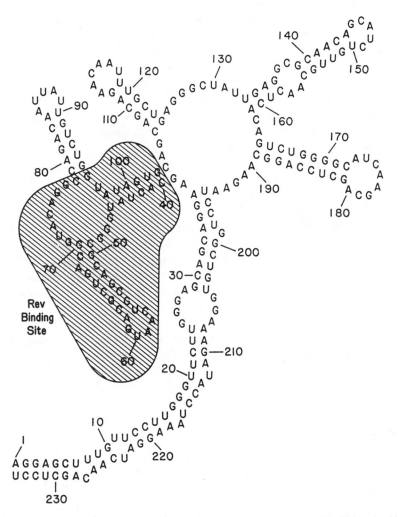

Figure 6 The Rev/RRE interaction. The sequence and predicted structure of the 234-nucleotide RRE RNA element are shown together with the approximate location of the primary binding site of the viral Rev protein (modified with permission from Ref. 94).

residues in vivo, but this posttranslational modification does not appear to be essential for Rev function (90). Two distinct protein domains essential for Rev function have been defined. The first is an ~40–amino acid N-terminal sequence characterized by an arginine-rich central core that functions as the Rev protein nuclear/nucleolar localization signal (16, 82, 90). This sequence also appears critical for the sequence-specific interaction of Rev with the RRE

(94, 109). Flanking the arginine-rich core are sequences that facilitate the multimerization of Rev, a process that appears important for in vivo Rev function (109). Mutations within any part of this sequence element result in Rev proteins that display a recessive negative phenotype (90, 109).

Rev probably also contains a protein sequence element that interacts directly with a component of the nuclear RNA transport or splicing machinery (90). Mutational analysis has suggested that a leucine-rich domain centered on amino acid 80 may serve this function (90). Rev proteins mutated in this latter domain retain full RRE binding and multimerization activity yet are not only defective but also inhibit wild-type Rev function *in trans* (90, 109). This *trans*-dominant inhibition could result from competition between wild-type and mutant Rev proteins for binding to the viral RRE, whereupon the bound, mutant Rev proteins are unable to interact with cellular factors involved in RNA transport from the nucleus. Alternatively, these mutant Rev proteins could inhibit wild-type Rev by forming inactive mixed multimers. In either case, the definition of the in vivo role of this leucine-rich motif appears critical to the full resolution of the mechanism of action of Rev.

At this point, I wish to discuss briefly the observation that both Rev and Tat concentrate in the nucleoli of over-expressing cells (34, 61, 90). The significance of this subcellular localization has been obscure, given the very different functions of these two RNA-sequence specific regulatory proteins in the HIV-1 replication cycle. In fact, this remarkable coincidence has rendered the hypothesis that the nucleoli are the site of action of either Tat or Rev considerably less attractive. Indeed, the mutationally defined minimal sequence within Tat that is sufficient to confer in vitro affinity for the TAR RNA element, i.e. the arginine-rich motif, is the same as the minimal sequence that is sufficient to act as an in vivo nucleolar localization signal when appended to a heterologous cytoplasmic protein (121, 122, 133, 151). Similarly, the basic domain of Rev appears both necessary and sufficient for localization to the nucleolus and binding to the RRE (82, 109). Hence, the nucleolar localization of both Tat and Rev is probably simply a surrogate marker for the affinity of these proteins for available structured RNA sequences. In over-expressing cells, this property is hypothesized to result in the concentration of Tat and Rev in the nuclear region with the highest concentration of structured RNA, i.e. the nucleolus. The observation that mutations of the arginine-rich motif that affect nucleolar localization also inhibit the in vivo function of Tat and Rev may therefore simply reflect the simultaneous inhibition of both the specific and the nonspecific RNA binding properties of these proteins (17, 122).

HIV-1 RNA Expression Patterns

As discussed above, HIV-1 transcripts can be divided into two classes based on their temporal expression in the HIV-1 replication cycle (Figure 5).

Multiply-spliced viral mRNA species are detected early in the HIV-1 replication cycle and encode the viral regulatory proteins (76). In contrast, expression of the unspliced or singly spliced mRNAs that encode the viral structural proteins occurs late in the viral replication cycle in response to the action of the viral Rev *trans*-activator (32, 33, 76). HIV-1 is therefore similar to many DNA tumor viruses, and distinct from MLV, in that it divides its replication cycle into early, regulatory, and late structural phases. However, HIV-1 differs from these DNA viruses in that the temporal regulation of gene expression in HIV-1 is regulated entirely at the posttranscriptional level.

Figure 7 outlines the HIV-1 mRNA species actually detected in vivo (33, 53, 101, 116, 125, 126). This figure shows the major splice donors and acceptors found within the HIV-1 genome (Figure 7A), the exons observed in the multiply spliced mRNA species (Figure 7B), and the structures of known early (Figure 7C) and late mRNAs (Figure 7D). Current evidence suggests that the selection of splice sites in the initial, genome-length HIV-1 transcript is determined by the interaction of *cis*-acting viral RNA sequences with host-cell splicing factors (53, 116). The first processing event is believed to utilize splice donor D1 and any one of the five splice acceptors A1 to A6. Evidence suggests an order of preference for this initial splicing event that is approximately A5 > A4 > A6 > A3 = A2 = A1 (53, 116). In the presence of Rev, these various singly spliced mRNAs can exit the nucleus and then be translated to yield the viral gene products indicated in Figure 7D. However, in the absence of Rev, these singly spliced mRNAs remain sequestered within the nucleus (Figure 5), presumably because of the continued presence of intact splice donor/acceptor combinations, and instead undergo additional processing. Although the temporal order of these subsequent splicing events is unclear, all multiply spliced viral transcripts appear to undergo splicing of the D4 splice donor to the A6 splice acceptor (33, 53, 101, 116, 125). Transcripts that were initially spliced between donor D1 and acceptor A1 also complete a third splicing event between donor D2 and acceptor A3, A4, or A5 to generate the small noncoding exon E2 (43, 125). Similarly, viral mRNAs spliced between D1 and A2 complete a third splice between donor D3 and either A3, A4, or A5 to generate the noncoding exon E3. These latter two splicing events preclude expression of the viral Vif and Vpr proteins in the absence of Rev, i.e. they make Vif and Vpr late viral gene products (43).

Each early viral gene product can therefore be expressed from multiple distinct viral mRNA species that differ by the presence or absence of the noncoding exons E2 and E3 (116, 125). All three such mRNAs are presented for Tat (Figure 7C). Therefore, at least 10 different mRNAs are in the early ~2-kb class of HIV-1 mRNAs (125). In fact, because both donor D2 and acceptor A4 actually consist of two closely spaced splice sites (43, 125), one can calculate that this class consists of up to 17 distinct mRNAs. However, these mRNAs actually only differ in the precise composition of their 5'

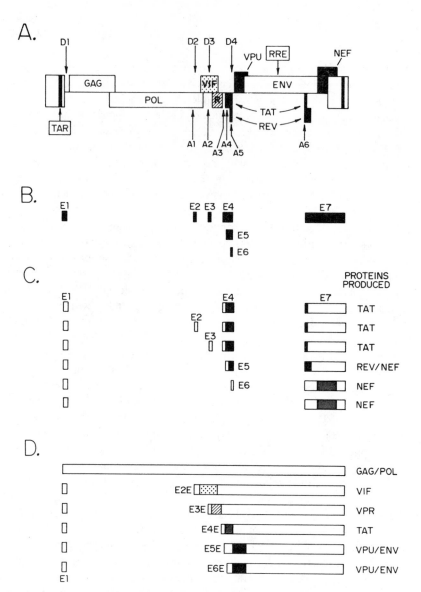

Figure 7 RNA expression patterns in HIV-1. (*A*) Genomic organization of HIV-1 showing the location of major splice donors (D1 to D4) and splice acceptors (A1 to A6). (*B*) HIV-1 exons observed in the multiply spliced viral mRNA species. Exons E1, E2, and E3 are noncoding. The exon nomenclature used here is similar to that previously proposed. (*C*) Structure of the early HIV-1 mRNA species. The noncoding E2 and E3 exons can occur in any early HIV-1 mRNA (with the probable exception of the smallest Nef mRNA). Only for the Tat mRNAs are all three variants shown. (*D*) Structure of the late HIV-1 mRNA species. The genomic RNA and the known singly spliced viral mRNAs are indicated together with the known translation products of each. These viral proteins are only expressed in the presence of the viral Rev *trans*-activator (see Figure 5).

noncoding region and, in total, only express the three proteins Tat, Rev, and Nef. Of interest, the multiply spliced mRNA species predicted to encode Rev (Figure 7C) also appear to be translated to yield Nef protein, apparently because of poor recognition of the initiation codon of Rev by the cell translation machinery (125).

As indicated in Figure 7D, there are at least five distinct singly spliced viral transcripts (101, 126). Of interest, the *env* gene does not appear to be translated from a monocistronic mRNA species but is instead translated from a set of two bicistronic mRNAs that encodes the viral Vpu protein as the 5'-most open reading frame (126). These two Vpu/Env mRNAs appear to comprise the majority (<90%) of the singly spliced class of viral mRNA species (53). A second singly spliced viral mRNA that is of interest is the transcript spliced between donor D1 and acceptor A3. This mRNA contains a highly conserved translation termination codon at the end of the first exon of Tat and therefore encodes a precisely truncated, single-exon form of the Tat protein that fully retains the ability to *trans*-activate the HIV-1 LTR (20, 92). The expression of this singly spliced Tat mRNA may therefore permit HIV-1 to maintain a significant level of Tat synthesis during the late phase of the replication cycle when expression of the various multiply spliced Tat mRNAs is inhibited by the action of the Rev protein (Figure 5).

HIV-1 Virion Assembly and Release

The late events in the HIV-1 replication cycle, i.e. virion assembly and release, remain relatively poorly understood. In general, however, this process appears similar for both HIV-1 and MLV. Both the Gag and Gag-Pol polyproteins of HIV-1 bear a N-terminal myristic acid residue that is essential for virion assembly (51). The HIV-1 genome again contains a specific packaging signal within the RNA leader region, and recognition of this sequence again requires the integrity of a zinc-finger motif within the nucleocapsid protein of Gag (2, 49, 87). As is the case with MLV, HIV-1 virions acquire an outer membrane studded with envelope glycoprotein spikes while budding out of the cell plasma membrane, and the subsequent cleavage of the HIV-1 Gag and Gag-Pol polyproteins is again accomplished by the action of an essential virus-encoded protease (81). Despite this general similarity, significant differences in this late phase of the HIV-1 and MLV replication cycles reflect the fact that HIV-1 encodes three additional late gene products that have no known equivalent in MLV.

The 23-kd Vif protein is required for the efficient transmission of cell-free HIV-1 virions in tissue culture (37, 142). Proviruses lacking Vif appear to express fully normal levels of the other viral proteins and can release virus from infected cells with normal efficiency. However, these released virions, despite their apparently normal morphological appearance, are up to 1000-

fold less infectious than virions released from Vif$^+$ provirus–infected cells (37, 142). Interestingly, Vif does not appear to affect the efficiency of direct cell-to-cell spread of HIV-1. Vif has not as yet been shown to be virion associated and its mechanism of action is therefore uncertain. Current possibilities include roles in virion maturation and/or morphogenesis (37, 142). However, the Vif open reading frame is conserved among the primate lentiviruses and also appears to be retained in visna virus, a distantly related ungulate lentivirus (Figure 1).

In marked contrast to Vif, the HIV-1 Vpu protein appears to have no equivalent in other primate lentiviruses, including the other human representative, HIV-2. The Vpu protein is 81 amino acids in length, is phosphorylated in vivo, and is associated with the cytoplasmic membranes of expressing cells (143). Expression of Vpu is not essential for HIV-1 replication in culture. However, the loss of a functional Vpu gene product results in a 5- to 10-fold drop in the production of progeny HIV-1 virions (80, 146). This reduction does not appear to reflect a decrease in the biosynthesis of any of the other HIV-1 proteins but instead results from a defect in virion release. Notably, lack of Vpu expression appears to result in an accumulation of cell-associated HIV-1 virions (80, 146). Again, the mechanism of action of this viral protein remains uncertain. Vpu may enhance budding of virions from the cell surface or, instead, inhibit budding of virions through intracytoplasmic membranes (80). In either case, why HIV-1 requires a *vpu* gene product for efficient virion release while related viruses, such as HIV-2, appear able to replicate and bud efficiently without an equivalent protein remains unclear.

The HIV-1 Vpr protein, like Nef, is dispensable for HIV-1 replication in culture (18, 108). Indeed, several replication-competent proviruses derived from the HTLV-IIIB substrain of HIV-1 lack functional copies of both of these viral genes (18, 108). Recent data suggest that viruses containing an intact *vpr* gene replicate slightly more rapidly in culture and may display enhanced cytopathicity (18, 108). The Vpr protein was recently shown to be virion associated and thus may be considered a structural protein (17). Surprisingly, data have also been presented suggesting that the Vpr protein can *trans*-activate HIV-1 LTR–specific gene expression by approximately two- to threefold in transient expression assays, thus suggesting that Vpr may enhance HIV-1 gene expression during the earliest phases of subsequent virus infections (18).

HIV-1 AS A PROTOTYPIC COMPLEX RETROVIRUS

Although the canonical retroviral replication cycle depicted in Figure 2 applies with equal force to both HIV-1 and MLV, the results presented above clearly show that HIV-1 has added several regulatory complexities to this basic scheme. This perception led to the suggestion that HIV-1 in particular, or perhaps human retroviruses in general, might be uniquely complex in terms of its genomic organization and gene regulation. More recently, work on other human retroviruses such as HTLV-I and HSRV (65, 75, 103, 136) and on animal retroviruses such as visna virus and equine infectious anemia virus (EIAV) (63, 140, 147) has shown, to the contrary, that HIV-1 is merely the most fully understood representative of a whole class of animal retroviruses that I refer to as "complex" retroviruses (Figure 1). These viruses are distinguished from simple retroviruses such as MLV and ALV not only by the greater complexity of their genomes but, more importantly, by the specific pattern of viral gene regulation displayed in the infected cell. Figure 8 depicts this regulatory pattern, which both requires and facilitates a more complex genomic organization.

At least four criteria distinguish the replication cycle of the complex retroviruses from that of the simple retroviruses: 1. Complex retroviruses encode a third, multiply spliced class of viral transcripts in addition to the singly spliced (Env) and unspliced (Gag-Pol) mRNA seen in the simple retroviruses. This class encodes at least two nuclear regulatory proteins. 2. The first of these regulatory proteins is a sequence-specific *trans*-activator of LTR-driven gene expression. 3. The second regulatory protein represses the expression of the early, regulatory mRNAs and induces the expression of the late, structural mRNA species. 4. The combined action of these two proteins divides the replication cycle of complex retroviruses into two temporal phases, a pattern not seen in simple retroviruses.

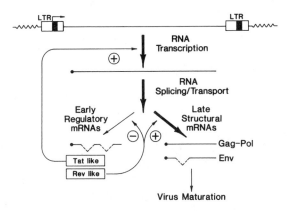

Figure 8   Gene regulation in complex retroviruses. Complex retroviruses, including HIV-1, are defined by a pattern of gene regulation that requires the action of a virally encoded Tat-like transcriptional activator and of a Rev-like posttranscriptional regulator. See text for detailed discussion (reproduced with permission from Ref. 22).

Retroviruses have customarily been divided into three subgroups based on the pattern of in vivo disease and, more recently, on the basis of sequence homology (144, 148). The four members of the proposed complex retrovirus classification described in Figure 1 were selected from all three of the historic taxonomic subgroups. HTLV-I is classified as an oncovirus. HIV-1 and visna virus are representative lentiviruses, the former a primate lentivirus and the latter an ungulate lentivirus. HSRV is included as a representative of the rather poorly understood spumavirus subgroup. These viruses have quite different genomic organizations and have very limited primary sequence homology. Yet these four viruses all appear to share a similar pattern of viral gene regulation (Figure 8) and can therefore be distinguished from MLV, ALV, and other simple retroviruses based on the criteria enumerated above.

The pattern of viral gene expression delineated in Figure 8 predicts that complex retroviruses should encode at least five distinct gene products. These are the *gag*, *pol*, and *env* genes, also seen in the simple retroviruses, as well as two regulatory proteins that serve functions comparable to the HIV-1 Tat and Rev *trans*-activators. This minimal pattern is seen in HTLV-I, which appears to encode precisely these five predicted gene products (65) (Figure 1). However, the regulatory proteins characteristic of the complex retroviruses can also accommodate the ordered expression of additional novel viral mRNAs and proteins, thus significantly increasing the potential genetic flexibility of this retroviral classification. As discussed above, this observation is clearest for HIV-1, which encodes 9 distinct viral gene products that are translated from over 20 different viral mRNA species. However, these other HIV-1 proteins are distinct from Tat and Rev in that their functional equivalents are not observed in all complex retroviruses.

The complex retroviruses are defined by a particular pattern of viral gene expression that depends upon the action of two regulatory proteins functionally equivalent to the Tat and Rev *trans*-activators of HIV-1 (Figure 8). Although all complex retroviruses are therefore predicted to encode, for example, a *trans*-activator of LTR-dependent transcription, these proteins are not required to act via the same mechanism. Thus, the Tat *trans*-activator of HIV-1, the Tax protein of HTLV-I, the S protein of visna, and the Bel-1 *trans*-activator of HSRV all appear to have distinct mechanisms of action yet all function as transcriptional *trans*-activators of their homologous LTR promoter element (21, 63, 75, 136). Although the replication cycle of complex retroviruses may therefore differ in detail, these viruses nevertheless share a common strategy for the regulation of viral gene expression (Figure 8). The primate immunodeficiency viruses may therefore serve as the prototype for a whole class of retroviruses that includes not only other human retroviruses but also many nonprimate retroviruses. Conversely, the interaction of these animal retroviruses with their hosts may also provide experimental models directly relevant to the understanding of retroviral latency and pathogenesis in humans. The suggested members of the complex retrovirus classification all produce persistent infections characterized by high levels of latently infected cells (144). In HIV-1, the level of Rev activity in the infected cell could be a primary determinant of this ability to establish a latent infection (113). Therefore, the determination of whether the similar pattern of gene regulation observed in other complex retroviruses could also underlie their similar patterns of in vivo pathogenesis will be interesting.

CONCLUDING REMARKS

This review briefly presented the current understanding of the HIV-1 replication cycle, focusing particularly on viral and cellular factors involved in regulating HIV-1 gene expression. Although an extraordinary amount of information about HIV-1 has accumulated over the last five years, this knowledge falls far short of painting a complete picture of the life cycle of this remarkable human pathogen. In particular, the cellular factors involved in mediating the action of the essential HIV-1 Tat and Rev proteins remain essentially undefined. The achievement of a more complete understanding of the mechanism of action of Tat, Rev, and the other novel HIV-1 gene products and, most importantly, the application of this information to the discovery of effective approaches to the chemotherapeutic intervention in HIV-1–induced disease appears likely to remain a major focus of biomedical research for the foreseeable future.

ACKNOWLEDGMENTS

I thank Sharon Goodwin for her assistance in the preparation of this manuscript.

Literature Cited

1. Ahmad, N., Venkatesan, S. 1988. *Nef* protein of HIV-1 is a transcriptional repressor of HIV-1 LTR. *Science* 241:1481-85
2. Aldovini, A., Young, R. A. 1990. Mutations of RNA and protein sequences involved in human immunodeficiency virus type 1 packaging result in production of noninfectious virus. *J. Virol.* 64:1920-26
3. Arrigo, S., Beemon, K. 1988. Regulation of rous sarcoma virus RNA splicing and stability. *Mol. Cell. Biol.* 8:4858-67
4. Arya, S. K., Guo, C., Josephs, S. F., Wong-Staal, F. 1985. *Trans*-activator gene of human T-lymphotropic virus type III (HTLV-III). *Science* 229:69-73
5. Bachelerie, F., Alcami, J., Hazan, U.,

Israel, N., Goud, B., et al. 1990. Constitutive expression of human immunodeficiency virus (HIV) *nef* protein in human astrocytes does not influence basal or induced HIV long terminal repeat activity. *J. Virol.* 64:3059-62
6. Baldwin, G. C., Fleischmann, J., Chung, Y., Koyanagi, Y., Chen, I. S. Y., et al. 1990. Human immunodeficiency virus causes mononuclear phagocyte dysfunction. *Proc. Natl. Acad. Sci. USA* 87:3933-37
7. Barre-Sinoussi, F., Chermann, J. C., Rey, F., Nugeybe, M. T., Chamaret, S., et al. 1983. Isolation of a T-lymphotropic retrovirus from a patient at risk of acquired immune deficiency syndrome (AIDS). *Science* 220:868-70

8. Berkhout, B., Gatignol, A., Rabson, A. B., Jeang, K.-T. 1990. TAR-independent activation of the HIV-1 LTR: evidence that *tat* requires specific regions of the promoter. *Cell* 62:757-67

9. Berkhout, B., Jeang, K.-T. 1989. *Trans*-activation of human immunodeficiency virus type 1 is sequence specific for both the single-stranded bulge and loop of the *trans*-acting-responsive hairpin: a quantitative analysis. *J. Virol.* 63:5501-4

10. Berkhout, B., Silverman, R. H., Jeang, K.-T. 1989. Tat *trans*-activates the human immunodeficiency virus through a nascent RNA target. *Cell* 59:273-82

11. Bohnlein, E., Lowenthal, J. W., Siekevitz, M., Ballard, D. W., Franza, B. R., et al. 1988. The same inducible nuclear proteins regulate mitogen activity of both the interleukin-2 receptor-alpha gene and type 1 HIV. *Cell* 53:827-36

12. Bohnlein, S., Hauber, J., Cullen, B. R. 1989. Identification of a U5 specific sequence required for efficient polyadenylation within the human immunodeficiency virus long terminal repeat. *J. Virol.* 63:421-24

13. Braddock, M., Thorburn, A. M., Chambers, A., Elliott, G. D., Anderson, G. J., et al. 1990. A nuclear translational block imposed by the HIV-1 U3 region is relieved by the Tat-TAR interaction. *Cell* 62:1123-33

14. Chang, D. D., Sharp, P. A. 1989. Regulation by HIV Rev depends upon recognition of splice sites. *Cell* 59:789-95

15. Cheng-Mayer, C., Iannello, P., Shaw, K., Luciw, P. A., Levy, J. A. 1989. Differential effects of *nef* on HIV replication: implications for viral pathogenesis in the host. *Science* 246:1629-32

16. Cochrane, A. W., Perkins, A., Rosen, C. A. 1990. Identification of sequences important in the nucleolar localization of human immunodeficiency virus Rev: relevance of nucleolar localization to function. *J. Virol.* 64:881-85

17. Cohen, E. A., Dehni, G., Sodroski, J. G., Haseltine, W. A. 1990. Human immunodeficiency virus *vpr* product is a virion-associated regulatory protein. *J. Virol.* 64:3097-99

18. Cohen, E. A., Terwilliger, E. F., Jalinoos, Y., Proulx, J., Sodroski, J. G., et al. 1990. Identification of HIV-1 *vpr* product and function. *J. Acquired Immune Defic. Syndr.* 3:11-18

19. Collman, R., Godfrey, B., Cutilli, J., Rhodes, A., Hassan, N. F., et al. 1990. Macrophage-tropic strains of human immunodeficiency virus type 1 utilize the CD4 receptor. *J. Virol.* 64:4468-76

20. Cullen, B. R. 1986. *Trans*-activation of human immunodeficiency virus occurs via a bimodal mechanism. *Cell* 46:973-82

21. Cullen, B. R. 1990. The HIV-1 Tat protein: an RNA sequence-specific processivity factor? *Cell* 63:655-57

22. Cullen, B. R. 1991. Human immunodeficiency virus as a prototypic complex retrovirus. *J. Virol.* 65:1053-56

23. Cullen, B. R., Greene, W. C. 1990. Functions of the auxiliary gene products of the human immunodeficiency virus type 1. *Virology* 178:1-5

24. Cullen, B. R., Malim, M. H. 1990. Regulation of HIV-1 gene expression. *Nucleic Acids Mol. Biol.* 4:176-84

25. Dalgleish, A. G., Beverly, P. C. L., Clapham, P. R., Crawford, D. H., Greaves, M. F., et al. 1984. The CD4 (T4) antigen is an essential component of the receptor for the AIDS retrovirus. *Nature (London)* 312:763-66

26. Daly, T. J., Cook, K. S., Gray, G. S., Maione, T. E., Rusche, J. R. 1989. Specific binding of HIV-1 recombinant Rev protein to the Rev-responsive element in vitro. *Nature* 342:816-19

27. Dayton, A. I., Sodroski, J. G., Rosen, C. A., Goh, W. C., Haseltine, W. A. 1986. The *trans*-activator gene of the human T cell lymphotropic virus type III is required for replication. *Cell* 44:941-47

28. Dickson, C., Eisenman, R., Fan, H., Hunter, E., Teich, N. 1982. Protein biosynthesis and assembly. See Ref. 152a, pp. 513-648

29. Dingwall, C., Ernberg, I., Gait, M. J., Green, S. M., Heaphy, S., et al. 1989. Human immunodeficiency virus 1 *tat* protein binds *trans*-activation-responsive region (TAR) RNA in vitro. *Proc. Natl. Acad. Sci. USA* 86:6925-29

30. Ellison, V., Abrams, H., Roe, T., Lifson, J., Brown, P. 1990. Human immunodeficiency virus integration in a cell-free system. *J. Virol.* 64:2711-15

31. Emerman, M., Vazeux, R., Peden, K. 1989. The *rev* gene product of the human immunodeficiency virus affects envelope-specific RNA localization. *Cell* 57:1155-65

32. Feinberg, M. B., Jarrett, R. F., Aldovini, A., Gallo, R. C., Wong-Staal, F. 1986. HTLV-III expression and production involve complex regulation at the levels of splicing and translation of viral RNA. *Cell* 46:807-17

33. Felber, B. K., Drysdale, C. M., Pavlakis, G. N. 1990. Feedback regulation of

human immunodeficiency virus type 1 expression by the Rev protein. *J. Virol.* 64:3734-41

34. Felber, B. K., Hadzopoulou-Cladaras, M., Cladaras, C., Copeland, T., Pavlakis, G. N. 1989. Rev protein of human immunodeficiency virus type 1 affects the stability and transport of the viral mRNA. *Proc. Natl. Acad. Sci. USA* 86:1495-99

35. Feng, S., Holland, E. C. 1988. HIV-1 *tat trans*-activation requires the loop sequence within tar. *Nature* 334:165-67

36. Feng, Y.-X., Copeland, T. D., Oroszlan, S., Rein, A., Levin, J. G. 1990. Identification of amino acids inserted during suppression of UAA and UGA termination codons at the gag-pol junction of Moloney murine leukemia virus. *Proc. Natl. Acad. Sci. USA* 87:8860-63

37. Fisher, A. G., Ensoli, B., Ivanoff, L., Chamberlain, M., Petteway, S., et al. 1987. The *sor* gene of HIV-1 is required for efficient virus transmission in vitro. *Science* 237:888-93

38. Fisher, A. G., Feinberg, M. B., Josephs, S. F., Harper, M. E., Marselle, L. M., et al. 1986. The *trans*-activator gene of HTLV-III is essential for virus replication. *Nature* 320:367-71

39. Frankel, A. D., Bredt, D. S., Pabo, C. O. 1988. Tat protein from human immunodeficiency virus forms a metal-linked dimer. *Science* 240:70-73

40. Fritsch, E., Temin, H. M. 1977. Inhibition of viral DNA synthesis in stationary chicken embryo fibroblasts infected with avian retroviruses. *J. Virol.* 24:461-69

41. Garcia, J. A., Harrich, D., Pearson, L., Mitsuyasu, R., Gaynor, R. B. 1988. Functional domains required for *tat*-induced transcriptional activation of the HIV-1 long terminal repeat. *EMBO J.* 7:3143-47

42. Garcia, J. A., Wu, F. K., Mitsuyasu, R., Gaynor, R. B. 1987. Interactions of cellular proteins involved in the transcriptional regulation of the human immunodeficiency virus. *EMBO J.* 6:3761-70

43. Garrett, E. D., Tiley, L. S., Cullen, B. R. 1991. Rev activates expression of the HIV-1 *vif* and *vpr* gene products. *J. Virol.* 65:1653-57

44. Gartner, S., Markovits, P., Markovitz, D. M., Kaplan, M. H., Gallo, R. C., et al. 1986. The role of mononuclear phagocytes in HTLV-III/LAV infection. *Science* 233:215-19

45. Gebhardt, A., Bosch, J. V., Ziemiecki, A., Friis, R. R. 1984. Rous sarcoma virus p19 and gp35 can be chemically crosslinked to high molecular weight complexes. *J. Mol. Biol.* 174:297-317

46. Gendelman, H. E., Phelps, W., Feigenbaum, L., Ostrove, J. M., Adachi, A., et al. 1986. *Trans*-activation of the human immunodeficiency virus long terminal repeat sequence by DNA viruses. *Proc. Natl. Acad. Sci. USA* 83:9759-63

47. Gilmore, T. D. 1990. NF-κB, KBF1, dorsal, and related matters. *Cell* 62:841-43

48. Gimble, J. M., Duh, E., Ostrove, J. M., Gendelman, H. E., Max, E. E., et al. 1988. Activation of the human immunodeficiency virus long terminal repeat by herpes simplex virus type 1 is associated with induction of a nuclear factor that binds to the NF-κB/core enhancer sequence. *J. Virol.* 62:4104-12

49. Gorelick, R. J., Nigida, S. M. Jr., Bess, J. W. Jr., Arthur, L. O., Henderson, L. E., et al. 1990. Noninfectious human immunodeficiency virus type 1 mutants deficient in genomic RNA. *J. Virol.* 64:3207-11

50. Gottlieb, M. S., Schroff, R., Schanler, H. M., Weisman, J. D., Fan, P. T., et al. 1981. *Pneumocystis carinii* pneumonia and mucosal candidiasis in previously healthy homosexual men: evidence of a new acquired cellular immuno-deficiency. *New Engl. J. Med.* 305:1426-31

51. Gottlinger, H. G., Sodroski, J. G., Haseltine, W. A. 1989. Role of capsid precursor processing and myristoylation in morphogenesis and infectivity of human immunodeficiency virus type 1. *Proc. Natl. Acad. Sci. USA* 86:5781-85

52. Griffin, G. E., Leung, K., Folks, T. M., Kunkel, S., Nabel, G. J. 1989. Activation of HIV gene expression during monocyte differentiation by induction of NF-κB. *Nature* 339:70-73

53. Guatelli, J. C., Gingeras, T. R., Richman, D. D. 1990. Alternative splice acceptor utilization during human immunodeficiency virus type 1 infection of cultured cells. *J. Virol.* 64:4093-98

54. Guy, B., Kieny, M. P., Riviere, Y., Peuch, C. L., Dott, K., et al. 1987. HIV F/3' *orf* encodes a phosphorylated GTP-binding protein resembling an oncogene product. *Nature* 330:266-69

55. Hadzopoulos-Cladaras, M., Felber, B. K., Cladaras, C., Athanassopoulos, A., Tse, A., et al. 1989. The *rev (trs/art)* protein of human immunodeficiency virus type 1 affects viral mRNA and protein expression via a *cis*-acting sequence in the *env* region. *J. Virol.* 63:1265-74

56. Hammarskjold, M.-L., Heimer, J.,

Hammarskjold, B., Sangwan, I., Albert, L., et al. 1989. Regulation of human immunodeficiency virus *env* expression by the *rev* gene product. *J. Virol.* 63:1959-66

57. Hammes, S. R., Dixon, E. P., Malim, M. H., Cullen, B. R., Greene, W. C. 1989. Nef protein of human immunodeficiency virus type 1: evidence against its role as a transcriptional inhibitor. *Proc. Natl. Acad. Sci. USA* 86:9549-53

58. Harrich, D., Garcia, J., Wu, F., Mitsuyasu, R., Gonzalez, J., et al. 1989. Role of SP1-binding domains in *in vivo* transcriptional regulation of the human immunodeficiency virus type 1 long terminal repeat. *J. Virol.* 63:2585-91

59. Hauber, J., Cullen, B. R. 1988. Mutational analysis of the *trans*-activation responsive region of the human immunodeficiency virus 1 long terminal repeat. *J. Virol.* 62:673-79

60. Hauber, J., Malim, M. H., Cullen, B. R. 1989. Mutational analysis of the conserved basic domain of the human immunodeficiency virus *tat* protein. *J. Virol.* 63:1181-87

61. Hauber, J., Perkins, A., Heimer, E. P., Cullen, B. R. 1987. *Trans*-activation of human immunodeficiency virus gene expression is mediated by nuclear events. *Proc. Natl. Acad. Sci. USA* 84:6364-68

62. Heaphy, S., Dingwall, C., Ernberg, I., Gait, M. J., Green, S. M., et al. 1990. HIV-1 regulator of virion expression (Rev) protein binds to an RNA stem-loop structure located within the Rev response element region. *Cell* 60:685-93

63. Hess, J. L., Small, J. A., Clements, J. E. 1989. Sequences in the visna virus long terminal repeat that control transcriptional activity and respond to viral *trans*-activation: involvement of AP-1 sites in basal activity and *trans*-activation. *J. Virol.* 63:3001-15

64. Huang, X., Hope, T. J., Bond, B. L., McDonald, D., Grahl, K., et al. 1991. Minimal *rev* response element for type-1 human immunodeficiency virus. *J. Virol.* 65:2131-34

65. Inoue, J.-I., Yoshida, M., Seiki, M. 1987. Transcriptional (p40^x) and post-transcriptional (p27^{x-III}) regulators are required for the expression and replication of human T-cell leukemia virus type I genes. *Proc. Natl. Acad. Sci. USA* 84:3653-57

66. Jacks, T., Power, M. D., Rasiarz, F. R., Luciw, P. A., Barr, P. J., et al. 1988. Characterization of ribosomal frameshifting in HIV-1 gag-pol expression. *Nature (London)* 231:280-83

67. Jacks, T., Varmus, H. E. 1985. Expression of rous sarcoma virus pol gene by ribosomal frameshifting. *Science* 230:1237-42

68. Jakobovits, A., Smith, D. H., Jakobovits, E. B., Capon, D. J. 1988. A discrete element 3' of human immunodeficiency virus 1 (HIV-1) and HIV-2 mRNA initiation sites mediates transcriptional activation by an HIV *trans*-activator. *Mol. Cell. Biol.* 8:2555-61

69. Jones, K. A., Kadonaga, J. T., Luciw, P. A., Tjian, R. 1986. Activation of the AIDS retrovirus promoter by the cellular transcription factor, Sp1. *Science* 232:755-59

70. Jones, K. A., Luciw, P. A., Duchange, N. 1988. Structural arrangements of transcription control domains within the 5'-untranslated leader regions of the HIV-1 and HIV-2 promoters. *Genes Dev.* 2:1101-14

71. Kaminchik, J., Bashan, N., Pinchasi, D., Amit, B., Sarver, N., et al. 1990. Expression and biochemical characterization of human immunodeficiency virus 1 *nef* gene product. *J. Virol.* 64:3447-54

72. Kao, S.-Y., Calman, A. F., Luciw, P. A., Peterlin, B. M. 1987. Anti-termination of transcription within the long terminal repeat of HIV-1 by *tat* gene product. *Nature* 330:489-93

73. Katoh, I., Yoshinaka, Y., Rein, A., Shibuya, M., Odaka, T., et al. 1985. Murine leukemia virus maturation: protease region required for conversion from "immature" to "mature" core form and for virus infectivity. *Virology* 145:280-92

74. Katz, R. A., Skalka, A. M. 1990. Control of retroviral RNA splicing through maintenance of suboptimal processing signals. *Mol. Cell. Biol.* 10:696-704

75. Keller, A., Partin, K. M., Lochelt, M., Bannert, H., Flugel, R. M., et al. 1991. Characterization of the transcriptional *trans*-activator of human foamy retrovirus. *J. Virol.* 65:2589-94

76. Kim, S., Byrn, R., Groopman, J., Baltimore, D. 1989. Temporal aspects of DNA and RNA synthesis during human immunodeficiency virus infection: evidence for differential gene expression. *J. Virol.* 63:3708-13

77. Kim, S., Ikeuchi, K., Byrn, R., Groopman, J., Baltimore, D. 1989. Lack of a negative influence on viral growth by the *nef* gene of human immunodeficiency virus type 1. *Proc. Natl. Acad. Sci. USA* 86:9544-48

78. Kim, S., Ikeuchi, K., Groopman, J., Baltimore, D. 1990. Factors affecting cellular tropism of human immunodeficiency virus. *J. Virol.* 64:5600-4

79. Klatzmann, D., Champagne, E., Chamaret, S., Gruest, J., Guetard, T., et al. 1984. T-lymphocyte T4 molecule behaves as the receptor for human retrovirus LAV. *Nature (London)* 312:767-68

80. Klimkait, T., Strebel, K., Hoggan, M. D., Martin, M. A., Orenstein, J. M. 1990. The human immunodeficiency virus type 1-specific protein *vpu* is required for efficient virus maturation and release. *J. Virol.* 64:621-29

81. Kohl, N. E., Emini, E. A., Schleif, W. A., Davis, L. J., Heimbach, J. C. 1988. Active human immunodeficiency virus protease is required for viral infectivity. *Proc. Natl. Acad. Sci. USA* 85:4686-90

82. Kubota, S., Siomi, H., Satoh, T., Endo, S.-I., Maki, M., et al. 1989. Functional similarity of HIV-1 *rev* and HTLV-I *rex* proteins: identification of a new nucleolar-targeting signal in *rev* protein. *Biochem. Biophys. Res. Commun.* 162:963-70

83. Laspia, M. F., Rice, A. P., Mathews, M. B. 1989. HIV-1 Tat protein increases transcriptional initiation and stabilizes elongation. *Cell* 59:283-92

84. Lazinski, D., Grzadzielska, E., Das, A. 1989. Sequence-specific recognition of RNA hairpins by bacteriophage antiterminators requires a conserved arginine-rich motif. *Cell* 59:207-18

85. Lenardo, M. J., Baltimore, D. 1989. NF-κB: a pleiotropic mediator of inducible and tissue-specific gene control. *Cell* 58:227-29

86. Leonard, J., Parrott, C., Buckler-White, A. J., Turner, W., Ross, E. K., et al. 1989. The NF-κB binding sites in the human immunodeficiency virus type 1 long terminal repeat are not required for virus infectivity. *J. Virol.* 63:4919-24

87. Lever, A., Gottlinger, H., Haseltine, W., Sodroski, J. 1989. Identification of a sequence required for efficient packaging of human immunodeficiency virus type 1 RNA into virions. *J. Virol.* 63:4085-87

88. Lu, Y., Touzjian, N., Stenzel, M., Dorfman, T., Sodroski, J. G., et al. 1990. Identification of *cis*-acting repressive sequences within the negative regulatory element of human immunodeficiency virus type 1. *J. Virol.* 64:5226-29

89. Lusso, P., Ensoli, B., Markham, P. D., Ablashi, D. V., Salahuddin, S. Z., et al. 1989. Productive dual infection of human CD4+ T lymphocytes by HIV-1 and HHV-6. *Nature* 337:370-73

90. Malim, M. H., Bohnlein, S., Hauber, J., Cullen, B. R. 1989. Functional dissection of the HIV-1 Rev *trans*-activator—derivation of a *trans*-dominant repressor of Rev function. *Cell* 58:205-14

91. Malim, M. H., Fenrick, R., Ballard, D. W., Hauber, J., Bohnlein, E., et al. 1989. Functional characterization of a complex protein:DNA binding domain located within the HIV-1 LTR leader region. *J. Virol.* 63:3213-19

92. Malim, M. H., Hauber, J., Fenrick, R., Cullen, B. R. 1988. Immunodeficiency virus *rev trans*-activator modulates the expression of the viral regulatory genes. *Nature* 335:181-83

93. Malim, M. H., Hauber, J., Le, S.-Y., Maizel, J. V., Cullen, B. R. 1989. The HIV-1 *rev trans*-activator acts through a structured target sequence to activate nuclear export of unspliced viral mRNA. *Nature* 338:254-57

94. Malim, M. H., Tiley, L. S., McCarn, D. F., Rusche, J. R., Hauber, J., et al. 1990. HIV-1 structural gene expression requires binding of the Rev *trans*-activator to its RNA target sequence. *Cell* 60:675-83

95. Marciniak, R. A., Calnan, B. J., Frankel, A. D., Sharp, P. A. 1990. HIV-1 Tat protein *trans*-activates transcription in vitro. *Cell* 63:791-802

96. Marciniak, R. A., Garcia-Blanco, M. A., Sharp, P. A. 1990. Identification and characterization of a HeLa nuclear protein that specifically binds to the *trans*-activation-response (TAR) element of human immunodeficiency virus. *Proc. Natl. Acad. Sci. USA* 87:3624-28

97. Masur, H., Michelis, M. A., Greene, J. B., Onovato, I., Van de Stowe, R. A., et al. 1981. An outbreak of community-acquired pneumocystis carinii pneumonia: initial manifestation of cellular immune dysfunction. *New Engl. J. Med.* 305:1431-38

98. McDougal, J. S., Kennedy, M., Sligh, J., Cort, S., Mowle, A., et al. 1986. Binding of the HTLV-III/LAV to T4+ T cells by a complex of the 110 K viral protein and the T4 molecule. *Science* 231:382-85

99. Meltzer, M. S., Skillman, D. R., Gomatos, P. J., Kalter, D. C., Gendelman, H. E. 1990. Role of mononuclear phagocytes in the pathogenesis of human immunodeficiency virus infection. *Annu. Rev. Immunol.* 8:169-94

100. Mosca, J. D., Bednarik, D. P., Raj, N. B. K., Rosen, C. A., Sodroski, J. G., et

al. 1987. Herpes simplex virus type-1 can reactivate transcription of latent human immunodeficiency virus. *Nature* 325:67-70

101. Muesing, M. A., Smith, D. H., Cabradilla, C. D., Benton, C. V., Lasky, L. A., et al. 1985. Nucleic acid structure and expression of the human AIDS/lymphadenopathy retrovirus. *Nature* 313:450-58

102. Muesing, M. A., Smith, D. H., Capon, D. J. 1987. Regulation of mRNA accumulation by a human immunodeficiency virus *trans*-activator protein. *Cell* 48:691-701

103. Muranyi, M., Flugel, R. M. 1991. Analysis of splicing patterns by polymerase chain reaction of the human spumaretrovirus reveals complex RNA structures. *J. Virol.* 65:727-35

104. Nabel, G., Baltimore, D. 1987. An inducible transcription factor activates expression of human immunodeficiency virus in T cells. *Nature* 326:711-13

105. Nabel, G. J., Rice, S. A., Knipe, D. M., Baltimore, D. 1988. Alternative mechanisms for activation of human immunodeficiency virus enhancer in T cells. *Science* 239:1299-1302

106. Niederman, T. M. J., Thielan, B. J., Ratner, L. 1989. Human immunodeficiency virus type 1 negative factor is a transcriptional silencer. *Proc. Natl. Acad. Sci. USA* 86:1128-32

107. O'Brien, W. A., Koyanagi, Y., Namazie, A., Zhao, J.-Q., Diagne, A., et al. 1990. HIV-1 tropism for mononuclear phagocytes can be determined by regions of gp120 outside the CD4-binding domain. *Nature* 348:69-73

108. Ogawa, K., Shibata, R., Kiyomasu, T., Higuchi, I., Kishida, Y., et al. 1989. Mutational analysis of the human immunodeficiency virus *vpr* open reading frame. *J. Virol.* 63:4110-14

109. Olsen, H. S., Cochrane, A. W., Dillon, P. J., Nalin, C. M., Rosen, C. A. 1990. Interaction of the human immunodeficiency virus type 1 Rev protein with a structured region in *env* mRNA is dependent on multimer formation mediated through a basic stretch of amino acids. *Genes Dev.* 4:1357-64

110. Olsen, H. S., Nelbock, P., Cochrane, A. W., Rosen, C. A. 1990. Secondary structure is the major determinant for interaction of HIV *rev* protein with RNA. *Science* 247:845-48

111. Perez, L. G., Davis, G. L., Hunter, E. 1987. Mutants of rous sarcoma virus envelope glycoprotein that lacks the transmembrane anchor and cytoplasmic domains: analysis of intracellular transport and assembly into virions. *J. Virol.* 61:2981-88

112. Peterlin, B. M., Luciw, P. A., Barr, P. J., Walker, M. D. 1986. Elevated levels of mRNA can account for the *trans*-activation of human immunodeficiency virus. *Proc. Natl. Acad. Sci. USA* 83:9734-38

113. Pomerantz, R. J., Trono, D., Feinberg, M. B., Baltimore, D. 1990. Cells nonproductively infected with HIV-1 exhibit an aberrant pattern of viral RNA expression: a molecular model for latency. *Cell* 61:1271-76

114. Popovic, M., Sarngadharan, M. G., Read, E., Gallo, R. C. 1984. Dectection, isolation, and continuous production of cytopathic retroviruses (HTLV-III) from patients with AIDS and pre-AIDS. *Science* 224:497-500

115. Ratner, L., Haseltine, W., Patarca, R., Livak, K. J., Starcich, B., et al. 1985. Complete nucleotide sequence of the AIDS virus, HTLV-III. *Nature* 313:277-84

116. Robert-Guroff, M., Popovic, M., Gartner, S., Markham, P., Gallo, R. C., et al. 1990. Structure and expression of *tat*-, *rev*-, and *nef*-specific transcripts of human immunodeficiency virus type 1 in infected lymphocytes and macrophages. *J. Virol.* 64:3391-98

117. Rosen, C. A., Sodroski, J. G., Goh, W. C., Dayton, A. I., Lippke, J., et al. 1986. Post-transcriptional regulation accounts for the *trans*-activation of the human T-lymphotropic virus type III. *Nature* 319:555-59

118. Rosen, C. A., Sodroski, J. G., Haseltine, W. A. 1985. The location of *cis*-acting regulatory sequences in the human T cell lymphotropic virus type III (HTLV-III/LAV) long terminal repeat. *Cell* 41:813-23

119. Rosen, C. A., Terwilliger, E., Dayton, A., Sodroski, J. G., Haseltine, W. A. 1988. Intragenic *cis*-acting art gene-responsive sequences of the human immunodeficiency virus. *Proc. Natl. Acad. Sci. USA* 85:2071-75

120. Roy, S., Delling, U., Chen, C.-H., Rosen, C. A., Sonenberg, N. 1990. A bulge structure in HIV-1 TAR RNA is required for Tat binding and Tat-mediated *trans*-activation. *Genes Dev.* 4:1365-73

121. Roy, S., Parkin, N. T., Rosen, C., Itovitch, J., Sonenberg, N. 1990. Structural requirements for *trans*-activation of human immunodeficiency virus type 1 long terminal repeat-directed gene expression by *tat*: importance of base pairing, loop sequence, and bulges in the

tat-responsive sequence. *J. Virol.* 64: 1402-6

122. Ruben, S., Perkins, A., Purcell, R., Joung, K., Sia, R., et al. 1989. Structural and functional characterization of human immunodeficiency virus *tat* protein. *J. Virol.* 63:1-8

123. Sanchez-Pescador, R., Power, M. D., Barr, P. J., Steimer, K. S., Stempien, M. M., et al. 1985. Nucleotide sequence and expression of an AIDS-associated retrovirus (ARV-2). *Science* 227:484-92

124. Schultz, A. M., Rein, A. 1989. Unmyristylated moloney murine leukemia virus Pr65^{gag} is excluded from virus assembly and maturation events. *J. Virol.* 63:2370-73

125. Schwartz, S., Felber, B. K., Benko, D. M., Fenyo, E.-M., Pavlakis, G. N. 1990. Cloning and functional analysis of multiply spliced mRNA species of human immunodeficiency virus type 1. *J. Virol.* 64:2519-29

126. Schwartz, S., Felber, B. K., Fenyo, E.-M., Pavlakis, G. N. 1990. Env and Vpu proteins of human immunodeficiency virus type 1 are produced from multiple bicistronic mRNAs. *J. Virol.* 64:5448-56

127. Schwartzberg, P., Colicelli, J., Goff, S. P. 1984. Construction and analysis of deletion mutations in the pol gene of moloney murine leukemia virus: a new viral function required for productive infection. *Cell* 37:1043-52

128. Selby, M. J., Bain, E. S., Luciw, P. A., Peterlin, B. M. 1989. Structure, sequence, and position of the stem-loop in *tar* determine transcriptional elongation by *tat* through the HIV-1 long terminal repeat. *Genes Dev.* 3:547-58

129. Selby, M. J., Peterlin, B. M. 1990. *Trans*-activation by HIV-1 Tat via a heterologous RNA binding protein. *Cell* 62:769-76

130. Seto, E., Yen, T. S. B., Peterlin, B. M., Ou, J.-H. 1988. *Trans*-activation of the human immunodeficiency virus long terminal repeat by the hepatitis B virus X protein. *Proc. Natl. Acad. Sci. USA* 85:8286-90

131. Sharp, P. A., Marciniak, R. A. 1989. HIV TAR: an RNA enhancer? *Cell* 59:229-30

132. Siekevitz, M., Josephs, S. F., Dukovich, M., Peffer, N., Wong-Staal, F., et al. 1987. Activation of the HIV-1 LTR by T cell mitogens and the *trans*-activator protein of HTLV-I. *Science* 238:1575-78

133. Siomi, H., Shida, H., Maki, M., Hatanaka, M. 1990. Effects of a highly basic region of human immunodeficiency virus Tat protein on nucleolar localization. *J. Virol.* 64:1803-7

134. Sodroski, J., Goh, W. C., Rosen, C., Dayton, A., Terwilliger, E., et al. 1986. A second post-transcriptional *trans*-activator gene required for HTLV-III replication. *Nature* 321:412-17

135. Sodroski, J., Patarca, R., Rosen, C., Wong-Staal, F., Haseltine, W. 1985. Location of the *trans*-activating region on the genome of human T-cell lymphotropic virus type III. *Science* 229:74-77

136. Sodroski, J. G., Rosen, C. A., Haseltine, W. A. 1984. *Trans*-acting transcriptional activation of the long terminal repeat of human T lymphotropic viruses in infected cells. *Science* 225:381-421

137. Somasundaran, M., Robinson, H. L. 1988. Unexpectedly high levels of HIV-1 RNA and protein synthesis in a cytocidal infection. *Science* 242:1554-57

138. Southgate, C., Zapp, M. L., Green, M. R. 1990. Activation of transcription by HIV-1 Tat protein tethered to nascent RNA through another protein. *Nature* 345:640-42

139. Stein, B. S., Gouda, S. D., Lifson, J. D., Penhallow, R. C., Bensch, K. G., et al. 1987. pH-Independent HIV entry into CD4-positive T cells via virus envelope fusion to the plasma membrane. *Cell* 49:659-68

140. Stephens, R. M., Derse, D., Rice, N. R. 1990. Cloning and characterization of cDNAs encoding equine infectious anemia virus Tat and putative Rev proteins. *J. Virol.* 64:3716-25

141. Stevenson, M., Stanwick, T. L., Dempsey, M. P., Lamonica, C. A. 1990. HIV-1 replication is controlled at the level of T cell activation and proviral integration. *EMBO J.* 9:1551-60

142. Strebel, K., Daugherty, D., Clouse, K., Cohen, D., Folks, T., et al. 1987. The HIV "A" (*sor*) gene product is essential for virus infectivity. *Nature* 328:728-30

143. Strebel, K., Klimkait, T., Maldarelli, F., Martin, M. A. 1989. Molecular and biochemical analyses of human immunodeficiency virus type 1 *vpu* protein. *J. Virol.* 63:3784-91

144. Teich, N. 1984. Taxonomy of retroviruses. In *RNA Tumor Viruses*, ed. R. Weiss, N. Teich, H. Varmus, J. Coffin, 2:25-207. Cold Spring Harbor: Cold Spring Harbor Lab.

145. Terwilliger, E., Burghoff, R., Sia, R., Sodroski, J., Haseltine, W., et al. 1988. The *art* gene product of human immunodeficiency virus is required for replication. *J. Virol.* 62:655-58

146. Terwilliger, E. F., Cohen, E. A., Lu,

Y., Sodroski, J. G., Haseltine, W. A. 1989. Functional role of human immunodeficiency virus type 1 *vpu*. *Proc. Natl. Acad. Sci. USA* 86:5163-67

147. Tiley, L. S., Brown, P. H., Le, S.-Y., Maizel, J. V., Clements, J. E., et al. 1990. Visna virus encodes a post-transcriptional regulator of viral structural gene expression. *Proc. Natl. Acad. Sci. USA* 87:7497-7501

148. Varmus, H., Brown, P. 1989. Retroviruses. In *Mobile DNA*, ed. D. E. Berg, M. M. Hose, pp. 53-108. Washington DC: Am. Soc. Microbiol.

149. Varmus, H. E., Padgett, T., Heasley, S., Simon, G., Bishop, J. M. 1977. Cellular functions are required for the synthesis and integration of avian sarcoma virus–specific DNA. *Cell* 11:307-19

150. Wain-Hobson, S., Sonigo, P., Danos, O., Cole, S., Alizon, M. 1985. Nucleotide sequence of the AIDS virus, LAV. *Cell* 40:9-17

151. Weeks, K. M., Ampe, C., Schultz, S. C., Steitz, T. A., Crothers, D. M. 1990. Fragments of the HIV-1 Tat protein specifically bind TAR RNA. *Science* 249:1281-85

152. Weiss, R. 1982. Experimental biology and assay of RNA tumor viruses. See Ref. 152a, pp. 209-60

152a. Weiss, R., Teich, N., Varmus, H., Coffin, J., eds. 1982. *RNA Tumor Viruses*, Vol. 1. Cold Spring Harbor: Cold Spring Harbor Lab.

153. Wright, C. M., Felber, B. K., Paskalis, H., Pavlakis, G. N. 1986. Expression and characterization of the *trans*-activator of HTLV-III/LAV virus. *Science* 234:988-92

154. Zack, J. A., Arrigo, S. J., Weitsman, S. R., Go, A. S., Haislip, A., et al. 1990. HIV-1 entry into quiescent primary lymphocytes: molecular analysis reveals a labile, latent viral structure. *Cell* 61:213-22

155. Zagury, D., Bernard, J., Leonard, R., Cheynier, R., Feldman, M., et al. 1986. Long-term cultures of HTLV-III-infected T cells: a model of cytopathology of T-cell depletion in AIDS. *Science* 231:850-53

156. Zapp, M. L., Green, M. R. 1989. Sequence-specific RNA binding by the HIV-1 Rev protein. *Nature* 342:714-16

Annu. Rev. Microbiol. 1991. 45:251–63

VIRUSES OF THE PROTOZOA

A. L. Wang and C. C. Wang

Department of Pharmaceutical Chemistry, University of California, San Francisco, California 94143

KEY WORDS: double-stranded RNA, *Giardia lamblia, Trichmonas vaginalis, Leishmania braziliensis*, RNA-dependent RNA polymerase

CONTENTS

INTRODUCTION 251
DOUBLE-STRANDED RNA VIRUSES OF *TRICHOMONAS VAGINALIS*
    AND *GIARDIA LAMBLIA* 253
  TVV, the First dsRNA Virus in Protozoa 253
  GLV, the Giardiavirus 255
  Comparison of TVV and GVV with Two Mycoviruses, ScV-L and UmV-P1 258
THE RNA VIRUSES OF *LEISHMANIA BRAZILIENSIS* 259
OTHER NEWLY IDENTIFIED VIRUSES IN PROTOZOA 260
CONCLUSIONS AND FUTURE PROSPECTS 261

INTRODUCTION

Viruses were first identified near the end of the last century as submicroscopic infectious agents derived from infected cell extracts. Over the next 100 years, viruses were identified in a wide variety of organisms, from simple pro-karyotes to multicellular animals and higher plants (26). As obligatory in-tracellular replicative entities, viruses often utilize aspects of the host biolog-ical machinery in order to propagate. Investigations of basic viral functions and the use of viruses as a tool for genetic manipulation have led to an understanding of many fundamental biological processes (20, 27). Despite early knowledge of viruses in a wide range of organisms, viruses in pro-

251

0066-4227/91/1001-0251$02.00

tozoa were not definitively identified until 1986 (36, 37). The lack of such viruses that could be used as transforming vectors has no doubt played a role in our relatively poor understanding of protozoan genetics compared with that of other microorganisms such as yeast or bacteria (27, 39).

Early reports of virus-like particles (VLP) in protozoa derived from electron micrographs of thin cell sections. Researchers observed VLPs in *Plasmodium* (15), *Naegleria* (30), *Leishmania* (25), and *Entamoeba* (8, 21, 22), but with the possible exception of those in *Entamoeba* these VLPs occurred at very limited frequencies and could not be differentiated from prokaryotic inclusions within the eukaryotic cell (20). In the absence of direct evidence that these particles depend on their host cells for protein synthesis and genome replication, their viral nature remained questionable.

In the case of *Entamoeba histolytica*, three distinct types of VLPs were observed (7). First, icosahedral VLPs of 75–80 nm were found in the cytoplasm, often associated with vacuoles or the cell membrane. These VLPs were maintained in culture for long periods in several clonally derived cell lines of *E. histolytica*. Crude extracts of VLP-containing *E. histolytica* could lyse indicator amoebae in vitro, leading to speculation that these VLPs were the causative agent of the hitherto unexplained spontaneous lysis of amoebae in culture (8). The second type of VLP, found in the nuclei of *E. histolytica*, was filamentous, with a diameter of 7 nm. The third, or beaded type of VLP, also found within the nucleus, was 17 nm in diameter. None of these three forms has been purified as yet, leaving the relationship among the three difficult to ascertain, and the viral nature of these VLPs unclear.

Several years after the report of VLPs in *E. histolytica*, Molyneux (25) found VLPs, using transmission electron microscopy, in sandfly-stage promastigotes of eight separate strains of *Leishmania hertigi*, a kinetoplastid that infects porcupines. These VLPs were cytoplasmic, 55–60 nm in diameter, and were found either clustered in paracrystals or associated with induced tubules. Promastigotes in culture seemed unaffected by the presence of VLPs and retained steady levels of VLPs over as long as three years of propagation in vitro, suggesting that viral replication had taken place within cultured cells. Nevertheless, VLPs isolated from crude extracts have never been shown to infect virus-free *Leishmania* spp. (5).

While early reports of VLPs were based almost exclusively on electron microscopic studies, more recent studies of viruses in protozoa have included molecular evidence. In most cases, further investigation of a novel nucleic acid species or an unusual enzymatic activity eventually pointed to a viral origin for these observations. For example, in 1985, we (35) discovered that a 5.5-kb nucleic acid species present in a hot phenol extract of *Trichomonas vaginalis* was in fact a linear double-stranded RNA (dsRNA). Closer examination of cellular fractions enriched for this novel nucleic acid led to the identification of the *T. vaginalis* virus (TVV), the first virus of protozoa to have its genome and capsid characterized biochemically (37). Shortly thereafter, a second dsRNA virus (GLV) was identified in *Giardia lamblia* in our laboratory (36). Our more recent studies have focused on GLV because it is readily purified from spent culture medium and efficiently infects many other virus-free strains (23, 24, 36). Many of these findings are discussed later in this review.

Additional VLPs have been observed in the last few years in the genera *Leishmania* (31–33, 42, 43), *Eimeria* (10, 29), and, most recently, in *Babesia* (17). These VLPs are all similar in size and morphology, and, in most cases, their genomes are dsRNA. In many instances, identification of VLPs followed the discovery of a novel RNA species in cell extracts. However, in one of the two cases where VLPs were found in *Leishmania braziliensis guyanensis*, the initial finding identified RNA-dependent RNA polymerase (RDRP) activity. Screening of cells for this enzymatic activity eventually led to isolation of the RNA virus (42, 43).

Interestingly, all of the aforementioned protozoa are themselves obligatory parasites. This bias is not surprising considering that parasitic protozoa probably enjoy more research attention than their free-living cousins. Perhaps, as protozoologists begin to examine extracts of free-living protozoa for the presence of unusual molecules or enzymatic activities, viruses will be discovered in free-living species as well. As to whether association of these viruses with protozoa is related to parasitic life style, the possibility remains that these viruses play a pivotal role in the delicate balance of the host-parasite interaction.

DOUBLE-STRANDED RNA VIRUSES OF *TRICHOMONAS VAGINALIS* AND *GIARDIA LAMBLIA*

TVV, the First dsRNA Virus in Protozoa

In 1985, we (35) observed a 5.5-kb nucleic acid molecule in a nucleic acid extract of *T. vaginalis* ATCC 30001 strain that was (*a*) refractory to enzymes such as DNase I, DNA polymerase I, or restriction endonucleases that utilized DNA as substrates and (*b*) resistant to bleomycin A2, which specifically cleaves double-stranded DNA. In contrast, this molecule was readily degraded by treatment with 0.2 M NaOH, ribonuclease (RNase) T1, or RNase A at room temperature, suggesting that this new species is comprised of RNA. Furthermore, sensitivity of this 5.5-kb RNA to RNases depended on the ionic strength of the reaction buffers: the lower the ionic strength, the faster the degradation. This susceptibility to RNases, together with a DNA-like buoyant density and hyperchromicity, led to the conclusion that the nucleic acid species was in fact dsRNA. Examination of this species using electron microscopy revealed a linear duplex 1.5 μm in length, which could be denatured by heat or 30% dimethyl sulfoxide to yield a single-stranded structure of the same length. The dsRNA nature of this molecule was further verified by its positive reactivity with anti-poly(I):poly(C) in ELISA and its ability to induce macrophage synthesis of γ-interferon in vitro (38).

Two lines of evidence indicated that the 5.5-kb dsRNA originated from a VLP: 1. The dsRNA remained stable in crude homogenates of *T. vaginalis* under conditions in which all other nucleic acids were degraded by endogenous nucleases. This protection of dsRNA from nucleases was readily reversible by treatment of the crude homogenate with either sodium dodecyl-sulfate or proteinase K, suggesting that the dsRNA is protected from digestion by a proteinaceous shell. 2. Although VLPs were not found in thin sections or crude cell homogenates (34), fractions enriched for this 5.5-kb dsRNA molecule through serial differential and CsCl density gradient centrifugations contained a surprisingly large, homogeneous population of VLPs 33 nm in diameter (37). By our calculations, on average 280–1350 such VLPs are present per infected cell. These VLPs have a buoyant density of 1.468 g/ml and contain a major protein of 85 kilodaltons (kd) in addition to the 5.5-kb dsRNA, which does not cross-hybridize with DNA isolated from infected cells (37). This VLP, named *T. vaginalis* virus (TVV), is believed to be the first virus positively identified and purified from a protozoan.

To determine the prevalence of viral infection among *T. vaginalis* strains, independent fresh isolates of *T. vaginalis* were examined for the presence of the TVV dsRNA. Of 28 isolates examined, 14 contained TVV indistinguishable from the original isolate, whereas the other 14 were free of the virus (40). Eight of the 14 infected isolates lost the TVV over several months of serial passage in in vitro culture. When isolates collected and stored at $-70°C$ before the loss of TVV were compared with cultures after the loss of virus, a curious correlation between the presence of TVV and the phenotypic variation of a 270-kd trichomonad surface antigen was observed. On the basis of reactivity of a monoclonal antibody towards this 270-kd antigen, *T. vaginalis* could be characterized as either homogeneously and stably negative or heterogeneously positive, comprising a mixed population of positive and negative cells. Cloned positive cells from this latter class would in turn segregate to give rise to trichomonads of mixed phenotypes in culture. This second class of cells, which can apparently vary the expression of this 270-kd protein, have been linked to enhanced cytadherence and cytotoxicity of *T. vaginalis* to epithelial cells in culture (1). Loss of TVV from the trichomonads and the termination of their capability for this phenotypic variation occur concomitantly. However, the 270-kd antigen and the 85-kd TVV protein did not cross-react immunologically. The significance of the correlation between surface antigen variation and the presence of TVV awaits elucidation.

Further studies on the infectivity of TVV indicate that the purified virus cannot infect other virus-free trichomonads, *Trichomonas foetus, G. lamblia, E. histolytica,* or *Trypanosoma brucei brucei* (37, 38). Additionally, virus particles are not detectable in filtered spent culture medium (A. L. Wang & C. C. Wang, unpublished observation).

GLV, the Giardiavirus

Soon after the identification of TVV, we (36) described a 7-kb nucleic acid species in *G. lamblia* Portland I. This nucleic acid was also a linear dsRNA as evidenced by: (*a*) its susceptibility to alkali treatment or nucleases that utilize either DNA or RNA as substrates, which was consistent with that of dsRNA; (*b*) its positive reactivity with an antiserum directed against poly(I):poly(C); and (*c*) its ability to induce the production of γ-interferon in vitro (36). Cellular fractions enriched for dsRNA contained abundant quantities of icosahedrons 33 nm in diameter, thereby linking this dsRNA to potential viral particles. In a manner similar to the TVV dsRNA, addition of detergent or proteinase K abolished protection of the *Giardia* dsRNA from nuclease degradation in crude extracts of infected cells. This finding suggested that the dsRNA is encapsidated by protein and does not exist as a free molecule within the cell. Isolation of GLV from infected cells indicates that GLV-infected *G. lamblia* trophozoites can harbor as many as 5×10^5 GLV per cell without affecting their rate of growth (24).

GLV particles were isolated as dsRNA-enriched fractions using CsCl buoyant density gradient centrifugation of infected *G. lamblia* cell-free extracts and from the spent culture medium of the infected cells (24, 36). Virus-like particles of the same diameter as GLV were also detectable in thin sections from both nuclei of infected *G. lamblia* (36). Viruses purified from either infected cell-free extracts or filtered spent culture medium could infect virus-free *G. lamblia* at a multiplicity of infection (m.o.i.) of as low as 10 virus particles per cell (24). While established infected cell lines showed the same cell-doubling time as uninfected cells, infection of uninfected cells at a high m.o.i. of 10^5 resulted in an increase in the number of nonadhering cells and cessation of growth, but not cell lysis (24). Of 76 strains and isolates of *G. lamblia* examined for the presence or absence of any dsRNA in the crude nucleic acid extract (6, 23), 28 contained the 7-kb dsRNA, presumably from the same GLV, while 48 were virus-free. Most of the virus-free isolates could be readily infected by purified GLV. However, nine were refractory to GLV infection even at a m.o.i. of 10^6 (23). These resistant isolates may lack a membrane receptor for GLV or differ taxonomically from the susceptible *Giardia*. The isolates that contained the 7-kb dsRNA were derived from humans as well as other mammals, including beaver, cat, guinea pig, and sheep. This suggests that viral tropism is targeted to the protozoan rather than the mammalian host. Further studies indicated that GLV could not infect the other species of protozoa tested, as well as two transformed human intestinal epithelial cell lines (34).

Further characterization of the GLV genome showed that the dsRNA is a linear duplex of approximately 1.5 μm as measured by electron microscopy. The molecule was readily radiolabeled with ^{32}pCp and T4 RNA ligase (36), suggesting that at least one of the two strands has a free hydroxyl group at the 3' end. Denatured dsRNA subjected to oligo(dT) column chromatography detected in the flow-through fraction indicates that GLV dsRNA does not possess a poly(A) tail. Direct RNA sequencing results confirm that the GLV dsRNA lacks poly(A) tracts at its 3' termini (A. L. Wang, E. Furfine, & C. C. Wang, unpublished observations). GLV dsRNA does not cross-hybridize with either TVV-dsRNA or the DNA of infected G. lamblia (38), suggesting, in the first case, that the two viruses are not highly related, and, in the second case, that neither free nor integrated DNA copies of the GLV genome exist in infected cells (36, 38).

In addition to the 7-kb dsRNA, GLV also contains a major protein of 100 kd (p100) (24). Antisera raised against purified virus particles reacted strongly with p100 but not with the dsRNA. Virus preincubated with this antiserum is no longer infectious. Furthermore, when virus-infected G. lamblia is incubated with antiserum-containing medium for three days, GLV dsRNA is no longer detectable in the nucleic acid fraction of the cell extract (34). The ability of an antiserum that recognizes p100 to block viral infection strongly suggests that p100 is a viral capsid protein necessary for the initiation of infection and subsequent assembly of progeny viral particles.

A GLV-related RNA molecule (SS) was recently detected in extracts of GLV-infected cells (14). This RNA, in contrast to the GLV dsRNA, is quite labile and migrates faster than the dsRNA in native agarose gel electrophoresis. Under denaturing conditions, however, its estimated size is 7 kb, comigrating with the denatured dsRNA. SS is not detectable in either the culture medium or the purified viral particles. During the course of viral infection, SS is detectable before any GLV dsRNA or GLV particles are found in cells or culture supernatant. Rather high levels of SS persist before finally diminishing as infected cells reach stationary phase, concomitant with release of GLV particles into the medium. Strand-specific probes derived from a partial cDNA clone, pG30, of GLV dsRNA show that while the probe corresponding to one strand of GLV dsRNA hybridizes to both SS and dsRNA, the probe corresponding to the opposite strand hybridizes to only the dsRNA. These results indicate that SS is homologous to only one strand of GLV dsRNA. To test if SS is a single-stranded (ss) RNA identical to one of the two strands of dsRNA, radiolabeled dsRNA was denatured, then reannealed in the presence or absence of unlabeled SS. SS displaces one of the duplex strands in this experiment, and therefore represents a full-length transcript of the viral genome. To conclusively demonstrate that SS contains a complete GLV genome, gel-purified SS was introduced into virus-free *G. lamblia* by electroporation. Surviving cells became infected and, after further culture, extruded infectious GLV particles into the medium (13). SS was therefore proven to be the viral message of the GLV genome, and capable of serving as a functional replicative intermediate of GLV.

The availability of SS has allowed its use as a template for cDNA synthesis by primer extension, resulting in several partial cDNA clones ranging from 120 nucleotides to 1 kb in size (A. L. Wang & C. C. Wang, in preparation). Complete sequencing of these clones reveals that at least one, pG30 (14), encodes a polypeptide with some homology to the consensus motifs of the known RDRPs encoded by other RNA viruses (28). The degree of homology of this 66–amino acid GLV polypeptide with other viral RDRPs is, respectively: Sindbis virus (SNSV), 19.7%; yeast killer virus (ScV), 16.7%; and polio virus, 18.2%, where percent homology reflects identical residues. While the overall amino acid identity of the potential polypeptide encoded by pG30 with those of known RDRPs is modest, the FLDD motif in pG30 may be functionally equivalent to YGDD, the most conserved region of all RDRPs (28). Figure 1 shows the alignments of these sequences.

Consistent with the presence of RDRP motifs in the genomic GLV sequence, RDRP activity itself was found in GLV-infected cell-free extracts as well as in purified GLV particles (41). The polymerase activity displays many characteristics common to other RNA polymerases such as a strict requirement for divalent cations and all four ribonucleoside triphosphates. The RNA polymerase activity was not inhibited by agents specific for DNA-dependent RNA polymerases, such as α-amanitin, rifampicin, and actinomycin D. Hybridization studies indicated that the nascent RNAs synthesized by this polymerase are predominantly of the same strand as SS. A polypeptide corresponding to the GLV RDRP activity is not detectable in SDS-PAGE

```
SNSV    2333 MFLTL..FVNT..VLNVVIASR.V..LE.....ERLKT.SRC.AA..FIGDDNI
ScV      557 WRLTT..FMNT..VLNWAYM.K.L..AG....VFDLDD.VQD.SV..HNGDDVM
Polio    290 CSGTS..IFNS..MINNLII.RTL..LLKTYKGIDLDH.L.K.MI..AYGDDVI
pG30       1 WIPTSGPAWKVPYLENVVK..RSGRRLL.....AELRIASNNGSGDRTFLDDVI


SNSV    2377 DKEMAE.RCATWLNMEVKI
ScV      720 HRVCGGISTDTWAPVETKI
Polio    333 ......ASYP..HEVDASL
pG30      49 DKKGNAFCYFS.AALGGKI
```

Figure 1 Alignment of computer-generated amino acid sequence from pG30, a partial cDNA clone derived from GLV dsRNA (14), with RDRPs of Sindbis virus (SNSV), yeast killer virus (ScV), and polio virus. Amino acids conserved are shown in bold face. Alignment of SNSV, ScV, and polio virus is adopted from Ref. 9.

analysis of purified GLV particles, which reveals only a single species, p100. However, when a Western blot of purified GLV is probed with the antiviral serum, a 200-kd cross-reactive species is detectable in addition to the p100 capsid protein (A. L. Wang & C. C. Wang, unpublished observation). In this context, it is useful to consider a well-characterized small, nonsegmented dsRNA virus also associated with a RDRP activity, the yeast killer virus ScV L-A. In this case, the yeast virus dsRNA encodes an 80-kd major coat protein, as well as a minor polypeptide of 180 kd believed to be a RDRP. The nucleotide sequence of L-A cDNAs reveals two different open reading frames (ORFs) that overlap by 130 nucleotides. The first open reading frame (ORF-1) encodes the 80-kd coat protein, whereas the 180-kd polypeptide is most likely encoded by a fusion between ORF-1 and ORF-2 that contains a (-1) frameshift somewhere within the 130-nucleotide overlap (9, 16). If the organization of the GLV genome is analogous to that of the yeast killer virus ScV-L, the 200-kd cross-reactive species observed could represent a p100/RDRP fusion protein.

Comparison of TVV and GLV with Two Mycoviruses, ScV-L and UmV-P1

TVV and GLV are distinct viruses whose RNAs do not cross-hybridize, and their capsid polypeptides do not cross-react immunologically, either against each other, or with mycoviruses such as ScV (36, 38). Nevertheless, many of the physical and biological characteristics of TVV and GLV are quite similar to those of the killer yeast virus or *Ustilago maydis* virus (UmV) (3, 4, 18, 19, 33). All four are isometric particles that lack lipids and comprise a single segment of dsRNA and one major polypeptide. Table 1 lists some of their properties. The similarity between these two groups of viruses extends beyond their physical and biochemical characteristics to their replicative cycles. For example, none of these viruses is believed to go through an intermediary DNA stage (36, 37). Three of these viruses, GLV (14), TVV (A. L. Wang, & C. C. Wang, unpublished observation) and ScV-L1 (12), overproduce a ssRNA in the infected cell that could function both as a viral message and replicative intermediate. These findings prompted the International Committee on the Taxonomy of Viruses in 1990 to recognize and accept GLV as the first fully identified virus of protozoa. GLV is classified in the family *Totiviridae*, which includes other nonsegmented dsRNA viruses such as the mycoviruses, and is assigned the genus *Giardiavirus*.

Mycoviruses such as ScV-L or UmV-P1 are often found associated with smaller, toxin-encoding defective VLPs that depend on the former for their capsids (3, 4, 11, 33). In contrast, polymorphic dsRNAs of varying sizes that could represent defective VLPs or killer toxin–encoding elements have yet to be detected in the protozoan systems. Considering the enormous number of virus particles supported at the expense of these protozoan hosts with no

Table 1 Physical characteristics of TVV, GLV, ScV-L and UmV-P1

Virus	TVV[a]	GLV[b]	ScV-L[c]	UmV-P1[d]
Shape	Isometric	Isometric	Isometric	Isometric
Diameter (nm)	33	33	33–41	41–43
Density in CsCl	1.468	1.400–1.420	1.368	1.418
dsRNA, length (μm)	1.5	1.5	1.31	—
Est. size (kb)	5.5	7.0–7.5	4.3–4.8	6.3
Major capsid protein (kd)	85	100	88	73

[a](37).
[b](36).
[c](3).
[d](2).

apparent selective advantage involved, the retention of such viruses over the course of evolution remains intriguing.

THE RNA VIRUSES OF *LEISHMANIA BRAZILIENSIS*

Recently, Tarr et al (32) identified a candidate RNA virus LR-1, present in promastigotes of *L. braziliensis guyanensis* CUMC1-1A but not in a second *L. braziliensis guyanensis* subspecies nor in ten other *Leishmania* species. The potential viral RNA has a size of approximately 6 kb, and, as isolated from infected parasites, appears to be single stranded. The RNA is associated with spherical particles 32 nm in diameter that are detected in the cytoplasmic fraction of cellular extracts and have an estimated sedimentation coefficient of 130S in sucrose density gradients. These particles were not detectable in either culture supernatants or by electron microscopic analysis of sectioned cells. Further studies identified other 6-kb RNAs from *L. braziliensis guyanensis* M4147, M1142, and two other stocks. However, this 6-kb RNA did not hybridize to the LR-1-derived cDNA clone Lp5-30, suggesting that these multicopy small RNAs prevalent in New World *Leishmania* may be genetically divergent (31). Using isolated 6-kb RNA as template for cDNA synthesis, investigators have cloned segments of LR-1 and have determined over 2000 nucleotides of sequence information. The largest single segment, 886 nucleotides in length, contains an intact ORF that does not bear any nucleotide or protein sequence homology with any known sequence in sequence databases (31).

In 1989, Widmer et al (42, 43) identified a viral RDRP activity in lysates from *L. braziliensis guyanensis* M4147 and WR677 (a derivative of M4147), the only isolates examined harboring a 6-kb RNA species. As assayed by native or denaturing agarose gel electrophoresis, the polymerase reaction products included species up to 6 kb in length as well as many smaller RNAs.

Radiolabeled polymerase-reaction products derived from WR677 and M4147 were used to probe blots of total RNAs from WR677, M4147, and PH8, a *Leishmania mexicana amazonensis* strain that lacks the 6-kb RNA. The results showed that probes derived from either WR677 or M4147 annealed only to the 6-kb band of WR677 and M4147, and not to the RNA from PH8. Virus-like particles 33 nm in size and similar in morphology to LR-1 were isolated and found to be associated with this RDRP activity (42). Both single-stranded and double-stranded 6-kb RNAs were found in the virions, so whether the viral genome consists of a ds- or ssRNA is unclear. However, Tarr et al (32) found that LR-1 does not cross-hybridize with genomic DNA isolated from infected cells, indicating that no copies of LR-1 are integrated into the cellular genome and ruling out the possibility that LR-1 is a retrovirus.

OTHER NEWLY IDENTIFIED VIRUSES IN PROTOZOA

Within the past year, three new reports have surfaced describing virus-like particles and possibly virus-associated RNA molecules in protozoa. Revets et al (29) isolated a 6.5-kb linear dsRNA measuring 1.63 μm from sporozoites of *Eimeria stiedae*. This dsRNA is associated with spherical (probably icosahedral) virus-like particles with a diameter of 35 nm present in sporozoite lysates. RNA-RNA hybridization experiments revealed that the RNA associated with the *E. stiedae* virus-like particle cross-hybridizes strongly to the giardiavirus RNA, whereas no cross-hybridization could be detected between this potential viral genome and that of TVV. It will be interesting to see if further studies confirm that this virus in *E. stiedae* sporozoites is highly similar or even identical to the giardiavirus.

Along similar lines, Ellis & Revets (10) recently identified two RNA species in the oocysts and sporozoites of *Eimeria necatrix,* as well as a 5.8-kb RNA in the oocysts and sporozoites of *Eimeria maxima*. The latter appears to be a linear dsRNA measuring 1.13 μm by electron microscopy and is detected in all four isolates of *E. maxima* examined. This RNA does not hybridize with the dsRNA of *E. stiedae* virus-like particles and has not as yet been found associated with any virus-like particle. However, its relative insensitivity to exogenous ribonuclease A added to crude lysates of *E. maxima* oocysts under conditions in which all ribosomal RNAs are degraded suggests that the RNA is protected in a nucleoprotein complex, which may comprise a viral particle.

Most recently, Johnston et al (17) found using agarose gel electrophoresis a nucleic acid species of about 5.5 kb in the nucleic acid fraction of two isolates of *Babesia bovis*. Further characterization using DNase I, RNase, and mung bean nuclease indicated that the nucleic acid is a dsRNA that is associated with spherical VLPs of an average density of 1.358 g/ml and a diameter of 38 nm.

CONCLUSIONS AND FUTURE PROSPECTS

Rapid progress in the discovery of new and potential viruses among parasitic protozoa during the past few years has brought us to the threshold of a new era in molecular parasitology. Interesting new findings made among the anaerobic flagellates *T. vaginalis* and *G. lamblia*, the kinetoplastidae *L. braziliensis*, and the sporozoa family of *Eimeria* and *Babesia* spp. suggest that a wide variety of parasitic protozoa can harbor viruses. All the viruses of protozoa share several common features: (*a*) all are RNA viruses and most, if not all, are dsRNA viruses; (*b*) all are spherical or icosahedral in shape; (*c*) all have a diameter of 30 to 40 nm; and (*d*) the dsRNA genomes are all nonsegmented, with a size between 5 and 7 kb. These common features suggest that these viruses may be closely related to one another evolutionarily. In addition, these viruses bear a close resemblance to the yeast dsRNA killer virus (33) as well as some of the dsRNA viruses of various fungi (4, 18, 19), which generally exert no lytic action on infected cells and allow normal growth. However, in the case of yeast killer virus as well as many other mycoviruses (4, 18, 19, 33), the virus is often associated with defective particles that encode toxins lethal to other sensitive strains, thereby offering its host a selective advantage.

Our success in introducing the isolated giardiavirus mRNA into *G. lamblia* trophozoites to generate infectious virus represents, to our knowledge, the first time such a study has been accomplished on a dsRNA virus. This technique could be most beneficially extended to those viruses that are incapable of infecting cells as isolated virions, such as the yeast dsRNA killer virus and TVV. Electroporation of viral mRNA into other species of parasitic protozoa or into mammalian cells can be also tested. Successful viral replication in an unnatural host after mRNA electroporation would suggest that these cells can regulate viral gene expression in a fashion similar to that of the natural host. The only difference between a natural and unnatural host could then be that the latter lack a surface receptor for viral infection. Once infected, however, these unnatural hosts may allow viral propagation with cell division as in the case of yeast dsRNA killer virus. Thus, for those protozoa for which no natural virus has yet been identified, artificial infection with a foreign virus mRNA could be used for the purpose of gene transfection. This approach could potentially result in the ability to manipulate protozoa genetically, thus opening a whole new avenue of research.

Using the positive-strand ssRNA of a dsRNA virus as a template for synthesis of cDNAs in the 5' direction via primer extension may lead to eventual identification of the viral promoter region. Foreign genes could be linked downstream of the promoter cDNA fragment, cloned into an appropriate vector, and transcribed in vitro. In the case of GLV, such a transcript, when electroporated into GLV-infected *G. lamblia* strains, should be able to utilize the endogenous intact virus as a helper virus. The engineered defective virus would thus be transcribed, translated, and encapsulated into GLV-like particles as a dsRNA. These GLV-like particles, carrying foreign genes, could then infect *G. lamblia*. Expression of the foreign gene in the parasite could be accomplished with help from an endogenous GLV. Selection of a foreign gene whose expression happens to be lethal for *G. lamblia* would result in a potential anti-giardiasis therapy.

ACKNOWLEDGMENTS

Research conducted in the authors' laboratory was supported by NIH grant AI19391.

Literture Cited

1. Alderete, J. F., Suprun-Brown, L., Kasmala, L., Smith, J., Spence, M. 1985. Heterogeneity of *Trichomonas vaginalis* and discrimination among trichomonal isolates and subpopulations by sera of patients and experimentally infected mice. *Infect. Immun.* 49:463–69
2. Bozarth. R. F., Koltin, Y., Weissman, M. B., Parker, R. L., Dalton, R. E., et al. 1981. The molecular weight and packaging of dsRNAs in the mycovirus from *Ustilago maydis* killer strains. *Virology* 113:492–502
3. Bruenn, J. A. 1980. Virus-like particles of yeast. *Annu. Rev. Microbiol.* 34:49–68
4. Bruenn, J. A. 1986. The killer systems of *Saccharomyces cerevisiae* and other yeasts. In *Fungal Virology*, ed. K. W. Buck, pp. 85–108. Boca Raton, FL: CRC Press
5. Croft, S. L., Molyneux, D. H. 1979. Studies on the ultrastructure, virus-like particles and infectivity of *Leishmania hertigi*. *Ann. Trop. Med. Parasitol.* 73:213–26
6. De Jonckeheere, J. F., Gordts, B. 1987. Occurrence and transfection of a *Giardia* virus. *Mol. Biochem. Parasitol.* 23:85–89
7. Diamond, L. S., Mattern, C. F. T. 1976. Protozoal viruses. *Adv. Virus Res.* 20:87–112
8. Diamond, L. S., Mattern, C. F. T., Bartgis, T. L. 1972. Viruses of *Entamoeba histolytica*. I. Identification of transmissible virus like agents. *J. Virol.* 9:326–41
9. Diamond, M. E., Dowhanick, J. J., Nemeroff, M. E., Pietras, D. F., Tu, C. I., et al. 1989. Overlapping genes in a yeast double-stranded RNA virus. *J. Virol.* 63:3983–90
10. Ellis, J., Revets, H. 1990. *Eimeria* species which infect the chicken contain virus-like RNA molecules. *Parasitology* 101:163–69
11. El-Sherbeini, M., Tipper, D. J., Mitchell, D. J., Bostian, K. A. 1984. Virus-like particle capsid proteins encoded by different L double-stranded RNAs of *Saccharomyces cerevisiae:* their roles in maintenance of M double-stranded killer plasmids. *Mol. Cell Biol.* 4:2818–27
12. Esteban, R., Kujimura, T., Wickner, R. B. 1988. Site-specific binding of viral plus single-stranded RNA to replicase-containing open virus-like particles of yeast. *Proc. Natl. Acad. Sci. USA* 85:4411–15
13. Furfine, E. S., Wang, C. C. 1990. Transfection of the *Giardia lamblia* double-stranded RNA virus into *Giardia lamblia* by electroporation of a single-stranded RNA copy of the viral genome. *Mol. Cell. Biol.* 10:3659–63
14. Furfine, E. S., White, T. C., Wang, A. L., Wang, C. C. 1989. A single-stranded RNA copy of the *Giardia lamblia* virus double-stranded RNA genome is present in the infected *Giardia lamblia*. *Nucleic Acids Res.* 17:7453–67
15. Garnham, P. C., Bird, R. G., Baker, J. R. 1962. Electron microscope studies of motile stages of malaria parasites. III. The ookinetes of *Haemamoeba* and *Plasmodium*. *Trans. R. Soc. Trop. Med. Hyg.* 56:116–20
16. Icho, T., Wickner, R. B. 1989. The double-stranded RNA genome of yeast virus L-A encodes its own putative RNA polymerase by fusing two open reading frames. *J. Biol. Chem.* 264:6716–23
17. Johnston, R. C., Farias, N. A. R., Gonzales, J. C., Dewes, H., Masuda, A., et al. 1990. A putative RNA virus in *Babesia bovis*. *Mol. Biochem. Parasitol.* 45:155–58
18. Kandel, J., Koltin, Y. 1978. Killer phenomenon in *Ustilago maydis:* compari-

son of the killer proteins. *Exp. Mycol.* 2:270–78

19. Koltin, Y., Kandel, J. S. 1978. Killer phenomenon in *Ustilago maydis:* the organization of the viral genome. *Genetics* 88:267–76

20. Lemke, P. A. 1976. Viruses of eukaryotic microorganisms. *Annu. Rev. Microbiol.* 30:105–45

21. Mattern, C. F. T., Diamond, L. S., Daniel, W. A. 1972. Viruses of *Entamoeba histolytica.* II. Morphogenesis of the polyhedral particle $(ABRM)^2 \rightarrow HK-9 \rightarrow HB-301$ and the filamentous agent $(ABRM)^2 \rightarrow HK-9$. *J. Virol.* 9:342–58

22. Mattern, C. F. T., Hruska, J. F., Diamond, L. S. 1974. Viruses of *Entamoeba histolytica.* V. Ultrastructure of the polyhedral virus V_{301}. *J. Virol.* 13:247–49

23. Miller, R. L., Wang, A. L., Wang, C. C. 1988. Identification of *Giardia lamblia* strains susceptible and resistant to infection by the double-stranded RNA virus. *Exp. Parasitol.* 66:118–23

24. Miller, R. L., Wang, A. L., Wang, C. C. 1988. Purification and characterization of the *Giardia lamblia* double-stranded RNA virus. *Mol. Biochem. Parasitol.* 28:189–96

25. Molyneux, D. H. 1974. Virus-like particles in *Leishmania* parasites. *Nature (London)* 249:588–89

26. Murphy, F. A., Kingsbury, D. W. 1990. Virus taxonomy. In *Virology*, Vol. 1, ed. B. N. Fields, pp. 9-35. New York: Raven. 2nd ed.

27. Patterson, J. L. 1990. Viruses of protozoan parasites. *Exp. Parasitol.* 70: 111–13

28. Poch, O., Sauvaget, I., Delarue, M., Tordo, N. 1989. Identification of four conserved motifs among the RNA-dependent polymerase encoding elements. *EMBO J.* 8:3867–74

29. Revets, H., Dekegel, D., Deleersnijder, W., De Jonckheere, J., Peeters, J., et al. 1989. Identification of virus-like particles in *Eimeria stiedae. Mol. Biochem. Parasitol.* 36:209–16

30. Schuster, F. L. 1969. Intranuclear virus-like bodies in the amoeboflagellate *Naegleria gruberi. J. Protozool.* 16: 724–27

31. Stuart, K., Weeks, R., Tripp, C., Smiley, B., Aline, R. F. Jr. 1990. Viruses and episomes of *Leishmania.* In *Immune Recognition and Evasion: Molecular Aspects of Host-Parasite Interaction*, ed. L. H. T. van der Ploeg, C. Cantor, H. J. Vogel, pp. 269–78. New York: Academic. 315 pp.

32. Tarr, P. I., Aline, R. F. Jr., Smiley, B. L., Scholler, J., Keithly, J., et al. 1988. LR1: a candidate RNA virus of *Leishmania. Proc. Natl. Acad. Sci. USA* 85: 9572–75

33. Tipper, D. J., Bostian, K. A. 1984. Double-stranded ribonucleic acid killer systems in yeasts. *Microbiol. Rev.* 48:125–56

34. Wang, A. L., Miller, R. L., Wang, C. C. 1988. Antibodies to the *Giardia lamblia* double-stranded RNA virus major protein can block the viral infection. *Mol. Biochem. Parasitol.* 30:225–32

35. Wang, A. L., Wang, C. C. 1985. A linear double-stranded RNA in *Trichomonas vaginalis. J. Biol. Chem.* 260: 3697–3702

36. Wang, A. L., Wang, C. C. 1986. Discovery of a specific double-stranded RNA virus in *Giardia lamblia. Mol. Biochem. Parasitol.* 21:269–76

37. Wang, A. L., Wang, C. C. 1986. The double-stranded RNA in *Trichomonas vaginalis* may originate from virus-like particles. *Proc. Natl. Acad. Sci. USA* 83:7956–60

38. Wang, A. L., Wang, C. C. 1988. Viruses of parasitic protozoa. In *Molecular Basis of the Action of Drugs and Toxic Substances*, ed. T. P. Singer, N. Castagnoli, C. C. Wang, pp. 126-37. Berlin/New York: de Gruyter. 248 pp.

39. Wang, A. L., Wang, C. C. 1990. Viruses of parasitic protozoa. *Parasitol. Today.* 7:76–80

40. Wang, A. L., Wang, C. C., Alderete, J. F. 1987. *Trichomonas vaginalis* phenotypic variation occurs only among trichomonads infected with the double-stranded RNA virus. *J. Exp. Med.* 166:142–50

41. White, T. C., Wang, C. C. 1990. RNA dependent RNA polymerase activity associated with the double-stranded RNA virus of *Giardia lamblia. Nucleic Acids Res.* 18:553–59

42. Widmer, G., Comeau, A. M., Furlong, D. B., Wirth, D. F., Patterson, J. L. 1989. Characterization of an RNA virus from the parasite *Leishmania. Proc. Natl. Acad. Sci. USA* 86:5979–82

43. Widmer, G., Keenan, M. C., Patterson, J. L. 1990. RNA polymerase activity is associated with viral particles isolated from *Leishmania braziliensis* subsp. *guyanensis. J. Virol.* 64:3712–15

Annu. Rev. Microbiol. 1991. 45:265–82

VARICELLA-ZOSTER VIRUS LATENCY[1]

Kenneth D. Croen

Department of Medicine, University of Cincinnati College of Medicine, Cincinnati, Ohio 45267

Stephen E. Straus

Medical Virology Section, Laboratory of Clinical Investigation, National Institutes of Allergy and Infectious Diseases, Bethesda, Maryland 20893

KEY WORDS: herpesvirus, reactivation, transcription, genes

CONTENTS

INTRODUCTION 265
THE MOLECULAR BIOLOGY OF VZV 267
PATHOGENESIS OF PRIMARY AND RECURRENT DISEASE 269
    Varicella 269
    Zoster 269
ANIMAL MODELS OF VZV INFECTION 270
LATENCY 271
    Overview of Herpesvirus Latency 271
    VZV Latency 272
REACTIVATION 276
CONCLUSIONS 277

INTRODUCTION

The herpesviruses are ubiquitous pathogens of the animal kingdom. Their abilities to establish and maintain latent infections and to reactivate

---

periodically during the life of their host are central features of their biology. Of the seven known human herpesviruses (23), six are extremely prevalent, including varicella-zoster virus (VZV), herpes simplex viruses types 1 and 2 (HSV-1 and -2), Epstein-Barr virus (EBV), cytomegalovirus (CMV), and human herpesvirus number 6 (HHV-6). Substantial progress has been made, particularly in recent years, toward understanding the pathogenesis of latency for many of the viruses in this family (12, 73).

The frequency with which reactivation punctuates latency varies significantly from one herpesvirus to another. HSV-1 and -2 reactivate often and may cause as many as 20–25 clinical recurrences per year (11). Asymptomatic recurrences are well recognized and contribute greatly to disease transmission (46, 65). Clinically evident recurrences of EBV, CMV, and HHV-6 are generally limited to hosts with impaired cellular immunity. However, asymptomatic shedding of EBV and CMV from the oropharynx occurs frequently and is the primary source of infection for susceptible hosts. In the normal host, reactivation of HHV-6 has not yet been documented, but the epidemiology of roseola infantum associated with primary infection is consistent with asymptomatic transmission from latently infected adults to susceptible children (4). Thus, reactivation from latency plays an important role in securing the dissemination of most human herpesviruses.

In contrast, VZV rarely reactivates and usually does so only once during the lifetime of an infected individual. Transmission of this virus occurs primarily in an epidemic fashion via respiratory tract inoculation of aerosolized particles shed by individuals during the incubation period of their primary infection, varicella (28, 78). Patients with reactivated VZV infection, known as zoster, are contagious, but the low viral burden and usual lack of virus in the respiratory tract limits the mechanism of spread predominantly to one of direct contact. Asymptomatic shedding of VZV following the establishment of latency has not been reported. Thus, reactivation from latency plays a far less significant role in the spread of VZV than it does for the other members of the herpesvirus family.

Vast differences in the reactivation patterns of the human herpesviruses imply different strategies for the establishment and maintenance of latent infections. Contributions by the cell in which the virus persists are undoubtedly fundamental to the pathogenesis of latency, though, at this time, little is known about the mechanics of this interaction. Other host factors, such as the immune response, may also influence the latent state.

Most of the work to date on herpesvirus latency has focused on defining the status of the virus in terms of its transcriptional activity and the structure of its genome during latency (12, 73). In the pages that follow, we review what is known about VZV latency and contrast these observations with those of other neurotropic herpesviruses.

THE MOLECULAR BIOLOGY OF VZV

The herpesviruses are large, enveloped viruses containing a linear double-stranded DNA genome. Varicella-zoster virus is approximately 125,000 base pairs in length, making it the smallest of the human herpesviruses (16). The base composition of the genome is 46% guanine plus cytosine (G + C), indicating a major evolutionary divergence from the other neurotropic herpesviruses; HSV-1 and -2 are 67% and 69% G + C, respectively.

The VZV genome contains unique sequences of approximately 100 and 5.4 kb (U_L and U_S, respectively), which are flanked by inverted repeats as shown in Figure 1b. The short repeats (IR_S and TR_S) are 6.8 kb in length and allow the U_S to invert during the course of viral replication such that both orientations may be found with equal frequency in mature virions (16, 18, 38, 79). In contrast, the long repeats (IR_L and TR_L) are vestigial structures and do not facilitate isomerization as readily as the short repeats; at most 5% of viral genomes have an inverted U_L segment. An unpaired nucleotide at each 3' terminus of the virus permits circularization of the genome. The presence of circular forms was suggested by electron microscopic observations and verified using southern hybridization of restriction digests of virion DNA (38, 77). Although the pathogenetic significance of these structural features is not known, they represent fundamental differences from those of the HSV genome, which may contribute to differences in the pathogenesis of these viruses.

The complete sequence of the VZV genome has been determined and predicts approximately 70 unique genes (16). Transcript mapping of both total cellular and polyadenylated RNA from infected cells has identified the positions of 77 discrete viral transcripts (43, 54, 62). By analogy to related sequences in other herpesviruses and by direct analyses, functions have been assigned to many of the viral gene products, although the majority remain undefined. Figure 1b shows the map locations of key structural and nonstructural gene products. Of particular note is the absence of a VZV equivalent of the HSV ICP0 gene (16). As discussed below, this region of the HSV genome appears to impact the pathogenesis of HSV latency and reactivation (12, 73). Therefore, its absence in VZV may account for some of the differences that are observed in the reactivation patterns of these two viruses.

Studies that elucidated the temporal order of viral gene expression during the replicative cycle for HSV were done with high titers of cell-free virus that facilitated synchronous infection of a cell monolayer. From these studies, four classes of genes were identified; immediate-early, early, delayed-early, and late (10, 33, 34). These classes of genes are expressed in sequential fashion during the lytic replication cycle. Identification of the regulatory factors for each class of genes provided important insights into the pathogenesis of HSV infections. Unfortunately, the inability to generate adequate titers of cell-free

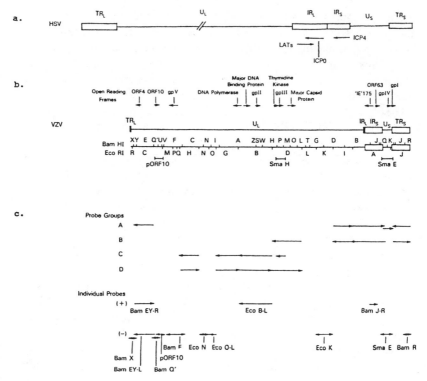

Figure 1 Maps of the HSV-1 and VZV genomes show their structural similarities including positions of the long and short unique regions (U_L and U_S) and the internal (I) and terminal (T) inverted repeats flanking the U_S (IR_S and TR_S) and U_L (IR_L and TR_L). Viral genes that map within the repeats are shown only in the internal repeats. (*a*) Map of the HSV-1 genome showing the location of specific HSV-1 genes relevant to this discussion of latency. (*b*) Map of the VZV genome showing the location of key viral genes and relevant restriction sites. Selected gene products and open reading frames (ORFs) of the genome are shown. ORF4 and IE175 encode the VZV equivalents of the HSV-1 immediate-early infected cell proteins 27 and 4, respectively. ORF 10 encodes the equivalent of the HSV-1 α-*trans*-inducing factor. (*c*) RNA probes were transcribed in either direction (*arrows*) from templates spanning the VZV genome and were divided into four pool groups, A–D. Hybridization signals were detected with each of the probe groups. Individual RNA probes that detected [(+) probes] or that failed to detect [(−) probes] VZV-specific latency transcripts are shown. R and L refer to right- and left-oriented probes.

stocks of the highly cell-associated VZV has precluded an extensive analysis of VZV gene regulation (70). Indeed, putative VZV IE genes [VZV open reading frames (ORFs) 4, 62, and 63] have been identified primarily through sequence homology to HSV genes (16, 70). Complementation studies of HSV ICP4 mutants have confirmed their functional similarity to the VZV ORF62 gene (IE175) (21, 22).

For the purpose of studying the function of individual viral genes, specific mutations have been readily engineered in HSV by exploiting its ability to undergo efficient homologous recombination. VZV, in contrast, has proven to be highly refractory to these recombinant strategies and, consequently, only a single mutant virus has been constructed in this manner (42).

Additional limitations in the study of VZV pathogenesis are the failure of the virus to replicate well in nonhuman cell lines and, more importantly, the absence of useful animal models that closely mimic any phase of the disease in humans (discussed below). Thus, studies of viral pathogenesis and latency have been confined primarily to human subjects.

PATHOGENESIS OF PRIMARY AND RECURRENT DISEASE

Varicella

Primary infection with VZV generally occurs via inhalation of virus-containing aerosolized particles leading to an initial nidus of infection in the respiratory epithelium and local reticuloendothelial system (RES). Dissemination of the virus to distant cells of the RES ensues wherein further amplification of the infection occurs. Ultimately, viremia leads to infection of the skin resulting in the classic exanthem of chickenpox (3, 20, 48, 55, 56, 82). Concurrently, viremic infection may occur in all viscera, but clinical recognition of this event is largely limited to immune-deficient patients. In a manner analogous to HSV, cutaneous infection with VZV, followed by retrograde transport of the virus, provides one route by which the virus reaches sensory nerve ganglia. This hypothesis is supported by the observation that the location of recurrent VZV infections (zoster) mirrors the distribution of lesions during a typical episode of varicella (72). Viremia provides an alternate route by which the virus may establish its residence in the sensory ganglion. In situ hybridizations of tissues from a child that died with progressive varicella revealed a pattern suggestive of viremic seeding of the ganglia (14). The presence of viral sequences within some nonneuronal cells whose adjacent neurons lacked evidence of infection argues that retrograde transport of virus may not be the only means by which VZV reaches the ganglion. HSV, in contrast, appears to reach sensory ganglia primarily, if not entirely, by ascent of sensory nerves. Thus, in animal models of acute disease, infection of satellite cells has only been observed adjacent to infected neurons (39).

Zoster

Clinical experience reveals that the latent state of VZV is tightly maintained and only rarely disturbed, as only about 10–20% of seropositive individuals ever develop even a single episode of zoster (Table 1). This figure contrasts with the hundreds of episodes of HSV recurrence that may occur in a given

Table 1 Features of VZV and HSV reactivation infections

	VZV	HSV
Frequency of recurrences	Usually once in lifetime	Up to several hundred in a lifetime
Likelihood of recurrence	Increases with age	Decreases over time
Percent of seropositives with symptomatic recurrences	10–20%	20–47%
Distribution	Dermatome	Focal lesion
Associated symptoms	Severe pain	Mild dysesthesias
Time to recurrence after the onset of immunosuppression	2–6 months	1–4 weeks
Reactivation induced by UV light	No	Yes
Asymptomatic shedding	No	Yes

individual's lifetime. Another obvious difference between VZV and HSV reactivation patterns is the age at which such recurrences are observed. Zoster is predominantly a disease of the elderly, with an increasing annual incidence from <50 episodes per 100,000 individuals below the age of 15 years to >400 episodes per 100,000 individuals above age 75 (60). Recurrences of HSV, on the other hand, are most frequent in the first few years after primary infection and are seen less often in the elderly.

Waning of immune surveillance for VZV has long been implicated as an important predisposing factor for zoster in the elderly. Early studies suggested that the senescence of humoral immune recognition of VZV was responsible for the reactivation of this infection in the elderly (35). The advent of more sensitive serologic assays enabled investigators to prove that these observations were incorrect (2, 6, 25). Impaired cellular immune responses, however, have been clearly linked to VZV reactivation (7). The decline in peripheral lymphocyte responses to VZV antigens in the elderly is inversely related to the rising incidence of zoster in this population. The T cells of patients with Hodgkin's disease and those on immunosuppressive therapies who are at increased risk for zoster exhibit a significant reduction in their ability to respond to VZV antigens (2, 41, 61). The reduced rate of exposure of elderly individuals to acute VZV infections may be one factor that accounts for the decline in T cell recognition of this virus.

ANIMAL MODELS OF VZV INFECTION

The pathogenesis of HSV infections have been elucidated considerably through the use of animal models that closely mimic the disease in humans. In terms of latency, observations on the state of the virus in mice, rabbits, and guinea pigs have been essentially identical to the findings in humans (8, 13, 64, 75). Comparable models for VZV infection do not exist. The common marmoset can be infected with VZV by an oral/nasal route of inoculation, resulting in an immune response and mild pneumonitis but no other stigmata of disease (59). Naturally occurring varicella of a gorilla has been documented with virus recovered from vesicular lesions (51). This model was predictably too unfriendly to pursue further.

The most promising model is that of the guinea pig infected with VZV adapted to fetal guinea pig tissues in culture. Several investigators have demonstrated infection of weanling strain 2 guinea pigs following inoculation through intranasal, intratracheal, subcutaneous, intramuscular (IM), corneal, or intracranial routes (45, 49, 52, 57). One study reported a high rate of disseminated infection following IM inoculation, but latency was not explored (52). This same group recently reported the use of congenitally hairless Hartley guinea pigs that develop a more evident exanthem during the acute illness (50). Studies on the status of the virus within the sensory ganglia are in progress.

Another recently described, potentially useful system uses adult rats infected by subcutaneous injection with cell associated virus (67). Although the animals in this study failed to develop any signs of an acute illness other than an immune response, following in vitro cultivation, the dorsal root ganglia reportedly contained viral nucleic acids and proteins up to nine months after infection.

LATENCY

Overview of Herpesvirus Latency

As indicated, the herpesviruses persist within their hosts primarily in a state of latency, with only occasional interruptions in the form of lytic infections. Latency is defined operationally as the inability to recover infectious particles from disrupted cells that harbor the virus. This condition should be distinguished from a persistent infection in which a low level of viral replication and infectious particles are recoverable from disrupted cells. Examples of the latter include subacute sclerosing panencephalitis (SSPE), progressive multifocal leukoencephalopathy (PML), chronic hepatitis B, and HIV infections (1).

Once thought to be completely dormant, latent herpesvirus genomes are now recognized to be transcriptionally active. In every case studied thus far, a few viral genes are expressed during the latent state (12, 73). As many as 10 viral transcripts in EBV and as few as one in HSV have been identified during latency. The contribution made to the latent state by the expressed genes have not yet been elucidated but are the focus of intensive investigation.

The neurotropic (alpha) herpesviruses include many naturally occurring pathogens of nonhuman hosts. In addition to HSV and VZV, pseudorabies virus (PRV) and bovine herpesvirus (BHV) are among the most widely studied members of this group (Table 2). A pattern of latency-associated transcription common to most of these viruses is emerging. HSV-1 and -2, PRV, and BHV express large quantities of RNA from a single region of their genomes during latency (9, 15, 63, 75, 81). For HSV-1, the transcripts are referred to as LATs (latency-associated transcripts). In each instance, the abundant transcripts overlap one of the viral IE genes in an antisense manner. This juxtaposition makes feasible the occurrence of significant RNA-RNA (antisense) interactions, although adequate proof of this phenomenon is lacking at the present time. Preliminary reports suggest that a protein may be encoded by the the LATs of HSV-1 and BHV (30; C. Doerig, L. I. Pizer, C. L. Wilcox, submitted). A precise function has not yet been assigned to any of these latency genes. Deletion mutants lacking the LATs gene of HSV-1 are fully capable of establishing latent infections, yet they reactivate in vitro and in animal models with reduced efficiency (32, 37, 40, 68, 71). Thus, the HSV LATs are not involved in the establishment or maintenance of latency but may facilitate the process of reactivation.

VZV Latency

Many aspects of the latent state of VZV are unique among the neurotropic herpesviruses (see Table 2). As discussed below, some of these differences may help explain the pattern of recurrent disease characteristic of VZV.

The demonstration by Head & Campbell (31) in 1900 that the cutaneous lesions of zoster correlate with the distribution of pathologic lesions within sensory ganglia led to the first mapping of cutaneous dermatomes. Garland (24) proposed in 1943 that zoster represents a recrudescence of the chickenpox virus. Hope-Simpson (35) hypothesized in 1965 that VZV lay dormant within the sensory ganglia following primary infection and could reactivate

Table 2 Characteristics of the latent phase of neurotropic herpesviruses

	VZV	HSV	PRV	BHV
Virus recovered through cocultivation or explantation	−	+	+	+
Multiple spontaneous reactivations	−	+	+	+
Abundant LATs-like transcript	−	+	+	+
Location of latency transcripts	Nonneuronal cells	Neuron	Neuron	Neuron

from them to produce zoster. Proof of this hypothesis did not come until Straus et al (80) demonstrated using DNA restriction endonuclease analysis that a single VZV isolate caused both varicella and zoster infections in a child with Wiskott-Aldrich syndrome.

HSV can be readily recovered from latently infected ganglia through cocultivation or explantation (5, 74), but VZV has never been isolated in this way (47, 58). Methodologies such as the introduction of demethylating agents optimize the recovery of HSV from latency. Systematic studies using these techniques for VZV have not been reported, however. A novel approach was taken recently by Vafai et al (83). Rather than use the recovery of infectious particles as the end point of the assay, they sought viral proteins and transcripts in explanted ganglia. As early as 24 h after explantation, they detected VZV-specific proteins in protein extracts of ganglion tissue. However, they could not detect late proteins using their immunoprecipitation assay. In situ hybridization of ganglia 12 days after explantation showed a low level of transcription from the one viral immediate-early gene investigated, ORF63. These authors concluded that the failure to recover infectious particles from latently infected ganglia results from a block in viral gene expression within sensory ganglion cells. They hypothesized that these genes may also be expressed during the latent state, although at a lower, undetectable level.

Over the past eight years, several reports described the presence of viral nucleic acids within human sensory ganglia during latency. In situ hybridizations of human trigeminal ganglia by Hyman and coworkers (36) revealed VZV transcripts overlying cells that were felt to be neurons. The pool of radiolabeled DNA probes used in that study spanned the entire viral genome and thus did not identify individual transcriptionally active regions. Later, Southern blot hybridizations of genomic DNA from human sensory ganglia led Gilden et al (27) to suggest that as many as one copy of the viral genome/cell was dormant within latently infected trigeminal ganglia. More recently this same group used the polymerase chain reaction (PCR) to assess the distribution and frequency of sensory ganglion involvement during the latent stage of the VZV infection (44). Trigeminal ganglia from 13 of 15 seropositive individuals contained VZV DNA sequences (see Figure 2). Thoracic ganglia were positive from 9 of 17 individuals, but not all ganglia from a single host were positive. These data suggest that latency is more readily established within trigeminal ganglia than in thoracic dorsal root ganglia, a finding consistent with the observation that the trigeminal ganglia are those most likely to be involved in reactivation. In all but one case, widely separated regions of the genome were detected by amplification, suggesting that the entire genome probably persists within latently infected ganglia. Efforts are now underway by these investigators and others to amplify RNA

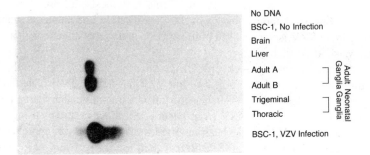

Figure 2 PCR amplification and Southern blot hybridization of the VZV origin of replication. One μg of human tissue DNA and 1 ng of DNA from uninfected and infected BSC-1 cells were amplified. Reprinted with permission (44).

within sensory ganglia using reverse transcriptase in the first step of the PCR procedure. These methods should further enhance the ability to detect and map VZV transcripts expressed within human ganglia during latency.

Several reports in the literature have used in situ hybridization to identify the transcriptional activity of latent VZV. As mentioned above, Hyman et al (36) found signals for VZV RNA using DNA probes spanning almost the entire genome. Gilden and coworkers (26) observed hybridization signals in two of four thoracic ganglia from a single individual when they were probed with a segment from the short repeats (SalP, includes portions of ORFs 63 and 64). In both of these reports, the cells bearing the hybridization signal were believed to be neurons.

More recently, we (14) examined trigeminal ganglia from thirty subjects and thoracic ganglia from four using in situ hybridization with ^{35}S-labeled single-stranded RNA probes prepared from VZV-recombinant DNA templates. We detected hybridization signals in ganglia from 15 of 30 individuals with probes from at least 5 regions of the VZV genome. Surprisingly, no signals were detected overlying the neuronal cells of the ganglia, but, rather, they were found over the small nonneuronal cells that typically surround neurons (see Figure 3). These include satellite cells, endothelial cells, and fibroblast-like cells. In contrast to the large number of such cells and neurons that appeared acutely infected in the ganglia from the child that died during an episode of varicella (see discussion above), in latently infected ganglia only a small fraction of the nonneuronal cells contained detectable VZV-specific sequences (0.01–0.15% of cells). Trigeminal ganglia from only half of the seropositive individuals hybridized to the VZV probes, suggesting that latency may not be established in all sensory ganglia. Alternatively, limited involvement of any single ganglion may account for the negative results. The

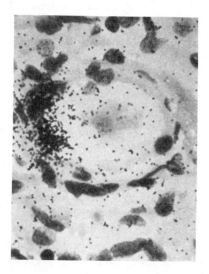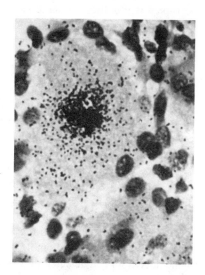

Figure 3   In situ hybridization of human trigeminal ganglia probed with ^{35}S-labeled RNA probes for VZV (*left*) transcripts (pool group A, see Figure 1c) or for HSV-1 LATs (*right*). Silver grains indicate cells with specific signals. Large neuronal cells are surrounded by small nonneuronal cells in sensory ganglia (×570). Reprinted with permission (14).

detection of VZV signals in only one of eight thoracic ganglia is further evidence that latent VZV may be sparsely distributed.

These initial hybridization experiments were performed with pooled groups (see Figure 1c) of single-stranded RNA probes spanning approximately 80% of the viral genome (14). Each of four groups of probes yielded signals on the latently infected ganglia. In an effort to determine which regions of the genome account for the hybridization, individual probes were ultimately used and have thus far identified three regions from two of the probe groups that can detect VZV sequences. As shown in Figure 1c, Bam EY-R, Eco B-L, and Bam J-R were hybridization positive. Subclones of probes spanning hybridization-positive regions of the genome are being used to determine specific ORFs that are actively expressed during latency. Some of the genes that appear to be expressed in latency include ORFs 29, 62, and 63 (R. P. Holman & S. E. Straus, unpublished observations). At least one other region of the VZV genome from each of the two probe groups that have not yet been studied individually (groups B and C, Figure 1c) also must be actively transcribed in latency. Thus, a total of at least five regions of the genome are active during VZV latency. Until a more complete picture of latent VZV gene expression emerges, what phase of the viral gene regulatory cascade is interrupted within these nonneuronal cells during latency cannot be established. For that matter, until all specific VZV transcripts are identified, the possibility remains that these include products of unrecognized genes, some of which may be antisense to genes that have already been mapped.

The signals for VZV sequences were found to represent hybridization to viral transcripts rather than the viral genome based on results following the pretreatment of tissues with either RNase, DNase, or both (14). Because the latent viral genome is not detected with in situ hybridization [which is also true for HSV (13, 75)], the possibility that a transcriptionally inactive VZV genome resides within the neuron cannot be excluded.

Studies to date confirm that VZV lacks a gene comparable to the LATs of HSV-1 and -2, BHV, or PRV. Moreover, VZV, BHV, and PRV each lack a gene equivalent to the ICP0 gene of HSV. Nevertheless, the latency transcripts of BHV and PRV are antisense to another immediate-early gene, in each case one equivalent to the ICP4 gene of HSV. As mentioned above, VZV possesses an ICP4 homologue (IE175), but transcripts antisense to this gene have not been detected during latent VZV infections (14; R. P. Holman, & S. E. Straus, unpublished observations). Although the literature contains some discrepancies about the sites of latent VZV transcription, this virus clearly has a unique pattern of gene activity that sets it apart from the other neurotropic herpesviruses.

REACTIVATION

Very little is known about the pathogenesis of reactivation for any of the herpesviruses. A gene that induces the lytic cycle for EBV (BZLF1) has been identified (12, 73). Similarly, the ICP0 gene of HSV is the only gene needed to induce reactivation of HSV from an in vitro latency model (29, 66, 84). Both of these herpesvirus genes function as transactivators of gene expression. Whether these genes ultimately prove to be relevant to the reactivation process in vivo remains to be determined.

Numerous and varied stimuli trigger reactivation of HSV from its latent state. Among these are fever, trauma, UV light, and immunosuppression. VZV, in contrast, is not consistently induced by any stimuli other than, perhaps, immunosuppression. Recurrences of VZV are observed after 2–4 months of immunosuppression, while HSV typically reactivates within 1–4 weeks. Therefore, the regulatory apparatus involved in VZV latency is apparently more potent than that for HSV. Several explanations may account for this observation:

1. VZV does not replicate well within sensory neurons and thus has greater difficulty in reactivating and spreading to the periphery. The block in viral

gene expression in explanted human ganglia indicates this lack of efficiency, which may account for the failure to recover VZV from latently infected tissues (83).

2. VZV is latent within nonneuronal cells and must reactivate from these cells. Transmission to the neuron may be an inefficient process, which could be blocked by components of the immune system. The failure of VZV to reactivate following exposure to stimuli that induce HSV replication (i.e. UV light) may also reflect the fact that the virus does not reside within the neuron. Consequently, VZV is not subject to the altered intraneuronal environment that arises with these varied stimuli.

3. The absence of a VZV gene equivalent to the LATs gene of HSV may diminish its ability to reactivate. As noted above, LAT deletion mutants of HSV-1 reactivate less efficiently than wild-type virus (32, 37, 40, 68, 71).

4. The absence of an ICP0 equivalent in VZV may account for its reduced reactivation frequency. The possible role of ICP0 in facilitating reactivation is based on in vitro studies (29, 66, 84).

5. The many regions of VZV transcriptionally active during latency may each contribute to the stability of the latent virus, perhaps through an antisense mechanism.

One can propose a model, based on the cumulative observations, that accounts for several features of VZV latency and reactivation. Following a stimulus for viral replication, the infection spreads from its host nonneuronal cell through the ganglion via a network of nonneuronal cells (Figure 4). In the process, however, many cells within the ganglion, including endothelium, are destroyed by the infection, resulting in a hemorrhagic, necrotizing lesion that typifies the histology of the ganglion during VZV reactivation (19, 69, 76). Eventually, the virus enters numerous neuronal cells including ones that may not have been infected previously. This acute process involving many neurons may account for the severe pain that often accompanies this infection. Having entered neuronal cells, the virus migrates along the axon to the skin and produces an exanthem confined to a single dermatome.

CONCLUSIONS

In many respects, varicella-zoster virus is a unique member of the herpesvirus family. Its potential for epidemic dissemination and its tendency to produce protracted pain syndromes in the elderly after an episode of zoster are two of its unique and most troublesome clinical features. In the research laboratory, the limited host range, cell-associated behavior, and unwillingness of VZV to undergo homologous recombination impede studies of its biology. Neverthe-

VARICELLA-ZOSTER VIRUS: LATENCY

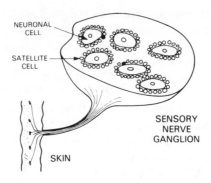

VARICELLA-ZOSTER VIRUS: REACTIVATION

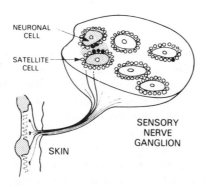

Figure 4 Sketch of latent VZV within a sensory ganglion and the hypothetical pattern of infection during reactivation. Large cells are neurons; small cells are nonneuronal cells (including satellite, endothelial, and fibroblast-like cells). Blackened cells contain latent virus. Stippling indicates area of active viral replication. Reprinted with permission (76).

less, recent progress has been made in defining several aspects of VZV latency in its human host. Here again, VZV appears to be unique at least among the neurotropic herpesviruses. Multiple transcriptionally active regions within nonneuronal cells, and undetectable transcription within neurons of sensory ganglia are two features that distinguish VZV latency from that of other neurotropic herpesviruses. Current investigations must ascertain whether the observed activity of the latent virus contributes to the pathogenesis of latency.

Literature Cited

1. Ahmed, R., Stevens, J. G. 1990. Viral persistence. In *Virology*, ed. B. N. Fields, pp.241-65. New York: Raven. 2nd ed.
2. Arvin, A. M., Pollard, R. B., Rasmussen, L. E., Merigan, T. C. 1980. Cellular and humoral immunity in the pathogenesis of recurrent herpes viral infections in patients with lymphoma. *J. Clin. Invest.* 68:869–78
3. Asano, Y., Itakura, N., Hiroishi, Y., Hirose, S., Nagai, T., et al. 1985. Viremia is present in incubation period in nonimmunocompromised children with varicella. *J. Pediatr.* 106:69–71
4. Balachandra, K., Ayuthaya, P. I. N., Auwanit, W., Jayavasu, C., Okuno, T., et al. 1989. Prevalence of antibody to human herpesvirus 6 in women and children. *Microbiol. Immunol.* 33:515–18
5. Bastian, F. O., Rabson, A. S., Yee, C. L., Tralka, T. S. 1972. Herpesvirus hominis: isolation from human trigeminal ganglia. *Science* 178:306–7
6. Brunell, P. A., Gershon, A. A., Uduman, S. A., Steinberg, S. 1975. Varicella-zoster immunoglobulins during varicella, latency, and zoster. *J. Infect. Dis.* 132:49–54.
7. Burke, B. L., Steele, R. W., Beard, O. W., Wood, J. S., Cain, T. D., et al. 1982. Immune responses to varicella-zoster in the aged. *Arch. Intern. Med.* 142:291–93
8. Burke, R. L., Hartog, K., Croen, K. D., Ostrove, J. M. 1991. Detection and characterization of latent HSV 2 RNA by in-situ and northern blot hybridizations in guinea pigs immunized with a herpes simplex subunit vaccine. *Virology*. In press
9. Cheung, A. K. 1989. Detection of Pseudorabies virus transcripts in trigeminal ganglia of latently infected swine. *J. Virol.* 63:2908–13
10. Clements, J. B., Watson, R. J., Wilkie, N. M. 1977. Temporal regulation of herpes simplex virus type 1 transcription: location of transcripts on the viral genome. *Cell* 12:275–85
11. Corey, L., Spear, P. G. 1986. Infections with herpes simplex viruses. *New Engl. J. Med.* 314:686–91, 749–57
12. Croen, K. D. 1991. Latency of the human herpesviruses. *Annu. Rev. Med.* 42:In press
13. Croen, K. D., Ostrove, J. M., Dragovic, L. J., Smialek, J. E., Straus, S. E. 1987. Latent herpes simplex virus in human trigeminal ganglia: Detection of an immediate early gene "anti-sense" transcript. *New Engl. J. Med.* 317:1427–32
14. Croen, K. D., Ostrove, J. M., Dragovic, L. J., Straus, S. E. 1988. Patterns of gene expression and sites of latency in human nerve ganglia are different for varicella-zoster and herpes simplex viruses. *Proc. Natl. Acad. Sci. USA* 85:9773–77
15. Croen, K. D., Ostrove, J. M., Dragovic, L. J., Straus, S. E. 1991. Characterization of herpes simplex virus type 2 latency-associated transcription in human sacral ganglia and in cell culture. *J. Infect. Dis.* 163:23–28
16. Davison, A. J., Scott, J. E. 1986. The complete DNA sequence of varicella-zoster virus. *J. Gen. Virol.* 67:1759–1816
17. Deleted in proof
18. Ecker, J. R., Hyman, R. W. 1986. Varicella zoster virus DNA exists as two isomers. *Proc. Natl. Acad. Sci. USA* 79:156–60
19. Esiri, M. M., Tomlinson, A. H. 1972. Herpes zoster: demonstration of virus in trigeminal nerve and ganglion by immunofluorescence and electron microscopy. *J. Neurol. Sci.* 15:35–48
20. Feldman, S., Epp, E. 1979. Detection of viremia during incubation of varicella. *J. Pediatr.* 94:746–48
21. Felser, J. M., Straus, S. E., Ostrove, J. M. 1987. Varicella-zoster virus complements herpes simplex virus type 1 temperature-sensitive mutants. *J. Virol.* 61:225–28
22. Felser, J. M., Kinchington, P. R., Inchauspe, G. I., Straus, S. E., Ostrove, J. M. 1988. Cell lines containing varicella-zoster virus open reading frame 62 and expressing the "IE" 175 protein complement ICP4 mutants of herpes simplex virus type 1. *J. Virol.* 62:2076–82
23. Frenkel, N., Schirmer, E. C., Wyatt, L. S., Katsafanas, G., Roffman, E., et al. 1990. Isolation of a new herpesvirus from human CD4+ T cells. *Proc. Natl. Acad. Sci. USA* 87:748–52
24. Garland, J. 1943. Varicella following exposure to herpes zoster. *New Engl. J. Med.* 228:336–37
25. Gershon, A. A., Steinberg, S. P. 1981. Antibody responses to varicella-zoster virus and the role of antibody in host defense. *Am. J. Med. Sci.* 282:12–17
26. Gilden, D. H., Rozenman, Y., Murray, R., Devlin, M., Vafai, A. 1987. Detection of varicella-zoster virus nucleic acid

in neurons of normal human thoracic ganglia. *Ann. Neurol.* 22:377–80

27. Gilden, D. H., Vafai, A., Shtram, Y., Becker, Y., Devlin, M., et al. 1983. Varicella-zoster virus DNA in human sensory ganglia. *Nature* 306:478–80

28. Grose, C. 1981. Variation on a theme by Fenner: the pathogenesis of chickenpox. *Pediatrics* 68:735–37

29. Harris, R. A., Everett, R. D., Zhu, X., Silverstein, S., Preston, C. M. 1989. Herpes simplex virus type 1 immediate-early protein Vmw110 reactivates latent herpes simplex virus type 2 in an in-vitro latency system. *J. Virol.* 63:3513–15

30. Hayes, M. K., Rock, D. L. 1989. Characterization of a putative latency related protein of BHV-1. *14th Int. Herpesvirus Workshop*, p. 49. Denmark: Nyborg Strand

31. Head, H., Campbell, A. W. 1900. The pathology of herpes zoster and its bearing on sensory localization. *Brain* 23:353–523

32. Hill, J. M., Sedarati, F., Javier, R. T., Wagner, E. K., Stevens, J. G. 1990. Herpes simplex virus latent phase transcription facilitates in vivo reactivation. *Virology* 174:117–25

33. Honess, R. W., Roizman, B. 1974. Regulation of herpesvirus macromolecular synthesis. I. Cascade regulation of the synthesis of three groups of viral proteins. *J. Virol.* 14:8–19

34. Honess, R. W., Roizman, B. 1975. Regulation of herpesvirus macromolecular synthesis: Sequential transition of polypeptide synthesis requires functional viral polypeptides. *Proc. Natl. Acad. Sci. USA* 72:1276–80

35. Hope-Simpson, R. E. 1965. The nature of herpes zoster: a long-term study and a new hypothesis. *Proc. R. Soc. Med.* 58:9–20

36. Hyman, R. W., Ecker, J. R., Tenser, R. B. 1983. Varicella-zoster virus RNA in human trigeminal ganglia. *Lancet* 2:814–16

37. Javier, R. T., Stevens, J. G., Dissette, V. B., Wagner, E. K. 1988. A herpes simplex virus transcript abundant in latently infected neurons is dispensable for establishment of the latent state. *Virology* 166:254–57

38. Kinchington, P. R., Reinhold, W. C., Casey, T. A., Straus, S. E., Hay, J., et al. 1985. Inversion and circularization of the varicella-zoster virus genome. *J. Virol.* 56:194–200

39. Knotts, F. B., Cook, M. L., Stevens, J. G. 1974. Pathogenesis of herpetic encephalitis in mice after ophthalmic inoculation. *J. Infect. Dis.* 130:16–27

40. Leib, D. A., Bogard, C. L., Kosz-Vnenchak, M., Hicks, K. A., Coen, D. M., et al. 1989. A deletion mutant of the latency-associated transcript of herpes simplex virus type 1 reactivates from the latent state with reduced frequency. *J. Virol.* 63:2893–2900

41. Locksley, R. M., Flournoy, N., Sullivan, K. M., Meyers, J. D. 1985. Infection with varicella-zoster virus after marrow transplantation. *J. Infect. Dis.* 152:1172–81

42. Lowe, R. S., Keller, P. M., Keech, B. J., Davison, A. J., Whang, Y., et al. 1987. Varicella-zoster virus as a live vector for the expression of foreign genes. *Proc. Natl. Acad. Sci. USA* 84:3896–3900

43. Maguire, H. F., Hyman, R. W. 1986. Polyadenylated, cytoplasmic transcripts of varicella-zoster virus. *Intervirology* 26:181–91

44. Mahalingam, R., Wellish, M., Wolf, W., Dueland, A. N., Cohrs, R., et al. 1990. Latent varicella-zoster viral DNA in human trigeminal and thoracic ganglia. *New Engl. J. Med.* 323:627–31

45. Matsunaga, Y., Yamanishi, K., Takahashi, M. 1982. Experimental infection and immune response of guinea pigs with varicella-zoster virus. *Infect. Immun.* 37:407–12

46. Mertz, G. J., Coombs, R. W., Ashley, R., Jourden, J., Remington, M., et al. 1988. Transmission of genital herpes in couples with one symptomatic and one asymptomatic partner: A prospective study. *J. Infect. Dis.* 157:1169–77

47. Meurisse, E. V. 1969. Laboratory studies on the varicella-zoster virus. *J. Med. Microbiol.* 2:317–25

48. Myers, M. G. 1979. Viremia caused by varicella-zoster virus: association with malignant progressive varicella. *J. Infect. Dis.* 140:229–33

49. Myers, M. G., Duer, H. L., Hausler, C. K. 1980. Experimental infection of guinea pigs with varicella-zoster virus. *J. Infect. Dis.* 142:414–20

50. Myers, M. G., Harrison, C. J., Stanberry, L. R. 1988. Expression of exanthem in varicella zoster virus (VZV) infected hairless guinea pigs. *Ped. Res.* 23:377A

51. Myers, M. G., Kramer, L. W., Stanberry, L. R. 1987. Varicella in a gorilla. *J. Med. Virol.* 23:317–22

52. Myers, M. G., Stanberry, L. R., Edmond, B. J. 1985. Varicella-zoster virus infection of strain 2 guinea pigs. *J. Infect. Dis.* 151:106–13

53. Deleted in proof

54. Ostrove, J. M., Reinhold, W., Fan, C., Zorn, S., Hay, J., Straus, S. E. 1985.

Transcription mapping of the varicella-zoster virus genome. *J. Virol.* 56:600–6

55. Ozaki, T., Ichikawa, T., Matsui, Y., Nagai, T., Asano, Y., et al. 1984. Viremic phase in nonimmunocompromised children with varicella. *J. Pediatr.* 104:85–87

56. Ozaki, T., Ichikawa, T., Yoshiharu, M., Kondo, H., Nagai, T., et al. 1986. Lymphocyte-associated viremia in varicella. *J. Med. Virol.* 19:249–54

57. Pavan-Langston, D., Dunkel, E. C. 1989. Ocular varicella-zoster virus infection in the guinea pig. *Arch. Ophthalmol.* 107:1068–72

58. Plotkin, S. A., Stein, S., Snyder, M., Immesoete, P. 1977. Attempts to recover varicella virus from ganglia (letter). *Ann. Neurol.* 2:249

59. Provost, P. J., Keller, P. M., Banker, F. S., Keech, B. J., Klein, H. J., et al. 1987. Successful infection of the common marmoset with human varicella-zoster virus. *J. Virol.* 61:2951–55

60. Ragozzino, M. W., Melton L. J. III, Kurland L. T., Chu C. P., Perry, H. O. 1982. Population based study of herpes zoster and its sequelae. *Medicine* 61:310–16

61. Rand, K. H., Rasmussen, L. E., Pollard, R. B., Arvin, A., Merigan, T. C. 1976. Cellular immunity and herpesvirus infection in cardiac transplant patients. *New Engl. J. Med.* 296:1372–77

62. Reinhold, W. C., Straus, S. E., Ostrove, J. M. 1988. Directionality and further mapping of varicella-zoster virus transcripts. *Virus Res.* 9:249–61

63. Rock, D. L., Beam, S. L., Mayfield, J. E. 1987. Mapping bovine herpesvirus type 1 latency-related RNA in trigeminal ganglia of latently infected rabbits. *J. Virol.* 61:3827–31

64. Rock, D. L., Nesburn, A. B., Ghiasi, H., Ong, J., Lewis, T. L., et al. 1987. Detection of latency-related viral RNAs in trigeminal ganglia of rabbits latently infected with herpes simplex virus type 1. *J. Virol.* 61:3820–26

65. Rooney, J. F., Felser, J. M., Ostrove, J. M., Straus, S. E., 1986. Acquisition of genital herpes from an asymptomatic sexual partner. *New Engl. J. Med.* 314:1561–64

66. Russell, J., Stow, N. D., Stow, E. C., Preston, C. M. 1987. Herpes simplex virus genes involved in latency in-vitro. *J. Gen. Virol.* 68:3009–18

67. Sadzot-Delvaux, C., Merville-Louis, M. P., Delree, P., Piette, J., Moonen, G., et al. 1990. An in-vivo model of varicella-zoster virus latent infection of

dorsal root ganglia. *J. Neurosci. Res.* 26:83–89

68. Sedarati, F., Izumi, K. M., Wagner, E. K., Stevens, J. G. 1989. Herpes simplex virus type 1 latency-associated transcription plays no role in establishment or maintenance of a latent infection in murine sensory neurons. *J. Virol.* 63:4455–58

69. Shibuta, H., Ishikawa, T., Hondo, R., Aoyama, Y., Kurata, K., et al. 1974. Varicella virus isolation from spinal ganglia. *Arch. Gesamte Virusforsch.* 45:382–85

70. Shiraki, K., Hyman, R. W. 1987. The immediate early proteins of varicella-zoster virus. *Virology* 156:423–26

71. Steiner, I., Spivack, J. G., Lirette, R. P., Brown, S. M., MacLean, A. R., et al. 1989. Herpes simplex virus type 1 latency-associated transcripts are evidently not essential for latent infection. *EMBO J.* 8:505–11

72. Stern, E. S. 1937. The mechanism of herpes zoster and its relation to chicken pox. *Br. J. Dermatol. Syph.* 49:264–71

73. Stevens, J. G. 1989. Human herpesviruses: a consideration of the latent state. *Microbiol. Rev.* 53:318–32

74. Stevens, J. G., Cook, M. L. 1971. Latent herpes simplex virus in spinal ganglia of mice. *Science* 173:843–5

75. Stevens, J. G., Wagner, E. K., Devi-Rao, G. B., Cook, M. L., Feldman, L. T. 1987. RNA complementary to a herpesvirus α gene mRNA is prominent in latently infected neurons. *Science* 235:1056–59

76. Straus, S. E. 1989. Clinical and biological differences between recurrent herpes simplex virus and varicella-zoster virus infections. *J. Am. Med. Assoc.* 262:3455–58

77. Straus, S. E., Aulakh, H. S., Ruyechan, W. T., Hay, J., Casey, T. A., et al. 1981. Structure of varicella-zoster virus DNA. *J. Virol.* 40:516–25

78. Straus, S. E., Ostrove, J. M., Inchauspe, G., Felser, J. M., Freifeld, A., et al. 1988. Varicella-zoster virus infections: biology, natural history, treatment and prevention. *Ann. Intern. Med.* 108:221–37

79. Straus, S. E., Owens, J., Ruyechan, W. T., Takiff, H. E., Casey, T. A., et al. 1982. Molecular cloning and physical mapping of varicella-zoster virus DNA. *Proc. Natl. Acad. Sci. USA* 79:993–97

80. Straus, S. E., Reinhold, W., Smith H., Ruyechan, W. T., Henderson, D. K., et al. 1984. Endonuclease analysis of viral DNA from varicella and subsequent zos-

ter infection in the same patient. *New Engl. J. Med.* 311:1362–64

81. Suzuki, S., Martin, J. R. 1989. Herpes simplex virus type 2 transcripts in trigeminal ganglia during acute and latent infection in mice. *J. Neurol. Sci.* 93:239–51

82. Twomey, J. J., Gyorkey, F., Norris, S. M. 1974. The monocyte disorder with herpes zoster. *J. Lab. Clin. Med.* 83: 768–77

83. Vafai, A., Murray, R. S., Wellish, M., Devlin, M., Gilden, D. 1988. Expression of varicella-zoster virus and herpes simplex virus in normal human trigeminal ganglia. *Proc. Natl. Acad. Sci. USA* 85:2362–66

84. Zhu, X., Chen, J., Young, C. S. H., Silverstein, S. 1990. Reactivation of latent herpes simplex virus by adenovirus recombinants encoding mutant IE-0 gene products. *J. Virol.* 64:4489–98

Annu. Rev. Microbiol. 1991. 45:283–99

BIOCHEMICAL DIVERSITY OF TRICHLOROETHYLENE METABOLISM

B. D. Ensley

Envirogen, Inc., Lawrenceville, New Jersey 08648

KEY WORDS: hazardous waste, cometabolism, chlorinated aliphatics, oxygenases

CONTENTS

INTRODUCTION... 283
ANAEROBIC DECHLORINATION 284
   Metabolism in Soils and Sediments 284
   Dechlorination by Microbial Consortia and Pure Cultures 285
AEROBIC OXIDATION 286
   Oxidation by Cytochrome P-450.. 286
   Oxidation by Ammonia Monooxygenase.. 288
   TCE Oxidation by Aromatic Oxygenases... 288
   TCE Oxidation by Methane Monooxygenase and Propane Monooxygenase 292
   Propane Monooxygenase 295

INTRODUCTION

Trichloroethylene (TCE) belongs to a family of synthetic chlorinated hydro-carbons manufactured as solvents with a greatly reduced potential for fire or explosion. These halogenated organics may have served their purposes all too well; the stability and solvent properties of these compounds led to their application in degreasing metals, electronic components, and dry cleaning, as fumigants for insect and rodent control, for the cleaning of septic tanks and military hardware, and in the manufacture of plastics. The widespread use of

283

0066-4227/91/1001-0283$02.00

these compounds and concomitant careless handling, storage, and disposal coupled with the chemical stability designed into them make TCE and related molecules among the most frequently detected groundwater contaminants in the United States. Many instances of drinking and well water contamination by haloorganics have been documented (16, 30). The widespread nature of groundwater contamination by TCE and its persistence in the environment causes concern because TCE can be both directly toxic and carcinogenic (34, 43). Ironically, the relatively stable nature of TCE has doubtlessly saved many lives that would have been lost to fire or explosion in industrial accidents, but these same properties have led to widespread groundwater contamination that carries its own consequences for human health. Fortunately, both aerobic and anaerobic biological processes can degrade TCE in the environment. Enzymes with a broad substrate specificity react with TCE and can reductively dechlorinate or oxidize this molecule. Under the proper environmental conditions, TCE can be rapidly converted to less chlorinated products. The diverse biochemical processes for conversion of TCE are the subject of this review and include some fairly well-defined mechanisms in oxidative enzyme systems and less well-defined anaerobic processes involving microbial consortia and pure isolates of some microorganisms.

ANAEROBIC DECHLORINATION

Metabolism in Soils and Sediments

Some of the earliest processes observed for the biological metabolism of TCE and other halogenated organics relied upon studies of fairly undefined biological systems such as soils, sediments from aquifer materials, and primary sewage sludges. An early study using sewage sludge under denitrifying conditions demonstrated putative reductive dehalogenation of chloroform but no activity against molecules such as trichloroethane (5). Similar experiments conducted under methanogenic conditions failed to demonstrate dechlorination of TCE or perchloroethylene (PCE), but a significant finding of these studies was that 50% of ^{14}C-labeled 1,2-dichloroethylene (DCE) was converted to CO_2 (6). The finding that DCE can be converted to CO_2 using ^{14}C-labeled tracer studies is important because of the speculation that the anaerobic metabolism of PCE and TCE results in the formation of vinyl chloride, a potent carcinogen in its own right. If DCE, a proposed intermediate in the dehalogenation process, can be converted to CO_2, vinyl chloride may not be the end product of TCE metabolism under the appropriate conditions, and gradual mineralization of TCE under anaerobic conditions may occur.

Researchers have used TCE labeled with ^{13}C in soil studies to demonstrate the anaerobic conversion of this molecule to DCE by recovery as ^{13}C-DCE

(20). The issue that vinyl chloride may not be the final product of anaerobic TCE metabolism has also been raised with a laboratory study of authentic contaminated aquifer material (48). This research revealed that TCE disappeared from methanogenic aquifer material over a period of 16–40 weeks while only traces of vinyl chloride could be detected at the end of the experiment. Although other workers have demonstrated the sequential biotransformation of TCE to 1,2-dichloroethylene and then to vinyl chloride, Barrio-Lage et al (2, 3) proposed that the mechanism of anaerobic TCE conversion to DCE, vinyl chloride, or other products is a reductive dehalogenation after experiments using well-defined microcosms including one made of crushed rock and water. A recent study of an anoxic aquifer contaminated with halocarbons showed a conversion of PCE to TCE and DCE with little or no vinyl chloride formed (39). By adding methanol, glucose, H_2, and other electron donors, Friedman & Gossett (15) demonstrated the reductive dechlorination of PCE and TCE to ethylene, an environmentally acceptable product. Studies with ^{14}C-labeled PCE showed that [^{14}C] ethylene was the final product. No conversion of this alkene to CO_2 or CH_4 was observed. These authors propose a pathway for reductive dechlorination that follows the course PCE→TCE→1,2-DCE→vinyl chloride→ethylene. The dechlorination process was significantly stimulated by electron donors such as hydrogen and was inhibited by 2-bromoethane sulfonic acid, a methanogen inhibitor, indicating that these organisms may play a key role in the anaerobic biotransformation of PCE and TCE.

Dechlorination by Microbial Consortia and Pure Cultures

A clearer picture of the microorganisms and enzymes involved in reductive dechlorination emerges with studies using pure cultures. Reductive dehalogenation of molecules such as dibromoethane and dichloroethane has been demonstrated with pure culture of methanogens (4). These cultures did not display activity against 1,2-dichloroethylene, and TCE was a fairly potent growth inhibitor. Boyd and coworkers (9) demonstrated the role of methanogens in the dechlorination of PCE and to a lesser extent TCE. Several methanogens were observed to convert PCE to TCE under the appropriate conditions. The most active microorganism was a dechlorinating bacterium called DCB-1 (35). Interestingly, both the dechlorination of PCE and the subsequent rapid metabolism of TCE by DCB-1 required the presence of a methanogenic consortium including a methanospirillum and a benzoate degrader. Apparently, the more favorable growth conditions of the methanogenic consortium enhance the ability of DCB-1 to dechlorinate PCE and TCE. Fathepure & Boyd (8) showed that the reductive dechlorination of PCE requires an electron-donating substrate using a pure culture of a *Methanosarsina* species strain DSM. These studies strengthen the hypothesis that reductive dechlorination by anaerobes involves the transfer of electrons to chlorinated ethylenes via biochemical processes in which the reduction of the chlorinated hydrocarbon is coupled to the oxidation of electron transfer agents involved in methane biosynthesis. Fathepure & Boyd (8) proposed a scheme for linking reductive dechlorination to methanogenesis. This scheme defines what is known about the anaerobic processes involved in the biochemical reduction of PCE or TCE.

The biochemistry of anaerobic TCE metabolism is still not well-defined. Some studies with methanogens and dechlorinating microorganisms suggest that electron-transfer processes are coupled to reductive dechlorination. A clearer understanding of the processes involved in reductive dechlorination is very important to the elimination of these compounds in the environment. To date, anaerobes are the only organisms known to degrade tetrachloroethylene; none of the known aerobic pathways will attack this molecule. In addition, many aquifers are anaerobic or oxygen is the limiting nutrient, and in situ degradation of PCE or TCE requires anaerobic processes. Finally, the dechlorination of PCE or TCE to vinyl chloride is an undesirable process. The literature hints that vinyl chloride can be further dechlorinated to ethylene at least and more precise control of this biochemical pathway could avoid the potential problems associated with vinyl-chloride formation. Further work aimed at the elucidation of the anaerobic dechlorination process of PCE and TCE will be central in devising ways to mediate the biological removal of these compounds from the environment.

AEROBIC OXIDATION

Oxidation by Cytochrome P-450

The metabolism of TCE in mammals is the basis for a good deal of the concern about its widespread contamination of drinking water. Unaltered TCE may have no carcinogenic activity. The products of its partial degradation by cytochrome P-450 may cause observed mutagenic effects. The history of human exposure to TCE in various environments is considerable, and, in fact, TCE was once widely used as an anesthetic (7). The adverse long-term effects, if any, from acute exposure to TCE are unknown. At the same time, the chronic effects of exposure may be profound, particularly if TCE is activated by oxidation with cytochrome P-450. A study of the toxic and mutagenic effects of TCE on the yeast *Saccharomyces cerevisiae* found that TCE is a powerful mutagen in yeast only after activation. After activation by mouse liver microsomes, TCE appeared to induce frame shift and base substitution mutations in yeast. In addition, this study showed that TCE is directly toxic to yeast at concentrations as low as 10 μl/ml (34). The activation of TCE by mammalian microsomes and its subsequent covalent binding to proteins was demonstrated as early as 1976. The hypothesis at that time was that TCE epoxide could be responsible for covalent interactions with microsomal proteins and mutagenic effects (43).

Several studies have provided evidence that some molecules are indirect-acting carcinogens and are metabolized to their activated carcinogenic intermediate by cytochrome P-450. These compounds are frequently epoxides, and the hypothesis was raised that an epoxide intermediate was responsible for ^{14}C-labeled TCE binding to microsomal proteins. TCE binding was inhibited by classic inhibitors of cytochrome P-450, providing indirect evidence that a metabolite of TCE catalyzed by cytochrome P-450 was responsible for microsomal protein binding and potential mutagenicity. Further work has shown that both microsomal proteins and exogenous DNA can be covalently bound to TCE in liver microsomal preparations (42). This study indicated that TCE binds covalently to both microsomal proteins and DNA in vitro and that metabolic activation mediated by microsomes is required for this binding. These authors proposed a metabolic scheme of TCE activation by cytochrome P-450, including formation of TCE epoxide, TCE dihydrodiol, trichloroacetaldehyde, trichloroethanol, and trichloroacetic acid. Later studies have shown the oxidation of TCE by liver microsomal cytochrome P-450, including the formation of chloral, glyoxylic and formic acids, and TCE epoxide (23). Both microsomal preparations and a reconstituted enzyme system containing purified rat liver P-450, P-450 reductase, phospholipid, and NADPH oxidized TCE. The use of *para*-nitrobenzylpyridine to trap the epoxide in the reconstituted enzyme system demonstrated the formation of TCE epoxide. The rate of TCE oxidation by the enzyme system was in the range of 25 nmol of various TCE products formed per minute per nmol of cytochrome P-450. These workers (23) proposed that TCE epoxide is not an obligate intermediate in the formation of chloral and presented an alternative model in which chlorine migration occurs in an oxygenated TCE cytochrome P-450 transition state. The authors also mention studies not presented in which the heme of cytochrome P-450 was destroyed during oxidative metabolism of TCE. The metabolic inactivation of the catalyzing enzyme is a common theme in this review of TCE metabolism.

Further studies of TCE metabolism in isolated rat hepatocytes and microsomal preparations demonstrated the formation of chloral; TCE oxide, which decomposes to CO and glyoxylate; and metabolites that bind irreversibly to protein, DNA, and RNA (22). As in the previous study, TCE-mediated cytochrome P-450 heme destruction occurred to the extent that 40% of the heme in a microsomal system was destroyed within 30 min at 37°C. The heme destruction was determined through analysis of radioactive heme from rats in which cytochrome P-450 was labeled by the addition of gamma [^{14}C] aminolevulinic acid. The authors postulated that the destruction occurs through attack by the pyrrolic nitrogen of the heme on an oxidized intermediate.

To date, research on TCE metabolism by cytochrome P-450 suggests that TCE is metabolized to oxidized intermediates including TCE epoxide and chloral. Apparently, TCE metabolites rather than TCE itself are responsible for the observed carcinogenicity and mutagenicity of this compound. TCE metabolism appears to be destructive to the cytochrome P-450 catalyzing the reaction. Either TCE itself or one of its active oxidized products is responsible for damaging the catalyzing enzyme. Taken together, these data suggest a possible mechanism for TCE mutagenicity in that this molecule is activated by cytochrome P-450 in tissues and forms a reactive intermediate capable of binding to the catalytic enzyme, to other cellular proteins, and to DNA or RNA. These data demonstrate a basis for concern about TCE contamination in drinking water. If this compound is activated by the liver and combines with DNA, it is prudent to be concerned about chronic exposure to TCE in drinking water or even vapor.

Oxidation by Ammonia Monooxygenase

Ammonia-oxidizing denitrifying bacteria such as *Nitrosomonas europaea* oxidize ammonia to nitrite for growth via an enzyme system known as ammonia monooxygenase. These microorganisms, presumably via their ammonia monooxygenase system, catalyze the oxidation of carbon monoxide, methane, methanol, ethylene, propylene, and bromoethane. These compounds are substrates for other broad-specificity monooxygenases such as the methane monooxygenase. The broad–substrate specificity ammonia monooxygenase system is presumed to be responsible for observed degradation of TCE by whole cells of *N. europaea* (1). Whole cells of this organism catalyzed the disappearance of TCE at a rate of 1 nmol/min per mg of whole cell protein, and this rate continued for many hours. The metabolism of TCE by these cells was stimulated by ammonia, suggesting the requirement of a cosubstrate as a reductant, and was inhibited by ammonia monooxygenase inhibitors such as acetylene. Whole cells of *N. europaea* also oxidize *cis*- and *trans*-DCE and vinyl chloride in addition to TCE. Vinyl chloride is the chlorinated ethylene most rapidly degraded by this microorganism, with rates about fivefold higher than those observed for TCE oxidation (44). Ammonia monooxygenase in whole cells also oxidizes brominated analogs of ethane and ethylene as well as fluoro-, chloro-, bromo, and iodo- methanes and ethanes. Tetrachloroethylene is not a substrate for ammonia monooxygenase (32).

TCE Oxidation by Aromatic Oxygenases

In 1986, Nelson et al (27) documented the first pure culture of a microorganism capable of metabolizing TCE under aerobic conditions. They noted that oxygen and an unidentified component in naval air station water were essential for TCE oxidation by this microorganism. Studies with [^{14}C]-labeled TCE demonstrated that 60% of the total ^{14}C-TCE was converted to CO_2 and 35% remained as an unidentified nonvolatile product. Later studies with this strain, designated G4, demonstrated that the essential component in naval air station water was phenol (26, 28). TCE-oxidizing activity could be stimulated by phenol, toluene, and meta- or *ortho*-cresol. These studies were the first reports implicating an aromatic degradative pathway in the cometabolism of TCE. Degradation by strain G4 appeared to require an aromatic substrate both as an inducer and as a cosubstrate. Also demonstrated was that *Pseudomonas putida* strain F1 containing a toluene dioxygenase enzyme system would oxidize TCE. A mutant organism lacking this enzyme system would not oxidize TCE, indicating that the initial oxygenase in these organisms was responsible for TCE oxidation. Researchers later found that strain G4 does not possess a toluene dioxygenase enzyme system, but rather employs a novel toluene degradative pathway involving the *ortho*-monohydroxylation of toluene by a new enzyme system; toluene *ortho*-monooxygenase (36). Kinetic analysis of the toluene *ortho*-monooxygenase in whole cells demonstrated that this enzyme had an apparent K_s and V_{max} for phenol oxidation of 8.5 μM and 466 nmol/min per mg of protein, respectively. The K_s and V_{max} values for TCE were 3 μM and 8 nmol/min per mg of protein (12). The fortuitous oxidation of TCE by toluene *ortho*-monooxygenase should be inhibited by the presence of molecules such as phenol or toluene, but, at the same time, these compounds are necessary inducers of the enzyme pathway and also stimulate TCE oxidation. The relationship between cosubstrates such as phenol and TCE is complicated by the mutually competitive inhibition potentially observed with these two molecules. This conjecture is born out by the observation that TCE inhibits phenol degradation by approximately 50% when both compounds are present at equal concentrations (28). Theoretically, phenol will also inhibit TCE degradation by approximately the same amount.

The microorganism containing toluene *ortho*-monooxygenase has been used in a first step towards an in situ treatment process. Strain G4 was injected within a clean oxygenated water stream directly into a TCE plume in a contaminated aquifer. Essential nutrients were added to the injection stream and TCE concentrations in the contaminated plume were measured. The concentration of TCE within the aquifer declined within 8 hours after injection, and the TCE concentration was reduced from 3 ppm to 78 ppb during a 20-day period (25).

Toluene dioxygenase, as observed by Wackett & Gibson (46), degrades TCE after growth of *P. putida* F1 in the presence of toluene. Toluene dioxygenase was shown to be the enzyme responsible for TCE oxidation in *P. putida* F1 by the use of mutants deficient in this enzyme. A series of mutants deficient in toluene dioxygenase enzyme activity could not oxidize TCE, while a mutant deficient in catechol 2,3-dioxygenase activity oxidized TCE as rapidly as the wild-type. The rate of TCE oxidation with the toluene dioxygenase enzyme system was initially fairly rapid with a rate of 1.8 nmol/min per mg of protein at an initial TCE concentration of 80 μM. No TCE oxidation at all could be measured when the initial TCE concentration was increased to 320 μM. TCE oxidation by this enzyme system also displayed a rapid loss of activity. The initial rate of oxidation decreased rapidly after approximately 10 nmol of TCE had been degraded over 20 min, and a much slower rate prevailed for the next six hours. This decrease in activity was attributed to toxic effects of TCE or TCE metabolites, and subsequent work demonstrated a toxic effect mediated by TCE and toluene dioxygenase on *P. putida* F1 as measured by growth-rate effects (47). The toluene dioxygenase enzyme system has a broad substrate specificity and could degrade TCE and *cis*-1,2-dichloroethylene at similar rates. *Trans*-1,2-dichloroethylene and 1,1-dichloroethylene were also oxidized at much lower rates. Tetrachloroethylene, vinyl chloride, and ethylene were not measurably oxidized by this enzyme system.

The role of toluene dioxygenase in the degradation of TCE was confirmed with experiments involving a recombinant *Escherichia coli* containing the genes encoding the components of toluene dioxygenase (53). The recombinant *E. coli* degraded TCE at a lower rate than *P. putida* F1. However, a linear rate of TCE disappearance over at least six hours was catalyzed by the recombinant *E. coli,* in contrast to the toluene dioxygenase enzyme system in *P. putida*. The authors speculated here that there may be a difference in cytotoxic effects of TCE metabolites between *E. coli* and *P. putida*.

In addition to the toluene *ortho*-monooxygenase and toluene dioxygenase enzyme systems, a strain of *Pseudomonas mendocina* contains a pathway for toluene oxidation involving the *para*-monooxygenation of toluene to form *para*-cresol (33, 52). Toluene *para*-monooxygenase oxidizes TCE when *P. mendocina* KR-1 is grown in the presence of toluene (51). The role of toluene *para*-monooxygenase in TCE oxidation was confirmed by transferring the genes encoding this enzyme system into *E. coli*. The recombinant *E. coli* also oxidized TCE. The rate of TCE oxidation by this enzyme system was between 1 and 2 nmol/min per mg of whole cell protein. Washed cells of *P. mendocina* KR-1 oxidized TCE at a high initial rate that decreased over time. The extent of TCE degradation could be extended if glutamate were added to the incubation mixture. TCE oxidation by cells incubated in the presence of toluene displayed a complex interaction between substrates. At toluene concentrations of approximately 1 mM, no TCE oxidation was observed to occur for some time. TCE concentrations then rapidly declined until approximately 90% of the TCE was oxidized within three hours and the rate again decreased. These data indicate that the concentration of toluene, which acts both as a substrate and an inducer of enzyme synthesis, is an important determinant of TCE metabolism by *P. mendocina* KR-1. Insufficient toluene will not stimulate TCE oxidation, while higher concentrations inhibit this reaction, presumably by competitive inhibition. Some of these speculations are confirmed by the performance of the recombinant *E. coli*. When this organism was incubated in the presence of TCE and glucose, TCE was rapidly and completely degraded, and no competitive inhibition or decrease in oxidation rates was observed.

Recently, another toluene monooxygenase enzyme system, a toluene *meta*-monooxygenase, was discovered in an organism isolated by Olsen and colleagues (17). This organism initially oxidizes toluene in the *meta*-position to form *meta*-cresol and also has been observed to oxidize TCE (R. Olsen & B. Kaphammer, personal communication).

The toluene oxygenases, in spite of some obvious differences, have properties in common. These enzymes all have a broad substrate specificity and fortuitously oxidize TCE. The toluene dioxygenase and toluene *para*-monooxygenase enzyme systems have been characterized in cell-free assays and both require NADH as a cofactor for enzyme activity. Presumably all the toluene oxygenases require some form of electron donating factor to function. TCE oxidation by toluene dioxygenase from *P. putida* F1 and toluene *para*-monooxygenase by *P. mendocina* both proceed at initial high rates that decrease over time. While the decrease in activity with the toluene dioxygenase enzyme system has been attributed to toxicity, it may also result from depletion of reducing power in the cells (47). TCE appears to produce little or no NADH during its initial oxidation or subsequent metabolism to regenerate the NADH used in the initial oxidative attack. Recombinant *E. coli* containing either the toluene dioxygenase or toluene *para*-monooxygenase enzyme systems, when incubated in the presence of glucose, rapidly and continuously oxidize TCE. While we may again attribute this observation to differences in toxic effects of TCE on various hosts, it also could be explained by the replenishment of reducing power through glucose oxidation as a cosubstrate during the oxidation of TCE. The requirement for a continuous source of reducing power during TCE oxidation complicates the degradation of this molecule in the environment. Nelson et al (25) added nutrients including a source of reducing equivalents to *Pseudomonas cepacia* G4 in a field trial involving injection of the organisms and nutrients directly into a contaminated aquifer. If an exogenous source of reducing power is degraded by non-TCE-oxidizing microorganisms present in the environment, then TCE oxidation will cease even though the right organisms are present along with the TCE. This situation can be relieved somewhat by the use of genetically engineered microorganisms (GEMs) so that molecules such as phenol or toluene are no longer required as inducing cosubstrates, but even the GEM must presumably have some source of reducing power for TCE oxidation to proceed.

TCE Oxidation by Methane Monooxygenase and Propane Monooxygenase

Wilson & Wilson (50) presented some of the first evidence that methanotrophic microorganisms may be involved in aerobic TCE metabolism in 1985. Sandy soil was exposed to natural gas to enrich for methanotrophs and organisms that oxidize other small alkanes. The soil was then examined for its capacity to remove TCE from infiltrating water. An air stream containing a natural gas mixture of 77% methane and 17% ethane and propane was passed through a soil column. The natural gas–treated soil column lowered the TCE concentration by roughly one order of magnitude during a two-day residence time with water containing 150 μg/liter of TCE flowing through the column. Soil columns not exposed to natural gas removed no TCE above that found for volatilization (49). A liquid culture grown with methane as the sole carbon source also oxidizes TCE (11). This culture oxidized TCE at an initial concentration of 80 μg/liter at a rate of 2 nmol/h per mg whole-cell protein. The culture also oxidized vinyl chloride and cis- and trans-1,2-dichloroethylene. Tetrachloroethylene was not oxidized. Experiments with [^{14}C] TCE demonstrated that 57% of the labeled TCE was released as $^{14}CO_2$ and ^{14}C-labeled biomass. These authors (11) explained TCE incorporation by assuming that TCE is oxidized by these organisms to TCE epoxide through action of methane monooxygenase. The degradation of highly concentrated chlorinated ethenes has been examined using methanogenic consortia (19). At concentrations of 30–80 μM chlorinated ethylenes, inhibition of growth on methane but not methanol was observed, suggesting that the inhibition process was specific for enzymes involved in methane oxidation. Of the compounds tested, trans-1,2-dichloroethylene showed measurable rates of degradation. An unknown metabolite accumulated in culture fluid during the degradation of this compound. This metabolite was identified using ^{3}H-NMR and mass spectrometry as trans-1,2-dichloroethylene oxide, lending credence to earlier speculation that TCE epoxide may be a product of TCE oxidation by methane monooxygenase.

Subsequent studies have demonstrated that microbial consortia isolated from a variety of environments can aerobically degrade more than 99% of TCE at concentrations as high as 50 mg/liter (10). TCE could not be used by the microbial consortia as a sole energy source, suggesting that cometabolism was taking place. Tryptone, yeast extract, glucose, acetate, methanol, and methane all supported degradation of TCE. Although this study does not provide substantial evidence that a methanotroph was involved in TCE degradation, other studies showed that a methane-utilizing mixed culture containing a type II methanotroph was responsible for TCE degradation (41). This culture required methane and oxygen for TCE degradation but methanol or formic acid could not substitute for methane.

Methanotrophic bacteria have also been used in the degradation of *trans*-dichloroethylene (18). Not only would a mixed methanotrophic culture oxidize dichlorethylene in this study, but *Methylomonas methanica* and *Methylosinus trichosporium* OB3b degraded *trans*-1,2-dichloroethylene when grown with methane as a sole carbon source. The degradation of *trans*-DCE by methane-utilizing bacteria has also been observed in a study utilizing an aquifer simulator (24). The aquifer studies showed that DCE concentrations decreased over time and that the unstable DCE metabolite, DCE oxide, appeared transiently. Methane-utilizing bacteria were added to the model aquifer, and DCE oxidation was stimulated by amending the aquifer water with mineral nutrients, oxygen, and methane. Methane increased the degradation of DCE, but some activity was observed even after methane starvation. The authors (24) speculated that energy for DCE oxidation could be obtained by the methanotrophs from their energy storage product, poly-β-hydroxybutarate.

The degradation of trichloroethylene and *trans*-1,2-dichloroethylene by a methanotrophic consortium has also been examined in packed- and expanded-bed bioreactors. A methane-utilizing consortium was established in a packed-bed bioreactor and fed TCE at concentrations of approximately 1 mg/liter. Greater than 50% of the TCE and 90% of DCE could be degraded in a single pass through this reactor (38). The system was fed methane and air, and, although no competitive inhibition of TCE metabolism was observed, shutting off the methane gas stream resulted in TCE degradation rates remaining constant for approximately 4 h and then decreasing by about one-third. Studies with a continuous-recycle expanded-bed bioreactor system have shown substantial TCE degradation in a reactor fed either methane or propane (31). Up to 95% removal of TCE was observed after 5 days of incubation in the recycled expanded-bed reactor. The reactor was fed various carbon sources in both a continuous and pulsed mode. TCE was degraded in reactors that were either fed in the pulse mode or fed daily, but little degradation was observed during periods of starvation, again demonstrating a cosubstrate requirement. A reactor fed in the pulse configuration consumed a calculated 55 mol of substrate/mol of TCE degraded, while 100 mol of substrate were required per mole of TCE degraded in continuously fed experiments. When methane was used as the sole energy source, total TCE degradation decreased by approximately 60% compared with experiments in which both methane and propane were fed at concentrations of 5% and 3% by volume, respectively. With propane as the sole carbon and energy source, TCE degradation was very similar to that observed when methane plus propane was fed into the reactor. Propane-fed reactors are the most efficient on a continuous feed basis, requiring only 80–100 mol of substrate per mole of TCE. The increased efficiency of propane mixed with methane or propane alone suggests that the microbial consortia in the reactor used propane more efficiently as a growth substrate or that propane does not compete as effectively as methane with TCE-transforming enzymes.

Other pure cultures of methane-oxidizing bacteria have been used to demonstrate TCE degradation (21). One report describes a microorganism called strain 46-1 containing a methane monooxygenase enzyme system. TCE could be degraded to CO_2 and water-soluble metabolites as demonstrated by radioisotope experiments. The maximum rate of TCE degradation depended on the presence of methane or methanol to stimulate activity. TCE degradation ceased after cosubstrate was depleted, demonstrating the dependence of cometabolism on TCE degradation by methanotrophs. Under the best of circumstances, methane-degrading strain 46-1 degraded approximately 40% of the added TCE at an initial concentration of 400 μg/liter.

Pure cultures of methanotrophs degrade TCE as well as a wide variety of other chlorinated alkanes. Studies have shown that rapid TCE degradation by methanotrophs depends upon the presence of the soluble form of the methane monooxygenase (29, 40), an enzyme that is derepressed only with growth of cells under strict copper limitation (37). TCE degradation by *M. trichosporium* OB3b can be extremely rapid, displaying activities as high as 150 nmol/min per mg of cell protein. TCE degradation under these conditions was strictly cometabolic, and formate supported the highest rates of TCE degradation and complete inhibition of TCE oxidation by methanol (29). In addition to TCE, *M. trichosporium* containing the soluble form of the methane monooxygenase also oxidized dichloromethane, chloroform, dichloroethane, cis- and trans-DCE, and 1,2-dichloropropane. Neither carbon tetrachloride nor perchloroethylene could be oxidized by this enzyme system. Hanson and coworkers (40) also measured TCE degradation by this same organism with some additional observations. They observed a decrease in TCE oxidation rates over time with both resting cell suspensions and purified enzyme preparations, suggesting that TCE may interfere with its own oxidation. These experiments also correlated the presence of soluble methane monooxygenase with TCE degradation. Only samples of cells containing soluble methane monooxyenase as demonstrated by immunological blotting oxidized TCE at measurable rates. The presence of soluble methane monooxygenase in the cells was manipulated by changing the concentrations of copper during growth. The soluble form of methane monooxygenase is synthesized under copper-limited growth conditions (37).

Fox et al (13) published the most definitive study to date of any enzyme system involved in TCE metabolism (13). They measured the oxidation of halogenated ethylenes, including TCE, in reaction systems containing each of three separately purified components comprising the enzyme system methane monooxygenase (MMO) (14). The purified enzyme system in the presence of NADH very rapidly oxidized chloroalkenes including vinyl chloride, DCE, and TCE. TCE was oxidized at a rate of 680 nmol/min per mg of protein with a K_m of 35 μM. Similar rates and kinetic constants were measured for the other chlorinated alkenes. As with other aerobic oxygenases, tetrachloroethylene is not oxidized by purified methane monooxygenase. TCE is oxidized by MMO to formate, CO, glyoxylate, dichloroacetic acid, and chloral. The use of p-nitrobenzylpyridine to trap epoxides demonstrated the formation of TCE epoxide in the reaction. These studies also showed that haloalkene oxidation resulted in intramolecular hydrogen or hydride migration similar to reactions observed with cytochrome P-450 (23). These data suggest that the iron cluster of MMO hydroxylase generates an activated oxygen species with reactivity similar to the heme of cytochrome P-450. Another similarity to cytochrome P-450 was also observed with MMO. The catalysis of TCE results in the destruction of enzyme activity. TCE oxidation–dependent enzyme inactivation was observed with the purified MMO system. Complete inactivation of the enzyme was observed after approximately 200 molecules of TCE had been oxidized per molecule of hydroxylase component. Studies with [^{14}C] TCE showed that inactivation of the enzyme is accompanied by the covalent modification of all of the components of methane monooxygenase, including all three subunits of the hydroxylase. The distribution of radioactive label is roughly in proportion to the estimated exposed surface area of each peptide, supporting the idea that a diffusible modifying form of TCE is responsible for covalent binding.

Propane Monooxygenase

In a survey of TCE oxidation by a variety of microbial oxygenases, Wackett et al (45) dispelled the notion that any microbial oxygenase can catalyze the oxidation of TCE. This study showed that nitropropane dioxygenase, cyclohexanone monooxygenase, two different bacterial cytochrome P-450s, 4-methoxybenzoate monooxygenase, two different preocene monooxygenases, and two hexane monooxygenases would not measurably oxidize TCE. This same study, however, identified propane monooxygenase enzyme systems from five different bacteria that would oxidize TCE after growth in the presence of propane. In addition, propane inhibited TCE oxidation when present in incubation mixtures. Following consumption of the propane, TCE oxidation resumed. These results implicate proprane monooxygenase as the enzyme involved in TCE degradation by these organisms. In addition to TCE, the propane monooxygenase in *Mycobacterium vaccae* JOB5 oxidized vinyl chloride and *cis*- and *trans*-DCE, but not tetrachloroethylene. This observation of propane-oxidizing bacteria degrading TCE correlates with studies of the natural gas–stimulated, continuous-cycled bioreactor discussed earlier in this review (31).

The data available to date concerning aerobic oxidation processes for TCE and the other chlorinated alkenes contain a considerable amount of promise for the eventual biological treatment of these groundwater contaminants. At the same time, characteristics of the oxidation process present formidable challenges to practical use in environmental applications, and in situ treatment of TCE contamination by aerobic microorganisms will never be a simple operation. The best news is that TCE, DCE, and vinyl chloride can definitely be biologically degraded by microorganisms. Broad–substrate specificity oxygenases can bind to and attack TCE and other halogenated ethylenes. In many instances, the rate of TCE oxidation is trivial compared to the oxidation rate for the natural substrate. This fact is particularly evident with ammonia monooxygenase and the various toluene oxygenases for which the relative rates have been measured. The soluble form of the methane monooxygenase oxidizes TCE at approximately the same rate as methane, and this reaction is extraordinarily rapid. An oxidation rate of 150 nmol/min per mg of protein measured with whole cells of *M. trichosporium* OB3b expressing the soluble methane monooxygenase has very promising environmental implications. At this oxidation rate, a suspension of microorganisms at 1 mg/ml of protein would eliminate TCE contamination at 20 mg/liter (20 ppm), a fairly high contamination level, within 1 minute. This ideal degradation rate contrasts much with the persistence of TCE in the environment and emphasizes the difficulty of obtaining observed laboratory degradation rates in the environment.

TCE is persistent because its oxidation requires a competitive cosubstrate. Ammonia-oxiding microorganisms will not sustain TCE oxidation without ammonia present, and ammonia is a competitive inhibitor. The same is true for the toluene oxidizers, the propane oxidizers, and the methane-oxidizing microorganisms. In each of these cases, the cosubstrate must be present in the environment at high enough concentration to induce the necessary oxygenase and regenerate reducing power in the cells lost during the oxidation of TCE. At the same time, the concentration of cosubstrate must be low enough that it does not completely inhibit TCE oxidation through competition for the active site on the enzyme. Apparently, the proper set of cosubstrate-concentration conditions are so rare in the environment that TCE persists.

Another problem emerging from these studies is that the catalysis of TCE usually results in destruction of the catalytic enzyme. The best-studied example is the purified methane monooxygenase study: 200 turnovers of TCE were sufficient for complete inactivation of the enzyme. Toxic effects have also been observed with the toluene dioxygenase enzyme system, and heme destruction was measured during oxidation by cytochrome P-450. Some enzymes may be more resistant to inactivation than others; the toluene monooxygenase enzyme systems appear less sensitive than toluene dioxygenase, but no known enzyme seems completely resistant. All of these proteins are probably inactivated at some rate by reactive TCE metabolites. Environmental implications of this catalytic inactivation are profound. If a methane-oxidizing microorganism is degrading TCE and TCE metabolites inactivate the MMO, less MMO is available to oxidize methane, regenerate reducing power, and convert methane to biomass and fresh MMO. This kind of interaction is highly unstable: the situation would probably quickly result in the replacement of an original population of methanotrophs with a new population of microorganisms that could grow at the expense of methane but could no longer rapidly oxidize TCE. The biochemical characteristics of aerobic TCE oxidation mean that only carefully devised strategies, taking into account all that is known about the enzymatic oxidation or reduction of TCE, will be successful in environmental applications of biological processes for TCE metabolism.

Literature Cited

1. Arciero, D., Vannelli, T., Logan, N., Hooper, A. B. 1989. Degradation of trichloroethylene by the ammonia-oxidizing bacterium *Nitrosomonas europaea. Biochem. Biophys. Res. Commun.* 159:640–43
2. Barrio-Lage, G. A., Parsons, F. Z., Nassar, R. S., Lorenzo, P. A. 1987. Biotransformation of trichloroethylene in a variety of subsurface materials. *Environ. Toxicol. Chem.* 6:571–78
3. Barrio-Lage, G. A., Parsons, F. Z., Nassar, R. S., Lorenzo, P. A. 1986. Sequential dehalogenation of chlorinated ethenes. *Environ. Sci. Technol.* 20:96–99
4. Belay, N., Daniels, L. 1987. Production of ethane and ethylene from halogenated hydrocarbons by methanogenic bacteria. *Appl. Environ. Microbiol.* 53:1604–10
5. Bouwer, E. J., McCarty, P. L. 1983. Transformation of halogenated organic compounds under denitrification conditions. *Appl. Environ. Microbiol.* 45:1295–99
6. Bouwer, E. J., McCarty, P. L. 1983. Transformations of 1- and 2-carbon halogenated aliphatic organic compounds under methanogenic conditions. *Appl. Environ. Microbiol.* 45:1286–94
7. Defalque, R. J. 1961. Pharmacology and toxicology of trichloroethylene: a critical review of the world literature. *Chem. Pharmacol. Ther.* 2:665–88
8. Fathepure, B. Z., Boyd, S. A. 1988. Dependence of tetrachloroethylene dechlorination on methanogenic substrate consumption by *Methanosarsina* sp. strain DSM. *Appl. Environ. Microbiol.* 54:2976–80
9. Fathepure, B. Z., Nengu, J. P., Boyd, S. A. 1987. Anaerobic bacteria that dechlorinate perchloroethylene. *Appl. Environ. Microbiol.* 53:2671–74
10. Fliermans, C. B., Phelps, T. J., Ringelberg, D., Mikell, A. T., White, D. C. 1988. Mineralization of trichloroethylene by heterotrophic enrichment cultures. *Appl. Environ. Microbiol.* 54:1709–14
11. Fogel, M. M., Taddeo, A. R., Fogel, S. 1986. Biodegradation of chlorinated ethenes by a methane-utilizing mixed culture. *Appl. Environ. Microbiol.* 51:720–24
12. Folsom, B. R., Chapman, P. J., Pritchard, P. H. 1990. Phenol and trichloroethylene degradation by *Pseudomonas cepacia* G4: Kinetics and interactions between substrates. *Appl. Environ. Microbiol.* 56:1279–85
13. Fox, B. G., Borneman, J. G., Wackett, L. P., Lipscomb, J. D. 1990. Haloalkene oxidation by the soluble methane monooxygenase from *Methylosinus trichosporium* OB3b: Mechanistic and environmental implications. *Biochemistry* 29:6419–27

14. Fox, B. G., Froland, W. A., Deje, J. E., Lipscomb, J. D. 1989. Methane monooxygenase from *Methylosinus trichosporium* OB3b. *J. Biol. Chem.* 264:10023–33

15. Friedman, D. L., Gossett, J. M. 1989. Biological reductive dechlorination of tetrachloroethylene and trichloroethylene to ethylene under methanogenic conditions. *Appl. Environ. Microbiol.* 55:2144–51

16. Geiger, W., Molner-Kubica, E. 1977. Tetrachlorolethylene in contaminated ground and drinking waters. *Bull. Environ. Contam. Toxicol.* 19:475–580

17. Gibson, T. L., Abdul, A. S., Olsen, R. H. 1988. Microbial degradation of aromatic hydrocarbons in hydrogeologic material: Microcosm studies. In *Proc. 2nd Natl. Outdoor Action Conf. Aquifer Restoration: Groundwater and Geophysical Methods* 1:53–69. Dublin, OH: Natl. Water Well Association

18. Janssen, D. B., Grobben, G., Hoekstra, R., Oldenhuis, R., Witholt, B. 1988. Degradation of *trans*-1,2-dichloroethene by mixed and pure cultures of methanotrophic bacteria. *Appl. Microbiol. Biotechnol.* 29:392–99

19. Janssen, D. B., Grobben, G., Witholt, B. 1987. Toxicity of chlorinated aliphatic hydrocarbons and degradation by methanotrophic consortia. *Proc. 4th Eur. Congr. Biotechnology*, ed. O. M. Neijssel, R. R. Van der Meer, K. Ch. A. M. Luyben, 3:515–18. Amsterdam: Elsevier

20. Kleopfer, R. D., Easley, D. M., Haas, B. B., Deihl, T. G., Jackson, D. E., Wurrey, C. J. 1985. Anaerobic degradation of trichloroethylene in soil. *Environ. Sci. Technol.* 19:277–80

21. Little, C. D., Palumbo, A. V., Herbes, S. E., Lidstrom, M. V., Tyndall, R. L., Gilmen, P. J. 1988. Trichloroethylene biodegradation by a methane-oxidizing bacterium. *Appl. Environ. Microbiol.* 54:951–56

22. Miller, R. E., Guengerich, F. P. 1983. Metabolism of trichloroethylene in isolated hepatocytes, microsomes and reconstituted enzyme systems containing cytochrome P-450. *Cancer Res.* 43:1145–52

23. Miller, R. E., Guengerich, F. P. 1982. Oxidation of trichloroethylene by liver microsomal cytochrome P-450; Evidence for chlorine migration in a transition state not involving trichlorethylene oxide. *Biochemistry* 21:1090–97

24. Moore, A. T., Vira, A., Fogel, S. 1989. Biodegradation of *trans*-1,2-dichloroethylene by methane-utilizing bacteria

25. Nelson, M. J., Kinsella, J. V., Montoya, T. 1990. *In situ* biodegradation of TCE contaminated groundwater. *Environ. Prog.* 9:190–96

26. Nelson, M. J. K., Montgomery, S. O., Mahaffey, W. R., Pritchard, P. H. 1987. Biodegradation of trichloroethylene: An involvement of an aromatic biodegradative pathway. *Appl. Environ. Microbiol.* 53:949–54

27. Nelson, M. J. K., Montgomery, S. O., O'Neill, E. J., Pritchard, P. H. 1986. Aerobic metabolism of trichloroethylene by a bacterial isolate. *Appl. Environ. Microbiol.* 52:383–84

28. Nelson, M. J. K., Montgomery, S. O., Pritchard, P. H. 1988. Trichloroethylene metabolism by microorganisms that degrade aromatic compounds. *Appl. Environ. Microbiol.* 54:604–6

29. Oldenhuis, R., Vink, R. L. J. M., Janssen, D. B., Witholt, B. 1989. Degradation of chlorinated aliphatic hydrocarbons by *Methylosinus trichosporium* OB3b expressing soluble methane monooxygenase. *Appl. Environ. Microbiol.* 55:2819–26

30. Petura, J. C. 1981. Trichloroethylene and methylchloroform in ground water: A problem assessment. *J. Am. Waterworks Assoc.* 73:200–5

31. Phelps, T. J., Herbes, S. E., White, D. C. 1990. Biodegradation of trichloroethylene in continuous-recycled expanded-bed bioreactors. *Appl. Environ. Microbiol.* 56:1702–9

32. Rasche, M. E., Hicks, R. E., Heiman, M. R., Arp. D. J. 1990. Oxidation of monohalogenated ethanes and *n*-chlorinated alkanes by whole cells of *Nitrosomonas europaea*. *J. Bacteriol.* 172:5368–73

33. Richardson, K. L., Gibson, D. T. 1984. A novel pathway for toluene oxidation in *Pseudomonas mendocina*. *Abstr. Annu. Meet. Am. Soc. Microbiol.* 84:K54

34. Shahin, M. N., Von Borstel, R. C. 1977. Mutagenic and lethal effects of alpha-benzyne hexochloride, dibutyl phthalate and trichloroethylene in *Saccharomyces cerevisiae*. *Mutat. Res.* 48:173–80

35. Shelton, D. R., Tiedje, J. M. 1984. General method for determining anaerobic biodegradation potential. *Appl. Environ. Microbiol.* 47:850–57

36. Shields, M. S., Montgomery, S. O., Chapman, P. J., Cuskey, S. M., Pritchard, P. H. 1989. Novel pathway of toluene catabolism in the trichloroethylene degrading bacterium G4.

Appl. Environ. Microbiol. 55:1624–29

37. Stanley, S. H., Prior, S. D., Leak, D. J., Dalton, H. 1983. Copper stress underlies the fundamental change in intracellular location of methane monooxygenase in methane-oxidizing organisms. *Biotechnol. Lett.* 5:487–92

38. Strandberg, G. W., Donaldson, T. L., Farr, L. L. 1989. Degradation of trichloroethylene and *trans*-1,2-dichloroethylene by a methanotrophic consortium in a fixed film, packed-bed bioreactor. *Environ. Sci. Technol.* 23:1422–25

39. Suflita, J. M., Gibson, S. A., Demon, R. E. 1988. Anaerobic biotransformations of pollutant chemicals in aquifers. *J. Ind. Microbiol.* 3:179–94

40. Tsien, H.-C., Brusseau, G. A., Hanson, R. S., Wackett, L. P. 1989. Biodegradation of trichloroethylene by *Methylosinus trichosporium* OB3b. *Appl. Environ. Microbiol.* 55:3155–61

41. Uchiyama, H., Nakajima, T., Yagi, O., Tabuchi, T. 1989. Aerobic degradation of trichloroethylene at high concentrations by a methane-utilizing mixed culture. *Agric. Biol. Chem.* 53:1019–24

42. Van Duren, B. L., Banerjee, S. 1978. Covalent binding of the carcinogen trichloroethylene to hepatic microsomal proteins and to exogenous DNA in vitro. *Cancer Res.* 38:776–80

43. Van Duren, B. L., Banerjee, S. 1976. Covalent interaction of metabolites of the carcinogen trichloroethylene in rat hepatic microsomes. *Cancer Res.* 36:2419–22

44. Vannelli, T., Logan, M., Arciero, D., Hooper, A. B. 1990. Degradation of halogenated aliphatic compounds by the ammonia-oxidizing bacterium, *Nitrosomonas europaea*. *Appl. Environ. Microbiol.* 56:1169–71

45. Wackett, L. P., Brusseau, G. A., Householder, S. R., Hanson, R. S. 1989. Survey of microbial oxygenases: Trichloroethylene degradation by propane oxidizing bacteria. *Appl. Environ. Microbiol.* 55:2960–64

46. Wackett, L. P., Gibson, D. T. 1988. Degradation of trichloroethylene by toluene dioxygenase in whole cell studies with *Pseudomonas putida* F1. *Appl. Environ. Microbiol.* 54:1703–8

47. Wackett, L. P., Householder, S. R. 1989. Toxicity of trichloroethylene to *Pseudomonas putida* F1 is mediated by toluene dioxygenase. *Appl. Environ. Microbiol.* 55:2723–25

48. Wilson, B. H., Smith, G. B., Rees, J. F. 1986. Biotransformations of selected alkyl benzenes and halogenated aliphatic hydrocarbons in methanogenic aquifer material: a microcosm study. *Environ. Sci. Technol.* 20:997–1002

49. Wilson, J. T., Wilson, B. H. 1987. Biodegradation of halogenated aliphatic hydrocarbons. *US Patent No. 4,713,343*

50. Wilson, J. T., Wilson, B. H. 1985. Biotransformation of trichloroethylene in soil. *Appl. Environ. Microbiol.* 49:242–43

51. Winter, R. B., Yen, K. M., Ensley, B. D. 1989. Efficient degradation of trichloroethylene by a recombinant *Escherichia coli*. *Bio/Technology* 7:282–85

52. Wited, G. M. 1986. *Metabolism of toluene and aromatic acids by strains of* Pseudomonas. PhD dissertation. Austin, TX: Univ. Texas

53. Zylstra, G. J., Wackett, L. P., Gibson, D. T. 1989. Trichloroethylene degradation by *Escherichia coli* containing the cloned *Pseudomonas putida* F1 toluene dioxygenase genes. *Appl. Environ. Microbiol.* 55:3162–66

Annu. Rev. Microbiol. 1991. 45:301–25

THE UNIVERSALLY CONSERVED Groe (Hsp60) CHAPERONINS

Jill Zeilstra-Ryalls, Olivier Fayet[1], and Costa Georgopoulos

Department of Cellular, Viral and Molecular Biology, University of Utah Medical Center, Salt Lake City, Utah 84132

KEY WORDS: chaperone, heat-shock proteins, protein folding, common antigen

CONTENTS

INTRODUCTION 301
THE *groE* OPERON 303
THE GroE PROTEINS 303
EVOLUTIONARY CONSERVATION OF *groES* AND *groEL* 305
FUNCTION OF THE *groE* GENES IN BACTERIOPHAGE MORPHOGENESIS 308
    The Bacteriophage T4 Case 309
    An In Vitro System for λ Preconnector Assembly 310
FUNCTION OF THE GroE PROTEINS IN *E. COLI* PHYSIOLOGY 311
    Phenotypes Associated with groE 312
    Function of the groE *Gene Products in Protein Folding, Oligimerization,*
        and Export 313
DEFINING SUBSTRATES OF GroE CHAPERONINS 314
    Folding and/or Export of Pre-β-Lactamase 315
A MODEL FOR GroES-GroEL ACTION 317

INTRODUCTION

The *groE* genes of *Escherichia coli* were first identified through mutations that block λ (26, 70) or T4 bacteriophage growth (9, 27, 65, 72), and, therefore, allowed colony formation in the presence of the corresponding

[1]Permanent Address: Centre de Recherche de Biochimie et de Genetique Cellulaires du Centre National de la Recherche Scientifique, 31062 Toulouse, France

0066-4227/91/1001-0301$02.00

bacteriophage. The rationale behind the original selection screen is as follows: If an infected bacterium is wild-type, progeny bacteriophage will form and proceed to infect neighboring cells, thus limiting the size of the colony. However, if the infected cell is mutated in a host function essential for bacteriophage growth, such that the bacteriophage lytic cycle is blocked at some stage, the infected cell may be killed, but no viable bacteriophage progeny will be produced. Because the sibling cells remain uninfected, a colony will be formed. Bacteria with mutations that block bacteriophage growth at a postadsorption or injection stage were originally designated as *gro* (22, 28). Those *gro* mutations that block bacteriophage morphogenesis have been called *groE, mop, tabB,* or *hdh* (9, 27, 66, 72), but we use the term *groE* to refer to them throughout this review. All of these terms specify a single operon, comprising the *groES* and *groEL* genes, located at 94 min on the *E. coli* genetic map (1). Many of the *groES* mutants isolated at 30°C were subsequently shown to be temperature sensitive for growth, suggesting that GroE is essential for *E. coli* growth, at least at temperatures greater than 42°C. Transduction experiments, coupled with the analysis of temperature-resistant revertants, confirmed that a single mutation is responsible for both the block imposed on bacteriophage growth at all temperatures and that imposed on *E. coli* growth at 42°C (25, 74, 77).

Extensive analysis of the *groE* requirements for bacteriophage growth has shown that *groES* mutations block assembly of the bacteriophage particles. Table 1 lists the GroE requirements for several bacteriophages. This list reveals that, although the GroE requirement is consistently associated with particle assembly, the form this blockage takes varies. For bacteriophage λ and T4, GroE participation is required primarily during head assembly, whereas for T5 and 186 bacteriophage, it is required primarily during tail assembly (38, 91). Table 1 also lists the bacteriophage genes whose products potentially interact with GroE, in that mutations in these genes allow the bacteriophage to overcome the GroE-imposed block to growth. Unlike the other bacteriophages listed in Table 1, T4 bacteriophage growth is blocked only by mutations in the *groEL* gene; the *groES* gene product appears to be nonessential for T4 growth (see below). The interaction of GroE with a variety of bacteriophage proteins implied from these analyses, together with the fact that GroE is apparently required in assembly or oligomerization of these proteins, suggests one potential host function for GroE: participation in assembly or oligomerization of host proteins.

This conclusion has been substantiated in the last few years by a series of elegant biochemical analyses that took advantage of the structural and functional conservation of the GroE proteins throughout evolution. Ellis and coworkers (3) identified a protein that functions analogously to the *groE* gene products in assisting the assembly of the oligomeric enzyme ribulose bisphosphate carboxylase-oxygenase (Rubisco), which catalyzes photosynthetic CO_2

Table 1 Effect of *E. coli groE* mutations on bacteriophage growth[a]

Mutation	λ	T4	T4	186
groES	Head assembly; genes *B* and *E*	No effect	Tail assembly; gene *D19*	Tail assembly; gene *H*
groEL	Head assembly; genes *B* and *E*	Head assembly; gene *31*	Tail assembly; gene *D19*	Tail assembly; gene *H*

[a]The various *groE* mutations block either head assembly (λ and T4) or tail assembly (T5 and 186). Also shown are the bacteriophage genes in which mutations can occur, thus allowing a bypass of the *groE*-imposed block. See text for details and references.

fixation in higher plants. Sequence analysis subsequently revealed that this Rubisco binding protein is 46% identical (at the amino acid level) to the GroEL protein (35). Furthermore, it turned out that the *E. coli* GroEL protein could also promote, in vivo and in vitro, the assembly of prokaryotic Rubisco (for review, see 20). In addition, GroEL-related proteins, termed Hsp60, were found in mitochondria of a variety of organisms (42, 56, 65). Then it became clear that these highly conserved proteins represent a class of proteins that have a general and essential cellular function. These proteins are called molecular chaperones (13). Those chaperones found in chloroplasts, mitochondria, and prokaryotes are termed chaperonins (14, 35).

THE *groE* OPERON

The *groE* locus maps at 94 min on the *E. coli* genetic map (1). An extensive deletion analysis of λ*groE* transducing bacteriophages established that the operon is composed of two genes, *groES* and *groEL*, where *groES* is the first gene of the *groE* operon (74, 76, 77). Extensive genetic studies demonstrated that both *groEL* and *groES* function are essential at all temperatures (16), and further, that deletions of *rpoH* (*htpR*) can be tolerated in *E. coli* at temperatures below 20°C (47, 89). Expression in all conditions is guaranteed by the two promoters that have been identified for this operon (32, 89), arranged as shown in Figure 1. At physiological temperatures, the operon is primarily transcribed from the $E\sigma^{32}$-directed promoter, which occludes the $E\sigma^{70}$-directed promoter. The presence of the $E\sigma^{70}$-directed promoter probably ensures the constitutive transcription of the *groE* operon at all temperatures. The $E\sigma^{32}$-directed promoter confers to the operon the typical pattern of heat-shock expression. Thus, the overall expression of *groE* is such that more GroE chaperonins are produced as the temperature increases (58).

THE GroE PROTEINS

The *groES* gene encodes a 97-residue polypeptide of M_r 10,368 (35). During SDS-polyacrylamide gel electrophoresis (SDS-PAGE), the monomer mi-

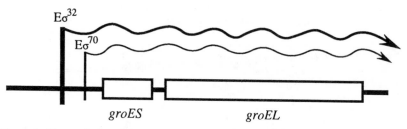

Figure 1   The regulation of the *groE* operon. The *groE* operon is under the control of two promoters. One is transcribed by the $E\sigma^{32}$ and the other by the $E\sigma^{70}$ RNA polymerase holoenzyme (89). Use of the $E\sigma^{32}$-directed promoter leads to an occlusion of the $E\sigma^{70}$-directed promoter at normal *E. coli* growth temperatures (see text for details). The figure is taken from Ref. 23 with permission from the publisher and the authors.

grates with an apparent molecular weight of approximately 15,000 (76, 77). Chromatographic and sedimentation behavior, as well as crosslinking experiments with purified protein, indicate that the native form is composed of seven identical subunits (7; R. Hendrix, G. Lorimer, & T. Ziegelhoffer, personal communication). The oligomer is apparently very stable, as it is not disrupted in the presence of either 2 M urea or 600 mM KCl, nor by heating at temperatures up to 60°C (S. Landry & L. Gierasch, personal communication).

The substantially larger *groEL* gene encodes a 548-residue polypeptide of M_r 57,259 (35). The monomer migrates with an apparent molecular weight of 65,000 in SDS-polyacrylamide gels (29, 37). The 14 subunits of the native protein are identical, and the GroEL particle has a sevenfold axis of symmetry (36, 39). The ring-shaped "double donut" is 125–130 Å in diameter and 100–155 Å in height. This large particle is readily observable using electron microscopy, and its unique shape has frequently been used as a means to identify GroEL homologues isolated from other organisms (40, 56, 63, 92). The weak ATPase activity of GroEL, approximately one molecule of ATP per GroEL 14-mer per second, has been well documented (7, 36). Recent experiments (80) have confirmed this result, and have also determined the precise in vitro ionic requirements of the ATPase activity. Potassium ion was clearly required, not only for the ATPase activity of GroEL, but for its chaperonin function of ATP-dependent reconstitution of unfolded Rubisco (see below).

GroEL and GroES protein-protein interaction has been demonstrated both genetically and biochemically. The strongest genetic evidence in support of the interaction between GroES and GroEL proteins consists of the isolation of missense mutations in the *groEL* gene that compensate, in an allele-specific manner, for the temperature-sensitive phenotypes of certain *groES* mutations (74, 75). In agreement with these results, mutations have also been obtained in the *groES* gene that can suppress the temperature-sensitivity phenotype of certain *groEL* mutations (J. Zeilstra-Ryalls & C. Georgopoulos, unpublished data). Biochemical evidence supporting the protein-protein interaction between GroEL and GroES consists of the following analyses: First, the smaller GroES particle (4.5S) cosediments with the larger GroEL particle (25S) in glycerol gradients in the presence of Mg^{2+} and ATP (7). Second, the presence of GroES protein inhibits the weak ATPase activity of GroEL (7, 80). Third, GroES protein is specifically retained on a GroEL-affinity column, again in the presence of ATP and Mg^{2+} (7). Such evidence clearly indicates functional protein-protein interaction between the GroES and GroEL chaperonins. This interaction provides an explanation for the fact that mutations in either the *groEL* or *groES* gene frequently give rise to similar phenotypes for bacterial and bacteriophage growth.

Hallet et al (33) recently described a GroEL-like protein in *E. coli*. These authors showed that (*a*) a 60,000-M_r protein was massively overproduced in ciprofloxacin-resistant mutants that overproduce the DNA gyrase A protein, and (*b*) the sequence of the sixteen N-terminal amino acids was strikingly homologous to GroEL (10 amino acids identical and 4 similar). This finding strongly suggests the existence of a second GroEL-like protein in *E. coli*. No other evidence for this GroEL-like protein exists. Surprisingly, Zwickl et al (92) found an identical N-terminal amino acid sequence when they sequenced a GroEL-like protein from *Comamonas acvidovorans*. This last finding raises the possibility that the GroEL-like protein of Hallet et al (33) may have been isolated from a bacterial contaminant.

EVOLUTIONARY CONSERVATION OF *groES* AND *groEL*

GroEL has been remarkably conserved across evolution. Homologues (called Hsp60 or Cpn-60) have been identified in organisms as diverse as bacteria, fungi, plants, and humans. Figure 2 illustrates this conservation (kindly provided by R. Gupta), presenting an amino acid sequence comparison of some of the sequenced homologues, together with a prediction of secondary structural motifs, and points out the highly conserved nature of GroEL. Table 2 shows similarities at the amino acid level of several GroEL homologues [data taken from Martel et al (55)].

The known prokaryotic GroES proteins are also highly conserved (2, 86), as one would suspect from the fact that in *E. coli* this protein functionally interacts with GroEL (2, 86). Recently, GroES analogs have been isolated from both bovine and rat liver mitochondria (54). Such conservation identifies these two proteins as fulfilling a universally important function. Martel et al (55) have compared the amino acid sequences of several GroEL homologues to GroES sequences from various organisms. They identified a common

Table 2   Amino acid sequence similarity among various Hsp60 homologues

Species[a]		Sequence similarity[b]								
		A	B	C	D	E	F	G	H	I
A *Brassica napus*	Hsp60α	—								
B *Triticum aes-* *tivum*	Hsp60α	81.4	—							
C *B. napus*	Hsp60β	49.1	49.9	—						
D *Homo sapiens*	Hsp60m	44.1	42.1	45.7	—					
E *Saccharomyces* *cerevisiae*	Hsp60m	44.2	41.6	43.5	54.1	—				
F *Escherchia coli*	Hsp60(GroEL)	46.7	46.3	51.8	49.1	53.0	—			
G *Mycobacterium* *tuberculosis*	Hsp60(GroEL)	51.1	48.7	51.8	47.6	46.9	58.3	—		
H *C. burnetii*	Hsp60(GroEL)	48.3	47.2	53.1	48.6	51.8	75.6	59.8	—	
I *Synechococcus* 6301	Hsp60(GroEL)	58.3	52.7	57.3	47.7	50.7	60.0	63.3	59.0	—

[a] The predicted mature coding regions of five eukaryotic sequences (A–E), the complete coding regions of three prokaryotic sequences (F–H), and partial coding region of a fourth (I), were aligned with the introduction of a small number of gaps of one to three residues. (A) Martel et al (55), (B) Hemmingsen et al (35), (C) Martel et al (55), (D) Jindal et al (42), (E) Reading et al (65), Johnson et al (43), (F) Hemmingsen et al (35), (G) Shinnick (68), (H) Vodkin & Williams (81), (I) Cozens & Walker (10).

[b] The values are the number of positions (%) at which identical a.a. residues are found for each pairwise comparison. Data taken from Ref. 55, with permission from the publisher and the authors.

amino acid sequence motif present in both the GroES and GroEL proteins. By searching for consensus sequences, they have identified a region of the GroEL proteins that resembles an ATPase domain. This region is within the GroES motif, but corresponds to one of two gaps they introduced into the GroES alignment. Thus, this weak ATPase consensus sequence found within GroEL is absent in GroES. Biochemical analyses have shown that GroEL protein binds avidly (at 10–20 μM) to the ATP analog 8-azidoadenosine 5'-triphosphate (K. McEntee & C. Georgopoulos, unpublished experiments). A careful examination of the kinetics of GroEL's ATPase activity has shown that the apparent K_m of the reaction is approximately 10–20 μM ATP (90). The correlation between this activity and the potential ATPase motif remains to be established.

Other experiments have demonstrated that proteins from this family are not only homologous in sequence, but are also highly conserved functionally. For example, *E. coli* GroEL, together with GroES, functions in the assembly of cyanobacterial Rubisco in vivo when the Rubisco and *groE* genes are expressed in *E. coli* (31). In vitro refolding of the active, dimeric form of Rubisco, from *Rhodospirillum rubrum,* can be obtained in a system consisting of purified GroEL from *E. coli,* or chloroplast Rubisco binding protein, or mitochondrial Hsp60 in conjunction with either GroES from *E. coli* or its mitochondrial analog (31, 32, 80). Furthermore, recent studies have shown that the wheat chloroplast α protein homologue to GroEL, when expressed in

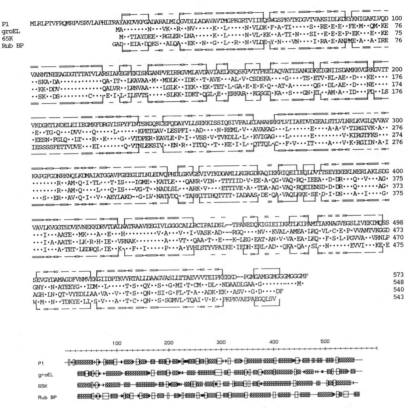

Figure 2 (*Top*) Multiple sequence alignment of the human mitochondrial protein, designated P1 (42*;). *E. coli* GroEL (35); the 65-kilodalton (kd) major antigen from *Mycobacterium bovis* BCG, designated 65K (73); and the Rubisco large-subunit binding protein from wheat (*Triticum aestivum*), designated as Rub BP (35). Dots indicate residues identical to the corresponding P1 sequence. Positions with identical residues in three or all four proteins are boxed with single or double lines, respectively. To indicate conservative changes based on amino acid similarity or common codon replacements, an ad hoc grouping of residues was used. Positions in which all four amino acids belong to one of the following groups are also boxed with a single line: (F, I, L, M, V), (F, Y, W), (H, N, Q), (D, E, G, N, Q, S, T), (K, R), or (A, P, G). Dashes indicate gaps in the sequence alignment. (*Bottom*) Comparison of the secondary-structure predictions of P1, GroEL, *M. bovis* 65-kd protein (65K), and the Rubisco large-subunit binding protein (Rub BP). Structures are predicted using the method of Garnier et al (19). α helix (*hatched boxes*), β sheet (*open boxes*), and turns (*solid boxes*) are aligned as shown in the top panel but without gaps. Reproduced from Ref. 42, with permission from the publisher and the authors.

E. coli forms mixed 14-mers consisting of subunits encoded by the wheat gene and the chromosomal *groEL* gene (78).

The high degree of conservation of GroEL has led to its identification as a common antigen among a wide variety of bacterial species, many of which are human pathogens (reviewed in 87, 88). Recent experiments using γδ

T-cells suggested an even greater degree of conservation. Studies designed to investigate the possible function(s) of $\gamma\delta$ T-cells revealed that proliferation of every spontaneous producer of interleukin-2 (IL-2) among a series of $\gamma\delta$ T-cell surface positive hybridomas was further stimulated by a purified protein derivative of *Mycobacterium tuberculosis* (60). A second study found that an enrichment of $\gamma\delta^+$ T-cells was obtained upon exposure of a lymphoid population first to mycobacterial antigens in vivo then to heat shock in vitro (64). Recently, the putative stimulatory epitope for $\gamma\delta$ T-cells was mapped for several organisms (5). For the *E. coli* GroEL protein, the epitope was mapped to amino acids 181–197, which is within the GroEL sequence previously identified as the common antigen. The important conclusion from all of this work is that $\gamma\delta$ T-cells recognize not only heterologous but also autologous stress proteins. Two recent reviews of this topic (87, 88) present the hypothesis that the common antigen might be a causative agent of autoimmune disease. Most recently, a study showed that the $V_\gamma 9/V_\delta 2$ subset of human $\gamma\delta$ T-cells proliferate in response to a GroEL homologue found on the surface of Daudi Burkitt's lymphoma cells (17). This result is striking for two reasons: First, it is evidence for a direct relationship between the recognition of common antigen by T-cells and neoplasia. Second, this GroEL homologue is the first to be found at the cell surface. All others have been localized either internally, for prokaryotic homologues, or found in mitochondria or chloroplasts, for eukaryotic homologues. Perhaps this homologue is the first to be identified of a new family of GroEL homologues that, by virtue of its location on the cell surface, has a different function from the intracellularly localized GroEL homologues. Surprisingly, the GroEL peptides that stimulated murine $\gamma\delta$ T-cell hybridomas (5, 60) did not stimulate the human $\gamma\delta$ T-cells (17), suggesting that different epitopes are recognized in the two systems.

FUNCTION OF THE *groE* GENES IN BACTERIOPHAGE MORPHOGENESIS

Although GroE clearly assists in particle assembly in bacteriophage morphogenesis, it is not obvious why the components of the particle using GroE-mediated assembly vary. Thus, for λ and T4 bacteriophages, the *groE* blocks head assembly, whereas the block is in tail assembly for bacteriophages T5 and 186 (see also Table 1). Other chaperones, host- or bacteriophage-coded, are perhaps needed for tail assembly in λ and T4 and for head assembly in 186 and T5 bacteriophage. Evidence for this possibility comes from a study of *E. coli rpoH* (*htpR*) mutants, which cannot initiate a proper heat-shock response (84, 85). Bacteriophage λ infection in these mutant strains is blocked at both the head and tail assembly level. Head assembly is blocked presumably as a consequence of insufficient levels of GroE protein synthesis. That tail assembly is blocked as well is consistent with the hypothesis that another σ^{32}-regulated transcription product(s) is required for this process.

The Bacteriophage T4 Case

T4 bacteriophage alone among the bacteriophages requiring GroE function for assembly apparently does not require the *groES* gene product. This conclusion is based on the normal growth of T4 on *groES* mutant strains (44). Because *groES* is an essential gene at all temperatures (16), it is not possible to determine the ability of T4 to grow in the absence of GroES protein. The most straightforward explanation for *groES* mutations' lack of effect on T4 bacteriophage growth is that T4 gene *31* and the *groES* gene encode functionally homologous proteins, making GroES redundant in the assembly of T4 bacteriophage. As a first step towards understanding what allows T4 bacteriophage to bypass the GroES requirement, Keppel et al (44) analyzed T4 gene *31–groE* complementarity. Table 3 presents the results of this analysis. The allele-specific complementation exhibited by the gene *31* mutations with respect to the different *groEL* mutations strongly suggests protein-protein interaction between these two gene products.

The gene *31* product (M_r 12,064) and GroES are similar in size, and both are acidic (pI 4.88 for gp31 and 4.71 for GroES). However, although

Table 3 Plaque-forming ability of T4ϵ mutants on various *Escherichia coli groE* hosts

E. coli hosts[a]	B178groE+			groES619			groEL44			groEL59			groEL764 groEL515		
Phage T4 mutants (°C)[b]	30	37	42	30	37	42	30	37	42	30	37	42	30	37	42
T4D$_o$wt	+[c]	+	+	+	+	+	±	−	−	+	+	+	+	+	+
31ϵ1	+	+	+	+	+	+	+	+	+	+	+	+	−	−	−
31ϵ711	+	+	+	+	+	+	−	−	−	+	±	−	+	+	+
31ϵ714	+	+	+	+	+	+	+	+	+	+	+	+	−	−	−
31ϵ4211	+	+	+	+	+	+	−	−	−	±	−	−	+	+	+
31ϵ9723	+	+	+	+	+	+	−	−	−	+	±	−	+	+	+
31ϵ9725	+	+	±	+	+	+	−	−	−	−	−	−	+	±	−

[a] The bacterial hosts are described in Refs. 25, 26, and 76.

[b] Phage T4D$_o$ is the wild type parent for all *31ϵ* mutants isolated (at frequencies of 10^{-5}–10^{-7}), except ϵ9725, whose parent is phage T4D$_o$$\epsilon$1. Phage mutants ϵ711 and ϵ714 were isolated as plaque formers of T4D$_o$ on bacterial mutant *groES7* Tr$^+$1 (25). Phage mutant ϵ4211 was isolated as a plaque former of T4D$_o$ on bacterial mutant *groES42* Tr$^+$1 (25). Phage mutants ϵ9723 and ϵ9725 were isolated as plaque formers of T4D$_o$ and T4D$_o$$\epsilon$1, respectively, on bacterial mutant *groES97* Tr$^+$2 (25).

[c] The + symbol indicates an eop of approx. 1.0 and good plaque size. The ± symbol indicates an efficiency of plating of 0.1–1.0, and small plaque size. The − symbol indicates an effciency of plating of < 10^{-4}, and no visible plaque formation (except for occasional ϵ mutants). Reproduced in part from Ref. 44 with the permission from the publisher and authors.

inspection by eye has revealed that appropriate rearrangement of the gp31 sequence allows identification of groups of amino acids that are similar in both proteins, computer analysis of gp31 and GroES sequences failed to reveal significant homology at the amino acid level, nor any similarity in predicted secondary structures (44, 59). These results seem to indicate that GroES and gp31 do not interact with GroEL through the recognition of specific amino acid sequences. What exactly comprises the features of these two proteins that are necessary for recognition and interaction with GroEL are, as yet, undetermined. Surprisingly, most of the gene *31* mutations that allow bacteriophage growth on *groEL* mutant hosts result in subtle amino acid substitutions, e.g. the T4ε1 mutation changes a leucine to an isoleucine, yet results in pronounced plating differences on the various bacterial hosts (44) (Table 3). This suggests that the interaction between the GroEL and gp31 proteins is primarily hydrophobic in nature. Whatever model arises to explain the apparent lack of GroES requirement in T4 bacteriophage assembly must also account for another observation with respect to T4 morphogenesis: so-called bypass single–amino acid substitution mutations in T4 gene *23*, which encodes the major capsid protein, have been isolated (11, 69) that can partially alleviate both the GroEL and gp31 requirements for assembly. Perhaps these gp23* mutant proteins can fold properly without the aid of the GroE proteins or fold with help from another chaperone. The existence of these *23** bypass mutations suggests that the primary role of gp31 is to assist in the correct folding of gp23. We propose the following hypothesis based on these observations: because bacteriophage T4 possesses a lytic life-style, it must grow fast, "putting its head together quickly." To ensure the rapid and correct assembly of its capsid, bacteriophage T4 has evolved the specialized chaperonin-like protein gp31 to replace GroES and to interact with GroEL, leading to efficient capsid assembly.

An In Vitro System for λ Preconnector Assembly

The participation of the GroE chaperonins in bacteriophage λ prohead assembly has been studied in great detail (45, 46). Sophisticated in vitro mixing experiments using combinations of cell-free extracts, which alone cannot assemble proheads, have allowed the identification of protein donor capabilities of different mutant extracts (46). Further experiments have defined the order in which assembly occurs (45). Figure 3 shows a scheme for λ prohead assembly based on this work. The GroE chaperonins, with the help of the λNu3 scaffolding protein, assemble the head-tail connector, consisting of 12 subunits of λB protein. This process in turn leads to the eventual correct assembly of the λ prohead. The ability to follow the assembly pathway, leading to the formation of a biologically active bacteriophage particle, provides a powerful tool to explore the chaperonin activity of GroEL and GroES. Mutants are first isolated based on the inability to propagate

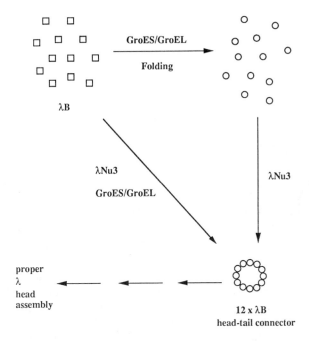

Figure 3   The role of GroE chaperonins in λ morphogenesis. The GroES and GroEL chaperonins, in conjunction with the λNu3 scaffolding protein, promote the oligomerization of the λB protein (45, 46). In turn, the head-tail connector allows the correct assembly of the λ prohead structure. The λ DNA is packaged into the prohead. Subsequently, a tail is attached, resulting in the formation of a viable bacteriophage (18). Reproduced from Ref. 24, with permission from the publisher and authors.

bacteriophage; subsequently, suppressor mutations that restore activity can be obtained.

Recently, Ziegelhoffer (90) showed that denatured λB monomers bind to wild-type GroEL, as evidenced by their cosedimentation in glycerol gradients. This GroEL-λB complex dissociates upon the addition of hydrolyzable ATP. However, the released λB protein behaved as a monomer. No conversion of λB monomers to a 12-mer preconnector structure was seen, even when purified GroES and λNu3 were present during the dissociation of λB from GroEL. Another host- or bacteriophage-coded factor is perhaps needed for the assembly of the 12-mer preconnector structure (see Figure 3).

FUNCTION OF THE GroE PROTEINS IN *E. COLI* PHYSIOLOGY

All of the *groE* mutations studied thus far, with one exception (57) (discussed below), were isolated on the basis of blocking bacteriophage growth. As mentioned above, the *groE* gene functions are essential for *E. coli* growth (16). Hence, these *groE* mutant alleles must still retain activity at some level. Furthermore, mutations isolated in this way may not necessarily identify all of the properties with respect to host function.

Phenotypes Associated with groE

Many of the *groES* and *groEL* alleles display temperature sensitivity. This feature has allowed an analysis of the phenotypes conferred by these mutations at the nonpermissive temperature. Three phenotypes have been identified in *groE* temperature-sensitive strains: (*a*) a reduction in the overall rates of both DNA and RNA syntheses at the nonpermissive temperature (83); (*b*) a blockage of cell division at the nonpermissive temperature, leading in some instances to the formation of long filaments without septa (25); and (*c*) a display by *groE* mutants of altered protease activity (12, 71).

Various genetic studies confirm and extend the observed phenotypes of the *groE* temperature-sensitive strains. One type of analysis consists of the isolation and characterization of extragenic suppressor mutations that compensate for the temperature-sensitive phenotype of these *groE* strains. Mutations in the *rpoA* gene, coding for the α-subunit of RNA polymerase, suppress the temperature sensitivity of certain *groES* mutant strains (82). This observation clearly suggests a relationship between RNA synthesis and *groE* function. However, whether this relationship is direct or indirect is unknown.

The overproduction of GroEL and GroES leads to the suppression of the temperature-sensitive phenotypes of mutations in several other genes. The suppression of temperature-sensitive alleles of *dnaA* (15, 41), whose product is essential for the initiation of *E. coli* DNA replication, provides further evidence of the role of *groE* in DNA synthesis. Other examples of this type of *groE* suppression of temperature sensitive mutations are discussed below (see next section).

An indirect consequence of the altered proteolytic activity in *groES* or *groEL* mutant strains is the defect exhibited by these mutants in *umuDC*-dependent UV mutagenesis (12, 53). A recent study pointed out this relationship by demonstrating an almost threefold decrease in the half-life of the UmuC protein in the *groEL100* mutant strain relative to a wild-type strain (12). The consequence of this altered protein stability is that *groE* mutant strains are severely deficient in their capacity to undergo error-prone mutagenesis following UV irradiation. This altered protein stability may result from a decrease in the chaperonin function of the mutant *groE* gene products; the *groE* mutants are less able to correctly bring about complex formation between UmuC protein and other proteins thought to associate in order to carry out UV mutagenesis. The incorrectly folded or aggregated UmuC protein is then subject to faster degradation (12).

Experiments by Miki et al (57) suggest that the GroES protein of *E. coli* may be one of the targets of the lethal action of the F-factor–encoded CcdB protein. The evidence consists of the isolation of mutations in the *groES* gene that dampen the lethal effect of the CcdB protein (57).

Finally, both wild-type and *groEL* mutant bacteria grow poorly at all temperatures when GroES is overproduced from high-copy-number plasmids. However, overproduction of both wild-type gene products or GroEL alone does not noticeably affect bacterial growth (J. Zeilstra-Ryalls, O. Fayet, C. Georgopoulos, unpublished observations). Such features associated with the *groE* products must be accounted for by models invoked to explain chaperonin activity (see below).

Function of the groE Gene Products in Protein Folding, Oligomerization, and Export

The GroE proteins play roles in the process of protein export. Bochkareva et al (4) conducted the key study that identified an interaction between GroEL and an exported protein. These authors demonstrated the formation of a transient complex between GroEL and nascent polypeptide chains of pre-β-lactamase and chloramphenicol acetyltransferase. Such transient complexes were destroyed in the presence of hydrolyzable ATP. Furthermore, this complex formation was not observed with the mature form of β-lactamase, and the association of pre-β-lactamase with GroEL allowed more efficient translocation across membranes (4).

Using purified components, another study analyzed the interaction between several molecular chaperones and a variety of exported proteins (51). This study revealed that the strength of substrate binding, for the substrates tested, varied among the chaperones. Thus, the chaperones GroEL, SecB, and trigger factor all bound to the unfolded form of pro-OmpA polypeptide; GroES and DnaK chaperones did not bind. GroEL and SecB, but not trigger factor, bound to the unfolded form of pre-PhoE. None of the chaperones bound any of the folded proteins tested. Competition reactions defined the relative affinities of the three chaperones for the substrate pro-OmpA. For this substrate, the order of decreasing affinity was SecB, GroEL, and trigger factor. In addition to its higher binding affinity to the unfolded substrates tested, the SecB protein also facilitates protein export through its demonstrated interaction with the SecA protein (34). The SecA protein in turn facilitates protein export through its interaction with the secretory protein pathway located at the inner membrane (34). Thus, SecB could be a chaperone specialized for exporting proteins. The GroEL and trigger-factor chaperones do not directly interact with SecA (34); hence, their role in protein export could be of secondary importance.

Other evidence demonstrating a role for GroE proteins in the process of protein export comes from the observation that high-copy expression of GroE chaperonins (as well as DnaK) results in quantitative export of a LamB-LacZ hybrid polypeptide (62). The chimaeric protein cannot be properly exported under normal conditions and causes a lethal jamming of the membrane when overproduced. However, strains that contain high-copy plasmids bearing *groE* (or *dnaK*) overcome this lethality. An interpretation of these observations is that when overproduced, the GroEL protein can maintain more polypeptide substrates in the unfolded conformation. Under normal growth conditions, i.e. a single *groE* locus, the amount of GroEL synthesized is such that it is saturated with its preferred substrates and, hence, is not available to maintain the LamB-LacZ hybrid polypeptide in the unfolded conformation required for export.

There is appreciable evidence that the *groE* gene products play roles in the processes of protein folding and export. In addition to the genetic studies mentioned in the previous section, other studies showed that overexpression of the GroE chaperonins could also suppress temperature-sensitive mutations in several *Salmonella* genes coding for metabolic proteins, such as *hisC*, *hisD*, and *ilvGM*, and in genes involved with protein export, such as *secA* (79). In all of these cases, as with suppression of the *dnaA* temperature-sensitive alleles mentioned above, both GroEL and GroES are strictly required (15, 79). One apparently common feature among the alleles affected by *groE* expression is that many of these genes encode proteins that function as oligomeric structures. Oligomeric structures are required in a wide variety of cellular functions, such as the biosynthesis of some amino acids, RNA synthesis, DNA replication, protein translocation, and morphogenesis of bacteriophage particles.

A recent in vitro study (52) demonstrated a new role for the GroE chaperonins in the process of self-assembly. The investigators showed that the process of assembly of GroEL 14-mers from monomers (*a*) is assisted by already assembled 14-mers, (*b*) requires ATP hydrolysis for high efficiency, and (*c*) is stimulated by GroES. This series of experiments is nicely complemented by the in vitro and in vivo studies of Cheng et al (8) in yeast. These authors demonstrated that in the absence of functional Hsp60 in mitochondria, the import of wild-type Hsp60 subunits occurs normally, but their assembly into functional Hsp60 14-mers is inhibited. Thus, wild-type Hsp60 is needed to assemble itself. All of these observations are consistent with other reconstitution assays, such as the assembly of prokaryotic Rubisco (31, 32), mammalian citrate synthase (6), and pre-β-lactamase (50) (see Table 4, below).

DEFINING SUBSTRATES OF GroE CHAPERONINS

That such widely varying proteins interact at some level with GroE proteins points out one of the major unanswered questions with respect to all molecular chaperones: what constitutes a substrate for these proteins? Several systems provide models with which to begin an exploration of this question. For example, Ruben et al (67) isolated a *groEL411* mutation as an extragenic suppressor of the *ssb1* mutation (*ssb* codes for the single-stranded DNA binding protein essential for *E. coli* DNA replication). The *groEL411* mutation is allele specific, in as much as it can suppress the *ssb1* but not the *ssb113* mutation (67). A likely explanation is that the *groEL411* protein helps the mutant *ssb1* polypeptide to form tetramers at the nonpermissive temperature. Overproduction of the wild-type *groE* proteins does not suppress *ssb1*, suggesting that the *groEL411* suppressor polypeptide has acquired a new property not shared by the wild-type *groEL* chaperonin. Determining the mechanism by which the *groEL411* mutation allows *groEL* to acquire a new function will undoubtedly contribute towards our understanding of how chaperonins recognize and bind to various protein surfaces. Table 4 summarizes the ability of GroEL/GroES (Hsp60/Hsp10) chaperonins to facilitate the refolding or reconstitution of several different protein molecules. The following section is a more detailed presentation of one of these systems, which has already been mentioned in other sections of this review, the folding and/or export of pre-β-lactamase.

Folding and/or Export of Pre-β-Lactamase

Both in vivo (48) and in vitro analyses (4, 49) showed that GroE proteins function in the folding and export of pre-β-lactamase, a substrate that was identified first by Bochkareva et al (4). The in vivo analysis consisted of pulse-chase experiments in which several known exported proteins were analyzed for their ability to be exported in bacteria containing temperature-sensitive *groE* mutations (48). The results, shown in Table 5 (reproduced with kind permission of the authors), demonstrated that among the six exported proteins analyzed, β-lactamase was the only protein to be significantly retarded in export in these mutants, relative to wild-type. The others were affected in export by a mutation in another chaperone, SecB.

The in vitro analysis consisted of a refolding assay using purified components (50). This study demonstrated the following (see also Figure 4, reproduced with the authors' consent): (*a*) The refolding of pre-β-lactamase is completely inhibited in the absence of ATP, at an approximate molar ratio of 14 subunits of GroEL per molecule of pre-β-lactamase. (*b*) This folding arrest, mediated by GroEL, is released by ATP; the addition of GroES to the reaction causes a twofold acceleration in the initial rate of release from arrest over that observed in the presence of GroEL and ATP alone. And (*c*) not only does GroEL cause folding arrest, but the presence of GroEL alone or the GroES-GroEL complex leads to a net unfolding of pre-β-lactamase in the absence of ATP; when ATP is subsequently added to this mixture, more

Table 4 In vitro GroE (Hsp60) chaperonin-facilitated reconstitution of native proteins

	Reconstitution	References
E. coli GroEL		
+ prokaryotic Rubisco	0%	32, 80
+ Mg^{2+}ATP	0%	32, 80
+ *E. coli* GroES	80%	32, 80
E. coli GroEL		
+ prokaryotic Rubisco	0%	54
+ Mg^{2+}ATP	0%	54
+ beef mitochondrial Hsp10	60%	54
Yeast Hsp60		
+ prokaryotic Rubisco	n.d.[a]	32
+ Mg^{2+}ATP	n.d.	32
+ *E. coli* GroES	8%	32
Plant chloroplast Rubisco binding protein		
+ prokaryotic Rubisco	n.d.	32
+ Mg^{2+}ATP	n.d.	32
+ *E. coli* GroES	20%	32
E. coli GroEL		
+ pre-β-lactamase	——[b]	50
+ Mg^{2+}ATP	+++[c]	50
+ *E. coli* GroES	+++[d]	50
E. coli GroEL		
+ mammalian citrate synthase	0%	6
+ Mg^{2+}ATP	16%	6
+ *E. coli* GroES	28%	6
Yeast Hsp60-Su9-DHFR complex[e]		
+ Mg^{2+}ATP	60%[f]	61
E. coli GroEL		
+ *E. coli* GroEL monomers	< 0.3%	52
+ Mg^{2+}ATP	35.6%	52
+ *E. coli* GroES	35.0%	52

[a] Not determined.
[b] Complete inhibition of folding of substrate.
[c] The yield of folded protein is higher than that obtained in the absence of GroEL.
[d] No measurable effect on the folding reaction, but a small acceleration in the initial rate of folding over that observed in the presence of GroEL and Mg^{2+}ATP alone.
[e] Yeast Hsp60-Su9-DHFR complexes were isolated from ATP-depleted mitochondria, then partially purified.
[f] Folding of the Su9-DHFR fusion protein was determined as the level of resistance to protease.

β-lactamase enzymatic activity is obtained than was recovered in the absence of chaperonins. Thus, chaperonin-assisted folding produces a higher yield of correctly folded active enzyme. These results show by both genetic and biochemical criteria that pre-β-lactamase is an in vivo substrate for the GroE chaperonins. This system should therefore allow for a well-defined exploration of the substrate requirements for recognition by GroE.

Table 5 Export of envelope proteins[a]

Protein		secB::Tn5	Genetic lesion groES619	groEL44
MalE		X	O	O
OmpA		X	O	O
OmpF		X	O	O
Bla		O	X	X
Lpp		O	O	O
PhoA	(42°C)	O	O	O
	(30°C)	X		

[a] Pulse-chase experiments were carried out and results are summarized. X represents significant retardation in comparison to the wild-type strain, and O represents negligible effects of the mutation. Experiments were performed at 42°C unless otherwise indicated. The MalE protein was induced by 0.4% maltose. Reproduced from Ref. 48, with permission from the publisher and the authors.

A MODEL FOR GroES-GroEL ACTION

Consideration of the genetic and biochemical data available has led to formulation of the model shown in Figure 5 for the action of the GroE chaperonins. This model incorporates the following information: (a) GroEL binds to many but not all unstructured, unfolded polypeptides; (b) GroES alone does not bind to such unfolded polypeptides; (c) GroES and GroEL interact only in the presence of ATP (7, 80), and (d) mutations in either groES or groEL often cause identical phenotypes with respect to bacterial and bacteriophage growth (26).

The first step in this model is the binding of GroEL to the unfolded form of a polypeptide. This step is apparently reversible in that either the binding is weak, or that it is possible to compete for unfolded protein by addition of other chaperones. With respect to the nature of the unfolded peptide, perhaps it is bound to GroEL before it is completely synthesized, as Bochkareva et al demonstrated (4). This association is thought to prevent the incorrect or premature folding of the polypeptide. The work of Goloubinoff et al (30) and Buchner et al (6), on the assembly of prokaryotic Rubisco and mammalian citrate synthase, respectively, has clearly shown that the primary role of GroEL is to assist correct folding by preventing protein aggregation. In principle, an unfolded polypeptide that is still bound to GroEL could begin the processes leading to correct intramolecular or intermolecular folding, protein export or membrane integration, or proteolytic processing. Folding/release from GroEL is accompanied by ATP hydrolysis. GroES would then act as a cogwheel, displacing the unfolded polypeptide for which ATP hydrolysis is also required. Thus, GroES could in a sense be considered a catalytic agent

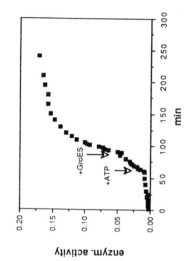

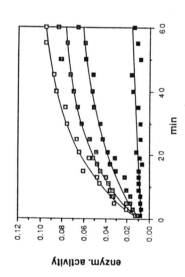

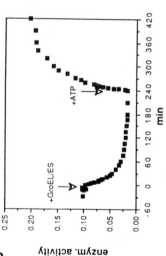

Figure 4 (*A*) Stoichiometry of interaction of GroEL with pre-β-lactamase. (*open boxes*) no GroEL; (*dotted boxes*) 25 mol% GroEL; (*boxed circles*) 50 mol% GroEL; (*closed boxes*) 100 mol% GroEL, where 100 mol% refers to 14 subunits of GroEL per molecule of pre-β-lactamase. The enzymatic activity is given in arbitrary units. (*B*) Effect of the addition of first ATP then GroES to a GroEL-arrested folding reaction of pre-β-lactamase. (*C*) Apparent net unfolding of refolded pre-β-lactamase in the presence of GroEL/ES. The precursor was refolded for 4 h and reached a plateau value of enzymatic activity before an equivalent amount (by particle molarity) of GroEL/ES was added at time 0. At the time indicated by the second arrow, ATP was added. Under the assumption that the refolded precursor has the same specific activity as the mature reduced β-lactamase (49), the first plateau corresponds to 8% and the second plateau to 16% folding yield. The true specific activity of the precursor may be lower than this estimate, and the true folding yield would then be higher. Data are taken from Ref. 50 with permission from the publisher and authors.

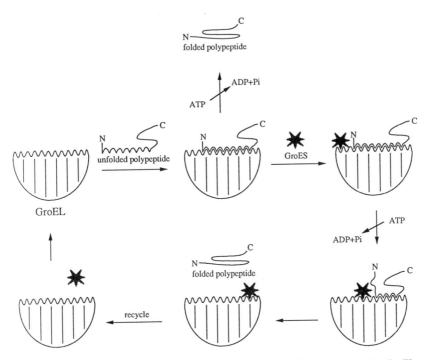

Figure 5 A model for the intracellular action of the GroEL and GroES chaperonins. The GroEL chaperonin can bind to many, but perhaps not all, unfolded polypeptides, some of which may still be nascent (4). The bound polypeptide is either not released or released very slowly. The envisioned role of the GroES protein is as a cogwheel, displacing the bound polypeptides. The hydrolysis of ATP by GroEL provides the energy for such a displacement. The released polypeptide may undergo further intra- or intermolecular folding. Eventually, the GroE chaperonins dissociate, allowing GroEL to recycle (figure kindly provided by Debbie Ang).

for the activity of GroEL. This analogy is quite reasonable, based on the studies of GroE action in the pre-β-lactamase folding assay in which GroEL, in the presence of ATP, results in an increase in β-lactamase activity, and addition of GroES increases the rate at which the activity is recovered (50). Furthermore, this analogy also accounts for the observation that purified GroEL alone allows pro-OmpA to translocate through urea-treated inner membranes (51). Finally, this model predicts that overproduction of GroES alone may be inhibitory for GroEL activity, in that it may cause the premature release of some of the bound polypeptides from GroEL. This prediction is supported by the observed toxicity when GroES is expressed from high-copy plasmids in the absence of GroEL overproduction (J. Zeilstra-Ryalls, O. Fayet, C. Georgopoulos, unpublished observations).

This model does not address questions of stoichiometry, such as how many molecules of unfolded polypeptide can associate with a GroE particle, or whether GroEL can function in vivo as a heptamer, dimer, or monomer. Other details, such as the identification of substrate-interactive regions and polypeptide folding–ATPase kinetics are lacking as well.

Figure 5 shows that, following dissociation of the bound polypeptide, the GroEL and GroES proteins also dissociate. Given that the intracellular concentration of ATP is 2–4 mM, the model is perhaps simplistic in its depiction of GroES as ever being dissociated from GroEL, because GroEL and GroES form a stable complex in the presence of ATP. Hence, GroES and GroEL may always be found in a complex intracellularly. An additional role for GroES would then be to inhibit GroEL's ATPase activity, thus preventing the premature, unproductive release of the bound polypeptide. In this scenario, GroES plays a role in both productive binding of the unfolded polypeptide and in its eventual release. As mentioned before, Martel et al (55) have pointed out the presence of certain conserved protein sequences in both GroEL and GroES. The existence of such conserved, repeated polypeptide sequences may facilitate GroES movement on the surface of GroEL through the making and breaking of semi-equivalent contacts.

A potentially important factor that may have to be considered is the role of the polypeptide bound to the chaperonin. Partial folding, occurring at this stage, could promote in turn minor structural changes in the GroES/GroEL complex, thus abolishing the GroES-imposed block on the ATPase activity of GroEL and liberating the polypeptide (now in a state where folding can be achieved without further assistance).

Another question that has recently been addressed (52) is whether GroEL is required for the formation of the GroEL 14-mer. Evidence that this is indeed the case comes from work by Lissin et al (52), which has been discussed above (see section on function of the *groE* gene products). Interestingly, these workers found that the GroEL monomer becomes more disordered as the temperature decreases, a process they call cold denaturation. They point out that hydrophobic interactions, being the only kinds of protein interaction that decrease with decreasing temperature, may have an important role in maintaining GroEL 14-mer structures (52).

We wish to point out again the catalytic nature of GroE chaperonin function in the process of protein folding. A fine discussion of folding vs aggregation can be found in a review by Gatenby et al (21) and in the paper by Buchner et al (6). The most salient point of their discussion is that temperature and protein concentration strongly influence the partitioning of folding intermediates between aggregation and the folded native state. Viewed in this light, GroE chaperonins could be considered to act like molecular ice in the folding process.

Finally, the identification of mutants other than those that have been isolated on the basis of their inability to support bacteriophage λ growth may lead to new insights into the mechanism of GroE chaperonin activity. The GroEL protein probably consists of several domains that could include an ATPase domain, a region that interacts with GroES, an oligomerization domain, and areas that interact with other proteins. Identification of these various regions of the GroEL molecule should also improve our understanding of chaperonin function.

ACKNOWLEDGMENTS

We thank Kit Tilly, G. N. Chandrasekhar, Tom Ziegelhoffer, Helios Murialdo, Carol Woolford, Roger Hendrix, Debbie Ang, Fred Neidhardt, Ruth VanBogelen, France Keppel, Barbara Lipinska, Stuart Lecker, William Wickner, Axel Laminet, and Andreas Plückthun for their contributions to the GroE project over the years; France Keppel, Andreas Plückthun, Debbie Ang, Rodney Gupta, Sean Hemmingsen, and Koreaki Ito for permission to use tables or figures from their publications; our many colleagues who provided us with reprints and unpublished information (cited in the text); Debbie Ang and Kit Tilly for a critical reading of the manuscript; Jeni Urry for expert and cheerful editing of the manuscript, and the National Institutes of Health for continuous support (Grants GM23917 and AI21029).

Literature Cited

1. Bachmann, B. J. 1990. Linkage map of *Escherichia coli* K-12, Edition 8. *Microbiol. Rev* 54:130–97

2. Baird, P. N., Hall, L. M. C., Coates, A. R. M. 1989. Cloning and sequence analysis of the 10 kDa antigen gene of *Mycobacterium tuberculosis*. *J. Gen. Microbiol.* 135:931–39

3. Barraclough, R., Ellis, R. J. 1980. Protein synthesis in chloroplasts. IX. Assembly of newly-synthesized large subunits into ribulose bisphosphate carboxylase in isolated intact pea chloroplasts. *Biochim. Biophys. Acta* 608:19–31

4. Bochkareva, E. S., Lissin, N. M., Girshovich, A. S. 1988. Transient association of newly synthesized unfolded proteins with the heat-shock GroEL protein. *Nature* 336:254–57

5. Born, W., Hall, L., Dallas, A., Boymel, J., Shinnick, T., et al. 1990. Recognition of a peptide antigen by heat shock-reactive γδ T lymphocytes. *Science* 249:67–69

6. Buchner, J., Schmidt, M., Fuchs, M., Jaenicke, R., Rudolph, R., et al. 1991. GroE facilitates refolding of citrate synthase by suppressing aggregation. *Biochemistry* 30:1586–91

7. Chandrasekhar, G. N., Tilly, K., Woolford, C., Hendrix, R., Georgopoulos, C. 1986. Purification and properties of the groES morphogenetic protein of *Escherichia coli*. *J. Biol. Chem.* 261:12414–19

8. Cheng, M. Y., Hartl, F.-U., Horwich, A. L. 1990. The mitochondrial chaperonin hsp60 is required for its own assembly. *Nature* 348:455–58

9. Coppo, A., Manzi, A., Pulitzer, J. F., Takahashi, H. 1973. Abortive bacteriophage T4 head assembly in mutants of *Escherichia coli*. *J. Mol. Biol.* 76:61–87

10. Cozens, A. L., Walter, J. E. 1987. The organization and sequence of the genes for ATP synthase subunits in the cyanobacterium *Synechococcus* 6301. *J. Mol. Biol.* 194:359–83

11. Doermann, A. H., Simon, L. D. 1984. Bacteriophage T4 *bypass31* mutations that make gene 31 nonessential for bacteriophage T4 replication: mapping *bypass31* mutations by UV rescue experiments. *J. Virol.* 51:315–20

12. Donnelly, C. E., Walker, G. C. 1989.

groE mutants of *Escherichia coli* are defective in *umuDC*-dependent UV mutagenesis. *J. Bacteriol.* 171:6117–25

13. Ellis, J. 1987. Proteins as molecular chaperones. *Nature* 328:378–79

14. Ellis, R. J., Hemmingsen, S. M. 1989. Molecular chaperones: proteins essential for the biogenesis of some macromolecular structures. *TIBS* 14:339–42

15. Fayet, O., Louarn, J.-M., Georgopoulos, C. 1986. Suppression of the *Escherichia coli dnaA46* mutation by amplification of the *groES* and *groEL* genes. *Mol. Gen. Genet.* 202:435–45

16. Fayet, O., Ziegelhoffer, T., Georgopoulos, C. 1989. The *groES* and *groEL* heat shock genes of *Escherichia coli* are essential for bacterial growth at all temperatures. *J. Bacteriol.* 171:1379–85

17. Fisch, P., Malkovsky, M., Kovats, S., Sturm, E., Braakman, E., et al. 1990. Recognition by human V$_\gamma$9/V$_\delta$4 T cells of a GroEL homolog on Daudi Burkitt's lymphoma cells. *Science* 250:1269–73

18. Friedman, D. I., Olson, E. R., Tilly, K., Georgopoulos, C., Herskowitz, I., Banuett, F. 1984. Interactions of bacteriophage and host macromolecules in the growth of bacteriophage λ. *Microbiol. Rev.* 48:299–325

19. Garnier, J., Osguthorpe, D. J., Robson, B. 1978. Analysis of the accuracy and implications of simple methods of predicting the secondary structure of globular proteins. *J. Mol. Biol.* 120:97–120

20. Gatenby, A. A., Ellis, R. J. 1990. Chaperone function: the assembly of ribulose bisphosphate carboxylase-oxygenase. *Annu. Rev. Cell Biol.* 6:125–49

21. Gatenby, A. A., Viitanen, P. V., Lorimer, G. H. 1990. Chaperonin assisted polypeptide folding and assembly: implications for the production of functional proteins in bacteria. *Trends Biotechnol.* 8:354–58

22. Georgopoulos, C. 1971. Bacterial mutants in which the gene N function of bacteriophage lambda is blocked have an altered RNA polymerase. *Proc. Natl. Acad. Sci. USA* 68:2977–81

23. Georgopoulos, C., Ang, D. 1990. The *Escherichia coli* groE chaperonins. In *Molecular Chaperones*, ed. R. J. Ellis, pp. 19–25. London: Saunders Scientific

24. Georgopoulos, C., Ang, D., Liberek, K., Zylicz, M. 1990. Properties of the *Escherichia coli* heat shock proteins and their role in bacteriophage λ growth. In *Stress Proteins in Biology and Medicine,*

ed. R. Morimoto, A. Tissieres, C. Georgopoulos, pp. 191–221. Cold Spring Harbor, NY: Cold Spring Harbor Lab.

25. Georgopoulos, C. P., Eisen, H. 1974. Bacterial mutants which block phage assembly. *J. Supramol. Struct.* 2:349–59

26. Georgopoulos, C. P., Hendrix, R. W., Casjens, S. R., Kaiser, A. D. 1973. Host participation in bacteriophage lambda head assembly. *J. Mol. Biol.* 76:45–60

27. Georgopoulos, C. P., Hendrix, R. W., Kaiser, A. D., Wood, W. B. 1972. Role of the host cell in bacteriophage morphogenesis: Effects of a bacterial mutation on T4 head assembly. *Nature New Biol.* 239:38–42

28. Georgopoulos, C., Herskowitz, I. 1971. *Escherichia coli* mutants blocked in lambda DNA synthesis. In *The Bacteriophage Lambda,* ed. A. D. Hershey, pp. 553–65. Cold Spring Harbor, NY: Cold Spring Harbor Lab.

29. Georgopoulos, C. P., Hohn, B. 1978. Identification of a host protein necessary for bacteriophage morphogenesis (the *groE* gene product). *Proc. Natl. Acad. Sci. USA* 75:131–35

30. Goloubinoff, P., Christeller, J. T., Gatenby, A. A., Lorimer, G. H. 1989. Reconstitution of active dimeric ribulose bisphosphate carboxylase from an unfolded state depends on two chaperonin proteins and Mg-ATP. *Nature* 342:884–89

31. Goloubinoff, P., Gatenby, A. A., Lorimer, G. H. 1989. GroE heat shock proteins promote assembly of foreign prokaryotic ribulose bisphosphate carboxylase oligomers in *Escherichia coli*. *Nature* 337:44–47

32. Grossman, A. D., Straus, D. B., Walter, W. A., Gross, C. A. 1987. σ32 synthesis can regulate the synthesis of heat shock proteins in *Escherichia coli*. *Genes Dev.* 1:179–84

33. Hallet, P., Mehlert, A., Maxwell, A. 1990. *Escherichia coli* cells resistant to the DNA gyrase inhibitor ciprofloxacin overproduce a 60 kDa protein homologous to GroEL. *Mol. Microbiol.* 4:345–53

34. Hartl, F.-U., Kecker, S., Schiebel, E., Hendrick, J. P., Wickner, W. 1990. The binding cascade of SecB to SecA to SecY/E mediates preprotein targeting to the E. coli plasma membrane. *Cell* 63:269–79

35. Hemmingsen, S. M., Woolford, C., van der Vies, S. M., Tilly, K., Dennis, D. T., et al. 1988. Homologous plant and

bacterial proteins chaperone oligomeric protein assembly. *Nature* 333:330–34

36. Hendrix, R. W. 1979. Purification and properties of GroE, a host protein involved in bacteriophage assembly. *J. Mol. Biol.* 129:375–92

37. Hendrix, R. W., Tsui, L. 1978. Role of the host in virus assembly: cloning of the *Escherichia coli groE* gene and identification of its protein product. *Proc. Natl. Acad. Sci. USA* 75:136–39

38. Hocking, S. M., Egan, J. B. 1982. Genetic studies of coliphage 186. I. Genes associated with phage morphogenesis. *J. Virol.* 44:1056–67

39. Hohn, T., Hohn, B., Engel, A., Wurtz, M., Smith, P. R. 1979. Isolation and characterization of the host protein GroE involved in bacteriophage lambda assembly. *J. Mol. Biol.* 129:359–73

40. Hutchinson, E. G., Tichelaar, W., Hofhaus, G., Weiss, H., Leonard, K. R. 1989. Identification and electronmicroscopic analysis of a chaperonin oligomer from *Neurospora crassa* mitochondria. *EMBO J.* 8:1485–90

41. Jenkins, A. J., Marsh, J. B., Oliver, I. R., Masters, M. 1986. A DNA fragment containing the *groE* genes can suppress mutations in the *Escherichia coli dnaA* gene. *Mol. Gen. Genet.* 202:446–54

42. Jindal, S., Dudani, A. K., Singh, G., Harley, C. B., Gupta, R. S. 1989. Primary structure of a human mitochondrial protein homologous to the bacterial and plant chaperonins and to the 65-kilodalton mycobacterial antigen. *Mol. Cell. Biol.* 9:2279–83

43. Johnson, R. B., Earon, K., Mason, T., Jindal, S. 1989. Cloning and characterization of the yeast chaperonin HSP60 gene. *Gene* 84:295–302

44. Keppel, F., Lipinska, B., Ang, D., Georgopoulos, C. 1990. Mutational analysis of the phage T4 morphogenetic 31 gene, whose product interacts with the *Escherichia coli* GroEL protein. *Gene* 86:19–25

45. Kochan, J., Carrascosa, J. L., Murialdo, H. 1984. Bacteriophage lambda preconnectors; purification and structure. *J. Mol. Biol.* 174:433–47

46. Kochan, J., Murialdo, H. 1983. Early intermediates in bacteriophage lambda prohead assembly. II. Identification of biologically active intermediates. *Virology* 131:100–15

47. Kusukawa, N., Yura, T. 1988. Heat shock protein GroE of *Escherichia coli:* key protective roles against thermal stress. *Genes Dev.* 2:874–82

48. Kusukawa, N., Yura, T., Ueguchi, C., Akiyama, Y., Ito, K. 1989. Effects of mutations in heat-shock genes *groES* and *groEL* on protein export of *Escherichia coli. EMBO J.* 8:3517–21

49. Laminet, A. A., Plückthun, A. 1989. The precursor of β-lactamase: purification, properties and folding kinetics. *EMBO J.* 8:1469–77

50. Laminet, A. A., Ziegelhoffer, T., Georgopoulos, C., Plückthun, A. 1990. The *Escherichia coli* heat shock proteins GroEL and GroES modulate the folding of the β-lactamase precursor. *EMBO J.* 9:2315–19

51. Lecker, S., Lill, R., Ziegelhoffer, T., Georgopoulos, C., Bassford, P. J. Jr., et al. 1989. Three pure chaperone proteins of *Escherichia coli*, secB, trigger factor and groEL, form soluble complexes with precursor proteins in vitro. *EMBO J.* 8:2703–9

52. Lissin, N. M., Venyaminov, S. Yu., Girshovich, A. S. 1990. (Mg-ATP)-dependent self-assembly of molecular chaperone GroEL. *Nature* 348:339–42

53. Liu, S.-K., Tessman, I. 1990. *groE* genes affect SOS repair in *Escherichia coli. J. Bacteriol.* 172:6135–38

54. Lubben, T. H., Gatenby, A. A., Donaldson, G. K., Lorimer, G. H., Viitanen, P. V. 1990. Identification of a groES-like chaperonin in mitochondria that facilitates protein folding. *Proc. Natl. Acad. Sci. USA* 87:7683–87

55. Martel, R., Cloney, L. P., Pelcher, L. E., Hemmingsen, S. M. 1990. Unique composition of plastid chaperonin-60: α and β polypeptide-encoding genes are highly divergent. *Gene* 94:181–87

56. McMullin, T. W., Hallberg, R. L. 1988. A highly evolutionarily conserved mitochondrial protein is structurally related to the protein encoded by the *Escherichia coli groEL* gene. *Mol. Cell. Biol.* 8:371–80

57. Miki, T., Orita, T., Funruno, M., Horiuchi, T. 1988. Control of cell division by sex factor F in *Escherichia coli. J. Mol. Biol.* 201:327–38

58. Neidhardt, F. C., VanBogelen, R. A. 1987. Heat shock response. In *Escherichia coli and Salmonella typhimurium: Cellular and Molecular Biology,* ed. F. C. Neidhardt, J. L. Ingraham, K. B. Low, B. Magasanik, M. Schaechter, H. E. Umbarger, p. 1334–45. Washington, DC: Am. Soc. Microbiol.

59. Nivinskas, R., Black, L. W. 1988. Cloning, sequence, and expression of the temperature dependent phage T4

capsid assembly gene 31. *Gene* 73:251–57

60. O'Brien, R. L., Happ, M. P., Dallas, A., Palmer, E., Kubo, R., Born, W. K. 1989. Stimulation of a major subset of lymphocytes expressing T cell receptor γδ by an antigen derived from Mycobacterium tuberculosis. *Cell* 57:667–74

61. Ostermann, J., Horwich, A. L., Neupert, W., Hartl, F.-U. 1989. Protein folding in mitchondria requires complex formation with hsp60 and ATP hydrolysis. *Nature* 341:125–30

62. Phillips, G. J., Silhavy, T. J. 1990. Heat-shock proteins DnaK and GroEL facilitate export of LacZ hybrid proteins in *E. coli*. *Nature* 344:882–84

63. Pushkin, A. V., Tsuprun, V. L., Solovjeva, N. A., Shubin, V. V., Evstigneeva, Z. G., Kretovich, W. L. 1982. High molecular weight pea leaf protein similar to the *groE* protein of *Escherichia coli*. *Biochim. Biophys. Acta* 704:379–84

64. Rajasekar, R., Sim, G.-K., Augustin, A. 1990. Self heat shock and γδ T-cell reactivity. *Proc. Natl. Acad. Sci. USA* 87:1767–71

65. Reading, D. S., Hallberg, R. L., Myers, A. M. 1989. Characterization of the yeast HSP60 gene coding for a mitochondrial assembly factor. *Nature* 337:655–59

66. Revel, H. R., Stitt, B. L., Lielausis, I., Wood, W. B. 1980. Role of the host cell in bacteriophage T4 development. I. Characterization of host mutants that block T4 head assembly. *J. Virol.* 33:366–76

67. Ruben, S. M., VanDenBrink-Webb, S. E., Rein, D. C., Meyer, R. R. 1988. Suppression of the *ssb-1* mutation by an allele of *groEL*. *Proc. Natl. Acad. Sci. USA* 85:3767–71

68. Shinnick, T. M. 1987. The 65-kDa antigen of *M. tuberculosis*. *J. Bacteriol.* 169:1080–88

69. Simon, L. D., Randolph, B. 1984. Bacteriophage T4 *bypass31* mutations that make gene 31 nonessential for bacteriophage T4 replication: isolation and characterization. *J. Virology* 51:321–28

70. Sternberg, N. 1973. Properties of a mutant of *Escherichia coli* defective in bacteriophage λ head formation (*groE*) II. The propagation of phage λ. *J. Mol. Biol.* 76:25–44

71. Straus, D. B., Walter, W. A., Gross, C. A. 1988. *Escherichia coli* heat shock gene mutants are defective in proteolysis. *Genes Dev.* 2:1851–58

72. Takano, T., Kakefuda, T. 1972. Involvement of a bacterial factor in morphogenesis of bacteriophage capsid. *Nature New Biol.* 239:34–37

73. Thole, J. E. R., Keulen, W. J., Kolk, A. H. J., Groothuis, D. G., Berwald, L. G., et al. 1987. Characterization, sequence determination and immunogenicity of a 64-kilodalton protein of *Mycobacterium bovis* BCG expressed in *Escherichia coli* K-12. *Infect. Immun.* 55:1466–75

74. Tilly, K. 1982. *Studies on bacteriophage and host genes involved in morphogenesis*. PhD thesis. Salt Lake City: Univ. Utah

75. Tilly, K., Georgopoulos, C. 1982. Evidence that the two *Escherichia coli groE* morphogenetic gene products interact in vivo. *J. Bacteriol.* 149:1082–88

76. Tilly, K., Murialdo, H., Georgopoulos, C. 1981. Identification of a second *Escherichia coli groE* gene whose product is necessary for bacteriophage morphogenesis. *Proc. Natl. Acad. Sci. USA* 78:1629–33

77. Tilly, K., VanBogelen, R. A., Georgopoulos, C., Neidhardt, F. C. 1983. Identification of the heat inducible protein C15.4, as the *groES* gene product in *Escherichia coli*. *J. Bacteriol.* 154:1505–7

78. van der Vies, S. M. 1989. *Isolation and expression of the plastid* alpha *chaperonin cDNA sequence from* Triticum aestivum. PhD thesis. Coventry, UK: Univ. Warwick

79. Van Dyk, T. K., Gatenby, A. A., LaRossa, R. A. 1989. Demonstration by genetic suppression of interaction of GroE products with many proteins. *Nature* 342:451–53

80. Viitanen, P. V., Lubben, T. H., Reed, J., Goloubinoff, P., O'Keefe, D. P., Lorimer, G. H. 1990. Chaperonin-facilitated refolding of ribulosebisphosphate carboxylase and ATP hydrolysis by chaperonin 60 (groEL) are K^+ dependent. *Biochemistry* 29:5665–71

81. Vodkin, M. H., Williams, J. C. 1988. A heat shock operon in *Coxiella burnetii* produces a major antigen homologous to a protein in both mycobacteria and *E. coli*. *J. Bacteriol.* 170:1227–34

82. Wada, M., Fujita, H., Itikawa, H. 1987. Genetic suppression of a temperature-sensitive *groES* mutation by an altered subunit of RNA polymerase of *Escherichia coli* K-12. *J. Bacteriol.* 169:1102–6

83. Wada, M., Itikawa, H. 1984. Participation of *Escherichia coli* K-12 *groE* gene products in the synthesis of cellular

DNA and RNA. *J. Bacteriol.* 157:694–96

84. Waghorne, C., Fuerst, C. R. 1985. Identification of a temperature-sensitive mutation in the *htpR* (*rpoH*) gene of *Escherichia coli* K-12. *J. Bacteriol.* 164:960–63

85. Waghorne, C., Fuerst., C. R. 1985. Involvement of the *htpR* gene product of *Escherichia coli* in phage lambda development. *Virology* 141:51–64

86. Webb, R., Reddy, K. J., Sherman, L. A. 1990. Regulation and sequence of the *Synechococcus* sp. strain PCC 7942 *groESL* operon, encoding a cyanobacterial chaperonin. *J. Bacteriol.* 172:5079–88

87. Young, D. B. 1990. Chaperonins and the immune response. *Semin. Cell Biol.* 1:27–35

88. Young, R. A. 1990. Stress proteins and immunology. *Annu. Rev. Immunol.* 8:401–20

89. Zhou, Y., Kusukawa, N., Erickson, J. W., Gross, C. A., Yura, T. 1988. Isolation and characterization of *Escherichia coli* mutants that lack the heat shock sigma factor (σ^{32}). *J. Bacteriol.* 170:3640–49

90. Ziegelhoffer, T. 1991. *Characterization of the GroEL chaperonin of Escherichia* coli *and its role in bacteriophage λ morphogenesis*. PhD thesis. Salt Lake City: Univ. Utah

91. Zweig, M., Cummings, D. J. 1973. Cleavage of head and tail proteins during bacteriophage T5 assembly: selective host involvement in the cleavage of a tail protein. *J. Mol. Biol.* 80:505–18

92. Zwickl, P., Pfeifer, G., Lottspeich, F., Kopp, F., Dahlmann, B., Baumeister, W. 1990. Electron microscopy and image analysis reveal common principles of organization in two large protein complexes: groEL-type proteins and proteasomes. *J. Struct. Biol.* 103:197–203

Annu. Rev. Microbiol. 1991. 45:327–44
Copyright © 1991 by Annual Reviews Inc. All rights reserved

RNA EDITING IN TRYPANOSOMATID MITOCHONDRIA

K. Stuart

Seattle Biomedical Research Institute, Seattle, Washington 98109-1651

KEY WORDS: RNA processing, mitochondrion, Kinetoplastida, gene regulation

CONTENTS

INTRODUCTION 327
kDNA 328
   Maxicircles 329
   Minicircles 329
   kDNA Mutations 331
RNA EDITING IS TRANSCRIPT AND TRANSCRIPT-REGION SPECIFIC 332
   Editing of Restricted Regions 332
   Extensive Editing 332
CONSEQUENCES OF EDITING 334
GUIDE RNA 335
   gRNA Characteristics 335
   gRNA Coding Sequences 335
PARTIALLY EDITED mRNAs 337
   Junctions 337
   Models of gRNA Usage 339
   The Editing Machinery 340
DEVELOPMENTAL REGULATION 340
PERSPECTIVE 341

INTRODUCTION

Studies of mitochondrial gene organization and expression in kinetoplastid protozoans led to the discovery of a form of RNA processing called RNA

327

0066-4227/91/1001-0327$02.00

editing. However, RNA editing in kinetoplastids is distinct from other types of RNA processing, some of which are also termed RNA editing (13, 43), and perhaps should have a distinctive designation such as K-RNA editing. K-RNA editing is characterized by the addition and removal of uridines, probably employs a different mechanism, and has been the subject of several reviews (4, 5, 19, 20, 48, 51, 53, 54, 58, 66). RNA editing changes the coding sequence of mRNAs and can be so extensive that it produces most of the mRNA sequence. All RNA processing involves catalytic activity and recognition of the molecule and site that is processed. These activities include specific endonucleolytic cleavage as in rRNA maturation (27) or cleavage combined with RNA ligation to excise introns in RNA splicing (38). Other catalytic activities add nucleotides to RNA termini as in polyadenylation (37) or modify nucleotides as in the case of tRNA maturation (9). The recognition and catalytic activities may occur in a single molecule such as poly(A) polymerase and may even be inherent to the processed molecule as in the case of self-splicing RNA (14). Other RNA processing employs a macromolecular complex, such as the spliceosome, which is composed of several RNAs and proteins (36). The mechanism of RNA editing is not known but appears to employ small guide RNAs (gRNAs) to direct the editing, perhaps within a macromolecular complex.

kDNA

The mitochondrial DNA of trypanosomatids, kinetoplast DNA (kDNA), is the hallmark of the order Kinetoplastida and has unusual characteristics that reflect the presence of RNA editing. The kDNA is composed of 20–50 maxicircles and 5000–10,000 minicircles. These numerous molecules are catenated together into a single DNA network that is located across from the base of the flagellum within the single large mitochondrion. Maxicircles are between 20 and 39 kb in size, depending on species, but are all identical within each network. The minicircles are between about 0.5 and 2.5 kb in size, depending on species, and are heterogeneous in sequence within each network; the total heterogeneity varies widely among species. The significance of the organization of kDNA into a network is not known, but if related to editing, it may keep newly synthesized pre-mRNAs and gRNAs in physical proximity and enhance their opportunity for interactions that occur during RNA editing, or it may serve as a scaffold that binds other components of the editing machinery. The location of the kDNA network opposite the flagellar basal body may allow the basal body to function analogously to a centriole and segregate the duplicated kDNA at cell division. Several authors have reviewed the characteristics of kDNA (3, 42, 47, 52).

Maxicircles

Maxicircles encode mitochondrial rRNAs and components of the mitochondrial respiratory system, as do all other mitochondrial DNAs that have been examined (Table 1). However, some maxicircle genes are compact, overlap at their ends, contain frame-shifts, or have pronounced G vs C strand bias that reflects the presence of RNA editing. Several genes of the maxicircle encode proteins whose functions are not yet identified, in some cases because of extensive editing of the mRNA. These include the maxicircle unidentified reading frames (MURFs) 1 and 2 that are conserved among species, an open reading frame (ORF) adjacent to the ND7 gene, and six G vs C strand–biased sequences (CR1–6) whose positions but not sequences are conserved among species (31, 50). These genes may specify proteins encoded by the mitochondrial genomes of other organisms such as subunits of the ATPase (or ATP synthase) complex, the NADH dehydrogenase complex, or mitochondrial ribosomal proteins. More tantalizing, from the perspective of RNA editing, is the possibility that they may encode components of the RNA editing machinery. This would not be unprecedented since some mitochondria encode RNA processing activities such as maturase and self-splicing RNA. The maxicircle also contains a large variable region (VR) that differs in size and sequence among species and isolates (18, 41, 57). The VR is primarily composed of repeated A + T–rich sequences, but the VR sequence adjacent to the rRNA genes is not repeated. The VR does not appear to encode proteins but encodes guide RNAs (gRNAs) as discussed below.

Minicircles

Minicircle function was a mystery until the discovery that these DNA molecules encode gRNAs (8, 35, 40, 60). Minicircles have approximately 120 bp of sequence that is conserved among minicircles within a single species and 12 bp that are conserved in minicircles of all kinetoplastid species. This conserved region is probably the origin of DNA replication because it is single stranded in replicating molecules and a potential RNA primer for replication has been identified (47). The size, organization, and total sequence diversity of minicircles vary among species. The significance of the variation in size and organization among species is not yet apparent. Among different species, however, minicircle diversity is correlated with the extent of RNA editing, as discussed below. Minicircle kinetic complexity is high (~300 kb) in *Trypanosoma brucei* in which extensive editing occurs and low (~3 kb) in *Leishmania tarentolae* in which editing is less extensive (52). *L. tarentolae* contains six CR regions, which if extensively edited might exceed the gRNA coding capacity of the minicircles estimated from the kinetic complexity. These analyses do not provide a precise measure of the number of different minicir-

Table 1 Summary of RNA editing

gene[a]	strand[b]	*T. brucei* size ed	uned	U's edited add	rem	DR[e]	result[f]	*L. tarentolae* size ed	uned	U's edited add	rem	result	*C. fasciculata* size ed	uned	U's edited add	rem	result
rRNA	R																
12S		NE[g]	1141					NE	1172				NE	1141			
9S	R	NE	610					NE	613				NE	612			
CR1	R	562	349	259	46	A	I,T,ORF	P	348[h]				P	364[h]			
CR2	O	+	270[h]					P	303[h]				P	309[h]			
ORF	O		226[k]						303[k]					247[k]			
ND7	R	1238	774	553	89	B	I,T,ORF	1199[i]	1174[i]	25	0	ORF	1198	1171	27	0	I^-,ORF
5'				71	13	A				20	0				22	0	
3'				482	76					5					5		
COIII	R	969	463	547	41	B	I,T,ORF	904[i]	890[i]	29	15	I,ORF	912	882	32	2	I,ORF
CYb	R	1151	1117	34	0	V	I,ORF	1150[i]	1111[i]	39	0	I,ORF	ND	ND	39	0	I,ORF
A6	R	811	392	447	28	B	I,T,ORF	746	645	106	5	I,ORF					
MURF1	O	NE	1352[i]					NE	1332[i]				ND				
CR3	R	P	75[h]						72[h]				ND				
ND1	O	NE	1046[i]					NE	941[i]				ND				
COII	R	663[i]	659[i]	4	0	V	ORF	670[i]	666[i]	4	0	ORF	643[i]	639[i]	4	0	ORF
MURF2	R	1111[i]	1089[i]	26	4	B	I,ORF	1099[i]	1075[i]	28	4	I,ORF	1117	1089	28	0	ORF
COI	O	NE	1680[i]					NE	1684[i]				ND				
ND4	O	+	249[h]					P	251[h]				ND				
CR4	O	NE	1358[i]					NE	1345[i]				ND				
CR5	O	P	186[h]					P	191[h]				ND				
CR6	R	+	221[h]					P	202[h]				ND				
ND5	R	NE	1801[i]					NE	1812				ND				

[a] CR1-6, G versus C strand biased gene sequences 1–6; ORF, open reading frame whose position but not sequence is conserved among species; ND1,4,5, and 7, NADH dehydrogenase subunits 1,4,5 and 7; COI,II and III, cytochrome *c* oxidase subunits I, II and III; CYb, apocytochrome *b*; A6, ATP synthase subunit 6; MURF1 and 2, maxicircle unidentified reading frames 1 and 2 with homology conserved among species.

[b] Coding strand the same as ribosomal RNA (R) or opposite to ribosomal RNA (O).

[c] Sizes of edited (ed) and unedited (uned) mRNAs (not including the most 3' A or U nucleotides).

[d] Number of Us added (add) and removed (rem) in fully edited mRNA compared to DNA.

[e] Developmental regulation of editing where editing occurs in animal host (A), insect vector (V), or both animal and insect (B).

[f] Result of editing creating (I) or deleting (I^-) initiation and termination (T) codons and creating or extending an open reading frame (ORF).

[g] NE, no editing detected; +, editing detected but not fully characterized; P, editing is probable from G versus C strand bias but not yet demonstrated; ND, gene sequence not yet completely determined, unable to assess extent of editing.

[h] Estimated from G versus C strand bias and location of surrounding genes.

[i] 5' end from RNA sequencing and 3' end from ORF analysis (stop codon).

[j] 5' end from ORF analysis (start codon) and 3' end from cDNA.

[k] Both 5' and 3' ends from ORF analysis.

cles and probably underestimate minicircle diversity; the 14.5-kb VR of *L. tarentolae* may also encode numerous gRNAs.

Minicircle sequence organization varies substantially among species. The minicircles of *T. brucei* and *L. tarentolae* are organized quite differently. *T. brucei* minicircles contain three gRNA coding cassettes between 18-bp inverted repeats in addition to the conserved region (33, 34). The 0.9-kb minicircles of *L. tarentolae* do not have this repeat organization and may only encode one gRNA per molecule (60). The 1.4-kb minicircles of *Trypanosoma cruzi* are organized into four-fold repeats (47), but RNA editing and gRNAs have not yet been reported in this species. The significance of the variation in minicircle organization among species is not known, but the differences may reflect the substantial differences in the developmental regulation of the respiratory system. For example, cytochromes and Krebs cycle enzymes are present in *L. tarentolae* in both the animal and insect phases of the life cycle but are only present in the insect stages in *T. brucei* (65).

kDNA Mutations

Mutations that delete or modify kDNA occur spontaneously in kinetoplastids and can be induced with intercalating agents such as ethidium bromide and acridines (30, 52). Mutants that are devoid of kDNA or have substantial kDNA alterations are conditionally lethal in African trypanosomes; they survive in the animal host where mitochondrial respiration is not essential but not in the insect host where this respiration is essential. *Trypanosoma evansi, Trypanosoma equiperdum,* and *Trypanosoma equinum* are classified as separate species but may be considered variants or mutants of *T. brucei*. These three species are morphologically indistinguishable from *T. brucei* but lack developmental stages in an insect host, probably because of partial or total kDNA deletions, and are transmitted venereally or mechanically. *T. evansi* lacks maxicircles but retains a single class of microheterogeneous minicircles, and mutants of *T. evansi* are devoid of kDNA (12). Similarly, *T. equiperdum* retains a single class of microheterogeneous minicircles but also retains maxicircles (26). Some sequences are deleted in these maxicircles. These mutants of African trypanosomes may be useful tools for the study of RNA editing. Intercalators can also induce kDNA loss in *Leishmania* spp. and other kinetoplastids, but these mutants are not viable for extended periods of time (61), presumably because of the requirement for mitochondrial respiration.

Editing has been most extensively studied in *T. brucei, L. tarentolae,* and *Crithidia fasciculata,* but it also occurs in other *Leishmania* species, including those causing human disease (55). It may occur in all species that contain kDNA minicircles. However, although *T. equiperdum* contains minicircles that encode gRNAs, we find maxicircle transcripts but not edited RNA in this species (K. Stuart, unpublished data). This lack of editing may result from loss of specific maxicircle and/or minicircle sequences. It is uncertain if RNA editing occurs in *Bodo caudatus,* which has atypical kDNA that contains 10–12 kb circles that may be the equivalent of minicircles (10). The absence of minicircles is not an inherent constraint since some gRNAs are encoded in maxicircles (10). No evidence yet indicates K-RNA-type editing outside the mitochondrion of kinetoplastids.

RNA EDITING IS TRANSCRIPT AND TRANSCRIPT-REGION SPECIFIC

Editing of Restricted Regions

Only certain mRNAs are edited, and the editing is restricted to specific regions of edited transcripts. The COII genes of three kinetoplastid species contain homology to the COII genes of other organisms in two different reading frames (17, 29, 39). The finding of this frameshift set the stage for the discovery of RNA editing. Benne and colleagues (7) and others (24, 44) showed that COII mRNA contains four Us that are not encoded in the COII gene. These additional Us eliminate the frameshift in mRNA, implying that it is the edited mRNA that is translated and a candidate protein has been detected (46). Other mRNAs are edited near, but not at, their 5' terminus by the addition and in some cases deletion of Us. In most cases, the 5' editing creates an AUG in frame with an ORF that is homologous to those of other organisms. No AUG is encoded in the 5' region of the gene in most cases, and thus editing may function as a translational control mechanism because unedited transcripts would not be translated. Nevertheless, no editing has been detected in the 5' end of ND1 transcripts of *T. brucei* and *C. fasciculata* that lack encoded AUGs; editing of ND7 transcripts in *C. fasciculata* shifts an AUG out of frame; and ND7 is edited in *L. tarentolae,* but no in-frame AUG is produced (45, 63, 64). This finding suggests that noncanonical initiation codons may be used as previously proposed (6) or that a small or undetected fraction of transcripts may contain the in-frame AUG. Many maxicircle transcripts have been only partially sequenced but some have been entirely sequenced (summarized in Table 1). Editing has not been detected in the 5' region of the COI and II, ND1, 4, and 5, and MURF1 transcripts; in rRNA of *T. brucei* and *L. tarentolae;* nor in rRNA of *C. fasciculata* (54). Editing of ND1 and ND7 transcripts of *C. fasciculata* appears restricted to the regions indicated in Table 1 (62, 63), and we only detected RNA editing in the 5' regions of *T. brucei* CYb and *L. tarentolae* A6 transcripts (K. Stuart, unpublished results).

Extensive Editing

Perhaps most startling are the cases of extensive editing that occur in *T. brucei* in which these transcripts are completely remodeled such that mRNA sequence is determined as much by editing as it is by transcription. RNA editing changes all but the farthest 5' and 3' sequences of the COIII (21; K. Stuart, unpublished results) and A6 (8) transcripts of *T. brucei*. The added Us comprise 56 and 55% of the fully edited mRNA sequence, respectively, and editing also removes tens of encoded Us from these transcripts. The CR1, 2, 4, and 6 transcripts of *T. brucei* are edited to a similar extent (L. Simpson, unpublished data; K. Stuart, unpublished data). The 5' region of the A6 transcript of *L. tarentolae* is also extensively edited but to a lesser extent than in *T. brucei* (8). The most complex case to date is the ND7 transcript of *T. brucei*, which is completely edited except at the 5' and 3' terminal regions and in a 59-nucleotide region that separates two extensively and independently edited domains (35). All cases of editing examined create continuous ORFs, most create initiation codons, and many create termination codons. Interestingly, the 5' terminus of the two ND7 editing domains in *T. brucei* correspond in position to the regions of editing in *L. tarentolae* (45) and *C. fasciculata* (64). Indeed, the same transcripts are edited in the same regions in all three species but the editing is more extensive in *T. brucei*.

All of the extensively edited regions exhibit prominent G vs C strand bias in the DNA sequence such that the Gs are present in the transcripts (22, 31, 32, 50). Based on this observation, we predicted that transcripts from the six CR regions are extensively edited (58). This hypothesis was confirmed for four CR transcripts of *T. brucei* (K. Stuart, unpublished data). Edited CR1 mRNA appears to encode a protein with two iron sulfur binding domains and thus may be a component of the respiratory chain, perhaps complex I (A. Sousa, unpublished data). Preliminary studies indicate the CR2, 4, and 6 transcripts of *T. brucei* (K. Stuart, unpublished data) and the CR5 transcript of *L. tarentolae* (L. Simpson, personal communication) are edited. Several cDNAs corresponding to a G vs C strand–biased region of *T. brucei* COI that were cloned using polymerase chain reaction are not edited, implying that this region of the RNA is not edited (K. Stuart, unpublished data). Thus, the strand bias is a useful but not infallible indicator of RNA editing. In all cases, at least 16 encoded 3' and at least 32 encoded 5' nucleotides are not edited in the final RNA, probably reflecting the requirements of gRNA utilization as discussed below.

The definition of the fully edited mRNA sequence is somewhat operational. The fully edited mRNA sequence is the consensus of several cDNA sequences that are in agreement with sequence obtained through direct RNA sequencing. All these fully edited transcripts appear to be the functional mRNAs. They contain continuous ORFs that predict proteins that are homologous to proteins encoded by mRNAs that are edited less or not edited in other species. In addition, a protein of the predicted size is detected with antibodies prepared with a synthetic peptide predicted from the edited COII mRNA of *L. tarentolae* (44). Small sequence variations occur in discrete regions of the fully edited RNA sequence of some mRNAs as detected by cDNAs and/or RNA sequencing (8, 35). These variations may not affect protein function because they predict conservative replacements of a few amino acids or occur upstream of the initiation codon sequences (8, 35). These variations might reflect the use of multiple gRNAs (59) or some flexibility in the editing process.

CONSEQUENCES OF EDITING

Edited genes can be compact, especially in *T. brucei* in which editing is extensive. These genes are so encrypted that homology to related genes cannot be detected without knowing the edited sequence. The CR1–6 genes that are G vs C strand biased and conserved in position but not sequence among species are compact and may encode proteins that are highly homologous among kinetoplastids (but this possibility cannot be discerned from the DNA sequence) (50). The G vs C and A vs T strand bias and the general lack of Ts in the coding sequences also reflect the U addition and deletion and use of wobble base-pairing (see below) aspects of RNA editing. The predicted consequences of editing at the protein level are intriguing, although few studies have directly examined the protein products of edited mRNA. In most cases, unless noncanonical initiation codons are used, unedited versions of edited RNAs would produce no product because they lack an initiation codon. However, initiation codons occur in unedited transcripts of COII in *T. brucei, C. fasciculata,* and *L. tarentolae;* CYb in *T. brucei*; and ND7 in *C. fasciculata,* and thus these transcripts could conceivably be translated, although their association with mitochondrial ribosomes has not been tested. Particularly intriguing is that editing of these three transcripts is developmentally regulated in *T. brucei* (23, 24, 35) raising the possibility that unedited transcripts may be translated to produce truncated proteins perhaps with modified functions.

RNA editing is posttranscriptional and proceeds in the 3' to 5' direction. A variety of approaches have shown that unedited RNA is invariably present along with fully edited RNA, and partially edited RNA is abundant. Numerous cDNAs, probably derived from RNA that was in the process of editing when isolated, have edited 3' and unedited 5' sequences (1, 16, 21, 35, 58, 59). The presence of both edited and unedited sequences on the same molecules is strong evidence that editing is posttranscriptional and indicates that editing proceeds in the 3' to 5' direction. The detection with probes for 5' edited sequences of transcripts that are larger and hence more edited than those with 3' probes reinforces this conclusion (35). In addition, PCR analysis of total cellular RNA detects only partially edited RNA that is edited on the 3' and not the 5' side (1). The partially edited RNAs from extensively edited mRNAs are more abundant than the fully edited mRNA according to Northern analysis results (1, 8, 21, 35). This finding is not surprising given the numerous events that must occur during the editing of these molecules. Us are present in mRNA poly(A) tails (21, 25, 64). Both the positions and numbers of these U additions vary even in transcripts from the same gene, suggesting that their addition is not directed by gRNA. These Us may be added by the enzyme that adds Us during editing and/or by poly(A) polymerase.

GUIDE RNA

gRNA Characteristics

The discovery of gRNA (10) revealed the likely repository of the edited sequence and provided substantial insight into the RNA editing process. The gRNAs (8, 10, 11, 35, 40) are small (~60 nucleotides) and are complementary to the edited RNA sequence. The predicted complementarity at the 5' end of the gRNA with mRNA is primarily, if not entirely, Watson-Crick base-pairing, while the remaining complementarity entails some wobble (G-U) base-pairing. It is important to recognize that the wobble base-pairing in gRNA-mRNA interactions indicates that gRNA is not functioning as a conventional template because gRNA Gs would specify Cs and gRNA Us would specify As; however, Us are specified during editing by Gs and As. The 5' Watson-Crick complementarity suggests that a duplex initially forms between mRNA and the 5' region of the gRNA. Approximately 15 noncoded Us are added to the 3' end of the gRNAs. These Us may stabilize the gRNA-mRNA association during editing (11). An alternate possibility is that the 3' Us create a secondary structure that leaves the 5' end of the gRNA single stranded and hence available to duplex with mRNA (U. Goeringer, personal communication). Of the numerous gRNAs identified directly or as coding sequences, only those for the farthest 3' and hence initial region of an editing domain can form a duplex between the gRNA 5' end and unedited RNA (8, 10, 35; K. Stuart, unpublished data). The other gRNAs must be edited to provide the sequence with which the 5' region of the gRNA can duplex, which suggests that the order in which gRNAs are utilized is determined by the ability of their 5' ends to form a duplex with the mRNA. This suggestion explains the overall 3' to 5' direction of editing and provides a mechanism for the order of gRNA utilization.

gRNA Coding Sequences

The gRNAs are encoded in both maxicircles and minicircles, but the number of gRNA coding sequences and their distribution among the maxicircles and minicircles differs between T. brucei and L. tarentolae. Most gRNAs identified to date in *L. tarentolae* are encoded in the maxicircle (10), but some are also encoded in minicircles (60; K. Stuart, unpublished data). All of the known gRNA coding sequences in *T. brucei* are present in minicircles (8, 35, 40). Potential gRNA coding sequences have been identified in the maxicircle of *T. brucei*, but the gRNAs have not been demonstrated. Some gRNA coding sequences identified in the maxicircle of *L. tarentolae* do not appear to be encoded in the maxicircle of *T. brucei*. For example, the gRNA genes for CYb are not in *T. brucei* maxicircles, at least not at the same position as in *L. tarentolae* (K. Stuart, unpublished data). This absence may reflect either the developmental regulation of editing that occurs in *T. brucei* and not *L. tarentolae* or the more extensive editing in *T. brucei*.

   T. brucei kDNA has adequate coding capacity for all gRNAs needed for all editing detected and predicted in this species. The total number of Us known to be added/removed by editing in *T. brucei* and *L. tarentolae* is 1870/208 and 256/24, respectively (Table 1). These changes approximately double the sizes of the edited regions. Net increases of about 750 and 1000 Us in *T. brucei* and *L. tarentolae*, respectively, are required to account for the remaining editing predicted if the CR transcripts are extensively edited in both species. The large minicircle diversity of *T. brucei* can easily encode sufficient gRNAs to direct this editing. Approximately 175 gRNAs, each adding 15 Us, could account for all the observed and predicted editing in *T. brucei*, allowing about 5 copies of each gRNA gene, since at least 300 different minicircles each encode 3 gRNAs. The repetition frequency could be higher because this minicircle complexity estimate is based on minimal minicircle sequence diversity. The lower minicircle diversity of *L. tarentolae* at first glance cannot account for the approximately 80 gRNAs estimated for the anticipated editing in this species. Only single gRNA coding sequences have been found on each *L. tarentolae* minicircle to date. However, editing of *L. tarentolae* CR RNAs may be less extensive than anticipated, thus requiring fewer gRNAs. Minicircle diversity may also be greater than estimated by renaturation kinetic and other analyses, and the ~14-kb VR of *L. tarentolae* may encode several gRNAs. Thus, *L. tarentolae* can encode all its gRNAs in kDNA.

   Multiple gRNAs with different sequences that can specify the same editing, because of wobble base-pairing, have been detected (K. Stuart, unpublished data). These occur in minicircles from two different stocks of *T. brucei*, which indicates minicircle divergence and/or redundancy of gRNA coding sequences. Thus, minicircle abundance and diversity, especially in *T. brucei*, reflect gRNA gene copy number, different gRNAs that specify the same edited sequence, and different gRNAs that specify editing to similar but not identical sequences, i.e. conservative differences.

   Little is known about the transcription of maxicircles or minicircles. No promoters have been identified in either molecule, but both strands of both molecules are transcribed. Detection of transcripts that span more than one maxicircle gene in steady-state RNA indicates that polycistronic maxicircle transcripts occur with some abundance (56), but no polycistronic minicircle transcripts have been reported. All *T. brucei* minicircle gRNAs are encoded in the same minicircle DNA strand and between inverted 18-bp repeats, including cases in which multiple gRNAs are encoded in the same minicircle (8, 35, 40; K. Stuart, unpublished data). This strand is opposite to that which encodes transcripts from near the conserved sequence and opposite to the strand encoding gRNAs in *L. tarentolae* (K. Stuart, unpublished data). Several transcripts from maxicircles and minicircles can be radiolabeled using guanyltransferase, indicating that the most-5' nucleotide has a 5' di- or triphosphate and suggesting that these are primary transcripts (11, 40, 49). Thus, maxicircles and minicircles may have multiple promoters, but the compactness of the genes and the presence of apparent polycistronic transcripts suggest that each maxicircle gene does not have its own promoter. Polycistronic precursors may be processed in the mitochondrion of kinetoplastids as in other organisms. The inverted 18-bp repeats that flank gRNA coding sequences in *T. brucei* may have a role in transcript processing. Further study is needed to identify promoters and primary transcripts and to determine if kDNA transcripts undergo processing in addition to RNA editing and polyadenylation.

PARTIALLY EDITED mRNAs

Junctions

Several studies have examined partially edited mRNAs in detail (1, 16, 21, 35, 58, 59; D. J. Koslowsky, unpublished data) because they are likely to be molecules undergoing the process of editing and thus may provide insight into this process. All partially edited RNAs, or their editing domains, are edited on their 3' but not their 5' side. Their unedited sequence is identical to the gene sequence, and the fully edited sequence is identical among edited cDNAs and to the RNA sequence determined directly from RNA sequencing. In some molecules, the RNA sequence switches directly from edited to unedited sequence. Importantly, the great majority of molecules contains a short region of edited sequence that does not match the fully edited RNA sequence at the junction of the edited and unedited sequence (Figure 1). The simplest interpretation is that the junction is the region of active editing. Most partially edited RNAs are probably end products of an editing cycle at a site rather than of editing of reaction intermediates. Such intermediates with 5' Us have been observed as cDNAs (1, 23) and may be products of the cleavage associated with editing, or some may reflect cDNA cloning artifacts (64).

The junctions (sequences that are edited but do not match fully edited RNA) vary in size, and their positions often overlap. Junction size varies from

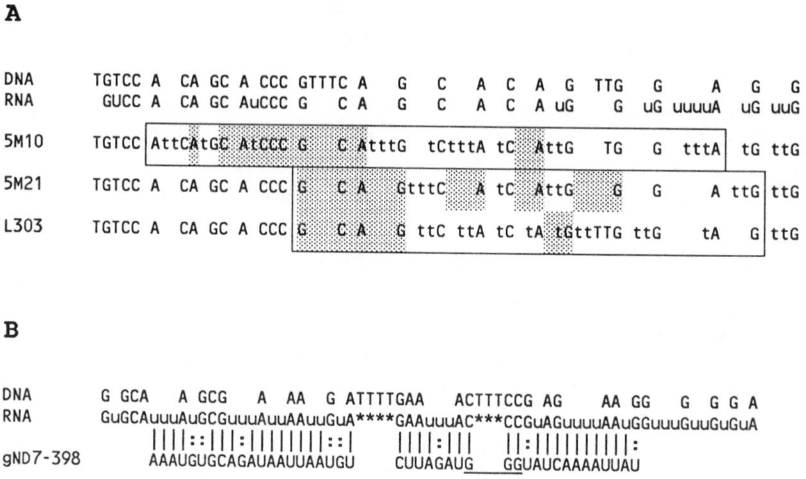

A

```
DNA    TGTCC A  CA GC A CCC GTTTC A   G   C   A  C  A G  TTG   G     A    G   G
RNA    GUCC A  CA GC AuCCC G    C A   G   C   A  C  A uG    G  uG uuuuA  uG uuG

5M10   TGTCC AttCAtGC AtCCC G  C AtttG  tCtttA tC AttG   TG   G  tttA  tG ttG

5M21   TGTCC A  CA GC A CCC G  C A  GtttC  A tC AttG    G   G     A ttG ttG

L303   TGTCC A  CA GC A CCC G  C A  G ttC ttA tC tA tGttTTG ttG    tA   G ttG
```

B

```
DNA      G GCA   A GCG   A  AA  G ATTTTGAA   ACTTTCCG AG   AA GG   G  G G A
RNA      GuGCAuuuAuGCGuuuAuuAAuuGuA****GAAuuuAC***CCGuAGuuuuAAuGGuuuGuuGuGuA
         |||::|||:||||||||::|    ||||:|||   ||:|||||||||:
gND7-398     AAAUGUGCAGAUAAUUAAUGU   CUUAGAUG   GGUAUCAAAAUUAU
```

Figure 1 (A) Junctions of partially edited RNA (*boxed*) compared to gene (DNA) and fully edited (RNA) sequences. Shaded regions in the junctions match the fully edited sequence while unshaded regions do not. (B) A gRNA sequence compared to fully edited (RNA) and unedited (DNA) sequences. The underlined site contains, 3' to a C, Ts that are removed by editing.

3 to 109 nucleotides. The sizes of some junctions exceed the size of any gRNA detected to date, implying that a junction may represent the utilization of more than one gRNA or that some gRNAs may be large. Numerous junctions have been found for limited regions of editing such as the 5' regions of CYb and COIII (16, 58, 59; K. Stuart, unpublished data). Numerous junctions have also been observed for extensively edited RNAs. Some of these junctions may represent molecules that are not destined to become fully edited, but some, perhaps many and possibly all, must be edited to the final mRNA sequence. This observation indicates an extensive diversity of partially edited molecules, suggesting that many events must transpire in the editing of mRNAs, especially in the extensively edited RNAs. The relationship between junctions and gRNAs, where both have been characterized, has not been determined. The 3' boundary of most junctions is usually identical to that of one or more other junctions, but the 3' boundaries can occur at adjacent editing sites (see Figure 1).

The junctions contain numerous sites with the same number of Us (16, 35, 58, 59; K. Stuart, unpublished data) as the final RNA sequence interspersed with sites that have either more or fewer Us than present in the final RNA and thus require further editing (Figure 1). Commonly, many sites contain Us where none are present in unedited or fully edited mRNA. This finding suggests that most, if not all, sites in an editing domain undergo editing to achieve the final edited sequence. It also suggests that Us are added to many sites and subsequently removed, implying that sites are reedited. The distribution of the sites requiring further editing among those that match the final edited sequence does not have a regular pattern progressing precisely 3' to 5'. Thus, the characteristics of junctions may reflect gRNA diversity, overlapping gRNAs, and/or an editing process that does not proceed precisely 3' to 5'.

Models of gRNA Usage

No studies have yet been published that demonstrate that gRNAs determine the edited sequence. However, the existence of this class of small RNAs that matches the edited sequence strongly indicates this role. Analyses of partially edited RNAs led to two different hypotheses to explain how gRNAs are used to produce the edited sequence. One hypothesis (10), which I term *mismatch recognition,* proposes rounds of (*a*) cleavage of the mRNA at the mismatch immediately 5' (mRNA perspective) of the gRNA-mRNA duplex, (*b*) U addition or deletion to eliminate the mismatch, and (*c*) religation; this process continues until the mRNA region matches the gRNA. The other hypothesis (16), which I term *match protection,* proposes random U addition and deletion within a restricted region of the mRNA until the gRNA and mRNA match, thus protecting the mRNA from further editing. Probably neither model is correct exactly as proposed. For example, neither model can adequately explain how to accommodate sequences of the form 5' CU 3' in mRNA where Us are either deleted or added 3' to the C. For example, the gRNA in Figure 1 contains a G at a position where three encoded Us are deleted, which would prevent recognition of the mismatch according to the first model and could produce inappropriate protection of a sequence according to the second model. The mismatch recognition model does not fully explain the distribution of sites that require further editing in junctions of numerous partially edited mRNAs, although utilization of gRNAs that do not produce the final RNA sequence may explain some of these molecules. The match protection model does not provide insight into the enzymology of the process. Thus, substantial modification of these models or an alternate model is required.

Editing may proceed precisely 3' to 5' but use a variety of gRNAs covering the same region, thus explaining the characteristics of the junction sequences. Another possibility, which does not preclude multiple gRNAs, is that editing does not proceed precisely 3' to 5'. The secondary structures assumed by gRNA and/or mRNA could explain the order of editing site selection because sites could be presented to the catalytic machinery in a non-3'-to-5' order. This mechanism would allow for reediting of sites using the same gRNA. The progressive change of the mRNA sequence during editing might result in a succession of secondary structures that could be very specific. Studies of the means of gRNA utilization would be aided by an in vitro editing system.

The Editing Machinery

The study of the mechanism of RNA editing is at such an early stage that no molecules that participate in the process have been identified, other than gRNA and mRNA. Other molecules probably catalyze this intricate process, and such molecules have been suggested to occur as a macromolecular complex, provisionally termed the editosome, although its existence has not been demonstrated. Nevertheless, by analogy to RNA splicing, RNA editing may be catalyzed by a macromolecular complex perhaps composed of RNA and/or protein. The precise reactions and the sequence in which they occur during editing have not been identified. Endoribonuclease, uridine addition and deletion, and RNA ligase activities have been predicted to account for addition and deletion of Us within mRNAs (4, 21, 23, 51, 53). Candidate 3′ terminal uridylyltransferase (TUTase) and RNA ligase activities have been identified in lysates of whole cells (67) and isolated mitochondria (2, 28), but these activities have not been shown to be associated with editing. Chimeric molecules of gRNAs, joined by their 3′ ends to internal regions of edited ND7 and COII mRNAs of *L. tarentolae* (68) and ND7 and CR6 mRNAs of *T. brucei* (K. Stuart, unpublished data), document the association between gRNA and mRNA and suggest that uridines may be added and removed by transesterification as also suggested by Cech (69). The gRNAs may have a role in the recognition of the mRNA and region to be edited. The complex may contain the catalytic molecules and other molecules that function in stabilization and RNA translocation. The number of components of such a complex could be as numerous as those of the spliceosome, and their genes may reside in nuclear and/or mitochondrial DNA. A nuclear location of some editosome genes seems possible since most of the kDNA genes are identified. This possibility is intriguing because the products of such genes might have a role in processing nuclear transcripts.

DEVELOPMENTAL REGULATION

RNA editing is developmentally regulated in *T. brucei,* indicating the existence of a regulatory system that controls the editing activity. Interestingly, the editing is transcript specific: some transcripts are constitutively edited; others are only edited in the animal stage of the life cycle; while others are only edited in the insect stage of the life cycle. In the animal host, slender bloodstream form (Sl-BF) *T. brucei* have no cytochromes nor a Krebs cycle; they produce ATP by glycolysis that occurs at a prodigious rate in the glycosome, an organelle that contains glycolytic enzymes. The nondividing stumpy bloodstream forms (St-BF), a less discrete stage than the Sl-BF, have a somewhat enlarged mitochondrion and an additional mitochondrial oxido-reductive enzyme activity that has been detected only through cytochemical staining with tetrazolium dyes. The insect procyclic forms (PF) have a full complement of cytochromes, a Krebs cycle, and produce ATP primarily by mitochondrial oxidative phosphorylation (65). *L. tarentolae* and *C. fasciculata* have less complex life cycles and do not regulate their mitochondrial composition in such a dramatic fashion.

The COIII, A6, and MURF2 mRNAs are edited in both Sl-BF and PF, indicating that editing activity is present in both life-cycle stages (8, 21, 24). The CYb and COII mRNAs are edited in PF and St-BF but not in Sl-BF (23, 24). The abundance of edited transcripts is less in St-BF than in PF. The actual amount appears to differ among stocks, presumably reflecting differences among stocks and among cell populations of the same stock in the production of these life-cycle stages. Editing of these transcripts in PF is consistent with the greater mitochondrial activity in PF and St-BF than in Sl-BF (K. Stuart, unpublished data). The CR1 transcripts are edited in Sl-BF but not PF. Although the function of the CR1 protein is unknown, its iron-sulfur center motif suggests that it may be part of the respiratory chain, perhaps complex I. The significance of its editing in Sl-BF and not PF is unclear. However, ND5 transcripts are more abundant in Sl-BF than in PF (32), indicating that components of respiratory complex I may be more abundant in BF than PF. The 5' domain of ND7 is edited in both BF and PF but the larger 3' domain is preferentially edited in BF (35). Thus, editing is developmentally regulated in a transcript-specific fashion. This regulation is not controlled at the gRNA-abundance level because gRNAs that have been identified for developmentally regulated regions are present in similar abundance in life-cycle stages whether or not they are edited (K. Stuart, unpublished data). Hence, some system must control editing during the life cycle, but how it functions is unknown.

PERSPECTIVE

The raison d'etre and the selective value of such a baroque process as RNA editing are not intuitively obvious. However, editing does provide an additional genetic regulatory capability. It could be an evolutionary residuum of processes that originated in the era of the RNA genome but no longer exists or is not extensively utilized in many organisms. While it is distinct from other types of RNA processing, some activities appear superficially similar and thus may have an evolutionary origin common to these other types. RNA editing appears superficially similar to RNA splicing because both entail recognition of specific regions of transcripts, cleavage, and religation. RNA editing may be catalyzed by a complex analogous to the spliceosome. The RNA editing reported in *Physarum polycephalum* resembles RNA editing in kinetoplastids since it occurs in the mitochondrion and primarily involves addition of single Cs (D. Miller, personal communication). Elucidation of gRNA interactions with mRNA may extend our knowledge of the importance of RNA interactions beyond their role in splicing (38). These interactions may include the postulated role of small RNAs in poly(A) site selection (15) and the significance of the recently discovered enzymes that specifically modify double-stranded RNA (13). RNA editing may be the harbinger of other as yet undiscovered RNA processing phenomena.

ACKNOWLEDGMENTS

I thank Drs. P. Myler, M. Parsons, and J. Feagin for helpful discussions and critical reading of the manuscript. This work received support from NIH AI14102 and GM42188. The author is a Burroughs-Wellcome Scholar in Molecular Parasitology.

Literature Cited

1. Abraham, J. M., Feagin, J. E., Stuart, K. 1988. Characterization of cytochrome c oxidase III transcripts that are edited only in the 3' region. *Cell* 55:267–72

2. Bakalara, N., Simpson, A. M., Simpson, L. 1989. The *Leishmania* kinetoplast-mitochondrion contains terminal uridylyltransferase and RNA ligase activities. *J. Biol. Chem.* 264:18679–86

3. Benne, R. 1985. Mitochondrial genes in trypanosomes. *Trends Genet.* 1:117–21

4. Benne, R. 1989. RNA editing in trypanosome mitochondria. *Biochim. Biophys. Acta* 1007:131–39

5. Benne, R. 1990. RNA editing in trypanosomes: Is there a message? *Trends Genet.* 6:177–81

6. Benne, R., van den Burg, J., Brakenhoff, J., deVries, B., Nederlof, P., et al. 1985. Mitochondrial genes in trypanosomes: abnormal initiator triplets, a conserved frameshift in the gene for cytochrome oxidase subunit II and evidence for a novel mechanism of gene expression. In *Achievements and Perspectives of Mitochondrial Research*, ed. E. Quagliariello, E. C. Slater, F. Palmierei, C. Saccone, A. M. Kroon, pp. 325–36. Amsterdam: Elsevier

7. Benne, R., van den Burg, J., Brakenhoff, J. P., Sloof, P., Van Boom, J. H., et al. 1986. Major transcript of the frameshifted coxII gene from trypanosome mitochondria contains four nucleotides that are not encoded in the DNA. *Cell* 46:819–26

8. Bhat, G. J., Koslowsky, D. J., Feagin, J. E., Smiley, B. L., Stuart, K. 1990. An extensively edited mitochondrial transcript in kinetoplastids encodes a protein homologous to ATPase subunit 6. *Cell* 61:885–94

9. Bjork, G. R., Erickson, J. U., Gustafsson, C. E. D., Hagervall, T. G., Jonsson, Y. H., et al. 1989. Transfer RNA modification. *Annu. Rev. Biochem.* 58: 263–87

10. Blum, B., Bakalara, N., Simpson, L. 1990. A model for RNA editing in kinetoplastid mitochondria: "guide" RNA molecules transcribed from maxicircle DNA provide the edited information. *Cell* 60:189–98

11. Blum, B., Simpson, L. 1990. Guide RNAs in kinetoplastid mitochondria have a nonencoded 3' oligo(U) tail involved in recognition of the preedited region. *Cell* 62:391–97

12. Borst, P., Fase-Fowler, F., Gibson, W. C. 1987. Kinetoplast DNA of *Trypanosoma evansi*. *Mol. Biochem. Parasitol.* 23:31–38

13. Cattaneo, R. 1990. Messenger RNA editing and the genetic code. *Experientia* 46:1142–48

14. Cech, T. R. 1990. Self-splicing of group I introns. *Annu. Rev. Biochem.* 59:543–68

15. Cotten, M., Gick, O., Vasserot, A., Schaffner, G., Birnstiel, M. L. 1988. Specific contacts between mammalian U7 SnRNA and histone precursor RNA are indispensible for the in vitro 3' RNA processing reaction. *EMBO. J.* 7:801–8

16. Decker, C. J., Sollner-Webb, B. 1990. RNA editing involves indiscriminate U changes throughout precisely defined editing domains. *Cell* 61:1001–11

17. de la Cruz, V. F., Neckelman, N., Simpson, L. 1984. Sequences of six genes and several open reading frames in the kinetoplast maxicircle DNA of *Leishmania tarentolae*. *J. Biol. Chem.* 259:15136–47

18. de Vries, B. F., Mulder, E., Brakenhoff, J. P., Sloof, P., Benne, R. 1988.

The variable region of the *Trypanosoma brucei* kinetoplast maxicircle: sequence and transcript analysis of a repetitive and a non-repetitive fragment. *Mol. Biochem. Parasitol.* 27:71–82

19. Eisen, H. 1988. RNA editing: who's on first?. *Cell* 53:331–32
20. Feagin, J. E. 1991. RNA editing in kinetoplastid mitochondria. *J. Biol. Chem.* 265:19373–76
21. Feagin, J. E., Abraham, J. M., Stuart, K. 1988. Extensive editing of the cytochrome c oxidase III transcript in Trypanosoma brucei. *Cell* 53:413–22
22. Feagin, J. E., Jasmer, D. P., Stuart, K. 1985. Apocytochrome *b* and other mitochondrial DNA sequences are differentially expressed during the life cycle of *Trypanosoma brucei*. *Nucleic Acids Res.* 13:4577–96
23. Feagin, J. E., Jasmer, D. P., Stuart, K. 1987. Developmentally regulated addition of nucleotides within apocytochrome b transcripts in Trypanosoma brucei. *Cell* 49:337–45
24. Feagin, J. E., Stuart, K. 1988. Developmental aspects of uridine addition within mitochondrial transcripts of *Trypanosoma brucei*. *Mol. Cell. Biol.* 8:1259–65
25. Feagin, J. E., Stuart, K. 1989. Transcript alteration by mRNA editing in kinetoplastid mitochondria. In *Molecular Biology of RNA*, ed. T. Cech, pp. 187–97. New York: Liss
26. Frasch, A. C. C., Borst, P., Hajduk, S. L., Hoeijmakers, J. H. J., Brunel, F., et al. 1980. The kinetoplast DNA of *Trypanosoma equiperdum*. *Biochim. Biophys. Acta* 607:397–401
27. Gegenheimer, P., Apirion, D. 1981. Processing of prokaryotic ribonucleic acid. *Microbiol. Rev.* 45:502–41
28. Harris, M. E., Moore, D. R., Hajduk, S. L. 1990. Addition of uridines to edited RNAs in trypanosome mitochondria occurs independently of transcription. *J. Biol. Chem.* 265:11368–76
29. Hensgens, L. A., Brakenhoff, J., de Vries, B. F., Sloof, P., Tromp, M. C., et al. 1984. The sequence of the gene for cytochrome c oxidase subunit I, a frameshift containing gene for cytochrome c oxidase subunit II and seven unassigned reading frames in *Trypanosoma brucei* mitochondrial maxicircle DNA. *Nucleic Acids Res.* 12: 7327–44
30. Hoare, C. A. 1954. The loss of the kinetoplast in trypanosomes, with special reference to *Trypanosoma evansi*. *J. Protozool.* 1:28–33
31. Jasmer, D. P., Feagin, J. E., Payne, M., Stuart, K. 1987. Variation of G-rich mitochondrial transcripts among stocks of Trypanosoma brucei. *Mol. Biochem. Parasitol.* 22:259–72
32. Jasmer, D. P., Feagin, J. E., Stuart, K. 1985. Diverse patterns of expression of the cytochrome c oxidase subunit 1 gene and unassigned reading frames 4 and 5 during the life cycle of *Trypanosoma brucei*. *Mol. Cell. Biol.* 5:3041–47
33. Jasmer, D. P., Stuart, K. 1986. Sequence organization in African trypanosome minicircles is defined by 18 base pair inverted repeats. *Mol. Biochem. Parasitol.* 18:321–31
34. Jasmer, D. P., Stuart, K. 1986. Conservation of kinetoplastid minicircle characteristics without nucleotide sequence conservation. *Mol. Biochem. Parasitol.* 18:257–69
35. Koslowsky, D. J., Bhat, G. J., Perrollaz, A. L., Feagin, J. E., Stuart, K. 1990. The MURF3 gene of Trypanosoma brucei contains multiple domains of extensive editing and is homologous to a subunit of NADH dehydrogenase. *Cell* 62:901–11
36. Maniatis, T., Reed, R. 1987. The role of small nuclear ribonucleoprotein particles in pre-mRNA splicing. *Nature* 325:673–78
37. Manley, J. L. 1988. Polyadenylation of mRNA precursors. *Biochim. Biophys. Acta* 950:1–12
38. Padgett, R. A., Grabowski, P. J., Konarska, M. M., Seiler, S., Sharp, P. A. 1986. Splicing of messenger RNA precursors. *Annu. Rev. Biochem.* 55:1119–50
39. Payne, M., Rothwell, V., Jasmer, D. P., Feagin, J. E., Stuart, K. 1985. Identification of mitochondrial genes in *Trypanosoma brucei* and homology to cytochrome c oxidase in two different reading frames. *Mol. Biochem. Parasitol.* 15:159–70
40. Pollard, V. W., Rohrer, S. P., Michelotti, E. F., Hancock, K., Hajduk, S. L. 1990. Organization of minicircle genes for guide RNAs in Trypanosoma brucei. *Cell* 63:783–90
41. Roberts, T. M., Kacich, R., Ptashne, M. 1979. A general method for maximizing the expression of a cloned gene. *Proc. Natl. Acad. Sci. USA* 76:760–64
42. Ryan, K. A., Shapiro, T. A., Rauch, C. A., Englund, P. T. 1988. Replication of kinetoplast DNA in trypanosomes. *Annu. Rev. Microbiol.* 42:339–58
43. Scott, J. 1989. Messenger RNA editing and modification. *Curr. Opin. Cell Biol.* 1:1141–47
44. Shaw, J. M., Campbell, D., Simpson, L. 1989. Internal frameshifts within the mitochondrial genes for cytochrome oxidase subunit II and maxicircle un-

identified reading frame 3 of *Leishmania tarentolae* are corrected by RNA editing: Evidence for translation of the edited cytochrome oxidase II mRNA. *Proc. Natl. Acad. Sci. USA* 86:6220–24

45. Shaw, J. M., Feagin, J. E., Stuart, K., Simpson, L. 1988. Editing of kinetoplastid mitochondrial mRNAs by uridine addition and deletion generates conserved amino acid sequences and AUG initiation codons. *Cell* 53:401–11

46. Shaw, J. M., Simpson, L. 1989. Characterization of a protein fraction containing cytochromes *b* and *c1* from mitochondria of *Leishmania tarentolae*. *Exp. Parasitol.* 68:443–49

47. Simpson, L. 1987. The mitochondrial genome of kinetoplastid protozoa: genomic organization, transcription, replication and evolution. *Annu. Rev. Microbiol.* 41:363–82

48. Simpson, L. 1990. RNA editing—a novel genetic phenomenon? *Science* 250:512–13

49. Simpson, L., Neckelman, N., de la Cruz, V. F., Muhich, M. 1985. Mapping and 5′ end determination of kinetoplast maxicicle gene transcripts from *Leishmania tarentolae*. *Nucleic Acids Res.* 130:5977–93

50. Simpson, L., Neckelmann, N., de la Cruz, V. F., Simpson, A. M., Feagin, J. E., et al. 1987. Comparison of the maxicircle (mitochondrial) genomes of *Leishmania tarentolae* and *Trypanosoma brucei* at the level of nucleotide sequence. *J. Biol. Chem.* 262:6182–96

51. Simpson, L., Shaw, J. 1989. RNA editing and the mitochondrial cryptogenes of kinetoplastid protozoa. *Cell* 57:355–66

52. Stuart, K. 1983. Kinetoplast DNA: mitochondrial DNA with a difference. *Mol. Biochem. Parasitol.* 9:93–104

53. Stuart, K. 1989. RNA editing: new insights into the storage and expression of genetic information. *Parasitol. Today* 5:5–8

54. Stuart, K. 1991. RNA editing in mitochondrial RNA of trypanosomatids. *Trends Biochem. Sci.* 16:68–72

55. Stuart, K., Feagin, J. E. 1988. Transcript alteration in *Leishmania*. In *Leishmaniasis: The Current Status and New Strategies for Control*, ed. D. T. Hart, pp. 937–45. New York: Plenum

56. Stuart, K., Feagin, J. E., Jasmer, D. P. 1985. Regulation of mitochondrial gene expression in *Trypanosoma brucei*. In *Sequence Specificity in Transcription and Translation*, ed. R. Calender, L. Gold, pp. 621–31. New York: Liss

57. Stuart, K., Feagin, J. E., Jasmer, D. P. 1987. Mitochondrial gene expression during development in *Trypanosoma*

brucei. In *Molecular Strategies of Parasite Invasion*, ed. N. Agabian, H. Goodman, N. Nogueira, pp. 145–55. New York: Liss

58. Stuart, K., Koslowsky, D. J., Bhat, G. J., Feagin, J. E. 1990. The implications of selective and extensive RNA editing. In *Parasites: Molecular Biology, Drug and Vaccine Design*, ed. N. Agabian, A. Cerami, pp. 111–22. New York: Wiley-Liss

59. Sturm, N. R., Simpson, L. 1990. Partially edited mRNAs for cytochrome b and subunit III of cytochrome oxidase from *Leishmania tarentolae* mitochondria: RNA editing intermediates. *Cell* 61:871–78

60. Sturm, N. R., Simpson, L. 1990. Kinetoplast DNA minicircles encode guide RNAs for editing of cytochrome oxidase subunit III mRNA. *Cell* 61:879–84

61. Trager, W., Rudzinska, M. A. 1964. The riboflavin requirement and the effects of acriflavin on the fine structure of the kinetoplast of *Leishmania tarentolae*. *J. Protozool.* 11:133–45

62. van der Spek, H., Arts, G.-J., van den Burg, J., Sloof, P., Benne, R. 1989. The nucleotide sequence of mitochondrial maxicircle genes of *Crithidia fasciculata*. *Nucleic Acids Res.* 17:4876

63. van der Spek, H., Speijer, D., Arts, G.-J., van den Burg, J., Steeg, H., et al. 1990. RNA editing in transcripts of the mitochondrial genes of the insect trypanosome *Crithidia fasciculata*. *EMBO J.* 9:257–62

64. van der Spek, H., van den Burg, J., Croiset, A., van den Broek, M., Sloof, P., et al. 1988. Transcripts from the frameshifted MURF3 gene from *Crithidia fasciculata* are edited by U insertion at multiple sites. *EMBO J.* 7:2509–14

65. Vickerman, K. 1985. Developmental cycles and biology of pathogenic trypanosomes. *Br. Med. Bull.* 41:105–14

66. Weiner, A. M., Maizels, N. 1990. RNA editing: Guided but not templated?. *Cell* 61:917–20

67. White, T. C., Borst, P. 1987. RNA end-labeling and RNA ligase activities can produce a circular rRNA in whole cell extracts from trypanosomes. *Nucleic Acids Res.* 15:3275–90

68. Blum, B., Sturm, N., Simpson, A. M., Simpson, L. 1991. Chimeric gRNA/mRNA molecules with oligo[U] tails covalently attached at sites of RNA suggest that uridine addition occurs by transesterification. *Cell* 65:1–8

69. Cech, T. R. 1991. RNA editing: worlds smallest introns? *Cell* 64:667–69

Annu. Rev. Microbiol. 1991. 45:345–82

PLANT GENETIC CONTROL
OF NODULATION

Gustavo Caetano-Anollés and Peter M. Gresshoff

Plant Molecular Genetics, Institute of Agriculture and Center for Legume Research, University of Tennessee, Knoxville, Tennessee 37901

KEY WORDS: nitrogen fixation, symbiosis, molecular genetics, legumes, *Rhizobium, Bradyrhizobium*

CONTENTS

INTRODUCTION 345
LEGUME NODULATION 346
ROLE OF THE BACTERIAL SYMBIONT: SIGNAL EXCHANGE 348
NODULATION AS A DEVELOPMENTALLY REGULATED PHENOMENON 354
PLANT NODULATION MUTANTS 357
NODULATION CONTROL IN LEGUMES 361
AUTOREGULATION 362
    What Is the Signal Transduction Mechanism? an Example of Systemic
        Root-Shoot Interaction. 363
    How Is Nodulation Suppressed? 364
    What Triggers the Systemic Response? 365
    A Working Hypothesis 367
NODULATION IN THE ABSENCE OF *RHIZOBIUM* SPP. 368
PERSPECTIVES 370

INTRODUCTION

The interaction of *Rhizobium* and *Bradyrhizobium* bacterial species with roots of leguminous plants results in the development of a new organ, the legume root nodule. Within this morphologically defined structure, the bacteria re-

345

duce atmospheric nitrogen to ammonia, which is then internally assimilated by the plant.

The symbiosis is an excellent example of how the plant adapts to the changing environment by allowing a carefully regulated and evolved biological process to occur. Whether subject to microbial attack or stress, the plant responds to any environmental cue with the careful control of its biochemical processes. Usually this action involves a signal-transduction apparatus that perceives the changing environment and exerts a defined response that influences gene expression or a defined biomolecular process. The final outcome can be a change in development or cell behavior or the onset of cell division. The establishment of the symbiotic association involves signal exchange and cellular recognition between the symbionts, essential components of pathogenesis, and defense and developmental processes. The mutual induction of gene expression and metabolic function induces cell division and alters cell development and morphology, which finally leads to the formation of the nodule. A comprehensive coverage of the field can be found in two recent symposium proceedings (119, 129).

Considerable progress has been made during the past few years in characterizing the way the plant controls nodule formation at the biochemical, genetic, physiological, and ultrastructural levels in several symbiotic associations. However, we need to understand the molecular basis of nodulation control in future efforts of manipulating the symbiosis to maximize its efficiency and potential and expand the range of plants that can establish the symbiotic relationship.

LEGUME NODULATION

The symbiosis between legume plants and bacteria offers an interesting model to study the intricacy of the various mechanisms that control plant cell division and development. Though little is known about the underlying biochemical events influencing the establishment and function of the symbiosis, more than fifty bacterial genes and several plant loci have been identified and characterized in detail. Nodule initiation as well as infection development involve a highly complex series of interactions between the plant and the bacterium, which has been extensively studied (for reviews, see 16, 104, 178, 196, 197, 199, 226). In general, the bacterial symbiont is known to form nodules only on a restricted number of hosts, and each host is only nodulated by a restricted number of microsymbionts. Thus, the development of the nodule symbiosis is highly specific. Some exceptions exist; for example, *Rhizobium* strain NGR234 nodulates a variety of legumes, ranging from woody plants to annuals. The host secretes substances that act as chemoattractants of *Rhizobium* and *Bradyrhizobium* spp., inducing active chemotaxis towards defined regions of the roots (19, 120, 150, 214). The bacteria are similarly attracted to flavonoid compounds (1, 8, 32), which are themselves inducers of bacterial gene expression (217). Both motility and chemotaxis are not required for nodulation but provide a competitive advantage to the bacteria, probably by allowing their successful establishment in the rhizosphere in close association with the root surface (6, 38, 120). Firm bacterial attachment follows and is frequently polar (25, 267), involves pili (273, 274), bacterial lectin (132, 133), and adhesin molecules (245), and requires specific plant signals (277). Studies of cell-surface interaction suggest that plant lectins bind polysaccharide components of bacterial origin and mediate attachment of the rhizobia to the root hair (62, 123). A recent study furthers the involvement of lectin in the infection process, though this subject is still controversial. A lectin gene from pea was introduced into the genome of clover roots using *Agrobacterium rhizogenes* transformation (76). The clover roots could then nodulate both with the clover and the pea microsymbionts, suggesting that the lectin glycoproteins could play a crucial role in determining specificity. At the surface of the root, bacteria secrete substances that induce root hairs to branch, deform, and curl (21, 280). Only young root hairs can be induced to curl sufficiently to entrap bacterial cells in a pocket of host-cell walls. In soybean, such entrapment occurs within 12 h after contact and seems required for subsequent penetration and infection (267, 268). This process is followed by the generation of tubular structures, the infection threads, that grow through the root hair cell and into the root cortex where they ramify and finally release the bacteria within the host cytoplasm enclosed in a peribacteroid host-derived membrane (199). At this point, the bacteria differentiate into bacteroids and begin to fix atmospheric nitrogen into ammonia in exchange for fixed carbon sources (107, 199, 226).

Even before the infection thread is initiated, root cortical cells begin to divide, giving rise to a nodule primordium (41, 84, 107, 174, 267, 268). This process is one of the earliest induced morphological events that happens during infection, and appears to be requisite (but is not sufficient) for successful infection-thread development. In soybean, a plant that develops spherical (determinate) nodules, the first divisions occur in the hypodermal layer (41). In pea and alfalfa, temperate legumes that develop cylindrical or indeterminate nodules, the earliest divisions occur in the inner cortex (84, 174). Several other different strategies of infection occur in legumes (226, 250). Bacteria can also enter the plant through cracks or middle lamellae. While in some associations bacteria induce cell divisions, in others they take advantage of already dividing cells or use the emergence of a lateral root to enter the host. Such is the case with peanut, *Parasponia, Casuarina,* and the stem-nodulating *Sesbania* symbioses.

Although nodulation responses vary among plant species, one finds amazing similarities. Comparison of nodule initiation in legume, actinorhizal nonlegume, and *Parasponia* nonlegume symbioses shows the common feature of an initial induction of cell division in the cortical region. In the legume symbiosis, these initial cell divisions lead to the induction of pericycle cell division, which in turn results in a nodule with tissues of two distinct origins, the cortex, which leads to the infected zone and perhaps part of the inner nodule parenchyma, and the pericycle-derived tissues. The presence of two regions of cell growth results in the characteristic peripheral vascular tissue arrangement of the legume nodule. The nonlegume nodule ontogeny as in *Frankia*-induced *Alnus* or *Bradyrhizobium*-induced *Parasponia* (223) also starts with cortical cell divisions. These subside, but lead to the induction of pericycle-derived cell divisions. Hence these nodules show only a single tissue-lineage and possess a lateral root type of vascular (i.e. central) arrangement.

Nodules formed in alfalfa in the absence of *Rhizobium* spp. possess the same ontogeny as *Rhizobium*-induced nodules (149) (see later discussion). Likewise, one finds *Rhizobium*-induced nodule-like structures on rice and rape seed plants (4, 52) that have a central vascular cylinder and may be of lateral root or root-cap origin. Many functions associated with lateral root emergence are probably common to nodule initiation (205). Thus, some genes involved in lateral root induction and emergence should be functional homologues.

A decade ago, J. M. Vincent (276a) proposed several phenotypic codes to permit the classification of symbiotic mutants in plants and bacteria. Since then the understanding of the nodulation process has grown, and additional categories should be included in Vincent's postulates. Table 1 shows an updated version of the proposed phenotypic stages needed to achieve legume nodulation. However, specific blockages at any one of the phenotypic points may be impossible because of multiple phenotypes and developmental pleiotropy. Furthermore, nodulation proceeds along several ontogenetic pathways (250), and alternative codes may be needed for specialized symbioses like those in *Parasponia* or *Andira* spp.

THE ROLE OF THE BACTERIAL SYMBIONT: SIGNAL EXCHANGE

During recent years, our understanding of the organization and expression of bacterial symbiotic genes has increased considerably (178, 226). The fast-growing *Rhizobium* species usually have large plasmids of about 200 to 1500 kb, some of which carry nodulation-related genes, the so-called *nod, nol, syr, exo, lps, ndv, nif,* and *fix* genes. In other symbionts like *Bradyrhizobium* spp., symbiotic genes are chromosomal. For a list of nodulation genes see Stacey

Table 1 Phenotypic codes of legume nodule development

Stage	Abridged description	Phenotypic code
Preinfection		
Chemotaxis	Chemotaxis	Che
Multiplication and colonization of the root surface	Root colonization	Roc
Adsorption to the roots	Root adsorption	Roa
Induction of *nod* gene expression	*nod* gene induction	Ngi
Increase in Ngi	Increased *nod* gene induction	Ini
Division and multiplication of cortical cells	Cortical cell division	Ccd
Deformation of root hairs	Hair deformation	Had
Branching of root hairs	Hair branching	Hab
Marked curling of root hairs	Hair curling	Hac
Infection and nodule formation		
Infection thread formation	Infection	Inf
Infection thread branching	Infection thread branching	Inb
Host blockage of sustained cell division	Autoregulation	Aut
Pericycle cell division	Pericycle cell division	Pcd
Intracellular bacterial release from infection threads	Bacterial release	Bar
Intracellular bacterial multiplication and development of full bacteroid form	Bacteroid development	Bad
Nodule function		
Reduction of gaseous nitrogen (nitrogenase activity)	Nitrogen fixation	Nif
Complementary biochemical and physiological functions	Complementary functions	Cof
Persistence of nodule function	Nodule persistence	Nop

(251). Several other gene loci have also been identified in the chromosome or in plasmids though their function still remains unclear. Despite all efforts, our knowledge of the role of nodulation genes in symbiosis is limited to sequence homology and a few biochemical studies that point to the genes' possible involvement in hormone metabolism, membrane transport, and lipid and polysaccharide biosynthesis.

In fast-growing *Rhizobium* spp., nodulation genes are basically organized in two clusters: (*a*) the common *nodABC* genes, which are essential for both root hair curling and the initiation of cell division, are functionally interchangeable among *Rhizobium* spp., are followed immediately downstream by *nodIJ* and are preceded by a divergently transcribed regulatory *nodD* gene (63, 80, 83, 89, 90, 98, 139, 144, 227, 233, 237, 264) and (*b*) the host-specific nodulation genes required for the correct induction of root hair curling and cell division in the appropriate legume host, which are downstream of *nodABC* in *Rhizobium meliloti* (*nodH, nodFEG,* and *nodPQ*) and downstream of *nodD* in *Rhizobium leguminosarum* bv. *trifolii* and bv. *viciae* (*nodFELMN* and *nodO*) (47, 63, 64, 73, 78, 82, 88, 91, 139, 161, 236, 238, 242, 257, 259). In *R. leguminosarum* bv. *viciae,* a gene, *nodX,* confers the ability to nodulate Afghanistan peas (55). Moreover, different strains of *Rhizobium* have a different number of regulatory (*nodD* and other) genes (13, 111, 121, 137, 194).

The organization of *nod* genes in slow-growing bacteria like *Bradyrhizobium japonicum* differs from that of fast-growers (128). *B. japonicum* carries a set of common *nodABC* genes preceded by an open reading frame termed *nodY* and a conserved sequence (*nod* box), responsible for the *nodABC* genes' transcription (12, 112, 122, 167). Downstream of these genes, two genes *nodSU* are closely followed by *nodIJ* (110). Apparently there are two regulatory *nodD* genes (7). Three DNA regions have been identified in *B. japonicum* that encode host-specificity functions important for nodulation of soybean, *Vigna radiata,* siratro, cowpea, and mung bean (109, 122, 200). A soybean genotype–specific nodulation gene, *nolA,* has also been identified and sequenced (228a). In other broad–host range *Rhizobium* strains, researchers have also made progress in defining nodulation genes controlling host specificity (9, 14, 15, 172, 173, 198, 240).

Another group of bacterial genes is related to the synthesis of surface and extracellular polysaccharides. These polysaccharides are believed to be involved in the actual infection process (16, 63, 123). Extracellular heteropolysaccharides (EPS), capsular polysaccharides, the periplasmic cyclic oligosaccharide β-(1→2)-glucan, and lipopolysaccharides (LPS) could all play roles in root nodule entry. Their involvement in symbiosis is not reviewed here. However, polysaccharides like the acidic EPS could determine host range (219). The acylation pattern of the acidic EPS of *R. leguminosarum* bv. *viciae* can be modified by the introduction of host-range genes from *R. leguminosarum* bv. *trifolii,* which confer to the bacteria the ability to interact with clover lectin (220). Mutants deficient in the production of acidic EPS (*exo* mutants) have been described for several *Rhizobium* strains (26, 48–50, 81, 95, 103, 169, 192, 283) and in most cases induce empty nodule-like structures that cannot fix nitrogen. In some cases, mutants fail to nodulate or appear to induce normal nodule formation (26, 229). In alfalfa, *exo* mutants are blocked early in infection development and fail to invade the nodules they induce (95, 157, 169), suggesting that nodulation can be uncoupled from infection and supporting the concept that nodule morphogenesis can be triggered from a distance (266). Mutations responsible for these phenotypes were clustered on a 22-kb region on a second megaplasmid different from the one that carries the *nod* genes, and some *exo* genes were located on the bacterial chromosome (96, 180). Interestingly, chromosomal mutations in *R. meliloti* genes related to virulence genes in *Agrobacterium tumefaciens* rendered the bacteria capable of inducing nodules without infection threads and bacteroids (87). These *ndv* mutants produced normal amounts of exopolysaccharides but no cyclic oligosaccharide β-(1→2)-glucan.

The ability of *Rhizobium* and *Bradyrhizobium* spp. to induce cell responses in their host depends on the expression of certain nodulation genes in the bacterium, like the *nodABC* genes (178). Expression of the *nod* genes depends in turn on the activation by phenolic compounds, secreted by the host root (reviewed in 217). This chain of signal-and-response events has been observed in several symbioses in which the expression of several nodulation genes is induced by compounds exuded from the host root surface and requires *nodD* (143, 193, 228). The inducing compounds have been identified as plant flavonoids for the alfalfa-*R. meliloti* (126, 127, 188, 189, 215), clover-*R. leguminosarum* bv. *trifolii* (78, 225), and pea-*R. leguminosarum* bv. *viciae* (97, 282) associations and as isoflavonoids for the soybean-*B. japonicum* symbiosis (12, 113, 163). Related phenolic compounds also antagonize *nod* gene induction by inducers (79, 97, 164, 216, 225). Flavonoids and isoflavonoids are involved in mammalian cell regulation and growth control. For example, the isoflavonoid genistein inhibits specifically tyrosine protein kinases (2), and psi-tectorigenin inhibits cellular phosphatidylinositol turnover, both implicated in the cellular response to growth factors (142). Interestingly, the *R. meliloti nodG* gene product shows homology to human placental 17β-hydroxysteroid dehydrogenase (10).

In alfalfa, *nod*-gene-inducing compounds are exuded from the portion of the root with emerging root hairs (216) that is susceptible to infection by *R. meliloti* (20). However, while alfalfa root exudates contain the *nod*-gene inducers 4,4'-dihydroxy-2'-methoxychalcone, 4',7-dyhydroxyflavone, and 4',7-dihydroxyflavanone (228), the seed exudates contain a different set of inducers: luteolin, 3',4',5,7-tetrahydroxyflavone, 3'-methoxy-4',5,7-trihy-droxyflavone, and chrysoeriol (127, 215). Results suggest that the adequate balance of *nod*-gene inducing compounds and their timely synthesis and exudation determines whether symbiotic genes will be appropriately expressed to induce plant responses in the host.

On the bacterial side, the specificity of the response to different flavonoids correlates with the source of *Rhizobium nodD* gene and can determine host range (14, 121, 138, 248). The NodD protein contains two distinct domains, one involved in the regulation of its synthesis, the other determining flavonoid specificity (27, 138, 247, 249). The domain that determines specificity is not conserved and differs between species. An additional level of complexity in the response to host exudates by the bacteria is the ability of the different *nodD* genes to be induced by different flavonoid compounds from different hosts (121, 136). The different levels in which specificity is expressed suggests that *Rhizobium* spp. will only induce its symbiotic genes when the adequate plant signals are sensed by the appropriate *nodD* genes. This process probably occurs in particular regions of the roots and at a particular plant developmental stage. Recently, a heat-stable factor from *R. leguminosarum* bv. *viciae* was shown to increase specifically the *nod* gene–inducing activity of root exudate from *Vicia sativa* subsp. *nigra* (269). The *nodDABCIJ* and *nodFEL* genes were all important for the expression of the biovar-specific extracellular signal. These observations show a new level of signal exchange between symbionts, in which bacteria precondition the root to secrete adequate sets of *nod*-gene inducers or optimizes their production.

Only a small region close to the zone of elongation of the host root appears to be susceptible to infection and nodulation by rhizobia (20, 22). In general, nodule formation in this susceptible region of the roots is a transient property, in that nodule emergence results from infections that have been initiated within a relatively short period after inoculation. Although little is known about the mechanisms that determine and control nodule initiation, evidence indicates that *nod* gene–related extracellular signaling is required to elicit appropriate host responses (11, 29, 31, 93, 94, 135, 170). A recent study showed that *nodA* and *nodB* were involved in generating extracellular factors that could induce host responses leading to cortical cell division (235). The *nodA* gene product resided within the bacterial cell (234) while the *nodC* protein was associated with the cell membrane (148). Additional evidence supports the extracellular nature of the bacterial signals involved in cell division. *Rhizobium* and *Bradyrhizobium* spp. secrete cytokinins (221, 255). The exogenous application of the cytokinin benzyladenine induced pseudoinfections in soybean (17). Empty nodule structures were also formed in alfalfa by auxin transport inhibitors (131) or when *R. meliloti* was separated from the roots using filter membranes (151). Recently, Lerouge et al (170) found that a sulfated and acylated glucosamine lipo-oligosaccharide symbiotic signal, the so-called NodRm-1, whose activity on alfalfa depended on the host-range *nodH* and *nodQ* genes, required the *nodABC* genes for its synthesis. NodRm-1 triggered root hair deformation on alfalfa at very low concentration (10^{-11} M) and cortical cell division and the formation of empty nodules at higher concentrations (171). The NodP and NodQ proteins had ATP sulphurylase activity (239) that with NodH could activate inorganic sulphate and introduce it into a precursor molecule, turning it from vetch-specific to alfalfa-specific (171). Figure 1 depicts a model developed from the one by Faucher et al (93) that illustrates how NodRm-1 is synthesized. This signal probably is not the only one required for the induction of host responses. Different *nod* mutants synthesize different but complementary sets of symbiotic effectors (31). Pairs of host-specificity mutants help wild-type *R.*

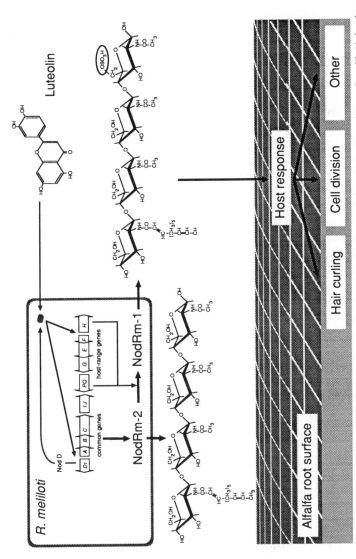

Figure 1 Model developed by Faucher et al (93, 94). The lengthy exposure of alfalfa and vetch seedlings to culture filtrates from wild-type *R. meliloti* induced root hair branching on alfalfa but not on vetch. However, culture filtrates from *nodH* and *nodQ* mutants did not induce branching on alfalfa but could do so in vetch. Based on these and other results, the model proposes that the common *nodABC* genes direct the synthesis of signal precursor molecules, active on vetch but not alfalfa, that are converted to active alfalfa signals by the action of host-specificity genes like *nodH* and *nodQ*. The active signal molecule on alfalfa, NodRm-1, is a N-acyl tri N-acetyl-β-1,4-D-glucosamine tetrasaccharide, bearing a sulphate group on C-6 of the reducing sugar and a 2,9-hexadecadienoic N-acyl group in the reducing terminal sugar residue (170). The active signal molecule on vetch, NodRm-2, has the same structure as NodRm-1 but lacks the sulphate moiety (171). The common *nodABC* genes could mediate NodRm-2 production either directly through de novo synthesis from N-acetyl-D-glucosamine or through the degradation or modification of preexisting cell wall components. The host-range *nodH* and *nodPQ* genes could introduce the sulphate group into the NodRm-2 molecule, turning it into the active alfalfa signal (239). The tetraglucosamine backbone of the molecule is acylated and acetylated and carries a fatty acid residue. Thus, genes like *nodF*, *nodE*, or *nodL* could be involved in the synthesis of the factor because their gene products are homologous to acyl-carrier protein (242), β-ketoacyl synthase (the condensing enzyme activity of fatty acid synthase) (23), and acetyltransferase (82), respectively. Moreover, the *nodM* gene product is homologous to an enzyme involved in the synthesis of glucosamine phosphate, an intermediate of the pathway to N-acetyl-D-glucosamine (256).

meliloti initiate nodule formation, apparently by providing a sustained supply of these extracellular signals that act synergistically to favor nodule initiation (31). Moreover, other flavonoid-inducible signal molecules secreted by *R. leguminosarum* bv. *trifolii,* like N-acetylglutamic acid, elicit root hair and cell division responses in clover (135).

The question of how cell division is caused at a distance from the actual site of infection remains unanswered. Two clear alternatives have been postulated (179). A small molecule could diffuse to the root cells and stimulate cell divisions directly, or alternatively, the bacteria could trigger a secondary signal in the epidermal cells, which then cause the response. Though arguments can be in favor of or against these two general models, our understanding of the underlying cellular and biochemical mechanisms and the role of the plant in this initial interaction is meager. Another puzzling question is whether root-hair curling and plant-cell division are coupled mechanistically. Dissection of the nodulation process using *exo* mutants showed that root hair deformation without marked curling can occur with full nodule morphogenesis, while *nodABC* genes are not only required for cell division but also for minimal deformation of root hairs. Recently, Dudley & Long (85), analyzing these phenomena in a nonnodulating alfalfa line, suggested that root-hair curling and cell division are triggered by related mechanisms, or are causally linked. Results in soybean do not appear to support this alternative. Two nonnodulating soybeans belonging to the same complementation group exhibited subepidermal cell divisions but no root hair curling (183–185, 187). However, a third soybean nonnodulating mutant had no cell division and root-hair curling and thus appears similar to the one mutant studied in alfalfa (85). Similarly, a mutation in a loci downstream of *nodD* made *B. japonicum* incapable of inducing subepidermal cell division without affecting the ability to curl root hairs (74). This discrepancy may reflect different nodulation strategies in temperate and tropical legumes. Alternatively, root hair curling and cortical cell division may be controlled by an arrangement of extracellular (such as NodRm-1) and intercellular (receptors, positional gradients, membrane leakage, etc) plant functions. Thus, multiple mutant phenotypes of both plant and bacterial origin showing different combinations of developmental responses will most probably be detected.

NODULATION AS A DEVELOPMENTALLY REGULATED PHENOMENON

Plants represent a diverse group of organisms with relatively simple but unique reproductive, developmental, and physiological processes (106). Despite their morphological simplicity and totipotential, the plant cell is as complex as the animal cell in its genetic trebling of development. Physical and functional analysis of plant genes in transformed plants indicate that gene expression is highly regulated and controlled much as it is in the animal kingdom (155). Plant genomes are large and complex with genetic potential comparable to that of mammals. Since plants depend greatly on the environment to trigger developmental events, much of that genetic complexity may be used for an array of signals that activate and repress specific genes involved in unique adaptive physiological phenomena. For instance, a complex group of signal transduction mechanisms are used to activate plant defenses against microbial attack (166). These mechanisms require disease-resistance genes also under developmental regulation. For example, chitinase and glucanase genes are under hormonal control (190, 244), the biosynthetic genes of the phenylpropanoid pathway are regulated by both developmental and environmental stimuli, and hydroxyproline-rich glycoproteins (HRGPs) accumulate in cell walls as a result of stress or normally during cell maturation (166). Comparatively, the interaction between plants and the environment can lead to either injury or acclimation and may involve the release of hormones and hormonal-like substances that act as long-range effectors of stress-resistance (224). An excellent and interesting example is the recent discovery that a volatile signal compound, the lipid-derived molecule methyl jasmonate, can induce the accumulation of wound-response proteinase inhibitor proteins in plant leaves (92). The gaseous signal molecules mediate interplant communication but also intracellular signaling in response to wounding or pathogenic attack. Several genes that respond to external influences, such as heat-shock, wounding, and anaerobiosis have been isolated and characterized (100) and appear to be developmentally regulated.

Few genes that control nodulation and nitrogen fixation have been studied in legumes (196, 271, 272). Expression of several of these genes occurs preferentially in nodules, and the codified nodule-specific plant proteins, termed *nodulins,* can be detected and studied (68). Nodulin genes are genes expressed almost exclusively in the nodular tissue. Several nodulins are key polypeptides in the soybean symbiosis including uricase (202), leghemoglobin (141), sucrose synthetase (263), and proteins of the peribacteroid membrane (152). Nodule-specific glutamine synthetase has been characterized from bean (54), alfalfa (86), and soybean (241). Most of these genes are expressed late in the infection process when nodules are already visible but not in nodules lacking infection threads and intracellular bacteria (86, 191). Conversely, the presence of nodulins expressed early in development (Enod) has been shown in soybean, peas, and alfalfa (77, 99, 114). In particular, the gene for N-75 of soybean, *enod2,* appears to encode two 75-kilodalton (kd) structural HRGPs (99). At least four soybean nodulins (N-75, N-44, N-41, and N-38) were already expressed at the time of the formation of the nodule primordium (105). The presence of these nodulins could be correlated with nodular meristematic activity. The precise time along nodule ontogeny in which these nodulin genes begin expressing themselves is yet to be determined. The isolation of cDNA clones of several nodulin genes has not allowed study of their biochemical function; at present this function is only intimated through derived amino acid sequences or by homology to previously characterized genes (196). The use of plant transformation and antisense strand mutagenesis will help to elucidate the role of these symbiotic plant genes (67).

A nodulin gene that has received considerable attention is *enod2*, which codes for HRGPs (99). It has been discovered in nodules of several legumes, although its sequence suggests that it may be part of a wide family of HRGPs expressed in different plant tissues (197). Expression of *enod2* has been documented in empty nodules produced by *exo* mutants, pseudonodules induced by auxin transport inhibitors (131, 270), and nodules formed in the absence of *Rhizobium* spp. (265). In situ hybridization to transcripts from the gene indicates preferential expression of Enod2 in nodule tissue that is pericycle-derived (cf 226 for analysis of cortical versus pericycle origins of nodule tissues).

Other HRGPs involved in the actual infection process have been identified. The early nodulin Enod5 (232), a hydroxyproline-rich cell-wall protein, and Enod12 (231), an arabinogalactan-related protein, are expressed during infection-thread development. In particular, while the Enod12 gene is expressed in all cells of the nodule primordium, the Enod5 is expressed only in cells containing growing infection threads. Application of a NodRm-1-like purified extracellular factor from *R. leguminosarum* bv. *viciae* induced the expression of Enod12 in pea root hairs (197), suggesting that Nod factors can also induce responses of infection.

The discovery of similar HRGPs in the pericycle-associated tissues of emerging lateral roots of tobacco is significant (154). Likewise, transgenic tobacco plants containing the chimeric *Parasponia* hemoglobin promoter/*gus* gene construct expressed this gene in pericycle-associated tissue at the time of lateral root emergence (24). This observation showed that (*a*) the nonlegume tobacco has the necessary *trans*acting factors to express the *Parasponia* leghemoglobin gene and (*b*) its expression is possible in a tissue where active cell division of a lateral root apex generates high oxygen requirement, while the intact endodermis (including the Casparian strip) restricts oxygen diffusion.

Cloned nodulin genes can also serve as tools to study signal transduction. For example, one can transform chimeric gene constructs of 5' DNA regulatory regions fused to reporter genes (like *cat* or *gus*) to monitor activation of the transgene in either homologous or heterologous plants. The pioneering work of de Bruijn, Marcker, and coworkers illustrated that the soybean leghemoglobin promoter, fused to a *cat* gene, can be expressed in a tissue-specific fashion in transgenic nodules of *Lotus* (65, 66, 147, 254, 260). Similar work was carried out with the *Parasponia* hemoglobin promoter and *gus* gene fusions in transgenic *Lotus* and tobacco. Transgenic plants may be further investigated using mutagenesis to isolate mutants either unable to induce the transgene or able to express it constitutively or with tissue nonspecificity. Such mutants would define genetic elements of the signal transduction chain, and as such would provide an approach to study genes that are controlling, rather than controlled by, nodulation.

PLANT NODULATION MUTANTS

The standard mutagenic approach for defining genetic loci has produced interesting germplasm for use in physiological and developmental studies. Nonnodulating and supernodulating plant mutants have been isolated in several legumes such as soybeans (28, 44–46, 115), pea (145, 146, 158, 159, 278), french bean (213), and chickpeas (57, 58). Mutations in soybean, bean, and pea were induced after ethyl methane sulfonate (EMS) mutagenesis. The number of plant symbiotic mutants has also expanded to other legumes including alfalfa and peanut (226). Genetic analysis of these mutants has shown that several plant loci are involved in controlling nodulation. Table 2 summarizes the plant genetic components characterized so far in legume species.

In soybean, several nonnodulating and supernodulating mutants have been isolated after EMS mutagenesis and M2 family selection (44–46, 115). Initial physiological, biochemical, agronomic, and genetic characterization of some of the mutants (5, 42, 44–46, 59–61, 69–72, 117, 118, 124, 183–187, 212) have shown that mutations are controlled by single recessive Mendelian genes and affect different stages of the symbiosis.

Three of the several nonnodulating mutants that have been isolated (46) are now better characterized. These are nod49, nod772, and nod139. Complementation analysis indicated that the *nod49, nod772* and *rj₁* loci are located in a same complementation group, while the *nod139* locus defines a new mutant class and group (185). The mutants represent single, nuclear recessive mutations that epistatically suppress supernodulation if placed into a double mutant configuration (186). Serial sectioning of pouch-grown roots showed that mutants nod49, nod772, and rj₁ all shared a similar phenotype. These mutants could induce few subepidermal cell divisions with no infection threads (pseudoinfections). In contrast, mutant nod139 caused neither pseudoinfections nor actual infections. All mutants could not induce root hair curling. The cytological analysis of the mutants suggests that pseudoinfections may precede actual infections, and that the pseudoinfection potentiates

Table 2 Symbiotic legume mutants

Gene[a]	Origin[b]	Inheritance	Phenotype; comments	Reference
Soybean [*Glycine max* (L.) Merr.]				
rj_1	—	Monogenic recessive	Nonnodulation	165, 279
Rj_2	—	Monogenic dominant	Ineffective nodulation with several strains; linked to RFLP probe pA-233	39, 40
Rj_3	—	Monogenic dominant	Ineffective nodulation	275
Rj_4	—	Monogenic dominant	Ineffective nodulation	276
Rj_5	—	Monogenic dominant	Ineffective nodulation with fast growing *Rhizobium fredii* USDA205	75
nod2 (nts)	EMS induced	Monogenic recessive	Supernodulation; defective in autoregulation; linkage to RFLP probe pA-132	44, 45
nod1	EMS induced	Monogenic recessive	Nonnodulation; allelic to rj_1	46
nod3	EMS induced	Monogenic recessive	Nonnodulation; nonallelic to nod1	46
Alfalfa (*Medicago sativa* L.)				
nn_1nn_2	Induced	Double tetrasomic	Nonnodulation; requires homozygous recesive alleles at all loci	218
in_1	Induced	Single tetrasomic	Ineffective nodulation	218
in_2	Induced	Single tetrasomic	Ineffective nodulation	218
in_3	Induced	Single tetrasomic	Ineffective nodulation	218
in_4in_5	Induced	Double recessive	Ineffective nodulation; requires nulliplex condition at both loci	218
Red clover (*Trifolium pratense* L.)				
r	—	Monogenic recessive	Nodulation resistance; interacts with citoplasmic factor σ; homozygous rr is lethal in the absence of σ	204
i_1	—	Monogenic recessive	Ineffective nodulation with some strains; prevents Bar; a recessive suppressor (m_1) restores effectiveness to the i_1i_1.	18, 206
ie	—	Monogenic recessive	Ineffective nodulation with several strains	207
n	—	Monogenic recessive	Ineffective nodulation with some strains	209
d	—	Monogenic recessive	Ineffective nodulation with some strains; similar to n	209

Table 2 (*Continued*)

Gene[a]	Origin[b]	Inheritance	Phenotype; comments	Reference
Crimson clover (*Trifolium incarnatum* L.)				
n_1	—	Monogenic recessive	Ineffective nodulation; nonstrain specific	246
Pea (*Pisum sativum* L.)				
sym-1	—	Monogenic recessive	Nodulation resistance to some strains below 20°C in cultivar Iran	175
sym-2	—	Monogenic recessive	Nodulation resistance in cv. Afghanistan; infected by *R. leguminosarum* bv. *viciae* Middle East strains like TOM; maps to chromosome 1 near *d* and *Idh*	134, 159, 175, 278, 281
sym-3	—	Monogenic recessive	Ineffective nodulation	134
sym-4	—	Monogenic recessive	Nodulation resistance in cv. Iran and Afghanistan	176
sym-5	Induced	Monogenic recessive	Nonnodulation; nodulates at lower temperatures; possible ethylene sensitivity mutants; maps to chromosome 1 near *d* and *Idh*	158, 278
sym-6	Induced	Monogenic recessive	Ineffective nodulation in cv. Afghanistan	177
sym-7	Induced	Monogenic recessive	Nonnodulation; maps to chromosome 3 near *Lap-1*	160
sym-8	Induced	Monogenic recessive	Nonnodulation; maps to chromosome 6 near *Arg*	160
sym-9	Induced	Monogenic recessive	Nonnodulation	160
sym-10	Induced	Monogenic recessive	Nonnodulation; maps to chromosome 1 close to *I*	160
sym-11	Induced	Monogenic recessive	Nonnodulation; maps to chromosome 7 near *Skdh*	160
sym-12	Induced	Monogenic recessive	Nonnodulation	160
sym-13	Induced	Monogenic recessive	Ineffective nodulation; maps to chromosome 2 near *Skdh*	160a
sym-14	Induced	Monogenic recessive	Nonnodulation	278
sym-15	Induced	Monogenic recessive	Decreased nodulation; maps to chromosome 7	278
sym-16	Induced	Monogenic recessive	Decreased nodulation; maps to chromosome 5 near *coh*	278
sym-17	Induced	Monogenic recessive	Decreased nodulation	278
sym-18	Induced	Semidominant	Nodulation resistance to some strains; late flowering maps to chromosome 1 near *d* and *Idh*	278

Table 2   (*Continued*)

Gene[a]	Origin[b]	Inheritance	Phenotype; comments	Reference
sym-19	Induced	Monogenic recessive	Nonnodulation; resistant to mycorrhizal infection; maps to chromosome 1 near *d* and *Idh*	145, 278
nod₁	—	Monogenic recessive	Decreased nodulation in cv. Parvus	101
nod₂	—	Monogenic recessive	Decreased nodulation in cv. Parvus	101
nod₃	Induced	Monogenic recessive	Supernodulation; nitrate tolerant	146
Chickpea (*Cicer arietinum* L.)				
rn₁	Induced	Monogenic recessive	Nodulation resistance	57, 58
rn₂	Induced	Monogenic recessive	Nonnodulation	57, 58
rn₃	Induced	Monogenic recessive	Nonnodulation	57, 58
rn₄	Induced	Monogenic recessive	Ineffective nodulation	56
rn₅	Induced	Monogenic recessive	Ineffective nodulation	56
Peanut (*Arachis hypogaea* L.)				
—	—	Not monogenic recessive	Nonnodulation	108
—	—	Duplicate recessive	Nonnodulation	201

[a] Not officially recognized as yet.
[b] Dash indicates natural occurrence.

the epidermal site to become an actual infection site (226). While there were no differences in colonization and adsorption of *B. japonicum* to the roots of wild-type and mutant soybeans, root extracts and exudates had similar *nod* gene–inducing activity over the first three days after inoculation (187, 258). Thus, the nonnodulation phenotypes are not the result of alterations in very early preinfection events or signal exchange interactions involving flavonoids. The analysis of a nonnodulating alfalfa mutant supports this conclusion (85), as does recent research with a separately isolated nonnodulation mutant of soybean (51).

Several soybean mutants with the ability to form large numbers of nodules even in the presence of nitrate have been isolated. These nitrate-tolerant symbiotic *(nts)* mutants usually form 3 to 40 times as many nodules as the parent (44, 45), have increased nitrogen fixation ability in the presence of nitrate (124), and are partially tolerant to the inhibitory effects of soil acidity (5). Twelve independent *nts* mutants were characterized using complementation analysis to define a single supernodulation locus (69). The *nts* mutation is recessive and unlinked to the nonnodulation *nod49* and *nod139* loci, and its expression is epistatically suppressed in double mutants homozygous for the *nts* and *nod* alleles (186). Cosegregation of several restriction fragment length polymorphisms (RFLPs) with the supernodulation *nts* locus in F2 families from crosses between nts382 and *Glycine soja* (PI468.397) allowed the location of the *nts* locus on a genetic linkage group, 10 centimorgans (cM) distant from marker pA-36, and less than 1 cM from pA-132 (168). These markers are part of a soybean RFLP linkage map (USDA-ARS/ISU) that now contains over 300 polymorphic markers spanning about 2800 cM at an average distance of 9.3 cM (153). The close molecular mapping of the *nts* locus is the first step towards the isolation of the supernodulation gene by a reverse genetic approach. The isolation of the gene will involve the use of pulse field gel electrophoresis and chromosome jumping, and of a novel technique for dense mapping of amplification fragment length polymorphisms (AFLPs) generated using single arbitrary oligonucleotide primers (28a).

NODULATION CONTROL IN LEGUMES

The adaptive response to environmental stimuli is a common phenomenon in nature and is expressed in both unicellular and multicellular organisms from bacteria and fungi to plants and animals. Basically, the adaptive response involves either a transient effect in cell behavior or a long-term global reorganization of gene expression and cell morphology. Signals from the environment or neighboring cells are used to control a cellular activity that ultimately results in a defined response. For example, a stimulus-response coupling mechanism that involves protein phosphorylation controls nitrogen and phosphorous regulation, chemotaxis, osmoregulation, and virulence in bacteria (253). In multicellular organisms like *Dictyostelium discoideum*, the response involves cyclic adenosine monophosphate (cAMP) as the main effector of cell aggregation (156). During differentiation of eukaryotic cells, growth and cell proliferation are carefully regulated by an evolutionarily conserved mitotic trigger mechanism whose key component appears to be a protein kinase (195, 210) and several control mechanisms that act as check-points along the cell-division cycle (125).

In legume nodulation, the plant can control and optimize the formation of nodules. This adaptive response occurs when fixed nitrogen is readily available in the soil (i.e. nitrate inhibition of nodulation), but is also expressed in its absence (i.e. autoregulation of nodule formation). Exogenous application of nitrate suppresses nodulation and nitrogen fixation through multiple and complex effects during the establishment and function of the symbiosis. Some exhaustive reviews on the subject are available (43, 252). Nitrate has its greatest inhibiting effects on infection events that are completed during the first 18 h after inoculation of soybean (182). Previous studies with alfalfa and clover indicate that nitrate can affect several infection steps, such as bacterial attachment, root hair emergence and deformation, and infection-thread initiation. The contribution of each of these steps to the overall suppressive effect on infection has not been assessed. However, nitrate itself does not appear to be the active effector of the suppressive response because of the isolation of supernodulation mutants tolerant to otherwise inhibitory levels of nitrate.

AUTOREGULATION

The susceptible region of the roots cannot support further nodulation after the establishment of first infections in a phenomenon known as autoregulation or feedback control of nodule formation (222). Ample evidence indicates that nodulation in legumes is controlled by a signal-and-response mechanism that suppresses nodule emergence in younger parts of the root system once a critical number of nodules has formed (20, 22, 30, 36, 41, 44, 130, 162, 181, 212, 222, 230, 261, 262). The formation of nodules is a complex and costly process for the plant, so one should not be surprised to find that nodule number is strictly regulated and that the establishment and function of the symbiosis is controlled by fixed nitrogen in the soil (252). The availability of nitrogen to metabolic pools per se is not the regulatory mechanism. Thus, early nodulation is not repressed by the nitrogen-fixing activity of other nodules, but by the presence of the nodules themselves. Nitrate may slow development of cortical cell division, so that the endogenous autoregulation of nodulation response can suppress further nodule development. Thus a nitrate tolerant symbiosis, expressed in the supernodulating nts mutants, is thought to result from diminished autoregulation.

It was primarily the early work of Nutman that showed that the extent of nodulation is regulated by the host plant (203, 205, 208). Nutman (205) found that surgical excision of functional nodules or root tips in red clover stimulated the formation of new nodules. He interpreted these results as an expression of the ability of established root meristematic foci to inhibit new nodule production. The common observation that nodules are clustered near the crown of the roots of soybean plants grown in the field (3) prompted Bhuvaneswari et al (22) to study nodulation in growth pouches and to suggest that reduced nodulation in younger parts of the primary root might reflect the effects of a host-mediated autoregulatory mechanism. Pierce & Bauer (222) extended these findings by showing that a second inoculation of the primary root, applied 15 h after the first, resulted in the formation of few if any additional nodules in the young regions of the roots. Similar evidence to suggest such a mechanism was subsequently obtained in alfalfa, clover, and cowpea (20, 29, 30, 130, 230). In soybean, feedback regulation was also shown to control nodulation in the basal region of the roots (261, 262). When a large second inoculum was applied 10–17 h after the first inoculum, nodulation in the initially susceptible region of the root was suppressed. Basipetal suppression appears to be another expression of autoregulatory phenomena.

Little is known about the mechanisms by which legumes sense formation of the first nodules, transduce this information in the plant, and exert the suppression of nodule formation. Several basic questions can be sought along each of the steps of the adaptive response. What is the symbiotic event that triggers the response? Does it require the concerted action of the plant and the bacteria? If so, what are the signal molecule(s) or sensory information required by the plant? Once the critical symbiotic event is established in the roots, what kind of signal transduction mechanism transfers the local information of the infection site to other tissues and exerts the general response? How is this response exerted? Finally, how are all responses integrated within the host biochemistry and development? Despite our ignorance, enough evidence is available to give us some clues on how the adaptive response may operate.

What Is the Signal-Transduction Mechanism? an Example of Systemic Root-Shoot Interaction

Some evidence suggests unequivocally that suppression of nodulation occurs systemically. When roots of an intact plant were separated in two different compartments, inoculation of one side of this split-root system strongly inhibited nodule formation on the other. This inhibition occurred in soybean (162, 212), subterranean clover (230), and alfalfa (30, 36). The total number of nodules formed on both sides of the split-root system remained constant despite changes in time and placement of the inoculum (162, 212), suggesting a careful homeostatic control of nodule number throughout the root system. Other studies provided similar results (33, 140, 243).

Additional evidence to suggest the systemic nature of the elicitors of responses comes from the study of supernodulating mutants. Grafting studies (70–72) showed that nine supernodulation and one hypernodulation mutant controlled their primary phenotype (i.e. the formation of nodules) through the action of the shoot. In other words, when mutant shoots were grafted to parental rootstocks, profuse nodulation occurred upon inoculation, whereas parental shoots grafted to mutant roots developed normal nodule numbers. This was not the case for the two nonnodulating soybeans nod49 and nod139, where reciprocal grafting showed that the root genotype controlled the plant phenotype (72). Recent apex-removal experiments by A. Delves (personal communication) suggest that the inhibitory factors from the wild-type plant do not require the presence of the shoot apex. Shoot control of the supernodulation phenotype was even extended subspecifically to *G. soja* (71). These results are consistent with the responses observed in split-root experiments and strongly suggest the involvement of the shoot in the regulatory response. Furthermore, split-root experiments using supernodulating soybean plants showed that nodulation on one side of a split-root system of mutant nts382 was not affected by nodulation on the other side in the presence of low levels of nitrogen (212).

How Is Nodulation Suppressed?

Anatomical and physiological studies in soybean indicate that nodule formation in younger regions of the root is blocked during infection development rather than during infection initiation (37, 41, 184). Serial section analysis showed that nodule suppression did not result from a decreased number of infections, but rather from an increase in the number of infections that became arrested or aborted. While Calvert et al (41) found that blocked infections were observed in all stages of development 10 days after inoculation, our studies using roots harvested 13 days after inoculation indicate that the blockage occurs relatively early during nodule ontogeny in a stage that occurs usually 72 h postinoculation (102). This difference may be an expression of different rates of nodule development in the two soybean cultivars examined. Nevertheless, the maturation of nodule meristems into emergent nodules appears to be the target of the regulatory suppressive response. Recently, basipetal suppression of nodulation was also shown to result from the failure of cell division foci to enlarge rather than from a change in the number of those foci (262). That nodule suppression is not exerted exclusively through the abortion of nodule development but most probably involves the arrest of infections comes from a recent study in which we excised nodules formed on the primary root of wild-type and supernodulating soybeans (37). Surgical removal of mature nodules induced nodules to reappear in those regions from which they were originally excised and that harbored the original inoculum. These nodules did not result from new infection events but from the maturation of arrested infections. This phenomenon also occurred in supernodulating plants, indicating that additional mechanisms different from the autoregulatory response and not part of the supernodulating phenotype control nodulation in soybean. In principle, the putative autoregulatory mechanisms still active in the *nts* mutants are not systemic. We hypothesize that nodules develop a suppressive field around themselves, which is released when mature nodules are removed. In parallel experiments, excision of lateral root tips increased nodule formation on the primary root of wild-type soybean but not on the primary root of a *nts* mutant (37). This result suggests that apical root meristems behave as nodule primordia in that both control nodulation at a distance, probably through systemic elicitors, and confirms previous experiments in red clover (205).

Serial sectioning of inoculated roots of Bragg and the supernodulating mutant nts382 five days after inoculation showed that the number of actual infections and pseudoinfections were more or less similar in the two genotypes (184). However, infection events in nts382 reached more advanced stages of nodule development. These findings suggest that mutant nts382 fails to regulate its nodulation because of a diminished ability to arrest cell divisions in the cortex and the pericycle in a stage of development that occurs 72 h after inoculation. Alternatively, mutant nts382 may fail to slow down the development of cortical nodule primordia (characterized by dividing but not expanding cells), so that a plant developmental response makes the primordia unable to proceed further.

In alfalfa, anatomical analysis of nodule development and nodule excision experiments indicated that feedback suppression of nodule formation occurs through the blockage of nodule initiation and not during nodule development (34). Examination of roots 13 or 21 days after inoculation showed that almost all infections developed into mature nodules and that few if any cortical cell division foci harboring infection threads were arrested early during ontogeny. Furthermore, the excision of both primary or lateral nodules resulted in nodules reappearing only in those regions of the roots susceptible to infection at the time of excision, usually on primary lateral roots. Thus, in alfalfa, suppression occurs through the blockage of an event that occurs most probably during pre-infection. It is really surprising that feedback regulation can be exerted in legumes through completely divergent mechanisms. Whether both mechanisms occur concomitantly but one of them is selectively favored in a particular legume remains to be established.

What Triggers the Systemic Response?

Several bacterial genes can have important effects on the elicitation of systemic feedback responses (30). Mutations in the *nodABC, nodE,* and *nodH* genes of *R. meliloti* all prevented elicitation of autoregulation in alfalfa split root assays. Mutation in the *nodIJ* genes induced a weak suppressive response, only 20% as strong as the response elicited by the parent or other mutant bacteria, suggesting a crucial role of these bacterial genes in some aspect of nodule development involved in the elicitation of the response. Mutations in other genes, like *nodPQ,* did not affect the systemic response but had profound effects on efficiency during nodule development (30). To summarize, only *R. meliloti* isolates capable of initiating nodules (but not those unable to nodulate) were capable of feedback regulation. In two other symbioses, nonnodulating bacterial mutants failed to elicit inhibitory responses. Split-root experiments with subterranean clover showed that nonnodulating (*nodD* and symbiotic plasmid-cured) mutants of *R. leguminosarum* bv. *trifolii* could not suppress nodulation by wild-type bacteria (230). Transposon Tn5 mutants in the *nodABC* genes of *B. japonicum* did not alter the distribution of nodules in soybean primary roots produced by a first inoculum of wild-type bacteria, an indication that basipetal autoregulation requires host responses induced by these genes (262). Collectively, these results suggest the importance of some aspect of nodule development, which could involve cortical cell division activity and/or infection threads.

Additional evidence indicates that feedback control of nodulation is triggered without requiring the presence of infection threads or the invasion of the host cells by the rhizobia. Using split-root assays, *R. meliloti exo* mutants could still induce a rapid and sustained systemic response in spite of producing empty nodules and no infection threads (36). These nodule-like structures were also subject to feedback regulation (36). Moreover, plants harboring spontaneous nodules generated in the absence of *Rhizobium* spp. (265) suppressed further nodulation when these plants were inoculated with wild-type *R. meliloti* (35). These results favor the idea that the formation of a nodule primordium constitutes the only and single event that triggers the autoregulatory response.

In soybean, we used a different approach. Wild-type Bragg and nonnodulating mutants were approach-grafted just below the hypocotyls and their roots kept separate from each other (33). The root systems of the approach-grafted plants were inoculated simultaneously or the inoculation of one of them delayed for 72 h. Using this chimaeric split-root system, we showed that while mutant nod49 induced the systemic suppression of nodulation in Bragg, nod139 could not do so. Again, these results suggest that subepidermal cell divisions of early ontogeny trigger the autoregulatory mechanism that ultimately results in the suppression of further symbiotic cell divisions in ontogenetically younger root tissue.

Using this same experimental set-up, we were able to show that inoculation of approach-grafted nod139 mutants induced nodules to appear 4 to 6 days earlier in Bragg (33). This evidence suggests that during preinfection *B. japonicum* cells are also able to stimulate nodule formation. This stimulatory mechanism appears to be systemic, fast, and should exert its effects at the level of nodule initiation. In preliminary experiments, we found that a *B. japonicum* mutant harboring a *nodC*::Tn5 insertion could generate a transient and systemic suppressive response in Bragg when inoculated to approach-grafted Bragg and nod49 plants. This same phenomenon was observed in alfalfa split-root assays with *R. meliloti nodABC* mutants (G. Caetano-Anollés & W. D. Bauer, unpublished results). The possibility that the bacterial common *nod* genes could be involved in a stimulatory response early during pre-infection is tempting and is further suggested by the ability of inoculated nod139 to speed up the appearance of nodules in approach-grafted plants (33).

That spontaneous nodules formed in the absence of *Rhizobium* spp. in alfalfa, or cortical cell division primordia with no infection threads in soybean, trigger the systemic response does not rule out the involvement of some important component provided by the bacteria. A careful study using nanoliter spot inoculations on very localized areas of the root (not more than 500 μ^2) suggests the existence of a signal threshold determined by the concentration of the bacteria in the inoculum (G. Caetano-Anollés & W. D. Bauer, in preparation). While nodulation was substantial with inoculum levels of 10–100 bacteria/spot and linearly proportional to the inoculum concentration in this range, only if more than 500 bacteria were spot inoculated in the infectible region of the roots was it possible to observe suppression of nodule emergence in younger regions of the roots when a second unrestricted inoculum was supplied 24 h later. Apparently, to trigger the response, not only must a particular number of cortical cell division centers be generated, but a particular bacterial concentration must be sustained.

A Working Hypothesis

The research on autoregulation is of interest because it demonstrates a progression of thought and insight that goes from the analysis of the specific to the general. In the late 1970s our interest focused on the inhibition of nodulation and nitrogen fixation by nitrate. Here was a simple molecule, whose structure and metabolism in the plant were known, yet it had significant, but not understood, effects on the symbiotic development in legumes. The isolation of *nts* mutants that nodulate in the presence of nitrate led to the realization that the *nts* condition was coupled with supernodulation; that is, plants could have plenty of nodules in the absence of nitrate. Ironically, *nts* mutants would have been isolated even if we had never known about the nodulation-inhibitory effect of nitrate.

The work of Bauer and coworkers made quickly apparent the fact that soybean plants autoregulate nodulation, so that the *nts* mutants now were viewed as autoregulatory. While autoregulation functions in part through the shoot of the plant (72, 116), at the cellular level cell divisions in the preemergent nodule were clearly arrested to control overall nodule formation (see 41, 184). Our recent research extended the understanding of that process. We now know that the autoregulation process is activated by a developmental stage involving the early nodule-related cell divisions of the cortex (33). Furthermore, the availability of the autoregulation mutants allowed us to detect another nodulation-controlling process working separately from the systemic response altered in *nts* mutants.

The analysis of the nitrate inhibition phenomenon in soybean has thus matured beyond the specific questions and now relates to broader plant phenomena such as intertissue communication and the systemic regulation of cell division clusters. Understanding such processes can give important insight into plant growth in general.

Basing it on the evidence accumulated so far, we propose the following general model for autoregulation, derived from the one previously proposed for soybean (33). Adequate signaling between the microsymbiont and the epidermal cells triggers a response in the plant that leads to cortical cell division that in turn results in the systemic release of an inducer of responses in the shoot. We term this first systemic messenger the *root synthesized inducer* or Q. A complex set of changes, probably a cascade of events associated with a metabolic pathway now result in the production of a second systemic messenger, SDI, a *shoot-derived inhibitor* that will finally arrest development of further infections or block nodule initiation. Evidence suggests that in soybean the proposed systemic shoot-derived inhibitor, and not elicitor Q, is nodulation-rate limiting and closely regulated and that its suppressive activity depends on the volume of the plant in which it is diluted (33, 211). Moreover, cortical cell divisions are able to trigger an apparently normal suppression of nodule formation even if the number of cell divisions is considerably reduced as in mutant nod49 (33). Figure 2 shows variations of the general model to accommodate the different responses observed in soybean and alfalfa.

NODULATION IN THE ABSENCE OF *RHIZOBIUM* SPP.

Only recently was the existence of genuine nodules formed in the absence of *Rhizobium* spp. recognized (265). Cytological studies showed that spontaneous nodules formed in alfalfa were organized structures rather than abnormal lateral root outgrowths, had no inter- or intracellular bacteria, but retained the histological characteristics of a normal indeterminate nodule (35, 265). Presumably they occur in many legumes, but were discarded over the years as accidentally contaminated plants. Nodulation in the absence of *Rhizobium* spp. (Nar) occurs in the same region of the primary root that is normally nodulated, but the appearance of spontaneous nodules is delayed (35). This delay probably results in suppression of the spontaneous nodules in inoculated roots by *Rhizobium*-induced nodules. Nitrate inhibits the formation of spontaneous nodules (35, 265), and spontaneous nodules elicit and are themselves subject to autoregulation (35). The ontogeny of spontaneous nodules was

Soybean:

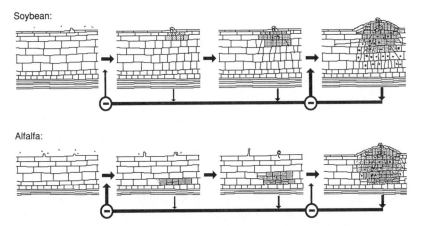

Alfalfa:

Figure 2   A general model for the regulation of nodule formation in legumes. *Rhizobium* or *Bradyrhizobium* cells induce cell division in the root cortex. Legumes that develop spherical determinate nodules, like soybean, induce the earliest cell divisions in the hypodermal layer, while legumes with cylindrical or indeterminate nodules, like alfalfa or clover, do so in the inner cortex. Cell division clusters produce a translocatable signal, which acts systemically either directly or via the shoot to suppress cortical cell division activity. Suppression in legumes such as soybean occurs mainly through the arrest of developing infections while in legumes such as alfalfa occurs mainly during the onset of cell division, early during pre-infection. Whether other legumes different from soybean require the shoot to exert the autoregulatory response is un-known, and thus the model may or may not involve shoot-derived inhibitors.

identical to that of *Rhizobium*-induced nodules, starting with cell divisions in the inner cortex and not the pericycle (150). Spontaneous nodules contained different cell types just like *Rhizobium*-induced nodules, some of which were enlarged with numerous starch deposits (149). The preferential deposition of starch in some nodule cells suggests that the ancestral nodule may have functioned as a carbon-storage organ.

All progeny from self-fertilized Nar$^+$ plants formed spontaneous nodules (G. Caetano-Anollés, unpublished data). The number of nodules and their location within the root system remained the same, possibly because of strong genetic control over the Nar phenotype. The mode of inheritance indicated that a single dominant genetic element could control Nar in the tetraploid alfalfa. Most features of a nodule are not under the inductive control of *Rhizobium* spp., but represent an internal developmental program, whose expression is presumably optimized in some homozygous recessive plant genotypes by *Rhizobium* spp. Spontaneous nodulation has not been reported in other legumes, although it is likely to occur in white clover (53). The question whether the heterogeneous nature of the alfalfa population favors the development of spontaneous nodules needs to be addressed. Will other heterozygous legumes like clover or primitive *Glycine* cultivars produce nodules in the absence of *Rhizobium* or *Bradyrhizobium* spp?

PERSPECTIVES

The recent identification of a signal molecule secreted by the microsymbiont capable of inducing the early host responses of root hair curling and cortical cell division now provides a way to examine the underlying mechanisms that control nodulation in legumes. The oligosaccharide signal must control plant morphogenesis either directly or indirectly through more or less complicated transducing mechanisms. The plant should control the activity of these signal molecules at different levels, for example, by regulating the availability of the putative receptor, by altering the release of secondary signals, or through plant factors that modulate the overall response. In this context, autoregulation may represent the way the plant curbs the activity of the bacterial signal molecules, and nodulation in the absence of *Rhizobium* spp. may be just the endogenous expression of those same control mechanisms in selected plants. Our developing knowledge on the physiology and genetics of nodulation will certainly aid in our understanding of how bacterial and plant signals intermingle to control morphogenesis.

Literature Cited

1. Aguilar, J. M. M., Ashby, A. M., Richards, A. J. M., Loake, G. J., Watson, M. D., Shaw, C. H. 1988. Chemotaxis of *Rhizobium leguminosarum* biovar *phaseoli* towards flavonoid inducers of the symbiotic nodulation genes. *J. Gen. Microbiol.* 134:2741–46
2. Akiyama, T., Ishida, J., Nakagawa, S., Ogawara, H., Watanabe, S., et al. 1987. Genistein, a specific inhibitor of tyrosine-specific protein kinases. *J. Biol. Chem.* 262:5592–95
3. Allen, O. N., Allen, E. K. 1981. *The Leguminosae, a Source Book of Characteristics, Uses and Nodulation.* Madison, WI: Univ. Wisconsin Press
4. Al-Mallah, M. K., Davey, M. R., Cocking, E. C. 1989. Formation of nodular structures on rice seedlings by rhizobia. *J. Exp. Bot.* 40:473–78
5. Alva, A. K., Edwards, D. G., Carroll, B. J., Asher, C. J., Gresshoff, P. M. 1988. Effects of soil infertility factors on

nodulation and growth of soybean mutants with increased nodulation capacity. *Agron. J.* 80:836–41
6. Ames, P., Bergman, K. 1981. Competitive advantage provided by bacterial motility in the formation of nodules by *Rhizobium meliloti*. *J. Bacteriol.* 148:728–29
7. Appelbaum, E. R., Thompson, D. V., Idler, K., Chartrain, N. 1988. *Rhizobium japonicum* USDA 191 has two *nodD* genes that differ in primary structure and function. *J. Bacteriol.* 170:12–20
8. Armitage, J. P., Gallagher, A., Johnston, A. W. B. 1988. Comparison of the chemotactic behavior of *Rhizobium leguminosarum* with and without the nodulation plasmid. *Mol. Microbiol.* 1:743–48
9. Bachem, C. W. B., Banfalvi, Z., Kondorosi, E., Schell, J., Kondorosi, A. 1986. Identification of host range determinants in the *Rhizobium* species

MPIK-3030. *Mol. Gen. Genet.* 203:42–48

10. Baker, M. E. 1989. Human placental 17β-hydroxysteroid dehydrogenase is homologous to NodG protein of *Rhizobium meliloti. Mol. Endocrinol.* 3:881–84

11. Banfalvi, Z., Kondorosi, A. 1989. Production of root hair deformation factors by *Rhizobium meliloti* nodulation genes in *Escherichia coli: hsnD (nodH)* is involved in the plant host-specific modification of the NodABC factor. *Plant Mol. Biol.* 13:1–12

12. Banfalvi, Z., Niewkoop, A., Schell, M., Besl, L., Stacey, G. 1988. Regulation of *nod* gene expression in *Bradyrhizobium japonicum. Mol. Gen. Genet.* 214:420–24

13. Barnet, M. J., Long, S. R. 1990. DNA sequence and translational product of a new nodulation-regulatory locus: SyrM has sequence similarity to NodD proteins. *J. Bacteriol.* 172:3695–3700

14. Bassam, B. J., Djordjevic, M. A., Redmond, J. W., Batley, M., Rolfe, B. G. 1988. Identification of a *nodD*-dependent locus in the *Rhizobium* strain NGR234 activated by phenolic factors secreted by soybeans and other legumes. *Mol. Plant-Microbe Interact.* 1:161–68

15. Bassam, B. J., Rolfe, B. G., Djordjevic, M. A. 1986. *Macroptilium atropurpureum* (siratro) host specificity determinants are linked to a *nodD*-like gene in the broad host range *Rhizobium* strain NGR234. *Mol. Gen. Genet.* 203:49–57

16. Bauer, W. D. 1981. Infection of legumes by rhizobia. *Annu. Rev. Plant Physiol.* 32:407–49

17. Bauer, W. D., Bhuvaneswari, T. V., Calvert, H. E., Law, I. J., Malik, N. S. A., Vesper, S. J. 1985. Recognition and infection by slow-growing rhizobia. See Ref. 90a, pp. 247–53

18. Bergersen, F. J., Nutman, P. S. 1957. Symbiotic effectiveness in nodulated red clover. IV. The influence of the host factors i_l and *ie* upon nodule structure and cytology. *Heredity* 11:175–84

19. Bergman, K., Gulash-Hofee, M., Hoverstadt, R. E., Larosiliere, R. C., Ronco, P. G., Su, L. 1988. Physiology of behavioral mutants of *Rhizobium meliloti:* evidence for a dual chemotaxis pathway. *J. Bacteriol.* 170:3249–54

20. Bhuvaneswari, T. V., Bhagwat, A. A., Bauer, W. D. 1981. Transient susceptibility of root cells in four common legumes to nodulation by rhizobia. *Plant Physiol.* 68:1144–49

21. Bhuvaneswari, T. V., Solheim, B. 1985. Root hair deformations in the white clover/*Rhizobium trifolii* symbiosis. *Physiol. Plant.* 63:25–34

22. Bhuvaneswari, T. V., Turgeon, B. G., Bauer, W. D. 1980. Early stages in the infection of soybean (*Glycine max* L. Merr.) by *Rhizobium japonicum.* I. Localization of infectible root cells. *Plant Physiol.* 66:1027–31

23. Bibb, M. J., Biro, S., Motamedi, H., Collins, J. F., Hutchinson, C. R. 1989. Analysis of the nucleotide sequence of the *Streptomyces glaucescens tcml* genes provides key information about the enzymology of polyketide antibiotic biosynthesis. *EMBO J.* 8:2727–36

24. Bogusz, D., Llewellyn, D. J., Craig, S., Dennis, E. S., Appleby, C. A., Peacock, W. J. 1990. Nonlegume hemoglobin genes retain organ-specific expression in heterologous transgenic plants. *Plant Cell* 2:633–41

25. Bohlool, B. B., Schmidt, E. L. 1976. Immunofluorescent polar tips of *Rhizobium japonicum:* possible site of attachment of lectin binding. *J. Bacteriol.* 125:1188–94

26. Borthakur, D., Barber, C. E., Lamb, J. W., Daniels, M. J., Downie, J. A., Johnston, A. W. B. 1986. A mutation that blocks exopolysaccharide synthesis prevents nodulation of peas by *Rhizobium leguminosarum* but not of beans by *R. phaseoli* and is corrected by cloned DNA from *Rhizobium* or the phytopathogen *Xanthomonas. Mol. Gen. Genet.* 203:320–23

27. Burn, J., Rossen, L., Johnston, A. W. B. 1987. Four classes of mutations in the *nodD* gene of *Rhizobium leguminosarum* biovar *viciae* that affects its ability to autoregulate and/or activate other *nod* genes in the presence of flavonoid inducers. *Genes Dev.* 1:456–64

28. Buzzell, R. I., Buttery, B. R., Ablett, G. 1990. Supernodulation mutants in Elgin 87 soybean. See Ref. 119, p. 726

28a. Caetano-Anollés, G., Bassam, B. J., Gresshoff, P. M. 1991. DNA amplification fingerprinting using very short arbitrary oligonucleotide primers. *Bio/Technology.* 9:553–57

29. Caetano-Anollés, G., Bauer, W. D. 1988. Enhanced nodule initiation on alfalfa by wild-type *Rhizobium meliloti* co-inoculated with *nod* gene mutants and other bacteria. *Planta* 174:385–95

30. Caetano-Anollés, G., Bauer, W. D.

1988. Feedback regulation of nodule formation in alfalfa. *Planta* 175:546–57

31. Caetano-Anollés, G., Bauer, W. D. 1990. Host-specificity mutants of *Rhizobium meliloti* have additive effects in situ on initiation of alfalfa nodules. *Planta* 181:109–16

32. Caetano-Anollés, G., Christ-Estes, D. K., Bauer, W. D. 1988. Chemotaxis of *Rhizobium meliloti* to the plant flavone luteolin requires functional nodulation genes. *J. Bacteriol.* 170:3164–69

33. Caetano-Anollés, G., Gresshoff, P. M. 1990. Early induction of feedback regulatory responses governing nodulation in soybean. *Plant Sci.* 71:69–91

34. Caetano-Anollés, G., Gresshoff, P. M. 1991. Alfalfa controls nodulation during the onset of *Rhizobium*-induced cortical cell division. *Plant Physiol.* 95:366–73

35. Caetano-Anollés, G., Joshi, P. A., Gresshoff, P. M. 1991. Spontaneous nodules induce feedback suppression of nodulation in alfalfa. *Planta* 183:77–82

36. Caetano-Anollés, G., Lagares, A., Bauer, W. D. 1990. *Rhizobium meliloti exopolysaccharide* mutants elicit feedback regulation of nodule formation in alfalfa. *Plant Physiol.* 92:368–74

37. Caetano-Anollés, G., Paparozzi, E. T., Gresshoff, P. M. 1991. Mature nodules and root tips control nodulation in soybean. *J. Plant Physiol.* 137:389–96

38. Caetano-Anollés, G., Wall, L. G., DeMicheli, A. T., Macchi, E. M., Bauer, W. D., Favelukes, G. 1988. Role of motility and chemotaxis in efficiency of nodulation by *Rhizobium meliloti*. *Plant Physiol.* 86:1228–35

39. Caldwell, B. E. 1966. Inheritance of a strain-specific ineffective nodulation in soybean. *Crop Sci.* 6:427–28

40. Caldwell, B. E., Hinson, K., Johnson, H. W. 1966. A strain-specific ineffective nodulation reaction in the soybean *Glycine max* L. Merrill. *Crop Sci.* 6:495–96

41. Calvert, H. E., Pence, M. K., Pierce, M., Malik, N. S. A., Bauer, W. D. 1984. Anatomical analysis of the development and distribution of *Rhizobium* infections in soybean roots. *Can. J. Bot.* 62:2375–84

42. Carroll, B. J., Gresshoff, P. M., Delves, A. C. 1988. Inheritance of supernodulation in soybean and estimation of the genetically effective cell number. *Theor. Appl. Genet.* 76:54–58

43. Carroll, B. J., Mathews, A. 1990. Nitrate inhibition of nodulation in legumes. See Ref. 115a, pp. 159–80

44. Carroll, B. J., McNeil, D. L., Gress-

hoff, P. M. 1985. Isolation and properties of soybean *(Glycine max)* mutants that nodulate in the presence of high nitrate concentrations. *Proc. Natl. Acad. Sci. USA* 82:4164–66

45. Carroll, B. J., McNeil, D. L., Gresshoff, P. M. 1985. A supernodulation and nitrate tolerant symbiotic *(nts)* soybean mutant. *Plant Physiol.* 78:34–40

46. Carroll, B. J., McNeil, D. L., Gresshoff, P. M. 1986. Mutagenesis of soybean *(Glycine max* (L.) Merr.) and the isolation of non-nodulating mutants. *Plant Sci.* 47:109–14

47. Cervantes, E., Sharma, S. B., Maillet, F., Vasse, J., Truchet, G., Rosenberg, C. 1989. The *Rhizobium meliloti* host range *nodQ* gene encodes a protein which shares homology with translation, elongation and initiation factors. *Mol. Microbiol.* 3:745–55

48. Chakravorty, A. K., Zurkowski, W., Shine, J., Rolfe, B. G. 1982. Symbiotic nitrogen fixation: molecular cloning of *Rhizobium* genes involved in exopolysaccharide synthesis and effective nodulation. *J. Mol. Appl. Genet.* 1:585–96

49. Chen, H., Batley, M., Redmond, J., Rolfe, B. G. 1985. Alteration of the effective nodulation properties of a fast-growing broad host range *Rhizobium* due to changes in exopolysaccharide synthesis. *J. Plant Physiol.* 120:331–49

50. Chen, H., Gray, J. X., Nayudu, M. A., Djordjevic, M. A., Batley, M., et al. 1988. Five genetic loci involved in the synthesis of acidic exopolysaccharide are closely linked in the genome of *Rhizobium* sp. strain NGR234. *Mol. Gen. Genet.* 212:310–16

51. Cho, M. J., Harper, J. E. 1991. Effect of inoculation and nitrogen on isoflavonoid concentration in wild-type and nodulation mutant soybean roots. *Plant Physiol.* 95:435–42

52. Cocking, E. C., Al-Mallah, M. K., Benson, E., Davey, M. R. 1990. Nodulation of non-legumes by rhizobia. See Ref. 212a, pp. 813–23

53. Collins, J. M. 1983. *Nodule initiation in white clover.* Botany Honors thesis. Canberra: Australian Natl. Univ.

54. Cullimore, J. V., Gebhardt, C., Saarelainen, R., Miflin, B. J., Idler, K. B., Barker, R. F. 1984. Glutamine synthetase of *Phaseolus vulgaris* L.: organ specific expression of a multigene family. *J. Mol. Appl. Gen.* 2:589–99

55. Davis, E. O., Evans, I. J., Johnston, A. W. B. 1988. Identification of *nodX*, a gene that allows *Rhizobium leguminosarum* bv. *viciae* strain TOM to nodulate

Afghanistan peas. *Mol. Gen. Genet.* 212:531–35
56. Davis, T. M. 1985. Host genes affecting root nodule formation and function in chickpea (*Cicer arietinum* L.). See Ref. 90a, p. 40
57. Davis, T. M., Foster, K. W., Phillips, D. A. 1985. Non-nodulation mutants of chickpea. *Crop Sci.* 25:345–48
58. Davis, T. M., Foster, K. W., Phillips, D. A. 1986. Inheritance and expression of three genes controlling root nodule formation in chickpea. *Crop Sci.* 26: 719–23
59. Day, D. A., Carroll, B. J., Delves, A. C., Gresshoff, P. M. 1989. The relationship between autoregulation and nitrate inhibition of nodulation in soybeans. *Physiol. Plant.* 75:37–42
60. Day, D. A., Lambers, H., Bateman, J., Carroll, B. J., Gresshoff, P. M. 1986. Growth comparisons of a supernodulating soybean mutant and its wildtype parent. *Physiol. Plant.* 68:375–82
61. Day, D. A., Price, G. D., Schuller, K. A., Gresshoff, P. M. 1987. Nodule physiology of a supernodulating soybean (*Glycine max*) mutant. *Aust. J. Plant Physiol.* 14:527–38
62. Dazzo, F. B., Truchet, G. 1983. Interaction of lectins and their saccharide receptors in the *Rhizobium*-legume symbiosis. *J. Membr. Biol.* 73:1–16
63. Debellé, F., Rosenberg, C., Vasse, J., Maillet, F., Martinez, E., et al. 1986. Assignment of symbiotic developmental phenotypes to common and specific nodulation *(nod)* genetic loci of *Rhizobium meliloti*. *J. Bacteriol.* 168:1075–86
64. Debellé, F., Sharma, S. B. 1986. Nucleotide sequence of *Rhizobium meliloti* RCR2011 genes involved in host-specificity of nodulation. *Nucleic Acids Res.* 14:7453–72
65. de Bruijn, F. J., Felix, G., Grunenberg, B., Hoffman, H. J., Metz, B., et al. 1989. Regulation of plant genes specifically induced in nitrogen fixing nodules: role of *cis*-acting elements and *trans*-acting factors in leghemoglobin gene expression. *Plant Mol. Biol.* 13:319–25
66. de Bruijn, F. J., Szabados, L., Schell, J. 1990. Chimeric genes and transgenic plants to study the regulation of genes involved in symbiotic plant-microbe interactions. *Dev. Genet.* 11:182–96
67. Delauney, A. J., Tabaeizadeh, Z., Verma, D. P. S. 1988. A stable bifunctional antisense transcript inhibiting gene expression in transgenic plants. *Proc. Natl. Acad. Sci. USA* 85:4300–4

68. Delauney, A. J., Verma, D. P. S. 1988. Cloned nodulin genes for symbiotic nitrogen fixation. *Plant Mol. Biol. Rep.* 6:279–85
69. Delves, A. C., Carroll, B. J., Gresshoff, P. M. 1988. Genetic analysis and complementation studies on a number of mutant supernodulating soybeans. *J. Genet.* 67:1–8
70. Delves, A. C., Higgins, A., Gresshoff, P. M. 1987. Shoot control of nodulation in a number of mutant soybeans (*Glycine max* L. Merr.). *Aust. J. Plant. Physiol.* 14:689–94
71. Delves, A. C., Higgins, A., Gresshoff, P. M. 1987. Supernodulation in interspecific grafts between *Glycine max* (soybean) and *Glycine soja*. *J. Plant Physiol.* 128:473–78
72. Delves, A. C., Mathews, A., Day, D. A., Carter, A. S., Gresshoff, P. M. 1986. Regulation of the soybean-*Rhizobium* nodule symbiosis by shoot and root factors. *Plant Physiol.* 82:588–90
73. de Maagd, R. A., Wijfjes, A. H. M., Spaink, H. P., Ruiz-Sainz, J. E., Wijffelman, C. A., et al. 1989. *nodO*, a new *nod* gene of the *Rhizobium leguminosarum* biovar *viciae* Sym plasmid pRL1JI, encodes a secreted protein. *J. Bacteriol.* 171:6764–70
74. Deshmane, N., Stacey, G. 1989. Identification of *Bradyrhizobium nod* genes involved in host-specific nodulation. *J. Bacteriol.* 171:3324–30
75. Devine, T. E. 1984. Inheritance of soybean nodulation response with a fast-growing strain of *Rhizobium*. *J. Heredity* 75:359–61
76. Díaz, C. L., Melchers, L. S., Hooykaas, P. J. J., Lugtenberg, B. J. J., Kijne, J. W. 1989. Root lectin as a determinant of host-plant specificity in the *Rhizobium*-legume symbiosis. *Nature* 338:579–81
77. Dickstein, R., Bisseling, T., Reinhold, V. N., Ausubel, F. M. 1988. Expression of nodule-specific genes in alfalfa root nodules blocked at an early stage of development. *Genes Dev.* 2:677
78. Djordjevic, M. A., Innes, R. W., Wijffelman, C. A., Schofield, P. R., Rolfe, B. G. 1986. Nodulation of specific legumes is controlled by several distinct loci in *Rhizobium trifolii*. *Plant Mol. Biol.* 6:389–402
79. Djordjevic, M. A., Redmond, J. W., Batley, M., Rolfe, B. G. 1987. Clovers secrete specific phenolic compounds which stimulate or repress *nod* gene expression in *Rhizobium trifolii*. *EMBO J.* 6:1173–79
80. Djordjevic, M. A., Schofield, P. R.,

Rolfe, B. G. 1985. Tn5 mutagenesis of *Rhizobium trifolii* host-specific nodulation genes result in mutants with altered host-range ability. *Mol. Gen. Genet.* 200:463–71

81. Djordjevic, S. P., Chen, H., Batley, M., Redmond, J. W., Rolfe, B. G. 1987. Nitrogen fixation ability of exopolysaccharide synthesis mutants of *Rhizobium* sp. strain NGR234 and *Rhizobium trifolii* is restored by the addition of homologous exopolysaccharides. *J. Bacteriol.* 169:53–60

82. Downie, J. A. 1989. The *nodL* gene from *Rhizobium leguminosarum* is homologous to the acetyltransferases encoded by *lacA* and *cysE*. *Mol. Microbiol.* 3:1649–51

83. Downie, J. A., Knight, C. D., Johnston, A. W. B., Rossen, L. 1985. Identification of genes and gene products involved in the nodulation of peas by *Rhizobium leguminosarum*. *Mol. Gen. Genet.* 198: 255–62

84. Dudley, M. E., Jacobs, T. W., Long, S. R. 1987. Microscopic studies of cell divisions induced in alfalfa roots by *Rhizobium meliloti*. *Planta* 171:289–301

85. Dudley, M., Long, S. R. 1989. A nonnodulating alfalfa mutant displays neither root hair curling nor early cell division in response to *Rhizobium meliloti*. *Plant Cell* 1:65–72

86. Dunn, K., Dickstein, R., Feinbaum, R., Burnett, B. K., Peterman, T. K., et al. 1988. Developmental regulation of nodule-specific genes in alfalfa root nodules. *Mol. Plant-Microbe Interact.* 1:66–74

87. Dylan, T., Ielpi, L., Stanfield, S., Kashyap, L., Douglas, C., et al. 1986. *Rhizobium meliloti* genes required for nodule development and related to chromosomal virulence genes in *Agrobacterium tumefaciens*. *Proc. Natl. Acad. Sci. USA* 83:4403–7

88. Economou, A., Hamilton, W. D. O., Johnston, A. W. B., Downie, J. A. 1990. The *Rhizobium* nodulation gene *nodO* encodes a Ca^{2+}-binding protein that is exported without N-terminal cleavage and is homologous to haemolysin and related proteins. *EMBO J.* 9:349–54

89. Egelhoff, T. T., Fisher, R. F., Jacobs, T. W., Mulligan, J. T. Long, S. R. 1985. Nucleotide sequence of *Rhizobium meliloti* 1021 nodulation genes: *nodD* is read divergently from *nodABC-DNA* 4:241–48

90. Egelhoff, T. T., Long, S. R. 1985. *Rhizobium meliloti* nodulation genes: identification of *nodDABC* gene prod-

ucts, purification of nodA protein, and expression of *nodA* in *Rhizobium meliloti*. *J. Bacteriol.* 164:591–99

90a. Evans, H. J., Bottomley, P. J., Newton, W. E., eds. 1985. *Nitrogen Fixation Research Progress*. Dordrecht: Nijhoff

91. Evans, I. J., Downie, J. A. 1986. The *nodI* gene product of *Rhizobium leguminosarum* is closely related to the ATP-binding bacterial transport proteins: nucleotide sequence analysis of the *nodI* and *nodJ* genes. *Gene* 43:95–102

92. Farmer, E. E., Ryan, C. A. 1990. Interplant communication: airborne methyl jasmonate induces synthesis of proteinase inhibitors in plant leaves. *Proc. Natl. Acad. Sci. USA* 87:7713–16

93. Faucher, C., Camut, S., Dénarié, J., Truchet, G. 1989. The *nodH* and *nodQ* host range genes of *Rhizobium meliloti* behave as avirulence genes in *R. leguminosarum* bv. *viciae* and determine changes in the production of plant-specific extracellular signals. *Mol. Plant-Microbe Interact.* 2:291–300

94. Faucher, C., Maillet, F., Vasse, J., Rosenberg, C., vanBrussel, A. N., et al. 1988. *Rhizobium meliloti* host range *nodH* gene determines production of an alfalfa-specific extracellular signal. *J. Bacteriol.* 170:5489–99

95. Finan, T. M., Hirsch, A. M., Leigh, J. A., Johansen, E., Kuldau, G. A., et al. 1985. Symbiotic mutants of *Rhizobium meliloti* that uncouple plant from bacterial differentiation. *Cell* 40:869–877

96. Finan, T. M., Kunkel, B., DeVos, G. F., Signer, E. R. 1986. Second symbiotic megaplasmid in *Rhizobium meliloti* carrying exopolysaccharide and thiamine synthesis genes. *J. Bacteriol.* 167:66–72

97. Firmin, J. L., Wilson, K. E., Rossen, L., Johnston, A. W. B. 1986. Flavonoid activation of nodulation genes in *Rhizobium* reversed by other compounds present in plants. *Nature* 324:90–92

98. Fisher, R. F., Tu, J. K., Long, S. R. 1985. Conserved nodulation genes in *Rhizobium meliloti* and *Rhizobium trifolii*. *Appl. Environ. Microbiol.* 49:1432–35

99. Franssen, H. J., Nap, J. P., Gloudemans, T., Stiekema, W., VanDam, H., et al. 1987. Characterization of cDNA for nodulin-75 of soybean: gene product involved in early stages of root nodule development. *Proc. Natl. Acad. Sci. USA* 84:4495–99

100. Gasser, C. S., Fraley, R. T. 1989. Genetically engineering plants for crop improvement. *Science* 244:1293–99

101. Gelin, O., Blixt, S. 1964. Root nodulation in peas. *Agric Hort. Genet.* 22:149–59

102. Gerahty, N., Caetano-Anollés, G., Joshi, P. A., Gresshoff, P. M. 1990. Distribution of *Bradyrhizobium*-induced cell divisions in soybean. See Ref. 119, p. 737

103. Glazebrook, J., Walker, G. C. 1989. A novel exopolysaccharide can function in place of the calcofluor-binding exopolysaccharide in nodulation of alfalfa by *Rhizobium meliloti*. *Cell* 56:661–72

104. Gloudemans, T., Bisseling, T. 1989. Plant gene expression in early stages of *Rhizobium*-legume symbiosis. *Plant Sci.* 65:1–14

105. Gloudemans, T., De Vries, S. C., Bussink, H. J., Malik, N. S. A., Franssen, H. J., et al. 1987. Nodulin gene expression during soybean (*Glycine max*) nodule development. *Plant Mol. Biol.* 8:395–403

106. Goldberg, R. B. 1988. Plants: novel developmental processes. *Science* 240:1460–67

107. Goodchild, D. J., Bergerson, F. J. 1966. Electron microscopy of the infection and subsequent development of soybean nodule cells. *J. Bacteriol.* 92:204–13

108. Gorbet, D. W., Burton, J. C. 1979. A non-nodulating peanut. *Crop Sci.* 19:727–28

109. Göttfert, M., Grob, P., Hennecke, H. 1990. Proposed regulatory pathway encoded by the *nodV* and *nodW* genes, determinants of host-specificity in *Bradyrhizobium japonicum*. *Proc. Natl. Acad. Sci. USA* 87:2680–84

110. Göttfert, M., Hitz, S., Hennecke, H. 1990. Identification of *nodS* and *nodU*, two inducible genes inserted between the *Bradyrhizobium japonicum nodYABC* and *nodIJ* genes. *Mol. Plant-Microbe Interact.* 3:308–16

111. Göttfert, M., Horvath, B., Kondorosi, E., Putnoky, P., Rodriguez-Quiñones, F., Kondorosi, A. 1986. At least two *nodD* genes are necessary for efficient nodulation of alfalfa by *Rhizobium meliloti*. *J. Mol. Biol.* 191:411–20

112. Göttfert, M., Lamb, J. W., Gasser, R., Semeza, J., Hennecke, H. 1989. Mutational analysis of the *Bradyrhizobium japonicum* common *nod* genes and further *nod* box-linked genomic DNA regions. *Mol. Gen. Genet.* 215:407–15

113. Göttfert, M., Weber, J., Hennecke, H. 1988. Induction of a *nodA-lacZ* fusion in *Bradyrhizobium japonicum* by an isoflavone. *J. Plant Physiol.* 132:394–97

114. Govers, F., Moerman, M., Downie, J. A., Hooykas, P., Franssen, H. J., et al. 1986. *Rhizobium nod* genes are involved in inducing an early nodulin gene. *Nature* 323:564–66

115. Gremaud, M. F., Harper, J. E. 1989. Selection and initial characterization of partially nitrate tolerant nodulation mutants of soybean. *Plant Physiol.* 89:169–73

115a. Gresshoff, P. M., ed. 1990. *Molecular Biology of Symbiotic Nitrogen Fixation.* Boca Raton, FL: CRC

116. Gresshoff, P. M., Delves, A. C. 1986. Plant genetic approaches to symbiotic nodulation and nitrogen fixation in legumes. In *Plant Gene Research 3*, ed. A. D. Blonstein, P. J. King, pp. 159–206. Vienna: Springer-Verlag

117. Gresshoff, P. M., Krotzky, A., Mathews, A., Day, D. A., Schuller, K. A., et al. 1988. Suppression of the symbiotic supernodulation symptoms of soybean. *J. Plant Physiol.* 132:417–23

118. Gresshoff, P. M., Mathews, A., Krotzky, A., Olsson, J. E., Carroll, B. J., et al. 1988. Supernodulation and non-nodulation mutants of soybean. See Ref. 212a, pp. 364–69

119. Gresshoff, P. M., Roth, E., Stacey, G., Newton, W. E., eds. 1990. *Nitrogen Fixation: Achievements and Objectives.* New York: Chapman and Hall

120. Gulash, M., Ames, P., LaRosiliere, R. C., Bergman, K. 1984. Rhizobia are attracted to localized sites in legume roots. *Appl. Environ. Microbiol.* 48:149–52

121. Györgypal, Z., Iyer, N., Kondorosi, A. 1988. Three regulatory *nodD* alleles of diverged flavonoid-specificity are involved in host-dependent nodulation by *Rhizobium meliloti*. *Mol. Gen. Genet.* 212:85–92

122. Hahn, M., Hennecke, H. 1988. Cloning and mapping of a novel nodulation region from *Bradyrhizobium japonicum* by genetic complementation of a deletion mutant. *Appl. Environ. Microbiol.* 54:55–61

123. Halverson, L. J., Stacey, G. 1986. Signal exchange in plant-microbe interactions. *Microbiol. Rev.* 50:193–225

124. Hansen, A. P., Peoples, M. B., Gresshoff, P. M., Atkins, C. A., Pate, J. S., Carroll, B. J. 1989. Symbiotic performance of supernodulating soybean (*Glycine max* (L.) Merr.) mutants during development of different nitrogen regimes. *J. Exp. Bot.* 40:715–24

125. Hartwell, L. H., Weinert, T. A. 1989. Checkpoints: controls that ensure the order of cell cycle events. *Science* 246:629–34

126. Hartwig, U. A., Maxwell, C. A., Joseph, C. M., Phillips, D. A. 1990. Effects of alfalfa *nod* gene-inducing flavonoids on *nodABC* transcription in *Rhizobium meliloti* strains containing different *nodD* genes. *J. Bacteriol.* 172:2769–73

127. Hartwig, U. A., Maxwell, C. A., Joseph, C. M., Phillips, D. A. 1990. Chrysoeriol and luteolin released from alfalfa seeds induce *nod* genes in *Rhizobium meliloti*. *Plant Physiol.* 92:116–22

128. Hennecke, H., Meyer, L., Göttfert, M., Fischer, H. M. 1988. Genetics of the *Bradyrhizobium japonicum*–soybean symbiosis: recent developments on genes for nodulation, bacteroid respiration, and regulation of nitrogen fixation. See Ref. 212a, pp. 118–23

129. Hennecke, H., Verma, D. P. S. 1991. *Advances in Molecular Genetics of Plant-Microbe Interaction*, Vol. 1, Boston: Kluwer Academic. In press

130. Heron, D. S., Pueppke, S. G. 1987. Regulation of nodulation in the soybean-*Rhizobium* symbiosis. Strain and cultivar variability. *Plant Physiol.* 84:1391–96

131. Hirsch, A. M., Bhuvaneswari, T. V., Torrey, J. G., Bisseling, T. 1989. Early nodulin genes are induced in alfalfa root outgrowths elicited by auxin transport inhibitors. *Proc. Natl. Acad. Sci. USA* 86:1244–48

132. Ho, S., Schindler, M., Wang, J. L. 1990. Carbohydrate binding activities of *Bradyrhizobium japonicum*. II. Isolation and characterization of a galactose-specific lectin. *J. Cell Biol.* 111:1639–43

133. Ho, S., Wang, J. L., Schindler, M. 1990. Carbohydrate binding activities of *Bradyrhizobium japonicum*. I. Saccharide-specific inhibition of homotypic and heterotypic adhesion. *J. Cell Biol.* 111:1631–38

134. Holl, F. B. 1975. Host plant control of the inheritance of dinitrogen fixation in the *Pisum-Rhizobium* symbiosis. *Euphytica* 24:767–70

135. Hollingsworth, R. I., Philip-Hollingsworth, S., Dazzo, F. B. 1990. Isolation, characterization, and structural elucidation of a "*nod* signal" excreted by *Rhizobium trifolii* ANU843 which induces root hair branching and nodule-like primordia in axenic white clover seedlings. See Ref. 119, pp. 193–98

136. Honma, M. A., Asomaning, M., Ausubel, F. M. 1990. *Rhizobium meliloti nodD* genes mediate host-specific activation of *nodABC*. *J. Bacteriol.* 172: 901–11

137. Honma, M. A., Ausubel, F. M. 1987. *Rhizobium meliloti* has three functional copies of the *nodD* symbiotic regulatory gene. *Proc. Natl. Acad. Sci. USA* 84: 8558–62

138. Horvath, B., Bachem, C. W., Schell, J., Kondorosi, A. 1987. Host-specific regulation of nodulation genes in *Rhizobium* is mediated by a plant-signal interacting with the *nodD* gene product. *EMBO J.* 6:841–48

139. Horvath, B., Kondorosi, E., John, M., Schmidt, J., Török, I., et al. 1986. Organization structure and symbiotic function of *Rhizobium meliloti* nodulation genes determining host specificity for alfalfa. *Cell* 46:335–43

140. Hunt, P. G., Kasperbauer, M. J., Matheny, T. A. 1987. Nodule development in a split-root system in response to red and far-red light treatment of soybean roots. *Crop Sci.* 27:973–976

141. Hyldig-Nielsen, J. J., Jensen, E. O., Paludan, K., Wiborg, O., Garret, R., et al. 1982. The primary structures of two LB genes from soybean. *Nucleic Acids Res.* 10:689–701

142. Imoto, M., Yamashita, T., Sawa, T., Kurasawa, S., Naganawa, H., et al. 1988. Inhibition of cellular phosphatidylinositol turnover by psi-tectorigenin. *FEBS Lett.* 230:43–46

143. Innes, R. W., Kuempel, P. L., Plazinski, J., Canter-Cremers, H., Rolfe, B. G., Djordjevic, M. A. 1985. Plant factors induce expression of nodulation and host-range genes in *Rhizobium trifolii*. *Mol. Gen. Genet.* 201:426–32

144. Jacobs, T. W., Egelhoff, T. T., Long, S. R. 1985. Physical and genetic map of a *Rhizobium meliloti* nodulation gene region and nucleotide sequence of *nodC*. *J. Bacteriol.* 162:469–76

145. Jacobsen, E. 1984. Modification of symbiotic interaction *(Pisum sativum)* and *Rhizobium leguminosarum* by induced mutation. *Plant Soil* 82:427–38

146. Jacobsen, E., Feenstra, W. J. 1984. A new pea mutant with efficient nodulation in the presence of nitrate. *Plant Sci. Lett.* 33:337–44

147. Jensen, E. O., Marcker, K. A., Schell, J., de Bruijn, F. J. 1988. Interaction of a nodule specific, transacting factor with distinct DNA elements in the soybean leghemoglobin *lbc3* 5' upstream region. *EMBO J.* 7:1265–71

148. John, M., Schmidt, J., Wieneke, U., Krussmann, H. D., Schell, J. 1988. Transmembrane orientation and receptor-like structure of the *Rhizobium meliloti* common nodulation protein nodC. *EMBO J.* 7:583–88

149. Joshi, P. A., Caetano-Anollés, G., Graham, E., Gresshoff, P. M. 1991. Ontogeny and ultrastructure of spontaneous nodules in alfalfa (Medicago sativa). Protoplasma. In press

150. Kape, R., Parniske, M., Werner, D. 1991. Chemotaxis and nod gene activity of Bradyrhizobium japonicum in response to hydroxycinnamic acids and isoflavonoids. Appl. Environ. Microbiol. 57:316–19

151. Kapp, D., Niehaus, K., Quandt, J., Müller, P., Pühler, A. 1990. Cooperative action of Rhizobium meliloti nodulation and infection mutants during the process of forming mixed infected alfalfa nodules. Plant Cell 2:139–51

152. Katinakis, P., Verma, D. P. S. 1985. Nodulin-24 gene of soybean codes for a polypeptide of the peribacteroid membrane and was generated by tandem duplication of a sequence resembling an insertion element. Proc. Natl. Acad. Sci. USA 82:4157–61

153. Keim, P., Diers, B., Olson, T., Shoemaker, R. 1990. RFLP mapping in soybean: association between marker loci and variation in quantitative traits. Genetics 126:735–42

154. Keller, B., Lamb, C. J. 1989. Specific expression of a novel cell wall hydroxyproline-rich glycoprotein gene in lateral root initiation. Genes Dev. 3:1639–46

155. Klee, H., Horsch, R., Rogers, S. 1987. Agrobacterium-mediated plant transformation and its further applications to plant biology. Annu. Rev. Plant. Physiol. 38:467–86

156. Klein, P. S., Sun, T. J., Saxe, C. L. III, Kimmel, A. R., Johnson, R. L., Devreotes, P. N. 1988. A chemoattractant receptor controls development in Dictyostelium discoideum. Science 241:1467–72

157. Klein, S., Hirsch, A. M., Smith, C. A., Signer, E. R. 1988. Interaction of nod and exo Rhizobium meliloti in alfalfa nodulation. Mol. Plant-Microbe Interact. 1:94–100

158. Kneen, B. E., LaRue, T. A. 1984. Nodulation resistant mutant of Pisum sativum (L.). J. Hered. 75:238–40

159. Kneen, B. E., LaRue, T. A. 1984. Peas (Pisum sativum L.) with strain specificity for Rhizobium leguminosarum. Heredity 52:383–89

160. Kneen, B. E., Vam Vikites, D., LaRue, T. A. 1986. Nodulation mutants of Pisum sativum. In Genetics of Plant-Microbe Interactions, ed. D. P. S. Verma, N. Brisson, pp. 79–84. Dordrecht: Martinus Nijhoff

160a. Kneen, B. E., LaRue, T. A., Hirsch, A. M., Smith, C. A., Weeden, N. F. 1990. sym13—A gene conditioning ineffective nodulation in Pisum sativum. Plant Physiol. 94:899–905

161. Kondorosi, E., Banfalvi, Z., Kondorosi, A. 1984. Physical and genetic analysis of a symbiotic region of Rhizobium meliloti: identification of nodulation genes. Mol. Gen. Genet. 193:445–52

162. Kosslak, R. M., Bohlool, B. B. 1984. Suppression of nodule development of one side of a root system of soybeans caused by prior inoculation of the other side. Plant Physiol. 75:125–30

163. Kosslak, R. M., Bookland, R., Barkei, J., Paaren, H., Appelbaum, E. 1987. Induction of Bradyrhizobium japonicum common nod genes by isoflavones isolated from Glycine max. Proc. Natl. Acad. Sci. USA 84:7428–32

164. Kosslak, R. M., Joshi, R. S., Bowen, B. A., Paaren, H. E., Appelbaum, E. R. 1990. Strain-specific inhibition of nod gene induction in Bradyrhizobium japonicum by flavonoid compounds. Appl. Environ. Microbiol. 56:1333–41

165. La Favre, J. S., Eaglesham, A. R. J. 1984. Increased nodulation of "nonnodulating" (rj₁rj₁) soybeans by high dose inoculation. Plant Soil 80:297–300

166. Lamb, C. J., Lawton, M. A., Dron, M., Dixon, R. A. 1989. Signals and transduction mechanisms for activation of plant defenses against microbial attack. Cell 56:215–24

167. Lamb, J. W., Hennecke, H. 1986. In Bradyrhizobium japonicum the common nodulation genes nodABC are linked to nifA and fixA. Mol. Gen. Genet. 202:512–17

168. Landau-Ellis, D., Shoemaker, R., Angermüller, S., Gresshoff, P. M. 1991. The genetic locus controlling supernodulation co-segregates tightly with a cloned molecular marker. Mol. Gen. Genet. In press

169. Leigh, J. A., Signer, E. R., Walker, G. C. 1985. Exopolysaccharide-deficient mutants of Rhizobium meliloti that form ineffective nodules. Proc. Natl. Acad. Sci. USA 82:6231–35

170. Lerouge, P., Roche, P., Faucher, C., Maillet, F., Truchet, G., et al. 1990. Symbiotic host-specificity of Rhizobium meliloti is determined by a sulphated and acylated glucosamine oligosaccharide signal. Nature 344:781–84

171. Lerouge, P., Roche, P., Promé, J. C., Faucher, C., Vasse, J., et al. 1990. Rhizobium meliloti nodulation genes specify the production of an alfalfa-specific sulphated lipo-oligosaccharide signal. See Ref. 119, pp. 177–86

172. Lewin, A., Cervantes, E., Chee-Hong, W., Broughton, W. J. 1990. *nodSU*, two new *nod* genes of the broad host range *Rhizobium* strain NGR234 encode host-specific nodulation of the tropical tree *Leucaena leucocephala*. *Mol. Plant-Microbe Interact.* 3:317–26

173. Lewin, A., Rosenberg, C., Meyer, H., Wong, C. H., Nelson, L., et al. 1987. Multiple host-specificity loci of the broad host-range *Rhizobium* sp. NGR234 selected using the widely compatible legume *Vigna unguiculata*. *Plant Mol. Biol.* 8:447–59

174. Libbenga, K. R., Harkes, P. A. A. 1973. Initial proliferation of cortical cells in the formation of root nodules in *Pisum sativum*. *Planta* 114:17–28

175. Lie, T. A. 1971. Temperature-dependent root-nodule formation in pea cv. Iran. *Plant Soil* 34:751–52

176. Lie, T. A. 1984. Host genes in *Pisum sativum* conferring resistance to European *Rhizobium leguminosarum*. *Plant Soil* 82:415–25

177. Lie, T. A., Timmermans, P. C. J. M. 1983. Host genetic control of nitrogen fixation in the legume-*Rhizobium* symbiosis: complication in the genetic analysis due to maternal effects. *Plant Soil* 75:449–53

178. Long, S. R. 1989. *Rhizobium*-legume nodulation: life together in the underground. *Cell* 56:203–14

179. Long, S. R., Cooper, J. 1988. Overview of symbiosis. See Ref. 212a, pp. 163–78

180. Long, S., Reed, J. W., Himawan, J., Walker, G. C. 1988. Genetic analysis of a cluster of genes required for synthesis of the calcofluor-binding exopolysaccharide of *Rhizobium meliloti*. *J. Bacteriol.* 170:4239–48

181. Malik, N. S. A., Bauer, W. D. 1988. When does the self-regulatory response elicited by soybean roots after inoculation occur? *Plant Physiol.* 88:537–39

182. Malik, N. S. A., Calvert, H. E., Bauer, W. D. 1987. Nitrate induced regulation of nodule formation in soybean. *Plant Physiol.* 84:266–71

183. Mathews, A., Carroll, B. J., Gresshoff, P. M. 1987. Characterization of non-nodulation mutants of soybean (*Glycine max* (L.) Merr.): *Bradyrhizobium* effects and absence of root hair curling. *J. Plant Physiol.* 131:349–61

184. Mathews, A., Carroll, B. J., Gresshoff, P. M. 1989. Development of *Bradyrhizobium* infections in a supernodulating and non-nodulating mutant of soybean (*Glycine max*. (L.) Merr.). *Protoplasma* 150:40–47

185. Mathews, A., Carroll, B. J., Gresshoff, P. M. 1989. A new non-nodulation gene in soybean. *J. Hered.* 80:357–60

186. Mathews, A., Carroll, B. J., Gresshoff, P. M. 1990. The genetic interaction between non-nodulation and supernodulation in soybean: an example of developmental epistasis. *Theor. Appl. Genet.* 79:125–30

187. Mathews, A., Kosslak, R. M., Sengupta-Gopalan, C., Appelbaum, E. R., Carroll, B. J., Gresshoff, P. M. 1989. Biological characterization of root exudates and extracts from non-nodulating and supernodulating soybean mutants. *Mol. Plant-Microbe Interact.* 2:283–90

188. Maxwell, C. A., Hartwig, U. A., Joseph, C. M., Phillips, D. A. 1989. A chalcone and two related flavonoids released from alfalfa roots induce *nod* genes of *Rhizobium meliloti*. *Plant Physiol.* 91:842–47

189. Maxwell, C. A., Phillips, D. A. 1990. Concurrent synthesis and release of *nod*-gene-inducing flavonoids from alfalfa roots. *Plant Physiol.* 93:1552–58

190. Memelink, J., Hoge, J. H. C., Schilperoort, R. A. 1987. Cytokinin stress changes the developmental regulation of several defense related genes in tobacco. *EMBO J.* 6:3579–84

191. Morrison, N., Verma, D. P. S. 1987. A block in the endocytosis of *Rhizobium* allows cellular differentiation in nodules but affects the expression of some peribacteroid membrane nodulins. *Plant Mol. Biol.* 9:185–96

192. Müller, P., Hynes, M., Kapp, D., Niehaus, K., Pühler, A. 1988. Two classes of *Rhizobium meliloti* infection mutants differ in exopolysaccharide production and in coinoculation properties with nodulation mutants. *Mol. Gen. Genet.* 211:17–26

193. Mulligan, J. T., Long, S. R. 1985. Induction of *Rhizobium meliloti nodC* expression by plant exudate requires *nodD*. *Proc. Natl. Acad. Sci. USA* 82:6609–13

194. Mulligan, J. T., Long, S. R. 1989. A family of activator genes regulates expression of *Rhizobium meliloti* nodulation genes. *Genetics* 122:7–18

195. Murray, A. W., Kirschner, M. W. 1989. Dominoes and clocks: the union of two views of the cell cycle. *Science* 246:614–21

196. Nap, J. P., Bisseling, T. 1990. Nodulin function and nodulin gene regulation in root nodule development. See Ref. 115a, pp. 181–229

197. Nap, J. P., Bisseling, T. 1990. Developmental biology of a plant-prokaryote symbiosis: the legume root nodule. *Science* 250:948–54

198. Nayudu, M., Rolfe, B. G. 1987. Analysis of R-primes demonstrates that genes for broad host range nodulation of *Rhizobium* strain NGR234 are dispersed on the Sym plasmid. *Mol. Gen. Genet.* 206:326–37

199. Newcomb, W. 1981. Nodule morphogenesis and differentiation. In *Biology of Rhizobiaceae, Int. Rev. Cytol. Suppl. 13*, ed. K. L. Giles, A. G. Atherly, pp. 246–98. New York: Academic

200. Niewkoop, A. J., Banfalvi, Z., Deshmane, N., Gerhold, D., Schell, M. G., et al. 1987. A locus encoding host range is linked to the common nodulation genes of *Bradyrhizobium japonicum*. *J. Bacteriol.* 169:2631–38

201. Nigam, S. N., Arunachalam, V., Gibbons, R. W., Bandyopadhyay, A., Nambiar, P. T. C. 1980. Genetics of nodulation in groundnut *(Arachis hypogaea L.)*. *Oleagineux* 35:453–55

202. Nguyen, T., Zelechowska, M., Foster, V., Bergmann, H., Verma, D. P. S. 1985. Primary structure of the soybean nodulin-35 gene encoding uricase II localized in the peroxisomes of uninfected cells of nodules. *Proc. Natl. Acad. Sci. USA* 82:5040–44

203. Nutman, P. S. 1945. A factor in clover nodule formation associated with the volume of the medium occupied by the roots. *Nature* 156:20–21

204. Nutman, P. S. 1949. Nuclear and cytoplasmic inheritance of resistance to infection by nodule bacteria in red clover. *Heredity* 3:263–91

205. Nutman, P. S. 1952. Studies on the physiology of nodule formation. III. Experiments on the excision of root-tips and nodules. *Ann. Bot.* 16:80–102

206. Nutman, P. S. 1954. Symbiotic effectiveness in nodulated red clover. II. A major gene for ineffectiveness in the host. *Heredity* 8:47–60

207. Nutman, P. S. 1957. Symbiotic effectiveness in nodulated red clover. III. Further studies on inheritance of ineffectiveness in the host. *Heredity* 11:157–73

208. Nutman, P. S. 1962. The relation between root hair infection by *Rhizobium* and nodulation in *Trifolium* and *Vicea*. *Proc. R. Soc. London Ser. B* 156:122–37

209. Nutman, P. S. 1968. Symbiotic effectiveness in nodulated red clover. V. The *n* and *d* factors for ineffectiveness. *Heredity* 23:537–51

210. O'Farrell, P. H., Edgar, B. A., Lakish, D., Lehner, C. F. 1989. Directing cell division during development. *Science* 246:635–40

211. Olsson, J. E. 1988. *Systemic control of soybean nodule autoregulation.* PhD thesis. Canberra, Australia: Australian Natl. Univ.

212. Olsson, J. E., Nakao, P., Bohlool, B. B., Gresshoff, P. M. 1989. Lack of systemic suppression of nodulation in split root systems of supernodulating soybean *(Glycine max* (L.) Merr.). *Plant Physiol.* 90:1347–52

212a. Palacios, R., Verma, D. P. S., eds. 1988. *Molecular Genetics of Plant-Microbe Interactions.* St. Paul, MN: APS Press

213. Park, S. J., Buttery, B. R. 1988. Nodulation mutants of white bean *(Phaseolus vulgaris* L.) induced by ethyl-methane sulphonate. *Can. J. Plant Sci.* 68:199–202

214. Parke, D., Rivelli, M., Ornston, L. N. 1985. Chemotaxis to aromatic and hydroaromatic acids: comparison of *Bradyrhizobium japonicum* and *Rhizobium trifolii*. *J. Bacteriol.* 163:417–22

215. Peters, K., Frost, J., Long, S. R. 1986. A plant flavone, luteolin, induces expression of *Rhizobium meliloti* nodulation genes. *Science* 233:977–80

216. Peters, K., Long, S. R. 1988. *Rhizobium meliloti* nodulation genes inducers and inhibitors. *Plant Physiol.* 88:396–400

217. Peters, N. K., Verma, D. P. S. 1990. Phenolic compounds as regulators of gene expression in plant-microbe interactions. *Mol. Plant-Microbe Interact.* 3:4–8

218. Peterson, M. A., Barnes, D. K. 1981. Inheritance of ineffective nodulation and non-nodulation traits in alfalfa. *Crop Sci.* 21:611–16

219. Philip-Hollingsworth, S., Hollingsworth, R. I., Dazzo, F. B. 1989. Host-range related structural features of the acidic extracellular polysaccharides of *Rhizobium trifolii* and *Rhizobium leguminosarum*. *J. Biol. Chem.* 264:1461–66

220. Philip-Hollingsworth, S., Hollingsworth, R. I., Dazzo, F. B., Djordjevic, M. A., Rolfe, B. G. 1989. The effect of interspecies transfer of *Rhizobium* host-specific nodulation genes on acidic polysaccharide structure and *in situ* binding by host lectin. *J. Biol. Chem.* 264:5710–14

221. Phillips, D. A., Torrey, J. G. 1971. Studies on cytokinin production by *Rhizobium*. *Plant Physiol.* 49:11–15

222. Pierce, M., Bauer, W. D. 1983. A rapid regulatory response governing nodulation in soybean. *Plant Physiol.* 73:286–90

223. Price, G. D., Mohapatra, S. S., Gress-hoff, P. M. 1984. Structure of nodules formed by *Rhizobium* strain ANU289 in the non-legume *Parasponia* and legume siratro *(Macroptilium atropurpureum)*. *Bot. Gaz.* 145:444–51
224. Randall, D. D., Blevins, D. G. 1989. *Current Topics in Plant Biochemistry and Physiology.* Columbia: Univ. Missouri
225. Redmond, J. W., Batley, M., Djordjevic, M. A., Innes, R. W., Kuempel, P. L., Rolfe, B. G. 1986. Flavones induce expression of nodulation genes in *Rhizobium*. *Nature* 323:632–35
226. Rolfe, B. G., Gresshoff, P. M. 1988. Genetic analysis of legume nodulation. *Annu. Rev. Plant Physiol. Plant Mol. Biol.* 39:297–319
227. Rossen, L., Johnston, A. W. B., Downie, J. A. 1984. DNA sequence of the *Rhizobium leguminosarum* nodulation genes *nodAB* and *C* required for root hair curling. *Nucleic Acids Res.* 12:9497–9508
228. Rossen, L., Shearman, C. A., Johnston, A. W. B., Downie, J. A. 1985. The *nodD* gene of *Rhizobium leguminosarum* is autoregulatory and in the presence of plant exudate induces the *nodA, B, C* genes. *EMBO J.* 4:3369–73
228a. Sadowsky, M. J., Cregan, P. B., Gottfert, M., Sharma, A., Gerhold, D., et al. 1991. The *Bradyrhizobium japonicum nolA* gene and its involvement in the genotype-specific nodulation of soybean. *Proc. Natl. Acad. Sci. USA* 88:637–41
229. Sanders, R., Raleigh, E., Signer, E. R. 1981. Lack of correlation between extracellular polysaccharide and nodulation ability in *Rhizobium*. *Nature* 292:148–49
230. Sargent, L., Huang, S. Z., Rolfe, B. G., Djordjevic, M. A. 1987. Split-root assays using *Trifolium subterraneum* shows that *Rhizobium* infection induces a systemic response that can inhibit nodulation of another invasive *Rhizobium* strain. *Appl. Environ. Microbiol.* 53:1611–19
231. Scheres, B., van de Wiel, C., Zalensky, A., Horvath, B., Spaink, H., et al. 1990. The ENOD12 gene product is involved in the infection process during the pea-*Rhizobium* interaction. *Cell* 60:281–94
232. Scheres, B., van Engelen, F., van der Knapp, E., van de Wiel, C., van Kammen, A., Bisseling, T. 1990. Sequential induction of nodulin gene expression in the developing pea nodule. *Plant Cell* 2:687–700

233. Schmidt, J., John, M., Kondorosi, E., Kondorosi, A., Weineke, U., et al. 1984. Mapping of the protein coding regions of *Rhizobium meliloti* common nodulation genes. *EMBO J.* 3:1705–11
234. Schmidt, J., John, M., Wieneke, U., Krussmann, H. D., Schell, J. 1986. Expression of the nodulation gene *nodA* in *Rhizobium meliloti* and localization of the gene product in the cytosol. *Proc. Natl. Acad. Sci. USA* 83:9581–85
235. Schmidt, J., Wingender, R., John, M., Wieneke, U., Schell, J. 1988. *Rhizobium meliloti nodA* and *nodB* genes are involved in generating compounds that stimulate mitosis of the host plant cells. *Proc. Natl. Acad. Sci. USA* 85:8578–82
236. Schofield, P. R., Ridge, R. W., Rolfe, B. G., Shine, J., Watson, J. M. 1984. Host-specific nodulation is encoded on a 14 kb DNA fragment in *Rhizobium trifolii*. *Plant Mol. Biol.* 3:3–11
237. Schofield, P. R., Watson, J. M. 1986. DNA sequence of *Rhizobium trifolii* nodulation genes reveals a reiterated and potentially regulatory sequence preceding *nodABC* and *nodFE*. *Nucleic Acids Res.* 14:2891–2903
238. Schwedock, J., Long, S. R. 1989. Nucleotide sequence and protein products of two new nodulation genes of *Rhizobium meliloti*, *nodP* and *nodQ*. *Mol. Plant-Microbe Interact.* 2:181–94
239. Schwedock, J., Long, S. R. 1989. ATP sulphurylase activity of the *nodP* and *nodQ* gene products of *Rhizobium meliloti*. *Nature* 348:644–47
240. Scott, K. F. 1986. Conserved nodulation genes from the non-legume symbiont *Bradyrhizobium* sp. Parasponia. *Nucleic Acids Res.* 14:2905–19
241. Sengupta-Gopalan, C., Pitas, J. W. 1986. Expression of nodule specific glutamine synthetase genes during nodule development in soybeans. *Plant Mol. Biol.* 7:189–99
242. Shearman, C. A., Rossen, L., Johnston, A. W. B., Downie, J. A. 1986. The *Rhizobium leguminosarum* nodulation gene *nodF* encodes a polypeptide similar to acyl-carrier protein and is regulated by *nodD* plus a factor in pea root exudate. *EMBO J.* 5:647–52
243 Singleton, P. W., Van Kessel, C. 1987. Effect of localized nitrogen availability to soybean half-root systems on photosynthate partitioning to roots and nodules. *Plant Physiol.* 83:552–56
244. Sinshi, H., Mohnen, D., Meins, F. Jr. 1987. Regulation of a plant pathogenesis-related enzyme: inhibition of chitinase and chitinase mRNA accumulation in cultured tobacco tissues by auxin and

cytokinin. *Proc. Natl. Acad. Sci. USA* 84:89–92

245. Smit, G., Logman, T. J. J., Boerrigter, M. E. T. I., Kijne, J. W., Lugtenberg, B. J. J. 1989. Purification and partial characterization of the *Rhizobium leguminosarum* biovar *viciae* Ca^{2+}-dependent adhesin, which mediates the first step in attachment of cells of the family *Rhizobiaceae* to plant root hair tips. *J. Bacteriol.* 171:4054–62

246. Smith, G. R., Knight, W. E. 1984. Inheritance of ineffective nodulation in crimson clover. *Crop Sci.* 24:601–4

247. Spaink, H. P., Okker, R. J. H., Wijffelman, C. A., Tak, T., Goosen-de Roo, L., et al. 1989. Symbiotic properties of rhizobia containing a flavonoid-independent hybrid *nodD* product. *J. Bacteriol.* 171:4045–53

248. Spaink, H. P., Wijffelman, C. A., Pees, E., Okker, R. J. H., Lugtenberg, B. J. J. 1987. *Rhizobium* nodulation gene *nodD* as determinant of host specificity. *Nature* 328:337–39

249. Spaink, H. P., Wijffelman, C. A., Pees, E., Okker, R. J. H., Lugtenberg, B. J. J. 1989. Localization and functional regions of the *Rhizobium nodD* product using hybrid *nodD* genes. *Plant Mol. Biol.* 12:59–73

250. Sprent, J. I. 1990. Evolution, structure and function of nitrogen-fixing root nodules: confessions of ignorance. See Ref. 119, pp. 45–54

251. Stacey, G. 1990. Workshop summary: compilation of the *nod, fix,* and *nif* genes of rhizobia and information concerning their function. See Ref. 212a, pp. 239–44

252. Streeter, J. 1988. Inhibition of legume nodule formation and nitrogen fixation by nitrate. *CRC Crit. Rev. Plant Sci.* 7:1–23

253. Stock, J. B., Ninfa, A. J., Stock, A. M. 1989. Protein phosphorylation and regulation of adaptive responses in bacteria. *Microbiol. Rev.* 53:450–90

254. Stougaard, J., Petersen, T. E., Marcker, K. A. 1987. Expression of a complete soybean leghemoglobin gene in root nodules of transgenic *Lotus corniculatus. Proc. Natl. Acad. Sci. USA* 84:5754–57

255. Sturtevant, D. B., Taller, B. J. 1989. Cytokinin production by *Bradyrhizobium japonicum. Plant Physiol.* 89:1247–52

256. Surin, B. P., Downie, J. A. 1988. Characterization of the *Rhizobium leguminosarum* genes *nodLMN* involved in efficient host specific nodulation. *Mol. Microbiol.* 2:173–83

257. Surin, B. P., Watson, J. M., Hamilton, W. D. O., Economou, A., Downie, J. A. 1990. Molecular characterization of the nodulation gene, *nodT*, from two biovars of *Rhizobium leguminosarum. Mol. Microbiol.* 4:245–52

258. Sutherland, T., Bassam, B. J., Schuller, L. J., Gresshoff, P. M. 1990. Early nodulation signals of wild type and symbiotic mutants of soybean *(Glycine max). Mol. Plant-Microbe Interact.* 3:122–28

259. Swanson, J., Tu, J. K., Ogawa, J. M., Sanga, R., Fisher, R., Long, S. R. 1987. Extended region of nodulation genes in *Rhizobium meliloti* 1021. I. Phenotypes of Tn5 insertion mutants. *Genetics* 117:181–89

260. Szabados, L., Ratet, P., Grunenberg, B., Schell, J., de Bruijn, F. J. 1990. Functional analysis of the *Sesbania rostrata* leghemoglobin *glb3* gene 5' upstream region in transgenic *Lotus corniculatus* and *Nicotiana tabacum* plants. *Plant Cell* 2:973–86

261. Takats, S. T. 1986. Suppression of nodulation in soybeans by superoptimal inoculation with *Bradyrhizobium japonicum. Physiol. Plant.* 66:669–73

262. Takats, S. T. 1990. Early autoregulation of symbiotic root nodulation in soybeans. *Plant Physiol.* 94:865–69

263. Thummler, F., Verma, D. P. S. 1987. Nodulin-100 of soybean is the subunit of sucrose synthase regulated by the availability of free heme in nodules. *J. Biol. Chem.* 262:14730–36

264. Török, I., Kondorosi, E., Stepkowski, T., Posfai, J., Kondorosi, A. 1984. Nucleotide sequence of *Rhizobium meliloti* nodulation genes. *Nucleic Acids Res.* 12:9509–24

265. Truchet, G., Barker, D. G., Camut, S., de Billy, F., Vasse, J., Huguet, T. 1989. Alfalfa nodulation in the absence of *Rhizobium. Mol. Gen. Genet.* 219:65–68

266. Truchet, G., Michel, M., Dénarié, J. 1980. Sequential analysis of the organogenesis of lucerne *(Medicago sativa)* root nodules using symbiotic-defective mutants of *Rhizobium meliloti. Differentiation* 16:163–72

267. Turgeon, B. G., Bauer, W. D. 1982. Early events in the infection of soybean by *Rhizobium japonicum. Can. J. Bot.* 60:152–61

268. Turgeon, B. G., Bauer, W. D. 1985. Ultrastructure of infection-thread development during infection of soybean by *Rhizobium japonicum. Planta* 163:328–49

269. van Brussel, A. N. N., Recourt, K.,

Pees, E., Spaink, H. P., Tak, T., et al. 1990. A biovar-specific signal of *Rhizobium leguminosarum* bv. *viciae* induces increased nodulation gene-inducing activity in root exudate of *Vicia sativa* subsp. *nigra*. *J. Bacteriol.* 172:5394–5401

270. Van de Wiel, C., Norris, J. H., Bochenek, B., Dickstein, R., Bisseling, T., Hirsch, A. M. 1990. Nodulin gene expression and ENOD2 localization in effective, nitrogen fixing and ineffective, bacteria-free nodules of alfalfa. *Plant Cell* 2:1009–17

271. Verma, D. P. S. 1989. Plant genes involved in carbon and nitrogen assimilation. In *Plant Nitrogen Metabolism*, ed. J. E. Poulton, J. T. Romeo, E. E. Conn, pp. 43–76. New York: Plenum

272. Verma, D. P. S., Fortin, M. G. 1989. Nodule development and formation of the endosymbiotic compartment. In *Cell Culture and Somatic Cell Genetics of Plants*, 6:329–53. New York: Academic

273. Vesper, S. J., Bauer, W. D. 1986. Role of pili (fimbriae) in attachment of *Bradyrhizobium japonicum* to soybean roots. *Appl. Environ. Microbiol.* 52:134–41

274. Vesper, S. J., Malik, N. S. A., Bauer, W. D. 1987. Transposon mutants of *Bradyrhizobium japonicum* altered in attachment to host roots. *Appl. Environ. Microbiol.* 53:1959–61

275. Vest, G. 1970. *Rj₃*: a gene controlling ineffective nodulation in soybean. *Crop Sci.* 10:34–35

276. Vest, G., Caldwell, B. E. 1972. *Rj₄*: a gene controlling ineffective nodulation in soybean. *Crop Sci.* 12:692–93

276a. Vincent, J. M. 1980. Factors control-

ling the legume-Rhizobium symbiosis. In *Nitrogen Fixation*, Vol. 2, ed. W. E. Newton, W. H. Orme-Johnson, pp. 103–29. Baltimore: Univ. Park Press

277. Wall, L. G., Giménez, M. C., Favelukes, G. 1990. Stimulation of early adsorption of *Rhizobium meliloti* to alfalfa roots, and their nodulation, by previous specific interaction with root exudate protein factor or seed agglutinin. See Ref. 119, p. 279

278. Weeden, N. F., Kneen, B. E., LaRue, T. A. 1990. Genetic analysis of *sym* genes and other nodule-related genes in *Pisum sativum*. See Ref. 119, p. 323–30

279. Williams, L. F., Lynch, D. L. 1954. Inheritance of a non-nodulating character in the soybean. *Agron. J.* 46:28–29

280. Yao, P. Y., Vincent, J. M. 1969. Host specificity in the root hair "curling factor" of *Rhizobium* sp. *Aust. J. Biol. Sci.* 22:413–23

281. Young, J. P. W., Johnston, A. W. B., Brewin, N. J. 1982. A search for peas (*Pisum sativum* L.) showing strain specificity for symbiotic *Rhizobium leguminosarum*. *Heredity* 48:197–201

282. Zaat, S. A. J., Wijffelman, C. A., Spaink, H. P., VanBrussel, A. A. N., Okker, J. H., Lugtenberg, B. J. J. 1987. Induction of the *nodA* promoter of *Rhizobium leguminosarum* Sym plasmid PRL1J1 by plant flavanones and flavones. *J. Bacteriol.* 169:198–204

283. Zahn, H., Levery, S. B., Lee, C. C., Leigh, J. A. 1989. A second exopolysaccharide of *Rhizobium meliloti* strain SU47 that can function in root nodule invasion. *Proc. Natl. Acad. Sci. USA* 86:3055–59

Annu. Rev. Microbiol. 1991. 45:383–415

CHAPERONE-ASSISTED ASSEMBLY AND MOLECULAR ARCHITECTURE OF ADHESIVE PILI

Scott J. Hultgren and Staffan Normark

Department of Molecular Microbiology, Washington University School of Medicine, St. Louis, Missouri 63110

Soman N. Abraham

Department of Pathology and Molecular Microbiology, Washington University School of Medicine and Jewish Hospital, St. Louis, Missouri 63110

KEY WORDS: bacterial adhesins, periplasmic chaperones, PapD, phase and antigenic
            variation, post-secretional assembly, biogenesis

CONTENTS

INTRODUCTION 384
   P and Type 1 Pili of Escherichia coli 384
POSTSECRETIONAL ASSEMBLY 387
   Periplasmic Chaperones 388
   Structure-Function Properties of PapD 391
   Polymerization of Pilus Subunits and Chaperone Release 392
STRUCTURE OF P AND TYPE 1 PILI 393
RECEPTOR BINDING AND ASSEMBLY DOMAINS OF PILUS ADHESINS 398
ASSEMBLY OF TYPE 4 PILI 401
   Pili of Neisseria gonorrhoeae 402
   TCP Pili of Vibrio cholerae 405
   Pseudomonas aeruginosa Pili 406
   Biogenesis Model for Type 4 Pili 406
SUMMARY 406

383

0066-4227/91/1001-0383$02.00

INTRODUCTION

Bacterial-mediated hemagglutination was first reported (48) in the same year that the Chicago Cubs last won the baseball World Series, in 1908. Over the past 83 years, much has been learned about the molecular details of bacterial attachment and its role in initiating disease. Most bacterial adhesins are assembled into polymeric surface structures. The assembly of adhesive surface organelles thus provides powerful models for detailed analyses of the folding and assembly of protein protomers after their translocation across the cytoplasmic membrane. In addition, these model systems allow us to investigate the requirement of chaperone proteins in the periplasm to guide protein subunits along biologically productive pathways. In this review, we discuss how genetics and biochemistry together with glycolipid chemistry, X-ray crystallography, and physical chemistry have been blended to study the surfaces of a periplasmic chaperone and structural proteins that interact with one another to form adhesive heteropolymers. In addition, the intriguing new concept of how the regulation of pilus assembly machinery may trigger antigenic variation in *Neisseria gonorrhoeae* is presented. We do not intend to describe all of the bacterial pilus systems and compare them to one another, as this has already been done in several recent reviews (72, 108, 115, 146, 148). Instead, we focus on the P, type 1, and type 4 pilus systems as models to introduce several new and exciting concepts in the biology of the bacterial pili.

P and Type 1 Pili of Escherichia coli

Escherichia coli is possibly the best-studied free-living organism. It is the most frequent cause of many of the most common bacterial infections in humans, including urinary tract infections, bacteremia, and bacterial-related travelers' diarrhea (30, 63, 71, 86). It is also a leading cause of neonatal meningitis (71) and can cause a variety of other clinical manifestations including pneumonia (30). The initiation of many of these infections is thought to be mediated by molecular recognition between adhesins on the bacterial cell surface and specific receptor molecules on mucosal cells of the host (9, 118). *E. coli* express long, thin filamentous protein appendages known as pili or fimbriae that are usually 5–10 nm in diameter and up to 2 μm in length (14, 25–27). Historically, pili expressed by *E. coli* have been differentiated according to their sensitivities in hemagglutination reactions to specific sugar inhibitors (26). Most uropathogenic *E. coli* isolated from humans express P pili that mediate Galα(1-4)Gal–sensitive hemagglutination of human erythrocytes (66, 85). Type 1 pili, which are expressed by many strains of pathogenic as well as nonpathogenic *E. coli,* are characterized by their D-mannose–sensitive agglutinatination of guinea pig erythrocytes (25, 37, 42, 64, 119).

Several genes are involved in the biosynthesis and expression of functional P and type 1 pili (115). These genes reside in clusters at different sites in the *E. coli* chromosome (60, 95, 123). Both the *pap* and type 1 gene clusters from the same human urinary tract *E. coli* isolate J96 have been cloned (59) and extensively characterized (88, 89, 92, 106, 113, 115, 116, 120). The DNA sequence of the entire *pap* operon has been determined, and it consists of eleven genes (see Figure 1).

The functions of the various gene products were determined by inactivating each gene and then examining the effect of the mutation on expression or function of the pili. The bulk of the pilus fiber is composed of PapA, the product of the *papA* gene (8), which is located at the promoter proximal end of the *pap* operon. Inactivation of *papA* abolished pilus expression, but the hemagglutinating ability of the bacterium was still retained (89, 115, 149). Since the general view at this time was that the major subunit protein of pili was responsible for their adhesiveness, this observation was the first indication that the adhesive property of P pili was not determined by the structural subunit. Subsequent studies showed that the Galα(1-4)Gal binding property of P pili depended on the expression of a 35-kilodalton (kd) protein that was the product of *papG*, the gene located at the distal end of the *pap* operon (62, 87–89, 93, 113). It was also shown that PapG, together with the products of two other genes in the *pap* operon, *papE* and *papF*, were minor components of the P pilus fiber (88) located exclusively at the tip (87). PapE and PapF are pilin-like proteins that are similar in primary structure (88). PapE apparently functions as an adaptor that couples the PapG adhesin to the pilus filament because inactivation of *papE* results in reduced hemagglutination titers of purified pili. Inactivation of *papF* results in drastically reduced levels of

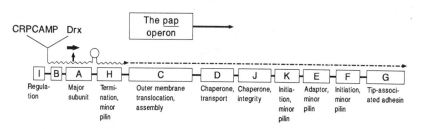

Figure 1 Summary of the structure, function, and regulation of the *E. coli pap* operon. The established and postulated functions of the various gene products are indicated. The messenger RNA transcripts eminating from the *papB* promoter are depicted by a wavy line followed by a dashed line. Regulatory targets of the CRP, protein DRX, and cAMP are also shown. A transcriptional terminator *(circle on stilts)* occurs between *papA* and *papH*.

piliation (88), suggesting that it plays an important role in initiating the assembly of the pilus filament (87, 88). Genes dispensable for piliation but required for adhesion have also been found in the other P pilus systems (126, 150).

The products of two genes, *papC* and *papD*, play crucial roles in translocation and/or assembly of pili; genetic inactivation of either of these two genes abolishes piliation (62, 112, 113, 115). PapC is an 88-kd outer-membrane protein thought to form the assembly center for pilus polymerization. The gene product of *papD* encodes a 28.5-kd protein located in the periplasmic space (90). A mutation in *papD* results in a rapid proteolytic degradation of the major and minor pilus subunits (90) as well as limited degradation of PapG (62). This finding suggests that PapD interacts with the different subunits of the P pilus in the periplasm, stabilizing them in an assembly-competent form. A detailed account of the three-dimensional structure of PapD and how it relates to its function is discussed elsewhere in this review. The role of PapJ is unclear but it may also be involved in pilus assembly (147). Finally, *papI* and *papB* regulate pilus expression because inactivation of either of these genes dramatically affects the transcription of the *pap* operon (6, 38, 47).

The genetic organization of the type 1 pilus gene cluster is similar to the *pap* operon (17, 18, 41, 76, 120, 146). Although fewer genes compose the type 1 gene cluster, their functions are extremely similar to corresponding genes in the *pap* operon, suggesting that the biosynthesis of these supramolecular structures is similar. The *E. coli* type 1 *fim* gene cluster includes, in addition to the structural gene *fimA*, two regulatory genes *fimB* and *fimE*, which direct the phase-dependent expression of the *fimA* gene (73). The mechanism of the phase variation phenomenon involves the inversion of a 300–base pair DNA segment harboring the promoter for the *fimA* gene (1, 23, 29). In addition to FimA and its regulators, *fimC* and *fimD* have been identified and are neccesary for the transport and assembly of pili (76, 120). FimC is thought to be a periplasmic protein (76, 120) and possibly functions in the translocation and assembly of the fimbrial proteins (61) as suggested for PapD in the *pap* operon (62, 90, 113). FimC is also required for the surface localization of the mannose-binding adhesin moiety even in the absence of the major FimA subunit (61). FimD resides in the outer membrane and might serve the same function as PapC in pilus assembly (75). Three genes distal to the structural gene have been identified, and their corresponding gene products appear to be minor components of the type 1 pilus (3, 53, 74). The product of one of these genes, FimH, has been specifically implicated in mediating D-mannose–specific binding (2, 3, 5, 78, 98, 99).

Recently, a third type of pilus now referred to as Prs was detected on *E. coli* strain J96 (67, 93, 95). The Prs pili are characterized by their ability to hemagglutinate sheep erythrocytes and by their inability to agglutinate human erythrocytes, clearly exhibiting a different binding specificity from P pili (95). However, Prs pili resemble P pili in several respects; the Prs pilus filament expressed by E. *coli* J96 is serologically indistinguishable from the P pilus filament expressed by the same strain, and the *prs* operon is homologous to the *pap* operon (95). Subsequent studies have revealed that the only detectable difference between the *pap* and *prs* operons is limited to their respective PapG molecules (139; B.-I. Stromberg, in preparation). This finding suggests that alterations in the receptor binding component of pili can result in significant changes in binding specificity. In summary, pathogenic E. *coli,* such as J96, can express a variety of adhesive pili with distinct receptor binding properties that may be important in increasing the range of hosts and tissues that the organism can potentially colonize.

POSTSECRETIONAL ASSEMBLY

The occurrence of specialized proteins in both eukaryotes and prokaryotes that assist in the posttranslational assembly of oligomeric protein structures is emerging as a general cellular phenomenon (33). Much has recently been learned about a class of proteins called chaperones, including such proteins as GroEL, SecB, and DnaK (45, 110, 125, 137), that are found in the cytoplasm of bacteria. The role of these proteins is to assist other polypeptides to maintain or to assume conformations that permit their correct assembly into oligomeric structures or their secretion across the cytoplasmic membrane (12, 19, 20, 54, 83, 84). These proteins are thought to bind to folding intermediates, thus stabilizing them and allowing them to proceed along biologically productive pathways (83). The secretion of proteins across the cytoplasmic membrane is a complex process (15, 28, 110, 124, 156) and is assisted by chaperones that prevent their aggregation into secretion-deficient conformations (83). Does another family of proteins in the periplasm receive translocated proteins and continue to chaperone them along biologically productive pathways? The pilus biogenesis pathway provides an excellent model to understand the biological principles involved in postsecretional folding and assembly pathways. The exposure of interactive surfaces of protein protomers at the wrong time during intermediate stages of postsecretional assembly could cause biologically nonproductive interactions that lead to kinetically dead-end pathways and aggregation. However, if these surfaces are protected by a chaperone, the protomer would be stabilized in an assembly-competent state.

Periplasmic Chaperones

The assembly of pili in the *Enterobacteriaceae* requires periplasmic chaperone proteins. Mutations in such proteins render the organisms assembly deficient and thereby bald of that particular pilus. The genes *papD, fimC, sfaE, faeE, f17-D,* and *fanE* encode pilus chaperones required for the assembly of P, type 1, S, K88, F17, and K99 pili of *E. coli* (21a, 24, 51, 76, 91, 108, 115, 120, 121, 127, 151). The assembly of type 3 pili of *Klebsiella pneumoniae* (40) and *Haemophilus influenzae* type b pili (A. Smith; personal communication) requires the *mrkB* and *hifB* gene products, respectively. Several studies have provided insight into the role of these proteins in pilus assembly (62, 109a, 129, 153). Molecular details concerning the structure-function properties of such a protein have come from the analysis of PapD, which is required for P pilus assembly. PapD is discussed in this review as a representative of this family of periplasmic pilus chaperones.

Holmgren & Branden (57) solved the three-dimensional structure of the PapD periplasmic protein that forms transient complexes with the adhesin and the other pilus subunit proteins (see Figure 2). PapD consists of two globular domains oriented towards one another in a way that gives the molecule a boomerang shape. Each domain is a beta-barrel structure formed by two antiparallel beta pleated sheets and has the topology identical to an immunoglobulin fold. The C-terminal domain, domain 2, has structural features analogous to the HIV receptor, CD4. Domain 1 of PapD is most similar to immunoglobulin variable domains.

The structures of FanE, FaeE, SfaE, F17-D, HifB, and MrkB were analyzed using their amino acid sequences and the known PapD crystal structure (A. Holmgren, M. J. Kuehn, C. I. Branden & S. J. Hultgren, submitted). These researchers found that all seven proteins were 30–40% identical and approximately 60% similar. In addition, all residues that form the hydrophobic core of PapD are conservatively substituted in all members of the family. This alignment is in agreement with the data showing that all of these proteins have similar functions and confirms that they belong to the same family of proteins.

Overall, 23 of 218 residues in PapD were identical in all seven chaperones. Fifty-eight additional residues are identical in a majority of the proteins. Amino acids at 12 other positions are structurally homologous in that they are either aliphatic, aromatic, basic, or acidic at that position in all of the proteins. The structural and functional significance of the invariant residues was investigated by superimposing the consensus sequence onto the known three-dimensional structure of PapD (A. Holmgren, M. J. Kuehn, C. I. Branden & S. J. Hultgren, submitted). Most residues were found to be conserved to maintain the overall structure of the immunoglobulin-like domains.

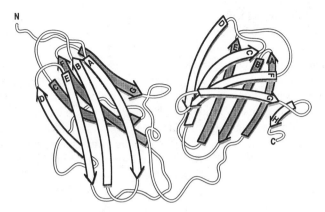

Figure 2   Schematic diagram of the PapD molecule showing the arrangement of the beta strands in the two domains [courtesy of Holmgren & Branden (57)]. Strands A, B, and E form one beta sheet, and strands C, F, G, and D form a second beta sheet that is packed against the first sheet. In domain 1, both strands D and A are shared between the two sheets.

One class of invariant residues are those that occupy critical points in loops or are involved in intramolecular interactions that serve to orient loops. For example, four conserved asparagines form hydrogren bonds to an amino acid in the main chain to correctly position the loop regions. Other conserved amino acids are important in the formation of bends in the loop regions or in the disruption of beta strands. A conserved glycine allows the beta strand to fold back on itself between betaF and betaG of the second domain. A second group of conserved residues are involved in internal salt bridge formation that serves to orient the two domains towards one another, which creates a cleft region. The last group of conserved residues are surface exposed, and the side chains are oriented towards the solvent. Their function to a large extent is unknown, but is predicted to be involved in interactions with pilus proteins or other assembly proteins like PapC or PapJ (A. Holmgren, M. J. Kuehn, C. I. Branden & S. J. Hultgren, submitted).

In summary, the majority of conserved residues are concentrated within the beta strands in the region between the domains while the loop regions are composed mostly of variable residues. Two of the variable regions in domain 1 occur at the same relative positions in a chaperone molecule as hypervariable regions occur in an immunoglobulin variable domain. Residues in the variable loop regions may be important in providing chaperone binding specificity as is the case in immunoglobulins.

Recently, insight was gained into the role of PapD in pilus biogenesis by investigating the protein-protein interactions that occur after the pilus subunits are translocated across the cytoplasmic membrane and before they are assembled into a pilus. By using galabiose-sepharose in affinity chromatography, the PapG adhesin was isolated in a preassembly complex with PapD from the periplasmic space (62), showing that after PapG is translocated across the cytoplasmic membrane it forms a complex with PapD.

The PapD preassembly complexes are easily isolated from the periplasm of *pap* proficient *E. coli* for study in vitro (62, 90). The PapD-PapG complex migrates as a single homogenous moiety on native polyacrylamide gels and is composed of an equimolar ratio of PapD and PapG (M. J. Kuehn, S. Normark & S. J. Hultgren, submitted). The complex also migrates as a single homogeneous unit on isoelectric focusing gels to an isoelectric point of 7.4 (M. J. Kuehn, S. Normark & S. J. Hultgren, submitted), which is intermediate between the pIs of PapD (9.4) and PapG (5.14) (58). The intermediate pI of 7.4 supports the argument that PapD associates with PapG in an equimolar ratio to form a distinct complex. Also, the opposite charge of those proteins at a physiological pH suggests that some of the atomic bonds formed when PapD binds to PapG may be ionic in nature. Although the complex that PapD forms with PapG is stable, it must be transient in vivo since PapD must be released upon incorporation of PapG into the pilus because PapD is not a component of the final structure. The dynamic nature of the preassembly complex has been demonstrated by showing that ^{125}I-PapD can displace unlabeled PapD from the PapD-PapG complex (M. J. Kuehn, S. Normark & S. J. Hultgren, submitted). PapD-PapE preassembly complexes have also been isolated, demonstrating the importance of these protein-protein interactions prior to the assembly of a pilus (90).

The PapD-PapG complex is stable in the presence of 6 M urea but is destroyed under reducing conditions, probably because of the unfolding of the proteins (M. J. Kuehn, S. Normark & S. J. Hultgren, submitted). When the urea is diluted away, the homogeneous complex does not reform; instead, large-molecular-weight polyaggregates are formed. One possible explanation for this result is that the site recognized by PapD is the same surface of PapG that is destined to be polymerized to adjacent subunits in the pilus, so that the urea treatment (which destroys the PapD-PapG interactions) would presumably result in the exposure of this interactive surface of PapG. The exposure of this interactive surface leads to the formation of large-molecular-weight aggregates upon dialysis or dilution of the urea. However, aggregation is prevented if the urea-treated PapD-PapG (PapD$_U$-PapG$_U$) is diluted or dialyzed in the presence of purified native PapD (M. J. Kuehn, S. Normark & S. J. Hultgren, submitted). In this environment, the excess native PapD is able to bind to the surface of PapG to reform the complex and prevent aggregation.

Periplasmic chaperone proteins such as PapD probably recognize and cap interactive surfaces of pilus proteins that are exposed as the polypeptides emerge from the cytoplasmic membrane (M. J. Kuehn, S. Normark, & S. J. Hultgren, submitted). This surface may in part be composed of carboxy-terminal residues exposed on the native molecule and/or on a compact folding intermediate with a high content of secondary structure and fluctuating tertiary structure. Supporting this hypothesis are the data showing that unlike other chaperone-substrate complexes PapG is in a highly folded state within the preassembly complex since its two disulfide bridges are intact and it possesses its native binding specificity (62, 70). In addition, all known pilins produced by the *Enterobacteriaceae* contain several highly conserved amino acids in the carboxy terminus, (88, 115) so that the entire pilus chaperone family may recognize similar surfaces. In summary, PapD may function as a reversible capping protein that modulates polymerization. When PapD is bound to the subunits, aggregation is prevented, whereas its release results in polymerization of the pilus rod. The binding and release of PapD is apparently orchestrated to occur at distinct sites within the cell, guiding the protein protomers along biologically productive pathways.

Many of the most interesting molecular features of postsecretional folding and assembly remain unsolved. For example, when does the periplasmic PapD protein bind to PapG and what drives its release? It is intriguing that mutations in either a cytoplasmic chaperone (SecB) (79–81) or a periplasmic chaperone (PapD) can result in analogous phenotypes (a block in secretion and accumulation of precursor polypeptides) (62). Other chaperone-assisted events may include the refolding of the pilus subunit proteins that occurs after their translocation across the membrane, the association of polypeptides into multisubunit complexes, changes in protein chemistry during the normal functioning of a complex, and subsequent polymerization of protein units to one another, possibly involving the dissociation of PapD.

Structure-Function Properties of PapD

Studying PapD as a representative model for this class of periplasmic chaperone proteins has many advantages. For example, the genetics of the *pap* locus have been extensively elucidated facilitating the manipulation of *pap* gene products and the analysis of chaperone target proteins; the three-dimensional structure of PapD is known, permitting the precise design and molecular analysis of site-directed mutations; the PapD and PapD-complexes have been easily isolated, and in vitro assays have been established to measure its activity. This information has been used to construct a point mutation in the proposed active cleft of PapD to begin mapping active surfaces of this protein (L. N. Slonim, J. S. Pinkner, A. Holmgren & S. J. Hultgren, submitted).

Glutamic acid-167 is part of a hypervariable loop positioned between beta strands C and D in domain 2 that protrudes into the solvent at the lip of the cleft (57). The importance of this residue in subunit binding was tested by changing Glu167 to a histidine by using site-directed mutagenesis (L. N. Slonim, J. S. Pinkner, A. Holmgren & S. J. Hultgren, submitted). The effect of this mutation on piliation was determined in a complementation analysis by supplying the wild-type PapD, (PapD$_{wt}$) or the mutant PapD (PapD$_{his}$), *in trans* into a strain of HB101 that contained the entire *pap* operon with an *xhoI* linker insertion in the *papD* gene. In this way, the two strains constructed were isogenic except for the single codon change in *papD* from GAG to CAC.

The effect of this mutation on piliation was determined using transmission electron microscopy (TEM) and by quantitating pilus antigen on the surface of the wild-type and mutant cells (L. N. Slonim, J. S. Pinker, A. Holmgren & S. J. Hultgren, submitted). The results showed that the *papD*$_{his}$ mutation caused kinetic alterations in pilus assembly as demonstrated by showing that an overnight culture of the PapD$_{wt}$ strain produced twofold more pili than the isogenic *PapD*$_{his}$ strain (L. N. Slonim, J. S. Pinker, A. Holmgren & S. J. Hultgren, submitted). This demonstration was the first to show how an alteration in a periplasmic chaperone can cause a corresponding alteration in the phenotype of a supramolecular structure—a significant observation considering that PapD is not a component of the final pilus structure. In summary, it seems that PapD's structural framework contains putative binding regions reminiscent of immunoglobulin domains, making it well suited to bind the structural subunits of the pilus.

Polymerization of Pilus Subunits and Chaperone Release

A feature common to all pilus gene clusters that have been examined in genetic detail is that they encode a high-molecular-weight outer-membrane protein essential for the assembly and surface localization of pili including FimD (75), SfaF (121, 127), FanD (128), and FaeD (109, 153) as well as nonfimbrial adhesins, including AfaC (82). In the P pilus system, assembly requires the expression of the 88.3-kd PapC protein. The *papC* nucleotide sequence has been determined and the deduced primary sequence analyzed (112). Cell fractionation experiments revealed that PapC was an outer-membrane protein. The number of pili formed per cell is directly related to the amount of PapC produced. The current hypothesis is that PapC plays an active role in the dissociation of PapD from pilus proteins as they are assembled into the pilus. However, very little is known about the molecular details of the release of PapD from its periplasmic complexes except that it is apparently ATP-independent. In contrast, cytoplasmic chaperones such as GroEL require ATP for release (45, 54). We can predict with high probability that PapD does not require ATP for release during assembly because the PapD structure does not contain an ATP binding domain. A typical ATP binding domain as has been found in adenyl cyclase (131) consists of a sheet of parallel beta strands with alpha helices on both sides and the nucleotide binding site on the carboxyl end of the beta sheet.

STRUCTURE OF P AND TYPE 1 PILI

Both the P and type 1 pilus filaments consist of a quaternary assembly of several thousand copies of the structural subunit that typically weighs 20 kd for P pili and 17 kd for type 1 pili. X-ray crystallography of the type 1 pilus filament by Brinton (13) has revealed that the filament is comprised of subunits that are arranged in a simple, tight right-handed helix with a central axial hole. He predicted that each turn of the helix consisted of 3.14 subunits and the helical pitch distance was 2.32 nm (13). Since these studies were undertaken long before the presence of minor subunits in the pilus was known, he did not account for these subunits in his predictions. X-ray crystallographic data are not available on the arrangement of subunits in the P pilus, but the arrangement of the structural subunits is probably similar to that of the type 1 pilus.

Lindberg et al (87) undertook the first studies to localize minor components in the pilus structure. They prepared monospecific antiserum against each of the minor pilus components to probe the surface of the P pilus filament. Immunogold electron microscopy revealed that three of the minor proteins of the P pilus including PapG, the Galα(1-4)Gal binding moiety, were exclusively located at the distal tips of the pili (87). Recent investigations revealed that the tip of the P pilus was morphologically distinct from the rest of the filament (M. J. Kuehn, J. Heuser, S. Normark & S. J. Hultgren, submitted) (Figure 3). The distal ends of P pili contain short thin fibers (approximately one third the diameter of the pilus filament) composed mainly of PapE. This finding demonstrates for the first time that the architecture of the P pilus tip is different from the main pilus filament and may imply that the assembly of this structure is different than the assembly of PapA. The diameter of the tip suggests that its subunits are arranged in a linear polymeric array. In conclusion, the pilus tip is a structure that resembles K88 pili: thin filaments arranged in linear polymeric arrays. This model argues that architectural differences amongst the pili produced by the *Enterobacteriaceae* may be determined by the ability or inability of the respective pilus subunits to pack into a right-handed helical rod.

In contrast to P pili, the receptor-binding component of type 1 pili, FimH, is not located exclusively at the tips (2, 3, 5). Immune electron microscopy with FimH-specific monoclonal antibodies revealed that FimH was also located along the length of the pilus filament. The location of FimH along the

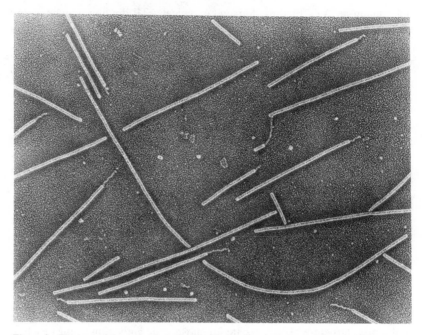

Figure 3 Electron micrograph of purified P pili showing the unique tip structure at the distal ends of some of the pili.

pilus filament did not appear to have any regular periodicity (2, 3). However, even if a periodic pattern of FimH localization existed, it would probably not have been detected with routine immunoelectron microscopy because of the limited amount of FimH in the pilus and because the helical arrangement of the pilus subunits could render some of the FimH molecules inaccessible to antibodies. No information is currently available on the location of the other ancillary pilus proteins FimF and FimG.

Although FimH is undoubtedly associated with the type 1 pilus filament, whether it is intercalated into the filament or merely tightly associated with the lateral sides of the pili is unknown. Some evidence, albeit of an indirect nature, suggests that FimH is an integral part of the pilus filament. For example, pili from a hyperadhesive mutant that contains five times more FimH than wild-type appear distorted and fragmented (2). Furthermore, pili from a FimH$^-$ mutant appear longer and less fragmented than wild-type (74, 98). Both of these observations imply that the association of FimH with the pilus filament enhances its destabilization and fragmentation, which is most consistent with a model of physical insertion of FimH rather than a lateral association with the filament. The notion that the presence of FimH in the pilus filament leads to increased fragility was tested by subjecting wild-type and mutant FimH⁻ pili to several cycles of freezing and thawing. Electron microscopic measurements of both pilus types before and after freeze-thawing revealed that wild-type pili were at least five times more fragmented than mutant pili (S. Ponniah, R. Endres, D. L. Hasty & S. N. Abraham, submitted). Even more intriguing was the finding associated with this study that the hemagglutination titers of wild-type pili were at least sixteen times greater after freeze-thawing (S. Ponniah, R. Endres, D. L. Hasty & S. N. Abraham, submitted). These data argue that fragmentation increased the total number of available receptor-binding FimH molecules. This increase can be explained if only the FimH proteins exposed at the tips of pili are functional or if they at least have a higher hemagglutination activity than FimH molecules integrated within the pilus structure. The idea that FimH exposed at the pilus tips are functionally more active has been supported by other observations that show increased potency of fragmented pili in mediating other FimH-associated functions of type 1 pili (S. Ponniah, R. Endres & S. N. Abraham, unpublished data).

Very little is known about the composition of the base of the pilus filament. Although no structure resembling the hook that couples flagella to the cell surface (102) has yet been identified on pili, it has been suggested that the product of the *papH* gene in the *pap* operon is located at the base of the pilus filament. PapH is a pilin-like protein believed to be the last pilus subunit incorporated into the pilus filament (7). Its presence at the base of the pilus is thought to signal termination of further pilus growth. The average length of a P pilus appears to be controlled by the relative stoichiometry of PapH to the structural subunit PapA. When an eightfold overproduction of PapH was induced relative to the wild-type situation, unusually short P pili were produced. Conversely, when PapH was underproduced relative to PapA, extremely long pili were expressed that were secreted into the culture supernatant (7). These data suggested that PapH may form interactions with the cell wall (or with PapC) to anchor the pilus to the cell surface. A subunit with a comparable function in type 1 pili may be FimF. This protein has been associated with the pilus filament and inactivation of *fimF* results in extremely long pili (74, 98).

Valuable information regarding the molecular arrangement of pilus subunits and the conditions that affect subunit polymerization were derived by completely dissociating pili into their subunits and then determining if and how reconstitution can best take place. Such studies have been undertaken with type 1 pili of *E. coli* (4, 34), 987P pili of enteroxigenic *E. coli* (130), PAK pili of *Pseudomonas aeruginosa* (155), and type 2 pili of *Actinomyces naeslundii* (J. P. Babu & S. N. Abraham, submitted). The quaternary structure of type 1 pili is extremely stable and, with the exception of guanidine hydrochloride, is resistant to actions of all common dissociating agents (13,

22, 101). Saturated guanidine hydrochloride, however, completely dissociates type 1 pili without evoking irreversible structural damage to the
subunits. Eshdat et al (34) showed that type 1 pili depolymerized by guanidine
hydrochloride can be reconstituted by the removal of the denaturant. They
found that the reconstituted pili had the same thickness but were often shorter
than native pili as determined by electron microscopy. Abraham et al (4)
monitored the denaturation and renaturation of type 1 pili by using a panel of
monoclonal antibodies that were directed towards conformation-specific epitopes. They demonstrated that depolymerization of pili resulted in the loss of
several quaternary structural-specific epitopes and in the exposure of several
new epitopes on the structural subunit that were previously buried in the
quaternary pilus conformation (4). In addition, reconstituted pili exhibited the
same level of reactivity as did native pili when probed with a panel of
monoclonal antibodies (4) supporting Eshdat's findings that reconstituted pili
were morphologically similar to wild-type pili. For example, monoclonal
antibodies specific for quaternary structural epitopes displayed the same
periodicity and spiral pattern of binding to reconstituted pili as with native
pili, indicating that the highly ordered subunit packing in the native pilus was
restored in the in vitro reconstituted pili. While no systematic study was
undertaken, it was found that pH, temperature, and ionic conditions were
critical factors in determining the rate of pilus repolymerization in vitro.
These reconstitution studies also highlighted the requirement for divalent
cations in the polymerization of type 1 pili; magnesium ions greatly enhanced
assembly whereas EDTA inhibited this process (4, 34). Similarly interesting
is that in vitro polymerization of pilus subunits does not require ATP. An
intriguing question is whether reconstituted pili retain any of the adhesive
capability of native pili.

Recently, a study found that certain concentrations of glycerol and guanidine hydrochloride selectively disrupted the hydrophobic and hydrogen bonds
that create the helical conformation of the pilus polymer (S. N. Abraham &
D. L. Hasty, unpublished data). This treatment resulted in the removal of the
quaternary structure of the pilus by unraveling the helices without significant
depolymerization (Figure 4). This linearized polymer of pilus subunits lends
itself ammenably to several investigations including the mapping of antigenic
determinants on the linearized polymer of type 1 pili that are normally buried
in the quaternary pilus conformation (4). In addition, attempts are currently
being made to localize the minor pilus components by immunoelectron
microscopy using specific antibodies. Any periodicity in the localization of
these minor components should be readily discerned.

In summary, our current understanding of the molecular architecture of P
and type 1 pili is that although they are heteropolymers, over 99% of the pilus
is comprised of the structural subunit. Therefore, the predictions of Brinton

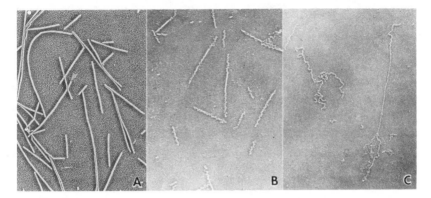

Figure 4   Electron micrograph of rotary shadowed preparations of type 1 pili after exposure to glycerol and guanidine hydrochloride showing unraveling of tight helical conformation of pilus subunits: (*A*) control, (*B*) partially unraveled, and (*C*) completely unraveled type 1 pili.

concerning the right-handed helical arrangement of the structural subunits in the filament could, for the most part, be correct. At least four proteins are associated with the P pilus fiber. Three of these, PapE, PapF, and the adhesin moiety PapG, are exclusively located at the pilus tips. These proteins are arranged in a linear polymeric spike structure that can be discerned on the tips of P pili. PapH appears to be inserted at the base of the pilus and serves as a terminator of pilus assembly and anchors the structure to the cell surface. Similarly, three minor proteins are associated with type 1 pilus fiber. Unlike PapG of the P pilus, however, the FimH adhesin moiety of the type 1 pilus is inserted at long intervals into the tight helical arrangement of the structural subunits. Since the size of FimH approximates two structural subunits, it possibly occupies the space of two structural subunits on the helix. The D-mannose binding domain on FimH is either buried or inaccessible when the molecule is intercalated in the pilus structure because only FimH molecules presented on the pilus tips appear able to mediate mannose-sensitive adhesive interactions. Interestingly, sites of FimH insertion within the pilus also appear to be the preferred sites for fragmentation. Information on the other minor proteins of type 1 pili is limited, and predictions on their location and function must await further study.

RECEPTOR BINDING AND ASSEMBLY DOMAINS OF PILUS ADHESINS

Pilus-associated bacterial adhesins necessarily have at least two activities. In addition to their receptor binding activity, they must contain assembly sites (or surfaces) necessary for their incorporation into a pilus. Initial investigations into the amino acid sequences of PapG involved in receptor binding tested the ability of carboxy-terminal deletion mutants of PapG to bind to Galα(1-4)Gal-sepharose (62). Periplasmic extracts from labeled minicells containing plasmids carrying two carboxy-terminal *papG* deletions were tested in a binding assay to Galα(1-4)Gal-sepharose. The carboxy-terminal deletions reduced the molecular weight of the native form of PapG and of three lower-molecular-weight polypeptides, identifying them as PapG truncates. Consequently, the receptor-binding properties of these PapG truncates were also analyzed. This analysis showed that a PapG peptide containing amino acids 1–142 did not bind to the receptor; however, a PapG truncate that was approximately 13 amino acids longer retained its galabiose binding specificity, identifying this region as one that has a critical role in binding to the receptor. However, a truncate of PapG that contained those 13 amino acids important in binding but was missing the amino terminus of PapG did not bind to the receptor, indicating that the amino-terminal third of PapG must also contain information necessary for binding (62).

The studies described above make clear that the interaction between PapG and PapD must be such that the galabiose-binding region of PapG is exposed because the complex retains the receptor-binding specificity. Deletion of the carboxy-terminal 13 amino acids of PapG abolished its ability to form a complex with PapD. This observation indicated that the carboxyl terminus of PapG forms part of an assembly site that is recognized by PapD (62).

Commensal and pathogenic bacteria display a remarkable selectivity for certain hosts and tissues (43, 118). This tropism is thought to result from the expression of adhesins with different binding specificities for cell surfaces (107, 118). Glycosides of galabiose (70) and binding assays to glycolipids immobilized on chromatograms have been used to develop a model illustrating the general features of adhesin-carbohydrate interactions and to begin to study the fine molecular details of host and tissue tropisms and of pili biogenesis.

We are currently analyzing the fine molecular details of adhesin-receptor interactions for three *pap* clones that bind human erythrocytes and one *prs* clone that binds sheep erythrocytes. The *pap* clones, pPAP5 (89), pPIL110-35 (152), and pDC1(16), cloned from strains AD110, J96, and IA2, express pili of serotypes F13, $F7_2$, and F11, respectively. The *prs* clone (95) also expresses pili of serotype F13. We refer to these four alleles as $papG_{AD110}$, $papG_{J96}$, $papG_{IA2}$, and $prsG_{J96}$, respectively. The respective adhesin gene (named G in all four cases) has been sequenced from each respective operon. $PapG_{J96}$ is only 50% homologous to both $PapG_{IA2}$ and $PapG_{AD110}$, but $PapG_{IA2}$ and $PapG_{AD110}$ differ from each other by only five amino acids (94,

139). The putative carboxy-terminal assembly surface of the PrsG$_{J96}$ adhesin is highly homologous to both PapG$_{IA2}$ and PapG$_{AD110}$, but the amino-terminal region of PrsG$_{J96}$ is strikingly different from all of the other three PapG proteins.

The ability of the four pili clones to bind to a panel of erythrocytes from 30 different animal sources was analyzed to gain insight into the correlation between amino acid sequence and binding specificity (N. Stromberg, P. G. Nyholm, I. Pascher & S. Normark, submitted). The three *pap* clones hemag-glutinated human and goat erythrocytes but not sheep erythrocytes. PapG$_{J96}$ unlike PapG$_{IA2}$ and PapG$_{AD110}$ also agglutinated rabbit erythrocytes. The *prs* clone agglutinated only a restricted number of erythrocytes from the species panel including sheep erythrocytes.

Interestingly, although all three classes of G adhesins bind the Forssman glycolipid in vitro, only PrsG$_{J96}$ could bind to this glycolipid when present in the sheep erythrocyte membrane. Similarly, on artificial surfaces, globotri-asyl ceramide is a high-affinity receptor for both PapG$_{AD110}$ and PapG$_{J96}$ but only PapG$_{J96}$ mediates agglutination of rabbit erythrocytes, which contain globotriasyl ceramide as the dominating isoreceptor (N. Stromberg, P. G. Nyholm, I. Pascher & S. Normark, submitted). These findings are true examples of *crypticity,* i.e. failure to participate in ligand-receptor in-teractions in spite of high concentrations in the membrane, and suggest a distinct functional isoreceptor for each G adhesin.

In an attempt to determine if any of the tip-located Pap proteins could alter the binding specificity mediated by the *prs* gene cluster, a frameshift mutation was first introduced into a position equivalent to a site within *papG$_{J96}$* of pPAP5. Cells harboring this *prsG* mutant no longer agglutinated sheep erythrocytes but instead could be made to agglutinate human P1 erythrocytes by the presence of a plasmid carrying an intact copy of *papG$_{J96}$*. The involvement of PapF in this phenomenon was excluded by comparing the effect of complementing the *prsG* mutation with plasmids containing muta-tions in *papF* or *papG$_{J96}$* (95). In this way, PapG was identified as the Galα(1-4)Gal-specific adhesin of the J96 P pilus. These data suggest that the receptor binding to the globoseries of glycolipids and the variation in isoreceptor recognition depends solely on the G adhesin and that sequence variations in the amino-terminal half of the protein determine the receptor binding specificity. In addition, the conserved carboxy terminii of these proteins may create homologous assembly surfaces, allowing them to use the same assembly machinery to be incorporated into pili. Supporting this view is the recent observation that the mannose-resistant *Klebsiella* adhesin (MR/K encoded by *mrkD*) can use the P pilus machinery to be incorporated into a P pilus. The most significant homology between the MR/K adhesin and PapG occurs in the carboxyl end of the molecule, which perhaps creates a conserved assembly surface that can be recognized by the P pilus assembly machinery and structural proteins (40).

The hypothesis that PapG solely determines isoreceptor specificity was tested further by comparing the interactions of the preassembled and tip-located $PapG_{J96}$ adhesins to the receptor. Receptor analogs were synthesized, in which hydroxyl groups crucial for bacterial binding to erythrocytes were exchanged for either a hydrogen, methoxy, or flourine group, (21, 39, 69, 70). These receptor analogs were then tested for their ability to block interactions between the pilus-tip-located $PapG_{J96}$ and erythrocytes in a hemagglutination inhibition assay and for their ability to elute the preassembled $PapG_{J96}$ adhesin from $Gal\alpha(1-4)Gal$-sepharose. In general, compounds that were either poor, intermediate, or good inhibitors of hemagglutination had correspondingly poor, intermediate, and good eluting powers (62). These results suggested that the adhesin possesses its binding specificity prior to its incorporation into the pilus and that the $PapG_{J96}$ adhesin possesses virtually the same galabiose-binding specificity in its preassembled state as when present at the pilus tip.

Interesting insight into differences in binding specificities in type 1 pili was recently obtained by evaluating the binding characteristics of clones expressing *E. coli* and *K. pneumoniae* type 1 pili (B. Madison, I. Ofek, E. H. Beachey & S. N. Abraham, submitted). Although their respective FimH proteins were structurally and antigenically similar, several distinct differences in the binding specificities between the two type 1 piliated clones were noted, including the observation that type 1 pili of *K. pneumoniae* but not *E. coli* mediated mannose-sensitive agglutination of sheep erythrocytes. Since the putative mannose-binding moiety of type 1 pili is the FimH protein, an attempt was made to convert the binding characteristics of *E. coli* into that of *K. pneumoniae* and vice versa by exchanging their respective FimHs with each other by deleting the *fimH* gene in each *fim* cluster and then complementing each deletion *in trans* with the heterologous *fimH* borne on a compatible plasmid. In this manner, two hybrid forms of type 1 pili were generated; in one case the *E. coli* FimH was presented on a filament of *K. pneumoniae* structural subunits (EcFimH-KpFimA); in the other case the *K. pneumoniae* FimH was presented on a filament of *E. coli* structural subunits (KpFimH-EcFimA). When the adhesive properties of these hybrid pili were evaluated, the workers found that EcFimH-KpFimA pili but not KpFimH-EcFimA pili mediated mannose-sensitive agglutination of sheep erythrocytes (B. Madison, I. Ofek, E. H. Beachey & S. N. Abraham, submitted). This finding was unexpected because it suggested that the sheep agglutinating property of *K. pneumoniae* was apparently not linked to its FimH protein but, rather, appeared to be associated with the filament composed of the *K. pneumoniae* structural subunits. However, FimH$^-$ mutant pili of *K. pneumoniae* have no hemagglutinating activity, arguing that the *K. pneumoniae* pilus filament, in the absence of FimH, does not contain a sheep erythrocyte–binding adhesin moiety. One possible explanation for the unexpected agglutination reactions is that the filament can indirectly affect the adhesin moiety by altering the conformation or presentation of the heterologous *E. coli* FimH molecule. For example, since the structural subunits of *K. pneumoniae* and *E. coli* are different, *E. coli* FimH must undergo some conformational alteration to fit the quaternary constraints of the *K. pneumoniae* pilus. Regions of the heterologous FimH molecule that are possibly altered could include the mannose-binding site. This model was supported by the data showing that some of the FimH-specific monoclonal antibodies had a dramatically lower reactivity to isolated EcFimH-KpFimA hybrid pili compared to the wild-type EcFimH-EcFimA (S. N. Abraham, unpublished observations). Experiments are underway to determine if the D-mannose binding pocket of the hybrid EcFimH-KpFimA was converted into a receptor-binding pocket that mimics the wild-type *K. pneumoniae* pilus (KpFimH-KpFimA) by probing their respective combining sites with various analogs of D-mannose as described previously by Firon et al (36, 37). The notion that the pilus filament can influence the binding properties of the adhesin moiety by modulating its configuration is novel and contrasts with the P pilus system in which PapG is the sole determinant of binding specificity.

ASSEMBLY OF TYPE 4 PILI

Several bacterial species such as *Neisseria gonorrhoeae*, *Moraxella bovis*, *Bacteroides nodosus*, and *Pseudomonas aeruginosa* express related pilins referred to as type 4 pilins (31, 96, 100, 103, 122). The pilins of both *B. nodosus* and *M. bovis* can be assembled into extracellular pilus fibers when the respective subunit gene is expressed in *P. aeruginosa* (10, 32, 97), implying a common pathway for the assembly of type 4 pili. These pilins all contain a conserved amino terminal hydrophobic domain beginning with an amino-terminal phenylalanine that is methylated upon processing and secretion of the pilin (55). Another characteristic feature of type 4 pilins is that in the propilin form they all contain similar six– or seven–amino acid–long leader peptides, which are much shorter than typical signal sequences. The role of these leader peptides as signal sequences involved in secretion has not yet been established. It appears from *phoA* fusion analyses of the *P. aeruginosa* pilin that the conserved amino-terminal hydrophobic region of the mature pilin may be involved in secretion (138). The Tcp pilin of *Vibrio cholerae* is highly homologous to type 4 pilins. Tcp pilin contains the characteristic amino-terminal hydrophobic domain as well as having a modified N-terminal amino acid that in this case is apparently a modified methionine because the Tcp pilin gene encodes a methionine residue at the position where all the others encode a phenylalanine. Precursor TcpA contains a much longer leader sequence than typical type 4 propilins but retains homology in the region surrounding the processing site (35, 136).

Pili of Neisseria gonorrhoeae

In the gonococcus, transition from a pilus$^+$ to a pilus$^-$ phenotype occurs at a high frequency (the switching rate ranges from 10^{-4} to 10^{-3}). These transitions are accompanied by changes in colonial morphology, which has greatly facilitated studies on phase variation of the gonococcal pilus (68, 143). Most strains of N. gonorrhoeae contain one copy of pilE, the expressed pilin gene, and multiple copies of pilS, which are transcriptionally silent incomplete pilin loci carrying variant sequences (49, 104). Intragenic recombination between silent and expressed loci leads to the formation of diverse pilins (52, 105, 133). One mechanism to explain the pathway by which this diversity is generated in pilE is transformation-mediated recombination of DNA that is released from lysing gonococci and taken up by surviving cells (44, 114, 134). A second pathway is thought to be the result of reciprocal recombination between a silent and an expressed locus of the same chromosome (44). Recently, however, Hill et al (56) presented data that argue that pilE undergoes an intragenomic gene-conversion event initiated by DNA deletions in pilE involving direct repeats. These investigators proposed that these deletions are subsequently repaired by pilS sequences creating the observed pilin diversity. The genetic mechanisms or combination of mechanisms by which pilE varies therefore remains controversial.

Mechanisms such as those described above that generate pilus antigenic diversity may also cause pilus phase variation from pilus$^+$ (P$^+$) to pilus$^-$ (P$^-$) and vice versa. Three different P$^-$ phenotypes have been defined. One P$^-$ phenotype is nonreverting (P$^-$n). These are gonococci that carry deletions in the pilE locus and therefore produce no pilin and no pilin-specific mRNA (141). Another class of P$^-$ variants are those that express pilin mRNA but no immunologically detectable pilin (P$^-$rp$^-$). Such variants can arise by frameshift mutations that change the number of C nucleotides in a C-tract located within the pilE gene, causing truncated pilins (11). The last class of P$^-$ variants are those that express both pilin mRNA and pilin and can revert to a pilus$^+$ phenotype (P$^-$rp$^+$). Sequence analyses revealed that the P$^-$rp$^+$ variants contained nucleotide changes in the pilin gene (P$^-$rp$^+$) relative to the P$^+$ parental clone. The nonpiliated phenotypes of P$^-$rp$^+$ variants may be the result of pilins that are defective in pilus assembly (142). Thus the same mechanisms that generate pilus antigenic diversity could also cause pilus phase variation.

No observations have indicated that genes closely linked to *pilE* are involved in the biogenesis of gonococcal pili. This complication together with the rapid occurrence of nonpiliated variants has made it extremely difficult to identify putative assembly genes for gonococcal pili. Since the frequency of pili phase variation is greatly reduced in *recA* mutants of *N. gonorrhoeae* (77), one approach was to investigate mutants defective in piliation in a $recA^-$ background in an attempt to identify assembly genes.

A biochemical approach has recently been used to identify genes and gene products required for gonococcal pilus assembly (65). Highly purified preparations of gonococcal pili were found to contain minor amounts of a 110-kd large outer-membrane protein. Two complete nonidentical copies for the corresponding structural gene, *pilC,* were identified and found located at different positions on the chromosome (J. Cannon, personal communication). Expression of *pilC* from each of the loci was controlled at the level of translation by frequent frameshift mutations occurring in a tract of G nucleotides positioned in the region encoding the signal peptide. These frameshift mutations occurred independently in each *pilC* locus, giving rise to variants that expressed only PilC1 or only PilC2 or both proteins. When both *pilC1* and *pilC2* were shifted out of frame, PilC expression was completely abolished. Several P^+ variants that switched to a nonpiliated pilin-producing phenotype were examined for their expression of PilC. All lacked PilC expression, but when P^+ revertants were examined from such clones, all had regained expression of PilC. Insertional inactivation of both *pilC1* and *pilC2* resulted in a stable nonpiliated phenotype. Genetic inactivation by the minitransposon mTn*cm* (135) of the expressed *pilC* locus abolished piliation, while inactivation of the nonexpressed locus had no effect on piliation. Taken together these data strongly argue that expression of PilC is required for the biogenesis of gonococcal pili. Supporting this hypothesis was the finding that the *pilE* sequence in one nonpiliated PilC$^-$ variant was identical to the sequence in one isogenic piliated backswitcher that was PilC$^+$, showing that the unassembled pilin in the P$^-$ variant is structurally assembly proficient.

Interestingly, most reported pilin antigenic variants in gonococci have been obtained via a phaseshift from one P^+ state to another via a P$^-$ transition state. The frequency with which the outer-membrane protein PilC is turned on and off has not yet been exactly determined but is in the order of magnitude of 10^{-4}. If the PilC off switch was unrelated to the structural change in the pilin, most, if not all, of the PilC off switchers would produce a pilin identical to the PilC$^+$ parent variant. In contrast, all pilins that have been sequenced in such PilC$^+$→PilC$^-$ pairs have an alteration in the pilin gene. Likewise most P$^+$, PilC$^+$ revertants from P$^-$, PilC$^-$ variants also expressed an altered pilin (A.

B. Jonsson, J. Pfeifer & S. Normark, submitted). The possibility therefore exists that the on and off transitions of PilC expression cause a selection for pilin variation. In a recent review article, Scocca (132) presented several arguments for a programmed mechanism of pilin variation. Silent *pilS* sequences are physically separated from transformation uptake sequences (46), suggesting that *pilS* loci would be taken up poorly by competent cells. Moreover, homology is limited at the recombination sites between silent and expression loci, and the efficiency of RecA-mediated recombination greatly depends on the length of perfectly matched homologies (154). Based on these considerations, Scocca (132) speculated that incoming DNA may induce a global regulatory circuit–enhancing recombination between *pilE* and *pilS*.

An alternative explanation is that the frequent structural diversity in *pilE* results from programmed selection at the level of pilus assembly. For example, a turn off of PilC expression would result in the accumulation of unassembled pilin. We observed that all PilC off switchers expressed both the full-length pilin and a short 16-kd pilin truncate, which most likely represents the S-pilin previously described by Haas et al (50). S-pilin is derived from full-length pilin by a proteolytic cleavage after amino acid residue 39. As a result, it is more hydrophilic than full-length pilin and is secreted into the medium by an unknown mechanism. An intriguing possibility is that an accumulation in PilC⁻ cells of unassembled full-length pilin is toxic, whereas the S form is not since it is readily secreted. Thus, pilin variants that arise which can be processed to an S-pilin form would be selected for in the PilC⁻ background. Many or most of these pilin variants (that can be processed to the S-form) may be assembly defective even when PilC is switched back on (backswitchers). Consequently, P⁺, PilC⁺ backswitchers must necessarily be revertants containing novel pilin alterations that yield assembly proficient pilin variants. This selective model for structural diversity in *pilE* is supported by recent studies in which a *pilC1, pilC2* double "knock out" mutant was created (A. B. Jonsson, J. Pfeifer & S. Normark, submitted). The double mutant initially expressed pilin but grew poorly. Upon subculturing, faster-growing colonies were observed and subsequently shown to contain deletions in *pilE* and thus no longer produced pilin. The best interpretation of these results is that in the double knock out mutant, pilin expression is toxic to the cells because of the accumulation of unassembled subunits, and this toxicity results in a strong selection for deletions in *pilE*. Further evidence for the selective model comes from the finding that identical pilins, depending on whether they were assembled via PilC1 or PilC2, give rise to markedly different degrees of piliation, suggesting that different pilin variants may be assembled with different efficiencies depending on whether *pilC1, pilC2,* or both loci are expressed.

Translational frameshifting in *pilC* is a *recA*-independent process probably generated by slipped-strand mispairing during DNA-replication or DNA-repair (111). In contrast, phase variation of gonococcal pili expression is dramatically decreased in a *recA⁻* background (77). The selective model described here would argue that most PilC⁻ off switchers are lethal in a *recA⁻* background because of the accumulation of toxic unassembled pilin. Recent experiments supporting this view have shown that P⁻, PilC⁻ off switchers in a *recA⁻* background are not expressing pilin, in contrast to the *recA⁺* situation in which all tested P⁻, PilC⁻ variants expressed an altered pilin. Furthermore, one P⁻, PilC⁻ pilin-producing off switcher from a *recA⁻* strain contained a point mutation altering leucine 39 to a phenylalanine. This alteration generated an S-pilin processing site (A. B. Jonsson & S. Normark, in preparation).

TCP Pili of Vibrio cholerae

The *toxR* regulated pilin gene of *V. cholerae, tcpA,* is part of a gene cluster involved in regulation and assembly of TCP pili (144, 145). Most of the *tcp* gene products are likely to be secreted proteins because translational fusions with *phoA* give PhoA⁺ phenotypes. Some of the functions of the *tcp* gene products and their subcellular locations have recently been assessed. One of these, the *tcpJ* gene product, is required for processing of the TcpA propilin and may therefore be a specific signal peptidase (R. Taylor, personal communication). The *tcpB* gene is located immediately downstream of the *tcpA* pilin subunit gene in the *tcp* gene cluster and contains a short sequence highly homologous to leader sequences of the type 4 pilins of *N. gonorrhoeae* and other species (P. Manning, personal communication). In addition, both mature TcpA and TcpB have very similar hydrophobic N termini. Therefore, TcpJ could act as a signal peptidase for both TcpA and TcpB. Whether or not TcpB is a minor pilus-associated protein in the Tcp pilus fiber has not yet been shown but seems likely. Another gene product encoded within the *tcp* gene cluster, TcpC, is an outer membrane lipoprotein (J. Mekalanos, personal communication). Available data suggest that the functional binding properties of TCP pili are mediated by the major pilin protein itself and not a minor component (140). Another gene, *tcpG,* is located outside of the *tcp* gene cluster, which has been shown to encode a product required for efficient biogenesis of TCP pili. This gene product shares homology with thioredoxin and disulfide isomerase and has similar in vitro activities to these proteins, suggesting that it may act as a chaperone in TCP pilus assembly (R. Taylor, personal communication).

Pseudomonas aeruginosa *Pili*

In *P. aeruginosa*, three genes (*pilB, pilC,* and *pilD*) have been located adjacent to the *pilA* pilin subunit gene but found to be transcribed in the opposite direction (117). Transposon insertion mutants in any of these *pil* genes abolished piliation but expressed pilin subunits, suggesting that *pilB, pilC,* and *pilD* are involved in pilus assembly. PilB may be a cytoplasmic protein while PilC and PilD may be integral membrane proteins. Insertion inactivation of *pilD* resulted in an accumulation of the *P. aeruginosa* propilin, suggesting that PilD may be a signal peptidase (117, 157, 158). PilD shares homology in one region with the TcpJ product of *V. cholerae*, suggesting that these proteins are functionally related (R. Taylor, personal communication). None of the three accessory *pil* genes seem to have any structural counterparts in gene clusters expressing different types of *E. coli* pili. Therefore, secretion of type 4 pilins across the cytoplasmic membrane may require a unique secretion apparatus not used by *E. coli* major and minor pilins. However, the accessory Pil proteins of *P. aeruginosa* show homologies with those proteins involved in DNA transport in *Bacillus subtilis* and secretion of pullulanase in *Klebsiella oxytoca* (159).

Biogenesis Model for Type 4 Pili

By combining the available data from *N. gonorrhoeae, V. cholerae,* and *P. aeruginosa*, we can deduce a highly tentative model for the biogenesis of type 4 pili. The secretion of the type 4 pilin subunit across the cytoplasmic membrane may involve a unique signal peptidase and other proteins that target the pilin to a secretory route. Protection of interactive surfaces during pilin secretion may be achieved by periplasmic chaperones or by outer-membrane proteins similar to PilC of *N. gonorrhoeae*. In addition, pili anchoring to the outer membrane may involve one or more specific outer-membrane lipoproteins. Whether or not type 4 pili are homopolymers or heteropolymers with associated minor subunit proteins is yet unresolved.

SUMMARY

The assembly of bacterial pili as exemplified here by P and type 1 pili of *E. coli* is a complex process involving specific molecular interactions between structural and chaperone proteins (see Figure 5). The assembly process occurs postsecretionally, i.e. after the subunits are translocated across the cytoplasmic membrane. In a single cell, hundreds of thousands of interactive subunits are typically surface localized and assembled into pili.

Periplasmic chaperones are generally required to bind to the interactive subunits and partition them into assembly-competent complexes. The binding of the chaperone to the subunits apparently protects the interactive surfaces and prevents them from aggregating at the wrong time and place within the cell. Pili are most likely assembled into linear polymers that package into right-handed helices after their translocation through specific outer-membrane channels. Each pilus filament is a quaternary assembly of the structural subunit and several minor subunits including the adhesin moiety. Although the assembly and organization of P and type 1 pili are very similar, there are some notable differences. For example, the P pilus adhesin is located ex-clusively at the tips of the pilus filament and forms part of a morphologically distinct structure. In contrast, the adhesin moiety of type 1 pili is inserted into the pilus filament at intervals, but only the adhesin molecule exposed at the pilus tip is functional. The variability in isoreceptor recognition amongst P pili has been solely ascribed to structural differences in the respective adhesin molecules, whereas in type 1 pili, variability in binding specificity has been attributed to the pilus filament that influences the conformation of the adhesin moiety.

Less is known about the structure or assembly of type 4 pili, which are a unique class of pili expressed by several different species of gram-negative bacteria. The phase variation of the *pilC* assembly gene in *N. gonorrheae* to the off state results in the accumulation of unassembled subunits toxic to the cells. This process exerts a strong selection pressure on the cells that triggers

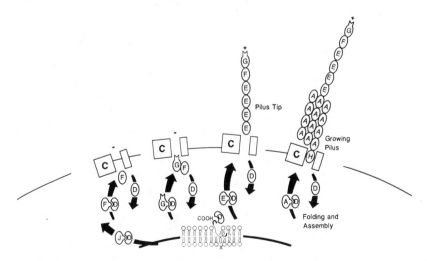

Figure 5   Model of postsecretional pilus assembly. The details of this figure are discussed in the text.

alterations in the pilin structural gene. Thus, antigenic variation of pili in this organism may be regulated at the level of assembly.

Finally, the concept of periplasmic chaperones in postsecretional assembly is most likely a general phenomenon in the biology of gram-negative bacteria. The investigations of pilus assembly will continue to provide insight into the details of how macromolecular assembly reactions are coordinated in the bacterial cell and how the regulation of assembly genes can profoundly affect biological processes.

ACKNOWLEDGMENTS

Dr. Normark's work was supported by grants from the Swedish Medical Research Council (B87-16X-04769-12A and B86-16P-06893-03A), the Swedish Natural Sciences Research Council (B-BU-3373-112), and the National Institute of Health (1 R01 GM4465501) and Symbicom. Dr. Hultgren's work was supported by grants from the National Institute of Health (1 R01 AI 29549 01A1), Symbicom, and the Lucille P. Markey Charitable Trust. Dr. Abraham's work was supported by research funds from the US Veterans Administration and from a Public Health Service Grant (AI-13550) from the National Institute of Health.

Literature Cited

1. Abraham, J. M., Freitag, C. S., Clements, J. R., Eisenstein, B. I. 1985. An invertible element of DNA controls phase variation of type 1 fimbriae of *Escherichia coli*. *Proc. Natl. Acad. Sci. USA* 82:5724–27

2. Abraham, S. N., Goguen, J. D., Beachey, E. H. 1988. Hyperadhesive mutant of type 1 fimbriated *Escherichia coli* associated with the formation of FimH organelles (fimbriosomes). *Infect. Immun.* 56:1023–29

3. Abraham, S. N., Goguen, J. D., Sun, D., Klemm, P., Beachey, E. H. 1987. Identification of two ancillary subunits of *Escherichia coli* type 1 fimbriae by using antibodies against synthetic oligopeptides of *fim* gene products. *J. Bacteriol.* 169:5530–35

4. Abraham, S. N., Hasty, D. L., Simpson, W. A., Beachey, E. H. 1983. Antiadhesive properties of a quaternary structure-specific hybridoma antibody against type 1 fimbriae of *Escherichia coli*. *J. Exp. Med.* 158:1128–44

5. Abraham, S. N., Sun, D., Dale, J. B., Beachey, E. H. 1988. Conservation of the D-mannose-adhesion protein among type 1 fimbriated members of the family *Enterobactericeae*. *Nature (London)* 336:682–84

6. Baga, M., Goransson, M., Normark, S., Uhlin, B. E. 1985. Transcriptional activation of a Pap pilus virulence operon from uropathogenic *Escherichia coli*. *EMBO J.* 4:3887–93

7. Baga, M., Norgren, M., Normark, S. 1987. Biogenesis of *E. coli* Pap-pili: PapH, a minor pilin subunit involved in cell anchoring and length modulation. *Cell* 49:241–51

8. Baga, M., Normark, S., Hardy, J., O'Hanley, P., Lark, D., et al. 1984. Nucleotide sequence of the gene encoding the *papA* pilus subunit of human uropathogenic *Escherichia coli*. *J. Bacteriol.* 157:330–33

8a. Beachey, E. H., ed. 1980. *Bacterial Adherence Receptors and Recognition*. London: Chapman & Hall

9. Beachey, E. H. 1981. Bacterial adherence: Adhesin-receptor interactions mediating the attachment of bacteria to mucosal surfaces. *J. Infect. Dis.* 143:325–45

10. Beard, M. K. M., Mattick, J. S., Moore, M. R., Marrs, C. F., Egerton, J. R. 1990. Morphogenic expression of *Moraxella bovis* fimbiae (pili) in *Pseudomonas aeruginosa*. *J. Bacteriol.* 172:2601–7

11. Bergstrom, S., Robbins, K., Koomey,

J. M., Swanson, J. 1986. Piliation control mechanism in *Neisseria gonorrhoeae*. *Proc. Natl. Acad. Sci. USA* 83:3890–94

12. Bochkareva, E. S., Lissin, N. M., Girshovich, A. S. 1988. Transient association of newly synthesized unfolded proteins with the heat-shock GroEL protein. *Nature* 336:254–57

13. Brinton, C. C. 1965. The structure, function, synthesis, and genetic control of bacterial pili and a model for DNA and RNA transport in gram negative bacteria. *Trans. N. Y. Acad. Sci.* 27:1003–1165

14. Brinton, C. C. Jr. 1959. Non-flagellar appendages of bacteria. *Nature* 183:782–86

15. Brundage, L., Hendrick, J. P., Schiebel, E., Driessen, A. J. M., Wickner, W. 1990. The purified *E. coli* integral membrane protein SecY/E is sufficient for reconstitution by SecA dependent precursor protein translocation. *Cell* 62:649–57

16. Clegg, S. 1982. Cloning of genes determining the production of mannose-resistant fimbriae in a uropathogenic *Escherichia coli* belonging to serogroup 06. *Infect. Immun.* 38:739–44

17. Clegg, S., Hull, S., Hull, R., Pruckler, J. 1985. Construction and comparison of recombinant plasmids encoding type 1 fimbriae of members of the family *Enterobacteriacae*. *Infect. Immun.* 48:275–79

18. Clegg, S., Pruncler, J., Purcell, B. K. 1985. Complementation analyses of recombinant plasmids encoding type 1 fimbriae of members of the family *Enterobacteriacae*. *Infect. Immun.* 50:338–40

19. Crooke, E., Brundage, L., Rice, M., Wickner, W. 1988. Pro OmpA spontaneously folds into a membrane assembly competent state which trigger factor stabilizes. *EMBO J.* 7:1831–35

20. Crooke, E., Guthrie, B., Lecker, S., Lil, R., Wickner, W. 1988. Pro OmpA is stabilized for membrane translocation by either purified *E. coli* trigger factor or canine signal recognition particle. *Cell* 54:1003–11

21. Dahmen, J., Frejd, T., Magnusson, G., Noori, G., Carlstrom, A. S. 1984. 2-Bromoethyl glycosides in glycoside synthesis: preparation of glycoproteins containing α-L-Fuc-(1→2)-D-Gal and β-D-Gal-(1→4)-D-GlcNAc. *Carbohydr. Res.* 125:237–45

21a. De Graaf, F. K., Krenn, B. E., Klaasen, P. 1984. Organization and expression of genes involved in the biosythesis of K99 fimbrae. *Infect. Immun.* 43:508–14

22. Dodd, D. C., Eisenstein, B. I. 1982. Antigenic quantitation inhibition assay of type 1 fimbriae on the surface of *Escherichia coli* cells by an enzyme linked immunosorbent inhibition assay. *Infect. Immun.* 38:764–69

23. Dorman, C. J., Higgins, C. F. 1987. Fimbrial phase variation in *Escherichia coli:* Dependence on integration host factor and homologies with other site-specific recombinases. *J. Bacteriol.* 169:3840–43

24. Dougan, G., Dowd, G., Kehoe, M. 1983. Organization of K88ac-encoded polypeptides in the *Escherichia coli* cell envelope: use of minicells and outer membrane protein mutants for studying assembly of pili. *J. Bacteriol.* 153:364–70

25. Duguid, J. P., Clegg, S., Wilson, M. I. 1979. The fimbrial and non-fimbrial haemagglutinins of *Escherichia coli*. *J. Med. Microbiol.* 12:213–27

26. Duguid, J. P., Old, D. C. 1980. Adhesive properties of *Enterobacteriacae*. See Ref. 8a, pp. 187–217

27. Duguid, J. P., Smith, I. W., Dempster, G., Edmunds, P. N. 1955. Non-flagellar filamentous appendages ("fimbriae") and hemagglutinating activity in *Bacterium coli*. *J. Pathol. Bacteriol.* 70:335–48

28. Eilers, M., Schatz, G. 1988. Protein unfolding and the energetics of protein translocation across biological membranes. *Cell* 52:481–83

29. Eisenstein, B. I. 1981. Phase variation of type 1 fimbriae in *Escherichia coli* is under transcriptional control. *Science* 214:337–39

30. Eisenstein, B. J. 1990. Enterobacteriacae. In *Enterobacteriacae in Principles and Practice of Infectious Diseases*, ed. G. L. Mandell, R. Gordon Danglers, J. E. Bennet. pp. 1658–73. New York: Churchill Livingston

31. Elleman, T. C., Hoyne, P. A. 1984. Nucleotide sequence of the gene encoding pilin of *Bacteroides nodosus,* the causal organism of bovine foot rot. *J. Bacteriol.* 160:1184–87

32. Elleman, T. C., Hoyne, P. A., Stewart, D. J., McKern, N. M., Peterson, J. E. 1986. Expression of pili from *Bacteroides nodosus* in *Pseudomonas aeruginosa*. *J. Bacteriol.* 168:574–80

33. Ellis, R. J., Hemmingson, S. M. 1989. Molecular chaperones: proteins essential for the biogenesis of some macromolecular structures. *Trends Biochem. Sci.* 14:339–42

34. Eshdat, Y., Silverblatt, F. J., Sharon, N. 1981. Dissociation and reassembly of *Escherichia coli* type 1 pili. *J. Bacteriol.* 148:308–14

35. Faast, R., Ogierman, A., Stroeher, U. H., Manning, P. A. 1989. Nucleotide sequence of the structural gene, *tcpA*, for a major pilin subunit of *Vibrio cholerae. Gene* 85:227–31

36. Firon, N., Ashkenazis, S., Mirelman, D., Ofek, I., Sharon, N. 1987. Aromatic α-glycosides of mannose are powerful inhibitors of the adherence of type 1 fimbriated *Escherichia coli* to yeast and intestinal cells. *Infect. Immun.* 55:472–76

37. Firon, N., Ofek, I., Sharon, N. 1983. Carbohydrate specificity of the surface lectins of *Escherichia coli, Klebsiella pneumoniae* and *Salmonella typhimurium. Carbohydr. Res.* 120:235–49

38. Forsman, K., Goransson, M., Uhlin, B. E. 1989. Autoregulation and multiple DNA interactions by a transcriptional regulatory protein in *E. coli* pili biogenesis. *EMBO J.* 8:1271–78

39. Garegg, P. J., Oscarsson, S. 1985. Synthesis of 6- and 6'-deoxy derivatives of methyl 4-*O*-α-D-galatopyranosyl-β-D-galactopyranoside for studies of inhibition of pyelonephritogenic fimbriated *E. coli* adhesion to urinary epithelium-cell surfaces. *Carbohydr. Res.* 137:270–75

40. Gerlach, G. D., Clegg, S., Allen, B. L. 1989. Identification and characterization of the genes encoding the type 3 and type 1 fimbrial adhesins of *Klebsiella pneumoniae. J. Bacteriol.* 171:1262–70

41. Gerlach, G. D., Clegg, S., Ness, N. J., Swenson, D. L., Allen, B. L., Nichols, W. D. 1989. Expression of type 1 fimbriae and mannose-sensitive hemagglutinin by recombinant plasmids. *Infect. Immun.* 57:764–70

42. Giampapa, C. S., Abraham, S. N., Chiang, T. M., Beachey, E. H. 1988. Isolation and characterization of the receptor for type 1 fimbriae of *Escherichia coli* from guinea pig erythrocytes. *J. Biol. Chem.* 5362–67

43. Gibbons, R. J., Van Houte, I. 1975. Bacterial adherence in oral microbial ecology. *Annu. Rev. Microbiol.* 29:19–44

44. Gibbs, C. P., Reimann, B. Y., Schultz, E., Kaufmann, A., Haas, R., Meyer, T. F. 1989. Reassortment of pilin genes in *Neisseria gonorrhoeae* occurs by two distinct mechanisms. *Nature* 338:651–52

45. Goloubinoff, P., Christeller, J. T., Gatenby, A. A., Lorimer, G. H. 1989. Reconstitution of active dimeric ribulose biphosphate carboxylase from an unfolded state depends on two chaperonin proteins and Mg-ATP. *Nature* 342:884–89

46. Goodman, S. D., Scocca, J. J. 1988. Identification and arrangement of the DNA sequence recognized in specific transformation of *Neisseria gonorrhoeae. Proc. Natl. Acad. Sci. USA* 85:6982–86

47. Goransson, M., Forsman, K., Uhlin, B. E. 1989. Regulatory genes in the thermoregulation of *Escherichia coli* pili gene transcription. *Genes Dev.* 3:123–30

48. Guyot, G. 1908. Uber die bakterielle Haemagglutination (Bacterio-Haemagglutination). *Zentralbl. Bakteriol. Parasitenkd. Infektionskr. Hyg. Abt. 1: Orig.* 47:640–53

49. Haas, R., Meyer, T. 1986. The repertoire of silent pilus genes in *Neisseria gonorrhoeae:* Evidence for gene conversion. *Cell* 44:107–15

50. Haas, R., Schwartz, H., Meyer, T. F. 1987. Release of soluble pilin antigen coupled with gene conversion in *Neisseria gonorrhoeae. Proc. Natl. Acad. Sci. USA* 84:9079–83

51. Hacker, J., Schmidt, G., Hughes, C., Knapp, S., Marget, M., Goebel, W. 1985. Cloning and characterization of genes involved in production of mannose-resistant neuraminidase-susceptible (X) fimbriae from a uropathogenic 06:K15:H31 *Escherichia coli* strain. *Infect. Immun.* 47:434–40

52. Hagblom, P., Segal, E., Billyard, E., So, M. 1985. Intragenic recombination leads to pilus antigenic variation in *Neisseria gonorrhoeae. Nature* 315:156–58

53. Hansen, M. S., Brinton, C. C. 1988. Identification and characterization of *E. coli* type 1 pilus tip adhesion protein. *Nature (London)* 332:265–68

54. Hemmingsen, S. M., Woolford, C., van der Vies, S. M., Tilly, K., Dennis, D. T., et al. 1988. Homologous plant and bacterial proteins chaperone oligomeric protein assembly. *Nature* 333:330–34

55. Hermodson, M. A., Chenk, K. C. S., Buchanan, T. M. 1978. *Neisseria* pili proteins: amino-terminal amino acid sequences and identification of an unusual amino acid. *Biochemistry* 17:442–45

56. Hill, S. A., Morrison, S. G., Swanson, J. 1990. The role of direct oligonucleotide repeats in gonococcal pilin gene variation. *Mol. Microbiol.* 4(8):1341–52

57. Holmgren, A., Branden, C. I. 1989. Crystal structure of chaperone protein

PapD reveals an immunoglobulin fold. *Nature* 342:248–51

58. Hoschutzky, H., Lottspeich, F., Jann, K. 1989. Isolation and characterization of the α-galactosyl-1, 4-β galactosyl-specific adhesin (P Adhesin) from fimbriated *Escherichia coli*. *Infect. Immun.* 57:76–81

59. Hull, R. A., Gill, R. E., Hsu, P., Minshaw, B. H., Falkow, S. 1981. Construction and expression of recombinant plasmids encoding type 1 and D-mannose-resistant pili from a urinary tract infection *Escherichia coli* isolate. *Infect. Immun.* 33:933–38

60. Hull, R. A., Hull, S. I., Falkow, S. 1984. Frequency of gene sequences necessary for pyelonephritis-associated pili expression among isolates of *Enterobacteriaceae* from human extraintestinal infections. *Infect. Immun.* 43:1064–67

61. Hultgren, S. J., Duncan, J. L., Schaeffer, A. J., Amundsen, S. K. 1990. Mannose-sensitive hemagglutination in the absence of piliation in *Escherichia coli*. *Mol. Microbiol.* 4:1311–18

62. Hultgren, S. J., Lindberg, F., Magnusson, G., Kihlberg, J., Tennent, J. M., Normark, S. 1989. The PapG adhesin of uropathogenic *Escherichia coli* contains separate regions for receptor binding and for the incorporation into the pilus. *Proc. Natl. Acad. Sci. USA* 86:4357–61

63. Hultgren, S. J., Porter, T. N., Schaeffer, A. J., Duncan, J. L. 1985. Role of type 1 pili and effects of phase variation on lower urinary tract infections produced by *Escherichia coli*. *Infect. Immun.* 50:370–77

64. Hultgren, S. J., Schwan, W. R., Schaeffer, A. J., Duncan, J. L. 1986. Regulation of production of type 1 pili among urinary tract isolates of *Escherichia coli*. *Infect. Immun.* 54:613–20

65. Jonsson, A. B., Nyberg, G., Normark, S. 1991. Phase variation of gonococcal pili by frameshift mutation in *pilC*, a novel gene for pilus assembly. *EMBO J.* 10:477–88

66. Kallenius, G., Mollby, R., Svenson, S. B., Windberg, J., Lundblud, A., et al. 1980. The P^K antigen as receptor for the haemagglutinin of pyelonephritogenic *Escherichia coli*. *FEMS Microbiol. Lett.* 8:297–302

67. Karr, J. F., Nowicki, B., Truong, L. D., Hull, R. A., Hull, S. I. 1989. Purified P fimbriae from two cloned gene clusters of a single pyelonephritogenic strain adhere to unique structures in the human kidney. *Infect. Immun.* 57:3594–3600

68. Kellogg, D. S., Peacock, W. L., Dea-con, W. E., Brown, L., Pirkle, C. I. 1963. *Neisseria gonorrhoeae*. I. Virulence genetically linked to clonal variation. *J. Bact.* 85:1274–79

69. Kihlberg, J., Frejd, T., Jansson, K., Sundin, A., Magnusson, G. 1988. Synthetic Receptor Analogues: Preparation and Calculated Conformations of the 2-Deoxy, 6-0-Methyl, 6-Deoxy and 6-Deoxy-6-Fluoro Derivatives of Methyl 4-O-α-D-Galactopyranoside (Methyl β-D-Galabioside). *Carbohydr. Res.* 176:271–86

70. Kihlberg, J., Hultgren, S. J., Normark, S., Magnusson, G. 1989. Probing of the Combining Site of the PapG Adhesin of Uropathogenic *Escherichia coli* Bacteria by Synthetic Analogues of Galabiose. *J. Am. Chem. Soc.* 111:6364–6368

71. Klein, J. O., Marcy, S. M. 1976. Bacterial infections. (A.) Sepsis and meningitis. In *Infectious Diseases of the Fetus and Newborn Infant*, ed. J. S. Remington, J. O. Klein, pp. 747–802. Philadelphia: Saunders

72. Klemm, P. 1985. Fimbrial adhesins of *Escherichia coli*. *Review Infect. Dis.* 7:321–339

73. Klemm, P. 1986. Two regulatory *fim* genes, *fimB* and *fimE*, control the phase variation of type 1 fimbriae in *Escherichia coli*. *EMBO J.* 5:1389–93

74. Klemm, P., Christensen, G. 1987. Three *fim* genes required for the regulation of length and mediation of adhesion of *Escherichia coli* isolate. *Infect. Immun.* 33:933–38

75. Klemm, P., Christiansen, G. 1990. The *fimD* gene required for cell surface localization of *Escherichia coli* type 1 fimbriae. *Mol. Gen. Genet.* 220:334–38

76. Klemm, P., Jorgensen, B. J., van Die, I., de Ree, H., Bergman, H. 1985. The *fim* genes responsible for synthesis of type 1 fimbriae in *Escherichia coli* cloning and genetic organization. *Mol. Gen. Genet.* 199:410–14

77. Koomey, J. M., Gotschlich, E. C., Robbins, K., Bergstrom, S., Swanson, J. 1987. Effects of *recA* mutations on pilus antigenic variation and phase transitions in *Neisseria gonorrhoeae*. *Genetics* 117:391–98

78. Krogfelt, K. A., Bergmans, H., Klemm, P. 1990. Direct evidence that the FimH protein is the mannose specific adhesin of *Escherichia coli* type 1 fimbriae. *Infect. Immun.* 58:1995–99

79. Kumamoto, C. A. 1990. SecB protein-A cytosolic export factor that associates with nascent exported proteins. *J. Bioenerg. Biomembr.* 22:337–51

80. Kumamoto, C. A., Beckwith, J. 1983. Mutations in a new gene, *secB*, cause defective protein localization in *Escherichia coli*. *J. Bacteriol.* 154:253–60

81. Kumamoto, C. A., Beckwith, J. 1985. Evidence for specificity at an early step in protein export in *Escherichia coli*. *J. Bacteriol.* 163:267–74

82. Labigne-Roussel, A. F., Schmidt, M. A., Walz, W., Falkow, S. 1985. Genetic organization of the AFA operon and nucleotide sequence from a uropathogenic *Escherichia coli* gene encoding an afimbrial adhesin (AFA-1). *J. Bacteriol.* 162:1285–92

83. Lecker, S., Driessen, A. J. M., Wickner, W. 1990. ProOmpA contains secondary and tertiary structure prior to translocation and is shielded from aggregation by association with SecB protein. *EMBO J.* 9:2309–14

84. Lecker, S., Lill, R., Ziegelhoffer, T., Bassford, P. J. Jr., Kumamoto, C. A., Wickner, W. 1989. Three pure chaperone proteins of *Escherichia coli*, SecB, trigger factor, and Gro EL, form soluble complexes with precursor proteins in vitro. *EMBO J.* 8:2703–9

85. Leffler, H., Svanborg-Eden, C. 1980. Chemical identification of a glycosphingolipid receptor for *Escherichia coli* attaching to human urinary tract epithelial cells and agglutinating human erythrocytes. *FEMS Microbiol. Lett.* 8:127–34

86. Levine, M. M., Kaper, J. B., Black, R. E., Clements, M. L. 1983. New knowledge on pathogenesis of bacterial enteric infections as applied to vaccine development. *Microbiol. Rev.* 47:510–50

87. Lindberg, F. P., Lund, B., Johansson, L., Normark, S. 1987. Localization of the receptor-binding protein at the tip of the bacterial pilus. *Nature* 328:84–87

88. Lindberg, F. P., Lund, B., Normark, S. 1986. Gene products specifying adhesion of uropathogenic *Escherichia coli* are minor components of pili. *Proc. Natl. Acad. Sci. USA* 83:1891–95

89. Lindberg, F. P., Lund, B., Normark, S. 1984. Genes of pyelonephritogenic *E. coli* required for digalactoside-specific agglutination of human cells. *EMBO J.* 3:1167–73

90. Lindberg, F. P., Tennent, J. M., Hultgren, S. J., Lund, B., Normark, S. 1989. PapD, a periplasmic transport protein in P-pilus biogenesis. *J. Bacteriol.* 171:6052–58

91. Lintermans, P. 1990. *Karakterizatie van de F17 en F111 fimbriae van Escherichia coli en genetische analyse van de F17 genkluster.* PhD thesis. Ghent, Belgium: Rijksuniversiteit gent

92. Lund, B., Lindberg, F. P., Baga, M., Normark, S. 1985. Globoside-specific adhesins of uropathogenic *Escherichia coli* are encoded by similar transcomplementable gene clusters. *J. Bacteriol.* 162:1293–1301

93. Lund, B., Lindberg, F. P., Marklund, B. I., Normark, S. 1987. The PapG protein is the α-D-galactopyranosyl-(1-4)-β-D-galactopyranose-binding adhesin of uropathogenic *Escherichia coli*. *Proc. Natl. Acad. Sci. USA* 84:5898–5902

94. Lund, B., Lindberg, F., Normark, S. 1988. The structure and antigenic properties of the tip-located P-pili proteins of uropathogenic *Escherichia coli*. *J. Bacteriol.* 170:1887–94

95. Lund, B., Marklund, B. I., Stromberg, N., Lindberg, F., Karlsson, K. A., Normark, S. 1988. Uropathogenic *Escherichia coli* express serologically identical pili with different receptor binding specifities. *Mol. Microbiol.* 2:255–63

96. Marrs, C. F., Schoolnik, G., Koomey, J. M., Hardy, J., Rothbard, J., Falkow, S. 1985. Cloning and sequencing of a *Moraxella bovis* pilin gene. *J. Bacteriol.* 163:132–39

97. Mattick, J. S., Bills, M. M., Anderson, B. J., Dalrymple, B., Mott, M. R., Egerton, J. R. 1987. Morphogenic expression of *Bacteroides nodosus* fimbriae in *Pseudomonas aeruginosa*. *J. Bacteriol.* 169:33–41

98. Maurer, L., Orndorff, P. E. 1987. Identification and characterization of genes determining receptor binding and pilus length of *Escherichia coli* type 1 pili. *J. Bacteriol.* 169:640–45

99. Maurer, L., Orndorff, P. E. 1985. A new locus, *pilE*, required for the binding of type 1 piliated *Escherichia coli* to erythrocytes. *FEMS Microbiol. Lett.* 30:59–66

100. McKern, N. M., O'Donnell, I. J., Inglis, A. S., Stewart, D. J., Clark, B. L. 1983. Amino acid sequence of pilin from *Bacteroides nodosus* (strain 198), the causative organism of bovine foot rot. *FEBS Lett.* 164:149–53

101. McMichael, J. C., Ou, J. T. 1979. Structure of common pili from *Escherichia coli*. *J. Bacteriol.* 138:969–75

102. McNab, R. M. 1987. Flagella. In *Escherichia coli and Salmonella typhimurium: Cellular and Molecular Biology*, ed. F. C. Neidhardt, 1:70–83. Washington, DC: Am. Soc. Microbiol.

103. Meyer, T. F., Billyyard, E., Haas, R.,

Storzbach, S., So, M. 1984. Pilus genes of *Neisseria gonorrhoeae:* Chromosomal organization and DNA sequence. *Proc. Natl. Acad. Sci. USA* 81:6110–14

104. Meyer, T. F., Gibbs, C. P., Haas, R. 1990. Variation and control of protein expression in *Neisseria. Annu. Rev. Microbiol.* 44:451–77

105. Meyer, T., Mlawer, N., So, M. 1982. Pilus expression in *Neisseria gonorrhoeae* involves chromosomal rearrangements. *Cell* 30:45–52

106. Minion, F. C., Abraham, S. N., Beachey, E. H., Goguen, J. D. 1986. The genetic determinant of adhesive function in type 1 fimbriae of *Escherichia coli* is distinct from the gene encoding the fimbrial subunit. *J. Bacteriol.* 165:1033–36

107. Mirelman, D., ed. 1986. *Microbial Lectins and Agglutinins.* New York: Wiley

108. Mooi, F. R., De Graaf, F. K. 1985. Molecular biology of fimbriae of enterotoxigenic *Escherichia coli. Curr. Top. Microbiol. Immunol.* 118:119–38

109a. Mooi, F. R., Wijfies, A., DeGraaf, F. K. 1983. Identification of precursors in the biosynthesis of the K88ab fimbriae. *J. Bacteriol.* 154:41–49

109. Mooi, F. R., Classen, I., Baaker, D., Kuipers, H., de Graaf, F. K. 1986. Regulation and structure of an *Escherichia coli* gene coding for an outer membrane protein involved in export of K88ab fimbrial subunits. *Nucleic Acids Res.* 14:2443–57

110. Morimoto, R. I., Tissieres, A., Georgopoulos, C. 1990. *Stress Proteins in Biology and Medicine.* Cold Spring Harbor: Cold Spring Harbor Lab.

111. Murphy, G. L., Connell, T. D., Barritt, D. S., Koomey, M., Cannon, J. G. 1989. Phase variation of gonococcal protein II: regulation of gene expression by slipped strand mispairing of a repetitive DNA sequence. *Cell* 56:539–47

112. Norgren, M., Baga, M., Tennent, J. M., Normark, S. 1987. Nucleotide sequence, regulation and functional analysis of the *papC* gene required for cell surface localization of Pap pili of uropathogenic *Escherichia coli. Mol. Microbiol.* 1:169–178

113. Norgren, M., Normark, S., Lark, D., O'Hanley, P., Schoolnik, G., et al. 1984. Mutations in *E. coli* cistrons affecting adhesion to human cells do not abolish Pap pili fiber formation. *EMBO J.* 3:1159–65

114. Norlander, L., Davies, J., Norqvist, A., Normark, S. 1979. Genetic basis for colonial variation in *Neisseria gonorrhoeae. J. Bacteriol.* 138:762–69

115. Normark, S., Baga, M., Goransson, M., Lindberg, F. P., Lund, B., et al. 1986. Genetics and biogenesis of *Escherichia coli* adhesins. In *Microbial Lectins and Agglutinins: Properties and Biological Activity,* ed. D. Mirelman, pp. 113–43. New York: Wiley Intersci.

116. Normark, S., Lark, D., Hull, R., Norgren, M., Baga, M., et al. 1983. Genetics of digalactoside-binding adhesin from a uropathogenic *Escherichia coli* strain. *Infect. Immun.* 41:942–49

117. Nunn, D., Bergman, S., Lory, S. 1990. Products of three accessory genes, *pilB, pilC* and *pilD,* are required for biogenesis of *Pseudomonas aeruginosa* pili. *J. Bacteriol.* 172:2911–19

118. Ofek, I., Beachey, E. H. 1980. General concepts and principles of bacterial adherence. See Ref. 8a, pp. 1–29

119. Old, D. C. 1972. Inhibition of the interaction between fimbrial hemagglutinins and erythrocytes by *D*-mannose and other carbohydrates. *J. Gen. Microbiol.* 71:149–57

120. Orndorff, P. E., Falkow, S. 1984. Organization and expression of genes responsible for type 1 piliation in *Escherichia coli. J. Bacteriol.* 159:736–44

121. Ott, M., Hoschutzky, H., Jann, K., Van Die, I., Hacker, J. 1988. Gene clusters for S fimbrial adhesin *(sfa)* and F1C fimbriae *(foc)* of *Escherichia coli:* Comparative aspects of structure and function. *J. Bacteriol.* 170:3983–90

122. Pasloske, B. L., Finlay, B., Paranchych, W. 1985. Cloning and sequencing of the *Pseudomonas aeruginosa* PAK pilin gene. *FEBS Lett.* 183:408–12

123. Plos, K., Carter, T., Hull, S., Hull, R., Svanborg-Eden, C. 1990. Frequency and organization of *pap* homologous DNA in relation to clinical origin of uropathogenic *Escherichia coli. J. Infect. Dis.* 161:518–24

124. Randall, L. L., Hardy, S. J. S., Thom, J. R. 1987. Export of protein: a biochemical view. *Annu. Rev. Microbiol.* 41:507–41

125. Randall, L. L., Topping, T. B., Hardy, S. J. S. 1990. No specific recognition of leader peptide by SecB, a chaperone involved in protein export. *Science* 248:860–63

126. Rhen, M., Tenhunen, J., Vaisanen-Rhen, U., Pere, A., Baga, M., Korhonen, T. 1986. Fimbriation and P-antigen recognition of *Escherichia coli* strains harboring mutated recombinant plasmids encoding fimbrial adhesins of

the uropathogenic *E. coli* strain KS71. *J. Gen. Microbiol.* 132:71–77

127. Riegman, N., Kusters, R., Van Veggel, H., Bergmans, H., Van Bergen en Henegouwen, P., et al. 1990. FIC fimbriae of a uropathogenic *Escherichia coli* strain: genetic and functional organization of the *foc* gene cluster and identification of minor subunits. *J. Bacteriol.* 172:1114–20

128. Roosendaal, B., De Graff, F. K. 1989. The nucleotide sequence of the *fanD* gene encoding the large outer membrane protein involved in the biosynthesis of K99 fimbriae. *Nucleic Acids. Res.* 17:1263–64

129. Roosendaal, B., van Bergen en Henegouwen, P. M., De Graaf, F. K. 1986. Subcellular localization of K99 fimbrial subunits and effect of temperature on subunit synthesis and assembly. *J. Bacteriol.* 165:1029–32

130. Schifferli, D. M., Abraham, S. N., Beachey, E. H. 1987. Use of monoclonal antibodies to probe subunit- and polymer-specific epitopes of 987P fimbriae of *Escherichia coli*. *Infect. Immun.* 55:923–30

131. Schulz, G. E., Elzinga, M., Marx, F., Schirmer, R. H. 1974. Three-dimensional structure of adenyl kinase. *Nature* 250:120–23

132. Scocca, J. J. 1990. The role of transformation in the variability of the *Neisseria gonorrhoeae* cell surface. *Mol. Microbiol.* 4:321–27

133. Segal, E., Billyyard, E., So, M., Storzbach, S., Meyer, T. F. 1985. Role of chromosomal rearrangements in *N. gonorrhoeae* pilus phase variation. *Cell* 40:293–300

134. Seifert, H. S., Ajioka, R. S., Marchal, C., Sparling, P. F., So, M. 1988. DNA transformation leads to pilin antigenic variation in *Neisseria gonorrhoeae* pilin variation. *Nature* 336:392–95

135. Seifert, H. S., Ajioka, R. S., Parachuri, D., Heffron, F., So, M. 1990. Shuttle mutagenesis of *Neisseria gonorrhoeae*: Pilin null mutations lower DNA transformation competence. *J. Bacteriol.* 172:40–46

136. Shaw, C. E., Taylor, R. K. 1990. *Vibrio cholerae* O395 *tcpA* pilin gene sequence and comparison of predicted protein structural features to those of type 4 pilins. *Infect. Immun.* 58:3042–49

137. Skowyra, D., Georgopolous, C., Zylicz, M. 1990. The *E. coli dnak* gene product, the hsp70 homolog can reactivate heat-inactivated RNA polymerase in an ATP hydrolysis-dependent manner. *Cell* 62:939–44

138. Strom, M. A., Lory, S. 1987. Mapping of export signals of *Pseudomonas aeruginosa* pilin with alkaline phosphatase fusions. *J. Bacteriol.* 169:3181–3388

139. Stromberg, N., Marklund, B. I., Lund, B., Ilver, D., Hamers, A., et al. 1990. Host-specificity of uropathogenic *Escherichia coli* depends on differences in binding specificity to Galα1-4Gal containing isoreceptors. *EMBO J.* 9:2001–10

140. Sun, D., Seyer, J. M., Kovari, I., Sumrada, R. A., Taylor, R. K. 1991. Localization of protective epitopes within the pilin subunit of the *Vibrio cholerae* toxin-coregulated pilus. *Infect. Immun.* 59:In press

141. Swanson, J., Bergstrom, S., Barrera, O., Robbins, K., Corwin, D. 1985. Pilus-gonococcal variants. Evidence for multiple forms of piliation control. *J. Exp. Med.* 162:729–44

142. Swanson, J., Bergstrom, S., Robbins, K., Barrera, O., Corwin, D., Koomey, J. M. 1986. Gene conversion involving the pilin structural gene correlates with pilus$^+$ to pilus$^-$ changes in *Neisseria gonorrhoeae*. *Cell* 47:267–76

143. Swanson, J., Stephen, M. D., Kraus, J., Gotschlich, E. C. 1971. Studies on gonococcus infection. Pili and zones of adhesion: their relation to gonococcal growth patterns. *J. Exp. Med.* 134:886–906

144. Taylor, R., Shaw, C., Peterson, K., Spears, P., Mekalanos, J. 1988. Safe, live *Vibrio cholerae* vaccines? *Vaccine* 6:151–54

145. Taylor, R. K., Miller, V. L., Furlong, D. B., Mekalanos, J. J. 1987. Use of *phoA* gene fusions to identify a pilus colonization factor coordinately regulated with cholera toxin. *Proc. Natl. Acad. Sci. USA* 84:2833–37

146. Tennent, J. M., Hultgren, S., Forsman, K., Goransson, M., Marklund, B. I., et al. 1990. Genetics of adhesin expression in *Escherichia coli*. In *The Bacteria: Molecular Basis of Pathogenesis*, ed. B. H. Iglewski, V. C. Clark, pp. 79–110. San Diego: Academic

147. Tennent, J. M., Lindberg, F., Normark, S. 1990. Integrity of *Escherichia coli* P pili during biogenesis: properties and role of PapJ. *Mol. Microbiol.* 4:747–58

148. Uhlin, B. E., Baga, M., Goransson, M., Lindberg, F. P., Lund, B., et al. 1985. Genes determining adhesin formation in uropathogenic *Escherichia coli*. *Curr. Topics Microbiol. Immunol.* 118:163–78

149. Uhlin, B. E., Nogren, M., Baga, M., Normark, S. 1985. Adhesion to human cells by *Escherichia coli* lacking the ma-

jor subunit of a digalactoside-specific pilins adhesions. *Proc. Natl. Acad. Sci. USA* 82:1800–4

150. Van Die, I., Spierings, G., van Meyen, I., Zuidweg, E., Hoekstra, W., Bergman, H. 1985. Cloning and genetic organization of the gene cluster encoding F7, fimbriae of a uropathogenic *Escherichia coli* and comparison with $F7_2$ gene cluster. *FEMS Microbiol. Lett.* 28:329–34

151. Van Die, I., Van Megen, I., Hoekstra, W., Bergmans, H. 1984. Molecular organization of the genes involved in the production of $F7_2$ fimbriae, causing mannose resistant hemagglutination of a uropathogenic *Escherichia coli* 06:K2:H1:F7 strain. *Mol. Gen. Genet.* 194:528–33

152. Van Die, I. C., van den Hondel, C., Hamstra, H. S., Hoekstra, W., Bergmans, H. 1983. Studies on the fimbriae of an *Escherichia coli* 06: K2: H1: F7 strain: molecular cloning of a DNA fragment encoding a fimbrial antigen responsible for mannose-resistant hemagglutination of human erythrocytes. *FEMS Microbiol. Lett.* 19:77–82

153. Van Doorn, J., Oudega, B., Mooi, F. R., De Graaf, F. K. 1982. Subcellular localization of polypeptides involved in the biosynthesis of K88ab fimbriae. *FEMS Microbiol. Lett.* 13:99–104

154. Watt, V. M., Ingles, C. J., Urdea, M. S., Rutter, W. J. 1985. Homology requirements for recombination in *Escherichia coli*. *Proc. Natl. Acad. Sci. USA* 82:4768–72

155. Watts, T. H., Scraba, D. G., Paranchych, W. 1982. Formation of 9-nm filaments from pilin monomers obtained by octyl-glucoside dissociation of *Pseudomonas aeruginosa* pili. *J. Bacteriol.* 151:1508–13

156. Zimmerman, R., Meyer, D. I. 1986. 1986: A year of new insights into how proteins cross membranes. *Trends Biochem. Sci.* 11:512–15

157. Nunn, D. N., Lory, S. 1991. Product of *Pseudomonas aeruginosa* gene *pilD* is a prepilin leader peptidase. *Proc. Natl. Acad. Sci. USA* 88:3281–85

158. Strom, M. S., Nunn, D., Lory, S. 1991. Multiple roles of the pilus biogenesis protein of PilD: Involvement of PilD in excretion of enzymes from *Pseudomonas aeruginosa*, *J. Bacteriol.* 173:1175–80

159. Whitchurch, C. B., Hobbs, M., Livingston, S. P., Krishnapillai, V., Mattick, J. S. 1991. Characterization of a *Pseudomonas aeruginosa* twitching motility gene and evidence for a specialized protein export system widespread in eubacteria. *Gene.* In press

Annu. Rev. Microbiol. 1991. 45:417–44

GENE AMPLIFICATION IN *LEISHMANIA*

Stephen M. Beverley

Department of Biological Chemistry and Molecular Pharmacology, Harvard Medical School, Boston, MA 02115

KEY WORDS: drug resistance, karyotypic change, P-glycoprotein, DNA rearrangement, protozooan parasites

CONTENTS

INTRODUCTION 417
   A Leishmania *Primer* 418
   The Leishmania *Genome and Circular DNAs* 419
MULTIPLE MECHANISMS OF DRUG RESISTANCE 420
GENES AMPLIFIED IN RESPONSE TO DRUG PRESSURE 421
   Dihydrofolate Reductase–Thymidylate Synthase 421
   The H Region: a Complex Multiple Drug–Resistance Element 422
   Tunicamycin and Glycosyltransferase 425
   ODC, IMPDH, and Classic MDR 425
MISCELLANEOUS AMPLIFIED GENES 426
   T and D DNAs 426
   Miniexon 427
   Subchromosomal Amplifications 427
   What Leads to the Emergence of Apparently Nonfunctional Amplified
      DNAs? 428
FREQUENCY OF GENE AMPLIFICATION 429
STRUCTURE OF EXTRACHROMOSOMAL AMPLIFIED DNAs 429
   Simple, Time-Invariant Direct and Inverted Amplifications 430
   Unstable and Stable Amplification 430
   Recurrence of Rearrangements Involving Repetitive DNA Sequences 431
   Functional Genetic Elements Within Amplified DNAs 431
   Comparisons with Amplified DNAs in Cultured Mammalian Cells 432
   Three Chromosomal Types of Amplification 432
MECHANISM OF GENE AMPLIFICATION 433
ROLE OF GENE AMPLIFICATION IN *LEISHMANIA* BIOLOGY
      AND EVOLUTION 436
   Clinical Drug Resistance 436
   Amplified Genes in Leishmania*: a Bridge Between Prokaryotic Resistance*
      Factors and Mammalian Gene Amplifications 437
   Role of Amplification in Shaping the Parasite Genome 438
PROSPECTUS 439

417

0066-4227/91/1001-0417$02.00

INTRODUCTION

Trypanosomatid protozoa provide amazingly fertile ground for the discovery of novel molecular phenomena such as RNA editing (102), *trans*-splicing (16), and bent DNA (77) that have subsequently been observed in metazoans. Studies of drug-resistant *Leishmania* spp. have similarly yielded new perspectives on the mechanism of gene amplification, in which a limited portion of the genome selectively increases in copy number. De novo circular amplifications mediating drug resistance, including direct and inverted amplification, were first discovered in *Leishmania* spp. (7). These parasites continue to offer simple model systems for the study of gene amplification in higher eukaryotes, including cultured mammalian cells (reviewed in 51, 93–96, 105, 106).

Since gene amplification in *Leishmania* spp. was last reviewed (10), progress in this field has been rapid. Amplified DNAs have been modified to generate prototypic DNA transfection vectors for *Leishmania* spp. (60), which can be used to directly test gene function. This approach has permitted the identification of the drug resistance genes contained within amplified DNA (H. L. Callahan & S. M. Beverley, in preparation) and will allow identification of *cis*-acting elements mediating gene expression, replication, and maintenance. Current data indicate that gene amplification is widespread in drug-resistant *Leishmania*, occurring in many different species in response to a wide spectrum of compounds. One amplification, the H region, is a complex drug-resistance element widely conserved during *Leishmania* spp. evolution, encoding at least two different drug-resistance genes. The region appears to be an amplification-prone segment of the *Leishmania* spp. genome that combines elements of prokaryotic drug resistance factors and gene amplification. Surprisingly, gene amplification is a common phenomenon in unselected laboratory stocks, although the role of most of these amplifications is often unknown.

A Leishmania *Primer*

The eukaryotic *Leishmania* is a genus of pathogenic protozoan parasites belonging to the family Trypanosomatidae (Order Kinetoplastida). Depending upon the particular species, *Leishmania* infection can result in a mild cutaneous lesion, a disfiguring mucocutaneous disease, or a fatal visceral infection. Approximately 10 million cases are estimated worldwide, but this figure is probably an underestimate (119). Current methods for treatment of the parasite involve pentavalent antimony complexes; however, these drugs are antiquated and better chemotherapeutic agents are urgently needed (2, 30, 119). Several studies of gene amplification in fact arose from investigations focused upon proteins that may prove to be excellent targets for selective chemotherapy in the future.

Leishmania are digenetic parasites with two basic life stages. An insect vector, the phlebotomine sand fly, transmits the flagellated promastigote stage. After introduction by the bite of the fly, promastigotes are taken up into the phagolysosome of macrophages. Despite the hostile cellular environment, the infective promastigotes resist the action of complement, hydrolytic enzymes, and oxidizing agents, and in some manner mitigate the response of the immune system. Differentiation into the aflagellate amastigote stage ensues, followed by growth and cell division. The developmental cycle is complete when a feeding sand fly takes up cells containing amastigotes, which then differentiate back into promastigotes in the fly gut. Promastigotes are grown in defined or semidefined media in vitro, and quantities are generally not limiting (58). Colonies can readily be obtained on the surface of semisolid media, greatly facilitating genetic analysis and the recovery of drug resistant mutants.

The Leishmania *Genome and Circular DNAs*

One of the attractive features of *Leishmania* spp. is the small size of its genome, approximately 50,000 kb (75); current data indicate that the parasite is diploid at most loci (10, 31, 56, 57, 75). Because amplified DNA often constitutes as much as 5–10% of total parasite DNA (27), amplified DNA fragments are readily detected as abundant DNA fragments in restriction-enzyme digests of total genomic DNA and can be directly isolated and molecularly cloned (10, 27). Many *Leishmania* spp. amplifications arise as extrachromosomal circular DNAs, so preparative quantities can be obtained by biochemical fractionations such as CsCl density gradient centrifugation, alkaline lysis, or differential NaCl/SDS precipitation (7, 32, 117).

Leishmania spp. contain 25–30 small chromosomes that are readily separable by pulsed field electrophoresis (28, 42, 44, 91, 98, 113). Amplified supercoiled circular DNAs exhibit migration properties distinct from those of linear DNAs, such as pulse time–independent absolute mobility (pulse time–dependent relative to linear markers) (4, 42). In many apparatuses, supercoiled circular DNAs tend to migrate along a somewhat different track than the linear chromosomes because of the variable response of DNAs of differing topology under alternating electric fields of different strengths (4). These diagnostic properties have been used to establish the circularity of *Leishmania* DNA amplifications, and can be manipulated to purify circular DNAs that are free of the chromosomes (4, 22, 42). Large (> 200 kb), nicked, relaxed, or concatenated circular DNAs are frequently trapped in the sample well and must be distinguished from amplified DNA that has integrated into larger linear chromosomes. One can use γ-irradiation to introduce limited numbers of double-strand breaks, thereby releasing the circular molecules as linear DNAs whose size can readily be measured (5, 88, 90, 112).

MULTIPLE MECHANISMS OF DRUG RESISTANCE

Most amplifications studied in *Leishmania* spp. arose in response to multiple rounds of stepwise drug selection. Schimke et al (96) have suggested that, in mammalian cells, the stepwise selection protocol, which employs relatively small increases in drug pressure, greatly increases the likelihood of gene amplification. No data addressing this point have been obtained for *Leishmania* species. Lines derived by multiple serial steps often contain multiple alterations contributing to drug resistance, although this effect depends greatly upon the particular drug and cell line studied (96). Selection with methotrexate (MTX) has yielded clonal lines of *Leishmania major* possessing two different functional gene amplifications [dihydrofolate reductase–thymidylate synthase (DHFR-TS) and the H region] and alterations in MTX uptake, as well as lines exhibiting various combinations of these three mutations (36, 38). These data suggest that even when gene amplification is a potential resistance mechanism, it is not necessarily the favored event. For example, selections of clonal derivatives of *L. major* have yielded DHFR-TS or H amplifications in about 30–40% of the MTX-resistant lines (S. M. Beverley, J. Cordingley, & D. D. Rogers, in preparation). MTX-resistant lines of *Leishmania donovani* and *Leishmania mexicana amazonensis* did not exhibit gene amplification (64, 100), nor did MTX-resistant *Leishmania tarentolae* selected from a line lacking pre-existing H amplification (117). Thus, any given resistant line may fail to include amplification in its spectrum of resistance mechanisms.

One often-overlooked factor is the effect of the specific culture medium utilized on the spectrum of drug-resistance mutations obtained. In MTX selections, the external folate concentration can modulate the potency of MTX over a factor of 100,000 in *Leishmania* spp., whereas the effect of external folate is small in mammalian cells (64, 89). Whether this potency modulation affects the type of resistance mechanisms elicited is unknown. However, the recovery of mutants exhibiting severe deficiencies in MTX and folate uptake could probably be enhanced in several commonly utilized media that contain folate levels nearly 1000 times normal physiological concentrations (64, 117). Similarly, to obtain sensitivity to low concentrations of mycophenolic acid, an inhibitor of inosine monophosphate dehydrogenase (IMPDH), Wilson et al (118) used a defined medium containing hypoxanthine as the sole source of purine (trypanosomatids are obligate purine auxotrophs); resistant mutants then arose by amplification of the IMPDH structural gene.

The occurrence of multiple resistance mechanisms means that one must demonstrate a causal association between molecular alterations such as gene amplification and inferred biochemical mechanism of resistance. Prior to the availability of genetic tests, most workers relied upon correlative studies, associating amplifications with phenotypes in resistant lines obtained by different methods, with different drugs, or in different species (33, 37, 53, 62, 63, 88, 117). Surprisingly, this kind of analysis also revealed the presence of several amplifications whose presence does not correlate with drug resistance. These apparently nonfunctional amplifications are discussed in a later section and underscore the need for functional analysis.

The advent of stable transfection and expression vectors for *Leishmania* spp. (26, 60, 69, 71) and methods of specific gene targeting (31) will enable functional tests of the genes encoded within amplifications. These techniques have already enabled direct demonstration of the functional role of the H region in drug resistance in both *L. major* and *L. tarentolae* (H. L. Callahan & S. M. Beverley, in preparation). As the use of this powerful technology is explored, progress will be rapid on many of the questions raised in this review.

GENES AMPLIFIED IN RESPONSE TO DRUG PRESSURE

Several drug-resistant *Leishmania* spp. have been obtained, but for many of these the causal biochemical mechanism or molecular changes associated with resistance have not been characterized. This section considers only those drug-selected lines in which amplification of genes known or strongly suspected to mediate resistance has been observed.

Dihydrofolate Reductase–Thymidylate Synthase

MTX is a stoichiometric inhibitor of DHFR from most sources, and MTX-resistant mutants in many species frequently exhibit overproduction of DHFR as well as structural alterations and reductions in MTX accumulation. In eukaryotes, overproduction is mediated by amplification of the DHFR structural gene. Many MTX-resistant lines of *L. major* selected for resistance to MTX show elevated DHFR activity and amplification of the structural gene contained within a segment of DNA termed the R region (7, 9, 10, 27; S. M. Beverley, J. Cordingley, & D. D. Rogers, in preparation). In *Leishmania* spp. and all protozoan parasites studied to date, DHFR is encoded in a fusion polypeptide that contains the structural gene for thymidylate synthase (TS) appended to the carboxy terminus (9, 49). DHFR-TS amplification has thus been observed in lines resistant to the TS inhibitor 10-propargyl-5,8-deazafolate (CB3717) (41). Because MTX-resistant lines always exhibit additional metabolic alterations, a transfection-based approach was employed to test whether DHFR-TS amplification alone was sufficient to confer MTX resistance. A multicopy molecular construct containing the DHFR-TS structural gene was introduced into wild-type cells without employing MTX treatment. DHFR-TS transfectants were MTX-resistant, while control trans-fectants were not (86).

Depending upon the specific amplification, upwards of 30 kb of DNA flanking the DHFR-TS structural gene are additionally co-amplified (7, 10, 54; S. M. Beverley, J. Cordingley, & D. D. Rogers, in preparation). The DNAs found within the most commonly amplified 30-kb segment (the pro-totypic R region) (7, 10) are extensively transcribed into at least nine poly-somal polyadenylated RNAs, but sequencing of the genomic copy of several of these has not revealed significant open reading frames (59, 61). No function nor role in drug resistance for these additional RNAs has been shown.

The H Region: a Complex Multiple Drug–Resistance Element

The first MTX-resistant line of *L. major* (R1000) contained another DNA amplification in addition to the DHFR-TS/R region amplification, termed the H region amplification (7). Analysis of clonal derivatives revealed that the H amplification occurred within the same cells bearing DHFR-TS/R region amplification, the first example of cells bearing two unrelated amplifications. Initially, the H region was a puzzle: amplification of genes other than DHFR-TS in antifolate-resistant mutants from other species had not been reported; no data causally implicated this amplification in MTX resistance; and it might have represented an amplification not functionally mediating drug resistance (examples of which are discussed in a later section).

Subsequent studies showed a correlation between drug resistance and H region amplification in numerous independent lines and species. First, in-dependent selections of *L. major* with the drugs primaquine and terbinafine, which are structurally and mechanistically unrelated to MTX, yielded lines bearing only H amplification that were 10- to 20-fold cross-resistant to MTX (38). Second, independent MTX selections of *L. major* and *Leishmania tropica* (including clonal derivatives) have yielded lines bearing H but not DHFR-TS amplification (36, 38, 53; S. M. Beverley, J. Cordingley, & D. D. Rogers, in preparation; Beverley, S. M. Iovannisci, P. F. Kamitsuka, J. Manning, & N. Mukhopadhyay, in preparation). Third, several unselected laboratory stocks of the lizard parasite *L. tarentolae* contained an unselected amplification that turned out to be the equivalent of the *L. major* H region amplification, with extensive sequence homology and the characteristic in-verted repeat structure (88, 117) (Figure 1). These lines exhibited up to 20-fold resistance to MTX, and the H region copy number could be elevated by MTX pressure. Fourth, selection of *L. mexicana amazonensis* with sodium arsenite yielded lines bearing amplification of the H region of this species. These lines were highly cross-resistant to MTX (33, 62). Correspondingly, H-amplified *L. major* exhibit varying levels of arsenite resistance (37; H. L. Callahan & S. M. Beverley, in preparation).

Direct Amplification   Inverted Amplification

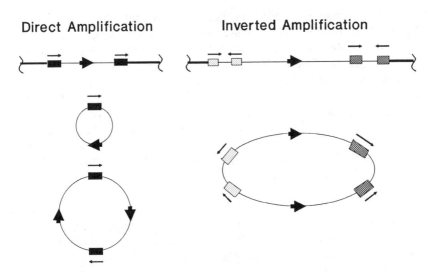

Figure 1 Amplified DNA structures characterized in *Leishmania* species. The boxes indicate repetitive DNA sequences whose orientations are indicated by small arrows and the heavy lines flanking chromosomal DNA.

The data summarized above reveal a clear correlation of H amplification with drug resistance, especially MTX resistance. However, the use of lines obtained by serial stepwise selection introduced an element of uncertainty resulting from the possibility of multiple mechanisms of MTX resistance discussed earlier. One approach to this problem was to focus on lines selected with structurally unrelated drugs because the MTX resistance of these lines could probably be attributed solely to the H region amplification. Biochemical studies of the MTX resistant, H-amplified *L. major* obtained by terbinafine and primaquine selection revealed no alterations in MTX uptake, accumulation, or efflux (37) or increased MTX hydrolase activity (38). In contrast, alterations in MTX uptake were observed in all MTX-selected lines including those lacking H region amplification (36, 64). Thus far, no biochemical change likely to mediate MTX resistance has been associated with H region amplification, suggesting that this region of DNA encodes a novel mode of resistance.

Molecular studies of the H-amplified lines of *L. major* have shown that the 45-kb H region is transcribed into at least 20 polyadenylated RNAs and encodes at least one protein (35, 83). The relative levels of these molecules do not vary in response to heat shock or drug pressure (35). Interestingly, a homologue of the P-glycoprotein or multiple drug–resistance (MDR) genes implicated in multiple drug resistance in cultured mammalian cells (47) has been identified within the H amplification of both *L. tarentolae* (*ltpgA*) (83) and *L. major* (*lmpgpA*) (H. L. Callahan & S. M. Beverley, in preparation).

Some P-glycoproteins mediate resistance by increasing drug export, and P-glycoprotein relatives in *Drosophila melanogaster* control the accumulation of pterin derivatives (34, 82) (recall that MTX is a pterin derivative). However, a comparable role for P-glycoprotein genes in MTX resistance seems unlikely because (*a*) MTX accumulation was not altered in the H-amplified lines selected by unrelated drugs (37); (*b*) MTX resistance was not reversed by verapamil, which does reverse the toxicity of many P-glycoprotein substrates (37; H. L. Callahan & S. M. Beverley, in preparation); and (*c*) the H-amplified *L. tarentolae* was not resistant to a variety of compounds normally considered to be substrates of the mammalian P-glycoprotein, such as puromycin, vincristine, or adriamycin (83).

H REGION AMPLIFICATION CONFERS DRUG RESISTANCE   Recently DNA transfection approaches have been used to assess the coding potential of the H region (H. L. Callahan & S. M. Beverley, in preparation). A series of DNA fragments encompassing the wild-type *L. major* H region were inserted into multicopy transfection vectors bearing the neomycin (NEO)-resistance gene, introduced into *Leishmania* by electroporation and G418 selection, and amplified by increasing G418 pressure (60). When tested for drug resistance, a single segment of the H region was shown to confer resistance to arsenite by this protocol, and deletion studies localized the resistance gene to the MDR gene homologue *lmpgpA* mentioned previously. Consistent with previous work, *lmpgpA* constructs did not confer MTX resistance, and preliminary data indicate that the MTX resistance gene maps to another part of the H region (H. Callahan and S. M. Beverley, unpublished data). These data provide the first evidence that the H region encodes drug resistance determinants that are functional following gene amplification. Moreover, it suggests that the *lmpgpA* gene is functionally divergent from P-glycoprotein genes involved in classical multiple drug resistance (49). Further studies are required to determine (*a*) if *lmpgpA* mediates arsenite resistance through reductions in arsenite accumulation, as expected for members of the P-glycoprotein gene family and (*b*) if point mutations in *lmpgpA* or other genes confer altered drug resistance specificities as observed in mammalian MDR genes (24). Studies of the MTX-resistance element encoded by the H region are currently underway.

Interestingly, reports of a parallel for the association of arsenite and MTX resistance with gene amplification in *Leishmania* spp. have emerged for metazoans. Treatment of cultured mammalian cells with arsenite increases the frequency of DHFR amplification (73) and induces the expression of P-glycoprotein mRNAs (23); however, P-glycoprotein expression alone does not confer MTX resistance. Whether these associations are functional or fortuitous is unknown.

While pre-existing amplification of the H region is clearly evident in unselected laboratory stocks of *L. tarentolae* (88, 117), some controversy surrounds the occurrence of pre-existing H region amplifications in the human pathogen *L. major*. One group (53) has reported that two independent stabilates of the unselected LT252 line possess H region amplification. However, our (37) studies of an early-passage stabilate of this line, prepared prior to selection of the first MTX-resistant line bearing R and H amplification (R1000) (7), have failed to detect any H amplification. Recent work employed a sensitive PCR amplification method to detect H amplification–specific rearrangements (S. M. Beverley, D. M. Iovannisci, P. F. Kamitsuka, J. Manning, & N. Mukhopadhyay, in preparation). It is possible that the instability of the H amplification may account for the discrepant findings (7). However, at present the existence of H-region amplification in unselected *L. major* is uncertain.

Tunicamycin and Glycosyltransferase

Chang and coworkers have studied a series of *Leishmania* spp. lines selected with tunicamycin (TUN), an inhibitor of the microsomal N-acetylglucosamine-1-phosphate transferase. In most species, this enzyme is the first step in the dolichol pathway for protein N-glycosylation. In other systems, TUN resistance results from altered uptake, structural alterations, or amplifications of the glycosyltransferase (68, 74, 99, 108). Although the first two mechanisms have not been tested in *Leishmania* spp., every TUN-resistant line of *Leishmania* obtained thus far contains a DNA amplification and elevated levels of a TUN-sensitive glycosyl transferase activity, regardless of whether mutagenesis was included in the selection process (32, 63, 65, 86). Examination of a variety of independent amplified lines from several species revealed the presence of a 20-kb homologous region common to all amplifications (63). The common region is transcribed into at least five abundant RNAs, which translate in vitro into several protein bands (63; K.-P. Chang, personal communication). The common region may contain the glycosyltransferase structural gene, but heterologous probing with the yeast gene has proven inconclusive despite early reports (63). The coding potential of the common region is currently being tested using DNA sequencing and transfection studies. This amplification is interesting because it appears to be associated with a small but significant increase in parasite virulence (65, 66), although it has not been encountered in unselected virulent strains.

ODC, IMPDH, and Classic MDR

Recent work by Ullman and coworkers suggests that gene amplification has been obtained in response to at least three different agents in *L. donovani*. They (118) have reported amplification of the *L. donovani* IMPDH gene in response to mycophenolic acid selection. Vinblastine-resistant lines contain an amplification of a P-glycoprotein homologue distinct from the *lmpgpA* gene present on the H region and show collateral resistance to many of the classical mammalian P-glycoprotein substrates (47; B. Ullman, personal communication). A line selected for resistance to α-difluoromethylornithine has been obtained that exhibits unstable overproduction of ornithine decarboxylase (ODC), a phenotype highly suggestive of gene amplification (29). These new amplifications are currently being characterized. Their occurrence emphasizes the fact that, as in mammalian cells, gene amplification in *Leishmania* spp. is probably a widespread phenomenon underlying many instances of drug resistance and is not restricted to any specific structural or functional class of compounds.

MISCELLANEOUS AMPLIFIED GENES

The powerful methods available for electrophoretic separation of *Leishmania* spp. chromosomes have revealed a variety of chromosomal alterations involving gene amplification that are distinct from those reported above. These include the T amplification of *L. tarentolae,* the D amplification of *L. tropica,* subchromosomal amplifications of the LD-1/715 class, and amplification of the miniexon. Current data suggest that such chromosomal changes may be common (6, 43, 56, 85; S. M. Beverley, J. Cordingley, & D. D. Rogers, in preparation). The four kinds of amplifications discussed below are those that have been characterized to date. These amplifications often do not involve DNAs of known function, and in most cases have not been associated with any phenotype.

T and D DNAs

The Trager line of *L. tarentolae* contains an amplified DNA, designated the T region (87). Hybridization studies revealed that the T amplification was distinct from other known amplifications, including the H region amplified in other lines of *L. tarentolae* (87). The amplified T region contains about 20 kb of DNA, amplified as a circular dimeric molecule. This amplification is unusually ephemeral in that examination of the Trager line obtained from other laboratories or following various periods of culture showed widely varying levels. T-amplified lines do not show drug resistance.

Electrophoretic surveys revealed the presence of an amplification termed D DNA in an unselected laboratory stock of *L. tropica* (53). This DNA contained approximately 75 kb of DNA and possessed an inverted repeat structure. Hybridization studies revealed that this DNA was distinct from both the H and R regions, and selection of these cells with MTX led to the emergence of H amplification but no changes in D DNA levels. Thus far, no phenotype has been ascribed to either T or D DNA amplification.

Miniexon

Studies of *L. major* revealed alterations in karyotype arising from amplifications occurring within the locus encoding the miniexon donor RNA (56). This RNA provides the 39-nucleotide leader sequence added by *trans*-splicing onto the 5' end of all known protein-coding mRNAs in trypanosomatids (16) and is encoded in the genome as a tandem repetitive array of 0.45-kb units in *Leishmania* spp. (56, 78). Chromosome 2 in *L. major* contains the miniexon array, and several lines exhibiting alterations in this chromosome contained expansions of the miniexon array. Clonal derivatives of the LT252Δ, in which the miniexon amplification was first observed, exhibit a growth advantage (56), although genetic tests are required to determine whether the miniexon amplification itself is responsible for the growth phenotype. Interestingly, amplification of the miniexon array has been observed in several *L. major* isolates (56; S. Beverley, unpublished data). Whether this amplification occurs in nature or represents an adaptation to in vitro culture is currently unknown.

Subchromosomal Amplifications

Karyotypic surveys of numerous *Leishmania* species have revealed the occasional occurrence of relatively small chromosomes (250 kb or less) absent in other isolates of the same species (6, 15, 40, 98, 107). These small linear DNAs (SLDs) can be distinguished from normal chromosomes by the fact that they occur in multiple copies, up to 40 per cell. In *L. donovani*, they were termed the "HU-3" minichromosome (15) or LD-1 (98), and in *L. major* they were designated the 715-class of SLDs (6). Hybridization studies revealed that these DNAs from different strains or species are similar but not identical in size or sequence content (6). Because SLDs occur in some but not all isolates from numerous *Leishmania* species, researchers initially proposed that they could represent the result of some form of horizontal transmission. Subsequent studies have revealed that all species of *Leishmania* contain a reservoir copy of the sequences present on the new small chromosomes (6, 14). Current data, though limited, are most consistent with the idea that the SLDs represent large, subchromosomal amplifications; as such they must have acquired at least one new telomere during their formation. Their greatly increased copy number suggests that they replicate autonomously, and somehow escape mechanisms normally limiting chromosome number. Interestingly, Stuart and coworkers (6, 40, 50, 107) have also described a multicopy circular DNA, CD-1, which exhibits a complex relationship with certain SLDs.

Although the antiquity of the SLDs detected in laboratory stocks of *L. donovani*, *L. braziliensis*, and *L. mexicana* (6, 15, 40, 107) is unknown, the de novo generation of SLDs may have occurred in *L. major* and *L. braziliensis* (including a WHO reference strain) during routine culture in vitro and in two clonal derivatives of *L. major* undergoing MTX selection. In lines not known to have undergone drug pressure that bear SLDs, drug resistance has not been observed, and to date no biological role for these SLDs has been demonstrated. Their recurrent emergence throughout most *Leishmania* species is provocative.

What Leads to the Emergence of Apparently Nonfunctional Amplified DNAs?

Why are amplified DNAs commonly observed in unselected laboratory stocks of *Leishmania* spp., and what is their significance to the parasite? This section discusses two models.

FUNCTIONAL SELECTION   These amplifications may be functional but confer a phenotype not yet tested. For example, they may provide some subtle growth advantage during adaptation to culture in vitro or conceivably in nature. This could provide a directed selective force responsible for the multiple independent occurrence of events such as amplification of the miniexon in *L. major* or SLDs in many *Leishmania* species. Recall that in the 1970s a variety of amplified DNAs of unknown function and origins were similarly observed in cultured mammalian tumor cells (93). Subsequently, many of these amplifications were shown to contain functional oncogenes.

A variant of this model is that these amplifications are part of more complex biochemical resistance mechanisms, obligatorily requiring the presence of another unlinked resistance gene. Segregation in the absence of selective pressure could produce cells bearing only the amplification, which would appear to be nonfunctional. The best candidates for this kind of model would be those amplifications discovered in unselected laboratory stocks, such as T and D DNA and certain SLDs. Studies of chloroquine-resistant malaria postulated an analogous two-step model (39, 81, 115); however, at present this model remains only a possibility for *Leishmania* species.

NEUTRAL CHROMOSOMAL MUTATIONS   Some chromosomal alterations and amplifications may be approximately functionally neutral, constituting chromosomal mutations with no functional significance. Because this model postulates no intrinsic selective force promoting fixation of these mutations, other mechanisms such as recurrent directed mutation and population forces involving genetic drift must be invoked. Although other creatures exhibit examples of these forces, their role and presence in *Leishmania* is unknown. Founder effects contributing to the emergence of variant phenotypes could arise from multiple serial passages or cloning (1). Another possibility is hitchhiking, i.e. the occurrence of an unlinked advantageous mutation (such as drug resistance) in a line containing a neutral chromosomal alteration or amplification. A similar phenomenon, termed periodic selection, has been reported in bacterial chemostat experiments (52, 67).

FREQUENCY OF GENE AMPLIFICATION

In cultured mammalian cells, the frequency of gene amplification in drug-selected cells has been estimated to be from 10^{-3} to less than 10^{-8}; this value depends on the specific cell line utilized (primary, established, or tumor), the methods of measurement, and whether positive or negative selection methods are utilized (96, 110, 120). In *Leishmania* spp., studies of 20 independent clonal lines of *L. major* undergoing MTX selection revealed a frequency of DHFR-TS or H region amplification of about 5×10^{-8} (S. M. Beverley, J. Cordingley, & D. D. Rogers, in preparation), a value considerably lower than estimates for DHFR amplification in tumorigenic or cultured mammalian cells using comparable methods (about 10^{-5}). The value for *Leishmania* spp. is consistent with studies showing that the frequency of gene amplification in normal human cells is very low (120). Gene amplification does not generally reduce the infectivity of *Leishmania* spp. to animals, cultured macrophages, and sand flies (10, 65, 86), and appears quite compatible with the normal infectious cycle.

Many of the amplifications currently thought to be unrelated to drug resistance have been detected in drug-selected lines. For example, in the 20 clonal derivatives of *L. major* described above that were selected for methotrexate resistance, 3 independent mutations apparently unrelated to methotrexate resistance were observed, 2 of which belonged to the 715-class of subchromosomal amplifications (6, 56; S. Beverley, unpublished data). Similarly, in 10 lines maintained over a period of at least 6 months, 2 mutations unrelated to drug resistance were observed, 1 involving the miniexon and 1 a SLD (6, 56). Although these data are not directly comparable (since hitchhiking effects will be greater in the drug-selected lines because of the low frequency of drug resistance), they provide no evidence for an elevated frequency of the apparently nonfunctional amplifications in *L. major* undergoing drug pressure.

STRUCTURE OF EXTRACHROMOSOMAL AMPLIFIED DNAs

The structures and properties of several *Leishmania* spp. amplifications are known in detail. The general features emerging from these studies are described below.

Simple, Time-Invariant Direct and Inverted Amplifications

Amplified DNA segments can be organized in a direct, head-to-tail orientation, or alternatively, in an inverted, head-to-head manner (Figure 1). To date, the DHFR-TS and TUN amplifications reported fall into the direct class, while the D and prototypic H region amplifications are inverted. Unlike mammalian amplifications, *Leishmania* spp. amplifications appear to be quite homogeneous and possess only the minimum number of DNA rearrangements necessary to generate each class from a chromosomal reservoir: one for direct amplification, two for inverted amplification (see Figure 1). Although oligomers of the amplified DNA may arise during in vitro culture (7, 42, 54), additional DNA rearrangements do not generally occur. This finding is quite important, for it means that the rearrangements observed are probably primary events associated with the initial formation of the amplified DNA (unlike most mammalian amplifications, discussed below).

CIRCULAR AND LINEAR AMPLIFICATIONS   Most DNA amplifications appear to consist of extrachromosomal circular DNAs, ranging in size from 30 to greater than 200 kb. However, SLDs are linear, subchromosomal amplifications, and MTX- and difluoromethylornithine (DFMO)-resistant *Leishmania* spp. have recently been developed that contain linear amplifications (S. M. Beverley, J. Cordingley, & D. D. Rogers, in preparation; B. Ullman, personal communication). Because linear DNAs are expected to contain telomeric ends, their emergence suggests the de novo formation of the characteristic telomeric DNA (114), presumably by the action of the leishmanial telomerase.

Unstable and Stable Amplification

As in cultured mammalian cells, many *Leishmania* drug resistance amplifications are initially unstable, rapidly declining in copy number in the absence of continued drug pressure (7, 29, 65, 118). After lengthy propagation in the presence of drug, amplified DNAs can become stable upon drug removal (7). Not surprisingly, most of the amplifications observed in unselected laboratory stocks of *Leishmania* spp. are stable. In cultured mammalian cells, the transition from unstable to stable amplification is usually associated with a relocalization of the extra-chromosomal amplified sequences into the chromosome (94, 106). In *Leishmania* spp., once extrachromosomal amplified DNAs are established, they do not appear to reinsert back into chromosomal DNA during the stabilization process (42; S. Beverley, unpublished data). Occasionally the number of amplification units per circle increases, but otherwise no structural alterations have been shown. This finding suggests that subtle mutations in the initially unstable circular DNA can confer stability, or that stability is conferred by factors or mutations acting in trans (11).

The lack of knowledge concerning chromosomal elements mediating karyotypic stability in *Leishmania* hinders studies of the stability of amplified *Leishmania* DNA. Mitotic chromosomes do not condense, and although structures resembling kinetochores have been reported in other trypanosomatids their role is dubious because their number is considerably less than the number of chromosomes detected using pulsed-field electrophoresis (45, 104). Whether *Leishmania* chromosomes possess functional localized centromeres or whether they are holocentric, with centromeric activity dispersed over the entire chromosome as in nematodes and some arthropods (116) is unknown.

Recurrence of Rearrangements Involving Repetitive DNA Sequences

Frequently, the same amplified DNA structures are observed in independent lines. Six of nine independent amplifications of the DHFR-TS region utilized the same site, and six of six independent amplifications of the H region of *L. major* have the same structure (10, 37; S. M. Beverley, J. Cordingley, & D. D. Rogers, in preparation; Beverley, S. M. Iovannisci, P. F. Kamitsuka, J. Manning, & N. Mukhopadhyay, in preparation). Current data indicate that these rearrangements occur within repetitive DNA sequences. The DHFR-TS gene is flanked by two 600-bp elements separated by 30 kb, and the circular amplified genes are preferentially formed by joining of these two elements (10; S. M. Beverley, J. Cordingley, & D. D. Rogers, in preparation) (Figure 1). Similarly, the H region of *L. major* is flanked by two different pairs of inverted repeats (Figure 1), which are joined during amplification to form the two new rearrangements required (S. M. Beverley, D. M. Iovannisci, P. F. Kamitsuka, J. Manning, & N. Mukhopadhyay, in preparation). Similar data were recently reported for *L. tarentolae* (84).

Functional Genetic Elements Within Amplified DNAs

The ability of the extrachromosomal amplified DNAs to persist and direct the synthesis of encoded gene products has led many workers to conclude that these are autonomous elements. Kapler et al (60) explicitly tested this conclusion in the R region amplification of *L. major,* where a modified version of this region introduced by DNA transfection replicated autonomously and directed the efficient formation of a correctly *trans*-spliced RNA. Smaller derivatives of this plasmid are also equivalently functional (71), and as these DNAs are dissected further the identification of *cis*-acting elements involved in DNA replication, segregation, initiation of transcription, and RNA processing should follow. Origins of replication would be especially interesting to study in an amplification context. Curiously, many *Leishmania* DNA segments can apparently replicate autonomously (60, 69, 71). Because linear amplifications may have acquired telomeres de novo, characterization of these should provide some insight into the structure and mechanism of telomere formation in *Leishmania* species.

Comparisons with Amplified DNAs in Cultured Mammalian Cells

Comparisons of the structural features of amplified *Leishmania* genes with those observed in cultured mammalian cells, summarized in several recent reviews (95, 96, 105), are interesting. One is immediately struck by the complexity of amplified mammalian DNA: large tracts of DNA can be amplified, possibly as much as 10 megabases. The structures of these amplified DNAs are usually quite heterogeneous, containing multiple rearrangements or novel joints. The structure of the amplified DNA also varies, both within and between different cell lines. As a function of increased drug pressure and time, additional DNA rearrangements accumulate, and occasionally smaller amplification units predominate. In contrast, secondary rearrangements are generally not observed in *Leishmania* species.

The simplicity of amplification in *Leishmania* spp. could be attributed to the small size of the *Leishmania* genome and chromosomes; a 30-kb amplification in *Leishmania* is proportionally 1.8 Mb in mammalian cells. Another source could be the propensity of *Leishmania* spp. to undergo homologous recombination (31, 111), accounting for the frequent occurrence of rearrangements joining homologous repetitive DNAs. Regardless of the cause, the relative simplicity of amplified DNAs in *Leishmania* spp. greatly facilitates their analysis.

Three Chromosomal Types of Amplification

Pulsed-field methods of chromosomal analysis have permitted an examination of the fate of the wild-type chromosomal genes during generation of the amplified DNAs. Thus far, three outcomes have been characterized (Figures 2 and 3):

1. In deletional amplification, a copy of the wild-type chromosomal locus is deleted, yielding a smaller chromosome. Because *Leishmania* spp. are diploid, the result is a heterozygous deletion line (10, 31; S. M. Beverley, J. Cordingley, & D. D. Rogers, in preparation).
2. In conservative amplification, no alterations in chromosomal structure or ploidy are detected (7, 10, 37, 88; S. M. Beverley, J. Cordingley, & D. D. Rogers, in preparation).
3. In duplicative amplification, several additional gene copies are found

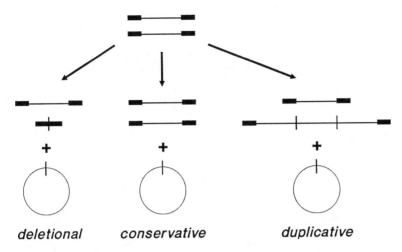

Figure 2   Three chromosomal types of amplification. The thick bars represent flanking chromosomal DNA, and the thin lines are the DNA segments that give rise to the extrachromosomal circular DNA in addition to being either deleted, retained, or duplicated.

inserted into the wild-type locus, yielding a larger chromosome in addition to the amplified extrachromosomal copies (S. M. Beverley, J. Cordingley, & D. D. Rogers, in preparation).

Thus far, the majority of events characterized fall into the conservative class; only one example each of the deletional and duplicative classes has been observed, both involving DHFR-TS (10; S. M. Beverley, J. Cordingley, & D. D. Rogers, in preparation). Chromosomal changes are evident in some arsenite-resistant *L. mexicana amazonensis*, but these have not been further characterized (33). Some cases of deletional amplification may have been missed because hybridization probes flanking the amplified region are not always employed to reveal deletion chromosomes obscured in ethidium bromide-stained gels.

MECHANISM OF GENE AMPLIFICATION

Several models have emerged from studies of amplification in cultured mammalian cells, including: (*a*) unscheduled rereplication of the wild-type chromosomal locus during a single cell cycle, followed by resolution into the final amplified DNA (51, 92, 94, 106); (*b*) duplications formed by unequal sister-chromatid exchange (46, 105, 106); and (*c*) models invoking recombinations in the absence of rereplication, such as the deletion plus episome model in which the wild-type chromosomal locus is converted into an ex-

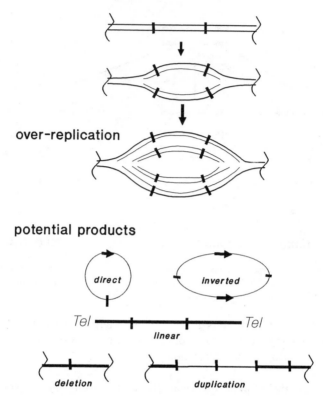

over-replication

potential products

Figure 3 Formation of the onionskin intermediate and potential products. Overreplication gives rise to the characteristic onionskin structure; both DNA strands are shown in the upper half of this figure. The vertical black bars indicate repetitive DNAs that are the sites of DNA rearrangement (see Figure 1 for an expanded view). Potential products formed by resolution of the onionskin intermediate by recombination among the repetitive DNAs or by branch migration and telomere addition are shown.

trachromosomal plasmid by intrachromosomal recombination (21, 97). The diversity of amplified structures has led some workers to postulate that mammalian cells may employ several different mechanisms that vary among loci or during different amplification steps (105).

If one considers only the *Leishmania* spp. amplifications that mediate drug resistance whose structures have been characterized, the majority appear conservative: changes in the wild-type chromosomal structure or ploidy are seen only rarely. This observation probably rules out models requiring alteration of the parental chromosome structure, such as sister chromatid exchange or recombination in the absence of rereplication (among others). Therefore, the amplified DNAs are likely generated from extra copies of the chromosomal locus, which are formed by some kind of rereplication occurring within a single cell cycle (92). One model for the initial structure of the rereplicated DNA is the "onionskin" model, in which one or more extra rounds of replication generate a hypothetical structure shown in Figure 3 (for another representation of the onionskin, see 105).

The onionskin model is quite flexible (97); by postulating different combinations of DNA rearrangements, one can obtain virtually all types of amplification structures. Examination of the onionskin intermediate reveals that rearrangements involving only the overreplicated DNA segments could lead to either direct or inverted amplification structures (factors affecting this choice are discussed below). In this case, DNA strands retaining the unrearranged wild-type information would be retained and could subsequently resolve into normal chromosome structure when the onionskin collapses, and so lead to conservative amplification. However, other structural outcomes of the onionskin are possible. Rearrangements within the wild-type chromosomal strand would lead to deletion plus episome formation, while rearrangements between the chromosomal strand and the overreplicated segment could lead to integrational or duplicative amplification. Although both of these structures could also arise by one or more of the other models discussed above, the only two cases of duplicative/integrational amplification observed in *Leishmania* spp. (at DHFR-TS) involved simultaneous formation of an episomal gene copy (10; S. M. Beverley, J. Cordingley, & D. D. Rogers, in preparation). Because many extra gene copies are generated in the onionskin intermediate, this model can easily accommodate the simultaneous formation of both integrated and circular amplified DNA. Another potential outcome of the onionskin intermediate is resolution by branch migrations, leading to the extrusion of linear gene copies that could either undergo rearrangements leading to circle formation or alternatively acquire telomeres by the action of a leishmanial telomerase; this process may be the source of linear amplifications (6). Thus, the onionskin model can readily account for all amplified structures observed in *Leishmania* spp. thus far, and, conversely, all types of possible structures postulated to arise from an onionskin intermediate have been observed. Although these data do not unambiguously rule out other mechanisms or combinations of mechanisms, they constitute perhaps the best evidence in support of overreplication and the onionskin intermediate in gene amplification. The preferential recovery of the conservative class of amplifications may signify that the rearrangements involving the overreplicated DNA are favored, perhaps because of its elevated copy number or the presence of nicks, gaps, and ends known to stimulate recombination in fungal systems.

However the nascent amplified DNAs are formed, they must ultimately resolve into amplified DNAs containing rearrangements. In *Leishmania* spp., the sites of DNA rearrangement are commonly within homologous repetitive sequences, "hotspots" often used in multiple independent lines; in contrast, in mammalian cells amplification rearrangements are not generally recurrent nor preferentially associated with homologous repetitive DNAs. This finding may reflect intrinsic differences in the activity of recombination pathways: *Leishmania* spp. and other unicellular eukaryotes appear to possess powerful systems mediating homologous recombination among DNAs as much as 1,000 times more active than those observed in mammalian cells when measured by the relative frequencies of homologous gene targeting (20, 31, 109). These systems could direct DNA rearrangements towards homologous repeated DNA sequences in *Leishmania* spp. and give rise to hotspots for DNA rearrangement. One prediction of this model is that genes flanked by direct repeats should undergo direct-type amplification, while genes flanked by inverted repeats should undergo inverted amplification. The amplifications characterized thus far have upheld this prediction: direct amplifications of the R region usually join flanking direct repeats, while inverted amplifications of the H region join two flanking sets of inverted repeats (Figure 1), and direct amplifications of DNA overlapping a portion of the H region join two directly repeating P-glycoprotein genes (84).

Thus, amplification in *Leishmania* spp. likely occurs by the over-replication/recombination model (3, 92, 94, 95), in which homologous repetitive DNA sequences usually direct the sites of recombination. White et al (117) proposed a similar model in which overreplication of the amplified region is initiated by DNA synthesis primed by the repetitive elements themselves (as opposed to initiating from an internal element as depicted in Figure 3—possibly a chromosomal origin of replication). Because most recombinational mechanisms require strand invasion and subsequent DNA resynthesis, the amplified DNAs are probably ultimately formed by a combination of these two mechanisms. The final step in the amplification mechanism is that the circular DNA, once formed, must increase in copy number. Whether this increase results from unequal segregation or an escape from normal mechanisms regulating copy number is currently unknown.

ROLE OF GENE AMPLIFICATION IN *LEISHMANIA* BIOLOGY AND EVOLUTION

Clinical Drug Resistance

Most of the agents used in laboratory studies of drug resistance and gene amplification are not employed in clinical treatment of leishmaniasis, although proteins such as DHFR-TS are likely to be targeted in the future (103). Recent studies of the H region amplification suggest that this region could be involved in the parasite's response to clinically utilized organic antimonial compounds. In addition to conferring resistance to arsenite, overexpression of the H region *lmpgpA* gene confers resistance to trivalent anti-monials [Sb(III)] when tested using DNA transfection (H. L. Callahan & S. M. Beverley, in preparation). Many workers believe that the pentavalent antimonial derivatives are not the active form and are metabolically altered into an active species, possibly into Sb(III); however, definitive evidence has not been presented. If the Sb(III) model is correct, the *lmpgpA* gene could modulate the toxicity of clinical antimonials, perhaps by altering Sb(III) accumulation. In a manner consistent with this model, agents such as ver-apamil that are known to inhibit the action of P-glycoprotein family members have been shown to reverse antimonial resistance in *L. donovani* (79). Moreover, monoclonal antibodies directed against the mammalian P-glycoprotein recognize proteins in *Leishmania* spp.—these proteins are more abundant in some antimonial-resistant lines (48). One might further speculate that the reportedly pre-existing H region amplifications in human-infecting *Leishmania* spp. may have been induced by clinical antimony treatment, although this idea has not been proven. Future studies are required to de-finitively address the role of the *lmpgpA* gene in antimony sensitivity and *lmpgpA* amplification in clinical antimony resistance.

Amplified Genes in Leishmania: *a Bridge Between Prokaryotic Resistance Factors and Mammalian Gene Amplifications*

In many ways, amplified *Leishmania* DNAs occupy a position intermediate between the drug-resistance plasmids of prokaryotes and the amplified DNAs of cultured mammalian cells. Like the prokaryotic plasmids (and some mammalian amplifications), they are generally extrachromosomal circular DNAs, occasionally bearing more than one drug-resistance element. Like mammalian amplifications, they arise from a chromosomal reservoir de novo, and can arise as unstable or stable forms. However, the differences are also instructive: unlike prokaryotic resistance factors, amplified *Leishmania* DNAs do not appear to contain gene functions that facilitate their transfer amongst cells. Unlike mammalian amplifications, frequently the same struc-ture is observed in independent amplifications in many *Leishmania* species.

One model for *Leishmania* DNA amplification is that these organisms contain within their genome amplification-prone cassettes that participate in an amplification and loss cycle. When subjected to selective stresses, in-formation built into the wild-type genome (such as flanking repeats) directs the formation of characteristic amplified DNA structures; although most cells perish, the small proportion undergoing amplification survive. Once the selective pressure abates, the extrachromosomal DNAs are lost, leaving behind the original locus. This kind of amplification and loss model in-corporates features of both prokaryotic and eukaryotic systems discussed above. However, for most loci we have little information about the obligatory role of specific flanking elements in directing the site of DNA amplification, and the amplification structures probably arise from utilization of fortuitously placed repeated sequences.

The H region seems like an excellent candidate for the amplification cassette model, as this model suggests a reason for the conservation of the unique wild-type structure (shown in Figure 1) in both *L. major* and *L. tarentolae* (84; S. M. Beverley, D. M. Iovannisci, P. F. Kamitsuka, J. Manning, & N. Mukhopadhyay, in preparation), which diverged as much as 50–100 million years ago (13; K. Nelson & S. M. Beverley, in preparation). The flanking inverted-repeat pairs evolve more rapidly than internal H region loci and have no known coding potential (S. M. Beverley, D. M. Iovannisci, P. F. Kamitsuka, J. Manning, & N. Mukhopadhyay, in preparation). Thus, their sole role may be in directing the site of H region amplification. The H region may then be seen as a reservoir of amplification-based drug resistance mechanisms, encoding at least two functional drug resistance genes (mediating resistance to certain metals and antifolates) and having the coding potential for many more (35) (genes mediating resistance to other agents known to induce H region amplification have not yet been sought). Because H region genes have been retained as readily amplified DNA segments during evolution, one can postulate that this persistence provides some evolutionary advantage to the parasite population. Thus, *Leishmania* spp. may be seen as possessing composite drug resistance factors analogous to those of prokaryotes.

Role of Amplification in Shaping the Parasite Genome

Gene amplification is a mechanism commonly employed during evolution, and it undoubtedly plays a similar role in shaping the parasite genome. Many workers have noted that most genes in trypanosomatid protozoa are present in multiple linked copies, including many genes normally present in one or a few copies in other taxa (25). A surprising fact is that in the current literature single-copy genes are the exception. In *Leishmania* spp., examples of repeated gene families include the miniexon and ribosomal RNA clusters (56, 75, 78), α- and β-tubulins (55, 70), a putative transporter (18), and proteins recognized by immune sera such as the surface antigens gp63 (17) and gp46 (76), and the 70- and 83-kilodalton (kd) heat shock proteins (72, 101). Amplification of genes provides not only abundant quantitative changes, but also new substrates for evolution because extra amplified copies can receive point mutations and evolve new functions while leaving the original copies unchanged.

Given the widespread occurrence of amplification in drug-resistant *Leishmania* spp., and the widespread occurrence of gene families in trypanosomatids, it is interesting that thus far gene amplification in drug-resistant African trypanosomes has not been reported. This fact may reflect fundamental molecular differences between these two genera of trypanosomatid protozoa or possibly the focus of many workers on drug-resistance mechanisms of *Leishmania* species.

PROSPECTUS

Originally, gene amplifications in *Leishmania* were sought as a simple approach towards protein and gene isolation, which remains an important application of this phenomenon. Although transfection-based methods now threaten to supplant amplification for this purpose, these genetic methods will aid future work on the mechanism of amplification as well as the functional elements within amplified DNA. The widespread occurrence of gene amplification in both drug resistant lines and unselected laboratory stocks, the advantages of studying simple amplifications that nonetheless resemble those of higher eukaryotes, and the existence of complex amplification-prone cassettes suggest that the study of this phenomenon will occupy the attention of molecular parasitologists for some time to come.

ACKNOWLEDGMENTS

I thank the following people for discussions and/or reading this manuscript: J. Berman, R. Berens, H. Callahan, K.-P. Chang, C. Coburn, A. Cruz, D. Dobson, T. Ellenberger, A. P. Fernandes, M. Grogl, G. Kapler, D. Iovannisci, M. Petrillo-Peixoto, D. D. Rogers, R. T. Schimke, and B. Ullman. This work was supported by grants from the NIH, March of Dimes, and Burroughs-Wellcome Fund.

Literature Cited

1. Bastien, P., Blaineau, C., Taminh, M., Rioux, J. A., Roizes, G., Pages, M. 1990.Interclonal variations in molecular karyotype in *Leishmania infantum* imply a "mosaic' strain structure. *Mol. Biochem. Parasitol.* 40:53–62
2. Berman, J. D. 1988. Chemotherapy for Leishmaniasis: biochemical mechanisms, clinical efficacy, and future strategies. *Rev. Infect. Dis.* 10:560–86
3. Beverley, S. M. 1988. Chromosomal basis of DHFR-TS amplification in *Leishmania major*. In *Molecular Genetics of Parasitic Protozoa*, ed. M. J. Turner, D. Arnot, pp. 48–51. Cold Spring Harbor, NY: Cold Spring Harbor Lab.
4. Beverley, S. M. 1988. Characterization of the "unusual" mobility of large circular DNAs in pulsed field-gradient electrophoresis. *Nucleic Acids Res.* 16:925–38
5. Beverley, S. M. 1989. Estimation of circular DNA size using gamma irradiation and pulsed-field gel electrophoresis. *Anal. Biochem.* 177:110–14
6. Beverley, S. M., Coburn, C. M. 1990. Recurrent de novo appearance of small linear DNAs in *Leishmania major* and relationship to extra-chromosomal DNAs in other species. *Mol. Biochem. Parasitol.* 42:133–42
7. Beverley, S. M., Coderre, J. A., Santi, D. V., Schimke, R. T. 1984. Unstable DNA amplifications in methotrexate-resistant *Leishmania* consist of extra-

440   BEVERLEY

chromosomal circles which relocalize during stabilization. *Cell* 38:431–39
8. Deleted in proof
9. Beverley, S. M., Ellenberger, T. E., Cordingley, J. S. 1986. Primary structure of the gene encoding the bifunctional dihydrofolate reductase-thymidylate synthase of *Leishmania major*. *Proc. Natl. Acad. Sci. USA* 83:2584–88
10. Beverley, S. M., Ellenberger, T. E., Iovannisci, D. M., Kapler, G. M., Petrillo-Peixoto, M., Sina, B. J. 1988. Gene amplification in *Leishmania*. In *The Biology of Parasitism*, ed. P. T. Englund, A. Sher, pp. 431–448. New York: Liss
11. Beverley, S. M., Ellenberger, T. E., Petrillo-Peixoto, M. 1989. Unstable and stable gene amplification in methotrexate-resistant *Leishmania major* and natural isolates of *Leishmania tarentolae*. See Ref. 51a, pp. 885–90
12. Deleted in proof
13. Beverley, S. M., Ismach, R. B., McMahon-Pratt, D. 1987. Evolution of the genus *Leishmania* as revealed by comparisons of nuclear DNA restriction fragment patterns. *Proc. Natl. Acad. Sci. USA* 84:484–88
14. Bishop, R. P. 1990. Extensive homologies between *Leishmania donovani* chromosomes of markedly different size. *Mol. Biochem. Parasitol.* 38:1–12
15. Bishop, R. P., Miles, M. A. 1987. Chromosome size polymorphisms of *Leishmania donovani*. *Mol. Biochem. Parasitol.* 24:263–72
16. Borst, P. 1986. Discontinuous transcription and antigenic variation in trypanosomes. *Annu. Rev. Biochem.* 55:701–32
17. Button, L. L., Russell, D. G., Klein, H., Medina-Acosta, E., Karess, R. E., McMaster, W. R. 1989. Genes encoding the major surface glycoprotein in *Leishmania* are tandemly linked at a single chromosomal locus and are constitutively transcribed. *Mol. Biochem. Parasitol.* 32:271–84
18. Cairns, B. R., Collard, M. W., Landfear, S. M. 1989. Developmentally regulated gene from *Leishmania* encodes a putative membrane transport protein. *Proc. Natl. Acad. Sci. USA* 86:7682–86
19. Deleted in proof
20. Capecchi, M. 1990. How efficient can you get?. *Nature* 348:109–9.
21. Carroll, S. M., DeRose, M. L., Gaudray, P., Moore, C. M., Needham-Vandevanter, D. R., et al. 1988. Double minute chromosomes can be produced from precursors derived from a chromosomal deletion. *Mol. Cell. Biol.* 8:1525–33

22. Chaudhuri, G., Chang, K. P. 1988. Acid protease activity of a major surface membrane glycoprotein (gp63) from *Leishmania mexicana* promastigotes. *Mol. Biochem. Parasitol.* 27:43–52
23. Chin, K.-V., Tanaka, S., Darlington, G., Pastan, I., Gottesman, M. M. 1990. Heat shock and arsenite increase expression of the multidrug resistance (MDR1) gene in human renals carcinoma cells. *J. Biol. Chem.* 265:221–26
24. Choi, K. C. J., Chen, M. K., Roninson, I. B. 1988. An altered pattern of cross-resistance in multidrug-resistant human cells results from spontaneous mutations in the *mdr1* (P-glycoprotein) gene. *Cell* 53:519–29
25. Clayton, C. E. 1988. The molecular biology of the Kinetoplastidae. *Genet. Eng.* 7:1–56
26. Coburn, C. M., Otteman, K., McNeely, T., Turco, S., Beverley, S. M. 1991. Stable transfection of a wide range of trypanosomatids. *Mol. Biochem. Parasitol.* In press
27. Coderre, J. A., Beverley, S. M., Schimke, R. T., Santi, D. V. 1983. Overproduction of a bifunctional thymidylate synthase-dihydrofolate reductase and DNA amplification in methotrexate-resistant *Leishmania*. *Proc. Natl. Acad. Sci. USA* 80:2132–36
28. Comeau, A. M., Miller, S. I., Wirth, D. F. 1986. Chromosome location of four genes in *Leishmania*. *Mol. Biochem. Parasitol.* 21:161–69
29. Coons, T., Bitonti, A. J., McCann, P. P., Ullman, B. 1990. α-Difluoromethylornithine resistance in *Leishmania donovani* associated with increased ornithine decarboxylase activity. *Mol. Biochem. Parasitol.* 39:77–89
30. Croft, S. L. 1986. In vitro screens in the experimental chemotherapy of leishmaniasis and trypanosomiasis. *Parasitol. Today* 2:64–69
31. Cruz, A., Beverley, S. M. 1990. Gene replacement in parasitic protozoa. *Nature* 348:171–74
32. Detke, S., Chaudhuri, G., Kink, J. A., Chang, K. P. 1988. DNA amplification in tunicamycin-resistant *Leishmania mexicana*. Multiple copies of a single 63 kilobase supercoiled molecule and their expression. *J. Biol. Chem.* 263:3418–24
33. Detke, S., Katakura, K., Chang, K. P. 1989. DNA amplification in arsenite-resistant *Leishmania*. *Exp. Cell Res.* 180:161–70
34. Dreesen, T. D., Johnson, D. H., Henikoff, S. 1988. The brown protein of *Drosophila melanogaster* is similar to the white protein and to components of

active transport complexes. *Mol. Cell. Biol.* 8:5206–15

35. Ellenberger, T. E. 1989. *Gene amplification and pleiotropic drug resistance in the human parasite* Leishmania. PhD Thesis. 1:1–196. Boston, MA: Harvard Univ.

36. Ellenberger, T. E., Beverley, S. M. 1987. Reductions in methotrexate and folate influx in methotrexate-resistant lines of *Leishmania major* are independent of R or H region amplification. *J. Biol. Chem.* 262:13501–6

37. Ellenberger, T. E., Beverley, S. M. 1989. Multiple drug resistance and conservative amplification of the H region in *Leishmania major*. *J. Biol. Chem.* 264:15094–103

38. Ellenberger, T. E., Wright, J. E., Rosowsky, A., Beverley, S. M. 1989. Wild-type and drug-resistant *Leishmania major* hydrolyze methotrexate to N-10-methyl-4-deoxy-4-aminopteroate without accumulation of methotrexate polyglutamates. *J. Biol. Chem.* 264:15960–66

39. Foote, S. J., Kyle, D. E., Martin, R. K., Oduola, A. M. J., Forsyth, K., et al. 1990. Several alleles of the multidrug-resistance gene are closely linked to chloroquine resistance in *Plasmodium falciparum*. *Nature* 345:255–58

40. Gajendran, N., Dujardin, J.-C., Ray, D. L., Matthyssens, G., Muyldermans, S., Hammers, R. 1989. Abnormally migrating chromosome identifies *Leishmania donovani* populations. See Ref. 51a, pp. 549–47

41. Garvey, E. P., Coderre, J. A., Santi, D. V. 1985. Selection and properties of *Leishmania* resistant to 10-propargyl-5,8-dideazafolate, an inhibitor of thymidylate synthase. *Mol. Biochem. Parasitol.* 17:79–91

42. Garvey, E. P., Santi, D. V. 1986. Stable amplified DNA in drug-resistant *Leishmania* exists as extrachromosomal circles. *Science* 233:535–40

43. Giannini, S. H., Curry, S. S., Tesh, R. B., Van der Ploeg, L. H. T. 1990. Size-conserved chromosomes and stability of molecular karyotype in cloned stocks of *Leishmania major*. *Mol. Biochem. Parasitol.* 39:9–22

44. Giannini, S. H., Schittini, M., Keithly, J. S., Warburton, P. W., Cantor, C. R., Van der Ploeg, L. H. T. 1986. Karyotype analysis of *Leishmania* species and its use in classification and clinical diagnosis. *Science* 232:762–65

45. Gibson, W. C., Miles, M. A. 1986. The karyotype and ploidy of *Trypanosoma cruzi*. *EMBO J.* 5:1299–305

46. Giulotto, E., Saito, I., Stark, G. R. 1986. Structure of DNA formed in the first step of CAD gene amplification. *EMBO J.* 5:2115–21

47. Gottesman, M. M., Pastan, I. 1988. The multidrug transporter, a double-edged sword. *J. Biol. Chem.* 263:12163–66

48. Grogl, M., Martin, R. K., Oduola, A. M. J., Milhous, W. K., Kyle, D. E. 1991. Characteristics of multidrug resistance in *Plasmodium* and *Leishmania*: detection of P-glycoprotein-like components. *Am. J. Trop. Med. Hyg.* In press

49. Grumont, R., Washtien, W. L., Caput, D., Santi, D. V. 1986. Bifunctional thymidylate synthase-dihydrofolate reductase from *Leishmania*: sequence homology with the corresponding monofunctional proteins. *Proc. Natl. Acad. Sci. USA* 83:5387–91

50. Hamers, R. N., Gajendran, N. J. C., Dujardin, K. S. 1989. Circular and linear forms of small nucleic acids in *Leishmania*. See Ref. 51a, pp. 985–88

51. Hamlin, J. L., Milbrandt, J. D., Heintz, N. H., Azizkhan, J. C. 1984. DNA sequence amplification in mammalian cells. *Int. Rev. Cytol.* 90:31–82

51a. Hart, D. T., ed. 1989. *Leishmaniasis: the Current Status and New Strategies for Control*. New York: Plenum

52. Hedrick, P. W. 1982. Genetic hitchhiking: a new factor in evolution? *Bioscience* 32:845–53

53. Hightower, R. C., Ruiz-Perez, L. M., Wong, M. L., Santi, D. V. 1988. Extrachromosomal elements in the lower eukaryote *Leishmania*. *J. Biol. Chem.* 263:16970–76

54. Hightower, R. C., Wong, M. L., Ruiz-Perez, L., Santi, D. V. 1987. Electron microscopy of amplified DNA forms in antifolate-resistant *Leishmania*. *J. Biol. Chem.* 262:14618–24

55. Huang, P. L., Roberts, B. E., McMahon-Pratt, D., David, J. R., Miller, J. S. 1984. Structure and arrangement of the β-tubulin genes of *Leishmania tropica*. *Mol. Cell. Biol.* 4:1372–83

56. Iovannisci, D. M., Beverley, S. M. 1989. Structural alterations of chromosome 2 in *Leishmania major* as evidence for diploidy, including spontaneous amplification of the mini-exon array. *Mol. Biochem. Parasitol.* 34:177–88

57. Iovannisci, D. M., Goebel, D., Allen, K., Kaur, K., Ullman, B. 1984. Genetic analysis of adenine metabolism in *Leishmania donovani* promastigotes. *J. Biol. Chem.* 259:14617–23

58. Jaffe, C. L., Grimaldi, G., McMahon-Pratt, D. 1984. The cultivation and clon-

ing of *Leishmania*. In *Genes and Antigens of Parasites*, ed. C. Morel, pp. 47–91. Rio de Janeiro: Fundacao Oswaldo Cruz

59. Kapler, G. M., Beverley, S. M. 1989. Transcriptional mapping of the amplified region encoding the DHFR-TS of *Leishmania major* reveals a high density of transcripts, including overlapping and antisense RNAs. *Mol. Cell. Biol.* 9: 3959–72

60. Kapler, G. M., Coburn, C. M., Beverley, S. M. 1990. Stable transfection of the human parasite *Leishmania* delineates a 30 kb region sufficient for extra-chromosomal replication and expression. *Mol. Cell. Biol.* 10:1084–94

61. Kapler, G. M., Zhang, K., Beverley, S. M. 1990. Nuclease mapping and DNA sequence analysis of transcripts from the dihydrofolate reductase–thymidylate synthase (R) region of *Leishmania major*. *Nucleic Acids Res.* 18:6399–408

62. Katakura, K., Chang, K. P. 1989. H DNA amplification in *Leishmania* resistant to both arsenite and methotrexate. *Mol. Biochem. Parasitol.* 34:189–92

63. Katakura, K., Peng, Y., Pithawalla, R., Detke, S., Chang, K. P. 1991. Tunicamycin-resistant variants from five species of *Leishmania* contain amplified DNA in extrachromosomal circles of different sizes with a transcriptionally active homologous region. *Mol. Biochem. Parasitol.* 44:233–44

64. Kaur, K., Coons, T., Emmett, K., Ullman, B. 1988. Methotrexate-resistant *Leishmania donovani* genetically deficient in the folate-methotrexate transporter. *J. Biol. Chem.* 263:7020–28

65. Kink, J. A., Chang, K. P. 1987. Tunicamycin-resistant *Leishmania mexicana amazonensis*: expression of virulence associated with an increased activity of N-acetylglucosaminyltransferase and amplification of its presumptive gene. *Proc. Natl. Acad. Sci. USA* 84:1253–57

66. Kink, J. A., Chang, K. P. 1988. N-glycosylation as a biochemical basis for virulence in *Leishmania mexicana amazonensis*. *Mol. Biochem. Parasitol.* 27:181–90

67. Koch, A. L. 1974. The pertinence of the periodic selection phenomenon to prokaryote evolution. *Genetics* 77:127–42

68. Kuwano, M., Tabuki, T., Akiyama, S., Mifune, K., Takatsuki, A., et al. 1981. Isolation and characterization of Chinese hamster ovary cell mutants with altered sensitivity to high doses of tunicamycin. *Somat. Cell Genet.* 7:507–21

69. Laban, A., Tobin, J. F., de Lafaille, M. A. C., Wirth, D. F. 1990. Stable expression of the bacterial neo[r] gene in *Leishmania enriettii*. *Nature* 343:572–74

70. Landfear, S. M., McMahon-Pratt, D., Wirth, D. F. 1983. Tandem arrangement of tubulin genes in the protozoan parasite *Leishmania enrietti*. *Mol. Cell. Biol.* 3:1070–76

71. LeBowitz, J. H., Coburn, C. M., McMahon-Pratt, D., Beverley, S. M. 1990. Development of a stable *Leishmania* expression vector and application to the study of parasite surface antigen genes. *Proc. Natl. Acad. Sci. USA* 87:9736–40

72. Lee, M. G. S., Atkinson, B. L., Gianni ni, S. H., Van der Ploeg, L. H. T. 1988. Structure and expression of the HSP70 gene family of *Leishmania major*. *Nucleic Acids Res.* 16:9567–85

73. Lee, T.-C., Tanaka, N., Lamb, P. W., Gilmer, T. M., Barrett, J. C. 1988. Induction of gene amplification by arsenic. *Science* 241:79–81

74. Lehrman, M. A., Zhu, X., Khounlo, S. 1988. Amplification and molecular cloning of the hamster tunicamycin-sensitive N-acetylglucosamine-1-phosphate transferase gene. *J. Biol. Chem.* 263:19796–803

75. Leon, W., Fouts, D. L., Manning, J. 1978. Sequence arrangement of the 16S and 26S rRNA genes in the pathogenic haemoflagellate *Leishmania donovani*. *Nucleic Acids Res.* 5:491–503

76. Lohman, K. L., Langer, P. J., McMahon-Pratt, D. 1990. Molecular cloning and characterization of the immunologically protective surface glycoprotein GP6/M-2 of *Leishmania amazonensis*. *Proc. Natl. Acad. Sci. USA* 87:8393–97

77. Marini, J. C., Levene, S. D., Crothers, D. M., Englund, P. T. 1982. Bent helical structure in kinetoplast DNA. *Proc. Natl. Acad. Sci. USA* 79:7664–68

78. Miller, S. I., Landfear, S. M., Wirth, D. F. 1986. Cloning and characterization of a *Leishmania enriettii* gene encoding an RNA spliced leader sequence. *Nucleic Acids.* 14:7341–60

79. Neal, R. A., van Buren, J., McCoy, N. G., Iwobi, M. 1989. Reversal of drug resistance in *Trypanosoma cruzi* and *Leishmania donovani* by verapamil. *Trans. Roy. Soc. Trop. Med. Hyg.* 83: 197–98

80. Deleted in proof

81. Newbold, C. 1990. The path of drug resistance. *Nature* 345:202–3

82. O'Hare, K., Murphy, C., Levis, R., Rubin, G. M. 1984. DNA sequence of the white locus of *D. melanogaster*. *J. Mol. Biol.* 180:437–55

83. Ouellette, M., Fase-Fowler, F., Borst, P. 1990. The amplified H circle of methotrexate-resistant *Leishmania tarentolae* contains a novel P-glycoprotein gene. *EMBO J.* 9:1027–33
84. Ouellette, M., Hettema, E., Wüst, D., Fase-Fowler, F., Borst, P. 1991. Direct and inverted DNA repeats associated with P-glycoprotein gene amplification in drug-resistant *Leishmania*. *EMBO J.* In press
85. Pages, M., Bastien, P., Veas, F., Rossi, V., Bellis, M., et al. 1989. Chromosome size and number polymorphisms in *Leishmania infantum* suggest amplification/deletion and possible genetic exchange. *Mol. Biochem. Parasitol.* 36:161–68
86. Panton, L. J., Tesh, R. B., Nadeau, K., Beverley, S. M. 1991. A test for genetic exchange in mixed infections of *Leishmania major* in the sand fly *Phlebotomus papatasi*. *J. Protozool.* In press
87. Petrillo-Peixoto, M., Beverley, S. M. 1989. Amplification of a new region of DNA in an unselected laboratory stock of *Leishmania tarentolae:* the T region. *J. Protozool.* 36:2257–61
88. Petrillo-Peixoto, M. L., Beverley, S. M. 1988. Amplified DNAs in laboratory stocks of *L. tarentolae:* extrachromosomal circles structurally and functionally similar to the inverted H region amplification of methotrexate-resistant *L. major*. *Mol. Cell. Biol.* 8:5188–99
89. Petrillo-Peixoto, M. P., Beverley, S. M. 1987. In vitro activity of sulfonamides and sulfones against *Leishmania major* promastigotes. *Antimicrob. Agents Chemother.* 31:1575–78
90. Ruiz, J. C., Choi, K., Hoff, D. D. vo, Roninson, I. B., Wahl, G. M. 1989. Autonomously replicating episomes contain *mdr1* genes in a multidrug-resistant human cell line. *Mol. Cell. Biol.* 9:109–15
91. Samaras, N., Spithill, T. W. 1987. Molecular karyotype of five species of *Leishmania* and analysis of gene locations and chromosomal rearrangements. *Mol. Biochem. Parasitol.* 25:279–91
92. Schimke, R. T. 1982. Gene amplification summary. See Ref. 93, pp. 317–33
93. Schimke, R. T., ed. 1982. *Gene Amplification*. Cold Spring Harbor: Cold Spring Harbor Lab. 339 pp.
94. Schimke, R. T. 1984. Gene amplification in cultured animal cells. *Cell* 37:705–13
95. Schimke, R. T. 1988. Gene amplification in cultured cells. *J. Biol. Chem.* 263:5989–92
96. Schimke, R. T., Roos, D. S., Brown, P. C. 1987. Amplification of genes in somatic mammalian cells. *Methods Enzymol.* 151:85–104
97. Schimke, R. T., Sherwood, S. W., Hill, A. B., Johnston, R. N. 1986. Over-replication and recombination of DNA in higher eukaryotes: potential consequences and biological implications. *Proc. Natl. Acad. Sci. USA* 83:2157–61
98. Scholler, J. K., Reed, S. G., Stuart, K. 1986. Molecular karyotype of species and subspecies of *Leishmania*. *Mol. Biochem. Parasitol.* 20:279–93
99. Scocca, J. R., Hartog, K. O., Krag, S. S. 1988. Evidence of gene amplification in tunicamycin-resistant Chinese hamster ovary cells. *Biochem. Biophys. Res. Commun.* 156:1063–69
100. Scott, D. A., Coombs, G. H., Sanderson, B. E. 1987. Effects of methotrexate and other antifolates on the growth and dihydrofolate reductase activity of *Leishmania* promastigotes. *Biochem. Pharmacol.* 36:2043–45
101. Shapira, M., Pinelli, E. 1989. Heat shock protein 83 of *Leishmania mexicana amazonensis* is an abundant cytoplasmic protein with a tandemly repeated genomic arrangement. *Eur. J. Biochem.* 185:231–36
102. Simpson, L., Shaw, J. 1989. RNA editing and the mitochondrial cryptogenes of kinetoplastid protozoa. *Cell* 57:355–66
103. Sirawaraporn, W., Sersrivanich, R., Booth, R. G., Hansch, C., Neal, R. A., Santi, D. V. 1988. Selective inhibition of *Leishmania* dihydrofolate reductase and *Leishmania* growth by 5-benzyl-2,4-diaminopyrimidines. *Mol. Biochem. Parasitol.* 31:79–86
104. Solari, A. J. 1980. The 3-dimensional fine structure of the mitotic spindle in *Trypanosoma cruzi*. *Chromosoma* 78:239–55
105. Stark, G. R., Debatisse, M., Giulotto, E., Wahl, G. M. 1989. Recent progress in understanding mechanisms of mammalian DNA amplification. *Cell* 57:901–8
106. Stark, G. R., Wahl, G. M. 1984. Gene amplification. *Annu. Rev. Biochem.* 53:447–91
107. Stuart, K., Karp, S., Aline, R. Jr., Smiley, B., Scholler, J., Keithly, J. 1989. Small nucleic acids in *Leishmania*. See Ref. 51a, pp. 555–62
108. Sudo, T., Onodera, K. 1979. Isolation and characterization of tunicamycin-resistant mutants from Chinese hamster ovary cells. *J. Cell. Physiol.* 101:149–56
109. Ten Asbroek, A. L. M. A., Ouellette,

M., Borst, P. 1990. Targeted insertion of the neomycin phosphotransferase gene into the tubulin gene cluster of *Trypanosoma brucei*. *Nature* 348:174–75

110. Tlsty, T. D., Margolin, B. H., Lum, K. 1989. Differences in the rates of gene amplification of nontumorigenic and tumorigenic cell lines as measured by Luria-Delbruck fluctuation analysis. *Proc. Natl. Acad. Sci. USA* 86:9441–45

111. Tobin, J. F., Laban, A., Wirth, D. F. 1991. Homologous recombination in *Leishmania enrietti*. *Proc. Natl. Acad. Sci. USA* 88:864–68

112. Van der Bliek, A. M., Lincke, C. R., Borst, P. 1988. Circular DNA of 3T6R50 double minute chromosomes. *Nucleic Acids Res.* 16:4841–52

113. Van der Ploeg, L. H. T., Cornelissen, A. W. C. A., Barry, J. D., Borst, P. 1984. Chromosomes of kinetoplastida. *EMBO J.* 3:3109–15

114. Van der Ploeg, L. H. T., Liu, A. Y. C., Borst, P. 1984. Structure of the growing telomeres of trypanosomes. *Cell* 36:459–68

115. Wellems, T. E., Panton, L. J., Gluzman, I. Y., do Rosario, V. E., Gwadz, R. W., et al. 1990. Chloroquine resistance not linked to *mdr*-like genes in a *Plasmodium falciparum* cross. *Nature* 345:253–55

116. White, M. J. D. 1973. *Animal Cytology and Evolution*. Cambridge: Cambridge Univ. Press. 961 pp.

117. White, T. C., Fase-Fowler, F., Luenen, H. va, Calafat, J., Borst, P. 1988. The H circles of *Leishmania tarentolae* are a unique amplifiable system of oligomeric DNAs associated with drug resistance. *J. Biol. Chem.* 263:16977–83

118. Wilson, K., Collart, F. R., Huberman, E., Stringer, J. R., Ullman, B. 1991. Amplification and molecular cloning of the IMP dehydrogenase gene of *Leishmania donovani*. *J. Biol. Chem.* 266:1665–71

119. World Health Organization Expert Committee. 1984. *The Leishmaniasis*. Geneva: WHO. 146 pp.

120. Wright, J. A., Smith, H. S., Watt, F. M., Hancock, M. C., Hudson, D. L., Stark, G. R. 1990. DNA amplification is rare in normal human cells. *Proc. Natl. Acad. Sci. USA* 87:1791–95

Annu. Rev. Microbiol. 1991. 45:445–74

IVERMECTIN AS AN ANTIPARASITIC AGENT FOR USE IN HUMANS

William C. Campbell

The Charles A. Dana Research Institute for Scientists Emeriti, Drew University, Madison, New Jersey 07940

KEY WORDS: chemotherapy, onchocerciasis, parasitic diseases, pharmacology, tropical medicine

CONTENTS

INTRODUCTION 446
INTESTINAL NEMATODES 446
    Ascaris lumbricoides 446
    Hookworms (Ancylostoma, Necator) 446
    Trichuris trichiura 447
    Enterobius vermicularis 448
    Strongyloides stercoralis 448
    Broad-Spectrum Potential 449
ONCHOCERCIASIS... 449
    Early Hospital-Based Probes (Phase I) 450
    Hospital-Based Trials with Reference Treatment (Phase II) 451
    Large-Scale Hospital-Based Trials (Phase III).................................... 453
    Large-Scale Community-Based Trials (Phase IV) 454
    Effect on the Parasite 455
    Effect on Transmission.. 459
    Causal Prophylaxis 461
OTHER FILARIAL INFECTIONS 461
    Wuchereria bancrofti 461
    Brugia, Mansonella, Loa 464
EFFICACY AGAINST OTHER PARASITES 464
SAFETY IN HUMANS... 465
    Safety and Tolerability in Onchocerciasis 465
    Safety in Other Infections 467
    Safety in General 467
CURRENT DRUG DISTRIBUTION... 468

0066-4227/91/1001-0445$02.00

INTRODUCTION

Ivermectin is a derivative of a family of macrocyclic lactones, the avermectins, that are produced by the filamentous bacterium *Streptomyces avermitilis*. Selective hydrogenation of avermectin B_1 yields 22-23-dihydroavermectin B_1, which bears the generic name ivermectin. Much has been written about ivermectin; hundreds of articles have appeared in the scientific literature, and the available information was summarized in a recent monograph (13). The preponderance of reports, however, deal with ivermectin in relation to animal health (and with its analog abamectin in relation to plant health). The present review deals with the efficacy and safety of ivermectin in the treatment and control of human parasitic infections.

INTESTINAL NEMATODES

Ascaris lumbricoides

Anecdotal evidence from onchocerciasis trials suggested that ivermectin may be active against *Ascaris lumbricoides*. This activity was recorded by Whitworth et al (102) who used ivermectin against onchocerciasis in a Sierra Leone community in which a third of the population had *Ascaris* infection. In that community the most common side-effect of treatment was the passage of *A. lumbricoides* in the stool (102).

In a trial in Peru, 20 patients infected with *Ascaris* were given single oral doses of ivermectin at 50–200 μg/kg (or 2 dosages at 100 μg/kg). After 3 days, only about half of them were cured, but by 30 days, fecal examinations revealed that all were totally free of *Ascaris* (59). Similarly, in a trial in Guatamala, 10 patients received single oral doses of ivermectin at 140–200 μg/kg, and all were completely cured after one month (39). In Gabon, 15 patients with *Ascaris* infection were completely cured when examined 23 days after receiving a single oral dose of ivermectin at 200 μg/kg (75). Complete cure was also obtained in 44 cases in Central African Republic (94).

Thus trials in Africa, Central America, and South America have indicated that ivermectin is highly effective against *Ascaris* at well-tolerated dosages.

Hookworms (Anclyostoma, Necator)

Incidental observations in the course of onchocerciasis trials indicated that ivermectin was not active against *Necator americanus* at 5 or 10 μg/kg (7) and "had no effect on hookworms" at dosages up to 200 μg/kg (6).

In a trial in Peru, little if any efficacy was recorded when 52 patients with *N. americanus* or *Ancylostoma duodenale* were given single oral doses of ivermectin at 50–200 μg/kg, or 2 doses at 200μg/kg (59). Similarly, in Guatamala, ivermectin was only slightly effective against hookworm (probably *N. americanus*) when given to 10 patients at 140–200 μg/kg (39). In both of these trials, the numbers of hookworm eggs in the stool of treated patients was reduced to about half of the pretreatment values. In Gabon, 15 patients with *N. americanus* received a single oral dose of 200 μg/kg, and none had stopped passing eggs after 23 days (75). Ivermectin was also found inactive against *N. americanus* in the Ivory Coast (52) and against *A. duodenale* in Central African Republic (94).

Ivermectin, as presently administered, thus seems to have little or no utility in the treatment of hookworm infection in humans, and is certainly less effective than other medications for this purpose.

The poor activity of ivermectin against human hookworm was surprising because the drug is extremely potent against canine hookworms (for review, see 13). In one study (99), a single oral dose at 10 μg/kg not only resulted in the expulsion of all *Ancylostoma caninum* from treated dogs, but also inhibited the development of eggs recovered from the affected worms. The difference in the human and canine experience may be related to differences in both parasite and host. *N. americanus* seems to be especially insensitive to ivermectin, and when this species is adapted to hamsters, extraordinarily high dosages of ivermectin are needed to remove them from treated animals (72).

The larvae of dog hookworm species cause skin disease, cutaneous larva migrans, in humans, and this condition often requires therapy. Ivermectin has not been studied systematically for efficacy against it, but a few patients have been treated informally. At a remote work camp in French Guayana, ivermectin was applied topically with apparent success (D. Barth & W. Rietschel, personal communication). The product used was probably the injectible cattle product, containing 1.0% ivermectin, and the solution was swabbed directly onto the affected skin. Ivermectin in such solutions does in fact penetrate mammalian skin to a considerable degree, and a topical formulation is used commercially in cattle. Thus, topical ivermectin could very well be an effective and well tolerated treatment for cutaneous larva migrans in humans, but the dosage and tolerability of such treatment are at present unknown. The infections in French Guayana were attributed to *Acylostoma braziliense*. Research has shown that the third-stage larvae of *A. caninum* are killed by ivermectin in vitro at a concentration of 0.025 μg/ml (99). Successful treatment of cutaneous larva migrans with one or two oral doses of ivermectin (12 mg per dose) was recently reported (87a).

Trichuris trichiura

In Peru, ivermectin was tested in 54 patients with *Trichuris trichiura* infection. Most received a single oral dose at 50–200 μg/kg, and efficacy was equivocal. The largest group, 17 patients, received a dosage of 200 μg/kg on two successive days; about 60% of them had negative stool samples after three days, and 100% were apparently cured after 30 days (59). In Guatamala, 12 patients were treated with ivermectin at 140–200 μg/kg, and only 50%

were cured (negative stool sample) within one month. Fecal egg numbers exhibited a mean 93% reduction but this decrease ranged from 75 to 100% in individual patients (39). In the Ivory Coast, dosages up to 200 μg/kg were inactive against *T. trichiura* (52). In Gabon, fecal examinations were done on patients 23 days after treatment with ivermectin at 200 μg/kg; only one of 15 patients had ceased to pass *T. trichiura* eggs (75). Clearly ivermectin is not particularly effective against whipworm *(Trichuris)* infections.

Enterobius vermicularis

In a trial in Peru, 88 patients were shown by the adhesive-tape test to have *Enterobius vermicularis* prior to treatment with ivermectin in single oral doses at 50–200 μg/kg, or doses of 100 or 200 μg/kg on two successive days. Prior to treatment, each patient received a placebo treatment; after treatment each patient received another placebo or a repeat dose of ivermectin. Cure, based on negative tape tests on three successive days, was recorded for 85% of the patients. There was no significant difference in the apparent efficacy of different dosages (59).

Strongyloides stercoralis

INTESTINAL   A trial in Peru, while providing data on various gastrointestinal nematodes (see above), was primarily concerned with *Strongyloides stercoralis*. Ivermectin was given to 110 patients with *S. stercoralis*, and efficacy data were obtained for all but 9 of them. All patients received placebo treatment 3 days before receiving ivermectin at dosages of 50–200 μg/kg and all received placebo (or a second dose of ivermectin) on the day following the ivermectin treatment (59). Treatments were coded, but no group of patients was left untreated. Efficacy was based on a comparison of the number of larvae in multiple stools collected before and after treatment. Cure rates at 30 days varied from 67% for the 50-μg/kg dosages to 100% for the subjects receiving two doses at 200 μg/kg; but these values represent to an unknown degree the efficacy of the drug and/or the spontaneous loss of infection. Patients not cured showed a large (>90%) reduction in the number of larvae passed in feces. The investigators considered it unlikely that complete cure had occurred spontaneously in the patients whose stools became negative after treatment. In heavily infected patients, the marked reduction in fecal larval output accompanied marked improvement in clinical condition.

In Guatamala, 10 patients with light *S. stercoralis* infection were given a single oral dose of ivermectin at 140–200 μg/kg. All were negative for *S. stercoralis* when their stools were examined one month later (39). As in the previous study, the protocol did not include any untreated control subjects. In Central African Republic, 53 patients were apparently cured with ivermectin at 200 μg/kg (94).

Thus, the evidence indicates that ivermectin is active against *S. stercoralis* in humans (as it is against *Strongyloides* spp. in other hosts), but definitive studies are needed. Control of this parasite may be a corollary benefit to mass treatment with ivermectin for the control of onchocerciasis (94).

DISSEMINATED   From the earliest days of ivermectin research, the question of its potential utility in disseminated strongyloidiasis has been considered, but this question remains essentially unanswered. It arises because of the continuing need for improved therapy for this dangerous condition; it is unanswered because the condition is relatively rare and because it is difficult to test drugs against it. In the trial conducted in *S. stercoralis* patients in Peru (see preceding section), three of the patients died from causes believed to be unrelated to the parasite or the treatment. They died within three weeks after treatment, and autopsy failed to reveal evidence of tissue-dwelling *S. stercoralis* larvae. However, in the absence of antemortem evidence indicating disseminated infection, the data are inconclusive with respect to the effect of treatment.

Broad-Spectrum Potential

The potential utility of ivermectin in the broad-spectrum control of gastrointestinal nematodes must be assessed in the light of the current armamentarium. Excellent drugs are presently available for such use. They are given orally and are well tolerated, although they differ in details of spectrum and in recommended regimen. None is highly active against all of the important nematodes when given as a single dose. None is dependably or highly curative in human hookworm infection, but ivermectin is unlikely to match these drugs at any dosage that could reasonably be projected. Conceivably ivermectin, if given in multidose regimen or in special formulation, would provide highly effective broad-spectrum activity, but present data and the existence of alternative drugs make exploration of this possibility unlikely.

Ivermectin might be employed with benefit in conjunction with other drugs. In mass treatment campaigns designed to control helminth diseases in children, ivermectin could be administered in conjunction with albendazole and praziquantel (100). Under such circumstances, the effect of ivermectin on intestinal nematodes might complement or even synergize that of albendazole. Because two different modes of action are involved, the effects might even be synergistic, but that remains speculative.

ONCHOCERCIASIS

Ivermectin has been evaluated in clinical trials that may be classified as Phase I (early hospital-based probes with open protocol), Phase II (hospital-based, double-blind trials with diethylcarbamazine as a reference standard), Phase III (hospital-based, double-blind trials comparing selected dosages and building an additional safety database) and Phase IV (community-based trials). Others have reviewed the subject previously (40, 42, 88, 89).

Early Hospital-Based Probes (Phase I)

Ivermectin was found effective against the skin-dwelling microfilariae of *Onchocerca cervicalis* in horses (36) and *Onchocerca* spp. in cattle in Australia (D. B. Copeman, personal communication), and a trial in human subjects was subsequently arranged. Because of the novelty of the drug and the idiosyncratic toxicity observed in mice, the first human trials were conducted with extreme caution. The initial dose was one twentieth (instead of the usual tenth) of the observed no-effect level of the drug when administered to the most sensitive animal species (11). Hence, the first subjects received a single oral dose of 5 μg/kg. Furthermore, the drug was given, not to noninfected volunteers as would normally be the case (11), but to young men with *Onchocerca volvulus* infections (and light hookworm infections) who stood to benefit directly from any diminution in microfilarial numbers. When neither efficacy nor toxicity was observed, higher dosages were tested (open, placebo-controlled, cross-over protocol). The evidence obtained from skin-snips indicated that single oral dosages of 30 or 50 μg/kg effectively reduced the number of microfilariae recoverable from the skin of treated patients (8, 31, 51). Adverse effects were minor and transient. Patients with high microfilarial densities or with ocular involvement had prudently been excluded from the trial, and thus the results did not indicate whether ivermectin treatment might elicit hypersensitivity reactions caused by the destruction of large numbers of microfilariae, or might mobilize microfilariae and induce ocular invasion, or might exacerbate ocular damage in patients with existing invasion of the eye. Such limitations of the protocol were recognized, as was the need for direct comparison of the new drug with the existing standard, diethylcarbamazine (DEC) (8, 81).

The real significance of the trial, not immediately appreciated by all concerned, was that a new chemical class was shown to reduce microfilarial skin density, without evidence of serious acute toxicity from the drug itself, and as a single oral dose. (The evidence of safety was, of course, very tentative because of the small number of subjects.) The structural novelty of the compound allowed the possibility, however unlikely, of diminished allergic reaction to dead microfilariae in heavily infected patients, and of efficacy against other stages (pre-adult and adult) of *O. volvulus*. In addition, the small single oral dosage of the new drug, even if it should prove inactive against the pre-adult or adult worms, might provide a microfilaricide that would be (even if only for logistical reasons) vastly more suitable than diethylcarbamazine for community use and for large-scale control programs. Additional trials were therefore undertaken.

Taking advantage of the presence in Paris of patients formerly resident in Senegal or Mali, the investigators undertook an open dose–ranging study. Patients without ocular involvement were given single oral doses at 50, 75, or 100 μg/kg (18), and subsequently, dosages of 150 or 200 μg/kg were given to patients, some of whom had ocular involvement (17). The main findings were "the rapid decrease in density of the skin microfilariae after a single oral 150 or 200 μg/kg dose of ivermectin, comparable with the effects of diethylcarbamazine; the persistence of low skin microfilaria density for up to a year in the seven patients followed up; the absence of severe ophthalmological side-effects (such as those seen with diethylcarbamazine); and the mild to moderate and transient nature of the adverse clinical and laboratory effects" (17).

At the same time, a similar open dose–ranging study was conducted in Ghana, using patients with moderate to heavy microfilarial densities (5, 6, 84). Dosages of 50, 100, 150, or 200 μg/kg were given, and "ivermectin slowly eliminated microfilariae from the skin and eye without serious adverse clinical or ocular reactions in all treated groups. . . . Very low levels of skin microfilariae were maintained for nine months. Microfilariae were not eliminated from the eye for at least three months" (6). The drug was not macrofilaricidal, nor was it embryotoxic for the worms. "However, it produced a dose-dependent stimulation of embryogenesis manifest at one month and succeeded by a suppression of embryogenesis at three months after therapy" (6). The three higher dosages were of approximately equal efficacy. Mobilization of microfilariae into blood or eyes was observed in some patients. There was some evidence of postural hypotension in treated patients, but systemic reactions in general were mild.

Hospital-Based Trials with Reference Treatment (Phase II)

Four randomized, double-blind studies, with placebo controls and reference treatment, were conducted in the endemic regions of West Africa. The patients, who were hospitalized during treatment, were adult males. They generally had moderate or heavy skin microfilarial (mf.) densities, and almost all had mild or moderate eye lesions. Treatment consisted of ivermectin (as a single oral dose of 200 μ/kg), or diethylcarbamazine (approximately 0.8 mg/kg $\times$ 2 days plus 1.6 mg/kg b.i.d. $\times$ 6 days), or matching placebo capsules.

SENEGAL   The study involved 30 patients; all had moderate or heavy skin microfilarial densities and some had mild or moderate eye lesions (28, 30, 32). Both medications resulted in about 98% reduction in skin mf. density by day 8. After 1 year, the density was still 82% less than pretreatment values in the DEC patients and 96% in the ivermectin patients (the difference between the drugs was significant).

GHANA   The trial was done in 59 patients with moderate to heavy infection and ocular involvement (4, 22). Treatment with DEC eliminated mf. from the anterior chamber in 8 days, whereas ivermectin eliminated them in 6 months. The authors found that DEC and ivermectin reduced the skin mf. counts to a similar extent over 6 months, but the subsequent rise in mf. count was significantly greater in the DEC group than in the ivermectin group. Both groups experienced some mobilization of mf. into the blood. It was suggested that the slower elimination in the ivermectin patients may have resulted partly from the inability of the larger ivermectin molecule to pass from blood to aqueous-humor.

MALI   The study was done on 30 patients with ocular involvement (10, 55, 98). In the DEC patients, the number of mf. in the anterior chamber was rapidly reduced to zero in some patients but rose again within 6 months. In the ivermectin patients, mf. were gradually eliminated over the 6-month period. Skin mf. density began to fall in both groups by day 2, and reached a low of 4% of pretreatment value on day 8 (DEC group) and a low of 1% of pretreatment value on day 28 (ivermectin group). At 1 year after treatment, the counts had risen to 45% of pretreatment (DEC group) or 9% of pretreatment (ivermectin group).

LIBERIA   The trial was done on 30 patients with moderate to severe infection and ocular involvement (41, 90). Both medications resulted in prompt reduction in skin mf. counts to almost zero; the lowest count was on day 8 for DEC and on day 14 for ivermectin. Numbers of mf. rose gradually in both groups. After 6 months, the counts in the ivermectin group (but not in the DEC group) were still significantly lower than in the placebo group. Treatment with DEC, but not ivermectin, resulted in more living and dead mf. in the cornea. Both medications reduced the numbers of mf. in the anterior chamber; the effect was slower in the ivermectin group. A separate trial, which departed from the standard protocol of the four primary Phase II trials, was conducted on 50 Liberian patients (1). The results of the Phase I ivermectin trials had raised the question of whether the clinical performance of DEC could be improved to match that of ivermectin simply by increasing the DEC dosage. Ivermectin, as a single oral dose at 150 μg/kg was therefore compared to high oral and/or cutaneous dosages of DEC, accompanied by corticosteroid treatment to suppress possible hypersensitivity reactions. Skin mf. counts were reduced by more than 90% following all treatments. After two months, the numbers of mf. had started to rise in the DEC patients, but not in the ivermectin patients.

The DEC treatment was associated with some apparent mobilization of mf. into the cornea and the urine, but the ivermectin treatment was not. Both medications resulted in reduced numbers of mf. in the anterior chamber of the eye after two months. The most striking difference between the two medications was that adverse systemic and ocular reactions were fewer and less severe with the use of ivermectin (see section on safety in humans).

Large-Scale Hospital-Based Trials (Phase III)

These studies involved larger numbers of patients (about 50 per group). The studies were double-blind, the patients were hospitalized for treatment, and the trials were done not only in Africa but also in Central America.

LIBERIA   A study was done on 200 patients with moderate to severe onchocerciasis (42, 60, 101), and detailed ophthalmological examinations were done on 39 persons who had severe ocular damage (92). The dosages used were 100, 150, and 200 μ/kg. All three dosages gave comparable reduction in mf. at 3, 6, or 12 months after treatment. The lowest counts were recorded at three months, at which time they were almost zero. At the 12-month interval, treatments (and placebo) were reassigned so as to give subgroups of patients receiving (a) treatment once a year for two years at 100, 150, or 200 μ/kg; (b) treatments at each of these dosages, given at a two-year interval; or (c) three treatments at 150 μ/kg given at six-month intervals (89). As expected, retreatment given when mf. counts began to rise resulted in renewed reduction. The investigators concluded that a dosage of 150 μ/kg, given yearly, represented the best regimen in terms of efficacy and safety. Treatment reduced the numbers of mf. in the cornea and in the anterior chamber of the eye. Even in patients with severe ocular involvement, lesions did not worsen (except perhaps in one patient), and the clinical condition of the eye generally improved.

GHANA   A study of 198 patients was conducted in the savannah region of Northern Ghana, where vector control had been successfully applied (3, 21). The patients, men and women, had moderate to heavy infections, but had dead and dying adult O. volvulus and diminishing numbers of skin and ocular mf. because of the prior interruption of transmission. Ivermectin dosages of 100, 150, or 200 μ/kg gave at least 97% reduction in skin mf., and the effect persisted for more than a year. The two higher dosages were superior to the lowest dosage. All three dosages eliminated mf. slowly (3–6 months) from the cornea and anterior of the eye.

MALI   A study was done on 234 patients with skin densities of at least 20 mf./mg and with moderate or severe ocular involvement (98). Ivermectin dosages of 100, 150, or 200 μg/kg were compared with placebo treatment. Skin mf. counts were reduced by 79% after 3 days and by 92% after six months (all dosages). After one year, the counts were reduced by 87% from pretreatment levels. The numbers of mf. in the placebo group also fell during the trial, but were always higher than in the ivermectin groups. Ocular mf. counts increased slightly in the first three days after ivermectin treatment, but then diminished gradually to give a reduction of more than 90% after three months.

IVORY COAST   A trial involving 220 male patients was conducted (52, 53, 54). The pretreatment skin mf. values were 59–64 mf./mg, and many patients had ocular involvement. By 4 days after treatment with ivermectin at 100, 150, or 200 μg/kg, the mf. count in the skin was significantly reduced, and after 3 months it had reached undetectable levels in almost all patients. The count then rose gradually and after 1 year had reached 10–18% of the original value. The number of mf. in the cornea and anterior chamber of the eye was significantly reduced at 3, 6, or 12 months after treatment.

Many of the patients in this trial were re-treated with ivermectin at half-yearly or yearly intervals, while others received repeated placebo treatment. Repeated ivermectin treatments were highly successful, and mf. were essentially eliminated in patients receiving three doses at 200 μg/kg at half-yearly intervals. For the reduction of mf. in the cornea or anterior chamber, two doses at a yearly interval were better than one (regardless of dosage).

TOGO   Trials have involved about 200 patients (44, 46, 47). Ivermectin dosages of 100, 150, or 200 μg/mg markedly reduced the numbers of mf. in skin and in the cornea and anterior chamber of the eye.

Large-Scale Community-Based Trials (Phase IV)

Ivermectin has been used in several community-based programs and mass treatment campaigns (25, 64, 68, 73, 77, 79, 97, 102). More than 600,000 patients have been treated, and the findings have been analyzed (74). Apart from exceptions noted below, the target dosage was 150 mg/kg, and recipients were weighed individually in order to adhere closely to this dosage. The emphasis in these trials, apart from the fundamental objective of disease control, was to monitor adverse reactions and to insure that the dosage could eventually be used without individual medical supervision (see section on safety in humans). Information was also gathered on the effect of treatment on infection status (on a community basis, not an individual basis) and on the status of vector infection (see section on effect on transmission).

Effect on the Parasite

MICROFILARIAE   The earliest clinical trials made clear that ivermectin treatment of onchocerciasis patients resulted in lower numbers of mf. recoverable from the skin. The investigators made this determination by counting the mf. that emerged from saline-soaked skin-snips taken from the patients before and after treatment. It was not clear whether the observed reduction reflected (a) paralysis of mf. and inability to migrate from the piece of tissue; (b) death of mf.; (c) inward retreat of mf. before snips were taken; or (d) failure to emerge from snips for reasons other than paralysis or death. Because the effect is apparent within 2 or 3 days after treatment, it can hardly be attributed to a suppression of larval output by affected adult worms and consequent failure to replace skin-dwelling mf. lost by natural attrition. A rapid posttreatment reduction in eosinophilia (57) further suggests a direct action on mf.

The reduction in mf. count in the eye, following ivermectin treatment, was associated with fewer local reactions (punctuate opacities) than in the case of DEC treatment, and the investigators (98) suggested that this result may occur because the mf. are paralyzed rather than immediately killed or because the mf. are affected only after they migrate out of the eye and become exposed to effective levels of the drug in other tissues. Migration out of the eye is unlikely to result from drug effect because ivermectin does not appreciably enter the eye. Chronic lesions in the cornea may in part be the result of autoantibodies induced by mf., but studies with *Onchocerca lienalis* in guinea pigs revealed no change in the production of such antibodies following treatment with ivermectin (33).

Early clinical observations suggested that ivermectin might kill mf. directly in the skin with consequent blood eosinophilia (4), but also that the slower elimination of mf. from the eye (requiring a few months instead of a few days) might be due to some indirect mechanism such as the wandering of mf. from the drug-free eye to the surrounding drug-laden tissue (23). Reductions of mf. numbers in both skin and eye were associated with fewer and milder hypersensitivity reactions, and this observation suggested that the mechanism, while not necessarily the same in both sites, was at least different from the mechanism of DEC in both sites.

Soboslay and his colleagues addressed the question of how ivermectin affects mf. by recovering mf. from treated patients and measuring their motility in an in vitro motility assay (85). The study was done in conjunction with the clinical trials in Liberia. When skin-snips were taken 24 hours after treatment, the mf. that emerged showed a clear and probably dose-related reduction in motility. At the same time, direct observation of mf. in the anterior chamber of the eye revealed abnormal motility in mf. from 24 of 94 ivermectin-treated patients but only 1 of 28 placebo-treated patients (85).

A difference in the effects of ivermectin and DEC on mf. was also suggested by observations made in the course of a Phase II study (9). Mobilization of mf. into blood was slower with ivermectin treatment (peak in 4 days) than with DEC treatment (peak in 2 days). Mobilization into the urine also occurred, but in the ivermectin patients, the mf. number remained very small.

When exposed to low concentrations of ivermectin in vitro, the mf. of *O. volvulus* exhibit an altered movement but not paralysis (58). In an attempt to demonstrate paralysis after in vitro treatment, skin-snips from patients were soaked in saline to allow emergence of mf., subsequently fixed and later digested with collagenase to reveal mf. that had failed to emerge. Before treatment, about 80% of mf. emerged during routine soaking (as in other studies). After treatment, the expected dramatic fall in mf. density in the skin occurred (as reflected by emergence into saline), but the percentage of mf. that emerged from the snips rather than remaining in situ was only slightly reduced. The reduction was statistically significant and dose-related, but even at the highest dosage of 200 μg/kg it was only 16%. The investigation concluded that this small reduction did not support the hypothesis that ivermectin acted primarily by paralyzing the mf.

The above investigation was conducted in Togo, and a similar study was done in Guatamala (77). Again skin-snips were soaked in saline in the usual way and were subsequently fixed and then digested in collagenase to reveal mf. that might not have emerged into saline. The patients had received ivermectin at 150 μg/kg. At 6 hours after treatment, the number of mf. emerging from skin-snips actually increased by about one third. At 48 hours, the number had fallen to only 13% of its original level. The numbers of mf. recovered from digested snips decreased very little in this period, so that the proportion that failed to emerge in saline increased from about 20% to about 50%. Nevertheless, the numbers in the digest were small at all times, and the lack of any absolute increase in their number indicated (as in the above study) that the decline in the number of mf. recovered by the usual saline method is not the result of immobilization of mf. in the skin. Indeed, the authors suggest that the mf. in the skin are mobilized by the treatment of the host, and retreat from the subepidermal layer of the skin into the deeper layers. If that is the case, their subsequent fate remains a mystery. (The authors noted a slight mobilization of mf. into blood and urine, but, like other investigators, they conclude that such mobilization is much less marked than in the case of DEC therapy.)

Attempts were made to titrate the concentration of ivermectin required to kill mf. when incubated in vitro at 37°C for 24–48 h. Concentrations comparable to those obtained in treated patients (10–50 ng/ml) had little effect. A concentration of 10,000 ng/ml killed about 50% of the mf., but 30,000 ng/ml was required to kill all of them. On the other hand, mf. that had been incubated for 30 min in cold solutions of ivermectin, at concentrations as low as 100 ng/ml, failed almost completely to develop when inoculated into susceptible black-flies (16).

It is apparent from the above studies that the effect of ivermectin on mf. in the skin is far from clear. Undoubtedly a direct effect reduces mf. numbers, as opposed to a lack of repopulation following natural attrition, and the reduction in the number of mf. that emerge from skin-snips does not seem to be attributable to the paralysis of affected mf. Possibly the mf. die and are quickly resorbed, and possibly they simply flee the scene for destinations unknown, but no direct evidence supports either conjecture.

THE ADULT WORMS   Following a single ivermectin dose, the numbers of mf. in the skin fall rapidly (suggesting, as stated, an effect on the mf. rather than the adult worm) and rise slowly after a lapse of several months, suggesting that the adult worms have not been killed. It does not follow, however, that the adult worms have been unaffected, and throughout the clinical efficacy trials the investigators attempted to document changes in the adults. The very slow reappearance of mf. in the skin could reflect a relatively rapid resumption of larviposition with a long period for the numbers of progeny to build up to reach the skin-snip detection threshold. Alternatively the observation could be attributed to an effect on the adult worms, resulting in a prolonged delay before the females resumed shedding mf. Almost all of the drug is excreted in the feces within 13 days after treatment (B. White-Guay, personal communication), so persistence of drug residues is unlikely to account for the prolonged suppression of microfilarodermia.

Data from the very first clinical trial of ivermectin suggested a "suppressive effect on worm reproduction," although the results were tentative and nothing indicated whether the effect was "macrofilaricidal activity or chemosterilization" (7). Almost immediately, further data, based on nodulectomy and collagenase digestion, indicated that "ivermectin was neither macrofilaricidal nor embryotoxic but there were changes in the numbers of developing embryos in the adult females . . ." (5). Many of the adult worms were apparently derived from old infections, and the level of reproductive activity was low even in worms taken from untreated control patients. Only 42% of the females contained embryos or mf. In worms recovered one month after treatment with ivermectin at 200 µg/kg, 67% of the females contained mf. and the numbers of mf. were much higher than in the controls. Thus, at first an apparent "stimulation of embryogenesis" occurred as had been seen with other medications. This process was followed by a marked decrease in reproductive activity at three months after treatment. The decrease did not result from chemosterilization because ova were still present in the uteri of the female worms, and spermatozoa were present in the testes of the males. There was, however, a drastic decline in the number and condition of embryos and mf. in the uteri, with many of them showing clear signs of degeneration. The investigators concluded that mf. develop normally after treatment, but that they "are not released" and that they "degenerate and are resorbed after several weeks or months in the uteri" (6, 84). Similar observations were made in conjunction with Phase II and Phase III trials (2, 28). At one month after treatment, worms from ivermectin and DEC patients had uteri with developing mf. that appeared normal. At six months, the developing mf. in the DEC group again appeared normal, but in the ivermectin group, inspection of the worms "appeared to show that developing forms of mf. had not been released and were deformed, dead or degenerating in the uterus" (28). In another Phase II study, ivermectin treatment was again followed by increased numbers of embryos in the female worms at one month, and by degeneration of mf. in the female worms at six months (4). Degeneration of intra-uterine mf. became a well confirmed feature of ivermectin treatment (55, 83, 84), as did the failure of the drug to kill the adult male or female worms (12, 28, 32, 41, 55, 84).

In one study, histological techniques were used to examine the effects of ivermectin on reproductive processes of the worms. The dosages used had been 150 or 220 μg/kg, and the effects were assessed on the basis of nodules taken at 10 months after treatment. No effect was observed on embryogenesis or early mf. development (up to the coiled stage), nor was an effect seen on spermatogenesis in the males. In examining worms with stretched (essentially fully developed) mf., the investigators found that the majority of mf. were dead in 7% of the control worms, and in 66% of the ivermectin worms. Nuclear remnants of mf. were seen in 4% of the control worms, but 52% of the ivermectin worms. Despite the degeneration of large numbers of mf., some had apparently survived and been shed by the maternal worm, because almost 30% of the nodules contained free mf. that appeared to be alive (12).

In the course of several clinical trials, nodules were excised from more than 100 patients, providing abundant data on the condition of adult worms following treatment with ivermectin or DEC (84). Neither drug killed the adult worms. In worms collected one month after ivermectin therapy, the intra-uterine mf. were viable and the proportion of early and late stages was normal. At 2 months, the number of mf. was elevated, but about half were dead or degenerate. At 3 and at 6 months, 85% of the mf. were dead or degenerate, and early stages were rare, although some worms showed signs of recent insemination. At 9 and at 12 months, some worms still contained mostly degenerate mf., but many had a normal mixture of embryos and mf. It was concluded that ivermectin treatment had not blocked embryogenesis but had caused mf. to be retained in the uteri until they degenerated and were resorbed. New cycles of the reproductive process had then begun.

The question remains of whether a more intense ivermectin therapy would kill adult *O. volvulus*, and this question is being addressed. In Liberia, 30 patients were given ivermectin at 150 μg/kg every 2 weeks for a total of 6 treatments. Preliminary data indicate little or no reduction in the number of live worms in nodules removed from these patients 4 months later (34).

Ivermectin inhibits the motility of adult *Onchocerca gutturosa* in vitro, but only at high levels (95). Combining ivermectin with various known macrofilaricides did not reveal any synergistic action against male adult *O. gutturosa* or female adult *O. volvulus* in vitro (96). Ivermectin by itself affects the behavior and metabolism of adult *O. volvulus* in vitro, but only at concentrations higher than those obtained in clinical use (87).

Effect on Transmission

The treatment of human populations with ivermectin could affect transmission in two ways. First, lowering the mf. density in the skin of treated individuals would diminish the pool of mf. available for pick-up by vector flies. Some flies would feed on persons with few mf. or even no mf. in their skin. Second, the mf. taken up from treated people might be defective and prove incapable of reaching the infection stage and infecting other human beings.

In the course of a Phase II trial in Liberia, patients were given ivermectin at 200 μg/kg and their ability to serve as a source infection for the local species of vector fly was assessed at three and six months after treatment (19). At both time periods, the mf. uptake by flies was significantly reduced, as was the number of mf. that reached their developmental site in the thorax of the flies. The effect was more pronounced than in the case of patients whose mf. load had been reduced by DEC therapy. These observations led to the conclusion that the ivermectin "could be effective in interrupting transmission of *Onchocerca volvulus* for epidemiologically important periods of time" (19).

A study in Ivory Coast also demonstrated a striking reduction in the percentage of flies that took up mf. from ivermectin-treated patients and in the numbers taken up (71). The number of mf. ingested by the flies was in fact even less than could be expected on the basis of the observed reduction in mf. density in skin.

This effect was also examined in Guatamala where patients were given 2 doses of ivermectin at 200 μg/kg, spaced 7 months apart (20). Treatment resulted in "almost complete suppression of developing or infective larvae in the vector population for a six month period" (20). The suppression of the infectiousness of patients for flies was evident not only in the group mean, but in the data for the individuals with the highest skin densities. It was concluded that regularly spaced ivermectin treatments at the community level would likely result in the elimination of infective flies.

The Phase IV trial conducted in Liberia provided another indication of the effect of treatment on transmission. Large numbers of children and adults were treated annually in a highly endemic area. Continued examination of mf.-negative children was of particular importance because it monitored the incidence of new patent infections in a community following general treatment of that community. By this means, the investigators showed that the incidence declined over two years by 35–45% (65, 91). They concluded that "ivermectin can be important in reducing the transmission of onchocerciasis" (91).

In this Liberian Phase IV trial, a detailed study of vector flies was also undertaken (97). The data were collected after the second of a series of annual ivermectin treatments (150 μg/kg). The number of flies landing and biting the members of this community remained the same as before treatment, but the number of flies harboring *O. volvulus* larvae fell by 94–95%. The number of flies in which the larvae had reached the infective (L_3) stage fell by 82–89%. The calculated monthly transmission potential fell by 75%. Also, the number of worm larvae in flies caught in neighboring districts where the mass treatment program was not in effect declined substantially. This reduction may have resulted from migration of flies or of people, but the explanation is uncertain.

The largest of the Phase IV trials was carried out in Ghana, where approximately 15,000 people were treated in a period of a few days, and here, too, entomological studies were conducted to assess the effect on transmission (73). The skin mf. density fell by 96% within two months, but rose earlier than expected, to give a decrease of 88% at four months after treatment. The total reservoir of mf. available for transmission (based on skin densities in treated and untreated members of the community) fell by about 70–80% at two months but was reduced very little at four months. Disection of more than 30,000 flies revealed a "dramatic and consistent reduction in vector infection" (73). Data on the number and developmental status of larvae in the flies led to the calculation that, within three months after treatment, the transmission of onchocerciasis had been reduced by 65% (based on infective larvae). It was concluded that transmission, under these circumstances, would continue at an unacceptably high level.

Reduction or elimination of microfilarodermia is clearly of potential clinical benefit to a treated individual. Further, the more people whose mf. load is lightened, the less likely it is that flies will acquire their infection and transmit it. The practical impact of community treatment, however, will depend on many factors. Treatment in one region (e.g. areas of Central America where *Simulium ochraceum* is the black-fly vector) may be more amenable to the interruption of transmission than others (e.g. areas of Africa where *Simulium yahense* is the vector). The impact of ivermectin programs on disease transmission will depend on the efficacy of vector control programs, the isolation of communities, and the ecological and climatic determinants of fly propagation. While the chief aim of the current distribution of ivermectin is the alleviation and prevention of disease in treated people, investigators are continuing to look for ways to make strategic treatment programs pay dividends in terms of epidemiological control.

Causal Prophylaxis

Ivermectin is used at very low dosage to prevent the maturation of *Dirofilaria immitis* in dogs, and it was thought that a similar prophylactic utility might be attainable in human onchocerciasis. Even if not used with prophylactic intent, regular treatment at, say, half-yearly intervals, might provide prophylaxis as well as therapeusis; that is, it might block the maturation of immature worms as well as exercising its effects on the adults and the mf. In both *D. immitis* and *O. volvulus,* the immature filarial worms (L_3 and L_4) migrate through subcutaneous tissues after entering the body via insect bite. In both instances, ivermectin is active against the mf. stage and affects the adult stage without killing it.

To test the prophylactic potential of ivermectin against *O. volvulus,* an experiment was carried out in chimpanzees (93). On day 0 of the experiment, chimpanzees were inoculated with infective larvae. Six of them received ivermectin at 200 μg/kg on day 0. Six received the same dosage on day 28. Six were left untreated. During the succeeding three months, skin-snips showed that one chimpanzee treated on day 0 had developed a patent infection, suggesting perhaps a variable efficacy against the L_3 developmental stage. Four animals treated on day 28, and four untreated controls also became patent, indicating a lack of activity against the L_4 state.

Thus, although ivermectin is being used for clinical prophylaxis, preventing the onset of dermal and ocular lesions, it is unlikely to offer causal prophylaxis. Daily medication might be effective if activity against L_3 larvae were to be confirmed or enhanced, but would hardly be practicable. Treatment at monthly intervals (and presumably at longer intervals) would evidently not provide prophylaxis at dosages currently considered acceptable.

OTHER FILARIAL INFECTIONS

Wuchereria bancrofti

About 400 patients with bancroftian filariasis have been treated with ivermectin at dosages ranging from 10 to 400 μg/kg. The results, summarized below, indicate that the drug is at least as potent against the blood-dwelling mf. of *Wuchereria bancrofti* as against the skin-dwelling mf. of *O. volvulus.*

SENEGAL   In an open trial involving 16 male patients, ivermectin was given as a single oral dose at 50 or 100 μg/kg. The mf. disappeared from the blood within three days (not examined in the higher-dose group until day 14) and reappeared within three months (29).

FRENCH POLYNESIA   In an open trial with 40 male patients, ivermectin was given at 50, 100, 150, or 200 μg/kg (once). At all dosages, mf. counts fell by more than 99% within six days (82). Counts started to rise again after one month, and by 6 months had reached 53% of pretreatment level (50 μg/kg) or 5–17% of pretreatment level (100–200 μg/kg).

In another trial in French Polynesia, healthy carriers of *W. bancrofti* (mf.-positive) were treated with ivermectin at 100 μg/kg or DEC at 3 mg/kg or DEC at 6 mg/kg. The efficacy of ivermectin in clearing mf. was superior to that of DEC at one week and one month after treatment, but not at three or six months (15). At the six-month mark, ivermectin offered no advantage over DEC in terms of mf. reduction, number or nature of adverse effects, or convenience (single oral dose in all cases). In French Polynesia, DEC is routinely given to carriers as single doses, at half-yearly intervals. The twelve-month data are pending.

Another French Polynesian study was designed to examine the effect of ivermectin on transmission as well as on mf. levels (14). Healthy carriers were given ivermectin at 50, 100, or 150 μg/kg. Dosages of 100 μg/kg, or higher, gave >99% reductions in mf., but the effect was temporary, as expected. Mosquitoes fed on treated carriers at six months after treatment were subsequently shown to have fewer infective larvae than mosquitoes fed on untreated carriers. The above experiment was extended by re-treating the same carriers with their respective dosages at one year after the initial treatment. The results suggested that the best strategy might be to treat entire populations every six months until mf. counts are substantially reduced, and then change to annual treatments.

INDIA   An open trial was conducted on 40 male patients, and the dosages used were 25, 50, 100, and 200 μg/kg (single oral dose). At all dosages, mf. disappeared within 5–12 days (49). Microfilaremia reappeared by three months and reached 14–32% of pretreatment level by six months, with all dosages giving similar results. The equivalent efficacy observed at 50 and especially at 25 μg/kg is remarkable, because the other trials (above) suggested that 100 μg/kg, or higher, was superior to lower dosages in curtailing the rise in mf. following the initial posttreatment decline.

To assess the potential value of ivermectin more thoroughly, a randomized, double-blind trial was conducted in India, and DEC was used as a reference (63). Forty male patients were included in the trial. Capsules of identical appearance were used to deliver (*a*) ivermectin at approximately 21 μg/kg followed by placebo daily for 12 days; (*b*) ivermectin at approximately 126 μg/kg followed by placebo for 12 days; (c) DEC at approximately 3 mg/kg followed by DEC at approximately 6 mg/kg daily for 12 days; (d) placebo for 5 days. All treatments (other than the placebo) were highly effective, clearing mf. from the blood by 12 days in all ivermectin patients and in most DEC patients. At 3 months after treatment, mf. counts were comparably low in ivermectin and DEC patients. By 6 months, the mf. counts in the ivermectin groups had risen to 18–20% of their pretreatment values, while in the DEC group the count had risen to 6% of the pretreatment value.

A third trial in India was carried out on 40 male patients to compare (a) ivermectin at 10 μg/kg, followed by placebo for 12 days; (b) ivermectin at 20 μg/kg, followed by placebo for 12 days; (c) DEC at 6 mg/kg for 12.5 days; or (d) placebo alone (63). All treatments except the placebo resulted in almost complete disappearance of mf. within 12 days. Inexplicably, the 10 μg/kg dosage of ivermectin appeared to be the most effective, based on the rate at which mf. reappeared after 1 month.

HAITI   Efficacy of a drug against the adult stage of *W. bancrofti* is usually assessed, for want of a more direct means, by following the mf. counts for a prolonged period after treatment. For such a purpose ivermectin was given to patients in Haiti and mf. levels were followed for a year (76). Ivermectin was given at 20 μg/kg and then, five days later, was given at 200 μg/kg once, or 200 μg/kg on two successive days. For comparison, DEC was given (in a conventional regimen of 72 mg/kg over 13 days) five days after the ivermectin 20-μg/kg dose. After the lapse of a year, the mf. counts in all groups were still reduced by more than 90% from pretreatment levels. The reappearance of mf. in the earlier clinical trials indicated the survival of adult worms. The remarkably long suppression of mf. seen with high ivermectin dosages in this trial raises the possibility that ivermectin, like DEC, may somehow affect adult *W. bancrofti*.

OTHER LOCALES   A dose-finding study is being carried out in Brazil, and preliminary results suggest high efficacy against mf. even at a dosage as low as 20 μg/kg. Other studies are in progress in Egypt, China, Sri Lanka, and Kenya (D. C. Neu, personal communication).

PRACTICAL UTILITY   In lymphatic filariasis, a drug with microfilaricidal activity presents perplexing problems in relation to practical utility. Removal of mf. may not prevent the progressive morbidity typical of filariasis because that is generally thought to be associated with the adult worms. Removal of mf. will, however, render a patient noninfectious to mosquitoes, and thus such a drug can be of immense value in public health programs in geographically circumscribed regions. The potential value of ivermectin in such situations is being assessed. Matters of potency and duration of effect still need to be clarified, and it is uncertain whether the drug would elicit fewer or milder adverse reactions than DEC, but ivermectin's one-dose treatment would doubtless represent a major advantage over the usual multidose regimen of DEC. In some circumstances, however, DEC, too, can be effective in a single oral dose (15). The critical issue is whether single-dose ivermectin treatment is superior to single-dose DEC treatment. Studies to address this question are in progress.

Brugia, Mansonella, Loa

Tests of ivermectin against *Brugia malayi* in leaf monkeys indicated that the mf. are sensitive to ivermectin but the adults are not (56). Trials against *B. malayi* in humans are in progress in India, Indonesia, and Malaysia. Results have not been published formally, but a preliminary communication indicates that ivermectin at 20 to 200 μg/kg, single oral dose, results in an 85–90% reduction in mf. over a three-month period (62).

In five patients with *Mansonella perstans,* ivermectin at 200 μg/kg did not reduce the mf. counts (75). This result was in keeping with observations made previously (6). On the other hand, a single dose, at 140 μg/kg, appeared to clear mf. in a patient with *Mansonella ozzardi,* and the absence of mf. even after nine months suggested an effect on the adult worm (61).

In a trial in Gabon, ivermectin was tested in 35 subjects with *Loa loa,* and in 17 subjects with *L. loa* plus one or two other filarial species (75). At dosages of 100, 150, or 200 μg/kg (but not at 50 μg/kg), numbers of mf. were greatly reduced, but the parasites were not eliminated.

EFFICACY AGAINST OTHER PARASITES

The avermectins have shown some activity against the intestinal phase of *Trichinella spiralis* infection at very high dosage in laboratory animals, but no activity against the muscle phase in mice or swine and enigmatic activity against the muscle phase in rats (13). Although these tests have not been definitive, ivermectin would probably not be useful in human trichinellosis.

The potent activity of ivermectin against several species of itch mite in various host species (13) has raised the possibility that the drug might be useful in human scabies.

Ivermectin at dosages up to 200 μg/kg was found inactive against *Plasmodium falciparum* in onchocerciasis patients (52). When administered in various dosage regimens, ivermectin was not active against *Schistosoma mansoni, Fasciola hepatica,* or *Hymenolepis diminuta* in laboratory rodents (D. A. Ostlind, personal communication).

Ivermectin paralyzed *Angiostrongylus cantonensis* in vitro at extremely low concentration, but in vivo tests have apparently not been reported (13).

SAFETY IN HUMANS

Evidence of the safety of ivermectin in humans has been obtained, not from studies in healthy subjects, but rather (a) indirectly from laboratory toxicological data (50) and (b) directly from the clinical efficacy trials. The overwhelming impression gained from the early clinical trials was that ivermectin was safe enough to justify more extensive trials, and the accumulated experience thus gained has led to its widespread use in community-based trials.

Safety and Tolerability in Onchocerciasis

Adverse reactions reported during the early probes included itching, dizziness, edema, mild Mazotti reaction, and minimal ocular inflammation in patients with ocular involvement. These effects were generally mild and transient.

In the Phase II trials, adverse reactions were milder and less frequent than in patients given DEC. This difference applied not only to the common systemic effects, but also to painful swelling of lymph nodes associated with mobilization of mf. into the nodes (1). One patient who received ivermectin at 245 μg/kg had a severe reaction including fever and scrotal swelling (28). Postural hypotension occurred in 4 of 19 patients in one of the open hospital-based trials (6), and hypotension was recorded in both ivermectin and DEC patients in a double-blind trial (4). These trials made apparent that, while certain reactions are common to both ivermectin and DEC, itching, painful swelling of lymph nodes, and rash tend to be more common with DEC therapy, whereas fever is more common with ivermectin (4).

In the Phase III trials, the investigators observed that ivermectin may slow the progression of ocular lesions and can be used even in patients with severe ocular lesions (42, 60, 92). In 39 patients with severe ocular onchocerciasis, "marked improvement was seen in the ocular status of the group as a whole" (92). It was also reported that severe postural hypotension (manifested by various signs, including dizziness, weakness, sweating, and tachycardia) occurred in some patients given ivermectin at 150 or 200 μg/kg, but not at 100 μg/kg (3). In 6% of 116 patients, mild ocular inflammation was seen, but it was resolved without treatment, and with no sequelae. In one trial, the number of patients with punctate keratitis was significantly reduced after ivermectin treatment (52). Treatment was well tolerated even when repeated at 6-month intervals (53).

Homeida et al (45) reported that ivermectin prolonged prothrombin time in the blood of certain treated patients in the Sudan and that this prolongation was associated with hematomatous swellings. However, review of data on the administration of more than 15,000 doses of ivermectin in Liberia failed to disclose any bleeding disorders (69), and a study in Haiti failed to demonstrate any prolongation of prothrombin time (78).

In Sierra Leone, a comparison was made of the side-effects in 629 ivermectin-treated subjects (100–200 μg/kg) and 623 placebo-treated controls (102). Data from this community-based trial yielded the startling figure of 34% "side-effects" in the ivermectin group and 11% in the placebo group. The most common side-effect, however, was the beneficial one of expulsion of *Ascaris lumbricoides* from ivermectin-treated persons. The most frequent adverse side-effects in the ivermectin group were itching/rash, muscle or joint pain, fever, and headache. Each of these effects occurred in 7–9% of the ivermectin subjects and in 1–4% of the placebo subjects (all figures to nearest whole number). The investigators concluded that "community-based treatment of onchocerciasis with ivermectin can cause substantial morbidity" (102). More than 95% of the reactions were reported in the first 3 days posttreatment.

Ivermectin was well tolerated by onchocerciasis patients even when given at 150 μg/kg every two weeks, for a total of six treatments (34). This regimen represents the most intensive ivermectin treatment so far reported in humans.

De Sole et al (25–27, 66) have thoroughly reviewed West African trials in which more than 60,000 people were treated (25–27). In one of these reviews, covering 50,929 persons, the authors (27) concluded: "Of those treated, 9% reported with adverse reactions, 2.4% with moderate reactions, and 0.24% with severe reactions. Most reactions were reported during the first day of follow-up, the most frequent severe reaction being severe symptomatic postural hypotension (in 49 cases). Three cases of transient but severe dyspnoea were considered life-threatening but their relationship with ivermectin treatment is uncertain. The incidence of adverse reactions was directly related to skin microfilarial load and was highest in the foci with the highest endemicity levels."

The observation that side-effects are more pronounced in patients with high mf. loads is consistent with the belief that side-effects are associated with mf. destruction rather than intrinsic toxicity. In this context, it is of interest that reactions seem to be more pronounced in Europeans who acquire onchocerciasis as adults living in Africa, and it has been suggested that this is because such individuals, having had less exposure to the parasite, have less tolerance to the antigens released by disintegrating microfilariae (24).

Almost nothing is known, however, about the disintegration of mf. following ivermectin therapy. The rate of adverse reactions may be related to the mechanism of parasite destruction. In an analysis of the overall clinical experience with ivermectin, the adverse reactions associated with both ivermectin and DEC have been tabulated in detail (37). The authors of this study noted that the Mazzotti reaction was mild or absent in ivermectin therapy; that mild or moderate hypotension occurred in 9 of 199 treated patients in 4 trials and was symptomatic in only 5 of them; and that such episodes have also been associated with DEC therapy. The investigators suggested that the lower rate of severe adverse reactions following the use of ivermectin rather than DEC may result from the spastic paralysis (even if only partial) of ivermectin-affected mf., followed by removal by the reticulo-endothelial system—as compared to the outright killing of mf. by immune effector cells that have been made more adherent as a result of DEC treatment of the host (37, 85). Clearly much remains to be discovered about the mechanism of mf. destruction and its relationship to adverse reactions.

A recent report warns that the rate of moderate or severe reactions may be higher when ivermectin is used in hyperendemic areas in which vector control has not been implemented. A reaction rate of 32% was recorded for a group of 87 patients in Sierra Leone, many of whom had severe ocular disease prior to treatment (80, 86).

Safety in Other Infections

In lymphatic filariasis, as in onchocerciasis, ivermectin treatment has been well tolerated (29, 49, 63). In general, fever, headache, and myalgia were more common than rash and tenderness of lymph nodes, whereas the opposite situation generally occurs in the use of DEC.

Treatment of other helminth infections has been too infrequent to yield meaningful safety data, but serious unexpected reactions have not been recorded in the trials reported thus far.

Safety in General

A few cases of accidental exposure to ivermectin have occurred. A man injected himself in the hand with about 4 ml cattle Ivomec, and developed pallor, nausea, and transient pain and numbness in the hand (43). The dosage would have been about 570 μg/kg. In other cases of accidental exposure, the reactions included irritation at injection site, nausea, vomiting, abdominal pain, tachycardia, hypotension, hypothermia, urticaria, and stinging sensation in the eye (43).

Pregnancy has been a basis for exclusion of women from ivermectin treatment programs, and this policy reflected a basic precaution rather than any anticipated fetal toxicity. In practice, however, women may be treated inadvertently before their pregnancy becomes known. In a study in Liberia involving some 14,000 persons who were treated annually for three years, a total of 203 children were born to women who had received ivermectin during pregnancy. The occurrence of birth defects in children from treated or untreated mothers, or from a reference population, did not differ significantly. Rates of miscarriage or stillbirth did not differ, nor was there any difference in the subsequent development or disease patterns of the babies (67). Because of the limited sample size, continued surveillance is considered necessary.

Ivermectin appears to be very safe, but safety is always relative. The therapeutic index of the drug appears to be high in those human applications for which it has been tested. Idiosyncratic or strain-related susceptibility to ivermectin occurs in mice and dogs in which fatal reactions have followed exposure to dosages that normally are well tolerated (50). Such reactions are therefore a possibility in other species, but there is no evidence of them in humans.

In communities with a high prevalence of onchocerciasis, ivermectin is being given to residents without screening for infection status. As mentioned, one report has suggested a risk of substantial morbidity in the use of ivermectin in onchocerciasis (102), but another commentator, emphasizing the safety of the drug and pointing out that the few serious reactions have developed slowly over several hours and have been amenable to clinical management, has called for a relaxation of the current controls on its use (70). In both instances, and in the other trials reviewed above, the real issue is not whether the drug is safe enough to be used on a community basis. Rather, the issue is the risk-benefit ratio and the degree of supervision that should be applied. Perhaps the current status is best summarized by the findings of a comprehensive review of onchocerciasis trials that covered approximately 51,000 people in West Africa: "Treatment resulted in 98% reductions in mean microfilarial loads at all endemicity levels. The benefit of treatment largely compensated for the discomfort due to adverse reactions, which were all transient and managed successfully. Ivermectin thus appears to be sufficiently safe for large-scale treatment but monitoring by resident nurses for at least 36 hours is recommended" (27). Further endorsing the safety of ivermectin in community use, a subcommittee of the World Health Organization estimated that more than 120,000 doses of ivermectin had been given to some 70,000 persons, and concluded that the "drug is extremely safe and is without known pharmacological side-effects in humans" (103). As distribution of ivermectin continues to expand, especially in areas with high microfilarial burdens, the need for medical or paramedical supervision will become more clearly defined.

CURRENT DRUG DISTRIBUTION

Late in 1987, Merck and Company announced that it would provide ivermectin (Mectizan®) free of charge for the treatment of onchocerciasis in humans. The Mectizan formulation of the drug is registered for human use only. Early in 1988, a Mectizan Expert Committee was formed "to devise and oversee a process for donating Mectizan to medically responsible and operationally sound community-wide, mass treatment programmes" (38). The members, who are recognized experts in tropical medicine, were appointed on the joint recommendation of Merck and Company and the World Health Organization.

The committee was set up as an independent body with a secretariat at the Carter Center in Atlanta, Georgia. The objectives and activities of the committee have been described (35).

Since September 1988, when applications were first received, the committee has granted approval for distribution of Mectizan in 30 of the 32 known endemic countries (20 in Africa, 5 in Latin America). Additional applications are under review. Mectizan is in the form of small tablets, each containing 6.0 mg ivermectin. For a 60 kg person, the prescribed dosage is one and a half tablets. More than three million such tablets have so far been shipped to the treatment programs, and this number will increase greatly as more applications are approved and more distribution programs are implemented. At least 600,000 persons have already been treated. Physicians and clinics with a need to treat small numbers of patients on an individual rather than community basis do not need to seek approval from the Mectizan Expert Committee. They may instead obtain the drug by applying directly to Merck and Company.

Clearly, the mass-treatment programs and the small-scale clinical administrations of Mectizan have not yet resulted in the treatment of all persons at risk of clinical onchocerciasis. To some [see, for example, Pond (70)] the distribution program seems too restrictive and cumbersome because of the degree of supervision demanded. As field experience accumulates, the restrictions may be eased to the extent that they remain compatible with responsible medical practice (37).

Mectizan is not currently approved for the treatment of any human disease other than onchocerciasis.

ACKNOWLEDGMENT

The author is much indebted to Mr. D. C. Neu of Merck and Company for helpful discussions, and to Mr. Neu, Dr. Kenneth R. Brown, and Dr. Brian White-Guay of Merck and Company for constructive criticism of the manuscript.

Literature Cited

1. Albiez, E. J., Newland, H. S., White, A. T., Kaiser, A., Greene, B. M., et al. 1988. Chemotherapy of onchocerciasis with high doses of diethylcarbamazine or a single dose of ivermectin: *Microfilaria* levels and side effects. *Trop. Med. Parasitol.* 39:19–24

2. Albiez, E. J., Walter, G., Kaiser, A., Ranque, P., Newland, H. S., et al. 1988. Histological examination of onchocercomata after therapy with ivermectin. *Trop. Med. Parasitol.* 39:93–99

3. Awadzi, K., Dadzie, K. Y., Klager, S., Gilles, H. M., 1989. The chemotherapy of onchocerciasis. XIII. Studies with ivermectin in onchocerciasis patients in northern Ghana, a region with long lasting vector control. *Trop. Med. Parasitol.* 40:361–66

4. Awadzi, K., Dadzie, K. Y., Schulz-Key, H., Gilles, H. M., Fulford, A. J., Aziz, M. A. 1986. The chemotherapy of onchocerciasis XI: A double-blind comparative study of ivermectin, diethyl-

470   CAMPBELL

carbamazine and placebo in human onchocerciasis in northern Ghana. *Ann. Trop. Med. Parasitol.* 80:433–42

5. Awadzi, K., Dadzie, K. Y., Schulz-Key, H., Haddock, D. R. W., Gilles, H. M., Aziz, M. A. 1984. Ivermectin in onchocerciasis. *Lancet* 2:921

6. Awadzi, K., Dadzie, K. Y., Schultz-Key, H., Haddock, D. R. W., Gilles, H. M., Aziz, M. A. 1985. The chemotherapy of onchocerciasis X. An assessment of four single dose treatment regimes of MK-933 (Ivermectin) in human onchocerciasis. *Ann. Trop. Med. Parasitol.* 79:63–78

7. Aziz, M. A., Diallo, S., Diop, I. M., Lariviere, M., Porta, M. 1982. Efficacy and tolerance of ivermectin in human onchocerciasis. *Lancet 2:* 171–73

8. Aziz, M. A., Diallo, S., Diop, I. M., Lariviere, M., Porta, M., Gaxotte, P. 1982. Ivermectin in onchocerciasis. *Lancet* 2:1456–57

9. Basset, D., Bouree, P., Basset, A., Lariviere, M. 1989. Effets de la di-ethylcarbamazine et le l'ivermectine sur la mobilisation des microfilaires d'onchocerca volvulus. *Pathol. Biol.* 37: 668–72

10. Bissan, Y., Vingtain, P., Doucoure, K., Doumbo, O., Dembele, D., et al. 1986. L'ivermectin (MK 933) dans le traitement de l'onchocercose, son incidence sur la transmission d'*Onchocerca volvulus* en savane soudanienne au Mali. *Med. Afr. Noire* 33:81–93

11. Brown, K. R., Neu, D. C. 1990. Ivermectin—clinical trials and treatment schedules in onchocerciasis. *Acta Leiden.* 59:285–96

12. Büttner, Ranque, P., Walter, G., Albiez, E. J. 1987. Histological studies on the effects of ivermectin on adult *Onchocerca volvulus* ten months after therapy. *Trop. Med. Parasitol.* 38:349

13. Campbell, W. C., ed. 1989. *Ivermectin and Abamectin.* New York: Springer Verlag. 363 pp.

14. Cartel, J. L., Celerier, P., Spiegel, A., Plichart, R., Roux, J. F. 1990. Effect of two successive annual treatments with single doses of ivermectin on microfilaremia due to *Wuchereria bancrofti* var. *pacifica. Trans. R. Soc. Trop. Med. Hyg.* 84:837–39

15. Cartel, J. L., Spiegel, A., Nguyen, L., Genelle, B., White-Guay, B., Roux, J. F. 1990. Double-blind study of single ivermectin and diethylcarbamazine (DEC) doses for treatment of Tahitian *Wuchereria bancrofti* carriers. *Bull. Soc. Fr. Parasitol.* 3:457 (Suppl.)

16. Chavasse, D. C., Davies, J. B. 1991. In vitro effects of ivermectin on *O. volvulus microfilariae* assessed by observation and by inoculation into *S. damnosum. Trans. R. Soc. Trop. Med. Hyg.* 84:707–8

17. Coulaud, J. P., Lariviere, M., Aziz, M. A., Gervais, M. C., Gaxotte, P., et al. 1984. Ivermectin in onchocerciasis. *Lancet* 2:526–27

18. Coulaud, J. P., Lariviere, M., Gervais, M. C., Gaxotte, P., Aziz, M. A., et al. 1983. Traitment de l'onchocercose humaine par l'ivermectine. *Bull. Soc. Pathol. Exot.* 76:681–88

19. Cupp, E. W., Bernardo, M. J., Kiszewski, A. E., Collins, R. C., Taylor, H. R., et al. 1986. The effects of ivermectin on transmission of *Onchocerca volvulus. Science* 231:740–42

20. Cupp, E. W., Ochoa, O., Collins, R. C., Ramberg, F. R., Zea, G. 1989. The effect of multiple ivermectin treatments on infection of *Simulium ochraceum* with *Onchocerca volvulus. Am. J. Trop. Med. Hyg.* 40:501–6

21. Dadzie, K. Y., Awadzi, K., Bird, A. C., Schulz-Key, H. 1989. Ophthalmological results from a placebo controlled comparative 3-dose ivermectin study in the treatment of onchocerciasis. *Trop. Med. Parasitol.* 40:355–60

22. Dadzie, K. Y., Bird, A. C., Awadzi, K., Schulz-Key, H., Gilles, H. M., Aziz, M. A. 1987. Ocular findings in a double-blind study of ivermectin versus diethylcarbamazine versus placebo in the treatment of onchocerciasis. *Br. J. Ophthalmol.* 71:78–85

23. Dadzie, K. Y., Remme, J., Rolland, A., Thylefors, B. 1986. The effect of 7–8 years of vector control on the evolution of ocular onchocerciasis in West African savanna. *Trop. Med. Parasitol.* 37:263–70

24. Davidson, R. N., Godfrey-Fausett, P., Bryceson, A. D. M. 1990. Adverse reactions in expatriates treated with ivermectin. *Lancet:* 336:1005

25. De Sole, G., Awadzi, K., Remme, J., Dadzie, K. Y., Ba, O., et al. 1989. A community trial of ivermectin in the onchocerciasis focus of Asubende, Ghana. II. Adverse Reactions. *Trop. Med. Parasitol.* 40:375–82

26. De Sole, G., Dadzie, K. Y., Giese, J., Remme, J. 1990. Lack of adverse reactions in ivermectin treatment of onchocerciasis. *Lancet* 335:1106–7

27. De Sole, G., Remme, J., Awadzi, K., Accorsi, S., Alley, E. S., et al. 1989. Adverse reactions after large-scale treatment of onchocerciasis with ivermectin:

Combined results from eight community trials. *Bull. WHO* 67:707–19

28. Diallo, S., Aziz, M. A., Lariviere, M., Diallo, J. S., Diop-Mar, I., et al. 1986. A double-blind comparison of the efficacy and safety of ivermectin and diethylcarbamazine in a placebo controlled study of senegalese patients with onchocerciasis. *Trans. R. Soc. Trop. Med. Hyg.* 80:927–34

29. Diallo, S., Aziz, M. A., N'dir, O., Badiane, S., Bah, I. B., Gaye, O. 1987. Dose-ranging study of ivermectin in treatment of filariasis due to *Wuchereria bancrofti. Lancet* 1:1030

30. Diallo, S., Lariviere, M., Diop-Mar, I., N'Dir, O., N'Diaye, O., et al. 1984. Conduite au senegal des premieres studes d'efficacite et de tolerance de l'ivermectine (MK-933) dans l'onchocercose humaine. *Bull. Soc. Pathol. Exot.* 77:196–205

31. Diop-Mar, I., Diallo, S., Aziz, M. A., Lariviere, M., N'diaye, M. R., et al. 1984. Essai de l'ivermectine dans le traitement de l'onchocercose humaine. *Dakar Med.* 29:19–26

32. Diop-Mar, I., Diallo, S., Diallo, J. S., N'dir, O., Badiane, S. 1986. L'experience senegalaise sur l'efficacite de l'ivermectine (MK-933 dans le traitement de l'onchocercose humaine (etude comparative en double aveugle avec le citrate de diethylcarbvamazine (dec.c)). *Bull. Acad. Nat. Med. Paris* 170:149–55

33. Donnelly, J. J., Xi, M. S., Haldar, J. P., Hill, D. E., Lok, J. B., et al. 1988. Autoantibody induced by experimental onchocerca infection: effect of different routes of administration of microfilariae and of treatment with diethylcarbamazine citrate and ivermectin. *Invest. Ophthalmol. Vis. Sci.* 29:827–31

34. Duke, B. O. L., Pacqué, M. C., Munoz, B., Greene, B. M., Taylor, H. R. 1991. Viability of adult *Onchocerca volvulus* after six 2-weekly doses of ivermectin. *Bull. WHO* In press

35. Dull, H. B. 1990. Mectizan donation and the Mectizan Expert Committee. *Acta Leiden.* 59:399–403

36. Egerton, J. R., Brokken, E. S., Suhayda, D., Eary, C. H., Wooden, J. W., Kilgore, R. L. 1981. The antiparasitic activity of ivermectin in horses. *Vet. Parasitol.* 8:83–88

37. Ette, E. I., Thomas, W. O. A., Achumba, J. I. 1990. Ivermectin: A long-acting microfiliaricdal agent DICP. *Ann. Pharmacother.* 24:426–33

38. Foege, W. H. 1990. Distributing ivermectin. *Lancet* 336:377

39. Freedman, D. O., Zierdt, W. S., Lujan, A., Nutman, T. B. 1989. The efficacy of ivermectin in the chemotherapy of gastrointestinal helminthiasis in humans. *J. Infect. Dis.* 159:1151–53

40. Greene, B. M., Brown, K. R., Taylor, H. R. 1989. Use of ivermectin in humans. See Ref. 13, pp. 311–23

41. Greene, B. M., Taylor, H. R., Cupp, E. W., Murphy, R. P., White, A. T., et al. 1985. Comparison of ivermectin and diethylcarbamazine in the treatment of onchocerciasis. *New Engl. J. Med.* 313:133–38

42. Greene, B. M., White, A. T., Newland, H. S., Keyvan-Larijani, E., Dukuly, Z. D., et al. 1987. Single dose therapy with ivermectin for onchocerciasis. *Trans. Assoc. Am. Physicians* 100:131–38

43. Hall, A. H., Spoerke, D. G., Bronstein, A. C., Kulig, K. W., Rumack, B. H. 1985. Human ivermectin exposure. *J. Emerg. Med.* 3:217–19

44. Helling, G., Adjamgba, A., Mossinger, J., Klager, S., Schultz-Key, H. 1987. Eine Phase III Therapiestudie mit ivermectin an Onchozerkosepatienten in Zentral-Togo. *Mitt. Österr. Ges. Tropenment. Parasitol.* 9:187–94

45. Homeida, M. M. A., Bagi, I. A., Ghalib, H. W., Sheikh, H. E., Ismail, A., et al. 1988. Prolongation of prothrombin time with ivermectin. *Lancet* 1:1346–47

46. Hussein, S., Bird, A., Jones, B. R. 1987. Ocular lesions seen in Phase III trial of ivermectin therapy of onchocerciasis in Togo. *Trop. Med. Parasitol.* 38:67

47. Klauss, V., Gerbert, M. 1988. Fortschritte in der onchozerkosebekampfung. *Klin. Monatsbl. Augenheilkd.* 193:224

48. Koo, J., Pien, F., Kliks, M. M. 1988. *Angiostrongylus (Parastrongylus) eosinophilic meningitis. Rev. Infect. Dis.* 10:1155–62

49. Kumaraswami, V., Ottesen, E. A., Vijayasekaran, V., Devi, S. U., Swaminathan, M., et al. 1988. Ivermectin for the treatment of *Wuchereria bancrofti* filariasis: Efficacy and adverse reactions. *J. Am. Med. Assoc.* 259:3150–53

50. Lankas, G. R., Gordon, L. R. 1989. Toxicology. See Ref. 13, pp. 89–112

51. Lariviere, M., Aziz, M. A., Diallo, S., Diop-Mar, I., Porta, M. 1982. Efficacité et tolérance de l'ivermectine (MK 933) dans l'onchocercose humaine. *Hosp. Claude Bernard* (no Vol.):227–33

52. Lariviere, M., Beauvais, B., Aziz, M., Garin, Y. J. F., Abeloos, J., et al. 1989. Etude en Cote-d'Ivoire (1985–1987) de l'effecacite et de la tolerance de l'ivermectine (mectizan) dans l'onchocercose

humaine. *Bull. Soc. Pathol. Exot.* 82:
35–47

53. Lariviere, M., Beauvais, B., Aziz, M.,
Garin, Y. J. F., Abeloos, J., et al. 1989.
Etude en Cote-d'Ivoire (1985–1987) de
l'efficacite et de la tolerance de l'ivermectin (mectizan) dans l'onchocercose
humaine. *Bull. Soc. Pathol. Exot.* 82:
48–57

54. Lariviere, M., Beauvais, B., Derouin,
F., Basset, D. A., Sarfati, C. 1986.
L'ivermectine dans le traitement et la
prophylaxie de l'onchocercose humaine.
Therapie 41:523

55. Lariviere, M., Vingtain, P., Aziz, M.,
Beuvais, B., Weimann, D., et al. 1985.
Double-blind study of ivermectin and di-
ethylcarbamazine in african onchocerci-
asis patients with ocular involvement.
Lancet 2:174–77

56. Mak, J. W., Lam, P. L., Rain, A. N.,
Suresh, K. 1988. Effect of ivermectin
against subperiodic *Brugia malayi* infection in the leaf monkey, *Presbytis crista-
ta. Parasitol. Res.* 74:383–85

57. Maso, M. J., Dapila, R., Schwartz, R.
A., Wiltz, H., Kaminski, Z. C., Lam-
bert, W. C. 1987. Cutaneous onchocerciasis. *Int. J. Dermatol.* 26(9):593–
96

58. Mössinger, J., Schulz-Key, H., Dietz,
K. 1988. Emergence of *Onchocerca volvulus* microfilariae from skin snips before and after treatment of patients with
ivermectin. *Trop. Med. Parasitol.*
39:313–16

59. Naquira, C., Jimenez, G., Guerra, J.
G., Bernal, R., Nalin, D. R., et al.
1989. Ivermectin for human strongyloidiasis and other intestinal helminths.
Am. J. Trop. Med. Hyg. 40:304–9

60. Newland, H. S., White, A. T., Greene,
B. M., D'Anna, S. A., Keyvan-
Larijani, E., et al. 1988. Effect of sing-
le-dose ivermectin therapy on human
Onchocerca volvulus infection with
onchocercal ocular involvement. *Br. J.
Ophthalmol.* 72:561–69

61. Nutman, T. B., Nash, T. E., Ottesen, E.
A. 1987 Ivermectin in the successful
treatment of a patient with *Mansonella
ozzardi* infection. *J. Infect. Dis.* 156:
662–65

62. Ottesen, E. A. 1990. Activity of ivermectin in human parasite infections
other than onchocerciasis. *Mectizan
Program Notes, Suppl. 2*, pp. 1–5.
Atlanta, GA: Mectizan Expert Comm.

63. Ottesen, E. A., Vijayasekaran, V.,
Kumaraswami, V., Perumal-Pillai, S.
V., Sadanandam, A., et al. 1990. Ivermectin and diethylcarbamazine: a
placebo-controlled, double-blind trial in

lymphatic filariasis. *New Engl. J. Med.*
322:1113–17

64. Pacqué, M. C., Dukuly, Z., Greene, B.
M., Munoz, B., Keyvan-Larijani, E., et
al. 1989. Community-based treatment of
onchocerciasis with ivermectin: Accep-
tability and early adverse reactions.
Bull. WHO 67:721–30

65. Pacqué, M., Munoz, B., Greene, B.
M., Taylor, H. R. 1990. The impact of
community-based ivermectin treatment
on the transmission of onchocerciasis.
Invest. Ophthalmol. Vis. Sci. 31:136

66. Pacqué, M., Munoz, B., Greene, B.
M., White, A. T., Dukuly, Z., Taylor,
H. R. 1990. Safety and compliance with
community-based ivermectin therapy.
Lancet 335:1377–80

67. Pacqué, M., Munoz, B., Poetschke, G.,
Foose, J., Greene, B. M., Taylor, H. R.
1990. Pregnancy outcome after in-
advertent ivermectin treatment during
community-based distribution. *Lancet*
336:1486–89

68. Pacqué, M. C., Munoz, B., White, A.
T., Taylor, H. R., Greene, B. M. 1989.
Mass treatment of *Onchocerca volvulus*
infection with ivermectin. *Clin. Res.*
37:436A

69. Pacqué, M. C., Munoz, B., White, A.
T., Williams, P. N., Greene, B. M.,
Taylor, H. R. 1989. Ivermectin and pro-
thrombin time. *Lancet* 1:1140

70. Pond, B. 1990. Distribution of ivermectin by health workers. *Lancet* 335:1939

71. Prod'Hon, J., Lardeux, F., Bain, O.,
Hebrard, G., Prud'Hom, J. M. 1987.
Ivermectine et modalites de la reduction
de l'infection des simulies dans un foyer
forestier d'onchocercose humain. *Ann.
Parasitol. Hum. Comp.* 62:590–98

72. Rajasekariah, G. R., Deb, B. N.,
Dhage, K. R., Bose, S. 1989 Response
of adult *Necator americanus* to some
known anthelmintics in hamsters. *Ann.
Trop. Med. Parasitol.* 83:279–85

73. Remme, J., Baker, R. H. A., DeSole,
G., Dadzie, K. Y., Walsh, J. F., 1989.
A community trial of ivermectin in the
onchocerciasis focus of Asubende, Ghana. *Trop. Med. Parasitol.* 40:367–74

74. Remme, J., De Sole, G., Dadzie, K. Y.,
Alley, E. S., Baker, R. H. A., et al.
1990. Large scale ivermectin distribution and its epidemiological consequences. *Acta Leiden.* 59:177–91

75. Richard-Lenoble, D., Kombila, M.,
Rupp, E. A., Pappayliou, E. S., Gax-
otte, P., et al. 1988. Ivermectin in
loiasis and concomitant *O. volvulus* and
M. perstans infections. *Am. J. Trop.
Med. Hyg.* 39:480–83

76. Richards, F. O., Eberhard, M. L.,

Bryan, R. T., McNeeley, D. F., Lammie, P. J., et al. 1991. Comparison of ivermectin and diethylcarbamazine for adulticidal activity in Haitian bancroftian filariasis. *Am. J. Trop. Med. Hyg.* 44:3–10

77. Richards, F. O. Jr., Flores Zea, R., Duke B. O. L. 1989. Dynamics of microfilariae of *Onchocerca volvulus* over the first 72 hours after treatment with ivermectin. *Trop. Med. Parasitol.* 40:299–303

78. Richards, F. O. Jr., McNeeley, M. B., Bryan, R. T., Eberhard, M. L., McNeeley, D. F., et al. 1989. Ivermectin and prothrombin time. *Lancet* 1:1139–40

79. Rivas Alcala, A. R., Schlie Guzman, M. A. 1987. La oncocercosis como problema de salud en el sureste de mexico. *Bol. Chil. Parasitol.* 42:58–63

80. Rothova, A., van der Lelij, A., Stilma, J. S., Wilson, W. R., Barbe, R. F. 1989. Side-effects of ivermectin in treatment of onchocerciasis. *Lancet* 1:1439–41

81. Rougemont, A. 1982. Ivermectin for onchocerciasis. *Lancet* 2:1158

82. Roux, J., Cartel, J., Perolat, P., Boputin, J., Sechan, Y., et al. 1989. Etude de l'ivermectine pour le traitement de la filariose lymphatique due a *Wuchereria bancrofti:* var Pacifica en Polynesie Francaise. *Rev. Soc. Pathol. Exot.* 82:72–81

83. Schultz-Key, H., Greene, B. M., Awadzi, K., Lariviere, M., Kläger, S., et al. 1986. Efficacy of ivermectin on the reproductivity of female *Onchocerca volvulus*. *Trop. Med. Parasit.* 37:89

84. Schultz-Key, H., Kläger, S., Awadzi, K., Diallo, S., Greene, B. M., et al. 1985. Treatment of human onchocerciasis: The efficacy of ivermectin on the parasite. *Trop. Med. Parasitol.* 36:20

85. Soboslay, P. T., Newland, H. S., White, A. T., Erttmann, K. D., Albiez, E. J., et al. 1987. Ivermectin effect on microfilariae of *Onchocerca volvulus* after a single oral dose in humans. *Tropenmed. Parasitol.* 28:8–10

86. Stilma, J. S., Rothova, A., van der Lelij, G., Eildon, E. T., Barbe, R. F. 1990. Ocular and systemic side effects following ivermectin treatment in onchocerciasis patients from Sierra Leone. *Acta Leiden.* 59:207–10

87. Strote, G., Wieland, S., Darge, K., Conley, J. D. W. 1990. In vitro assessment of the activity of anthelmintic compounds on adults of *Onchocerca volvulus*. *Acta Leiden.* 59:285–96

87a. Stupar, O. H., Arosemena, R. S.,

Monzón, H., Rondón Lugo, A. J. 1990. Larva migrans cutanea tratada con ivermectin. *Dermatol. Venez.* 26:72–76

88. Taylor, H. R. 1989. Ivermectin treatment of onchocerciasis. *Aust. N. Z. J. Ophthalmol.* 17:435–38

89. Taylor, H. R., Greene, B. M. 1989. The status of ivermectin in the treatment of human onchocerciasis. *Am. J. Trop. Med. Hyg.* 41:460–66

90. Taylor, H. R., Murphy, R. P., Newland, H. S., White, A. T., D'Anna, S. A. et al. 1986. Treatment of onchocerciasis: The ocular effects of ivermectin and diethylcarbamazine. *Arch. Ophthalmol.* 104:863–70

91. Taylor, H. R., Pacqué, M., Munoz, B., Greene, B. M. 1990. Impact of mass treatment of onchocerciasis with ivermectin on the transmission of infection. *Science* 250:116–18

92. Taylor, H. R., Semba, R. D., Newland, H. S., Keyvan-Larijani, E., White, A., et al. 1989. Ivermectin treatment of patients with severe ocular onchocerciasis. *Am. J. Trop. Med. Hyg.* 40:494–500

93. Taylor, H. R., Trpis, M., Cupp, E. W. 1988. Ivermectin prophlaxis against experimental *Onchocerca volvulus* infection in chimpanzees. *Am. J. Trop. Med. Hyg.* 39:86–90

94. Testa, J., Kizimandji-Coton, G., Delmont, J., DiCostanzo, B., Gaxotte, P. 1990. Traitement de l'anguillulose et de l'ascaridiose et de l'ankylostomiase par l'ivermectine (Mectizan) a Bangui (RCA). *Med. Afr. Noire* 37:283–84

95. Townson, S., Connelly, C., Dobinson, A., Muller, R. 1987. Drug activity against *Onchocerca gutturosa* males *in vitro*. *J. Helminthol.* 61:271–81

96. Townson, S., Dobinson, A. R., Townsend, J., Siemienska, L., Zea-Flores, G. 1990. The effects of ivermectin used in combination with other known antiparasitic drugs on adult *Onchocerca gutturosa* and *O. volvulus* in vitro. *Trans. R. Soc. Trop. Med. Hyg.* 84:411–16

97. Trpis, M., Childs, J. E., Fryauff, D. J., Greene, B. M., Williams, P. N., et al. 1990. Effect of mass treatment of a human population with ivermectin on transmission of *Onchocerca volvulus* by *Simulium vahense* in Liberia, West Africa. *Am. J. Trop. Med. Hyg.* 42:148–56

98. Vingtain, P., Pichard, E., Ginoux, J., Coulibaly, S., M., Bissan, Y., et al. 1988. Ivermectine et onchocercose humaine: A propos d'une etude portant sur 234 onchocerquiens en republique du mali. *Bull. Soc. Pathol. Exot.* 81:260–70

99. Wang, C., Huang, X. X., Zhang, Y. Q., Yen, Q. Y., Wen, Y. 1989. Efficacy of ivermectin in hookworms as examined in *Ancylostoma caninum* infections. *J. Parasitol.* 75:373–77

100. Warren, K. S. 1990. An integrated system for the control of the major human intestinal parasites. *Acta Leiden.* 59:433–22

101. White, A. T., Newland, H. S., Taylor, H. R., Erttmann, K. D., Keyvan-Larijani, E., et al. 1987. Controlled trial and dose-finding study of ivermectin for treatment of onchocerciasis. *J. Infect. Dis.* 156:463–70

102. Whitworth, J. A. G., Morgan, D., Maude, G. H., Taylor, D. W. 1988. Community-based treatment with ivermectin. *Lancet* 2:97–98

103. World Health Organization. 1989. *Report of a meeting of the TDR/OCP/OCT subcommittee for monitoring of community trials of ivermectin,* 89.3:1–16 Geneva: WHO

Annu. Rev. Microbiol. 1991. 45:475–508

HEPADNAVIRUSES AND HEPATOCELLULAR CARCINOMA[1]

Averell H. Sherker and Patricia L. Marion

Division of Infectious Diseases, Department of Medicine, Stanford University, Stanford, California 94305

KEY WORDS: hepatitis B virus, primary liver cancer, viral carcinogenesis, oncogenes, animal models

CONTENTS

INTRODUCTION 475
THE HEPADNAVIRUS FAMILY 477
MOLECULAR STRUCTURE OF HEPADNAVIRUSES AND THEIR GENE
 PRODUCTS 478
HEPADNAVIRUS REPLICATION 482
NONNEOPLASTIC DISEASE IN HEPADNAVIRAL INFECTION 483
SPONTANEOUS HCC IN THE HEPADNAVIRUS-INFECTED HOST 485
 HBV Infection of Humans 485
 HBV-Infected Chimpanzees 486
 WHV-Infected Woodchucks 487
 GSHV-Infected Ground Squirrels 487
 DHBV-Infected Ducks 489
 State of Hepadnaviral DNA in Hepatocellular Carcinoma 489
 Effects of Hepadnavirus on Cellular Genes in HCC 491
HEPADNAVIRUS-RELATED ONCOGENESIS IN EXPERIMENTAL SYSTEMS 495
 Cell Cultures 495
 Transgenic Mice 496
SUMMARY AND OUTLOOK 497

INTRODUCTION

Viruses were first associated with solid tumors in animals in 1911 when Peyton Rous showed that a filterable agent isolated from sarcomas in chickens

[1]This review is dedicated to the memory of Dr. Hans Popper.

475

0066-4227/91/1001-0475$02.00

could produce sarcomas in other chickens (137). This agent was later shown to contain RNA within mature virions and proved to be one of the earliest known members of the retrovirus family. In 1933, Shope (148) discovered a virus causing papillomas in cottontail rabbits. This virus was the first DNA-containing tumor virus and the first member of a novel family of viruses now known to be associated with cancer in humans. In the years since these early studies, many viruses in six virus families have been linked with tumors in animals or have been found to transform cultured cells. Of these viruses, only a few are associated with cancer in their natural host, and even fewer with cancer in humans. All of the viruses now thought to play a role in development of cancer in humans either contain DNA in the mature virions or, as with the retrovirus group, have a DNA intermediate as part of the viral life cycle. These viruses belong to only four virus families: the RNA-containing retroviruses and the DNA-containing herpesviruses, papillomaviruses, and hepadnaviruses. Of the three DNA virus families, the hepadnaviruses appear to be the most carcinogenic in the natural host.

The association of the hepadnaviruses with cancer is well established. The prototype member of the hepadnavirus family, hepatitis B virus (HBV) that infects humans, has been associated with at least 80% of one of the most common cancers in the world, primary liver cancer, or hepatocellular carcinoma (HCC) (6). Infection with HBV precedes development of the cancer. Related viruses can induce tumors in their animal hosts, albeit after a lengthy time span between initial infection and appearance of tumors, as is seen with HBV. The epidemiology of HCC is that expected of a tumor caused by an infectious agent. Whether vaccination against HBV in populations in high risk areas lowers the incidence of cancer remains to be determined. Such vaccination programs are currently in progress.

Hepatitis B virus was first distinguished from other hepatitis-inducing viruses following detection of its surface antigen by Blumberg and coworkers in 1965 (12). But the molecular and biological features that made HBV unique were difficult to study in a virus that infects only humans and higher primates. HBV-related viruses that infect woodchucks, ground squirrels, and ducks were discovered in 1978 and 1979. The genomes of these hepadnaviruses as well as that of HBV have been cloned, sequenced, and their features analyzed by several laboratories. Hepadnavirus replication and tissue tropism have been elucidated using the fresh tissues available in the animal models. The pathology associated with the three well-studied animal models has been observed, and commonalities of hepatitis and hepatocellular carcinoma have emerged from studies of persistent infection in the mammalian host. A high incidence of integrated viral DNA has been found in hepadnavirus-related liver carcinoma compared to nontumor liver tissue, and these integrations have been cloned and studied with respect to both viral and host DNA structure and gene location. Additional experimental models such as virus- and viral antigen–producing cell lines and transgenic mice have been developed in recent years. Experiments using all of these models have provided new insight into hepadnaviral replication and oncogenic potential.

Presently known data indicate that hepadnaviruses are not classic tumor viruses. Hepadnaviruses do not have a dominant oncogene like those associated with certain retroviruses. Hepadnavirus-associated oncogenesis apparently does not involve promoter activation of a specific cellular gene, as is seen with other retroviruses. The genome contains no strongly oncogenic region as is found in the adenoviruses or herpesviruses. There is no tumor antigen as in the polyomaviruses. It is not clear that virus-specific products, RNA and episomal DNA, and other factors specified by the virus even continue to be made in the cells of all hepadnavirus-associated tumors. Yet, as described below, elements of the above viral-specific mechanisms of carcinogenesis as well as other more general mechanisms may each play a role in the development of cancer in some of the hepadnavirus-infected livers and thus contribute to the total risk of cancer associated with this virus family.

THE HEPADNAVIRUS FAMILY

Hepatitis B virus, discovered in 1965, was the first known member of the hepadnaviruses. Exposure of an adult to HBV usually results in an acute infection lasting up to 20 weeks, followed by development of protective antibody to the virus (reviewed in 129). During active infection, virus and viral antigens are found in the blood and body fluids, with high amounts of viral antigens and nucleic acids in the liver. Transmission occurs by parenteral contact with body fluids containing the virus. Less than 10% of adults infected with HBV remain persistently infected with the virus, and complete virus or sometimes only viral surface antigen remains in the blood for decades. When infants are infected perinatally with HBV, nearly 95% develop persistent infection (6). Presently, there are over 250 million chronic carriers of HBV worldwide. Although several effective vaccines are now available to prevent HBV infection, there is no effective cure. An estimated 1–2 million deaths due to severe hepatitis, cirrhosis, or hepatocellular carcinoma are attributed to HBV infection per year (173a).

Woodchuck hepatitis virus (WHV) was the first animal hepadnavirus discovered, found by Summers, Smolec & Snyder (155) in sera of eastern woodchucks *(Marmota monax)*, a member of the Sciuridae, or squirrel family. Snyder had noted that the most frequent cause of death in a colony of woodchucks at the Philadelphia Zoo was hepatocellular carcinoma accompanied by a particular form of hepatitis with degenerative and regenerative changes. Sera from animals with active hepatitis were found to contain

HBV-like virus particles. Only a year later, during a search for an HBV-like virus in Californian relatives of the woodchuck (91), another hepadnavirus was found in a second member of the squirrel family: the ground squirrel hepatitis virus (GSHV) in the Beechey ground squirrel *(Spermophilus beecheyi)*. Discovery of the fourth member of the hepatitis virus family resulted, as with the woodchuck, from an observation of frequent hepatomas, this time in brown ducks from Qidong county of the People's Republic of China. J. Summers, W. T. London, S. Sun & B. S. Blumberg (unpublished data) found that sera from these ducks contained another HBV-like virus. Attempts to passage this virus in eggs from domestic Pekin ducks *(Anas domesticus)* led to the discovery by Mason and coworkers (97) that a similar virus was present in some 10% of· commercial flocks in the US. This virus was called duck hepatitis B virus (DHBV). In addition to these well-characterized viruses, researchers have reported other HBV-like viruses infecting tree squirrels (43, 44), kangaroos (35), snakes, domestic geese (R. Sprengel & H. Will, unpublished data), and herons (150). Of these viruses, the goose virus appears to be identical to DHBV (H. Will, personal communication), and only the heron virus DNA has been analyzed and shown to have the characteristic genome structure of the four well-studied hepadnaviruses. The remaining viruses were identified only on the basis of serological cross-reactivity or nucleic acid cross-hybridization with known hepadnaviruses, but have not yet been fully characterized as to genomic or physical structure. To date no hepadnaviruses infecting nonprimate laboratory animals have been identified.

The well-characterized hepadnaviruses are fairly species specific, infecting only the original host and a limited number of closely related species (see 87 for review). While both HBV and DHBV are found worldwide, WHV and GSHV are localized to specific regions of the east and west coasts of the United States, respectively.

MOLECULAR STRUCTURE OF HEPADNAVIRUSES AND THEIR GENE PRODUCTS

The hepatitis B virion has a diameter of approximately 42 nm, with a lipid-containing outer layer bearing the viral surface antigen (sAg) and an electron-dense core or nucleocapsid within (see 87, 131 for more detailed reviews of hepadnavirus molecular structure). The most abundant forms of virus particles in sera during HBV infections are spherical or filamentous and are defective, containing only viral envelope (sAg) and no nucleocapsid. The DNA of HBV virions is quite small, circular, and partly single stranded (see Figure 1). A viral-encoded DNA polymerase contained within the virion can repair the DNA to make fully double-stranded molecules approximately 3200 bp in length. The full-length strand is intact except for a nick at a specific site, and the other strand varies from approximately 1700 to 3000 nucleotides in length in different molecules. The 5' end of this shorter strand, now known to be the plus strand (or that with the same polarity as viral mRNA), has a fixed location approximately 300 bp from the nick in the long strand, creating a short, base-paired region that maintains the circular conformation of the DNA. A protein is covalently attached to the 5' end of the long DNA strand (57) and is referred to in this review as the terminal protein.

Each of the animal hepadnaviral DNAs has been cloned into bacteria, sequenced [WHV (52), DHBV (86), and GSHV (140)], and compared to earlier publications of HBV DNA sequences (e.g. 51, 53, 119). Sequence analysis shows that the genomic structure of the mammalian hepadnaviruses is nearly identical, with significant sequence homology among the three, and that the avian hepadnavirus is more divergent in genomic structure and sequence. The four major open reading frames (ORFs) of mammalian hepadnaviral DNA reside on the virion's long DNA strand (see Figure 1). The S and C ORFs encode the polypeptides bearing surface and core antigens of the virus coat and nucleocapsid respectively. A long ORF (P) encodes what is thought to be the viral polymerase and two other proteins or protein activities associated with the virus, the terminal protein and a RNAse H. Regions of the P gene product have amino acid sequence homology with the *pol* gene products of retroviruses and caulimoviruses (102, 160). The remaining short ORF is termed X because its gene product and function were completely unknown for several years. This gene is now known to encode a transactivating protein. The genomic structure shows considerable economy; the large P ORF overlaps each of the others and codes information contained within all three frames of the genome. The S and C ORFs are preceded by contiguous ORFs known as the pre-S and pre-C coding regions, respectively. The pre-S region is further divided into pre-S1 and pre-S2 regions. All known hepadnaviruses contain 11-base-pair direct repeats at either side of the cohesive ends, shown in Figure 1 as DR1 and DR2. These sequence features play an important role, discussed later, in viral replication. Other *cis*-acting regulatory elements of the genome include at least two enhancers (144, 181), at least three promoters (22, 78, 127, 178), a glucocorticoid-responsive regulatory element (162), and the conserved hexanucleotide TATAAA (AATAAA in DHBV and HHBV), which plays a role in the correct polyadenylation and processing of hepadnavirus RNA transcripts (54).

Calculations show an estimated 82% DNA homology between GSHV and WHV and about 55% between GSHV and HBV, with only scattered homology apparent between DHBV and the other hepadnaviruses (140). The genomes of WHV and GSHV are approximately 125 base pairs larger than HBV, with more coding present in the pre-S and P genes. The DHBV genome, in contrast, is smaller than HBV by 164 base pairs. The S gene of

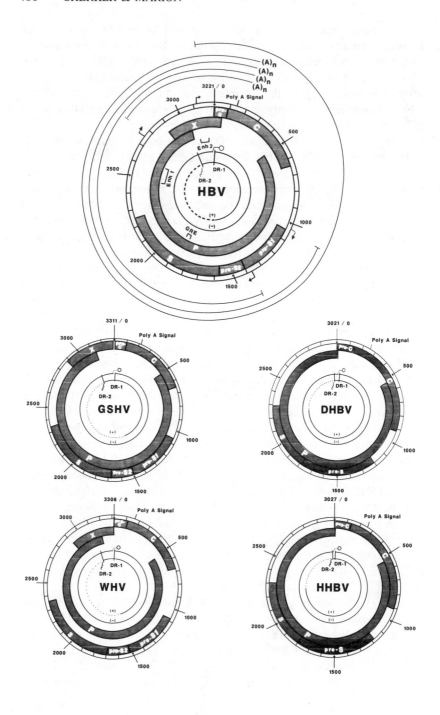

DHBV is smaller than that of the mammalian viruses, and most strikingly, the X ORF is absent (Figure 1).

The products of the structural hepadnaviral genes have been isolated and characterized. The S gene of each of the viruses encodes the sAg polypeptide, which appears in the viral envelopes and can elicit protective antibody. The sAg of HBV is found also in a glycosylated form, parallels of which are found in WHV and GSHV, but not in DHBV (reviewed in 93). Additional minor polypeptides of molecular weight greater than that of sAg are associated with all the hepadnaviruses. These polypeptides, some of which are glycosylated in the mammalian viruses, are gene products that use start codons in the pre-S region and terminate at the end of the S gene (61, 153, 174). Termed pre-S1 and pre-S2, these polypeptides are more abundant in complete virions than in the incomplete particles.

The nucleocapsid of HBV is formed of the other structural protein, the core polypeptide, upon which are found two distinct antigenic domains that elicit antibody during viral infection. The core polypeptide in undenatured form stimulates development of an antibody called anti-core or anti-HBc. When denatured with an ionic detergent, the same polypeptide displays additional antigenic epitopes termed e antigens and loses the conformational core anti-gen epitope. A truncated form of the C gene product displaying the eAg epitopes (and not the core epitope) is found in sera during active viral replication. Studies of in vitro expression of core gene products with and without the presence of the precore sequences indicate that the precore sequences are required for secretion of the eAg polypeptide. The core polypeptide has been isolated and analyzed in all the animal hepadnaviruses and corresponds to DNA sequence predictions of size (42, 122, 125).

The P gene product bearing DNA polymerase or reverse transcriptase activity still remains uncharacterized as to size and sequence. Work by Bosch

---

Figure 1   Comparison of the structure and genetic organization of the hepadnaviruses (see text for details). The inner circles represent the two strands of virion DNA, the complete minus strand, and the variable-length plus strand. A broken line denotes the gap. Features shown include: the direct repeats, DR-1 and DR-2; the polyadenylation signal; and the terminal protein *(small open circle)* and RNA oligomer *(wavy line)* at the 5' end of the minus and plus DNA strands, respectively. Nucleotides are numbered on the outer circle. The overlapping viral open reading frames are indicated, and the direction of transcription is clockwise in all cases. In the upper panel, the known *cis*-acting regulatory elements of hepatitis B virus (HBV) are shown, including promoters *(clockwise-pointing arrows)*, enhancers (Enh), and the glucocorticoid re-sponsive element (GRE). RNA transcripts are depicted by lines outside the circles; $(A)_n$ represents polyadenylation. Ground squirrel hepatitis virus (GSHV), woodchuck hepatitis virus (WHV), duck hepatitis B virus (DHBV), and heron hepatitis B virus (HHBV) are shown in the lower panel.

and colleagues (13) indicates that the terminal protein bound to the 5' end of the DHBV minus strand is encoded by the 5' end of the P gene. Several laboratories have described evidence for the coding of a RNase H by nucleotides downstream from the reverse transcriptase consensus sequences located in the middle and in the upstream C terminal portion of the gene (5, 25, 160).

After several years cloaked in mystery, the X gene is at last revealing some of its secrets. Antibody reacting to chemically or bacterially synthesized X gene product is found in both HBV-infected individuals (70, 100, 105) and in GSHV-infected squirrels (121), indicating that it is made during viral replication in the host. The X gene product has *trans*-acting properties that allow it to modulate the level of transcription of several host (166, 167) or viral (149, 165) regulatory sequences, either from HBV or heterologous viruses. A recent study by Wu and colleagues (175) indicates that the X gene product has a protein kinase activity and can phosphorylate serine and threonine residues on both the X-encoded protein as well as other substrates such as histone and caseine. Whether the kinase activity of X is essential to the transactivating function remains to be determined by genetic analysis.

HEPADNAVIRUS REPLICATION

The seminal studies of Summers & Mason (95, 154) using the duck-DHBV model showed that the key features of hepadnaviral replication are (*a*) conversion of incoming viral DNA to a supercoiled form, (*b*) synthesis of a RNA pregenome, (*c*) reverse transcription of the pregenome to make the viral DNA minus strand, and (*d*) synthesis of the plus strand using the minus strand as template.

The following is the scheme of viral infection as it is presently understood. The interested reader who desires a more in-depth accounting of molecular aspects of these agents is referred to a review by Ganem & Varmus (54).

When virus enters the hepatocyte, with the surface antigen removed by a yet unknown mechanism, virion DNA moves to the nucleus, probably still within the nucleocapsid. Either on the way to the nucleus or in the nucleus, the plus strand is extended and the virion DNA made fully double stranded. The terminal protein on the minus strand is removed, along with other features to be discussed below, and the DNA is converted into a covalently closed circular (CCC) supercoiled DNA molecule (163, 164). This CCC DNA is the first replicative intermediate to appear in experimental infections of ducklings with DHBV (96, 158) and is common to all the hepadnaviruses (101, 173). As it is the only replicative DNA form appearing prior to the appearance of viral RNAs, it is presumed to be the template for viral RNA transcription (96). Three different-sized major mRNA transcripts (and possibly other minor ones) with common 3' termini encode the viral proteins. The largest mRNA species (approximately 3.5 kb in length) is actually a group of mRNAs that are greater than genome length but whose 5' end varies within a range of 130–160 nucleotides. The smallest of these 3.5-kb RNAs is packaged in viral core particles along with viral polymerase and terminal protein, and functions as the pregenome. Synthesis of the viral minus strand then takes place using the terminal protein as a primer, with RNase H degradation of all but the most 5' region of the RNA pregenome. Plus-strand DNA synthesis then occurs, using the short residual oligoribonucleotide as a primer.

While some completed nucleocapsids may then be enveloped and exported, others appear to reenter the cycle of infection within the same cell. This movement of newly synthesized viral DNA to the nucleus was suggested by the work of Tuttleman and others (163), who showed that the amount of CCC DNA in the nucleus is amplified during an early stage in the infection by completion of relaxed circular DNA rather than by semiconservative replication of CCC DNA. In steady-state hepadnaviral infections in ducks, humans, and woodchucks, there are approximately 50 CCC DNA copies per cell (101, 163), as well as more numerous copies of protein-bound viral minus strands, ranging in size from the lowest limit of detection to full length, and relaxed circular DNA with variable amounts of repair of the short strand.

Though the scheme of hepadnavirus replication resembles that of retroviruses in its use of reverse transcription, no evidence suggests that integration of viral DNA into the host genome is an essential step as it is with retrovirus replication. Researchers have detected and cloned integrated viral DNA using lamboid vectors in chronically infected woodchuck liver (134), but not in ground squirrel (P. L. Marion, C. E. Rogler & J. Summers, unpublished data) or duck liver (C. E. Rogler & J. Summers, unpublished data). The integrated WHV DNA studied was not in a complete linear form, but was rearranged with inversions and deletions, and therefore unsuitable as a template for pregenome synthesis.

NONNEOPLASTIC DISEASE IN HEPADNAVIRAL INFECTION

In three of the four well-studied hepadnaviruses, an association of liver cancer with chronic infection has been demonstrated, and is described below. Because development of HCC in chronic infection may be linked to the severity of other forms of liver disease, one should understand what is known of the nonneoplastic disease in these infections. Liver disease associated with HBV has been well documented over the years. Acute HBV infection can be relatively silent or accompanied by severe, even fatal hepatitis. In chronic HBV infection of humans, liver involvement ranges from no detectable inflammation to a hepatitis confined to the portal areas of the liver (often called chronic persistent hepatitis) to a severe hepatitis termed chronic active hepatitis in which the inflammation spills out of the portal areas into the parenchyma. The fact that some individuals have minimal or absent histological liver damage, despite the presence of many virus-infected cells (60), suggests that HBV is not directly cytopathic but rather causes liver damage by inducing a host cellular immune response. This conclusion is supported by the lack of observed cytopathicity in cell cultures that produce mature virions (2, 58, 116, 164). Development of cirrhosis is a common and often fatal event in chronic infection of humans. In chronic HBV infection of chimpanzees, less inflammation is seen in the liver than in that of humans, and no cirrhosis has been observed. In general, more severe hepatitis is found in chronic HBV infection while viral replication is active. Later stages of infection, in which viral replication has waned and often only HBsAg rather than whole virus is secreted into the blood, are frequently accompanied by only insignificant to mild hepatitis (67).

When the animal hepadnaviruses were discovered, there was considerable interest in the liver disease of their hosts, as it was hoped that they would provide clues to better understand the effects of HBV on humans. WHV and DHBV were discovered in animal populations with a high incidence of hepatitis and hepatomas and were assumed to be the cause of the liver diseases. This has turned out to be the case with WHV. The ground squirrel virus was not discovered in the same manner, and early studies of relatively young squirrels indicated that little hepatitis accompanied GSHV infection and that no HCC developed (55, 90). Accumulated studies over the past eight years, however, indicate that chronic infection with GSHV is associated with both hepatitis and HCC (P. L. Marion & H. Popper, unpublished data). The extent of liver disease associated with DHBV infection is not yet as well defined as that of WHV and GSHV. Unexpectedly, only rare HCC has been detected in virus-infected ducks in 10 years of observation in several laboratories around the world.

The original pathological observations of WHV infection of naturally infected captive animals described a chronic hepatitis ranging from persistent to active (155) and have been confirmed by other laboratories. In studies of adult woodchucks that became chronically infected following experimental inoculation, only a persistent hepatitis was observed unless HCC developed (123, 168). When newborn woodchucks were injected with WHV and became chronic carriers, again, only a low level of hepatitis (persistent hepatitis) was observed. The greater range of liver inflammation seen in naturally infected woodchucks may be related to the greater period of virus infection or to a partial immunotolerance in woodchucks injected at birth. Cirrhosis is a rare event in WHV infection; only two cases of cirrhosis have been reported among the many cases of chronic WHV carriers studied (136; R. Snyder, personal communication).

In collaboration with our laboratory, Hans Popper (unpublished data) conducted a study under code of the liver histopathology of 79 captive ground squirrels at necropsy. He found that persistent hepatitis was present in the majority (59%) of 32 carrier animals examined at necropsy, while only 17% of 47 virus-negative animals exhibited any hepatitis above background level. Of those hepatitis cases rated significant or greater, the majority of the squirrels were over 4 years of age (58% of the carrier animals, 71% of the noncarriers). Active hepatitis was observed only in areas of liver adjacent to HCC. The severity of hepatitis was in general not as extensive as has been seen in some captive woodchucks. No cirrhosis was observed in any squirrel studied.

In the duck system, significant hepatitis has been observed in ducklings injected with DHBV, but not in congenitally infected ducklings at six weeks of age (89). The most common transmission of DHBV is vertical, through infected eggs. Viral replication begins during embryogenesis, and ducks are immunotolerant of viral antigens. Not all injected ducks with viremia exhibit significant hepatitis (88). The levels of inflammation may depend upon the genetics of the duck or, in part, upon the particular strain of virus injected. In Chinese ducks of unknown history from Qidong county, both persistent and active hepatitis have been noted (89, 118, 182), but in only one of the three studies was the more severe liver disease associated with the presence of DHBV in sera or liver.

SPONTANTEOUS HCC IN THE HEPADNAVIRUS-INFECTED HOST

HBV Infection of Humans

An association of HCC with viral hepatitis was postulated long before any of the specific viruses causing hepatitis had been identified (120, 152). Only after serological tests for hepatitis B surface antigen (HBsAg) were developed was this suspected association confirmed (145). Although HCC is an unusual malignancy in many parts of the world, it occurs commonly in several large, populous regions including sub-Saharan Africa and southeast Asia. With the exception of Japan, the annual incidence of HCC correlates with the HBV carrier rate of a region (8, 157). Recent research showed that the majority of patients with HCC in Japan have evidence of infection with hepatitis C virus (138).

Several large studies have been published comparing the risk of development of HCC in HBsAg-positive individuals with HBsAg-negative control populations (7, 83, 99, 114). All show a markedly increased risk for HCC among the HBV carriers. In the largest of these studies, 22,707 male Taiwanese government employees were followed prospectively for an average of 3.3 years (7). Of the 3454 men who were HBsAg-positive, 40 died from HCC, compared with only one of the 19,253 HBsAg-negative individuals: a relative risk of 223. HCC and/or cirrhosis accounted for over 50% of the deaths in the chronic carriers. Among those who had antibody to HBsAg upon entry into the study, the incidence of HCC was low and not statistically different from the cohort having no markers of current or past HBV infection (6), suggesting that individuals who recover from acute HBV infection have little or no excess risk of subsequent HCC development. Among Alaskan native HBV carriers, while the incidences of chronic active hepatitis and cirrhosis were comparable between males and females, males had an approximately sixfold incidence of HCC (99), suggesting that male sex is an independent risk factor in the development of HCC among HBsAg-positive individuals.

Although HCC has been described in an HBV carrier as young as eight months of age (176), the occurrence of this malignancy increases with age, with most cases presenting in the sixth through eighth decades of life (72). A still unexplained exception to this generality occurs among Mozambican Shangaan males who have a very high incidence of HCC with 50% of tumors presenting below age 30 (72). The histology of the HBV-linked HCCs is predominantly of the trabecular type.

Other etiologies associated with HCC in humans include ingestion of the mycotoxin aflatoxin B_1, infection with hepatitis C virus, pharmacological doses of anabolic steroids, various metabolic liver diseases, and other chronic liver diseases with associated necroinflammatory pathology (reviewed in 82).

HBV-Infected Chimpanzees

In contrast to humans, HCC has been observed only twice among chimpanzees infected with HBV, and in neither case was the infection chronic (108). Chimpanzees have served as models for studying HBV infection for 20 years. In one case, a chimpanzee was injected with HBV plus hepatitis delta antigen (HDV) and developed HCC two months after virus infection (108). HDV has not been linked with development of liver cancer in humans or chimpanzees. Another chimpanzee had antibody to HBsAg subsequent to an infection that occurred 8 years earlier, but had been injected with serum capable of transmitting non-A, non-B (NANB) hepatitis two years prior to the HBV infection. Two additional chimpanzees, entirely negative for markers of HBV infection, have developed HCC and are known carriers of NANB (109). Hepatitis C virus, now known to be associated with most cases of parenterally transmitted NANB, was recently linked to the development of HCC in humans (18, 34, 73, 138). These cases, therefore, provide little support for the association of HBV infection with HCC in the chimpanzee.

WHV-Infected Woodchucks

In the original study of a colony of captive WHV-infected woodchucks, HCC developed in animals ranging in age from 2.0 to 8.8 years, with an average of 5.0 years. The HCC was predominantly of the trabecular type histologically, as in the HBV-associated malignancies. Subsequent studies confirmed the presence of WHV in woodchucks developing HCC, with HCC appearing in some 30% of captive adult woodchucks of unspecified age per year. Other laboratories have confirmed the chronology of tumor development in captive carriers, and in most colonies observed, the incidence of HCC has approached 100%. Infection with WHV followed by seroconversion may carry increased risk of HCC. In a report on HCC development in a woodchuck colony (75), 5 of 92 (5.4%) convalescent animals developed HCC, while no liver carcinoma was detected in 167 uninfected controls. HCC has generally been observed in woodchucks in which viral replication is active [all of 29 animals (in 75)], whereas no active viral replication is seen in about 20% of human cases of HCC. The amount of HCC in virus-infected woodchucks may be linked to the amount of chronic active hepatitis in the populations studied: in three colonies of chronically infected woodchucks with 21, 43, and 87% HCC, 10, 29, and 67% chronic active hepatitis was detected, respectively; the remaining animals exhibited chronic persistent hepatitis (49, 124, 136). Unlike HBV infection in humans HCC appears to develop equally in woodchuck males and females.

Hepatocellular carcinoma develops even more rapidly when WHV is inoculated into newborn woodchucks. In the original study, Popper and colleagues (123) found that all of six newborn woodchucks that were injected with WHV and that became persistently infected developed HCC within two years. In these six animals, only chronic persistent hepatitis was observed, in contrast to the more severe hepatitis seen in the captive adult carrier. This finding, therefore, represents a departure from the association of severity of hepatitis with more rapid development of HCC.

GSHV-Infected Ground Squirrels

In our 9-year study of 24 GSHV-infected, 20 convalescent, and 26 GSHV marker–free ground squirrels over 4 years of age, we observed 18 cases of HCC (45% of all neoplasms). No tumors of any kind were detected in animals under 4 years of age. Eleven of the liver tumors were in carrier animals, 5 in convalescent, and 2 in GSHV-free animals. The association of HCC with the GSHV carrier state is significant ($p = 0.0016$). As in WHV-infected woodchucks, the incidence of HCC in postresolution animals was relatively high (20%). Convalescent squirrels developing tumors experienced only a brief period of viremia. As with the studies of WHV in woodchucks, no sex bias in HCC development was noted. Various tumors other than HCC have been observed, with no tumor type predominating. The average age of the squirrels when HCC was detected was 6.5 years, a year and a half older than the estimated average age of naturally infected WHV carriers when HCC develops, but considerably younger than that of HBV carriers. The average age of HCC detection in postresolution squirrels was similar (6.8 years), while that of the marker-free squirrels was considerably higher at 8.5 years, near the end of the 9.5-year maximum life span. Of the carrier animals developing HCC, one was an experimentally infected animal, while the others became GSHV carriers before capture. As with HCC in woodchucks, viral replication is active in the liver of ground squirrels that have developed HCC. High-molecular-weight viral DNA was detected in the tumor DNA of 3 of 7 carrier animals analyzed by Southern blots. This high-molecular-weight viral DNA is assumed to be integrated into host DNA, as has been observed in tumors associated with the other hepadnaviruses. As is seen with the bulk of HCCs associated with HBV and WHV infection, the histological type was trabecular and highly differentiated in all but one HCC. The remaining HCC was an anaplastic medullary hepatocellular carcinoma, and this tumor arose in one of the squirrels with anti-GSHs and not GSHsAg. Thus, infection of ground squirrels with GSHV carries a high risk of development of HCC, but at a slower rate than in WHV infection of adult woodchucks. As with the individual populations of woodchucks studied, a higher or more rapid incidence of HCC is associated with the animal model exhibiting the higher levels of liver inflammation.

This difference in rate of development of HCC in two hepadnavirus-infected hosts with equivalent life expectancies led Seeger and colleagues (139a) to test whether the rate difference results from the host or the virus. Taking advantage of the susceptibility of newborn woodchucks to both WHV and GSHV, Seeger and coworkers injected one group of newborn woodchucks with WHV and another with GSHV, and observed those that became chronically infected. After 51 months of observation, all of 16 WHV-infected animals developed HCC, while the carcinoma was detected in only 6 of 14 remaining GSHV-infected animals. Accumulated HCC incidence with time shows that GSHV causes HCC approximately two years later than WHV when studied in the same host, paralleling the differences seen in HCC development in the naturally infected captive hosts. Animals infected with GSHV have exhibited levels of sAg and viral DNA in the serum, and of viral DNA in the liver, similar to those infected with WHV. No difference between the two groups was noted in liver histopathology in biopsy specimens at two years after infection. These results indicate that the greater oncogenic potential of WHV lies in the virus itself, not in the level of virus expression or in the level of hepatocellular injury or regeneration. Similar experiments using recombinant chimeric genomes of WHV and GSHV should eventually reveal the portion of the WHV genome that enhances oncogenicity.

DHBV-Infected Ducks

The association of HCC with DHBV infection is less firm than that of the mammalian viruses. Although the virus was originally discovered in free-ranging flocks of ducks in China that exhibited a high occurrence of both hepatitis and HCC, the involvement of aflatoxin B_1 or other environmental carcinogens in both diseases cannot be discounted. Ducks are known to develop HCC after exposure to relatively low levels of the mycotoxin (20). In ten years of study in several laboratories around the world, no HCC has been observed in congenitally infected ducks, while development of HCC has been documented in only one of several studies of experimentally infected ducks (M. Omata, personal communication; J. Cullen, personal communication; P. Marion, unpublished data). Development of HCC in DHBV-infected ducks may depend upon the strain of virus used or the breed of ducks infected. If development of HCC occurs in the latter half of the life span of the host, as in humans and ground squirrels infected with hepadnaviruses, HCC may not develop in most of these long-lived ducks until they are seven years or older. However, as discussed below, intrinsic differences between the mammalian and avian viruses, such as the absence of an X gene, as well as the more subtle differences that appear to determine the oncogenic levels of WHV and GSHV, may lessen the level of oncogenicity of DHBV compared with the mammalian viruses.

State of Hepadnaviral DNA in Hepatocellular Carcinoma

As described above, HCC develops in woodchuck and ground squirrel livers in which virus is actively replicated. In contrast, HBV-associated HCC frequently develops in liver in which replication of virions is diminished or even absent, decades after the initiation of infection, though synthesis of HBsAg continues. When viral replication is ongoing and abundant in the liver, as in ground squirrels and woodchucks, replicating, free viral DNA is present in DNA extracted from tumors, but in reduced amounts compared to the surrounding liver. In HCC from late HBV infections, replicating free viral DNA does not appear in HCC cells (84, 126), while both integrated and free HBV are frequently seen in the nontumor cells in the same liver.

The existence of integrated HBV DNA was first demonstrated in analyses of a continuously growing cell line (PLC/PRF/5) from an HCC taken from an individual with circulating HBsAg (16, 24, 40, 94). Subsequent Southern blot analysis of numerous human and animal HCCs revealed that integrated viral sequences are found in the vast majority of seropositive patients tested and in a somewhat smaller fraction of the animal carriers (56, 92). Integrated viral DNA is found occasionally in the tumors of HB-antibody positive patients as well as in those from convalescent woodchucks (15, 75).

After the existence of integrated hepadnaviral DNA in HCC became known, Ogston and colleagues (117) achieved the initial cloning of an integrant in 1982 using the woodchuck system. As the hepadnaviruses are related to the retroviruses by their common reverse transcription step, researchers thought that integration of the hepadnaviral DNA might follow the orderly retroviral sequence of steps, including integration at a specific viral sequence. This has proven to not be the case, and more recent examination of homology between the polymerase genes of the two virus groups indicates that the integrase protein essential to the directed integration of retroviruses is absent in hepadnaviruses. The earliest study of integrated WHV DNA indicated that it was highly rearranged, with random deletions. Subsequent studies have shown that the host target is also rearranged and frequently deleted in areas. This type of integration of foreign DNA is typical of illegitimate recombination, and junction sites exhibit little specificity of viral or host sequence.

The pattern of viral integration in individual HCCs is generally identical from cell to cell within the tumor, suggesting a clonal origin (3, 11, 27, 41). Occasionally, more than one clonal tumor may coexist in the same liver (27, 41). Metastases have the same clonal integration pattern as the primary tumor (11, 41), and recurrent tumors may exhibit the original integration pattern or a novel one (27).

At least 40 different HBV integrations have been cloned and characterized from at least 15 different tumors or cell lines (32, 38, 65, 74, 98, 104, 110, 177, 184, 185). With one possible exception (38), none of the integrants contain an intact, contiguous, whole HBV genome. Complete nucleotide sequencing was not performed for the exception, so a small deletion, duplication, or insertion could have been overlooked. The patterns of viral integration are heterogeneous, with virus-cell junctions distributed through the genome. However, viral integration sites are clearly clustered; 18 of the 40 integrants have at least one junction within the short stretch between the beginning of DR1 and the end of DR2, which represents only about 7% of the viral genome. The integrants also contain virus-virus junctions at inverted repeats and duplications. These too are clustered in the same region, suggesting that properties of this region make it particularly recombination proficient. One theory proposed by Nagaya et al (110) is that single-stranded intermediates of replication may act as the "substrates of integration," and clustering in this area results from the fact that the 5' termini of the minus and plus strands are near DR1 and DR2, respectively. From what is known of normal viral infection, however, one would expect to find only two viral DNA forms in the nucleus: incoming relaxed circular virion DNA and CCC DNA. Rogler and coworkers (64) proposed that topoisomerase I may be involved in some cases of viral integration because four topoisomerase I cleavage sites have been mapped to the DR1-DR2 region in WHV. However, as the majority of virus-cell and virus-virus junctions do not map to this region, other mechanisms of integration must play a role as well. It is possible that deletions or rearrangement of integrated viral DNA may occur subsequent to the initial insertion.

No unique cellular sites of integration have yet been identified. HBV integrations into the human genome have been mapped to at least 12 different chromosomes (10, 14, 37, 65, 110, 133, 184), and chromosomes 3, 5, 6, 11, 17, and 18 are each represented in more than one integration. A few host junctions involve repeating *alu* (110) or satellite III (110, 143) sequences, and a single integration is flanked by 12-base-pair cellular direct repeats (177). No conclusions about the preferred sites of viral integration can be drawn from these few data.

Effect of Hepadnaviruses on Cellular Genes in HCC

Quantitative or qualitative alterations in the expression of cellular protooncogenes is believed to be an important antecedent to neoplasia in many malignancies. Protooncogenes are thought to encode tightly regulated proteins whose expression plays an important role in controlling cell growth. To date, the precise molecular pathway to oncogenesis has been elucidated in only a few experimental tumor model systems (reviewed in 132). An increasing body of scientific evidence, however, relates patterns of expression of specific oncogene(s) to specific human malignancies. Apparently, the activation of more than one oncogene is frequently necessary before the malignant phenotype is manifest (77). Studies have shown that the increased expression of one or both of the synergistic oncogenes, *ras* and *myc*, occurs in chemical hepatocarcinogenesis in rats (85), spontaneously occurring liver tumors in mice (128), rodent and human hepatoma cell lines (69, 85, 183), and HBV- and non-HBV-related human HCCs (59, 62, 80, 113). These observations suggest that the activation of these oncogenes may be common to the process of hepatocarcinogenesis in several species, regardless of underlying etiology.

In general terms, activation of protooncogenes may occur either through the abnormal expression of a normal protooncogene or the expression of an altered oncogene product. Demonstrated mechanisms by which the level of protooncogene expression may be altered include: integration of regulatory elements of nonacute transforming retroviruses (or lentiviruses) in proximity to protooncogenes [so called insertional mutagenesis (111)]; gene amplification (139); or chromosomal translocations resulting in altered transcriptional or posttranscriptional control of expression (79). An altered oncogene product may result from mutation of the normal protooncogene sequence (19) or chromosomal rearrangements and deletions (23). Another mechanism by which viruses may cause cancer is through transactivation (or inactivation) of important host regulatory genes (36, 112, 170). In a few hepadnavirus-related

HCCs of humans and animals, specific chromosomal alterations have been described that may be relevant to the molecular basis of hepatocarcinogenesis. We summarize these findings below.

INSERTIONAL MUTAGENESIS   Buendia and colleagues (46, 68, 107) presented evidence that either c-*myc* or the related protooncogene, N-*myc*, is activated in the HCCs of WHV-infected woodchucks. The increased expression of c-*myc* occurred in 3 of 33 HCCs (G. Fourel, personal communication). In one tumor, a rearrangement and translocation of the c-*myc* gene was remote from any viral integration site (107). In another, viral DNA integration was within a noncoding region of the third exon of the gene (68). In the third HCC, integration of viral sequences including enhancer regions was upstream from the host protooncogene. This WHV-c-*myc* chimera, isolated by cloning, has been used to create transgenic mice, which in turn develop HCC, but no other types of tumors (J. Etiemble, personal communication). However, this type of insertion and protooncogene activation is apparently a rare event. No enhanced c-*myc* expression was seen in 25 additional woodchuck tumors studied by another laboratory (O. Hino, personal communication). Increased expression of N-*myc* appeared in 6 of 30 woodchuck tumors examined, and occurred by insertional activation of either the classic N-*myc* gene or a previously unrecognized, normally silent cellular homologue of N-*myc* that lacks introns and likely represents a retroposon (46). Viral insertions were clustered in a short segment of the 3' untranslated region of N-*myc*, an area that coincides with a previously identified retroviral integration hotspot in T-cell lymphomas induced by murine leukemia virus (142, 169). Determining whether this is a common mechanism by which hepadnaviruses contribute to hepatocarcinogenesis will require systematic study of human and other animal tumors.

Study of viral DNA integration has revealed new potential protooncogenes. In a single integration found in a human HCC, a 1.4-kb viral DNA fragment ending with the first 29 codons of the pre-S region was found fused in frame with an exon of a previously unrecognized gene bearing considerable homology to members of the steroid/thyroid hormone receptor and *erb* oncogene families (37, 39). In this chimera, the putative DNA binding and hormone binding domains are present unaltered. Subsequent cloning, sequencing, and functional characterization of the entire gene led to the determination that it was a novel retinoic acid receptor (9, 39). Retinoids have many functions and are known to be involved with cellular proliferation and differentiation (179). Three of the four primary HCCs and the two HCC cell lines tested express a mRNA species that hybridizes to probes from this gene. An identical pattern of expression is seen in several other tissues but not normal adult or fetal hepatocytes (39). The aberrant expression of this retinoic acid receptor may play a role in hepatocarcinogenesis.

Another single integration in the region of a cellular gene has been identified in an early, well differentiated human HCC. This viral integration resulted in the increased expression of a cyclin A gene (172). The cyclins are a family of genes that are highly conserved through evolution, play an important role in the control of mitosis and meiosis, and could be involved in the development of some malignancies.

Other potentially important mediators of cell growth such as the mitogen, insulin-like growth factor II (50), and a protein kinase substrate, p36 (48), have been shown to have enhanced expression in several HBV-related HCCs. Research has not yet demonstrated that these findings are related to insertional mutagenesis.

CHROMOSOMAL TRANSLOCATIONS   As has been demonstrated in Burkitt's lymphoma, translocations resulting from the influence of heterologous host regulatory sequences that have been brought into the proximity of critical genes can contribute to carcinogenesis by altering the expression of these genes. How common a role this phenomenon may play in hepadnavirus-related HCC is uncertain as limited data are available because most investigators have focused on the regions adjacent to integrated virus. In one woodchuck HCC mentioned previously, rearrangement and translocation of the c-myc gene remote from any detectable WHV integration site resulted in the increased expression of the protooncogene. Integration of HBV DNA has been associated with the translocation of host chromosomes (65, 161). Each of the three translocations characterized involved a different pair of chromosomes. To date, however, no functional alteration in chromosomal expression has yet been ascribed to these translocations.

CHROMOSOMAL REARRANGEMENTS AND DELETIONS   The deletion or mutation of several tumor suppressor genes can be associated with the development of malignancy (summarized in 151). The hereditary embryonal tumor, retinoblastoma, is related to the loss or inactivation of both alleles of the gene RB-1 (23), which have been mapped to the q14 band of chromosome 13. Similarly, a locus within 11p13 appears to contain a recessive oncogene whose loss is associated with Wilms tumor, another embryonal malignancy (47).

The finding that the integration of HBV in one HCC resulted in deletion of at least 13.5 kb of chromosome 11p (133) triggered a search to see if deletions of host sequences were a common phenomenon in HCC. Wang & Rogler (171) studied the loss of heterozygosity of restriction fragment length polymorphisms (RFLP) in tumor tissue compared with surrounding nontumor liver tissue, using a number of probes to known loci on chromosomes 11p and 13q. They found a loss of heterozygosity of at least one marker on 11p in 6 of 14 tumors. Five of the 10 tumors evaluable on 13q showed loss of heterozygosity. Some tumors had deletions on both chromosomes, but no deletions were detected in five tumors. The fact that known tumor-suppressor genes reside on these chromosomal arms suggests that the deletion of host sequences associated with HBV integration may result in the loss or inactivation of tumor-suppressor genes and contribute to hepatocarcinogenesis.

The p53 gene product acts as a tumor suppressor (45). The gene is found on chromosome 17p, and its loss has been associated with colorectal cancer (4) and other malignancies. Point mutations can convert p53 from a tumor suppressor to a dominant oncogene (63). Zhou and colleagues (184) have mapped the site of one HBV DNA integration to chromosome 17p11.2-17p12, which is very close to the location of gene p53. The level of p53 expression was not quantified in that tumor. However, in HCC-derived cell lines, both with and without HBV integration, the molecular structure of p53 or its level of expression is frequently abnormal (17; C. Shih, personal communication). Similarly, mutation of p53 has also been seen in primary liver tumors. A loss of the 17p allele was observed in 42% of 19 HBV-associated HCCs from China (B. Slagle, personal communication). Two groups working independently (17a, 67a) have recently demonstrated tumor-specific mutations in the p53 gene of 13/26 primary HCCs from China and Southern Africa. In 11 cases, point mutations in the third base position of codon 249 resulted in an arginine-to-serine substitution. Ten of these mutations were due to $G \rightarrow T$ substitutions, which are known to be induced by aflatoxin B_1 in mutagenesis experiments (138a). These data suggest that alterations in p53 expression and/or other tumor suppressors may occur commonly in HCC and may be one of several factors leading to the development of malignancy.

TRANSACTIVATION   The X gene is frequently but not always found integrated into the host genome in HCC (26, 103, 110), although commonly in a 3' truncated state. The naturally occurring X gene–cell fusion product of at least some HCCs retains transactivating function (76, 159). Even in the absence of a functional X gene product in an HCC, integrated or episomal viral sequences in remote, nonmalignant hepatocytes could provide transactivation activity. This would be analogous to the situation seen in transgenic mice expressing the *tat* gene of human immunodeficiency virus (HIV) in whom the mRNA of the transactivator is not found within the dermal tumors but rather in nonmalignant cells of the surrounding skin (170).

Recent research has shown that 3' truncated preS/S sequences found in the huH-4 hepatoma cell line (71), cloned directly from a human HCC (21), or cloned from wild-type viral sequences (21, 71) can transactivate SV40 and c-*myc* regulatory elements in vitro. Thus, multiple, possibly complementary, transactivating genes may be generated as a result of HBV integration, and these could contribute to the transformation of liver cells.

HEPADNAVIRUS-RELATED ONCOGENESIS IN EXPERIMENTAL SYSTEMS

Cell Cultures

Recently, investigators have been able to produce not only viral antigens, but infectious hepadnavirus by transfection of viral DNA into cultured cells of liver origin (reviewed in 1). Both human hepatoblastoma and human and rat hepatoma cell lines have been found to produce infectious virions (141, 146, 156). Such transfections have made mutational analysis of the small hepadnaviral genomes readily accessible and have provided great advances in our understanding of the complexities of the compact and efficient hepadnaviral genome. Most of the cells that have been able to produce complete virus after transfection, however, have been completely transformed cells and unsuitable for studying the oncogenic potential of HBV. Primary hepatocytes, which are untransformed and which replicate the virus, display a low transfection efficiency. No evidence indicates that primary hepatocytes can be transformed during the normal events of viral replication, as those infected with WHV, GSHV, or DHBV do not divide any more than their uninfected counterparts. Experiments to examine the oncogenic potential of HBV DNA and its gene products have therefore been done using nonmalignant immortal cell lines such as mouse NIH3T3 cells, commonly used to detect the presence of oncogenes, and more recently, using a newly developed mouse hepatocyte line. These cell lines have undergone enough genetic changes to be on the verge of malignancy, and the addition of genetic material that moves the cells one step further in the progression of oncogenesis can convert them into fully malignant cells capable of growth in soft agar and tumor formation in nude mice or other hosts.

Robinson et al (130) observed a low level of malignant conversion of NIH3T3 cells transfected with an HBV dimer in a plasmid vector. In their experiments, transfected cells became malignant without the expression of HBV genes or even maintenance of detectable HBV DNA sequences. The transforming potential was found in one of two Bam HI fragments of HBV. Within this fragment (nucleotides 1403–0030), no gene product appeared essential because the transforming capability remained even when the genes (X, C, and the N-termini of P and pre-S) were cut with restriction enzymes. Other restriction enzymes, cutting some of the same genes in different locations, did eliminate the ability of the DNA to transform.

In contrast, Koike and colleagues (147) found that two clones of transfected NIH3T3 cells that strongly expressed the X gene were more tumorigenic in nude mice than one transfected clone in which X expression was weak or absent. In this experiment, the transfecting DNA was limited to the X gene and HBV enhancer downstream of the SV40 early promoter. A more extensive study of clones that are transfected with the X gene intact, enzyme restricted, and mutated to yield an inactive product will be necessary to determine if the X gene product can indeed be oncogenic in cells that have already undergone some of the steps in the progression to malignancy.

Hohne and coworkers (66) recently examined the oncogenic potential of HBV in a nonmalignant cell line in which complete replication of HBV can be demonstrated. They transfected HBV DNA into an immortal mouse hepatocyte line harboring the SV40 large tumor antigen gene under the control of the metallothionein promoter. Of 182 clones resistant to the cotransfected selectable marker, 21 secreted either HBsAg or HBcAg. Four clones secreting both antigens and very likely complete virions were then tested for growth in soft agar and malignancy in nude mice. All four of these clones caused tumors in mice and grew in soft agar, while clones resulting from a control experiment in which plasmid vector sequences without HBV DNA were transfected did not grow in agar. Interestingly, unusually high levels of X mRNA were expressed in the HBV-transfected clones, compared with the other viral mRNAs. Testing the remaining HBV-transfected clones that do not express HBV antigens for malignant properties and mutational or restriction enzyme analysis will be necessary to determine whether expression of the X gene alone or portions of the incoming HBV DNA, as seen in the experiment of Robinson and coworkers, are more important in causing malignancy in this useful cell line.

Similar transfection studies can be done to identify activated oncogenes in HCC. Several groups have transfected NIH3T3 cells with DNA from primary HCCs and liver cancer cell lines and obtained transformants (106, 115). In one experiment, the sequences responsible for transformation were characterized by restriction enzyme analysis. In four of 12 human HCC tissues tested, Ochiya and colleagues (115) found weakly transforming sequences. Of these, two sequences were identical, were of host origin, and did not hybridize with any of numerous known human transforming sequence probes. This potential oncogene was named *lca* and was localized to human chromosome 2. Primary sequence data have not yet been published, and whether this sequence is commonly activated in HCC remains to be seen.

In summary, transfection experiments suggest that both HBV DNA alone and expression of one of its gene products, the X-encoded protein, may trigger malignant transformation. No single oncogene has yet been identified with development of HCC using transfection experiments.

Transgenic Mice

Studies of transgenic mice have provided an interesting twist to the hepadnavirus carcinogenesis story. Mice have been made that express the S gene products, the X gene product, and even make complete virus (reviewed in part in 28, 180). Surprisingly, overexpression of both the S gene and the X gene can lead to development of HCC, while other constructs that may have lower expression do not lead to HCC development, nor is HCC observed in the one strain of mice that makes complete HBV.

Two lines of transgenic mice have been developed in which expression of viral envelope proteins is dysregulated due to the presence of a constitutively active albumin promoter upstream from the S ORF (29, 30). In these mice, a toxic accumulation of the largest S gene product, that including pre-S1, pre-S2, and S regions, occurs, with resultant nonimmunologic hepatocellular injury. Overexpression of this large envelope protein inhibits secretion of incomplete sAg particles composed predominantly of polypeptides containing the S region only. In these mouse lines, cell death and nodular regenerative hyperplasia eventually occurs, and almost all mice die with liver tumors before two years of age (31). Some accumulation of viral envelope proteins does occur in natural infection, though whether it is toxic and plays a role in development of HCC is unknown. Altered expression of structural proteins may occur with late aberrant infection or following viral integration. In lines of mice in which the large envelope protein is expressed, but at lower levels than that described above, no hepatocellular injury or HCC is seen, therefore the level of expression is a determining factor in hepatocellular injury.

Two strains of transgenic mice have been developed that carry the X gene of HBV under the control of its own promoter/enhancer region and have been shown to have liver-specific expression of the X gene product (G. Jay, personal communication). In these mice, malignant liver tumors develop in 78–90% of male mice and in 60–75% of females within the second half of the life span of the animals. These interesting results are analogous to those seen with transgenic mice carrying the transactivating *tax* gene of HTLV-1 (112) and *tat* gene of HIV (170), and suggest an important role for transactivators in viral carcinogenesis. Another laboratory (81) has also developed transgenic mice expressing the X gene product, and these mice have shown only rare minor hepatocellular pathology and/or nodular hyperplasia, but not HCC. Currently, the difference in these findings has not been explained, though the levels of expression may play a role in the pathogenesis, as with the over-expression of the large envelope protein.

As yet, no data indicate whether expression of products of the remaining genes, C and P, might lead to injury or tumor formation, though cellular toxicity has been noted in cell lines that produce core antigen alone (135).

SUMMARY AND OUTLOOK

As outlined in the foregoing review, no single unifying hypothesis explains the mechanism of hepatocarcinogenesis in chronic HBV infection. Apparently, both virus-specific and liver-specific factors contribute to the high incidence of HCC in chronically infected individuals. The fact that other viral and nonviral chronic liver diseases are associated with an excess incidence of HCC over the general population (but not to the level seen in HBV infection) suggests that liver neoplasia may result from longstanding hepatocellular necrosis and regenerative repair.

The recent findings that HCC can develop in transgenic mice overexpressing an HBV envelope protein and in chronic carriers of hepatitis C virus, a RNA virus with no known DNA intermediate, indicate that virus-associated HCC can develop in the absence of integration of viral DNA. Yet analysis of hepadnaviral DNA integrations in tumors shows that in some instances, viral integration can disrupt important cellular regulatory genes, including both dominant and recessive oncogenes, in a manner analogous to that observed in oncogenic retroviruses. Preliminary evidence from experimental systems suggests that overexpression of the transactivating X gene may favor malignant transformation. The fact that DHBV appears to be only weakly carcinogenic, if carcinogenic at all, is intriguing because one of the most striking genetic differences of the avian hepadnaviruses compared with the mammalian viruses is the apparent absence of the X gene or transactivating activity (33). To further elucidate the role of altered expression of oncogenes and tumor supressor genes, systematic study needs to be undertaken to compare tumor tissue to nonmalignant hepatic and extrahepatic tissues in individuals in various populations to arrive at meaningful conclusions. These studies will also help to determine the relevance of *cis*- and *trans*-acting viral elements in hepatocarcinogenesis. The existence of a liver-derived, nonmalignant immortal cell line with which to do transfection studies may now facilitate the study of liver-specific oncogenes.

Study of the rate of HCC development in the animal models raises several questions and suggests new approaches to understanding hepadnavirus carcinogenesis. Why does HCC develop faster with WHV and GSHV than with HBV infection? As there does not appear to be less inflammation with HBV than with WHV, either the squirrel family viruses carry more potential for oncogenesis, or there is a difference in host susceptibility to HCC formation. Though the correlation of time of HCC appearance with percent of life span of the hosts supports the latter, the former could be tested in the cell culture model systems or even in transgenic mice. Similarly, model systems could be used to identify regions of WHV DNA or encoded genes that might have more transformation potential than their GSHV counterparts. Explaining why HCC develops much more rapidly in WHV-injected newborns compared to adults requires another approach. Injected newborns exhibit less liver inflammation and regeneration during chronic infection than adults. Yet because infection takes place during a period of rapid growth of the liver, infection of actively dividing cells occurs, a situation analogous to the regenerative activity that occurs in response to hepatocellular necrosis. It will be important to compare the HCCs of newborn and adult injected woodchucks to observe differences in expression of oncogenes or tumor suppressor genes and in integration patterns that might provide clues to the earlier timetable of HCC in the newborn. More study of DHBV-infected ducks is needed to determine whether this avian virus is carcinogenic in its host. Simple exposure of the immunotolerant, growing, and congenitally infected hatchlings to virus infection does not appear to cause HCC in ducks, in contrast to the WHV-injected newborn. Whether injected ducks that have some inflammatory response to virus infection develop HCC remains to be determined through observation into the second half of their life span.

It is likely that a complex interplay of regenerative cell growth induced by hepatic inflammatory disease, molecular aspects of viral integration and chromosomal alterations, and genetic and environmental host factors may all participate in the development of the malignant phenotype. The relative contribution and chronological sequence of each of these factors remains to be determined and may vary among chronically infected individuals. We are now entering an era in hepadnaviral research in which we have new experimental tools with which to investigate the process of hepatocarcinogenesis, improve the diagnosis and treatment of HCC, and hopefully even prevent its occurrence.

ACKNOWLEDGMENTS

This work was supported by Public Health Services Grant AI-20551. A. H. S. is a research fellow of the Medical Research Council of Canada and is the recipient of a Veronica Volk Memorial Postdoctoral Research Fellowship from the American Liver Foundation.

Literature Cited

1. Acs, G., Price, P. M. 1990. Expression of hepatitis B virus DNA sequences in cell culture. Prog. Liver Dis. 9:379–89
2. Aldrich, C. E., Coates, L., Wu, T. T., Newbold, J., Tennant, B. C., et al. 1989. In vitro infection of woodchuck hepatocytes with woodchuck hepatitis virus and ground squirrel hepatitis virus. Virology 172:247–52
3. Aoki, N., Robinson, W. S. 1989. State of hepatitis B viral genomes in cirrhotic and hepatocellular carcinoma nodules. Mol. Biol. Med. 6:395–408
4. Baker, S. J., Fearon, E. R., Nigro, J. M., Hamilton, S. R., Preisinger, A. C., et al. 1989. Chromosome 17 deletions and p53 gene mutations in colorectal carcinomas. Science 244:217–21

5. Bartenschlager, R., Junker-Niepmann, M., Schaller, H. 1990. The P gene product of hepatitis B virus is required as a structural component for genomic RNA encapsidation. J. Virol. 64:5324–32
6. Beasley, R. P., Hwang, L.-Y. 1984. Epidemiology of hepatocellular carcinoma. See Ref. 170a, pp. 209–24
7. Beasley, R. P., Hwang, L.-Y., Lin, C.-C., Chien, C.-S. 1981. Hepatocellular carcinoma and hepatitis B virus. A prospective study of 22,707 men in Taiwan. Lancet 2:1129–32
8. Beasley, R. P., Lin C.-C., Chien, C.-S., Chen, C.-J., Hwang, L.-Y. 1982. Geographic distribution of HBsAg carriers in China. Hepatology 2:553–56
9. Benbrook, D., Lernhardt, E., Pfahl, M.

1988. A new retinoic acid receptor identified from a hepatocellular carcinoma. *Nature* 333:669–72

10. Blanquet, V., Garreau, F., Chenivesse, X., Brechot, C., Turleau, C. 1988. Regional mapping to 4q32.1 by in situ hybridization of a DNA domain rearranged in human liver cancer. *Hum. Genet.* 80:274–76

11. Blum, H. E., Offensperger W. B., Walter, E., Offensperger, S., Wahl, A., et al. 1987. Hepatocellular carcinoma and hepatitis B virus infection: molecular evidence for monoclonal origin and expansion of malignantly transformed hepatocytes. *J. Cancer Res. Clin. Oncol.* 113:466–72

12. Blumberg, B. S., Alter, J. H., Visnich, S. 1965. A "new" antigen in leukemia sera. *J. Am. Med. Assoc.* 191:541–46

13. Bosch, V., Bartenschlager, R., Radziwill, G., Schaller, H. 1988. The duck hepatitis B virus P-gene codes for protein strongly associated with the 5'-end of the viral DNA minus strand. *Virology* 166:475–85

14. Bowcock, A. M., Pinto, M. R., Bey, E., Kuyl, J. M., Dusheiko, G. M., Bernstein, R. 1985. The PLC/PRF/5 human hepatoma cell line. II. Chromosomal assignment of hepatitis B virus integration sites. *Cancer Genet. Cytogenet.* 18:19–26

15. Brechot, C., Degos, F., Lugassy, C., Thiers, V., Zafrani, S., et al. Hepatitis B virus DNA in patients with chronic liver disease and negative tests for hepatitis B surface antigen. *New Engl. J. Med.* 312:270–76

16. Brechot, C., Pourcel, C., Louise, A., Rain, B., Tiollais, P. 1980. Presence of integrated hepatitis B virus DNA sequences in cellular DNA of human hepatocellular carcinoma. *Nature* 286:533–35

17. Bressac, B., Galvin, K., Liang, T. J., Isselbacher, K. J., Wands, J. R., Ozturk, M. 1990. Abnormal structure and expression of p53 gene in human hepatocellular carcinoma. *Proc. Natl. Acad. Sci. USA* 87:1973–77

17a. Bressac, B., Kew, M., Wands, J., Ozturk, M. 1991. Selective G to T mutations of p53 gene in hepatocellular carcinoma from southern Africa. *Nature* 350:429–31

18. Bruix, J., Barrera, J. M., Calvet, X., Ercilla, G., Costa, J., et al. 1989. Prevalence of antibodies to hepatitis C virus in Spanish patients with hepatocellular carcinoma and hepatic cirrhosis. *Lancet* 2:1004–6

19. Capon, D. J., Seeburg, P. H., McGrath, J. P., Hayflick, J. S., Edman, U., et al. 1983. Activation of Ki-*ras* 2 gene in human colon and lung carcinomas by two different point mutations. *Nature* 304:507–13

20. Carnaghan, R. B. A. 1965. Hepatic tumours in ducks fed a low level of toxic groundnut meal. *Nature* 208:308

21. Caselmann, W. H., Meyer, M., Kekule, A. S., Lauer, U., Hofschneider, P. H., Koshy, R. 1990. A trans-activator function is generated by integration of hepatitis B virus *preS/S* sequences in human hepatocellular carcinoma DNA. *Proc. Natl. Acad. Sci. USA* 87:2970–74

22. Cattaneo, R., Will, H., Hernandez, N., Schaller, H. 1983. Signals regulating hepatitis B surface antigen transcription. *Nature* 305:336–38

23. Cavenee, W. K., Dryja, T. P., Phillips, R. A., Benedict, W. F., Godbout, R., et al. 1983. Expression of recessive alleles by chromosomal mechanisms in retinoblastoma. *Nature* 305:779–84

24. Chakraborty, P. R., Ruiz-Opazo, N., Shouval, D., Shafritz, D. A. 1980. Identification of integrated hepatitis B virus DNA and expression of viral RNA in an HBsAg-producing human hepatocellular carcinoma cell line. *Nature* 286:531–33

25. Chang, L.-J., Hirsch, R. C., Ganem, D., Varmus, H. E. 1990. Effects of insertional and point mutations on the functions of the duck hepatitis B virus polymerase. *J. Virol.* 64:5553–58

26. Chen, J. Y., Harrison, T. J., Lee, C. S., Chen, D. S., Zuckerman, A. J. 1988. Detection of hepatitis B virus DNA in hepatocellular carcinoma: analysis by hybridization with subgenomic DNA fragments. *Hepatology* 8:518–23

27. Chen, P. J., Chen, D. S., Lai, M. Y., Chang, M. H., Huang, G. T., et al. 1989. Clonal origin of recurrent hepatocellular carcinomas. *Gastroenterology* 96:527–29

28. Chisari, F. V. 1989. Hepatitis B virus gene expression in transgenic mice. *Mol. Biol. Med.* 6:143–49

29. Chisari, F. V., Filippi, P., Buras, J., McLachlan, A., Popper, H., et al. 1987. Structural and pathological effects of synthesis of hepatitis B virus large envelope polypeptide in transgenic mice. *Proc. Natl. Acad. Sci. USA* 84:6909–13

30. Chisari, F. V., Filippi, P., McLachlan, A., Milich, D. R., Riggs, M., et al. 1986. Expression of hepatitis B virus large envelope polypeptide inhibits hepatitis B surface antigen secretion in transgenic mice. *J. Virol.* 60:880–87

31. Chisari, F. V., Klopchin, K.,

Moriyama, T., Pasquinelli, C., Dunsford, H. A., et al. 1989. Molecular pathogenesis of hepatocellular carcinoma in hepatitis B virus transgenic mice. *Cell* 59:1145–56

32. Choo, K. B., Liu, M. S., Chang, P. C., Wu, S. M., Su, M. W., et al. 1986. Analysis of six distinct integrated hepatitis B virus sequences cloned from the cellular DNA of a human hepatocellular carcinoma. *Virology* 154:405–8

33. Colgrove, R., Simon, G., Ganem, D. 1989. Transcriptional activation of homologous and heterologous genes by the hepatitis B virus X gene product in cells permissive for viral replication. *J. Virol.* 63:4019–26

34. Colombo, M., Kuo, G., Choo, Q. L., Donato, M. F., Del Ninno, E., et al. 1989. Prevalence of antibodies to hepatitis C virus in Italian patients with hepatocellular carcinoma. *Lancet* 2:1006–8

35. Cossart, Y. E., Keirnan, E. 1984. Hepadna viruses of Australian animals (Abstract). See Ref. 170a, p. 647

36. Cross, S. L., Feinberg, M. B., Wolf, J. B., Holbrook, N. J., Wong-Staal, F., Leonard, W. J. 1987. Regulation of the human interleukin-2 receptor alpha chain promoter: activation of a nonfunctional promoter by the transactivator gene of HTLV-1. *Cell* 49:47–56

37. Dejean, A., Bougueleret, L., Grzeschik, K.-H., Tiollais, P. 1986. Hepatitis B virus DNA integration in a sequence homologous to v-erb-A and steroid receptor genes in a hepatocellular carcinoma. *Nature* 322:70–72

38. Dejean, A., Brechot, C., Tiollais, P., Wain-Hobson, S. 1983. Characterization of integrated hepatitis B viral DNA cloned from a human hepatoma and the hepatoma-derived cell line PLC/PRF/5. *Proc. Natl. Acad. Sci. USA* 80:2505–9

39. de The, H., Marchio, A., Tiollais, P., Dejean, A. 1987. A novel steroid thyroid hormone receptor-related gene inappropriately expressed in human hepatocellular carcinoma. *Nature* 330:667–70

40. Edman, J. C., Gray, P., Valenzuela, P., Rall, L. B., Rutter, W. J. 1980. Integration of hepatitis B virus sequences and their expression in a human hepatoma cell. *Nature* 286:535–38

41. Esumi, M., Aritaka, T., Arii, M., Suzuki, K., Tanikawa, K., et al. 1986. Clonal origin of human hepatoma determined by integration of hepatitis B virus DNA. *Cancer Res.* 46:5767–71

42. Feitelson, M. A., Marion, P. L., Robinson, W. S. 1982. Core particles of hepatitis B virus and ground squirrel hepatitis

virus. I. Relationship between hepatitis B core antigen- and ground squirrel hepatitis core antigen-associated polypeptides by sodium dodecyl sulfate-polyacrylamide gel electrophoresis and tryptic peptide mapping. *J. Virol.* 43:687–96

43. Feitelson, M. A., Millman, I., Blumberg, B. S. 1986. Tree squirrel hepatitis B virus: antigenic and structural characterization. *Proc. Natl. Acad. Sci. USA* 83:2994–97

44. Feitelson, M. A., Millman, I., Halbherr, T., Simmons, H., Blumberg, B. S. 1986. A newly identified hepatitis B type virus in tree squirrels. *Proc. Natl. Acad. Sci. USA* 83:2233–37

45. Finlay, C. A., Hinds, P. W., Levine, A. J. 1989. The p53 proto-oncogene can act as a suppressor of transformation. *Cell* 57:1083–93

46. Fourel, G., Trepo, C., Bougueleret, L., Henglein, B., Ponzetto, A., et al. 1990. Frequent activation of N-*myc* genes by hepadnavirus insertion in woodchuck liver tumours. *Nature* 347:294–98

47. Francke, U., Riccardi, V. M. 1979. Aniridia-Wilm's tumor association: evidence for specific deletion of 11p13. *Cytogenet. Cell. Genet.* 23:185–92

48. Frohlich, M., Motte, P., Galvin, K., Takahashi, H., Wands, J., Ozturk, M. 1990. Enhanced expression of the protein kinase substrate p36 in human hepatocellular carcinoma. *Mol. Cell. Biol.* 10:3216–23

49. Frommel, D., Crevat, D., Vitvitsky, L., Pichoud, C., Hantz, O., et al. 1984. Immunopathologic aspects of woodchuck hepatitis. *Am. J. Pathol.* 115:125–34

50. Fu, X. X., Su, C. Y., Lee, Y., Hintz, R., Biempica, L., et al. 1988. Insulin-like growth factor II expression and oval cell proliferation associated with hepatocarcinogenesis in woodchuck hepatitis virus carriers. *J. Virol.* 62:3422–30

51. Fujiyama, A., Miyanohara, A., Nozaki, C., Yoneyama, T., Ohtomo, N., Matsubara, K. 1983. Cloning and structural analyses of hepatitis B virus DNAs, subtype *adr*. *Nucleic Acids Res.* 11:4601–10

52. Galibert, F., Chen, T. N., Mandart, E. 1982. Nucleotide sequence of a cloned woodchuck hepatitis virus genome: comparison with the hepatitis B virus sequence. *J. Med. Virol.* 9:101–9

53. Galibert, F., Mandart, E., Fitoussi, F., Tiollais, P., Charnay, P. 1979. Nucleotide sequence of the hepatitis B virus genome (subtype *ayw*) cloned in *E. coli*. *Nature (London)* 281:646–50

54. Ganem, D., Varmus, H. E. 1987. The molecular biology of the hepatitis B viruses. *Annu. Rev. Biochem.* 56:651–93

55. Ganem, D., Weiser, B., Barchuk, A., Brown, R. J., Varmus, H. E. 1982. Biological characterization of acute infection with ground squirrel hepatitis virus. *J. Virol.* 44:366–73

56. Gerin, J. L., Tennant, B. C., Ponzetto, A., Purcell, R. H., Tyeryar, F. J. 1983. The woodchuck animal model of hepatitis B-like virus infection and disease. *Prog. Clin. Biol. Res.* 143:23

57. Gerlich, W. H., Robinson, W. S. 1980. Hepatitis B virus contains protein attached to the 5' terminus of its complete DNA strand. *Cell* 21:801–9

58. Gripon, P., Diot, C., Theze, N., Fourel, I., Loreal, O., et al. 1988. Hepatitis B virus infection of adult human hepatocytes cultured in the presence of dimethyl sulfoxide. *J. Virol.* 62:4136–43

59. Gu, J.-R., Hu, L.-F., Cheng, Y.-C., Wan, D.-F. 1986. Oncogenes in primary hepatic cancer. *J. Cell. Phys. Supp.* 4:13–20

60. Gudat, F., Bianchi, L., Sonnabend, W., Thiel, G., Aenishaenslin, W., Stalder, G. A. 1975. Pattern of core and surface expression in liver tissue reflects state of specific immune response in hepatitis B. *Lab. Invest.* 32:1–9

61. Heermann, K. H., Goldmann, U., Schwartz, W., Seyffarth, T., Baumgarten, H., Gerlich, W. H. 1984. Large surface proteins of hepatitis B virus containing the pre-s sequence. *J. Virol.* 52:396–402

62. Himeno, Y., Fukuda, Y., Hatanaka, M., Imura, H. 1988. Expression of oncogenes in human liver disease. *Liver* 8:208–12

63. Hinds, P., Finlay, C., Levine, A. J. 1989. Mutation is required to activate the p53 gene for cooperation with the *ras* oncogene and transformation. *J. Virol.* 63:739–46

64. Hino, O., Ohtake, K., Rogler, C. E. 1989. Features of two hepatitis B virus (HBV) DNA integrations suggest mechanisms of HBV integration. *J. Virol.* 63:2638–43

65. Hino, O., Shows, T. B., Rogler, C. E. 1986. Hepatitis B virus integration site in hepatocellular carcinoma at chromosome 17;18 translocation. *Proc. Natl. Acad. Sci. USA* 83:8338–42

66. Hohne, M., Schaefer, S., Seifer, M., Feitelson, M. A., Paul, D., Gerlich, W. H. 1990. Malignant transformation of immortalized transgenic hepatocytes after transfection with hepatitis B virus DNA. *EMBO J.* 9:1137–45

67. Hoofnagle, J. H., Shafritz, D. A., Popper, H. 1987. Chronic type B hepatitis and the "healthy" HBsAg carrier state. *Hepatology* 7:758–63

67a. Hsu, I. C., Metcalf, R. A., Sun, T., Welsh, J. A., Wang, N. J., et al. 1991. Mutational hotspot in the p53 gene in human hepatocellular carcinomas. *Nature* 350:328–28

68. Hsu, T.-Y., Moroy, T., Etiemble, J., Louise, A., Trepo, C., et al. 1988. Activation of c-*myc* by woodchuck hepatitis virus insertion in hepatocellular carcinoma. *Cell* 55:627–35

69. Huber, B. E., Dearfield, K. L., Williams, J. R., Heilman, C. A., Thorgeirsson, S. S. 1985. Tumorigenicity and transcriptional modulation of c-*myc* and N-*ras* oncogenes in a human hepatoma cell line. *Cancer Res.* 45:4322–29

70. Kay, A., Mandart, E., Trepo, C., Galibert, F. 1985. The HBV HBX gene expressed in *E. coli* is recognised by sera from hepatitis patients. *EMBO J.* 4:1287–92

71. Kekule, A. S., Lauer, U., Meyer, M., Caselmann, W. H., Hofschneider, P. H., Koshy, R. 1990. The *preS2/S* region of integrated hepatitis B virus DNA encodes a transcriptional transactivator. *Nature* 343:457–61

72. Kew, M. C. 1986. The development of hepatocellular cancer in humans. *Cancer Surv.* 5:719–39

73. Kew, M. C., Houghton, M., Choo, Q. L., Kuo, G. 1990. Hepatitis C virus antibodies in southern African blacks with hepatocellular carcinoma. *Lancet* 335:873–74

74. Koch, S., von Loringhoven, A. F., Kahmann, R., Hofschneider, P. H., Koshy, R. 1984. The genetic organization of integrated hepatitis B virus DNA in the human hepatoma cell line PLC/PRF/5. *Nucleic Acids Res* 12:6871–86

75. Korba, B. E., Wells, F. V., Baldwin, B., Cote, P. J., Tennant, B. C., et al. 1989. Hepatocellular carcinoma in woodchuck hepatitis virus-infected woodchucks: presence of viral DNA in tumor tissue from chronic carriers and animals serologically recovered from acute infections. *Hepatology* 9:461–70

76. Koshy, R., Hofschneider, P. H. 1989. Transactivation by hepatitis B virus may contribute to hepatocarcinogenesis. *Curr. Top. Microbiol. Immunol.* 144:265–81

77. Land, H., Parada, L. F., Weinberg, R.

A. 1983. Cellular oncogenes and multi-step carcinogenesis. *Science.* 222:771–78

78. Laub, O., Treinin, M. 1987. Identification of a promoter element located upstream from the hepatitis B virus X gene. *Mol. Cell. Biol.* 7:545–48
79. Leder, P., Battey, J., Lenoir, G., Moulding, C., Murphy, W., et al. 1983. Translocations among antibody genes in human cancer. *Science* 222:765–71
80. Lee, H.-S., Rajagopalan, M. S., Vyas, G. N. 1988. A lack of direct role of hepatitis B virus in the activation of *ras* and c-*myc* oncogenes in human hepatocellular carcinogenesis. *Hepatology* 8:1116–20
81. Lee, T.-H., Finegold, M. J., Shen, R.-F., DeMayo, J. L., Woo, S. L. C., Butel, J. S. 1990. Hepatitis B virus *trans*activator X protein is not tumorigenic in transgenic mice. *J. Virol.* 64:5939–47
82. Lisker-Melman, M., Martin, P., Hoofnagle, J. H. 1989. Conditions associated with hepatocellular carcinoma. *Med. Clin. North Am.* 73:999–1009
83. Lohiya, G. S., Pirkle, H., Nguyen, H., Lohiya, S., Vuu, T. 1988. Hepatocellular carcinoma in hepatitis B surface antigen carriers in eight institutions. *West. J. Med.* 148:426–29
84. Loncarevic, I. F., Schranz, P., Zentgraf, H., Liang, X. H., Herrmann, G., et al. 1990. Replication of hepatitis B virus in a hepatocellular carcinoma. *Virology* 174:158–68
85. Makino, R., Hayashi, K., Sato, S., Sugimura, T. 1984. Expression of the c-Ha-*ras* and c-*myc* genes in rat liver tumors. *Biochem. Biophys. Res. Commun.* 119:1096–1102
86. Mandart, E., Kay, A., Galibert, F. 1984. Nucleotide sequence of a cloned duck hepatitis B virus genome: comparison with woodchuck and human hepatitis B virus sequences. *J. Virol.* 49:782–92
87. Marion, P. L. 1988. Use of animal models to study hepatitis B virus. *Prog. Med. Virol.* 35:43–75
88. Marion, P. L., Cullen, J. M., Azcarraga, R. R., Van Davelaar, M. J., Robinson, W. S. 1987. Experimental transmission of duck hepatitis B virus to Pekin ducks and to domestic geese. *Hepatology* 7:724–31
89. Marion, P. L., Knight, S. S., Ho, B. K., Guo, Y. Y., Robinson, W. S., Popper, H. 1984. Liver disease associated with duck hepatitis B virus infection of domestic ducks. *Proc. Natl. Acad. Sci. USA* 81:898–902

90. Marion, P. L., Knight, S. S., Salazar, F. H., Popper, H., Robinson, W. S. 1983. Ground squirrel hepatitis virus infection. *Hepatology* 3:519–27
91. Marion, P. L., Oshiro, L. S., Regnery, D. C., Scullard, G. H., Robinson, W. S. 1980. A virus in Beechey ground squirrels that is related to hepatitis B virus of humans. *Proc. Natl. Acad. Sci. USA* 77:2941–45
92. Marion, P. L., Popper, H., Azcarraga, R. R., Steevens, C., Van Davelaar, M. J., et al. 1987. Ground squirrel hepatitis virus and hepatocellular carcinoma. In *Hepadna Viruses,* ed. W. Robinson, K. Koike, H. Will, pp. 337–48. New York: Liss
93. Marion, P. L., Robinson, W. S. 1983. Hepadna viruses: hepatitis B and related viruses. *Curr. Top. Microbiol. Immunol.*105:99–121
94. Marion, P. L., Salazar, F. H., Alexander, J. J., Robinson, W. S. 1980. State of hepatitis B viral DNA in a human hepatoma cell line. *J. Virol.* 33:795–806
95. Mason, W. S., Aldrich, C., Summers, J., Taylor, J. M. 1982. Asymmetric replication of duck hepatitis B virus DNA in liver cells: Free minus-strand DNA. *Proc. Natl. Acad. Sci. USA* 79:3997–4001
96. Mason, W. S., Halpern, M. S., England, J. M., Seal, G., Egan, J., et al. 1983. Experimental transmission of duck hepatitis B virus. *Virology* 131:375–84
97. Mason, W. S., Seal, G., Summers, J. 1980. Virus of Pekin ducks with structural and biological relatedness to human hepatitis B virus. *J. Virol.* 36:829–36
98. Matsumoto, H., Yoneyama, T., Mitamura, K., Osuga, T., Shimojo, H., Miyamura, T. 1988. Analysis of integrated hepatitis B virus DNA and cellular flanking sequences cloned from hepatocellular carcinoma. *Int. J. Cancer* 42:1–6
99. McMahon, B. J., Alberts, S. R., Wainwright, R. B., Bulkow, L., Lanier, A. P. 1990. Heptatitis B-related sequelae. Prospective study in 1400 hepatitis B surface antigen-positive Alaska native carriers. *Arch. Int. Med.* 150:1051–54
100. Meyers, M. L., Trepo, L. V., Nath, N., Sninsky, J. J. 1986. Hepatitis B polypeptide X: expression in *Escherichia coli* and identification of specific antibodies in sera from hepatitis B virus-infected humans. *J. Virol.* 57:101–9
101. Miller, R. H., Marion, P. L., Robinson, W. S. 1984. Hepatitis B viral DNA-

RNA hybrid molecules in particles from infected liver are converted to viral DNA molecules during an endogenous DNA polymerase reaction. *Virology* 139:64–72

102. Miller, R. H., Robinson, W. S. 1986. Common evolutionary origin of hepatitis B virus and retroviruses. *Proc. Natl. Acad. Sci. USA* 83:2531–35

103. Miyaki, M., Sato, C., Gotanda, T., Matsui, T., Mishiro, S., et al. 1986. Integration of region X of hepatitis B virus genome in human primary hepatocellular carcinomas. *J. Gen. Virol.* 67:1449–54

104. Mizusawa, H., Taira, M., Yaginuma, K., Kobayashi, M., Yoshida, E., Koike, K. 1985. Inversely repeating integrated hepatitis B virus DNA and cellular flanking sequences in the human hepatoma-derived cell line huSP. *Proc. Natl. Acad. Sci. USA* 82:208–12

105. Moriarty, A. M., Alexander, H., Lerner, R. A., Thornton, G. B. 1985. Antibodies to peptides detect new hepatitis B antigen: serological correlation with hepatocellular carcinoma. *Science* 227:429–33

106. Morizane, T., Nakamura, T., Saito, H., Watanabe, T., Inagaki, Y., et al. 1987. Transformation of NIH/3T3 cells with DNA from a human hepatoma cell line with integrated hepatitis B virus DNA. *Eur. J. Cancer Clin. Oncol.* 23:163–69

107. Moroy, T., Marchio, A., Etiemble, J., Trepo, C., Tiollais, P., Buendia, M. A. 1986. Rearrangement and enhanced expression of c-*myc* in hepatocellular carcinoma of hepatitis virus infected woodchucks. *Nature* 324:276–79

108. Muchmore, E., Popper, H., Peterson, D. A., Miller, M. F., Lieberman, H. M. 1988. Non-A, Non-B hepatitis-related hepatocellular carcinoma in a chimpanzee. *J. Med. Primatol.* 17:235–46

109. Muchmore, E., Socha, W. W., Krawczynski, C. 1990. HCC in chimpanzees. In *Viral Hepatitis and Hepatocellular Carcinoma*, ed. J.-L. Sung, D.-S. Chen, pp. 698–702. Hong Kong: Exerpta Medica

110. Nagaya, T., Nakamura, T., Tokino, T., Tsurimoto, T., Imai, M., et al. 1987. The mode of hepatitis B virus DNA integration in chromosomes of human hepatocellular carcinoma. *Genes Dev.* 1: 773–82

111. Neel, B. G., Hayward, W. S., Robinson, H. L., Fang, J., Astrin, S. M. 1981. Avian leukosis virus-induced tumors have common proviral integration sites and synthesize discrete new RNAs: oncogenesis by promoter insertion. *Cell* 23:323–34

112. Nerenberg, M., Hinrichs, S. H., Reynolds, R. K., Khoury, G., Jay, G. 1987. The *tat* gene of human T-lymphotrophic virus type 1 induces mesenchymal tumors in transgenic mice. *Science* 237:1324–29

113. Nonamura, A., Ohta, G., Hayashi, M., Izumi, R., Watanabe, K., et al. 1987. Immunohistochemical detection of *ras* oncogene p21 product in liver cirrhosis and hepatocellular carcinoma. *Am. J. Gastroenterol.* 82:512–18

114. Obata, H., Hayashi, H., Motoike, Y., Hisamitsu, T., Okuda, H., et al. 1980. A prospective study on the development of hepatocellular carcinoma from liver cirrhosis with persistent hepatitis B infection. *Int. J. Cancer* 25:741–47

115. Ochiya, T., Fujiyama, A., Fukushige, S., Hatada, I., Matsubara, K. 1986. Molecular cloning of an oncogene from a human hepatocellular carcinoma. *Proc. Natl. Acad. Sci. USA* 83:4993–97

116. Ochiya, T., Tsurimoto, T., Ueda, K., Okubo, K., Shiozawa, M., Matsubara, K. 1989. An in vitro system for infection with hepatitis B virus that uses primary human fetal hepatocytes. *Proc. Natl. Acad. Sci. USA* 86:1875–79

117. Ogston, C. W., Jonak, G. J., Rogler, C. E., Astrin, S. M., Summers, J. 1982. Cloning and structural analysis of integrated woodchuck hepatitis virus sequences from hepatocellular carcinomas of woodchucks. *Cell* 29:385–94

118. Omata, M., Uchiumi, K., Ito, Y., Yokosuka, O., Mori, J., et al. 1983. Duck hepatitis B virus and liver diseases. *Gastroenterology* 85:260–67

119. Pasek, M., Goto, T., Gilbert, W., Zink, B., Schaller, H., et al. 1979. Hepatitis B virus genes and their expression in E. *coli. Nature (London)* 282:575–79

120. Payet, M., Camain, R., Pene, P. 1956. Le cancer primitif du foie, etude critique a propos de 240 cas. *Rev. Int. Hepatol.* 4:1–20

121. Persing, D. H., Varmus, H. E., Ganem, D. 1986. Antibodies to pre-S and X determinants arise during natural infection with ground squirrel hepatitis virus. *J. Virol.* 60:177–84

122. Ponzetto, A., Cote, P. J., Ford, E. C., Engle, R., Cicmanec, J., et al. 1985. Radioimmunoassay and characterization of woodchuck hepatitis virus core antigen and antibody. *Virus Res.* 2:301–15

123. Popper, H., Roth, L., Purcell, R. H., Tennant, B. C., Gerin, J. L. 1987.

Hepatocarcinogenicity of the woodchuck hepatitis virus. *Proc. Natl. Acad. Sci. USA* 84:866–70

124. Popper, H., Shih, J. W., Gerin, J. L., Wong, D. C., Hoyer, B. H., et al. 1981. Woodchuck hepatitis and hepatocellular carcinoma: correlation of histologic with virologic observations. *Hepatology* 1: 91–98

125. Pugh, J., Zweidler, A., Summers, J. 1989. Characterization of the major duck hepatitis B virus core particle protein. *J. Virol.* 63:1371–76

126. Raimondo, G., Burk, R. D., Lieberman, H. M., Muschel, J., Hadziyannis, S. J., et al. 1988. Interrupted replication of hepatitis B virus in liver tissue of HBsAg carriers with hepatocellular carcinoma. *Virology* 166:103–12

127. Rall, L. B., Standring, D. N., Laub, O., Rutter, W. J. 1983. Transcription of hepatitis B virus by RNA polymerase II. *Mol. Cell. Biol.* 3:1766–73

128. Reynolds, S. H., Stowers, S. J., Maronpot, R. R., Anderson, M. W., Aaronson, S. A. 1986. Detection and identification of activated oncogenes in spontaneously occurring benign and malignant hepatocellular tumors of the B6C3F1 mouse. *Proc. Natl. Acad. Sci. USA* 83:33–37

129. Robinson, W. S. 1984. Hepatitis B virus. In *Principles and Practice of Infectious Diseases*, ed. G. L. Mandell, R. G. Douglas, J. E. Bennett, pp. 1204–31. New York: Wiley

130. Robinson, W. S., Klote, L., Aoki, N. 1990. Hepadnaviruses in cirrhotic liver and hepatocellular carcinoma. *J. Med. Virol.* 31:18–32

131. Robinson, W. S., Marion, P. L. 1988. Biological features of hepadna viruses. In *Viral Hepatitis and Liver Disease*, ed. A. J. Zuckerman, pp. 449–58. New York: Liss

132. Rochlitz, C. F., Benz, C. C. 1984. Oncogenes in human solid tumors. In *Oncogenes*, ed. C. Benz, E. Liu, pp. 199–240. Boston: Kluwer Academic

133. Rogler, C. E., Sherman, M., Su, C. Y., Shafritz, D. A., Summers, J., et al. 1985. Deletion of chromosome 11p associated with a hepatitis B integration site in hepatocellular carcinoma. *Science* 230:319–22

134. Rogler, C. E., Summers, J. 1984. Cloning and structural analysis of integrated woodchuck hepatitis virus sequences from a chronically infected liver. *J. Virol.* 50:832–37

135. Roingeard, P., Romet-Lemonne, J.-L., Leturcq, D., Goudeau, A., Essex, M. 1990. Hepatitis B virus core antigen

(HBcAg) accumulation in an HBV nonproducer clone of HepG2-transfected cells is associated with cytopathic effect. *Virology* 179:113–20

136. Roth, L., King, J. M., Hornbuckle, W. E., Harvey, H. J., Tennant, B. C. 1985. Chronic hepatitis and hepatocellular carcinoma associated with persistent woodchuck hepatitis virus infection. *Vet. Pathol.* 22:338–43

137. Rous, P. 1911. Transmission of a malignant new growth by means of a cell free filtrate. *J. Am. Med. Assoc.* 56:198

138. Saito, I., Miyamura, T., Ohbayashi, A., Harada, H., Katayama, T., et al. 1990. Hepatitis C virus infection is associated with the development of hepatocellular carcinoma. *Proc. Natl. Acad. Sci. USA* 87:6547–49

138a. Sambamurti, K., Callahan, J., Luo, X., Perkins, C. P., Jacobsen, J. S., et al. 1988. Mechanisms of mutagenesis by a bulky DNA lesion at the guanine G7 position. *Genetics* 120:863–73

139. Schwab, M., Alitalo, K., Varmus, H. E., Bishop, J. M., George, D. 1983. A cellular oncogene (c-Ki-*ras*) is amplified, overexpressed, and located within karyotypic abnormalities in mouse adrenocortical tumour cells. *Nature* 303: 497–501

139a. Seeger, C., Baldwin, B., Hornbuckle, W. E., Yeager, A. E., Tennant, B. C., et al. 1991. Woodchuck hepatitis virus is a more efficient oncogenic agent than ground squirrel hepatitis virus in a common host. *J. Virol.* 65:1673–79

140. Seeger, C., Ganem, D., Varmus, H. E. 1984. Nucleotide sequence of an infectious molecularly cloned genome of ground squirrel hepatitis virus. *J. Virol.* 51:367–75

141. Sells, M. A., Chen, M. L., Acs, G. 1987. Production of hepatitis B virus particles in HepG2 cells transfected with cloned hepatitis B virus DNA. *Proc. Natl. Acad. Sci. USA* 84:1005–9

142. Setoguchi, M., Higuchi, Y., Yoshida, S., Nasu, N., Miyazaki, Y., et al. 1989. Insertional activation of N-*myc* by endogenous Moloney-like murine retrovirus sequences in macrophage cell lines derived from myeloma cell line–macrophage hybrids. *Mol. Cell. Biol.* 9:4515–22

143. Shaul, Y., Garcia, P. D., Schonberg, S., Rutter, W. J. 1986. Integration of hepatitis B virus DNA in chromosome-specific satellite sequences. *J. Virol.* 59:731–34

144. Shaul, Y., Rutter, W. J., Laub, O. 1985. A human hepatitis B viral enhancer element. *EMBO J.* 4:427–30

145. Sherlock, S., Fox, R. A., Niazi, S. P., Scheuer, P. J. 1970. Chronic liver disease and primary liver-cell cancer with hepatitis-associated (Australia) antigen in serum. *Lancet* 1:1243–47

146. Shih, C., Li, L.-S., Roychoudhury, S., Ho, M.-H. 1989. In vitro propagation of human hepatitis B virus in a rat hepatoma cell line. *Proc. Natl. Acad. Sci. USA* 86:6323–27

147. Shirakata, Y., Kawada, M., Fujiki, Y., Sano, H., Oda, M., et al. 1989. The X gene of hepatitis B virus induced growth stimulation and tumorigenic transformation of mouse NIH3T3 cells. *Jpn. J. Cancer Res.* 80:617–21

148. Shope, R. 1933. Infectious papillomatosis of rabbits. *J. Exp. Med.* 58:607–24

149. Spandau, D. F., Lee, C. H. 1988. Trans-activation of viral enhancers by the hepatitis B virus X protein. *J. Virol.* 62:427–34

150. Sprengel, R., Kaleta, E. F., Will, H. 1988. Isolation and characterization of a hepatitis B virus endemic in herons. *J. Virol.* 62:3832–39

151. Stanbridge, E. J. 1990. Identifying tumor suppressor genes in human colorectal cancer. *Science* 247:12–13

152. Steiner, P. E., Davies, J. N. 1957. Cirrhosis and primary liver cancer in Uganda Africans. *Br. J. Cancer* 11:523–34

153. Stibbe, W., Gerlich, W. H. 1983. Structural relationships between minor and major proteins of hepatitis B surface antigen. *J. Virol.* 46:626–28

154. Summers, J., Mason, W. S. 1982. Replication of the genome of a hepatitis B-like virus by reverse transcription of an RNA intermediate. *Cell* 29:403–15

155. Summers, J., Smolec, J. M., Snyder, R. 1978. A virus similar to human hepatitis B virus associated with hepatitis and hepatoma in woodchucks. *Proc. Natl. Acad. Sci. USA* 75:4533–37

156. Sureau, C., Romet-Lemonne, J.-L., Mullins, J. I., Essex, M. 1986. Production of hepatitis B virus by a differentiated human hepatoma cell line after transfection with cloned circular HBV DNA. *Cell* 47:37–47

157. Szmuness, W. 1978. Hepatocellular carcinoma and the hepatitis B virus: Evidence for a causal association. *Prog. Med. Virol.* 24:40–69

158. Tagawa, M., Omata, M., Yokosuka, O., Uchiumi, K., Imazeki, F., Okuda, K. 1985. Early events in duck hepatitis B virus infection. Sequential appearance of viral deoxyribonucleic acid in the liver, pancreas, kidney, and spleen. *Gastroenterology* 89:1224–29

159. Takada, S., Koike, K. 1990. Transactivation function of a 3' truncated X gene–cell fusion product from integrated hepatitis B virus DNA in chronic hepatitis tissues. *Proc. Natl. Acad. Sci. USA* 87:5628–32

160. Toh, H., Hayashida, H., Miyata, T. 1983. Sequence homology between retroviral reverse transcriptase and putative polymerases of hepatitis B virus and cauliflower mosaic virus. *Nature* 305: 827–29

161. Tokino, T., Fukushige, S., Nakamura, T., Nagaya, T., Murotsu, T., et al. 1987. Chromosomal translocation and inverted duplication associated with integrated hepatitis B virus in hepatocellular carcinomas. *J. Virol.* 61: 3848–54

162. Tur-Kaspa, R., Burk, R. D., Shaul, Y., Shafritz, D. A. 1986. Hepatitis B virus DNA contains a glucocorticoid-responsive element. *Proc. Natl. Acad. Sci. USA* 83:1627–31

163. Tuttleman, J. S., Pourcel, C., Summers, J. 1986. Formation of the pool of covalently closed circular viral DNA in hepadnavirus-infected cells. *Cell* 47: 451–60

164. Tuttleman, J. S., Pugh, J. C., Summers, J. W. 1986. In vitro experimental infection of primary duck hepatocyte cultures with duck hepatitis B virus. *J. Virol.* 58:17–25

165. Twu, J. S., Robinson, W. S. 1989. Hepatitis B virus X gene can transactivate heterologous viral sequences. *Proc. Natl. Acad. Sci. USA* 86:2046–50

166. Twu, J.-S., Schloemer, R. H. 1987. Transcriptional trans-activating function of hepatitis B virus. *J. Virol.* 61:3448–53

167. Twu, J.-S., Schloemer, R. H. 1989. Transcription of the human beta interferon gene is inhibited by hepatitis B virus. *J. Virol.* 63:3065–71

168. Tyler, G. V., Snyder, R. L., Summers, J. 1986. Experimental infection of the woodchuck (*Marmota monax monax*) with woodchuck hepatitis virus. *Lab. Invest.* 55:51–55

169. van Lohuizen, M., Breuer, M., Berns, A. 1989. N-*myc* is frequently activated by proviral insertion in MuLV-induced T cell lymphomas. *EMBO J.* 8:133–36

170. Vogel, J., Hinrichs, S. H., Reynolds, R. K., Luciw, P. A., Jay, G. 1988. The HIV *tat* gene induces dermal lesions re-

sembling Kaposi's sarcoma in transgenic mice. *Nature* 235:606–11

170a. Vyas, G. H., Dienstag, J. L., Hoofnagle, J. H., eds. 1984. *Viral Hepatitis and Liver Disease*. Orlando, FL: Grune & Stratton

171. Wang, H. P., Rogler, C. E. 1988. Deletions in human chromosome arms 11p and 13q in primary hepatocellular carcinomas. *Cytogenet. Cell Genet.* 48:72–78

172. Wang, J., Chenivesse, X., Henglein, B., Brechot, C. 1990. Hepatitis B virus integration in a cyclin A gene in a hepatocellular carcinoma. *Nature* 343:555–57

173. Weiser, B., Ganem, D., Seeger, C., Varmus, H. E. 1983. Closed circular viral DNA and asymmetrical heterogeneous forms in livers from animals infected with ground squirrel hepatitis virus. *J. Virol.* 48:1–9

173a. World Health Organization. 1990. WHO reports decry neglect of world health problems. *ASM News* 56:358–59

174. Wong, D. T., Nath, N., Sninsky, J. J. 1985. Identification of hepatitis B virus polypeptides encoded by the entire pre-s open reading frame. *J. Virol.* 55:223–31

175. Wu, J. Y., Zhou, Z.-Y., Judd, A., Cartwright, C. A., Robinson, W. S. 1990. The hepatitis B virus-encoded transcriptional transactivator hbx appears to be a novel protein serine/threonine kinase. *Cell* 63:687–95

176. Wu, T. C., Tong, M. J., Hwang, B., Lee, S.-D., Hu, M. M. 1987. Primary hepatocellular carcinoma and hepatitis B infection during childhood. *Hepatology* 7:46–48

177. Yaginuma, K., Kobayashi, M., Yoshida, E., Koike, K. 1985. Hepatitis B virus integration in hepatocellular carci-

noma DNA: duplication of cellular flanking sequences at the integration site. *Proc. Natl. Acad. Sci. USA* 82:4458–62

178. Yaginuma, K., Koike, K. 1989. Identification of a promoter region for 3.6-kilobase mRNA of hepatitis B virus and specific cellular binding protein. *J. Virol.* 63:2914–20

179. Yamamoto, K. R. 1985. Steroid receptor regulated transcription of specific genes and gene networks. *Annu. Rev. Genet.* 19:209–52

180. Yamamura, K., Araki, K. 1989. Transgenic mice as tools in the study of HBV-related liver diseases. *Cell Struct. Funct.* 14:509–13

181. Yee, J.-K. 1989. A liver-specific enhancer in the core promoter region of human hepatitis B virus. *Science* 246:658–61

182. Yokosuka, O., Omata, M., Zhou, Y. Z., Imazeki, F., Okuda, K. 1985. Duck hepatitis B virus DNA in liver and serum of Chinese ducks: integration of viral DNA in a hepatocellular carcinoma. *Proc. Natl. Acad. Sci. USA* 82:5180–84

183. Zhai, W.-R., Paronetto, F. 1989. Relationship between c-*myc* gene protein, nucleic acids and hepatitis B virus expression in hepatoma cell lines and their corresponding tumors in nude mice. *J. Exp. Path.* 4:213–25

184. Zhou, Y. Z., Slagle, B. L., Donehower, L. A., vanTuinen, P., Ledbetter, D. H., Butel, J. S. 1988. Structural analysis of a hepatitis B virus genome integrated into chromosome 17p of a human hepatocellular carcinoma. *J. Virol.* 62:4224–31

185. Ziemer, M., Garcia, P., Shaul, Y., Rutter, W. J. 1985. Sequence of hepatitis B virus DNA incorporated into the genome of a human hepatoma cell line. *J. Virol.* 53:885–92

Annu. Rev. Microbiol. 1991. 45:509–38

MECHANISMS OF NATURAL RESISTANCE TO HUMAN PATHOGENIC FUNGI

Juneann W. Murphy

Department of Microbiology and Immunology, University of Oklahoma Health Sciences Center, Oklahoma City, Oklahoma 73190

KEY WORDS: mycoses, resistance to mycotic agents, NK cells against fungi, PMN against fungi, monocytes/macrophages against fungi, host defenses

CONTENTS

INTRODUCTION.. 509
HOST-PARASITE INTERACTIONS IN FUNGAL DISEASES.......................... 510
    General Information Regarding Fungi and Fungal Diseases.......................... 510
    Host Factors That Affect Mycotic Diseases... 513
PHYSICAL, MECHANICAL, AND CHEMICAL BARRIERS TO INFECTION
    WITH PATHOGENIC FUNGI... 516
CELLULAR RESISTANCE MECHANISMS.. 517
    Phagocytic Cells—Professional... 518
    Phagocytic Cells—Nonprofessional.. 526
    Nonphagocytic Natural Effector Cells... 527
    Interactions of Natural Effector Cells... 531
SUMMARY... 531

INTRODUCTION

Effective host defense against mycotic disease-causing agents depends upon a combination of multiple mechanisms that include both natural and immune defensive measures. The array of host resistance mechanisms that participate in clearing the infection vary from one mycotic disease to another; therefore,

509

0066-4227/91/1001-0509$02.00

one cannot make sweeping assertions concerning host defenses against mycotic diseases. In fact, generalized statements frequently convey mistaken impressions, so this review, under each resistance mechanism, provides specific examples of mycotic diseases that are influenced by that specific mechanism. Although this review focuses primarily on natural or innate defensive measures that prevent establishment of a fungal infection or eliminate the organisms once they have colonized or infected the tissues, the reader should keep in mind that immune or acquired defenses are important and at times essential in preventing a fatal outcome of the mycotic disease.

Natural or innate defenses are defined as those resistance mechanisms that do not require induction and do not display specificity. They include (a) physical barriers such as the skin and mucous membranes; (b) chemical barriers such as the secretions, serum factors, and chemical components found in certain tissues; and (c) the natural effector (phagocytic and nonphagocytic) cells. The natural resistance mechanisms may be governed by the genetic characteristics of the individual, by hormonal factors, and by the general health and immune status of the host.

Natural or innate host defenses are important contributors to effective host resistance against all fungal agents, and in some cases, natural defenses are essential, but frequently not sufficient, for complete protection against fungal disease. The antifungal activities of natural defenses, especially the activities of the natural effector cells, can be augmented by immune mechanisms making the natural defenses essential players in the immune component of host defense.

HOST-PARASITE INTERACTIONS IN FUNGAL DISEASES

Typically, the factors that affect host-parasite interactions in any infection can be subdivided into two major categories. One is comprised of those features of the organism that allow it to enter the host tissues and cause disease, and the other category contains the features of the host that either limit the infectious agent or allow the infectious agent to remain and multiply in the host. Such features that favor the organism include a lack of infiltrating host cells that can kill the organism and the provision in specific tissues of essential nutrients or growth factors for the organism. In mycotic diseases, as with diseases caused by other types of agents, the outcome of the disease is based on the relative effectiveness of the fungal and host factors in play during the disease process.

General Information Regarding Fungi and Fungal Diseases

Mycotic disease-causing agents are complex eukaryotic organisms that do not segregate into any one taxonomic group but rather are scattered broadly through the kingdom Mycota (93). The majority of fungal species that cause disease in humans are saprophytic organisms, and only those that can adapt to the temperature of the human body and survive in the environment provided by living tissue are threatening pathogens to the human host (118). *Candida albicans,* the organism that causes the most frequently encountered mycotic disease (candidiasis) in humans is one of the few fungi found in the normal flora of humans. The saprophytic mycotic agents that cause disease in humans occasionally cause problems in "normal" individuals; however, most saprophytic mycotic agents are opportunistic and cause infection only when the host is compromised in some way. The dimorphic fungi, such as *Histoplasma capsulatum, Coccidioides immitis, Blastomyces dermatitidis, Paracoccidioides brasiliensis,* and *Sporothrix schenckii,* which have a normal habitat in soil or are associated with vegetation, are good examples of organisms that have adapted to survive in the human host. These latter organisms grow well in the saprophytic form at 25°C, but by changing form can also exist effectively in living tissue at 37°C. The ability of the dimorphic organisms to transform into a parasitic stage allows the dimorphic organisms to produce the most serious systemic mycotic diseases in humans. In contrast, dermatophytes, the fungi that cause less serious infections of the skin, hair, and nails, are filamentous at both 25°C and 37°C. In fact, the optimal temperature for growth of most dermatophytes is 25°C, and typically, the dermatophytes colonize only the outer dead layers of the skin, hair, and nails where the temperature may be slightly below body temperature. The limited ability of the dermatophytes to cause disease in viable tissues may, in part, result from their inability to adapt by converting to alternative growth forms.

Many of the fungi gain entrance into the human host by taking advantage of weaknesses in or damage to the outer protective surfaces of the body, such as the skin or mucous membranes, whereas other mycotic agents enter the body by being inhaled into the lung alveoli. Superficial fungal infections and dermatophytoses are examples of diseases that are acquired because of alterations in the normal skin secretions, flora, or integrity. Mucocutaneous or cutaneous infections such as those caused by *C. albicans,* an endogenous organism, occur when natural host defenses, normal flora, or host physiology are disrupted. Subcutaneous mycotic diseases, such as chromomycosis, mycetoma, and sporotrichosis, are acquired by traumatic implantation of saprophytic mycotic organisms into the tissue, while the most serious systemic mycotic diseases (histoplasmosis, coccidioidomycosis, blastomycosis, paracoccidioidomycosis, and cryptococcosis) are acquired through inhalation of the infectious fungal particles. The array and effectiveness of the natural defenses at the entry site of the fungus are extremely important in determining whether the organism is restricted to that tissue or whether the fungus disseminates to other areas of the body. Since natural host resistance mechanisms vary among different tissues, the route of entry of the mycotic agent will bias the array of natural defenses that confront the entering fungus. Generally, the regional host defenses can limit the fungal infections to superficial, cutaneous, or subcutaneous tissues. The main exceptions to this rule occur with the fungi that enter through the respiratory route.

Fungi are not usually invasive organisms (118), although some produce enzymes that may enhance their ability to cause disease. For example, dermatophytes produce keratinases that allow them to penetrate the stratum corneum (129). C. albicans and C. immitis produce proteinases that may enhance their virulence (81, 147). Characteristically, fungi cause disease by taking advantage of weaknesses in the host's repertoire of defensive mechanisms or they evade or overwhelm host defenses. Although some pathogenic fungi can cause serious disease in apparently normal individuals, and thus are considered primary pathogens, most mycotic agents that infect humans are opportunistic pathogens because they only infect individuals who are immunologically compromised or debilitated by other conditions. Natural host resistance mechanisms contribute significantly in protecting against the opportunistic fungi, and though important, natural defenses play a lesser role in protection against the primary fungal pathogens. The natural resistance mechanisms form the host's first-line defenses, and under conditions of normal exposure to a fungal pathogen, these defenses generally can significantly reduce or completely eliminate the population of infectious particles. If, on the other hand, the natural defenses fail to clear the organism by the time the immune responses against the etiological agent become active, then the second-line defenses, the immune mechanisms, begin to function in limiting dissemination of the infectious agent or in completely eliminating it. Frequently, the combined host defenses are sufficient to contain the disease in the tissue that originally encountered the organism. However, if first- and second-line defenses fail or if the host is initially exposed to a large number of infective particles of a pathogenic fungus that overwhelms the host's natural defenses before the immune responses develop sufficiently to aid in protection, the organisms can become disseminated and cause progressive disease. In some instances, a minimal number of infectious particles can initiate progressive disease, if the pathogenic fungus has acquired ways of evading the natural host defensive mechanisms. Should the defensive repertoire of the host have generalized serious weaknesses, the host may succumb to the systemic infection even when the disease is being treated aggressively with antifungal drugs. This latter fact suggests that researchers should consider developing the means by which the host's natural and immune defenses can be reconstituted or augmented because such replacement or augmenting therapies may hold the most promise for successful treatment of the life-threatening fungal diseases.

The morphological characteristics and size of fungi present a challenge to host defensive mechanisms. Fungi can be unicellular or multicellular organisms (118). The multicellular or filamentous forms often produce spores that are very resistant to adverse environmental conditions and thus may not be damaged by some of the basic host defenses. Fungal cells are large in comparison to bacterial cells; therefore, the fungi are not as readily eliminated from host tissues by phagocytic cells as bacteria are. The large size of fungi contributes to the fact that the phagocytic cells have frequently been observed to kill fungal organisms through extracellular mechanisms (34, 121). In addition to having a size and shape that makes phagocytosis difficult, fungal cells are protected by relatively thick cell walls made of chitin with polymers of α- or β-glucan, mannan, galactose, and/or galactosamine (118). Some of the fungi have coverings over the cell wall, and those outer layers protect the organism from some of the natural host defenses. For example, *C. neoformans* blastoconidia have a large capsule comprised of high-molecular-weight polysaccharides that resist phagocytosis (76, 97), and *C. albicans* blastoconidia and hyphae have a mucous cell wall coat that may affect adherence to host cells and phagocytosis of the fungus by host cells (48).

Host Factors That Affect Mycotic Diseases

GENETIC PREDISPOSITION OF THE HOST TO FUNGAL DISEASES   The genetic characteristics of the host clearly impact on the host's natural and immune resistance status and thus influence susceptibility to fungal diseases. The specific defects in host natural and immune resistance mechanisms that are genetically acquired are discussed later in relation to the specific resistance mechanism affected. In some cases however, susceptibility to fungal infections cannot be attributed to a specific defect in natural or immune mechanisms of resistance or to factors other than the genetic background of the host. These as yet undefined genetic factors that predispose individuals to fungal infections may modify, either directly or indirectly, the natural defenses of the host. However, further investigations are necessary to acquire sufficient information to completely understand the genetic implications in fungal diseases.

Coccidioidomycosis is probably the best example of a fungal disease in which the propensity for dissemination is influenced by the ancestry of the host (24, 43, 107, 108), yet the specific genetic factor responsible for the susceptibility to progressive disease has not been elucidated. Several epidemiological studies have shown that Filipinos and blacks are 5–20 times more likely to develop disseminated coccidioidomycosis than are Caucasians (43, 107, 108). The factors that potentially could account for the increased incidence of disseminated coccidioidomycosis in the dark-skinned races have not been thoroughly examined; however, some observations impact this problem. It does not seem likely that the groups who are most susceptible to disseminated coccidioidomycosis are predisposed to the progressive disease because they are incapable of developing cell-mediated immunity to coccidioidal antigens, since anti-*Coccidioides* T-cell responses of blacks and Filipinos after immunization with a killed-spherule vaccine are similar to the responses of immunized Caucasians (24). On the other hand, features of specific major histocompatibility complex (MHC) antigen phenotypes and blood groups may influence susceptibility to disseminated coccidioidomycosis. This idea has been proposed because the HLA-A9 antigen and blood group B have been associated with the increased incidence of disseminated coccidioidomycosis and are found in increased frequencies in Filipinos and blacks as compared to Caucasians (24).

Additional information on the influence of genetic factors on susceptibility or resistance to systemic fungal diseases emerged from studies with inbred mice (Table 1). Although mouse strains differ with respect to their susceptibility and resistance to the various fungi, those differences do not appear to be controlled by the MHC (16, 25, 69, 70, 92, 116, 117). In murine coccidioidomycosis, resistance is the dominant phenotype and is determined by a gene designated as CmS (70). The exact role of CmS gene expression in resistance to coccidioidomycosis is not known; however, it does not appear to control the ability of the animals to mount a cell-mediated immune response as detected by the delayed-type hypersensitivity reaction (25). The effects of the CmS gene are most notable by day 10 of an infection (24, 25, 70), so the gene probably does not influence natural cellular resistance mechanisms.

In the murine model of cryptococcosis, resistance has been associated with the ability of the mouse strain to produce the complement component C5 (116, 117). Specific host resistance factors have not been identified with the other mycotic diseases. Clearly, sufficient attention has not been given to genetic control of resistance mechanisms in mycotic diseases. The limited

Table 1   Susceptibility and resistance of different mouse strains to various mycotic agents

	Mouse strain H-2 (KAED)					
	BALB/c	A	C57BL/6 or C57BL/10	CBA	DBA/2	
Mycotic agent	(dddd)	(kkkd)	(bb-b)	(kkkk)	(dddd)	Reference
C. immitis	S[a]	S	S	I[b]	R[c]	25, 69, 70
H. capsulatum	N/A[d]	R	S	N/A	N/A	144
P. brasiliensis	S	R	S	S	N/A	16
C. neoformans	I	S	R	I-R	S	117
C. albicans	S/R	I	R	I	S	1, 53, 92

[a] S = susceptible, [b] I = intermediate, [c] R = resistant, [d] N/A = data not available.

preliminary data suggest that gaining a better understanding of the genetic contributions to host resistance and susceptibility may be essential for the development of effective protective measures against mycotic agents.

HORMONAL FACTORS INFLUENCING SUSCEPTIBILITY TO MYCOTIC DISEASES ΛAt the present time, some data suggest hormonal factors in the host influence the establishment or progression of disease in at least three mycotic infections. For instance, the incidence of coccidioidomycosis in endemic areas is higher in pregnant females than in the population as a whole (52). Although this higher frequency of coccidioidomycosis during pregnancy may be due in part to the general immunosuppression associated with pregnancy (27), the growth of the organism is probably enhanced in the changed hormonal environment of the host. The latter concept is supported by the findings of Drutz and collaborators (35, 112, 113), who showed that the tissue phase (spherules/endospores) of *C. immitis* is stimulated to mature in vitro in the presence of progesterone and 17-β-estradiol at concentrations found in sera during the advanced stages of pregnancy.

Another dimorphic fungus affected by mammalian steroid hormones is *P. brasiliensis*. With this fungus, transition from the mycelial or saprophytic form to the yeast or parasitic form is inhibited by 17-β-estradiol (115). The inhibition of mycelium-to-yeast conversion in the lungs by estrogen may account for the less frequent occurrence of paracoccidioidomycosis in females than in males (115).

The third mycotic disease seemingly influenced by hormones is vaginal candidiasis, which occurs most often during pregnancy and in the late luteal phase of the menstrual cycle (65, 68, 127). Hormones can affect numerous mechanisms that influence the course of vaginal candidiasis. For example, estrogen can alter the vaginal epithelium, leukocyte influx, and other vaginal environmental factors, such as pH and glycogen content, which may affect adherence, proliferation, and/or differentiation of the blastoconidia (68, 127). Estrogen may directly interact with the organism by binding to hormone receptors in *C. albicans,* in turn affecting yeast-to-mycelium conversion, which is important in the establishment of infection (68, 127). Sex hormones also can affect the immune potential of the host (8). With the rat model, Kinsman & Collard (68) showed that at the end of the menstrual cycle when the level of serum progesterone is markedly elevated and the level of estradiol is decreasing, the lymphocyte proliferation response to *C. albicans* is low in comparison to the response at other times during the cycle, and serum obtained during this stage is more stimulatory in germination of *C. albicans* yeast cells than is serum taken at other times during the cycle. Their data support the concept that several mechanisms involved in the disease process may be affected by the hormonal state of the host. Although the information available on hormonal factors that influence mycotic diseases is minimal, the data are sufficient to suggest that these factors should be considered more frequently.

PHYSICAL, MECHANICAL, AND CHEMICAL BARRIERS TO INFECTION WITH PATHOGENIC FUNGI

As mentioned earlier, the skin and mucous membranes serve as excellent physical barriers against fungi; however, the exact mechanisms by which these tissues prevent establishment of fungal diseases have not been elucidated. The secretions associated with skin and mucous membranes most likely contribute to the barrier protection against mycotic agents. The protective nature of the skin and mucous membranes is evident by the fact that the organisms that cause subcutaneous mycotic disease do not establish an infection unless they are implanted into the deeper tissues by introduction with intravascular devises or through trauma to the skin or mucous membranes. Furthermore, even after the mycotic infection is initiated, the chemical and cellular defenses of the host play an important role in preventing the spread of the fungus to other tissues.

In the case of the systemic mycotic pathogens, which typically enter the host through the respiratory tract, the action of mucous and cilia in the respiratory tract prevent or limit the numbers of infective particles that gain entrance to the alveolar spaces. If they do not get into the lungs, the systemic mycotic pathogens are usually less of a threat to the host; therefore, the host's physical and mechanical barriers are clearly essential first-line protective defenses. If the entering organism evades the physical and mechanical barriers, then it is subjected to the chemical and cellular defenses of the tissues. Examples of chemical defenses are substances in human saliva and serum that inhibit the growth of *Cryptococcus neoformans* (3, 4, 60, 62). Although the factors in serum that prevent cryptococci from replicating have not been specifically defined, they clearly are not components of complement or an immunoglobulin (3, 60). Other mycotic pathogens such as *C. albicans* and *H. capsulatum* reportedly are limited in their ability to multiply in vitro in the presence of serum (14, 17, 71, 130, 145). Iron-binding proteins in serum such as transferrin inhibit replication of these iron-dependent mycotic agents (145). The sequestering of iron by transferrin in vivo may prevent extracellular multiplication of iron-dependent fungal pathogens. Chemical mechanisms certainly have the potential to limit the number of the infecting mycotic agent; however, certain pathogenic fungi have developed means of escaping from such defenses. For instance, *H. capsulatum* avoids the inhibitory threat of serum by entering phagocytic cells where the microenvironment is generally more favorable for growth.

Physical, mechanical, and chemical defenses of the host are definitely important in protection against fungi; however, our current understanding of the nature and mechanisms of these defenses is sketchy. Additional research is certainly warranted.

CELLULAR RESISTANCE MECHANISMS

When mycotic agents evade the physical, mechanical, and chemical barriers and gain entrance into the tissues, then the cellular defenses become involved. Two main groups of cells have the potential to interact with the entering organism. One group is comprised of the phagocytic cells, both professional, i.e. polymorphonuclear leukocytes (PMNL), monocytes, and macrophages, and nonprofessional, such as endothelial cells. The other major group of effector cells is composed of nonphagocytic cells such as natural killer (NK) cells (134), natural cytotoxic (NC) cells (82), and possibly MHC-nonrestricted cytotoxic T-cells (132).

As a general rule, effective cellular resistance cannot be attributed to any one of these host cell types alone, but rather the natural effector cells function together in a coordinated fashion to restrict fungal targets. An equation to express natural cellular defenses against mycotic agents would be extremely complex with many variables. Furthermore, the equation would be different for each fungal pathogen. Investigators studying the fungal diseases have found that the elimination of a single natural effector cell population in an infected animal model does not result in a dramatic change in fungal cell numbers in the tissues, just as one might expect with multiple-variable systems. Similarly, single effector cell populations do not sterilize cultures of fungal organisms in vitro. Because of the complexities of the organisms, the defenses, and the interactions of the effector and target cells, gaining an understanding of the role(s) of the various effector cell types in the elimination of fungal targets has been difficult.

Which host effector cell type(s) is the first to contact the organism once it enters the host depends somewhat on the site of entry. Thus, the differences in natural cellular defenses in different regions of the body may influence the establishment and progression of fungal disease. Other important factors in orchestrating the natural cellular defenses are the type(s), numbers, and sequence of effector cells stimulated to enter the infected tissue.

The infecting fungus controls, to some extent, the influx of natural effector cells into the region. Fungi or their products can be directly chemotactic to host effector cells, or the organism may fix complement by the alternative pathway, resulting in production of complement byproducts such as C5a that are chemotactic to natural effector cells. Fungi can also trigger an influx of effector cells by inducing changes in the endothelial cells lining the blood vessels, thereby controlling the types and numbers of infiltrating cells.

Since most fungal diseases do not display an acute onset, the initial stages of fungal infections in humans often go unobserved. As a result, investigators have rarely studied the natural effector cell functions during infections in humans. Our current understanding of natural effector cell function against mycotic agents is based predominantly on results from in vitro studies with human and animal cells and on data from in vivo experiments in animal models.

Phagocytic Cells—Professional

Professional phagocytic cells contribute in a very active way to natural cellular resistance against most mycotic diseases; however, their contributions vary with the fungal agent. Although the professional phagocytes may kill fungal cells intracellularly, they can also kill fungal target cells extracellularly. In fact, extracellular killing of fungi is more pronounced than intracellular killing because the large size of many of the fungal elements precludes engulfment by the phagocytes. Both intracellular and extracellular killing generally require that the phagocytic cells bind to the target cell, in this case the fungal cell. Binding of effector and target cells can be mediated through one or more of several different receptor-ligand interactions that are determined by the surface characteristics of the cells involved. Therefore, the binding interactions will depend on the stage of the fungus, whether or not the fungus is opsonized, the opsonizing substance, and the receptor expression on the effector cell. The signal resulting from binding of the target cell to the effector cell depends on the specific receptor-ligand interactions occurring and possibly the extent of those interactions. The signal transmitted to the effector cell could result in several outcomes. One would be phagocytosis followed by the associated cascade of events leading to killing of the target cell. Another might be exocytosis of granules or other cellular components that have killing or inhibitory powers extracellularly. And still another could be cytokine production by the phagocytic cell. One might imagine PMNL also playing a more passive role in target-cell killing by releasing cytoplasmic and granule components, not as a result of signaling, but of death and lysis of the phagocytic cells. The released PMNL components could be lethal to the fungal cells in the immediate area. In support of this possibility, Sohnle and coinvestigators have shown that lysed PMNL can suppress directed growth of *C. albicans* pseudohyphae and proliferation of *C. albicans* yeast cells (94, 128).

POLYMORPHONUCLEAR LEUKOCYTES   PMNL clearly play a significant role in host defense against *Aspergillus* spp. and systemic *C. albicans* infections (20, 23, 39, 84). Persons with chronic granulomatous disease, neutropenic patients, and individuals who have myeloperoxidase deficiencies (hereditary or acquired) are extremely suscpetible to infection with either of these two opportunistic mycotic agents (20, 23, 39, 84). PMNL also contribute to protection against other mycotic agents; however, their role is less critical because in the absence of PMNL other natural effector cells can assume PMNL functions (98). As a general rule, however, PMNL are the most effective killers of mycotic agents when compared to other natural effector cells (95, 98, 135). For specific information on the relative effectiveness of PMNL in killing the various forms of the different pathogenic fungi, the reader is referred to recent reviews (12, 98).

Typically PMNL are not the first natural effector cells to engage the infecting fungal agent because they are not normally present in high numbers in tissues. The PMNL must be stimulated to penetrate the infected tissues. Most mycotic agents are not invasive; therefore host-cell injury is not responsible for the influx of PMNL unless the fungus has been traumatically introduced into the tissue. Instead, PMNL are attracted to the site of the introduced fungus by chemotactic substances produced by the fungus or by generation of chemotactic complement products resulting from the fungus fixing complement through the alternative pathway. *C. albicans, B. dermatitidis,* and *Rhizopus oryzae* produce chemotactic factors, and several pathogenic fungi including *C. albicans, C. neoformans, C. immitis, H. capsulatum,* and *P. brasiliensis* reportedly fix complement by the alternative pathway (15, 19, 26, 29, 30, 47, 114, 133, 138, 141). Other mechanisms may potentiate the influx of PMNL into the infected tissues. Although the following scenario has not been completely documented in a fungal infection at the present time, it is a possible means by which mycotic agents could stimulate an influx of PMNL into the tissue. For example, upon entering the tissue, a fungus could stimulate local macrophages or other cells to produce cytokines. [In fact, spherules of *C. immitis* do trigger macrophages to produce tumor necrosis factor alpha (TNFα) (123).] Certain cytokines, including interleukin-1 and TNFα, can stimulate expression of adhesion molecules such as GMP-140, ELAM-1, and ICAM-1 on the vascular endothelium (111). The increased density of these adhesion molecules on the endothelial cells enhances the binding of PMNL to the endothelial cells, which is prerequisite to the entrance of PMNL into the tissues (7, 50, 125). Based on the limited information available in the case of coccidioidomycosis, this scenario would not be expected to occur until the *C. immitis* arthroconidia, which are the infective particles, have converted to spherules. However, like spherules, the arthroconidia may be able to induce adhesion molecule–stimulating cytokines that aid in getting neutrophils to the site of infection. Such a mechanism as this, in conjunction with the chemotactic substances in *C. immitis* cells, could account for the observations of heavy infiltrates of PMNL in *C. immitis*–infected tissues (61).

Once at the site of the infection, the PMNL must be signaled to kill the fungal target. Signaling is usually accomplished through fungal-cell binding to surface receptors on the PMNL. Although PMNL receptors are relatively well defined, studies on PMNL receptor-fungal target interactions are minimal. Schnur & Newman (122) recently reported that CD18 (β-chain of the CR3 receptor, LFA-1, and p150,95) is the ligand on human neutrophils responsible for binding unopsonized *H. capsulatum* yeast cells. Binding through CD18 stimulates the PMNL to phagocytize the *H. capsulatum* blastoconidia (122). By opsonizing *H. capsulatum* yeast cells with heat-labile and heat-stable serum components, binding and phagocytosis by PMNL was greatly augmented (122).

PMNL receptor-fungal cell ligand interactions in the absence of serum opsonins have not been completely defined for other fungi. However, in the presence of fresh serum, the deposition of C3bi and C3d on the surface of cryptococci through the alternative complement pathway enhances binding and phagocytosis of cryptococci by neutrophils (77, 80). In fact, opsonization with C3 fragments is essential for phagocytosis of encapsulated cryptococci (77, 80). These findings indicate that CR3s (receptor for C3bi) on PMNL are important for phagocytosis of *C. neoformans*. This concept is supported by the finding that up-regulation of CR3 expression on PMNL markedly increases phagocytosis of serum-opsonized cryptococcal yeast cells (79). Viability of the cryptococcal cells was not presented in this report (79); therefore, the influence of increased CR3 expression on killing of cryptococci is unknown at this time.

The signaling pathways in PMNL that are initiated by fungal attachment and result in the respiratory burst and release of cytotoxic components are complex and have been investigated in some detail by Diamond and collaborators (73, 74, 91, 146) with *C. albicans* hyphae, the predominate form found in tissues of infected individuals. The findings of these investigators were recently reviewed (28, 99), so only conclusions from their studies are discussed here. They found that serum-opsonized hyphae and unopsonized hyphae binding to PMNL signal through two separate pathways that lead to the respiratory burst (73, 74, 91, 146). Furthermore, the two pathways have different requirements for completion; therefore, opsonized and unopsonized *C. albicans* hyphae are likely to have different fates in tissue depending upon the microenvironmental conditions (146). This example depicts a signaling event that results in exocytosis of PMNL granules and therefore may be different from the sequence of events involved in phagocytosis and intracellular killing or fungistatic effects that occur with some of the smaller fungal forms. As more fungal cell–natural effector cell interactions are studied in detail, we should find that the form and/or surface characteristics of the organism and the maturation or activation state of the effector cells along with the factors in the microenvironment are critical in determining the signaling pathway, and the signaling pathway followed in the effector cell will make the difference in whether or not the fungal cell survives.

The mechanism(s) by which the PMNL kill the fungal targets can be divided into two broad categories. One consists of the oxygen-dependent mechanisms and the other of the oxygen-independent mechanisms. Products of the oxygen-dependent system with the potential to kill fungi are hydrogen peroxide, superoxide anions, singlet oxygen, hydroxyl radicals, hypochlorous acid, and chloramines (41, 119, 136). After stimulation of PMNL from normal individuals, NADPH oxidase is activated, resulting in production of superoxide anions that can be fungicidal. The effectiveness of superoxide anions is limited because superoxide anions rapidly combine with hydrogen to form H_2O_2, another toxic molecule. Normal PMNL also have myeloperoxidase (MPO) in their azurophilic granules, and upon stimulation, the PMNL degranulate and release MPO. MPO catalyzes reactions involving H_2O_2 and halide ions, resulting in toxic products such as hypochlorous acid and chloramines. Components of the PMNL that are fungicidal or fungistatic and do not depend on oxygen are lysozyme, lactoferrin, serine proteases, and defensins (41, 86). Oxidative mechanisms tend to contribute more to protection against fungi than nonoxidative mechanisms (120), as evidenced by the increased incidence of *C. albicans* and *Aspergillus* spp. infections in individuals with deficiencies in PMNL oxidative mechanisms (20, 23, 39, 84). Another finding that supports the idea that oxidative products are valuable assets in antifungal host defense is that neutrophils and monocytes that contain myeloperoxidase are more effective in killing fungal targets than are macrophages that lack the myeloperoxidase component of the oxygen-dependent killing system (22, 137). Although not as important as oxidative products, the components that do not depend on oxygen to kill microbes impact on the overall reduction in numbers of certain mycotic agents such as *C. neoformans* (46).

Mycotic disease-causing agents vary greatly in their susceptibility to components of both the oxygen-dependent and the oxygen-independent defenses of the PMNL (120). Thus, the effectiveness of PMNL in eliminating the fungal agent depends on which agent and infecting form is involved (98). PMNL killing of fungal cells has been reported to be as high as 80% and as low as 0%, but most results fall in the range of 30–60% (98). The effectiveness of PMNL killing of mycotic agents can be modified by a wide array of factors. For instance, certain characteristics of the fungi may block PMNL activity. The fungal agent may have a surface that is not conducive to PMNL recognition. The capsule of *C. neoformans* is an example. Highly encapsulated cryptococci are not phagocytized by PMNL, presumably because the capsule prevents binding of the cryptococcal cell to receptors on PMNL (78). *C. immitis* spherules have an extracellular fibrillar coating that does not permit PMNL attachment (44). Another way fungi avoid damage by PMNL is to produce substances that inhibit PMNL function. Smail et al (124) reported that *C. albicans* hyphae produce a *Candida* hyphal inhibitory product (CHIP) that selectively inhibits PMNL degranulation. *C. albicans* isolates that are capable of producing CHIP in vivo might restrict PMNL-mediated killing of *Candida* spp. (124). The effectiveness in killing of *C. albicans* yeast cells by PMNL can also be suppressed by a different mechanism. When *C. albicans* blastoconidia are phagocytized by PMNL, the blastoconidia are contained in either sealed or unsealed phagolysosomes (18). The organisms in unsealed phagolysosomes are not killed as readily as the organisms in the sealed vacuoles (18). The inefficiency in closing of the phagolysosomes is most likely responsible for the relatively low percent killing (30–50%) reported for *C. albicans* yeast cells (18).

H. capsulatum yeast cells affect PMNL function in yet another way (122). Upon phagocytosis of serum-opsonized *H. capsulatum* yeast cells, PMNL apparently undergo an oxidative burst response as measured by intracellular reduction of nitroblue tetrazolium, reduction of cytochrome c in the presence of cytochalasin D, oxygen consumption, chemiluminescence, and H_2O_2 production; however, the PMNL do not release superoxide anion to the exterior of the cell (122). Because the PMNL that have phagocytized *H. capsulatum* can be subsequently triggered with stimuli such as opsonized zymosan and PMA (phorbol myristate acetate) to produce superoxide anion, the lack of superoxide anion production after ingestion of *H. capsulatum* probably cannot be attributed to inhibition of the superoxide-generating system or to scavenging of superoxide by the phagocytized yeast cells (122). Rather, superoxide anion seems to be entrapped in the PMNL after phagocytosis of opsonized *H. capsulatum* yeast cells (122). These few examples indicate the complexity and diversity of the interactions of fungi with PMNL. Much remains to be done in this area to complete our understanding of PMNL-fungus interactions.

ALVEOLAR MACROPHAGES   Alveolar macrophages are the first natural effector cells to encounter the infectious particles or forms of the mycotic agents that enter through the respiratory route. Therefore, the fungistatic and fungicidal capabilities of these macrophages can be important in determining whether or not the fungal agent establishes an infection. The alveolar macrophages phagocytize fungi such as *Aspergillus* conidia (138), *H. capsulatum* microconidia and yeast (104), *C. immitis* arthroconidia and endospores (5), *C. neoformans* (10, 88, 143), *C. albicans* yeast (109), *P. brasiliensis* yeast (13), and *B. dermatitidis* yeast (11).

After phagocytosis, alveolar macrophages display differences in their capacity to kill various mycotic agents. This variation is best illustrated by examining how alveolar macrophages deal with several different fungi. Alveolar macrophages are fairly efficient in preventing the establishment of the relatively rare disease, pulmonary aspergillosis. The infectious particles of *Aspergillus* spp., conidia, once in the lungs are phagocytized by the alveolar macrophages and are either killed or prevented from germinating (138). Since the conidia must germinate, to form hyphae, for the disease to be established, the alveolar macrophages rank high on the list of natural cellular defenses effective against *Aspergillus* spp. The action of the alveolar macrophages may account, in part, for pulmonary aspergillosis occurring so rarely in normal hosts (138). Furthermore, the effectiveness of natural host defenses most likely accounts for aspergillosis being classified as an opportunistic disease.

Another disease frequently categorized as an opportunistic infection is cryptococcosis (118). Alveolar macrophages, the first natural effector cells encountered by cryptococci as they enter the lungs, are fairly efficient at limiting the growth of *C. neoformans* both intracellularly and extracellularly (10, 88, 143). Different strains of *C. neoformans* appear to have different levels of susceptibility to killing by alveolar macrophages, and opsonization with normal serum enhances killing (10, 88, 143). One hypothesis on how alveolar macrophages interact with *C. neoformans* stems from the studies of Levitz & DiBenedetto (88), who showed that murine bronchoalveolar macrophages (BAM) phagocytize serum-opsonized, acapsular strains of *C. neoformans* better than they phagocytize serum-opsonized, encapsulated isolates (88). However, BAM did not kill serum-opsonized, acapsular strains as well as they killed serum-opsonized, encapsulated isolates (88). Because of their small size, weakly encapsulated *C. neoformans* yeast are most likely the forms that reach the alveolar spaces and therefore are considered to be the infectious particles (97). After being in tissue for a time, the weakly encapsulated yeast become more encapsulated. Under these conditions, the alveolar macrophages would be expected to phagocytize the weakly encapsulated forms but would not restrict their growth. The weakly encapsulated *C. neoformans* cells that escaped phagocytosis would develop a larger capsule, become opsonized, and be phagocytized through binding to receptors that signal production of fungicidal components. In support of this scenario, Levitz & DiBenedetto (88) showed that BAM which had had CR1 (receptor for C3b, C4b, and C3bi) modulated off were no longer able to phagocytize the encapsulated isolate but could still phagocytize the acapsular isolate (88). Removal of CR3 (receptor for C3bi) or FcRII (receptor for IgG_1 and IgG_{2b} immune complexes) did not alter phagocytosis of either isolate. Thus, CR1 rather than CR3 may be the receptor for the opsonized, encapsulated cryptococci, and binding to CR1 signals the release of fungicidal components by the

BAM (88). The authors indicated other plausible explanations for the data (88), so further investigations are necessary to fully understand the complex interactions between alveolar macrophages and serum-opsonized, encapsulated *C. neoformans* cells.

In contrast to the opportunistic fungi, the infective particles of *C. immitis*, the arthroconidia, although phagocytized by alveolar macrophages, are not killed. This pathogenic fungus may remain viable because of the inability of the phagosomes containing the arthroconidia to fuse with the lysosomes (5). Within the alveolar macrophage, the arthroconidia can convert to spherules that are relatively resistant to killing and develop into large structures containing numerous endospores (5). In a *C. immitis* infection, the second phase of natural effector cells entering the lungs are PMNL that have weak killing power against *C. immitis* arthroconidia and spherules (34). Therefore, it is not surprising that pulmonary coccidioidomycosis occurs frequently in endemic areas (24). With a mouse model, coccidioidomycosis can be established with as few as 7 arthroconidia (75), confirming that the natural effector mechanisms against this mycotic agent are not very competent. Another example of the very limited capability of the alveolar macrophages to prevent establishment of a fungal infection is seen with *H. capsulatum* (67). Microconidia of *H. capsulatum* are the infectious particles, and they are phagocytized by normal nonactivated alveolar macrophages but are not killed by them. Within the alveolar macrophages, *H. capsulatum* microconidia convert to yeast cells that replicate inside the effector cells (12). The mechanisms by which the *H. capsulatum* microconidia and yeast cells avoid death in the alveolar macrophages are yet to be elucidated.

Alveolar macrophages are important in natural host defense against some of the fungi that enter through the lungs. The ability of the natural effector cells in the lungs to eliminate a given fungal agent correlates with infectivity of the organism and appears to make the difference in whether the fungal agent is classified as an opportunistic organism or a primary pathogen.

MONOCYTES AND MACROPHAGES   The antifungal effects of monocytes and macrophages have been studied in vitro and in vivo and were recently reviewed for the dimorphic fungi (12). Solid conclusions as to the effectiveness of these phagocytic cells in natural resistance against fungi are difficult to make because the results from one laboratory often do not corroborate results from another. The reasons for the varying results and thus the confusion on the roles of monocytes and macrophages in natural resistance against fungi are numerous. Researchers have studied monocytes, monocyte-derived macrophages, peritoneal macrophages, splenic macrophages, and alveolar macrophages from several animal species, making comparisons in activities difficult even when the same fungal target was used. The microenvironment in which the macrophages are found can modulate their activities; resident macrophages usually perform differently from induced macrophages, and these factors contribute to the disorder. Since fungal targets are complex and may be in different stages when studied, the fungus presents another set of variables in the experiments. The species of fungus, the fungal structure being studied, and the opsonized state of the fungus can alter the results obtained in experiments on antifungal activities of monocytes and macrophages. Not only do the experimental conditions and the effector-to-target ratios vary greatly from one laboratory to another, but the possible contamination of reagents with endotoxin, which can influence the activity of the effector cell populations, may produce different results in each study. In spite of all the variables, one consistent pattern has emerged: monocytes and macrophages from naive animals have limited abilities to kill systemic mycotic agents when compared with the antifungal activities of monocytes and macrophages activated with cytokines (12).

Like the PMNL, monocytes and macrophages must bind to their target before phagocytizing and attempting to kill the target intracellularly, or before exocytosis of cytotoxic components that kill the target extracellularly. Monocyte- and macrophage-receptor interactions with several fungi have been defined, and the receptor(s) engaged on the effector cells varies with the organism. In the case of *H. capsulatum,* the family of adhesion receptors that have CD18 β-chains (LFA-1, CR3, and p150,95) serve as the attachment site for unopsonized *H. capsulatum* yeast and microconidia on human alveolar and monocyte-derived macrophages (104). In contrast, the binding sites on human monocytes for unopsonized *C. albicans* yeast cells are the β-glucan receptors (63). *Aspergillus fumigatus* conidia attach to the mannosyl-fucosyl receptors on murine alveolar macrophages (66). The cell walls of fungi are composed of chitin with α- and β-glucan, mannan, galactose, and/or galactosamine (118), and the saccharide-containing molecules could serve as receptors to which lectin-like molecules on the effector cells bind. The fungal organisms could also have lectin-like surface components that would be recognized by effector cell receptors. Because both of these possibilities could occur, it is not surprising that the fungi bind readily to natural effector cells and signal the effector cells via different pathways.

Monocytes and macrophages differ with respect to their available antimicrobial mechanisms (41, 98). Monocytes from normal human subjects can generate oxidative products in a manner similar to that described for PMNL (41, 83, 98). Hence, monocytes can generate superoxide anions and H_2O_2, and they have an intact myeloperoxidase-H_2O_2-halide system that can generate additional active oxygen-dependent products (41, 83, 85, 98). Monocytes also have other active molecular species independent of oxygen, such as lysozyme and cationic proteins (85). Cathepsin G is missing, however, in the monocytes (85). As might be expected, monocytes are similar to PMNL in their abilities to kill fungal agents (98). Macrophages, on the other hand, are not generally as effective in damaging fungi as monocytes or PMNL (98).

Although normal macrophages can kill microbes through the oxygen-dependent NADPH oxidase pathway, they lack the myeloperoxidase component of the oxygen-dependent antimicrobial system. The absence of myeloperoxidase may, in part, be responsible for the reduced ability of unstimulated macrophages to kill fungal cells (41, 85, 98). Other possible macrophage mechanisms of antifungal activity have been described using in vitro models; however, the relevance of these mechanisms in vivo will require additional investigation. Levitz & Diamond (87) have described one such fungicidal system. It is comprised of ferrous ions, H_2O_2, and iodide and is active in vitro against *C. albicans* blastoconidia and spores of *A. fumigatus* and *R. oryzae* (87). Granger et al (51) reported another possible mechanism by which activated murine peritoneal macrophages may exert fungistatic effects on *C. neoformans*. The anticryptococcal effects they (51) studied were mediated through a deimination pathway that requires metabolism of L-arginine by macrophages to produce nitrite and citrulline.

Much work remains to be done with each of the mycotic agents to establish which of the professional phagocytes contribute to clearance of the organism and what mechanism(s) each cell uses to facilitate the clearance. Furthermore, studies on the influence of one effector cell population on another effector cell population will be necessary to gain a satisfactory understanding of natural host defensive measures.

Phagocytic Cells—Nonprofessional

Only a few investigations have been performed on the role of nonprofessional phagocytic cells in mycotic diseases (36, 37, 49). Frequently, to gain entrance into tissues, the infecting fungus must adhere to vascular endothelial cells and penetrate them. *C. albicans* is a fungus that adheres to and is internalized by vascular endothelial cells (72). In the absence of PMNL, *C. albicans* yeast cells germinate to hyphae, which eventually disrupt endothelial-cell monolayers (36). When PMNL are present in the cocultures of endothelial-cell monolayers and *C. albicans,* the PMNL attach to and spread over the *C. albicans* hyphal surfaces and eventually kill the *C. albicans* (36). *C. albicans* may stimulate modulation of endothelial-cell surface receptors, which in turn may influence the interactions of host cells with each other or with the fungal agent. *H. capsulatum* is another organism that reportedly interacts with nonprofessional phagocytes (9, 37, 49, 131). *H. capsulatum* yeast cells are phagocytized by human umbilical vein and murine lung endothelial cells as well as by hamster tracheal epithelial cells (9, 37, 49, 131). In two studies, the endothelial cells reduced the population of *H. capsulatum* yeast cells during the first 2–6 h in culture, but by 24 h, the numbers of *H. capsulatum* cells in the cocultures were equal to or greater than the original number of *H. capsulatum* cells (9, 131). Another study showed that strains of *H. capsulatum* with cell walls void of α-(1,3)-glucan but not isolates containing α-(1,3)-glucan were ingested by cultured respiratory epithelial cells and multiplied within the host cells (37). Exactly how these phenomena relate to the fungal disease and the host defenses is not understood at this time. Studies on nonprofessional phagocytes in regard to fungal disease have only recently begun. This is, however, a fascinating area of research, and future studies on nonprofessional phagocytes and fungi are expected to make significant contributions to our overall understanding of the pathobiology of fungal diseases.

Nonphagocytic Natural Effector Cells

Three types of cells fall into the category of nonphagocytic natural effector cells. They are natural killer cells, natural cytotoxic cells, and MHC-nonrestricted cytotoxic T-cells (82, 132, 134). These three types of cells have several characteristics in common. All can recognize and damage multiple types of target cells. Their activities are not restricted by MHC antigens, and they inflict damage on the target cell by first binding to the target cell and then either secreting or exocytosing toxic compounds. Although experimental evidence is fairly strong that NK cells can damage certain fungi (6, 21, 64, 96, 101, 110), one can only speculate on the abilities of the other two nonphagocytic cell types to damage fungal targets and thus contribute to natural resistance.

NATURAL KILLER CELLS   NK cells are a population of $CD3^-$, $CD16^+$, $CD56^+$, and asialo-GM_1^+ large granular lymphocytes (LGL) that kill their targets directly by exocytosis of granules that contain cytotoxic components such as perforin (cytolysin) and serine proteases (granzyme A), by secreting other toxic substances such as $TNF\alpha$, or by triggering DNA fragmentation in the target cell (106, 134). NK cells are best known for their ability to kill tumor or virus-infected cells; however, they also have the ability to damage targets other than tissue cells (membrane-bound eukaryotic cells) (6, 21, 64, 96, 101, 110, 134). NK cells reportedly have inhibitory effects on several mycotic agents including *C. neoformans, P. brasiliensis, C. immitis, H. capsulatum,* and *C. albicans* hyphae (6, 21, 64, 96, 101, 110). NK cell–fungal cell interactions have been studied in some detail using *C. neoformans* and *C. albicans* yeast cells as targets, and two patterns of NK cell–mediated antifungal activity have emerged. One is direct killing of target cells by NK cells (54–59, 90, 96, 100–103). The second is a NK cell-mediated indirect effect on fungal targets (31–33, 139). The latter mechanism involves fungal targets binding to NK cells and thereby simulating the NK cells to produce lymphokines such as TNF, IFNγ, and/or granulocyte-macrophage colony-stimulating factor (GM-CSF) (31, 33, 148). The lymphokines in turn up-regulate the fungicidal activity of other natural effector cells such as PMNL, monocytes or macrophages (32, 139).

Direct killing of a fungal target by NK cells has been studied most extensively with *C. neoformans* yeast cells, so the discussion here centers around that model. In vitro, murine, rat, and human NK cells bind to and kill cryptococcal cells (56, 59, 96, 100—103; J. W. Murphy, unpublished data). Recently, Miller et al (96) reported that human NK cells mixed with *C. neoformans* at effector-to-target (E:T) ratios of 500:1 and 100:1 did not inhibit the growth of cryptococci unless anticryptococcal antibody was included in the in vitro assay. In contrast, human NK cells bound to and significantly inhibited the growth of *C. neoformans* when an E:T ratio of 2:1 was used (Figure 1) (J. W. Murphy, unpublished data). Although the data are limited, they indicate that human NK cells can kill *C. neoformans* target cells providing the correct signal(s) is given to the effector cells.

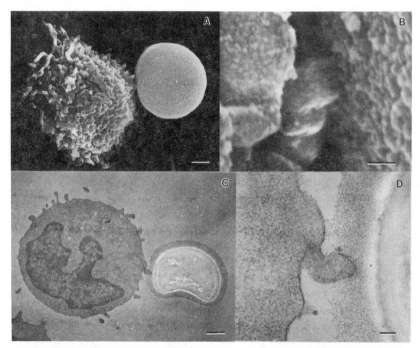

Figure 1   Scanning (*A, B*) and transmission (*C, D*) electron micrographs of human NK cells bound to *C. neoformans* cells. The NK cells are on the left and *C. neoformans* cells are on the right in each panel. Note the microvilli of the NK cells making contact with the cryptococcal cells and penetrating the capsule of the yeast cells (*C, D*). Bars in panels *A* and *C* = 1.0 μm and in panels *B* and *D* = 0.1 μm.

Murine NK cell–*C. neoformans* interactions have been assessed in some detail, and the main findings are briefly reviewed here. With murine NK cells, binding and growth-inhibitory activity against *C. neoformans* do not depend on the presence of serum or on the size or serospecificity of the cryptococcal capsule (98, 101). As in most natural effector cell interactions with their targets, binding of NK cells to cryptococcal cells is a prerequisite to killing of the cryptococcal cells (54, 56, 58, 59). NK cells associate with *C. neoformans* cells through many microvilli, which contrasts to the broad membrane-membrane contact made by NK cells interacting with a standard tumor cell target such as YAC-1 (100). Binding of NK cells to *C. neoformans* is Mg^{2+} dependent and not affected by temperatures below 37°C providing the time allowed for binding is not less than 2.5 h (56). Maximum conjugate formation between NK cells and *C. neoformans* is reached after 2 h when the cells are incubated at 37°C. The earliest that killing of the cryptococcal cells can be detected is 6 h after mixing the effector and target cells (100). Actin filaments of the NK-cell cytoskeletal network must be intact for the NK cells to bind to cryptococci, and it appears that disulfide bonding plays a role in NK cell–*C. neoformans* interactions (100).

Binding of NK cells to cryptococcal cells signals the NK cells to rearrange their cytoplasmic organelles (54). For example, after binding to *C. neoformans,* the nucleus of the NK cell moves away from the attachment site of the cryptococcal cell, and the Golgi apparatus and microtubule-organizing center of the NK cell can be seen in the cytoplasm adjacent to the site of binding of the cryptococcal cell (54). Focusing of the NK-cell cytoplasmic organelles toward the bound cryptococcal target depends on assembly of NK-cell microtubules and occurs only when Ca^{2+} is present (54). Reorientation of the Golgi apparatus and the microtubule-organizing center into the NK cell cytoplasm adjacent to the bound target cell is an important prerequisite for the secretion of toxic products into the region of the cryptococcal target (54). When granule exocytosis and secretion are blocked in the NK cells with the drug monensin, NK cells do not kill *C. neoformans,* demonstrating that movement of Golgi-derived vesicles to the cell membrane is necessary for NK cell–mediated damage to cryptococci (58). Granules from NK cells and cytolysin isolated from the granules inhibit the growth of *C. neoformans* (58). Taken together, these findings indicate that NK cells mediate their lethal effect on *C. neoformans* by exocytosis of cytolysin-containing granules into the region of the attached cryptococcal cell, and the granule contents then damage the cryptococcal cell (58). NK-cell cytoplasmic fractions other than the granules have also been found to inhibit the growth of cryptococci; therefore, there may be cytoplasmic components in addition to the granules that can damage *C. neoformans* (58).

Anticryptococcal activities of human and mouse NK cells are significantly augmented in the presence of anticryptococcal antibody, suggesting that in immune animals antibody-dependent, cell-mediated cytotoxicity (ADCC) may be another way in which NK cells participate in host defense against fungal targets (96, 103). ADCC in cryptococcosis may be minimal, however, because anticryptococcal antibodies are not usually present (97).

Murine NK cells not only limit the growth of *C. neoformans* in vitro, they also function in vivo (55, 57, 90). Hidore & Murphy (55) have shown that beige (bg/bg) mice that have reduced NK-cell activity and abnormally large granules in their PMNL do not clear *C. neoformans* from their tissues as effectively as do their heterozygote (bg/+) littermates. The reduced clearance of *C. neoformans* from tissues of bg/bg mice was shown to result from the NK-cell defect rather than abnormalities in the other natural effector cells because PMNL from beige mice inhibited the growth of *C. neoformans* in vitro better than did PMNL from the bg/+ mice, and splenic macrophages from bg/bg and bg/+ mice were equivalent in their ability to kill cryptococci in vitro (55). When *C. neoformans* was injected into the peritoneal cavity of bg/bg and bg/+ mice, the influxes of PMNL and macrophages were similar in the two groups of animals, demonstrating that the natural effector cells of the bg/bg mice did not have reduced chemotactic abilities in response to *C. neoformans* as compared to bg/+ mice (55). Findings with the beige mouse model demonstrated that NK cells were effective in inhibiting cryptococci in vivo, and those findings have been confirmed in two additional mouse models (57, 90). The combined studies make clear that NK cells contribute to early clearance of *C. neoformans* cells from the lungs of infected mice; however, the anticryptococcal activity of NK cells, at least in nonimmune mice, is not sufficient for sustained clearance of the organsims (55, 57, 90).

Djeu and coworkers (31–33, 139) have described an indirect role for NK cells in augmenting protection against the fungal target *C. albicans*. These investigators showed that human NK cells stimulated with *C. albicans* produce lymphokines that can activate PMNL and monocytes to more aggressively kill *C. albicans* (31–33, 139). Considering that NK cells can produce several different lymphokines, i.e. TNFα, GM-CSF, IFNγ, provided the cells are given an appropriate signal, an indirect role of NK cells in resistance against other fungal agents seems very feasible and should be evaluated.

OTHER NATURAL EFFECTOR CELLS   NC and MHC-nonrestricted T-cells can inhibit or even kill fungal targets; however, studies on the interactions of these cells with fungal targets are just beginning, so little more than preliminary data are available at this time. In fact, there are no reports on NC cell effectiveness against fungal targets, although TNFα and other lymphokines produced by NC cells could directly affect fungal targets or could modulate natural antifungal host defenses. This may be a fertile area of research to explore. The concept that MHC-nonrestricted T-cells can inhibit the growth of fungi or kill them is justified on the basis that T-cells from immunized mice have been shown to inhibit the growth of *C. neoformans* (45). Furthermore, recent preliminary data indicate that human T-cells can bind to *C. neoformans* targets (J. W. Murphy, unpublished data). Also, purified populations of human peripheral blood T lymphocytes inhibit the growth of *C. neoformans* in vitro (J. W. Murphy, unpublished data).

Interactions of Natural Effector Cells

Natural effector cells can produce many cytokines when appropriately stimulated, and the binding of fungi to the effector cells may provide the signal(s) necessary for cytokine production. If one links these ideas to the facts that IFNγ activates macrophages to aggressively kill fungal targets (2, 12, 13, 42, 89, 105, 140, 145) and that TNFα and GM-CSF boost the antifungal activity of PMNL, monocytes, and macrophages (2, 31–33, 38, 40, 89, 126, 139), then one can reasonably predict that effector cells can stimulate one another via cytokines to have increased antifungal activity. Only a few examples of such interactions have been experimentally validated, and most are discussed earlier in this review. The interactions of natural effector cells could also negatively affect host resistance. For example, Wei et al (142) recently reported that interleukin-2-activated NK (LAK) cells suppress human monocyte activity against *C. albicans*. Currently, it is not clear how these in vitro phenonena translate to the in vivo situation, but elucidating the in vivo interactions of natural effector cells is a challenging problem for the future.

SUMMARY

Natural host-resistance mechanisms are essential first-line defenses against most mycotic agents; however, these defenses are often not sufficient for complete protection. The host relies on the immune responses to provide the additional antifungal activity necessary for maximum protection. In systemic mycotic diseases, the immune system must be functional to prevent the host from succumbing to the disease. Natural resistance mechanisms act together in a coordinated manner early in the disease process to either kill or prevent the fungal agent from proliferating and gaining entrance to other tissues. The early defensive measures of the natural effector mechanisms are usually sufficiently effective to provide time for the generally more effective immune defenses to develop. Together, the natural defenses and the immune defenses regulate each other through cytokine networks, and generally these systems provide the host with adequate protection against threatening mycotic agents.

Literature Cited

1. Ashman, R. B., Papadimitriou, J. M. 1987. Murine candidiasis. Pathogenesis and host responses in genetically distinct inbred mice. *Immunol. Cell Biol.* 65: 163–71
2. Bancroft, G. J., Gunn, E. 1990. Macrophage activation by TNF and GM-CSF overcomes the anti-phagocytic effects of encapsulated *Cryptococcus neoformans*. *J. Leuk. Biol. Supp.* 1:97 (Abstr. 275)
3. Baum, G. L., Artis, D. 1963. Characterization of the growth inhibition factor for *Cryptococcus neoformans* (GIFc) in human serum. *Am. J. Med. Sci.* 246:53–57
4. Baum, G. L., Artis, D. 1961. Growth inhibition of *Cryptococcus neoformans* by cell free human serum. *Am. J. Med. Sci.* 241:613–16
5. Beaman, L., Holmberg, C. A. 1980. In vitro response of alveolar macrophages to infection with *Coccidioides immitis*. *Infect. Immun.* 28:594–600
6. Beno, D. W. A., Mathews, H. L. 1990. Growth inhibition of *Candida albicans* by interleukin-2-induced lymph node cells. *Cell. Immunol.* 128:89–100
7. Bevilacqua, M. P., Pober, J. S., Mendrick, D. L., Cotran, R. S., Gimbrone, M. A. Jr. 1987. Identification of an inducible endothelial leukocyte adhesion molecule, ELAM-1. *Proc. Natl. Acad. Sci. USA* 84:9238–42
8. Bhalla, A. K. 1989. Hormones and the immune response. *Ann. Rheum. Dis.* 48:1–6
9. Bhardwaj, G., Gatchel, S. L., Tewari, R. P. 1988. Fate of phagocytized *Histoplasma capsulatum* (HC) in human endothelial cells (EC) in culture. *FASEB J.* 2:5069
10. Bolanos, B., Mitchell, T. G. 1989. Killing of *Cryptococcus neoformans* by rat alveolar macrophages. *J. Med. Vet. Mycol.* 27:219–28
11. Bradsher, R. W., Balk, R. A., Jacobs, R. F. 1987. Growth inhibition of *Blastomyces dermatitidis* in alveolar and peripheral macrophages from patients with blastomycosis. *Am. Rev. Respir. Dis.* 135:412–17
12. Brummer, E. 1989. The role of neutrophils and macrophages in host resistance to systemic fungal infections. See Ref. 80a, pp. 273–89
13. Brummer, E., Hanson, L., Restrepo, A., Stevens, D. A. 1988. In vivo and in vitro activation of alveolar macrophages by gamma-interferon for enhanced killing of *Paracoccidioides brasiliensis* or *Blastomyces dermatitidis*. *J. Immunol.* 140:2786–89
14. Caldwell, C. W., Sprouse, R. F. 1982. Iron and host resistance to histoplasmosis. *Am. Rev. Respir. Dis.* 125:674–77
15. Calich, V. L. G., Kipnis, T. L., Mariano, M., Neto, C. F., da Silva, W. D. 1979. The activation of the complement system by *Paracoccidioides brasiliensis* in vitro: its opsonic effect and possible significance for an in vivo model of infection. *Clin. Immunol. Immunopath.* 12:20–30
16. Calich, V. L. G., Singer-Vermes, L. M., Siqueira, A. M., Burger, E. 1985. Susceptibility and resistance of inbred mice to *Paracoccidioides brasiliensis*. *Br. J. Exp. Path.* 66:585–94
17. Caroline, L., Taschdjian, C. L., Kozinn, P. J., Schade, A. L. 1964. Reversal of serum fungistasis by addition of iron. *J. Invest. Dermatol.* 42:415–19
18. Cech, P., Lehrer, R. I. 1984. Heterogeneity of human neutrophil phagolysosomes: functional consequences for candidacidal activity. *Blood* 64:147–51
19. Chinn, R. Y. W., Diamond, R. D. 1982. Generation of chemotactic factors by *Rhizopus oryzae* in the presence and absence of serum: relationship to hyphal damage mediated by human neutrophils and effects of hyperglycemia and ketoacidosis. *Infect. Immun.* 38:1123–29
20. Cho, Y. S., Choi, H. Y. 1979. Opportunistic fungal infection among cancer patients: a ten year autopsy study. *Am. J. Clin. Pathol.* 72:617–20
21. Choudhury, C., Raman, C., Gallagher, M. T., Tewari, R. P. 1989. Restoration of natural killer cell activity and immune competence against *Histoplasma capsulatum* in hairy-cell leukemia following treatment with recombinant alpha interferon. *Curr. Ther. Res.* 45:179–87
22. Cohen, A. B., Cline, M. J. 1971. The human alveolar macrophage: isolation, cultivation in vitro, and studies of morphologic and functional characteristics. *J. Clin. Invest.* 50:1390–98
23. Cohen, M. S., Isturiz, R. E., Malech, H. L., Root, R. K., Wilfert, C. M., et al. 1981. Fungal infection in chronic granulomatous disease. *Am. J. Med.* 71:59–66
24. Cox, R. A. 1989. Coccidioidomycosis. See Ref. 24a, pp. 166–97
24a. Cox, R. A., ed. 1989. *Immunology of*

the *Fungal Diseases*. Boca Raton, FL: CRC

25. Cox, R. A., Kennell, W., Boncyk, L., Murphy, J. W. 1988. Induction and expression of cell-mediated immune responses in inbred mice infected with *C. immitis*. *Infect. Immun.* 56:13–17

26. Cutler, J. E. 1977. Chemotactic factor produced by *Candida albicans*. *Infect. Immun.* 18:568–73

27. Deresinski, S. C., Stevens, D. A. 1975. Coccidioidomycosis in compromised hosts. Experience at Stanford University Hospital. *Medicine* 54:377–95

28. Diamond, R. D. 1988. Fungal surfaces: effects of interactions with phagocytic cells. *Rev. Infect. Dis.* 10(Suppl. 2): S428–31

29. Diamond, R. D., Erickson, N. F. III. 1982. Chemotaxis of human neutrophils and monocytes induced by *Cryptococcus neoformans*. *Infect. Immun.* 38:380–82

30. Diamond, R. D., May, J. E., Kane, M., Frank, M. M., Bennett, J. E. 1973. The role of late complement components and the alternate complement pathway in experimental cryptococcosis. *Proc. Soc. Exp. Biol. Med.* 144:312–15

31. Djeu, J. Y., Blanchard, D. K. 1987. Regulation of human polymorphonuclear neutrophil (PMN) activity against *Candida albicans* by large granular lymphocytes via release of a PMN-activating factor. *J. Immunol.* 139:2761–67

32. Djeu, J. Y., Blanchard, D. K., Halkias, D., Friedman, H. 1986. Growth inhibition of *Candida albicans* by human polymorphonuclear neutrophils: activation by interferon-γ and tumor necrosis factor. *J. Immunol.* 137:2980–84

33. Djeu, J. Y., Blanchard, D. K., Richards, A. L., Friedman, H. 1988. Tumor necrosis factor induction by *Candida albicans* from human natural killer cells and monocytes. *J. Immunol.* 141: 4047–52

34. Drutz, D. J., Huppert, M. 1983. Coccidioidomycosis: Factors affecting the host-parasite interaction. *J. Infect. Dis.* 147:372–90

35. Drutz, D. J., Huppert, M., Sun, S. H., McGuire, W. L. 1981. Human sex hormones stimulate the growth and maturation of *Coccidioides immitis*. *Infect. Immun.* 32:897–907

36. Edwards, J. E. Jr., Rotrosen, D., Fontaine, J. W., Haudenschild, C. C., Diamond, R. D. 1987. Neutrophil-mediated protection of cultured human vascular endothelial cells from damage by growing *Candida albicans* hyphae. *Blood* 69:1450–57

37. Eissenberg, L. G., Klimpel, K. R., Goldman, W. E. 1989. Invasion of respiratory epithelial cells by *Histoplasma capsulatum*: an alternative strategy for intracellular parasitism. *Abstr. Annu. Meet. Am. Soc. Microbiol.* F122:478

38. Ferrante, A. 1989. Tumor necrosis factor alpha potentiates neutrophil antimicrobial activity: increased fungicidal activity against *Torulopsis glabrata* and *Candida albicans* and associated increases in oxygen radical production and lysosomal enzyme release. *Infect. Immun.* 57:2115–22

39. Fietia, A., Sacchi, F., Mangiarotti, P., Manara, G., Grassi, G. 1984. Defective phagocyte *Aspergillus* killing associated with recurrent pulmonary *Aspergillus* infections. *Infection* 12:10–13

40. Fleischmann, J., Chung, Y., Golde, D. W., Baldwin, G. C. 1989. Granulocyte-macrophage colony stimulating factor (GM-CSF) activates human macrophages to kill *Cryptococcus neoformans*. *Int. Conf. Cryptococcus and Cryptococcosis.* Abstr. P-19, p. 300

41. Fleischmann, J., Lehrer, R. I. 1983. Phagocytic mechanisms in host response. In *Fungi Pathogenic for Humans and Animals*, ed. D. H. Howard, 2:123–49. New York: Dekker

42. Flesch, I. E. A., Schwamberger, G., Kaufmann, S. H. E. 1989. Fungicidal activity of IFN-γ-activated macrophages. Extracellular killing of *Cryptococcus neoformans*. *J. Immunol.* 142: 3219–24

43. Flynn, N. M., Hoeprich, P. D., Kawachi, M. M., Lee, K. K., Lawrence, R. M., et al. 1979. An unusual outbreak of windborne coccidioidomycosis. *New Engl. J. Med.* 301:358–63

44. Frey, C. L., Drutz, D. J. 1986. Influence of fungal surface components on the interaction of *Coccidioides immitis* with polymorphonuclear neutrophils. *J. Infect. Dis.* 153:933–43

45. Fung, P. Y. S., Murphy, J. W. 1982. In vitro interactions of immune lymphocytes and *Cryptococcus neoformans*. *Infect. Immun.* 36:1128–38

46. Gadebusch, H. H., Johnson, A. G. 1966. Natural host resistance to infection with *Cryptococcus neoformans*. IV. The effect of some cationic proteins on the experimental disease. *J. Infect. Dis.* 116:551–65

47. Galgiani, J. N., Yam, P., Petz, L. D., Williams, P. L., Stevens, D. A. 1980. Complement activation by *Coccidioides immitis*: in vitro and clinical studies. *Infect. Immun.* 28:944–49

48. Garzon, S., Marquis, G., Montplaisir,

S., Kurstak, E. 1989. Antigenic structure of *Candida albicans:* electron microscopic localization of polysaccharide and immunodeterminants in the cell wall. See Ref. 80a, pp. 3–36

49. Gatchel, S. L., Shigematsu, M. L., Maciag, T., Tewari, R. P. 1986. Interactions of *Histoplasma capsulatum* with human endothelial cells in culture. *Abstr. Annu. Meet. Am. Soc. Microbiol.* F15:400

50. Geng, J. G., Bevilacqua, M. P., Moore, K. L., Prescott, S. M., Kim, J. M., et al. 1990. Rapid neutrophil adhesion to activated endothelium by GMP-140. *Nature* 343(6260):757–60

51. Granger, D. L., Hibbs, J. B. Jr., Perfect, J. R., Durack, D. T. 1988. Specific amino acid (L-arginine) requirement for the microbiostatic activity of murine macrophages. *J. Clin. Invest.* 81:1129–36

52. Harvey, R. P. 1980. Coccidioidomycosis in pregnancy. See Ref. 129a, pp. 241–44

53. Hector, R. F., Domer, J. E., Carrow, E. W. 1982. Immune responses to *Candida albicans* in genetically distinct mice. *Infect. Immun.* 38:1020–28

54. Hidore, M. R., Mislan, T. W., Murphy, J. W. 1991. Responses of murine natural killer cells to binding of the fungal target, *Cryptococcus neoformans. Infect. Immun.* 59:1489–99

55. Hidore, M. R., Murphy, J. W. 1986. Natural cellular resistance of beige mice against *Cryptococcus neoformans. J. Immunol.* 137:3624–31

56. Hidore, M. R., Murphy, J. W. 1989. Murine natural killer cell interactions with a fungal target, *Cryptococcus neoformans. Infect. Immun.* 57:1990–97

57. Hidore, M. R., Murphy, J. W. 1986. Correlation of natural killer cell activity and clearance of *Cryptococcus neoformans* from mice after adoptive transfer of splenic nylon wool nonadherent cells. *Infect. Immun.* 51:547–55

58. Hidore, M. R., Nabavi, N., Reynolds, C. W., Henkart, P. A., Murphy, J. W. 1990. Cytoplasmic components of natural killer cells inhibit the growth of *Cryptococcus neoformans. J. Leuk. Biol.* 45:15–26

59. Hidore, M. R., Nabavi, N., Sonleitner, F., Murphy, J. W. 1991. Murine natural killer cells are fungicidal to *Cryptococcus neoformans. Infect. Immun.* 59: In press

60. Howard, D. H. 1961. Some factors which affect the initiation of growth of *Cryptococcus neoformans. J. Bacteriol.* 82:430–35

61. Huppert, M., Sun, S. H., Gleason-Jordan, I., Vukovich, K. R. 1976. Lung weight parallels disease severity in experimental coccidioidomycosis. *Infect. Immun.* 14:1356–68

62. Igel, H. J., Bolande, R. P. 1966. Humoral defense mechanisms in cryptococcosis: substances in normal human serum, saliva, and cerebrospinal fluid affecting the growth of *Cryptococcus neoformans. J. Infect. Dis.* 116:75–83

63. Janusz, M. J., Austen, K. F., Czop, J. K. 1988. Phagocytosis of heat-killed blastospores of *Candida albicans* by human monocyte β-glucan receptors. *Immunology* 65:181–85

64. Jimenez, B. E., Murphy, J. W. 1984. In vitro effects of natural killer cells against *Parracoccidioides brasiliensis* yeast phase. *Infect. Immun.* 46:552–58

65. Kalo-Klein, A., Witkin, S. S. 1989. *Candida albicans:* cellular immune system interactions during different stages of the menstrual cycle. *Am. J. Obstet. Gynecol.* 161:1132–36

66. Kan, V. L., Bennett, J. E. 1988. Lectin-like attachment sites on murine pulmonary alveolar macrophages bind *Aspergillus fumigatus* conidia. *J. Infect. Dis.* 158:407–14

67. Kimberlin, C. L., Hariri, A. R., Hempel, H. O., Goodman, N. L. 1981. Interactions between *Histoplasma capsulatum* and macrophages from normal and treated mice: comparison of the mycelial and yeast phases in alveolar and peritoneal macrophages. *Infect. Immun.* 34:6–10

68. Kinsman, O. S., Collard, A. E. 1986. Hormonal factors in vaginal candidiasis in rats. *Infect. Immun.* 53:498–504

69. Kirkland, T. N., Fierer, J. 1983. Inbred mouse strains differ in resistance to lethal *Coccidioides immitis* infection. *Infect. Immun.* 40:912–16

70. Kirkland, T. N., Fierer, J. 1985. Genetic control of resistance to *Coccidioides immitis:* a single gene that is expressed in spleen cells determines resistance. *J. Immunol.* 135:548–52

71. Kirkpatrick, C. H., Green, I., Rich, R. R., Schade, A. L. 1971. Inhibition of growth of *Candida albicans* by iron-unsaturated lactoferrin: relation to host-defense mechanisms in chronic mucocutaneous candidiasis. *J. Infect. Dis.* 124:539–44

72. Klotz, S. A., Drutz, D. J., Harrison, J. L., Huppert, M. 1983. Adherence and penetration of vascular endothelium by *Candida* yeast. *Infect. Immun.* 42:374–84

73. Kolotila, M. P., Diamond, R. D. 1988.

Stimulation of neutrophil actin polymerization and degranulation by opsonized and unopsonized *Candida albicans* hyphae and zymosan. *Infect. Immun.* 56:2016–22

74. Kolotila, M. P., Diamond, R. D. 1990. Effects of neutrophils and in vitro oxidants on survival and phenotypic switching of *Candida albicans* WO-1. *Infect. Immun.* 58:1174–79

75. Kong, Y. M., Levine, H. B., Madin, S. H., Smith, C. E. 1964. Fungal multiplication and histopathologic changes in vaccinated mice infected with *Coccidioides immitis*. *J. Immunol.* 92:779–90

76. Kozel, T. R. 1989. Antigenic structure of *Cryptococcus neoformans* capsular polysaccharides, See Ref. 80a, pp. 63–86

77. Kozel, T. R., Pfrommer, G. S. T., Guerlain, A. S., Highison, B. A., Highison, G. J. 1988. Strain variation in phagocytosis of *Cryptococcus neoformans:* dissociation of susceptibility to phagocytosis from activation and binding of opsonic fragments of C3. *Infect. Immun.* 56:2794–2800

78. Kozel, T. R., Pfrommer, G. S. T., Guerlain, A. S., Highison, B. A., Highison, G. J. 1988. Role of the capsule in phagocytosis of *Cryptococcus neoformans*. *Ref. Infect. Dis.* 10:S436–39

79. Kozel, T. R., Pfrommer, G. S. T., Redelman, D. 1987. Activated neutrophils exhibit enhanced phagocytosis of *Cryptococcus neoformans* opsonized with normal human serum. *Clin. Exp. Immunol.* 70:238–46

80. Kozel, T. R., Wilson, M. A., Pfrommer, G. S. T., Schlageter, A. M. 1989. Activation and binding of opsonic fragments of C3 on encapsulated *Cryptococcus neoformans* by using an alternative complement pathway reconstituted from six isolated proteins. *Infect. Immun.* 57:1922–27

80a. Kurstak, E., ed. 1989. *Immunology of Fungal Diseases*, Immunology Series 47. New York: Dekker

81. Kwon-Chung, K. J., Lehman, D., Good, C., Magee, P. T. 1985. Genetic evidence for role of extracellular proteinase in virulence of *Candida albicans*. *Infect. Immun.* 49:571–75

82. Lattime, E. C., Stoppacciaro, A., Khan, A., Stutman, O. 1988. Human natural cytotoxic activity mediated by tumor necrosis factor: regulation by interleukin-2. *J. Natl. Cancer Inst.* 80:1035–38

83. Lehrer, R. I. 1975. The fungicidal mechanisms of human monocytes. I. Evidence for myeloperoxidase-linked

and myeloperoxidase-independent candidacidal mechanisms. *J. Clin. Invest.* 55:338–46

84. Lehrer, R. I., Cline, M. J. 1969. Leukocyte myeloperoxidase deficiency and disseminated candidiasis: the role of myeloperoxidase in resistance to *Candida* infection. *J. Clin. Invest.* 48:1478–88

85. Lehrer, R. I., Fleischmann, J. 1982. Antifungal defense by macrophages. In *Microbiology 1982*, ed. D. Schlessinger, pp. 385–87. Washington, DC:Am. Soc. Microbiol.

86. Lehrer, R. I., Ganz, T. 1990. Antimicrobial polypeptides of human neutrophils. *Blood* 76:2169–81

87. Levitz, S. M., Diamond, R. D. 1984. Killing of *Aspergillus fumigatus* spores and *Candida albicans* yeast phase by the iron-hydrogen peroxide-iodide cytotoxic system: comparison with the myeloperoxidase-hydrogen peroxide-halide system. *Infect. Immun.* 43:1100–2

88. Levitz, S. M., DiBenedetto, D. J. 1989. Paradoxical role of capsule in murine bronchoalveolar macrophage-mediated killing of *Cryptococcus neoformans*. *J. Immunol.* 142:659–65

89. Levitz, S. M., Farrell, T. P. 1990. Growth inhibition of *Cryptococcus neoformans* by cultured human monocytes: role of the capsule, opsonins, the culture surface, and cytokines. *Infect. Immun.* 58:1201–9

90. Lipscomb, M. F., Alvarellos, T., Toews, G. B., Tompkins, R., Evans, Z., et al. Role of natural killer cells in resistance to *Cryptococcus neoformans* infections in mice. *Am. J. Pathol.* 128:354–61

91. Lyman, C. A., Simons, E. R., Melnick, D. A., Diamond, R. D. 1988. Induction of signal transduction in human neutrophils by *Candida albicans* hyphae: the role of pertussis toxin-sensitive guanosine triphosphate-binding proteins. *J. Infect. Dis.* 158:1056–64

92. Marquis, G., Montplaisir, S., Pelletier, M., Mousseau, S., Auger, P. 1986. Strain-dependent differences in susceptibility of mice to experimental candidosis. *J. Infect. Dis.* 154:906–9

93. McGinnis, M. R. 1980. In *Laboratory Handbook of Medical Mycology*, pp. 46–55. New York: Academic

94. McNamara, P. M., Wiessner, J. H., Collins-Lech, C., Hahn, B. L., Sohnle, P. G. 1988. Neutrophil death as a defence mechanism against *Candida albicans* infections. *Lancet* 2:1163–65

95. Miller, M. F., Mitchell, T. G. 1991. Killing of *Cryptococcus neoformans*

strains by human neutrophils and monocytes. *Infect. Immun.* 59:24–28
96. Miller, M. F., Mitchell, T. G., Storkus, W. J., Dawson, J. R. 1990. Human natural killer cells do not inhibit growth of *Cryptococcus neoformans* in the absence of antibody. *Infect. Immun.* 58:639–45
97. Murphy, J. W. 1989. Cryptococcosis. See Ref. 24a, pp. 93–138
98. Murphy, J. W. 1989. Natural host resistance mechanisms against systemic mycotic agents. In *Functions of the Natural Immune System.* ed. C. W. Reynolds, R. H. Wiltrout, pp. 149–84. New York: Plenum
99. Murphy, J. W. 1990. Immunity to fungi. *Curr. Opin. Immun.* 2:360–67
100. Murphy, J. W., Hidore, M. R., Nabavi, N. 1991. Binding interactions of murine natural killer cells with the fungal target, *Cryptococcus neoformans. Infect. Immun.* 59:1476–88
101. Murphy, J. W., McDaniel, D. O. 1982. In vitro effects of natural killer (NK) cells against *Cryptococcus neoformans. J. Immunol.* 128:1577–83
102. Nabavi, N., Murphy, J. W. 1985. In vitro binding of natural killer cells to *Cryptococcus neoformans* targets. *Infect. Immun.* 50:50–57
103. Nabavi, N., Murphy, J. W. 1986. Antibody-dependent natural killer cell mediated growth inhibition of *Cryptococcus neoformans. Infect. Immun.* 51:556–62
104. Newman, S. L., Bucher, C., Rhodes, J., Bullock, W. E. 1990. Phagocytosis of *Histoplasma capsulatum* yeasts and microconidia by human cultured macrophages and alveolar macrophages. *J. Clin. Invest.* 85:223–30
105. Newman, S. L., Gootee, L., Bucher, C., Bullock, W. E. 1991. Inhibition of intracellular growth of *Histoplasma capsulatum* yeast cells by cytokine-activated human monocytes and macrophages. *Infect. Immun.* 59:737–41
106. Ortaldo, J. R., Hiserodt, J. C. 1989. Mechanisms of target cell killing by natural killer cells. *Curr. Opin. Immun.* 2:39–42
107. Pappagianis, D. 1980. Epidemiology of coccidioidomycosis. See Ref. 129a, pp. 63–85
108. Pappagianis, D., Lindsay, S., Beall, S., Williams, P. 1979. Ethnic background and the clinical course of coccidioidomycosis. *Am. Rev. Respir. Dis.* 120:959–61
109. Peterson, E. M., Calderone, R. A. 1977. Growth inhibition of *Candida albicans* by rabbit alveolar macrophages. *Infect. Immun.* 15:910–15

110. Petkus, A. F., Baum, L. L. 1987. Natural killer cell inhibition of young spherules and endospores of *Coccidioides immitis. J. Immunol.* 139:3107–11
111. Pober, J. S., Gimbrone, M. A., Lapierre, L. A., Mendrick, D. L., Fiers, W., et al. 1986. Overlapping patterns of antigenic modulation by interleukin 1, tumor necrosis factor, and immune interferon. *J. Immunol.* 137:1893–96
112. Powell, B. L., Drutz, D. J. 1984. Identification of high affinity binder for estradiol and a low-affinity binder for testosterone in *Coccidioides immitis. Infect. Immun.* 45:784–86
113. Powell, B. L., Drutz, D. J., Huppert, M., Sun, S. H. 1983. Relationship of progesterone- and estradiol-binding proteins in *Coccidioides immitis. Infect. Immun.* 40:478–85
114. Ratnoff, W. D., Pepple, J. M., Winkelstein, J. A. 1980. Activation of the alternative complement pathway by *Histoplasma capsulatum. Infect. Immun.* 30:147–49
115. Restrepo, A., Salazar, M. E., Cano, L. E., Stover, E. P., Fledman, D., Stevens, D. A. 1984. Estrogens inhibit mycelium-to-yeast transformation in the fungus *Paracoccidioides brasiliensis:* implications for resistance of females to paracoccidioidomycosis. *Infect. Immun.* 46:346–53
116. Rhodes, J. C. 1985. Contribution of complement component C5 to the pathogenesis of experimental murine cryptococcosis. *Sabouraudia: J. Med. Vet. Mycol.* 23:225–34
117. Rhodes, J. C., Wicker, L. S., Urba, W. J. 1980. Genetic control of susceptibility to *Cryptococcus neoformans* in mice. *Infect. Immun.* 29:494–99
118. Rippon, J. W. 1988. In *Medical Mycology,* pp. 121–53 Philadelphia: Saunders. 3rd ed.
119. Sawyer, D. W., Donowitz, G. R., Mandel, G. L. 1989. Polymorphonuclear neutrophils: an effective antimicrobial force. *Rev. Infect. Dis.* 11(Suppl. 7): S1532–44
120. Schaffner, A., Davis, C. E., Schaffner, T., Markert, M., Douglas, H., et al. 1986. In vitro susceptibility of fungi to killing by neutrophil granulocytes discriminates between primary pathogenicity and opportunism. *J. Clin. Invest.* 78:511–24
121. Schneerson-Porat, S., Shahar, A., Aronson, M. 1965. Formation of histiocyte rings in response to *Cryptococcus neoformans* infection. *J. Reticuloendothel. Soc.* 2:249–55
122. Schnur, R. A., Newman, S. L. 1990.

The respiratory burst response to *Histoplasma capsulatum* by human neutrophils. Evidence for intracellular trapping of superoxide anion. *J. Immunol.* 144: 4765–72

123. Slagle, D. C., Cox, R. A., Kuruganti, U. 1989. Induction of tumor necrosis factor alpha by spherules of *Coccidioides immitis*. *Infect. Immun.* 57: 1916–21

124. Smail, E. H., Melnick, D. A., Ruggeri, R., Diamond, R. D. 1988. A novel natural inhibitor from *Candida albicans* hyphae causing dissociation of the neutrophil respiratory burst response to chemotactic peptides from other postactivating events. *J. Immunol.* 140: 3893–99

125. Smith, C. W., Marlin, S. D., Rothlein, R., Toman, C., Anderson, D. C. 1989. Cooperative interactions of LFA-1 and Mac-1 with intercellular adhesion molecule 1 in facilitating adherence and transendothelial migration of human neutrophils in vitro. *J. Clin. Invest.* 83:2008–17

126. Smith, P. D., Lamerson, C. L., Banks, S. M., Saini, S. S., Wahl, L. M., et al. 1990. Granulocyte-macrophage colony-stimulating factor augments human monocyte fungicidal activity for *Candida albicans*. *J. Infect. Dis.* 161:999–1005

127. Sobel, J. D. 1985. Epidemiology and pathogenesis of recurrent vulvovaginal candidiasis. *Am. J. Obstet. Gynecol.* 152:924–35

128. Sohnle, P. E., Collins-Lech, C. 1990. Comparison of candidacidal and candidastatic activities of human neutrophils. *Infect. Immun.* 58:2696–98

129. Sohnle, P. G. 1989. Dermatophytosis. See Ref. 24a, pp. 1–27

129a. Stevens, D. A., ed. 1980. *Coccidioidomycosis. A Text.* New York: Plenum

130. Sutcliffe, M. C., Savage, A. M., Alford, R. H. 1980. Transferrin-dependent growth inhibition of yeast-phase *Histoplasma capsulatum* by human serum and lymph. *J. Infect. Dis.* 142:209–19

131. Tewari, R. P., Bhardwaj, G., Kondoh, Y., Raman, C. 1988. Fate of phagocytized *Histoplasma capsulatum* (HC) in murine lung endothelial cells (EC) in culture. *Congr. Int. Soc. for Human and Animal Mycoses Barcelona.* Barcelona: Prous Sci. Publ. Abstr. O-52

132. Thiele, D. L., Lipsky, P. E. 1989. The role of cell surface recognition structures in the initiation of MHC-unrestricted "promiscuous" killing by T cells. *Immunol. Today* 10:375–81

133. Thurmond, L. M., Mitchell, T. G. 1984. *Blastomyces dermatitidis* chemotactic factor: kinetics of production and biological characterization evaluated by a modified neutrophil chemotaxis assay. *Infect. Immun.* 46:87–93

134. Trinchieri, G. 1989. Biology of natural killer cells. *Adv. Immunol.* 47:187–375

135. van't Wout, J. W., Linde, I., Leijh, P. C. J., van Furth, R. 1988. Contribution of granulocytes and monocytes to resistance against experimental disseminated *Candida albicans* infection. *Eur. J. Clin. Microbiol. Infect. Dis.* 7:736–41

136. Wagner, D. K., Collins-Lech, C., Sohnle, P. G. 1986. Inhibition of neutrophil killing of *Candida albicans* pseudohyphae by substances which quench hypochlorous acid and chloramines. *Infect. Immun.* 51:731–35

137. Waldorf, A. R. 1989. Pulmonary defense mechanisms against opportunistic fungal pathogens. See Ref. 80a, pp. 243–71

138. Waldorf, A. R., Diamond, R. D. 1985. Neutrophil chemotactic responses induced by fresh and swollen *Rhizopus oryzae* spores and *Aspergillus fumigatus* conidia. *Infect. Immun.* 48:458–563

139. Wang, M., Friedman, H., Djeu, J. Y. 1989. Enhancement of human monocyte function against *Candida albicans* by the colony-stimulating factors (CSF): IL-3, granulocyte-macrophage-CSF, and macrophage-CSF. *J. Immunol.* 143:671–77

140. Watanabe, K., Kagaya, K., Yamada, T., Fukazawa, Y. 1991. Mechanism for candidacidal activity in macrophages activated by recombinant gamma interferon. *Infect. Immun.* 59:521–28

141. Weeks, B. A., Escobar, M. R., Hamilton, P. B., Fueston, V. M. 1976. Chemotaxis of polymorphonuclear neutrophilic leukocytes by mannan-enriched preparations of *Candida albicans*. *Adv. Exp. Med. Biol.* 73:161–69

142. Wei, S., Serbousek, D., McMillen, S., Blanchard, D. K., Djeu, J. Y. 1991. Suppression of human monocyte function against *Candida albicans* by autologous IL-2 induced lymphokine-activated killer cells. *J. Immunol.* 146:337–42

143. Weinberg, P. B., Becker, S., Granger, D. L., Koren, H. S. 1987. Growth inhibition of *Cryptococcus neoformans* by human alveolar macrophages. *Am. Rev. Respir. Dis.* 136:1242–47

144. Wu-Hsieh, B. 1989. Relative susceptibilities of inbred mouse strains C57BL/6

and A/J to infection with *Histoplasma capsulatum*. *Infect. Immun.* 57:3788–92

145. Wu-Hsieh, B., Howard, D. H. 1989. Histoplasmosis. See Ref. 24a, pp. 199–225

146. Wysong, D. R., Lyman, C. A., Diamond, R. D. 1989. Independence of neutrophil respiratory burst oxidant generation from the early cytosolic calcium response after stimulation with unopsonized *Candida albicans* hyphae. *Infect. Immun.* 57:1499–1505

147. Yuan, L., Cole, G. T. 1987. Isolation and characterization of an extracellular proteinase of *Coccidioides immitis*. *Infect. Immun.* 55:1970–78

148. Zunino, S. J., Hudig, D. 1988. Interactions between human natural killer (NK) lymphocytes and yeast cells: human NK cells do not kill *Candida albicans* although *C. albicans* blocks NK lysis of K562 cells. *Infect. Immun.* 56:564–69

Annu. Rev. Microbiol. 1991. 45:539–67

NUCLEAR FUSION IN YEAST

Mark D. Rose

Department of Molecular Biology, Princeton University, Princeton, New Jersey 08544-1014

KEY WORDS: karyogamy, *Saccharomyces cerevisiae*, microtubule, conjugation

CONTENTS

PERSPECTIVES 539
PATHWAY OF NUCLEAR FUSION 540
   Mating and Nuclear Fusion 540
   Mutations That Block Nuclear Fusion 544
   Assays for Nuclear Fusion 545
   Unilaterality Versus Bilaterality 546
GENES REQUIRED FOR NUCLEAR FUSION 549
   KAR1 549
   KAR3 552
   BIK1 555
   KAR2 556
   CDC4 558
   KEM *Genes* 558
   CIN1 559
   CIK *Genes* 560
   CDC28, CDC34, *and* CDC37 560
MODELS FOR NUCLEAR FUSION 561
CONCLUSION 563

PERSPECTIVES

One of the major questions in cell biology concerns the identification of the regulatory information responsible for specifying the variety of microtubule structures and functions throughout the cell cycle. Clearly, both temporal and spatial regulation control the assembly, stabilization, and disassembly of the microtubule array. However, an array is not merely assembled; the research-

539

0066-4227/91/1001-0539$02.00

er's investigation of microtubules must include the identification of the motor proteins responsible for movement on the array and the sources of their functional specificity.

Yeasts and other simple eukaryotes that have facile methods for genetic analysis provide ideal systems for the identification of regulatory information because first, although regulatory proteins may be biochemically minor components of the cell, the genes specifying them should represent a fraction of the genome comparable to, if not greater than, that encoding the structural elements their products control. Therefore, any genetic screen for mutations affecting a microtubule-dependent process should identify regulatory and structural elements with equal probability. Second, although the microtubule arrays in yeasts are less extensive than in other eukaryotes, many microtubule-dependent processes have been conserved among all eukaryotes. Finally, extremely powerful and sensitive genetic selections and screens can be applied for the isolation of mutations that specifically affect microtubule-dependent processes.

This review focuses on current research to identify the components responsible for one specific microtubule-dependent process, nuclear fusion (karyogamy) in the yeast *Saccharomyces cerevisiae*.

PATHWAY OF NUCLEAR FUSION

Mating and Nuclear Fusion

In yeast, as in other fungi, the nuclear envelope remains intact throughout all phases of the life cycle (9), which has two important consequences for the purpose of this review. First, during conjugation a mechanism exists to fuse two haploid nuclei to produce a diploid nucleus in the zygote. Second, the microtubule organizing center, which is thought to be responsible for the assembly of most if not all microtubules in the cell (for reviews, see 7, 40, 80), is physically embedded in the nuclear envelope (10, 11, 58, 59). The significance of this location will become apparent when the mechanism of nuclear fusion is discussed.

That a specific mechanism for nuclear fusion must exist is not immediately apparent. During fertilization in most (although not all) animal and plant cells, nuclear fusion does not occur until after the pronuclear envelopes disassemble as part of the first zygotic mitosis. Both parental genomes enter the same nucleus through the subsequent reformation of the nuclear envelope. In contrast, in most fungi (particularly the filamentous fungi), the nuclear envelope remains intact, and cells bearing more than one nucleus (heterokaryons) may be quite stable throughout multiple mitoses. In these fungi, nuclear fusion typically occurs as part of the process leading to meiosis and sexual sporulation.

In *S. cerevisiae*, the introduction of two nuclei into the same cell normally occurs only during mating, which is independent of sporulation. Spheroplasts prepared from haploid cells of the same (*MAT*a) mating type were artificially fused to test whether nuclear fusion is simply a constitutive property of nuclei or is specific to conjugation. With mitotic cells, the rate of nuclear fusion is approximately 10^{-5} among viable spheroplasts. In contrast, pretreatment with mating pheromone produced by cells of the opposite mating type (α-factor) increases the frequency of nuclear fusion by as much as 10,000-fold (15, 64). This stimulation does not merely result from cell synchrony; a mutation that causes cells to arrest at the same stage of the cell cycle does not simultaneously activate them for nuclear fusion. However, the arrested mutant cells retain the ability to be stimulated for nuclear fusion by mating pheromone.

A second argument for the existence of a pathway of nuclear fusion is based on the relatively specific mutations that block it (12, 60). Certain mutations can drastically reduce nuclear fusion without measurably affecting the normal cell-division cycle. Therefore, a specific pathway of nuclear fusion probably exists, which is at least partially activated in response to mating pheromone.

As mentioned above, the other important corollary of a stable nuclear envelope is the location of the yeast microtubule organizing center, called the spindle pole body or SPB. The SPB is a planar, disc-shaped, multilamellar structure embedded in the plane of the nuclear envelope. Extending through the nuclear envelope, it has both an intranuclear and cytoplasmic face (9–11, 58, 59, 80). At various stages of the cell cycle, different sets of microtubules emanate from the two opposite faces of the SPB. The nuclear microtubules are responsible for the events of mitosis, including spindle formation and elongation and chromosome segregation (40–42, 66, 73). The cytoplasmic microtubules are thought to be responsible for the movement and positioning of the nucleus within the cell (16, 40–42, 73). They may also contribute to spindle elongation.

Electron microscopic examination of mating cells reveals that the SPB and the cytoplasmic microtubules appear to play critical roles in nuclear fusion (Figure 1) (11). As yeast cells exchange specific peptide pheromones, they induce a mating reaction in cells of the opposite mating type (for recent reviews, see 13, 37). Stimulated cells form cellular projections and are frequently called *shmoos*. In wild-type shmoos, the nuclei are normally found near the point of the projection, and short cytoplasmic microtubules extend towards the point. The cell wall is broken down where the two mating cells come into close contact (11, 56). The shmoo projection probably corresponds to the region where cells would fuse to form the zygote (27, 74). The plasma membrane between the two mating cells breaks down, effectively making a continuous cytoplasm. As a result of their previous location, the nuclei

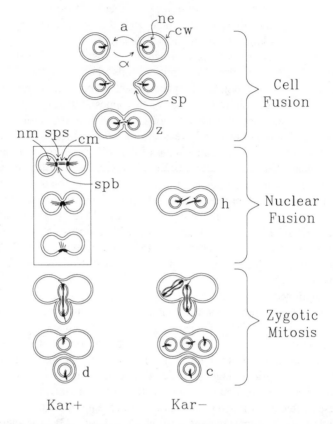

Figure 1 Schematic pathway of nuclear fusion during *Saccharomyces cerevisiae* conjugation. *Cell Fusion:* Cells of opposite mating type exchange peptide mating pheromones, indicated by arrows. Responding cells arrest in G1 and develop cellular projections (shmoos). Cell wall and plasma membrane dissolution allows the cells to fuse, forming the zygote. *Nuclear Fusion:* In Kar⁺ zygotes (box encloses enlarged depiction of nuclei only), the haploid nuclei rapidly become associated by interdigitating cytoplasmic microtubules arising from the two spindle pole bodies (SPB). Nuclei move together and subsequent nuclear envelope fusion initiates along one edge of the SPB. The resulting diploid nucleus has a novel zygotic SPB bearing a crease marking the site of fusion. In Kar⁻ zygotes, (e.g. *kar3* deletion mutants) the microtubules fail to interact; the nuclei remain separate; and a heterokaryotic zygote is formed. In both *kar1* and *kar3* mutant zygotes, long cytoplasmic microtubules are observed. *Zygotic Mitosis:* In Kar⁺ zygotes, a normal mitotic division ensues yielding both a diploid bud and a diploid zygote, each of which may go through multiple subsequent mitotic divisions. In a Kar⁻ zygote, both haploid nuclei undergo mitotic divisions. Usually one but often two haploid nuclei may then enter the zygotic bud. The haploid bud containing cytoplasmic genetic determinants derived from the opposite parent is called a cytoductant. Symbols are: a, **a**-factor; α, α-factor; ne, nuclear envelope; cw, cell wall; sp, shmoo projection; z, zygote; nm, nuclear microtubules; sps, spindle pole body satellite; cm, cytoplasmic microtubules; spb, spindle pole body; h, heterokaryon; c, haploid cytoductant; d, diploid.

are positioned close to the region of cell fusion with their SPBs directly opposed to one another. The cytoplasmic microtubules interconnect the two SPBs; the nuclei move together; and nuclear envelope fusion initiates along one edge of the two SPBs (11). Ultimately a single fused SPB, bearing a central crease, is formed, embedded in the envelope of the diploid nucleus. The zygote then enters a normal mitotic cycle. After DNA replication, the nucleus divides and a diploid nucleus enters the bud. The zygote is normally competent to undergo several subsequent mitotic divisions.

From the above description, several distinct elements of the nuclear fusion pathway can be discerned. First, microtubules may be required at more than one step. They may initially position the nuclei near the site of cell fusion. Subsequently they may serve in the congression of the nuclei in the zygote. Several studies have demonstrated that polymerized microtubules are indeed required for nuclear fusion. Drugs that depolymerize microtubules (e.g. benomyl or nocodazole) specifically block nuclear fusion but not cell fusion (16). Interestingly, when zygotes formed in the presence of benomyl or nocodazole are removed from the drug, the nuclei remain separate and the binucleate zygote proceeds through mitosis. Moreover, cold-sensitive mutations in the yeast β-tubulin gene *(TUB2)* block nuclear fusion but not cell fusion at the nonpermissive temperature (41, 73). In fact, several *tub2* alleles that preferentially affect the cytoplasmic microtubules have specific defects in both nuclear positioning and nuclear fusion (41). In addition, several of the genes discussed below have clear effects either on the stability or morphology of the cytoplasmic microtubules in shmoos and zygotes.

The second element in nuclear fusion is the spindle pole body. The SPB also plays several roles in nuclear fusion, serving not only as the nucleating center for the cytoplasmic microtubules that are critical for nuclear fusion, but also as the site where fusion initiates (11).

Finally, the third element of nuclear fusion is the membrane-fusion event, about which the least is known. Current theory assumes that a membrane fusogen catalyzes this step (71). Either specific nuclear fusion proteins or proteins shared with the secretory pathway might be utilized. Furthermore, it is not known exactly how many membranes must fuse to effect nuclear fusion because the cytology of the membrane in the SPB is particularly indistinct. Possibly, both the two outer membranes and the two inner ones must fuse. However, as the SPB is apparently embedded in the nuclear envelope in a manner similar to the nuclear pores (58), the edge of the SPB is a site where the inner membrane is continuous with the outer membrane. Therefore, a single membrane-fusion event, along with subsequent membrane flow, would suffice to join the two nuclei.

The above discussion makes clear that mutations affecting nuclear fusion should serve as sensitive probes for genes that specify structural elements and functions of the cytoplasmic microtubules, the SPB, and the nuclear envelope.

Mutations That Block Nuclear Fusion

Nuclear fusion is mediated by several cellular components, including microtubules and the SPB, that are required for essential mitotic pathways in the cell. In contrast to mitosis, however, nuclear fusion is not an essential function. Because yeasts propagate asexually, a defect in diploid formation has little consequence. Moreover, when cells mate without nuclear fusion, the consequence to the zygote is minimal; they simply proceed to the next round of mitosis with two nuclei instead of one. Usually single haploid nuclei then segregate into the buds so that heterokaryons mostly have uninucleate progeny (44).

Indeed, the utility of the nuclear fusion pathway for genetic studies arises from the fact that it is a nonessential process. Therefore, strong mutations can be isolated that greatly reduce nuclear fusion. Nevertheless, such mutations have frequently proven to be alleles of genes that are also involved in essential mitotic functions. Having identified such genes, researchers can use subsequent molecular genetic analysis to determine the mitotic roles of the genes and classical suppressor analysis to identify other interacting gene products.

Mutations that block nuclear fusion have been identified in three ways: by deliberate selection, by screening known mutations that affect related processes, and by serendipity. A deliberate selection scheme, devised by Conde & Fink (12), enriched for mutants that gave rise to a high frequency of cytoductants during mating. Cytoductants are the haploid progeny from heterokaryotic zygotes that have the nucleus of one parent but a cytoplasmic genetic element derived from the other parent. Cytoductants can be selected using a special strain that bears a nuclear gene for recessive drug resistance (e.g. cycloheximide resistance) but lacks mitochondrial DNA. Such a strain can grow in the presence of the drug but cannot grow on a nonfermentable carbon source (e.g. glycerol). In a cross to a wild-type strain, neither parent can grow on cycloheximide glycerol media. The diploid product of the cross also cannot grow because of the recessive nature of the drug resistance. Only a haploid cytoductant containing the drug resistant nucleus and an intact mitochondrial genome from the other cell can grow. By this route Conde & Fink (12) and later Polaina & Conde (60) isolated several mutations, all of which fell into three complementation groups; *KAR1*, *KAR2*, and *KAR3* (for *kar*yogamy defective).

The selection for Kar⁻ mutations is limited by the requirement that nuclear fusion fail if only one parent is a mutant. This phenotype is referred to as a unilateral karyogamy defect. In contrast, a bilateral karyogamy defect is one in which both parents must share the same defect for fusion to fail; nuclear fusion is normal when the mutants are mated to wild-type strains.

Berlin et al (4) described a screen specifically designed to identify bilateral mutations. In this protocol, the *HO* gene is used to switch the mating type of mutagenized spores. *HO* causes the progeny derived from the same haploid founder spore to have opposite mating types (37). Wild-type progeny quickly mate to form $\mathbf{a}/\alpha$ diploids, which grow into pure colonies of nonmating cells. Progeny of bilateral karyogamy defective mutants mate but give rise to mixed cytoductant colonies. Such colonies contain cells capable of mating with tester strains of both mating types.

In addition to the above screens, nuclear fusion defects have been found associated with mutations in several genes. These include mutations in a number of cell division cycle genes (*CDC4, CDC28, CDC34,* and *CDC37*) (18, 19) as well as the gene encoding β-tubulin (*TUB2*) (41, 73).

Finally, the *BIK1* gene (for *bi*lateral *k*aryogamy defect) was serendipitously discovered because of its location close to the *HIS4* gene (74). A deletion that removed material between *HIS4* and *LEU2* caused very poor rates of diploid formation in crosses in which both parents contained the deletion. Subsequent analysis demonstrated that the deletion had removed two genes required for efficient mating. The *FUS1* gene is required for normal cell fusion (46, 74) whereas the *BIK1* gene is required for efficient nuclear fusion (5, 74).

It is extremely unlikely that all of the genes affecting nuclear fusion have been identified. Current research focuses on identification of the specific roles that the known genes play in nuclear fusion and the isolation of new mutations that produce a bilateral karyogamy defect.

Assays for Nuclear Fusion

Several assays have been employed to measure the efficiency of nuclear fusion. The cytoduction assay used for the selection of Kar⁻ mutants provides a convenient quantitative assay for the efficiency of nuclear fusion. In this assay, researchers measure the frequency of cytoductants relative to the number of diploids (*C/D* ratio) produced in a mass mating. Different recessive auxotrophic mutations are included in each parent, and the efficiency of mating and nuclear fusion is determined by measuring the frequency of prototrophic diploids formed. Up to 60% of the cells of wild-type strains mate to form diploids, and the *C/D* ratio is typically below 0.001. The *kar* mutants typically yield efficiencies of diploid formation in the range of 1–5% (i.e. 10- to 20-fold decrease relative to wild-type), and the *C/D* ratio is in the range of 3 to 6.

However, because buds inherit variable amounts of cytoplasm from each parent and the drug resistance markers are recessive, some of the genetically resistant cytoductant buds will remain phenotypically sensitive. Therefore the

C/D ratio may seriously undercount the frequency of cytoduction. Moreover, as the frequencies of diploid and cytoductant formation are not independent variables, the ratio approximates linearity only at low levels of cytoductant formation.

Because of the inadequacies of the cytoduction assays, two more direct assays for nuclear fusion are also employed. One involves direct microscopic examination of zygotes after fixing and staining with a DNA-specific dye (e.g. the fluorescent dye DAPI). Before the appearance of the first bud, greater than 98% of wild-type zygotes contain a single fused nucleus. With *kar⁻* mutants, only 5–15% of the unbudded zygotes contain a fused nucleus; the remainder contain two nuclei. After a bud has formed, more than two nuclei may be present in *kar⁻* zygotes due to the mitosis of both parental nuclei.

The second assay requires the micromanipulation of several budded zygotes from a mating mixture to defined positions on a slab of nutrient agar. Close to 100% of the wild-type zygotes isolated in this way will give rise to diploid colonies. In contrast, the *kar⁻* mutant zygotes produce only 5–15% diploid colonies. The remaining zygotes give rise to a variety of colony genotypes, either essentially pure clones of one parental genotype or mixtures of the two parents. If a cytoplasmic genetic marker is included in the cross, one can show that even the pure haploid colonies have arisen from zygotes in which cell fusion has occurred. Due to the small numbers of zygotes that can be examined, the direct assays are of utility only when the mutation causes a large decrease in the frequency of nuclear fusion.

The efficiency of diploid formation can also be readily scored in a qualitative assay in which patches of cells growing on an agar plate are mated to a lawn of cells by replica plating. After a few hours, the mating mixture is again replica plated to media that selects for the prototrophic diploids. The 10- to 20-fold reduction in diploid formation that occurs with *kar* mutants is more than adequate to distinguish mutant from wild-type strains.

Unilaterality Versus Bilaterality

Unilateral mutations block nuclear fusion even when the mutant is mated to a wild-type strain. In other words, the wild-type gene product fails to complement the mutant defect in the zygote. In principle, this situation may arise in several ways. The simplest explanation is that the mutation is dominant, but this explanation is inadequate. Although some alleles of *KAR3* are in fact semidominant, mutations in *KAR1* and *KAR2* are completely recessive.

Other explanations of unilaterality require that the gene products act in a way somehow restricted to the nucleus that encodes them. Either temporal or spatial limitation could cause this restriction (19, 24).

Temporal limitation implies the gene must function before the cells fuse.

Mutations in a regulatory gene that is part of the pathway of response to mating pheromone or in a gene required for the proper assembly of some structure in the prior cell cycle may cause temporal limitation. In either case, the protein would be a diffusible factor that reaches the other nucleus too late to act productively. Such a protein need not be directly required for nuclear fusion or active after cell fusion.

In contrast, spatial limitation might arise for a nuclear envelope or SPB protein that cannot diffuse after assembly into the mature structure. Unlike in temporal limitation, the active protein can be active after cell fusion, but must be physically associated with both nuclei. Spatial limitation may also involve some degree of temporal limitation, as the nascent proteins should be accessible to both nuclei. For example, some proteins might be synthesized only before the cells fuse, or if made constitutively, wild-type function might require accumulation to higher levels than can be accomplished in the small window of time when nuclei are competent to fuse.

Lastly, the gene products produced in the zygote might remain associated with the nucleus of origin if the mRNA remains localized to the nearest nucleus and the nascent protein is transported back to the same nucleus. Subcellular localization of mRNA has been reported in mammalian cells, in the case of some cytoskeletal proteins (69), and in *Drosophila* spp. during early development (3, 28). In principle, the specific transport systems could include the secretory system for nuclear envelope proteins, or the nuclear transport system for internal nuclear proteins.

The interpretation of bilateral mutations seems more straightforward. A simple explanation is that the protein is present, active, and diffusible at the time of nuclear fusion. For example, recessive mutations in β-tubulin that cause depolymerization cause a Bik$^-$ defect at the nonpermissive temperature. Presumably, unassembled wild-type tubulin heterodimer is present in excess as a soluble pool and is readily available for assembly onto the mutant nucleus. Therefore, any recessive mutation that affects microtubule stability will probably affect nuclear fusion in a bilateral fashion.

An alternate explanation for bilaterality is that the protein is functionally redundant. That is, even if the protein is temporally or spatially limited as suggested for the unilateral mutations, only one nucleus need be wild-type for nuclear fusion to occur. Although this paradigm has not yet been identified in nuclear fusion, a prototype example does occur in cell fusion. Recessive mutations in the *FUS1* gene have little effect when the mutant is mated to wild-type cells but have a strong effect when mutant is mated to other *fus1* mutants (46, 74). Because FUS1 is required to break down the patch of cell wall between the mating cells, no diffusion of the protein can occur until after cell fusion. Apparently, the cell wall can be broken down from either side, implying that the protein is functionally redundant in the zygote.

Few experiments have been designed to directly test the various models that explain unilaterality and bilaterality. The models differ as to the time of action of the protein, its location and diffusibility, and whether it is required to act in both cells.

Determination of the time of action is best addressed through the use of appropriate conditional mutations. For many of the genes that strongly affect nuclear fusion, appropriate conditional mutations have only recently become available. Even with ideal mutations, however, the detailed characteristics of mating may make precise temporal experiments very difficult to achieve. Mating occurs at one particular stage of the cell cycle, is relatively inefficient, and takes place on a time scale similar to that of the cell cycle. Therefore, precise timing measurements will require that mating cells be in synchrony in the preceding cell cycle and throughout the course of mating.

One report (19) addressed a different issue by examining whether the *KAR1* gene product is accessible (and therefore diffusible) to the mutant nucleus. In this experiment, *kar1-1* mutant cells were mated to appropriately marked wild-type cells. The cytoductants containing the *kar1-1* nucleus were then tested for the ability to fuse nuclei upon remating to wild-type cells. Although cytoductants were initially refractory to mating, their progeny could mate. Under these conditions, the *kar1-1* nuclei were partially restored to a Kar$^+$ phenotype. These results indicate that the KAR1 protein is accessible to both nuclei in the zygote. Therefore, the authors suggested that the protein must be temporally limited. Since the mutant cytoductant nucleus replicated in the zygote, however, this experiment does not indicate whether it is the nascent or mature protein that is diffusible. Hence, these results are also consistent with KAR1 protein being a spatially limited structural protein. Similar results were obtained for mutations in the *cdc28* and *cdc37* genes (19).

Implicit in the preceding discussion is the fact that nuclei normally have only a small window of opportunity to fuse in the zygote. This notion is supported by experiments in which the buds are separated from the zygote by micromanipulation (44; M. D. Rose, unpublished observations). The subsequent buds are not more likely to contain diploid nuclei than the initial buds. Although, as discussed above, mutant cytoductant nuclei may be partially restored to the wild-type phenotype, this complementation is not observable in the zygote. One explanation of this finding is that the pheromone-induced competence for nuclear fusion is short lived. Perhaps as cells reenter the mitotic cycle they either stop the synthesis of the induced components, which then decay, or actively inhibit their activity. The zygote is the equivalent of a *MATa/α* diploid and therefore resistant to further induction by mating pheromone.

Ultimately, our understanding of the mechanistic basis of the unilateral and bilateral mutant classes will depend upon a detailed characterization of the biochemical properties of the proteins themselves. Until then, this method of classification remains a useful way to orient our thoughts about the mechanism.

GENES REQUIRED FOR NUCLEAR FUSION

KAR1

KAR1 IS ESSENTIAL FOR MITOSIS   *KAR1* was the first gene to be described that is required for nuclear fusion (12, 24). Several recessive mutant alleles were isolated, all of which resulted in a similar unilateral defect, an approximately 10-fold decrease in the frequency of nuclear fusion with no defect observed in either mitosis or meiosis. Strikingly, in mutant shmoos and zygotes, the cytoplasmic microtubules are greatly elongated and frequently dissociated from the SPB (62). Other cytoskeletal elements, such as the nuclear microtubules and the actin network, are normally arrayed, suggesting that the mutant phenotype might arise from a defect in the structure or function of the cytoplasmic microtubules.

Subsequent cloning of the gene and construction of deletion alleles demonstrated that *KAR1* plays an essential role during the normal mitotic cycle (62). The isolation of temperature-sensitive conditional mutations identified a specific cell-cycle block, apparently arising from a failure in SPB duplication. Even at the permissive temperature, mutants rapidly increase in ploidy, suggesting that DNA synthesis occurs without subsequent mitosis. Mutations in one other cell-division-cycle gene, *CDC31*, cause this same phenotype (8).

Placing the *KAR1* gene under the control of the inducible *GAL1* promoter allows greatly increased levels of wild-type KAR1 protein expression. However, overexpression of *KAR1* results in rapid lethality and apparently also causes cell-cycle arrest, the result of a failure in SPB duplication (62). The observation that both reduced function and increased levels give rise to the same defect suggests that the protein might be a structural part of a macromolecular complex that is sensitive to the stoichiometry of its components. Given that the various mutations interfere with SPB duplication and the structure of the associated microtubules, the SPB is a likely candidate for the complex containing KAR1.

LOCALIZATION OF KAR1 HYBRID PROTEINS   The normally very low level of the KAR1 protein, and its toxicity when overproduced, have hampered direct efforts to determine its location in the cell. To overcome this problem hybrid proteins containing portions of KAR1 fused to a marker protein, *Escherichia coli* β-galactosidase, were expressed in yeast. The hybrids can be produced at levels high enough to detect using immunological methods, and in many cases do not result in toxicity. KAR1 contains at least two regions that specify the localization of hybrid proteins. One region, 70 residues in the center of the protein, is both necessary and sufficient for localization of the hybrid proteins to the SPB (E. Vallen & M. Rose, manuscript in preparation). Immuno-electron microscopy confirmed that the hybrid protein is associated with the outer face of the SPB (T. Scherson & M. Rose, manuscript in preparation). A second region, at the carboxy terminus, causes the hybrid protein to localize to the nuclear envelope (K. van Zee & M. Rose, unpublished observations).

The localization of the hybrids is assumed to represent the normal affinity of the KAR1 protein. As discussed below, these regions correspond to essential parts of the protein. However, certainty on this point will require more sensitive methods of detection that will allow localization of wild-type protein under normal levels of expression.

Remarkably, the hybrid proteins containing the first region localize exclusively to only one of the two SPBs present after duplication. The labeled SPB is usually (90%) the one that enters the bud (E. Vallen & M. Rose, manuscript in preparation). A conditional mutation in the *NDC1* gene is thought to allow the distinction between the old (functional) and the newly synthesized (nonfunctional, aploid) SPB (72). In the *ndc1* mutant, the KAR1– β-galactosidase hybrids localized exclusively to the new, defective SPB (E. Vallen & M. Rose, manuscript in preparation). Two conclusions may be drawn from these data. First, nuclear division is nonrandom; the new SPB normally segregates into the bud. This fact has important implications for nuclear elements that are asymmetrically distributed between mother and daughter cells (e.g. *ARS* plasmids) (54). Second, the interaction of the hybrid proteins with the SPB is sensitive to the age of the SPB. Possibly, KAR1 is required for formation of the new SPB but is not normally a component of the mature SPB. Alternatively, authentic KAR1 protein may always be present in the SPB, but the localization of the hybrid protein reflects a regulated change in the affinity of another component of the SPB for a domain of KAR1.

Mating (leading to nuclear fusion) and mitosis (where the next step is SPB duplication) are alternate events that begin at the same point in the cell cycle. At this point, (called START and defined by the *cdc28* mutation; for review see 61) a satellite structure is present on the cytoplasmic face of the SPB (10, 11). Some have suggested that the satellite structure is the precursor to the new SPB (9, 11). The hybrid proteins associate with the SPB in *cdc28*-arrested and α factor–treated cells at times when the satellite is present (E. Vallen & M. Rose, manuscript in preparation). In contrast, in *cdc31* mutants, which neither form a satellite nor duplicate the SPB (8), the hybrid proteins do not localize to the SPB (E. Vallen & M. Rose, manuscript in preparation). These results suggest that KAR1 may be a part of the satellite or first associate with the SPB when the satellite is formed.

Hybrid proteins containing a second region of KAR1 (carboxyl terminal 40 residues) fused to the carboxy terminus of β-galactosidase localize to the nuclear periphery (K. van Zee & M. Rose, unpublished observations). Immuno-electron microscopy confirmed that the hybrid proteins are present on the outside surface of the nuclear envelope (T. Scherson & M. Rose, manuscript in preparation). This region of KAR1 contains 20 contiguous hydrophobic residues flanked by charged residues, characteristics of a membrane-spanning domain (34). Both the hybrids containing the carboxy terminus (but not those containing only amino-terminal portions) and the intact KAR1 protein behave as integral membrane proteins (T. Scherson & M. Rose, unpublished observations). These results suggest that KAR1 protein is anchored to the nuclear envelope via the hydrophobic carboxy terminus. In support of this idea, disruption of the hydrophobic stretch by insertion of a charged residue inactivates all functions of the *KAR1* gene (M. Hiller & M. Rose, manuscript in preparation).

DELETION ANALYSIS DEFINES KAR1 DOMAIN STRUCTURE   Construction of internal in-frame deletions has allowed the independent definition of several specific functional regions within KAR1 (E. Vallen & M. Rose, manuscript in preparation). One region, in the center of the protein and comprised of no more than about 70 residues, is essential to the mitotic function of KAR1. The internal essential domain corresponds to the region required for localization of the hybrid proteins to the SPB. This location suggests that the essential function of KAR1 is mediated through interaction with the SPB.

The deletion analysis of KAR1 also defined a region required only for nuclear fusion. The karyogamy region is comprised of no more than 70 residues and maps to the amino-terminal half of the protein, adjacent to the essential mitotic region. Deletions in the karyogamy region cause a unilateral defect in nuclear fusion, identical in severity to the original point mutation. All known karyogamy defective point mutations in KAR1 map to this region and create the same proline-to-serine change. One clue to the function of this region is that the localization of KAR3–β-galactosidase hybrids to the SPB depends on KAR1. The significance of this result is discussed in the section on models for nuclear fusion.

Deletions of the essential domain and deletions of the karyogamy domain show intragenic complementation for both nuclear fusion and mitosis. These data taken together demonstrate that the functions of the two regions are completely independent and indicate that they form separate structural domains.

Deletion and insertion analysis shows that the KAR1 protein is remarkably tolerant to large structural alterations. A simple model of KAR1 is that it is comprised of a linear array of a few independent protein binding domains tethered to the nuclear envelope via a membrane-spanning domain. Two domains (making up about 30% of the protein) have been identified, one required for interaction with and duplication of the SPB and the second for nuclear fusion. Possibly, other parts of the protein are involved with binding to other proteins. Any other functions are either redundant (performed either by other proteins or other parts of KAR1) or are required in as yet un-recognized processes.

The suggestion that KAR1 is an SPB component provides a ready explana-tion for the unilaterality of the karyogamy defective mutations. Clearly, a protein tethered to the nuclear envelope and embedded in the SPB should not be readily diffusible except as a nascent protein. The behavior of hybrid proteins suggest that KAR1 is assembled into the SPB prior to cell fusion. Either no assembly can occur at later times, or the presence of preassembled mutant protein precludes further assembly onto the SPB. If both wild-type and the mutant proteins are present in the cell at the time of assembly, then both can apparently be assembled into the structure. This phenomenon would account for both the recessiveness of the deletions and their capacity to show intragenic complementation.

KAR3

PLEIOTROPIC MUTANT PHENOTYPES   Mutations in the *KAR3* gene were identified by the Kar⁻ mutant selection scheme (60). Several different alleles were isolated, each of which caused a roughly 10-fold decrease in karyogamy in unilateral crosses. The alleles of *KAR3* were unusual in that they caused a much worse defect if both parents were mutant (J. Conde, personal com-munication; P. Meluh & M. Rose, unpublished data). Additionally, in di-ploids, the original mutations were partially dominant in their nuclear fusion defect (60). These results were explained when null mutations (deletions) were constructed in vitro and placed back in the genome (50). The null mutations were both completely recessive and strictly bilateral in their nuclear fusion defect. These findings led to the conclusion that the original mutations resulted in mutant proteins that poison nuclear fusion. As the rate of authentic nuclear fusion in bilateral crosses is undetectable, the *KAR3* gene is unique in being absolutely essential for nuclear fusion.

In addition to effects on nuclear fusion, all the *KAR3* mutations cause a variety of pleiotropic defects (50, 60). Although strains carrying null alleles are viable, their growth rate is roughly 60% slower, and strains carrying the original semidominant alleles (e.g. *kar3-1*) grow at least twice as slowly. Cultures of the mutant strains accumulate a high frequency of inviable cells (as many as 44%) arrested in the cell cycle with a large bud, an undivided nucleus, and a short spindle spanning the nucleus. FACS analysis indicates that the cultures contain an elevated fraction of cells with a G2 DNA content, presumably because of the arrested cells (P. Meluh & M. Rose, unpublished observations). Thus, the *KAR3* gene is clearly important for normal progression in mitosis; in mutants a significant fraction of cells terminally arrests during mitosis prior to or during spindle elongation.

Homozygous diploid null mutants, in which chromosome segregation can be easily examined, lost chromosome III at least 10-fold more frequently than in wild-type. However, chromosome loss cannot explain the inviability of the mutant cells. Diploids should be resistant to the lethal effects of chromosome loss, but for *kar3* null alleles, the frequency of inviability is the same for haploids and diploids.

Diploid cells are more sensitive to the toxic effects of the semidominant mutation *kar3-1*. For example, although haploid strains bearing *kar3-1* are viable, diploid strains homozygous for *kar3-1* are inviable. In contrast, both haploids and homozygous diploids containing *kar3* null alleles are viable. Therefore, the *kar3-1* mutation blocks diploid formation at two levels: one is the defect in karyogamy and the second is the inviability of homozygous diploids.

In addition to their effects on growth rate, the *kar3* mutations affect the resistance of cells to microtubule-destabilizing drugs, such as benomyl (P. Meluh & M. Rose, unpublished observations). Although the *kar3-1* mutants are more sensitive to benomyl than wild-type cells, the growth defect of the null alleles is remediated by benomyl. That is, the mutants grow better at some concentrations of benomyl than without benomyl. Remarkably, the presence of benomyl reduces the fraction of inviable cells in the *kar3* null mutant cultures. Nonetheless, the mutants are not resistant to benomyl; they do not grow at concentrations above that which is lethal to the wild-type. These results imply that the function of *KAR3* in mitotic cells is intimately connected with the structure and function of the microtubules.

In addition to effects on microtubule function, *kar3* mutants also show a puzzling sensitivity to ionizing radiation. Whether the sensitivity reflects a subtle defect in the recombination or repair processes or whether it bespeaks an indirect and unappreciated role for microtubule function in certain types of radiation repair is unclear.

Finally, *KAR3* is essential for meiosis. The homozygous null diploid fails to progress even to the formation of the first meiotic spindle. It is not yet known which if any early events of meiosis do occur in the mutant diploid.

KAR3 IS RELATED TO KINESIN   The DNA sequence of the *KAR3* gene (50) revealed that the protein is related to a well-known microtubule-dependent mechanochemical motor protein called kinesin (82). Kinesin was first found in neurons of the squid *Loligo pealii* (75, 76). It has since been isolated from several different metazoan sources [see recent reviews (49, 77)]. Kinesin most likely functions as a motor responsible for fast axonal transport of secretory vesicles and other organelles. Kinesin's properties in vitro indicate that it is specifically responsible for movement towards the distal end of the axon (68, 76).

Detailed analysis of the predicted structure of KAR3 showed that it differs from kinesin in several significant features. First, sequence similarity (about 40% identity) extends only over the domain in kinesin that is responsible for microtubule-dependent movement (67, 83). Second, the homologous domains are at different ends of the molecules, at the N terminus of kinesin, but at the C terminus of KAR3. Nevertheless, both proteins are predicted to be structurally similar, with long internal coiled-coil domains and small globular domains at the ends opposite the motor domains. The globular nonmotor end of kinesin is thought to be responsible for its interaction with organelles (38, 82). By analogy, the biological specificity of KAR3 function probably at least partially results from interactions via the nonmotor domain.

Recently, the kinesin-related genes were found to compose a large and complex family (21, 22, 33, 47, 57, 85). The kinesin-related genes have been implicated in several microtubule-dependent processes, including SPB separation, spindle elongation, meiosis, chromosome segregation, and nuclear fusion. Of particular interest is the *Drosophila ncd* gene, which encodes a protein whose motor domain is most closely related to that of KAR3 (45% identity) and that is also at the C terminus (21, 47). The remainder of the *ncd* gene is unrelated to *KAR3*. Unlike kinesin, which moves exclusively towards the plus end of a microtubule, the *ncd* protein moves towards the minus end (48, 79). The molecular basis for the difference in orientation is unknown. The direction of KAR3 movement on microtubules has not yet been determined.

DOMINANT MUTATIONS IN *KAR3*   The basis for dominant mutations in *KAR3* can be understood from a consideration of the biochemical behavior of kinesin. Kinesin couples the energy of ATP hydrolysis into directed movement along microtubules. In the absence of nucleotide or in the presence of nonhydrolyzable ATP analogs, kinesin binds tightly to microtubules (rigor binding). In the presence of ATP, kinesin releases from microtubules (75). The dissociation is thought to be part of the normal cycle of movement.

By extension, mutations in the ATP binding–hydrolysis site for a kinesin-like protein should produce a constitutive state of rigor binding. In the cell, the stable binding of mutant protein to microtubules might interfere with the movement of other wild-type kinesin-like proteins. Therefore, such mutations would be expected to be dominant. Four of the original dominant mutations in *KAR3* have been cloned and sequenced; as predicted, all are in the conserved ATP binding–hydrolysis site (50; P. Meluh & M. Rose, unpublished observations).

Initial attempts to localize the wild-type KAR3 protein were inconclusive, as it exhibited a diffuse distribution. In contrast, when the *kar3-1* mutant was examined, the protein was found to be concentrated along the length of the cytoplasmic microtubules in shmoos and zygotes, which was consistent with the mutant protein showing constitutive microtubule binding (50; P. Meluh & M. Rose, unpublished observations). These data support the idea that KAR3 is a kinesin-like motor protein that interacts with the cytoplasmic microtubules in mating cells.

A SECOND MICROTUBULE-ASSOCIATION DOMAIN   The specific function of KAR3 is probably determined by the protein complexes that interact with the nonmotor domain. In shmoos, hybrid proteins containing all or part of KAR3 fused to β-galactosidase localize to two regions along the cytoplasmic microtubules (50). Staining is most prominent at the distal ends of the microtubules and gradually diminishes in intensity towards the SPB. In some 40% of the cells, a second fainter site of staining can be discerned in the vicinity of the SPB. In strains with higher levels of hybrid protein expression, staining at the SPB is observed more frequently. Therefore, all of the cells probably contain hybrid protein at the SPB, but in some cells the staining is too faint to be detected.

The localization of the hybrid proteins to the cytoplasmic microtubules and to SPB does not depend on the motor domain of KAR3 because hybrids lacking it show precisely the same pattern of localization (50). Moreover, the same pattern is obtained if the authentic KAR3 protein is deleted from the cell. Therefore, KAR3 contains a second region allowing it to associate with the microtubules. It is not known whether the association is direct, in that the protein binds tubulin, or indirect, so that the protein binds to a microtubule-associated protein.

The presence of a second microtubule and SPB-association domain immediately suggests a KAR3 function. One end of the protein would bind stably to a microtubule or SPB component, while the motor domain translates along a second microtubule. Hence, the microtubules would slide with respect to one another. Such microtubule-dependent movements are likely to be central components of the complex mechanisms of mitosis, meiosis, and nuclear fusion.

BIK1

The *BIK1* gene was discovered serendipitously because a deletion next to *HIS4* resulted in a bilateral karyogamy defect (74). The *bik1* deletion causes an approximately 10-fold decrease in nuclear fusion. In mutant zygotes, the nuclei are initially found closely opposed but ultimately fail to move together. The pronounced cytoplasmic microtubules seen in *kar1* and *kar3* mutant zygotes are not present in *bik1* mutant zygotes (5).

Although the BIK1 protein is not essential in mitosis, the *bik1* deletion affects a variety of microtubule-dependent functions (5). First, combination of the *bik1* deletion with mutant alleles of the tubulin genes or with mutations that cause increased chromosome instability (*CIN* genes, see below) (39, 70) results in lethality or very slow growth. Second, the *bik1* deletion causes a cold-sensitive defect in microtubule morphology. At 14°C, the cytoplasmic microtubules are absent or very short, and the anaphase spindle only partially elongates. The nuclei frequently fail to move to the bud neck and often divide wholly within the mother cell. Third, homozygous diploid *bik1* null mutants show a 10-fold elevation in the frequency of chromosome loss. Fourth, overexpression of the wild-type protein is toxic. Initially, long cytoplasmic microtubules form, but, eventually, the phenotype becomes similar to that of the null alleles. Finally, in zygotes, the *bik1* mutation suppresses the formation of the abnormally long cytoplasmic microtubules associated with the *kar1-1* mutation.

The variety of pleiotropic defects suggest that the *BIK1* gene is generally required for microtubule stability in yeast. The requirement for BIK1 is somewhat greater in the cold, which may reflect the intrinsic cold sensitivity of microtubule polymerization in vitro. In addition, BIK1 appears particularly important for the cytoplasmic microtubule functions. This might mean that BIK1 specifically stabilizes the cytoplasmic microtubules, or that the cytoplasmic microtubules are inherently less stable.

The *BIK1* gene encodes a 58-kilodalton (kd) protein that appears to be a microtubule-associated protein in vivo. This protein is cytoplasmic in un-budded cells but shows variable colocalization with the nuclear microtubules early in mitosis. Staining is frequently observed on short spindles but rarely on long spindles. Researchers have not yet observed colocalization with cytoplasmic microtubules. The protein is predicted to have three domains. The amino terminal domain is globular, basic, and shows some limited sequence similarity to MAP2 and tau. Studies also predict that the central region forms an alpha helical coiled-coil, suggesting that the protein is oligomeric. Finally, the carboxy-terminal domain includes a small metal binding motif frequently observed in retroviral nucleocapsid proteins.

KAR2

The original *KAR2* mutations result in an approximately 10-fold unilateral decrease in nuclear fusion (60). The block in nuclear fusion is different from that imposed by mutations in *KAR1* and *KAR3*. Whereas the latter mutations appear to affect the functions of the cytoplasmic microtubules and result in nuclei that remain separate, the *KAR2* mutants have morphologically normal cytoplasmic microtubules and the nuclei move close together in the zygote (L. J. Stasenko & M. Rose, unpublished observations). *KAR2* likely functions in the membrane or SPB fusion event that must occur after nuclear congression.

DNA sequence analysis revealed that *KAR2* is a member of the HSP70 gene family (55, 63). Specifically, it encodes the HSP70 protein resident in the lumen of the endoplasmic reticulum (ER), known in mammalian cells as BiP (binding protein), or GRP78, (glucose regulated protein). BiP was initially described based upon its property of binding to mutant and unassembled secretory protein precursors in the ER (6, 30, 32, 52). Independently, GRP78 was discovered as a protein that is induced by glucose starvation and other treatments that interfere with glycosylation and thereby cause abnormally modified proteins to accumulate in the ER (reviewed in 45).

Subsequently, in mammalian systems, BiP was shown to bind transiently to secretory proteins during the normal course of assembly, as well as to peptides in vitro. Both the binding to abnormal proteins (52) and binding to peptides in vitro (25) are sensitive to ATP. It has been proposed that BiP and other HSP70s bind to unfolded proteins and aid in their normal folding and assembly (reviewed in 65).

Using temperature sensitive mutations, researchers showed that *KAR2* was absolutely required for the import of secreted proteins into the lumen of the ER (78). However, *KAR2* mutations probably do not affect nuclear fusion because of a defect in protein translocation. This conclusion comes from several observations. First, mutations in other genes that block protein translocation (e.g. *SEC61, SEC62,* and *SEC63*) (78) do not affect nuclear fusion as well. Second, several mutations in *KAR2* severely block nuclear fusion but do not noticeably affect protein translocation. Third, although the *KAR2* mutations that block protein translocation also affect nuclear fusion, they are defective for nuclear fusion at temperatures that are permissive for translocation. These data suggest that the role of KAR2 in nuclear fusion involves either a separate function of KAR2 or a related one (such as protein assembly) that acts on proteins after translocation.

The finding that an ER resident protein is involved in nuclear fusion is at first surprising. However, both immunofluorescent and immunoelectron microscopy demonstrate that KAR2 is associated with the nuclear envelope. One should remember that, in yeast, the nuclear envelope comprises the largest part of the ER membrane. Thus any given ER protein might be simultaneously required for secretory as well as other ostensibly nuclear functions.

Two functions for KAR2 in nuclear fusion have been suggested. The first is that it acts only indirectly; perhaps it is required for the folding or assembly of some other protein required for nuclear fusion. Such other proteins might be identified from mutations that either suppress or enhance the karyogamy defect associated with mutations in *KAR2*. Alternatively, KAR2 might be directly required for nuclear fusion. As nuclei fuse, the SPB must be remodeled to allow the formation of a single diploid SPB from the two single haploid SPBs. Normally the SPB is a relatively stable structure changing neither size nor gross morphology throughout the cell cycle. SPB fusion is therefore an unusual event. SPB fusion may require the action of a molecular chaperone to stabilize subunits of the reassembling SPB.

CDC4

During vegetative growth, temperature-sensitive mutations in the *CDC4* gene block the mitotic cycle after SPB duplication but before SPB separation and the initiation of DNA synthesis (35). Mutant cells produce multiple abnormal buds at the high temperature, with kinetics similar to the production of normal buds by a wild-type cell. When mated at the nonpermissive temperature, mutants produce a strong unilateral karyogamy defect (80–90% failure in nuclear fusion) (18).

The *cdc4* karyogamy defect is remarkable for several reasons. First, ordering experiments have suggested that *CDC4* acts in mitosis after the point that cells can mate (61). Indeed, *cdc4* cells that have already arrested are not competent for mating (18). In contrast, the karyogamy defect implies the gene must also act at an earlier point in the cell cycle for normal mating to occur. Second, although the karyogamy defect is not complemented in the zygote, the mitotic defect is (20). Thus in a cross, the protein from the wild-type parent enables replication of the mutant nucleus. One elegant model to explain these results is the suggestion that the *CDC4* gene product is required for SPB assembly (20). As only preexisting SPBs fuse in the zygote, for karyogamy *CDC4* would be required to act prior to cell fusion. Complementation in the zygote would then reflect the assembly of a new SPB under the influence of the wild-type CDC4 protein during the subsequent mitotic replication. Alternatively, CDC4 might simply have different functions in karyogamy and mitosis, so the fact that it appears to act at different times would not be surprising.

The *CDC4* gene has been cloned and sequenced. The predicted protein contains significant sequence and structural homology to the β-subunit of trimeric G-proteins (26, 84). This observation suggests that the protein is not simply a structural component of the SPB but rather is part of a signaling pathway that allows the SPB to respond to cell-cycle and mating-pheromone signals. The identities of putative α and γ subunits that would interact with CDC4 protein are unknown.

KEM *Genes*

Mutations that diminish the residual nuclear fusion observed in *kar1-1* mutant crosses might identify components of an alternative *KAR1*-independent pathway of nuclear fusion. The simple experiment of measuring nuclear fusion in strains completely lacking KAR1 protein is complicated by the essential mitotic function of KAR1. Nonetheless, when the karyogamy domain of KAR1 is deleted, the residual nuclear fusion is not reduced below that observed for *kar1-1*. These results suggest the possible existence of a second mechanism of nuclear fusion.

The three *KEM* (*KAR* enhancing mutation) genes were specifically identified through mutations that further reduce nuclear fusion (43). Regardless of whether the *kem* mutations are in a *kar1-1* mutant and mated to wild-type or in a *KAR1* strain and mated to a *kar1-1* mutant, residual nuclear fusion is reduced by at least 10- to 100-fold. In contrast, when neither parent contains the *kar1-1* mutation, the *kem* mutations do not affect nuclear fusion in unilateral crosses.

If the *kem* mutations define a second pathway of nuclear fusion, then it may seem paradoxical that these mutations do not block karyogamy in crosses to wild-type. Conceivably, the alternate pathway might be much less important in wild-type crosses. The *KAR1* pathway might suppress the alternate pathway, either by competition or because the alternate pathway is mediated by abnormal structures that are unique to *kar1-1* cells. In that regard, knowing whether the *kem* mutations affect the residual fusion arising from mutations in other *KAR* genes would be interesting. Alternatively, the *kem* mutations might only cause a bilateral nuclear fusion defect in *KAR1* crosses. Indeed, *kem1-1* mutations do show a partial bilateral defect, causing nuclear fusion to fail in about 20–30% of zygotes (43). The unilateral *kem⁻* defect observed in *kar1-1* crosses can be understood if both *kem1-1* and *kar1-1* decrease the robustness of the SPB or the microtubules, and this effect is amplified by presence of both mutations.

Mutation in at least two of the *KEM* genes have pleiotropic defects. The *kem3-1* allele is temperature sensitive for growth, suggesting that the gene is essential for vegetative growth. Two different alleles of *KEM1* are benomyl sensitive and increase chromosome loss 20-fold in homozygous diploids. Although a *kem1* null allele is viable, the strains are extremely slow growing and show an increased frequency of abnormal cells including some in which SPB duplication or separation has failed and others containing two nuclei. The preceding data suggest that the *kem1* mutations cause a general defect in microtubule or SPB function. However, all *kem1* mutants show decreased viability after nitrogen starvation, and homozygous *kem1* mutant diploids are defective for sporulation. These latter results suggest that KEM1 may have regulatory functions and affect the SPB and microtubules only indirectly.

Cloning and sequencing of the *KEM1* gene predict that it encodes a 175-kd protein. Comparison with previously sequenced genes has been uninformative.

CIN1

The *CIN* genes were identified through mutations causing both increased chromosome instability and increased sensitivity to benomyl (39, 70). These screens identified the three genes encoding tubulin subunits and three new genes affecting chromosome stability (*CIN1, CIN2,* and *CIN4*). The *CIN* genes are not essential but are needed for growth at low temperature. In the cold, mutants show a cell cycle arrest indicative of a general defect in both nuclear and cytoplasmic microtubule function and stability. A variety of genetic interactions with mutations in the tubulin genes support this interpretation of the mutant defect.

Although mutations in the *CIN1* gene do cause a measurable increase in the frequency of cytoductant formation (20- to 30-fold in a bilateral cross at 11°C) (39), this increase corresponds to a failure in nuclear fusion in less than 5% of the zygotes. Given the much greater effect in mitosis than in nuclear fusion, the role of *CIN1* in stabilizing microtubules may be specific to vegetative cells.

CIK *Genes*

The *CIK* (for *c*hromosome *i*nstability and *k*aryogamy) genes were identified by repeating the karyogamy mutant selection procedure of Conde & Fink (12) and screening the resultant cytoductants for chromosome loss and temperature sensitivity (B. D. Page & M. Snyder, personal communication). Five mutations were obtained in four genes (*CIK1, 2, 3,* and *4*). All the mutations cause a 10- to 100-fold increase in the formation of cytoductants, although, as noted above, this corresponds to only a small decrease in nuclear fusion. The mutations also cause a 10- to 50-fold decrease in the fidelity of chromosome segregation. *CIK1* is not an essential gene, although disruption does result in temperature-sensitive growth. These results are consistent with a general defect in the functions of the SPB and/or microtubules. Interestingly, *CIK1-lacZ* hybrids localize to the vicinity of the SPB.

CDC28, CDC34, *and* CDC37

An exhaustive analysis of the temperature-sensitive *cdc* mutations revealed that, in addition to *cdc4* (see above), several confer a karyogamy defect at the nonpermissive temperature. Recessive mutations in three genes (*CDC28, CDC34,* and *CDC37*) result in a weak unilateral nuclear fusion defect (10- to 100-fold increase in cytoductant to diploid ratio) (18, 19). However, because the cytoduction assay requires the zygote to progress through the cell cycle at the nonpermissive temperature, the mutants could only be tested in the unilateral configuration. Microscopic examination of bilateral zygotes produced at the nonpermissive temperature indicated that both the *cdc28* and *cdc37* mutations may cause a strong bilateral defect. Each of the genes blocks the cell cycle at G1.

The *CDC28* gene encodes the *S. cerevisiae* homologue of the p34 subunit of mitosis promoting factor (MPF) (2, 17, 23, 29). Several recent reviews discuss the role of the MPF protein kinase in the cell cycle (14, 53). With respect to cell-cycle progression, treatment with mating pheromone causes cells to arrest at the same point they do in *cdc28⁻* mutants (36). As *cdc28*-arrested cells remain capable of mating, this gene is required neither for the initial response to mating pheromone nor for cell fusion. The *CDC28* protein kinase may be required for the activation of some function required for nuclear fusion. Dutcher & Hartwell (19) suggested, based upon the unilateral effect of the mutation, and suppression of the nuclear fusion defect in cytoductants, that CDC28 must act prior to cell fusion to prepare the nucleus for fusion. However, given that the mutant phenotype is much more severe in a bilateral cross, the gene may act after cell fusion. In that case, the slight mutant defect might reflect a partial limitation in the diffusion of the wild-type gene product. This observation would be consistent with the reported partial inability of the wild-type *CDC28* gene product to complement the mutant nucleus for mitosis in zygotes in which nuclear fusion is blocked (20). Support for the spatial limitation of the CDC28 protein comes from the observation that the homologous CDC2 protein of *Schizosaccharomyces pombe* is nuclear and becomes concentrated at the SPB at certain stages of the cell cycle (1). However, the CDC28 protein itself is reported to be cytoplasmic (81).

The *CDC34* gene encodes a ubiquitin-conjugating enzyme (31). The role for this function in either the cell cycle or nuclear fusion is unclear. Presumably a substrate of the enzyme is degraded by the ubiquitin-dependent protein degradation pathway. The substrate protein may act as a negative regulator of nuclear fusion or a step in the cell cycle.

The *CDC37* gene encodes a predicted protein of 51 kd (23). The protein shares no sequence relationships with other known proteins. A high degree of alpha-helical character suggested that the protein may be a cytoskeletal component.

MODELS FOR NUCLEAR FUSION

Any model for nuclear fusion must ultimately take into account all of the elements so far described: a SPB component, a G-protein subunit, the cytoplasmic microtubules, a variety of microtubule-associated or stabilizing proteins, a microtubule motor protein, and a component of the ER-nuclear envelope. Within these constraints, a rough model of the pathway can be proposed.

As cells respond to mating pheromone, they become synchronized at the G1 stage of the cell cycle. Specific cell and nuclear fusion functions are induced. Possibly, CDC4 and CDC28 are part of the signaling mechanism to prepare the SPB for karyogamy. At least one gene required for nuclear fusion, *KAR3*, is transcriptionally induced by mating pheromone (50). In addition, the location of the KAR3 protein shifts from the nucleus to the cytoplasm (P. Meluh & M. Rose, unpublished observations).

A short bundle of cytoplasmic microtubules forms that runs from the SPB to the tip of the shmoo projection. These microtubules are abnormally long in *kar1* and *kar3* mutants. As the cell wall and plasma membrane break down, cytoplasmic microtubules from the two nuclei interact. In *KAR3* null mutant zygotes, the cytoplasmic microtubules fail to interact. In *KAR3* dominant mutant zygotes, the two nuclei become connected by a microtubule bridge. The mutant *kar3-1* protein is associated with the microtubule bridge. The geometry of nuclear fusion, assuming that each nucleus contributes microtubules, suggests that the bridge must be composed of a bundle of overlapping antiparallel microtubules. The mutant phenotypes indicate that KAR3 is responsible for the interaction between the two sets of microtubules. This proposal is consistent with the structural model of KAR3, discussed above, in which both ends of the protein would interact with microtubules. In the null mutant, the cross-bridging KAR3 protein is absent and the microtubules remain separate. In the dominant mutant, the cross-bridging occurs, but because of loss of motor activity, the nuclei remain separate. Thus the KAR3 protein appears to be responsible both for cross-bridging the antiparallel cytoplasmic microtubules and also for moving them relative to one another.

At this point the model diverges, as the orientation of KAR3 motor activity is unknown. For the sake of the discussion, the cytoplasmic microtubules are assumed to be in the plus-end-out orientation with respect to the SPB. This orientation has been found for microtubules associated with the organizing centers in a number of systems (reviewed in 7). If KAR3 acts solely to slide overlapping antiparallel microtubules relative to one another, then nuclear congression requires it to be a minus-end-oriented motor. This orientation is contrary to that of authentic kinesin, but is the same as the *Drosophila* ncd protein (48, 79). *KAR3* and *ncd* are more closely related to each other than to other members of the family (P. Meluh, D. Roof & M. Rose, unpublished observations), suggesting that KAR3 may also be a minus-end-oriented motor.

A somewhat more complicated model can also be constructed in which KAR3 acts as a plus-end-oriented motor. The justification for this model is that KAR3 hybrid molecules were observed to localize both to the distal ends of the cytoplasmic microtubules and to the SPB. The latter localization suggests that the authentic KAR3 protein is also anchored at the SPB via the nonmotor domain. The motor domain would then be free to interact with the microtubules from the same nucleus. A plus-end-oriented motor at the SPB would tend to pull cytoplasmic microtubules into the SPB. Allowing that microtubules can depolymerize at their minus ends, this process would create a microtubule flux towards the SPB. Just such a microtubule flux towards the MTOC has been observed in mammalian prometaphase (51). Unlike the previous model, however, sliding in the overlap region would tend to separate the two nuclei. Nevertheless, the interconnection between the two nuclei is maintained. This connection might be maintained nonspecifically by inter-ference between counter-moving KAR3 molecules or specifically by addition-al proteins. Thus, the plus-end-oriented model proposes that the cytoplasmic microtubules from the two nuclei become connected and subsequently shorten due to depolymerization at the SPB. The flux of microtubules into the SPB would be the source of the movement that is responsible for nuclear congres-sion.

Two observations support the plus-end-oriented model. First, the model predicts that a specific protein is required to anchor the KAR3 motor to the SPB. The protein should be a component of the SPB, be required for nuclear fusion, and be required for the localization of KAR3 hybrids to the SPB. KAR1 fulfills all three conditions. Second, if a flux of microtubules into the SPB really exists, then mutations that affect the motor protein should block the flux. Decreased flux would be manifest by increased polymerization and therefore length of the cytoplasmic microtubules, which provides a ready explanation for the increased length of the cytoplasmic microtubules in *kar1* and *kar3* mutant zygotes. Although KAR3 could affect microtubule length by interactions at either end, increased cytoplasmic microtubule length in the *KAR1* mutants is difficult to understand except in the context of interactions at the SPB. A direct determination of the orientation of KAR3 movement will be required to distinguish between the two models.

After nuclear congression, the SPBs and nuclear envelopes must fuse. The mechanism of this step is unknown, largely because mutations in only one gene, *KAR2,* have been observed to affect it. However, that mutations can affect this latter step without affecting nuclear congression suggests, first, that proximity is insufficient for nuclear fusion, and second, a specific mechanism for envelope fusion probably exists. Cytological observations indicate that a specific element of the SPB is required to catalyze the fusion. Perhaps the molecules that catalyze the later steps of fusion are functionally redundant, and their genes will only be found by analysis of bilateral karyogamy de-fective mutations.

CONCLUSION

The yeast nuclear fusion pathway provides a remarkably facile system for the analysis of a wide variety of problems in cell biology. Several issues of central importance influence karyogamy, including, but not limited to: the determinants of cell polarity, microtubule-dependent movement, microtubule structure and the specificity of microtubule function, organelle biogenesis, targeting of proteins to subcellular compartments, and membrane fusion. The utility of a sensitive genetic system has allowed the definition of many cell components that are not only required for efficient nuclear fusion but that are also involved in other integral cellular processes.

The current challenge is the identification of the remaining genes required for nuclear fusion and the determination of the precise role played by each component in nuclear fusion and cell division.

ACKNOWLEDGMENTS

I thank Pam Meluh, Elizabeth Vallen, and Joe Vogel for their critical reading of the manuscript and for their help in preparing this paper. I also thank them and all of the members of my laboratory for many stimulating discussions about the mechanism of nuclear fusion. Finally, I thank my colleagues for sharing their results and allowing me to discuss them prior to publication. This work was supported by grants from the National Institutes of Health (GM779), National Science Foundation Presidential Young Investigator Award (DCB8657497), and the James S. McDonnell Foundation.

Literature Cited

1. Alfa, C. E., Ducommun, B., Beach, D., Hyams, J. S. 1990. Distinct nuclear and spindle pole body populations of cyclin-cdc2 in fission yeast. *Nature* 347:680–82

2. Beach, D., Durkacz, B., Nurse, P. 1982. Functionally homologous cell cycle control genes in budding and fission yeast. *Nature* 300:706–9

3. Berleth, T., Burri, M., Thoma, D., Bopp, D., Richstein, S. et al. 1988. The role of localization in *bicoid* RNA in localizing the anterior pattern of the *Drosophila* embryo. *EMBO J.* 7:1749–56

4. Berlin, V., Brill, J. A., Trueheart, J., Boeke, J. D., Fink, G. R. 1991. Genetic screens and selections for cell and nuclear fusion mutants. *Methods Enzymol.* 194:774–92

5. Berlin, V., Styles, C. A., Fink, G. R. 1990. *BIK1*, a protein required for microtubule function during mating and mitosis in *Saccharomyces cerevisiae,* colocalizes with tubulin. *J. Cell Biol.* 111:2573–86

6. Bole, D. G., Hendershot, L. M., Kearney, J. F. 1986. Posttranslational association of immunoglobulin heavy chains in nonsecreting and secreting hybridomas. *J. Cell. Biol.* 102:1558–66

7. Brinkley, B. R. 1985. Microtubule organizing centers. *Annu. Rev. Cell Biol.* 1:145–72

8. Byers, B. 1981. Multiple roles of the spindle pole bodies in the life cycle of *Saccharomyces cerevisiae*. In *Molecular Genetics of Yeast, Alfred Benzon Symp. 16,* ed. D. von Wittstein, J. Friis, M.

Kielland-Brandt, A. Stenderup, pp. 119–31. Copenhagen: Munksgaard

9. Byers, B. 1981. Cytology of the yeast life cycle. See Ref. 71a, pp. 59–96

10. Byers, B., Goetsch, L. 1974. Duplication of spindle plaques and integration of the yeast cell cycle. *Cold Spring Harbor Symp. Quant. Biol.* 38:123–31

11. Byers, B., Goetsch, L. 1975. Behavior of spindles and spindle plaques in the cell cycle and conjugation in *Saccharomyces cerevisiae*. *J. Bacteriol.* 124:511–23

12. Conde, J., Fink, G. R. 1976. A mutant of *Saccharomyces cerevisiae* defective for nuclear fusion. *Proc. Natl. Acad. Sci. USA* 73:3651–55

13. Cross, F., Hartwell, L. H., Jackson, C., Konopka, J. B. 1988. Conjugation in *Saccharomyces cerevisiae*. *Annu. Rev. Cell Biol.* 4:429–57

14. Cross, F., Roberts, J., Weintraub, H. 1989. Simple and complex cell cycles. *Annu. Rev. Cell Biol.* 5:341–95

15. Curran, B. P. G., Carter, B. L. A. 1986. α-Factor enhancement of hybrid formation by protoplast fusion in *Saccharomyces cerevisiae* II. *Curr. Genet.* 10:943–45

16. Delgado, M. A., Conde, J. 1984. Benomyl prevents nuclear fusion in *Saccharomyces cerevisiae*. *Mol. Gen. Genet.* 193:188–89

17. Dunphy, W. G., Brizuela, L., Beach, D., Newport, J. 1988. The Xenopus cdc2 protein is a component of MPF, a cytoplasmic regulator of mitosis. *Cell* 54:423–31

18. Dutcher, S. K., Hartwell, L. H. 1982.

The role of *Saccharomyces cerevisiae* cell division cycle genes in nuclear fusion. *Genetics* 100:175–84

19. Dutcher, S. K., Hartwell, L. H. 1983. Genes that act prior to conjugation to prepare the *Saccharomyces cerevisiae* nucleus for caryogamy. *Cell* 33:203–10

20. Dutcher, S. K., Hartwell, L. H. 1983. Test for temporal or spatial restrictions in gene product function during the cell division cycle. *Mol. Cell. Biol.* 3:1255–65

21. Endow, S. A., Henikoff, S., Soler-Niedziela, L. 1990. Mediation of meiotic and early mitotic chromosome segregation in *Drosophila* by a protein related to kinesin. *Nature* 345:81–3

22. Enos, A. P., Morris, N. R. 1990. Mutation of a gene that encodes a kinesin-like protein blocks nuclear division in *A. nidulans*. *Cell* 69:1019–27

23. Ferguson, J., Ho, J.-Y., Peterson, T. A., Reed, S. I. 1986. Nucleotide sequence of the yeast cell division cycle start genes *CDC28, CDC36, CDC37*, and *CDC39*, and a structural analysis of the predicted products. *Nucleic Acids Res.* 14:6681–97

24. Fink, G. R., Conde, J. 1976. Studies on *KAR1*, a gene required for nuclear fusion in yeast. In *International Cell Biology 1976–1977*, ed. B. R. Brinkley, K. R. Porter, pp. 414–19 New York: The Rockefeller Univ. Press

25. Flynn, G. C., Chappell, T. G., Rothmann, J. E. 1989. Peptide binding and release by proteins implicated as catalysts of protein assembly. *Science* 245:385–90

26. Fong, H. K. W., Hurley, J. B., Hopkins, R. S., Miake, R., Johnson, M. S., et al. 1986. Repetitive segmental structure of the transducin beta subunit: homology with the *CDC4* gene and identification of related mRNAs. *Proc. Natl. Acad. Sci. USA* 83:2162–66

27. Ford, S., Pringle, J. 1986. Development of spatial organization during the formation of zygotes and shmoos in *Saccharomyces cerevisiae*. *Yeast* 2:S114

28. Frigerio, G., Burri, M., Bopp, D., Baumgartner, S., Noll, M. 1986. Structure of the segmentation gene *paired* and the *Drosophila PRD* gene set as part of a gene network. *Cell* 47:735–46

29. Gautier, J., Norbury, C., Lohka, M., Nurse, P., Maller, J. 1988. Purified maturation-promoting factor contains the product of a Xenopus homolog of the fission yeast cell cycle control gene *cdc2⁺*. *Cell* 54:433–39

30. Gething, M.-J., McGammon, K., Sambrook, J. 1986. Expression of wild-type

and mutant forms of influenza hemagglutinin: the role of folding in intracellular transport. *Cell* 46:939–50

31. Goebl, M. G., Yochem, J., Jentsch, S., McGrath, J. P., Varshavsky, A., Byers, B. 1988. The yeast cell cycle gene *CDC34* encodes a ubiquitin-conjugating enzyme. *Science* 241:1331–35

32. Haas, I. G., Wabl, M. 1984. Immunoglobulin heavy chain binding protein. *Nature* 306:387–89

33. Hagan, I., Yanagida, M. 1990. Novel potential mitotic motor protein encoded by the fission yeast *cut7⁺* gene. *Nature* 347:563–66

34. Hartmann, E., Rapoport, T. A., Lodish, H. F. 1989. Predicting the orientation of eukaryotic membrane-spanning proteins. *Proc. Natl. Acad. Sci. USA* 86:5786–90

35. Hartwell, L. H., Mortimer, R. K., Culotti, J., Culotti, M. 1973. Genetic control of the cell division cycle in yeast: V. Genetic analysis of cdc mutants. *Genetics* 74:267–86

36. Hereford, L. M., Hartwell, L. H. 1974. Sequential gene function in the initiation of *Saccharomyces cerevisiae* DNA synthesis. *J. Mol. Biol.* 84:445–61

37. Herskowitz, I. 1988. Life cycle of the budding yeast *Saccharomyces cerevisiae*. *Microbiol. Rev.* 52:536–53

38. Hirokawa, N., Pfister, K. K., Yorifuji, H., Wagner, M. C., Brady, S. T., Bloom, G. S. 1989. Submolecular domains of bovine brain kinesin identified by electron microscopy and monoclonal antibody decoration. *Cell* 56:867–78

39. Hoyt, M. A., Stearns, T., Botstein, D. 1990. Chromosome instability mutants of *Saccharomyces cerevisiae* that are defective in microtubule-mediated processes. *Mol. Cell. Biol.* 10:223–34

40. Huffaker, T. C., Hoyt, M. A., Botstein, D. 1987. Genetic analysis of the yeast cytoskeleton. *Annu. Rev. Genet.* 21:259–84

41. Huffaker, T. C., Thomas, J. H., Botstein, D. 1988. Diverse effects of β-tubulin mutations on microtubule formation and function. *J. Cell Biol.* 106:1997–2010

42. Jacobs, C. W., Adams, A. E. M., Szaniszlo, P. J., Pringle, J. R. 1988. Functions of microtubules in the *Saccharomyces cerevisiae* cell cycle. *J. Cell Biol.* 107:1409–26

43. Kim, J., Ljungdahl, P. O., Fink, G. R. 1990. *kem* mutations affect nuclear fusion in *Saccharomyces cerevisiae*. *Genetics* 126:799–812

44. Lancashire, W. E., Mattoon, J. R. 1979. Cytoduction: a tool for mito-

chondrial genetic studies in yeast. *Mol. Gen. Genet.* 170:333–44

45. Lee, A. S. 1987. Coordinated regulation of a set of genes by glucose and calcium ionophores in mammalian cells. *Trends Biochem. Sci.* 12:20–23

46. McCaffrey, G., Clay, F. J., Kelsay, K., Sprague, G. F. Jr. 1987. Identification and regulation of a gene required for cell fusion during mating of the yeast *Saccharomyces cerevisiae. Mol. Cell. Biol.* 7:2680–90

47. McDonald, H. B., Goldstein, L. S. B. 1990. Identification and characterization of a gene encoding a kinesin-like protein in *Drosophila. Cell* 61:991–1000

48. McDonald, H. B., Stewart, R. J., Goldstein, L. S. B. 1990. The kinesin-like *ncd* protein of *Drosophila* is a minus end-directed motor. *Cell* 63:1159–65

49. McIntosh, J. R., Porter, M. E. 1989. Enzymes for microtubule-dependent motility. *J. Biol. Chem.* 264:6001–4

50. Meluh, P. B., Rose, M. D. 1990. *KAR3,* a kinesin-related gene required for yeast nuclear fusion. *Cell* 60:1029–41

51. Mitchison, T. J. 1989. Polewards microtubule flux in the mitotic spindle: evidence from photoactivation of fluorescence. *J. Cell Biol.* 109:637–52

52. Munro, S., Pelham, H. R. 1986. An hsp70-like protein in the ER: identity with the 78 kD glucose-regulated protein and immunoglobulin heavy chain binding protein. *Cell* 46:291–300

53. Murray, A. W., Kirschner, M. W. 1989. Dominoes and clocks: the union of two views of the cell cycle. *Science* 246:614–21

54. Murray, A. W., Szostak, J. W. 1983. Pedigree analysis of plasmid segregation in yeast. *Cell* 34:961–70

55. Normington, K., Kohno, K., Kozutsumi, Y., Gething, M.-J., Sambrook, J. 1989. *S. cerevisiae* encodes an essential protein homologous in sequence and function to mammalian BiP. *Cell* 57:1223–36

56. Osumi, M., Shimoda, C., Yanagishima, N. 1974. Mating reaction in *Saccharomyces cerevisiae.* V. Changes in the fine structure during the mating reaction. *Arch. Microbiol.* 97:27–38

57. Otsuka, A. J., Jeyaprakash, A., Garcia-Anoveros, J., Tang, L. V., Fisk, G., et al. 1991. The *C. elegans unc104* gene encodes a putative kinesin heavy chain-like protein. *Neuron* 6:113–22

58. Peterson, J. B., Gray, R. H., Ris, H. 1972. Meiotic spindle plaques in *Saccharomyces cerevisiae. J. Cell Biol.* 53:837–41

59. Peterson, J. B., Ris, H. 1976. Electron-microscopic study of the spindle and chromosome movement in the yeast *Saccharomyces cerevisiae. J. Cell Sci.* 22:219–42

60. Polaina, J., Conde, J. 1982. Genes involved in the control of nuclear fusion during the sexual cycle of *Saccharomyces cerevisiae. Mol. Gen. Genet.* 186:253–58

61. Pringle, J. R., Hartwell, L. H. 1981. The *Saccharomyces cerevisiae* cell cycle. See Ref. 71a, pp. 97–142

62. Rose, M. D., Fink, G. R. 1987. *KAR1,* a gene required for function of both intranuclear and extranuclear microtubules in yeast. *Cell* 48:1047–60

63. Rose, M. D., Misra, L., Vogel, J. P. 1989. *KAR2,* a karyogamy gene, is the yeast homolog of the mammalian BiP/ GRP78 gene. *Cell* 57:1211–21

64. Rose, M. D., Price, B., Fink, G. R. 1986. Yeast nuclear fusion requires prior activation by alpha factor. *Mol. Cell Biol.* 6:3490–97

65. Rothman, J. E. 1989. Polypeptide chain binding proteins: catalysts of protein folding and related processes in cells. *Cell* 59:591–601

66. Schatz, P. J., Solomon, F., Botstein, D. 1988. Isolation and characterization of conditional-lethal mutations in the *TUB1* α-tunulin gene of the yeast *Saccharomyces cerevisiae. Genetics* 120:680–95

67. Scholey, J. M., Heuser, J., Yang, J. T., Goldstein, L. S. B. 1989. Identification of globular mechanochemical heads of kinesin. *Nature* 338:355–57

68. Schroer, T. A., Schnapp, B. J., Reese, T. S., Sheetz, M. P. 1988. The role of kinesin and other soluble factors in organelle movement along microtubules. *J. Cell Biol.* 107:1785–92

69. Singer, R. H., Langevin, G. L., Lawrence, J. B. 1989. Ultrastructural visualization of cytoskeletal mRNAs and their associated proteins using double-label *in situ* hybridization. *J. Cell Biol.* 108:2343–53

70. Stearns, T., Hoyt, M. A., Botstein, D. 1990. Yeast mutants sensitive to antimicrotubule drugs define three genes that affect microtubule function. *Genetics* 124:251–62

71. Stegmann, T., Doms, R. W., Helenius, A. 1989. Protein-mediated membrane fusion. *Annu. Rev. Biophys. Biophys. Chem.* 18:187–211

71a. Strathern, J. N., Jones, E. W., Broach, J. R., eds. 1981. *The Molecular Biology of the Yeast* Saccharomyces: *Life Cycle and Inheritance.* Cold Spring Harbor, NY: Cold Spring Harbor Lab.

72. Thomas, J. H., Botstein, D. 1986. A gene required for separation of chromosomes on the spindle apparatus in yeast. *Cell* 44:65–76

73. Thomas, J. H., Novick, P., Botstein, D. 1984. Genetics of the yeast cytoskeleton. In *Molecular Biology of the Cytoskeleton*, ed. G. G. Borisy, D. W. Cleveland, D. B. Murphy, pp. 153–74. Cold Spring Harbor, NY: Cold Spring Harbor Lab. 512 pp.

74. Trueheart, J., Boeke, J. D., Fink, G. R. 1987. Two genes required for cell fusion during yeast conjugation: evidence for a pheromone-induced surface protein. *Mol. Cell. Biol.* 7:2316–28

75. Vale, R. D., Reese, T. S., Sheetz, M. P. 1985. Identification of a novel force-generating protein, kinesin, involved in microtubule-based motility. *Cell* 42:39–50

76. Vale, R. D., Schnapp, B. J., Mitchison, T., Steuer, E., Reese, T. S., Sheetz, M. P. 1985. Different axoplasmic proteins generate movement in opposite directions along microtubules *in vitro. Cell* 43:623–32

77. Vallee, R. B., Shpetner, H. S. 1990. Motor proteins of cytoplasmic microtubules. *Annu. Rev. Biochem.* 59:909–32

78. Vogel, J. P., Misra, L. M., Rose, M. D. 1990. Loss of BiP/GRP78 function blocks translocation of secretory proteins in yeast. *J. Cell Biol.* 110:1885–95

79. Walker, R. A., Salmon, E. D., Endow, S. A. 1990. The *Drosophila* claret segregation protein is a minus-end directed motor molecule. *Nature* 347:780–82

80. Winey, M., Byers, B. 1991. The spindle pole body of *Saccharomyces cerevisiae:* a model for genetic analysis of the centrosome cycle. In *The Centrosome,* ed. V. Kalins. Orlando, FL: Academic. In press

81. Wittenberg, C., Richardson, S. L., Reed, S. I. 1987. Subcellular localization of a protein kinase required for cell cycle initiation in *Saccharomyces cerevisiae:* evidence for an association between the *CDC28* gene product and the insoluble cytoplasmic matrix. *J. Cell Biol.* 105:1527–38

82. Yang, J. T., Laymon, R. A., Goldstein, L. S. B. 1989. A three-domain structure of kinesin heavy chain revealed by DNA sequence and microtubule binding analyses. *Cell* 56:879–89

83. Yang, J. T., Saxton, W. M., Stewart, R. J., Raff, E. C., Goldstein, L. S. B. 1990. Evidence that the head of kinesin is sufficient for force generation and motility *in vitro. Science* 249:42–47

84. Yochem, J., Byers, B. 1987. Structural comparison of the yeast cell division cycle gene *CDC4* and a related pseudogene. *J. Mol. Biol.* 195:233–45

85. Zhang, P., Knowles, B. A., Goldstein, L. S. B., Hawley, R. S. 1990. A kinesin-like protein required for distributive chromosome segregation in *Drosophila. Cell* 62:1053–62

Annu. Rev. Microbiol. 1991. 45:569–606
Copyright © 1991 by Annual Reviews Inc. All rights reserved

PROKARYOTIC OSMOREGULATION:
Genetics and Physiology

Laszlo N. Csonka

Department of Biological Sciences, Purdue University, West Lafayette, Indiana 47907

Andrew D. Hanson

MSU-DOE Plant Research Laboratory, Michigan State University, East Lansing Michigan 48824-1312; Institut de Recherche en Biologie Végétale, 4101 Rue Sherbrooke Est, Montréal, Québec H1X 2B2, Canada

KEY WORDS: osmotic control of gene expression, compatible solutes, turgor regulation, volume regulation, growth in high osmolality

CONTENTS

INTRODUCTION 570
MECHANISMS UNDERLYING OSMOREGULATORY RESPONSES 571
   Homeostasis vs Adaptation to Change 571
   Examination of Possible Signals 573
PHYSIOLOGY OF OSMOTIC REGULATION 581
   Compatible Solutes Synthesized and/or Transported 581
   Osmoregulation of the Periplasm 588
GENES AND PROTEINS 588
   The EnvZ/OmpR-Dependent Expression of the ompF *and* ompC *Genes of*
     E. coli *K-12* 589
   The kdpABC *operon of* E. coli 592
   The proU *Operon of* E. coli *and* S. typhimurium 593
   Other Osmoregulated Genes 597

Sed quis custodiet ipsos custodes [But who is to guard the guards themselves?]

Decimus Junius Juvenal, Satires VI, 347

0066-4227/91/1001-0569$02.00

INTRODUCTION

The membranes that encompass cells are readily permeable to water but present a more effective barrier to most other solutes. Therefore, when the external concentration (strictly speaking, activity) of water changes because of increases or decreases in the concentrations of extracellular solutes that are excluded by the membrane, water moves out of or into the cells. This movement of water results in changes in the cellular volume (and hence, intracellular solute concentration) and/or pressure. Cells can carry out adaptive processes to restore these parameters to acceptable values. Because changes in the extracellular osmolality have the same physicochemical effects on cells from all biological kingdoms, the responses to osmotic shifts have considerable similarities in all organisms. In eukaryotes, the main experimental approaches with osmoregulation have, necessarily, been physiological ones. Prokaryotic osmoregulation, however, is amenable to biochemical-genetic analysis, making bacteria excellent model organisms for studying osmoregulation as a basic biological process.

Current interest in bacterial osmoregulation is very strong. Various aspects of this topic have been covered in several recent reviews (19, 44, 95, 133) and in a book by Brown (28), and new findings continually emerge. The study of osmoregulation has important applications in food microbiology (161, 168), plant-microbe interactions (32, 54, 55, 204), and medical microbiology (16, 17, 35, 36, 49, 50, 71). Although recent interest has generated a great deal of information about the physiological and genetic responses to the osmolality of the environment in both bacteria and higher organisms, the signals that regulate these responses are understood poorly. This review discusses concepts underlying the perception of osmoregulatory signals. The reader can consult the book by Brown (28) for a different treatment of this topic. We also summarize recent results in osmoregulation in mesophilic bacteria not dealt with in an earlier review (44), but we do not cover in detail osmoregulation in the extreme halophilic bacteria, which has been reviewed by Brown (28) and Vreeland (195a).

In this review, *osmoregulation* refers to active processes carried out during adaptation to the osmotic strength of the environment. There are two types of osmoregulatory phenomena: long-term or steady-state responses that are manifested during the growth of organisms at a constant osmolality, and short-term or transient responses that occur soon after changes in the external osmolality. By hyperosmotic shock, or osmotic shiftup, we mean an increase in the external osmolality, and by hypoosmotic shock or osmotic shiftdown, the opposite. Interestingly, all of the studies of osmoregulation have involved sudden shifts in osmolality; much information might be derived from gradual shift experiments.

MECHANISMS UNDERLYING OSMOREGULATORY RESPONSES

The regulation of most biological responses depends on the recognition of signal molecules by specific receptors (for example, the induction of the *lac* operon by lactose). However, osmoregulation differs in that the information from the environment is not a specific molecule but a physicochemical parameter: the water activity of the exterior (111). Regulation by physical rather than chemical signals occurs in only a few other systems in bacteria, such as the regulation of expression of genes by pressure (14), viscosity (126), and temperature (138). In all these cases, very little concrete information on the signal transduction is available.

This section concerns the physical and chemical parameters that change in an osmotically stressed cell and how these may be used as signals to trigger osmoregulatory responses. The question of the signals for osmoregulation and allied responses is common to the physiology of prokaryotes and eukaryotes and has prompted work on animals, higher plants, algae, and fungi (28, 40, 77, 200).

Accordingly, we first note some useful generalizations about osmoregulation and cellular homeostatic mechanisms that have emerged from work on these organisms and point out a conceptual difficulty that bedevils studies of osmoregulation. We then give a brief classical treatment of the physicochemical changes in osmotically stressed cells, drawing on comparative physiology. In the final section, we consider the evidence for the response of specific bacterial systems to some of these changes.

Homeostasis vs Adaptation to Change

For active metabolism to occur, the intracellular milieu of any organism must remain relatively constant with respect to ionic composition, pH, and metabolite levels; comparative work shows the limits to be strikingly similar among most species (175). These requirements, particularly that for an intracellular K^+ concentration of 100–150 mM (40, 175), set a minimum cytoplasmic osmolality of approximately 250 mosmol/kg (osmotic pressure 0.6 MPa). Thus, in media of low osmolality, those homeostatic mechanisms that keep the ion concentration, pH, and metabolite levels of the cytoplasm within the required limits dominate in the maintenance of intracellular osmolality (28, 199). Therefore, osmoregulation is inseparable from general ionic and metabolic regulation, i.e. cytoplasmic osmolality is controlled by a diverse set of homeostatic feedback mechanisms that respond to various intracellular signals.

Upon transfer to hyperosmotic medium, osmotic adaptation to change is required. The metabolism-imposed limits referred to above constrain the extent to which most metabolites and inorganic ions can be used to fill the role of osmoregulatory solute (199, 202). Thus, following a shiftup in medium osmolality, accumulation of specialized osmolytes that are nontoxic ("compatible") at high concentrations is required (see below) (29, 199, 202). Two general points about these adaptation responses are important. First, although the triggering of such responses at the level of gene expression or protein activity can be dramatic, it may be quite simple mechanistically—say the transient lifting of a negative control—compared to the homeostatic mechanisms that maintain the steady state (28). Second, the short-term responses to a shiftup in external osmolality must eventually be re-engaged with these homeostatic mechanisms to achieve the maintenance of a new osmotic steady state (40). Summarizing, comparative physiology leads to the ideas that osmoregulatory mechanisms are inextricably linked to other cellular homeostatic mechanisms and that they are therefore likely to respond to more than one cellular signal. These generalizations are borne out by recent work in bacteria, as we shall see.

Only a few studies have examined the transient responses to osmotic shifts in bacteria (8, 9, 48, 97, 147, 158), perhaps largely for technical reasons. In these organisms, adaptation to osmotic shifts occurs in a much shorter time frame than subsequent exponential growth in the media of the new osmolality, so that it is simpler to study the long-term responses after the cells have completed osmotic adaptation than the transient responses that occur during the seconds or minutes required for adaptation to a new osmolality. However, our understanding of even the long-term osmoregulatory signals is unsatisfactory.

There is a conceptual difficulty in the long-term regulation of an osmoadaptive process in cells that are in complete osmotic equilibrium with their environment. We illustrate this with the ProP transport system of *Escherichia coli,* but it should be emphasized that all the other long-term osmotically regulated phenomena entail the same conceptual problem. The ProP system, which is a permease for proline and glycine betaine, is synthesized at a nearly constitutive level, but its activity is stimulated in cells growing exponentially in media of high osmolality (31, 53, 131). Interestingly, stimulation of the ProP system by high osmolality can be reproduced in vitro with membrane vesicles (101, 131). Because such vesicles can withstand only very small pressures, less than 1% of the turgor pressure in whole cells (143), this observation suggests that turgor pressure is probably not the regulator of the activity of the ProP system. The signal is more likely to be membrane tension or some related parameter, which we address in more detail in the next section. In whole cells, the accumulation of compatible solutes (carried out in part by the ProP system itself) restores pressure and membrane tension to values very similar to those before the osmotic upshift, but nevertheless the

ProP system remains in its activated state after the cells have completed osmotic adjustment. While one can envision that some change in membrane structure upon the loss of tension, such as an alteration in the contact of the ProP transport protein with lipids, might result in transient stimulation of the activity of this permease both in whole cells and in cell-free vesicles, it is more difficult to imagine how the ProP system could remain activated after the membrane has returned to its original condition as a result of osmotic adaptation. An additional regulator that responds to some persistent osmoregulatory signal is needed to explain the maintenance of the ProP system in its active form; Figure 1 schematically shows this control as an effector molecule that locks the proline porter in its active conformation. But herein lies the conceptual difficulty: whatever the signal is for the long-term regulation of the ProP system, it must itself be subject to regulation by the osmolality of the medium.

A unifying hypothesis proposed that the primary osmoregulatory mechanism is a homeostatic control circuit that maintains turgor within a range that can support cell growth (19, 59). Self-regulation of turgor was postulated to result from the regulation of the intracellular K^+ concentration, such that a drop in turgor pressure below a critical value would trigger increased uptake of K^+, and its excessive buildup would stimulate the excretion of this cation. A second part of the model proposed that the concentration of K^+ is the regulatory signal for all the other osmoregulatory responses, including the stimulation of the steady state activity of the ProP system in cells growing in media of high osmolality. However, the increase in the intracellular concentration of K^+ with increasing external osmolality is also one of the long-term osmoregulatory responses that persists after the turgor has been restored near or equal to its value prior to the osmotic shift. There is one additional level of complexity. Turgor has been proposed to regulate the rate of cell elongation (108). Because the growth rate of cells depends on other factors besides osmolality, such as the carbon or nitrogen source, temperature, etc, K^+ accumulation must also be regulated by growth rate (181a). Consequently, additional tiers of control must be invoked, deferring the question of what is the osmoregulatory signal. This deferral prompted the choice the quote from Juvenal as the theme for this review.

Examination of Possible Signals

Figures 2 and 3 illustrate some physicochemical changes that might be used by gram-negative bacteria for osmoregulatory responses; they are examined below. In this discussion, we make the simplifying assumption that the physicochemical changes schematized in these two figures occur very rapidly after hyperosmotic shock, before any active processes of osmotic adaptation are initiated by the cell.

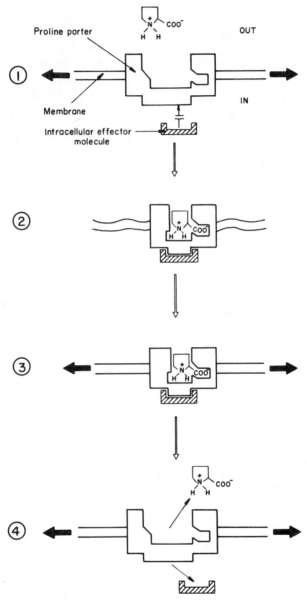

Figure 1 A scheme based on the activation of the ProP proline transport system by a hyperosmotic shift. It illustrates how a change in membrane stretch might switch on a process, and how this process might be maintained by another, persistent signal. The other signal in this scheme is an effector molecule whose ability to bind to the proline porter depends on high osmolality. (*Frame 1*) The membrane is in an expanded (stretched) state and causes the proline porter to adopt a conformation in which it is inactive. (*Frame 2*) The membrane relaxes following

ISOTROPIC PRESSURE   Within the bulk liquid of the cell interior, changes in hydrostatic pressure are isotropic (i.e. they are of uniform magnitude in all directions). As shown in Figure 3, these changes are ≤ 0.5 MPa, which is so low compared with pressures having marked direct effects on biological processes that researchers view intracellular baroreceptors (Figure 2A) as unlikely in relation to osmoregulation (40, 91). Nevertheless, small changes in hydrostatic pressure (< 1 MPa) can bring about measurable changes in protein-protein and protein-ligand interactions (88), and these might be amplified by cooperativity (109). It is therefore interesting that in the barophilic gram-negative bacterium SS9, the *ompH* gene is substantially induced by a hydrostatic pressure of only 7 MPa (14), as this implies that the threshold pressure for response may be much lower. Overall, isotropic pressure changes may deserve some investigation as potential signals, for which pressure chambers should prove useful tools.

PRESSURE DIFFERENTIAL ACROSS THE INNER MEMBRANE-PEPTIDOGLY-CAN COMPLEX   In this case, the pressure is anisotropic, acting normal to the wall. We refer to it as turgor pressure. It could be detected by a pressure (turgor) sensor located in the inner membrane, which responds to compression against the peptidoglycan sacculus (Figure 2B). The large tangential forces that develop within the wall to contain or oppose turgor pressure could also be used for its detection (70) (Figure 2C), as has been proposed for a peptidoglycan cleavage enzyme sensitive to bond angles in the substrate (108). Hydrostatic pressure acting outwards against the wall has been proposed to be fundamental to cell growth and rigidity in bacteria, plants, and algae (40, 91, 108), and so appears at first sight an attractive candidate as a signal in osmoregulation. Nevertheless, wall-less algae (40), many naked animal cells (77, 110), and vacuoles within plant cells (86) can also osmoregulate to control their volume in anisotonic media. Furthermore, as we discuss below, in gram-negative bacteria, the cytoplasmic membrane may not be in extensive contact with the peptidoglycan sacculus (106, 178). Therefore, one should keep in mind other possible signals when interpreting responses that apparently correlate with turgor changes. We now raise some relevant considerations.

← _____

a hyperosomotic shift; the proline porter assumes a new configuration that imparts increased transport activity and allows the intracellular effector molecule to bind to it. (*Frame 3*) The membrane returns to its original level of stretch as osmoregulation restores normal cell volume, but the porter resists the stretch because it is locked into the active configuration by the bound effector. The effector remains bound as long as the cells are kept in the medium of high osmolality. (*Frame 4*) On return to medium of low osmolality, the effector dissociates from the porter, and the stretched membrane forces the porter back into the inactive conformation.

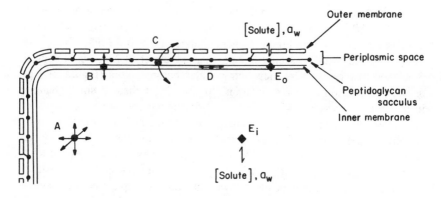

Figure 2   Some physicochemical parameters that change in a gram-negative bacterial cell subjected to an osmotic upshock, and possible sensors of such changes. (*A*) Hydrostatic pressure in the bulk liquid phase, detected by a baroreceptor. (*B*) Pressure differential across the inner membrane-peptidoglycan complex, detected by a turgor pressure sensor. (*C*) Tangential stress within the peptidoglycan layer, sensed by a wall stretch receptor. (*D*) Membrane surface area, sensed by a stretch receptor. (E_i and E_o) Internal and external solute concentration or water activity, sensed by chemoreceptors.

The first of these concerns the relationship between turgor pressure and cellular volume, which according to the analogy of Brown (28), are as inseparable as space and time in relativity theory. We consider two situations: a hypothetical one in which the peptidoglycan sacculus is completely rigid (Figure 3, lines labeled R), and a second, more realistic one, in which the sacculus is elastic (Figure 3, lines labeled E) so that it can shrink and swell along with the cytoplasm upon osmotic shifts. In the first case, the decline in pressure upon a hyperosmotic shock would be proportional to external osmolality; the cytoplasmic volume, internal osmolality and membrane area would change very little until turgor fell to zero (Figure 3A, *inset*). In this scenario, turgor is the only one of these parameters that could be used to sense a modest shiftup (< 0.5 MPa) in medium osmolality. Although previous treatments of osmoregulation in bacteria generally assumed that the sacculus is rigid (44, 196), several lines of evidence (see Figure 3 legend) indicate that this is not the case, and the sacculus may perhaps reach a state of zero tension only when more than half the cell water has been withdrawn. In this situation, turgor pressure would decline less steeply as the peptidoglycan shrank in step with the cytoplasm, with the relationship between the cellular volume and the external osmolality set by the volumetric elastic modulus of the sacculus. For simplicity in Figure 3 (lines labeled E), the volumetric elastic modulus of the sacculus is assumed to be constant, although it seems likely to increase as maximum cell volume is approached, as occurs in algal and plant cell walls (40). If the peptidoglycan sacculus is elastic, turgor will decline gradually with increasing external osmolality (Figure 3A), and cytoplasmic volume, the concentration of internal solutes (Figure 3B), and membrane area (Figure 3C) will all change as soon as medium osmolality is raised. Contrast this with the buffering effect that a rigid sacculus has on these parameters. The point here is that if—as is most probably the case—the sacculus is elastic, then appreciable changes in internal solute concentration and membrane area will occur as well and at the same time as a decline in turgor, so that the cell might monitor three or more types of signals simultaneously.

Complexities also arise from the osmotic regulation of the periplasmic space in gram-negative bacteria. The periplasm contains anionic polysaccharides that generate a Donnan potential across the outer membrane (107, 178; see section on osmoregulation of the periplasm). Hydrostatic pressure is generated in the periplasm by the accumulation of counterions (e.g. K^+, Na^+) for anionic polysaccharides, and it is presumably resisted externally by the wall on one side and the cytoplasm on the other. Perhaps one way to visualize this difficult concept is that the isotonic Donnan space in the periplasm behaves as an incompressible gel surrounding the cytoplasm (106). The presence of such a space would not change the hydrostatic pressure exerted on the wall, but it would mean that the main pressure differential would not be at the inner membrane-peptidoglycan interface, but rather across the whole inner membrane–periplasm–outer membrane complex. As a corollary, the pressure in the periplasm must be nearly equal to the pressure in the cytoplasm (178), except for an insignificant pressure differential of ~0.003 MPa that can be supported by the lipid bilayer itself (143). If osmotic signal-sensing proteins are localized in the portions of the cytoplasmic membrane that contact the periplasm (as has been proposed for the transcriptional regulatory proteins EnvZ and KdpE; see below), then whether such proteins could indeed sense turgor pressure is questionable. However, our understanding of the structure of the periplasm is very tenuous, especially concerning whether the cytoplasmic membrane is in contact with the peptidoglycan sacculus over much (25, 64) or over very little of its surface area (106).

INTERNAL SOLUTE LEVEL OR WATER ACTIVITY   As noted above, in cells with elastic walls, cytoplasmic volume would change with external osmolality as a continuous function, but in cells with rigid walls, it would decrease only after turgor is lost completely. In either case, once turgor is lost the cytoplasmic compartment follows the Boyle-Van't Hoff law, behaving as an osmometer (132). Thus, in principle, either the cytoplasmic volume itself, the accompanying changes in the concentration of one or more solutes, or the activity (concentration) of water could serve as signals. These are the parameters available as osmoregulatory signals to wall-less algal and animal cells, and evidence indicates sensing of the first two quantities in animals.

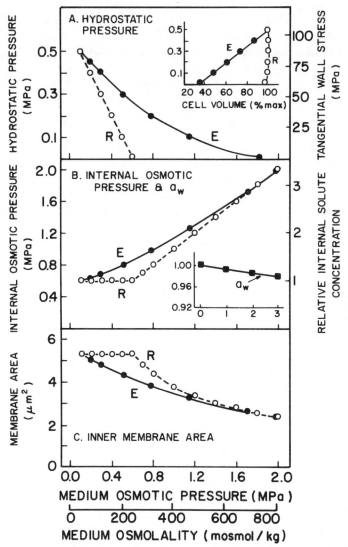

Figure 3 Idealized scheme to show the magnitude of some of the physicochemical changes occurring in a gram-negative bacterial cell upon transfer from minimal medium (osmotic pressure 0.1 MPa) to media of higher osmolality (0.2–2.0 MPa). The cytoplasmic compartment is assumed to behave as a perfect osmometer. Two scenarios are developed, for cells with a rigid (R) or elastic (E) sacculus. For the rigid cell, the hydrostatic pressure is assumed to decline rapidly to zero as water leaves the cell; for the elastic cell, the volumetric elastic modulus is assumed to remain constant so that hydrostatic pressure falls as a linear function of volume, reaching zero at 35% of the initial volume (*inset, Frame A*). This scenario is based on the estimate of Koch (108) that the area of the extended wall is twofold greater than that of the unstressed wall,

Because volume sensing in animals is probably associated with the plasma membrane, we discuss this process in a later section. Evidence points to sensing of the internal solute level (Figure 2, E_i) for K^+ and Na^+ in cultured kidney cells (191), and for Na^+ in the vertebrate hypothalamus (171). As discussed before, K^+ has been proposed to be a key osmoregulatory signal in *E. coli* (19, 59). Because in these instances, the signals are particular solutes, their receptors are chemoreceptors and osmosensors (see below). These systems can be very sensitive (e.g. to < 10 mM in kidney cells), and so provide precedents for the sensing of changes in ion concentrations of the magnitude likely to occur in the cytoplasm of bacterial cells given a moderate osmotic upshock.

The activity of water a_w is effectively the concentration (or mole fraction) of water in a solution. It is related to osmotic pressure Π as follows:

$$\Pi = (RT/V_w) \ln a_w$$

where R is the gas constant, T is absolute temperature, and V_w is the partial molal volume of water. Thus, as the medium osmolality is raised, the cytoplasmic a_w falls proportionally (Figure 3B, inset), but the cytoplasmic a_w changes much less, relatively, than the cytoplasmic osmotic pressure. For example, while an increase of 1.9 MPa in the external osmolality decreases a_w only by 2%, it raises Π more than threefold. Because of the relative insensitivity of a_w to changes in osmolality, it has been suggested to be unlikely as a signal (e.g. 91). However, what is valid for water in simple solutions may not be so for intracellular water. Evidence indicates that some fraction of

←——————————————————————————————————————

and is broadly consistent with observations on plasmolysis (132) and cell volume (12, 178). The internal osmolality of cells grown on minimal medium was taken as 0.24 mosmol/kg (osmotic pressure 0.6 MPa), which in minimal medium would generate a hydrostatic pressure of 0.5 MPa. Cells were assumed to be spherical, with a radius of 0.8 μm, and the periplasmic volume was taken to be 20% (194). The solutes were assumed to behave ideally. (A) Changes in internal hydrostatic pressure. Note that pressure declines steeply in the rigid cell, gradually in the elastic cell, and that these changes are accompanied by large reductions in the tangential forces in the cell wall (*right hand axis*). (B) Changes in internal osmotic pressure, or in the concentration of individual solutes. Note that in the rigid cell no changes occur until turgor is completely lost. In contrast, the volume decrease undergone by the elastic cell in response to moderate osmotic upshock results in appreciable increases in solute concentration. The inset compares the small changes in the activity of water (a_w) with the much larger changes in osmotic pressure; the differences between the a_w in rigid and in elastic cells would be very small and so are not shown. (C) Changes in the area of the inner membrane. In the rigid cell, membrane area does not change until turgor is lost, whereas area decreases substantially in the elastic cell even with slight increases in the osmolality of the medium.

cytoplasmic water has altered properties because of its association with macromolecules (38, 166, 197a), and cooperativity effects might transduce changes in the a_w of such bound water into a biologically useful output. In any case, to invoke an "osmosensor" (i.e. a sensor that measures osmolality regardless of the nature of the solutes) is to invoke a sensor that responds to a_w, and if such a sensor could be demonstrated it could have profound importance for our understanding of the structure of intracellular water.

EXTERNAL SOLUTE LEVEL OR WATER ACTIVITY   In principle, a transmembrane protein with an outward-facing binding site could sense the level of a solute in the periplasmic space (or the medium) (Figure 2, E_o). Many precedents for such chemoreceptors, including bacterial chemotactic receptors (117), can be found in biology. For sensing of extracellular a_w, the considerations are similar to those for intracellular water, with the following addition. If an a_w sensor faced the periplasmic space, its output would be influenced by the osmolality of the external medium, and also by the content of fixed anions and their counterions in the periplasm. If the anionic polysaccharides, which are down-regulated in cells grown in high-osmolality medium (107) (see below), are the main sources of periplasmic fixed anions, then the a_w sensor would be unable to measure medium a_w (osmolality). Rather, it would respond to some derivative thereof, which would itself be subject to genetic and environmental control.

INNER MEMBRANE AREA   As for cytoplasmic volume, the cytoplasmic membrane area could change considerably following moderate osmotic upshock, e.g. by around 7% in an elastic cell for a rise in medium osmolality of 100 mosmol/kg (Figure 3C). These changes could be detected by a stretch receptor in the membrane (Figure 2D). Many animals cells and tissues sense volume or pressure changes via such stretch receptors, which in some cases are very sensitive. Thus, the "baroreceptors" of vertebrate blood vessels are stretch-sensitive nerve endings embedded in the vessel walls. Increased arterial pressure distends the receptors, excites the sensory endings, and leads to an increase in firing rate. These receptors respond markedly to pressure changes as small as 10^{-3} MPa, corresponding to an area change of 5% (172). The stretch receptors of vertebrate airways are even more sensitive (167).

Small changes in membrane area ($< 1\%$) may also signal an increase in K^+ uptake after osmotic upshock in giant algal cells (40). Membrane area changes in plant and animal cells have been shown to affect stretch-activated ion channels (111). The study of stretch-activated channels in bacteria is in its infancy, but they have been found in the outer membrane of $E.\ coli$ (111, 118, 119) and in the cytoplasmic membrane of $Bacillus\ subtilis$ (119, 203). As these channels allow the bidirectional traffic of solutes, they probably do not have a direct role in the active transport of compatible solutes, but they could mediate their excretion. However, regardless of the function of the stretch-activated channels in bacteria that have been described thus far, the presence of the channels raises the possibility that membrane stretch could control cytoplasmic membrane-bound channels, solute pumps, or perhaps even transcriptional regulatory proteins that are important for osmoregulation.

PHYSIOLOGY OF OSMOTIC REGULATION

Compatible Solutes Synthesized and/or Transported

Increases or decreases in the extracellular osmolality commonly elicit corresponding changes in the intracellular concentrations of compatible solutes (28, 40, 44, 73). As a result of this adaptive response, cells tend to keep their volume fairly constant over a large range of external osmolality. Although compatible solutes are not unduly toxic at high concentrations (29), they do seem to affect biochemical processes because high osmolality has been shown not only to overcome temperature-sensitive mutations (i.e. the osmoremedial phenotype) (see 44), but also has been found to increase the high temperature limit of growth of many bacteria (168, 183, 185). Table 1 summarizes recent results concerning bacterial compatible solutes. The cytoplasmic concentration of putrescine is also subject to osmotic control, but unlike the solutes listed in Table 1, the concentration of this diamine decreases with increasing osmolality (136, 201). This decrease may provide a mechanism for the electroneutral exchange of two K^+ ions for one putrescine, enabling cells to increase their osmolality without disturbing the ionic balance (136). Bacteria also have mechanisms of avoidance of unfavorable conditions (117); E. coli can swim away from media of excessively low and high solute concentrations (116, 152).

Even though the intracellular concentration of a solute might depend on the extracellular osmolality, this dependence is of little significance for osmotic adaptation if the concentration of the solute is low compared with the external osmolality. Thus, although the levels of glutamine, glutathione, and γ-glutamylglutamine are proportional to the external osmolality in E. coli (127), they are present at less than 10% of the intracellular concentration of K^+, and therefore they can make only a modest contribution to the cellular osmolality. Because glutamine can be a precursor of glutamate, a major osmolyte in bacteria, the increase in glutamine pool size may be simply a metabolic consequence of the higher flux to glutamate. Similarly, glycine betaine has been found at 10–20 mM concentration in halophilic archaebacteria (141), which is ~100-fold less than the concentration of K^+ and Cl^-, the major osmolytes in this organism (28). In these organisms, the glycine betaine

Table 1 Recent reports of compatible solutes in bacteria[a]

Solute	Bacterial species	Mode of accumulation[b]	Reference
K$^+$	*Escherichia coli*	T	127
	Rhizobium meliloti	T	22
Amino acids			
Glutamate	*Methanogenium anulus,*	?	163
	Methanogenium cariaci,		
	Methanococcus igneus,		
	Methanococcus jannaschii,		
	Methanococcus thermolitho-		
	trophicus,		
	R. meliloti	S, T	22
	Rhizobium sp.	T	57
β-Glutamate	*M. anulus,*	?	163
(β-Aminoglutarate)	*M. cariaci,*		
	M. igneus,		
	M. jannaschii,		
	M. lithotrophicus		
Glutamine	*E. coli*	S	127
	E. coli	T	74
Proline	*Brevibacterium lactofer-*	S	104, 104a
	mentum		
	Streptomyces clavuligerus	T	15
Disaccharides			
Trehalose	*Ectothiorhodospira halo-*	S	72, 186, 187
	chloris		
	E. coli	S	18, 24
	Mixococcus xanthus	S	125
	Rhizobium sp.	S	58
	Sulfolobus solfataricus	?	140
Mannosucrose	*Agrobacterium tumefaciens*	S	174
(β-furanosyl-α-mannopyranoside)			
N-methyl substituted amino acids			
Glycine betaine	*Azospirillum brasiliense*	T	160a
	Ba$_1$, *Vibrio costicola*	T	159
	Bradyrhizobium japonicum RCR 3407	T	57
	Brevibacterium lactoferentum	T	104a
	E. halochloris	T	72, 186, 187

Table 1   *(Continued)*

Solute	Bacterial species	Mode of accumulation[b]	Reference
	M. anulus,	?	162
	M. cariaci,		
	Methanococcus voltae,		
	Methanohalophilus mahii,		
	Methanohalophilus zhilinae		
	Methanosarcinia thermophila	T	176
	R. meliloti	S[c]	149
		T	68
	Rhodobacter sphaeroides	S[c], T	1
Proline betaine	*R. meliloti*	T	78
(Stachydrine)			
Taurine betaine	*Klebsiella pneumoniae*	T	121
γ-Amino butyric acid betaine	*K. pneumoniae*	T	121
β-Alanine betaine	*E. coli,*	T	87
	Salmonella typhimurium		
Carnitine	*E. coli*	T	98a
γ-Aminocrotonic acid betaine	*E. coli*	T	98a
Peptides			
γ-Glutamylglutamine	*E. coli*	S	127
Glutathione	*E. coli*	S	56, 127
N-Acetylglutamylgluta-mine	*R. meliloti*	S	173
Others			
Ectoine (1,4,5,6-tetra-hydro-2-methyl-4-pyrimidine carboxylic acid)	Ba₁ *V. costicola*	S	159
	E. halochloris	S	72, 186, 187
	Deleye halophila,	S	198
	Halomonas elongata,		
	Halomonas halinophila		
N^ε-acetyl-β-lysine	*M. thermophila* and other methanogenic archaebacteria	S	176
3-Dimethylsulpho-niopropionate	*K. pneumoniae*	T	121
3-(N-Morpholino)pro-panesulphonate	*E. coli*	T	34
Choline-O-sulphate	*K. pneumoniae*	T	121
	E. coli, S. typhimurium	T	87

[a]For previous reports, see Ref. 44.
[b]S = synthesis; T = transport from medium; ? = mechanism not known.
[c]Synthesis of glycine betaine only from choline.

was apparently complexed with anionic lipids, and so it may have some other function besides acting as a cytoplasmic compatible solute. Trehalose, which is used as a compatible solute in many species of bacteria (Table 1), is synthesized constitutively in archaebacteria (140) and in the spores of eubacteria (124, 125); this compound has also been proposed to act as a stabilizer of membranes under desiccation (41).

Some compatible solutes can alleviate the inhibitory effects of high osmolality when they are present in the culture medium, suggesting that they can accumulate to high concentrations by transport but not by de novo synthesis. Compounds that have this ability are called osmoprotectants. Two mechanisms have been proposed for their modes of action: to establish the intracellular osmolality or to stabilize biological macromolecules in environments of low water activity (for discussion, see 44). These two effects are not mutually exclusive, and it is not clear which is more important for a given osmoprotectant. Choline deserves special mention in this regard: although it is a potent alleviator of osmotic stress in several bacterial species (1, 121, 180), it is not itself a compatible solute and needs to be oxidized to glycine betaine. Several compounds that have osmoprotectant activities for *Enterobacteriaceae* have been described recently. These include the sulfonium compounds 3-dimethylsulphoniopropionate (121) and dimethylthetin (37), the quaternary amines β-alanine betaine (87), taurine betaine, γ-aminobutyric acid betaine (121), carnitine, γ-aminocrotonic acid betaine (98a), and the sulfate ester choline-O-sulfate (87, 121). Certain compatible solutes, notably trehalose (18, 76) and in most cases glutamate (42, 44, 115), do not alleviate osmotic inhibition when added exogenously (but see 22). As these compounds can be taken up from the medium, this observation suggests that the cellular capacity to synthesize them does not limit osmotic adaptation. Trehalose is synthesized by the condensation of the glucose from UDP-glucose with glucose-6-phosphate forming trehalose-6-phosphate, which is hydrolyzed to trehalose (18). In *E. coli,* mutations inactivating the enzymes for these two steps or the reactions leading to the formation of UDP-glucose and glucose-6-phosphate result in sensitivity to high osmolality, which can be relieved by glycine betaine (18, 76). This observation is consistent with a requirement for trehalose in maintaining the osmotic balance in media of high osmolality, although this phenotype could result from the accumulation of a toxic intermediate in the mutants (69).

The major anionic organic solute in most eubacteria, glutamate, can be synthesized by two reactions: glutamate dehydrogenase and glutamate synthase (182). Glutamate dehydrogenase has a low affinity for NH_4^+ ($K_m \approx 1$ mM), and therefore one can limit synthesis of glutamate by growing glutamate synthase mutants with < 1 mM concentrations of NH_4^+ (182). In the presence of excess NH_4^+, single mutations in either glutamate dehydrogenase (*gdh*) or glutamate synthase (*gltB*) in *S. typhimurium* did not prevent accumulation of glutamate in response to high osmolality (S. Kustu, personal communication). However, in media containing 1 mM NH_4^+, the *gltB* mutants were sensitive to high osmolality, and unlike the control *gltB*$^+$ strains, they could not increase their glutamate levels upon a hyperosmotic shock. These results not only demonstrate that in *S. typhimurium* both glutamate synthase and glutamate dehydrogenase are under osmotic control, but they also provide direct proof that the accumulation of glutamate is necessary for growth in media of high osmolality. Besides synthesis, the catabolism of glutamate or its utilization in protein synthesis and in biosynthetic reactions could potentially be subject to osmotic regulation. The last mechanism has been proposed to occur in *Rhizobium meliloti* (22).

In *E. coli*, the intracellular levels of K^+ are determined by the combined effects of several uptake systems, Kdp, TrkA, TrkF, and Kup (20, 21, 60, 196, 197), and at least two efflux systems, KefB and KefC (56); the interactions between these uptake and efflux systems need to be further characterized. Buurman et al (30) reported that in K^+-limited chemostat cultures of *Klebsiella pneumoniae* and *Bacillus stearothermophilus*, NH_4^+ ions can partially replace K^+, with a progressively increased effectiveness with increasing pH. These observations could raise questions concerning the proposed role of K^+ as an osmoregulatory signal (19, 59), but one should note that Buurman et al (30) used only a medium of low osmolality and did not test whether the NH_4^+ could substitute for K^+ in media of high osmolality.

HIERARCHIES OF COMPATIBLE SOLUTES   Most bacterial species can accumulate several compatible solutes, but seem to prefer some over others. In a thorough study of the kinetic profile of compatible solute accumulation, Dinnbier et al (48) found that adaptation of *E. coli* to hyperosmotic shock occurred in two phases. First, K^+ was taken up rapidly and glutamate was synthesized. In the second phase, the concentration of these two solutes fell as a result of excretion of K^+ and by excretion and/or catabolism of glutamate. The synthesis of trehalose began at the onset of the second phase, and as the cells completed their osmotic adaptation, this disaccharide replaced K^+ and glutamate as the major compatible solute. Apparently, a regulatory interplay occurs between the accumulation of compatible solutes, because mutants unable to synthesize trehalose exhibited enhanced K^+ accumulation (11, 113). Conversely, mutants defective in K^+ uptake (because of mutations in both the TrkA and Kdp K^+-transport systems) accumulated trehalose more rapidly and to a higher concentration than the wild-type cells (48), in apparent contradiction of the model in which K^+ is the triggering signal for all other osmoregulatory responses (19, 59).

Several observations suggest that in most eubacteria glycine betaine is preferred over all other compatible solutes. This substance is a more potent alleviator of osmotic stress than most other osmoprotectants in *Enterobacteriaceae* (115). It also suppresses the accumulation of other compatible solutes in several species of bacteria. Thus, the addition of glycine betaine to cultures of *E. coli* grown in media of high osmolality in the absence of any osmoprotectants elicited a rapid excretion of K^+ (11, 48, 181), a depletion of trehalose (48), and an inhibition of the uptake of 3-(N-morpholino)-propane sulfonate (34). Likewise, glycine betaine inhibited the accumulation of proline in *Brevibacterium lactoterentum* (104), ectoine in the bacterium Ba_1 and in *Vibrio costicola* (159), mannosucrose in *Agrobacterium tumefaciens* (174), and N^ϵ-acetyl-β-lysine in *Methanosarcina thermophila* (176). However, other environmental factors can affect accumulation of compatible solutes, because in *Ectothiorhodospira halochloris,* nitrogen limitation in media of high osmolality resulted in the preferential synthesis of trehalose over the nitrogen-containing compatible solutes glycine betaine and ectoine (72).

Solutes that carry a net electric charge are generally more deleterious to protein stability than nonpolar or zwitterionic solutes (10), and the in vivo preference for glycine betaine over K^+ and glutamate for the maintenance of the cellular osmolality suggests that glycine betaine is more compatible than K^+ and glutamate. Proline reportedly is very similar, if not identical, to glycine betaine in eliciting the efflux of K^+ and the depletion of trehalose in *E. coli* grown in high osmolality (48, 181), even though proline is not as potent an osmoprotectant as glycine betaine (115). Thus, the osmoprotecting efficacy of solutes apparently depends not only on their ability to replace K^+ and glutamate but also on other factors, such as their interactions with macromolecules (202).

ENVIRONMENTAL SOURCES OF OSMOPROTECTANTS   As defined above, osmoprotectants are solutes that alleviate osmotic inhibition when present in the medium. In the bacterial kingdom, only a few photoautotrophic species can carry out the complete synthesis of glycine betaine (1, 143a, 186); other species depend on exogenous glycine betaine (or its precursor, choline). Curiously, proline is an osmoprotectant for several bacteria that are nevertheless capable of producing it for protein synthesis (Table 1) (44). Proline-overproducing mutants that acquired increased tolerance of osmotic stress have been isolated in *S. typhimurium* (42), so in principle these organisms could make their own proline in sufficient amounts to overcome osmotic inhibition. Nevertheless, in wild-type *Enterobacteriaceae,* neither the synthesis (23, 43, 62) nor the catabolism of proline (43, 47) is subject to osmotic control, and these organisms depend on exogenous proline for an osmoprotectant (44).

That many bacteria depend on transport for the accumulation of osmoprotectants implies that these substances should be present in the natural environment of the organisms. Glycine betaine, proline betaine, and 3-dimethylsul-phoniopropionate are synthesized by cyanobacteria or algae and are found in fresh or salt water environments as a result of excretion or leakage from the producing organisms (121, 143a, 157). Glycine betaine has been detected in marine sediments (26, 75), where it enhances the survival of enteric contaminants (120, 137, 164). Because they are abundant plant metabolites, proline, glycine betaine, and proline betaine are present in the diet of many animals and thus available to intestinal bacteria. Glycine betaine, which is used for the maintenance of the osmotic balance of kidney cells (36, 73), is excreted in urine and can be taken up by uropathogenic bacteria (35, 36).

REGULATION OF CATABOLISM OF COMPATIBLE SOLUTES   Because some compatible solutes can be used as nitrogen or carbon sources, their catabolism needs to be regulated to prevent their degradation as long as they are needed as osmotic balancers. Accordingly, in *R. meliloti,* conditions of high osmolality inhibit the catabolism of choline, glycine betaine, and proline betaine, which can be used as nitrogen sources in media of low osmolality (78, 149). In *E. coli* grown in media of low osmolality, the catabolic pathway of trehalose consists of its uptake and phosphorylation by a trehalose-specific component of the phosphotransferase system and the conversion of the product, trehalose-6-phosphate, to glucose and a long chain glucose polymer by amylotrehalase (18). Under high osmolality, the organism uses a different pathway in which trehalose is hydrolyzed to glucose outside the cytoplasm by a periplasmic trehalase. High osmolality induces the periplasmic trehalase and represses the enzymes that normally mediate the catabolism of trehalose under conditions of low osmolality (18), and therefore the catabolism of trehalose does not interfere with its synthesis in media of high osmolality. In *E. coli,* L-carnitine can be converted under anaerobic conditions to γ-aminocrotonic acid betaine, which can be used as a terminal electron acceptor in anaerobic respiration, generating γ-aminobutyric acid betaine (98a). Conditions of high osmolality inhibit the synthesis of L-carnitine dehydrase and γ-aminocrotonic acid betaine reductase (98a).

ADAPTATION TO HYPOOSMOTIC SHOCK   A decrease in extracellular osmolality results in an influx of water into the cells, which would lead to a build up of turgor pressure in cells with inelastic cell walls. Because bacterial cell walls can withstand pressures of 10 MPa without rupturing (33), increases in turgor pressure may not be particularly deleterious. Nevertheless, bacteria possess active processes for dissipating excessive turgor by decreasing the concentrations of compatible solutes. In principle, this can be accomplished by four processes: dilution by growth, catabolism to osmotically inert molecules (such as H_2O or CO_2), polymerization, and excretion into the medium. Literature is scant on these processes in bacteria, but the most extensively characterized example is the excretion of K^+ via the KefB and KefC systems in *E. coli* (56). Hypoosmotic shock results in a depletion of the trehalose content in several species of cyanobacteria, partly as a result of excretion but mainly as a result of catabolism (156, 157). Specific export systems for glycine betaine and ectoine were suggested for *E. halochloris* (187). Hypoosmotic shock causes a rapid excretion of glycine betaine in cyanobacteria (156, 157) and *S. typhimurium* (V. J. Prange & L. Csonka, unpublished results). However, dilution of the cells into media of low osmolality may confer a generalized leakiness to the membranes without causing cell death (27, 157), so that the loss of intracellular solutes upon hypoosmotic shock could be a passive process.

Osmoregulation of the Periplasm

The periplasmic space of gram-negative bacteria contains oligosaccharides known as membrane-derived oligosaccharides that have been proposed to be involved in the osmoregulation of the periplasm. These oligosaccharides are called membrane-derived oligosaccharides (MDOs) in *E. coli* (107) and β-glucans in *Agrobacterium, Rhizobium* (129), and *Bradyrhizobium* (190a) strains. Unlike intracellular compatible solutes, the levels of these oligosaccharides decrease with increasing external osmolality (129). The MDOs of *E. coli* and the β-glucans of *A. tumefaciens* (130), *Bradyrhizobium japonicum* (190a), and some *R. meliloti* (128a) strains are negatively charged, and therefore can generate a Donnan potential across the outer membrane. Consequently, the concentration of cations is greater in the periplasm than in the medium, giving rise to an osmotic pressure in the periplasm. Mutational blocks in the synthesis of β-glucans result in sensitivity to low osmolality in *R. meliloti* (54, 55) and *A. tumefaciens* (32, 204), but these mutations have additional pleiotropic effects including impairment of the invasion of the hosts (51, 54, 55). Surprisingly, MDO-deficient *E. coli* mutants are not sensitive to media of low osmolality (107). There is inconsistency in the literature concerning the electrical charge of β-glucans in *R. meliloti,* because they were reported to be anionic in some strains (128a, 130) and neutral in others (54). These oligosaccharides could be directly responsible for the osmotic pressure in the periplasm because long-chain polyols can generate osmotic pressures excessively greater than the ideal value predicted from their concentrations (135).

GENES AND PROTEINS

Changes in extracellular osmolality generally bring about changes in the expression of few genes, which for the most part encode proteins involved in the synthesis or transport of compatible solutes. Biochemical (96) and genetic analyses in *Enterobacteriaceae* (reviewed in 44) revealed only about twenty genes that are subject to osmotic control at the level of transcription. NaCl increased the transcription of ~100 genes in a salt-tolerant cyanobacterium, *Anabaena torulosa* (7). The observation that osmotic shifts change the transcriptional rate of a particular gene is not sufficient evidence that this gene is subject to osmotic control, because its transcription may depend on some other aspect of cell physiology affected indirectly by the osmolality. For example, the expression of many genes in *E. coli* depends on growth rate (148), which is affected by the external osmolality. A more specific instance of apparent osmotic control of transcription is the complex regulation of expression of the *ompF* and *ompC* genes of enteric bacteria. The transcription of these two genes responds to the osmolality of the medium (see below), but studies have not firmly established that this response is significant to the ability of the organism to grow in media of high vs low osmolality. Although simultaneous loss of both the OmpC and OmpF porins in *E. coli* K-12 results in a growth impairment owing to a reduction of the diffusion rate of nutrients across the outer membrane (25), single mutations in either the *ompF* or *ompC* gene do not cause any sensitivity to the osmolality of the growth medium under laboratory conditions. In fact, *E. coli* B, a close relative of *E. coli* K-12, lacks the OmpC porin and synthesizes only the OmpF porin constitutively, regardless of the osmolality (134). In *S. typhimurium,* the synthesis of the OmpF and OmpC porins is regulated as in *E. coli* K-12, but this organism has a third porin, OmpD, whose synthesis is not under osmotic control (142). Because the cellular signals responsible for the transcriptional control of the *ompC* and *ompF* genes of *E. coli* K-12 and *S. typhimurium* are unknown (see below), the apparent osmoregulation of these genes may be the consequence of other physiological factor(s) that depend in part on the external osmolality.

The EnvZ/OmpR-Dependent Expression of the ompF *and* ompC Genes of E. coli *K-12*

The transcription of these two genes, which encode two similar outer membrane channel proteins or porins, responds in a reciprocal fashion to the external osmolality; the expression of the *ompF* gene is depressed and that of the *ompC* gene is enhanced with increasing osmolality. However, other factors, such as the carbon source, oxygen availability, temperature, and the pH of the medium, also influence the expression of the *ompF* and *ompC* genes (82). Recent reviews by Mizuno & Mizushima (133) and Igo et al (95) have summarized the transcriptional control of the *ompC* and *ompF* genes; we discuss only the main features of this process and new results not included in these reviews.

The cardinal transcriptional regulator of the *ompC* and *ompF* genes is the phosphoprotein OmpR. This protein can be phosphorylated by the osmotic signal sensing protein, EnvZ protein, which spans the cytoplasmic membrane and has both periplasmic and cytoplasmic domains (4, 66, 94, 94a, 184). The EnvZ and OmpR proteins belong to the so-called two-component family of regulatory proteins, in which one partner is a sensor of some environmental signal and the second is the signal transducer that regulates response (5, 177). In addition to its function as a kinase, the EnvZ protein can also dephosphorylate the OmpR protein (2, 3, 102). The steady-state level of phosphorylation of the latter protein could be determined by the net of the rates of phosphorylation and dephosphorylation, but at present it is not known which of these two reactions is under osmotic control. In vivo, the steady-state level of phosphorylation of the OmpR protein is stimulated by high osmolality (65, 67). This result suggests that the induction of the *ompC* gene and repression of the *ompF* gene in media of high osmolality are the consequences of increased phosphorylation of the OmpR protein, but whether these processes result from phosphorylation of more OmpR monomers or from the incorporation of more than one phosphate moiety into each monomer is unclear. Procaine is a nonphysiological regulator of the synthesis of the porins that mimics conditions of high osmolality in that it increases the expression of the *ompC* gene and decreases the expression of the *ompF* gene (184, 195). This compound inhibits the in vitro dephosphorylation of the OmpR protein by the intact EnvZ protein (184).

The OmpR protein binds to multiple sites upstream of the *ompF* and *ompC* promoters both in vitro (95, 103, 133) and in vivo (189, 190). Depending on its state of phosphorylation, it activates the transcription of the *ompC* and *ompF* genes, probably by enhancing the binding of RNA polymerase to otherwise weak promoters (190). In vitro experiments showed that both unphosphorylated and phosphorylated OmpR protein could bind to the same sequences upstream of the *ompC* and the *ompF* promoters, but the latter form had higher affinity for its target sites than the former (65, 95, 133). However, even though unphosphorylated OmpR protein can bind to its target sites, in this form it is not a transcriptional activator even for the *ompF* gene because null mutations in the *envZ* gene drastically decrease the expression of both porin genes in media of any osmolality (95, 133). The OmpR protein also functions as the repressor of the *ompF* gene in media of high osmolality (65, 95, 171a; J. Slauch, personal communication). The presence of multiple OmpR-binding sites in front of the *ompC* and *ompF* genes suggests that the transcriptional control of these genes could entail cooperative interactions between several OmpR molecules (possibly with different states of phosphorylation), but how these interactions are related to the transcriptional control of expression of the two porin genes is unclear. Mutations inactivating the multifunctional histone-like DNA-binding protein IHF lead to increased expression of both the *ompF* (188) and *ompC* genes (92). Also, the expression of both porin genes is sensitive to supercoiling (82). In view of the strong dependence of the expression of the two porin genes on the OmpR protein, the IHF protein and supercoiling seem to have secondary roles in the transcription of these two genes, which could involve assisting the proper contacts between the DNA and the transcriptional complex.

As mentioned above, the transcription of the OmpC and OmpF genes is also subject to regulation by temperature. In the case of the *ompF* gene, temperature regulation is mediated in part by a posttranscriptional mechanism involving the *mic* RNA, which is a natural antisense RNA complementary to the 5' portion of the *ompF* mRNA (see 44 for references). The OmpR protein is required for maximal synthesis of the *mic* RNA at 24°C, but at 37°C this RNA could be made independently of the OmpR protein (39).

CONTROL BY PERIPLASMIC SOLUTE LEVEL?   Although the signal transduction pathway for the transcriptional control of the *ompC* and *ompF* genes has been well characterized with respect to the structures and interactions of its components, the issues of what the signal is and how it is sensed have been difficult to tackle. Isotropic pressure differential and wall or membrane stretch are not strong candidates for the signal because the change in relative levels of the OmpF and OmpC proteins is not a transient response to a change in medium osmolality, but a long-term one (193). Also, the permeant solute glycerol elicits the response, at least to some extent (85). Hence, the only possible signals are the levels of specific solutes or the cytoplasmic, periplasmic, or extracellular a_w. The localization and structure of the EnvZ protein (see above), taken with its strong overall resemblance to the Tar and Tsr chemotactic receptor proteins (165, 192), point strongly to its being a sensor of conditions in the periplasm rather than in the cytoplasm or outside the cell. That the response is elicited both by polar and nonpolar solutes argues at first sight against EnvZ being a specific chemoreceptor, leaving a_w in the periplasm as a candidate parameter. However, some observations are not consistent with this. Kawaji et al (105) showed that sugars and dextrans of molecular weight above 600–700 (the cutoff size corresponding to the exclusion limit for outer membrane pores) were more effective on a molal basis in switching porin expression than those of lower molecular weight. These results do not fit with the expected effects of these solutes on a_w but they do reinforce the idea that EnvZ senses some parameter in the periplasmic space that changes with medium osmolality. Whatever this parameter is, it must change rapidly because changes in the differential rates of synthesis of the OmpF and OmpC porins could be detected within 3 and 10 min, respectively, after an osmotic upshift (65, 97).

Other observations on the OmpF-OmpC system are not easily reconciled

592   CSONKA & HANSON

with a_w sensing and/or indicate a more complex picture. First, glycine betaine antagonizes the osmotic repression of the *ompF* gene (13), and procaine represses the *ompF* gene and induces the *ompC* gene in low osmolality (184, 195). Because procaine also affects the stretch-activated channels in the outer membrane of *E. coli* (118), the change in the expression of the *ompC* and *ompF* genes by this amphipathic compound may result from procaine's perturbation of membranes rather than from a direct interaction with the EnvZ protein. Second, as we discussed above, the expression of *ompF* and *ompC* genes is affected by cultural conditions unrelated to osmolality, i.e. temperature and carbon source. Third, substantial osmoregulation of *ompC* (but not *ompF*) production during long-term growth can occur in the absence of EnvZ (67), which indicates that the regulatory circuit that includes the EnvZ protein is not the only one involved in the control of porin expression. Therefore, while the EnvZ protein is not strictly an osmosensor (a_w sensor), it does respond in some fashion to medium osmolality, and perhaps to other culture conditions as well. On comparative physiological and biochemical grounds, one may reasonably suppose that the EnvZ protein is a chemoreceptor for some factor in the periplasm that is itself under genetic and environmental control. In this connection, sensing of the MDOs present in the periplasmic space has been proposed (63). Although this sensing is broadly consistent with the effects on porin expression of NaCl and nonionic solutes of various molecular weights and with the consequences of MDO mutations, it does not appear to be supported by the rapid kinetics of induction of the *ompC* gene and repression of the *ompF* gene after hyperosmotic shocks (65, 97).

The kdpABC *operon of* E. coli

The *kdpABC* operon of *E. coli* specifies a high-affinity K^+ transport system. The energy for the uptake of K^+ via this system is supplied by ATP, and a complex consisting of the KdpA, B, and C proteins has been shown to have a K^+-dependent ATPase activity (169). This complex has been purified (169), and the hydrolysis of ATP has been shown to involve the phosphorylation of the KdpB protein (170).

CONTROL BY PRESSURE? The *kdpABC* operon of *E. coli* is induced by high osmolality, but it is unusual among the osmoreglated genes because it is induced only transiently by osmotic upshock (112, 196). The transcription of the *kdpABC* operon is under the control of two positive regulatory proteins, KdpD and KdpE. Nucleotide sequence analysis of the *kdpD* gene revealed that the protein product resembles the transcriptional activator proteins in the family of the two component regulatory proteins (5); the KdpE protein is presumably its signal-sensing partner (60). Induction of the *kdpABC* operon can be triggered with medium osmotic pressure increases of ≥ 0.2 MPa; it is elicited by ionic as well as nonpolar solutes that are excluded by the inner membrane, but not by glycerol. The latter observation rules out sensing of intra- or extracellular a_w, so that isotropic pressure, tangential wall stress, the intracellular concentration of critical solutes, turgor pressure, and membrane stretch remain as possibilities. The first three of these seem not to have been addressed, at least in relation to short-term osmotic upshock (see below). Attention has been focussed on the last two, particularly turgor pressure. The response certainly occurs with kinetics and osmolality dependence consistent with a response to turgor, although this observation in itself is inconclusive because several other parameters may show correlated changes (Figure 3). Since the KdpE protein is membrane-associated, it is a plausible turgor-pressure sensor (112, 196). As mentioned earlier, however, it is not clear whether there is a significant pressure drop across the inner membrane to be sensed. Note that a membrane stretch receptor would also be membrane-associated, as might a sensor of tangential stress in the peptidoglycan layer, or even a chemosensor for an intracellular or periplasmic solute. Overall, evidence is fairly good that the *kdpABC* operon can respond to turgor pressure or some close correlate thereof, such as membrane area—but the precise nature of the signal remains hypothetical. In this connection, experiments with wall-less cells or spheroplasts could be informative.

In the experiments implicating turgor as a signal, *kdpABC* expression was measured after osmotic upshock. Other protocols involving long term growth provide evidence for greater complexity. Thus, the *kdpABC* operon could be induced by K^+-limitation in media of high osmolality to the same, if not higher, level in the presence of glycine betaine as that in its absence (181). Since glycine betaine is used preferentially over K^+ as a compatible solute, turgor is apparently not the sole regulatory signal for the *kdpABC* operon, but the availability or intracellular concentration of K^+ also regulates the expression of this operon, as was originally indicated by the experiments of Rhoads et al (160) and later work by Gowrishankar (80).

The proU *Operon of* E. coli *and* S. typhimurium

The *proU* operon of *E. coli* and *S. typhimurium,* which specifies a high-affinity transport system for glycine betaine and a low-affinity transport system for proline, exhibits a 200- to 700-fold transcriptional induction in response to high osmolality (44). NiBhriain et al (139) reported that in *S. typhimurium* the osmotic induction of the *proU* operon could be potentiated by anaerobiosis, but this effect was not seen in *E. coli* (116a, 153). The osmotic induction of this operon is very rapid: it has been detected within 4 min after hyperosmotic shock (147). A combination of genetic, biochemical, and nucleotide sequence analyses (45, 81, 123, 146, 179) revealed that the

ProU transport system belongs to a family of structurally related permeases that utilize a periplasmic protein for the initial binding of the substrate (6). The ProU system is made up of two membrane-associated proteins, specified by the *proV* and *proW* genes, and a periplasmic binding protein specified by the *proX* gene. These three genes, which comprise the *proU* operon, are transcribed in the order *proV, proW, proX*. The nucleotide sequence of the entire *proU* operon of *E. coli* (81) and of a ~2 kbp region containing the promoter and the 5' end of the operon of *S. typhimurium* have been determined (146, 179). Comparable regions of the *proU* operons of the two organisms have > 80% nucleotide sequence identity.

Nuclease S1 mapping and primer extension analysis revealed that the transcription initiation site of the *proU* operon is at position +61[1] upstream of the *proV* gene in *E. coli* (81, 123) and at positions +63 to +64 in *S. typhimurium* (146, 179). Bacterial promoters are made up of two hexameric elements, the so-called −10 and −35 sequences (90), which provide the recognition sites for RNA polymerase. Sequence motifs at the proper distance upstream of the transcription initiation site that serve as the −10 and −35 sequences are present in the *proU* operon. However, the nucleotide sequences and the spacing between these elements differ enough from the canonical −10 and −35 elements (90) to suggest that the *proU* promoter might not be recognized efficiently by RNA polymerase without some activator factor. This possibility is substantiated by the observations that mutations that brought the *proU* promoter closer to the cannonical promoter led to increased expression of the *proU* operon (116a, 123).

The entire *cis*-acting information required for the normal osmotic control of transcription of the *proU* promoter is contained in the sequences from positions −207 to +48 in *E. coli* (147) and −60 to +200 in *S. typhimurium* (144, 145). In *E. coli*, there is a transcriptional activatory element within ~200 bp upstream of the *proU* promoter (116a). This element is required for full expression of the promoter under conditions of both low and high osmolality, but is not involved in the osmotic control per se. Deletion analysis of the *S. typhimurium proU* operon indicated that an important negative control element is downstream of the *proU* promoter located at least partially between nucleotide positions +95 to +200, because deletions removing this region caused up to a 75-fold increase in the transcription of the *proU* promoter in media of low osmolality (144–146). The role of this element in the transcriptional control of the *proU* operon has not yet been established, but it could be the binding site for a protein, which in cells grown in media of low osmolality

---

[1]According to the usual convention, the nucleotides of the *proU* operon are numbered such that position +1 denotes the start site of transcription, with positive and negative numbers denoting nucleotides downstream and upstream of the transcription start site, respectively.

makes the promoter inaccessible to RNA polymerase either by forming a DNA loop or by winding up the DNA into some chromatin-like structure (144). However, the transcriptional control of the *proU* operon may differ between *S. typhimurium* and *E. coli* because apparently all the *cis*-acting elements required for the proper transcriptional control of this operon in *E. coli* are upstream of position +48 (147).

In an attempt to identify transcriptional regulatory factors of the *proU* operon, several groups carried out selections in *E. coli* and *S. typhimurium* for mutations resulting in increased expression of this operon in media of low osmolality. These selections did not yield any mutations in any specific transcriptional regulatory protein, but only *cis*-acting promoter mutations (52, 89, 123, 146) and pleiotropic mutations that affected DNA supercoiling. The latter type of mutations were in two genes: *topA*, the structural gene for topoisomerase I, and *osmZ*, which was subsequently shown to encode a histone-like DNA-binding protein H-NS (or H1) (79, 93, 122). Higgins et al (89) reported that high osmolality increased the supercoiling reporter plasmids. On the basis of this observation and the finding that unlinked mutations resulting in increased expression of the *proU* operon were only in genes governing supercoiling, Higgins et al (89) put forward the model that the recognition of the *proU* promoter by RNA polymerase does not involve any ancillary transcriptional regulatory factors but only changes in the supercoiling of the *proU* promoter. They proposed that the changes in supercoiling could result from effects of K^+ and/or glutamate on the binding of the OsmZ or other histone-like proteins to the DNA, or from changes in the activities of topoisomerases or gyrases. However, some observations are not consistent with this hypothesis. Plasmids carrying the *proU* operon isolated from *E. coli* cultures grown in media of low and high osmolality had very similar abilities to direct both the in vitro transcription (150) and the coupled transcription-translation of the *proU* operon in cell-free (S30) extracts (153). Because the transcription of many other *E. coli* genes besides the *proU* operon is sensitive to supercoiling, perhaps the effects of supercoiling on the expression of the *proU* operon should be seen as an indication of pleiotropic effects of supercoiling on transcription, rather than proof that supercoiling is a specific osmoregulatory signal (151). In addition to the *topA* and *osmZ* genes, a third locus, $mprA^+$, may play a role in the regulation of the *proU* operon. When placed on high copy plasmids, this gene resulted in a 10-fold reduction in the expression of the *proU* operon both in media of low and high osmolality (46).

CONTROL BY CYTOPLASMIC K^+ LEVEL?   As with the *kdp* operon, the *proU* operon can be induced only by high concentrations of solutes that do not cross the inner membrane (53, 81, 181). These findings make regulation by intra- or extracellular a_w improbable. Regulation by pressure, tangential wall stress, or membrane stretch are also unlikely to be signals because these parameters presumably return towards their previous values as growth resumes after an osmotic upshock. By elimination, the signal could be the concentration of a specific intracellular solute or solutes. Two kinds of evidence suggest that K^+ concentration might be a link between the *kdp* and *proU* systems in overall osmoregulation. The first type of evidence is essentially correlative. The expression of *proU* in media of high osmolality was greatly reduced if K^+ was limiting because of K^+ starvation or *kdp* mutations (181). Similarly, the expression of the *proU* operon in media of high osmolality was reduced by glycine betaine, along with a concomitant decrease in the intracellular K^+ level (181). However, surprisingly proline did not cause a comparable reduction in the expression of the *proU* operon, even though it resulted in almost the same reduction in the K^+ concentration as glycine betaine (181).

The second and more direct type of evidence comes from in vitro studies of the expression of the *proU* operon. The coupled transcription-translation of the *proU* operon in S30 systems was stimulated specifically by physiological concentrations of the glutamate or acetate salts of K^+, but Na^+ salts, sugars, and glycine betaine were ineffective (98, 153, 154). Furthermore, S30 extracts prepared from cells grown in media of high osmolality supported more rapid transcription of the *proU* operon than those prepared from cells grown in low osmolality; this result suggested that either the extract from the cells grown in high osmolality contained a transcriptional activator or the extract of the cells grown in the low osmolality contained a repressor for the *proU* operon (98). The stimulation of the expression of the *proU* operon seen in the coupled transcription-translation systems was confirmed in an assay of the in vitro transcription of this operon by σ^{70}-RNA polymerase (150). In this simplified system, the transcription of the *proU* operon was stimulated by similar concentrations of K^+-glutamate as were found to be effctive in the coupled transcription-translation assays.

Although the above in vitro studies are consistent with K^+, by itself or together with glutamate, as the signal for the transcriptional control of the *proU* operon, they do not necessarily prove that this is the case. Because the minimum K^+ concentration in *E. coli* is ~0.1 M (127), the in vitro results would predict that the *proU* operon should always be induced, which is clearly not the case. Because K^+ and glutamate are the prevalent ions in bacteria, probably most enzymes have evolved to function most efficiently in the presence of fairly high concentrations of these ions. Many other processes are stimulated by K^+, including the recognition of phage λ or *lac* promoters by RNA polymerase (114) and the activities of restriction enzymes (114) and of DNA polymerase III (83). The dependence of the transcription of the *proU* operon on K^+-glutamate may therefore be a reflection of a stimulatory effect of these ions on enzymatic reactions in general, rather than evidence for a specific osmoregulatory signal.

Other Osmoregulated Genes

In this section, we give a brief account of other results on the molecular biology of osmoregulation published since the review by Csonka (44). One study reported the purification of glycine betaine aldehyde dehydrogenase of *E. coli* (61). A regulatory locus, *proQ*, which affects the functioning of the ProP transport system of *E. coli*, was identified (131a). Meyer et al (128) observed that the *phoE* gene, which encodes a phosphate-regulated outer membrane porin related structurally to the OmpF and OmpC porins, is under osmotic regulation: it could be induced by phosphate starvation in media of low but not high osmolality. The nucleotide sequence of the *treA* gene of *E. coli*, which encodes the osmotically inducible trehalase, has been has been determined (84). Jenkins et al (96) proposed an overlap between osmoregulation and growth phase–dependent control of gene expression, because five of the osmotically inducible genes were also induced by stationary phase in *E. coli*. One of the genes exhibiting this dual control is the *osmB*, which specifies a lipoprotein (99, 100). Genes involved in or associated with pathogenesis have been reported to be under osmotic control in *S. typhimurium* (49, 71), *Shigella dysenteriae* (16), and *Pseudomonas aeruginosa* (17).

ACKNOWLEDGMENTS

We thank Drs. J. M. Brass, M. Burg, D. G. Fraenkel, R. Kolter, C. Kung, S. G. Kustu, and K. J. Miller for stimulating discussions, and C. Kung and J. M. Slauch for insightful comments on the manuscript. Research in our laboratories on osmoregulation has been funded by grants from The Corporation for Science and Technology, Public Health Service (#R01-GM 3194401), and the US Department of Agriculture (#87 CRCR-1-2495) to L. N. C., and from the US Department of Energy, the US Department of Agriculture (#87-CRCR-1-2460), and the National Science and Engineering Research Council of Canada (#OGP-0043713) to A. D. H.

Literature Cited

1. Abee T., Palmen R., Hellingwerf, K. J., Konings, W. N. 1990. Osmoregulation in *Rhodobacter sphaeroides*. *J. Bacteriol* 172:149–54
2. Aiba, H., Mizuno, T., Mizushima, S. 1989. Transfer of phosphoryl group between two regulatory proteins involved in osmoregulatory expression of the *ompF* and *ompC* genes in *Escherichia coli*. *J. Biol. Chem.* 264:8563–67
3. Aiba, H., Nakasai, F., Mizushima, S., Mizuno, T. 1989. Evidence for the physiological importance of the phosphotransfer between the two regulatory components EnvZ and OmpR in

osmoregulation in *Escherichia coli*. *J. Biol. Chem.* 264:14090–94
4. Aiba, H., Nakasai, F., Mizushima, S., Mizuno, T. 1989. Phosphorylation of a bacterial activator protein OmpR by a protein kinase EnvZ results in stimulation of its DNA-binding ability. *J. Biochem. (Tokyo)* 106:5–7
5. Albright, L. M., Huala, E., Ausubel, F. M. 1989. Prokaryotic signal transduction mediated by sensor and regulator protein pairs. *Annu. Rev. Genet.* 23: 311–36
6. Ames, G. F.-L. 1986. Bacterial periplasmic transport systems: structure,

mechanism, and evolution. *Annu. Rev. Biochem.* 55:397–425

7. Apte, S. K., Haselkorn, R. 1990. Cloning of salinity-stress induced genes from the salt-tolerant nitrogen-fixing cyanobacterium *Anabaena torulosa. Plant Mol. Biol.* 15:723–33

8. Apte, S. K., Reddy, B. R., Thomas, J. 1987. Relationship between sodium influx and salt tolerance of nitrogen-fixing cyanobacteria. *Appl. Env. Microbiol.* 53:1934–39

9. Apte, S. K., Thomas, J. 1986. Membrane electrogenesis and sodium transport in filamentous nitrogen-fixing cyanobacteria. *Eur. J. Biochem.* 154:395–401

10. Arakawa, T., Timasheff, S. N. 1985. The stabilization of proteins by osmolytes. *Biophys. J.* 47:411–14

11. Bakker, E. P., Booth, I. R., Dinnbier, U., Epstein, W., Gajewska, A. 1987. Evidence for multiple K⁺ export systems in *Escherichia coli. J. Bacteriol.* 169:3743–49

12. Baldwin, W. W., Sheu, M.-J. T., Bankston, P. W., Woldringh, C. L. 1988. Changes in buoyant density and cell size of *Escherichia coli* in response to osmotic shocks. *J. Bacteriol.* 170:452–55

13. Barron, A., May, G., Bremer, E., Villarejo, M. 1986. Regulation of envelope protein compositon during adaptation to osmotic stress in *Escherichia coli. J. Bacteriol.* 167:433–38

14. Bartlett, D., Wright, M., Yayanos, A. A., Silverman, M. 1989. Isolation of a gene regulated by hydrostatic pressure in a deep-sea bacterium. *Nature* 342:572–74

15. Bascaran, V., Hardisson, C., Brana, A. F. 1990. Proline uptake in *Streptomyces clavuligerus. FEMS Microbiol. Lett.* 69:27–30

16. Bernardini, M. L., Fontaine, A., Sansonetti, P. J. 1990. The two-component regulatory system OmpR-EnvZ controls the virulence of *Shigella flexneri. J. Bacteriol.* 172:6274–81

17. Berry, A., DeVault, J. D., Chakrabarty, A. M. 1989. High osmolarity is a signal for enhanced *algD* transcription in mucoid and nonmucoid *Pseudomonas aeruginosa* strains. *J. Bacteriol.* 171:2312–17

18. Boos, W., Ehmann, U., Forkl, H., Klein, W., Rimmele, M., Postma, P. 1990. Trehalose transport and metabolism in *Escherichia coli. J. Bacteriol.* 172:3450–61

19. Booth, I. R., Higgins, C. F. 1990. Enteric bacteria and osmotic stress: in-

tracellular potassium glutamate as a secondary signal of osmotic stress. *FEMS Microbiol. Rev.* 75:239–46

20. Bossemeyer, D., Borchard, A., Dosch, D. C., Helmer, G. C., Epstein, W., et al. 1989. K⁺-transport protein TrkA of *Escherichia coli* is a peripheral membrane protein that requires other *trk* gene products for attachment to the cytoplasmic membrane. *J. Biol. Chem.* 264:16403–10

21. Bossemeyer, D., Schloesser, A., Bakker, E. P. 1989. Specific cesium transport via the *Escherichia coli* Kup (TrkD) K⁺ uptake system. *J. Bacteriol.* 171:2219–21

22. Botsford, J. L., Lewis, T. A. 1990. Osmoregulation in *Rhizobium meliloti:* production of glutamic acid in response to osmotic stress. *Appl. Environ. Microbiol.* 56:488–94

23. Brady, R. A., Csonka, L. N. 1988. Transcriptional regulation of the *proC* gene of *Salmonella typhimurium. J. Bacteriol.* 170:2379–82

24. Brand, B., Boos, W. 1989. Convenient preparative synthesis of [¹⁴C]trehalose from [¹⁴C]glucose by intact *Escherichia coli* cells. *Appl. Environ. Microbiol.* 55:2414–15

25. Brass, J. M. 1986. The cell envelope of gram-negative bacteria: new aspects of its function in transport and chemotaxis. *Curr. Top. Microbiol.* 129:1–92

26. Breitmayer, V., Gauthier, M. J. 1990. Influence of glycine betaine on the transfer of plasmid RP4 between *Escherichia coli* strains in marine sediments. *Lett. Appl. Microbiol.* 10:65–68

27. Britten, R. J., McClure, F. T. 1962. The amino acid pool in *Escherichia coli. Bacteriol. Rev.* 26:292–335

28. Brown, A. D. 1990. *Microbial Water Stress Physiology: Principles and Perspectives.* Chichester: Wiley

29. Brown, A. D., Simpson, J. R. 1972. Water relations of sugar-tolerant yeasts: the role of intracellular polyols. *J. Gen. Microbiol.* 72:589–91

30. Buurman, E. T, Pennock, J., Tempest, D. W., Teixeira de Matos, M. J., Neijssel, O. 1989. Replacement of potassium ions by ammonium ions in different micro-organisms grown in potassium-limited chemostat culture. *Arch. Microbiol.* 152:58–63

31. Cairney, J., Booth, I. R., Higgins C. F. 1985. *Salmonella typhimurium proP* gene encodes a transport system for the osmoprotectant betaine. *J. Bacteriol.* 164:1218–23

32. Cangelosi, G. A., Martinetti, G., Nester, E. W. 1990. Osmosensitivity phe-

notypes of *Agrobacterium tumefaciens* mutants that lack periplasmic β-1,2 glucan. *J. Bacteriol.* 172:2172–74

33. Carpita, N. C. 1985. Tensile strength of cell walls of living cells. *Plant Physiol.* 79:485–88

34. Cayley, S., Record, M. T. Jr., Lewis, B. A. 1989. Accumulation of 3-(N-morpholino)-propanesulfonate by osmotically stressed *Escherichia coli* K-12. *J. Bacteriol.* 171:3597–602

35. Chambers, S. T., Kunin, C. 1987. Isolation of glycine betaine and proline betaine from human urine: assessment of their role as osmoprotective agents for bacteria and the kidney. *J. Clin. Invest.* 79:731–37

36. Chambers, S. T., Kunin, C. 1987. Osmoprotective activity for *Escherichia coli* in mammalian renal inner medulla and urine: correlation of glycine and proline betaines and sorbitol with response to osmotic loads. *J. Clin. Invest.* 80:1255–60

37. Chambers, S. T., Kunin, C. M., Miller, D., Hamada, A. 1987. Dimethylthetin can substitute for glycine betaine as an osmoprotectant molecule for *Escherichia coli*. *J. Bacteriol.* 169:4845–47

38. Clegg, J. S. 1984. Properties and metabolism of the aqueous cytoplasm and its boundaries. *Am. J. Physiol.* 246:R133–51

39. Coyer, J., Andersen, J., Forst, S. A., Inouye, M., Delihas, N. 1990. *micF* RNA in *ompB* mutants of *Esherichia coli:* different pathways regulate *micF* RNA levels in response to osmolarity and temperature change. *J. Bacteriol.* 172:4143–50

40. Cram, W. J. 1976. Negative feedback regulation of transport in cells. The maintenance of turgor, volume and nutrient supply. In *Encyclopedia of Plant Physiology, New Series*, Vol. 2A, ed. U. Luttge, M. G. Pitman, pp. 284–316. Berlin/New York: Springer

41. Crowe, J. H., Crowe, L. M., Chapman, D. 1984. Preservation of membranes in anhydrobiotic organisms: the role of trehalose. *Science* 223:701–3

42. Csonka, L. N. 1981. Proline overproduction results in enhanced osmotolerance in *Salmonella typhimurium*. *Mol. Gen. Genet.* 182:82–86

43. Csonka, L. N. 1988. Regulation of cytoplasmic proline levels in *Salmonella typhimurium:* effect of osmotic stress on synthesis, degradation, and cellular retention of proline. *J. Bacteriol.* 170:2374–78

44. Csonka, L. N. 1989. Physiological and genetic responses of bacteria to osmotic stress. *Microbiol. Rev.* 53:121–47

45. Dattanada, C. S., Gowrishankar, J. 1989. Osmoregulation in *Escherichia coli:* complementation analysis and gene-protein relationships in the *proU* locus. *J. Bacteriol.* 171:1915–22

46. del Castillo, I., Gómez, J. M., Moreno, F. 1990. *mprA*, an *Escherichia coli* gene that reduces growth-phase dependent synthesis of microcins B17 and C7 and blocks osmoinduction of *proU* when cloned on a high-copy-plasmid. *J. Bacteriol.* 172:437–45

47. Deutch, C. E., Hasler, J. M., Houston, R. M., Sharma, M., Stone, V. J. 1989. Nonspecific inhibition of proline dehydrogenase synthesis in *Escherichia coli* during osmotic stress. *Can. J. Microbiol.* 35:779–85

48. Dinnbier, U., Limpinsel, E., Schmid, R., Bakker, E. P. 1988. Transient accumulation of potassium glutamate and its replacement by trehalose during adaptation of growing cells of *Escherichia coli* K-12 to elevated sodium chloride concentrations. *Arch. Microbiol.* 150:348–57

49. Dorman, C. J., Chatfield, S., Higgins, C. F., Hayward, C., Dougan, G 1989. Characterization of porin a⊢ ⅃ *ompR* mutants of a virulent strain of *Salmonella typhimurium: ompR* mutants are attenuated in vivo. *Infect. Immun.* 57:2136–40

50. Dorman, C. J., NiBhriain, N., Higgins, C. F. 1990. DNA supercoiling and environmental regulation of virulence gene expression in *Shigella flexneri*. *Nature (London)* 334:789–92

51. Douglas, C. J., Staneloni, R. J., Rubin, R. A., Nester, E. W. 1985. Identification and genetic analysis of an *Agrobacterium tumefaciens* chromosomal virulence region. *J. Bacteriol.* 161:850–60

52. Druger-Liotta, J., Prange, V. J., Overdier, D. G., Csonka, L. N. 1987. Selection of mutations that alter osmotic control of transcription of the *Salmonella typhimurium proU* operon. *J. Bacteriol.* 169:2449–59

53. Dunlap, V. J., Csonka, L. N. 1985. Osmotic regulation of L-proline transport in *Salmonella typhimurium*. *J. Bacteriol.* 163:296–304

54. Dylan, T., Helinski, D. R., Ditta, G. S. 1990. Hypoosmotic adaptation in *Rhizobium meliloti* requires β-(1→2)-glucan. *J. Bacteriol.* 172:1400–8

55. Dylan, T., Nagpal, P., Helinski, D. R., Ditta, G. S. 1990. Symbiotic pseudorevertants of *Rhizobium meliloti ndv* mutants. *J. Bacteriol.* 172:1409–17

56. Elmore, M. J., Lamb, A. J., Ritchie, G. Y., Douglas, R. M., Munro, A., et al. 1990. Activation of potassium efflux from *Escherichia coli* by glutathione metabolites. *Mol. Microbiol.* 4:405–12

57. Elsheikh, E. A. E., Wood, M. 1989. Response of chickpea and soybean rhizobia to salt: osmotic and specific ion effects of salts. *Soil. Biol. Biochem.* 21:889–96

58. Elsheikh, E. A. E., Wood, M. 1990. Rhizobia and bradyrhizobia under salt stress: possible role of trehalose in osmoregulation. *Lett. Appl. Microbiol.* 10:127–30

59. Epstein, W. 1986. Osmoregulation by potassium transport in *Escherichia coli*. *FEMS Microbiol. Rev.* 39:73–78

60. Epstein, W., Walderhaug, M. O., Polarek, J. W., Hesse, J. E., Dorus, E., Daniel, J. M. 1990. The bacterial Kdp K^{2+}-ATPase and its relation to other transport ATPases, such as the Na^+/K^+- and Ca^{2+}-ATPases in higher organisms. *Phil. Trans. R. Soc. London Ser. B.* 326:479–87

61. Falkenberg, P., Strøm, A. R. 1990. Purification and characterization of osmoregulatory betaine aldehyde dehydrogenase of *Escherichia coli*. *Biochim. Biophys. Acta* 1034:253–59

62. Fernández, M. F., Cobos, A., Hoz, L., Hernández, P. E., Sanz, B. 1989. Operon fusions of Mu d1(Ap,*lac*) to the L-proline biosynthetic genes of *Escherichia coli* K-12. *Curr. Microbiol.* 18:113–18

63. Fiedler, W., Rottering, M. 1988. Properties of *Escherichia coli* mutants lacking membrane-derived oligosaccharides. *J. Biol. Chem.* 263:14684–89

64. Foley, M., Brass, J. M., Birmingham, J., Cook, W. R., Garland, P. B., et al. 1989. Compartmentation of the periplasm at cell division sites in *Escherichia coli* as shown by fluorescence photobleaching experiments. *Mol. Microbiol* 3:1329–36

65. Forst, S., Delgado, J., Inouye, M. 1989. DNA-binding properties of the transcription activator (OmpR) for the upstream sequences of *ompF* in *Escherichia coli* are altered by *envZ* mutations and medium osmolarity. *J. Bacteriol.* 171:2949–55

66. Forst, S., Delgado, J., Inouye, M. 1989. Phosphorylation of OmpR by the osmosensor EnvZ modulates expression of the *ompF* and *ompC* genes in *Escherichia coli*. *Proc. Natl. Acad. Sci. USA* 86:6052–56

67. Forst, S., Delgado, J., Rampersaud, A.,

Inouye, M. 1990. In vivo phosphorylation of OmpR, the transcription activator of the *ompF* and *ompC* genes in *Escherichia coli*. *J. Bacteriol.* 172:3473–77

68. Fougère, F., Le Rudulier, D. 1990. Uptake of glycine betaine and its analogues by bacteroids of *Rhizobium meliloti*. *J. Gen. Microbiol.* 136:157–64

69. Fraenkel, D. G. 1987. Glycolysis, pentose phosphate pathway, and Entner-Douderoff pathway. See Ref. 137a, pp. 142–50

70. Frey-Wyssling, A. 1957. *Macromolecules in Cell Structure*. Cambridge: Harvard Univ. Press. 112 pp.

71. Galán, J. E., Curtiss, R. III. 1990. Expression of *Salmonella* genes required for invasion is regulated by changes in DNA supercoiling. *Infect. Immun.* 58: 1879–85

72. Galinski, E. A., Herzog, R. M. 1990. The role of trehalose as a substitute for nitrogen-containing compatible solutes *Ectothiorhodospira halochloris*. *Arch. Microbiol.* 153:607–13

73. Garcia-Perez, A., Burg, M. B. 1990. Importance of organic osmolytes for osmoregulation by renal medullary cells. *Hypertension* 16:595–602

74. Gehring, K., Hofnung, M., Nikaido, H. 1990. Stimulation of glutamine transport by osmotic stress in *Escherichia coli* K-12. *J. Bacteriol.* 172:4741–43

75. Ghoul, M., Bernard, T., Cormier, M. 1990. Evidence that *Escherichia coli* accumulates glycine betaine from marine sediments. *Appl. Environ. Microbiol.* 56:551–54

76. Giæver, H. M., Styrvold, O. B., Kaasen, I., Strøm, A. R. 1988. Biochemical and genetic characterization of osmoregulatory trehalose synthesis in *Escherichia coli*. *J. Bacteriol.* 170: 2841–49

77. Gilles, R., Kleinzeller, A., Bolis, L., eds. 1987. *Cell Volume Control: Fundamental and Comparative Aspects in Animal Cells. Current Topics in Membranes and Transport*, Vol. 30. San Diego: Academic. 289 pp.

78. Gloux, K., Le Rudulier, D. 1989. Transport and catabolism of proline betaine in salt-stressed *Rhizobium meliloti*. *Arch. Microbiol.* 151:143–48

79. Göransson, M., Sonden, B., Nilsson, P., Dagberg, B., Forsman, K., et al. 1990. Transciptional silencing and thermoregulation of gene expression in *Escherichia coli*. *Nature (London)* 344: 682–85

80. Gowrishankar, J. 1987. A model for the regulation of expression of the potas-

sium-transport operon, *kdp*, in *Escherichia coli. J. Genet.* 66:87–92

81. Gowrishankar, J. 1989. Nucleotide sequence of the osmoregulatory *proU* operon of *Escherichia coli. J. Bacteriol.* 171:1923–31

82. Graeme-Cook, K. A., May, G., Bremer, E., Higgins, C. F. 1989. Osmotic regulation of porin expression: role for DNA supercoiling. *Mol. Microbiol.* 3:1287–94

83. Griep, M. R., McHenry, C. S. 1989. Glutamate overcomes the salt inhibition of DNA polymerase III holoenzyme. *J. Biol. Chem.* 264:11294–301

84. Gutierrez, C., Ardourel, M., Bremer, E., Middendorf, A., Boos, W. 1989. Analysis and DNA sequence of the osmoregulated *treA* gene encoding the periplasmic trehalase of *Escherichia coli* K-12. *Mol. Gen. Genet.* 217:347–54

85. Gutierrez, C., Barondess, J., Manoil, C., Beckwith, J. 1987. The use of transposon Tn*phoA* to detect genes for cell envelope proteins subject to a common regulatory stimulus. *J. Mol. Biol.* 195: 289–97

86. Gutknecht, J. 1968. Salt transport in *Valenia*: inhibition of potassium uptake by small hydrostatic pressures. *Science* 160:68–70

87. Hanson. A. D. 1991. Compatible solute synthesis and compartmentation in higher plants. See Ref. 175a. In press

88. Heremans, K. 1982. High pressure effects on proteins and other biomolecules. *Annu. Rev. Biophys. Bioeng.* 11: 1–21

89. Higgins, C. F., Dorman, C. J., Stirling, D. A., Wadell, L., Booth, I. R., et al. 1988. A physiological role for DNA supercoiling in the osmotic regulation of gene expression in *S. typhimurium* and *E. coli. Cell* 52:569–84

90. Hoopes, B. C., McClure, W. R. 1987. Strategies in regulation of initiation. See Ref. 137a, pp. 1231–40

91. Hsiao, T. C. 1973. Plant responses to water stress. *Annu. Rev. Plant Physiol.* 24:519–70

92. Huang, L., Tsui, P., Freundlich, M. 1990. Integration host factor is a negative effector of in vivo and in vitro expression of *ompC* in *Escherichia coli. J. Bacteriol.* 172:5293–98

93. Hulton, C. S. J., Seirafi, A., Hinton, J. C. D., Sidebotham, J. M., Waddell, L., et al. 1990. Histone-like protein H1 (H-NS), DNA supercoiling, and gene expression in bacteria. *Cell* 63:631–42

94. Igo, M. M., Ninfa, A. J., Silhavy, T. J. 1989. A bacterial environmental sensor that functions as a protein kinase and stimulates transcriptional activation. *Genes Dev.* 3:598–605

94a. Igo, M. M., Silhavy, T. J. 1988. EnvZ, a transmembrane environmental sensor of *Escherichia coli* K-12 is phosphorylated in vitro. *J. Bacteriol.* 170: 5971–73

95. Igo, M. M., Slauch, J. M., Silhavy, T. J. 1990. Signal transduction in bacteria: kinases that control gene expression. *New Biol.* 2:5–9

96. Jenkins, D. E., Chaisson, S. A., Matin, A. 1990. Starvation-induced cross protection against osmotic challenge in *Escherichia coli. J. Bacteriol.* 172:2779–81

97. Jovanovich, S. B., Martinell, M., Record, M. T. Jr., Burgess, R. B. 1988. Rapid response to osmotic upshift by osmoregulated genes in *Escherichia coli* and *Salmonella typhimurium. J. Bacteriol.* 170:534–39

98. Jovanovich, S. B., Record, M. T. Jr., Burgess, R. R. 1989. In an *Escherichia coli* coupled transcription-translation system, expression of the osmoregulated gene *proU* is stimulated at elevated potassium concentrations and by an extract from cells grown at high osmolality. *J. Biol. Chem.* 264:7821–25

98a. Jung, H., Jung, K., Kleber, H.-P. 1990. L-Carnitine metabolization and osmotic stress response in *Escherichia coli. J. Basic Microbiol.* 30:409–13

99. Jung, J. U., Gutierrez, C., Martin, F., Ardourel, M., Villarejo, M. 1990. Transcription of *osmB*, a gene encoding an *Escherichia coli* lipoprotein, is regulated by dual signals osmotic stress and stationary phase. *J. Biol. Chem.* 265: 10574–81

100. Jung, J. U., Gutierrez, C., Villarejo, M. R. 1989. Sequence of an osmotically inducible lipoprotein gene. *J. Bacteriol.* 171:511–20

101. Kaback, H. R., Deuel. T. F. 1969. Proline uptake by disrupted membrane preparations from *Escherichia coli. Arch. Biochem. Biophys.* 132:118–29

102. Kanamaru, K., Aiba, H., Mizushima, S., Mizuno, T. 1989. Signal transduction and osmoregulation in *Escherichia coli*: a single amino acid change in the protein kinase *envZ* results in loss of its phosphorylation and dephosphorylation abilities with respect to the activator protein OmpR. *J. Biol. Chem.* 264:21633–37

103. Kato, M., Aiba, H., Mizuno, T. 1989. Molecular analysis by deletion and site-directed mutagenesis of the *cis*-acting upstream sequence involved in activation of the *ompF* promoter in *Es-*

cherichia coli. J. Biochem 105:341–47

104. Kawahara, Y., Yoshihara, T. O. Y., Ikeda, S. 1989. Proline in the osmoregulation of *Brevibacterium lactofermentum. Agric. Biol. Chem.* 53:2475–80

104a. Kawahara, Y., Yoshihara, Y., Ikeda, S., Hirose, Y. 1990. Effect of glycine betaine, an osmoprotective compound, on the growth of *Brevibacterium lactoferentum. Appl. Microbiol. Biotechnol.* 33:574–77

105. Kawaji, H., Mizuno, T., Mizushima, S. 1979. Influence of molecular size and osmolarity of sugars and dextrans on the synthesis of outer membrane proteins O–8 and O–9 of *Escherichia coli* K-12. *J. Bacteriol.* 140:843–47

106. Kellenberger, E. 1990. The "Bayer bridges" confronted with results from improved electron microscopy methods. *Mol. Microbiol.* 4:697–705

107. Kennedy, E. P. 1987. Membrane-derived oligosaccharides. See Ref. 137a, pp. 672–79

108. Koch, A. L. 1983. The surface stress theory of microbial morphogenesis. *Adv. Microb. Physiol.* 24:301–66

109. Koshland, D. E. Jr. 1987. Switches, thresholds and ultra-sensitivity. *Trends Biochem. Sci.* 12:225–29

110. Kregenow, F. M. 1981. Osmoregulatory salt transporting mechanisms: control of cell volume in anisotonic media. *Annu. Rev. Physiol.* 43:493–505

111. Kung, C., Saimi, Y., Martinac, B. 1990. Mechano-sensitive ion channels in microbes and the early evolutionary origin of solvent sensing. *Curr. Top. Membr. Transp.* 36:145–53

112. Laimins, L. A., Rhoads, D. B., Epstein, W. 1981. Osmotic control of *kdp* operon expression in *Escherichia coli. Proc. Natl. Acad. Sci. USA* 78:464–68

113. Larsen, P. I., Sydnes, L. K., Landfald, B., Strøm, A. R. 1987. Osmoregulation in *Escherichia coli* by accumulation of organic osmolytes: betaines, glutamic acid, and trehalose. *Arch. Microbiol.* 147:1–7

114. Leirmo, S., Harrison, C., Cayley, D. S., Burgess, R. R., Record, M. T. Jr. 1987. Replacement of KCl by K glutamate dramatically enhances protein-DNA interactions in vitro. *Biochemistry* 26:7157–64

115. Le Rudulier, D., Bouillard, L. 1983. Glycine betaine, an osomotic effector in *Klebsiella pneumoniae* and other members of the *Enterobacteriaceae. Appl. Environ. Microbiol.* 46:152–59

116. Li, C., Boileau A. J., Kung, C., Adler, J. 1988. Osmotaxis in *Escherichia coli.*

Proc. Natl. Acad. Sci. USA 85:9451–55

116a. Lucht, J. M., Bremer, E. 1991. Characterization of mutations affecting the osmoregulated *proU* promoter of *Escherichia coli* and identification of 5' sequences required for high-level expression. *J. Bacteriol.* 173:801–9

117. Macnab, R. M. 1987. Motility and chemotaxis. See Ref. 137a, pp. 732–59

118. Martinac, B., Adler, J., Kung, C. 1990. Mechanosensitive ion channels of *E. coli* activated by amphipaths. *Nature (London)* 348:261–63

119. Martinac, B., Delcour, A. H., Buechner, M., Adler, J., Kung, C. 1991. Mechanosensitive ion channels in bacteria. In *Comparative Aspects of Mechanoreceptor Systems,* ed. F. Ito. Berlin: Springer-Verlag. In press

120. Marthi, B., Lighthart, B. 1990. Effects of betaine on enumeration of airborne bacteria. *Appl. Environ. Microbiol.* 56:1286–89

121. Mason, T. G., Blunden, G. 1989. Quaternary ammonium and tertiary sulfonium compounds of algal origin as alleviators of osmotic stress. *Bot. Mar.* 32:313–16

122. May, G., Dersch, P., Haardt, M., Middendorf, A., Bremer, E. 1990. The *osmZ* (*bglY*) gene encodes the DNA-binding protein H-NS (H1a), a component of the *Escherichia coli* K12 nucleoid. *Mol. Gen. Genet.* 224:81–90

123. May, G., Faatz, E., Lucht, J. M., Haardt, M., Bollinger, M., Bremer, E. 1989. Characterization of the osmoregulated *Escherichia coli proU* promoter and identification of ProV as a membrane-associated protein. *Mol. Microbiol.* 3:1521–31

124. McBride, M. J., Ensign, J. C. 1990. Regulation of trehalose metabolism by *Streptomyces griseus* spores. *J. Bacteriol.* 172:3637–43

125. McBride, M. J., Zusman, D. R. 1989. Trehalose accumulation in vegetative cells and spores of *Myxococcus xanthus. J. Bacteriol.* 171:6383–86

126. McCarter, L., Silverman, M. 1990. Surface-induced swarmer cell differentiation in *Vibrio parahaemolyticus. Mol. Microbiol.* 4:1057–62

127. McLaggan, D., Logan, T. M., Lynn, D. G., Epstein, W. 1990. Involvement of γ-glutamyl peptides in osmoadaptation of *Escherichia coli. J. Bacteriol.* 172:3631–36

128. Meyer, S. E., Granett, S., Ung, J. U., Villarejo, M. R. 1990. Osmotic regulation of PhoE porin synthesis in *Es-*

cherichia coli. J. Bacteriol. 172:5501–2

128a. Miller, K. J., Gore, R. S., Benesi, A. J. 1988. Phosphoglycerol substituents present on the cyclic β-1,2-glycans of *Rhizobium meliloti* 1021 are derived from phosphatidylglycerol. *J. Bacteriol.* 170:4569–75

129. Miller, K. J., Kennedy, E. P., Reinhold, V. N. 1986. Osmotic adaptation by gram-negative bacteria: possible role for periplasmic oligosaccharides. *Science* 231:48–51

130. Miller, K. J., Reinhold, V. N., Weissborn, A. C., Kennedy, E. P. 1987. Cyclic glucans produced by *Agrobacterium tumefaciens* are substituted with sn-1-phophoglycerol residues. *Biochem. Biophys. Acta* 901:112–18

131. Milner, J. L., Grothe, S., Wood, J. M. 1988. Proline porter II is activated by a hyperosmotic shift in both whole cells and membrane vesicles of *Escherichia coli* K-12. *J. Biol. Chem.* 263:14900–5

131a. Milner, J. L., Wood, J. M. 1989. Insertion *proQ*::Tn*5* alters regulation of proline porter II, a transporter of proline and glycinebetaine in *Escherichia coli*. *J. Bacteriol.* 171:947–51

132. Mitchell, P., Moyle, J. 1956. Osmotic function and structure in bacteria. *Symp. Soc. Gen. Microbiol.* 6:150–80

133. Mizuno, T., Mizushima, S. 1990. Signal transduction and gene regulation through the phosphorylation of two regulatory components: the molecular basis for the osmotic regulation of the porin genes. *Mol. Microbiol.* 4:1077–82

134. Mizuno, T., Shinkai, A., Matsui, K., Mizushima, S. 1990. Osmoregulatory expression of porin genes in *Escherichia coli*: a comparative study on strains B and K-12. *FEMS Microbiol. Lett.* 68: 289–94

135. Money, N. P. 1989. Osmotic pressure of aqueous polyethylene glycols: relationship between molecular weight and vapor pressure deficit. *Plant Physiol.* 91:766–69

136. Munro, G. F., Hercules, K., Morgan, J., Sauerbier, W. 1972. Dependence of putrescine content of *Escherichia coli* on the osmotic strength of the medium. *J. Biol. Chem.* 247:1272–80

137. Munro, P. M., Gauthier, M. J., Breittmayer, V. A., Bongiovanni, V. A. 1989. Influence of osmoregulation processes on starvation survival of *Escherichia coli* in seawater. *Appl. Environ. Microbiol.* 55:2017–24

137a. Neidhardt, F. C., Ingraham, J. L., Low, K. B., Magasanik, B., Schaechter, M., Umbarger, H. E., eds. 1987.

Escherichia coli and Salmonella typhimurium: Cellular and Molecular Biology. Washington, DC: Am. Soc. Microbiol.

138. Neidhardt, F. C., VanBogelen, R. A. 1987. Heat shock response. See Ref. 137a, pp.1334–45

139. NiBhriain, N., Dorman, C. J., Higgins, C. F. 1989. An overlap between osmotic and anaerobic stress responses: a potential role for DNA supercoiling in the coordinate regulation of gene expression. *Mol. Microbiol.* 3:933–42

140. Nicolaus, B., Gambacorta, A., Basso, A. L., Riccio, R., De Rosa, M., Grant, W. D. 1988. Trehalose in archaebacteria. *Syst. Appl. Microbiol.* 10:215–17

141. Nicolaus, B., Lanzotti, V., Trincone, A., De Rosa, M., Gambacorta, A. 1989. Glycine betaine and polar lipid composition in halophilic archaebacteria in response to growth in different salt concentrations. *FEMS Microbiol. Lett.* 59:157–60

142. Nikaido, H., Vaara, M. 1987. Outer membrane. See Ref. 137a, pp. 7–27

143. Nobel, P. S. 1983. *Biophysical Plant Physiology and Ecology.* San Francisco: Freeman

143a. Oren, A. 1990. Formation and breakdown of glycine betaine and trimethylamine in hypersaline environments. *Antonie van Leeuwenhoek* 58:291–98

144. Overdier, D. G. 1990. *Genetic and molecular analysis of the osmotically regulated proU operon of Salmonella typhimurium.* PhD thesis. West Lafayette, IN: Purdue Univ.

145. Overdier, D. G., Fletcher, S., Csonka, L. N. 1991. The osmotic control of transcription of the *proU* operon of *Salmonella typhimurium*. See Ref. 175a. In press

146. Overdier, D. G., Olson, E. R., Erickson, B. D., Ederer, M. M., Csonka, L. N. 1989. Nucleotide sequence of the transcriptional control region of the osmotically regulated *proU* operon of *Salmonella typhimurium* and identification of the 5' endpoint of the *proU* mRNA. *J. Bacteriol.* 171:4694–706

147. Park, S. F., Stirling, D. A., Hulton, C. S. J., Booth, I. R., Higgins, C. F., Stewart, G. S. A. B. 1989. A novel, non-invasive promoter probe vector: cloning of the osmoregulated *proU* promoter of *Escherichia coli* K12. *Mol. Microbiol.* 3:1011–23

148. Pedersen, S., Bloch, P. L., Reeh, S., Neidhardt, F. C. 1978. Patterns of protein synthesis in *E. coli*: a catalog of the amounts of 140 individual proteins at

different growth rates. *Cell* 14:179–90

149. Pocard, J.-A., Bernard, T., Smith, L. T., Le Rudulier, D. 1989. Characterization of three choline transport activities in *Rhizobium meliloti:* modulation by choline and osmotic stress. *J. Bacteriol.* 171:531–37

150. Prince, W. S., Villarejo, M. R. 1990. Osmotic control of *proU* transcription is mediated through direct action of potassium glutamate on the transcription complex. *J. Biol. Chem.* 265:17673–79

151. Pruss, G. J., Drlica, K. 1989. DNA supercoiling and prokaryotic transcription. *Cell* 56:521–23

152. Qi, Y., Adler, J. 1989. Salt taxis in *Escherichia coli* bacteria and its lack in mutants. *Proc. Natl. Acad. Sci. USA* 86:8358–62

153. Ramirez, R. M., Prince, W. S., Bremer, E., Villarejo, M. 1989. In vitro reconstitution of osmoregulated expression of *proU* of *Escherichia coli*. *Proc. Natl. Acad. Sci. USA* 86:1153–57

154. Ramirez, R. M., Villarejo, M. 1991. Osmotic signal transduction to *proU* is independent of DNA supercoiling in *Escherichia coli*. *J. Bacteriol.* 173:879–85

155. Rampersaud, A., Norioka, S., Inouye, M. 1989. Characterization of OmpR binding sequences in the upstream region of the *ompF* promoter essential for transcriptional activation. *J. Biol. Chem.* 264:18693–700

156. Reed, R. H., Stewart, W. D. P. 1983. Physiological responses of *Rivularia atra* to salinity: osmotic adjustment in hypersaline media. *New Phytol.* 95:595–603

157. Reed, R. H., Warr, S. R. C., Kerby, N. W, Stewart, W. D. P. 1986. Osmotic shock-induced release of low molecular weight metabolites from free-living and immobilized cyanobacteria. *Enzyme Microb. Technol.* 8:101–4

158. Reed, R. H., Warr, S. R. C., Richardson, D. L., Moore, D. J., Stewart, W. D. P. 1985. Multiphasic osmotic adjustment in a euryhaline cyanobacterium. *FEMS Microbiol. Lett.* 28:225–29

159. Regev, R., Peri, I., Gilboa, H., Avidor, Y. 1990. ^{13}C NMR study of the interrelation between synthesis and uptake of compatible solutes in two moderately halophilic eubacteria: bacterium Ba_1 and *Vibrio costicola*. *Arch. Biochem. Biophys.* 278:106–12

160. Rhoads, D. B., Waters, F. B., Epstein, W. 1976. Cation transport in *Escherichia coli*. VIII. Potassium transport mutants. *J. Gen. Physiol.* 67:325–41

160a. Riou, N., Le Rudlier, D. 1990. Osmoregulation in *Azospirillum brasilense:* glycine betaine transport enhances growth and nitrogen fixation under salt stress. *J. Gen. Microbiol.* 136:1455–62

161. Roberts, T. A., Skinner, F. A. 1983. *Food Microbiology: Advances and Prospects*. London/New York: Academic

162. Robertson, D. E., Noll, D., Roberts, M. F., Menaia, J. A. G. F., Boone, D. R. 1990. Detection of the osmoregulator betaine in methanogens. *Appl. Environ. Microbiol.* 56:563–65

163. Robertson, D. E., Roberts, M. F., Belay, N., Stetter, K. O., Boone, D. R. 1990. Occurrence of β-glutamate, a novel osmolyte in marine methanogenic bacteria. *Appl. Environ. Microbiol* 56:1504–8

164. Roth, W. G., Leckie, M. P., Dietzler, D. N. 1988. Restoration of colony-forming activity in osmotically stressed *Escherichia coli* by betaine. *Appl. Environ. Microbiol.* 54:3142–46

165. Russo, A. F., Koshland, D. E. Jr. 1983. Separation of signal transduction and adaptation functions of the aspartate receptor in bacterial sensing. *Science* 220:1016–20

166. Saenger. W. 1987. Structure and dynamics of water surrounding biomolecules. *Annu. Rev. Biophys. Biophys. Chem.* 16:93–114

167. Sant'Ambrogio, G. 1987. Nervous receptors of the tracheobronchial tree. *Annu. Rev. Physiol.* 49:611–27

168. Scott, V. N. 1989. Integration of factors to control microbial spoilage of refrigerated foods. *J. Food Prot.* 52:431–35

169. Siebers, A., Altendorf, K. 1988. The K^+-translocating Kdp-ATPase from *Escherichia coli:* purification, enzymatic properties and production of complex- and subunit-specific antisera. *Eur. J. Biochem.* 178:131–40

170. Siebers, A., Altendorf, K. 1989. Characterization of the phosphorylated intermediate of the K^+-translocating Kdp-ATPase from *Escherichia coli*. *J. Biol. Chem.* 264:5831–38

171. Simon, E., Hammel, H. T., Simon-Oppermann, C. 1980. Properties of the body fluids affecting nasal salt gland secretion and urine formation in birds. *Adv. Physiol. Sci.* 18:43–51

171a. Slauch, J. M., Silhavy, T. M. 1989. Genetic analysis of the switch that controls porin gene expression in *Escherichia coli* K-12. *J. Mol. Biol.* 210:281–92 (Erratum: 1990. *J. Mol. Biol.* 212:429)

172. Sleight, P., ed. 1980. *Arterial Barore-ceptors and Hypertension.* Oxford: Oxford Univ. Press. 540 pp.
173. Smith, L. T., Smith, G. M. 1989. An osmoregulated dipeptide in stressed *Rhizobium meliloti. J. Bacteriol.* 171:4714–17
174. Smith L. T., Smith, G. M., Madkour, M. A. 1990. Osmoregulation in *Agrobacterium tumefaciens:* accumulation of a novel disaccharide is controlled by osmotic strength and glycine betaine. *J. Bacteriol.* 172:6848–55
175. Somero, G. N. 1986. Protons, osmolytes, and fitness of internal milieu for protein function. *Am. J. Physiol.* 251: R197-R213
175a. Somero, G. N., Osmond, C. B., Bolis, C. L., eds. 1992. *Water and Life: A Comparative Analysis of Water Relationships at the Organismic, Cellular, and Molecular Levels.* Berlin: Springer-Verlag. In press
176. Sowers, K. R., Robertson, D. E., Noll, D., Gunsalus, R. P., Roberts, M. F. 1990. N$^\epsilon$-Acetyl-β-lysine: an osmolyte synthesized by methanogenic archaebacteria. *Proc. Natl. Acad. Sci. USA* 87: 9082–87
177. Stock, J. B., Ninfa, A., Stock, A. M. 1989. Protein phosphorylation and regulation of adaptive responses in bacteria. *Microbiol. Rev.* 53:450–90
178. Stock, J. B., Rauch, B., Roseman, S. 1977. Periplasmic space in *Salmonella typhimurium* and *Escherichia coli. J. Biol. Chem.* 252:7850–61
179. Stirling, D. A., Hulton, C. S. J., Waddell, L., Park, S. F., Stewart, G. S. A. B., et al. 1989. Molecular characterization of the *proU* loci of *Salmonella typhimurium* and *Escherichia coli* encoding osmoregulated glycine betaine transport systems. *Mol. Microbiol.* 3:1025–38
180. Strøm, A. R., Falkenberg, P., Landfald, B. 1986. Genetics of osmoregulation in *Escherichia coli:* uptake and biosynthesis of organic osmolytes. *FEMS Microbiol. Rev.* 39:79–86
181. Sutherland, L., Cairney, J., Elmore, M. J., Booth, I. R., Higgins, C. F. 1986. Osmotic regulation of transcription: induction of the *proU* betaine transport gene is dependent on accumulation of intracellular potassium. *J. Bacteriol.* 168:805–14
181a. Tempest, D. W., Meers, J. L. 1968. The influence of NaCl concentration of the medium on the potassium content of *Aerobacter aerogenes* and on the interrelationships between potassium, magnesium and ribonucleic acid in the growing bacteria. *J. Gen. Microbiol.* 54:319–25
182. Tempest, D. W., Meers, J. L., Brown, C. M. 1970. Synthesis of glutamate in *Aerobacter aerogenes* by a hiterto unknown route. *Biochem. J.* 117:405–7
183. Tesone, S., Hughes, A., Hurst, A. 1981. Salt extends the upper temperature limit for growth of food-poisoning bacteria. *Can. J. Microbiol.* 27:970–72
184. Tokoshita, S., Yamada, H., Aiba, H., Mizuno, T. 1990. Transmembrane signal transduction and osmoregulation in *Escherichia coli:* II. The osmotic sensor, EnvZ, located in the isolated cytoplasmic membrane displays its phosphorylation and dephosphorylation abilities as to the activator protein, OmpR. *J. Biochem.* 109:488–93
185. Troller, J. A. 1986. Water relations of foodborne bacterial pathogens—an updated review. *J. Food Prot.* 49:656–70
186. Trüper, H. G., Galinski, E. A. 1990. Biosynthesis and fate of compatible solutes in extremely halophilic phototrophic eubacteria. *FEMS Microbiol. Rev.* 75:247–54
187. Tschichholz, I., Trüper, H. G. 1990. Fate of compatible solutes during dilution stress in *Ectothiorhodospira halochloris. FEMS Microbiol. Ecol.* 73:181–86
188. Tsui, P., Helu, V., Freundlich, M. 1988. Altered osmoregulation of *ompF* in integration host factor mutants of *Escherichia coli. J. Bacteriol.* 170:4950–53
189. Tsung, K., Brissette, R. E., Inouye, M. 1989. Identification of the DNA-binding domain of the OmpR protein required for transcriptional activation of the *ompF* and *ompC* genes of *Escherichia coli* by in vivo DNA foot printing. *J. Biol. Chem.* 264:10104–9
190. Tsung, K., Brisette, R. E., Inouye, M. 1990. Enhancement of RNA polymerase binding to promoters by a transcriptional activator, OmpR, in *Escherichia coli:* its positive and negative effects on transcription. *Proc. Natl. Acad. Sci. USA* 87:5940–44
190a. Tully, R. A., Keister, D. L., Gross, K. C. 1990. Fractionation of the β-linked glucans of *Bradyrhizobium japonicum* and their response to osmotic potential. *Appl. Environ. Microbiol.* 56:1518–22
191. Uchida, S., Garcia-Perez, A., Murphy, H., Burg, M. 1989. Signal for induction of aldose reductase in renal medullary cells by high external NaCl. *Am. J. Physiol.* 256:C614–20
192. Utsumi, R., Brisette, R. E., Rampersaud, A., Forst, S. A., Oosawa, K.,

Inouye, M. 1989. Activation of bacterial porin gene expression by a chimeric signal transducer in response to asparate. *Science* 245:1246–49

193. Van Alphen, W., Lugtenberg, B. 1977. Influence of osmolarity of the growth medium on the outer membrane protein pattern of *Escherichia coli*. *J. Bacteriol.* 131:623–30

194. Van Wielink, J. E., Duine, J. A. 1990. How big is the periplasmic space? *Trends Biochem. Sci.* 15:136–37

195. Villarejo, M., Case, C. C. 1984. *envZ* mediates transcriptional control by local anesthetics but is not required for osmoregulation in *Escherichia coli*. *J. Bacteriol.* 159:883–87

195a. Vreeland, R. H. 1987. Mechanisms of halotolerance in microorganisms. *CRC Crit. Rev. Microbiol.* 14:311–56

196. Walderhaug, M. O., Dosch, D. C., Epstein, W. 1987. Potassium transport in bacteria. In *Ion Transport in Prokaryotes*, ed. B. P. Rosen, S. Silver, pp. 85–129. San Diego: Academic

197. Walderhaug, M. O., Litwack, E. D., Epstein, W. 1989. Wide distribution of homologs of *Escherichia coli* Kdp K$^+$-ATPase among gram-negative bacteria. *J. Bacteriol.* 171:1192–95

197a. Wiggins, P. M. 1990. Role of water in some biological processes. *Microbiol. Rev.* 54:432–49

198. Wohlfarth, A., Severin, J., Galinski, E.

A. 1990. The spectrum of compatible solutes in heterotrophic halophilic eubacteria of the family Halomonadaceae. *J. Gen. Microbiol.* 136:705–12

199. Wyn Jones, R. G. 1984. Phytochemical aspects of osmotic adaptation. *Recent Adv. Phytochem.* 18:55–78

200. Wyn Jones, R. G., Gorham, J. 1983. Osmoregulation. In *Encyclopedia of Plant Physiology, New Series*, Vol. 12C, ed. O. L. Lange, C. B. Osmond, H. Ziegler, pp. 35–58. Berlin/New York: Springer

201. Yamamoto, S., Yamasaki, K., Takashina, K., Katsu, T., Shinoda, S. 1989. Characterization of putrescine production in nongrowing *Vibrio parahaemolyticus* cells in response to external osmolality. *Microbiol. Immunol.* 33:11–22

202. Yancey, P. H., Clark, M. E., Hand, S. C., Bowlus, R. D., Somero, G. N. 1982. Living with water stress: the evolution of osmolyte systems. *Science* 217:1214–22

203. Zorati, M., Petronilli, V., Szabo, I. 1990. Stretch-activated composite ion channels in *Bacillus subtilis*. *Biochem. Biophys. Res. Commun.* 168:443–50

204. Zorreguieta, A., Cavaignac, S., Geremia, R. A., Ugalde, R. A. 1990. Osmotic regulation of $\beta(1-2)$ glucan synthesis in members of the family *Rhizobiaceae*. *J. Bacteriol.* 172:4701–4

Annu. Rev. Microbiol. 1991 45:607–35

PROPER AND IMPROPER FOLDING OF PROTEINS IN THE CELLULAR ENVIRONMENT

Björn Nilsson

KabiGen AB, S-112 87, Stockholm, Sweden

Stephen Anderson

Center for Advanced Biotechnology and Medicine, 679 Hoes Lane, Piscataway, New Jersey 08854

KEY WORDS: disulfides, prolyl isomerase, heat-shock proteins, proteolysis

CONTENTS

INTRODUCTION... 608
  Principles from In Vitro Folding Studies 608
  From Nascent Chain to Folded Protein In Vivo 612
INTRACELLULAR FOLDING 613
  Binding of Molecular Chaperones to Nascent Polypeptides............................. 613
  Aggregation and Inclusion Body Formation.. 615
  Prolyl Isomerase 627
PROTEOLYSIS... 618
SECRETION AND FOLDING 619
  Signal Sequences.. 620
  Protein Factors that Contribute to Secretion Competency.............................. 621
  Protein Disulfide Isomerase and Thioredoxin.. 623
MOLECULAR CHAPERONES—HOW DO THEY WORK?.. 625
  Interactions Between Molecular Chaperones and Unfolded Proteins.................. 625
  Translational Pausing and Protein Folding In Vivo..................................... 628
SUMMARY 628

607

0066-4227/91/1001-0607$02.00

INTRODUCTION

Not long ago, protein folding seemed to be a somewhat arcane subject that occupied a relatively small number of physical biochemists. Recently, however, interest and experimentation in this field have increased enormously, with much of this attention driven by the profound technological improvements that have reshaped biology in the past two decades. Especially important have been the revolutionary improvements in biosynthetic methodologies, including recombinant DNA and peptide synthesis, and the new tools for protein structure determination such as multidimensional NMR. Protein sequences can now be varied systematically and the resultant perturbations of folding behavior accurately determined. These advances have made the immense complexities of protein folding seem palpably less daunting. It is no longer foolhardy for one to hope that a detailed molecular description of the folding process, for at least some proteins, will be available in one's lifetime.

In parallel to the renaissance in protein-folding biophysics, other facets of protein folding manifest primarily in vivo have emerged in the past several years. *Molecular chaperones, foldases,* and *inclusion bodies* are relatively recent terms that were coined as investigators grappled with the problem of describing in vivo folding phenomena. If describing protein folding in vitro is difficult, detailing such a reaction in vivo would seem to be impossible. Yet this need not be true if one assumes that the underlying physical principles, derived from in vitro studies, also hold in vivo.

Unfortunately, the literature relevant to the topic of in vivo protein folding is already large enough to preclude a comprehensive survey here. We have therefore chosen instead to present a selective and somewhat more personal view of this area. Our aim is to illuminate the process of protein folding in living cells as much as possible in terms that are familiar to microbiologists. At all times, however, we have tried to maintain enough rigor in the interpretation to satisfy a biophysicist.

Principles from In Vitro Folding Studies

FORCES THAT STABILIZE PROTEINS   Four basic forces contribute to the stabilization of the native state of proteins: electrostatic interactions, hydrogen bonding, van der Waals interactions, and the hydrophobic effect. The nature and relative contributions of each of these is discussed briefly below.

Electrostatic interactions   Electrostatic effects arise from the forces of attraction or repulsion between ionized groups on the protein. In the physiological pH range, the relevant amino acids are Glu and Asp (negatively charged) and Lys, Arg, and His (positively charged). The partial charges at the ends of α-helices, which result from the helix macrodipole (62), may also contribute significantly to the total electrostatic field of a given protein. In general, charge-charge interactions tend to occur predominantly at the surfaces of proteins because ionizable groups are rarely found buried in the hydrophobic core (4), presumably because of the extremely unfavorable free energy that would arise from such an arrangement of atoms.

Hydrogen bonding   Hydrogen bonds, involving the sharing of a proton between a suitable donor group and the unpaired electrons on an acceptor atom (or the π orbitals of an aromatic group), have more directionality than any other type of noncovalent interaction in proteins. Protein hydrogen bonds occur most prominently in the regular pairings of amide groups in the polypeptide backbone that give rise to α-helix and β-sheet secondary structure, but side chain–side chain and side chain–backbone hydrogen bonds are not uncommon in proteins. Hydrogen bonding between water molecules also plays a major role in protein stability (see below).

van der Waals interactions   van der Waals interactions are the short-range dispersion forces that result from induced dipole effects in atoms that are near each other. The extremely steep positive potential energy change that occurs at small separations allows atoms to be approximated as hard spheres, each with a characteristic van der Waals radius.

Hydrophobic effect   The hydrophobic effect is not so much a true force as a thermodynamic consequence of the fact that a soluble globular protein is a large organic molecule with many apolar residues that must exist in a highly polar solvent, water. The free energies of solvation in aqueous buffers of the large hydrophobic side chains such as phenylalanine, leucine, isoleucine, valine, and methionine are positive, presumably because they force the water molecules to adopt a clathrate-like hydrogen bonding network that results in a large and unfavorable drop in the solvent entropy. Thus, when one views the protein plus solvent as a complete system, one can see that much energy can be gained by having the hydrophobic side chains sequestered in the core of the protein in contact with each other and inaccessible to solvent. This tendency of the hydrophobic side chains to pack together in the center of the protein and exclude water is thought to be the primary driving force behind protein folding (30, 116).

Chain entropy   Folding into a relatively fixed native structure unfavorably affects the conformational entropy of the polypeptide chain. This of course opposes all the positive forces that give rise to protein folding and this effect, in addition to the fact that groups on the protein can form favorable electrostatic, H-bonding, and van der Waals interactions with solvent molecules as well as with other groups on the same protein, means that proteins have marginal stability. Large opposing enthalpic and entropic effects on protein conformation generally produce only small net free energies of stabilization (on the order of 5–15 kcal/mol), and even then over only a relatively small range of temperatures (25).

STRUCTURAL HIERARCHY OF FOLDING UNITS   *Domain,* in the sense it is used in this review, refers to a segment of a polypeptide chain that can fold into a stable, unique, and globular conformation using only the sequence information contained within the same segment. Although this definition is open to many qualifications because interactions with ligands, prosthetic groups, or other polypeptide segments can provide additional stability to a domain, it nonetheless leads to little confusion in practice. Inspection of three-dimensional models of proteins derived from, for example, X-ray crystallography, can usually identify domains. Domains are also thought to be the basic modules that are swapped about combinatorially during the course of evolution, giving rise to much diversity in protein structure and function based on relatively few fundamental folding units (111). Subdomain structures such as α-helices, β-sheets, turns, and Ω-loops can form in solution under some conditions and may also behave as autonomous folding units (73). At least part of the process of assembling a polypeptide domain during folding may consist of packing together such preformed subdomain structures (73). In isolation and under physiological conditions, however, these putative folding units exhibit only marginal stability, and typically only a fraction of the population of such units exists in the folded state at any given time.

Multidomain proteins consist of two or more globular polypeptide domains linked together. Generally, cleaving proteins in these linker regions or, in the case of recombinantly expressed proteins, deleting, truncating, or making insertions in the gene at points corresponding to the linker regions does not destroy the folding integrity of the individual domains. *Proproteins* may be single domain or multidomain; in some instances, excision of the propeptide [e.g. subtilisin and α-lytic protease (see 138, 159)] may dramatically affect the ability of a protein to fold. *Preproteins* are proteins that are targeted for membrane insertion or secretion by virtue of the attachment of an N-terminal signal peptide. The signal peptide seems to regulate protein folding by retarding the folding rate (see below). In general, then, propeptides can be thought of as up-regulating (accelerating) protein folding and signal peptides as down-regulating the same process. Propeptides may act as autonomous folding units and provide a crucial bit of structure or template for the rest of the protein to pack against; signal peptides, according to the same paradigm, may disrupt the folding process by competing with the productive interactions among the autonomous folding units that make up the mature protein.

THE PROCESS OF PROTEIN FOLDING   In vitro studies of protein folding have indicated that it is, at least for many single-domain globular proteins, a highly cooperative reaction. In other words, it can be approximated as a two-state phenomenon: folded vs unfolded, in which partly folded intermediate states are only negligibly populated. If K_{eq} is the equilibrium constant that defines this transition, then the free energy of stabilization of the protein can be calculated as $\Delta G = -RT\ln K_{eq}$, where R is the universal gas constant and T is the absolute temperature in Kelvin.

As discussed above, an early event in protein folding may be the formation of some subdomain elements, including regular α-helix and β-sheet secondary structure, followed by the packing of these into a higher order domain-type structure. This process has been termed the *framework hypothesis* (72), and it is supported by experimental data on the time course of protection of exchangeable hydrogens during refolding of RNase A, cytochrome c, and barnase (15, 63, 125, 150). One should realize, however, that not all secondary structure in a protein necessarily forms early or at the same rate (125). Other features besides regular secondary structure may also form early during the folding process, but methods are not yet available to detect such elements. A final caveat is that the protein secondary structure that forms early on in folding may differ from that which is present in the final native protein.

On approximately the same time scale (~ 10 ms) that inital secondary structure forms during folding, the unfolded protein is thought to also undergo hydrophobic collapse (30). One can think of this process as analogous to micelle formation, in which the polypeptide chain becomes more compact as the hydrophilic residues turn outward and the hydrophobic residues interact in the center of the molecule away from solvent. This intermediate, though it may contain some secondary structure and be relatively compact, is probably still disordered in its core. A third state, distinct from the native or the unfolded states and termed the *molten globule,* is adopted by some proteins under mildly denaturing conditions; this state has properties similar to those envisioned for transient protein folding intermediates that have undergone hydrophobic collapse (5, 50, 117).

The final and rate-limiting phase of protein folding is the transition from the molten globule–like intermediate to the native folded structure. This process may involve the packing together of the hydrophobic residues in the core into a three-dimensional jigsaw puzzle arrangement [the *tertiary template* (116)]. The term *protein folding pathway* is often used to describe events at this stage because a limited number of intermediates seem to suffice to describe the kinetically most prominent route to the fully folded form (3, 26). Such intermediates may not be obligatory, however, especially where folding in vivo is concerned (99).

From Nascent Chain to Folded Protein In Vivo

No doubt protein folding, as complex as it appears in vitro, is even more problematical in vivo where many other factors, compartments, timing issues, competing degradative processes, etc come into play. Comparison of folding data from in vitro experiments, where denaturants are often employed, with in vivo folding phenomena, where denaturants per se do not play a role, must be done with care. Moreover, folding in vivo, at least for some proteins, may occur vectorially (starting from the N terminus) as a polypeptide emerges from a ribosome or from a secretion pore in a membrane.

After evolution has produced a certain minimal degree of stability for a given protein in a given cell, the main selective pressure from the standpoint of protein folding may be to ensure that the kinetics of folding and unfolding for that protein are attuned to the rates of other relevant processes in the cell. A newly synthesized polypeptide chain may face many competing pathways (Figure 1) in a cell, including folding, secretion, nonspecific aggregation, proteolytic degradation, sorting to various compartments, binding of molecular chaperones, and posttranslational modification. In general, these various

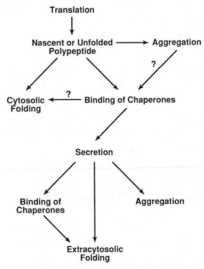

Figure 1 Some of the steps relevant to folding in vivo of a hypothetical protein. The relative importance of each event for a given protein depends on its expression level, its intrinsic folding rate, the solubility of the unfolded form, the availability of molecular chaperones, and so on (see text). Not all possible pathways are shown. Those marked ? have only been observed in vitro but are presumed to operate in vivo.

processes have to be coordinately regulated and synchronized (or avoided) in order to achieve efficient delivery of a properly folded and modified native protein to the correct location within or without the cell.

INTRACELLULAR FOLDING

Binding of Molecular Chaperones to Nascent Polypeptides

The term "molecular chaperones" was first used to describe proteins that aid in macromolecular assembly reactions by suppressing undesirable side reactions (83, 102). Now clear is that such proteins (reviewed in 31, 32, 126) have multiple functions in the cell in addition to their roles in oligomer assembly/disassembly. In particular, several of the molecular chaperones and accessory proteins participate in protein folding reactions in vivo. Different terms have been used to describe different subsets of the molecular chaperones, including chaperonins, polypeptide chain binding proteins, foldases, unfoldases, etc. In this review, we use "molecular chaperones" in a narrow sense, mainly to refer to the heat shock–related proteins of the hsp60/GroEL and the hsp70/DnaK classes, because the term seems to be especially descriptive of the functionalities these proteins exhibit in vivo. We also discuss the folding functions of other accessory factors but refer to these by their proper names rather than generically.

HSP70/DnaK   Nascent, unfolded polypeptides probably associate with molecular chaperones as soon as they emerge from the ribosome. Hsp72/73 proteins have been shown to cosediment with Hela cell polysomes, indicating that chaperone binding can occur cotranslationally (6). Under some conditions of stress, the cellular abundance of the hsp70/DnaK class of chaperones is comparable to that of elongation factors. This stoichiometry is consistent with a role for hsp70/DnaK that is a function of the absolute rate of protein synthesis. Studies with protein synthesis inhibitors have indeed shown that levels of such chaperones in the cell are correlated with translation rates under some conditions (6).

What do these observations have to do with protein folding and the properties of unfolded proteins? Unfolded proteins are typically very insoluble and one primary role of this class of molecular chaperones may be to solubilize and prevent precipitation of nascent polypeptides in the immediate vicinity of the ribosome, where they necessarily exist at the highest concentration in the cell. The turnover time for binding of hsc70 (a member of the hsp70/DnaK family) to peptides is on the order of minutes (38, 126). This period would give the soluble complex of nascent polypeptide and chaperones time to diffuse away from the ribosome before the unfolded protein was released. Hence, molecular chaperone is an especially appropriate term in this case; these molecules quite literally chaperone young proteins to prevent them from aggregating too early in life.

Using variants of λ repressor with known thermostabilities and turnover rates, Parsell & Sauer (108) showed that heat-shock proteins in *Escherichia coli* are regulated by the absolute level of unfolded protein in the cell, independent of protein degradation. Thus, the cell may have a general mechanism of sensing when unfolded polypeptides are approaching a critical concentration at which they are in danger of precipitating. Operating directly or indirectly through σ^{32}, this mechanism would cause transcription of the heat-shock genes to increase and result in the overproduction of molecular chaperones (47, 52, 108, 143). In general, the role of the hsp70/DnaK class of molecular chaperones may be simply to keep all the protein constituents in the cell in solution until they can fold, assemble, be secreted, be disposed of, etc (112, 128). Recently, direct catalysis of disaggregation and protein solubilization, coupled to ATP hydrolysis, was demonstrated for DnaK (139). This result may explain the previously puzzling observation that *dnaK* mutants are actually deficient in proteolysis (144) because intracellular precipitation (inclusion body formation) protects sensitive proteins from proteolytic attack (18). By preventing such a sequestration, DnaK would facilitate degradation of abnormal proteins.

HSP60/GroEL   The products of the *E. coli groE* locus, GroEL and GroES, were first identified as host factors that were required for efficient capsid assembly during lytic phage infections (43, 142). The 57-kilodalton (kd) GroEL monomers assemble, under appropriate conditions and in the presence of Mg-ATP, into a doughnut-shaped 14-mer made up of two stacked rings of seven monomers each (60, 61, 93). GroES is a much smaller 10-kd protein that interacts with the multimeric ring form of GroEL with a stoichiometry of one molecule of GroES for every two of GroEL. The genes of the *groE* locus are essential for growth in *E. coli* (34). Recently, GroEL was found to be structurally and functionally homologous to a binding protein required for Rubisco subunit assembly in chloroplast stroma (59) and to the heat-shock protein hsp60 (17). The family resemblances in this group of large, oligomeric molecular chaperones were reviewed recently (31).

Screening a set of yeast mutants for those that exhibited a specific defect in the assembly of multimeric mitochondrial proteins produced nuclear mutations in a complementation group termed *mif4* (17). Such mutants were pleiotropic with respect to the assembly of different mitochondrial proteins, and molecular cloning of the *mif4* gene demonstrated that it coded for yeast hsp60. Using a heterologous preprotein, F_o-ATPase presubunit 9 from *Neurospora crassa* fused to murine dihydrofolate reductase, Ostermann et al (106) developed a mitochondrial import assay in which the state of folding of imported polypeptide could be monitored. With this system, Ostermann and his colleagues observed that urea-denatured preSu9-DHFR was imported, processed, and folded into a proteinase K–resistant state within several minutes. Folding, but not import, was blocked if nonhydrolyzable ATP analogs were present or if mitochondria were preincubated with N-ethylmaleimide (NEM). Imported proteins whose folding had been blocked by low levels of ATP were found to be associated with hsp60; this association could be broken, and folding restarted, by the addition Mg-ATP. In contrast, much of the imported DHFR in NEM-pretreated mitochondria (or in mitochondria from *mif4* yeast mutants) ended up in insoluble, misfolded aggregates (106).

Although mitochondria represent a relatively complex in vitro system, studies with a better-defined in vitro system reconstituted from purified components have supported the above view of hsp60 activity. Laminet et al (81) showed that when purified GroEL is added to pre-β-lactamase in a stoichiometric ratio of 14:1, folding of the preprotein is strongly inhibited. GroEL also binds to already-folded pre-β-lactamase and unfolds it. Addition of Mg-ATP to the GroEL (or GroEL/ES):pre-β-lactamase complex results in the release and folding of the preprotein. Folding mediated by GroEL/ES, at least with this system, results in an increase in the yield but not the rate of folding, compared to the reaction carried out in the absence of accessory factors. These results are not inconsistent with the observations outlined above for hsp60 in isolated mitochondria. Hence, the hsp60/GroEL ATPase cannot yet be formally considered a folding catalyst or foldase. Rather, one can for the moment conclude that this class of molecular chaperones acts by providing unfolded proteins with a specialized environment in which they can fold productively, unhindered by aggregation or other side reactions, at their own intrinsic rates. The energy of ATP hydrolysis may only be required to drive the binding/release cycle as the chaperones repeatedly interact with different newly synthesized or unfolded polypeptide domains.

Aggregation and Inclusion Body Formation

In many of the early attempts to express recombinant eukaryotic proteins in bacteria, researchers discovered that high-level intracellular expression was often accompanied by the formation of aggregates, termed *inclusion bodies,* of inactive recombinant protein in the cytoplasm of the bacterial cell (131). Typical protocols for recovering active protein from these aggregates have included solubilization in high concentrations of urea or guanidine-HCl and reduction, if necessary, of the polypeptide sulfhydryls followed by refolding in vitro. Yields of native protein from such procedures can range from nearly quantitative to virtually negligible. Because many instances of inclusion-body formation were observed during attempts to produce in the cytoplasm of *E. coli* recombinant proteins normally found as extracellular, disulfide-bonded, mammalian proteins in nature, investigators initially felt that this phenomenon might be limited to such cases. However, it is now known to be a more general phenomenon of bacterial expression, involving for example secreted as well as intracellularly expressed proteins (20), proteins without cysteines or disulfide bonds (100) as well as those with cytoplasmic as well as extracytoplasmic proteins [e.g. Rhesus monkey alcohol dehydrogenase (D. Light & M. Dennis, personal communication)], and bacterial as well as mammalian proteins (54).

Phage P22 tailspike endorhamnosidase, which King and his collaborators have studied extensively, forms intracellular inclusion bodies when synthesized at temperatures above 30°C (48, 54, 140). A class of temperature-sensitive (ts) mutants of this protein (74) exhibit a greatly enhanced tendency to form such aggregates at elevated temperatures. Both wild-type and mutant P22 tailspike trimers are quite thermostable when folded into the native conformation (145); thus these ts mutations seem to divert newly synthesized proteins down a path towards aggregation and away from the productive folding pathway. This diversion may result from destabilization of thermolabile folding intermediates (54). Such mutations could also affect the kinetics of folding without affecting stability (65, 105), slowing down productive folding and thus allowing the off-pathway aggregation route to predominate. A third possibility is that these mutations generate nucleation sites for aggregation in the P22 tailspike folding intermediates that are not present in the wild-type protein and are unusually sensitive to small changes in temperature (54). Interestingly, for a broad range of proteins, inclusion-body formation in vivo is suppressed by lowering the temperature of the culture (131).

One way to unify the observations on misfolding and aggregation of proteins in vivo is to view folding as an intramolecular recognition process governed by the intrinsic rate constants of the various folding steps as well as by the intrinsic solubilities of various regions of the polypeptide chain. According to this view, if a protein is given enough time and is in the presence of other parts of the same folding domain, it should fold spontaneously. Folding probably proceeds via collisions of parts of the chain to create marginally stable subdomain structures that, if they contain enough stabilizing interactions, persist and eventually assemble into the complete domain (56, 71, 73). Excessive aggregation will potentially become a problem if the rate of folding is retarded, if the solubility of the unfolded chain is decreased, or if the concentration of the nascent chain is increased. Any of these three factors will accentuate intermolecular interactions at the expense of folding. One example of this dynamic is the effect of expression levels on the folding of protein A–IGF-I fusions. At higher expression levels, a significant proportion of the fusion protein is diverted into inactive, multimeric forms (129). Thus, aggregation (Figure 1) may occur if proteins do not have enough time to fold at their own intrinsic rates before they collide with another unfolded chain.

Prolyl Isomerase

Most peptide bonds in proteins, because of resonance and steric effects, exist predominantly in the *trans* configuration (25). Proline, however, because its five-membered ring relieves some of the steric constraints, can isomerize readily about its peptide bond. At equilibrium and in the absence of other interactions, roughly 10–20% of proline residues have the *cis* configuration with respect to the peptide bond (103). Typical rate constants for proline *cis-trans* isomerization about this bond are on the order of minutes at room temperature.

Proline isomerization is important for protein folding because prolines are usually free to isomerize when polypeptide chains are in the unfolded state, but are constrained when these chains fold up. Some proteins may be completely unable to fold when particular prolines are in the wrong isomeric configuration because of the unfavorable packing interactions made by the isomer in the native conformation of the protein [termed type III prolines by Levitt (89)]. Since proline isomerization is in general much slower than protein folding, this step becomes rate-limiting in the folding process [reviewed by Nall (103)], which leads to a subpopulation of unfolded molecules that exhibit slow-phase kinetics during in vitro refolding experiments (12, 64, 65, 68, 103, 132).

Do proline isomerization events impact folding reactions in vivo? Some nascent proteins may fold up so rapidly after synthesis that proline isomerization would not have enough time to appreciably affect the outcome (105). On the other hand, if molecular chaperones hold nascent proteins in an unfolded state for more than a minute or so (126), and if in doing so they do not inhibit proline isomerization, then equilibration to a nonnative proline conformer could retard folding significantly. In particular, the folding of proteins with more than a few type III prolines would become problematic in the absence of any catalysis of the isomerization reaction.

Such catalysts exist in the form of peptidyl-prolyl *cis-trans* isomerases (35, 92). However, the exact role that these enzymes play during protein folding in vivo is unclear. The *ninaA* gene of *Drosophila melanogaster* codes for a protein that is homologous to the known prolyl isomerase, cyclophilin (133). These mutants have reduced levels of rhodopsin in R1-R6 photoreceptor cells. It is not known whether this defect is caused by a missing prolyl isomerase activity or even whether the *ninaA* gene product exhibits such an activity, but the lesion appears to be posttranscriptional with respect to opsin gene expression, consistent with a block in protein folding or maturation (133). Perhaps, rather than acting as general housekeeping folding factors, specific prolyl isomerases facilitate the folding of specific classes of proteins in certain specialized cells. In lower eukaryotes, none of the known prolyl isomerases appear to be essential for cell viability (149, 158).

The recent discovery that the receptor proteins for the potent immunosuppressants, cyclosporin A and FK506, are prolyl isomerases has generated much excitement (36, 55, 137, 146). These binding proteins (cyclophilin and FK506 rotamase) are thought to be the receptors that mediate the action of cyclosporin A and FK506, and the prolyl isomerization activity of each of the cognate binding proteins is competitively inhibited by binding of the respective drugs. However, the immunosuppressant activity of these compounds seems to result from an effect on T-cell transcription (148) rather than from a blockage of protein folding. Moreover, studies with model compounds related to FK506 have suggested that these immunosuppressants exert their effects in vivo by mimicking endogenous effector ligands rather than by preventing the enzymatic catalysis of proline isomerization (10).

PROTEOLYSIS

Proteolytic degradation of polypeptides in vivo is a matter of considerable practical and theoretical importance [reviewed recently for $E.$ $coli$ by Gottesman (51) and for eukaryotic cells by Dice (29)]. Analyses of well-characterized mutants of λ repressor have shown that susceptibility to proteolytic degradation in vivo is highly correlated with thermal stability measured in vitro (109). The turnover rates for λ repressor mutants generally fit a model in which proteolysis is envisioned to proceed from attack on the unfolded state only (109). Thus, destabilizing mutations increase the proportion of polypeptide chain that is in the unfolded configuration and thereby increase the rate of turnover; stabilizing mutations have the opposite effect. In agreement with this overall scheme, second-site mutations that repress ts mutations elsewhere in the protein appear to do so either by enhancing stability or by increasing the affinity of the folded form for DNA (and thus pulling the folding equilibrium away from the unfolded state) (109). Indeed, in a well-characterized system such as λ repressor or bovine pancreatic trypsin inhibitor, resistance to in vivo proteolysis can be used as a powerful and useful screening method for mutants with altered folding properties (23, 91).

For a given protein in the nascent or unfolded state, the rate of proteolysis in vivo may be so great that, even with high rates of transcription and translation, net synthesis of mature protein may be virtually nil (152). For example, screens for temperature-sensitive folding mutants yield variants falling into four phenotypic classes: 1. extra stable; 2. stability indistinguishable from wild-type; 3. ts mutants; and 4. null mutants [note: temperature-sensitive synthesis (tss) mutants fall into a special class in which no appreciable thermolability of the native form is observed (see 74)]. Besides encompassing nonsense and frameshift mutants, class 4 also includes extremely destabilizing missense mutants (49, 91). Therefore, one should keep in mind that both the type of screen employed and the fundamental stability of the target protein affect the relative distribution of the resulting mutants in the four phenotypic classes. Two major studies on collections of randomly generated destabilizing point mutations have produced a conundrum of apparently opposing conclusions: in T4 lysozyme, *ts* mutations are predominantly found in those residues making up the hydrophobic core of the protein, which has been interpreted to mean that the primary effect of these mutations is the destabilization of the native state (1, 101); in staphylococcal nuclease, on the other hand, many *ts* mutations were isolated that seemed to exert their primary effects on the structure and free energy of the denatured state (134, 135). These results may not be as contradictory as they first appear because of the markedly different thermal stabilities of these two proteins: at neutral pH, staphylococcal nuclease has a T_m of 53.3°C (136), whereas at pH 6.5, T4 lysozyme has a T_m of 65°C (157). Hence, T4 lysozyme may require mutations that are more severely destabilizing, compared with mutations in staphylococcal nuclease, to show an observable phenotype. This requirement may have resulted in a preponderance of core mutants being scored in T4 lysozyme because these are generally more destabilizing than mutations at the protein surface (57, 124).

Some aspects of proteolytic degradation in vivo, however, seem to operate independent of the global thermodynamic stability of the affected protein. Determinants at the N terminus (2) or the C terminus (11, 110) also affect the in vivo turnover rate. Also, mutants of λ repressor that incorporate the P78A mutation seem to have an unusually short half-life in vivo (123), and [C14A, C38A]BPTI is remarkably temperature sensitive in vivo at 37°C (104) even though it is a rather stable protein with a T_m of 78°C at neutral pH (G. Liu, K. Breslauer & S. Anderson, unpublished data). These observations may mean that local modes of unfolding in a protein, altered by mutation, also govern somewhat the susceptibility to proteolytic attack in vivo.

SECRETION AND FOLDING

The mechanisms of protein translocation across the cytoplasmic membrane in prokaryotes and across the endoplasmic reticulum in eukaryotes exhibit many common features. Even though the secretory machinery in humans and in bacteria have important differences, the systems are similar enough for one organism to secrete some precursor proteins with components from the other. The process of protein secretion has been perhaps most fully characterized in *E. coli,* in part because of the development of elegant genetic screens for secretory mutants [reviewed by Bieker et al (8)] and of advanced methods for studying protein translocation biochemically in vivo and in vitro (33, 121). Presently, many of the necessary components of the secretion apparatus have been identified in *E. coli*. In fact, a functional in vitro protein translocation system was recently reconstituted from purified proteins and membrane components (13). Almost all secreted proteins have a *cis*-acting element, namely the signal peptide, attached at the N terminus; this form of the protein is called the preform. This peptide is of similar structure in all organisms. It is responsible for the recognition of the preprotein by the secretory machinery, and it is cleaved off during or after translocation. Several recent reviews have covered protein secretion (7–9, 33, 120, 121). Below, we discuss the interplay between protein folding and protein secretion, drawing mostly on data from *E. coli*.

In prokaryotes, protein translation and protein secretion are independent but simultaneous processes. Entry into the secretory pathway is normally rapid, before the completion of polypeptide chain synthesis, so secretion may appear to be fully cotranslational. However, recognition of the nascent preprotein by the secretory machinery is kinetically determined and is not coupled to polypeptide chain elongation. Thus, posttranslational as well as cotranslational secretion can occur.

Protein folding is relevant to protein secretion because the fully folded form of some preproteins is not secretion-competent, as first described by Randall & Hardy (119). This restriction has not been characterized fully at the molecular level, but it is likely that there are steric constraints governed by the dimensions and/or the deformability of the membrane pores through which the secreted protein must pass. Additionally, successful export may require that the secreted molecule transiently occupy only a limited subset of all its possible conformational states, and thermodynamic or kinetic barriers may affect such a transition. Even though these limitations are not fully understood, the observation that for some proteins the folded native structures are not readily exportable implies mechanisms must exist in vivo to keep preproteins in a secretion-competent state.

The folding rates of preproteins are modulated in vivo by two independent mechanisms. First, the signal sequence per se slows down the rate of folding of the precursor molecule, as demonstrated for premaltose binding protein (pre-MBP) (107) and pre-β-lactamase (80), respectively. Second, some proteins in the cell bind to preproteins and prevent folding, thus maintaining them in a secretion-competent state. In bacterial systems, several such molecular chaperones have been identified: SecB, trigger factor, DnaK, and GroEL.

Signal Sequences

The signal sequences of preproteins are involved in many steps in protein secretion: protein folding inhibition (120), recognition of the secretion apparatus (42), and participation in the actual translocation event across the membrane (147). As the primary structures of signal sequences are not highly constrained, other structural features must endow signal sequences with their characteristic properties. One approach to understanding the mode of action of signal sequences has been to study their structures in aqueous as well as in nonpolar media. These studies, performed mainly with circular dichroism spectroscopy, but most recently also with NMR (for reviews, see 44, 67), have shown that signal peptides tend to adopt β-strand or random coil structures in aqueous medium but exhibit a significant content of α-helix in nonpolar solvents. This helix-forming potential has been correlated with the ability of the signal peptide to mediate translocation across a membrane (67). Though it has not been demonstrated, the function of the signal sequence in the aqueous medium (recognition of the secretory machinery and/or retardation of protein folding) is possibly correlated with its propensity to form β-structure or random coil in that medium.

The folding retardation property of signal sequences was first demonstrated for pre-MBP (107), based on the kinetics of refolding of guanidine hydrochloride–denatured material. In these experiments, pre-MBP was found to refold more slowly in vitro than mature MBP, but the unfolding rates were similar. Because the export of posttranslationally secreted MBP is SecB dependent (see below), these results were interpreted in terms of a model in which the retarded folding rate of the MBP precursor facilitates the binding of SecB to the unfolded state (120). Secretion behavior consistent with this model has been observed in vivo (95), and this scheme is further supported by results showing that second-site suppressors of defective signal sequence mutations, located in the mature region of MBP, show retarded folding (24, 94). In addition, one class of suppressors of defective MBP secretion in $secB^-$ E. coli cells consists of signal sequence mutants that enter the secretory apparatus significantly more rapidly (22). Recently, marked folding suppression in vitro by the signal sequence of prenuclease from Staphylococcus aureus was also demonstrated (S. Chatterjee, personal communication). Circular dichroism studies on purified mature nuclease and prenuclease have shown that both the mature and the preprotein have nearly identical secondary structure, but the prenuclease exhibits significant disorder in its aromatic core residues (S. Chatterjee, personal communication). This characteristic of the preprotein structure is strikingly similar to the signature expected for a molten globule state (5, 50, 117), and it suggests that the mechanism of folding retardation by the signal peptide may involve partitioning of the peptide into the hydophobic core and consequent hindrance of proper packing of the core residues during folding (116).

Protein Factors that Contribute to Secretion Competency

THE FOLDING MODULATOR SecB   Evidence for a direct involvement of the cytosolic protein SecB in protein translocation in E. coli comes from both genetic studies (8, 76) and from biochemical analyses (75, 153). According to the current view of SecB's function in protein translocation, it binds to protein precursors and thereby keeps them in a secretion-competent state, but it acts only on a subset of proteins (77). SecB is not essential for growth on minimal medium, but *secB* null mutants are inviable on complex medium (8). The reason for this selective-growth defect is not known. The nucleotide sequence of the *secB* gene was recently determined (78), and it shows a deduced amino acid sequence of 155 residues. Thus, SecB is a rather small 16.7-kd protein that reportedly exists in a tetrameric form (75, 154).

The best-studied protein precursor that shows a SecB-dependent secretion is MBP. The binding site of SecB to the MBP precursor has been a subject of dispute. The binding site was first suggested to be in the mature portion of MBP and not in the signal peptide as might have been expected, based on the absence of SecB binding to deletion mutants of MBP (21). Later, a specific SecB interaction with the signal sequence was proposed based on exclusive binding to pre-MBP* and not to MBP* (MBP* is MBP with a short C-terminal deletion) (154). Recent experiments with purified components showed that SecB indeed interacts with the mature portion of the preprotein and may interact with the signal peptide as well, but if so this interaction is not preferential (122, 155).

What is the actual significance of SecB binding to precursor proteins? Collier et al (21) suggested that it acts primarily as a folding inhibitor, and many studies support this hypothesis (79, 153, 154). However, other hypotheses exist in the literature. One model proposes that SecB binds to the mature portion of preproteins to keep the signal sequence exposed for subsequent recognition by the secretory machinery (120). An alternative explanation for SecB binding to preforms of secreted proteins comes from an in vitro study of proOmpA (the precursor of OmpA), which suggested that the secretion-competent precursor shows significant folding in the presence of SecB. These conclusions are based on circular dichroism and tryptophan fluorescence measurements (86). In the absence of SecB, proOmpA aggregated and became secretion incompetent. The conclusion from this study was that one role of SecB may be to prevent aggregation of preproteins by binding to hydrophobic stretches on the precursor polypeptide. This hypothesis is supported by the finding that temperature-dependent intracellular aggregation limits the secretion of a mutant human tumor necrosis factor in *E. coli* (88).

Interestingly, only a subset of the secreted proteins in *E. coli* depends on SecB (77), perhaps implying that other SecB-like activities occur in the cell that have not yet been discovered. This possibility was recently addressed in an experiment in which different portions of pre-MBP were fused to alkaline phosphatase (41). MBP secretion is SecB dependent while alkaline phosphatase secretion is completely independent of SecB. The secretion of these fusion proteins became SecB dependent, even when as little as 74 amino acids of MBP were fused to alkaline phosphatase. The results indicate that no factor that stimulates the secretion of alkaline phosphatase can replace SecB under these conditions and that only a small portion of MBP is needed to induce SecB binding. If SecB is utilized as an antifolding factor in this case, then the 74 N-terminal amino acids of MBP probably fold into a relatively stable, secretion-incompetent, structure.

OTHER HOST FACTORS   Other *E. coli* proteins have been shown to bind to precursors of secreted proteins and stimulate their translocation, possibly by inhibiting folding or aggregation. Trigger factor was first discovered because of its ability to bind to proOmpA and stimulate its secretion in an in vitro system (28). Trigger factor is an abundant ribosome-associated protein in *E. coli* and has a molecular weight of approximately 63 kd (27, 90). However, a physiological role for trigger factor in protein translocation has not been completely established as trigger factor depletion has no obvious effect on secretion in vivo (53). In addition, SecB efficiently out-competes the binding of trigger factor to proOmpA, indicating a much stronger interaction of SecB with proOmpA (85). The observed effects of overproduction or depletion of trigger factor in *E. coli* relate to filamentous growth, and the phenotype caused by the overproduction of trigger factor could be suppressed by cooverproduction of FtsZ, which is the product of a gene involved in cell division (53). Thus, the activity of trigger factor in keeping proOmpA in a secretion-competent state may not reflect its major activity in the cell.

Another *E. coli* protein chaperone that may be involved in maintaining the secretion competence of some precursor proteins is DnaK. DnaK belongs to the hsp70 family of proteins (see above), members of which stimulate protein secretion in eukaryotic cells across the endoplasmic reticulum as well as into mitochondria (19). In *E. coli,* overproduction of DnaK stimulates the secretion of β-galactosidase fused to a signal sequence (113). The secretion incompetency of β-galactosidase, an intracellular protein, has been well studied (87), and this property was originally used to screen for the *sec⁻* mutant strains of *E. coli* (8). The ability of DnaK to partially suppress the secretion blockage of this intracellular protein is interesting as multiple regions of β-galactosidase are responsible for its secretion incompetence (87). However, the full significance of DnaK's role in the export of proteins from *E. coli* remains to be clarified.

GroEL, a member of the hsp60 heat shock protein family (see above), interacts with many proteins in the cell (151). Members of this protein family, although they primarily seem to be involved in folding and assembly reactions, have also been observed to stimulate secretion in some model systems (17, 113).

Protein Disulfide Isomerase and Thioredoxin

For many proteins, especially secreted ones, formation of disulfide bonds is coupled to protein folding (25). The mechanism(s) of protein disulfide bond formation in vivo, however, remains a mystery. Direct oxidation by metal ions or oxygen may represent a major route to the formation of proper and improper disulfide bonds in over-expressed recombinant proteins [for example, in periplasmic inclusion bodies (20)], but this process is not likely to be significant for the formation of disulfides during biosynthesis of endogenous proteins. Protein folding and formation of proper disulfide bonds proceeds much more efficiently in an environment that promotes reversible thiol/disulfide exchange, with redox conditions that favor correct disulfides and disfavor incorrect ones (114, 130). Protein disulfide formation and breakage in vivo probably occurs via such an exchange mechanism, catalyzed by some combination of glutathione and protein factors such as thioredoxin or protein disulfide isomerase. Protein disulfide formation is thought to occur in the lumen of the endoplasmic reticulum in eukaryotes and in the periplasm (for gram negatives) or the extracellular medium (for gram positives) of prokaryotes, because premature disulfide bond formation in the cytosol appears to block secretion (97, 105).

Protein disulfide isomerase, a 114-kd homodimer, is an abundant protein found in the lumen of the ER that has many of the characteristics one would expect for a protein whose role is to promote proper formation of disulfides in secreted proteins (39, 40). For example, protein disulfide isomerase levels in cells are closely correlated with secretion activity (39, 40). Moreover, depletion of dog pancreas microsomes of soluble lumenal proteins renders them deficient with respect to the formation of protein disulfide bonds, although they are still translocation competent (14). Reconstitution in vitro with purified protein disulfide isomerase restores the ability of these pH 9–stripped microsomes to catalyze the formation of disulfide bonds in nascent proteins; oxidized glutathione can not substitute for protein disulfide isomerase in this system (14). One intriguing twist to the protein disulfide isomerase story is the finding that it is identical to the β subunit of prolyl-4-hydroxylase (115), although no evidence indicates that it acts in coordination with prolyl isomerase (82).

Thioredoxins are small ($\sim$12-kd) proteins found both in E. coli and in mammalian cells that have an active-site sequence similar to that of protein disulfide isomerases and that appear to have similar functional properties (96). In E. coli, subcellular fractionation studies have shown that thioredoxin, although it is a soluble protein, does not copurify with known cytosolic proteins or with periplasmic markers (46); thus it may reside in a somewhat specialized third compartment in the cell. E. coli thioredoxin is an electron donor in nucleotide metabolism (84), a necessary subunit of the replicative T7 DNA polymerase (98), and is involved in filamentous phage coat protein assembly (127), but none of these roles seem to involve disulfide bond rearrangements. However, secretion studies with BPTI disulfide mutants in *trx*$^+$ and *trx*$^-$ strains of *E. coli* have led to the postulate that one additional role for thioredoxin may be the reduction of prematurely formed disulfides in proteins that have entered the secretion pathway (105).

Mechanistically, thioredoxin and protein disulfide isomerase may function by providing an electrostatically controlled microenvironment where disulfide bond reduction or formation can proceed efficiently at physiological pH values. Sulfhydryl groups are normally only reactive when ionized to the thiolate species, and the acid dissociation constant (pKa) of an unperturbed cysteine thiol is 8.7 (141). Thus, at neutral pH, uncatalyzed thiol/disulfide exchange reactions are relatively slow. Thioredoxin, however, has a reactive thiol group with a pKa shifted to 6.7 (70); such a thiol would be almost fully ionized and reactive at physiological pH values. This may explain in part the roughly 1000-fold rate enhancement of the intramolecular thiol/disulfide exchange reaction catalyzed by such proteins (45, 114).

MOLECULAR CHAPERONES—HOW DO THEY WORK?

Interactions Between Molecular Chaperones and Unfolded Proteins

A reasonable postulate is that the binding of molecular chaperones to unfolded proteins must be relatively nonspecific with respect to the sequences of the bound polypeptides; otherwise many proteins would not react. An analogy can be made to the interaction of a broad-specificity serine protease, subtilisin, with proteinaceous substrates. Subtilisin has a single primary specificity pocket, S1, that can accept a spectrum of different side chains at the P1 position in the substrate (156). Subtilisin also has a series of secondary sites, S2, S3, and S4, that interact with the P2, P3, and P4 residues in the substrate. The K_m values exhibited by subtilisin for a spectrum of different peptide substrates are in the range of 10–100 μM (156). This is in the same range as the affinity constants of hsc70 and BiP for a variety of small peptides (38). Thus, the binding of a molecular chaperone monomer to its ligand, unfolded protein may be no more sequence-dependent than the binding of subtilisin to its substrates. Additionally, the phenomenon of substrate recognition by subtilisin exhibits other features that are analogous to some of the presumed properties of molecular chaperones: a preference for hydrophobic sites on proteins and heightened activity against denatured proteins compared to native ones.

A multimer of the hsp60/GroEL class of chaperones could associate very strongly with an unfolded protein if several of the subunits in such a structure were to bind to the unfolded polypeptide simultaneously. In the multimeric complex, relatively weak binding free energies of individual interacting monomers should, to a first approximation, behave in an additive fashion, resulting in a very favorable free energy of binding for the complex itself. Similarly, molecular chaperones of the hsp70/DnaK class may also acquire extra affinity by acting cooperatively under some conditions. Hsp70/DnaK monomers may bind adjacent regions of polypeptide chain while forming intersubunit contacts with each other, perhaps even forming an ordered structure like a linear array. In this regard, the recently discovered structural homology between the hsc70 ATPase domain and actin (37, 69) is particularly suggestive, as actin is well-known for its ability to form helical fibers in solution in an ATP-dependent fashion. Support for a model involving cooperative binding of chaperones to unfolded proteins comes from recent in vitro studies on the interaction of purified *E. coli* DnaK with different staphylococcal protein A fusion proteins. Hellebust et al (58) found that an unfolded C-terminal tail of 24 amino acids on protein A had a much lower affinity for DnaK than a tail only twice as long (51 amino acids). Other lines of evidence, including coprecipitation studies (6), also indicate that extended polypeptide chains interact more strongly with molecular chaperones than do short peptides (38).

The interaction of hsp70/DnaK chaperones with unfolded proteins is normally a transient phenomenon, after which the proteins are released for folding (or secretion followed by folding). Release is accompanied by ATP hydrolysis (38), and, given the structural relatedness between this class of chaperones and actin (37, 69), the release process may be mechanistically related to the conformational transitions that accompany ATP hydrolysis in actin (66). Following release, the unfolded polypeptide can fold spontaneously or may bind to an hsp60/GroEL chaperone prior to folding. A reaction involving chaperone exchange, in which ATP hydrolysis and hsp70/DnaK release of the unfolded protein is coupled directly to hsp60/GroEL binding, is also possible (Figure 2).

Release of the bound, unfolded protein by hsp60/GroEL requires hydrolysis of ATP and is accompanied by folding, but the yield rather than the rate of folding is enhanced by the action of this chaperone, implying that the complex is not acting catalytically on the folding process per se (81). This observation is consistent with early conceptions that considered chaperones as primarily agents for masking regions of the polypeptide chain that might otherwise engage in unproductive or dead-end interactions (31, 112), a process that could be termed *molecular guidance*. The mechanism by which hsp60/GroEL accomplishes this task is unknown, but the occurrence of this chaperone as a double stacked disk, 14-subunit oligomer (60, 61) is highly suggestive; the structure of such a distinctive macromolecular assembly is almost certain to be related to its function.

A hypothesis consistent with the known properties of hsp60/GroEL is that the annular stacked disk of this chaperone is hollow (Figure 2), with an inside surface that can switch between two alternative states. In one state, the individual hsp60/GroEL monomers would bind to hydrophobic stretches of the unfolded polypeptide in a manner analogous to binding of hsp70/DnaK chaperones (see above). Conceivably, such binding could precede oligomerization of the hsp60/GroEL subunits. In the complex between the assembled 14mer and the unfolded protein, the model would place these binding sites on the inside surface of the double-disk structure (not all binding sites would need to be occupied, however). The unfolded protein would thus be held inside the disk structure (Figure 2), attached to the inside surface by its hydrophobic residues, which are thought to encode the fundamental information for the structure of the protein core and the overall protein fold (30, 116). Upon hydrolysis of ATP, the model envisions that a conformational change in hsp60/GroEL would result in the concerted release of the bound hydrophobics and in a shift in the properties of the inside reactive surface of the double stacked disk, converting it to an unreactive and relatively hydrophilic state. Hence, the encapsulated protein would be allowed to fold

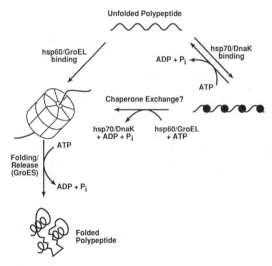

Figure 2 Interactions of molecular chaperones with unfolded proteins. An unfolded protein can interact directly with either hsp60/GroEL or hsp70/DnaK chaperones. Hydrolysis of ATP by both types of chaperone is accompanied by release of the bound protein. Release of the unfolded polypeptide by hsp70/DnaK may be coupled under some conditions to hsp60/GroEL binding. Hypothetically, the target protein domain could fold inside of the hsp60/GroEL oligomer (see text). In multidomain proteins, the N- and C-terminal amino acid stretches leading into or away from a given domain would then presumably protrude from the holes at each end of the annular stacked-disk structure. Translational pausing could phase the attachment of chaperones to specific segments of the polypeptide chain (see text), thus allowing domains in multidomain proteins to fold essentially independent of each other.

628   NILSSON & ANDERSON

spontaneously at its own inherent rate in a sequestered aqueous environment, shielded from most if not all nonnative hydrophobic interactions.

Translational Pausing and Protein Folding In Vivo

Some eukaryotic proteins, especially large multidomain ones, are notorious for their inability to fold properly when expressed in bacteria, and attempts to refold them in vitro often meet with limited success as well. In contrast, single domains of multidomain proteins can often be expressed in bacteria, either cytoplasmically or in secreted form, and the material can be refolded, if necessary, to its native conformation. What is it about eukaryotic proteins or eukaryotic gene expression that may account for this phenomenon? Perhaps relevant to this apparent paradox is the observation that translation rates in yeast, as governed by codon usage and message secondary structure, are not uniform across genes (118). Rather, pause points in protein synthesis occur that are correlated with domain boundaries. These may serve as temporal punctuation marks that synchronize the attachment of blocks of contiguous molecular chaperone monomers to stretches of unfolded polypeptide chain. The position of the punctuation marks in the sequence would ensure that these blocks corresponded to particular domains in the folded protein. Complexes of molecular chaperones with unfolded proteins may have an internal clock that causes them to dissociate after a predetermined length of time (126). Thus, this pausing mechanism would allow a segment of the polypeptide chain representing the folding information for a single domain to fold, guided by the chaperones, independent of possibly confounding information in adjacent segments (Figure 2). Rothman (126) proposed a similar model of programmed chaperone release to account for protein folding phenomena, but he postulated specific signals in the protein sequence itself to explain this process. Our model, in contrast, postulates phasing of chaperones en bloc by means of signals embedded in the string of codons that make up the gene. The encoding of translation pause points by clusters of codons representing low-abundance tRNAs (118) could explain the observation that in vivo folding of recombinant multidomain proteins is often inefficient, since the limiting tRNAs in the heterologous host may be different from those in the cell where the gene is naturally expressed. The general notion that signals in the messenger RNA may regulate protein folding in the cellular environment, via the coordination of molecular chaperone binding to newly synthesized polypeptides as they emerge from the ribosome or cross a membrane, is in principle experimentally testable.

SUMMARY

Protein folding in the cellular environment involves an interplay between the intrinsic biophysical properties of a protein, in both its folded and unfolded states, and various accessory proteins that aid the process. Factors such as peptidyl prolyl isomerase, protein disulfide isomerase, thioredoxin, and SecB may interact with the unfolded forms of specific classes of proteins, while members of the hsp70/DnaK and hsp60/GroEL molecular chaperone families may play a more general role in folding. Secretion, proteolysis, and aggregation are other in vivo processes that depend greatly on the folding behavior of a given protein. Intrinsic folding rates, or even translation rates, of nascent proteins may be optimized by natural selection to ensure smooth coordination with all the cellular components required for a successful folding reaction.

ACKNOWLEDGMENTS

We thank the Center for Advanced Biotechnology and Medicine, Kabi Gen AB, the US National Science Foundation, and the US National Institutes of Health for their support of this work.

Literature Cited

1. Alber, T., Dao-pin, S., Nye, J. A., Muchmore, D. C., Matthews, B. W. 1987. Temperature-sensitive mutations of bacteriophage T4 lysozyme occur at sites with low mobility and low solvent accessibility in the folded protein. *Biochemistry* 26:3754–58

2. Bachmair, A., Finley, D., Varshavsky, A. 1986. In vivo half-life of a protein is a function of its amino-terminal residue. *Science* 234:179–86

3. Baldwin, R. L. 1989. How does protein folding get started? *Trends Biochem. Sci.* 14:291–95

4. Barlow, D. J., Thornton, J. M. 1983. Ion-pairs in proteins. *J. Mol. Biol.* 168:867–85

5. Baum, J., Dobson, C. M., Evans, P. A., Hanley, C. 1989. Characterization of a partly folded protein by NMR methods: studies on the molten globule state of guinea pig α-lactalbumin. *Biochemistry* 28:7–13

6. Beckmann, R. P., Mizzen, L. A., Welch, W. J. 1990. Interaction of hsp70 with newly synthesized proteins: implications for protein folding and assembly. *Science* 248:850–54

7. Benson, S. A., Hall, M. N., Silhavy, T. J. 1985. Genetic analysis of protein export in *Escherichia coli* K12. *Annu. Rev. Biochem.* 54:101–34

8. Bieker, K. L., Phillips, G. J., Silhavy, T. J. 1990. The *sec* and *prl* genes of *Escherichia coli*. *J. Bioenenerg. Biomembr.* 22:291–310

9. Bieker, K. L., Silhavy, T. J. 1990. The genetics of protein secretion in *E. coli*. *Trends Genet.* 6:329–34

10. Bierer, B. E., Somers, P. K., Wandless, T. J., Burakoff, S. J., Schreiber, S. L. 1990. Probing immunosuppressant action with a non-natural immunophilin ligand. *Science* 250:556–59

11. Bowie, J. U., Sauer, R. T. 1989. Identification of C-terminal extensions that protect proteins from intracellular proteolysis. *J. Biol. Chem.* 264:7596–602

12. Brandts, J. F., Halvorson, H. R., Brennan, M. 1975. Consideration of the possibility that the slow step in protein denaturation reactions is due to cis-trans isomerism of proline residues. *Biochemistry* 14:4953–63

13. Brundage, L., Hendrick, J. P., Schiebel, E., Driessen, A. J. M., Wickner, W. 1990. The purified *E. coli* integral membrane protein SecY/E is sufficient for reconstitution of SecA-dependent precursor protein translocation. *Cell* 62:649–57

14. Bulleid, N. J., Freedman, R. B. 1988. Defective co-translational formation of disulfide bonds in protein disulfide isomerase-deficient microsomes. *Nature* 335:649–51

15. Bycroft, M., Matouschek, A., Kellis, J. T. Jr., Serrano, L., Fersht, A. R. 1990. Detection and characterization of a folding intermediate in barnase by NMR. *Nature* 346:488–90

16. Deleted in proof

17. Cheng, M. Y., Hartl, F.-U., Martin, J., Pollock, R. A., Kalousek, F., et al. 1989. Mitochondrial heat-shock protein hsp60 is essential for assembly of pro-

teins imported into yeast mitochondria. *Nature* 337:620–25

18. Cheng, Y. E., Kwoh, D., Kwoh, T. J., Soltvedt, B. C., Zipser, D. 1981. Stabilization of a degradable protein by its overexpression in *Escherichia coli*. *Gene* 14:121–30

19. Chirico, W. J., Waters, M. G., Blobel, G. 1988. 70k heat shock related proteins stimulate protein translocation into microsomes. *Nature* 332:805–10

20. Cleary, S., Mulkerrin, M. G., Kelley, R. F. 1989. Purification and characterization of tissue plasminogen activator kringle-2 domain expressed in *Escherichia coli*. *Biochemistry* 28:1884–91

21. Collier, D. N., Bankaitis, V. A., Weiss, J. B., Bassford, P. J. 1988. The antifolding activity of SecB promotes the export of the *E. coli* maltose-binding protein. *Cell* 53:273–83

22. Collier, D. N., Bassford, P. J. 1989. Mutations that improve export of maltose-binding protein in SecB-cells of *Escherichia coli*. *J. Bacteriol.* 171:4640–47

23. Coplen, L. J., Frieden, R. W., Goldenberg, D. P. 1990. A genetic screen to identify variants of bovine pancreatic trypsin inhibitor with altered folding energetics. *Proteins* 7:16–31

24. Cover, W. H., Ryan, J. P., Bassford, P. J., Walsh, K. A., Bollinger, J., Randall, L. L. 1987. Suppression of a signal sequence mutation by an amino acid substitution in the mature portion of the maltose-binding protein. *J. Bacteriol.* 169:1794–800

25. Creighton, T. E. 1984. *Proteins: Structures and Molecular Properties.* New York: Freeman. 515 pp.

26. Creighton, T. E. 1985. The problem of how and why proteins adopt folded conformations. *J. Phys. Chem.* 89:2452–59

27. Crooke, E., Guthrie, B., Lecker, S., Lill, R., Wickner, W. 1988. ProOmpA is stabilized for membrane translocation by either purified *E. coli* trigger factor or canine signal recognition particle. *Cell* 54:1003–11

28. Crooke, E., Wickner, W. 1987. Trigger factor: a soluble protein that folds proOmpA into a membrane-assembly-competent form. *Proc. Natl. Acad. Sci. USA* 84:5216–20

29. Dice, J. F. 1987. Molecular determinants of protein half-lives in eukaryotic cells. *FASEB J.* 1:349–57

30. Dill, K. A. 1990. Dominant forces in protein folding. *Biochemistry* 29:7133–55

31. Ellis, R. J. 1990. Molecular chaparones:

the plant connection. *Science* 250:954–59

32. Ellis, R. J., Hemmingsen, S. M. 1989. Molecular chaperones: proteins essential for the biogenesis of some macromolecular structures. *Trends Biochem. Sci.* 14:339–42

33. Fandl, J., Tai, P. C. 1990. Protein translocation in vitro: Biochemical characterization of genetically defined translocation components. *J. Bioenerg. Biomembr.* 22:369–87

34. Fayet, O., Ziegelhoffer, T., Georgopoulos, C. 1989. The *groES* and *groEL* heat shock gene products of *Escherichia coli* are essential for bacterial growth at all temperatures. *J. Bacteriol.* 171:1379–85

35. Fischer, G. 1984. Determination of enzymatic catalysis for the *cis-trans* isomerization of peptide binding in proline-containing peptides. *Biomed. Biochim. Acta* 43:1101–11

36. Fischer, G., Wittman-Liebold, B., Lang, K., Kiefhaber, T., Schmid, F. X. 1989. Cyclophilin and peptidylprolyl*cis-trans* isomerase are probably identical proteins. *Nature* 337:476–78

37. Flaherty, K. M., DeLuca-Flaherty, C., McKay, D. B. 1990. Three-dimensional structure of the ATPase fragment of a 70K heat-shock cognate protein. *Nature* 346:623–28

38. Flynn, G. C., Chappell, T. G., Rothman, J. E. 1989. Peptide binding and release by proteins implicated as catalysts of protein assembly. *Science* 245:385–90

39. Freedman, R. B. 1989. Protein disulfide isomerase: multiple roles in the modification of nascent secretory proteins. *Cell* 57:1069–72

40. Freedman, R. B., Bulleid, N. J., Hawkins, H. C., Paver, J. L. 1989. Role of protein disulfide isomerase in the expression of native proteins. *Biochem. Soc. Symp.* 55:167–92

41. Gannon, P. M., Li, P., Kumamoto, C. A. 1989. The mature portion of *Escherichia coli* maltose-binding protein (MBP) determines the dependence of MBP on SecB for export. *J. Bacteriol.* 171:813–18

42. Gennity, J., Goldstein, J., Inouye, M. 1990. Signal peptide mutants of *Escherichia coli*. *J. Bioenerg. Biomembr.* 22:233–69

43. Georgopoulos, C. P., Hendrix, R. W., Casjens, S. R., Kaiser, A. D. 1973. Host participation in bacteriophage lambda head assembly. *J. Mol. Biol.* 76:45–60

44. Gierasch, L. M. 1989. Signal sequences. *Biochemistry* 28:923–30
45. Gilbert, H. F. 1989. Catalysis of thiol/disulfide exchange: single-turnover reduction of protein disulfide isomerase by glutathione and catalysis of peptide disulfide reduction. *Biochemistry* 28:7298–305
46. Gleason, F. K., Holmgren, A. 1988. Thioredoxin and related proteins in prokaryotes. *FEMS Microbiol. Rev.* 4:271–97
47. Goff, S. A., Goldberg, A. L. 1985. Production of abnormal proteins in *E. coli* stimulates transcription of *lon* and other heat shock genes. *Cell* 41:587–95
48. Goldenberg, D. P., Berget, P. B., King, J. 1982. Maturation of the tail spike endorhamnosidase of *Salmonella* phage P22. *J. Biol. Chem.* 257:7864–71
49. Goldenberg, D. P., Frieden, R. W., Haack, J. A., Morrison, T. B. 1989. Mutational analysis of a protein folding pathway. *Nature* 338:127–32
50. Goto, Y., Calciano, L. J., Fink, A. L. 1990. Acid-induced folding of proteins. *Proc. Natl. Acad. Sci. USA* 87:573–77
51. Gottesman, S. 1989. Genetics of proteolysis in *Escherichia coli*. *Annu. Rev. Genet.* 23:163–98
52. Grossman, A. D., Erickson, J. W., Gross, C. A. 1984. The *htpR* gene product of *E. coli* is a sigma factor for heat-shock promoters. *Cell* 38:383–90
53. Guthrie, B., Wickner, W. 1990. Trigger factor depletion or overproduction causes defective cell division but does not block protein export. *J. Bacteriol.* 172:5555–62
54. Haase-Pettingell, C. A., King, J. 1988. Formation of aggregates from a thermolabile in vivo folding intermediate in P22 tailspike maturation. *J. Biol. Chem.* 263:4977–83
55. Harding, M. W., Galat, A., Uehling, D. E., Schreiber, S. L. 1989. A receptor for the immunosuppressant FK506 is a *cis-trans* peptidyl-prolyl isomerase. *Nature* 341:758–60
56. Harrison, S., Durbin, R. 1985. Is there a single pathway for the folding of a polypeptide chain? *Proc. Natl. Acad. Sci. USA* 82:4028–30
57. Hecht, M. H., Sturtevant, J. M., Sauer, R. T. 1984. Effect of single amino acid replacements on the thermal stability of the NH2-terminal domain of phage lambda repressor. *Proc. Natl. Acad. Sci. USA* 81:5685–89
58. Hellebust, H., Uhlen, M., Enfors, S.-V. 1990. Interaction between heat shock protein DnaK and recombinant staphylo-coccal protein A. *J. Bacteriol.* 172:5030–34
59. Hemmingsen, S. M., Woolford, C., van der Vies, S. M., Tilly, K., Dennis, D. T., et al. 1988. Homologous plant and bacterial proteins chaperone oligomeric protein assembly. *Nature* 333:330–34
60. Hendrix, R. W. 1979. Purification and properties of *groE*, a host protein involved in bacteriophage assembly. *J. Mol. Biol.* 129:375–92
61. Hohn, T., Hohn, B., Engel, A., Wurtz, M., Smith, P. R. 1979. Isolation and characterization of the host protein *groE* involved in bacteriophage lambda assembly. *J. Mol. Biol.* 129:359–73
62. Hol, W. G. J. 1985. The role of the α-helix dipole in protein function and structure. *Prog. Biophys. Mol. Biol.* 45:149–95
63. Hughson, F. M., Wright, P. E., Baldwin, R. L. 1990. Structural characterization of a partly folded apomyoglobin intermediate. *Science* 249:1544–48
64. Hurle, M. R., Anderson, S., Kuntz, I. D. 1991. Confirmation of the predicted source of a slow folding reaction: proline-8 of bovine pancreatic trypsin inhibitor. *Protein Eng.* 4:451–55
65. Hurle, M. R., Marks, C., Kosen, P. A., Anderson, S., Kuntz, I. D. 1990. Denaturant-dependent folding of bovine pancreatic trypsin inhibitor mutants with two intact disulfide bonds. *Biochemistry* 29:4410–19
66. Janmey, P. A., Hvidt, S., Oster, G. F., Lamb, J., Stossel, T. P., Hartwig, J. H. 1990. Effect of ATP on actin filament stiffness. *Nature* 347:95–99
67. Jones, J. D., McKnight, J., Gierasch, L. M. 1990. Biophysical studies of signal peptides: Implications for signal sequence functions and the involvement of lipid in protein export. *J. Bioenerg. Biomembr.* 22:213–32
68. Jullien, M., Baldwin, R. L. 1981. The role of proline residues in the folding kinetics of the bovine pancreatic trypsin inhibitor derivative RCAM(14–38). *J. Mol. Biol.* 145:265–80
69. Kabsch, W., Mannherz, H. G., Suck, D., Pai, E. F., Holmes, K. C. 1990. Atomic structure of the actin:DNase I complex. *Nature* 347:37–44
70. Kallis, G.-B., Holmgren, A. 1980. Differential reactivity of the functional sulfhydryl groups of cysteine-32 and cysteine-35 present in the reduced form of thioredoxin from *Escherichia coli*. *J. Biol. Chem.* 255:10261–65
71. Karplus, M., Weaver, D. 1976. Protein folding dynamics. *Nature* 260:404–6
72. Kim, P. S., Baldwin, R. L. 1982.

Specific intermediates in the folding reactions of small proteins and the mechanism of protein folding. *Annu. Rev. Biochem.* 51:459–89

73. Kim, P. S., Baldwin, R. L. 1990. Intermediates in the folding reactions of small proteins. *Annu. Rev. Biochem.* 59:631–60

74. King, J., Haase, C. A., Yu, M.-H. 1987. Temperature sensitive mutations affecting kinetic steps in protein folding pathways. In *Protein Engineering,* ed. D. Oxender, C. F. Fox, pp. 109–21. New York: Liss

75. Kumamoto, C. A. 1990. SecB protein: a cytosolic export factor that associates with nascent exported proteins. *J. Bioenerg. Biomembr.* 22:337–51

76. Kumamoto, C. A., Beckwith, J. 1983. Mutations in a new gene, *secB,* cause defective protein localization in *Escherichia coli. J. Bacteriol.* 154:253–60

77. Kumamoto, C. A., Beckwith, J. 1985. Evidence for specificity at an early step in protein export in *Escherichia coli. J. Bacteriol.* 163:267–74

78. Kumamoto, C. A., Nault, A. K. 1989. Characterization of the *Escherichia coli* protein-export gene *secB. Gene* 75:167–75

79. Kusters, R., de Vrije, T., Breukink, E., de Kruijff, B. 1989. SecB protein stabilizes a translocation-competent state of purified prePhoE protein. *J. Biol. Chem.* 264:20827–30

80. Laminet, A. A., Plückthun, A. 1989. The precursor of β-lactamase: purification, properties and folding kinetics. *EMBO J.* 8:1469–77

81. Laminet, A. A., Ziegelhoffer, T., Georgopoulos, C., Plückthun, A. 1990. The *Escherichia coli* heat shock proteins GroEL and GroES modulate the folding of the β-lactamase precursor. *EMBO J.* 9:2315–19

82. Lang, K., Schmid, F. X. 1988. Protein-disulfide isomerase and prolyl isomerase act differently and independently as catalysts of protein folding. *Nature* 331:453–55

83. Laskey, R. A., Honda, B. M., Mills, A. D., Finch, J. T. 1978. Nucleosomes are assembled by an acidic protein which binds histones and transfers them to DNA. *Nature* 275:416–20

84. Laurent, T. C., Moore, E. C., Reichard, P. 1964. Enzymatic synthesis of deoxyribonucleotides. IV. Isolation and characterization of thioredoxin, the hydrogen donor from *Escherichia coli* B. *J. Biol. Chem.* 239:3436–44

85. Lecker, S., Lill, R., Ziegelhoffer, T., Georgopoulos, C., Bassford, P. J., et al.

1989. Three pure chaperone proteins of *Escherichia coli*—SecB, trigger factor and GroEL—form soluble complexes with precursor proteins in vitro. *EMBO J.* 8:2703–9

86. Lecker, S. H., Driessen, A. J. M., Wickner, W. 1990. ProOmpA contains secondary and tertiary structure prior to translocation and is shielded from aggregation by association with SecB. *EMBO J.* 9:2309–14

87. Lee, C., Li, P., Inouye, H., Brickman, E. R., Beckwith, J. 1989. Genetic studies of the inability of β-galactosidase be translocated across the *Escherichia coli* cytoplasmic membrane. *J. Bacteriol.* 171:4609–16

88. Leemans, R., Remaut, E., Fiers, W. 1989. Correlation between temperature-dependent cytoplasmic solubility and periplasmic export of a heterologous protein in *Escherichia coli. Gene* 85:99–108

89. Levitt, M. 1981. Effect of proline residues on protein folding. *J. Mol. Biol.* 145:251–63

90. Lill, R., Crooke, E., Guthrie, B., Wickner, W. 1988. The "trigger factor cycle" includes ribosomes, presecretory proteins, and the plasma membrane. *Cell* 54:1013–18

91. Lim, W. A., Sauer, R. T. 1989. Alternative packing arrangements in the hydrophobic core of λ repressor. *Nature* 339:31–36

92. Lin, L.-N., Brandts, J. F. 1984. Involvement of prolines-114 and -117 in the slow refolding phase of ribonuclease A as determined by isomer-specific proteolysis. *Biochemistry* 23:5713–23

93. Lissin, N. M., Venyaminov, S. Y., Girshovich, A. S. 1990. (Mg-ATP)-dependent self-assembly of molecular chaperone GroEL. *Nature* 348:339–42

94. Liu, G., Topping, T. B., Cover, W. H., Randall, L. L. 1988. Retardation of folding as possible means of suppression of a mutation in the leader sequence of an exported protein. *J. Biol. Chem.* 263:14790–93

95. Liu, G., Topping, T. B., Randall, L. L. 1989. Physiological role during export for the retardation of folding by the leader peptide of maltose-binding protein. *Proc. Natl. Acad. Sci. USA* 86:9213–17

96. Lundström, J., Holmgren, A. 1990. Protein disulfide isomerase is a substrate for thioredoxin reductase and has thioredoxin-like activity. *J. Biol. Chem.* 265:9114–20

97. Maher, P. A., Singer, S. J. 1986. Disulfide bonds and the translocation of

proteins across membranes. *Proc. Natl. Acad. Sci. USA* 83:9001–5

98. Mark, D. F., Richardson, C. C. 1976. *Escherichia coli* thioredoxin: a subunit of bacteriophage T7 DNA polymerase. *Proc. Natl. Acad. Sci. USA* 73:780–84

99. Marks, C. B., Naderi, H., Kosen, P. A., Kuntz, I. D., Anderson, S. 1987. Mutants of bovine pancreatic trypsin inhibitor lacking cysteines 14 and 38 can fold properly. *Science* 235:1370–73

100. Marston, F. A. 0. 1986. The purification of eukaryotic polypeptides synthesized in *Escherichia coli. Biochem. J.* 240:1–12

101. Matthews, B. W. 1987. Genetic and structural analysis of the protein stability problem. *Biochemistry* 26:6885–87

102. Musgrove, J. E., Ellis, R. J. 1986. The Rubisco large subunit binding protein. *Phil. Trans. R. Soc. London Ser. B* 313:419–28

103. Nall, B. T. 1985. Proline isomerization and protein folding. *Commun. Mol. Cell Biophys.* 3:123–43

104. Nilsson, B., Kuntz, I. D., Anderson, S. 1990. Expression and stabilization of bovine pancreatic trypsin inhibitor folding mutants in *Escherichia coli.* In *Protein Folding: Deciphering the Second Half of the Genetic Code,* ed. L. M. Gierasch, J. King, pp. 117–22. Washington, DC: Am. Assoc. Advancement Sci.

105. Nilsson, B., Marks, C. B., Kuntz, I. D., Anderson, S. 1991. Secretion incompetence of bovine pancreatic trypsin inhibitor expressed in *Escherichia coli. J. Biol. Chem.* 266:2970–77

106. Ostermann, J., Horwich, A. L., Neupert, W., Hartl, F.-U. 1989. Protein folding in mitochondria requires complex formation with hsp60 and ATP hydrolysis. *Nature* 341:125–30

107. Park, S., Liu, G., Topping, T. B., Cover, W. H., Randall, L. L. 1988. Modulation of folding pathways of exported proteins by the leader sequence. *Science* 239:1033–35

108. Parsell, D. A., Sauer, R. T. 1989. Induction of a heat shock–like response by unfolded protein in *Escherichia coli:* dependence on protein level not protein degradation. *Genes Dev.* 3:1226–32

109. Parsell, D. A., Sauer, R. T. 1989. The structural stability of a protein is an important determinant of its proteolytic susceptibility in *Escherichia coli. J. Biol. Chem.* 264:7590–95

110. Parsell, D. A., Silber, K. R., Sauer, R. T. 1990. Carboxy-terminal determinants of intracellular protein degradation. *Genes Dev.* 4:277–86

111. Patthy, L. 1987. Evolution of the proteases of blood coagulation and fibrinolysis by assembly from modules. *Cell* 41:657–63

112. Pelham, H. R. B. 1986. Speculations on the functions of the major heat shock and glucose-regulated proteins. *Cell* 46:959–61

113. Philips, G. J., Silhavy, T. J. 1990. Heat-shock proteins DnaK and GroEL facilitate export of LacZ hybrid proteins in *E. coli. Nature* 344:882–84

114. Pigiet, V. P., Schuster, B. J. 1986. Thioredoxin-catalyzed refolding of disulfide-containing proteins. *Proc. Natl. Acad. Sci. USA* 83:7643–47

115. Pihlajaniemi, T., Helaakoski, T., Tasanen, K., Myllylä, R., Huhtala, M.-L., et al. 1987. Molecular cloning of the β-subunit of human prolyl-4-hydroxylase. This subunit and protein disulfide isomerase are products of the same gene. *EMBO J.* 6:643–49

116. Ponder, J. W., Richards, F. M. 1987. Tertiary templates for proteins: use of packing criteria in the enumeration of allowed sequences for different structural classes. *J. Mol. Biol.* 193:775–91

117. Ptitsyn, O. B. 1987. Protein folding: hypotheses and experiments. *J. Protein Chem.* 6:272–93

118. Purvis, I. J., Bettany, A. J. E., Santiago, T. C., Coggins, J. R., Duncan, K., et al. 1987. The efficiency of folding of some proteins is increased by controlled rates of translation in vivo: a hypothesis. *J. Mol. Biol.* 193:413–17

119. Randall, L. L., Hardy, S. J. S. 1986. Correlation of competence for export with lack of tertiary structure of the mature species: a study in vivo of maltose-binding protein in *E. coli. Cell* 46:921–28

120. Randall, L. L., Hardy, S. J. S. 1989. Unity in function in the absence of consensus in sequence: Role of leader peptides in export. *Science* 243:1156–59

121. Randall, L. L., Hardy, S. J. S., Thom, J. R. 1987. Export of protein: a biochemical view. *Annu. Rev. Microbiol.* 41:507–41

122. Randall, L. L., Topping, T. B., Hardy, S. J. S. 1990. No specific recognition of leader peptide by SecB, a chaperone involved in protein export. *Science* 248:860–63

123. Reidhaar-Olson, J. F., Parsell, D. A., Sauer, R. T. 1990. An essential proline in λ repressor is required for resistance to intracellular proteolysis. *Biochemistry* 29:7563–71

124. Reidhaar-Olson, J. F., Sauer, R. T. 1988. Combinatorial cassette mutagene-

sis as a probe of the informational content of protein sequences. *Science* 241: 53–57

125. Roder, H., Elove, G. A., Englander, S. W. 1988. Structural characterization of folding intermediates in cytochrome *c* by H-exchange labelling and proton NMR. *Nature* 335:700–4

126. Rothman, J. E. 1989. Polypeptide chain binding proteins: catalysts of protein folding and related processes in cells. *Cell* 59:591–601

127. Russel, M., Model, P. 1985. Thioredoxin is required for filamentous phage assembly. *Proc. Natl. Acad. Sci. USA* 82:29–33

128. Sambrook, J., Gething, M.-J. 1989. Chaperones, paperones. *Nature* 342: 224–25

129. Samuelsson, E., Wadensten, H., Hartmanis, M., Moks, T., Uhlen, M. 1991. Facilitated in vitro refolding of human recombinant insulin-like growth factor I using a solubilizing fusion partner. *Bio/Technology* 9:363–66

130. Saxena, V. P., Wetlaufer, D. B. 1970. Formation of three dimensional structure in proteins. I. Rapid nonenzymic reactivation of reduced lysozyme. *Biochemistry* 9:5015–23

131. Schein, C. H. 1989. Production of soluble recombinant proteins in bacteria. *Bio/Technology* 7:1141–49

132. Schmid, F. X., Baldwin, R. L. 1978. Acid catalysis of the formation of the slow-folding species of RNase A: evidence that the reaction is proline isomerization. *Proc. Natl. Acad. Sci. USA* 75:4764–68

133. Shieh, B.-H., Stamnes, M. A., Seavello, S., Harris, G. L., Zuker, C. S. 1989. The *ninaA* gene required for visual transduction in *Drosophila* encodes a homologue of cyclosporin A–binding protein. *Nature* 338:67–70

134. Shortle, D., Meeker, A. K. 1986. Mutant forms of staphylococcal nuclease with altered patterns of guanidine hydrochloride and urea denaturation. *Proteins* 1:81–89

135. Shortle, D., Meeker, A. K. 1989. Residual structure in large fragments of staphylococcal nuclease: effects of amino acid substitutions. *Biochemistry* 28:936–44

136. Shortle, D., Meeker, A. K., Freire, E. 1988. Stability mutants of staphylococcal nuclease: large compensating enthalpy-entropy changes for the reversible denaturation reaction. *Biochemistry* 27: 4761–68

137. Siekierka, J. J., Hung, S. H. Y., Poe, M., Lin, C. S., Sigal, N. H. 1989. A cytosolic binding protein for the immunosuppressant FK506 has peptidyl-prolyl isomerase activity but is distinct from cyclophilin. *Nature* 341:755–57

138. Silen, J. L., Agard, D. A. 1989. The α-lytic protease pro-region does not require a physical linkage to activate the protease domain in vivo. *Nature* 341: 462–64

139. Skowyra, D., Georgopoulos, C., Zylicz, M. 1990. The *E. coli dnaK* gene product, the hsp70 homolog, can reactivate heat-inactivated RNA polymerase in an ATP hydrolysis-dependent manner. *Cell* 62:939–44

140. Smith, D. H., King, J. 1981. Temperature-sensitive mutants blocked in the folding or subunit assembly of the bacteriophage P22 tail spike protein. III. Inactive polypeptide chains synthesized at 39°C. *J. Mol. Biol.* 145:653–76

141. Snyder, G. H. 1984. Free energy relationships for thiol-disulfide interchange reactions between charged molecules in 50% methanol. *J. Biol. Chem.* 259: 7468–72

142. Steinberg, N. J. 1973. Properties of a mutant of *Escherichia coli* defective in bacteriophage lambda head formation (*groE*). II. The propagation of phage lambda. *J. Mol. Biol.* 76:25–44

143. Strauss, D. B., Walter, W. A., Gross, C. A. 1987. The heat shock response of *E. coli* is regulated by changes in the concentration of σ^{32}. *Nature* 329:348–51

144. Strauss, D. B., Walter, W. A., Gross, C. A. 1988. *Escherichia coli* heat shock gene mutants are defective in proteolysis. *Genes Dev.* 2:1851–58

145. Sturtevant, J. M., Yu, M., Haase-Pettingell, C., King, J. 1989. Thermostability of temperature-sensitive folding mutants of the P22 tailspike protein. *J. Biol. Chem.* 264:10693–98

146. Takahashi, N. J., Hayano, T., Suzuki, M. 1989. Peptidyl-prolyl *cis-trans* isomerase is the cyclosporin A binding protein cyclophilin. *Nature* 337:473–75

147. Thom, J. R., Randall, L. L. 1988. Role of the leader peptide of maltose-binding protein in two steps of the export process. *J. Bacteriol.* 170:5654–61

148. Tocci, M. J., Matkovich, D. A., Collier, K. A., Kwok, P., Dumont, F., et al. 1989. The immunosuppressant FK506 selectively inhibits expression of early T cell activation genes. *J. Immunol.* 143:718–26

149. Tropschug, M., Barthelmess, I. B., Neupert, W. 1989. Sensitivity to cyclosporin A is mediated by cyclophilin in

Neurospora crassa and *Saccharomyces cerevisiae*. *Nature* 342:953–55

150. Udgaonkar, J. B., Baldwin, R. L. 1988. NMR evidence for an early framework intermediate on the folding pathway of ribonuclease A. *Nature* 335:694–99

151. van Dyk, T. K., Gatenby, A. A., LaRossa, R. A. 1989. Demonstrating by genetic suppression of interaction of GroE products with many proteins. *Nature* 342:451–53

152. von Wilcken-Bergmann, B., Tils, D., Sartorius, J., Auerswald, E. A., Schröder, W., Müller-Hill, B. 1986. A synthetic operon containing 14 bovine pancreatic trypsin inhibitor genes is expressed in *E. coli. EMBO J.* 5:3219–25

153. Watanabe, M., Blobel, G. 1989. Cytosolic factor purified from *Escherichia coli* is necessary and sufficient for the export of a preprotein and is a homotetramer of SecB. *Proc. Natl. Acad. Sci. USA* 86:2728–32

154. Watanabe, M., Blobel, G. 1989. SecB functions as a cytosolic signal recognition factor for protein export in *E. coli. Cell* 58:695–705

155. Weiss, J. B., Bassford, P. J. 1990. The folding properties of the *Escherichia coli* maltose-binding protein influence its interaction with SecB *in vitro. J. Bacteriol.* 172:3023–29

156. Wells, J. A., Cunningham, B. C., Graycar, T. P., Estell, D. A. 1987. Recruitment of substrate-specificity properties from one enzyme into a related one by protein engineering. *Proc. Natl. Acad. Sci. USA* 84:5167–71

157. Wetzel, R., Perry, L. J., Baase, W. A., Becktel, W. J. 1988. Disulfide bonds and thermal stability in T4 lysozyme. *Proc. Natl. Acad. Sci. USA* 85:401–5

158. Wiederrecht, G., Brizuela, L., Elliston, K., Sigal, N. H., Siekierka, J. J. 1991. *FKBI* encodes a nonessential FK506-binding protein in *Saccharomyces cerevisiae* and contains regions suggesting homology to the cyclophilins. *Proc. Natl. Acad. Sci. USA* 88:1029–33

159. Zhu, X., Ohta, Y., Jordan, F., Inouye, M. 1989. Pro-sequence of subtilisin can guide the refolding of denatured subtilisin in an intermolecular process. *Nature* 339:483–84

SUBJECT INDEX

A

Abraham, S. N., 383-408
Acetate
  synthesis of pyruvate from, 6
Acetobacterium kivui, 25
Acetobacterium woodii, 25
Acetoin
  metabolism in *Bacillus subtilis*, 117-18
Acquired immunodeficiency syndrome, 219-20
Actinomyces naeslundii
  type 2 pili of
    subunit polymerization and, 396
Actinomycin D
  giardiavirus and, 257
Adenosine triphosphate
  methylreductase reaction and, 18
Adhesins, 384
  receptor binding and assembly domains of, 398-401
Aflatoxin B1
  hepatocellular carcinoma and, 486
Agrobacterium
  β-glucans in, 588
Agrobacterium rhizogenes, 347
Agrobacterium tumefaciens
  osmoregulation in, 586
AIDS
  See Acquired immunodeficiency syndrome
β-Alanine betaine
  osmoprotectant activities of, 584
Albendazole
  for helminth infection, 449
Aldobiuronic acid, 23
Alfalfa
  nodulation of, 347
    feedback suppression of, 365
    inhibition of, 363
    regulation of, 362
  nodule-specific glutamine synthetase from, 355
Alkalophiles
  isolation of, 96-97
Allantoin
  degradation pathway of, 22

Alveolar macrophages
  host defense against mycotic agents and, 522-24
α-Amanitin
  giardiavirus and, 257
Amino acids
  catabolite repression in *Bacillus subtilis* and, 123-24
γ-Aminobutyric acid betaine
  osmoprotectant activities of, 584
γ-Aminocrotinic acid betaine
  osmoprotectant activities of, 584
Ammonia monooxygenase
  trichloroethylene oxidation by, 288
Anabaena torulosa
  gene transcription in
    osmotic control of, 589
Anabolic steroids
  hepatocellular carcinoma and, 486
Ancylostoma braziliense
  ivermectin activity against, 447
Ancylostoma caninum
  ivermectin activity against, 447
Ancylostoma duodenale
  ivermectin activity against, 446-47
Anderson, S., 607-29
Angiostrongylus cantonensis
  ivermectin activity against, 464
Anticarsia gemmatalis
  baculovirus insecticide for, 75
Antimony complexes
  pentavalent
    for *Leishmania* infection, 418, 437
Antiparasitic agents
  for human use, 445-69
Archaebacteria, 11-14
Aromatic oxygenases
  trichloroethylene oxidation by, 288-92
Arthrobacter crystallopoietes, 23
Ascaris lumbricoides
  ivermectin activity against, 446
Asparaginase
  in *Bacillus subtilis*, 123

Aspartyl acid proteinase
  Candida albicans virulence and, 198-200
Aspergillosis
  alveolar macrophages and, 523
Aspergillus
  conidia of
    alveolar macrophages and, 522
  host defense against
    polymorphonuclear leukocytes and, 518-19
Atlas, R. M., 137-56
ATP
  See Adenosine triphosphate
Autographa californica, 71
Avermectins
  detection of, 100
  production of, 446
  for *Trichinella spiralis*, 464
Aztreonam, 57

B

Babesia
  virus-like particles in, 253
Babesia bovis
  RNA viruses in, 260
Bacillus cereus
  β-lactamase of, 47
Bacillus licheniformis
  asparaginase expression in, 123
  β-lactamase of, 39-40
  penicillin-binding domain of, 39, 47
Bacillus macerans
  pyruvate reactions in, 7
Bacillus stearothermophilus
  osmoregulation in, 585
Bacillus subtilis
  ammonia assimilation systems in, 120-23
    glutamate synthase and, 123-24
    glutamine synthetase and, 120-23
  carbohydrate metabolism genes in, 113-19
  carbon catabolite repression in, 108-19
    mutants and, 112-13

cytoplasmic membrane of
stretch-activated channels
in, 580
msDNA and, 165
nitrogen catabolite repression
in amino acids and, 123-
24
penicillin-binding proteins of,
57
sporulation in
catabolite repression of,
124-29
sugar transport in, 109-12
urease, asparaginase, nrg gene
expression in, 123
Bacteria
compatibile solutes in, 582-83
hepadnaviral DNA cloned in,
479
osmoregulation in, 569-97
genes and proteins in, 588-
97
mechanisms of, 571-81
physiology of, 581-88
See also specific type
Bacterial symbiont
legume nodulation and, 348-
54
Bacteriophage λ
assembly of
GroE chaperonins and,
310-11
Bacteriophage morphogenesis
GroE genes and, 308-11
Bacteriophage P22
tailspide endorhamnosidase of
synthesis of, 616
Bacteriophage T4
assembly of
groES gene product and,
309-10
Bacteroides nodosus
type 4 pilins of, 401-2
Baculoviruses, 69-85
classification and properties
of, 70-71
expression vector system of,
78-80
infection and replication in insects, 71-74
as viral insecticides, 74-75
Baculovirus insecticides, 74-75
environment and, 80-81
field-release testing of, 81-83
Barnase
refolding of
framework hypothesis and,
611
Bean
nodulation mutants of, 357
nodule-specific glutamine synthetase from, 355

Beggiatoa, 22
Beverley, S. M., 417-39
Bio-assays, 100-1
Blastomyces dermatitidis, 190
chemotactic factors produced
by, 519
compromised host and, 511
yeast of
alveolar macrophages and,
522
Blastomycosis
acquisition of, 511
Bleomycin A2
dsRNA viruses and, 253
Bodo caudatus
RNA editing in, 332
Bombyx mori
"jaundice disease" of, 69-70
Bovine herpesvirus, 272
Bradyrhizobium
β-glucans in, 588
symbiotic genes of, 348-50
Bradyrhizobium japonicum
nod gene organization in, 350
Brevibacterium lactoterentum
osmoregulation in, 586
Bromethanesulfonate
methanogenesis and, 11
Brufia malayi
ivermectin activity against,
464
Budded virus, 71
Burkitt's lymphoma
chromosomal translocations
in, 493

C

Caetano-Anolles, G., 345-70
Campbell, W. C., 445-69
Cancer
colorectal
p53 gene product and, 494
Candida albicans
adherence of, 203-7
antigenic variability of, 208-9
blastoconidia and hyphae of,
513
chemical defenses to, 516
chemotactic factors produced
by, 519
chromosomal instability of,
208
complement fixation by, 519
host defense against
polymorphonuclear leuko-
cytes and, 518-19
hyphal production by, 190-97
natural killer cells and, 527,
530
in normal flora of humans,
511

proteinase activity of, 197-
203, 512
receptor-ligand molecules of,
203-6
spherules of
polymorphonuclear leuko-
cytes and, 522
variability potential of, 207-9
virulence factors of, 187-210
virulence genes in, 188
yeast of
alveolar macrophages and,
522
Candida immitis
arthroconidia and endospores
of
alveolar macrophages and,
522
complement fixation by, 519
proteinases produced by, 512
tissue phase of
hormones and, 515
Candida neogromans
complement fixation by,
519
Candida parapsilosis, 198
Candidia immitis
natural killer cells and, 527
Candidiasis, 187-88, 511
vaginal
hormones influencing, 515-
16
Carbamyl phosphate
oxalurate phosphorolysis and,
22
Carbon
metabolism in Bacillus subtilis, 107-19
Carbon dioxide
methanogenesis from
enzymology of, 17-20
synthesis of pyruvate from, 6
Carbon dioxide reduction factor,
16
Carcinogenesis
chromosomal translocation
and, 493
Carcinoma
hepatocellular
hepadnaviral DNA in, 489-
91
hepadnaviruses and, 475-99
Carnitine
osmoprotectant activities of,
584
Casuarina
nodulation of, 347
Catabolite repression
in Bacillus subtilis, 108-24
Cell cultures
hepadnavirus-related
oncogenesis in, 495-96

Cellular immunity
  impaired
    herpesvirus transmission
      and, 266
Cellular resistance
  mycotic agents and, 517-31
Cellular transcription factors
  human immunodeficiency
    virus-1 replication and,
    225-27
Cephalexin, 59
Chain entropy
  protein stability and, 609-10
Chaperones
  molecular
    bonding to nascent
      polypeptides, 613-15
    interactions with unfolded
      proteins, 625-28
  pilus assembly and, 387-93
  release of
    polymerization of pilus sub-
      units and, 392-93
Chaperonins
  GroE, 301-21
    model for action of, 317-21
    substrates of, 314-16
Chickenpox
  pathogenesis of, 269
Chimpanzees
  hepatitis B virus-infected, 486
Chitinase genes
  developmental regulation of,
    355
Chloramphenicol
  msDNA biosynthesis and, 172
Choline-O-sulfate
  osmoprotectant activities of,
    584
Chromatium, 21
Chromatophores, 21
Chromomycosis
  acquisition of, 511
Chromosomal translocation
  carcinogenesis and, 493
Chronic granulomatous disease
  opportunistic mycotic infec-
    tion and, 520
Circular DNA
  in Leishmania, 419
Cirrhosis
  hepatitis B virus infection
    and, 484-85
Citrate
  metabolism in Bacillus sub-
    tilis, 118-19
Citrobacter freundi
  msDNA and, 165
Citrobacter freundii
  β-lactamase of, 39-40
Clostridium pasteurianum
  pyruvate reactions in, 6-7

Clostridium tetanomorphum, 23
Clover
  nodulation of, 362
  inhibition of, 363
Coccidioides immitis
  compromised host and, 511
Coccidioidomycosis, 524
  acquisition of, 511
  genetic predisposition to, 513-
    14
  pregnancy and, 515
Coenzyme F$_{420}$, 14
Coenzyme F$_{430}$, 15-16
Coenzyme M, 10-11
Coleoptera
  baculovirus infection in, 71
Colorectal cancer
  p53 gene product and, 494
Compatible solutes
  bacterial, 582-83
Complement fixation
  pathogenic fungi and, 519
Corrins
  methylreductase reaction and,
    18
Cotton
  baculovirus insecticide for,
    75
Cowpea
  nodulation of, 350, 362
Crenothrix, 21
Crithidia fasciculata
  RNA editing in, 331
Croen, K. D., 265-78
Crypticity, 399
Cryptococcosis
  acquisition of, 511
  alveolar macrophages and,
    523
Cryptococcus neoformans
  alveolar macrophages and,
    522
  blastoconidia of, 513
  capsule of
    polymorphonuclear leuko-
      cytes and, 521-22
  chemical defenses to, 516
  natural killer cells and, 527-
    30
Csonka, L. N., 569-97
Cullen, B. R., 219-43
Cutler, J. E., 187-210
Cyanobacteria
  hypoosmotic shock and, 588
Cyclohexanone monooxygenase
  trichloroethylene oxidation
    and, 295
Cyclophilin, 617
Cyclosporin A
  receptor proteins for, 618
Cystobacter ferrugineus
  msDNA in, 165

Cystobacter fuscus
  msDNA in, 165
Cystobacter virolaceus
  msDNA in, 165
Cytochrome c
  refolding of
    framework hypothesis and,
      611
Cytochrome P-450
  trichloroethylene oxidation by,
    286-88
Cytomegalovirus
  recurrence of
    cellular immunity and, 266
Cytoplasmic membrane
  protein translocation across
    mechanisms of, 619-20

D

Deazaflavin, 14
Decoyinine
  sporulation in Bacillus subtilis
    and, 125-28
Deletion analysis
  yeast KAR1 gene domain
    structure and, 551-52
Dermatophytes
  growth of
    optimal conditions for, 511
  keratinases produced by, 512
Dermatophytoses, 201
  acquisition of, 511
Dibromoethane
  reductive dehalogenation of,
    285
Dichlorethylene
  methanotrophic oxidation of,
    293
Dichloroethane
  reductive dehalogenation of,
    285
Dictyostelium discoideum, 361
Diethylcarbamazine
  for onchocherciasis, 450
α-Difluoromethylornithine
  Leishmania resistant to, 426
Dihydrofolate reductase
  Leishmania drug resistance
    and, 421-22
3-Dimethylsulphoniopropionate
  osmoprotectant activities of,
    584
Dimethylthetin
  osmoprotectant activities of,
    584
Diptera
  baculovirus infection in, 71
DNA
  amplified
    drug resistance genes in,
      418

circular
  in *Leishmania*, 419
cloning of
  polymerase chain reaction
    and, 153-55
hepadnaviral
  in hepatocellular carcinoma,
    489-91
See also kDNA; msDNA
DNA polymerase I
  dsRNA viruses and, 253
  reverse transcriptase activity
    of, 178
DNase I
  dsRNA viruses and, 253
DNA sequence analysis
  yeast *KAR2* gene and, 557
DNA target sequences
  quantification of
    polymerase chain reaction
      and, 149-50
DNA transvection vectors
  for *Leishmania*, 418
Douglas-fir tussock moth
  baculovirus insecticide for, 74
Drosophila melanogaster
  ninA gene of
    coding for cyclophilin, 617
Drug resistance
  in *Leishmania*, 418
  mechanisms of, 420-21
Drug resistance genes
  in amplified DNA, 418
dsRNA viruses, 253-59
Duck hepatitis B virus, 478
  homology with other hepadna-
    viruses, 479-82
  infection due to, 489
  transmission of, 485

E

Ectothiorhodospira halochloris
  export systems of, 588
  osmoregulation in, 586
Edwardsiella tarda
  msDNA and, 165
Eimeria
  virus-like particles in, 253
Eimeria maxima
  oocysts and sporozoites of
    RNA viruses in, 260
Eimeria necatrix
  oocysts and sporozoites of
    RNA viruses in, 260
Eimeria stiedae
  sporozoites of
    dsRNA virus in, 260
Electrostatic interactions
  protein stability and, 608-9
Endoplasmic membrane
  protein translocation across
    mechanisms of, 619-20

Ensley, B. D., 283-97
Entamoeba
  virus-like particles in, 252
Entamoeba histolytica
  virus-like particles in, 252
Enterobacteriaceae
  osmoprotectant activities for
    compounds with, 584
Enterobius vermicularis
  ivermectin activity against,
    448
Enterococcus hirae
  penicillin-resistant, 60
Epstein-Barr virus
  reactivation of, 276
  recurrence of
    cellular immunity and, 266
Equine infectious anemia virus,
    241
Erwinia amylovora
  msDNA and, 165
Escherichia coli
  carbon catabolite control in,
    108
  glycine betaine aldehyde de-
    hydrogenase of
      purification of, 597
  groE operon of, 303
  heat-shock proteins in
    regulation of, 614
  kdpABC operon of, 592-93
  membrane-derived oligosac-
    charides in, 588
  msDNA in, 164-65
  outer membranes of
    stretch-activated channels
      in, 580
  P and type 1 pili of, 384-87
  physiology of
    GroE proteins and, 311-14
  ProP transport system of,
    572-73, 597
  protein translocation in
    cytosolic protein SecB and,
      621-23
  proU operon of, 593-96
  retrons in, 180
  thioredoxins in, 624-25
  trigger factor in, 623
  type 1 pili of
    binding specificities of,
      400-1
    subunit polymerization and,
      396
Escherichia coli K-12
  ompF and *ompC* genes of
    expression of, 589-92
17-β-Estradiol
  tissue phase of *Candida im-
    mitis* and, 515
Ethyl methane sulfonate
  plant nodulation mutants and,
    357

Eukaryotes
  endoplasmic membrane in
    protein translocation across,
      619-20
  retroelements in, 164

F

Factor 342, 14-15
Fasciola hepatica
  ivermectin activity against,
    464
Fayet, O., 301-21
Ferredoxin, 5-7
Fever
  herpesvirus reactivation and,
    276
Filarial infection
  ivermectin for, 461-64
Filariasis
  lymphatic
    ivermectin for, 463-64
    ivermectin safety and
      tolerability in, 465-67
Fisher, S. H., 107-29
FK506
  receptor proteins for, 618
Flavin adenine dinucleotide, 6
Flexibacter elegans
  msDNA in, 165
Formaldehyde
  methanogenesis from, 15
Formaldehyde activation factor,
    15
Formylation
  coenzyme of, 16
Formylmethanofuran, 19-20
Formylmethanofuran de-
    hydrogenase, 19
Framework hypothesis, 611
Fungal disease
  cellular resistance to, 517-31
  genetic predisposition to, 513-
    15
  host factors affecting, 513-16
  host-parasite interactions in,
    510-16
  susceptibility to
    hormonal factors in, 515-16
Fungi
  natural resistance to, 509-31
  pathogenic
    barriers to infection with,
      516-17
  retroelements in, 164

G

Gallionella, 21
Gas chromatography
  microbial screening and, 100

Gene amplification
  in *Leishmania*, 417-39
  frequency of, 429
  mechanism of, 433-36
  role in biology and evolution, 436-39
  protooncogene expression and, 491
Gene probes
  creation of
    polymerase chain reaction and, 153-55
Geodermatophilus, 23-24
Georgopoulos, C., 301-21
Ghuysen, J.-M., 37-60
Giardia lamblia
  dsRNA viruses in, 253, 255-58
Giardiavirus, 255-58
  comparison with mycoviruses, 258-59
Glucanase genes
  developmental regulation if, 355
Gluconate
  metabolism in *Bacillus subtilis*, 115
Glutamate
  osmoprotectant activities of, 584
Glutamate synthase
  Bacillus subtilis ammonia assimilation systems and, 123-24
Glutamine synthetase
  Bacillus subtilis ammonia assimilation systems and, 120-23
  nodule-specific, 355
Glycine betaine aldehyde dehydrogenase
  Escherichia coli
    purification of, 597
Glycosyltransferase
  Leishmania resistant to, 425
Gram-negative bacteria
  periplasmic space in
    osmotic regulation of, 577
Granados, R. R., 69-85
Granulosis viruses, 70-71
Gresshoff, P. M., 345-70
gRNA, 335-37
  characteristics of, 335
  coding sequences of, 335-37
  models of, 339
GroE chaperonins
  action of
    model for, 317-21
  substrates of, 314-16
GroE genes
  bacteriophage morphogenesis and, 308-11

GroEL proteins
  evolutionary conservation of, 305-8
GroE proteins, 303-5
  Escherichia coli physiology and, 311-14
GroES proteins
  evolutionary conservation of, 305-8
Ground squirrel hepatitis virus, 478
  homology with other hepadnaviruses, 479-82
  infection due to, 487-88
Guanidine hydrochloride
  type 1 pili and, 396-97
Guide RNA
  See gRNA
Gypsy moth
  baculovirus insecticide for, 74

H

Haemophilus influenzae
  type b pili of
    assembly of, 388
Hanson, A. D., 569-97
Heat-shock proteins
  Escherichia coli
    regulation of, 614
Helminth infection
  combined chemotherapy for, 449
  ivermectin safety and tolerability in, 465-67
Hemagglutination
  bacterial-mediated, 384
Hepadnaviral DNA
  in hepatocellular carcinoma, 489-91
Hepadnaviruses
  gene products of, 478-82
  hepatocellular carcinoma and, 475-99
  infection due to
    nonneoplastic disease and, 483-85
  molecular structure of, 478-82
  oncogenesis in experimental systems related to, 495-97
  replication of, 482-83
Hepatitis
  non-A, non-B, 486
Hepatitis B, 271
Hepatitis B virus
  homology with other hepadnaviruses, 479-82
  infection in chimpanzees, 486
  molecular structure of, 478-82
  surface antigen of, 485-86
  transmission of, 477

Hepatitis C virus
  hepatocellular carcinoma and, 486
Hepatitis V virus
  surface antigen of, 476
Hepatocarcinogenesis
  insertional mutagenesis and, 492-93
  retinoic acid receptor and, 493
Hepatocellular carcinoma
  hepadnaviral DNA in, 489-91
  hepadnaviruses and, 475-99
Hepatoma
  hepatitis B virus infection and, 484
Herpes simplex viruses
  reactivation of
    disease transmission and, 266
Herpesviruses
  carcinogenicity of, 476
  latency of, 271-72
  reactivation infections due to
    features of, 270
  reactivation of, 276-77
    disease transmission and, 266
Hexane monooxygenases
  trichloroethylene oxidation and, 295
High-performance liquid chromatography
  microbial screening and, 100
Hippicurase, 3
Histidine
  metabolism in *Bacillus subtilis*, 119
Histoplasma capsulatum, 190
  chemical defenses to, 516
  complement fixation by, 519
  compromised host and, 511
  microconidia and yeast of
    alveolar macrophages and, 522
  natural killer cells and, 527
Histoplasmosis
  acquisition of, 511
Homeostasis
  prokaryotic osmoregulation and, 571-73
Hookworm infection
  ivermectin activity against, 446-47
Hormones
  susceptibility to mycotic disease and, 515-16
Hultgren, S. J., 383-408
Human immunodeficiency virus-1
  gene expression in infected cells, 227-32

mRNAs of, 232-36
as prototypic complex retrovirus, 240-43
replication of, 219-43
 cellular transcription factors
  and, 225-27
 cycle of, 223-40
 proviral synthesis and integration in, 223-25
 virion assembly and release
  in, 239-40
RNA expression patterns in,
 236-39
Hydrogen
 interspecies transfer of, 8-10
 methanogenesis from
  enzymology of, 17-20
Hydrogen bonding
 protein stability and, 609
Hydrophobic effect
 protein stability and, 609
Hydroxyproline-rich glycoproteins, 355
 nodulin gene coding for, 356
Hymenolepsis diminuta
 ivermectin activity against,
  464
Hymenoptera
 baculovirus infection in, 71
Hypotension
 ivermectin therapy and, 465

I

Immunity
 cellular
  herpesvirus transmission
   and, 266
 host-acquired specific
  Candida albicans and, 209
Immunocompromised host
 candidiasis and, 187-88
Immunosuppression
 herpesvirus reactivation and,
  276
Inclusion bodies
 protein folding and, 615-17
Inouye, M., 163-84
Inouye, S., 163-84
Insecticides
 baculovirus
  environment and, 80-81
  field-release testing of, 81-
   83
 detection of
  bio-assays and, 100
Insects
 baculorvirus infection and
  replication in, 71-74
 retroelements in, 164
Insertional mutagenesis
 hepatocarcinogenesis and,
  492-93

Intestinal nematodes
 ivermectin activity against,
  446-49
Introns
 retroelements in, 164
Isoptera
 baculovirus infection in, 71
Itch mite
 ivermectin activity against,
  464
Ivermectin, 445-69
 current distribution of, 468-69
 for filarial infections, 461-64
 for intestinal nematodes, 446-
  49
 for onchocerciasis, 449-61
 safety in humans, 465-68

K

kDNA, 328-32
 maxicircles in, 329
 minicircles in, 329-31
 mutations in, 331-32
Keratitis
 punctate
  ivermectin therapy and, 465
Killer yeast virus
 dsRNA viruses compared,
  258-59
Kinesin
 yeast KAR3 gene and, 553-54
Kinetoplast DNA
 See kDNA
Klebiella pneumoniae
 osmoregulation in, 585
Klebsiella aerogens
 msDNA and, 165
Klebsiella pneumoniae
 type 1 pili of
  binding specificities of,
   400-1
 type 3 pili of
  assembly of, 388

L

β-Lactamases, 37-60
 pre-folding and export of,
  315-16
Lactose
 metabolism in Staphylococcus
  aureus, 119
Leghemoglobin
 soybean symbiosis and, 355
Legionella pneumophila
 detection of
  polymerase chain reaction
   and, 149
Legume nodulation, 345-70
 in absence of Rhizobium,
  368-70

autoregulation of, 362-68
 bacterial symbiont and, 348-
  54
 control of, 361-62
 developmental regulation of,
  354-57
Leishmania
 chromosomal mutations in
  neutral, 428-29
 drug resistance in
  dihydrofolate reductase-
   thymidylate synthase
   and, 421-22
  glycosyltransferase and,
   425
  H region and, 422-25
  mechanisms of, 420-21
  tunicamycin and, 425
 extrachromosomal amplified
  DNAs in
  structure of, 429-33
 gene amplification in, 417-39
  frequency of, 429
  mechanism of, 433-36
  role in biology and evolution, 436-39
 life stages of, 419
 nonfunctional amplified DNAs
  in, 428-29
 small linear DNAs in, 427-28
 virus-like particles in, 252-53
Leishmania braziliensis
 RNA viruses of, 259-60
 small linear DNAs in, 427-28
Leishmania braziliensis
  guyanensis
 virus-like particles in, 253
Leishmania donovani
 antimonial resistance in
  reversal of, 437
 gene amplification in
  agents causing, 424-25
 methotrexate-resistant, 420
 small linear DNAs in, 427-28
Leishmania genome, 419
Leishmania hertigi
 virus-like particles in, 252
Leishmania major
 chromosome 2 in
  miniexon array in, 427
 drug resistance in
  gene amplification and, 420
  H region and, 421
  H region amplification in,
   422
  multiple-drug resistance
   genes in, 423
  R region amplification in, 431
  small linear DNAs in, 427-28
Leishmania mexicana
 small linear DNAs in, 427-28
Leishmania mexicana ama-
  zonensis, 260

arsenite-resistant
  chromosomal changes in,
    433
methotrexate-resistant, 420
Leishmaniasis, 436
Leishmania tarentolae
  drug resistance in
    H region and, 421
  grna coding sequences of,
    335-37
  H amplification of
    multiple-drug resistance
      genes in, 423
  methotrexate-resistant, 420
  minicircle kinetic complexity
    in, 329
  minicircle sequence organiza-
    tion in, 331
  RNA editing in, 333
  T amplification in, 426
Leishmania tropica
  D amplification of, 426
Lentiviruses, 242
Lepidoptera
  baculovirus infection in, 71
Leptothrix, 21
Leukocytes
  polymorphonuclear
    host defense against myco-
      tic agents and, 516-22
Leukoencephalopathy
  progressive multifocal, 271
Liver disease
  hepatitis B virus and, 483-85
Loa loa
  ivermectin activity against,
    464
Lymantria dispar
  baculovirus insecticide for,
    74
Lymphatic filariasis
  ivermectin for, 463-64
  ivermectin safety and
    tolerability in, 465-67
Lymphoma
  Burkitt's
    chromosomal translocations
      in, 493
  T-cell
    murine leukemia virus-
      inducing, 493

M

Macrophages
  alveolar
    host defense against myco-
      tic agents and, 522-24
  host defense against mycotic
    agents and, 524-26
Mammals
  retroelements in, 164

Mansonella ozzardi
  ivermectin activity against,
    464
Mansonella perstans
  ivermectin activity against,
    464
Marion, P. L., 475-99
Mass spectometry
  microbial screening and, 100
Maxicircles, 329
2-Mercaptoethanesulfonic acid,
    10-11
7-Mercaptoheptanoylthreonine
  phosphate, 17
Methane monooxygenase
  trichloroethylene oxidation by,
    292-95
Methanobacillus omelianskii
  methanogenesis in, 7-8
Methanobacterium thermoauto-
  trophicum, 18, 24
Methanobrevibacter ruminantium
  growth factor required by, 11
Methanococcus jannaschii, 24
Methanococcus voltae, 24
Methanofuran, 16
Methanogenesis, 7-8
  enzymology of, 17-20
Methanogenium cariacii, 24
Methanogenium marisnigri, 24
Methanogenium thermophilum,
    24
Methanogens
  perchloroethylene dechlorina-
    tion and, 285
Methanomicroboium mobile
  growth factor required by,
    17
Methanopterin, 14-15
Methanosarcina barkeri
  methanofuran of, 16
Methanosarcina thermophila
  osmoregulation in, 586
Methanospirillum hungatei, 25
Methanotrophs
  trichloroethylene degradation
    due to, 292-93
Methenyl-tetra-
  hydromethanopterin, 15
Methicillin
  bacterial resistance to, 60
Methotrexate
  Leishmania resistant to, 420-
    25
4-Methoxybenzoate monooxyge-
  nase
  trichloroethylene oxidation
    and, 295
Methylcobalamin
  reduction to methane, 8
Methylmonas methanica
  dichlorethylene oxidation due
    to, 293

Methylosinus trichosporium
  dichlorethylene oxidation due
    to, 293
Microbial screening, 89-103
  primary, 98-102
Microorganisms
  commercial applications of,
    92
  genetically engineered
    detection with polymerase
      chain reaction, 147-48
Milbemycins
  detection of, 100
Minicircles, 329-31
Miniexon
  in Leishmania, 427
Mitochondria
  GroEL-related proteins in,
    303
  rRNA of
    maxicircles encoding, 329
  trypanosomatid
    RNA editing in, 327-42
Moenomycin
  peptide crosslinking and, 56
Molecular chaperones
  bonding to nascent
    polypeptides, 613-15
  interactions with unfolded
    proteins, 625-28
Molten globule, 611
Monocytes
  host defense against mycotic
    agents and, 524-26
Moraxella bovis
  type 4 pilins of, 401-2
mRNA
  partially edited, 337-40
  quantification of
    polymerase chain reaction
      and, 150-52
msDNA, 163-75
  biosynthesis of, 171-75
    pathway of, 172-73
    reverse transcriptase and,
      171-72
    termination of, 175
  discovery of, 164-65
  features of, 168-70
  genetic locus of, 170-71
  structure of, 166-68
Mung bean
  nodulation of, 350
Murine leukemia virus
  T-cell lymphomas induced by,
    493
Murphy, J. W., 509-31
Mutagenesis
  insertional
    hepatocarcinogenesis and,
      492-93
Mycetoma
  acquisition of, 511

Mycobacterium vaccae JOB5
  propane monooxygenase system of
    vinyl chloride oxidation and, 295
Mycotic disease
  cellular resistance to, 517-31
  genetic predisposition to, 513-15
  host factors affecting, 513-16
  host-parasite interactions in, 510-16
  susceptibility to
    hormonal factors in, 515-16
Mycoviruses
  dsRNA viruses compared, 258-59
Myeloperoxidase deficiency
  opportunistic mycotic infection and, 520
Myxobacter AL-1 protease I, 23
Myxobacter AL-1 protease II, 23
Myxococcus coralloides
  msDNA in, 165
Myxococcus xanthus
  msDNA in, 164-65
  retrons in, 180

N

Naegleria
  virus-like particles in, 252
Nalidixic acid
  msDNA biosynthesis and, 172
Nannocystis exedens
  msDNA in, 165
Natural effector cells
  interactions of, 531
  pathogenic fungi and, 530-31
Natural killer cells
  pathogenic fungi and, 527-30
Necator americanus
  ivermectin activity against, 446-47
Neisseria gonorrhoeae
  msDNA and, 165
  penicillin and, 59
  pili of, 402-5
  type 4 pili of
    biogenesis model for, 406
  type 4 pilins of, 401-2
Neisseria meningitidis
  penicillin-resistant, 59-60
Nematodes
  intestinal
    ivermectin activity against, 446-49
Neutropenia
  opportunistic mycotic infection and, 520

Neutrophils
  Candida albicans hyphae and, 191
Nicotinamide adenine dinucleotide, 6
Nikkomycins
  detection of, 100
Nilsson, B., 607-29
Nitrate
  legume nodulation and, 361-62
Nitrogen
  metabolism in *Bacillus subtilis*, 119-24
Nitropropane dioxygenase
  trichloroethylene oxidation and, 295
Nitrosomonas europaea
  ammonia monooxygenase system of, 288
Nodulin genes, 355-56
Normark, S., 383-408
Nuclear magnetic resonance
  spectrometry
    microbial screening and, 100
Nuclear polyhedoris viruses
  cellular infection cycle of, 72
Nuclear polyhedrosis viruses, 70
Nucleic acids
  environmental
    isolation for polymerase chain reaction, 142-43

O

Onchocerca cervicalis
  ivermectin activity against, 450
Onchocerca lienalis
  ivermectin activity against, 455
Onchocerca volvulus
  ivermectin activity against, 456, 459
Onchocerciasis, 446, 449-61
  ivermectin safety and tolerability in, 465-67
Oncogenesis
  hepadnavirus-associated, 477
  hepadnavirus-related in experimental systems, 495-97
  protooncogene activation and, 491-92
Oncoviruses, 242
Orgyia pseudotsugata
  baculovirus insecticide for, 74
Ornithine decarboxylase
  Leishmania drug resistance and, 426
Orthoptera
  baculovirus infection in, 71

Osmoprotectants
  environmental sources of, 586-87
Osmoregulation
  prokaryotic, 569-97
    genes and proteins in, 588-97
    mechanisms of, 571-81
    physiology of, 581-88
Oxalurate
  phosphorolysis of, 22
Oxamate
  oxalurate phosphorolysis and, 22
Oxamic transcarbamylase
  allantoin degradation and, 22
Oxygenases
  aromatic
    trichloroethylene oxidation by, 288-92

P

Panencephalitis
  subacute sclerosing, 271
PapD proteins
  pilus assembly and, 388-91
  structure-function properties of, 391-92
Papillomaviruses
  carcinogenicity of, 476
Paracoccidioides brasiliensis, 190
  complement fixation by, 519
  compromised host and, 511
  mammalian steroid hormones and, 515
  natural killer cells and, 527
  yeast of
    alveolar macrophages and, 522
Paracoccidioidomycosis
  acquisition of, 511
  occurrence of
    estrogen and, 515
Parasponia
  nodulation of, 347
Pathogens
  detection of
    polymerase chain reaction and, 148-49
Pea
  nodulation mutants of, 357
  nodulation of, 347
Peanut
  nodulation of, 347
Penicillin
  bacterial resistance to, 59-60
  peptide crosslinking and, 56
Penicillin-binding proteins, 37-60
  high-Mr, 54-60
  low-Mr, 45-47

Pentavalent antimony complexes
for *Leishmania* infection, 418,
437
Perchloroethylene
dechlorination of
methanogens and, 285
Periplasm
osmoregulation of, 588
Pest control
baculoviruses as agents for,
69-85
Pesticides
viral
genetically enhanced, 76-
78
P-glycoprotein genes
methotrexate resistance in
Leishmania and, 424
Phagocytic cells
mycotic agents and, 518-27
Phagocytosis
Candida albicans hyphae and,
191
Pili, 383-408
Escherichia coli P and type
1, 384-87
Neisseria gonorrhoeae, 402-5
P and type 1
structure of, 393-98
postsecretional assembly of,
387-93
Pseudomonas aeruginosa, 406
subunit polymerization, 392-
93
type 4
assembly of, 401-6
biogenesis model for, 406
Vibrio cholerae TCP, 405-6
Pilins
type 4
expression of, 401-2
Pilus adhesins
receptor binding and assembly
domains of, 398-401
Plant nodulation mutants, 357-
361
Plants
retroelements in, 164
Plasmids
retroelements in, 164
Plasmodium
virus-like particles in, 252
Plasmodium falciparum
ivermectin activity against,
464
Polyhedrin, 70
Polymerase chain reaction, 137-
56
analysis of ribosomal RNA
sequences and, 152-53
detection of genetically engineered microorganisms
and, 147-48

detection of indicator organisms and pathogens and,
148-49
DNA cloning and, 153-55
gene probe creation and, 153-
55
isolation of environmental
nucleic acids for, 142-43
products of
detection of, 144-47
quantification of, 149-52
varicella-zoster virus latency
and, 273
Polymorphonuclear leukocytes
host defense against mycotic
agents and, 518-22
Polypeptides
nascent
molecular chaperones binding to, 613-15
proteolytic degradation in
vivo, 618-19
Postural hypotension
ivermectin therapy and, 465
Praziquantel
for helminth infection, 449
Pregnancy
coccidioidomycosis and, 515
ivermectin therapy and, 467
Preocene monooxygenases
trichloroethylene oxidation
and, 295
Preproteins, 610
signal sequences of, 620-21
Primaquine
Leishmania major selection
with, 422
Progesterone
tissue phase of *Candida immitis* and, 515
Progressive multifocal
leukoencephalopathy, 271
Prokaryotes
cytoplasmic membrane in
protein translocation across,
619-20
osmoregulation in, 569-97
genes and proteins in, 588-
97
mechanisms of, 571-81
physiology of, 581-88
Proline isomerization
protein folding and, 617
Prolyl isomerase
protein folding and, 617-18
Propane monooxygenase
trichloroethylene oxidation by,
295-97
Propedtides, 610-11
Protein disulfide isomerase
protein folding and, 623-25
Protein folding, 607-29
aggregation and, 615-17

inclusion bodies and, 615-17
intracellular, 613-18
from nascent chain in vivo,
612-13
process of, 611-12
prolyl isomerase and, 617-18
protein disulfide isomerase
and, 623-25
protein secretion and, 619-25
thioredoxin and, 623-25
translational pausing and, 628
Protein folding pathway, 611
Proteins
GroE, 303-5
Escherichia coli physiology
and, 311-14
GroEL
evolutionary conservation
of, 305-8
GroES
evolutionary conservation
of, 305-8
heat-shock
regulation of, 614
PapD
pilus assembly and, 388-91
structure-function properties
of, 391-92
penicillin-binding, 37-60
high-Mr, 54-60
low-Mr, 45-47
prokaryotic osmoregulation
and, 588-97
stability of
chain entropy and, 609-10
electrostatic interactions
and, 608-9
hydrogen bonding and, 609
hydrophobic effect and, 609
van der Waals interactions
and, 609
unfolded
interactions with molecular
chaperones, 625-28
See also specific protein
Proteolysis
in vivo, 618-19
Proteus mirabilis
msDNA and, 165
Prothrombin time
ivermectin therapy and, 465
Protooncogenes
activation of
oncogenesis and, 491-92
Protozoa
viruses of, 251-62
Pseudomonas aeruginosa
msDNA and, 165
PAK pili of
subunit polymerization and,
396
pathogenic genes in
osmotic control of, 597

pili of, 406
type 4 pili of
biogenesis model for, 406
type 4 pilins of, 401-2
Pseudomonas cepacia
detection of
polymerase chain reaction
and, 147-48
Pseudomonas mendocina
toluene oxidation pathway of,
290-91
Pseudomonas putida strain F1
trichloroethylene oxidation by,
289
Pseudorabies virus, 272
Psychrophiles
isolation of, 97
Punctate keratitis
ivermectin therapy and, 465
Pyruvate
synthesis of, 5-6
Pyruvate oxidation factor, 4

Q

Quaternary amines
osmoprotectant activities of,
584

R

Restriction endonucleases
dsRNA viruses and, 253
Retinoblastoma
gene RB-1 and, 493
Retinoic acid receptor
hepatocarcinogenesis and, 493
Retinoids
cellular proliferation and, 493
Retroelements, 164
Retrons, 178-83
chromosomal integration site
of, 180-81
function of, 183
phylogenetic relationships of,
181-83
structure and distribution of,
178-89
Retrotransposons
retroelements in, 164
Retroviruses
carcinogenicity of, 476
life cycle of, 221-23
retroelements in, 164
Reverse hybridization
polymerase chain reaction
and, 146-47
Reverse transcriptase, 175-78
codon usage of, 178
enzymatic specificity of, 178
genetic locus of, 175-76
msDNA biosynthesis and,
171-72

structural diversity of, 176-78
Reverse transcription
hepadnavirus replication and,
483
Rhizobium
β-glucans in, 588
nodulation in absence of,
368-70
symbiotic genes of, 348-50
Rhizobium meliloti
osmoregulation in, 585
Rhizobium strain NGR234
legume nodulation and, 346
Rhizopus oryzae
chemotactic factors produced
by, 519
Rhodomicrobium vannielii, 21
Rhodopseudomonas palustris, 22
Rhodopseudomonas sphaeroides,
21
Rhodospirillum rubrum, 21
Rifampicin
giardiavirus and, 257
msDNA biosynthesis and, 172
RNA
See also dsRNA; gRNA;
mRNA; rRNA
RNA editing, 327-42
consequences of, 334-35
developmental regulation of,
340-41
transcript-region specific, 332-
34
RNA polymerase II
retrovirus replication and, 222
RNase A
refolding of
framework hypothesis and,
611
RNA sequences
ribosomal
polymerase chain reaction
and, 152-53
RNA viruses
of *Leishmania braziliensis*,
259-60
Rose, M. D., 539-64
Roseola infantum
transmission of, 266
rRNA
mitochondrial
maxicircles encoding, 329

S

Saccharomyces cerevisiae
effects of trichloroethylene
on, 286
nuclear fusion in
assays for, 545-46
BIK1 gene in, 555-56
CDC28 gene in, 560-61
CDC34 gene in, 560-61

CDC37 gene in, 560-61
CDC4 gene in, 558
CIK genes in, 560
CIN1 gene in, 559-60
genes required for, 549-61
KAR1 gene in, 549-52
KAR2 gene in, 556-58
KAR3 gene in, 552-55
KEM genes in, 558-59
models for, 561-63
mutations blocking, 544-45
Saccharomyces cervisiae
nuclear fusion in, 539-64
pathway of, 540-49
Salmonella typhimurium
β-lactamase of, 49
hypoosmotic shock and, 588
msDNA and, 165
osmoregulation in, 585
pathogenic genes in
osmotic control of, 597
proU operon of, 593-96
Sarcina ventriculi, 22
Scabies
ivermectin activity against,
464
Schistosoma mansoni
ivermectin activity against,
464
Sediment
isolation of nucleic acids
from, 143
trichloroethylene metabolism
in, 284-85
Serratia marcescens
msDNA and, 165
Sesbania
nodulation of, 347
Sherker, A. H., 475-99
Shigella dysenteriae
msDNA and, 165
pathogenic genes in
osmotic control of, 597
Signal sequences
protein folding and, 620-21
Siratro
nodulation of, 350
Sodium arsenite
*Leishmania mexicana ama-
zonensis* and, 422
Soil
isolation of nucleic acids
from, 143
trichloroethylene metabolism
in, 284-85
Solutes
compatible
bacterial, 582-83
Sonenshein, A. L., 107-29
Soybean
nodulation of, 347, 350, 362
inhibition of, 363
nitrate and, 361-62

nodulation mutants of, 357
nodule-specific glutamine synthetase from, 355
Soybean symbiosis
nodulins and, 355
Sphaerotilus natans, 22-23
Sporothrix schenckii
compromised host and, 511
Sporotrichosis
acquisition of, 511
Staphylococcus auerus
prenuclease of
signal sequence of, 621
Staphylococcus aureus
β-lactamase of, 39-40
lactose metabolism in, 119
methicillin-resistant, 60
Starch
metabolism in *Bacillus subtilis*, 115-17
Steele, D. B., 89-103
Steffan, R. J., 137-56
Stigmatella aurantiaca
msDNAs in, 164-65
Stowers, M. D., 89-103
Straus, S. E., 265-78
Streptococcus allantoicus, 22
Streptomyces albus
β-lactamase of, 39-40
Streptomyces avermitilis
avermectins produced by,
446
Streptomyces venezuelae
carbon catabolite control in,
108
Strongyloides stercoralis
ivermectin activity against,
448-49
Strongyloidiasis
ivermectin for, 449
Stuart, K., 327-42
Subacute sclerosing pan-
encephalitis, 271
Sucrose
metabolism in *Bacillus subtilis*, 113-15
Sucrose synthetase
soybean symbiosis and, 355
Sugar phosphotransferase system
phophoenolpyruvate-dependent
in *Bacillus subtilis*, 109-12
Sulfate esters
osmoprotectant activities of,
584
Sulfonium compounds
osmoprotectant activities of,
584

T

Taurine betaine
osmoprotectant activities of,
584

T cells
helper
human immunodeficiency
virus-1 replication and,
223-25
Terbinafine
Leishmania major selection
with, 422
Tertiary template, 611
Tetrahydrocorphin, 16
Tetrahydromethanopterin
methanogenesis and, 15
Tetranactin
detection of, 100
Thermophiles
isolation of, 97
Thioredoxin
protein folding and, 623-
25
Thymidylate synthase
Leishmania drug resistance
and, 421-22
Toluene dioxygenase
trichloroethylene degradation
by, 289-90
Topoisomerase I
hepadnaviral integration and,
490-91
Transgenic mice
hepadnavirus-related
oncogenesis in, 496-
97
Trauma
herpesvirus reactivation and,
276
Trehalose
osmoprotectant activities of,
584
Trichenellosis
ivermectin activity against,
464
Trichinella spiralis
avermectins and, 464
Trichloroethylene
ammonia monooxygenase
oxidation of, 288
aromatic oxygenase oxidation
of, 288-92
cytochrome P-450 oxidation
of, 286-88
metabolism of, 283-97
anaerobic, 284-86
methane monooxygenase oxidation of, 292-95
propane monooxygenase oxidation of, 295-97
Trichodesmium theibautii
nitrogen fixation genes of
amplification of, 154-
55
Trichomonas vaginalis
dsRNA in, 252-53
dsRNA viruses of, 253-55

Trichomonas vaginalis virus,
253-55
comparison with mycoviruses,
258-59
identification of, 253
Trichophyton mentagrophytes,
201
Trichoptera
baculovirus infection in, 71
Trichuris trichiura
ivermectin activity against,
447-48
Trigger factor, 623
Trypanosoma brucei
gRNA coding sequences of,
335-37
minicircle kinetic complexity
in, 329
minicircle sequence organization in, 331
RNA editing in, 332-33
Trypanosoma equinum
kDNA deletions in, 331
Trypanosoma equiperdum
kDNA deletions in, 331
Trypanosoma evansi
kDNA deletions in, 331
Trypanosomatids
mitochondria of
RNA editing in, 327-42
Tunicamycin
Leishmania resistant to, 425

U

Ultraviolet light
herpesvirus reactivation and,
276
Urease
in *Bacillus subtilis*, 123
Ureidoglycolate synthetase
allantoin degradation and, 22
Uricase
soybean symbiosis and, 355
Ustilago maydis virus
dsRNA viruses compared,
258-59

V

Vaginal candidiasis
hormones influencing, 515-16
van der Waals interactions
protein stability and, 609
Varicella, 266
pathogenesis of, 269
Varicella-zoster virus, 265-78
infections due to
animal models of, 270-71
latency of, 272-76
molecular biology of, 267-69
reactivation infections due to
features of, 270

reactivation of, 276-77
Velvetbean caterpillar
   baculovirus insecticide for, 75
Vibrio cholerae
   TCP pili of, 405-6
   Tcp pilin of, 402
   type 4 pili of
      biogenesis model for, 406
Vibrio costicola
   osmoregulation in, 586
Vigna radiata
   nodulation of, 350
Vinblastine
   Leishmania resistance to,
      426
Vinyl chloride
   propane monooxygenase
      oxidation of, 295
Viruses
   budded, 71
   dsRNA, 253-59
   granolosis, 70-71
   nuclear polyhedrosis, 70
      cellular infection cycle of,
         72
   protozoan, 251-62
   RNA
      of *Leishmania braziliensis*,
         259-60

See also specific virus
Visna virus, 241-42

W

Wang, A. L., 251-62
Wang, C. C., 251-62
Water
   isolation of nucleic acids
      from, 142-43
Whipworm infection
   ivermectin activity against,
      447-48
Wilms' tumor, 493
Wiskott-Aldrich syndrome, 273
Wolfe, R. S., 1-28
Wood, H. A., 69-85
Woodchuck hepatitis virus, 477-
   78
   infection due to, 484-85, 487
Wuchereria bancrofti
   ivermectin activity against,
      461-64

X

Xylose
   metabolism in *Bacillus sub-
      tilis*, 115

Y

Yeast
   effects of trichloroethylene
      on, 286
   nuclear fusion in, 539-64
      assays for, 545-46
      BIK1 gene in, 555-56
      CDC28 gene in, 560-61
      CDC34 gene in, 560-61
      CDC37 gene in, 560-61
      CDC4 gene in, 558
      CIK genes in, 560
      CIN1 gene in, 559-60
      genes required for, 549-61
      KAR1 gene in, 549-52
      KAR2 gene in, 556-58
      KAR3 gene in, 552-55
      KEM genes in, 558-59
      models for, 561-63
      mutations blocking, 544-45
      pathway of, 540-49

Z

Zeilstra-Ryalls, J., 301-21
Zoster
   pathogenesis of, 269-70

CUMULATIVE INDEXES

CONTRIBUTING AUTHORS, VOLUMES 41–45

A

Abraham, S. N., 45:383–415
Alano, P., 44:429–49
Almond, J. W., 41:153–80
Anders, R. F., 41:181–208
Anderson, S., 45:607–35
Atlas, R. M., 45:137–61
Auger, E. A., 43:293–316

B

Baltz, R. H., 42:547–74
Barbour, A. G., 44:155–71
Beguin, P., 44:219–48
Benz, R., 42:359–93
Beveridge, T., 43:147–72
Beverley, S. M., 45:417–44
Binns, A. N., 42:575–606
Black, F. L., 41:677–701
Black, L. W., 43:267–92
Blum, P. H., 43:293–316
Boeke, J. D., 43:403–34
Boman, H. G., 41:103–26
Boom, T. V., 43:317–44
Braun, M. M., 44:555–77
Brennan, P. J., 41:645–75
Bruce, M. G., 43:503–36

C

Caetano-Anollés, G., 45:345–82
Campbell, W. C., 45:445–74
Campbell-Burk, S. L., 41:595–615
Carlow, C. K. S., 42:685–716
Caron, F., 43:23–42
Carter, R., 44:429–49
Chambers, T. J., 44:649–88
Chang, K.-P., 44:499–529
Chaudhuri, G., 44:499–529
Cheng, K.-J., 41:435–64
Childers, N., 43:503–36
Compans, R. W., 42:489–516
Coppel, R. L., 41:181–208
Corces, V. G., 43:403–34
Costerton, J. W., 41:435–64
Cozzone, A. J., 42:97–125
Crawford, I. P., 43:567–600
Croen, K. D., 45:265–82
Cronan, J. E., 43:317–44
Cruden, D. L., 41:617–43
Csonka, L. N., 45:569–606
Cullen, B. R., 45:219–50
Cundliffe, E., 43:207–34
Curran, J. W., 44:555–77
Cutler, J. E., 45:187–218

D

Dagley, S., 41:1–23
Dales, S., 44:173–92
Dasgupta, M., 41:435–64
Davis, T. B., 42:685–716
Desrosiers, R. C., 42:607–25
Dick, J. D., 44:249–69
Dybvig, K., 44:81–104

E

Emmons, R. W., 42:49–64
Englund, P. T., 42:339–58
Ensley, B. D., 45:283–99
Epstein, J. S., 43:629–60
Evans, H. J., 41:335–61
Evans, W. C., 42:289–317

F

Fainstein, V., 42:395–419
Farrell, R. L., 41:465–505
Fayet, O., 45:301–25
Firshein, W., 43:89–120
Fisher, S. H., 45:107–35
Fong, D., 44:499–529
Frank, D. W., 44:335–63
Fuchs, G., 42:289–317

G

Galler, R., 44:649–88
Gaylord, H., 41:645–75
Geesey, G. G., 41:435–64
Geesey, G. G., 44:579–602
Georgopoulos, C., 45:301–25
Ghuysen, J.-M., 45:37–67
Gibbs, C. P., 44:451–77
Girard, M., 42:745–63
Granados, R. R., 45:69–87
Gresshoff, P. M., 45:345–82
Grose, C., 44:59–80
Guffanti, A. A., 43:435–64

H

Haas, R., 44:451–602
Hahn, C. S., 44:649–88
Hanson, A. D., 45:569–606
Hanus, F. J., 41:335–61
Hardy, S. J. S., 41:507–41
Harker, A. R., 41:335–61
Heim, J., 41:51–75
Hermansson, M., 41:25–49
Heyward, W. L., 44:555–77
Hochstein, L. I., 42:231–61

Holland, J. J., 41:409–33
Hultgren, S. J., 45:383–415
Hultmark, D., 41:103–26

I

Iandolo, J. J., 43:375–402
Iglewski, B. H., 44:335–63
Inouye, M., 45:163–86
Inouye, S., 45:163–86

J

Jabbar, M. A., 43:465–502
James, W. D., 42:441–64
Joiner, K. A., 42:201–30
Jones, G. W., 41:25–49

K

Kaufman, L., 41:209–25
Keen, N. T., 42:421–40
Kemp, D. J., 41:181–208
Kennedy, C., 41:227–58
Khardori, N., 42:395–419
Kirk, T. K., 41:465–505
Kjelleberg, S., 41:25–49
Kleinkauf, H., 41:259–89
Klier, A. F., 42:65–95
Knackmuss, H.-J., 42:263–87
Kokjohn, T. A., 44:365–94
Kolenbrander, P. E., 42:627–56
Krulwich, T. A., 43:435–64

L

Ladd, T. I., 41:435–64
Lai, M. M. C., 44:303–33
Layton, A. C., 44:625–48
Lidstrom, M. E., 44:27–58
Liras, P., 43:173–206

M

Mårdén, P., 41:25–49
Marion, P. L., 45:475–508
Markovetz, A. J., 41:617–43
Marrie, T. J., 41:435–64
Marrs, B. L., 41:703–26
Martín, J. F., 43:173–206
Matin, A., 43:293–316
Maurelli, A. T., 42:127–50
McConkey, G. A., 44:479–98
McCutchan, T. F., 44:479–98
McGee, Z. A., 41:291–300
McGeoch, D. J., 43:235–66
McGhee, J., 43:503–36

650 CONTRIBUTING AUTHORS

Meighen, E. A., 42:151–76
Meyer, E., 43:23–42
Meyer, T. F., 44:451–77
Miller, L. K., 42:177–99
Miller, R. V., 44:365–94
Misra, T. K., 42:717–43
Moir, A., 44:531–53
Moller-Zinkhan, D., 43:43–68
Monaghan, R. L., 44:271–301
Müller, M., 42:465–88
Murphy, J. W., 45:509–38
Murray, R. G. E., 42:1–34

N

Nayak, D. P., 43:465–502
Newton, A., 44:689–719
Nickel, J. C., 41:435–64
Nilsson, B., 45:607–35
Normark, S., 45:383–415
Novick, R. P., 43:537–66
Nüesch, J., 41:51–75

O

Ohta, N., 44:689–719
Opperdoes, F. R., 41:127–51
Ourisson, G., 41:301–33

P

Palmenberg, A. C., 44:603–23
Papen, H., 41:335–61
Philipp, M., 42:685–716
Pittman, M., 44:1–25
Pizzo, P. A., 42:517–45
Poralla, K., 41:301–33
Prusiner, S. B., 43:345–74

R

Randall, L. L., 41:507–41
Rapoport, G., 42:65–95
Rauch, C. A., 42:339–58
Reineke, W., 42:263–87

Rest, R. F., 43:121–46
Rice, C. M., 44:649–88
Riley, L. W., 41:383–407
Rohmer, M., 41:301–33
Roizman, B., 41:543–71
Rose, M. D., 45:539–67
Roth, R. R., 42:441–64
Russell, S. A., 41:335–61
Ryan, K. A., 42:339–58

S

Sanders, C. C., 41:573–93
Sansonetti, P. J., 42:127–50
Sayler, G. S., 44:625–48
Schlessinger, D., 44:105–29
Schochetman, G., 43:629–60
Schultz, J. E., 43:293–316
Scolnik, P. A., 41:703–26
Sears, A. E., 41:543–71
Seno, E. T., 42:547–74
Setlow, P., 42:319–38
Shafer, W. M., 43:121–46
Shapiro, T. A., 42:339–58
Sherker, A. H., 45:475–508
Shulman, R. G., 41:595–616
Silver, S., 42:717–43
Simpson, L., 41:363–82
Singer, B., 41:677–701
Siporin, C., 43:601–28
Smith, C. A., 41:77–101
Smith, D. A., 44:531–53
Smith, H., 43:1–22
Sonenshein, A. L., 45:107–35
Spormann, A. M., 43:43–68
Srivastava, A. K., 44:105–29
Standard, P. G., 41:209–25
Staskawicz, B., 42:421–40
Steele, D. B., 45:89–106
Steffan, R. J., 45:137–61
Steinhauer, D. A., 41:409–33
Stephens, E. B., 42:489–516
Stirling, D. I., 44:27–58
Storey, D. G., 44:335–63
Storey, N., 42:685–716

Stowers, M. D., 45:89–106
Straus, S. E., 45:265–82
Strauss, E. G., 42:657–83
Strauss, J. H., 42:657–83
Stuart, K., 45:327–44
Sutherland, I. W., 39:243–70

T

Thauer, R. K., 43:43–68
Thom, J. R., 41:507–41
Thomas, C. M., 41:77–101
Thomashow, M. F., 42:575–606
Tkacz, J. S., 44:271–301
Tomlinson, G. A., 42:231–61
Toukdarian, A., 41:227–58
Treichler, H.-J., 41:51–75
Tyrrell, D. A. J., 42:35–47

V

van der Waaij, D., 43:69–88
Vining, L. C., 44:395–427
von Döhren, H., 41:259–89

W

Wales, M. E., 44:193–218
Walsh, T. J., 42:517–45
Wang, A. L., 45:251–63
Wang, C. C., 45:251–63
Waters, A. P., 44:479–98
White, D. C., 44:579–602
Wick, M. J., 44:335–63
Wild, J. R., 44:193–218
Winkler, H., 44:131–53
Wolfe, R. S., 45:1–35
Wood, H. A., 45:69–87
Woods, M. L. Jr., 41:291–300

Z

Zeilstra-Ryalls, J., 45:301–25
Zuber, M., 41:335–61
Zuck, T. F., 43:629–60

CHAPTER TITLES, VOLUMES 41–45

PREFATORY CHAPTERS
Lessons from Biodegradation   S. Dagley   41:1–23
A Structured Life   R. G. E. Murray   42:1–34
The Mounting Interest in Bacterial and Viral
    Pathogenicity   H. Smith   43:1–22
A Life With Biological Products   M. Pittman   44:1–25
My Kind of Biology   R. S. Wolfe   45:1–35

DIVERSITY AND SYSTEMATICS
Microbial Ecology of the Cockroach Gut   D. L. Cruden, A. J. Markovetz   41:617–43
Intergeneric Coaggregation Among Human
    Oral Bacteria and Ecology of Dental Plaque P. E. Kolenbrander   42:627–56
Rickettsia Species (as Organisms)   H. H. Winkler   44:131–53
General Microbiology of recA: Environmental
    and Evolutionary Significance   R. V. Miller, T. A. Kokjohn   44:365–94
Variation and Control of Protein Expression
    in Neisseria   T. F. Meyer, C. P. Gibbs, R. Haas   44:451–77
Biochemical Diversity of Trichloroethylene
    Metabolism   B. D. Ensley   45:283–99
The Universally Conserved GroE (Hsp60)
    Chaperonins   J. Zeilstra-Ryalls, O. Fayet,
                                                    C. Georgopoulos   45:301–25

MORPHOLOGY, ULTRASTRUCTURE, AND DIFFERENTIATION
Prokaryotic Hopanoids and Other
    Polyterpenoid Sterol Surrogates   G. Ourisson, M. Rohmer, K.
                                                    Poralla   41:301–33
Bacterial Biofilms in Nature and Disease   J. W. Costerton, K.-J. Cheng,
                                                    G. G. Geesey, T. I. Ladd,
                                                    J. C. Nickel, M. Dasgupta,
                                                    T. J. Marrie   41:435–64
Microbial Ecology of the Cockroach Gut   D. L. Cruden, A. J. Markovetz   41:617–43
Small, Acid-Soluble Spore Proteins of
    Bacillus Species: Structure, Synthesis,
    Genetics, Function, and Degradation   P. Setlow   42:319–38
Role of Cellular Design in Bacterial Metal
    Accumulation and Mineralization   T. Beveridge   43:147–72
Structural Domains and Organizational
    Conformation Involved in the Sorting and
    Transport of Influenza Virus
    Transmembrane Proteins   D. P. Nayak, M. A. Jabbar   43:465–502
Structure, Function, and Regulation of
    Pseudomonas aeruginosa Exotoxin A   M. J. Wick, D. W. Frank,
                                                    D. G. Storey, B. H. Iglewski   44:335–63
Sexual Differentiation in Malaria Parasites   P. Alano, R. Carter   44:429–49
Molecular Determinants of Leishmania
    Virulence   K.-P. Chang, G. Chaudhuri,
                                                    D. Fong   44:499–529
Regulation of the Cell Division Cycle and
    Differentiation in Bacteria   A. Newton, N. Ohta   44:689–719
Serine β-Lactamases and Penicillin-Binding
    Proteins   J.-M. Ghuysen   45:37–67

msDNA and Bacterial Reverse Transcriptase   M. Inouye, S. Inouye   45:163–86
The Universally Conserved GroE (Hsp60)
  Chaperonins   J. Zeilstra-Ryalls, O. Fayet,
                 C. Georgopoulos   45:301–25
Chaperone-Assisted Assembly and Molecular
  Architecture of Adhesive Pili   S. J. Hultgren, S. Normark,
                                    S. N. Abraham   45:383–415
Proper and Improper Folding of Proteins in
  the Cellular Environment   B. Nilsson, S. Anderson   45:607–35

ANIMAL PATHOGENS AND DISEASES
  Cell-Free Immunity in Insects   H. G. Boman, D. Hultmark   41:103–26
Compartmentation of Carbohydrate
  Metabolism in Trypanosomes   F. R. Opperdoes   41:127–51
The Attenuation of Poliovirus Neurovirulence   J. W. Almond   41:153–80
Repetitive Proteins and Genes of Malaria   D. J., Kemp, R. L. Coppel,
                                             R. F. Anders   41:181–208
Specific and Rapid Identification of Medically
  Important Fungi by Exoantigen Detection   L. Kaufman, P. G. Standard   41:209–25
Use of Organ Cultures in Microbiological
  Research   Z. A. McGee, M. L. Woods, Jr.   41:291–300
The Epidemiologic, Clinical, and
  Microbiologic Features of Hemorrhagic
  Colitis   L. W. Riley   41:383–407
Bacterial Biofilms in Nature and Disease   J. W. Costerton, K.-J. Cheng,
                                             G. G. Geesey, T. I. Ladd,
                                             J. C. Nickel, M. Dasgupta,
                                             T. J. Marrie   41:435–64
Leprosy and the Leprosy Bacillus: Recent
  Developments in Characterization of
  Antigens and Immunology of the Disease   H. Gaylord, P. J. Brennan   41:645–75
Elaboration Versus Simplification in Refining
  Mathematical Models of Infectious Disease   F. L. Black, B. Singer   41:677–701
Hot News on the Common Cold   D. A. J. Tyrrell   42:35–47
Ecology of Colorado Tick Fever   R. W. Emmons   42:49–64
Genetic Determinants of Shigella
  Pathogenicity   A. T. Maurelli, P. J. Sansonetti   42:127–50
Complement Evasion by Bacteria and
  Parasites   K. A. Joiner   42:201–30
Replication of Kinetoplast DNA in
  Trypanosomes   K. A. Ryan, T. A. Shapiro,
                   C. A. Rauch, P. T. Englund   42:339–58
Aeromonas and Plesiomonas as Etiological
  Agents   N. Khardori, V. Fainstein   42:395–419
Nosocomial Fungal Infections: A
  Classification for Hospital-Acquired Fungal
  Infections and Mycoses Arising from
  Endogenous Flora or Reactiv   T. J. Walsh, P. A. Pizzo   42:517–45
Simian Immunodeficiency Viruses   R. C. Desrosiers   42:607–25
Intergeneric Coaggregation Among Human
  Oral Bacteria and Ecology of Dental Plaque   P. E. Kolenbrander   42:627–56
The Mounting Interest in Bacterial and Viral
  Pathogenicity   H. Smith   43:1–22
Molecular Basis of Surface Antigen Variation
  in Paramecia   F. Caron, E. Meyer   43:23–42
The Ecology of the Human Intestine and Its
  Consequences for Overgrowth by Pathogens
  Such as Clostridium difficile   D. van der Waaij   43:69–88
Interactions of Gonococci with Phagocytic
  Cells   W. M. Shafer, R. F. Rest   43:121–46
Scrapie Prions   S. B. Prusiner   43:345–74
Genetic Analysis of Extracellular Toxins of
  Staphylococcus aureus   J. J. Iandolo   43:375–402

Transcription and Reverse Transcription of
  Retrotransposons   J. D. Boeke, V. G. Corces   43:403–34
Alkalophilic Bacteria   T. A. Krulwich, A. A. Guffanti   43:435–64
Serodiagnosis of Infection with the AIDS
  Virus and Other Human Retroviruses   G. Schochetman, J. S. Epstein,
                                                        T. F. Zuck   43:629–60

Antigenic Variation of a Relapsing Fever
  Borrelia Species   A. G. Barbour   44:155–71
Reciprocity in the Interactions between the
  Poxviruses and Their Host Cells   S. Dales   44:173–92
Helicobacter (Campylobacter) pylori: A New
  Twist to an Old Disease   J. D. Dick   44:249–69
Sexual Differentiation in Malaria Parasites   P. Alano, R. Carter   44:429–49
The Generation of Genetic Diversity in
  Malaria Parasites   G. A. McConkey, A. P. Waters,
                                                        T. F. McCutchan   44:479–98

Molecular Determinants of *Leishmania*
  Virulence   K.-P. Chang, G. Chaudhuri,
                                                        D. Fong   44:499–529

The Global Epidemiology of HIV Infection
  and AIDS   M. M. Braun, W. L. Heyward,
                                                        J. W. Curran   44:555–77

Putative Virulence Factors of *Candida*
  albicans   J. E. Cutler   45:187–218
Varicella-Zoster Virus Latency   K. D. Croen, S. E. Straus   45:265–82
Hepadnaviruses and Hepatocellular Carcinoma   A. H. Sherker, P. L. Marion   45:475–508
Mechanisms of Natural Resistance to Human
  Pathogenic Fungi   J. W. Murphy   45:509–38

PLANT-BACTERIA INTERACTIONS
  Physiology, Biochemistry, and Genetics of
    the Uptake Hydrogenase in Rhizobia   H. J. Evans, A. R. Harker,
                                                        H. Papen, S. A. Russell,
                                                        F. J. Hanus, M. Zuber   41:335–61

  Enzymatic "Combustion": The Microbial
    Degradation of Lignin   T. K. Kirk, R. L. Farrell   41:465–505
  Host Range Determinants in Plant Pathogens
    and Symbionts   N. T. Keen, B. Staskawicz   42:421–40
  Cell Biology of *Agrobacterium* Infection and
    Transformation of Plants   A. N. Binns, M. F. Thomashow   42:575–606
  Molecular Biology of Cellulose Degradation   P. Beguin   44:219–48
  Plant Genetic Control of Nodulation   G. Caetano-Anollés, P. M.
                                                        Gresshoff   45:345–82

IMMUNOLOGY
  Cell-Free Immunity in Insects   H. G. Boman, D. Hultmark   41:103–26
  Repetitive Proteins and Genes of Malaria   D. J., Kemp, R. L. Coppel,
                                                        R. F. Anders   41:181–208
  Specific and Rapid Identification of Medically
    Important Fungi by Exoantigen Detection   L. Kaufman, P. G. Standard   41:209–25
  Leprosy and the Leprosy Bacillus: Recent
    Developments in Characterization of
    Antigens and Immunology of the Disease   H. Gaylord, P. J. Brennan   41:645–75
  Complement Evasion by Bacteria and
    Parasites   K. A. Joiner   42:201–30
  Immunity in Filariasis: Perspectives for
    Vaccine Development   M. Philipp, T. B. Davis, N. Storey,
                                                        C. K. S. Carlow   42:685–716
  Interactions of Gonococci with Phagocytic
    Cells   W. M. Shafer, R. F. Rest   43:121–46
  Molecular Mechanisms of Immunoglobulin: A
    Defense   N. Childers, M. G. Bruce,
                                                        J. McGhee   43:503–36

VIROLOGY

Rapid Evolution of RNA Viruses	D. A. Steinhauer, J. J. Holland	41:409–33
An Inquiry into the Mechanisms of Herpes Simplex Virus Latency	B. Roizman, A. E. Sears	41:543–71
Assembly of Animal Viruses at Cellular Membranes	E. B. Stephens, R. W. Compans	42:489–516
Simian Immunodeficiency Viruses	R. C. Desrosiers	42:607–25
Evolution of RNA Viruses	J. H. Strauss, E. G. Strauss	42:657–83
The Pasteur Institute's Contributions to the Field of Virology	M. Girard	42:745–63
The Genomes of the Human Herpesviruses: Contents, Relationships,	D. J. McGeoch	43:235–66
DNA Packaging in dsDNA Bacteriophages	L. W. Black	43:267–92
Transcription and Reverse Transcription of Retrotransposons	J. D. Boeke, V. G. Corces	43:403–34
Structural Domains and Organizational Conformation Involved in the Sorting and Transport of Influenza Virus Transmembrane Proteins	D. P. Nayak, M. A. Jabbar	43:465–502
Serodiagnosis of Infection with the AIDS Virus and Other Human Retroviruses	G. Schochetman, J. S. Epstein, T. F. Zuck	43:629–60
Glycoproteins Encoded by Varicella-Zoster Virus: Biosynthesis, Phosphorylation, and Intracellular Trafficking	C. Grose	44:59–80
Reciprocity in the Interactions between the Poxviruses and Their Host Cells	S. Dales	44:173–92
Coronavirus: Organization, Replication, and Expression of Genome	M. M. C. Lai	44:303–33
Proteolytic Processing of Picornaviral Polyprotein	A. C. Palmenberg	44:603–23
Flavivirus Genome Organization, Expression, and Replication	T. J. Chambers, C. S. Hahn, R. Galler, C. M. Rice	44:649–88
Genetically Engineered Baculoviruses as Agents for Pest Control	H. A. Wood, R. R. Granados	45:69–87
Regulation of Human Immunodeficiency Virus Replication	B. R. Cullen	45:219–50
Viruses of the Protozoa	A. L. Wang, C. C. Wang	45:251–63
Varicella-Zoster Virus Latency	K. D. Croen, S. E. Straus	45:265–82
Hepadnaviruses and Hepatocellular Carcinoma	A. H. Sherker, P. L. Marion	45:475–508

CHEMOTHERAPY AND CHEMOTHERAPEUTIC AGENTS

The Biosynthesis of Sulfur-Containing β-Lactam Antibiotics	J. Nüesch, J. Heim, H.-J. Treichler	41:51–75
Biosynthesis of Peptide Antibiotics	H. Kleinkauf, H. von Döhren	41:259–89
Chromosomal Cephalosporinases Responsible for Multiple Resistance to Newer β-Lactam Antibiotics	C. C. Sanders	41:573–93
Genetics of Streptomyces fradiae and Tylosin Biosynthesis	R. H. Baltz, E. T. Seno	42:547–74
Immunity in Filariasis: Perspectives for Vaccine Development	M. Philipp, T. B. Davis, N. Storey, C. K. S. Carlow	42:685–716
Organization and Expression of Genes Involved in the Biosynthesis of Antibiotics and Other Secondary Metabolites	J. F. Martín, P. Liras	43:173–206
How Antibiotic-Producing Organisms Avoid Suicide	E. Cundliffe	43:207–34
The Evolution of Fluorinated Quinolones: Pharmacology, Microbiological Activity, Clinical Uses, and Toxicities	C. Siporin	43:601–28
Bioactive Microbial Products: Focus upon Mechanism of Action	R. L. Monaghan, J. S. Tkacz	44:271–301

Functions of Secondary Metabolites | L. C. Vining | 44:395–427
Ivermectin as an Antiparasitic Agent for Use in Humans | W. C. Campbell | 45:445–74

GENETICS

Incompatibility Group P Plasmids: Genetics, Evolution, and Use in Genetic Manipulation | C. M. Thomas, C. A. Smith | 41:77–101
Repetitive Proteins and Genes of Malaria | D. J., Kemp, R. L. Coppel, R. F. Anders | 41:181–208

Genetics of Azotobacters: Applications to Nitrogen Fixation and Related Aspects of Metabolism | C. Kennedy, A. Toukdarian | 41:227–58
Physiology, Biochemistry, and Genetics of the Uptake Hydrogenase in Rhizobia | H. J. Evans, A. R. Harker, H. Papen, S. A. Russell, F. J. Hanus, M. Zuber | 41:335–61

The Mitochondrial Genome of Kinetoplastid Protozoa: Genomic Organization, Transcription, Replication, and Evolution | L. Simpson | 41:363–82
Rapid Evolution of RNA Viruses | D. A. Steinhauer, J. J. Holland | 41:409–33
Genetic Research with Photosynthetic Bacteria | P. A. Scolnik, B. L. Marrs | 41:703–26
Genetics and Regulation of Carbohydrate Catabolism in *Bacillus* | A. F. Klier, G. Rapoport | 42:65–95
Genetic Determinants of *Shigella* Pathogenicity | A. T. Maurelli, P. J. Sansonetti | 42:127–50
Enzymes and Genes From the *lux* Operons of Bioluminescent Bacteria | E. A. Meighen | 42:151–76
Baculoviruses as Gene Expression Vectors | L. K. Miller | 42:177–99
Small, Acid-Soluble Spore Proteins of *Bacillus* Species: Structure, Synthesis, Genetics, Function, and Degradation | P. Setlow | 42:319–38
Replication of Kinetoplast DNA in Trypanosomes | K. A. Ryan, T. A. Shapiro, C. A. Rauch, P. T. Englund | 42:339–58

Genetics of *Streptomyces fradiae* and Tylosin Biosynthesis | R. H. Baltz, E. T. Seno | 42:547–74
Plasmid-Mediated Heavy Metal Resistances | S. Silver, T. K. Misra | 42:717–43
Molecular Basis of Surface Antigen Variation in Paramecia | F. Caron, E. Meyer | 43:23–42
Role of the DNA/Membrane Complex in Prokaryotic DNA Replication | W. Firshein | 43:69–88
The Genomes of the Human Herpesviruses: Contents, Relationships, | D. J. McGeoch | 43:235–66
DNA Packaging in dsDNA Bacteriophages | L. W. Black | 43:267–92
Staphylococcal Plasmids and Their Replication | R. P. Novick | 43:537–66
Evolution of a Biosynthetic Pathway: The Tryptophan Paradigm | I. P. Crawford | 43:567–601
Methylotrophs: Genetics and Commercial Applications | M. E. Lidstrom, D. I. Stirling | 44:27–58
Mycoplasmal Genetics | K. Dybvig | 44:81–104
Mechanism and Regulation of Bacterial Ribosomal RNA Processing | A. K. Srivastava, D. Schlessinger | 44:105–29
Molecular Evolution and Genetic Engineering of Protein Domains Involving Aspartate Transcarbamoylase | J. R. Wild, M. E. Wales | 44:193–218
General Microbiology of *recA*: Environmental and Evolutionary Significance | R. V. Miller, T. A. Kokjohn | 44:365–94
The Generation of Genetic Diversity in Malaria Parasites | G. A. McConkey, A. P. Waters, T. F. McCutchan | 44:479–98
The Genetics of Bacterial Spore Germination | A. Moir, D. A. Smith | 44:531–53

Flavivirus Genome Organization, Expression,
and Replication   T. J. Chambers, C. S. Hahn,
   R. Galler, C. M. Rice   44:649–88
msDNA and Bacterial Reverse Transcriptase   M. Inouye, S. Inouye   45:163–86
Regulation of Human Immunodeficiency
   Virus Replication   B. R. Cullen   45:219–50
RNA Editing in Trypanosomatid Mitochondria   K. Stuart   45:327–44
Plant Genetic Control of Nodulation   G. Caetano-Anollés,
   P. M. Gresshoff   45:345–82
Gene Amplification in *Leishmania*   S. M. Beverley   45:417–44
Nuclear Fusion in Yeast   M. D. Rose   45:539–67
Prokaryotic Osmoregulation: Genetics and
   Physiology   L. N. Csonka, A. D. Hanson   45:569–606

PHYSIOLOGY, GROWTH, AND NUTRITION
Lessons from Biodegradation   S. Dagley   41:1–23
The Transient Phase Between Growth and
   Nongrowth of Heterotrophic Bacteria, With
   Emphasis on the Marine Environment   S. Kjelleberg, M. Hermansson,
   P. Mårdén, G. W. Jones   41:25–49
Compartmentation of Carbohydrate
   Metabolism in Trypanosomes   F. R. Opperdoes   41:127–51
Genetics of Azotobacters: Applications to
   Nitrogen Fixation and Related Aspects of
   Metabolism   C. Kennedy, A. Toukdarian   41:227–58
Prokaryotic Hopanoids and Other
   Polyterpenoid Sterol Surrogates   G. Ourisson, M. Rohmer,
   K. Poralla   41:301–33
Physiology, Biochemistry, and Genetics of
   the Uptake Hydrogenase in Rhizobia   H. J. Evans, A. R. Harker,
   H. Papen, S. A. Russell,
   F. J. Hanus, M. Zuber   41:335–61
Enzymatic "Combustion": The Microbial
   Degradation of Lignin   T. K. Kirk, R. L. Farrell   41:465–505
Export of Protein: A Biochemical View   L. L. Randall, S. J. S. Hardy,
   J. R. Thom   41:507–41
High-Resolution NMR Studies of
   Saccharomyces cerevisiae   S. L. Campbell-Burk, R. G.
   Shulman   41:595–616
Genetics and Regulation of Carbohydrate
   Catabolism in *Bacillus*   A. F. Klier, G. Rapoport   42:65–95
Protein Phosphorylation in Prokaryotes   A. J. Cozzone   42:97–125
The Enzymes Associated With Denitrification   L. I. Hochstein, G. A. Tomlinson   42:231–61
Microbial Degradation of Haloaromatics   W. Reineke, H.-J. Knackmuss   42:263–87
Anaerobic Degradation of Aromatic
   Compounds   W. C. Evans, G. Fuchs   42:289–317
Structure and Function of Porins From
   Gram-Negative Bacteria   R. Benz   42:359–93
Energy Metabolism of Protozoa Without
   Mitochondria   M. Müller   42:465–88
Biochemistry of Acetate Catabolism in
   Anaerobic Chemotrophic Bacteria   R. K. Thauer, D. Moller-Zinkhan,
   A. M. Spormann   43:43–68
Organization and Expression of Genes
   Involved in the Biosynthesis of Antibiotics
   and Other Secondary Metabolites   J. F. Martin, P. Liras   43:173–206
How Antibiotic-Producing Organisms Avoid
   Suicide   E. Cundliffe   43:207–34
Genetic Basis of Starvation Survival in
   Nondifferentiating Bacteria   A. Matin, E. A. Auger,
   P. H. Blum, J. E. Schultz   43:293–316
Genetics and Regulation of Bacterial Lipid
   Metabolism in Bacteria   T. V. Boom, J. E. Cronan, Jr.   43:317–44
Alkalophilic Bacteria   T. A. Krulwich, A. A. Guffanti   43:435–64

ANNUAL REVIEWS INC.

A NONPROFIT SCIENTIFIC PUBLISHER

 4139 El Camino Way
P.O. Box 10139
Palo Alto, CA 94303-0897 • USA

ORDER FORM

ORDER TOLL FREE
1-800-523-8635
(except California)

FAX: 415-855-9815

Annual Reviews Inc. publications may be ordered directly from our office; through booksellers and subscription agents, worldwide; and through participating professional societies. Prices subject to change without notice. ARI Federal I.D. #94-1156476

- **Individuals:** Prepayment required on new accounts by check or money order (in U.S. dollars, check drawn on U.S. bank) or charge to credit card — American Express, VISA, MasterCard.
- **Institutional buyers:** Please include purchase order.
- **Students:** $10.00 discount from retail price, per volume. Prepayment required. Proof of student status must be provided (photocopy of student I.D. or signature of department secretary is acceptable). Students must send orders direct to Annual Reviews. Orders received through bookstores and institutions requesting student rates will be returned. You may order at the Student Rate for a maximum of 3 years.
- **Professional Society Members:** Members of professional societies that have a contractual arrangement with Annual Reviews may order books through their society at a reduced rate. Check with your society for information.
- **Toll Free Telephone orders:** Call 1-800-523-8635 (except from California) for orders paid by credit card or purchase order and customer service calls only. California customers and all other business calls use 415-493-4400 (not toll free). Hours: 8:00 AM to 4:00 PM, Monday-Friday, Pacific Time. **Written confirmation** is required on purchase orders from universities before shipment.
- **FAX: 415-855-9815   Telex: 910-290-0275**
- **We do not ship on approval.**

Regular orders: Please list below the volumes you wish to order by volume number.
Standing orders: New volume in the series will be sent to you automatically each year upon publication. Cancellation may be made at any time. Please indicate volume number to begin standing order.
Prepublication orders: Volumes not yet published will be shipped in month and year indicated.
California orders: Add applicable sales tax. **Canada:** Add GST tax.
Postage paid (4th class bookrate/surface mail) by **Annual Reviews Inc.** UPS domestic ground service available (except Alaska and Hawaii) at $2.00 extra per book. Airmail postage or UPS air service also available at prevailing costs. UPS must have street address. P.O. Box, APO or FPO not acceptable.

ANNUAL REVIEWS SERIES	Prices postpaid, per volume USA & Canada / elsewhere		Regular Order Please Send Vol. Number:	Standing Order Begin With Vol. Number:
	Until 12-31-90	After 1-1-91		
Annual Review of ANTHROPOLOGY				
Vols. 1-16 (1972-1987)	$31.00/$35.00	$33.00/$38.00		
Vols. 17-18 (1988-1989)	$35.00/$39.00	$37.00/$42.00		
Vol. 19 (1990)	$39.00/$43.00	$41.00/$46.00		
Vol. 20 (avail. Oct. 1991)	$41.00/$46.00	$41.00/$46.00	Vol(s). _____	Vol. _____
Annual Review of ASTRONOMY AND ASTROPHYSICS				
Vols. 1, 5-14 (1963, 1967-1976)				
16-20 (1978-1982)	$31.00/$35.00	$33.00/$38.00		
Vols. 21-27 (1983-1989)	$47.00/$51.00	$49.00/$54.00		
Vol. 28 (1990)	$51.00/$55.00	$53.00/$58.00		
Vol. 29 (avail. Sept. 1991)	$53.00/$58.00	$53.00/$58.00	Vol(s). _____	Vol. _____
Annual Review of BIOCHEMISTRY				
Vols. 30-34, 36-56 (1961-1965, 1967-1987) ..	$33.00/$37.00	$35.00/$40.00		
Vols. 57-58 (1988-1989)	$35.00/$39.00	$37.00/$42.00		
Vol. 59 (1990)	$39.00/$44.00	$41.00/$47.00		
Vol. 60 (avail. July 1991)	$41.00/$47.00	$41.00/$47.00	Vol(s). _____	Vol. _____
Annual Review of BIOPHYSICS AND BIOPHYSICAL CHEMISTRY				
Vols. 1-11 (1972-1982)	$31.00/$35.00	$33.00/$38.00		
Vols. 12-18 (1983-1989)	$49.00/$53.00	$51.00/$56.00		
Vol. 19 (1990)	$53.00/$57.00	$55.00/$60.00		
Vol. 20 (avail. June 1991)	$55.00/$60.00	$55.00/$60.00	Vol(s). _____	Vol. _____

Annual Review of CELL BIOLOGY

Vols. 1-3	(1985-1987)	$31.00/$35.00	$33.00/$38.00	
Vols. 4-5	(1988-1989)	$35.00/$39.00	$37.00/$42.00	
Vol. 6	(1990)	$39.00/$43.00	$41.00/$46.00	
Vol. 7	(avail. Nov. 1991)	$41.00/$46.00	$41.00/$46.00	Vol(s). _____ Vol. _____

Annual Review of COMPUTER SCIENCE

Vols. 1-2	(1986-1987)	$39.00/$43.00	$41.00/$46.00	
Vols. 3-4	(1988, 1989-1990)	$45.00/$49.00	$47.00/$52.00	Vol(s). _____ Vol. _____

Series suspended until further notice. SPECIAL OFFER: Volumes 1-4 are available at the special promotional price of $100.00 USA & Canada / $115.00 elsewhere, when all 4 volumes are purchased at one time. Orders at the special price must be prepaid.

Annual Review of EARTH AND PLANETARY SCIENCES

Vols. 1-10	(1973-1982)	$31.00/$35.00	$33.00/$38.00	
Vols. 11-17	(1983-1989)	$49.00/$53.00	$51.00/$56.00	
Vol. 18	(1990)	$53.00/$57.00	$55.00/$60.00	
Vol. 19	(avail. May 1991)	$55.00/$60.00	$55.00/$60.00	Vol(s). _____ Vol. _____

Annual Review of ECOLOGY AND SYSTEMATICS

Vols. 2-18	(1971-1987)	$31.00/$35.00	$33.00/$38.00	
Vols. 19-20	(1988-1989)	$34.00/$38.00	$36.00/$41.00	
Vol. 21	(1990)	$38.00/$42.00	$40.00/$45.00	
Vol. 22	(avail. Nov. 1991)	$40.00/$45.00	$40.00/$45.00	Vol(s). _____ Vol. _____

Annual Review of ENERGY

Vols. 1-7	(1976-1982)	$31.00/$35.00	$33.00/$38.00	
Vols. 8-14	(1983-1989)	$58.00/$62.00	$60.00/$65.00	
Vol. 15	(1990)	$62.00/$66.00	$64.00/$69.00	
Vol. 16	(avail. Oct. 1991)	$64.00/$69.00	$64.00/$69.00	Vol(s). _____ Vol. _____

Annual Review of ENTOMOLOGY

Vols. 10-16, 18	(1965-1971, 1973)			
20-32	(1975-1987)	$31.00/$35.00	$33.00/$38.00	
Vols. 33-34	(1988-1989)	$34.00/$38.00	$36.00/$41.00	
Vol. 35	(1990)	$38.00/$42.00	$40.00/$45.00	
Vol. 36	(avail. Jan. 1991)	$40.00/$45.00	$40.00/$45.00	Vol(s). _____ Vol. _____

Annual Review of FLUID MECHANICS

Vols. 2-4, 7	(1970-1972, 1975)			
9-19	(1977-1987)	$32.00/$36.00	$34.00/$39.00	
Vols. 20-21	(1988-1989)	$34.00/$38.00	$36.00/$41.00	
Vol. 22	(1990)	$38.00/$42.00	$40.00/$45.00	
Vol. 23	(avail. Jan. 1991)	$40.00/$45.00	$40.00/$45.00	Vol(s). _____ Vol. _____

Annual Review of GENETICS

Vols. 1-21	(1967-1987)	$31.00/$35.00	$33.00/$38.00	
Vols. 22-23	(1988-1989)	$34.00/$38.00	$36.00/$41.00	
Vol. 24	(1990)	$38.00/$42.00	$40.00/$45.00	
Vol. 25	(avail. Dec. 1991)	$40.00/$45.00	$40.00/$45.00	Vol(s). _____ Vol. _____

Annual Review of IMMUNOLOGY

Vols. 1-5	(1983-1987)	$31.00/$35.00	$33.00/$38.00	
Vols. 6-7	(1988-1989)	$34.00/$38.00	$36.00/$41.00	
Vol. 8	(1990)	$38.00/$42.00	$40.00/$45.00	
Vol. 9	(avail. April 1991)	$41.00/$46.00	$41.00/$46.00	Vol(s). _____ Vol. _____

Annual Review of MATERIALS SCIENCE

Vols. 1, 3-12	(1971, 1973-1982)	$31.00/$35.00	$33.00/$38.00	
Vols. 13-19	(1983-1989)	$66.00/$70.00	$68.00/$73.00	
Vol. 20	(1990)	$70.00/$74.00	$72.00/$77.00	
Vol. 21	(avail. Aug. 1991)	$72.00/$77.00	$72.00/$77.00	Vol(s). _____ Vol. _____